# PRINCIPLES OF FINANCIAL ACCOUNTING

# PRINCIPLES OF FINANCIAL ACCOUNTING

## 5th Edition

### JERRY J. WEYGANDT Ph.D., CPA

Arthur Andersen Alumni Professor of Accounting
University of Wisconsin
Madison, Wisconsin

### DONALD E. KIESO Ph.D., CPA

KPMG Peat Marwick Emeritus Professor of Accountancy
Northern Illinois University
DeKalb, Illinois

### PAUL D. KIMMEL Ph.D., CPA

Associate Professor of Accounting
University of Wisconsin—Milwaukee
Milwaukee, Wisconsin

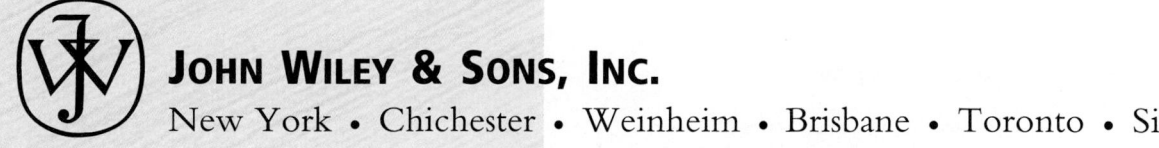

**JOHN WILEY & SONS, INC.**
New York • Chichester • Weinheim • Brisbane • Toronto • Singapore

Dedicated to
Walter G. Kell
Scholar–athlete, husband, father, teacher, author, gentleman, and friend

EXECUTIVE EDITOR   Susan Elbe
SENIOR DEVELOPMENT EDITOR   Nancy Perry
ASSOCIATE EDITOR   David B. Kear
SENIOR MARKETING MANAGER   Rebecca Hope
PRODUCTION COORDINATOR   Elm Street Publishing Services, Inc.
DESIGNER   Laura Boucher
PHOTO EDITORS   Alison Bamert, Hilary Newman
PHOTO RESEARCHER   Jennifer Atkins
ILLUSTRATION EDITOR   Anna Melhorn
ART STUDIO   Precision Graphics
COVER PHOTO   © Paul Souders/Tony Stone Images, New York

This book was set in 10.5/12 Palatino by Ruttle, Shaw & Wetherill, Inc. and printed and bound by Von Hoffmann Press. The cover was printed by Phoenix Color Corp.

Recognizing the importance of preserving what has been written, it is a
policy of John Wiley & Sons, Inc. to have books of enduring value published
in the United States printed on acid-free paper, and we exert our best
efforts to that end.

The paper in this book was manufactured by a mill whose forest management programs include sustained yield harvesting of its timberlands. Sustained yield harvesting principles ensure that the number of trees cut each year does not exceed the amount of new growth.

We are grateful for permission to use the following material: The image of *Tony the Tiger*™ thoughout the text: *™,® Kellogg Company © 1994 Kellogg Company. All rights reserved, used with permission. Appendix A Specimen Financial Statements of Kellogg Company and Kellogg's 1997 Annual Report: *Kellogg's®* is a registered trademark of Kellogg Company. All rights reserved, used with permission. Appendix B Specimen Financial Statements of General Mills, Inc.: Printed with permission of General Mills, Inc.

**Library of Congress Cataloging-in-Publication Data**
Weygandt, Jerry J.
    Principles of financial accounting.—5th ed. / Jerry J.
Weygandt, Donald E. Kieso, Paul D. Kimmel.
        p.   cm.
    Includes index.
    ISBN 0-471-19437-9 (pbk.   alk. paper)
    1. Accounting.   I. Kieso, Donald E.   II. Kimmel, Paul D.
III. Title.
HF5635.W5244   1998
657—dc21                                                                      98-25285
                                                                                 CIP

ISBN 0-471-19437-9

Printed in the United States of America

10  9  8  7  6  5  4  3  2

# STUDENT TO STUDENT

Hello!

Congratulations on the beginning of your accounting studies. I'd like to share with you a few ideas I found helpful when I took this course.

***Accounting is not only enjoyable but very exciting!*** As you continue your studies in accounting, you will gain an understanding of why accounting is vital to every business. Accounting gives you a solid background in financial statement analysis. This in turn will help you be a smarter investor. In short, accounting will open up the whole world of commerce and business to you.

Here are some tips I picked up while I used this text. Perhaps you can benefit from them.

- Accounting is a study of concepts and procedures. When studying, be sure you understand the concepts clearly. You might find that sometimes you have to review the text a few times until you fully understand the concepts. Look carefully at the illustrations; they will help you understand the main points of the text. When studying the journal entries, go over every entry until you fully understand it.

- Use the study aids in each chapter to help you understand the key concepts and learn the procedures. The *Feature Story*, list of *Study Objectives*, and *Preview* will help you understand what the chapter is about. Use the *Study Objectives* in the margins and the *Before You Go On* exercises to check whether you have understood and learned the material in each section.

- Use a highlighter. I found it very helpful both in studying and reviewing. Highlight whatever you feel is important.

- After you have done your homework, try some extra problems. Every chapter has two sets of problems on the same material. Try the alternative problems. They will help reinforce what you learned in each chapter.

- If possible, try to get some real-world practice, perhaps by doing some part-time work at an accounting office or just observing an accountant at work. It will bring alive what you study.

After a few short weeks, ***you will agree that accounting is exciting and enjoyable!***

Lots of success,

*Eli Oelbaum*

Eli Oelbaum
Ocean County College

# HOW TO USE THE STUDY AIDS IN THIS BOOK

Concepts for Review, listed at the beginning of each chapter from Chapter 2 on, are the accounting concepts you learned in previous chapters that you will need to know in order to understand the topics you are about to learn. Page references are provided if you need to review before reading the chapter.

## CONCEPTS FOR REVIEW

**Before studying this chapter, you should know or, if necessary, review:**

a. The cost principle (Ch. 1, p. 11) and matching principle of accounting. (Ch. 3, p. 94)

b. How to record purchases, sales, and cost of goods sold under a perpetual inventory system. (Ch. 5, pp. 191–199)

c. How to prepare financial statements for a merchandising company. (Ch. 5, pp. 199–201)

THE NAVIGATOR

## FEATURE STORY

### Keeping the Books on the Books

If you go to a large college or university, chances are that your bookstore or student union has state-of-the-art computer technology for tracking inventories. In an instant, the clerk at the check-out stand "whooshes" your purchases over a

scanning machine that automatically rings up the price and deducts the item from inventory.

Not all schools have such state-of-the-art technology. Some bookstores are even small enough that the person managing it can take a "mom-and-pop corner grocery" approach. One such bookstore is at Erie Community College in Buffalo, New York, which produces annual

sales of $500,000 per year. Instead of using "point-of-sale" computer technology, the bookstore uses an old-fashioned cash register. The inventory of textbooks, notebooks, art supplies, and so on is counted every month by Joel Damiani, manager. Because the quantity of inventory is relatively small, Damiani, or his two assistants, can specifically identify each item when sold. A larger bookstore would have too much inventory to use that approach; instead, they would use inventory costing methods that do not specifically match the cost of inventory to the actual sale of goods.

Damiani is candid, too, about some problems at his store. For one thing, the accounting records were in disarray when he took the job. "They told me it was going to be a challenge," he says. "And I like challenges." His challenges have included working with the school's accountant to produce a monthly balance sheet and income statement for the bookstore and making sure he has enough inventory of books and supplies on hand for the start of classes. "Sometimes, students say we're not quick enough."

THE NAVIGATOR

The Feature Story helps you picture how the chapter topic relates to the real world of accounting and business. You will find references to the story throughout the chapter and in the section called A Look Back at Our Feature Story toward the end of the chapter.

The **Navigator** is a learning system designed to guide you through each chapter and help you succeed in learning the material. It consists of (1) a checklist at the beginning of the chapter, which outlines text features and study skills you will need, and (2) a series of check boxes that prompt you to use the learning aids in the chapter and set priorities as you study.

# CHAPTER 9

# INVENTORIES

### THE NAVIGATOR

- Understand *Concepts for Review*
- Read *Feature Story*
- Scan *Study Objectives*
- Read *Preview*
- Read text and answer *Before You Go On*
  p. 370 ☐  p. 376 ☐  p. 385 ☐  p. 390 ☐
- Work *Demonstration Problem*
- Review *Summary of Study Objectives*
- Answer *Self-Study Questions*
- Complete assignments

## STUDY OBJECTIVES

**After studying this chapter, you should be able to:**

1. *Describe the steps in determining inventory quantities.*
2. *Prepare the entries for purchases and sales of inventory under a periodic inventory system.*
3. *Determine cost of goods sold under a periodic inventory system.*
4. *Identify the unique features of the income statement for a merchandising company using a periodic inventory system.*
5. *Explain the basis of accounting for inventories and describe the inventory cost flow methods.*
6. *Explain the financial statement and tax effects of each of the inventory cost flow methods.*
7. *Explain the lower of cost or market basis of accounting for inventories.*
8. *Indicate the effects of inventory errors on the financial statements.*
9. *Compute and interpret the inventory turnover ratio.*

**Study Objectives** at the beginning of each chapter give you a framework for learning the specific concepts and procedures covered in the chapter. You will also see each study objective in the margin where the concept is discussed. Finally, you can review all the study objectives in the **Summary** at the end of the chapter.

THE NAVIGATOR

365

The **Preview** starts with an introductory paragraph linking the feature story with the major topics of the chapter. It is followed by a graphic outline of major topics and subtopics that will be discussed. This preview gives you a mental framework upon which to arrange the new information you are learning.

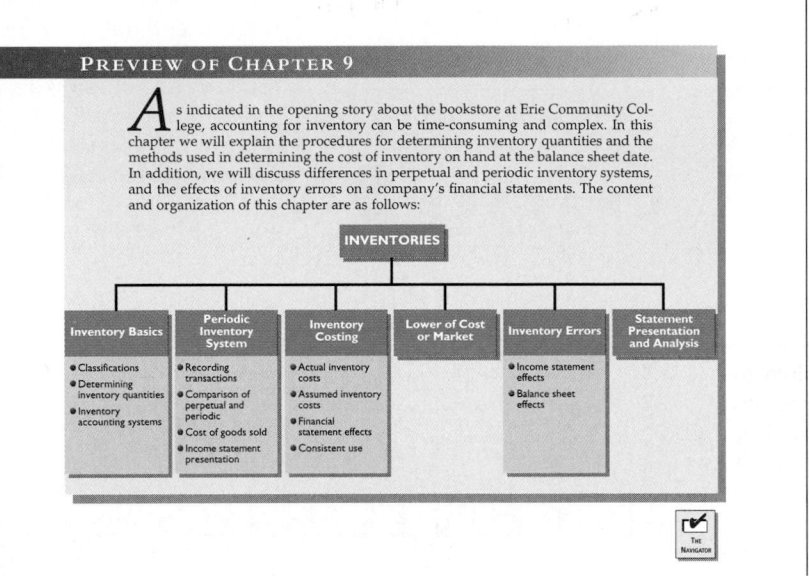

**The Accounting Equation** has been inserted in the margin next to key journal entries throughout the text. This new feature helps you understand the impact of an accounting transaction on the financial statements.

**Helpful Hints** in the margins help clarify concepts being discussed.

**Study Objectives** reappear in the margins at the point where the topic is discussed. End-of-chapter assignments are keyed to study objectives.

---

**PREVIEW OF CHAPTER 9**

A s indicated in the opening story about the bookstore at Erie Community College, accounting for inventory can be time-consuming and complex. In this chapter we will explain the procedures for determining inventory quantities and the methods used in determining the cost of inventory on hand at the balance sheet date. In addition, we will discuss differences in perpetual and periodic inventory systems, and the effects of inventory errors on a company's financial statements. The content and organization of this chapter are as follows:

INVENTORIES

| Inventory Basics | Periodic Inventory System | Inventory Costing | Lower of Cost or Market | Inventory Errors | Statement Presentation and Analysis |
|---|---|---|---|---|---|
| • Classifications<br>• Determining inventory quantities<br>• Inventory accounting systems | • Recording transactions<br>• Comparison of perpetual and periodic<br>• Cost of goods sold<br>• Income statement presentation | • Actual inventory costs<br>• Assumed inventory costs<br>• Financial statement effects<br>• Consistent use | | • Income statement effects<br>• Balance sheet effects | |

---

**372**    Chapter 9 • Inventories

$$A = L + OE$$
$$-3,430 \quad -3,500 \quad +70$$

| May 14 | Accounts Payable | 3,500 | |
| | Purchase Discounts | | 70 |
| | Cash | | 3,430 |
| | (To record payment to Highpoint Electronic within the discount period) | | |

Purchase Discounts is a temporary account whose normal balance is a credit.

### Recording Sales of Merchandise

The sale of $3,800 of merchandise to Chelsea Video on May 4 (sales invoice No. 731, Illustration 5-4) is recorded by the seller, Highpoint Electronic, as follows:

$$A = L + OE$$
$$+3,800 \quad +3,800$$

| May 4 | Accounts Receivable | 3,800 | |
| | Sales | | 3,800 |
| | (To record credit sales per invoice #731 to Chelsea Video) | | |

---

Inventory Basics    **367**

profit (net sales less cost of goods sold) is closely watched by management, owners, and other interested parties (as explained in Chapter 5).

### Classifying Inventory

How a company classifies its inventory depends on whether the firm is a merchandiser or a manufacturer. In a **merchandising enterprise**, inventory consists of many different items. For example, in a grocery store, canned goods, dairy products, meats, and produce are just a few of the inventory items on hand. These items have two common characteristics: (1) they are owned by the company, and (2) they are in a form ready for sale to customers in the ordinary course of business. Thus, only one inventory classification, **merchandise inventory**, is needed to describe the many different items that make up the total inventory.

In a **manufacturing enterprise**, inventories are also owned by the company, but some goods may not yet be ready for sale. As a result, inventory is usually classified into three categories: finished goods, work in process, and raw materials. For example, General Motors classifies automobiles completed and ready for sale as **finished goods**. The automobiles on the assembly line in various stages of production are classified as **work in process**. The steel, glass, upholstery, and other components that are on hand waiting to be used in the production of automobiles are identified as **raw materials**.

The accounting principles and concepts discussed in this chapter apply to inventory classifications of both merchandising and manufacturing companies. In this chapter we will focus on merchandise inventory.

### Determining Inventory Quantities

Many businesses take a physical inventory count on the last day of the year. Businesses using the periodic inventory system are required to take an end-of-the-period physical inventory to determine the inventory on hand at the balance sheet date and to compute cost of goods sold. Even businesses using a perpetual inventory system must take a physical inventory at some time during the year.

Determining inventory quantities consists of two steps: (1) taking a physical inventory of goods on hand, and (2) determining the ownership of goods.

**HELPFUL HINT**
An important inventory management concept is inventory turnover. Inventory that turns means sales and profit; inventory that doesn't turn means costs and losses.

**HELPFUL HINT**
Regardless of the classification, all inventories are reported under Current Assets on the balance sheet.

**1**
STUDY OBJECTIVE

Describe the steps in determining inventory quantities.

**ILLUSTRATION 9-1**
*Terms of sale*

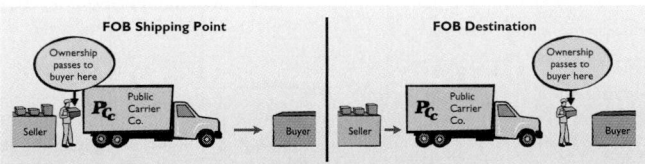

**Infographics,** a special type of illustration, pictorially link concepts to the real world and provide visual reminders of key concepts.

Significant errors may occur in determining inventory quantities if goods in transit at the statement date are ignored. Assume, for example, that Hargrove Company has 20,000 units of inventory on hand on December 31 and the following goods in transit: (1) **sales** of 1,500 units shipped December 31 FOB destination, and (2) **purchases** of 2,500 units shipped FOB shipping point by the seller on December 31. Hargrove has legal title to both the units sold and the units purchased. Consequently, inventory quantities would be understated by 4,000 units (1,500 + 2,500) if units in transit are ignored.

## TECHNOLOGY IN ACTION

**Technology in Action** boxes, identified by a CD icon, show how computers are used by accountants and users of accounting information.

 Many companies have invested large amounts of time and money in automated inventory systems. One of the most sophisticated is Federal Express' Digitally Assisted Dispatch System (DADS). This system uses hand-held "SuperTrackers" to transmit data about the packages and documents to the firm's computer system. Based on bar codes, the system allows the firm to know where any package is at any time to prevent losses and to fulfill the firm's delivery commitments. More recently, FedEx's newly developed software enables customers to track shipments on their own PCs.

**Financial statements** appear throughout the book. Those from real companies are identified by a logo or related photo. Often, numbers or categories are highlighted in colored type to draw your attention to key information.

**QUAKER OATS COMPANY**
**Notes to the Financial Statements**

**ILLUSTRATION 9-22**
*Disclosure of change in cost flow method*

**Note 1**   Effective July 1, the Company adopted the LIFO cost flow assumption for valuing the majority of U.S. Grocery Products inventories. The Company believes that the use of the LIFO method better matches current costs with current revenues. The effect of this change on the current year was to decrease net income by $16.0 million.

## ACCOUNTING IN ACTION
### International Insight

**Accounting in Action** boxes give you more glimpses into the real world of business. Each type of issue—business, ethics, and international—is identified by its own icon. Don't skip over the photos, figures, and tables.

U.S. companies typically choose between LIFO and FIFO. Many choose LIFO because it reduces inventory profits and taxes. However, the international community recently considered rules that would ban LIFO entirely and force companies to use FIFO. This proposal was defeated, but the issue will not go away.

The issue is sensitive. As John Wulff, controller for Union Carbide noted, "We were in support of the international effort up until the proposal to eliminate LIFO." Wulff says that if Union Carbide had been suddenly forced to switch from LIFO to FIFO, its reported $632 million pretax income would have jumped by $300 million. That would have increased Carbide's income tax bill by as much as $120 million. Given this, do you believe that accounting principles and rules should be the same around the world?

## BEFORE YOU GO ON . . .
### Review It

1. How do the cost and matching principles apply to inventoriable costs?
2. How are the three assumed cost flow methods applied in allocating inventoriable costs?
3. What factors should be considered by management in selecting an inventory cost flow method?
4. Which inventory cost flow method produces (a) the highest net income in a period of rising prices, and (b) the lowest income taxes?
5. What amount is reported by Kellogg Company in its 1997 Annual Report as inventories at December 31, 1997? Which inventory cost flow method does Kellogg Company use? The answer to this question is provided on p. 416.

### Do It

The accounting records of Shumway Ag Implement show the following data:

| | |
|---|---|
| Beginning inventory | 4,000 units at $3 |
| Purchases | 6,000 units at $4 |
| Sales | 5,000 units at $12 |

Determine the cost of goods sold during the period under a periodic inventory system using (a) the FIFO method, (b) the LIFO method, and (c) the average cost method.

*Reasoning:* Because the units of inventory on hand and available for sale may have been purchased at different prices, a systematic method must be adopted to allocate the costs between the goods sold and the goods on hand (ending inventory).

**Solution:**

(a) FIFO:   (4,000 @ $3) + (1,000 @ $4) = $12,000 + $4,000 = $16,000.
(b) LIFO:   5,000 @ $4 = $20,000.
(c) Average cost: [(4,000 @ $3) + (6,000 @ $4)] ÷ 10,000 = ($12,000 + $24,000) ÷ 10,000 = $3.60 per unit; 5,000 @ $3.60 = $18,000.

*Related exercise material:* BE9-6, BE9-7, E9-5, E9-6, E9-7.

**Accounting in Action** boxes give you more glimpses into the real world of business.

**Before You Go On** *Review It* questions serve as a learning check. If you cannot answer these questions, you should go back and read the section again.

*Review It* questions marked with the Tony the Tiger™ icon ask you to find information in Kellogg's 1997 Annual Report, which is packaged with this text and excerpted in Appendix A at the end of the text.

Brief *Do It* exercises help you apply what you are learning. They outline the *reasoning* necessary to complete the exercise, and their *solutions* help you see how the problem should be solved. (Keyed to homework exercises.)

The inventory turnover ratio measures the number of times on average the inventory is sold during the period. Its purpose is to measure the liquidity of the inventory. The inventory turnover is computed by dividing cost of goods sold by the average inventory during the period. Unless seasonal factors are significant, average inventory can be computed from the beginning and ending inventory balances. For example, Kellogg Company reported in its 1997 Annual Report a beginning inventory of $424,900,000, and cost of goods sold for the year 1997 of $3,270,100,000; its inventory turnover formula and computation are shown below:

**Key Terms** and concepts are printed in blue where they are first explained in the text and are defined again in the end-of-chapter glossary.

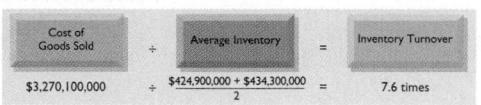

ILLUSTRATION 9-29

*Inventory turnover formula and computation for Kellogg Company*

| Cost of Goods Sold | ÷ | Average Inventory | = | Inventory Turnover |
|---|---|---|---|---|
| $3,270,100,000 | ÷ | $\frac{424,900,000 + \$434,300,000}{2}$ | = | 7.6 times |

One technique for determining the meaning of the information on financial statements is **ratio analysis.** Throughout this text, you will examine key financial ratios using data from Kellogg's financial statements.

A variant of the inventory turnover ratio is the **average days to sell inventory.** For example, the inventory turnover for Kellogg Company of 7.6 times divided into 365 is approximately 48 days. There are typical levels of inventory in every industry. However, companies that are able to keep their inventory at lower levels and higher turnovers and still satisfy customer needs are the most successful.

**Color illustrations** visually reinforce important concepts and therefore often contain material that may appear on exams.

---

390    Chapter 9 • Inventories

## BEFORE YOU GO ON . . .

### Review It

1. Why is it appropriate to report inventories at the lower of cost or market?
2. How do inventory errors affect financial statements?
3. What does the inventory turnover ratio reveal?

### A LOOK BACK AT OUR FEATURE STORY

Refer to the opening story concerning the bookstore at Erie Community College, and answer the following questions.
1. Why might a small bookstore use specific identification to determine inventory?
2. If the inventory is overstated at the end of the month, what effect does this error have on the balance sheet and the income statement?

*Solution:*
1. A small bookstore, as opposed to a large bookstore, might use specific identification because of:
   a. A smaller number of any one book in inventory.
   b. Fewer different books in inventory.
   c. The familiarity of the owner/manager (who handles sales) with the books being sold.
2. An end-of-month, inventory overstatement will result in overstated inventory in the balance sheet along with overstated stockholders' equity, due to overstated net income on the income statement. Cost of goods sold will be understated on the income statement. The next month's income statement will have overstated beginning inventory and understated net income.

The last **Before You Go On** exercise takes you back for a critical look at the chapter-opening feature story.

### DEMONSTRATION PROBLEM

Gerald D. Englehart Company has the following inventory, purchases, and sales data for the month of March.

| Inventory, March 1 | 200 units @ $4.00 | $ 800 |
|---|---|---|
| Purchases: | | |
| March 10 | 500 units @ $4.50 | 2,250 |
| March 20 | 400 units @ $4.75 | 1,900 |
| March 30 | 300 units @ $5.00 | 1,500 |
| Sales: | | |
| March 15 | 500 units | |
| March 25 | 400 units | |

The physical inventory count on March 31 shows 500 units on hand.

*Instructions*
Under a **periodic inventory system**, determine the cost of inventory on hand at March 31 and the cost of goods sold for March under the (a) first-in, first-out (FIFO) method, (b) last-in, first-out (LIFO) method, and (c) average cost method.

**PROBLEM-SOLVING STRATEGIES**
1. For FIFO, the latest costs are allocated to inventory.
2. For LIFO, the earliest costs are allocated to inventory.
3. For average costs, use a weighted average for periodic and a moving average for perpetual.
4. Remember, the costs allocated to cost of goods sold can be proved.
5. Total purchases are the same under all three cost flow methods.

### SOLUTION TO DEMONSTRATION PROBLEM

The cost of goods available for sale is $6,450:

| Inventory | 200 units @ $4.00 | $ 800 |
|---|---|---|
| Purchases: | | |
| March 10 | 500 units @ $4.50 | 2,250 |
| March 20 | 400 units @ $4.75 | 1,900 |
| March 30 | 300 units @ $5.00 | 1,500 |
| Total cost of goods available for sale | | $6,450 |

**Demonstration Problems** review the chapter material. These problems provide you with *problem-solving strategies* and with *solutions*.

## SUMMARY OF STUDY OBJECTIVES

**1.** *Describe the steps in determining inventory quantities.* The steps in determining inventory quantities are (1) taking a physical inventory of goods on hand and (2) determining the ownership of goods in transit.

**2.** *Prepare the entries for purchases and sales of inventory under a periodic inventory system.* In recording purchases, entries are required for (a) cash and credit purchases, (b) purchase returns and allowances, (c) purchase discounts, and (d) freight costs. In recording sales, entries are required for (a) cash and credit sales, (b) sales returns and allowances, and (c) sales discounts.

**3.** *Determine cost of goods sold under a periodic inventory system.* The steps in determining cost of goods sold are (a) recording the purchase of merchandise, (b) determining the cost of goods purchased, and (c) determining the cost of goods on hand at the beginning and end of the accounting period.

**4.** *Identify the unique features of the income statement for a merchandising company using a periodic inventory system.* The income statement for a merchandising company contains three sections: sales revenue, cost of goods sold, and operating expenses. The cost of goods sold section under a periodic inventory system generally shows more detail by reporting beginning and ending inventory, net purchases, and total goods available for sale.

**5.** *Explain the basis of accounting for inventories and describe the inventory cost flow methods.* The primary basis

of accounting for inventories is cost. Cost includes all expenditures necessary to acquire goods and place them in condition ready for sale. Inventoriable costs include (1) cost of beginning inventory and (2) the cost of goods purchased. The inventory cost flow methods are: specific identification, FIFO, LIFO, and average cost.

**6.** *Explain the financial statement and tax effects of each of the inventory cost flow methods.* The cost of goods available for sale may be allocated to cost of goods sold and ending inventory by specific identification or by a method based on an assumed cost flow. These methods have different effects on financial statements during periods of changing prices. When prices are rising, the first-in, first-out method (FIFO) results in lower cost of goods sold and higher net income than the average and the last-in, first-out (LIFO) methods. LIFO results in the lowest income taxes (because of lower net income). The reverse is true when prices are falling. In the balance sheet, FIFO results in an ending inventory that is closest to current value, whereas the inventory under LIFO is the farthest from current value.

**7.** *Explain the lower of cost or market basis of accounting for inventories.* The lower of cost or market basis (LCM) is used when the current replacement cost (market) is less than cost. Under LCM, the loss is recognized in the period in which the price decline occurs. LCM may be applied to individual inventory items, major categories of inventory, or to total inventory.

---

392    Chapter 9 • Inventories

**8.** *Indicate the effects of inventory errors on the financial statements.* In the income statement of the current year: (a) an error in beginning inventory will have a reverse effect on net income (overstatement of inventory results in understatement of net income) and (b) an error in ending inventory will have a similar effect on net income (overstatement of inventory results in overstatement of net income). If ending inventory errors are not corrected in the following period, their effect on net income for that period is reversed, and total net income for the two years will be correct. In the balance sheet, ending inventory errors will have the same

effect on total assets and total stockholders' equity and no effect on liabilities.

**9.** *Compute and interpret the inventory turnover ratio.* The inventory turnover ratio is calculated as cost of goods sold divided by average inventory. It can be converted to average days in inventory by dividing 365 days by the inventory turnover ratio. A higher turnover ratio or lower average days in inventory suggests that management is trying to keep inventory levels low relative to its sales level.

## GLOSSARY

**Average cost method** An inventory costing method that assumes the goods available for sale have the same (average) cost per unit; generally they are homogeneous. (p. 381).

**Consigned goods** Goods shipped by a consignor, who retains ownership, to another party called the consignee. (p. 369).

**Cost of goods available for sale** The sum of the beginning merchandise inventory plus the cost of goods purchased. (p. 374).

**Cost of goods purchased** The sum of net purchases plus freight-in. (p. 374).

**Cost of goods sold** The total cost of merchandise sold during the period, determined by subtracting ending inventory from the cost of goods available for sale. (p. 374).

**Current replacement cost** The amount that would be paid at the present time to acquire an identical item. (p. 386).

**First-in, first-out method (FIFO)** An inventory costing method that assumes that the costs of the earliest goods acquired are the first to be recognized as cost of goods sold. (p. 378).

**Inventoriable costs** The pool of costs that consists of two elements: (1) the cost of the beginning inventory and (2) the cost of goods purchased during the period. (p. 376).

**Inventory turnover ratio** A ratio that measures the number of times on average the inventory is sold during the period. It is computed by dividing cost of goods sold by the average inventory during the period. (p. 389).

**Last-in, first-out method (LIFO)** An inventory costing method that assumes that the costs of the latest units purchased are the first to be allocated to cost of goods sold. (p. 380).

**Lower of cost or market basis (LCM) (inventories)** A method of valuing inventory that recognizes the decline in the value when the current purchase price (market) is less than cost. (p. 386).

**Net purchases** Purchases less purchase returns and allowances and purchase discounts. (p. 374).

**Periodic inventory system** An inventory system in which inventoriable costs are allocated to ending inventory and cost of goods sold at the end of the period. Cost of goods sold is computed at the end of the period by subtracting the ending inventory (costs are assigned to a physical count of items on hand) from the cost of goods available for sale. (p. 370).

**Specific identification method** An actual physical flow costing method in which items still in inventory are specifically costed to arrive at the total cost of the ending inventory. (p. 377).

## APPENDIX 9A   ESTIMATING INVENTORIES

**10**
STUDY
OBJECTIVE

Describe the two methods of estimating inventories.

We have assumed throughout the chapter that a company would be able to do a physical count of its inventory. But what if it cannot, as in the example of the lumber inventory destroyed by fire? In that case, we would use an estimate.

Two circumstances explain the reasons for estimating rather than counting inventories. First, management may want monthly or quarterly financial statements but a physical inventory is taken only annually. Second, a casualty such as fire, flood, or earthquake may make it impossible to take a physical inventory. The need for estimating inventories is associated primarily with a periodic inventory system because of the absence of detailed inventory records.

There are two widely used methods of estimating inventories: (1) the gross profit method and (2) the retail inventory method.

---

*The **Summary of Study Objectives** relates the study objectives to the key points in the chapter. It gives you another opportunity to review as well as to see how all the key topics within the chapter are related.*

*The **Glossary** defines all the terms and concepts introduced in the chapter. Page references help you find any terms you need to study further.*

*End-of-Chapter Appendixes address topics considered optional by some instructors.*

400     Chapter 9 • Inventories

*Note: All asterisked Questions, Exercises, and Problems relate to material in the appendixes to the chapter.

# SELF-STUDY QUESTIONS

Answers are at the end of the chapter.

(SO 2)  1. When goods are purchased for resale by a company using a periodic inventory system:
  a. purchases on account are debited to Merchandise Inventory.
  b. purchases on account are debited to Purchases.
  c. purchase returns are debited to Purchase Returns and Allowances.
  d. freight costs are debited to Purchases.

(SO 3)  2. In determining cost of goods sold:
  a. purchases discounts are deducted from net purchases.
  b. freight-out is added to net purchases.
  c. purchase returns and allowances are deducted from net purchases.
  d. freight-in is added to net purchases.

8. In periods of rising prices, LIFO will produce:
  a. higher net income than FIFO.
  b. the same net income as FIFO.
  c. lower net income than FIFO.
  d. higher net income than average costing.

9. Factors that affect the selection of an inventory costing method do *not* include:
  a. tax effects.
  b. balance sheet effects.
  c. income statement effects.
  d. perpetual vs. periodic inventory system.

10. The lower of cost or market basis may be applied to:
  a. categories of inventories.
  b. individual items of inventories.
  c. total inventory.
  d. all of the above.

> **Self-Study Questions** are a practice test, keyed to Study Objectives, that gives you an opportunity to check your knowledge of important topics. Answers appear on the last page of the chapter.

---

# QUESTIONS

1. Goods costing $1,700 are purchased on account on July 15 with credit terms of 2/10, n/30. On July 18 a $200 credit memo is received from the supplier for damaged goods. Give the journal entry on July 24 to record payment of the balance due within the discount period.

2. Identify the accounts that are added to or deducted from purchases to determine the cost of goods purchased. For each account, indicate (a) whether it is added or deducted and (b) its normal balance.

3. In the following separate mini cases, using a periodic inventory system, identify the item(s) designated by letter.
  (a) Purchases − X − Y = Net purchases.
  (b) Cost of goods purchased − Net purchases = X.
  (c) Beginning inventory   X = Cost of goods available for sale.
  (d) Cost of goods available for sale − Cost of goods sold = X.

13. "The selection of an inventory cost flow method is a decision made by accountants." Do you agree? Explain. Once a method has been selected, what accounting requirement applies?

14. Which assumed inventory cost flow method:
  (a) usually parallels the actual physical flow of merchandise?
  (b) assumes that goods available for sale during an accounting period are homogeneous?
  (c) assumes that the latest units purchased are the first to be sold?

15. In a period of rising prices, the inventory reported in Jim Groat Company's balance sheet is close to the current cost of the inventory, whereas Greg Hanson Company's inventory is considerably below its current cost. Identify the inventory cost flow method being used by each company. Which company has probably been reporting the higher gross profit?

> **Questions** allow you to explain your understanding of concepts and relationships covered in the chapter.

---

402     Chapter 9 • Inventories

*25. Jana Kingston Company has net sales of $400,000 and cost of goods available for sale of $300,000. If the gross profit rate is 30%, what is the estimated cost of the ending inventory? Show computations.

*26. John Ross Shoe Shop had goods available for sale in 1999 with a retail price of $120,000. The cost of these goods was $84,000. If sales during the period were $90,000, what is the ending inventory at cost using the retail inventory method?

*27. "When perpetual inventory record[s] under the FIFO and LIFO method[s] would be in a periodic invento[ry] agree? Explain.

*28. How does the average method of [...] fer between a perpetual inventory [...] inventory system?

> **Brief Exercises** help you focus on one Study Objective at a time and thus help you build confidence in your basic skills and knowledge. (Keyed to Study Objectives.)

# BRIEF EXERCISES

*Journalize purchases transactions.*
(SO 2)

**BE9–1**  Prepare the journal entries to record the following transactions on Svenska Company's books using a periodic inventory system.
  (a) On March 2, Svenska Company purchased $900,000 of merchandise from Sing Tao Company, terms 2/10, n/30.
  (b) On March 6, Svenska Company returned $130,000 of the merchandise purchased on March 2 because it was defective.
  (c) On March 12, Svenska Company paid the balance due to Sing Tao Company.

*Compute net purchases and cost of goods purchased.*
(SO 3)

**BE9–2**  Assume that Shinhan Company uses a periodic inventory system and has the following account balances: Purchases $440,000, Purchase Returns and Allowances $11,000, Purchase Discounts $8,000, and Freight-in $16,000. Determine (a) net purchases and (b) cost of goods purchased.

## EXERCISES

**E9–1**   Presented below is the following information related to Brazil Co.

1. On April 5, purchased merchandise from Chile Company for $18,000 terms 2/10, net/30, FOB shipping point.
2. On April 6, paid freight costs of $800 on merchandise purchased from Chile.
3. On April 7, purchased equipment on account for $26,000.
4. On April 8, returned damaged merchandise to Chile Company and was granted a $3,000 allowance.
5. On April 15, paid the amount due to Chile Company in full.

*Journalize purchases transactions.*
*(SO 2)*

**Instructions**
(a) Prepare the journal entries to record these transactions on the books of Brazil Co. using a periodic inventory system.
(b) Assume that Brazil Co. paid the balance due to Chile Company on May 4 instead of April 15. Prepare the journal entry to record this payment.

**E9–2**   The trial balance of Colombia Company at the end of its fiscal year, August 31, 1999, includes the following accounts: Merchandise Inventory $17,200, Purchases $142,400, Sales $190,000, Freight-in $4,000, Sales Returns and Allowances $3,000, Freight-out $1,000, and Purchase Returns and Allowances $2,000. The ending (August 31, 1999) merchandise inventory is $27,000.

*Prepare cost of goods sold section.*
*(SO 3)*

**Instructions**
Prepare a cost of goods sold section for the year ending August 31 (periodic inventory).

**E9–3**   Presented is information related to Mexico Co. for the month of January 1999.

*Prepare an income statement.*
*(SO 4)*

| | | | |
|---|---|---|---|
| Freight-in | $10,000 | Rent expense | 19,000 |
| Freight-out | 5,000 | Salary expense | 61,000 |
| Insurance expense | 12,000 | Sales discounts | 8,000 |
| Purchases | 200,000 | Sales returns and allowances | 13,000 |
| Purchase discounts | 3,000 | Sales | 312,000 |
| Purchase returns and allowances | 6,000 | | |

Beginning merchandise inventory was $42,000 and ending inventory was $63,000.

> **Exercises, which are more difficult than Brief Exercises, help you continue to build your confidence. (Keyed to Study Objectives.)**

---

> **Spreadsheet Problems, identified by** **, are selected exercises and problems that can be solved using the spreadsheet software *Solving Principles of Accounting Problems Using Lotus 1-2-3 and Excel for Windows.***

**406**   Chapter 9 • Inventories

**Instructions**
Calculate the inventory turnover ratio, days in inventory, and gross profit rate (from Chapter 5) for Linda Wasicsko Corporation for 1997, 1998, 1999. Comment on any trends.

**\*E9–12**   The inventory of DeBeers Company was destroyed by fire on March 1. From an examination of the accounting records, the following data for the first 2 months of the year are obtained: Sales $51,000, Sales Returns and Allowances $1,000, Purchases $28,200, Freight-in $1,200, and Purchase Returns and Allowances $1,400.

*Determine merchandise lost using the gross profit method of estimating inventory.*
*(SO 10)*

**Instructions**
Determine the merchandise lost by fire, assuming:

(a) A beginning inventory of $20,000 and a gross profit rate of 30% on net sales.
(b) A beginning inventory of $25,000 and a gross profit rate of 25% on net sales.

**\*E9–13**   Swiss Shoe Store uses the retail inventory method for its two departments: Women's Shoes and Men's Shoes. The following information

*Determine ending inventory at cost using retail method.*
*(SO 10)*

| Item |
|---|
| Beginning inventory at cost |
| Cost of goods purchased at cost |
| Net sales |
| Beginning inventory at retail |
| Cost of goods purchased at retail |

> **Two sets of Problems—Sets A and B—help you pull together and apply several concepts from the chapter. Included in these are problems that help you develop the writing skills that are so important in business. (Keyed to multiple Study Objectives.)**

**Instructions**
Compute the estimated cost of the ending inve
inventory method.

**\*E9–14**   Morocco Appliance uses a perpetual in
sets, the January 1 inventory was four sets at $60
chase was made: Jan. 10, 6 units at $640 each. T
sales: Jan. 8, 2 units and Jan. 15, 4 units.

*Apply cost flow methods to perpetual records.*
*(SO 11)*

**Instructions**
Compute the ending inventory under (1) FIFO, (2) LIFO, and (3) average cost.

## PROBLEMS: SET A

**P9–1A**   Chi Chi Lopez, a former professional golf star, operates Chi Chi's Pro Shop at Bay Golf Course. At the beginning of the current season on April 1, 1999, the ledger of Chi Chi's Pro Shop showed Cash $2,500, Merchandise Inventory $3,500, and Capital $6,000. The following transactions were completed during April.

*Journalize, post, and prepare trial balance and partial income statement.*
*(SO 2, 3, 4)*

| Apr. | 5 | Purchased golf bags, clubs, and balls on account from Balata Co. $1,600, FOB shipping point, terms 2/10, n/60. |
|---|---|---|
| | 7 | Paid freight on Balata purchase $80. |
| | 9 | Received credit from Balata Co. for merchandise returned $100. |
| | 10 | Sold merchandise on account to members $900, terms n/30. |
| | 12 | Purchased golf shoes, sweaters, and other accessories on account from Arrow Sportswear $660, terms 1/10, n/30. |
| | 14 | Paid Balata Co. in full. |
| | 17 | Received credit from Arrow Sportswear for merchandise returned $60. |
| | 20 | Made sales on account to members $700, terms n/30. |
| | 21 | Paid Arrow Sportswear in full. |
| | 27 | Granted credit to members for clothing that did not fit $30. |
| | 30 | Made cash sales $600. |
| | 30 | Received payments on account from members $1,100. |

The chart of accounts for the pro shop includes the following: No. 101 Cash, No. 112 Accounts Receivable, No. 120 Merchandise Inventory, No. 201 Accounts Payable, No. 301 Capital, No. 401 Sales, No. 412 Sales Returns and Allowances, No. 510 Purchases, No. 512 Purchase Returns and Allowances, No. 514 Purchase Discounts, No. 516 Freight-in.

> **General Ledger Problems, identified by** 💾**, are selected problems that can be solved using the *General Ledger Software* package.**

The **Broadening Your Perspective** section helps you pull together various concepts covered in the chapter and apply them to real-world business decisions.

BROADENING YOUR PERSPECTIVE

# FINANCIAL REPORTING AND ANALYSIS

**FINANCIAL REPORTING PROBLEM: Kellogg Company**

BYP9–1   The notes that accompany a company's financial statements provide informative details that would clutter the amounts and descriptions presented in the statements. Refer to the financial statements of Kellogg Company and the Notes to Consolidated Financial Statements in Appendix A.

*Instructions*
Answer the following questions. Complete the requirements in millions of dollars, as shown in Kellogg's annual report.

(a) What did Kellogg report for the
     Sheet at December 31, 1997? Dec

A **Financial Reporting Problem** directs you to study various aspects of the financial statements in Kellogg Company's 1997 Annual Report, which is packaged with the text and excerpted in Appendix A at the end of the text.

A **Comparative Analysis Problem** offers the opportunity to compare and contrast the financial reporting of Kellogg with that of a competitor, General Mills, whose financial statements are excerpted in Appendix B.

                                              Financial Reporting and Analysis   413

                       does
Kellogg use?
(d) What is the cost of sales (cost of goods sold) reported by Kellogg for 1997, 1996, and 1995? Compute the percentage of cost of sales to net sales in 1997.

**COMPARATIVE ANALYSIS PROBLEM: Kellogg Company vs. General Mills**

BYP9–2   Kellogg's financial statements are presented in Appendix A; General Mills's financial statements are presented in Appendix B.

*Instructions*
(a) Based on the information contained in these financial statements, compute the following 1997 ratios for each company:
    1. Inventory turnover ratio
    2. Average days to sell inventory
(b) What conclusions concerning the management of the inventory can be drawn from these data?

**RESEARCH ASSIGNMENT**

BYP9–3   The September 23, 1994, edition of *The Wall Street Journal* includes an article entitled "CompUSA Auctions Notebook Computers Through Bulk Sale."

*Instructions*
Read the article and answer the following inventory-related questions.

(a) At what amount did CompUSA estimate the retail value of the computers? What was the estimate made by one of the bidders?
(b) What was wrong with the computers?
(c) What were the rules of the auction as specified by CompUSA?
(d) CompUSA had just recorded a $3 million inventory writedown in the preceding quarter. Based on the information in the article, does it appear that additional writedowns were called for?

**Research Assignments** lead you to reports and articles published in various popular business periodicals for further study and analysis of key topics.

**INTERPRETING FINANCIAL STATEMENTS: Nike and Reebok**

BYP9–4   Nike and Reebok compete head-to-head in the sport shoe and sport apparel business. For both companies, inventory is a significant portion of their total assets. The following information was taken from each company's financial statements and notes to those financial statements.

**NIKE, INC.**

**Inventory note**
Inventories are stated at the lower of cost or market. Cost is determined using the last-in, first-out (LIFO) method for substantially all U.S. inventories. Non-U.S. inventories are valued on a first-in, first-out (FIFO) basis.

Inventories by major classification are as follows (in thousands):

|                  | May 31 | |
| --- | --- | --- |
|                  | 1997 | 1996 |
| Finished goods   | $1,248,401 | $ 874,700 |
| Work-in-process  | 50,245 | 28,940 |
| Raw materials    | 39,994 | 27,511 |

Other information for Nike:

|                    | May 31 | |
| --- | --- | --- |
|                    | 1997 | 1996 |
| Inventory          | $1,338,640 | $ 931,151 |
| Cost of goods sold | 5,502,993 | 3,906,746 |

**Interpreting Financial Statements** ask you to read parts of financial statements of actual companies and to interpret that information in light of concepts presented in the chapter.

**REAL-WORLD FOCUS: General Motors Corporation**

**BYP9–5** **General Motors** is the largest producer of automobiles in the world, as well as the world's biggest industrial enterprise. After stumbling in the early 1990s, GM has enacted numerous cost-cutting measures, including downsizing and renegotiating contracts with suppliers. In addition, it has shifted more of its resources to the hot-selling truck market.

The annual report of General Motors Corporation disclosed the following information about its accounting for inventories:

**GENERAL MOTORS CORPORATION**
**Notes to the Financial Statements**

**Note 5.   Inventories**
Major Classes of Inventories (in millions)

|  | December 31 | |
|---|---|---|
|  | 1995 | 1994 |
| Productive material, work in process, and supplies | $ 6,570.4 | $5,478.3 |
| Finished product, service parts, etc. | 4,959.1 | 4,649.5 |
| Total | $11,529.5 | $10,127.8 |
| Memo: Increase in LIFO inventories if valued at FIFO | $ 2,424.4 | $2,535.9 |

Inventories are stated generally at cost, which is not in excess of market. The cost of substantially all U.S. inventories other than the inventories of Saturn Corporation (Saturn) and Hughes is determined by the last-in, first-out (LIFO) method. The cost of non-U.S., Saturn, and Hughes inventories is determined generally by the first-in, first-out (FIFO) or average cost methods.

> The **Real-World Focus** asks you to apply concepts presented in the chapter to specific situations faced by actual companies.

**Instructions**
(a) What is meant by "inventories are stated generally at cost, which is not in excess of market"?
(b) The company uses LIFO for most of its inventory. What impact does this have on reported ending inventory if prices are increasing?
(c) General Motors uses different inventory methods for different types of inventory. Why might it do this?

# CRITICAL THINKING

**GROUP DECISION CASE**

**BYP9–6** On April 10, 1998, fire damaged the office and warehouse of Gibson Company. Most of the accounting records were destroyed but the following account balances were determined as of March 31, 1998: Merchandise Inventory, January 1, 1998, $80,000; Sales (January 1–March 31, 1998), $150,000; Purchases (January 1–March 31, 1998), $84,000.

The company's fiscal year ends on December 31, and it uses a periodic inventory system.

From an analysis of the April bank statement you discover cancelled checks of $4,200 during the period April 1–10 for cash purchases. Deposits during the same period totaled $18,500 of which 60% were collections on accounts receivable and the balance was cash sales.

Correspondence with the company's principal suppliers revealed $12,400 of purchases on account from April 1 to April 10 of which $1,800 was for merchandise in transit on April 10 that was shipped FOB destination.

Correspondence with the company's principal customers produced acknowledgments of credit sales totaling $28,000 from April 1 to April 10. It was estimated that $4,600 of credit sales will never be acknowledged or recovered from customers.

Gibson Company reached an agreement with the insurance company that its fire-loss claim should be based on the average of the gross profit rates for the preceding 2 years. The financial statements for 1996 and 1997 showed the following data:

|  | 1997 | 1996 |
|---|---|---|
| Net sales | $600,000 | $480,000 |
| Cost of goods purchased | 416,000 | 356,000 |
| Beginning inventory | 60,000 | 40,000 |
| Ending inventory | 80,000 | 60,000 |

...cost of $19,000 was salvaged from the fire.

...vided into groups, answer the following:
...e the balances in (1) Sales and (2) Purchases at April 10.
...e the average profit rate for the years 1996 and 1997. (*Hint:* Find the gross
...e for each year and divide the sum by 2.)
*(c) Determine the inventory loss as a result of the fire, using the gross profit method.

**COMMUNICATION ACTIVITY**

**BYP9–7** You are the controller of Small Toys Inc. Joe Paisley, the president, recently mentioned to you that he found an error in the 1998 financial statements which he believes has corrected itself. He determined, in discussions with the Purchasing Department, that 1998 ending inventory was overstated by $1 million. Joe says that the 1999 ending inventory is correct, thus he assumes that 1999 income is correct. Joe says to you, "What happened has happened—there's no point in worrying about it anymore."

**Instructions**
You conclude that Joe is incorrect. Write a brief, tactful memo to Joe, clarifying the situation.

**ETHICS CASE**

**BYP9–8** Lonergan Wholesale Corp. uses the LIFO method of inventory costing. In the current year, profit at Lonergan is running unusually high. The corporate tax rate is also high this

> **Communication Activities** ask you to engage in real-world business situations using writing, speaking, or presentation skills.

> The **Group Decision Case** helps you build decision-making skills by analyzing accounting information in a less structured situation. These cases require evaluation of a manager's decision or lead to a decision among alternative courses of action. As group activities, they prepare you for the business world, where you will be working with many people, by giving you practice in solving problems with colleagues.

> Through the **Ethics Cases**, you will reflect on typical ethical dilemmas and decide on an appropriate course of action.

416    Chapter 9 • Inventories

year, but it is scheduled to decline significantly next year. In an effort to lower current year's net income and to take advantage of the changing income tax rate, the president of Lonergan Wholesale instructs the plant accountant to recommend to the purchasing department a large purchase of inventory for delivery 3 days before the end of the year. The price of the inventory to be purchased has doubled during the year and the purchase will represent a major portion of the ending inventory value.

> **Surfing the Net exercises guide you to Net sites where you can find and analyze information related to the chapter topic.**

f this transaction on this year's and next year's income statement
nse? Why?
ale had been using the FIFO method of inventory costing, would
e same directive?
countant order the inventory purchase to lower income? What are
ons of this order?

# SURFING THE NET

BYP9–9   A company's annual report usually will identify the inventory method used. Knowing that, you can analyze the effects of the inventory method on the income statement and balance sheet.

**Address:** http://www.cisco.com

**Steps:**
1. From Cisco System's homepage, use the **quick search**, type annual report.
2. Choose **Search**.
3. Choose **Cisco System Annual Report**.
4. Choose **Financial Review**.
5. Use the financial statements and relating notes to the financial statements to answer the questions below.

*Instructions*
Answer the following questions:
(a) At Cisco's fiscal year-end, what was the net i
(b) How has this changed from the previous fisc
(c) How much of the inventory was finished goo
(d) What inventory method do they use?

> **Answers to Self-Study Questions provide feedback on your understanding of concepts.**

*Answers to Self-Study Questions*
1. b    2. d    3. a    4. a    5. b    6. c    7. d    8. c    9. d    10. d    *11. b
12. b    13. d    *14. d

*Answer to Kellogg Review It Question 5, p. 385.*
Kellogg Company reported inventories of $434,300,000 at December 31, 1997. Kellogg reports in Note 1—Accounting Policies that it uses the **average cost method** in applying product costs to inventories and cost of goods sold.

**Remember to go back to the Navigator box on the chapter-opening page and check off your completed work.**

> **After you complete your homework assignments, it's a good idea to go back to The Navigator checklist at the start of the chapter to see if you have used all the study aids of the chapter.**

# HOW DO YOU LEARN BEST?

Now that you have looked at your Owner's Manual, take time to find out how you learn best. This quiz was designed to help you find out something about your preferred learning method. Research on left brain/right brain differences and also on learning and personality differences suggests that each person has preferred ways to receive and communicate information. After taking the quiz, we will help you pinpoint the study aids in this text that will help you learn the material based on your learning style.

Circle the letter of the answer that best explains your preference. If a single answer does not match your perception, please circle two or more choices. Leave blank any question that does not apply.

1. You are about to give directions to a person. She is staying in a hotel in town and wants to visit your house. She has a rental car. Would you
   V) draw a map on paper?
   R) write down the directions (without a map)?
   A) tell her the directions?
   K) pick her up at the hotel in your car?

2. You are staying in a hotel and have a rental car. You would like to visit friends whose address/location you do not know. Would you like them to
   V) draw you a map on paper?
   R) write down the directions (without a map)?
   A) tell you the directions by phone?
   K) pick you up at the hotel in their car?

3. You have just received a copy of your itinerary for a world trip. This is of interest to a friend. Would you
   A) call her immediately and tell her about it?
   R) send her a copy of the printed itinerary?
   V) show her on a map of the world?

4. You are going to cook a dessert as a special treat for your family. Do you
   K) cook something familiar without need for instructions?
   V) thumb through the cookbook looking for ideas from the pictures?
   R) refer to a specific cookbook where there is a good recipe?
   A) ask for advice from others?

5. A group of tourists has been assigned to you to find out about national parks. Would you
   K) drive them to a national park?
   R) give them a book on national parks?
   V) show them slides and photographs?
   A) give them a talk on national parks?

6. You are about to purchase a new stereo. Other than price, what would most influence your decision?
   A) A friend talking about it.
   K) Listening to it.
   R) Reading the details about it.
   V) Its distinctive, upscale appearance.

7. Recall a time in your life when you learned how to do something like playing a new board game. (Try to avoid choosing a very physical skill, e.g., riding a bike.) How did you learn best? By
   V) visual clues—pictures, diagrams, charts?
   A) listening to somebody explaining it?
   R) written instructions?
   K) doing it?

8. Which of these games do you prefer?
   V) *Pictionary*
   R) *Scrabble*
   K) Charades

9. You are about to learn to use a new program on a computer. Would you
   K) ask a friend to show you?
   R) read the manual that comes with the program?
   A) telephone a friend and ask questions about it?

10. You are not sure whether a word should be spelled "dependent" or "dependant." Do you
    R) look it up in the dictionary?
    V) see the word in your mind and choose the best way it looks?
    A) sound it out in your mind?
    K) write both versions down?

11. Apart from price, what would most influence your decision to buy a particular textbook?
    K) Using a friend's copy.
    R) Skimming parts of it.
    A) A friend talking about it.
    V) It looks OK.

12. A new movie has arrived in town. What would most influence your decision to go or not to go?
    A) Friends talked about it.
    R) You read a review of it.
    V) You saw a preview of it.

13. Do you prefer a lecturer/teacher who likes to use
    R) handouts and/or a textbook?
    V) flow diagrams, charts, slides?
    K) field trips, labs, practical sessions?
    A) discussion, guest speakers?

**Results:** To determine your learning preference, add up the number of individual Vs, As, Rs, and Ks you have circled. Match the letter you have recorded most frequently to the same letter in the Learning Styles Chart. Next to each letter in the Chart are suggestions that will refer you to different learning aids throughout this text.

# LEARNING STYLES CHART

## VISUAL

**V**

| WHAT TO DO IN CLASS | WHAT TO DO WHEN STUDYING | TEXT FEATURES THAT MAY HELP YOU THE MOST | WHAT TO DO PRIOR TO AND DURING EXAMS |
|---|---|---|---|
| Underline. Use different colors. Use symbols, charts, arrangements on the page. | Use the "In Class" strategies. Reconstruct images in different ways. Redraw pages from memory. Replace words with symbols and initials. | **The Navigator** **Feature Story** **Preview** **Infographics/Illustrations** **Photos** **Accounting in Action** **Accounting Equation Analyses** **Key Terms in blue** **Words in bold** **Questions/Exercises/ Problems** **Financial Reporting Problem** **Comparative Analysis Problem** **Interpreting Financial Statements** **Research Assignments** **Surfing the Net** | Recall the "pictures of the pages." Draw, use diagrams where appropriate. Practice turning visuals back into words. |

## AURAL

**A**

| WHAT TO DO IN CLASS | WHAT TO DO WHEN STUDYING | TEXT FEATURES THAT MAY HELP YOU THE MOST | WHAT TO DO PRIOR TO AND DURING EXAMS |
|---|---|---|---|
| Attend lectures and tutorials. Discuss topics with students. Explain new ideas to other people. Use a tape recorder. Describe overheads, pictures, and visuals to somebody not there. Leave space in your notes for later recall. | You may take poor notes because you prefer to listen. Therefore: Expand your notes. Put summarized notes on tape and listen. Read summarized notes out loud. Explain notes to another "aural" person. | **Infographics/Illustrations** **Accounting in Action** **Review It/Do It** **Summary of Study Objectives** **Glossary** **Demonstration Problem** **Self-Study Questions** **Questions/Exercises/ Problems** **Financial Reporting Problem** **Comparative Analysis Problem** **Real-World Focus** **Group Decision Case** **Communication Activity** **Ethics Case** | Listen to your "voices" and write them down. Speak your answers. Practice writing answers to old exam questions. |

*Source*: Adapted from Neil D. Fleming and Colleen Mills, "Not Another Inventory, Rather a Catalyst for Reflections," *To Improve the Academy*, Volume II (1992), pp. 137-155. Used by permission.

# READING/WRITING

| WHAT TO DO IN CLASS | WHAT TO DO WHEN STUDYING | TEXT FEATURES THAT MAY HELP YOU THE MOST | WHAT TO DO PRIOR TO AND DURING EXAMS |
|---|---|---|---|
| Use lists, headings. Use dictionaries and definitions. Use handouts and textbooks. Read. Use lecture notes. | Write out words again and again. Reread notes silently. Rewrite ideas into other words. Organize diagrams into statements. | **The Navigator** **Feature Story** **Study Objectives** **Preview** **Review It/Do It** **Summary of Study Objectives** **Glossary** **Self-Study Questions** **Questions/Exercises/ Problems** **Writing Problems** **Financial Reporting Problem** **Comparative Analysis Problem** **Real-World Focus** **Group Decision Case** **Communication Activity** **Ethics Case** **Research Assignment** | Practice with multiple-choice questions. Write out lists. Write paragraphs, beginnings and endings. |

# KINESTHETIC

| WHAT TO DO IN CLASS | WHAT TO DO WHEN STUDYING | TEXT FEATURES THAT MAY HELP YOU THE MOST | WHAT TO DO PRIOR TO AND DURING EXAMS |
|---|---|---|---|
| Use all your senses. Go to labs, take field trips. Use trial-and-error methods. Listen to real-life examples. Use hands-on approach. | You may take notes poorly because topics do not seem relevant. Therefore: Put examples in note summaries. Use pictures and photos to illustrate. Talk about notes with another "kinesthetic" person. | **The Navigator** **Feature Story** **Preview** **Infographics/Illustrations** **Review It/Do It** **Summary of Study Objectives** **Demonstration Problem** **Self-Study Questions** **Questions/Exercises/ Problems** **Financial Reporting Problem** **Comparative Analysis Problem** **Real-World Focus** **Group Decision Case** **Communication Activity** **Research Assignment** **Surfing the Net** | Write practice answers. Role-play the exam situation. |

# SPECIAL STUDENT SUPPLEMENTS THAT HELP YOU GET THE BEST GRADE YOU CAN

## Working Papers, Volume I: Chapters 1-13 and Volume II: Chapters 13-27

These partially completed accounting forms can be used for all end-of-chapter exercises, problems, and cases. They demonstrate how to set up solution formats correctly and are directly tied to textbook assignments.

## Student Study Guide, Volume I: Chapters 1-13 and Volume II: Chapters 13-27

The Student Study Guide is a comprehensive review of accounting. In addition to guiding you through chapter content, it provides resources for use during lectures. With additional opportunities to practice your knowledge and skills, this is an excellent resource when preparing for exams.

## Self-Study Problems/Solutions Book, Volume I: Chapters 1-13 and Volume II: Chapters 13-27

This tutorial is designed to improve your ability in solving accounting principles homework assignments and exam questions through a wide selection of multiple-choice questions, exercises, and cases. The Self-Study Book also provides additional insights on how to study accounting and tips to alert you to common pitfalls.

## PowerNotes, Volume I: Chapters 1-13 and Volume II: Chapters 13-27

This handy note-taking guide includes all the PowerPoint presentations printed out three to a page, with spaces next to them for you to take notes. PowerNotes allow you to focus on the discussions at hand, instead of focusing on copying down slides projected in class.

## Financial Accounting Tutor (FAcT)

FAcT is a self-paced CD-ROM tutorial designed to review financial accounting concepts. It uses simple examples that have been carefully crafted to introduce concepts gradually. Throughout, the program emphasizes the logic underlying the accounting process. FAcT uses interactive and graphical tools to enhance the learning process. Intuitive navigation and a powerful search mechanism allow you to easily follow the tutorial from start to finish or skip to the topics you want to complete. The discussions and examples are followed by brief, interactive problems that provide immediate feedback. Built-in tools, such as an on-line financial calculator, help solve the problems.

## On-Line Business Survival Guide in Accounting

The journey of 1,000 Web sites begins with one click, and this practical guide gets you on the road. The On-Line Business Survival Guide is a brief, clear introduction to using the World Wide Web as a business research tool. Starting with the basics, this manual covers everything you need to know to become a master sleuth at finding critical information on the Internet. In addition, the guide provides a hands-on guide to using the Wall Street Journal Interactive Edition, as well as a discount offer for a subscription to the Wall Street Journal Interactive on-line.

## Business Extra Web Site at http://www.wiley.com/college/businessextra

To complement the On-Line Business Survival Guide in Ac-

counting, the Business Extra Web Site gives you instant access to a wealth of current articles dealing with all aspects of financial accounting. The articles are organized by topic, and discussion questions follow each article. You will find a password inside the On-Line Business Survival Guide that will give you access to the Business Extra Web Site.

## The Accounting Principles Web Site at http://www.wiley.com/college/weygandt

As a resource and learning tool, the Accounting Principles Web Site serves as a launching pad to numerous activities, resources, and related sites. Available through the Web site are links to companies discussed in the text, additional cases and problems, and items such as the Checklist of Key Figures and PowerPoint Presentations for download. Sample chapters of the Student Study Guide, Self-Study Book, and PowerNotes are available for download from this site, for you to try out. The site also provides a link to the Wiley Business Extra site, discussed above. Visit the site often for updated and new materials.

## Practice Sets

Practice sets expose you to a real-world simulation of maintaining a complete set of accounting records for a business. You'll find that practice sets reinforce the concepts and procedures learned in each chapter of the textbook, and show you how they are brought together to generate the accounting information that is essential in assessing the financial position and operating results of a company. The practice sets available are
- **Campus Cycle Shop**
- **Heritage Home Furniture**
- **University Bookstore, Inc.**

## General Ledger Software

The General Ledger Software program allows you to solve selected end-of-chapter text problems using a computerized accounting system. The software also allows you to complete the Campus Cycle Shop, Heritage Home Furniture, and the University Bookstore, Inc., practice sets on a computer.

## Solving Accounting Principles Problems Using Lotus 1-2-3 and Solving Accounting Principles Problems Using Excel for Windows

These electronic spreadsheet templates (available in either Lotus or Excel) allow you to complete selected end-of-chapter exercises and problems. The manuals, which include the disks, guide you step-by-step from an introduction to computers and Lotus or Excel, to completing preprogrammed spreadsheets, to designing your own spreadsheets.

## MicroStudy, A Computerized Study Guide

A computerized version of the Student Study Guide, Micro-Study is designed to provide more flexible movement through the content of the Study Guide to meet your particular needs. You can select from a number of self-study options, including: chapter summaries, chapter study objectives, and self-test questions. Multiple-choice questions offer you explanations of why the wrong choices are not correct.

# ACKNOWLEDGMENTS

During the course of the development of *Accounting Principles*, Fifth Edition, the authors benefited greatly from feedback from numerous instructors and students of accounting principles courses throughout the country, including many users of the Fourth Edition of the text. This feedback (constructive suggestions and innovative ideas) helped focus the revision on the needs of the students. We are indebted to the contributions of the following accounting professionals.

## Reviewers and Focus Group Participants for Prior Editions of *Accounting Principles*

Hector Agostini, Middlesex Community College; Linda Alderson, Cabrillo College; Marilyn Allan, Central Michigan University; Walter Allen, North Virginia Community College; Melody Ashenfelter, Southwestern Oklahoma State University; Peter Barton, University of Wisconsin-Whitewater; Abdul Baten, North Virginia Community College; Don Baynham, Eastfield College; Steven Becker, University of Wisconsin-Platteville; Harold Bland, Roosevelt University; Dennis Bolen, Augustana College; Lana Bone, West Valley College; Eugene Braun, North Virginia Community College; Russell Breslaur, Chabot College; William Brooks, Southwestern Oklahoma State University; Virginia Brunell, Diablo Valley College; Jim Bryant, Catonsville Community College; Terry Bullock, College of Dupage; Ashley Burrowes, California State University-Bakersfield; Madeline Carlin, University of Pittsburgh; Janet Cassagio, Nassau Community College; Randy Castello, West Valley College; Barbara Chiapetta, Nassau Community College; John Corradetti, Joliet Junior College; Sharon Cotton, Schoolcraft College; Carolyn Craig, Shepherd College; Mark Dawson, Indiana University of Pennsylvania; Michael Deda, Fairleigh Dickinson University; Irene Douma, Montclair State College; Charles Downing, Massasoit Community College; Roger DuFresne, Northern Essex Community College; Dean Eiteman, Indiana University of Pennsylvania; David Erlich, Queens College; Carl Fisher, Foothills College; Michael Foland, Belleville Area College; Mary Kathryn Gardner, Johnson & Wales University; Angelo Gazzola, University of Wisconsin-Fox Valley; Robert Giacoletti, Eastern Kentucky University; Debra Goorbin, Westchester Community College; Ed Gordon, Triton College; W. Michael Gough, DeAnza College; Don Green, State University of New York-Farmingdale; Gloria Halpern, Montgomery College; Margie Hamilton, Lewis & Clark Community College; Clo Hampton, West Valley College; Ken Hardy, Catonsville Community College; Patricia Harrison, University of New Orleans; John Hartwick, Bucks County Community College; Nabil Hassan, Wright State University; Alene Helling, Stark Technical College; Keith Hendrick, Wallace State College; Sid Hyder, Indiana University of Pennsylvania; Lou Jacoby, Saginaw Valley State University; Joe Kederabek, Baldwin-Wallace College; Janice Kelley, St. Louis Community College; Robert Kirsch, Bowling Green State University; Carol Klinger, Queens College; Jeanette Klosterman, Hutchinson Community College; Roann Kopel, Eastern Illinois University; John Lannen, Salem State College; Doug Larson, Salem State College; Kathy Larson, Middlesex Community College; Larry Larson, Triton College; Marcella Lecky, University of Southwestern Louisiana; Henri LeClerc, Suffolk Community College; Garry Lym, Golden Gate University; Johnnie Mapp, Norfolk State University; Mary Maury, St. John's University; Jean McKenzie, Fergus Falls Community College; Noel McKeon, Florida Community College-Jacksonville; Greg Mostyn, Mission College; Rhonda Mulkonen, University of South Dakota; Deborah Niemer, Oakland Community College-Royal Oak; Betty Nolen, Floyd Junior College; Cletus O'Drobinak, South Suburban College; Lynn Mazzola Paluska, Nassau Community College; Sandra Penn, Wayne State University; Wayne Pfingsten, Belleville Area College; Rose Marie Pilcher, Abilene Christian University; Beverly Piper, Ashland University; Paul Polachek, Loyola University of Chicago; Kay Poston, Arizona State University-West Campus; Charles Reilly, Suffolk Community College; Bill Reynolds, St. Charles Community College; James Rosa, Queensborough Community College; Victoria Rymer, University of Maryland; Stephen Schaefer, Contra Costa College; Barry Smith, DeAnza College; Jerome Spallino, Westmoreland Community College; Carolyn Strikler, Ohlone College; John Sullivan, North Shore Community College; Karen Ulbrich, Parkland College; DuWayne Wacker, University of North Dakota; Janis Waivio, Delta College; Daniel Ward, Southwest Louisiana State University; Michael Watters, New Mexico State University; John Wells, Triton College; Robert Wernagel, College of the Mainland; Kathleen Wessman, Montgomery College; Steven Wong, San Jose City College

## Survey Respondents

James Abbott, Broome Community College; Jill Estes Bailey, Abilene Christian University; Peter Barton, University of Wisconsin, Whitewater; Chris Bennett, Taylor University; Mary Bochnak, Hamline University; Michael Brown, Abilene Christian University; M. Patrick Joseph Cahill, R.S.H.M., Marymount University; Joseph D'Adamo, Providence College; S. T. Desai, Cedar Village College; Pamela Druger, Augustana College; Jim Dunigan, University of Wisconsin, Stevens Point; Larry Edwards, Tarrant County South Junior College; Harold Goldde, Marshall University; Mary Greenawalt, The Citadel; Vicki Greshik, Jamestown College; Sue Gunkel, Albuquerque T-VI; John Hartwick, Bucks County Community College; Candie Humphrey, University of Dubuque; Thomas Kam, Hawaii Pacific University; Kenneth Koerber, Bucks County Community College; Teresa Mack, Loras College; Don McDaniel, Clatsop Community College; Jean McKenzie, Fergus Falls Community College; Noel McKeon, Florida Community College; Ben Milchman, Queensborough Community College; Charles Mitchell, Central Carolina Community College; Sally Nelson, Northeast Iowa Community College and University of Dubuque; Jon Nitschke, Montana State University; Daniel Oliveras, Inter American University; William Radig, Marshall University; Reed Reynolds, Sheldon Jackson College; S. C. Schaefer, Contra Costa College; Richard Seek, University of South Alabama; James Segar, Southern College of Seventh-Day Adventists; Robbie Sheffy, Tarrant County South Junior College; Frank Urbancic, University of South Alabama; Du Wayne Wacker, University of North Dakota; Bea Wallace, St. Phillips College; Jack Wiehler, San Joaquin Delta College; Carolyn Woodbury, University of Montana-Missoula

## Reviewers and Focus Group Participants for *Accounting Principles*, Fifth Edition

Janet Becker, University of Pittsburgh at Johnstown; Nancy Boyd, Middle Tennessee State University; Lloyd Carroll, Borough of Manhattan Community College; Ed Castelloe, Lincoln Land Community College; Joan Cook, Milwaukee Area Technical College; Cecelia Fewox, Trident Technical College; Jeannie Folk, College of Du Page; Janet Grange, Chicago State University; Thomas Hofmeister, Northwestern Business School; Shirly Kleiner, Johnson County Community College; Robyn Lawrence, University of Scranton; Bruce Leauby, LaSalle University; Paul Lisowski, Edinboro University; Deanne Pannell, Pellissippi State Technical College; Nancy Sheridan, Bucks County Community College; Jerome Spallino, Westmoreland County Community College; Melvin Stinnett, Oklahoma Christian University; Lynda Thompson, Massasoit Community College; Cynthia Tomes, Des Moines Area Community College-Urban Campus; Chris Widmer, Tidewater Community College

## Student Reviewers for Prior Editions of *Accounting Principles*—Schools

Appalachian State University; Hofstra University; Nassau Community College; North Carolina A & M University; Ohlone State College; Phoenix College; Providence College, Queensborough Community College; University of Maine-Bangor; University of Texas-San Antonio; Wake Forest Technical College

## Student Reviewers for *Accounting Principles*, Fifth Edition

College of Lake County—Professor: Sharon Grove, Student Reviewer: Sheila Anderson, Professor: John Mason, Student Reviewer: Scott Parkerson; Massasoit Community College—Professor: Lynda Thompson, Student Reviewer: Khris Hovagimian; Ocean County Community College—Student Reviewer: Eli Oelbaum; University of Scranton—Professor: Robyn Lawrence, Student Reviewers: Marissa Marsico, Jennifer Medalis; University of Southwestern Louisiana—Professor: Marc Giullian, Student Reviewer: Sloan Richard, Professor: Kathy Hsu, Student Reviewer: Michelle Bryant

## Reviewers of Supplements for *Accounting Principles*, Fifth Edition

Jim Benedum, Milwaukee Area Technical College; Joan Cook, Milwaukee Area Technical College; Gaspare DiLorenzo, Gloucester County College; David Erlach, Queens College; Mark Holtzman, Hofstra University; Phil Kishimori, Leeward Community College; Lynn Koshiyama, University of Alaska-Anchorage; Laura Ruff, Milwaukee Area Technical College; Nathan Saltzberg, Milwaukee Area Technical College; Anita Singer, Kings College; Daniel Small, Jay Sargeant Reynolds Community College; David Zaumeyer, Rutgers University

## General Ledger Software Advisory Board

Denise Bloom, Upper Iowa University; Kevin Dooley, Kapiolani Community College; Peter Doran, North Shore Community College; Jeannie Folk, College of DuPage; Carolyn Harris, University of Texas-San Antonio; Molly Linksz, Anne Arundel Community College; Shelly Ota, Leeward Community College; Patricia A. Robinson, Johnson & Wales University; Karen Russom, North Harris Community College; Lynda Thompson, Massasoit Community College; Anne Tippitt, Tarrant County Junior College-South Campus.

## Special Thanks

Special thanks go to Joey Brenner, University of Wisconsin–Madison; Deanne Pannell, Pellissippi State Technical College; David Ravetch, University of California–Los Angeles; Barbara Trenholm, University of New Brunswick; and a very special thank you for the outstanding editorial efforts of Ann Torbert.

We also sincerely appreciate the work of our supplement authors: Anne Lee Bain, St. Cloud State University; Marianne Bradford, The University of Tennessee; Joan Cook, Milwaukee Area Technical College; Larry Falcetto, Emporia State University; Candace Humphrey, University of Dubuque; Marilyn Hunt, University of Central Florida; Verne Ingram, Red Rocks Community College; Doug Kieso, University of California-Irvine; Greg Lowry, Macon Technical Institute; Gary Lubin, Merck; Sally Nelson, Northeast Iowa Community College; Dick Wasson, Southwestern College.

We also thank those who have assured the accuracy of our supplements: Jack Borke, University of Wisconsin-Platteville; James Benedum, Milwaukee Area Technical College-South; Ed Castelloe, Lincoln Land Community College; Marc Giullian, University of Southwestern Louisiana; Lee Higgins, Southeast Community College; Phil Kishimori, Leeward Community College; Jennifer Laudermilch, Coopers & Lybrand; Scott Peterson, Northern State University; Laura Ruff, Milwaukee Area Technical College-West; Anita Singer, King's College; Teresa Speck, St. Mary's University.

In addition, special recognition goes to Ivan Pagan of the University of Wisconsin-Madison and Jo Koehn of Central Missouri State University for their work in applying Bloom's Taxonomy, to Karen Huffman of Palomar College for her assessment of the text's pedagogy and suggestions on how to increase its helpfulness to students, to Nancy Galli of Palomar College for her work on learning styles and to Wayne Higley of Buena Vista College for his technical proofing.

We also thank the editorial, marketing, production, design, and illustration staff of John Wiley & Sons. The following individuals were particularly helpful: Susan Elbe, Nancy Perry, David Kear, Joe Heider, Kate Yung, Bridget O'Lavin, Evy Fakiris, Rebecca Hope, Susan Nave, Tracy Guyton, Robert Meador, Steve Kazlauskas, Charlotte Hyland, Barbara Russiello, Laura Boucher, Madelyn Lesure, Anna Melhorn, Hilary Newman, Jennifer Atkins, Mary Ann Benson and Alison Bamert. In addition, a note of gratitude to Martha Beyerlein, Barb Lange, Ingrid Mount, and Elizabeth Jahaske of Elm Street Publishing Services and Mike Klinman of Ruttle, Shaw & Wetherill for their help on this project.

Finally, our thanks for the support provided by Will Pesce, President and Chief Executive Officer, and Bonnie Lieberman, Senior Vice-President of the College Division. Suggestions and comments from users—instructors and students alike—will be appreciated.

Jerry J. Weygandt    Donald E. Kieso    Paul D. Kimmel

# BRIEF CONTENTS

# DETAILED CONTENTS

# FEATURE STORY

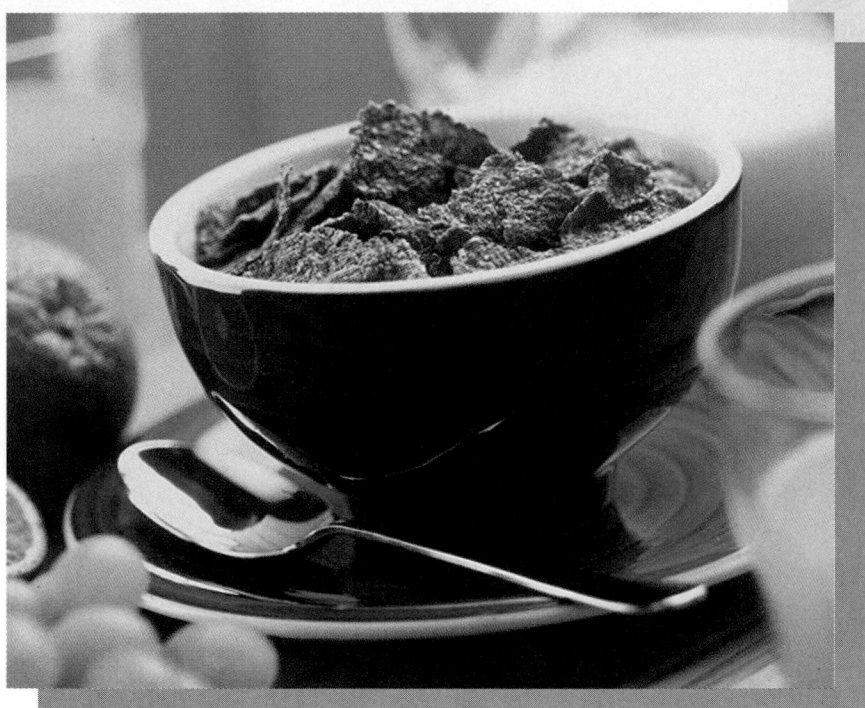

## The Best to You Each Morning

Sometimes it's better to be lucky than good. In 1894 two brothers were working on an experiment to introduce grain into the diet of sanitarium patients. Some of the grain got too wet, but they decided to roll it and toast it anyway. *Voilà*—the Kellogg brothers had just invented flaked cereal. At first they sold it by mail order, but in 1906 William Kellogg, believing he could serve a larger market, started his own company, the Battle Creek Toasted Corn Flake Company.

Today Kellogg produces 12 of the world's top 15 most popular cereals. It sells 40% of the cereal consumed in the world. How did it become so dominant? Kellogg's entrepreneurial vision was grounded in a clever marketing strategy. For example, one early promotion promised a box of cereal to any woman who winked at her grocer. Marketing has been a priority: Think about how many of Kellogg's cereal, slogans, or advertising jingles are ingrained in your memory such as *Tony the Tiger*™ *(Frosted Flakes®)* and *Snap! Crackle! and Pop!*™ *(Rice Krispies®)*. It is almost impossible to imagine growing up without *Rice Krispies Treats*™—those gooey globs of rice are a rite of passage for nearly every American child.

But it takes more than marketing to build a dominant company. Kellogg's success has also come from careful planning. Management must make many decisions: where to locate, whether to buy or rent properties, how to finance current operations and expansion, and what new products to sell. Kellogg's 14,000 employees manufacture its products in 19 countries and distribute them in 160 countries. Managing such a colossal business requires vast amounts of accounting information.

As a business becomes large, its financial needs often exceed the resources of the original owners. When this happens, the company looks for financing from lenders or from additional owners. Kellogg has approximately 27,000 owners, called shareholders. In addition, lenders and creditors have provided it with $3.8 billion. Lenders and investors will not provide financing unless they feel confident about a company's future. In order to obtain additional financing, Kellogg communicates its past performance and its plans for the future to lenders and investors through accounting information.

THE NAVIGATOR

*On the World Wide Web*
http://www.kelloggs.com

# CHAPTER 1

# ACCOUNTING IN ACTION

## THE NAVIGATOR ✔

- Understand *Concepts for Review* ☐
- Read *Feature Story* ☐
- Scan *Study Objectives* ☐
- Read *Preview* ☐
- Read text and answer *Before You Go On*
  p. 9 ☐ p. 15 ☐ p. 22 ☐ p. 26 ☐
- Work *Demonstration Problem* ☐
- Review *Summary of Study Objectives* ☐
- Answer *Self-Study Questions* ☐
- Complete assignments ☐

**The Navigator** is a learning system designed to prompt you to use the learning aids in the chapter and set priorities as you study.

## STUDY OBJECTIVES

Study Objectives give you a framework for learning the specific concepts covered in the chapter.

**After studying this chapter, you should be able to:**

1. Explain the meaning of accounting.
2. Identify the users and uses of accounting.
3. Understand why ethics is a fundamental business concept.
4. Explain the meaning of generally accepted accounting principles and the cost principle.
5. Explain the meaning of the monetary unit assumption and the economic entity assumption.
6. State the basic accounting equation and explain the meaning of assets, liabilities, and owner's equity.
7. Analyze the effect of business transactions on the basic accounting equation.
8. Prepare an income statement, owner's equity statement, balance sheet, and statement of cash flows.

THE NAVIGATOR

*T*he opening story about the Kellogg Company highlights the need for accurate and sound reporting of financial information. It follows that regardless of one's pursuits or occupation, the need for financial information is inescapable. You cannot earn a living, spend money, buy on credit, make an investment, or pay taxes without receiving, using, or dispensing financial information. Good decision making depends on good information.

The purpose of this chapter is to show you that accounting is the system used to provide useful financial information. The content and organization of the chapter are as follows:

The **Preview** describes and outlines the major topics and subtopics you will see in the chapter.

THE NAVIGATOR

# WHAT IS ACCOUNTING?

**1**

STUDY

OBJECTIVE

Explain the meaning of accounting.

As a financial information system, accounting is a process of three activities: **identifying**, **recording**, and **communicating** the economic events of an organization (business or nonbusiness) to interested users of the information. Let's take a closer look at these three activities:

Essential terms are printed in blue when they first appear, and are defined in the end-of-chapter glossary.

1. The first part of the process—**identifying**—involves selecting those events that are considered **evidence of economic activity relevant to a particular organization.** The sale of goods by Kellogg Company, the rendering of services by American Telephone & Telegraph, the payment of wages by Ford Motor Company, and the collection of ticket and broadcast money and the payment of expenses by major league sports teams are examples of economic events.

2. Once identified and measured in dollars and cents, economic events are **recorded** to provide a permanent history of the financial activities of the organization. Recording consists of keeping a **chronological diary of measured events in an orderly and systematic manner**. In recording, economic events are also classified and summarized.

3. This identifying and recording activity is of little use unless the information is **communicated** to interested users. The information is communicated through the **preparation and distribution of accounting reports**, the most common of which are called **financial statements**. To make the reported financial information meaningful, accountants describe and report the recorded data in a standardized way. Information resulting from similar transactions is accumulated and totaled. Such data are said to be reported **in the aggregate.** For example, all sales transactions of Kellogg Company are accumulated over a certain period of time and reported as one amount in the financial statements of Kellogg Company. By presenting the recorded data in the aggregate, the accounting process simplifies a multitude of transactions and renders a series of activities understandable and meaningful.

*References throughout the chapter tie the accounting concepts you are learning to the story that opened the chapter.*

A vital element in communicating economic events is the accountant's ability and responsibility to **analyze** and **interpret** the reported information. Analysis involves the use of ratios, percentages, graphs, and charts to highlight significant financial trends and relationships. Interpretation involves **explaining the uses, meaning, and limitations of reported data**. Appendix A of this textbook illustrates the financial statements and accompanying notes and graphs from Kellogg Company; Appendix B illustrates the financial statements of General Mills. We refer to these statements at various places throughout the text. At this point, they probably strike you as complex and confusing. By the end of this course, you'll be surprised at how much about them you understand.

In summary, the accounting process may be diagrammed as follows:

**ILLUSTRATION 1-1**

*Accounting process*

**Communication**

**Identification**

Select economic events (transactions)

**Recording**

Record, classify, and summarize

Prepare accounting reports

Analyze and interpret for users

Accounting should consider the needs of the users of financial information. As a consequence, you should know who these users are and something about their needs for information.

## Who Uses Accounting Data

Because it communicates financial information about a business enterprise, accounting is often called "the language of business." The information that a specific user of financial information needs depends upon the kinds of decisions that

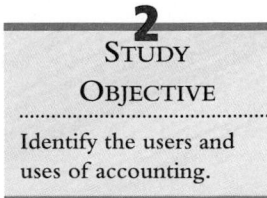

**2**
**STUDY**
**OBJECTIVE**

Identify the users and uses of accounting.

user makes. The differences in the decisions divide the users of financial information into two broad groups: internal users and external users.

## Internal Users

**ILLUSTRATION 1-2**

*Questions asked by internal users*

**Internal users** of accounting information are managers who plan, organize, and run a business. These include **marketing managers, production supervisors, finance directors, and company officers.** In running a business, managers must answer many important questions, as shown in Illustration 1-2.

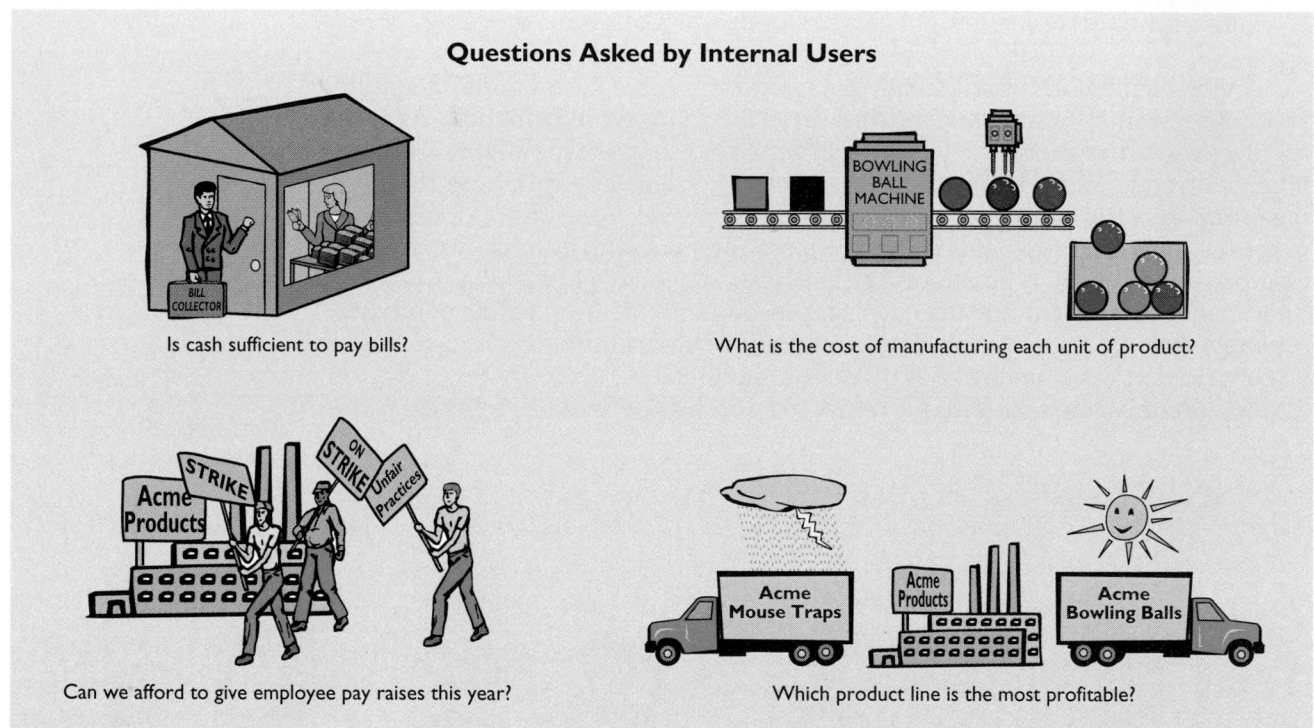

**Questions Asked by Internal Users**

Is cash sufficient to pay bills?

What is the cost of manufacturing each unit of product?

Can we afford to give employee pay raises this year?

Which product line is the most profitable?

To answer these and other questions, you need detailed information on a timely basis. For internal users, accounting provides internal reports, such as financial comparisons of operating alternatives, projections of income from new sales campaigns, and forecasts of cash needs for the next year. In addition, summarized financial information is presented in the form of financial statements.

## External Users

There are several types of **external users** of accounting information. **Investors** (owners) use accounting information to make decisions to buy, hold, or sell stock. **Creditors** such as suppliers and bankers use accounting information to evaluate the risks of granting credit or lending money. Some questions that may be asked by investors and creditors about a company are shown in Illustration 1-3.

The information needs and questions of other external users vary considerably. **Taxing authorities,** such as the Internal Revenue Service, want to know whether the company complies with the tax laws. **Regulatory agencies,** such as the Securities and Exchange Commission or the Federal Trade Commission, want to know whether the company is operating within prescribed rules. **Customers** are interested in whether a company will continue to honor product warranties

**HELPFUL HINT**
The IRS requires businesses to retain records that can be audited. Also, the Foreign Corrupt Practices Act requires public companies to keep records.

**ILLUSTRATION 1-3**
*Questions asked by external users*

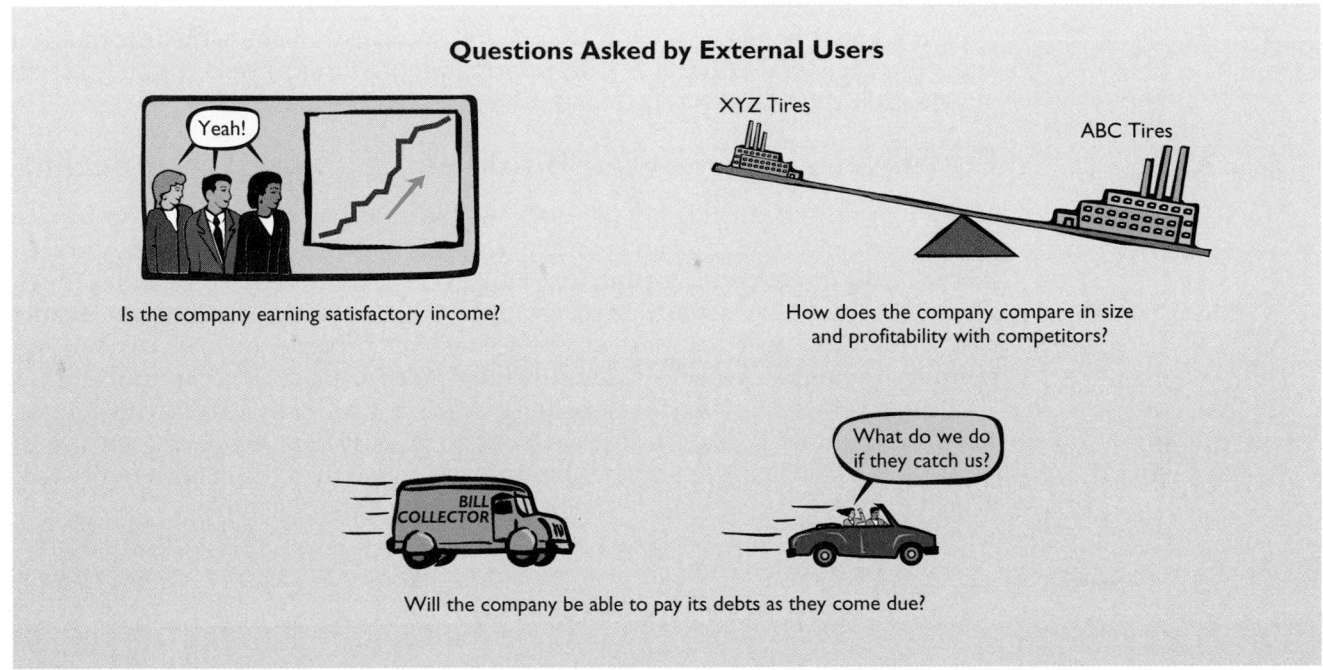

**Questions Asked by External Users**

Is the company earning satisfactory income?

How does the company compare in size and profitability with competitors?

Will the company be able to pay its debts as they come due?

and otherwise support its product lines. **Labor unions** want to know whether the owners have the ability to pay increased wages and benefits. **Economic planners** use accounting information to analyze and forecast economic activity.

# ACCOUNTING IN ACTION
## International Insight

When the chief engineer of Irkutsk Energo, a public utility in Moscow, addressed a gathering of international investors recently, he provided them with all kinds of financial information about the company. The reason: Russians are learning that corporate openness lures much-needed foreign investment. Foreign investors, however, have been reluctant to invest because Russian firms have been secretive (and sometimes deceptive) about their financial affairs. Now, however, things will probably change because firms such as Irkutsk Energo have enjoyed stock price surges after providing candid accounting information. In short, good accounting information may help Russia solve some of its economic problems.

*Source: The Wall Street Journal, June 9, 1995, p. A-6.*

Accounting in Action examples illustrate important and interesting accounting situations in business.

## Brief History of Accounting

The **origins of accounting** are generally attributed to the work of Luca Pacioli, a famous Italian Renaissance mathematician. Pacioli was a close friend and tutor to Leonardo da Vinci and a contemporary of Christopher Columbus. In his text *Summa de Arithmetica, Geometria, Proportione et Proportionalite*, Pacioli described a system to ensure that financial information was recorded efficiently and accurately.

With the advent of the **industrial age** in the nineteenth century and, later, the emergence of large corporations, a separation of the owners from the managers of businesses took place. As a result, the need to report the status of the business enterprise took on increasing importance, to ensure that managers acted in accord with owners' wishes. In addition, transactions between businesses became more complex, making necessary improved approaches for reporting financial information.

Our economy has now evolved into a post-industrial age—**the information age**—in which the "products" are information services. The computer, as the information processor, has been the driver of the information age.

## Distinguishing between Bookkeeping and Accounting

Many individuals mistakenly consider bookkeeping and accounting to be one and the same. This confusion is understandable because the accounting process **includes the bookkeeping function.** However, accounting also includes much more. Bookkeeping **usually involves only the recording of economic events** and is therefore just one part of the accounting process. In total, **accounting involves the entire process of identification, recording, and communication.**

The bookkeeping function is often performed by individuals with limited skills in accounting. As a result, it is not surprising that the increased use of computers by business enterprises has resulted in much of the detailed work that is part of the bookkeeping process being performed by machines.

## TECHNOLOGY IN ACTION

With the phenomenal growth in computers, more and more record keeping is being performed electronically. Businesses, small as well as large, are finding that through the use of the computer the entire recording process has become more efficient. However, it is important to know the procedures used in a manual system to understand the operations a computer performs.

**Technology in Action** examples show how computer technology is used in accounting and business.

## Accounting and You

One question frequently asked by students of accounting is, "How will the study of accounting help me?" It should help you a great deal, because a working knowledge of accounting is desirable for virtually every field of endeavor. Some illustrations of how accounting is used in other careers include:

**General management:** Imagine running General Motors, a major hospital, a school, a McDonald's franchise, a bike shop; all general managers need to understand and have access to accounting data in order to make wise business decisions.

**Marketing/Advertising:** A marketing specialist is someone who develops strategies to help the sales force be successful. But making a sale is meaningless unless it is a profitable sale. Marketing people must be sensitive to costs and benefits, which accounting helps them quantify and understand.

Marketing people are also involved in advertising. What would a flashy field such as advertising have to do with accounting? If you buy a commercial on a radio station, you'll want to know the cost per thousand listeners. You'll deal in ratings numbers and budgets all day. And ad agencies are always under pressure to cut costs, because their clients can be very fickle—particularly if the ad campaign doesn't work.

**Finance:** Do you want to be a banker, an investment analyst, a stock broker? These fields rely heavily on accounting. Suppose you decide to go into banking. You could become a lending officer, a money manager, a deal-maker, a foreign currency trader, or a retail branch supervisor. Whatever the situation, you will regularly examine and analyze financial statements. In fact, it is difficult to get a good job in a finance function without two or three courses in accounting.

**Real estate:** Perhaps the most prevalent career in real estate is that of a broker, a person who sells residential or commercial real estate. Because a third party—the bank—is almost always involved in financing a real estate transaction, brokers must understand the numbers involved: Can the buyer of the house afford to make the payments to the bank on a given salary? Does the cash flow from the industrial property justify the purchase price in this market? What are the tax benefits of making the purchase?

Accounting is useful even for occupations you might think completely unrelated. If you become a doctor, a lawyer, a social worker, a teacher, an engineer, an architect, or an entrepreneur—you name it—a working knowledge of accounting is relevant.

## The Accounting Profession

What would you do if you joined the accounting profession? You probably would apply your expertise in one of three major fields—public accounting, private accounting, or not-for-profit accounting.

### Public Accounting

In public accounting, you would offer expert service to the general public in much the same way that a doctor serves patients and a lawyer serves clients. A major portion of public accounting practice is involved with auditing. In this area, a certified public accountant (CPA) examines the financial statements of companies and expresses an opinion as to the fairness of presentation. When the presentation is fair, users consider the statements to be **reliable**. For example, Kellogg's investors and creditors would demand audited financial statements before extending it financing.

Taxation is another major area of public accounting. The work performed by tax specialists includes tax advice and planning, preparing tax returns, and representing clients before governmental agencies such as the Internal Revenue Service.

A third area in public accounting is management consulting. Management consulting ranges from the installing of basic computerized accounting systems to helping companies determine whether they should use the space shuttle for high-tech research and development projects.

### Private Accounting

Instead of working in public accounting, an accountant may be an employee of a business enterprise. In private (or managerial) accounting, you would be involved in one of the following activities:

1. **Cost accounting**—determining the cost of producing specific products.
2. **Budgeting**—assisting management in quantifying goals concerning revenues, costs of goods sold, and operating expenses.
3. **General accounting**—recording daily transactions and preparing financial statements and related information.
4. **Accounting information systems**—designing both manual and computerized data processing systems.

5. **Tax accounting**—preparing tax returns and engaging in tax planning for the company.
6. **Internal auditing**—reviewing the company's operations to determine compliance with management policies and evaluating the efficiency of operations.

From the above, you can see that within a specific company, private accountants perform as wide a variety of duties as the public accountant.

Illustration 1-4 presents the general career paths in public and private accounting.

**ILLUSTRATION 1-4**

*Career paths in public and private accounting*

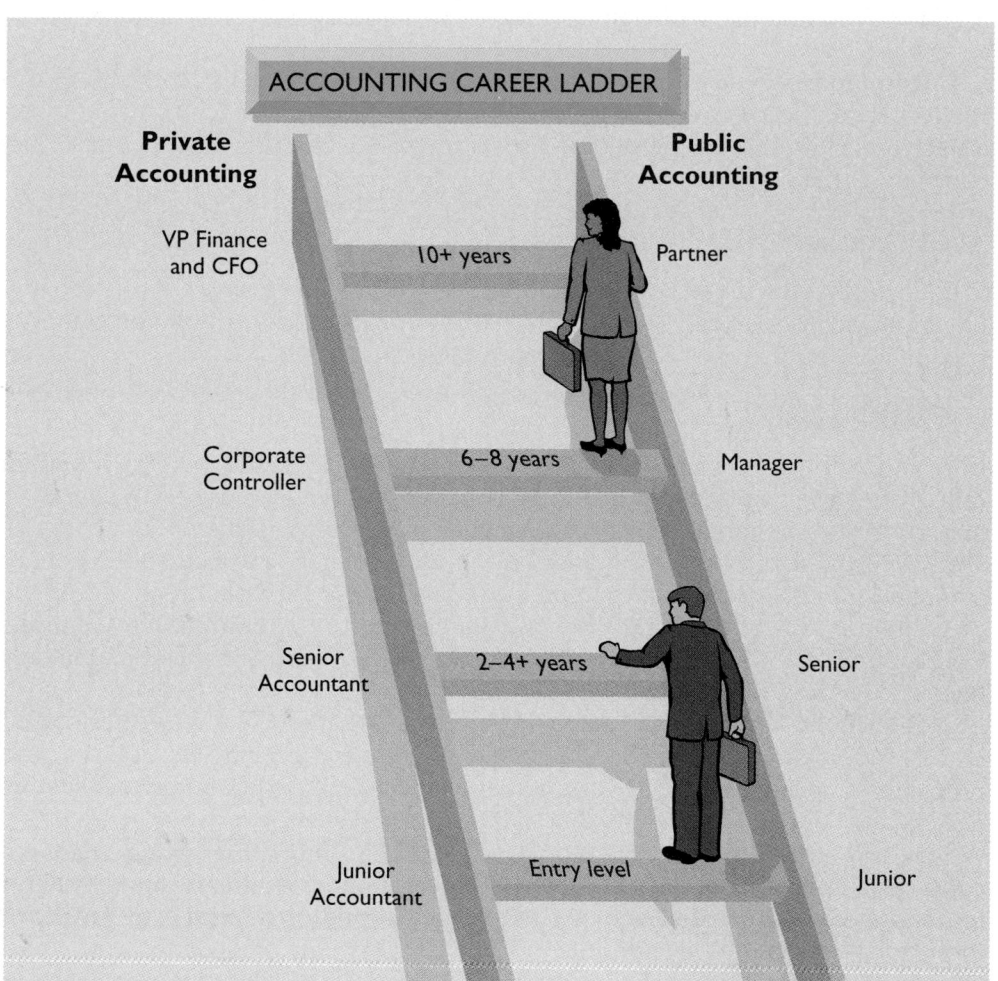

### Not-for-Profit Accounting

Like businesses that exist to make a profit, not-for-profit organizations also need sound financial reporting and control. Donors to such organizations as the United Way, the Ford Foundation, and the Red Cross want information about how well the organization has met its objectives and whether continued support is justified. Hospitals, colleges, and universities must make decisions about the allocation of funds. Local, state, and federal governmental units are continually providing financial information to legislators, citizens, employees, and creditors. At the federal level, the largest employers of accountants are the Internal Revenue Service, the General Accounting Office, the Federal Bureau of Investigation, and the Securities and Exchange Commission.

# ACCOUNTING IN ACTION
## Business Insight

### Help Wanted: Forensic CPAs

Tom Taylor's job at the FBI has changed. He used to pack a .357 magnum; now he wields a No. 2 pencil. Taylor, age 37, for two years an FBI agent, is a forensic accountant, somebody who sniffs through company books to ferret out white-collar crime. Demand for this service has surged in the past few years. In one recent year, a recruiter for San Diego's Robert Half International, a headhunting firm, had requests for more than 1,000 such snoops.

Qualification: a CPA with FBI, IRS, or similar government experience. Interestingly, despite its macho image, the FBI has long hired mostly accountants and lawyers as agents.

# BEFORE YOU GO ON . . .

## Review It

1. What is accounting?
2. Who uses accounting information?
3. What is the difference between bookkeeping and accounting?
4. How can you use your accounting knowledge?

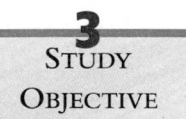

THE
NAVIGATOR

**Before You Go On** questions at the end of major text sections offer an opportunity to stop and reexamine the key points you have studied.

# THE BUILDING BLOCKS OF ACCOUNTING

Every profession develops a body of theory consisting of principles, assumptions, and standards. Accounting is no exception. Just as a doctor follows certain standards in treating a patient's illness, an accountant follows certain standards in reporting financial information. For these standards to work, however, a fundamental business concept is followed—ethical behavior.

## Ethics—A Fundamental Business Concept

Wherever you make your career—whether in accounting, marketing, management, finance, government, or elsewhere—your behavior and actions will affect other people and organizations. The standards of conduct by which one's actions are judged as right or wrong, honest or dishonest, fair or not fair, are **ethics**. Imagine trying to carry on a business, perform an audit, or invest money if you could not depend on the individuals you deal with to be honest. If managers, customers, investors, co-workers, and creditors all consistently lied, effective communication and economic activity would be impossible. Information would have no credibility.

Fortunately most individuals in business are ethical. Their actions are both legal and responsible, and they consider the organization's interests in their decision making. However, in some situations public officials, business executives, and respected leaders act unethically. For example, a former chief of the finance committee of the House of Representatives was indicted for possible illegal behavior; Sears was accused of widespread customer overcharging on car repairs; Woolworth Corp. executives were dismissed because they reported false income numbers. As one business leader noted: "We are all embarrassed by the events that make *The Wall Street Journal* read like the *Police Gazette*."

**3**
STUDY
OBJECTIVE
Understand why ethics is a fundamental business concept.

Many companies have developed corporate mission statements. Some of these mission statements include discussion of the company's ethical values. In its statement of company philosophy, for example, Kellogg Company has the following statement regarding integrity and ethics.

**ILLUSTRATION 1-5**

*Corporate ethics statement*

## KELLOGG COMPANY
### Statement of Company Philosophy

**Integrity and Ethics**
Integrity is the cornerstone of our business practice. We will conduct our affairs in a manner consistent with the highest ethical standards.
*To meet this commitment, we will:*

- Engage in fair and honest business practices.
- Show respect for each other, our consumers, customers, suppliers, shareholders and the communities in which we operate.
- Communicate in an honest, factual and accurate manner.

To sensitize you to ethical situations and to give you practice at solving ethical dilemmas, we have included in the book three types of ethics materials: (1) marginal notes that provide helpful hints for developing ethical sensitivity, (2) ethics in accounting boxes that highlight ethics situations and issues, and (3) an ethics case simulating a business situation at the end of the chapter. In the process of analyzing these ethics cases, you should apply the steps outlined in Illustration 1-6.

**ILLUSTRATION 1-6**

*Steps in analyzing ethics cases*

### Solving an Ethical Dilemma

**1. Recognize an ethical situation and the ethical issues involved.**

Use your personal ethics to identify ethical situations and issues. Some businesses and professional organizations provide written codes of ethics for guidance in some business situations.

**2. Identify and analyze the principal elements in the situation.**

Identify the *stakeholders*— persons or groups who may be harmed or benefited. Ask the question: What are the responsibilities and obligations of the parties involved?

**3. Identify the alternatives, and weigh the impact of each alternative on various stakeholders.**

Select the most ethical alternative, considering all the consequences. Sometimes there will be one right answer. Other situations involve more than one right solution; these situations require an evaluation of each and a selection of the best alternative.

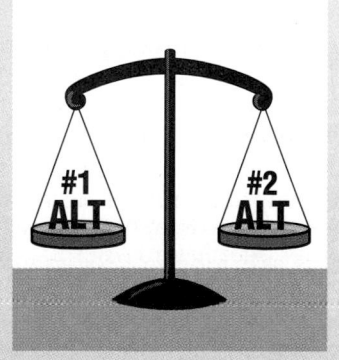

## Generally Accepted Accounting Principles

The accounting profession has attempted to develop a set of standards that is generally accepted and universally practiced. Its efforts have resulted in a common set of standards called **generally accepted accounting principles (GAAP)**. These standards indicate how to report economic events.

Two organizations are primarily responsible for establishing generally accepted accounting principles. The first is the **Financial Accounting Standards Board (FASB)**, a private organization that establishes broad reporting standards of general applicability as well as specific accounting rules. The second, the Securities and Exchange Commission (SEC), is a governmental agency that re-quires companies filing financial reports with it to follow generally accepted accounting principles. In situations where no principles exist, the SEC often mandates that certain guidelines be used. In general, the FASB and the SEC work hand in hand to assure that timely and useful accounting principles are developed.

One important principle is the cost principle, which states that assets should be recorded at their cost. **Cost is the value exchanged at the time something is acquired.** If you buy a house today, the cost is the amount you pay for it, say $100,000. If you sell the house in two years for $120,000, the sales price is its **market value**—the value determined by the market for homes at that time. At the time of acquisition, cost and fair market value are the same. In subsequent periods, cost and fair market value may vary, **but the cost amount continues to be used.**

For example, at one time, Greyhound Corporation had 128 bus stations nationwide that cost approximately $200 million. The current market value of the stations is approximately $1 billion. Under the cost principle, the bus stations are recorded and reported at $200 million, not $1 billion. Until the bus stations are actually sold, estimates of market values are considered too subjective.

As the Greyhound example indicates, cost has an important advantage over other valuations: it is reliable. Cost is definite and verifiable. The values exchanged at the time something is acquired generally can be objectively measured. To rely on the information supplied, users must know that the information is based on fact. However, critics argue that cost is often not relevant and that market values provide more useful information. Despite its shortcomings, cost continues to be used in the financial statements because of its reliability.

## Assumptions

In developing generally accepted accounting principles, certain basic assumptions are made. These assumptions provide a foundation for the accounting process. Two main assumptions are the **monetary unit assumption** and the **economic entity assumption.**

### Monetary Unit Assumption

The monetary unit assumption requires that only transaction data that can be expressed in terms of money be included in the accounting records of the economic entity. Because money is the commonly used medium of exchange, this assumption enables accounting to quantify (measure) the economic event. The monetary unit assumption is vital to applying the cost principle discussed earlier. This assumption prevents such relevant information as the health of the owner, the quality of service, and the morale of employees from being included in the accounting records because they cannot be quantified in terms of money.

**An important corollary to the monetary unit assumption is the added assumption that the unit of measure remains sufficiently constant over time.** However, the assumption of a stable monetary unit has been challenged because of the significant decline in the purchasing power of the dollar. For example, what used to cost $1.00 in 1960 costs over $4.00 in 1998. In such situations, adding, subtracting, or comparing 1960 dollars with 1998 dollars is highly questionable. The profession has recognized this problem and encourages companies to disclose the effects of changing prices.

### Economic Entity Assumption

**An economic entity can be any organization or unit in society.** It may be a business enterprise (such as General Electric Company), a governmental unit (such as the state of Ohio), a municipality (such as Seattle), a school district (such as St. Louis District 48), or a church (Southern Baptist). The economic entity assumption states that economic events can be identified with a particular unit of accountability. This assumption requires that the activities of the entity be kept separate and distinct from (1) the activities of its owner and (2) all other economic entities. To illustrate, if Sally Rider, owner of Sally's Boutique, charges any of her personal living costs as expenses of the Boutique, the economic entity assumption is violated. Similarly, the economic entity assumption assumes that the activities of Kellogg, General Mills, and Quaker Oats can each be segregated into separate economic entities for accounting purposes.

Although the economic entity assumption can be applied to any unit of accountability, we will generally discuss it in relation to a business enterprise, which may be organized as a proprietorship, partnership, or corporation.

## ACCOUNTING IN ACTION
### Ethics Insight

A violation of the economic entity assumption contributed to the resignation by the chief executive of W.R. Grace and Company. Investors were angered to learn that company funds were used for personal medical care, a Manhattan apartment, and a personal chef for the company's chief. Funds were also used to support a hotel interest owned by the chief executive's son.

**HELPFUL HINT**
Approximately 70% of United States companies are proprietorships; however, they account for only 6.5% of gross revenues. Corporations, on the other hand, are approximately 19% of all companies, but account for 90% of the revenues.

**Proprietorship.** A business owned by one person is generally a proprietorship. The owner is often the manager/operator of the business. Small service-type businesses (barber shops, law offices, plumbing companies, and auto repair shops), farms, and small retail stores (antique shops, clothing stores, and book stores) are often sole proprietorships. **Usually only a limited amount of money (capital) is necessary to start in business as a proprietorship, and the owner receives any profits, suffers any losses, and is personally liable for all debts of the business.** Although there is no legal distinction between the business as an economic unit and the owner, the records of the business activities are kept separate from the personal records and activities of the owner. Although sole proprietorships represent the largest number of businesses in the United States, they are typically the smallest in size and volume of business.

**Partnership.** A business owned by two or more persons associated as partners is a partnership. In most respects a partnership is similar to a sole proprietorship except that more than one owner is involved. When a partnership is created, an agreement (written or oral) should set forth such terms as initial investment of each partner, duties of each partner, division of net income (or net loss), and settlement to be made upon death or withdrawal of a partner. Each partner generally has unlimited personal liability for the debts of the partnership. **Like a proprietorship, for accounting purposes the partnership affairs must be kept separate from the personal activities of the partners.** Partnerships are often used to organize retail and service-type businesses, including professional practices (lawyers, doctors, architects, and certified public accountants).

**Corporation.**   A business organized as a separate legal entity under state corporation law and having ownership divided into transferable shares of stock is called a corporation. The holders of the shares (stockholders) **enjoy limited liability**; they are not personally liable for the debts of the corporate entity. Stockholders **may transfer all or part of their shares to other investors at any time** (i.e., sell their shares in the securities market). The ease with which ownership can change adds to the attractiveness of investing in a corporation. Because ownership can be transferred without dissolving the corporation, the corporation **enjoys an unlimited life**.

Although the combined number of proprietorships and partnerships in the United States is more than four times the number of corporations, the revenue produced by corporations is nine times greater. Most of the largest enterprises in the United States—for example, Exxon, General Motors, Sears Roebuck, Citicorp, and Kellogg Company—are corporations.

## Basic Accounting Equation

Other essential building blocks of accounting are the categories into which economic events are classified. The two basic elements of a business are what it owns and what it owes. **Assets** are the resources owned by a business. For example, Kellogg's competitor, General Mills, has total assets of approximately $3.9 billion. Liabilities and owner's equity are the rights or claims against these resources. Thus, a company such as General Mills that has $3.9 billion of assets also has $3.9 billion of claims against those assets. Claims of creditors are called **liabilities**. Claims of owners are called **owner's equity**. For example, General Mills has liabilities of $3.4 billion and owners' equity of $.5 billion. This equation can be expressed as follows:

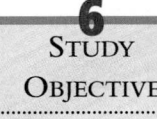

**6**
**STUDY OBJECTIVE**
State the basic accounting equation and explain the meaning of assets, liabilities, and owner's equity.

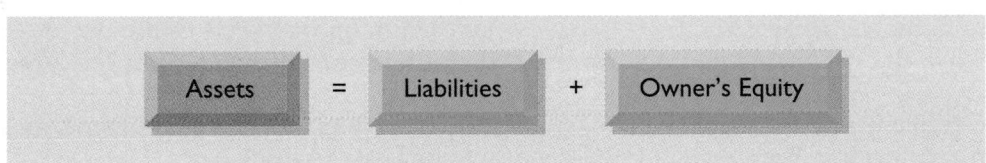

**ILLUSTRATION 1-7**

*The basic accounting equation*

This equation is referred to as the basic accounting equation. Assets must equal the sum of liabilities and owner's equity. Because creditors' claims are paid before ownership claims if a business is liquidated, liabilities are shown before owner's equity in the basic accounting equation.

The accounting equation applies to all **economic entities** regardless of size, nature of business, or form of business organization. Thus, it applies to a small proprietorship such as a corner grocery store as well as to a giant corporation such as Kellogg or General Mills. The equation provides the underlying framework for recording and summarizing the economic events of a business enterprise.

Let's look in more detail at the categories in the basic accounting equation.

**HELPFUL HINT**

In some places we use the term *owner's equity* and in others we use *owners' equity*. *Owner's* refers to one owner—the case with a sole proprietorship, and *owners'* refers to multiple owners—the case with partnerships or corporations.

### *Assets*

As indicated above, assets are resources owned by a business. Thus, they are the things of value used in carrying out such activities as production, consumption, and exchange. The common characteristic possessed by all assets is the capacity to provide future services or benefits to the entities that use them. In a business enterprise, that service potential or future economic benefit eventually results in cash inflows (receipts) to the enterprise.

For example, the enterprise Campus Pizza owns a delivery truck that provides economic benefits because it is used in delivering pizzas. Other assets of Campus Pizza are tables, chairs, jukebox, cash register, oven, mugs and silverware, and, of course, cash.

## Liabilities

Liabilities are claims against assets. Put more simply, **liabilities are existing debts and obligations**. For example, businesses of all sizes and degrees of success usually find it necessary to borrow money and to purchase merchandise on credit. Campus Pizza, for instance, purchases cheese, sausage, flour, and beverages on credit from suppliers; these obligations are called **accounts payable**. Additionally, Campus Pizza has a **note payable** to First National Bank for the money borrowed to purchase its delivery truck. Campus Pizza may also have **wages payable** to employees, and **sales and real estate taxes payable** to the local government. Persons or entities to whom Campus Pizza owes money are called **creditors**.

Most claims of creditors attach to **total** enterprise assets rather than to the specific assets provided by the creditor. In the event of nonpayment, creditors may legally force the liquidation of a business. In that case, the law requires that creditor claims be paid before ownership claims.

## Owner's Equity

The ownership claim on total assets is known as owner's equity. It is equal to total assets minus total liabilities. Here is why: The assets of a business are supplied or claimed by either creditors or owners. To determine what belongs to owners, we therefore subtract creditors' claims—the liabilities—from assets. The remainder—owner's equity—is the owner's claim on the assets of the business. Since the claims of creditors take precedence over ownership claims, the latter are often referred to as **residual equity**.

In a proprietorship, owner's equity is increased by owner's investments and revenues. It is decreased by owner's drawings and expenses.

**Investments by Owner.** Investments by owner are the assets put into the business by the owner. These investments in the business increase owner's equity.

**Drawings.** An owner may withdraw cash or other assets during the accounting period for personal use. These withdrawals could be recorded as a direct decrease of owner's equity. However, it is generally considered preferable to use a separate classification referred to as drawings to determine the total withdrawals for the accounting period. **Drawings decrease total owner's equity.**

**HELPFUL HINT**
The effect of revenues is positive—an increase in owner's equity coupled with an increase in assets or a decrease in liabilities.

**Revenues.** Revenues are the **gross increase in owner's equity resulting from business activities entered into for the purpose of earning income.** Generally, revenues result from the sale of merchandise, the performance of services, the rental of property, and the lending of money.

Revenues usually result in an increase in an asset. They may arise from different sources and are identified by various names depending on the nature of the business. Campus Pizza, for instance, has two categories of sales revenues—pizza sales and beverage sales. Other titles for and sources of revenue common to many businesses are: sales, fees, services, commissions, interest, dividends, royalties, and rent.

**Expenses.** Expenses are **the decreases in owner's equity that result from operating the business.** They are the cost of assets consumed or services used in the process of earning revenue. Expenses represent actual or expected cash outflows (payments). Like revenues, expenses take many forms and are identified by various names depending on the type of asset consumed or service used. For example, Campus Pizza recognizes the following types of expenses: cost of ingredients (meat, flour, cheese, tomato paste, mushrooms, etc.); cost of beverages; wages expense; utility expense (electric, gas, and water expense); telephone expense; delivery expense (gasoline, repairs, licenses, etc.); supplies expense (napkins, detergents, aprons, etc.); rent expense; interest expense; and property tax expense.

In summary, the principal sources (increases) of owner's equity are (1) investments by owners and (2) revenues from business operations. In contrast, reductions in owner's equity are a result of (1) withdrawals of assets by owners and (2) expenses. **Net income** results when revenues exceed expenses; conversely, a **net loss** occurs when expenses exceed revenues.

These relationships are shown in Illustration 1-8.

**HELPFUL HINT**
The effect of expenses is negative—a decrease in owner's equity coupled with a decrease in assets, or an increase in liabilities.

**ILLUSTRATION 1-8**

*Increases and decreases in owner's equity*

# BEFORE YOU GO ON . . .

## Review It

1. Why is ethics considered a fundamental business concept?
2. What are generally accepted accounting principles? Give an example of an accounting principle.
3. Explain the monetary unit and the economic entity assumptions.
4. What is the basic accounting equation? The accounting equation is: Assets = Liabilities + Owner's Equity. Replacing the words in that equation with dollar amounts, what is Kellogg's accounting equation at December 31, 1997? (*Hint:* Owner's equity is equivalent to stockholders' equity. The answer to this question is provided on page 43.)
5. What are assets, liabilities, and owner's equity?

Review It questions marked with this "Tony the Tiger" icon require that you use Kellogg's 1997 Annual Report.

## Do It

Classify the following items as investment by owner (I), owner's drawings (D), revenues (R), or expenses (E), and indicate whether these items increase or decrease owner's equity: (1) Rent Expense, (2) Service Revenue, (3) Drawings, and (4) Salaries Expense.

*Reasoning:* Both investments and revenue increase owner's equity; however, revenue arises from the sale of merchandise, the performance of services, the rental of property, or the lending of money. Investments are resources contributed to the business by the owner. Similarly, expenses and drawings decrease owner's equity; however, expenses arise from consuming assets or services. Drawings are withdrawals of cash or other assets from the business for personal use.

*Solution:*
(1) Rent Expense is classified as an expense (E); it decreases owner's equity.
(2) Service Revenue is classified as revenue (R); it increases owner's equity.
(3) Drawings is classified as owner's drawings (D); it decreases owner's equity.
(4) Salaries Expense is classified as an expense (E); it decreases owner's equity.

*Related exercise material:* BE1–1, BE1–2, BE1–3, BE1–4, BE1–5, BE1–6, BE1–7, BE1–9, E1–1, E1–2, E1–3, E1–4, E1–6, and E1–7.

THE NAVIGATOR

# USING THE BUILDING BLOCKS

**7**

STUDY
OBJECTIVE

Analyze the effect of
business transactions on
the basic accounting
equation.

Transactions (often referred to as business transactions) are the economic events of the enterprise that are recorded. Transactions may be identified as external or internal. **External transactions involve economic events between the company and some outside enterprise or party.** For example, for Campus Pizza the purchase of cooking equipment from a supplier, the payment of monthly rent to the landlord, and the sale of pizzas to customers are external transactions. **Internal transactions are economic events that occur entirely within one company.** The use of office supplies illustrates this type of transaction for Campus Pizza.

A company may carry on many activities that do not in themselves represent business transactions. Hiring employees, answering the telephone, talking with customers, and placing an order for merchandise with a supplier are examples. Some of these activities, however, may lead to a business transaction: employees will earn wages, and merchandise will be delivered by the supplier. Each transaction must be analyzed in terms of its effect on the components of the basic accounting equation. This analysis must identify the specific items affected and the amount of the change in each item. Illustration 1-9 demonstrates the transaction identification process.

**ILLUSTRATION 1-9**

*Transaction identification
process*

The equality of the basic equation must be preserved. Therefore, each transaction must have a dual effect on the equation. For example, if an individual asset is increased, there must be a corresponding:

1. Decrease in another asset, or
2. Increase in a specific liability, or
3. Increase in owner's equity.

It follows that two or more items could be affected when an asset is increased. For example, as one asset is increased $10,000, another asset could decrease $6,000, and a specific liability could increase $4,000. Note also that any change in an individual liability or ownership claim is subject to similar analysis.

## Transaction Analysis

The following examples are business transactions for a new computer programming business during its first month of operations. You will want to study these transactions until you are sure you understand them. They are not difficult but they are important to your success in this course. The ability to analyze transactions in terms of the basic accounting equation is essential for an understanding of accounting.

**Transaction (1).  Investment by Owner.**   Ray Neal decides to open a computer programming service. On September 1, 1999, he invests $15,000 cash in the business, which he names Softbyte. This transaction results in an equal increase in assets and owner's equity. In this case, there is an increase in the asset Cash, $15,000, and an equal increase in the owner's equity, R. Neal, Capital, $15,000. The effect of this transaction on the basic equation is:

| | Assets | = | Liabilities | + | Owner's Equity | |
|---|---|---|---|---|---|---|
| | Cash | = | | | R. Neal, Capital | |
| (1) | +$15,000 | = | | | +$15,000 | Investment |

Observe that the equality of the basic equation has been maintained. Note also that the source of the increase in owner's equity is indicated, to make clear that the increase is an investment rather than revenue from operations. Why does this matter? Because investments by the owner do not represent revenues, and they are excluded in determining net income.

**Transaction (2).  Purchase of Equipment for Cash.**   Softbyte purchases computer equipment for $7,000 cash. This transaction results in an equal increase and decrease in total assets, though the composition of assets is changed: Cash is decreased $7,000, and the asset Equipment is increased $7,000. Both the specific effect of this transaction and the cumulative effect of the first two transactions are:

| | | Assets | | | = | Liabilities | + | Owner's Equity |
|---|---|---|---|---|---|---|---|---|
| | | Cash | + | Equipment | = | | | R. Neal, Capital |
| | Old Bal. | $15,000 | | | | | | $15,000 |
| (2) | | −7,000 | | +$7,000 | | | | |
| | New Bal. | $ 8,000 | + | $7,000 | = | | | $15,000 |
| | | | $15,000 | | | | | |

Observe that total assets are still $15,000 and Neal's equity also remains at $15,000, the amount of his original investment.

**Transaction (3).   Purchase of Supplies on Credit.**   Softbyte purchases computer paper and other supplies expected to last several months from Acme Supply Company for $1,600. Acme Company agrees to allow Softbyte to pay this bill in October, a month later. This transaction is often referred to as a purchase on account or a credit purchase. Assets are increased by this transaction because of the expected future benefits of using the paper and supplies, and liabilities are increased by the amount due Acme Company. The asset Supplies is increased $1,600, and the liability Accounts Payable is increased by the same amount. The effect on the equation is:

|  | | Assets | | | = | Liabilities | + | Owner's Equity |
|---|---|---|---|---|---|---|---|---|
|  |  |  |  |  |  | Accounts |  | R. Neal, |
|  | Cash | + | Supplies | + | Equipment = | Payable | + | Capital |
| Old. Bal. | $8,000 | | | | $7,000 | | | $15,000 |
| (3) | | | +$1,600 | | | +$1,600 | | |
| New Bal. | $8,000 + | | $1,600 + | | $7,000 = | $1,600 | + | $15,000 |
|  | | | $16,600 | | | | $16,600 | |

Total assets are now $16,600. This total is matched by a $1,600 creditor's claim and a $15,000 ownership claim.

**Transaction (4).   Services Rendered for Cash.**   Softbyte receives $1,200 cash from customers for programming services it has provided. This transaction represents the principal revenue-producing activity of Softbyte. Recall that **revenue increases owner's equity**. Both assets and owner's equity are, then, increased by this transaction: In this case, Cash is increased $1,200, and R. Neal, Capital, is increased $1,200. The new balances in the equation are:

|  | | Assets | | | = | Liabilities | + | | Owner's Equity | |
|---|---|---|---|---|---|---|---|---|---|---|
|  |  |  |  |  |  | Accounts |  | R. Neal, | | |
|  | Cash | + | Supplies | + | Equipment = | Payable | + | Capital | | |
| Old Bal. | $8,000 | | $1,600 | | $7,000 | $1,600 | | $15,000 | | |
| (4) | +1,200 | | | | | | | +1,200 | | Service Revenue |
| New Bal. | $9,200 + | | $1,600 + | | $7,000 = | $1,600 | + | $16,200 | | |
|  | | | $17,800 | | | | $17,800 | | | |

The two sides of the equation balance at $17,800. Note that owner's equity is increased when revenues are earned. The source of the increase in owner's equity is indicated as service revenue. Service revenue is included in determining Softbyte's net income.

**Transaction (5).   Purchase of Advertising on Credit.**   Softbyte receives a bill for $250 from the *Daily News* for advertising the opening of its business but postpones payment of the bill until a later date. This transaction results in an increase in liabilities and a decrease in owner's equity. The specific items involved are Accounts Payable and R. Neal, Capital. The effect on the equation is:

|     |          | Assets | | | = | Liabilities | + | Owner's Equity | |
| --- | --- | --- | --- | --- | --- | --- | --- | --- | --- |
|     |          | Cash + | Supplies + | Equipment = | | Accounts Payable | + | R. Neal, Capital | |
|     | Old Bal. | $9,200 | $1,600 | $7,000 | | $1,600 | | $16,200 | |
| (5) |          |        |        |        | | +250 | | −250 | Advertising Expense |
|     | New Bal. | $9,200 + | $1,600 + | $7,000 | = | $1,850 | + | $15,950 | |
|     |          |          | $17,800 | | | | $17,800 | | |

The two sides of the equation still balance at $17,800. Observe that owner's equity is decreased when the expense is incurred, and the specific cause of the decrease (advertising expense) is noted. Expenses do not have to be paid in cash at the time they are incurred. When payment is made at a later date, the liability Accounts Payable will be decreased and the asset Cash will be decreased [see Transaction (8)]. The cost of advertising is considered an expense, as opposed to an asset, because the benefits have been used. This expense is included in determining net income.

**Transaction (6).  Services Rendered for Cash and Credit.**  Softbyte provides programming services of $3,500 for customers. Cash amounting to $1,500 is received from customers, and the balance of $2,000 is billed to customers on account. This transaction results in an equal increase in assets and owner's equity. Three specific items are affected: Cash is increased $1,500; Accounts Receivable is increased $2,000; and R. Neal, Capital is increased $3,500. The new balances are as follows:

|     |          | Assets | | | | = | Liabilities | + | Owner's Equity | |
| --- | --- | --- | --- | --- | --- | --- | --- | --- | --- | --- |
|     |          | Cash + | Accounts Receivable + | Supplies + | Equipment = | | Accounts Payable | + | R. Neal, Capital | |
|     | Old Bal. | $9,200 | | $1,600 | $7,000 | | $1,850 | | $15,950 | |
| (6) |          | +1,500 | +2,000 | | | | | | +3,500 | Service Revenue |
|     | New Bal. | $10,700 + | $2,000 + | $1,600 + | $7,000 | = | $1,850 | + | $19,450 | |
|     |          |           | $21,300 | | | | | $21,300 | | |

Why increase owner's equity by $3,500 when only $1,500 has been collected? Because the inflow of assets resulting from the earning of revenues does not have to be in the form of cash. Remember that owner's equity is increased when revenues are earned, and in Softbyte's case that is when the service is provided. When collections on account are received at a later date, Cash will be increased and Accounts Receivable will be decreased [see Transaction (9)].

**Transaction (7).  Payment of Expenses.**  Expenses paid in cash for September are store rent, $600, salaries of employees, $900, and utilities, $200. These payments result in an equal decrease in assets and owner's equity. Cash is decreased $1,700 and R. Neal, Capital is decreased by the same amount. The effect of these payments on the equation is:

| | | Assets | | | = Liabilities + | Owner's Equity | |
|---|---|---|---|---|---|---|---|
| | Cash + | Accounts Receivable + | Supplies + | Equipment = | Accounts Payable + | R. Neal, Capital | |
| Old Bal. | $10,700 | $2,000 | $1,600 | $7,000 | $1,850 | $19,450 | |
| (7) | −1,700 | | | | | −600 | Rent Expense |
| | | | | | | −900 | Salaries Expense |
| | | | | | | −200 | Utilities Expense |
| New Bal. | $ 9,000 + | $2,000 + | $1,600 + | $7,000 = | $1,850 + | $17,750 | |
| | | $19,600 | | | | $19,600 | |

The two sides of the equation now balance at $19,600. Three lines are required in the analysis to indicate the different types of expenses that have been incurred.

**Transaction (8). Payment of Accounts Payable.** Softbyte pays its *Daily News* advertising bill of $250 in cash. In analyzing the effect of this transaction, we must recall that the bill has previously been recorded in Transaction (5) as an increase in Accounts Payable and a decrease in owner's equity. Thus, this payment "on account" decreases both assets and liabilities. In this case, the asset Cash and the liability Accounts Payable are decreased by $250. The effect of this transaction on the equation is:

| | | Assets | | | = Liabilities + | Owner's Equity |
|---|---|---|---|---|---|---|
| | Cash + | Accounts Receivable + | Supplies + | Equipment = | Accounts Payable + | R. Neal, Capital |
| Old Bal. | $9,000 | $2,000 | $1,600 | $7,000 | $1,850 | $17,750 |
| (8) | −250 | | | | −250 | |
| New Bal. | $8,750 + | $2,000 + | $1,600 + | $7,000 = | $1,600 + | $17,750 |
| | | $19,350 | | | | $19,350 |

Observe that the payment of a liability related to an expense that has previously been recorded does not affect owner's equity.

**Transaction (9). Receipt of Cash on Account.** The sum of $600 in cash is received from customers who have previously been billed for services in Transaction (6). This transaction does not change total assets, but it changes the composition of Softbyte's assets. Cash is increased $600 and Accounts Receivable is decreased $600. The new balances are:

| | | Assets | | | = Liabilities + | Owner's Equity |
|---|---|---|---|---|---|---|
| | Cash + | Accounts Receivable + | Supplies + | Equipment = | Accounts Payable + | R. Neal, Capital |
| Old Bal. | $8,750 | $2,000 | $1,600 | $7,000 | $1,600 | $17,750 |
| (9) | +600 | −600 | | | | |
| New Bal. | $9,350 + | $1,400 + | $1,600 + | $7,000 = | $1,600 + | $17,750 |
| | | $19,350 | | | | $19,350 |

Note that a collection on account for services previously billed and recorded does not affect owner's equity. Revenue was already recorded in Transaction (6) and should not be recorded again.

**Transaction (10).  Withdrawal of Cash by Owner.**  Ray Neal withdraws $1,300 in cash from the business for his personal use. This transaction results in an equal decrease in assets and owner's equity. Thus, both Cash and R. Neal, Capital are decreased $1,300, as shown below:

|  |  | Cash | + | Accounts Receivable | + | Supplies | + | Equipment | = | Accounts Payable | + | R. Neal, Capital |  |
|---|---|---|---|---|---|---|---|---|---|---|---|---|---|
|  | Old Bal. | $9,350 |  | $1,400 |  | $1,600 |  | $7,000 |  | $1,600 |  | $17,750 |  |
| (10) |  | −1,300 |  |  |  |  |  |  |  |  |  | −1,300 | Drawings |
|  | New Bal. | $8,050 | + | $1,400 | + | $1,600 | + | $7,000 | = | $1,600 | + | $16,450 |  |

Assets = $18,050      Liabilities + Owner's Equity = $18,050

Observe that the effect of a cash withdrawal by the owner is the opposite of the effect of an investment by the owner. **Owner's drawings do not represent expenses.** Like owner's investment, they are not included in determining net income.

## Summary of Transactions

The transactions of Softbyte are summarized in Illustration 1-10 to show their cumulative effect on the basic accounting equation. The transaction number, the

**ILLUSTRATION 1-10**

*Tabular summary of Softbyte transactions*

| Transaction | Cash | + | Accounts Receivable | + | Supplies | + | Equipment | = | Accounts Payable | + | R. Neal, Capital |  |
|---|---|---|---|---|---|---|---|---|---|---|---|---|
| (1) | +$15,000 |  |  |  |  |  |  |  |  |  | +$15,000 | Investment |
| (2) | −7,000 |  |  |  |  |  | +$7,000 |  |  |  |  |  |
|  | 8,000 | + |  |  |  |  | 7,000 | = |  |  | 15,000 |  |
| (3) |  |  |  |  | +$1,600 |  |  |  | +$1,600 |  |  |  |
|  | 8,000 | + |  |  | 1,600 | + | 7,000 | = | 1,600 | + | 15,000 |  |
| (4) | +1,200 |  |  |  |  |  |  |  |  |  | +1,200 | Service Revenue |
|  | 9,200 | + |  |  | 1,600 | + | 7,000 | = | 1,600 | + | 16,200 |  |
| (5) |  |  |  |  |  |  |  |  | +250 |  | −250 | Advertising Expense |
|  | 9,200 | + |  |  | 1,600 | + | 7,000 | = | 1,850 | + | 15,950 |  |
| (6) | +1,500 | + | +$2,000 |  |  |  |  |  |  |  | +3,500 | Service Revenue |
|  | 10,700 | + | 2,000 | + | 1,600 | + | 7,000 | = | 1,850 | + | 19,450 |  |
| (7) | −1,700 |  |  |  |  |  |  |  |  |  | −600 | Rent Expense |
|  |  |  |  |  |  |  |  |  |  |  | −900 | Salaries Expense |
|  |  |  |  |  |  |  |  |  |  |  | −200 | Utilities Expense |
|  | 9,000 | + | 2,000 | + | 1,600 | + | 7,000 | = | 1,850 | + | 17,750 |  |
| (8) | −250 |  |  |  |  |  |  |  | −250 |  |  |  |
|  | 8,750 | + | 2,000 | + | 1,600 | + | 7,000 | = | 1,600 | + | 17,750 |  |
| (9) | +600 | | −600 |  |  |  |  |  |  |  |  |  |
|  | 9,350 | + | 1,400 | + | 1,600 | + | 7,000 | = | 1,600 | + | 17,750 |  |
| (10) | −1,300 |  |  |  |  |  |  |  |  |  | −1,300 | Drawings |
|  | $8,050 | + | $1,400 | + | $1,600 | + | $7,000 | = | $1,600 | + | $16,450 |  |

Assets = $18,050      Liabilities + Owner's Equity = $18,050 specific effects of the transaction, and the balances after each transaction are indicated. The illustration demonstrates a number of significant facts:

1. Each transaction must be analyzed in terms of its effect on:
   **a.** the three components of the basic accounting equation.
   **b.** specific types (kinds) of items within each component.
2. The two sides of the equation must always be equal.
3. The causes of each change in the owner's claim on assets must be indicated in the owner's equity column.

There! You made it through transaction analysis. If you feel a bit shaky on any of the transactions, it would probably be a good idea at this point to get up, take a short break, and come back again for a 10- to 15-minute review of the transactions, to make sure you understand them before you go on to the next section.

# BEFORE YOU GO ON . . .

## Review It

1. What is an example of an external transaction? What is an example of an internal transaction?
2. If an asset increases, what are the three possible effects on the basic accounting equation?

## Do It

A tabular analysis of the transactions made by Roberta Mendez & Co., a certified public accounting firm, for the month of August is shown below. Each increase and decrease in owner's equity is explained.

| | Assets | | | = | Liabilities | + | Owner's Equity | |
|---|---|---|---|---|---|---|---|---|
| | | | Office | | Accounts | | R. Mendez, | |
| | Cash | + | Equipment | = | Payable | + | Capital | |
| 1. | +$25,000 | | | | | | +25,000 | Investment |
| 2. | | | +7,000 | | +7,000 | | | |
| 3. | +8,000 | | | | | | +8,000 | Service Revenue |
| 4. | − 850 | | | | | | − 850 | Rent Expense |

Describe each transaction that occurred for the month.

*Reasoning:* The accounting equation must always be in balance. A change in an asset requires a change in another asset, in a liability, or in owner's equity. By analyzing the tabular analysis we can determine each transaction.

*Solution:*
1. The owner invested an additional $25,000 of cash in the business.
2. The company purchased $7,000 of office equipment on credit.
3. The company received $8,000 of cash in exchange for services performed.
4. The company paid $850 for this month's rent.

*Related exercise material:* BE1-4, BE1-5, BE1-6, BE1-7, E1-2, E1-3, E1-4, E1-6, and E1-7.

THE NAVIGATOR

# FINANCIAL STATEMENTS

After transactions are identified, recorded, and summarized, four financial statements are prepared from the summarized accounting data:

1. An income statement presents the revenues and expenses and resulting net income or net loss of a company for a specific period of time.
2. An owner's equity statement summarizes the changes in owner's equity for a specific period of time.
3. A balance sheet reports the assets, liabilities, and owner's equity of a business enterprise at a specific date.
4. A statement of cash flows summarizes information concerning the cash inflows (receipts) and outflows (payments) for a specific period of time.

Each statement provides management, owners, and other interested parties with relevant financial data. The financial statements of Softbyte and their interrelationships are shown in Illustration 1-11. The statements are interrelated: **(1) Net income of $2,750 shown on the income statement is added to the beginning balance of owner's capital in the owner's equity statement. (2) Owner's capital of $16,450 at the end of the reporting period shown in the owner's equity statement is reported on the balance sheet. (3) Cash of $8,050 on the balance sheet is reported on the statement of cash flows.**

Additionally, every set of financial statements is accompanied by explanatory notes and supporting schedules that are an integral part of the statements. Examples of these notes and schedules are illustrated in later chapters of this textbook.

Be sure to carefully examine the format and content of each statement. The essential features of each are briefly described in the following sections.

> **8**
> **STUDY**
> **OBJECTIVE**
> ..........................................
> Prepare an income statement, owner's equity statement, balance sheet, and statement of cash flows.

**HELPFUL HINT**
The income statement, owner's equity statement, and statement of cash flows are all for a *period* of time, whereas the balance sheet is for a *point* in time.

## ACCOUNTING IN ACTION
### Business Insight

Why do companies choose the particular year-ends that they do? For example, why doesn't every company use December 31 as the accounting year-end? Many companies choose to end their accounting year when inventory or operations are at a low. This is advantageous because compiling accounting information requires much time and effort by managers, so they would rather do it when they aren't as busy operating the business. Also, inventory is easier and less costly to count when it is low. Some companies whose year-ends differ from December 31 are Delta Air Lines, June 30; Walt Disney Productions, September 30; Kmart Corp., January 31; and Dunkin' Donuts, Inc., October 31.

## Income Statement

The income statement for Softbyte is prepared from the data appearing in the owner's equity column of Illustration 1-10. The heading of the statement identifies the company, the type of statement, and the time period covered by the statement. Note that the primary focus of the income statement is on reporting the success or profitability of the company's operations over a specified period of time. To indicate that it applies for a period of time, the income statement is dated "For the Month Ended September 30, 1999."

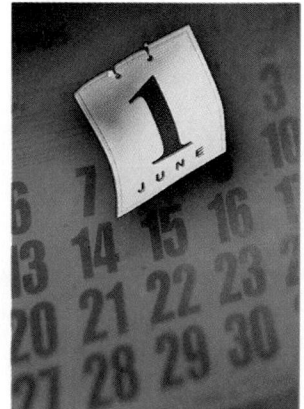

**ALTERNATIVE TERMINOLOGY**
The income statement is sometimes referred to as the *statement of operations, earnings statement,* or *profit and loss statement.*

**ILLUSTRATION 1-11**

*Financial statements and their interrelationships*

**SOFTBYTE**
**Income Statement**
**For the Month Ended September 30, 1999**

| | | |
|---|---:|---:|
| Revenues | | |
| Service revenue | | $4,700 |
| Expenses | | |
| Salaries expense | $900 | |
| Rent expense | 600 | |
| Advertising expense | 250 | |
| Utilities expense | 200 | |
| Total expenses | | 1,950 |
| Net income | | **$2,750** |

**HELPFUL HINT**

Note that final sums are double-underlined, and negative amounts are presented in parentheses.

**SOFTBYTE**
**Owner's Equity Statement**
**For the Month Ended September 30, 1999**

| | | |
|---|---:|---:|
| R. Neal, Capital, September 1 | | $   –0– |
| Add: Investments | $15,000 | |
| Net income | 2,750 | 17,750 |
| | | 17,750 |
| Less: Drawings | | 1,300 |
| R. Neal, Capital, September 30 | | **$16,450** |

**SOFTBYTE**
**Balance Sheet**
**September 30, 1999**

**Assets**

| | |
|---|---:|
| Cash | $ 8,050 |
| Accounts receivable | 1,400 |
| Supplies | 1,600 |
| Equipment | 7,000 |
| Total assets | $18,050 |

**Liabilities and Owner's Equity**

| | |
|---|---:|
| Liabilities | |
| Accounts payable | $ 1,600 |
| Owner's Equity | |
| R. Neal, Capital | **16,450** |
| Total liabilities and owner's equity | $18,050 |

**SOFTBYTE**
**Statement of Cash Flows**
**For the Month Ended September 30, 1999**

| | | |
|---|---:|---:|
| Cash flows from operating activities | | |
| Cash receipts from revenues | | $ 3,300 |
| Cash payments for expenses | | (1,950) |
| Net cash provided by operating activities | | 1,350 |
| Cash flows from investing activities | | |
| Purchase of equipment | | (7,000) |
| Cash flows from financing activities | | |
| Investments by owner | $15,000 | |
| Drawings by owner | (1,300) | 13,700 |
| Net increase in cash | | 8,050 |
| Cash at the beginning of the period | | 0 |
| Cash at the end of the period | | **$ 8,050** |

**HELPFUL HINT**

Net income is computed first and is needed to determine the ending balance in owner's equity. The ending balance in owner's equity is needed in preparing the balance sheet. The cash shown on the balance sheet is needed in preparing the statement of cash flows.

On the income statement, revenues are listed first, followed by expenses. Finally net income (or net loss) is determined. Although practice varies, we have chosen in our illustrations and homework solutions to list expenses in order of magnitude. Alternative formats for the income statement will be considered in later chapters.

Note that investment and withdrawal transactions between the owner and the business are not included in the measurement of net income. For example, the withdrawal by Ray Neal of cash from Softbyte was not regarded as a business expense, as explained earlier.

## Owner's Equity Statement

Data for the preparation of the owner's equity statement are obtained from the owner's equity column of the tabular summary (Illustration 1-10) and from the income statement. The heading of this statement identifies the company, the type of statement, and the time period covered by the statement. The time period is the same as that covered by the income statement and therefore is dated "For the Month Ended September 30, 1999." The beginning owner's equity amount is shown on the first line of the statement. Then, the owner's investments, net income, and the owner's drawings are identified in the statement. The information provided by this statement indicates the reasons why owner's equity has increased or decreased during the period.

What if Softbyte reported a net loss in its first month? Let's assume that during the month of September 1999, Softbyte lost $10,000. The presentation in the owner's equity statement of a net loss appears in Illustration 1-12.

**ILLUSTRATION 1-12**

*Presentation of net loss*

| SOFTBYTE | | |
|---|---:|---:|
| **Owner's Equity Statement** | | |
| **For the Month Ended September 30, 1999** | | |
| R. Neal, Capital, September 1 | | $  –0– |
| Add: Investments | | 15,000 |
| | | 15,000 |
| Less: Drawings | $ 1,300 | |
| Net loss | 10,000 | 11,300 |
| R. Neal, Capital, September 30 | | $3,700 |

If there are additional investments, they are reported as investments in the owner's equity statement.

## Balance Sheet

The balance sheet for Softbyte is prepared from the column headings and the month-end data shown in the last line of the tabular summary (Illustration 1-10). The heading of a balance sheet must identify the company, the statement, and the date. To indicate that the balance sheet is at a specific date, it is dated "September 30, 1999." Observe that the assets are listed at the top, followed by liabilities and owner's equity. Total assets must equal total liabilities and owner's equity. In the Softbyte illustration, only one liability, accounts payable, is reported on the balance sheet. In most cases, there will be more than one liability. When two or more liabilities are involved, a customary way of listing is as follows:

**ILLUSTRATION 1-13**

*Presentation of liabilities*

| Liabilities | |
| --- | --- |
| Notes payable | $10,000 |
| Accounts payable | 63,000 |
| Salaries payable | 18,000 |
| Total liabilities | $91,000 |

The balance sheet is like a snapshot of the company's financial condition at a specific moment in time (usually the month-end or year-end).

## Statement of Cash Flows

**HELPFUL HINT**

Investing activities pertain to investments made by the company, not investments made by the owner.

The primary purpose of a statement of cash flows is to provide financial information about the cash receipts and cash payments of an enterprise for a specific period of time. To achieve this purpose and to aid investors, creditors, and others in their analysis of cash, the statement of cash flows reports (1) the cash effects of a company's operations during a period, (2) its investing transactions, (3) its financing transactions, (4) the net increase or decrease in cash during the period, and (5) the cash amount at the end of the period.

Reporting the sources, uses, and net increase or decrease in cash is useful because investors, creditors, and others want to know what is happening to a company's most liquid resource. The statement of cash flows, therefore, provides answers to the following simple but important questions:

1. Where did the cash come from during the period?
2. What was the cash used for during the period?
3. What was the change in the cash balance during the period?

A statement of cash flows for Softbyte is provided in Illustration 1-11.

As shown in the statement, cash increased $8,050 during the year. This increase resulted because net cash flow provided from operating activities increased cash $1,350, cash flow from investing transactions decreased cash $7,000, and cash flow from financing transactions increased cash $13,700. At this time, you need not be concerned with how these amounts are determined. Chapter 18 will examine in detail how the statement is prepared.

## BEFORE YOU GO ON . . .

### Review It

1. What are the income statement, statement of owner's equity, balance sheet, and statement of cash flows?
2. Indicate how the financial statements are interrelated.

### A LOOK BACK AT OUR FEATURE STORY

Refer to the opening story about Kellogg Company, and answer the following questions:

1. If you were interested in investing in Kellogg Company, what would the balance sheet and income statement tell you?
2. Would you request audited financial statements? Explain.
3. Will the financial statements show the market value of the company? Explain.

*Solution:*

1. The balance sheet reports the assets, liabilities, and owners' equity of the company. The income statement presents the revenues and expenses and resulting net income (or net loss) for a specific period of time. The balance sheet is like a snapshot of the company's financial condition at a point in time. The income statement should give you a good indication of the profitability of the company. Also, the sources of the company's revenues and a picture of its expenses are provided in the income statement.
2. You should request **audited** financial statements—statements that a CPA has examined and expressed an opinion as to the fairness of presentation. You should not make decisions without having audited financial statements.
3. The financial statements will not show the market value of the company. As indicated, one important principle of accounting is the cost principle, which states that assets should be recorded at cost. Cost has an important advantage over other valuations: it is reliable.

**A Look Back** exercises refer to the chapter opening story. These exercises help you analyze that real-world situation in terms of the accounting topic of the chapter.

THE NAVIGATOR

# DEMONSTRATION PROBLEM

Mary Malone opens her own law office on July 1, 1999. During the first month of operations, the following transactions occurred:

1. Invested $10,000 in cash in the law practice.
2. Paid $800 for July rent on office space.
3. Purchased office equipment on account, $3,000.
4. Rendered legal services to clients for cash, $1,500.
5. Borrowed $700 cash from a bank on a note payable.
6. Rendered legal services to client on account, $2,000.
7. Paid monthly expenses: salaries, $500; utilities, $300; and telephone, $100.

*Instructions*

(a) Prepare a tabular summary of the transactions.

(b) Prepare the income statement, owner's equity statement, and balance sheet at July 31 for Mary Malone, Attorney at Law.

The **Demonstration Problems** are a final review of the section just completed. The Problem-Solving Strategies in the margin give you tips about how to approach the problem, and the solutions provided demonstrate both the form and content of complete answers.

# SOLUTION TO DEMONSTRATION PROBLEM

(a)

| Trans-action | | Assets | | = | Liabilities | + | Owner's Equity | |
| --- | --- | --- | --- | --- | --- | --- | --- | --- |
| | Cash | + Accounts Receivable | + Equipment | = Notes Payable | + Accounts Payable | + | Mary Malone, Capital | |
| (1) | +$10,000 | | | | | | +$10,000 | Investment |
| (2) | −800 | | | | | | −800 | Rent Expense |
| | 9,200 | | | = | | | 9,200 | |
| (3) | | | +$3,000 | | +$3,000 | | | |
| | 9,200 | + | 3,000 | = | | 3,000 | + 9,200 | |
| (4) | +1,500 | | | | | | +1,500 | Service Revenue |
| | 10,700 | + | 3,000 | = | | 3,000 | + 10,700 | |
| (5) | +700 | | | +$700 | | | | |
| | 11,400 | + | 3,000 | = | 700 | + 3,000 | + 10,700 | |
| (6) | | +$2,000 | | | | | +2,000 | Service Revenue |
| | 11,400 + | 2,000 | + 3,000 | = | 700 | + 3,000 | + 12,700 | |
| (7) | −900 | | | | | | −500 | Salaries Expense |
| | | | | | | | −300 | Utilities Expense |
| | | | | | | | −100 | Telephone Expense |
| | $10,500 + | $2,000 | + $3,000 | = | $700 | + $3,000 | + $11,800 | |

**PROBLEM-SOLVING STRATEGIES**

1. Remember that assets must equal liabilities and owner's equity after each transaction.
2. Investments and revenues increase owner's equity.
3. Expenses decrease owner's equity.
4. The income statement shows revenues and expenses for a period of time.
5. The owner's equity statement shows the changes in owner's equity for a period of time.
6. The balance sheet reports assets, liabilities, and owner's equity at a specific date.

(b)

**MARY MALONE**
**Attorney at Law**
**Income Statement**
**For the Month Ended July 31, 1999**

| | | |
|---|---:|---:|
| Revenues | | |
| Service revenue | | $3,500 |
| Expenses | | |
| Rent expense | $800 | |
| Salaries expense | 500 | |
| Utilities expense | 300 | |
| Telephone expense | 100 | |
| Total expenses | | 1,700 |
| Net income | | $1,800 |

**MARY MALONE**
**Attorney at Law**
**Owner's Equity Statement**
**For the Month Ended July 31, 1999**

| | | |
|---|---:|---:|
| Mary Malone, Capital, July 1 | | $   –0– |
| Add: Investments | $10,000 | |
| Net income | 1,800 | 11,800 |
| Mary Malone, Capital, July 31 | | $11,800 |

**MARY MALONE**
**Attorney at Law**
**Balance Sheet**
**July 31, 1999**

**Assets**

| | |
|---|---:|
| Cash | $10,500 |
| Accounts receivable | 2,000 |
| Equipment | 3,000 |
| Total assets | $15,500 |

**Liabilities and Owner's Equity**

| | | |
|---|---:|---:|
| Liabilities | | |
| Notes payable | | $   700 |
| Accounts payable | | 3,000 |
| Total liabilities | | 3,700 |
| Owner's equity | | |
| Mary Malone, Capital | | 11,800 |
| Total liabilities and owner's equity | | $15,500 |

THE
NAVIGATOR

This would be a good time to return to the **Student Owner's Manual** at the beginning of the book (or look at it for the first time if you skipped it before) to read about the various types of assignment materials that appear at the end of each chapter. Knowing the purpose of the different assignments will help you appreciate what each contributes to your accounting skills and competencies.

# SUMMARY OF STUDY OBJECTIVES

**1. Explain the meaning of accounting.** Accounting is the process of identifying, recording, and communicating the economic events of an organization (business or nonbusiness) to interested users of the information.

**2. Identify the users and uses of accounting.** The major users and uses of accounting are: (a) Management uses accounting information in planning, controlling, and evaluating business operations. (b) Investors (owners) judge the wisdom of buying, holding, or selling their financial interests on the basis of accounting data. (c) Creditors (suppliers and bankers) evaluate the risks of granting credit or lending money to particular businesses on the basis of the accounting information obtained about those businesses. Other groups are taxing authorities, regulatory agencies, customers, labor unions, and economic planners.

**3. *Understand why ethics is a fundamental business concept.*** Ethics are the standards of conduct by which one's actions—both personal and business—are judged as right or wrong. If you cannot depend on the honesty of the individuals you deal with, effective communication and economic activity would be impossible and information would have no credibility.

**4. *Explain the meaning of generally accepted accounting principles and the cost principle.*** Generally accepted accounting principles are a common set of standards used by accountants. One important principle is the cost principle, which states that assets should be recorded at their cost.

**5. *Explain the meaning of the monetary unit assumption and the economic entity assumption.*** The monetary unit assumption requires that only transaction data capable of being expressed in terms of money be included in the accounting records of the economic entity. The economic entity assumption states that economic events can be identified with a particular unit of accountability.

**6. *State the basic accounting equation and explain the meaning of assets, liabilities, and owner's equity.*** The basic accounting equation is:

$$Assets = Liabilities + Owner's\ Equity$$

Assets are resources owned by a business. Liabilities are creditorship claims on total assets. Owner's equity is the ownership claim on total assets. It is often referred to as residual equity.

**7. *Analyze the effect of business transactions on the basic accounting equation.*** Each business transaction must have a dual effect on the accounting equation. For example, if an individual asset is increased, there must be a corresponding (1) decrease in another asset, or (2) increase in a specific liability, or (3) increase in owner's equity.

**8. *Prepare an income statement, owner's equity statement, balance sheet, and statement of cash flows.*** An income statement presents the revenues and expenses of a company for a specified period of time. An owner's equity statement summarizes the changes in owner's equity that have occurred for a specific period of time. A balance sheet reports the assets, liabilities, and owner's equity of a business at a specific date. A statement of cash flows summarizes information concerning the cash inflows (receipts) and outflows (payments) for a specific period of time.

THE
NAVIGATOR

# GLOSSARY

**Accounting** The process of identifying, recording, and communicating the economic events of an organization to interested users of the information. (p. 2).

**Assets** Resources owned by a business. (p. 13).

**Auditing** The examination of financial statements by a certified public accountant in order to express an opinion as to the fairness of presentation. (p. 7).

**Balance sheet** A financial statement that reports the assets, liabilities, and owner's equity at a specific date. (p. 23).

**Basic accounting equation** Assets = Liabilities + Owner's equity. (p. 13).

**Bookkeeping** A part of accounting that involves only the recording of economic events. (p. 6).

**Corporation** A business organized as a separate legal entity under state corporation law having ownership divided into transferable shares of stock. (p. 13).

**Cost principle** An accounting principle that states that assets should be recorded at their cost. (p. 11).

**Drawings** Withdrawal of cash or other assets from an unincorporated business for the personal use of the owner(s). (p. 14).

**Economic entity assumption** An assumption that economic events can be identified with a particular unit of accountability. (p. 12).

**Ethics** The standards of conduct by which one's actions are judged as right or wrong, honest or dishonest, fair or not fair. (p. 9).

**Expenses** The cost of assets consumed or services used in the process of earning revenue. (p. 15).

**Financial Accounting Standards Board (FASB)** A private organization that establishes generally accepted accounting principles. (p. 10).

**Generally accepted accounting principles (GAAP)** A common set of standards that indicate how to report economic events. (p. 10).

**Income statement** A financial statement that presents the revenues and expenses and resulting net income or net loss of a company for a specific period of time. (p. 23).

**Investments by owner** The assets put into the business by the owner. (p. 14).

**Liabilities** Creditorship claims on total assets. (p. 14).

**Management consulting** An area of public accounting involving financial planning and control and the development of accounting and computer systems. (p. 7).

**Monetary unit assumption** An assumption stating that only transaction data that can be expressed in terms of money be included in the accounting records of the economic entity. (p. 11).

**Net income** The amount by which revenues exceed expenses. (p. 15).

**Net loss** The amount by which expenses exceed revenues. (p. 15).

**Owner's equity** The ownership claim on total assets. (p. 14).

**Owner's equity statement** A financial statement that summarizes the changes in owner's equity for a specific period of time. (p. 23).

**Partnership** An association of two or more persons to carry on as co-owners of a business for profit. (p. 12).

**Private (or managerial) accounting** An area of accounting within a company that involves such activities as cost accounting, budgeting, and accounting information systems. (p. 7).

**Proprietorship** A business owned by one person. (p. 12).

**Public accounting** An area of accounting in which the accountant offers expert service to the general public. (p. 7).

**Revenues** The gross increase in owner's equity resulting from business activities entered into for the purpose of earning income. (p. 14).

**Securities and Exchange Commission (SEC)** A governmental agency that requires companies to file financial reports in accordance with generally accepted accounting principles. (p. 10).

**Statement of cash flows** A financial statement that provides information about the cash inflows (receipts) and cash outflows (payments) of an entity for a specific period of time. (p. 23).

**Taxation** An area of public accounting involving tax advice, tax planning, and preparing tax returns. (p. 7).

**Transactions** The economic events of the enterprise recorded by accountants. (p. 16).

# SELF-STUDY QUESTIONS

Answers are on page 43.

(SO 1) 1. Which of the following is *not* a step in the accounting process?
   a. identification.
   b. verification.
   c. recording.
   d. communication.

(SO 2) 2. Which of the following statements about users of accounting information is *incorrect*?
   a. Management is considered an internal user.
   b. Taxing authorities are considered external users.
   c. Present creditors are considered external users.
   d. Regulatory authorities are considered internal users.

(SO 2) 3. Services provided by a public accountant include:
   a. auditing, taxation, and management consulting.
   b. auditing, budgeting, and management consulting.
   c. auditing, budgeting, and cost accounting.
   d. internal auditing, budgeting, and management consulting.

(SO 4) 4. The cost principle states that:
   a. assets should be initially recorded at cost and adjusted when the market value changes.
   b. activities of an entity are to be kept separate and distinct from its owner.
   c. assets should be recorded at their cost.
   d. only transaction data capable of being expressed in terms of money be included in the accounting records.

(SO 5) 5. Which of the following statements about basic assumptions is *incorrect*?
   a. Basic assumptions are the same as accounting principles.
   b. The economic entity assumption states that there should be a particular unit of accountability.
   c. The monetary unit assumption enables accounting to measure economic events.

   d. An important corollary to the monetary unit assumption is the stable monetary unit assumption.

6. Net income will result during a time period when: (SO 6)
   a. assets exceed liabilities.
   b. assets exceed revenues.
   c. expenses exceed revenues.
   d. revenues exceed expenses.

7. Performing services on account will have the following (SO 7) effects on the components of the basic accounting equation:
   a. increase assets and decrease owner's equity.
   b. increase assets and increase owner's equity.
   c. increase assets and increase liabilities.
   d. increase liabilities and increase owner's equity.

8. As of December 31, 1999, Stoneland Company has assets (SO 7) of $3,500 and owner's equity of $2,000. What are the liabilities for Stoneland Company as of December 31, 1999?
   a. $1,500.
   b. $1,000.
   c. $2,500.
   d. $2,000.

9. On the last day of the period, Genesis Company buys a (SO 8) $900 machine on credit. This transaction will affect the:
   a. income statement only.
   b. balance sheet only.
   c. income statement and owner's equity statement only.
   d. income statement, owner's equity statement, and balance sheet.

10. The financial statement that reports assets, liabilities, (SO 8) and owner's equity is the:
   a. income statement.
   b. owner's equity statement.
   c. balance sheet.
   d. statement of cash flow.

THE NAVIGATOR

# QUESTIONS

1. "Accounting is ingrained in our society and it is vital to our economic system." Do you agree? Explain.

2. Identify and describe the steps in the accounting process.

3. (a) Who are internal users of accounting data?
   (b) How does accounting provide relevant data to these users?

4. What uses of financial accounting information are made by external users (a) investors and (b) creditors?

5. "Bookkeeping and accounting are the same." Do you agree? Explain.

6. Joe Kirby Travel Agency purchased land for $85,000 cash on December 10, 1999. At December 31, 1999, the land's value has increased to $93,000. What amount should be reported for land on Joe Kirby's balance sheet at December 31, 1999? Explain.

7. What is the monetary unit assumption? What impact does inflation have on the monetary unit assumption?

8. What is the economic entity assumption?

9. What are the three basic forms of business organizations for profit-oriented enterprises?

10. Mary Stone is the owner of a successful printing shop. Recently her business has been increasing, and Mary has been thinking about changing the organization of her business from a proprietorship to a corporation. Discuss some of the advantages Mary would enjoy if she were to incorporate her business.

11. What is the basic accounting equation?

12. (a) Define the terms assets, liabilities, and owner's equity. (b) What items affect owner's equity?

13. Which of the following items are liabilities of Gilt Jewelry Stores?
   (a) Cash.
   (b) Accounts payable.
   (c) Drawings.
   (d) Accounts receivable.
   (e) Supplies.
   (f) Equipment.
   (g) Salaries payable.
   (h) Service revenue.
   (i) Rent expense.

14. Can a business enter into a transaction in which only the left side of the basic accounting equation is affected? If so, give an example.

15. Are the following events recorded in the accounting records? Explain your answer in each case.
   (a) The owner of the company dies.
   (b) Supplies are purchased on account.
   (c) An employee is fired.

   (d) The owner of the business withdraws cash from the business for personal use.

16. Indicate how the following business transactions affect the basic accounting equation.
   (a) Paid cash for janitorial services.
   (b) Purchased equipment for cash.
   (c) Invested cash in the business.
   (d) Paid an accounts payable in full.

17. Listed below are some items found in the financial statements of Kaustav Sen, M.D. Indicate in which financial statement(s) the following items would appear.
   (a) Service revenue.
   (b) Equipment.
   (c) Advertising expense.
   (d) Accounts receivable.
   (e) Kaustav Sen, Capital.
   (f) Wages payable.

18. In February 1999, John Alcorn invested an additional $10,000 in his business, Alcorn's Pharmacy, which is organized as a proprietorship. Alcorn's accountant, Terry Elliot, recorded this receipt as an increase in cash and revenues. Is this treatment appropriate? Why or why not?

19. A company's net income appears directly on the income statement and the owner's equity statement, and it is included indirectly in the company's balance sheet. Do you agree? Explain.

20. Sotero Enterprises had a capital balance of $168,000 at the beginning of the period. At the end of the accounting period, the capital balance was $198,000.
   (a) Assuming no additional investment or withdrawals during the period, what is the net income for the period?
   (b) Assuming an additional investment of $13,000 but no withdrawals during the period, what is the net income for the period?

21. Summarized operations for the Alberto Rivera Co. for the month of July are as follows:

   Revenues earned: for cash $35,000; on account $70,000.

   Expenses incurred: for cash $26,000; on account $40,000.

   Indicate for Alberto Rivera Co. (a) the total revenues, (b) the total expenses, and (c) net income for the month of July.

# BRIEF EXERCISES

•••••••••••••••••••••••••••••••••••••••••••••••••••••••••••••••••••••••••••••

*Use basic accounting equation.*
*(SO 6)*

**BE1–1**   Presented below is the basic accounting equation. Determine the missing amounts:

| | Assets | = | Liabilities | + | Owner's Equity |
|---|---|---|---|---|---|
| (a) | $80,000 | | $50,000 | | ? |
| (b) | ? | | $45,000 | | $70,000 |
| (c) | $94,000 | | ? | | $62,000 |

*Use basic accounting equation.*
*(SO 6)*

**BE1–2**   Given the accounting equation, answer each of the following questions:

1. The liabilities of Logan Company are $100,000 and the owner's equity is $240,000. What is the amount of Logan Company's total assets?
2. The total assets of Perez Company are $170,000 and its owner's equity is $80,000. What is the amount of its total liabilities?
3. The total assets of Bono Co. are $600,000 and its liabilities are equal to one half of its total assets. What is the amount of Bono Co.'s owner's equity?

*Use basic accounting equation.*
*(SO 6)*

**BE1–3**   At the beginning of the year, Leary Company had total assets of $800,000 and total liabilities of $500,000. Answer the following questions:

1. If total assets increased $150,000 during the year and total liabilities decreased $80,000, what is the amount of owner's equity at the end of the year?
2. During the year, total liabilities increased $100,000 and owner's equity decreased $70,000. What is the amount of total assets at the end of the year?
3. If total assets decreased $90,000 and owner's equity increased $120,000 during the year, what is the amount of total liabilities at the end of the year?

*Determine effect of transactions on basic accounting equation.*
*(SO 7)*

**BE1–4**   Presented below are three business transactions. On a sheet of paper, list the letters a, b, c with columns for assets, liabilities, and owner's equity. For each column, indicate whether the transactions increased ($+$), decreased ($-$) or had no effect (NE) on assets, liabilities, and owner's equity:

(a) Purchased supplies on account.
(b) Received cash for providing a service.
(c) Expenses paid in cash.

*Determine effect of transactions on basic accounting equation.*
*(SO 7)*

**BE1–5**   Follow the same format as BE1-4 above. Determine the effect on assets, liabilities, and owner's equity of the following three transactions:

(a) Invested cash in the business.
(b) Withdrawal of cash by owner.
(c) Received cash from a customer who had previously been billed for services provided.

*Determine effect of transactions on owner's equity.*
*(SO 7)*

**BE1–6**   Classify each of the following items as owner's drawing (D), revenue (R), or expense (E).

_____ Advertising expense          _____ B. Farve, Drawing
_____ Commission revenue           _____ Rent revenue
_____ Insurance expense            _____ Utilities expense
_____ Salaries expense

*Determine effect of transactions on owner's equity.*
*(SO 7)*

**BE1–7**   Presented below are three transactions. Mark each transaction as affecting owner's investment (I), owner's drawings (D), revenue (R), expense (E), or not affecting owner's equity (NOE):

_____ Received cash for services performed
_____ Paid cash to purchase equipment
_____ Paid employee salaries

*Prepare a balance sheet.*
*(SO 8)*

**BE1–8**   In alphabetical order below are balance sheet items for Yung Company at December 31, 1999. Kim Yung is the owner of Yung Company. Prepare a balance sheet, following the format of Illustration 1-11.

| | |
|---|---|
| Accounts payable | $80,000 |
| Accounts receivable | $71,000 |
| Cash | $40,500 |
| Kim Yung, Capital | $31,500 |

**BE1–9**  Indicate whether each of the following items is an asset (A), liability (L), or part of owner's equity (OE).

_____ Accounts receivable  _____ Office supplies
_____ Salaries payable  _____ Owner's investment
_____ Equipment  _____ Notes payable

*Identify assets, liabilities, and owner's equity.*
*(SO 6)*

**BE1–10**  Indicate whether the following items would appear on the income statement (IS), balance sheet (BS), or owner's equity statement (OE).

_____ Notes payable  _____ Cash
_____ Advertising expense  _____ Service revenue
_____ S. O'Reiley, Capital

*Determine where items appear on financial statements.*
*(SO 8)*

# EXERCISES

**E1–1**  The Otto Cleaners has the following balance sheet items:

| | |
|---|---|
| Accounts payable | Accounts receivable |
| Cash | Notes payable |
| Cleaning equipment | Salaries payable |
| Cleaning supplies | J. Otto, Capital |

*Classify accounts as assets, liabilities, and owner's equity.*
*(SO 6)*

*Instructions*
Classify each item as an asset, liability, or owner's equity.

**E1–2**  Selected transactions for Lush Lawn Care Company are listed below:

1. Made cash investment to start business.
2. Paid monthly rent.
3. Purchased equipment on account.
4. Billed customers for services performed.
5. Withdrew cash for owner's personal use.
6. Received cash from customers billed in (4).
7. Incurred advertising expense on account.
8. Purchased additional equipment for cash.
9. Received cash from customers when service was rendered.

*Analyze the effect of transactions.*
*(SO 6, 7)*

*Instructions*
List the numbers of the above transactions and describe the effect of each transaction on assets, liabilities, and owner's equity. For example, the first answer is: (1) Increase in assets and increase in owner's equity.

**E1–3**  Le Wong Computer Timeshare Company entered into the following transactions during May 1999.

1. Purchased computer terminals for $19,000 from Digital Equipment on account.
2. Paid $4,000 cash for May rent on storage space.
3. Received $15,000 cash from customers for contracts billed in April.
4. Provided computer services to Barto Construction Company for $3,000 cash.
5. Paid Southern States Power Co. $11,000 cash for energy usage in May.
6. Le Wong invested an additional $32,000 in the business.
7. Paid Digital Equipment for the terminals purchased in (1) above.
8. Incurred advertising expense for May of $1,000 on account.

*Analyze the effect of transactions on assets, liabilities, and owner's equity.*
*(SO 6, 7)*

*Instructions*
Indicate with the appropriate letter whether each of the transactions above results in:

(a) an increase in assets and a decrease in assets.
(b) an increase in assets and an increase in owner's equity.
(c) an increase in assets and an increase in liabilities.
(d) a decrease in assets and a decrease in owner's equity.
(e) a decrease in assets and a decrease in liabilities.
(f) an increase in liabilities and a decrease in owner's equity.
(g) an increase in owner's equity and a decrease in liabilities.

*Analyze transactions and compute net income.*
*(SO 7)*

**E1–4** A tabular analysis of the transactions made by Maria Mendoza & Co., a certified public accounting firm, for the month of August is shown below. Each increase and decrease in owner's equity is explained.

| | Cash | + Accounts Receivable | + Supplies | + Office Equipment | = Accounts Payable | + Owner's Equity M. Mendoza, Capital | |
|---|---|---|---|---|---|---|---|
| 1. | +$12,000 | | | | | +$12,000 | Investment |
| 2. | −2,000 | | | +$5,000 | +$3,000 | | |
| 3. | − 750 | | +$750 | | | | |
| 4. | +2,600 | +3,400 | | | | +6,000 | Service Revenue |
| 5. | −1,500 | | | | −1,500 | | |
| 6. | −2,000 | | | | | −2,000 | Drawings |
| 7. | − 650 | | | | | − 650 | Rent Expense |
| 8. | + 450 | −450 | | | | | |
| 9. | −2,900 | | | | | −2,900 | Salaries Expense |
| 10. | | | | | + 500 | − 500 | Utilities Expense |

**Instructions**

(a) ✏️➤ Describe each transaction that occurred for the month.

(b) Determine how much owner's equity increased for the month.

(c) Compute the amount of net income for the month.

*Prepare an income statement and owner's equity statement.*
*(SO 8)*

**E1–5** The tabular analysis of transactions for Maria Mendoza & Co. is presented in E1–4.

**Instructions**

Prepare an income statement and an owner's equity statement for August and a balance sheet at August 31, 1999.

*Determine net income (or loss).*
*(SO 7)*

**E1–6** The Dylan Company had the following assets and liabilities on the dates indicated:

| December 31 | Total Assets | Total Liabilities |
|---|---|---|
| 1999 | $400,000 | $250,000 |
| 2000 | $460,000 | $320,000 |
| 2001 | $590,000 | $400,000 |

Dylan began business on January 1, 1999, with an investment of $100,000.

**Instructions**

From an analysis of the change in owner's equity during the year, compute the net income (or loss) for:

(a) 1999, assuming Dylan's drawings were $15,000 for the year.

(b) 2000, assuming Dylan made an additional investment of $50,000 and had no drawings in 2000.

(c) 2001, assuming Dylan made an additional investment of $15,000 and had drawings of $20,000 in 2001.

*Analyze financial statements items.*
*(SO 6, 7)*

**E1–7** Two items are omitted from each of the following summaries of balance sheet and income statement data for two proprietorships for the year 1999, Anne Wyatt, D.D.S., and Rambo Enterprises.

| | Anne Wyatt, D.D.S. | Rambo Enterprises |
|---|---|---|
| Beginning of year: | | |
| Total assets | $ 95,000 | $125,000 |
| Total liabilities | 80,000 | (c) |
| Total owner's equity | (a) | 95,000 |
| End of year: | | |
| Total assets | 160,000 | 180,000 |
| Total liabilities | 120,000 | 50,000 |
| Total owner's equity | 40,000 | 130,000 |
| Changes during year in owner's equity: | | |
| Additional investment | (b) | 25,000 |
| Drawings | 24,000 | (d) |
| Total revenues | 215,000 | 100,000 |
| Total expenses | 175,000 | 85,000 |

*Instructions*

Determine the missing amounts.

**E1–8**  The following information relates to Dyna Seng Co. for the year 1999.

*Prepare income statement and owner's equity statement.*
*(SO 8)*

| | | | |
|---|---|---|---|
| Dyna Seng, Capital, January 1, 1999 | $48,000 | Advertising expense | 1,800 |
| Dyna Seng, Drawing, during 1999 | 5,000 | Rent expense | 10,400 |
| Service revenue | 55,000 | Utilities expense | 3,100 |
| Salaries expense | 28,000 | | |

*Instructions*

After analyzing the data, prepare an income statement and an owner's equity statement for the year ending December 31, 1999.

**E1–9**  Clare Gardner is the bookkeeper for Otago Company. Clare has been trying to get the balance sheet of Otago Company to balance. Otago's balance sheet is as follows:

*Correct an incorrectly prepared balance sheet.*
*(SO 8)*

## OTAGO COMPANY
### Balance Sheet
### December 31, 1999

| Assets | | Liabilities | |
|---|---|---|---|
| Cash | $20,500 | Accounts payable | $20,000 |
| Supplies | 8,000 | Accounts receivable | (10,000) |
| Equipment | 46,000 | Otago, Capital | 67,500 |
| Otago, Drawing | 3,000 | Total liabilities and | |
| Total assets | $77,500 | owner's equity | $77,500 |

*Instructions*

Prepare a correct balance sheet.

**E1–10**  Ian King is the sole owner of Bear Park, a public camping ground near the Lake Mead National Recreation Area. Ian has compiled the following financial information as of December 31, 1999.

*Compute net income and prepare a balance sheet.*
*(SO 8)*

| | | | |
|---|---|---|---|
| Revenues during 1999—camping fees | $160,000 | Market value of equipment | 140,000 |
| Revenues during 1999—general store | 40,000 | Notes payable | 60,000 |
| Accounts payable | 11,000 | Expenses during 1999 | 150,000 |
| Cash on hand | 20,000 | Supplies on hand | 2,500 |
| Original cost of equipment | 115,500 | | |

*Instructions*

(a)  Determine Ian King's net income from Bear Park for 1999.

(b)  Prepare a balance sheet for Bear Park as of December 31, 1999.

**E1–11**  Presented below is financial information related to the 1999 operations of Titanic Cruise Company.

*Prepare an income statement.*
*(SO 8)*

| | |
|---|---|
| Maintenance expense | $ 80,000 |
| Property tax expense (on dock facilities) | 10,000 |
| Salaries expense | 142,000 |
| Advertising expense | 3,500 |
| Ticket revenue | 325,000 |

*Instructions*

Prepare the 1999 income statement for Titanic Cruise Company.

**E1–12**  Presented below is information related to the sole proprietorship of Wayne Robinson, attorney.

*Prepare an owner's equity statement.*
*(SO 8)*

| | |
|---|---|
| Legal service revenue—1999 | $360,000 |
| Total expenses—1999 | 205,000 |
| Assets, January 1, 1999 | 85,000 |
| Liabilities, January 1, 1999 | 62,000 |
| Assets, December 31, 1999 | 168,000 |
| Liabilities, December 31, 1999 | 70,000 |
| Drawings—1999 | ? |

*Instructions*

Prepare the 1999 owner's equity statement for Wayne Robinson's legal practice.

# PROBLEMS: SET A

*Analyze transactions and compute net income.*
(SO 6, 7)

**P1–1A**  On April 1, Merle Peper established the Wayne State Travel Agency. The following transactions were completed during the month:

1. Invested $15,000 cash to start the agency.
2. Paid $400 cash for April office rent.
3. Purchased office equipment for $2,500 cash.
4. Incurred $300 of advertising costs in the Chicago Tribune, on account.
5. Paid $600 cash for office supplies.
6. Earned $9,000 for services rendered: Cash of $1,000 is received from customers, and the balance of $8,000 is billed to customers on account.
7. Withdrew $200 cash for personal use.
8. Paid Chicago Tribune amount due in transaction (4).
9. Paid employees' salaries, $2,200.
10. Received $8,000 in cash from customers who have previously been billed in transaction (6).

*Instructions*
(a) Prepare a tabular analysis of the transactions using the following column headings: Cash, Accounts Receivable, Supplies, Office Equipment, Accounts Payable, and Merle Peper, Capital.
(b) From an analysis of the column, Merle Peper, Capital, compute the net income or net loss for April.

*Analyze transactions and prepare income statement and owner's equity statement.*
(SO 6, 7, 8)

**P1–2A**  George Kanaan opened a law office, George Kanaan, Attorney at Law, on July 1, 1999. On July 31, the balance sheet showed Cash $4,000, Accounts Receivable $1,500, Supplies $500, Office Equipment $5,000, Accounts Payable $4,200, and George Kanaan, Capital, $6,800. During August the following transactions occurred:

1. Collected $1,400 of accounts receivable.
2. Paid $2,700 cash on accounts payable.
3. Earned revenue of $6,400, of which $3,000 is collected in cash and the balance is due in September.
4. Purchased additional office equipment for $1,000, paying $400 in cash and the balance on account.
5. Paid salaries $2,500, rent for August $900, and advertising expenses $350.
6. Withdrew $550 in cash for personal use.
7. Received $2,000 from Standard Federal Bank—money borrowed on a note payable.
8. Incurred utility expenses for month on account, $250.

*Instructions*
(a) Prepare a tabular analysis of the August transactions beginning with July 31 balances. The column heading should be as follows: Cash + Accounts Receivable + Supplies + Office Equipment = Notes Payable + Accounts Payable + George Kanaan, Capital.
(b) Prepare an income statement for August, an owner's equity statement for August, and a balance sheet at August 31.

*Prepare income statement, owner's equity statement, and balance sheet.*
(SO 8)

**P1–3A**  On June 1, Ann Okah started Secret Cosmetics Co., a company that provides individual skin care treatment to clients, by investing $26,200 cash in the business. Following are the assets and liabilities of the company at June 30 and the revenues and expenses for the month of June.

| | | | |
|---|---|---|---|
| Cash | $12,000 | Notes Payable | $13,000 |
| Accounts Receivable | 4,000 | Accounts Payable | 1,200 |
| Service Revenue | 7,500 | Supplies Expense | 1,200 |
| Cosmetic Supplies | 2,400 | Gas and Oil Expense | 800 |
| Advertising Expense | 500 | Utilities Expense | 300 |
| Equipment | 25,000 | | |

Ann made no additional investment in June, but withdrew $1,700 in cash for personal use during the month.

*Instructions*

(a) Prepare an income statement and owner's equity statement for the month of June and a balance sheet at June 30, 1999.

(b) Prepare an income statement and owner's equity statement for June assuming the following data are not included above: (1) $800 of revenue was earned and billed but not collected at June 30, and (2) $100 of gas and oil expense was incurred but not paid.

**P1–4A** Jessica Bell started her own consulting firm, Bell Consulting, on May 1, 1999. The following transactions occurred during the month of May:

*Analyze transactions and prepare financial statements. (SO 7, 8)*

| May | 1 | Bell invested $10,000 cash in the business. |
|---|---|---|
| | 2 | Paid $800 for office rent for the month. |
| | 3 | Purchased $500 of supplies on account. |
| | 5 | Paid $50 to advertise in the County News. |
| | 9 | Received $1,000 cash for services provided. |
| | 12 | Withdrew $700 cash for personal use. |
| | 15 | Performed $3,000 of services on account. |
| | 17 | Paid $2,500 for employee salaries. |
| | 20 | Paid for the supplies purchased on account on May 3. |
| | 23 | Received a cash payment of $2,000 for services provided on account on May 15. |
| | 26 | Borrowed $5,000 from the bank on a note payable. |
| | 29 | Purchased office equipment for $2,400 on account. |
| | 30 | Paid $150 for utilities. |

*Instructions*

(a) Show the effects of the previous transactions on the accounting equation using the following format:

|  | Assets | | | | Liabilities | | Owner's Equity |
|---|---|---|---|---|---|---|---|
| Date | Cash + | Accounts Receivable + | Supplies + | Office Equipment = | Notes Payable + | Accounts Payable + | J. Bell, Capital |

Include explanations for any changes in the J. Bell, Capital account in your analysis.

(b) Prepare an income statement for the month of May.

(c) Prepare a balance sheet at May 31, 1999.

**P1–5A** Financial statement information about four different companies is as follows:

*Determine financial statement amounts and prepare owner's equity statements. (SO 7, 8)*

| | Montreal Company | Calgary Company | Edmonton Company | Vancouver Company |
|---|---|---|---|---|
| January 1, 1999: | | | | |
| Assets | $ 75,000 | $90,000 | (g) | $150,000 |
| Liabilities | 50,000 | (d) | 75,000 | (j) |
| Owner's equity | (a) | 60,000 | 55,000 | 90,000 |
| December 31, 1999: | | | | |
| Assets | (b) | 120,000 | 180,000 | (k) |
| Liabilities | 55,000 | 62,000 | (h) | 80,000 |
| Owner's equity | 45,000 | (e) | 110,000 | 140,000 |
| Owner's equity changes in year: | | | | |
| Additional investment | (c) | 8,000 | 10,000 | 15,000 |
| Drawings | 10,000 | (f) | 12,000 | 10,000 |
| Total revenues | 350,000 | 400,000 | (i) | 500,000 |
| Total expenses | 335,000 | 385,000 | 360,000 | (l) |

*Instructions*

(a) Determine the missing amounts. (*Hint:* For example, to solve for (a), Assets − Liabilities = Owner's equity = $25,000.)

(b) Prepare the owner's equity statement for Montreal Company.

(c) ◼▐▐▭▭▭▶ Write a memorandum explaining the sequence for preparing financial statements and the interrelationship of the owner's equity statement to the income statement and balance sheet.

# PROBLEMS: SET B

·····································································································

*Analyze transactions and compute net income.*
*(SO 6, 7)*

**P1–1B** Kumar's Repair Shop was started on May 1 by U. Kumar. A summary of May transactions is presented below.

1. Invested $15,000 cash to start the repair shop.
2. Purchased equipment for $5,000 cash.
3. Paid $400 cash for May office rent.
4. Paid $500 cash for supplies.
5. Incurred $250 of advertising costs in the Beacon News on account.
6. Received $4,100 in cash from customers for repair service.
7. Withdrew $500 cash for personal use.
8. Paid part-time employee salaries $1,000.
9. Paid utility bills $140.
10. Provided repair service on account to customers, $400.
11. Collected cash of $120 for services billed in transaction (10).

**Instructions**

(a) Prepare a tabular analysis of the transactions, using the following column headings: Cash, Accounts Receivable, Supplies, Equipment, Accounts Payable, and U. Kumar, Capital. Revenue is called Service Revenue.

(b) From an analysis of the column, U. Kumar, Capital, compute the net income or net loss for May.

*Analyze transactions and prepare income statement and owner's equity statement.*
*(SO 6, 7, 8)*

**P1–2B** Bruce Smith opened a veterinary business in Mankato, Minnesota, on August 1. On August 31, the balance sheet showed Cash $9,000, Accounts Receivable $1,700, Supplies $600, Office Equipment $6,000, Accounts Payable $3,600, and B. Smith, Capital, $13,700. During September the following transactions occurred:

1. Paid $3,100 cash on accounts payable.
2. Collected $1,300 of accounts receivable.
3. Purchased additional office equipment for $2,100, paying $800 in cash and the balance on account.
4. Earned revenue of $5,900, of which $2,500 is paid in cash and the balance is due in October.
5. Withdrew $600 cash for personal use.
6. Paid salaries $700, rent for September $900, and advertising expense $300.
7. Incurred utility expenses for month on account, $170.
8. Received $7,000 from Hilldale Bank—money borrowed on a note payable.

**Instructions**

(a) Prepare a tabular analysis of the September transactions beginning with August 31 balances. The column headings should be as follows: Cash + Accounts Receivable + Supplies + Office Equipment = Notes Payable + Accounts Payable + B. Smith, Capital.

(b) Prepare an income statement for September, an owner's equity statement for September, and a balance sheet at September 30.

*Prepare income statement, owner's equity statement, and balance sheet.*
*(SO 8)*

**P1–3B** On May 1, Thomas Phillips started Ruston Flying School, a company that provides flying lessons to would-be pilots, by investing $45,000 cash in the business. Following are the assets and liabilities of the company on May 31, 1999, and the revenues and expenses for the month of May.

| | | | |
|---|---|---|---|
| Cash | $ 6,800 | Notes Payable | $30,000 |
| Accounts Receivable | 7,200 | Rent Expense | 1,200 |
| Equipment | 64,000 | Repair Expense | 400 |
| Lesson Revenue | 8,600 | Fuel Expense | 2,200 |
| Advertising Expense | 500 | Insurance Expense | 400 |
| | | Accounts Payable | 800 |

Thomas Phillips made no additional investment in May, but he withdrew $1,700 in cash for personal use.

### Instructions
(a) Prepare an income statement and owner's equity statement for the month of May and a balance sheet at May 31.
(b) Prepare an income statement and owner's equity statement for May assuming the following data are not included above: (1) $900 of revenue was earned and billed but not collected at May 31, and (2) $3,300 of fuel expense was incurred but not paid.

**P1–4B**  Peter Alex started his own delivery servcice, Alex Deliveries, on June 1, 1999. The following transactions occurred during the month of June:

*Analyze transactions and prepare financial statements. (SO 7, 8)*

June  1  Alex invested $15,000 cash in the business.
  2  Purchased a used van for deliveries for $10,000. Alex paid $2,000 cash and signed a note payble for the remaining balance.
  3  Paid $500 for office rent for the month.
  5  Performed $1,000 of services on account.
  9  Withdrew $200 cash for personal use.
  12  Purchased supplies for $150 on account.
  15  Received a cash payment of $750 for services provided on June 5.
  17  Purchased gasoline for $100 on account.
  20  Received a cash payment of $1,500 for services provided.
  23  Made a cash payment of $500 on the note payable.
  26  Paid $250 for utilities.
  29  Paid for the gasoline purchased on account on June 17.
  30  Paid $500 for employee salaries.

### Instructions
(a) Show the effects of the previous transactions on the accounting equation using the following format:

| | Assets | | | Liabilities | | Owner's Equity |
|---|---|---|---|---|---|---|
| Date | Cash + Accounts Receivable + Supplies + | | Delivery Van | = Notes Payable + | Accounts Payable + | P. Alex, Capital |

Include explanations for any changes in the P. Alex, Capital account in your analysis.
(b) Prepare an income statement for the month of June.
(c) Prepare a balance sheet at May 31, 1999.

**P1–5B**  Financial statement information about four different companies is as follows:

*Determine financial statement amounts and prepare owner's equity statements. (SO 7, 8)*

| | Loyola Company | Marshall Company | UNLV Company | UNC Company |
|---|---|---|---|---|
| **January 1, 1999:** | | | | |
| Assets | $ 80,000 | $110,000 | (g) | $170,000 |
| Liabilities | 50,000 | (d) | 75,000 | (j) |
| Owner's equity | (a) | 60,000 | 50,000 | 90,000 |
| **December 31, 1999:** | | | | |
| Assets | (b) | 145,000 | 200,000 | (k) |
| Liabilities | 55,000 | 65,000 | (h) | 80,000 |
| Owner's equity | 58,000 | (e) | 130,000 | 180,000 |
| **Owner's equity changes in year:** | | | | |
| Additional investment | (c) | 15,000 | 10,000 | 15,000 |
| Drawings | 25,000 | (f) | 14,000 | 20,000 |
| Total revenues | 350,000 | 420,000 | (i) | 520,000 |
| Total expenses | 320,000 | 385,000 | 350,000 | (l) |

### Instructions
(a) Determine the missing amounts.
(b) Prepare the owner's equity statement for Marshall Company.
(c) ▌▌▌▌► Write a memorandum explaining the sequence for preparing financial statements and the interrelationship of the owner's equity statement to the income statement and balance sheet.

## BROADENING YOUR PERSPECTIVE

# FINANCIAL REPORTING AND ANALYSIS

**FINANCIAL REPORTING PROBLEM: Kellogg Company**

**BYP1–1** The actual financial statements of Kellogg Company, as presented in the company's 1997 Annual Report, are contained in Appendix A (at the back of the textbook).

*Instructions*
Refer to Kellogg's financial statements and answer the following questions:
- (a) What were Kellogg's total assets at December 31, 1997? At December 31, 1996?
- (b) How much cash (and cash equivalents) did Kellogg have on December 31, 1997?
- (c) What amount of accounts payable did Kellogg report on December 31, 1997? On December 31, 1996?
- (d) What were Kellogg's net sales in 1995? In 1996? In 1997?
- (e) What is the amount of the change in Kellogg's net income from 1996 to 1997?

**COMPARATIVE ANALYSIS PROBLEM: Kellogg Company vs. General Mills**

**BYP1–2** Kellogg's financial statements are presented in Appendix A; General Mills's financial statements are presented in Appendix B.

*Instructions*
- (a) Based on the information contained in these financial statements, determine the following for each company;
    - (1) Total assets at December 31, 1997, for Kellogg and at May 25, 1997, for General Mills.
    - (2) Accounts (notes) receivable, less allowances at December 31, 1997, for Kellogg and at May 25, 1997, for General Mills.
    - (3) Net sales for 1997.
    - (4) Net income for 1997.
- (b) What conclusions concerning the two companies can be drawn from these data?

**RESEARCH ASSIGNMENT**

**BYP1–3** To do financial research, you need to know where to look. This assignment, in two parts, will familiarize you with two important resources.

Part 1: *The Wall Street Journal* (WSJ), published weekdays by Dow Jones & Company, Inc., is a premier source of business information.

*Instructions*
Examine a recent copy of the WSJ and answer the following questions:
- (a) How many separate sections are included in the WSJ? What are the contents of each?
- (b) An index of the companies referenced in each edition is included on page 2 of section B. Select a company from the index and read the associated article. What is the article about? Identify any accounting-related issues discussed in the article.

Part 2: Most libraries have company annual reports on file or available on microfiche.

*Instructions*
Examine copies of the financial statements of two companies and answer the following questions:
- (a) What were the total assets, total liabilities, and total stockholders' equity at the most recent balance sheet date?
- (b) Mathematically demonstrate the basic accounting equation for each company.
- (c) What were the total current assets and total current liabilities at the most recent balance sheet date?

(d) What were the net sales (or revenue) and net income in the most recent income statement?

## INTERPRETING FINANCIAL STATEMENTS: Lincoln Village Properties, Inc.

BYP1–4    Lincoln Village Properites, Inc., is a property management firm in Springfield, Missouri, that provides residential property management such as grounds maintenance, minor repair service, and trash collection for an annual fee. A portion of Lincoln Village's previous year's balance sheet follows:

---

### LINCOLN VILLAGE PROPERTIES, INC.
### Balance Sheet (partial)

#### Assets

| | |
|---|---|
| Cash | $ 10,000 |
| Accounts receivable | 2,000 |
| Supplies inventory | 8,000 |
| Machinery and equipment, net | 80,000 |
| Other noncurrent assets | 5,000 |
| Total assets | $105,000 |

---

During the current year, the following events occurred:
1. $25,000 of machinery, net, was sold for cash.
2. $100,000 was received from cash sales.
3. $115,000 was paid for cash expenses.
4. Customers contracted for $150,000 in services on credit.
5. Lincoln Village Properties collected $148,000 from accounts receivable.

### Instructions
Prepare the Assets portion of the current year's balance sheet for Lincoln Village Properties.

## REAL-WORLD FOCUS: Air Transportation Holding Company Inc.

BYP1–5    Founded in 1980, **Air Transportation Holding Company** operates contract cargo shipping, specializing in small, overnight deliveries throughout the eastern United States. The company flies approximately 80 routes, as specified in its contracts with Federal Express. It has hangars and maintenance facilities in North Carolina, Michigan, and South Carolina.

The specific assets, liabilities, and subdivisions of owner's equity of any business depend on the type of business being operated. Management of Air Transportation Holding Company explained the year's results of operations as follows:

---

### AIR TRANSPORTATION HOLDING COMPANY
### Management Discussion

Operating expenses increased $5,498,000 (29.9%) to $23,904,000 in a recent year compared to the prior year. The increase in operating expenses consisted of the following changes: cost of flight operations increased $2,313,000 (25.7%) as a result of increases in pilot and flight personnel and costs associated with travel and landing fees which were partially offset by decreased aircraft lease and fuel costs; maintenance expense increased $2,850,000 (42.9%) primarily as a result of increases in aircraft parts purchases and mechanic and maintenance personnel costs (due to start-up of satellite maintenance facility and the operation of additional aircraft); the general and administrative expense increase of $470,000 (17.3%) resulted from increases in operational and clerical staffing related to expansion of the aircraft fleet operated.

---

*Instructions*

(a) Recall the definition of an asset. Can you identify three specific types of assets owned by Air Transportation Holding Company?

(b) The discussion above is largely about the operating expenses of the company. Identify five expenses of operations that Air Transportation incurs.

(c) When this company renders service by providing air transportation, what account affecting owner's equity is increased?

# CRITICAL THINKING

## GROUP DECISION CASE

**BYP1-6**  Patsy and Perry Ross, local golf stars, opened the Long-Shot Driving Range on March 1, 1999, by investing $10,000 of their cash savings in the business. A caddy shack was constructed for cash at a cost of $4,000 and $800 was spent on golf balls and golf clubs. The Rosses leased five acres of land at a cost of $1,000 per month and paid the first month's rent. During the first month, advertising costs totaled $750 of which $150 was unpaid at March 31, and $400 was paid to members of the high school golf team for retrieving golf balls. All revenues from customers were deposited in the company's bank account. On March 15, Patsy and Perry withdrew a total of $800 in cash for personal living expenses. A $100 utility bill was received on March 31 but it was not paid. On March 31, the balance in the company's bank account was $7,550.

Patsy and Perry thought they had a pretty good first month of operations. However, their estimates of profitability ranged from a loss of $2,450 to net income of $2,100.

*Instructions*

With the class divided into groups, answer the following:

(a) How could the Rosses have concluded that the business operated at a loss of $2,450? Was this a valid basis on which to determine net income?

(b) How could the Rosses have concluded that the business operated at a net income of $2,100? *(Hint:* Prepare a balance sheet at March 31.) Was this a valid basis on which to determine net income?

(c) Without preparing an income statement, determine the actual net income for March.

(d) What was the revenue earned in March?

## COMMUNICATION ACTIVITY

**BYP1-7**  Lynn Bowen is the bookkeeper for Texas Company. Lynn has been trying to get the balance sheet of Texas Company to balance. The company's balance sheet is as follows:

### TEXAS COMPANY
### Balance Sheet
### For the Month Ended December 31, 1999

| Assets | | Liabilities | |
|---|---|---|---|
| Equipment | $21,500 | Thompson, Capital | $21,000 |
| Cash | 9,000 | Accounts receivable | 3,000 |
| Supplies | 2,000 | Thompson, Drawing | (2,000) |
| Accounts payable | (6,000) | Notes payable | 10,500 |
| | $37,500 | | $32,500 |

*Instructions*

Explain to Lynn Bowen in a memo why the original balance sheet is incorrect, and what should be done to correct it.

## ETHICS CASE

**BYP1–8**   After numerous campus interviews, Steve Pelli, a senior at Great Eastern College, received two office interview invitations from the Baltimore offices of two large firms. Both firms offered to cover his out-of-pocket expenses (travel, hotel, and meal). He scheduled the interviews for both firms on the same day, one in the morning and one in the afternoon. At the conclusion of each interview, he submitted to both firms his total out-of-pocket expenses for the trip to Baltimore, $244: mileage $70 (280 miles at $.25), hotel $120, meals $36, parking and tolls $18, for a total of $244. He believes this approach is appropriate. If he had made two trips, his cost would have been two times $244. He is also certain that neither firm knew he had visited the other on that same trip. Within ten days Steve received two checks in the mail, each in the amount of $244.

*Instructions*
- (a)  Who are the stakeholders (affected parties) in this situation?
- (b)  What are the ethical issues in this case?
- (c)  What would you do in this situation?

# SURFING THE NET

**BYP1–9**   This exercise will familiarize you with skill requirements, job descriptions, and salaries for accounting careers.

*Address:* http://www.cob.ohio-state.edu/dept/fin/jobsaccount.htm

*Instructions*
Go to the site shown above. Answer the following questions:

- (a)  What are the three broad areas of accounting?
- (b)  List four skills required in these areas.
- (c)  How do these areas differ in required skills?
- (d)  Explain one of the key job functions in accounting.
- (e)  Based on the *Smart Money* survey, what is the salary range for a junior staff accountant with Deloitte & Touche?

*Answers to Self-Study Questions*
1. b    2. d    3. a    4. c    5. a    6. d    7. b    8. a    9. b    10. c

*Answer to Kellogg Review It Question 4, p. 15*
Kellogg's accounting equation is:

| Assets | = | Liabilities | + | Owner's (Stockholders') Equity |
|---|---|---|---|---|
| $4,877,600,000 | = | $3,880,100,000 | + | $997,500,000 |

Remember to go back to the Navigator box on the chapter-opening page and check off your completed work.

Concepts for Review highlight accounting concepts that you need to understand from earlier chapters before starting the new chapter.

**Before studying this chapter, you should know or, if necessary, review:**

a. What are assets, liabilities, owner's capital, owner's drawings, revenues, and expenses. (Ch. 1, pp. 13–15)

b. Why assets equal liabilities plus owner's equity. (Ch. 1, pp. 12–13)

c. What transactions are and how they affect the basic accounting equation. (Ch. 1, pp. 16–22)

THE NAVIGATOR

## FEATURE STORY

# Her Classroom Is the Real World

Gabriella Torres of San Diego learned how to record transactions on a computer before she took her first accounting course. The reason: by day, she manages the office of Diabetes & Endocrine Associates, a medical practice with an office located near San Diego State University. The doctors' office uses a computer package that makes recording transactions quite easy for Gabriella. She attends night school and hopes to graduate within six years. "The doctors have really been accommodating to my school schedule."

Working during the day allows Gabriella to bring a real-world perspective to the classroom. In turn, studying business subjects at night makes her job easier. She is in charge of paying the bills for the medical practice, making sure the bank statement reconciles with the checkbook, hiring office staff, preparing patient bills, and maintaining accounts receivable. "I really love my job," she says, which is one reason she prefers to work days and go to school at night.

Taking her first accounting course helped Gabriella understand how the journal entries, the accounts, and financial statements fit together. Unlike doing homework assignments, though, the computer package at work catches some of her errors. "It won't let you proceed from one accounting entry to the next unless the entry balances," she says. In fact, there are no "books" at all, just diskettes and printouts.

THE NAVIGATOR

# CHAPTER 2

# THE RECORDING PROCESS

**THE NAVIGATOR** ✔

- Understand *Concepts for Review* ☐
- Read *Feature Story* ☐
- Scan *Study Objectives* ☐
- Read *Preview* ☐
- Read text and answer *Before You Go On*
  p. 51 ☐ p. 54 ☐ p. 64 ☐ p. 69 ☐
- Work *Demonstration Problem* ☐
- Review *Summary of Study Objectives* ☐
- Answer *Self-Study Questions* ☐
- Complete assignments ☐

## STUDY OBJECTIVES

**After studying this chapter, you should be able to:**

1. Explain what an account is and how it helps in the recording process.
2. Define debits and credits and explain how they are used to record business transactions.
3. Identify the basic steps in the recording process.
4. Explain what a journal is and how it helps in the recording process.
5. Explain what a ledger is and how it helps in the recording process.
6. Explain what posting is and how it helps in the recording process.
7. Prepare a trial balance and explain its purposes.

THE NAVIGATOR

*I*n Chapter 1, we analyzed business transactions in terms of the accounting equation and presented the cumulative effects of these transactions in tabular form. Imagine a medical practice such as Diabetes & Endocrine Associates using the same tabular format as Softbyte to keep track of every one of its transactions. In a single day, this medical practice engages in hundreds of business transactions. To record each transaction this way would be impractical, expensive, and unnecessary.

As a result, a set of procedures and records are used to make it possible to keep track of and accumulate transaction data more easily. In this chapter we will introduce and illustrate the basic procedures and records that are used. The content and organization of the chapter are as follows:

THE NAVIGATOR

**1**
STUDY
OBJECTIVE

Explain what an account is and how it helps in the recording process.

# THE ACCOUNT

An account is an individual accounting record of increases and decreases in a specific asset, liability, or owner's equity item. For example, Softbyte (discussed in Chapter 1) would have separate accounts for Cash, Accounts Receivable, Accounts Payable, Service Revenue, Salaries Expense, and so on. In its simplest form, an account consists of three parts: (1) the title of the account, (2) a left or debit side, and (3) a right or credit side. Because the alignment of these parts of an account resembles the letter T, it is referred to as a T account. The basic form of an account is shown in Illustration 2-1.

**ILLUSTRATION 2-1**

*Basic form of account*

| Title of Account | |
|---|---|
| Left or debit side | Right or credit side |
| Debit balance | Credit balance |

**T Account**

The T account is a standard shorthand in accounting that helps make clear the effects of transactions on individual accounts. This form of account will be used often throughout this book to explain basic accounting relationships.

# TECHNOLOGY IN ACTION

Computerized and manual accounting systems basically parallel one another. Most of the procedures are handled by electronic circuitry in computerized systems. They seem to occur invisibly. Therefore, to fully comprehend how computerized systems operate, it is necessary to illustrate and understand manual approaches for processing accounting data.

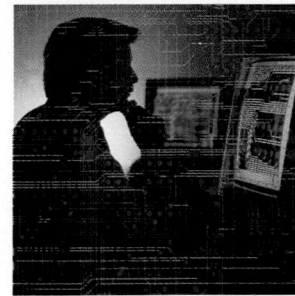

## Debits and Credits

The terms debit and credit mean left and right, respectively. They are commonly abbreviated as Dr. for debit and Cr. for credit.[1] These terms do not mean increase or decrease. The terms debit and credit are used repeatedly in the recording process. For example, the act of entering an amount on the left side of an account is called **debiting** the account, and making an entry on the right side is **crediting** the account. When the totals of the two sides are compared, an account will have a **debit balance** if the total of the debit amounts exceeds the credits. Conversely, an account will have a **credit balance** if the credit amounts exceed the debits.

The procedure of having debits on the left and credits on the right is an accounting custom, or rule. We could function just as well if debits and credits were reversed. However, the custom of having debits on the left side of an account and credits on the right side (like the custom of driving on the right-hand side of the road) has been adopted in the United States. **This rule applies to all accounts.**

The procedure of recording debits and credits in an account is shown in Illustration 2-2 for the cash transactions of Softbyte. The data are taken from the cash column of the tabular summary in Illustration 1-10.

**2**
STUDY
OBJECTIVE
...............................................
Define debits and credits and explain how they are used to record business transactions.

**ILLUSTRATION 2-2**

*Tabular summary compared to account form*

| Tabular Summary | Account Form |
|---|---|

| Cash | Cash | | | |
|---|---|---|---|---|
| $15,000 | (Debits) | 15,000 | (Credits) | 7,000 |
| −7,000 | | 1,200 | | 1,700 |
| 1,200 | | 1,500 | | 250 |
| 1,500 | | 600 | | 1,300 |
| −1,700 | Balance | 8,050 | | |
| −250 | (Debit) | | | |
| 600 | | | | |
| −1,300 | | | | |
| $ 8,050 | | | | |

**HELPFUL HINT**
The word credit has a different meaning in accounting than it has in everyday life. For accounting purposes, think of the terms debit and credit solely as directional signals. Debit—use the left side of the account; credit—use the right side.

Every positive item in the tabular summary represents a receipt of cash; every negative amount constitutes a payment of cash. Notice that in the account form the increases in cash are recorded as debits, and the decreases in cash are recorded as credits. Having increases on one side and decreases on the other helps

---

[1]These abbreviations come from the Latin words *debere* (Dr.) and *credere* (Cr.).

in determining the totals of each side of the account as well as the balance in the account. The account balance, a debit of $8,050, indicates that Softbyte has had $8,050 more increases than decreases in cash. That is, it has $8,050 in its Cash account.

## Debit and Credit Procedure

In Chapter 1 you learned the effect of a transaction on the basic accounting equation. Remember that each transaction must affect two or more accounts to keep the basic accounting equation in balance. In other words, for each transaction debits must equal credits in the accounts. The equality of debits and credits provides the basis for the double-entry system of recording transactions (sometimes referred to as double-entry bookkeeping).

Under the universally used double-entry system, the dual (two-sided) effect of each transaction is recorded in appropriate accounts. This system provides a logical method for recording transactions. It also offers a means of proving the accuracy of the recorded amounts. If every transaction is recorded with equal debits and credits, then the sum of all the debits to the accounts must equal the sum of all the credits.

The double-entry system for determining the equality of the accounting equation is much more efficient than the plus/minus procedure used in Chapter 1. There, it was necessary after each transaction to compare total assets with total liabilities and owner's equity to determine the equality of the two sides of the accounting equation.

**Assets and Liabilities.**   In the Softbyte illustration above, increases in cash—an asset—were entered on the left side, and decreases in cash were entered on the right side. We know that both sides of the basic equation (assets = liabilities + owner's equity) must be equal; it then follows that increases and decreases in liabilities will have to be recorded opposite from increases and decreases in assets. Thus, increases in liabilities must be entered on the right or credit side, and decreases in liabilities must be entered on the left or debit side. The effects that debits and credits have on assets and liabilities are summarized as follows:

**ILLUSTRATION 2-3**

*Debit and credit effects—assets and liabilities*

|  Debits  |  Credits  |
| --- | --- |
| Increase assets | Decrease assets |
| Decrease liabilities | Increase liabilities |

Debits to a specific asset account should exceed the credits to that account, and credits to a liability account should exceed debits to that account. Thus, asset accounts normally show debit balances, and liability accounts normally show credit balances. The normal balances may be diagrammed as follows:

**ILLUSTRATION 2-4**

*Normal balances—assets and liabilities*

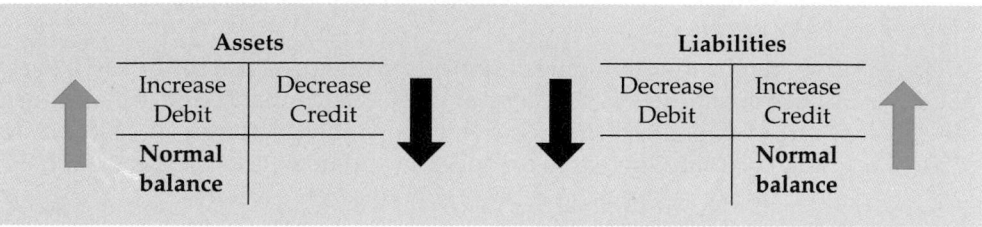

An awareness of the normal balance in an account may help you when you are trying to trace errors. For example, a credit balance in an asset account such as Land or a debit balance in a liability account such as Wages Payable would indicate errors in recording. Occasionally, however, an abnormal balance may be correct. The Cash account, for example, will have a credit balance when a company has overdrawn its bank balance (i.e., written a "bad" check).

**Owner's Equity.**    As indicated in Chapter 1, owner's equity is increased by owner's investments and revenues. It is decreased by owner's drawings and expenses. In a double-entry system, accounts are kept for each of these types of transactions, as explained below.

*Owner's Capital.*    Investments by owners are credited to the owner's capital account. The owner's capital account is increased by credits and decreased by debits. For example, when cash is invested in the business, cash is debited and owner's capital is credited. Conversely, owner's capital is debited when the owner's investment in the business is reduced.

The rules of debit and credit for the owner's capital account are stated as follows:

| Debits | Credits |
| --- | --- |
| Decrease owner's capital | Increase owner's capital |

**ILLUSTRATION 2-5**
*Debit and credit effects—owner's capital*

The normal balance in this account may be diagrammed as follows:

| Owner's Capital | |
| --- | --- |
| Decrease Debit | Increase Credit |
| | Normal balance |

**ILLUSTRATION 2-6**
*Normal balance—owner's capital*

*Owner's Drawing.*    An owner may withdraw cash or other assets for personal use. Withdrawals could be debited directly to owner's capital to indicate a decrease in owner's equity. However, it is preferable to establish a separate account, referred to as the owner's drawing account, in order to determine the total withdrawals for the accounting period. **The drawing account decreases owner's equity. It is not an income statement account like revenues and expenses.** Owner's drawing is increased by debits and decreased by credits. Normally, the drawing account will have a debit balance. The rules of debit and credit for the drawing account are stated as follows:

| Debits | Credits |
| --- | --- |
| Increase owner's drawing | Decrease owner's drawing |

**ILLUSTRATION 2-7**
*Debit and credit effects—owner's drawing*

The normal balance may be diagrammed as follows:

**ILLUSTRATION 2-8**

*Normal balance—owner's drawing*

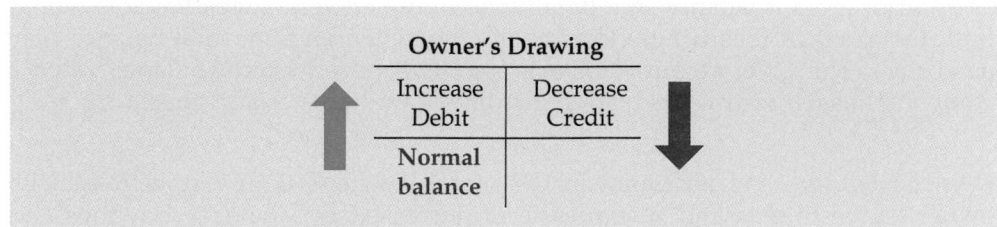

|  | Owner's Drawing |  |
|---|---|---|
| ↑ | Increase<br>Debit | Decrease<br>Credit | ↓ |
|  | Normal<br>balance |  |

**Revenues and Expenses.**  When revenues are earned, owner's equity is increased. Accordingly, **the effect of debits and credits on revenue accounts is identical to their effect on owner's capital**. Revenue accounts are increased by credits and decreased by debits.

On the other hand, expenses decrease owner's equity. As a result, expenses are recorded by debits. Since expenses are the negative factor in the computation of net income, and revenues are the positive factor, it is logical that the increase and decrease sides of expense accounts should be the reverse of revenue accounts. Thus, expense accounts are increased by debits and decreased by credits. The effect of debits and credits on revenues and expenses may be stated as follows:

**HELPFUL HINT**

Because revenues increase owner's equity, a revenue account has the same debit and credit rules as does the owner's capital account. Conversely, expenses have the opposite effect.

**ILLUSTRATION 2-9**

*Debit and credit effects—revenues and expenses*

| Debits | Credits |
|---|---|
| Decrease revenues | Increase revenues |
| Increase expenses | Decrease expenses |

Credits to revenue accounts should exceed the debits, and debits to expense accounts should exceed credits. Thus, revenue accounts normally show credit balances and expense accounts normally show debit balances. The normal balances may be diagrammed as follows:

**ILLUSTRATION 2-10**

*Normal balances—revenues and expenses*

|  | Revenues |  |  |  | Expenses |  |
|---|---|---|---|---|---|---|
| ↓ | Decrease<br>Debit | Increase<br>Credit | ↑ | ↑ | Increase<br>Debit | Decrease<br>Credit | ↓ |
|  |  | Normal<br>balance |  |  | Normal<br>balance |  |

## ACCOUNTING IN ACTION
### Business Insight

The Chicago Cubs baseball team has the following major revenue and expense accounts:

| Revenues | Expenses |
|---|---|
| Admissions (ticket sales) | Players' salaries |
| Concessions | Administrative salaries |
| Television and radio | Travel |
| Advertising | Ballpark maintenance |

## Expansion of Basic Equation

You have already learned the basic accounting equation. Illustration 2-11 expands this equation to show the accounts that comprise owner's equity. In addition, the debit/credit rules and effects on each type of account are illustrated. Study this diagram carefully. It will help you understand the fundamentals of the double-entry system. Like the basic equation, the expanded basic equation must be in balance (total debits equal total credits).

**ILLUSTRATION 2-11**

*Expanded basic equation and debit/credit rules and effects*

# BEFORE YOU GO ON . . .

## Review It

1. What do the terms debit and credit mean?
2. What are the debit and credit effects on assets, liabilities, and owner's capital?
3. What are the debit and credit effects on revenues, expenses, and owner's drawing?
4. What are the normal balances for Kellogg Company's cash, accounts payable, and interest expense accounts? The answers to this question are provided on page 88.

## Do It

Kate Browne has just rented space in a shopping mall for the purpose of opening and operating a beauty salon, to be called "Hair It Is." Long before opening day and before purchasing equipment, hiring assistants, and remodeling the space, Kate is strongly advised to set up a double-entry set of accounting records in which to record all of her business transactions.

Identify the balance sheet accounts that Kate will likely need to record the transactions necessary to establish and open her business. Also, indicate whether the normal balance of each account is a debit or a credit.

*Reasoning:* To start her business, Kate will need to have asset accounts for each different type of asset invested in the business. In addition, Kate will need liability accounts for debts incurred by the business. Kate will only need one owner's equity account, owner's capital, when she begins the business. The other owner's equity accounts will only be needed after business has commenced.

*Solution:* Kate would likely need the following accounts in which to record the transactions necessary to establish and ready her beauty salon for opening day: Cash (debit balance); Equipment (debit balance); Supplies (debit balance); Accounts Payable (credit balance); if she borrows money, Notes Payable (credit balance); K. Browne, Capital (credit balance).

*Related exercise material:* BE2–1, BE2–2, E2–1, E2–3, and E2–10.

THE
NAVIGATOR

# STEPS IN THE RECORDING PROCESS

Although it is possible to enter transaction information directly into the accounts, few businesses do so. In practically every business, the basic steps in the recording process are:

1. Analyze each transaction in terms of its effect on the accounts.
2. Enter the transaction information in a journal (book of original entry).
3. Transfer the journal information to the appropriate accounts in the ledger (book of accounts).

The actual sequence of events begins with the transaction. Evidence of the transaction comes in the form of a **business document**, such as a sales slip, a check, a bill, or a cash register tape. This evidence is analyzed to determine the effect of the transaction on specific accounts. The transaction is then entered in the journal. Finally, the journal entry is transferred to the designated accounts in the ledger. The sequence of events in the recording process can be diagrammed as follows:

**The Recording Process**

Analyze each transaction          Enter transaction in a journal          Transfer journal information to ledger accounts

**ILLUSTRATION 2-12**

*The recording process*

The basic steps in the recording process occur repeatedly in every business enterprise. The analysis of transactions has already been illustrated, and further examples of this step will be given in this and later chapters. The other steps in the recording process are explained in the next sections.

## The Journal

Transactions are initially recorded in chronological order in a journal before being transferred to the accounts. Thus, the journal is referred to as the book of original entry. For each transaction the journal shows the debit and credit effects on specific accounts. Companies may use various kinds of journals, but every company has the most basic form of journal, a general journal. Typically, a general journal has spaces for dates, account titles and explanations, references, and two money columns. Whenever the term journal is used in this textbook without a modifying adjective, it will mean the general journal.

The journal makes several significant contributions to the recording process:

1. It discloses in one place the complete effect of a transaction.
2. It provides a chronological record of transactions.

**3.** It helps to prevent or locate errors because the debit and credit amounts for each entry can be readily compared.

## Journalizing

Entering transaction data in the journal is known as journalizing. Separate journal entries are made for each transaction. A complete entry consists of: (1) the date of the transaction, (2) the accounts and amounts to be debited and credited, and (3) a brief explanation of the transaction.

To illustrate the technique of journalizing, the first two transactions of Softbyte are journalized in Illustration 2-13 using the first page (J1) of the general journal. These transactions were: September 1, Ray Neal invested $15,000 cash in the business, and computer equipment was purchased for $7,000 cash.

| Date | Account Titles and Explanation | Ref. | Debit | Credit |
|------|-------------------------------|------|-------|--------|
| 1999 | | | | |
| Sept. 1 | Cash | | 15,000 | |
| | R. Neal, Capital | | | 15,000 |
| | (Owner's investment of cash in business) | | | |
| 1 | Computer Equipment | | 7,000 | |
| | Cash | | | 7,000 |
| | (Purchase of equipment for cash) | | | |

GENERAL JOURNAL — J1

**ILLUSTRATION 2-13**
*Technique of journalizing*

The standard form and content of journal entries are as follows:

**1.** The date of the transaction is entered in the Date column. The date recorded should include the year, month, and day of the transaction.
**2.** The debit account title (that is, the account to be debited) is entered first at the extreme left margin of the column headed "Account Titles and Explanation," and the amount of the debit is recorded in the Debit column.
**3.** The credit account title (that is, the account to be credited) is indented and entered on the next line in the column headed "Account Titles and Explanation," and the amount of the credit is recorded in the Credit column.
**4.** A brief explanation of the transaction is given.
**5.** A space is left between journal entries. The blank space separates individual journal entries and makes the entire journal easier to read.
**6.** The column entitled Ref. (which stands for reference) is left blank at the time the journal entry is made. The Reference column is used later when the journal entries are transferred to the ledger accounts. At that time, the ledger account number is placed in the Reference column to indicate where the amount in the journal entry was transferred.

**It is important to use correct and specific account titles in journalizing.** Since most accounts appear later in the financial statements, erroneous account titles lead to incorrect financial statements. Some flexibility exists initially in selecting account titles. The main criterion is that each title must appropriately describe the content of the account. For example, the account title used for the cost of delivery trucks may be Delivery Equipment, Delivery Trucks, or Trucks.

Once a company chooses the specific title to use, all subsequent transactions involving the account should be recorded under that account title.[2]

If an entry involves only two accounts, one debit and one credit, it is considered a *simple entry*. For some transactions, however, it may be necessary to use more than two accounts in journalizing. Imagine, for example, the numerous accounts needed by General Electric to record the acquisition of all the assets and liabilities of RCA in what was one of the largest mergers ever completed. When three or more accounts are required in one journal entry, the entry is referred to as a *compound entry*. To illustrate, assume that on July 1, Butler Company purchases a delivery truck costing $14,000 by paying $8,000 cash and the balance on account (to be paid at a later date). The entry is as follows:

**ILLUSTRATION 2-14**

*Compound journal entry*

| GENERAL JOURNAL | | | | | J1 |
|---|---|---|---|---|---|
| Date | Account Titles and Explanation | Ref. | Debit | Credit |
| 1999 | | | | |
| July 1 | Delivery Equipment | | 14,000 | |
| | Cash | | | 8,000 |
| | Accounts Payable | | | 6,000 |
| | (Purchased truck for cash with balance on account) | | | |

**HELPFUL HINT**

Assume you find this compound entry:

Wages Expense 700
Cash 1,200
Advert. Expense 400
(Paid cash for wages and advertising)

Is the entry correct? No. It is incorrect in form because both debits should be listed before the credit. It is incorrect in content because the debit amounts do not equal the credit amount.

In a compound entry, it is important to determine that the total debit and credit amounts are equal. Also, the standard format requires that all debits be listed before the credits are listed.

## BEFORE YOU GO ON . . .

### Review It

1. What is the correct sequence of the steps in the recording process?
2. What contribution does the journal make to the recording process?
3. What is the standard form and content of a journal entry made in the general journal?

### Do It

In establishing her beauty salon, Hair It Is, Kate Browne engaged in the following activities:

1. Opened a bank account in the name of Hair It Is and deposited $20,000 of her own money in this account as her initial investment.
2. Purchased on account (to be paid in 30 days) equipment, for a total cost of $4,800.
3. Interviewed three persons for the position of beautician.

In what form (type of record) should Kate record these three activities? Prepare the entries to record the transactions.

---

[2]In homework problems, when specific account titles are given, they should be used. When account titles are not given, you may select account titles that identify the nature and content of each account. The account titles used in journalizing should not contain explanations such as Cash Paid or Cash Received.

*Reasoning:* Kate should record the transactions in a journal, which is a chronological record of the transactions. The record should be a complete and accurate representation of the transactions' effects on her business's assets, liabilities, and owner's equity.

*Solution:* Each transaction that is recorded is entered in the general journal. The three activities would be recorded as follows:

| | | |
|---|---|---|
| 1. Cash | 20,000 | |
|     K. Browne, Capital | | 20,000 |
|        (Owner's investment of cash in business) | | |
| 2. Equipment | 4,800 | |
|     Accounts Payable | | 4,800 |
|        (Purchase of equipment on account) | | |

3. No entry because no transaction has occurred.

*Related exercise material:* BE2–3, BE2–5, BE2–6, E2–2, E2–4, E2–6, E2–7, and E2–8.

THE NAVIGATOR

# The Ledger

The entire group of accounts maintained by a company is referred to collectively as the ledger. The ledger keeps in one place all the information about changes in specific account balances.

Companies may use various kinds of ledgers, but every company has a general ledger. A general ledger contains all the assets, liabilities, and owner's equity accounts, as shown in Illustration 2-15. A business can use a looseleaf binder or card file for the ledger with each account kept on a separate sheet or card. Whenever the term ledger is used in this textbook without a modifying adjective, it will mean the general ledger.

**5**
STUDY OBJECTIVE

Explain what a ledger is and how it helps in the recording process.

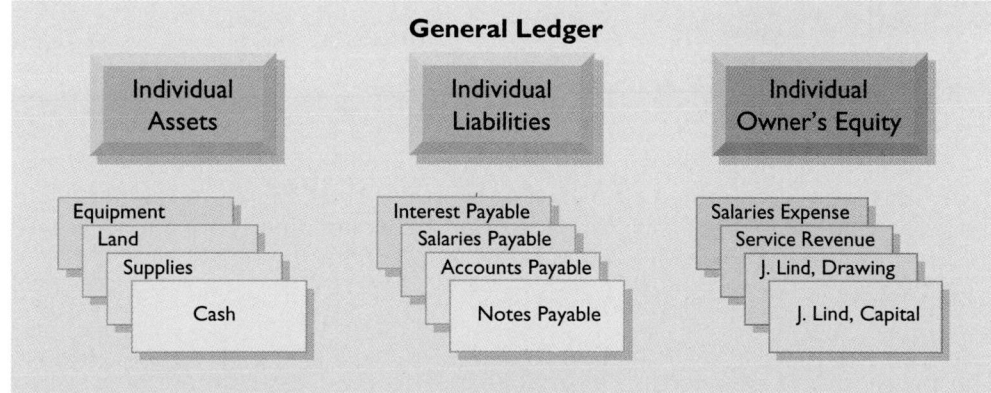

**ILLUSTRATION 2-15**
*The general ledger*

The ledger should be arranged in statement order beginning with the balance sheet accounts. First in order are the asset accounts, followed by liability accounts, owner's capital, owner's drawing, revenues, and expenses. Each account is numbered for easier identification.

The information in the ledger provides management with the balances in various accounts. For example, the Cash account enables management to determine the amount of cash that is available to meet current obligations. Amounts due from customers and the amounts owed to creditors can be determined by examining the Accounts Receivable and Accounts Payable accounts, respectively.

## ACCOUNTING IN ACTION
### Business Insight

In his autobiography Sam Walton described the double-entry accounting system he began the Wal-Mart empire with: "We kept a little pigeonhole on the wall for the cash receipts and paperwork of each [Wal-Mart] store. I had a blue binder ledger book for each store. When we added a store, we added a pigeonhole. We did this at least up to twenty stores. Then once a month, the bookkeeper and I would enter the merchandise, enter the sales, enter the cash, and balance it."

*Source:* Sam Walton, *Made in America* (New York: Doubleday, 1992), p. 53.

### Standard Form of Account

The simple T-account form of an account used in an accounting textbook is often very useful for illustration and analysis purposes. However, in practice, the account forms used in ledgers are much more structured. A form widely used in a manual system is shown in Illustration 2-16, using assumed data from a cash account.

**ILLUSTRATION 2-16**

*Three-column form of account*

| | | CASH | | | | No. 10 |
|---|---|---|---|---|---|---|
| **Date** | | **Explanation** | **Ref.** | **Debit** | **Credit** | **Balance** |
| 1999 | | | | | | |
| June | 1 | | | 25,000 | | 25,000 |
| | 2 | | | | 8,000 | 17,000 |
| | 3 | | | 4,200 | | 21,200 |
| | 9 | | | 7,500 | | 28,700 |
| | 17 | | | | 11,700 | 17,000 |
| | 20 | | | | 250 | 16,750 |
| | 30 | | | | 7,300 | 9,450 |

This form has three money columns—debit, credit, and balance. The balance in the account is determined after each transaction. Thus, this form is often called the three-column form of account. Note that the explanation space and reference columns are used to provide special information about the transaction.

### Posting

**6**
STUDY
OBJECTIVE
Explain what posting is and how it helps in the recording process.

The procedure of transferring journal entries to the ledger accounts is called posting. **This phase of the recording process accumulates the effects of journalized transactions in the individual accounts.**

Posting involves the following steps:

1. In the ledger, enter in the appropriate columns of the account(s) debited the date, journal page, and debit amount shown in the journal.
2. In the reference column of the journal, write the account number to which the debit amount was posted.
3. In the ledger, enter in the appropriate columns of the account(s) credited the date, journal page, and credit amount shown in the journal.
4. In the reference column of the journal, write the account number to which the credit amount was posted.

These four steps are diagrammed in Illustration 2-17 using the first journal entry of Softbyte. The boxed numbers indicate the sequence of the steps.

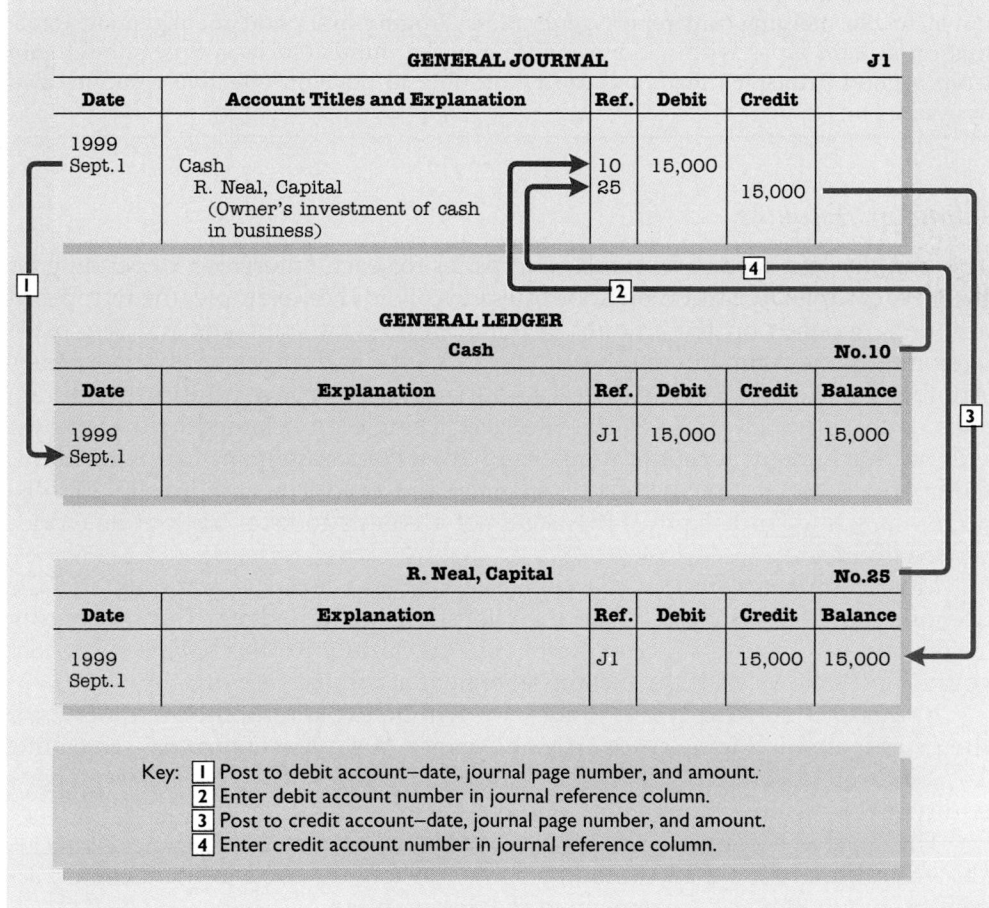

ILLUSTRATION 2-17

*Posting a journal entry*

Posting should be performed in chronological order. That is, all the debits and credits of one journal entry should be posted before proceeding to the next journal entry. Under the journalizing procedures described in this chapter, postings should be made on a timely basis to ensure that the ledger is up to date.[3]

The reference column **in the journal** serves several purposes. The numbers in this column indicate the entries that have been posted. After the last entry has been posted, the journal reference column should be scanned to see that all postings have been made.

The reference column **of a ledger** account indicates the journal page from which the transaction has been posted. The explanation space of the ledger account is used infrequently because an explanation already appears in the journal. It generally is used only when detailed analysis of account activity is required.

---

[3]In homework problems, it will be permissible to journalize all transactions before posting any of the journal entries.

# TECHNOLOGY IN ACTION

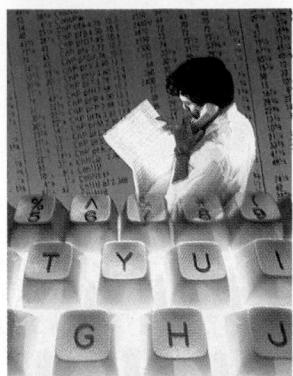

Determining what to record is the most critical (and for most businesses the most expensive) point in the accounting process. In computerized systems, after this phase is completed, your input and all further processing just boil down to file merging and report generation. Programmers and management information system types with good accounting backgrounds (such as they should gain from a good principles textbook) are better able to develop effective computerized systems.

## Chart of Accounts

The number and type of accounts used differ for each enterprise, depending on the size, complexity, and type of business involved. For example, the number of accounts depends on the amount of detail desired by management. The management of one company may want one account for all types of utility expense. Another may keep separate expense accounts for each type of utility expenditure, such as gas, electricity, and water. Similarly, a single proprietorship like Softbyte will not have many accounts compared with a corporate giant like Ford Motor Company. Softbyte may be able to manage and report its activities in 20 to 30 accounts, while Ford requires thousands of accounts to keep track of its worldwide activities.

Most companies have a chart of accounts that lists the accounts and the account numbers which identify their location in the ledger. The numbering system used to identify the accounts usually starts with the balance sheet accounts and follows with the income statement accounts.

In this and the next two chapters, we will be explaining the accounting for the proprietorship Pioneer Advertising Agency (a service enterprise). Accounts 1–19 indicate asset accounts; 20–39 indicate liabilities; 40–49 indicate owner's equity accounts; 50–59, revenues; and 60–69, expenses.

The chart of accounts for Pioneer Advertising Agency (C. R. Byrd, owner) is shown in Illustration 2-18. Accounts shown in red are used in this chapter; accounts shown in black are explained in later chapters.

**ILLUSTRATION 2-18**

*Chart of accounts*

## Chart of Accounts
### Pioneer Advertising Agency

| Assets | Owner's Equity |
| --- | --- |
| 1. Cash | 40. C. R. Byrd, Capital |
| 6. Accounts Receivable | 41. C. R. Byrd, Drawing |
| 8. Advertising Supplies | 49. Income Summary |
| 10. Prepaid Insurance | **Revenues** |
| 15. Office Equipment | |
| 16. Accumulated Depreciation—Office Equipment | 50. Service Revenue |
| **Liabilities** | **Expenses** |
| 25. Notes Payable | 60. Salaries Expense |
| 26. Accounts Payable | 61. Advertising Supplies Expense |
| 27. Interest Payable | 62. Rent Expense |
| 28. Unearned Revenue | 63. Insurance Expense |
| 29. Salaries Payable | 64. Interest Expense |
| | 65. Depreciation Expense |

You will notice that there are gaps in the numbering system of the chart of accounts for Pioneer Advertising. Gaps are left to permit the insertion of new accounts as needed during the life of the business.

## ACCOUNTING IN ACTION
### Business Insight

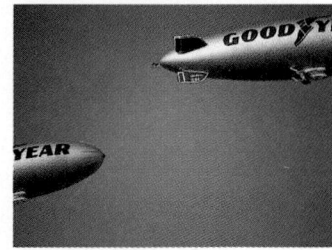

The numbering system used to identify accounts can be quite sophisticated or relatively simple. For example, at Goodyear Tire & Rubber Company an 18-digit system is used. The first three digits identify the division or plant. The second set of three-digit numbers contains the following account classifications:

| | |
|---|---|
| 100–199 Assets | 300–399 Revenues |
| 200–299 Liabilities and Owner's Equity | 400–599 Expenses |

Other digits describe the location of a specific plant, product line, region of the country, and so on. In practice, account numbers are not the same from company to company. Therefore, to reflect the situation you would find in the real world, account numbers in the text and in the homework materials also vary from company to company.

# THE RECORDING PROCESS ILLUSTRATED

Illustrations 2-19 through 2-28 show the basic steps in the recording process, using the October transactions of the Pioneer Advertising Agency. Its accounting period is a month. A basic analysis and a debit-credit analysis precede the

(text continues on page 64)

**ILLUSTRATION 2-19**

*Investment of cash by owner*

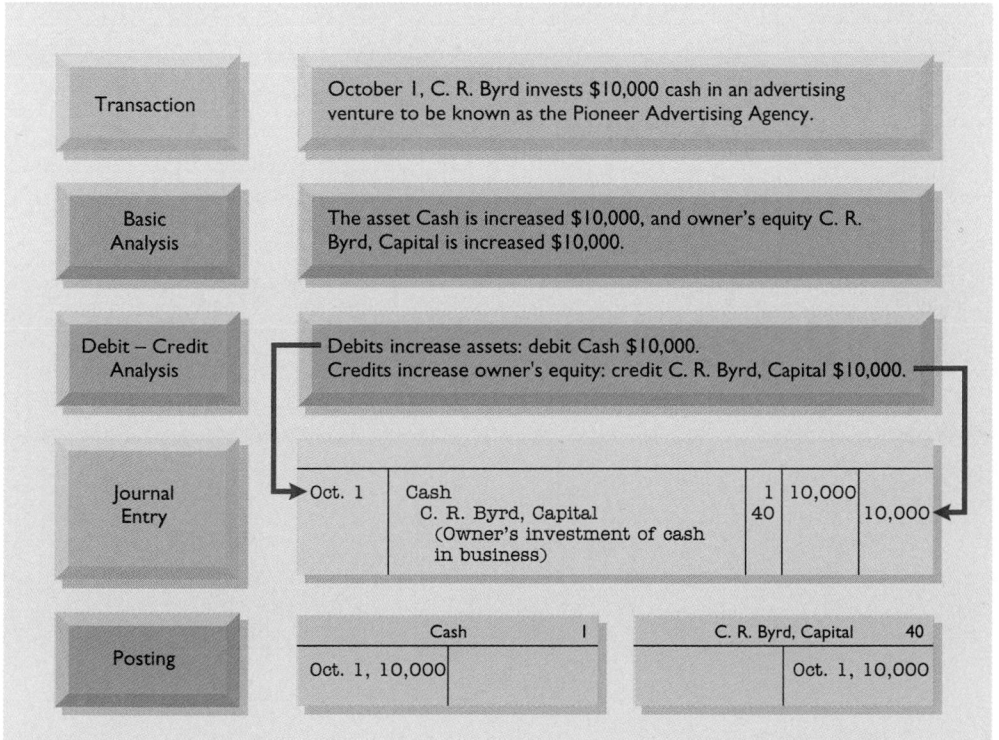

**HELPFUL HINT**
To correctly record a transaction, you must carefully analyze the event and translate that analysis into debit and credit language.
First: Determine what type of account is involved.
Second: Determine what items increased or decreased and by how much.
Third: Translate the increases and decreases into debits and credits.

**ILLUSTRATION 2-20**

*Purchase of office equipment*

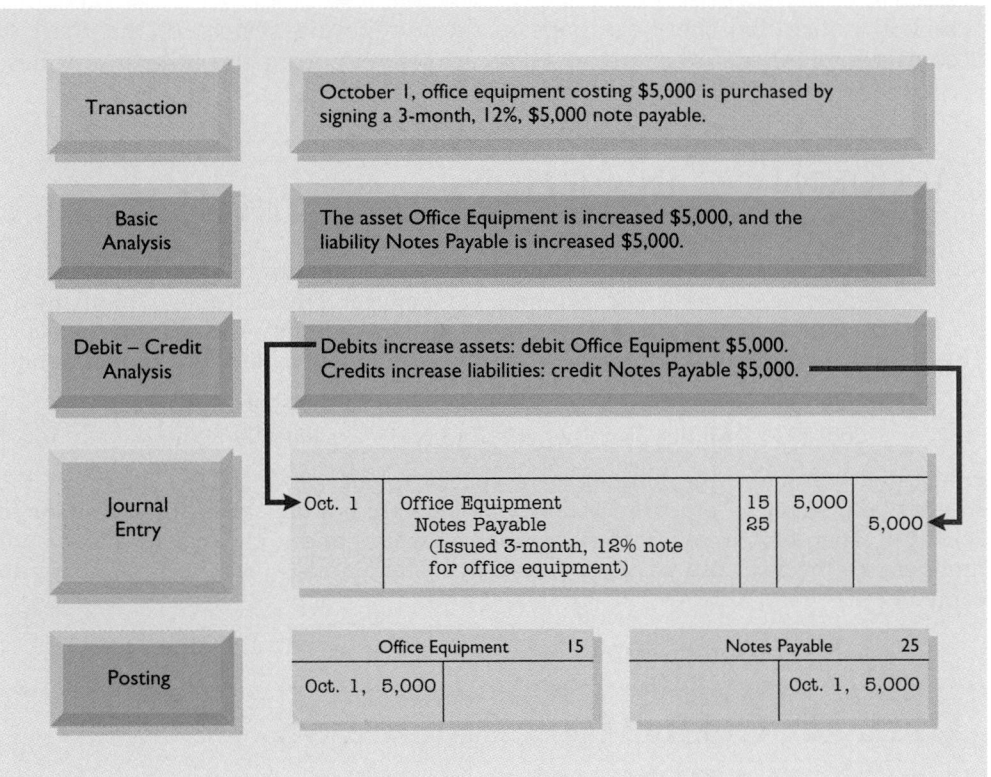

**ILLUSTRATION 2-21**

*Receipt of cash for future service*

**HELPFUL HINT**

When the revenue is earned, the unearned revenue account is debited, and an earned revenue account is credited.

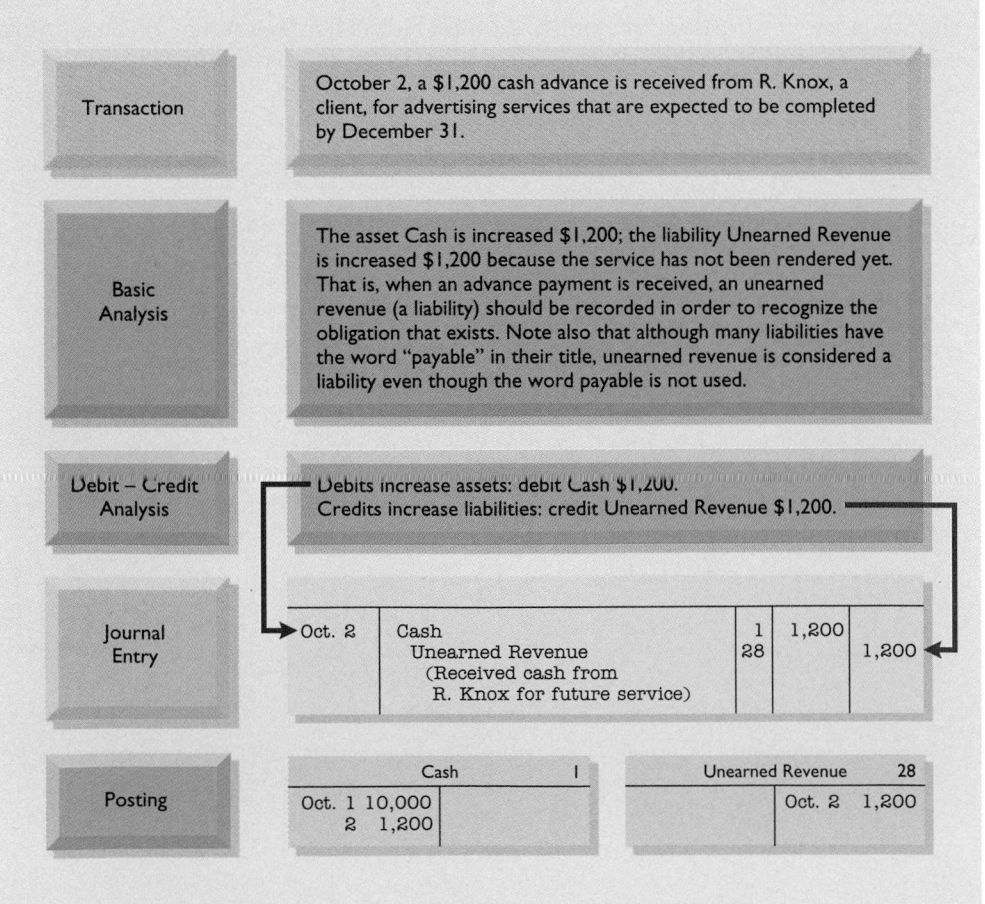

**ILLUSTRATION 2-22**

*Payment of monthly rent*

| Transaction | October 3, office rent for October is paid in cash, $900. |
| --- | --- |
| Basic Analysis | The expense Rent is increased $900 because the payment pertains only to the current month; the asset Cash is decreased $900. |
| Debit – Credit Analysis | Debits increase expenses: debit Rent Expense $900. Credits decrease assets: credit Cash $900. |

| Journal Entry | Oct. 3 | Rent Expense | 62 | 900 | |
| --- | --- | --- | --- | --- | --- |
| | | Cash | 1 | | 900 |
| | | (Paid October rent) | | | |

| Posting | Cash | | 1 | | Rent Expense | | 62 |
| --- | --- | --- | --- | --- | --- | --- | --- |
| | Oct. 1 10,000 | Oct. 3 | 900 | | Oct. 3 | 900 | |
| | 2  1,200 | | | | | | |

**ILLUSTRATION 2-23**

*Payment for insurance*

| Transaction | October 4, $600 is paid for a one-year insurance policy that will expire next year on September 30. |
| --- | --- |
| Basic Analysis | The asset Prepaid Insurance is increased $600 because the payment extends to more than the current month; the asset Cash is decreased $600. Note that payments of expenses that will benefit more than one accounting period are identified as prepaid expenses or prepayments. When a payment is made, an asset account is debited in order to show the service or benefit that will be received in the future. |
| Debit – Credit Analysis | Debits increase assets: debit Prepaid Insurance $600. Credits decrease assets: credit Cash $600. |

| Journal Entry | Oct. 4 | Prepaid Insurance | 10 | 600 | |
| --- | --- | --- | --- | --- | --- |
| | | Cash | 1 | | 600 |
| | | (Paid one-year policy; effective date October 1) | | | |

| Posting | Cash | | 1 | | Prepaid Insurance | | 10 |
| --- | --- | --- | --- | --- | --- | --- | --- |
| | Oct. 1 10,000 | Oct. 3 | 900 | | Oct. 4 | 600 | |
| | 2  1,200 | 4 | 600 | | | | |

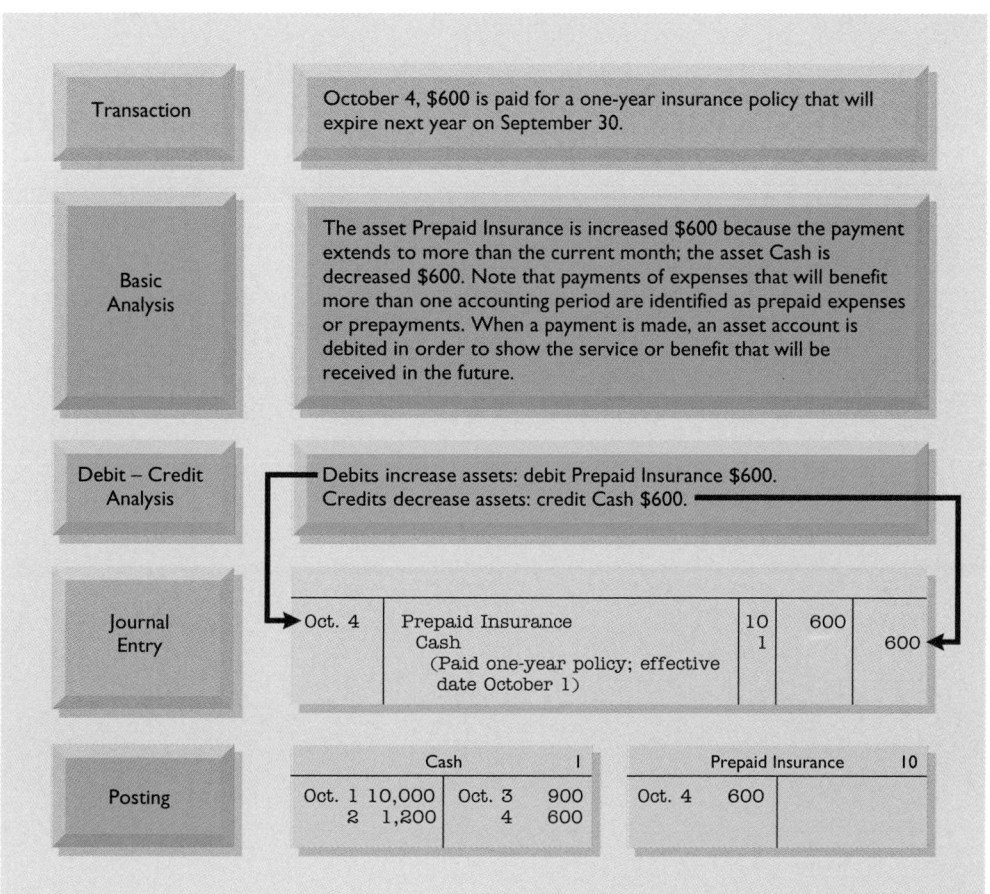

**ILLUSTRATION 2-24**

*Purchase of supplies on credit*

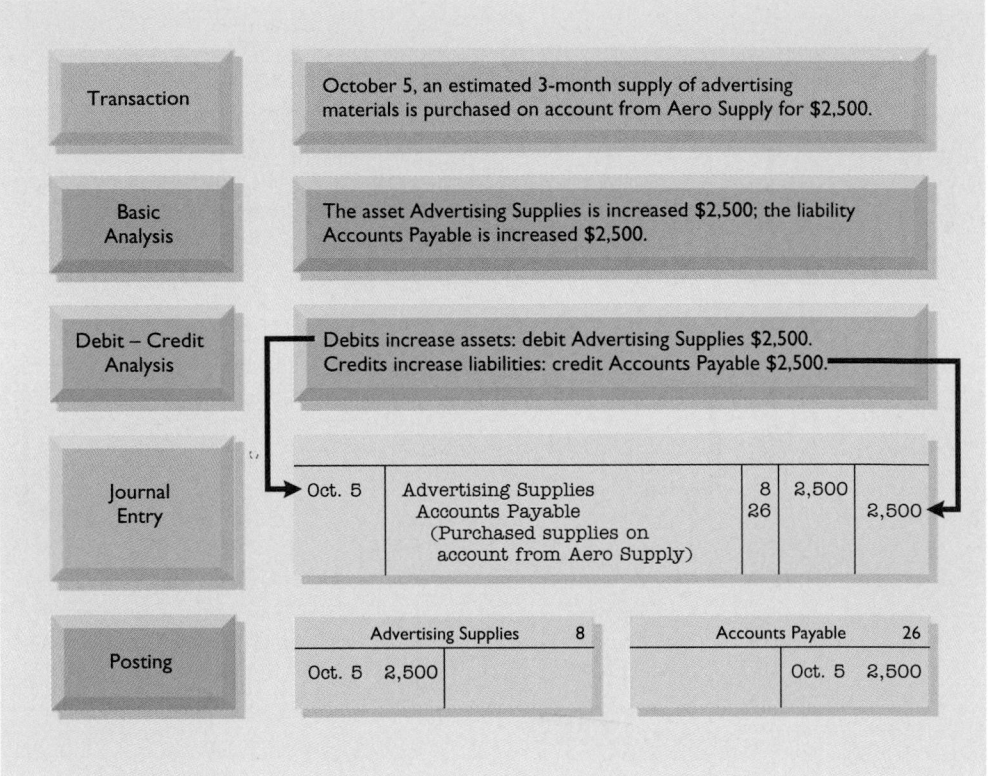

**ILLUSTRATION 2-25**

*Hiring of employees*

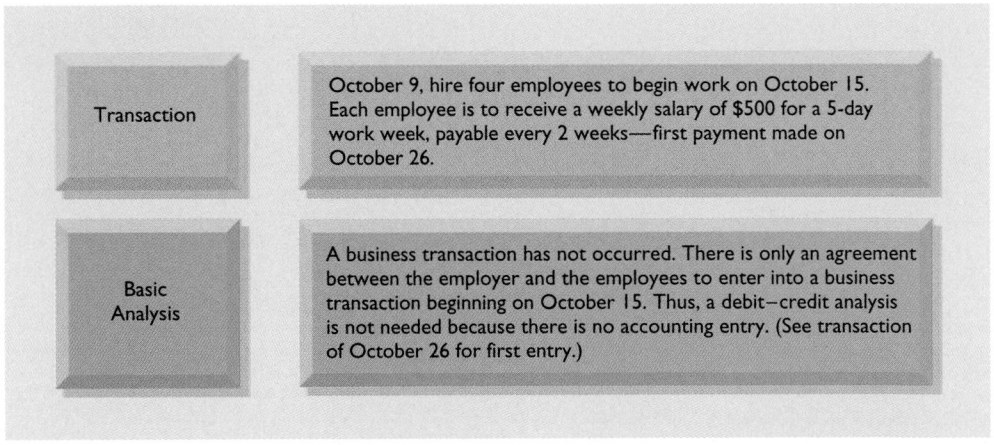

**ILLUSTRATION 2-26**
*Withdrawal of cash by owner*

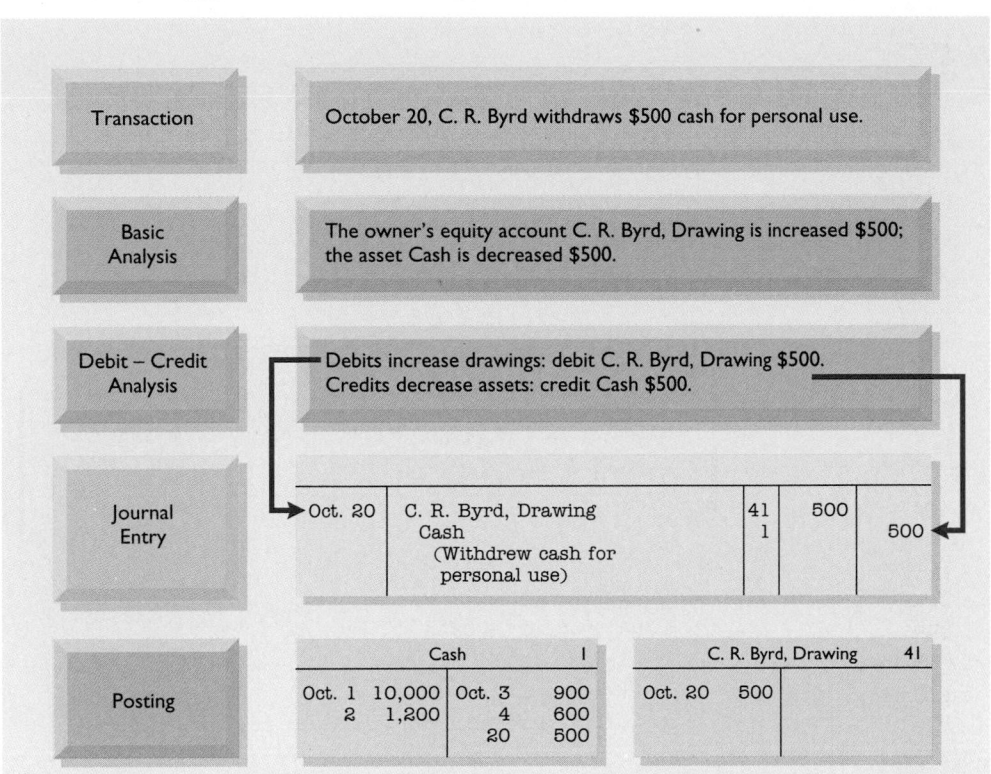

**ILLUSTRATION 2-27**
*Payment of salaries*

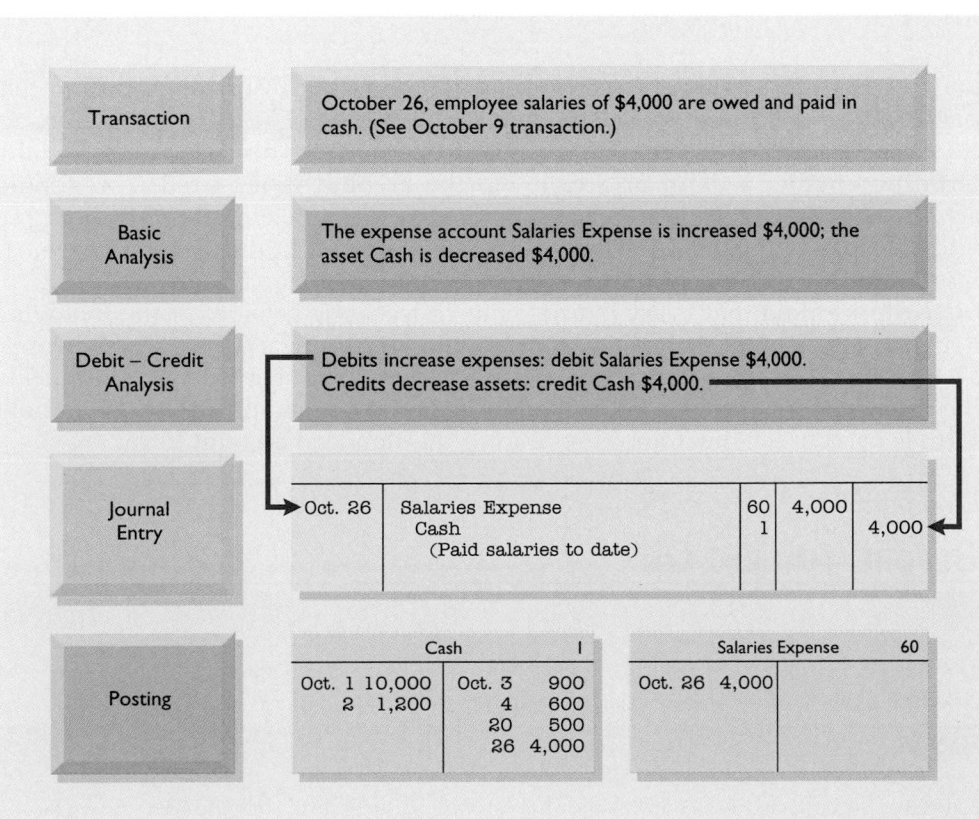

**ILLUSTRATION 2-28**

*Receipt of cash for fees earned*

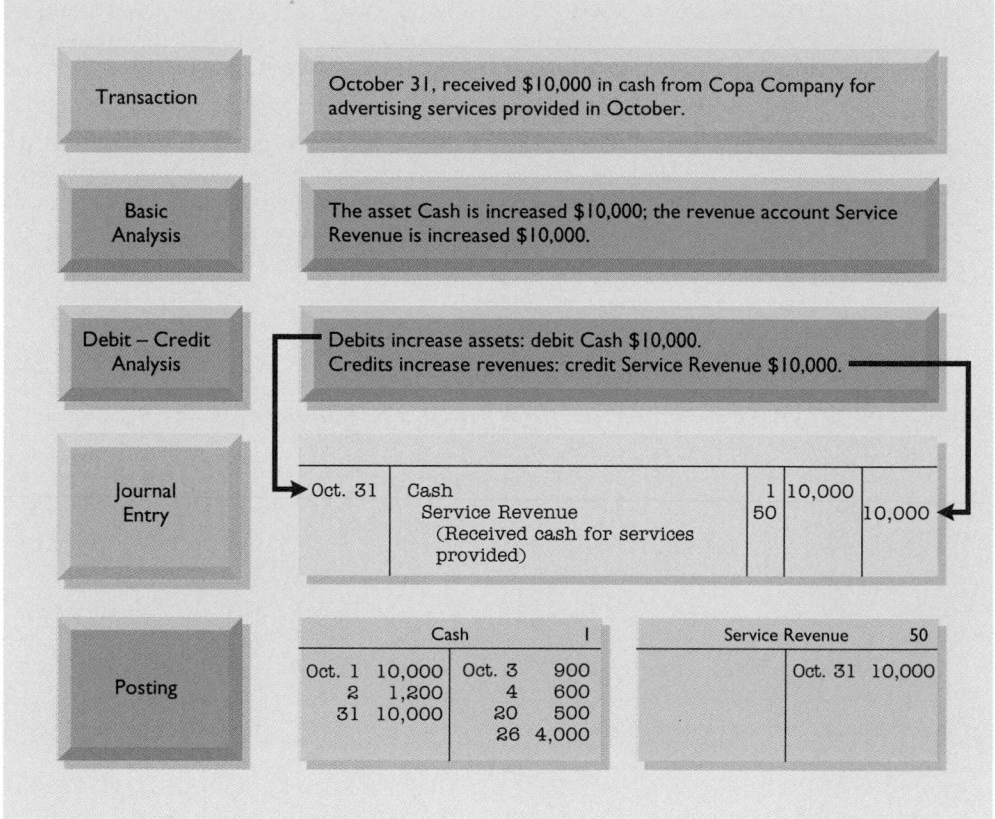

journalizing and posting of each transaction. Go back over the preceding five pages, and study these transaction analyses carefully. **The purpose of transaction analysis is first to identify the type of account involved, and then to determine whether a debit or a credit to the account is required.** You should always perform this type of analysis before preparing a journal entry. Doing so will help you understand the journal entries discussed in this chapter as well as more complex journal entries to be described in later chapters.

Keep in mind that every journal entry affects one or more of the following items: assets, liabilities, owner's capital, owner's drawing, revenues, or expenses. By becoming skilled at transaction analysis, you will be able to recognize quickly the impact of any transaction on these six items. For simplicity, the T-account form is used in the illustrations instead of the standard account form.

# BEFORE YOU GO ON . . .

## Review It

1. How does journalizing differ from posting?
2. What is the purpose of (a) the ledger and (b) a chart of accounts?

## Do It

Kate Browne collected $2,280 in cash for hair styling services, and she paid $400 in wages and $92 for utilities. Kate recorded these transactions in a general journal and posted the entries to the general ledger. Explain the purpose and process of journalizing and posting.

*Reasoning:* Every business must keep track of its financial activities (receipts, payments, receivables, payables, etc.); journalizing does this. However, just recording every transaction in chronological order does not make the entries useful. To be useful, the entries need to be classified and summarized; posting the entries to specific ledger accounts does this.

*Solution:* Journalizing records in chronological order every transaction. Journalizing involves dating every transaction, measuring the dollar amount, identifying or labeling each amount with account titles, and recording in a standard format equal debits and credits. Posting involves transferring the journalized debits and credits to specific accounts in the ledger.

*Related exercise material:* BE2–7, BE2–8, E2–2, E2–5, and E2–8.

## Summary Illustration of Journalizing and Posting

The journal for Pioneer Advertising Agency for the month of October is summarized in Illustration 2-29. The ledger is shown in Illustration 2-30, on page 66, with all balances in color.

| Date | | Account Titles and Explanation | Ref. | Debit | Credit |
|---|---|---|---|---|---|
| **1999** | | **GENERAL JOURNAL** — **Page J1** | | | |
| Oct. | 1 | Cash | 1 | 10,000 | |
| | | C. R. Byrd, Capital | 40 | | 10,000 |
| | | (Owner's investment of cash in business) | | | |
| | 1 | Office Equipment | 15 | 5,000 | |
| | | Notes Payable | 25 | | 5,000 |
| | | (Issued three-month, 12% note for office equipment) | | | |
| | 2 | Cash | 1 | 1,200 | |
| | | Unearned Revenue | 28 | | 1,200 |
| | | (Received cash for future services) | | | |
| | 3 | Rent Expense | 62 | 900 | |
| | | Cash | 1 | | 900 |
| | | (Paid October rent) | | | |
| | 4 | Prepaid Insurance | 10 | 600 | |
| | | Cash | 1 | | 600 |
| | | (Paid one-year policy; effective date, October 1) | | | |
| | 5 | Advertising Supplies | 8 | 2,500 | |
| | | Accounts Payable | 26 | | 2,500 |
| | | (Purchased supplies on account from Aero Supply) | | | |
| | 20 | C. R. Byrd, Drawing | 41 | 500 | |
| | | Cash | 1 | | 500 |
| | | (Withdrew cash for personal use) | | | |
| | 26 | Salaries Expense | 60 | 4,000 | |
| | | Cash | 1 | | 4,000 |
| | | (Paid salaries to date) | | | |
| | 31 | Cash | 1 | 10,000 | |
| | | Service Revenue | 50 | | 10,000 |
| | | (Received cash for services provided) | | | |

**ILLUSTRATION 2-29**
*General journal entries*

## GENERAL LEDGER

### Cash                                                                   No. 1

| Date | Explanation | Ref. | Debit | Credit | Balance |
|------|-------------|------|-------|--------|---------|
| 1999 | | | | | |
| Oct.    1 | | J1 | 10,000 | | 10,000 |
|         2 | | J1 | 1,200 | | 11,200 |
|         3 | | J1 | | 900 | 10,300 |
|         4 | | J1 | | 600 | 9,700 |
|        20 | | J1 | | 500 | 9,200 |
|        26 | | J1 | | 4,000 | 5,200 |
|        31 | | J1 | 10,000 | | **15,200** |

### Advertising Supplies                                                   No. 8

| Date | Explanation | Ref. | Debit | Credit | Balance |
|------|-------------|------|-------|--------|---------|
| 1999 | | | | | |
| Oct.    5 | | J1 | 2,500 | | **2,500** |

### Prepaid Insurance                                                      No. 10

| Date | Explanation | Ref. | Debit | Credit | Balance |
|------|-------------|------|-------|--------|---------|
| 1999 | | | | | |
| Oct.    4 | | J1 | 600 | | **600** |

### Office Equipment                                                       No. 15

| Date | Explanation | Ref. | Debit | Credit | Balance |
|------|-------------|------|-------|--------|---------|
| 1999 | | | | | |
| Oct.    1 | | J1 | 5,000 | | **5,000** |

### Notes Payable                                                          No. 25

| Date | Explanation | Ref. | Debit | Credit | Balance |
|------|-------------|------|-------|--------|---------|
| 1999 | | | | | |
| Oct.    1 | | J1 | | 5,000 | **5,000** |

### Accounts Payable                                                       No. 26

| Date | Explanation | Ref. | Debit | Credit | Balance |
|------|-------------|------|-------|--------|---------|
| 1999 | | | | | |
| Oct.    5 | | J1 | | 2,500 | **2,500** |

### Unearned Revenue                                                       No. 28

| Date | Explanation | Ref. | Debit | Credit | Balance |
|------|-------------|------|-------|--------|---------|
| 1999 | | | | | |
| Oct.    2 | | J1 | | 1,200 | **1,200** |

### C. R. Byrd, Capital                                                    No. 40

| Date | Explanation | Ref. | Debit | Credit | Balance |
|------|-------------|------|-------|--------|---------|
| 1999 | | | | | |
| Oct.    1 | | J1 | | 10,000 | **10,000** |

### C. R. Byrd, Drawing                                                    No. 41

| Date | Explanation | Ref. | Debit | Credit | Balance |
|------|-------------|------|-------|--------|---------|
| 1999 | | | | | |
| Oct.   20 | | J1 | 500 | | **500** |

### Service Revenue                                                        No. 50

| Date | Explanation | Ref. | Debit | Credit | Balance |
|------|-------------|------|-------|--------|---------|
| 1999 | | | | | |
| Oct.   31 | | J1 | | 10,000 | **10,000** |

### Salaries Expense                                                       No. 60

| Date | Explanation | Ref. | Debit | Credit | Balance |
|------|-------------|------|-------|--------|---------|
| 1999 | | | | | |
| Oct.   26 | | J1 | 4,000 | | **4,000** |

### Rent Expense                                                           No. 62

| Date | Explanation | Ref. | Debit | Credit | Balance |
|------|-------------|------|-------|--------|---------|
| 1999 | | | | | |
| Oct.    3 | | J1 | 900 | | **900** |

**ILLUSTRATION 2-30**

*General ledger*

# THE TRIAL BALANCE

**7**
**STUDY**
**OBJECTIVE**

Prepare a trial balance and explain its purposes.

A trial balance is a list of accounts and their balances at a given time. Customarily, a trial balance is prepared at the end of an accounting period. The accounts are listed in the order in which they appear in the ledger, with debit balances listed in the left column and credit balances in the right column. The totals of the two columns must be in agreement.

**The primary purpose of a trial balance is to prove the mathematical equality of debits and credits after posting.** Under the double-entry system this equality will occur when the sum of the debit account balances equals the sum of the credit account balances. **A trial balance also uncovers errors in journalizing and posting. In addition, it is useful in the preparation of financial statements**, as will be explained in the next two chapters. The procedures for preparing a trial balance consist of:

1. Listing the account titles and their balances.
2. Totaling the debit and credit columns.
3. Proving the equality of the two columns.

**HELPFUL HINT**
A trial balance is so named because it is a test to determine if the sum of the debit balances equals the sum of the credit balances.

The trial balance prepared from the ledger of Pioneer Advertising Agency is presented below:

**ILLUSTRATION 2-31**
*A trial balance*

| PIONEER ADVERTISING AGENCY | | |
|---|---|---|
| Trial Balance | | |
| October 31, 1999 | | |
| | Debit | Credit |
| Cash | $15,200 | |
| Advertising Supplies | 2,500 | |
| Prepaid Insurance | 600 | |
| Office Equipment | 5,000 | |
| Notes Payable | | $ 5,000 |
| Accounts Payable | | 2,500 |
| Unearned Revenue | | 1,200 |
| C. R. Byrd, Capital | | 10,000 |
| C. R. Byrd, Drawing | 500 | |
| Service Revenue | | 10,000 |
| Salaries Expense | 4,000 | |
| Rent Expense | 900 | |
| | $28,700 | $28,700 |

**HELPFUL HINT**
To sum a column of figures is sometimes referred to as to foot the column. The column is then said to be footed.

Note that the total debits $28,700 equal the total credits $28,700. Account numbers are sometimes shown to the left of the account titles in the trial balance.

A trial balance is a necessary check point before proceeding to other steps in the accounting process. For example, if only the debit portion of a journal entry has been posted, the trial balance would bring this error to light.

## Limitations of a Trial Balance

**A trial balance does not prove that all transactions have been recorded or that the ledger is correct.** Numerous errors may exist even though the trial balance columns agree. For example, the trial balance may balance even when (1) a transaction is not journalized, (2) a correct journal entry is not posted, (3) a journal entry is posted twice, (4) incorrect accounts are used in journalizing or posting, or (5) offsetting errors are made in recording the amount of a transaction. In other words, as long as equal debits and credits are posted, even to the wrong account or in the wrong amount, the total debits will equal the total credits.

## Locating Errors

The procedure for preparing a trial balance is relatively simple. However, in manual systems if the trial balance does not balance, locating an error can be

# TECHNOLOGY IN ACTION

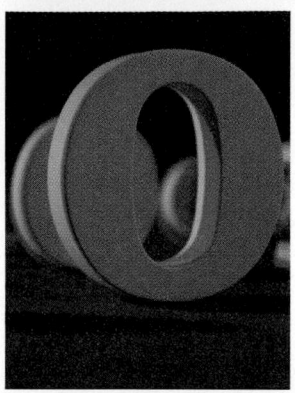

In a computerized system, the trial balance is often only one column (no debit or credit columns), and the accounts have plus and minus signs associated with them. The final balance therefore is zero. Any errors that develop in a computerized system will undoubtedly involve the initial recording rather than some error in the posting or preparation of a trial balance.

**ETHICS NOTE**

Auditors are required to differentiate errors from irregularities when evaluating the accounting system. An error is the result of an unintentional mistake; as such, it is neither ethical nor unethical. An irregularity, on the other hand, is an intentional misstatement, which is generally viewed as highly unethical.

time-consuming, tedious, and frustrating. The error(s) generally results from mathematical mistakes, incorrect postings, or simply transcribing the data incorrectly.

What happens if you are faced with a trial balance that does not balance? First determine the amount of the difference between the two columns of the trial balance. After this amount is known, the following steps are often helpful:

1. If the error is $1, $10, $100, or $1,000, re-add the trial balance columns and recompute the account balances.
2. If the error is divisible by two, scan the trial balance to see whether a balance equal to half the error has been entered in the wrong column.
3. If the error is divisible by nine, retrace the account balances on the trial balance to see whether they are incorrectly copied from the ledger. For example, if a balance was $12 and it was listed as $21, a $9 error has been made. Reversing the order of numbers is called a transposition error.
4. If the error is not divisible by two or nine (for example, $365), scan the ledger to see whether an account balance of $365 has been omitted from the trial balance, and scan the journal to see whether a $365 posting has been omitted.

# ACCOUNTING IN ACTION
## Business Insight

One minute it was flying high, the next minute its very survival was uncertain. That is the story of Informix. It was the best-performing software stock between 1990 and 1995. In early 1997 it seemed well positioned to rival the giants in the industry. But then serious accounting errors and irregularities were detected by the company's auditors. Simply stated, the company had recorded transactions as sales which actually were not sales. Thus its revenues were overstated by as much as $200 million. Problems like this can lead to the ultimate demise of the company. Customers become reluctant to buy from the company because they fear that the company might fail, and consequently won't be available to support the product. Suppliers are reluctant to sell to the company because they fear they won't be paid. Valuable employees begin to leave the company in search of job security. Shareholders are suing the company because of financial losses they sustained when the company's stock price dropped by 35% in a single day after the announcement of the accounting irregularities. The Nasdaq Stock Market threatened to "delist" the company which would mean the company could not trade its shares on that exchange anymore. The company's outside auditor brought in 30 additional staff persons to get to the bottom of the problem. The bottom line is that accounting errors, whether intentional or unintentional, can be very costly.

## Use of Dollar Signs

Note that dollar signs do not appear in the journals or ledgers. Dollar signs are usually used only in the trial balance and the financial statements. Generally, a dollar sign is shown only for the first item in the column and for the total of that column. A single line is placed under the column of figures to be added or subtracted; the total amount is double underlined to indicate the final sum.

# BEFORE YOU GO ON . . .

## Review It

1. What is a trial balance and how is it prepared?
2. What is the primary purpose of a trial balance?
3. What are the limitations of a trial balance?

## A LOOK BACK AT OUR FEATURE STORY

Now that you have learned the details of the recording process, think back to the beginning of the chapter to Gabriella Torres and her position as office manager at Diabetes & Endocrine Associates, and answer the following questions:

1. What accounting entries would Gabriella be likely to make to record (a) the rent payment, (b) billing a patient for services provided, and (c) collecting cash from a patient on account.
2. In what way might Gabriella's day-time job as office manager help in her studies as a night student in accounting and business?
3. Prepare a likely list of asset accounts Gabriella has in her general ledger at Diabetes & Endocrine Associates.

*Solution:*

1. Gabriella would likely make the following entries:
    (a)  Rent Expense
        Cash
            (Paid rent)
    (b)  Accounts Receivable
        Service Revenue
            (Billed a patient for services provided)
    (c)  Cash
        Accounts Receivable
            (Collected cash for amount due)
2. As a result of her office manager's position, Gabriella is able to relate the subject matter as well as much of the assignment material in her business courses to a real-world context. From her job she knows how bills are paid; how to reconcile a bank statement; how employees are hired, managed, evaluated, and paid; how the individual accounts receivable accounts are maintained; how accounting functions are performed on a computer; and much more.
3. A likely list of asset accounts is: Cash, Accounts Receivable, Medical Supplies, Land and Building (if owned), Medical Equipment, Office Furniture and Fixtures, and Prepaid Insurance.

THE
NAVIGATOR

# DEMONSTRATION PROBLEM

Bob Sample opened the Campus Laundromat on September 1, 1999. During the first month of operations the following transactions occurred:

Sept.  1  Invested $20,000 cash in the business.
2  Paid $1,000 cash for store rent for the month of September.
3  Purchased washers and dryers for $25,000 paying $10,000 in cash and signing a $15,000 6-month 12% note payable.
4  Paid $1,200 for one-year accident insurance policy.
10  Received bill from the Daily News for advertising the opening of the laundromat, $200.
20  Withdrew $700 cash for personal use.
30  Determined that cash receipts for laundry services for the month were $6,200.

The chart of accounts for the company is the same as in Pioneer Advertising Agency except for the following: No. 15 Laundry Equipment and No. 61 Advertising Expense.

### Instructions

(a) Journalize the September transactions. (Use J1 for the journal page number.)
(b) Open ledger accounts and post the September transactions.
(c) Prepare a trial balance at September 30, 1999.

## PROBLEM-SOLVING STRATEGIES

1. Separate journal entries are made for each transaction.
2. In journalizing, make sure debits equal credits.
3. In journalizing, use specific account titles taken from the chart of accounts.
4. Provide appropriate description of journal entry.
5. Arrange ledger in statement order, beginning with the balance sheet accounts.
6. Post in chronological order.
7. Numbers in the reference column indicate the amount has been posted.
8. The trial balance lists accounts in the order in which they appear in the ledger.
9. Debit balances are listed in the left column, and credit balances in the right column.

## SOLUTION TO DEMONSTRATION PROBLEM

(a)                          **GENERAL JOURNAL**                          **J1**

| Date | Account Titles and Explanation | Ref. | Debit | Credit |
|------|-------------------------------|------|-------|--------|
| 1999 | | | | |
| Sept. 1 | Cash | 1 | 20,000 | |
| | Bob Sample, Capital | 40 | | 20,000 |
| | (Owner's investment of cash in business) | | | |
| 2 | Rent Expense | 62 | 1,000 | |
| | Cash | 1 | | 1,000 |
| | (Paid September rent) | | | |
| 3 | Laundry Equipment | 15 | 25,000 | |
| | Cash | 1 | | 10,000 |
| | Notes Payable | 25 | | 15,000 |
| | (Purchased laundry equipment for cash and 6-month 12% note payable) | | | |
| 4 | Prepaid Insurance | 10 | 1,200 | |
| | Cash | 1 | | 1,200 |
| | (Paid one-year insurance policy) | | | |
| 10 | Advertising Expense | 61 | 200 | |
| | Accounts Payable | 26 | | 200 |
| | (Received bill from Daily News for advertising) | | | |
| 20 | Bob Sample, Drawing | 41 | 700 | |
| | Cash | 1 | | 700 |
| | (Withdrew cash for personal use) | | | |
| 30 | Cash | 1 | 6,200 | |
| | Service Revenue | 50 | | 6,200 |
| | (Received cash for services provided) | | | |

(b)

# GENERAL LEDGER

### Cash      No. 1

| Date | Explanation | Ref. | Debit | Credit | Balance |
|------|-------------|------|-------|--------|---------|
| 1999 | | | | | |
| Sept. 1 | | J1 | 20,000 | | 20,000 |
| 2 | | J1 | | 1,000 | 19,000 |
| 3 | | J1 | | 10,000 | 9,000 |
| 4 | | J1 | | 1,200 | 7,800 |
| 20 | | J1 | | 700 | 7,100 |
| 30 | | J1 | 6,200 | | 13,300 |

### Prepaid Insurance      No. 10

| Date | Explanation | Ref. | Debit | Credit | Balance |
|------|-------------|------|-------|--------|---------|
| 1999 | | | | | |
| Sept. 4 | | J1 | 1,200 | | 1,200 |

### Laundry Equipment      No. 15

| Date | Explanation | Ref. | Debit | Credit | Balance |
|------|-------------|------|-------|--------|---------|
| 1999 | | | | | |
| Sept. 3 | | J1 | 25,000 | | 25,000 |

### Notes Payable      No. 25

| Date | Explanation | Ref. | Debit | Credit | Balance |
|------|-------------|------|-------|--------|---------|
| 1999 | | | | | |
| Sept. 3 | | J1 | | 15,000 | 15,000 |

### Accounts Payable      No. 26

| Date | Explanation | Ref. | Debit | Credit | Balance |
|------|-------------|------|-------|--------|---------|
| 1999 | | | | | |
| Sept. 10 | | J1 | | 200 | 200 |

### Bob Sample, Capital      No. 40

| Date | Explanation | Ref. | Debit | Credit | Balance |
|------|-------------|------|-------|--------|---------|
| 1999 | | | | | |
| Sept. 1 | | J1 | | 20,000 | 20,000 |

### Bob Sample, Drawing      No. 41

| Date | Explanation | Ref. | Debit | Credit | Balance |
|------|-------------|------|-------|--------|---------|
| 1999 | | | | | |
| Sept. 20 | | J1 | 700 | | 700 |

### Service Revenue      No. 50

| Date | Explanation | Ref. | Debit | Credit | Balance |
|------|-------------|------|-------|--------|---------|
| 1999 | | | | | |
| Sept. 30 | | J1 | | 6,200 | 6,200 |

### Advertising Expense      No. 61

| Date | Explanation | Ref. | Debit | Credit | Balance |
|------|-------------|------|-------|--------|---------|
| 1999 | | | | | |
| Sept. 10 | | J1 | 200 | | 200 |

### Rent Expense      No. 62

| Date | Explanation | Ref. | Debit | Credit | Balance |
|------|-------------|------|-------|--------|---------|
| 1999 | | | | | |
| Sept. 2 | | J1 | 1,000 | | 1,000 |

(c)

## CAMPUS LAUNDROMAT
## Trial Balance
## September 30, 1999

| | Debit | Credit |
|---|-------|--------|
| Cash | $13,300 | |
| Prepaid Insurance | 1,200 | |
| Laundry Equipment | 25,000 | |
| Notes Payable | | $15,000 |
| Accounts Payable | | 200 |
| Bob Sample, Capital | | 20,000 |
| Bob Sample, Drawing | 700 | |
| Service Revenue | | 6,200 |
| Advertising Expense | 200 | |
| Rent Expense | 1,000 | |
| | $41,400 | $41,400 |

THE
NAVIGATOR

# SUMMARY OF STUDY OBJECTIVES

1. *Explain what an account is and how it helps in the recording process.* An account is an individual accounting record of increases and decreases in specific asset, liability, and owner's equity items.

2. *Define debits and credits and explain how they are used to record business transactions.* The terms debit and credit are synonymous with left and right. Assets, drawings, and expenses are increased by debits and decreased by credits. Liabilities, owner's capital, and revenues are increased by credits and decreased by debits.

3. *Identify the basic steps in the recording process.* The basic steps in the recording process are: (a) analyze each transaction in terms of its effect on the accounts, (b) enter the transaction information in a journal, (c) transfer the journal information to the appropriate accounts in the ledger.

4. *Explain what a journal is and how it helps in the recording process.* The initial accounting record of a transaction is entered in a journal before the data are entered in the accounts. A journal (a) discloses in one place the complete effect of a transaction, (b) provides a chronological record

of transactions, and (c) prevents or locates errors because the debit and credit amounts for each entry can be readily compared.

5. *Explain what a ledger is and how it helps in the recording process.* The entire group of accounts maintained by a company is referred to collectively as a ledger. The ledger keeps in one place all the information about changes in specific account balances.

6. *Explain what posting is and how it helps in the recording process.* Posting is the procedure of transferring journal entries to the ledger accounts. This phase of the recording process accumulates the effects of journalized transactions in the individual accounts.

7. *Prepare a trial balance and explain its purposes.* A trial balance is a list of accounts and their balances at a given time. The primary purpose of the trial balance is to prove the mathematical equality of debits and credits after posting. A trial balance also uncovers errors in journalizing and posting and is useful in preparing financial statements.

**THE NAVIGATOR**

# GLOSSARY

**Account**   An individual accounting record of increases and decreases in specific asset, liability, or owner's equity items. (p. 46).

**Chart of accounts**   A list of accounts and the account numbers which identify their location in the ledger. (p. 58).

**Compound entry**   An entry that involves three or more accounts. (p. 54).

**Credit**   The right side of an account. (p. 47).

**Debit**   The left side of an account. (p. 47).

**Double-entry system**   A system that records the dual effect of each transaction in appropriate accounts. (p. 48).

**General journal**   The most basic form of journal. (p. 52).

**General ledger**   A ledger that contains all asset, liability, and owner's equity accounts. (p. 55).

**Journal**   An accounting record in which transactions are initially recorded in chronological order. (p. 52).

**Journalizing**   The procedure of entering transaction data in the journal. (p. 53).

**Ledger**   The entire group of accounts maintained by a company. (p. 55).

**Posting**   The procedure of transferring journal entries to the ledger accounts. (p. 56).

**Simple entry**   An entry that involves only two accounts. (p. 54).

**T account**   The basic form of an account. (p. 46).

**Three-column form of account**   A form containing money columns for debit, credit, and balance amounts in an account. (p. 56).

**Trial balance**   A list of accounts and their balances at a given time. (p. 66).

# SELF-STUDY QUESTIONS

Answers are at the end of the chapter.

(SO 1)  1. Which of the following statements about an account is true?
   a. In its simplest form, an account consists of two parts.
   b. An account is an individual accounting record of increases and decreases in specific asset, liability, and owner's equity items.
   c. There are separate accounts for specific assets and liabilities but only one account for owner's equity items.

   d. The left side of an account is the credit or decrease side.

2. Debits:   (SO 2)
   a. increase both assets and liabilities.
   b. decrease both assets and liabilities.
   c. increase assets and decrease liabilities.
   d. decrease assets and increase liabilities.

3. A revenue account:   (SO 2)
   a. is increased by debits.
   b. is decreased by credits.

c. has a normal balance of a debit.
d. is increased by credits.

4. Accounts that normally have debit balances are:
   a. assets, expenses, and revenues.
   b. assets, expenses, and owner's capital.
   c. assets, liabilities, and owner's drawings.
   d. assets, owner's drawings, and expenses.

(SO 3) 5. Which of the following is *not* part of the recording process?
   a. Analyzing transactions.
   b. Preparing a trial balance.
   c. Entering transactions in a journal.
   d. Posting transactions.

(SO 4) 6. Which of the following statements about a journal is false?
   a. It is not a book of original entry.
   b. It provides a chronological record of transactions.
   c. It helps to locate errors because the debit and credit amounts for each entry can be readily compared.
   d. It discloses in one place the complete effect of a transaction.

(SO 5) 7. A ledger:
   a. contains only asset and liability accounts.
   b. should show accounts in alphabetical order.
   c. is a collection of the entire group of accounts maintained by a company.
   d. is a book of original entry.

8. Posting: (SO 6)
   a. normally occurs before journalizing.
   b. transfers ledger transaction data to the journal.
   c. is an optional step in the recording process.
   d. transfers journal entries to ledger accounts.

9. A trial balance: (SO 7)
   a. is a list of accounts with their balances at a given time.
   b. proves the mathematical accuracy of journalized transactions.
   c. will not balance if a correct journal entry is posted twice.
   d. proves that all transactions have been recorded.

10. A trial balance will not balance if: (SO 7)
   a. a correct journal entry is posted twice.
   b. the purchase of supplies on account is debited to Supplies and credited to Cash.
   c. a $100 cash drawing by the owner is debited to Owner's Drawing for $1,000 and credited to Cash for $100.
   d. a $450 payment on account is debited to Accounts Payable for $45 and credited to Cash for $45.

THE NAVIGATOR

# QUESTIONS

1. Describe a T account.
2. The terms *debit* and *credit* mean increase and decrease, respectively. Do you agree? Explain.
3. Omar Morena, a fellow student, contends that the double-entry system means each transaction must be recorded twice. Is Omar correct? Explain.
4. Kim Nguyen, a beginning accounting student, believes debit balances are favorable and credit balances are unfavorable. Is Kim correct? Discuss.
5. State the rules of debit and credit as applied to (a) asset accounts, (b) liability accounts, and (c) the owner's equity accounts (revenue, expenses, owner's drawing, and owner's capital).
6. What is the normal balance for each of the following accounts? (a) Accounts Receivable. (b) Cash. (c) Owner's Drawing. (d) Accounts Payable. (e) Service Revenue. (f) Salaries Expense. (g) Owner's Capital.
7. Indicate whether each of the following accounts is an asset, a liability, or an owner's equity account and whether it has a normal debit or credit balance: (a) Accounts Receivable, (b) Accounts Payable, (c) Equipment, (d) Owner's Drawing, (e) Supplies.
8. For the following transactions, indicate the account debited and the account credited:
   (a) Supplies are purchased on account.
   (b) Cash is received on signing a note payable.
   (c) Employees are paid salaries in cash.

9. Presented below is a series of accounts. Indicate whether these accounts generally will have (a) debit entries only, (b) credit entries only, (c) both debit and credit entries.
   (1) Cash.    (4) Accounts Payable.
   (2) Accounts Receivable.  (5) Salaries Expense.
   (3) Owner's Drawing.  (6) Service Revenue.
10. What are the basic steps in the recording process?
11. What are the advantages of using a journal in the recording process?
12. (a) When entering a transaction in the journal, should the debit or credit be written first?
   (b) Which should be indented, the debit or credit?
13. Describe a compound entry and provide an example of a compound entry.
14. (a) Should business transaction debits and credits be recorded directly in the ledger accounts?
   (b) What are the advantages of first recording transactions in the journal and then posting to the ledger?
15. The account number is entered as the last step in posting the amounts from the journal to the ledger. What is the advantage of this step?
16. Journalize the following business transactions.
   (a) Dana O'Shea invests $9,000 cash in the business.
   (b) Insurance of $800 is paid for the year.
   (c) Supplies of $1,500 are purchased on account.
   (d) Cash of $7,500 is received for services rendered.

17. (a) What is a ledger?
    (b) What is a chart of accounts and why is it important?

18. What is a trial balance and what are its purposes?

19. Ira Hirsch is confused about how accounting information flows through the accounting system. He believes the flow of information is as follows:
    (a) Debits and credits posted to the ledger.
    (b) Business transaction occurs.
    (c) Information entered in the journal.
    (d) Financial statements are prepared.
    (e) Trial balance is prepared.

Is Ira correct? If not, indicate to Ira the proper flow of the information.

20. Two students are discussing the use of a trial balance. They wonder whether the following errors, each considered separately, would prevent the trial balance from balancing.
    (a) The bookkeeper debited Cash for $600 and credited Wages Expense for $600 for payment of wages.
    (b) Cash collected on account was debited to Cash for $900 and Service Revenue was credited for $90. What would you tell them?

# BRIEF EXERCISES

*Indicate debit and credit effects and normal balance.*
*(SO 2)*

**BE2–1**   For each of the following accounts indicate the effects of (a) a debit and (b) a credit on the accounts and (c) the normal balance of the account.

1. Accounts Payable.
2. Advertising Expense.
3. Service Revenue.
4. Accounts Receivable.
5. B. C. Jardine, Capital.
6. B. C. Jardine, Drawing.

*Identify accounts to be debited and credited.*
*(SO 2)*

**BE2–2**   Transactions for the A. D. Ing Company for the month of June are presented below. Identify the accounts to be debited and credited for each transaction.

June  1  A. D. Ing invests $2,000 cash in a small welding business of which he is the sole proprietor.
      2  Purchase of equipment on account for $900.
      3  $500 cash is paid to landlord for June rent.
     12  Bills T. Sargento $300 for welding work done on account.

*Journalize transactions.*
*(SO 4)*

**BE2–3**   Using the data in BE2–2, journalize the transactions. (You may omit explanations.)

*Identify and explain steps in recording process.*
*(SO 3)*

**BE2–4**   ▰▰▰▰▱▶  M. Thompson, a fellow student, is unclear about the basic steps in the recording process. Identify and briefly explain the steps in the order in which they occur.

*Indicate basic and debit-credit analysis.*
*(SO 4)*

**BE2–5**   A. Fisher has the following transactions during August of the current year. Indicate (a) the effect on the accounting equation and (b) the debit-credit analysis illustrated on pages 59–64 of the text.

Aug.  1  Opens an office as a financial advisor, investing $6,000 in cash.
      4  Pays insurance in advance for 6 months, $1,800 cash.
     16  Receives $900 from clients for services rendered.
     27  Pays secretary $500 salary.

*Journalize transactions.*
*(SO 4)*

**BE2–6**   Using the data in BE2–5, journalize the transactions. (You may omit explanations.)

*Post journal entries to T accounts.*
*(SO 6)*

**BE2–7**   Selected transactions for the Fernandez Company are presented in journal form below. Post the transactions to T accounts. Make one T account for each item and determine each account's ending balance.

J1

| Date | Account Titles and Explanation | Ref. | Debit | Credit |
|------|-------------------------------|------|-------|--------|
| May  5 | Accounts Receivable | | 4,000 | |
|      | Service Revenue | | | 4,000 |
|      | (Billed for services provided) | | | |
| 12 | Cash | | 2,400 | |
|    | Accounts Receivable | | | 2,400 |
|    | (Received cash in payment of account) | | | |
| 15 | Cash | | 2,000 | |
|    | Service Revenue | | | 2,000 |
|    | (Received cash for services provided) | | | |

**BE2–8**   Selected journal entries for the Fernandez Company are presented in BE2–7. Post the transactions using the standard form of account.

*Post journal entries to standard form of account.*
(SO 6)

**BE2–9**   From the ledger balances given below, prepare a trial balance for the D. Beirsdorf Company at June 30, 1999. List the accounts in the order shown on page 67 of the text. All account balances are normal.

*Prepare a trial balance.*
(SO 7)

   Accounts Payable $5,000, Cash $4,800, D. Beirsdorf, Capital $20,000, D. Beirsdorf, Drawing $1,200, Equipment $17,000, Service Revenue $6,000, Accounts Receivable $3,000, Salaries Expense $4,000, and Rent Expense $1,000.

**BE2–10**   An inexperienced bookkeeper prepared the following trial balance that does not balance. Prepare a correct trial balance, assuming all account balances are normal.

*Prepare a correct trial balance.*
(SO 7)

### LOPEZ COMPANY
### Trial Balance
### December 31, 1999

|  | Debit | Credit |
|---|---|---|
| Cash | $16,800 | |
| Prepaid Insurance | | $ 3,500 |
| Accounts Payable | | 3,000 |
| Unearned Revenue | 2,200 | |
| P. Lopez, Capital | | 15,000 |
| P. Lopez, Drawing | | 4,500 |
| Service Revenue | | 25,600 |
| Salaries Expense | 18,600 | |
| Rent Expense | | 2,400 |
|  | $37,600 | $54,000 |

# EXERCISES

**E2–1**   Selected transactions for L. Visser, an interior decorator, in her first month of business, are as follows:

*Identify debits, credits, and normal balances.*
(SO 2)

Jan.  2  Invested $8,000 cash in business.
     3  Purchased used car for $4,000 cash for use in business.
     9  Purchased supplies on account for $500.
    11  Billed customers $1,800 for services performed.
    16  Paid $200 cash for advertising start of business.
    20  Received $700 cash from customers billed on January 11.
    23  Paid creditor $300 cash on account.
    28  Withdrew $500 cash for personal use of owner.

*Instructions*
For each transaction indicate (a) the basic type of account debited and credited (asset, liability, owner's equity); (b) the specific account debited and credited (cash, rent expense, service revenue, etc.); (c) whether the specific account is increased or decreased; and (d) the normal balance of the specific account. Use the following format, in which the January 2 transaction is given as an example:

| | Account Debited | | | | Account Credited | | | |
|---|---|---|---|---|---|---|---|---|
| Date | (a)<br>Basic<br>Type | (b)<br>Specific<br>Account | (c)<br><br>Effect | (d)<br>Normal<br>Balance | (a)<br>Basic<br>Type | (b)<br>Specific<br>Account | (c)<br><br>Effect | (d)<br>Normal<br>Balance |
| Jan. 2 | Asset | Cash | Increase | Debit | Owner's<br>Equity | L. Visser,<br>Capital | Increase | Credit |

**E2–2**   Data for L. Visser, interior decorator, are presented in E2–1.

*Journalize transactions and post using standard account form.*
(SO 4)

*Instructions*
Journalize the transactions using journal page J1. (You may omit explanations.)

*Analyze transactions and determine their effect on accounts.*
*(SO 2)*

**E2-3**   Presented below is information related to Sam Stine Real Estate Agency:

Oct. 1   Sam Stine begins business as a real estate agent with a cash investment of $15,000.
    2   Hires an administrative assistant.
    3   Purchases office furniture for $1,900, on account.
    6   Sells a house and lot for C. Clark; bills Clark $3,200 for realty services provided.
    27  Pays $700 on the balance related to the transaction of October 3.
    30  Pays the administrative assistant $1,050 in salary for October.

*Instructions*
Prepare the debit-credit analysis for each transaction as illustrated on pages 59–64.

*Journalize transactions.*
*(SO 4)*

**E2-4**   Transaction data for Stine Real Estate Agency are presented in E2-3.

*Instructions*
Journalize the transactions. Explanations may be omitted.

*Post journal entries and prepare a trial balance.*
*(SO 6, 7)*

**E2-5**   Selected transactions from the journal of J. L. Meche, investment broker, are presented below.

| Date | Account Titles and Explanation | Ref. | Debit | Credit |
|---|---|---|---|---|
| Aug.  1 | Cash | | 2,600 | |
| | J. L. Meche, Capital | | | 2,600 |
| | (Owner's investment of cash in business) | | | |
| 10 | Cash | | 2,400 | |
| | Service Revenue | | | 2,400 |
| | (Received cash for services provided) | | | |
| 12 | Office Equipment | | 4,000 | |
| | Cash | | | 1,000 |
| | Notes Payable | | | 3,000 |
| | (Purchased office equipment for cash and notes payable) | | | |
| 25 | Accounts Receivable | | 1,400 | |
| | Service Revenue | | | 1,400 |
| | (Billed for services provided) | | | |
| 31 | Cash | | 900 | |
| | Accounts Receivable | | | 900 |
| | (Receipt of cash on account) | | | |

*Instructions*
(a) Post the transactions to T accounts.
(b) Prepare a trial balance at August 31, 1999.

*Journalize transactions from account data and prepare a trial balance.*
*(SO 4, 7)*

**E2-6**   The T accounts below summarize the ledger of Doty Landscaping Company at the end of the first month of operations:

| Cash | | No. 101 |
|---|---|---|
| 4/1 | 6,000 | 4/15 | 600 |
| 4/12 | 900 | 4/25 | 1,500 |
| 4/29 | 400 | | |
| 4/30 | 800 | | |

| Unearned Revenue | | No. 205 |
|---|---|---|
| | 4/30 | 800 |

| Accounts Receivable | | No. 112 |
|---|---|---|
| 4/7 | 3,200 | 4/29 | 400 |

| D. Doty, Capital | | No. 301 |
|---|---|---|
| | 4/1 | 6,000 |

| Supplies | | No. 126 |
|---|---|---|
| 4/4 | 1,800 | |

| Service Revenue | | No. 400 |
|---|---|---|
| | 4/7 | 3,200 |
| | 4/12 | 900 |

| Accounts Payable | | No. 201 |
|---|---|---|
| 4/25 | 1,500 | 4/4 | 1,800 |

| Salaries Expense | | No. 726 |
|---|---|---|
| 4/15 | 600 | |

**Instructions**

   (a) Prepare the complete general journal (including explanations) from which the postings to Cash were made.

   (b) Prepare a trial balance at April 30, 1999.

**E2–7** Presented below is the ledger for McBride Co.

*Journalize transactions from account data and prepare a trial balance.*
*(SO 4, 7)*

| | | Cash | | No. 101 |
|---|---|---|---|---|
| 10/1 | 5,000 | 10/4 | 400 | |
| 10/10 | 650 | 10/12 | 1,500 | |
| 10/10 | 5,000 | 10/15 | 250 | |
| 10/20 | 500 | 10/30 | 300 | |
| 10/25 | 2,000 | 10/31 | 500 | |

| | | Accounts Receivable | | No. 112 |
|---|---|---|---|---|
| 10/6 | 800 | 10/20 | 500 | |
| 10/20 | 940 | | | |

| | | Supplies | | No. 126 |
|---|---|---|---|---|
| 10/4 | 400 | | | |

| | | Furniture | | No. 149 |
|---|---|---|---|---|
| 10/3 | 2,000 | | | |

| | | Notes Payable | | No. 200 |
|---|---|---|---|---|
| | | 10/10 | 5,000 | |

| | | Accounts Payable | | No. 201 |
|---|---|---|---|---|
| 10/12 | 1,500 | 10/3 | 2,000 | |

| | | McBride, Capital | | No. 301 |
|---|---|---|---|---|
| | | 10/1 | 5,000 | |
| | | 10/25 | 2,000 | |

| | | McBride, Drawing | | No. 306 |
|---|---|---|---|---|
| 10/30 | 300 | | | |

| | | Service Revenue | | No. 407 |
|---|---|---|---|---|
| | | 10/6 | 800 | |
| | | 10/10 | 650 | |
| | | 10/20 | 940 | |

| | | Store Wages Expense | | No. 628 |
|---|---|---|---|---|
| 10/31 | 500 | | | |

| | | Rent Expense | | No. 729 |
|---|---|---|---|---|
| 10/15 | 250 | | | |

**Instructions**

   (a) Reproduce the journal entries for the transactions that occurred on October 1, 10, and 20 and provide explanations for each.

   (b) Determine the October 31 balance for each of the accounts above and prepare a trial balance at October 31, 1999.

**E2–8** Selected transactions for the Tracy Lawrence Company during its first month in business are presented below.

*Prepare journal entries and post using standard account form.*
*(SO 4, 6)*

Sept.  1  Invested $12,000 cash in the business.

     5  Purchased equipment for $10,000 paying $5,000 in cash and the balance on account.

   25  Paid $3,000 cash on balance owed for equipment.

   30  Withdrew $500 cash for personal use.

Lawrence's chart of accounts shows: Cash, No. 101; Equipment, No. 157; and Accounts Payable, No. 201; Tracy Lawrence, Capital, No. 301; and Tracy Lawrence, Drawing, No. 306.

**Instructions**

   (a) Journalize the transactions on page J1 of the journal.

   (b) Post the transactions using the standard account form.

**E2–9** The bookkeeper for Gary Allen Equipment Repair made a number of errors in journalizing and posting, as described below:

*Analyze errors and their effects on trial balance.*
*(SO 7)*

   1. A credit posting of $400 to Accounts Receivable was omitted.

   2. A debit posting of $750 for Prepaid Insurance was debited to Insurance Expense.

   3. A collection on account of $100 was journalized and posted as a debit to Cash $100 and a credit to Service Revenue $100.

4. A credit posting of $300 to Property Taxes Payable was made twice.
5. A cash purchase of supplies for $250 was journalized and posted as a debit to Supplies $25 and a credit to Cash $25.
6. A debit of $465 to Advertising Expense was posted as $456.

**Instructions**
For each error, indicate (a) whether the trial balance will balance; if the trial balance will not balance, indicate (b) the amount of the difference, and (c) the trial balance column that will have the larger total. Consider each error separately. Use the following form, in which error (1) is given as an example.

| Error | (a) In Balance | (b) Difference | (c) Larger Column |
|---|---|---|---|
| (1) | No | $400 | debit |

*Prepare a trial balance.*
*(SO 2, 7)*

**E2–10** The accounts in the ledger of Always Late Delivery Service contain the following balances on July 31, 1999:

| | | | |
|---|---|---|---|
| Accounts Receivable | $ 7,642 | Prepaid Insurance | $ 1,968 |
| Accounts Payable | 8,396 | Repair Expense | 961 |
| Cash | ? | Service Revenue | 10,610 |
| Delivery Equipment | 49,360 | J. S. Bach, Drawing | 700 |
| Gas and Oil Expense | 758 | J. S. Bach, Capital | 44,636 |
| Insurance Expense | 523 | Salaries Expense | 4,428 |
| Notes Payable | 18,450 | Salaries Payable | 815 |

**Instructions**
Prepare a trial balance with the accounts arranged as illustrated in the chapter and fill in the missing amount for Cash.

# PROBLEMS: SET A
••••••••••••••••••••••••••••••••••••••••••••••••••••••••••••••••••••••••••••••••

*Journalize a series of transactions.*
*(SO 2, 4)*

**P2–1A** The Four Oaks Miniature Golf and Driving Range was opened on March 1 by Joe MacKey. The following selected events and transactions occurred during March:

Mar. 1 Invested $45,000 cash in the business.
3 Purchased Lee's Golf Land for $38,000 cash. The price consists of land, $23,000, building, $9,000, and equipment, $6,000. (Make one compound entry.)
5 Advertised the opening of the driving range and miniature golf course, paying advertising expenses of $1,600.
6 Paid cash $1,480 for a one-year insurance policy.
10 Purchased golf clubs and other equipment for $1,600 from Palmer Company payable in 30 days.
18 Received $800 in cash for golf fees earned.
19 Sold 100 coupon books for $15.00 each. Each book contains 10 coupons that enable the holder to one round of miniature golf or to hit one bucket of golf balls.
25 Withdrew $500 cash for personal use.
30 Paid salaries of $600.
30 Paid Palmer Company in full.
31 Received $500 cash for fees earned.

Joe MacKey uses the following accounts: Cash; Prepaid Insurance; Land; Buildings; Equipment; Accounts Payable; Unearned Revenue; Joe MacKey, Capital; Joe MacKey, Drawing; Golf Revenue; Advertising Expense; and Salaries Expense.

**Instructions**
Journalize the March transactions.

**P2–2A**  Maria Rojas is a licensed architect. During the first month of the operation of her business, the following events and transactions occurred.

*Journalize transactions, post, and prepare a trial balance.*
(SO 2, 4, 6, 7)

April  1   Invested $15,000 cash.

    1   Hired a secretary-receptionist at a salary of $300 per week payable monthly.

    2   Paid office rent for the month, $800.

    3   Purchased architectural supplies on account from Halo Company, $1,500.

  10   Completed blueprints on a carport and billed client $900 for services.

  11   Received $500 cash advance from R. Welk for the design of a new home.

  20   Received $1,500 cash for services completed and delivered to P. Donahue.

  30   Paid secretary-receptionist for the month, $1,200.

  30   Paid $600 to Halo Company on account.

Maria uses the following chart of accounts: No. 101 Cash, No. 112 Accounts Receivable, No. 126 Supplies, No. 201 Accounts Payable, No. 205 Unearned Revenue, No. 301 Maria Rojas, Capital, No. 400 Service Revenue, No. 726 Salaries Expense, and No. 729 Rent Expense.

*Instructions*
(a) Journalize the transactions.
(b) Post to the ledger accounts.
(c) Prepare a trial balance on April 30, 1999.

**P2–3A**  The trial balance of Judy's Laundry on September 30 is shown below:

*Journalize transactions, post, and prepare a trial balance.*
(SO 2, 4, 6, 7)

### JUDY'S LAUNDRY
### Trial Balance
### September 30, 1999

| Account No. | | Debit | Credit |
| --- | --- | --- | --- |
| 101 | Cash | $ 8,500 | |
| 112 | Accounts Receivable | 2,200 | |
| 126 | Supplies | 1,700 | |
| 157 | Equipment | 8,000 | |
| 201 | Accounts Payable | | $ 5,000 |
| 206 | Unearned Laundry Revenue | | 700 |
| 301 | Judy Kylie, Capital | | 14,700 |
| | | $20,400 | $20,400 |

The October transactions were as follows:

Oct.  5   Received $800 cash from customers on account.

  10   Billed customers for services performed $5,500.

  15   Paid employee salaries $1,200.

  20   Paid $1,600 to creditors on account.

  29   Withdrew $500 for personal use.

  31   Paid utilities $500.

*Instructions*
(a) Enter the opening balances in the ledger accounts as of October 1. Write "Balance" in the explanation space and insert a check mark (√) in the reference column. Provision should be made for the following additional accounts: No. 306 Judy Kylie, Drawing; No. 426 Laundry Revenue; No. 726 Salaries Expense; and No. 732 Utilities Expense.
(b) Journalize the transactions.
(c) Post to the ledger accounts.
(d) Prepare a trial balance on October 31, 1999.

*Prepare a correct trial balance.*
*(SO 7)*

**P2–4A**    The trial balance of Tim Winau Co. shown below does not balance.

## TIM WINAU CO.
## Trial Balance
## June 30, 1999

|  | Debit | Credit |
|---|---|---|
| Cash |  | $ 2,840 |
| Accounts Receivable | $ 3,231 |  |
| Supplies | 800 |  |
| Equipment | 3,000 |  |
| Accounts Payable |  | 2,666 |
| Unearned Revenue | 1,200 |  |
| T. Winau, Capital |  | 9,000 |
| T. Winau, Drawing | 800 |  |
| Service Revenue |  | 2,380 |
| Salaries Expense | 3,400 |  |
| Office Expense | 910 |  |
|  | $13,341 | $16,886 |

Each of the listed accounts has a normal balance per the general ledger. An examination of the ledger and journal reveals the following errors.

1. Cash received from a customer on account was debited for $470 and Accounts Receivable was credited for the same amount. The actual collection was for $740.
2. The purchase of a typewriter on account for $340 was recorded as a debit to Supplies for $340 and a credit to Accounts Payable for $340.
3. Services were performed on account for a client for $890. Accounts Receivable was debited for $890 and Service Revenue was credited for $89.
4. A debit posting to Salaries Expense of $600 was omitted.
5. A payment on account for $206 was credited to Cash for $206 and credited to Accounts Payable for $260.
6. The withdrawal of $500 cash for Winau's personal use was debited to Salaries Expense for $500 and credited to Cash for $500.

*Instructions*
Prepare a correct trial balance. *Hint:* It helps to prepare the correct journal entry for the transaction described and compare it to the mistake made.

*Journalize transactions, post,*
*and prepare a trial balance.*
*(SO 2, 4, 6, 7)*

**P2–5A**    The Starlite Theater, owned by Lee Baroni, will begin operations in March. The Starlite will be unique in that it will show only triple features of sequential theme movies. As of February 28, the ledger of Starlite showed: No. 101 Cash $16,000; No. 140 Land $42,000; No. 145 Buildings (concession stand, projection room, ticket booth, and screen) $18,000; No. 157 Equipment $16,000; No. 201 Accounts Payable $12,000; and No. 301 L. Baroni, Capital $80,000. During the month of March the following events and transactions occurred:

Mar.  2   Acquired the three *Star Wars* movies (*Star Wars, The Empire Strikes Back,* and *The Return of the Jedi*) to be shown for the first 3 weeks of March. The film rental was $9,000; $3,000 was paid in cash and $6,000 will be paid on March 10.

3   Ordered the first three *Star Trek* movies to be shown the last 10 days of March. It will cost $300 per night.

9   Received $6,500 cash from admissions.

10   Paid balance due on *Star Wars* movies rental and $3,000 on February 28 accounts payable.

11   Starlite Theater contracted with M. Brewer Company to operate the concession stand. Brewer is to pay 15% of gross concession receipts (payable monthly) for the right to operate the concession stand.

12   Paid advertising expenses $800.

20   Received $7,200 cash from admissions.

20   Received the *Star Trek* movies and paid the rental fee of $3,000.

31   Paid salaries of $3,800.

31   Received statement from M. Brewer showing gross receipts from concessions of
$8,000 and the balance due to Starlite Theater of $1,200 ($8,000 × 15%) for March.
Brewer paid one-half the balance due and will remit the remainder on April 5.

31   Received $12,500 cash from admissions.

In addition to the accounts identified above, the chart of accounts includes: No. 112 Accounts Receivable, No. 405 Admission Revenue, No. 406 Concession Revenue, No. 610 Advertising Expense, No. 632 Film Rental Expense, and No. 726 Salaries Expense.

### Instructions
(a)  Enter the beginning balances to the ledger. Insert a check mark (√) in the reference column of the ledger for the beginning balance.
(b)  Journalize the March transactions.
(c)  Post the March journal entries to the ledger. Assume that all entries are posted from page 1 of the journal.
(d)  Prepare a trial balance on March 31, 1999.

# PROBLEMS: SET B
......................................................

**P2–1B**  The Adventure Park was started on April 1 by Al Rossy. The following selected events and transactions occurred during April.

*Journalize a series of transactions.*
*(SO 2, 4)*

Apr.  1   Rossy invested $50,000 cash in the business.
4   Purchased land costing $30,000 for cash.
8   Incurred advertising expense of $1,800 on account.
11   Paid salaries to employees $1,500.
12   Hired park manager at a salary of $4,000 per month, effective May 1.
13   Paid $1,500 cash for a one-year insurance policy.
17   Withdrew $600 cash for personal use.
20   Received $5,700 in cash for admission fees.
25   Sold 100 coupon books for $25 each. Each book contains 10 coupons that entitle the holder to one admission to the park.
30   Received $5,900 in cash admission fees.
30   Paid $700 on account for advertising incurred on April 8.

Al Rossy uses the following accounts: Cash; Prepaid Insurance; Land; Accounts Payable; Unearned Admissions Revenue; Al Rossy, Capital; Al Rossy, Drawing; Admission Revenue; Advertising Expense; and Salaries Expense.

### Instructions
Journalize the April transactions.

**P2–2B**  Lisa Heins is a licensed CPA. During the first month of operations of her business, the following events and transactions occurred:

*Journalize transactions, post, and prepare a trial balance.*
*(SO 2, 4, 6, 7)*

May  1   Heins invested $32,000 cash.
2   Hired a secretary-receptionist at a salary of $1,000 per month.
3   Purchased $1,200 of supplies on account from Read Supply Company.
7   Paid office rent of $900 cash for the month.
11   Completed a tax assignment and billed client $1,100 for services rendered.
12   Received $3,500 advance on a management consulting engagement.
17   Received cash of $1,200 for services completed for H. Arnold Co.
31   Paid secretary-receptionist $1,000 salary for the month.
31   Paid 40% of balance due Read Supply Company.

Lisa uses the following chart of accounts: No. 101 Cash, No. 112 Accounts Receivable, No. 126 Supplies, No. 201 Accounts Payable, No. 205 Unearned Revenue, No. 301 Lisa Heins, Capital, No. 400 Service Revenue, No. 726 Salaries Expense, and No. 729 Rent Expense.

*Instructions*

(a) Journalize the transactions.

(b) Post to the ledger accounts.

(c) Prepare a trial balance on May 31, 1999.

*Journalize transactions, post, and prepare a trial balance.*
*(SO 2, 4, 6, 7)*

**P2–3B**    The trial balance of Steiner Dry Cleaners on June 30 is shown below.

### STEINER DRY CLEANERS
### Trial Balance
### June 30, 1999

| Account No. | | Debit | Credit |
|---|---|---|---|
| 101 | Cash | $12,532 | |
| 112 | Accounts Receivable | 10,536 | |
| 126 | Supplies | 4,844 | |
| 157 | Equipment | 25,950 | |
| 201 | Accounts Payable | | $15,878 |
| 206 | Unearned Revenue | | 1,730 |
| 301 | C. Steiner, Capital | | 36,254 |
| | | $53,862 | $53,862 |

The July transactions were as follows:

July  8    Collected $5,936 in cash related to June 30 accounts receivable.

    9    Paid employee salaries $2,100.

  11    Received $4,325 in cash for services rendered.

  14    Paid June 30 creditors $10,750 on account.

  17    Purchased supplies on account $554.

  22    Billed customers for services rendered, $5,700.

  30    Paid employee salaries $3,114, utilities $1,384, and repairs $692, all in cash.

  31    Withdrew $700 cash for personal use of owner.

*Instructions*

(a) Enter the opening balances in the ledger accounts as of July 1. Write "Balance" in the explanation space and insert a check mark (√) in the reference column. Provision should be made for the following additional accounts: No. 306 C. Steiner, Drawing; No. 428 Dry Cleaning Revenue; No. 622 Repair Expense; No. 726 Salaries Expense; and No. 732 Utilities Expense.

(b) Journalize the transactions.

(c) Post to the ledger accounts.

(d) Prepare a trial balance on July 31, 1999.

*Prepare a correct trial balance.*
*(SO 7)*

**P2–4B**    The trial balance of the Shawnee Company shown below does not balance.

### SHAWNEE COMPANY
### Trial Balance
### May 31, 1999

| | Debit | Credit |
|---|---|---|
| Cash | $ 5,850 | |
| Accounts Receivable | | $ 2,750 |
| Prepaid Insurance | 700 | |
| Equipment | 8,000 | |
| Accounts Payable | | 4,500 |
| Property Taxes Payable | 560 | |
| M. Flynn, Capital | | 11,700 |
| Service Revenue | 6,690 | |
| Salaries Expense | 4,200 | |
| Advertising Expense | | 1,100 |
| Property Tax Expense | 800 | |
| | $26,800 | $20,050 |

Your review of the ledger reveals that each account has a normal balance. You also discover the following errors.

1. The totals of the debit sides of Prepaid Insurance, Accounts Payable, and Property Tax Expense were each understated $100.
2. Transposition errors were made in Accounts Receivable and Service Revenue. Based on postings made, the correct balances were $2,570 and $6,960, respectively.
3. A debit posting to Salaries Expense of $200 was omitted.
4. A $700 cash drawing by the owner was debited to M. Flynn, Capital for $700 and credited to Cash for $700.
5. A $520 purchase of supplies on account was debited to Equipment for $520 and credited to Cash for $520.
6. A cash payment of $250 for advertising was debited to Advertising Expense for $25 and credited to Cash for $25.
7. A collection from a customer for $210 was debited to Cash for $210 and credited to Accounts Payable for $210.

*Instructions*
Prepare a correct trial balance. (Note: The chart of accounts includes the following: M. A. Flynn, Drawing; Supplies; and Supplies Expense.) *Hint:* It helps to prepare the correct journal entry for the transaction described and compare it to the mistake made.

**P2–5B** The Grand Theater is owned by Fran Holley. All facilities were completed on March 31. At this time, the ledger showed: No. 101 Cash $6,000; No. 140 Land $10,000; No. 145 Buildings (concession stand, projection room, ticket booth, and screen) $8,000; No. 157 Equipment $6,000; No. 201 Accounts Payable $2,000; No. 275 Mortgage Payable $8,000; and No. 301 Fran Holley, Capital $20,000. During April, the following events and transactions occurred.

*Journalize transactions, post, and prepare a trial balance.*
*(SO 2, 4, 6, 7)*

Apr. 2 Paid film rental of $800 on first movie.
    3 Ordered two additional films at $500 each.
    9 Received $1,800 cash from admissions.
    10 Made $2,000 payment on mortgage and $1,000 on accounts payable.
    11 Grand Theater contracted with R. Thoms Company to operate the concession stand. Thoms is to pay 17% of gross concession receipts (payable monthly) for the right to operate the concession stand.
    12 Paid advertising expenses $300.
    20 Received one of the films ordered on April 3 and was billed $500. The film will be shown in April.
    25 Received $5,200 cash from admissions.
    29 Paid salaries $1,600.
    30 Received statement from R. Thoms showing gross concession receipts of $1,000 and the balance due to The Lake Theater of $170 ($1,000 × 17%) for April. Thoms paid one-half of the balance due and will remit the remainder on May 5.
    30 Prepaid $700 rental on special film to be run in May.

In addition to the accounts identified above, the chart of accounts shows: No. 112 Accounts Receivable, No. 136 Prepaid Rentals, No. 405 Admission Revenue, No. 406 Concession Revenue, No. 610 Advertising Expense, No. 632 Film Rental Expense, and No. 726 Salaries Expense.

*Instructions*
(a) Enter the beginning balances in the ledger as of April 1. Insert a check mark (√) in the reference column of the ledger for the beginning balance.
(b) Journalize the April transactions.
(c) Post the April journal entries to the ledger. Assume that all entries are posted from page 1 of the journal.
(d) Prepare a trial balance on April 30, 1999.

## BROADENING YOUR PERSPECTIVE

# FINANCIAL REPORTING AND ANALYSIS

### FINANCIAL REPORTING PROBLEM: Kellogg Company

**BYP2–1**  The financial statements of Kellogg Company are presented in Appendix A and the notes accompanying the statements contain the following selected accounts, stated in millions of dollars:

| | | | |
|---|---|---|---|
| Accounts Payable | $   328.0 | Notes Payable | $368.6 |
| Accounts Receivable | 587.5 | Interest Expense | 108.3 |
| Property, net | 2,773.3 | Inventories | 434.3 |

*Instructions*
(a) Answer the following questions:
   1. What is the increase and decrease side for each account?
   2. What is the normal balance for each account?
(b) Identify the probable other account in the transaction and the effect on that account when:
   1. Accounts Receivable is decreased.
   2. Accounts Payable is decreased.
   3. Inventories are increased.
(c) Identify the other account(s) that ordinarily would be involved when:
   1. Interest Expense is increased.
   2. Property is increased.

### COMPARATIVE ANALYSIS PROBLEM: Kellogg Company vs. General Mills

**BYP2–2**  Kellogg's financial statements are presented in Appendix A; General Mills's financial statements are presented in Appendix B.

*Instructions*

(a) Based on the information contained in the financial statements, determine the normal balance of the listed accounts for each company:

| Kellogg's | General Mills's |
|---|---|
| 1. Inventories | 1. Accounts receivable |
| 2. Property, net | 2. Land |
| 3. Accounts payable | 3. Depreciation expense |
| 4. Interest expense | 4. Sales (revenue) |

(b) Identify the other account ordinarily involved when:
   1. Accounts receivable is increased.
   2. Accrued payroll is decreased.
   3. Property is increased.
   4. Interest expense is increased.

### RESEARCH ASSIGNMENT

**BYP2–3**  Several commonly available indexes enable individuals to locate articles previously included in numerous business publications and periodicals. Articles can generally be searched for by company or by subject matter. Four common indexes are *The Wall Street Journal Index*, *Business Abstracts* (formerly the *Business Periodical Index*), *Predicasts F&S Index*, and *ABI/Inform*. (*Note:* Your library may have hard copy or CD-ROM versions of these indexes.)

*Instructions*

Use one of these resources to find an article about a New York Stock Exchange company of your choosing. Read the article and answer the following questions.

(a) What is the article about?

(b) What company-specific information is included in the article?

(c) Is the article related to anything you read in Chapter 2 of your accounting textbook?

(d) Identify any accounting-related issues discussed in the article.

## INTERPRETING FINANCIAL STATEMENTS: Bob Evans Farms, Inc.

**BYP2–4**   Bob Evans Farms, Inc. operates 354 restaurants and several food processing plants. The food processing plants primarily process pork into sausage, some of which is used in the restaurants, and some of which is sold to grocery stores. The food processing plants also produce "fast-food"-type frozen sandwiches, which are marketed to grocery stores.

The balance sheet of Bob Evans Farms showed a cash balance of $10 million and trade accounts receivable of $16 million. The notes to the financial statements revealed that there was a line of credit available of $63 million, of which $26 million was then outstanding.

*Instructions*

(a) Explain why most of the trade accounts receivable would probably not pertain to the restaurant business.

(b) What kind of individuals or companies would you expect to find in the individual accounts receivable accounts?

(c) Why might Bob Evans Farms be keeping the $10 million in cash, instead of using most of it, for example $8 million, to help pay off the line of credit debt?

## REAL-WORLD FOCUS: Automated Security Holdings

**BYP2–5   Automated Security Holdings** operates multinationally, with principal markets in the United States and the United Kingdom. The company designs, produces, installs, and maintains security systems to safeguard life and property from a wide range of hazards. The markets for these security products include commercial, industrial, and residential customers.

The following notes to the financial statements identify a few of the accounts found in the general ledger.

| AUTOMATED SECURITY HOLDINGS Notes to the Financial Statements | | |
|---|---|---|
| | **November 30,** | |
| | Previous Year | Current Year |
| | (in thousands) | |
| Income Tax Payable | $ 3,929 | $ 3,919 |
| Accounts Payable | 6,499 | 9,620 |
| Salaries Expense | 16,353 | 9,213 |
| Cash | 4,749 | 2,869 |
| Unearned Revenue | 1,211 | 1,434 |
| Notes Payable | 52,000 | 40,000 |
| Prepaid Insurance | 1,333 | 2,000 |

*Instructions*

(a) Identify the accounts of Automated Security Holdings that have debit balances in the trial balance.

(b) What date has Automated Security Holdings adopted for its accounting year-end?

(c) Are the accounts listed above in the order in which they would appear in Automated Security Holdings' general ledger? Explain.

# CRITICAL THINKING
...................................................................................................................

## GROUP DECISION CASE

**BYP2–6**   Greg Daniels operates the Daniels Riding Academy. The academy's primary sources of revenue are riding fees and lesson fees, which are provided on a cash basis. Greg also boards horses for owners, who are billed monthly for boarding fees. In a few cases, boarders pay in advance of expected use. For its revenue transactions, the academy maintains the following accounts: No. 1 Cash, No. 5 Boarding Accounts Receivable, No. 27 Unearned Boarding Revenue, No. 51 Riding Revenue, No. 52 Lesson Revenue, and No. 53 Boarding Revenue.

The academy owns 10 horses, a stable, a riding corral, riding equipment, and office equipment. These assets are accounted for in accounts No. 11 Horses, No. 12 Building, No. 13 Riding Corral, No. 14 Riding Equipment, and No. 15 Office Equipment.

The academy employs stable helpers and an office employee who receive weekly salaries. At the end of each month, the mail usually brings bills for advertising, utilities, and veterinary service. Other expenses include feed for the horses and insurance. For its expenses, the academy maintains the following accounts: No. 6 Hay and Feed Supplies, No. 7 Prepaid Insurance, No. 21 Accounts Payable, No. 60 Salaries Expense, No. 61 Advertising Expense, No. 62 Utilities Expense, No. 63 Veterinary Expense, No. 64 Hay and Feed Expense, and No. 65 Insurance Expense.

Greg Daniels' sole source of income is the academy. Thus, he makes periodic withdrawals of cash for personal living expenses. To record Greg's equity in the business and his drawings, two accounts are maintained: No. 50 Greg Daniels, Capital, and No. 51 Greg Daniels, Drawing.

During the first month of operations an inexperienced bookkeeper was employed. Greg asks you to review the following eight entries of the 50 entries made during the month. In each case, the explanation for the entry is correct.

| Date | | Debit | Credit |
|---|---|---|---|
| May 1 | Cash | 15,000 | |
| | Greg Daniels, Capital | | 15,000 |
| | (Invested $15,000 cash in business) | | |
| 5 | Cash | 250 | |
| | Riding Revenue | | 250 |
| | (Received $250 cash for lessons provided) | | |
| 7 | Cash | 500 | |
| | Boarding Revenue | | 500 |
| | (Received $500 for boarding of horses beginning June 1) | | |
| 14 | Riding Equipment | 80 | |
| | Cash | | 800 |
| | (Purchased desk and other office equipment for $800 cash) | | |
| 15 | Salaries Expense | 400 | |
| | Cash | | 400 |
| | (Issued check to Greg Daniels for personal use) | | |
| 20 | Cash | 145 | |
| | Riding Revenue | | 154 |
| | (Received $154 cash for riding fees) | | |
| 30 | Veterinary Expense | 75 | |
| | Accounts Payable | | 75 |
| | (Received bill of $75 from veterinarian for services rendered) | | |
| 31 | Hay and Feed Expense | 1,700 | |
| | Cash | | 1,700 |
| | (Purchased an estimated two months' supply of feed and hay for $1,700 on account) | | |

*Instructions*

With the class divided into groups, answer the following:

(a) For each journal entry that is correct, so state. For each journal entry that is incorrect, prepare the entry that should have been made by the bookkeeper.

(b) Which of the incorrect entries would prevent the trial balance from balancing?

(c) What was the correct net income for May, assuming the bookkeeper reported net income of $4,500 after posting all 50 entries?

(d) What was the correct cash balance at May 31, assuming the bookkeeper reported a balance of $12,475 after posting all 50 entries (and the only errors occurred in the items listed above)?

## COMMUNICATION ACTIVITY

**BYP2–7**   Merlynn's Maid Company offers home cleaning service. Two recurring transactions for the company are billing customers for services rendered and paying employee salaries. For example, on March 15 bills totaling $6,000 were sent to customers and $2,000 was paid in salaries to employees.

*Instructions*

Write a memorandum to your instructor that explains and illustrates the steps in the recording process for each of the March 15 transactions. Use the format illustrated in the text under the heading, "The Recording Process Illustrated" (p. 59).

## ETHICS CASE

**BYP2–8**   Megan Menard is the assistant chief accountant at Staples Company, a manufacturer of computer chips and cellular phones. The company presently has total sales of $20 million. It is the end of the first quarter and Megan is hurriedly trying to prepare a general ledger trial balance so that quarterly financial statements can be prepared and released to management and the regulatory agencies. The total credits on the trial balance exceed the debits by $1,000. In order to meet the 4 p.m. deadline, Megan decides to force the debits and credits into balance by adding the amount of the difference to the Equipment account. She chose Equipment because it is one of the larger account balances: percentage-wise it will be the least misstated. Megan plugs the difference! She believes that the difference is quite small and will not affect anyone's decisions. She wishes that she had another few days to find the error but realizes that the financial statements are already late.

*Instructions*

(a) Who are the stakeholders in this situation?

(b) What are the ethical issues involved in this case?

(c) What are Megan's alternatives?

# SURFING THE NET

**BYP2–9**   Much information about specific companies is available on the World Wide Web. This information includes basic descriptions of the company's location, activities, industry, financial health, and financial performance.

**Address:** http://biz.yahoo.com/i (or go to the Wiley home page)

**Steps:**

1. Choose **Company.**

2. Type in a company name, or use index to find company name.

3. Choose **Profile.** Perform instructions (a)–(c) below.

4. Click on the company's specific industry to identify competitors. Perform instructions (d)–(g) below.

*Instructions*

Answer the following questions:

(a) What was the company's net income?
(b) What was the company's total sales?
(c) What is the company's industry?
(d) What are the names of four of the company's competitors?
(e) Choose one of these competitors.
(f) What is this competitor's name? What were its sales? What was its net income?
(g) Which of these two companies is larger by size of sales? Which one reported higher net income?

*Answers to Self-Study Questions*

1. b    2. c    3. d    4. d    5. b    6. a    7. c    8. d    9. a    10. c

*Answer to Kellogg Review It Question 4, p. 51*

Cash—debit; accounts payable—credit; interest expense—debit.

 **Remember to go back to the Navigator box on the chapter-opening page and check off your completed work.**

## CONCEPTS FOR REVIEW

Before studying this chapter, you should know, or, if necessary, review:

a. What a double-entry system is. (Ch. 2, p. 48)

b. How to increase or decrease assets, liabilities, and owner's equity using debit and credit procedures. (Ch. 2, pp. 48–50)

c. How to journalize a transaction. (Ch. 2, pp. 53–54)

d. How to post a transaction. (Ch. 2, pp. 56–59)

e. How to prepare a trial balance. (Ch. 2, pp. 66–67)

## FEATURE STORY

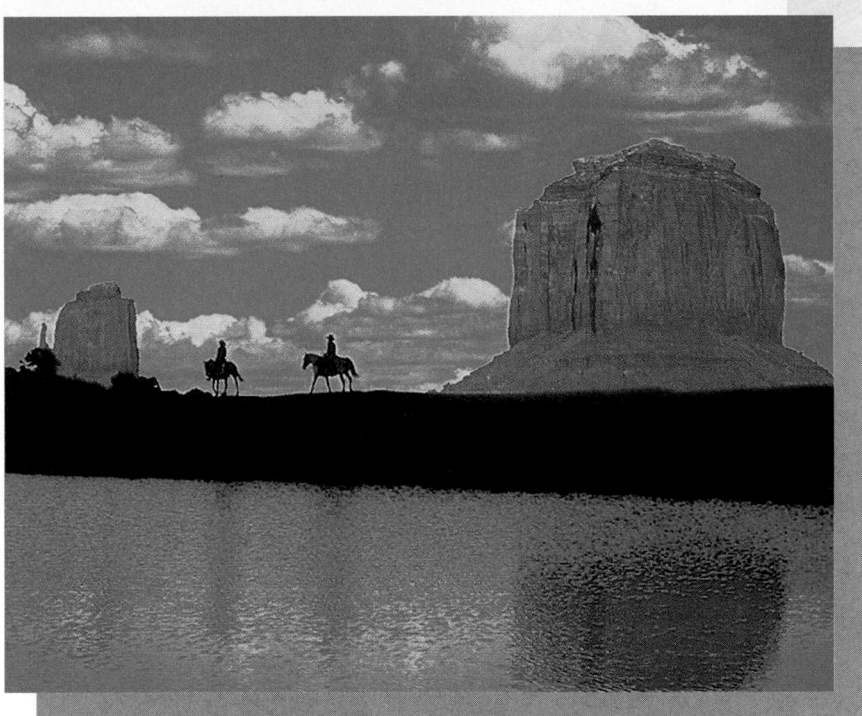

# When Students Leave Campus, This College Adjusts Its Books

Like many colleges, Arizona State University (ASU) uses a June 30 date as the end of its annual accounting period. Rather than using December 31, most colleges use the school year as their primary period of activity. Having an ending date like that seems neat and tidy—and it is in many respects. (If it were not, schools would choose an end-date that made more sense.) But colleges, just like any business organization, have some loose ends that need tying up at the end of the accounting period. For example, at ASU, the second summer session begins around July 5, but registration for the session takes place the prior February. The school collects tuition for the session in one accounting period but will provide the services in the next accounting period. "We have lots of students who are paying tuition in February for a session that begins in July," says Carol Balk, ASU's manager of student tuition payments. In the new accounting year, following completion of the summer session, "We have to account for the revenue collection of five months earlier."

Similarly, ASU has to account for supplies purchased in one accounting year but used the next. Supplies purchased on April 1 for use in the summer session will need to be reported as an expense in the new accounting year.

# CHAPTER 3

### THE NAVIGATOR ✔

- Understand *Concepts for Review* ☐
- Read *Feature Story* ☐
- Scan *Study Objectives* ☐
- Read *Preview* ☐
- Read text and answer *Before You Go On*
  p. 94 ☐ p. 102 ☐ p. 107 ☐ p. 113 ☐
- Work *Demonstration Problem* ☐
- Review *Summary of Study Objectives* ☐
- Answer *Self-Study Questions* ☐
- Complete assignments ☐

# ADJUSTING THE ACCOUNTS

## STUDY OBJECTIVES

**After studying this chapter, you should be able to:**

1. *Explain the time period assumption.*
2. *Distinguish between the revenue recognition principle and the matching principle.*
3. *Explain why adjusting entries are needed.*
4. *Identify the major types of adjusting entries.*
5. *Prepare adjusting entries for prepayments.*
6. *Prepare adjusting entries for accruals.*
7. *Describe the nature and purpose of an adjusted trial balance.*
8. *Explain the accrual basis of accounting.*

THE NAVIGATOR

*I*n Chapter 2 we examined the basic steps in the recording process through the preparation of the trial balance. Before we will be ready to prepare financial statements from the trial balance, additional steps need to be taken. The timing mismatch between revenues and expenses of Arizona State University illustrates the types of situations that make these additional steps necessary. For example, computer equipment purchased in the prior accounting year is being used to keep student records and accounts in the current year. What portion of the computer cost, if any, should be recognized as an expense of the current period? Before financial statements can be prepared, these and other questions relating to the recognition of revenues and expenses must be answered. With the answers in hand, the relevant account balances can then be adjusted.

The content and organization of the chapter are as follows:

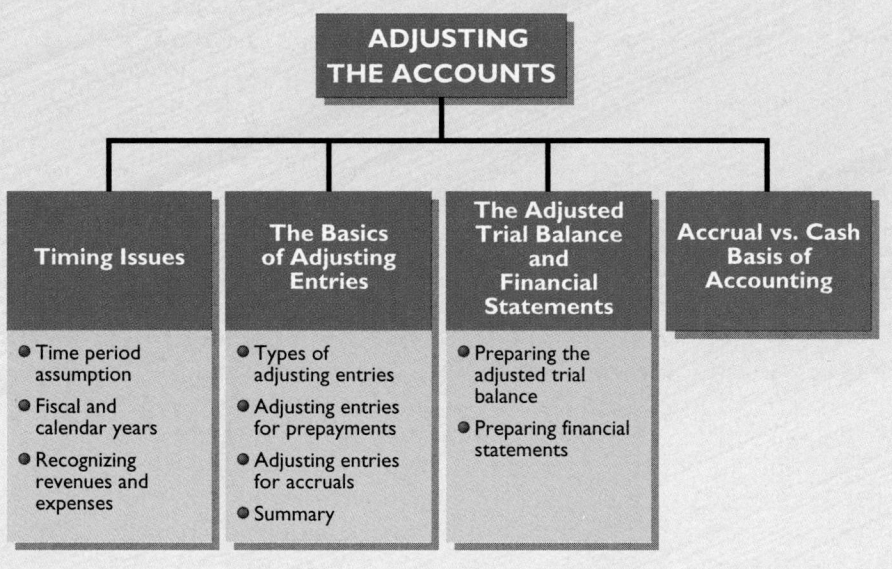

**ADJUSTING THE ACCOUNTS**

| Timing Issues | The Basics of Adjusting Entries | The Adjusted Trial Balance and Financial Statements | Accrual vs. Cash Basis of Accounting |
|---|---|---|---|
| ● Time period assumption <br> ● Fiscal and calendar years <br> ● Recognizing revenues and expenses | ● Types of adjusting entries <br> ● Adjusting entries for prepayments <br> ● Adjusting entries for accruals <br> ● Summary | ● Preparing the adjusted trial balance <br> ● Preparing financial statements | |

THE NAVIGATOR

# TIMING ISSUES

**1**

STUDY OBJECTIVE

Explain the time period assumption.

No adjustments would be necessary if we waited to prepare financial statements until a company ended its operations. At that point, we could readily determine its final balance sheet and the amount of lifetime income it earned. The following anecdote illustrates one way to compute lifetime income:

A grocery store owner from the old country kept his accounts payable on a spindle, accounts receivable on a note pad, and cash in a cigar box. His daughter, having just passed the CPA exam, chided the father: "I don't understand how you can run your business this way. How do you know what your profits are?"

"Well," the father replied, "when I got off the boat 40 years ago, I had nothing but the pants I was wearing. Today your brother is a doctor, your sister is a college professor, and you are a CPA. Your mother and I have a nice car, a well-furnished house, and a lake home. We have a good business and everything is paid for. So, you add all that together, subtract the pants, and there's your profit."

## Selecting an Accounting Time Period

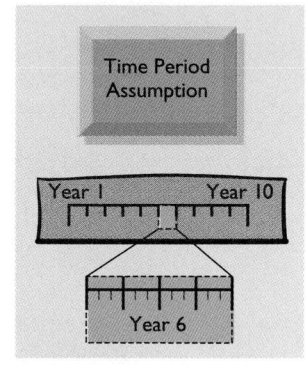

Although the old grocer may be correct in his evaluation, it is impractical to wait so long for the results of operations. All entities, from the corner grocery, to a global company like Kellogg, to your college or university, find it desirable and necessary to report the results of their activities more frequently. For example, management usually wants monthly financial statements, and the Internal Revenue Service requires all businesses to file annual tax returns. As a consequence, **accountants make the assumption that the economic life of a business can be divided into artificial time periods.** This assumption is referred to as the time period assumption.

Many business transactions affect more than one of these arbitrary time periods. For example, Farmer Brown's milking machine bought in 1998 and the airplanes purchased by Delta Air Lines 5 years ago are still in use today. Therefore it is necessary to determine the relevance of each business transaction to specific accounting periods. Doing so may involve subjective judgments and estimates. Generally, the shorter the time period (e.g., a month or a quarter of a year), the more difficult it becomes to determine the proper adjustments to be made.

**ALTERNATIVE TERMINOLOGY**
The time period assumption is also called the *periodicity assumption*.

## Fiscal and Calendar Years

Both small and large companies prepare financial statements on a periodic basis in order to assess their financial condition and results of operations. **Accounting time periods are generally a month, a quarter, or a year.** Monthly and quarterly time periods are often referred to as interim periods. Most large companies are required to prepare both interim (quarterly) and annual financial statements.

An accounting time period that is one year in length is referred to as a fiscal year. A fiscal year usually begins with the first day of a month and ends 12 months later on the last day of a month. The accounting period used by most businesses coincides with the calendar year (January 1 to December 31). Companies whose fiscal year differs from the calendar year include Delta Air Lines, June 30; Walt Disney Productions, September 30; Kmart Corp., January 31; and Dunkin' Donuts, Inc., October 31. Arizona State University's fiscal year is July 1 through June 30, which is typical of universities and governmental agencies.

## Recognizing Revenues and Expenses

**2**
STUDY
OBJECTIVE
.........................................
Distinguish between the revenue recognition principle and the matching principle.

Determining the amount of revenues and expenses to be reported in a given accounting period can be difficult. Therefore, accountants have developed two principles as part of generally accepted accounting principles (GAAP) that help in this determination: the revenue recognition principle and the matching principle.

The revenue recognition principle dictates that revenue be recognized in the accounting period in which it is earned. **In a service enterprise, revenue is considered to be earned at the time the service is performed.** To illustrate, assume that a dry cleaning business cleans clothing on June 30 but customers do not claim and pay for their clothes until the first week of July. Under the revenue recognition principle, revenue is earned in June when the service is performed and not in July when the cash is received. At June 30, the dry cleaner would report a receivable on its balance sheet and revenue in its income statement for the service performed.

In recognizing expenses, accountants follow the approach of "let the expenses follow the revenues." Thus, expense recognition is tied to revenue recognition. In the preceding example, this principle means that the salary expense

## ACCOUNTING IN ACTION
### Business Insight

Suppose you are a filmmaker and spend $15 million to produce a film. Over what period should the $15 million be expensed? Yes, it should be expensed over the economic life of the film. But what is its economic life? The filmmaker must estimate how much revenue will be earned from box office sales, video sales, and television—a period that easily can stretch five years or more. If a filmmaker allocates the cost over five years, and the film produces revenue in the sixth year, proper matching has not occurred. Furthermore, in some cases, films flop, and yet the costs are spread out over five years in the hopes that the films will eventually succeed. For example, in the mid-1980s Orion Pictures (now bankrupt) earned $7.3 million in one year, but lost $32 million the next year because it expensed 40 films that were not producing revenue. It was alleged that the company had overstated its income in earlier years because it did not expense these costs earlier. This case demonstrates the difficulty of properly matching expenses to revenues.

incurred in performing the cleaning service on June 30 should be reported in the income statement for the same period in which the service revenue is recognized. The critical issue in expense recognition is when the expense makes its contribution to revenue. This may or may not be the same period in which the expense is paid. If the salary incurred on June 30 is not paid until July, the dry cleaner would report salaries payable on its June 30 balance sheet. The practice of expense recognition is referred to as the matching principle because it dictates that efforts (expenses) be matched with accomplishments (revenues).

Once the assumption is made that the economic life of a business can be divided into artificial time periods, it follows that the revenue recognition and matching principles can be applied. This one assumption and two principles thus provide guidelines as to when revenues and expenses should be reported. These relationships are shown in Illustration 3-1.

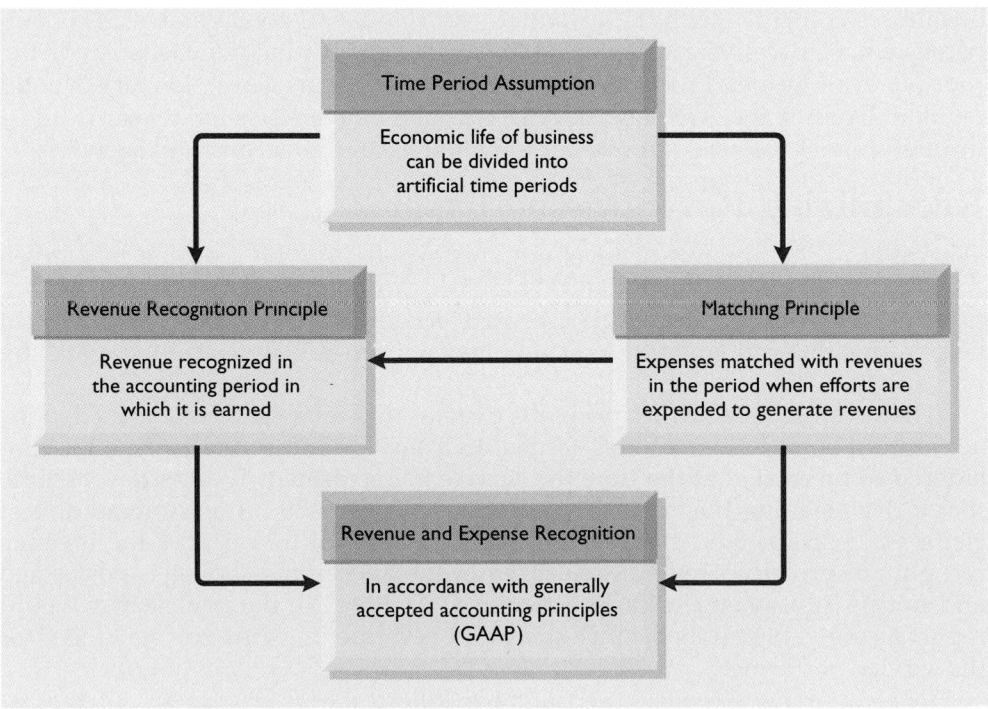

ILLUSTRATION 3-1

*GAAP relationships in revenue and expense recognition*

1. What is the relevance of the time period assumption to accounting?
2. What are the revenue recognition and matching principles?

THE
NAVIGATOR

# THE BASICS OF ADJUSTING ENTRIES

In order for revenues to be recorded in the period in which they are earned, and for expenses to be recognized in the period in which they are incurred, adjusting entries are made at the end of the accounting period. In short, adjusting entries **are needed to ensure that the revenue recognition and matching principles are followed.**

The use of adjusting entries makes it possible to report on the balance sheet the appropriate assets, liabilities, and owner's equity at the statement date and to report on the income statement the proper net income (or loss) for the period. However, the trial balance—the first pulling together of the transaction data—may not contain up-to-date and complete data. This is true for the following reasons:

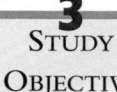

**3**
STUDY
OBJECTIVE

Explain why adjusting entries are needed.

1. Some events are not journalized daily because it is inexpedient to do so. Examples are the consumption of supplies and the earning of wages by employees.
2. Some costs are not journalized during the accounting period because these costs expire with the passage of time rather than as a result of recurring daily transactions. Examples of such costs are building and equipment deterioration and rent and insurance.
3. Some items may be unrecorded. An example is a utility service bill that will not be received until the next accounting period.

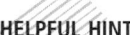

**HELPFUL HINT**
Adjusting entries are needed to enable financial statements to be in conformity with GAAP.

**Adjusting entries are required every time financial statements are prepared.** An essential starting point is an analysis of each account in the trial balance to determine whether it is complete and up-to-date for financial statement purposes. The analysis requires a thorough understanding of the company's operations and the interrelationship of accounts. The preparation of adjusting entries is often an involved process. In accumulating the adjustment data, the company may need to make inventory counts of supplies and repair parts. Also it may be desirable to prepare supporting schedules of insurance policies, rental agreements, and other contractual commitments. Adjustments are often prepared after the balance sheet date. However, the adjusting entries are dated as of the balance sheet date.

## Types of Adjusting Entries

Adjusting entries can be classified as either prepayments or accruals. Each of these classes has two subcategories as shown in Illustration 3-2:

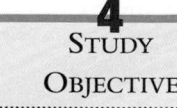

**4**
STUDY
OBJECTIVE

Identify the major types of adjusting entries.

**ILLUSTRATION 3-2**

*Categories of adjusting entries*

**Prepayments**

1. **Prepaid Expenses.** Expenses paid in cash and recorded as assets before they are used or consumed.
2. **Unearned Revenues.** Cash received and recorded as liabilities before revenue is earned.

**Accruals**

1. **Accrued Revenues.** Revenues earned but not yet received in cash or recorded.
2. **Accrued Expenses.** Expenses incurred but not yet paid in cash or recorded.

Specific examples and explanations of each type of adjustment are given in subsequent sections. Each example is based on the October 31 trial balance of Pioneer Advertising Agency, reproduced in Illustration 3-3 from Chapter 2.

**ILLUSTRATION 3-3**

*Trial balance*

**PIONEER ADVERTISING AGENCY**
**Trial Balance**
**October 31, 1999**

|  | Debit | Credit |
|---|---|---|
| Cash | $15,200 | |
| Advertising Supplies | 2,500 | |
| Prepaid Insurance | 600 | |
| Office Equipment | 5,000 | |
| Notes Payable | | $ 5,000 |
| Accounts Payable | | 2,500 |
| Unearned Revenue | | 1,200 |
| C. R. Byrd, Capital | | 10,000 |
| C. R. Byrd, Drawing | 500 | |
| Service Revenue | | 10,000 |
| Salaries Expense | 4,000 | |
| Rent Expense | 900 | |
| | $28,700 | $28,700 |

We assume that Pioneer Advertising uses an accounting period of one month. Thus, monthly adjusting entries will be made. The entries will be dated October 31.

## Adjusting Entries for Prepayments

**5**

**STUDY OBJECTIVE**

Prepare adjusting entries for prepayments.

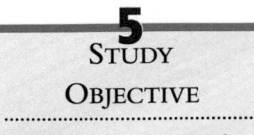

**HELPFUL HINT**

Remember that credits decrease assets and increase revenues. Debits increase expenses and decrease liabilities.

As indicated earlier, prepayments are either prepaid expenses or unearned revenues. Adjusting entries for prepayments are required at the statement date to record the portion of the prepayment that represents the **expense incurred or the revenue earned** in the current accounting period. Assuming an adjustment is needed for both types of prepayments, the asset and liability are overstated and the related expense and revenue are understated. For example, in the trial balance, the balance in the asset, Supplies, shows only supplies purchased. This balance is overstated; the related expense account, Supplies Expense, is understated because the cost of supplies used has not been recognized. Thus the adjusting entry for prepayments will decrease a balance sheet account and increase an income statement account. The effects of adjusting entries for prepayments are graphically depicted in Illustration 3-4.

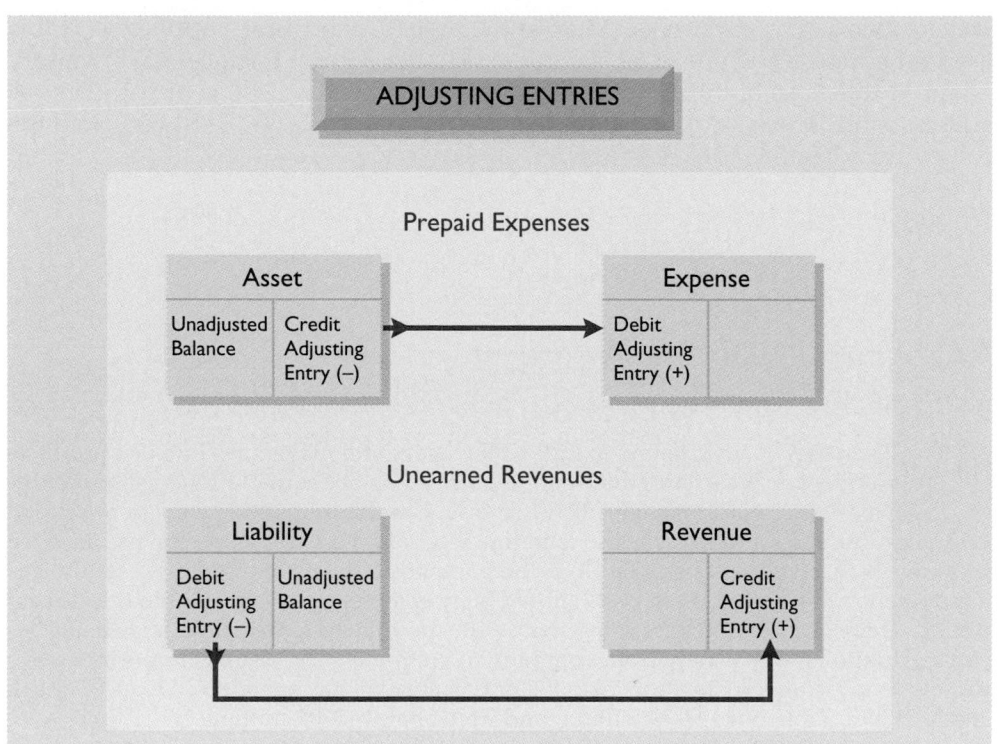

**ILLUSTRATION 3-4**

*Adjusting entries for prepayments*

## Prepaid Expenses

As stated on page 96, expenses paid in cash and recorded as assets before they are used or consumed are identified as prepaid expenses. When a cost is prepaid, an asset account is debited to show the service or benefit that will be received in the future. Prepayments often occur in regard to insurance, supplies, advertising, and rent. In addition, prepayments are made when buildings and equipment are purchased.

**Prepaid expenses expire either with the passage of time (e.g., rent and insurance) or through use and consumption (e.g., supplies).** The expiration of these costs does not require daily recurring entries, which would be unnecessary and impractical. Accordingly, it is customary to postpone the recognition of such cost expirations until financial statements are prepared. At each statement date, adjusting entries are made to record the expenses that apply to the current accounting period and to show the unexpired costs in the asset accounts.

Prior to adjustment, assets are overstated and expenses are understated. **Thus, the prepaid expense adjusting entry results in a debit to an expense account and a credit to an asset account.**

**Supplies.**   Several different types of supplies are used in a business enterprise. For example, a CPA firm will have **office supplies** such as stationery, envelopes, and accounting paper. In contrast, an advertising firm will have **advertising supplies** such as graph paper, video film, and poster paper. Supplies are generally debited to an asset account when they are acquired. During the course of operations, supplies are depleted or entirely consumed. However, recognition of supplies used is deferred until the adjustment process when a physical inventory (count) of supplies is taken. The difference between the balance in the Supplies (asset) account and the cost of supplies on hand represents the supplies used (expense) for the period.

Pioneer Advertising Agency purchased advertising supplies costing $2,500

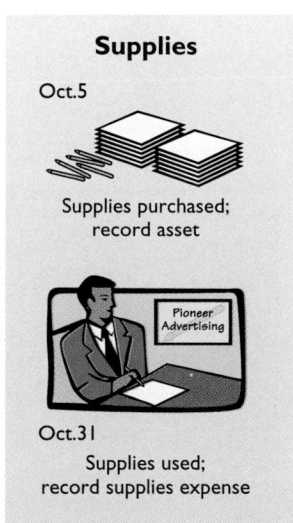

**Supplies**

Oct.5

Supplies purchased;
record asset

Oct.31

Supplies used;
record supplies expense

In the margins next to key journal entries are **equation analyses** that summarize the effects of the transaction on the three elements of the accounting equation.

| Equation Analysis | | |
|---|---|---|
| A | = L + | OE |
| − 1,500 | | − 1,500 |

on October 5. The debit was made to the asset Advertising Supplies, and this account shows a balance of $2,500 in the October 31 trial balance. An inventory count at the close of business on October 31 reveals that $1,000 of supplies are still on hand. Thus, the cost of supplies used is $1,500 ($2,500 − $1,000), and the following adjusting entry is made:

| Oct. 31 | Advertising Supplies Expense | 1,500 | |
|---|---|---|---|
| | Advertising Supplies | | 1,500 |
| | (To record supplies used) | | |

# ACCOUNTING IN ACTION
## Business Insight

The costs of advertising on radio, television, and magazines for such products as burgers, bleaches, athletic shoes, and so on are sometimes considered prepayments. As a manager for Procter & Gamble noted, "If we run a long ad campaign for soap and bleach, we sometimes report the costs as prepayments if we think we'll receive sales benefits from the campaign down the road." Presently it is a judgment call whether these costs should be prepayments or expenses in the current period. Developing guidelines consistent with the matching principle is difficult because situations vary widely from company to company. The issue is important since the outlays for advertising can be substantial. Recent big spenders: Sears Roebuck spent $1.28 billion, Nike $978 million, and McDonald's $503 million.

After the adjusting entry is posted, the two supplies accounts in T-account form show:

**ILLUSTRATION 3-5**

*Supplies accounts after adjustment*

| Advertising Supplies | | | | | Advertising Supplies Expense | | |
|---|---|---|---|---|---|---|---|
| 10/5 | 2,500 | 10/31 **Adj.** | **1,500** | | 10/31 **Adj.** | **1,500** | |
| 10/31 Bal. | 1,000 | | | | | | |

The asset account Advertising Supplies now shows a balance of $1,000, which is equal to the cost of supplies on hand at the statement date. In addition, Advertising Supplies Expense shows a balance of $1,500, which equals the cost of supplies used in October. **If the adjusting entry is not made, October expenses will be understated and net income overstated by $1,500. Moreover, both assets and owner's equity will be overstated by $1,500 on the October 31 balance sheet.**

**Insurance** Oct.4

Insurance purchased; record asset

| Insurance Policy | | | |
|---|---|---|---|
| Oct $50 | Nov $50 | Dec $50 | Jan $50 |
| Feb $50 | March $50 | April $50 | May $50 |
| June $50 | July $50 | Aug $50 | Sept $50 |
| I YEAR  $600 | | | |

Oct.31

Insurance expired; record insurance expense

**Insurance.**   Most companies have fire and theft insurance on merchandise and equipment, personal liability insurance for accidents suffered by customers, and automobile insurance on company cars and trucks. The cost of insurance protection is determined by the payment of insurance premiums. The term and coverage are specified in the insurance policy. The minimum term is usually one year, but three- to five-year terms are available and offer lower annual premiums. Insurance premiums normally are charged to the asset account Prepaid Insurance when paid. At the financial statement date it is necessary to debit Insurance Expense and credit Prepaid Insurance for the cost that has expired during the period.

On October 4, Pioneer Advertising Agency paid $600 for a one-year fire insurance policy. The effective date of coverage was October 1. The premium was charged to Prepaid Insurance when it was paid, and this account shows a balance of $600 in the October 31 trial balance. An analysis of the policy reveals that $50 ($600 ÷ 12) of insurance expires each month. Thus, the following adjusting entry is made:

| Oct. 31 | Insurance Expense | 50 | |
| | Prepaid Insurance | | 50 |
| | (To record insurance expired) | | |

| A | = | L | + | OE |
|---|---|---|---|---|
| −50 | | | | −50 |

After the adjusting entry is posted, the accounts show:

| Prepaid Insurance | | | | Insurance Expense | | |
|---|---|---|---|---|---|---|
| 10/4 | 600 | 10/31 **Adj.** | 50 | 10/31 **Adj.** | 50 | |
| 10/31 Bal. | 550 | | | | | |

**ILLUSTRATION 3-6**
*Insurance accounts after adjustment*

The asset Prepaid Insurance shows a balance of $550, which represents the unexpired cost applicable to the remaining 11 months of coverage. At the same time, the balance in Insurance Expense is equal to the insurance cost that has expired in October. **If this adjustment is not made, October expenses will be understated by $50 and net income overstated by $50. Moreover, both assets and owner's equity also will be overstated by $50 on the October 31 balance sheet.**

**Depreciation.**  A business enterprise typically owns a variety of productive facilities such as buildings, equipment, and motor vehicles. These assets provide service for a number of years. The term of service is commonly referred to as the useful life of the asset. Because an asset such as a building is expected to provide service for many years, it is recorded as an asset, rather than an expense, in the year it is acquired. As explained in Chapter 1, such assets are recorded at cost, as required by the cost principle.

**HELPFUL HINT**
Depreciation is an estimate— one of many estimates inherent in accounting.

According to the matching principle, a portion of the cost of a long-lived asset should be reported as an expense during each period of the asset's useful life. Depreciation is the process of allocating the cost of an asset to expense over its useful life in a rational and systematic manner.

***Need for Depreciation Adjustment.***  From an accounting standpoint, the acquisition of productive facilities is viewed essentially as a long-term prepayment for services. The need for making periodic adjusting entries for depreciation is, therefore, the same as described before for other prepaid expenses; that is, to recognize the cost that has expired (expense) during the period and to report the unexpired cost (asset) at the end of the period.

In determining the useful life of a productive facility, the primary causes of depreciation are actual use, deterioration due to the elements, and obsolescence. At the time an asset is acquired, the effects of these factors cannot be known with certainty, so they must be estimated. Thus, you should recognize that depreciation is an estimate rather than a factual measurement of the cost that has expired. A common procedure in computing depreciation expense is to divide the cost of the asset by its useful life. For example, if cost is $10,000 and useful life is expected to be 10 years, annual depreciation is $1,000.[1]

**Depreciation**

Oct. I

Office equipment purchased; record asset

| Office Equipment | | | |
|---|---|---|---|
| Oct | Nov | Dec | Jan |
| $40 | $40 | $40 | $40 |
| Feb | March | April | May |
| $40 | $40 | $40 | $40 |
| June | July | Aug | Sept |
| $40 | $40 | $40 | $40 |
| Depreciation = $480/year | | | |

Oct.31

Depreciation recognized; record depreciation expense

---

[1]Additional consideration is given to computing depreciation expense in Chapter 10.

For Pioneer Advertising, depreciation on the office equipment is estimated to be $480 a year, or $40 per month. Accordingly, depreciation for October is recognized by the following adjusting entry:

| A | = | L | + | OE |
|---|---|---|---|---|
| −40 | | | | −40 |

| Oct. 31 | Depreciation Expense | 40 | |
| |     Accumulated Depreciation—Office Equipment | | 40 |
| |     (To record monthly depreciation) | | |

After the adjusting entry is posted, the accounts show:

**ILLUSTRATION 3-7**

*Accounts after adjustment for depreciation*

The balance in the accumulated depreciation account will increase $40 each month. Therefore, after journalizing and posting the adjusting entry at November 30, the balance will be $80.

**HELPFUL HINT**
All contra accounts have increases, decreases, and normal balances opposite to the account to which they relate.

**Statement Presentation.** Accumulated Depreciation—Office Equipment is a contra asset account. A contra asset account is an account that is offset against an asset account on the balance sheet. This means that the accumulated depreciation account is offset against Office Equipment on the balance sheet and that its normal balance is a credit. This account is used instead of crediting Office Equipment in order to permit disclosure of **both the original cost** of the equipment **and the total cost that has expired to date**. In the balance sheet, Accumulated Depreciation—Office Equipment is deducted from the related asset account as follows:

**ILLUSTRATION 3-8**

*Balance sheet presentation of accumulated depreciation*

| Office equipment | $5,000 | |
| Less: Accumulated depreciation—office equipment | 40 | $4,960 |

The difference between the cost of any depreciable asset and its related accumulated depreciation is referred to as the book value of that asset. In Illustration 3-8, the book value of the equipment at the balance sheet date is $4,960. It is important to realize that the book value and the market value of the asset are generally two different values. The reason the two are different is that depreciation is not a matter of valuation but rather, a means of cost allocation.

**ALTERNATIVE TERMINOLOGY**
Book value is sometimes referred to as *carrying value* or *unexpired cost.*

Note also that depreciation expense identifies that portion of the asset's cost that has expired in October. As in the case of other prepaid adjustments, the omission of this adjusting entry would cause total assets, total owner's equity, and net income to be overstated and depreciation expense to be understated.

If additional equipment is involved, such as delivery or store equipment, or if the company has buildings, depreciation expense is recorded on each of these items. Related accumulated depreciation accounts also are established. These accumulated depreciation accounts would be described in the ledger as follows:

Accumulated Depreciation—Delivery Equipment; Accumulated Depreciation—Store Equipment; and Accumulated Depreciation—Buildings.

## Unearned Revenues

As stated on page 96, cash received and recorded as liabilities before revenue is earned is called **unearned revenues**. Such items as rent, magazine subscriptions, and customer deposits for future service may result in unearned revenues. Airlines such as United, American, and Delta treat receipts from the sale of tickets as unearned revenue until the flight service is provided. Similarly, tuition received prior to the start of a semester, as in the feature story about Arizona State University, is considered to be unearned revenue. Unearned revenues are the opposite of prepaid expenses. Indeed, unearned revenue on the books of one company is likely to be a prepayment on the books of the company that has made the advance payment. For example, if identical accounting periods are assumed, a landlord will have unearned rent revenue when a tenant has prepaid rent.

When the payment is received for services to be provided in a future accounting period, an unearned revenue (a liability) account should be credited to recognize the obligation that exists. Unearned revenues are subsequently earned through rendering service to a customer. During the accounting period it may not be practical to make daily recurring entries as the revenue is earned. In such cases, the recognition of earned revenue is delayed until the adjustment process. Then an adjusting entry is made to record the revenue that has been earned and to show the liability that remains. In the typical case, liabilities are overstated and revenues are understated prior to adjustment. Thus, **the adjusting entry for unearned revenues results in a debit (decrease) to a liability account and a credit (increase) to a revenue account**.

Pioneer Advertising Agency received $1,200 on October 2 from R. Knox for advertising services expected to be completed by December 31. The payment was credited to Unearned Revenue, and this account shows a balance of $1,200 in the October 31 trial balance. When analysis reveals that $400 of those fees has been earned in October, the following adjusting entry is made:

**Unearned Revenues**

Oct.2
Thank you in advance for your work
I will finish by Dec. 31
~$1,200~

Cash is received in advance; liability is recorded

Oct.31
Service is provided; revenue is recorded

**ALTERNATIVE TERMINOLOGY**
Unearned revenues is sometimes referred to as *deferred revenues*.

| Oct. 31 | Unearned Revenue | 400 | |
| | Service Revenue | | 400 |
| | (To record revenue for services provided) | | |

| A | = | L | + | OE |
|---|---|---|---|---|
| | | − 400 | | + 400 |

After the adjusting entry is posted, the accounts show:

| Unearned Revenue | | | | Service Revenue | | | |
|---|---|---|---|---|---|---|---|
| 10/31 **Adj.** | **400** | 10/2 | 1,200 | | | 10/31 Bal. | 10,000 |
| | | 10/31 Bal. | 800 | | | 31 **Adj.** | **400** |

**ILLUSTRATION 3-9**

*Revenue accounts after prepayments adjustment*

The liability Unearned Revenue now shows a balance of $800, which represents the remaining advertising services expected to be performed in the future. At the same time, Service Revenue shows total revenue earned in October of $10,400. **If this adjustment is not made, revenues and net income will be understated by $400 in the income statement. Moreover, liabilities will be overstated and owner's equity will be understated by $400 on the October 31 balance sheet.**

# BEFORE YOU GO ON . . .

## Review It

1. What are the four types of adjusting entries?
2. What is the effect on assets, owner's equity, expenses, and net income if a prepaid expense adjusting entry is not made?
3. What is the effect on liabilities, owner's equity, revenues, and net income if an unearned revenue adjusting entry is not made?

4. Using the Selected Financial Data section of Kellogg Company's financial statements what was the amount of depreciation and amortization expense for 1997 and 1996? The answer to this question is provided on page 136.

## Do It

The ledger of Hammond, Inc., on March 31, 1999, includes the following selected accounts before adjusting entries are prepared:

|  | Debit | Credit |
|---|---|---|
| Prepaid Insurance | 3,600 | |
| Office Supplies | 2,800 | |
| Office Equipment | 25,000 | |
| Accumulated Depreciation—Office Equipment | | 5,000 |
| Unearned Revenue | | 9,200 |

An analysis of the accounts shows the following:

1. Insurance expires at the rate of $100 per month.
2. Supplies on hand total $800.
3. The office equipment depreciates $200 a month.
4. One-half of the unearned revenue was earned in March.

Prepare the adjusting entries for the month of March.

***Reasoning:*** In order for revenues to be recorded in the period in which they are earned, and for expenses to be recognized in the period in which they are incurred, adjusting entries are made at the end of the accounting period. Adjusting entries for prepayments are required at the statement date to record the portion of the prepayment that represents the expense incurred or the revenue earned in the current accounting period. The failure to adjust for the prepayment leads to overstatement of the asset or liability and a related understatement of the expense or revenue.

***Solution:***

| | | |
|---|---|---|
| 1. Insurance Expense | 100 | |
|       Prepaid Insurance | | 100 |
|         (To record insurance expired) | | |
| 2. Office Supplies Expense | 2,000 | |
|       Office Supplies | | 2,000 |
|         (To record supplies used) | | |
| 3. Depreciation Expense | 200 | |
|       Accumulated Depreciation—Office Equipment | | 200 |
|         (To record monthly depreciation) | | |
| 4. Unearned Revenue | 4,600 | |
|       Service Revenue | | 4,600 |
|         (To record revenue for services provided) | | |

*Related exercise material:* BE3–3, BE3–4, BE3–5, BE3–6, E3–1, E3–2, E3–3, E3–4, E3–5, E3–6, E3–7, E3–8 and E3–9.

THE NAVIGATOR

## Adjusting Entries for Accruals

The second category of adjusting entries is **accruals**. Adjusting entries for accruals are required to record revenues earned and expenses incurred in the current accounting period that have not been recognized through daily entries. If an accrual adjustment is needed, the revenue account (and the related asset account) and/or the expense account (and the related liability account) is understated. Thus, the adjusting entry for accruals will **increase both a balance sheet and an income statement account**. Adjusting entries for accruals are graphically depicted in Illustration 3-10.

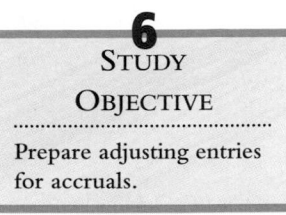

**6**

STUDY
OBJECTIVE

Prepare adjusting entries for accruals.

**ILLUSTRATION 3-10**

*Adjusting entries for accruals*

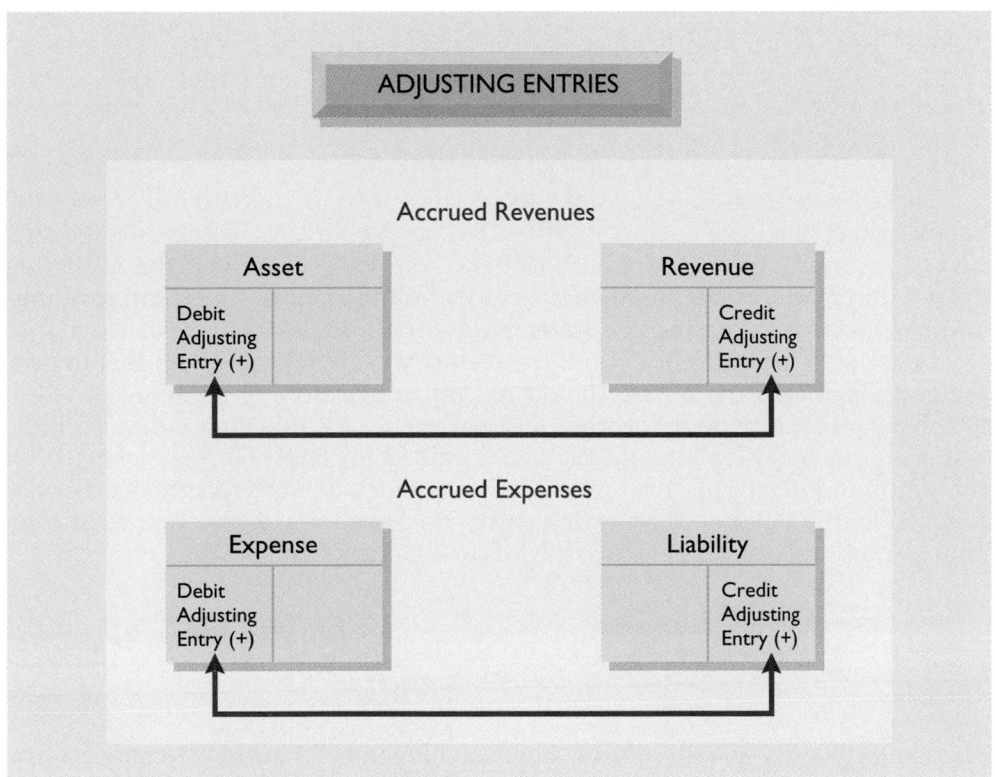

### *Accrued Revenues*

As explained on page 96, revenues earned but not yet received in cash or recorded at the statement date are accrued revenues. Accrued revenues may accumulate (accrue) with the passing of time, as in the case of interest revenue and rent revenue. Or they may result from services that have been performed but neither billed nor collected, as in the case of commissions and fees. The former are unrecorded because the earning of interest and rent does not involve daily transactions; the latter may be unrecorded because only a portion of the total service has been provided.

An adjusting entry is required to show the receivable that exists at the balance sheet date and to record the revenue that has been earned during the period. Prior to adjustment both assets and revenues are understated. Accordingly, **an adjusting entry for accrued revenues results in a debit (increase) to an asset account and a credit (increase) to a revenue account**.

In October Pioneer Advertising Agency earned $200 for advertising services that were not billed to clients before October 31. Because these services have not been billed, they have not been recorded. Thus, the following adjusting entry is made:

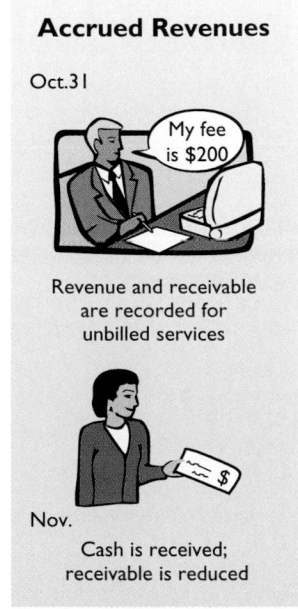

**Accrued Revenues**

Oct. 31

Revenue and receivable are recorded for unbilled services

Nov.

Cash is received; receivable is reduced

| A | = | L | + | OE |
|---|---|---|---|---|
| +200 | | | | +200 |

| Oct. 31 | Accounts Receivable | 200 | |
| |     Service Revenue | | 200 |
| |       (To record revenue for services provided) | | |

After the adjusting entry is posted, the accounts show:

**ILLUSTRATION 3-11**

*Receivable and revenue accounts after accrual adjustment*

| Accounts Receivable | | Service Revenue | |
|---|---|---|---|
| 10/31 **Adj.**   **200** | | 10/31 | 10,000 |
| | | 31 | 400 |
| | | 31 **Adj.** | **200** |
| | | 10/31 Bal. | 10,600 |

The asset Accounts Receivable shows that $200 is owed by clients at the balance sheet date. The balance of $10,600 in Service Revenue represents the total revenue earned during the month ($10,000 + $400 + $200). **If the adjusting entry is not made, assets and owner's equity on the balance sheet, and revenues and net income on the income statement, will all be understated.**

In the next accounting period, the clients will be billed. When this occurs, the entry to record the billing should recognize that $200 of revenue earned in October has already been recorded in the October 31 adjusting entry. To illustrate, assume that bills totaling $3,000 are mailed to clients on November 10. Of this amount, $200 represents revenue earned in October and recorded as Service Revenue in the October 31 adjusting entry. The remaining $2,800 represents revenue earned in November. Thus, the following entry is made:

**ALTERNATIVE TERMINOLOGY**

Accrued revenues are also called *accrued receivables*.

| A | = | L | + | OE |
|---|---|---|---|---|
| +2,800 | | | | +2,800 |

| Nov. 10 | Accounts Receivable | 2,800 | |
| |     Service Revenue | | 2,800 |
| |       (To record revenue for services provided) | | |

This entry records service revenue between November 1 and November 10. The subsequent collection of revenue from clients (including the $200 earned in October) will be recorded with a debit to Cash and a credit to Accounts Receivable.

### Accrued Expenses

As indicated on page 96, expenses incurred but not yet paid or recorded at the statement date are called accrued expenses. Interest, rent, taxes, and salaries can be accrued expenses. Accrued expenses result from the same causes as accrued revenues. In fact, an accrued expense on the books of one company is an accrued revenue to another company. For example, the $200 accrual of fees by Pioneer is an accrued expense to the client that received the service.

**ALTERNATIVE TERMINOLOGY**

Accrued expenses are also called *accrued liabilities*.

Adjustments for accrued expenses are necessary to record the obligations that exist at the balance sheet date and to recognize the expenses that apply to the current accounting period. Prior to adjustment both liabilities and expenses are understated. Therefore, **the adjusting entry for accrued expenses results in a debit (increase) to an expense account and a credit (increase) to a liability account.**

**Accrued Interest.**  Pioneer Advertising Agency signed a 3-month note payable in the amount of $5,000 on October 1. The note requires interest at an annual rate of 12%. The amount of the interest accumulation is determined by three factors: (1) the face value of the note, (2) the interest rate, which is always expressed as an annual rate, and (3) the length of time the note is outstanding. In this instance, the total interest due on the $5,000 note at its due date 3 months hence is $150 ($5,000 × 12% × 3/12), or $50 for one month. The formula for computing interest and its application to Pioneer Advertising Agency for the month of October[2] are shown in Illustration 3-12.

**HELPFUL HINT**
Interest is a cost of borrowing money that accumulates with the passage of time.

**ILLUSTRATION 3-12**

*Formula for computing interest*

Note that the time period is expressed as a fraction of a year. The accrued expense adjusting entry at October 31 is as follows:

| Oct. 31 | Interest Expense | 50 | |
| | Interest Payable | | 50 |
| | (To record interest on notes payable) | | |

| A | = | L | + | OE |
|---|---|---|---|---|
| | | +50 | | −50 |

After this adjusting entry is posted, the accounts show:

| Interest Expense | | Interest Payable | |
|---|---|---|---|
| 10/31   Adj.   50 | | | 10/31   Adj.   50 |

**ILLUSTRATION 3-13**

*Interest accounts after adjustment*

Interest Expense shows the interest charges applicable to the month of October. The amount of interest owed at the statement date is shown in Interest Payable. It will not be paid until the note comes due at the end of three months. The Interest Payable account is used instead of crediting Notes Payable to disclose the two types of obligations (interest and principal) in the accounts and statements. **If this adjusting entry is not made, liabilities and interest expense will be understated, and net income and owner's equity will be overstated.**

**Accrued Salaries.**    Some types of expenses, such as employee salaries and commissions, are paid for after the services have been performed. At Pioneer Advertising, salaries were last paid on October 26; the next payment of salaries will not occur until November 9. As shown in the calendar on page 106, three working days remain in October (October 29–31).

---

[2]The computation of interest will be considered in more depth in later chapters.

At October 31, the salaries for these days represent an accrued expense and a related liability to Pioneer Advertising. As explained on page 62, the employees receive total salaries of $2,000 for a five-day work week, or $400 per day. Thus, accrued salaries at October 31 are $1,200 ($400 × 3), and the adjusting entry is:

| A | = | L | + | OE |
|---|---|---|---|---|
|  |  | +1,200 |  | −1,200 |

| Oct. 31 | Salaries Expense | 1,200 | |
| | Salaries Payable | | 1,200 |
| | (To record accrued salaries) | | |

After this adjusting entry is posted, the accounts show:

**ILLUSTRATION 3-14**

*Salary accounts after adjustment*

| Salaries Expense | | | Salaries Payable | |
|---|---|---|---|---|
| 10/26 | 4,000 | | | 10/31 **Adj.** **1,200** |
| 31 **Adj.** | **1,200** | | | |
| 10/31 Bal. | 5,200 | | | |

After this adjustment, the balance in Salaries Expense of $5,200 (13 days × $400) is the actual salary expense for October. The balance in Salaries Payable of $1,200 is the amount of the liability for salaries owed as of October 31. **If the $1,200 adjustment for salaries is not recorded, Pioneer's expenses will be understated $1,200, and its liabilities will be understated $1,200.**

At Pioneer Advertising, salaries are payable every two weeks. Consequently, the next payday is November 9, when total salaries of $4,000 will again be paid. The payment consists of $1,200 of salaries payable at October 31 plus $2,800 of salaries expense for November (7 working days as shown in the November calendar × $400). Therefore, the following entry is made on November 9:

| A | = | L | + | OE |
|---|---|---|---|---|
| −4,000 |  | −1,200 |  | −2,800 |

| Nov. 9 | Salaries Payable | 1,200 | |
| | Salaries Expense | 2,800 | |
| | Cash | | 4,000 |
| | (To record November 9 payroll) | | |

This entry eliminates the liability for Salaries Payable that was recorded in the October 31 adjusting entry and records the proper amount of Salaries Expense for the period between November 1 and November 9.

## TECHNOLOGY IN ACTION

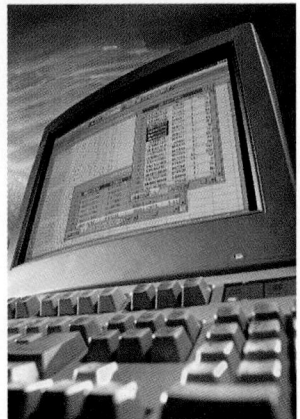

In many computer systems, the adjusting process is handled like any other transaction, with the accountant inputting the adjustment at the time required. The main difference between adjusting entries and regular transactions is that with adjusting entries, one part of the computer system may perform the required calculation for such items as depreciation or interest and then "feed" these figures to the journalizing process.

Such systems are also able to display information before and after changes were made. Management may be interested in such information to highlight the impact that adjustments have on the various accounts and financial statements.

## BEFORE YOU GO ON . . .

### Review It

1. What is the effect on assets, owner's equity, revenues, and net income if an accrued revenue adjusting entry is not made?
2. What is the effect on liabilities, owner's equity, and interest expense if an accrued expense adjusting entry is not made?

### Do It

Calvin and Hobbs are the new owners of Micro Computer Services. At the end of August 1999, their first month of ownership, Calvin and Hobbs are trying to prepare a monthly financial statement. The following information relates to August:

1. At August 31, Calvin and Hobbs owed their employees $800 in salaries that will be paid on September 1.
2. On August 1, Calvin and Hobbs borrowed $30,000 from a local bank on a 15-year mortgage. The annual interest rate is 10%.
3. Service revenue unrecorded in August totaled $1,100.

Prepare the adjusting entries needed at August 31, 1999.

*Reasoning:* Adjusting entries for accruals are required to record revenues earned and expenses incurred in the current accounting period that have not been recognized through daily entries. An adjusting entry for accruals will increase both a balance sheet and an income statement account.

*Solution:*

| | | |
|---|---|---|
| 1. Salaries Expense | 800 | |
|     Salaries Payable | | 800 |
|         (To record accrued salaries) | | |
| 2. Interest Expense | 250 | |
|     Interest Payable | | 250 |
|         (To record interest) | | |
|         ($30,000 \times 10\% \times 1/12 = $250) | | |
| 3. Accounts Receivable | 1,100 | |
|     Service Revenue | | 1,100 |
|         (To record revenue for services provided) | | |

*Related exercise material:* BE3–7, E3–1, E3–2, E3–3, E3–4, E3–5, E3–6, E3–7, E3–8, and E3–9.

THE NAVIGATOR

# Summary of Basic Relationships

ILLUSTRATION 3-15

*Summary of adjusting entries*

The four basic types of adjusting entries are summarized in Illustration 3-15. Take some time to study and analyze the adjusting entries shown in the summary. Be sure to note that **each adjusting entry affects one balance sheet account and one income statement account.**

| Type of Adjustment | Reason for Adjustment | Accounts before Adjustment | Adjusting Entry |
|---|---|---|---|
| 1. Prepaid expenses | (a) Prepaid expenses originally recorded in asset accounts have been used. | Assets overstated Expenses understated | Dr. Expenses Cr. Assets |
| 2. Unearned revenues | (b) Unearned revenues initially recorded in liability accounts have been earned. | Liabilities overstated Revenues understated | Dr. Liabilities Cr. Revenues |
| 3. Accrued revenues | (c) Revenues earned but not yet received in cash or recorded. | Assets understated Revenues understated | Dr. Assets Cr. Revenues |
| 4. Accrued expenses | (d) Expenses incurred but not yet paid in cash or recorded. | Expenses understated Liabilities understated | Dr. Expenses Cr. Liabilities |

The journalizing and posting of adjusting entries for Pioneer Advertising Agency on October 31 are shown in Illustrations 3-16 and 3-17. All adjustments are identified in the ledger by the reference J2 because they are journalized on page 2 of the general journal. A center caption entitled Adjusting Entries may be inserted between the last transaction entry and the first adjusting entry to identify these entries. When reviewing the general ledger in Illustration 3-17, note that the adjustments are highlighted in color.

ILLUSTRATION 3-16

*General journal showing adjusting entries*

**HELPFUL HINT**
(1) Remember that adjusting entries should not involve debits and credits to cash. (2) Evaluate whether the adjustment makes sense. For example, an adjustment to recognize supplies used should increase supplies expense. (3) Double-check all computations.

| | | GENERAL JOURNAL | | | J2 |
|---|---|---|---|---|---|
| **Date** | | **Account Titles and Explanation** | **Ref.** | **Debit** | **Credit** |
| 1999 | | Adjusting Entries | | | |
| Oct. | 31 | Advertising Supplies Expense | 61 | 1,500 | |
| | |   Advertising Supplies | 8 | | 1,500 |
| | |   (To record supplies used) | | | |
| | 31 | Insurance Expense | 63 | 50 | |
| | |   Prepaid Insurance | 10 | | 50 |
| | |   (To record insurance expired) | | | |
| | 31 | Depreciation Expense | 65 | 40 | |
| | |   Accumulated Depreciation—Office Equipment | 16 | | 40 |
| | |   (To record monthly depreciation) | | | |
| | 31 | Unearned Revenue | 28 | 400 | |
| | |   Service Revenue | 50 | | 400 |
| | |   (To record revenue for services provided) | | | |
| | 31 | Accounts Receivable | 6 | 200 | |
| | |   Service Revenue | 50 | | 200 |
| | |   (To record revenue for services provided) | | | |
| | 31 | Interest Expense | 64 | 50 | |
| | |   Interest Payable | 27 | | 50 |
| | |   (To record interest on notes payable) | | | |
| | 31 | Salaries Expense | 60 | 1,200 | |
| | |   Salaries Payable | 29 | | 1,200 |
| | |   (To record accrued salaries) | | | |

**ILLUSTRATION 3-17**

*General ledger after adjustment*

# GENERAL LEDGER

### Cash                                           No. 1

| Date | Explanation | Ref. | Debit | Credit | Balance |
|------|-------------|------|-------|--------|---------|
| 1999 | | | | | |
| Oct.  1 | | J1 | 10,000 | | 10,000 |
| 2 | | J1 | 1,200 | | 11,200 |
| 3 | | J1 | | 900 | 10,300 |
| 4 | | J1 | | 600 | 9,700 |
| 20 | | J1 | | 500 | 9,200 |
| 26 | | J1 | | 4,000 | 5,200 |
| 31 | | J1 | 10,000 | | 15,200 |

### Accounts Receivable                           No. 6

| Date | Explanation | Ref. | Debit | Credit | Balance |
|------|-------------|------|-------|--------|---------|
| 1999 | | | | | |
| Oct. 31 | Adj. entry | J2 | 200 | | 200 |

### Advertising Supplies                          No. 8

| Date | Explanation | Ref. | Debit | Credit | Balance |
|------|-------------|------|-------|--------|---------|
| 1999 | | | | | |
| Oct.  5 | | J1 | 2,500 | | 2,500 |
| 31 | Adj. entry | J2 | | 1,500 | 1,000 |

### Prepaid Insurance                             No. 10

| Date | Explanation | Ref. | Debit | Credit | Balance |
|------|-------------|------|-------|--------|---------|
| 1999 | | | | | |
| Oct.  4 | | J1 | 600 | | 600 |
| 31 | Adj. entry | J2 | | 50 | 550 |

### Office Equipment                              No. 15

| Date | Explanation | Ref. | Debit | Credit | Balance |
|------|-------------|------|-------|--------|---------|
| 1999 | | | | | |
| Oct.  1 | | J1 | 5,000 | | 5,000 |

### Accumulated Depreciation—Office Equipment No. 16

| Date | Explanation | Ref. | Debit | Credit | Balance |
|------|-------------|------|-------|--------|---------|
| 1999 | | | | | |
| Oct. 31 | Adj. entry | J2 | | 40 | 40 |

### Notes Payable                                 No. 25

| Date | Explanation | Ref. | Debit | Credit | Balance |
|------|-------------|------|-------|--------|---------|
| 1999 | | | | | |
| Oct.  1 | | J1 | | 5,000 | 5,000 |

### Accounts Payable                              No. 26

| Date | Explanation | Ref. | Debit | Credit | Balance |
|------|-------------|------|-------|--------|---------|
| 1999 | | | | | |
| Oct.  5 | | J1 | | 2,500 | 2,500 |

### Interest Payable                              No. 27

| Date | Explanation | Ref. | Debit | Credit | Balance |
|------|-------------|------|-------|--------|---------|
| 1999 | | | | | |
| Oct. 31 | Adj. entry | J2 | | 50 | 50 |

### Unearned Revenue                              No. 28

| Date | Explanation | Ref. | Debit | Credit | Balance |
|------|-------------|------|-------|--------|---------|
| 1999 | | | | | |
| Oct.  2 | | J1 | | 1,200 | |
| 31 | Adj. entry | J2 | 400 | | 800 |

### Salaries Payable                              No. 29

| Date | Explanation | Ref. | Debit | Credit | Balance |
|------|-------------|------|-------|--------|---------|
| 1999 | | | | | |
| Oct. 31 | Adj. entry | J2 | | 1,200 | 1,200 |

### C. R. Byrd, Capital                           No. 40

| Date | Explanation | Ref. | Debit | Credit | Balance |
|------|-------------|------|-------|--------|---------|
| 1999 | | | | | |
| Oct.  1 | | J1 | | 10,000 | 10,000 |

### C. R. Byrd, Drawing                           No. 41

| Date | Explanation | Ref. | Debit | Credit | Balance |
|------|-------------|------|-------|--------|---------|
| 1999 | | | | | |
| Oct. 20 | | J1 | 500 | | 500 |

### Service Revenue                               No. 50

| Date | Explanation | Ref. | Debit | Credit | Balance |
|------|-------------|------|-------|--------|---------|
| 1999 | | | | | |
| Oct. 31 | | J1 | | 10,000 | 10,000 |
| 31 | Adj. entry | J2 | | 400 | 10,400 |
| 31 | Adj. entry | J2 | | 200 | 10,600 |

### Salaries Expense                              No. 60

| Date | Explanation | Ref. | Debit | Credit | Balance |
|------|-------------|------|-------|--------|---------|
| 1999 | | | | | |
| Oct. 26 | | J1 | 4,000 | | 4,000 |
| 31 | Adj. entry | J2 | 1,200 | | 5,200 |

### Advertising Supplies Expense                  No. 61

| Date | Explanation | Ref. | Debit | Credit | Balance |
|------|-------------|------|-------|--------|---------|
| 1999 | | | | | |
| Oct. 31 | Adj. entry | J2 | 1,500 | | 1,500 |

### Rent Expense                                  No. 62

| Date | Explanation | Ref. | Debit | Credit | Balance |
|------|-------------|------|-------|--------|---------|
| 1999 | | | | | |
| Oct.  3 | | J1 | 900 | | 900 |

### Insurance Expense                             No. 63

| Date | Explanation | Ref. | Debit | Credit | Balance |
|------|-------------|------|-------|--------|---------|
| 1999 | | | | | |
| Oct. 31 | Adj. entry | J2 | 50 | | 50 |

### Interest Expense                              No. 64

| Date | Explanation | Ref. | Debit | Credit | Balance |
|------|-------------|------|-------|--------|---------|
| 1999 | | | | | |
| Oct. 31 | Adj. entry | J2 | 50 | | 50 |

### Depreciation Expense                          No. 65

| Date | Explanation | Ref. | Debit | Credit | Balance |
|------|-------------|------|-------|--------|---------|
| 1999 | | | | | |
| Oct. 31 | Adj. entry | J2 | 40 | | 40 |

**7**
STUDY
OBJECTIVE

Describe the nature and purpose of an adjusted trial balance.

# THE ADJUSTED TRIAL BALANCE AND FINANCIAL STATEMENTS

After all adjusting entries have been journalized and posted, another trial balance is prepared from the ledger accounts. This trial balance is called an adjusted trial balance. It shows the balances of all accounts, including those that have been adjusted, at the end of the accounting period. The purpose of an adjusted trial balance is to **prove the equality** of the total debit balances and the total credit balances in the ledger after all adjustments have been made. Because the accounts contain all data that are needed for financial statements, the adjusted trial balance is the primary basis for the preparation of financial statements.

## Preparing the Adjusted Trial Balance

The adjusted trial balance for Pioneer Advertising Agency presented in Illustration 3-18 has been prepared from the ledger accounts in Illustration 3-17. To facilitate the comparison of account balances, the trial balance data, labeled "Before Adjustment" (presented earlier in Illustration 3-3), are shown alongside the adjusted data, labeled "After Adjustment." In addition, the amounts affected by the adjusting entries are highlighted in color in the "After Adjustment" columns.

**ILLUSTRATION 3-18**

*Trial balance and adjusted trial balance compared*

| | Before Adjustment | | After Adjustment | |
|---|---|---|---|---|
| | **Dr.** | **Cr.** | **Dr.** | **Cr.** |
| Cash | $15,200 | | $15,200 | |
| Accounts Receivable | | | 200 | |
| Advertising Supplies | 2,500 | | 1,000 | |
| Prepaid Insurance | 600 | | 550 | |
| Office Equipment | 5,000 | | 5,000 | |
| Accumulated Depreciation— Office Equipment | | | | $    40 |
| Notes Payable | | $ 5,000 | | 5,000 |
| Accounts Payable | | 2,500 | | 2,500 |
| Interest Payable | | | | 50 |
| Unearned Revenue | | 1,200 | | 800 |
| Salaries Payable | | | | 1,200 |
| C. R. Byrd, Capital | | 10,000 | | 10,000 |
| C. R. Byrd, Drawing | 500 | | 500 | |
| Service Revenue | | 10,000 | | 10,600 |
| Salaries Expense | 4,000 | | 5,200 | |
| Advertising Supplies   Expense | | | 1,500 | |
| Rent Expense | 900 | | 900 | |
| Insurance Expense | | | 50 | |
| Interest Expense | | | 50 | |
| Depreciation Expense | | | 40 | |
| | $28,700 | $28,700 | $30,190 | $30,190 |

**PIONEER ADVERTISING AGENCY**
**Trial Balances**
**October 31, 1999**

# Preparing Financial Statements

**Financial statements can be prepared directly from an adjusted trial balance.** The preparation of financial statements from the adjusted trial balance of Pioneer Advertising Agency and the interrelationship of data are presented in Illustrations 3-19 and 3-20.

As shown in Illustration 3-19 the income statement is prepared from the revenue and expense accounts; the owner's equity statement is derived from the owner's capital and drawing accounts and the net income (or net loss) shown in the income statement. As shown in Illustration 3-20 the balance sheet is then prepared from the asset and liability accounts and the ending owner's capital balance as reported in the owner's equity statement.

**ILLUSTRATION 3-19**

*Preparation of the income statement and owner's equity statement from the adjusted trial balance*

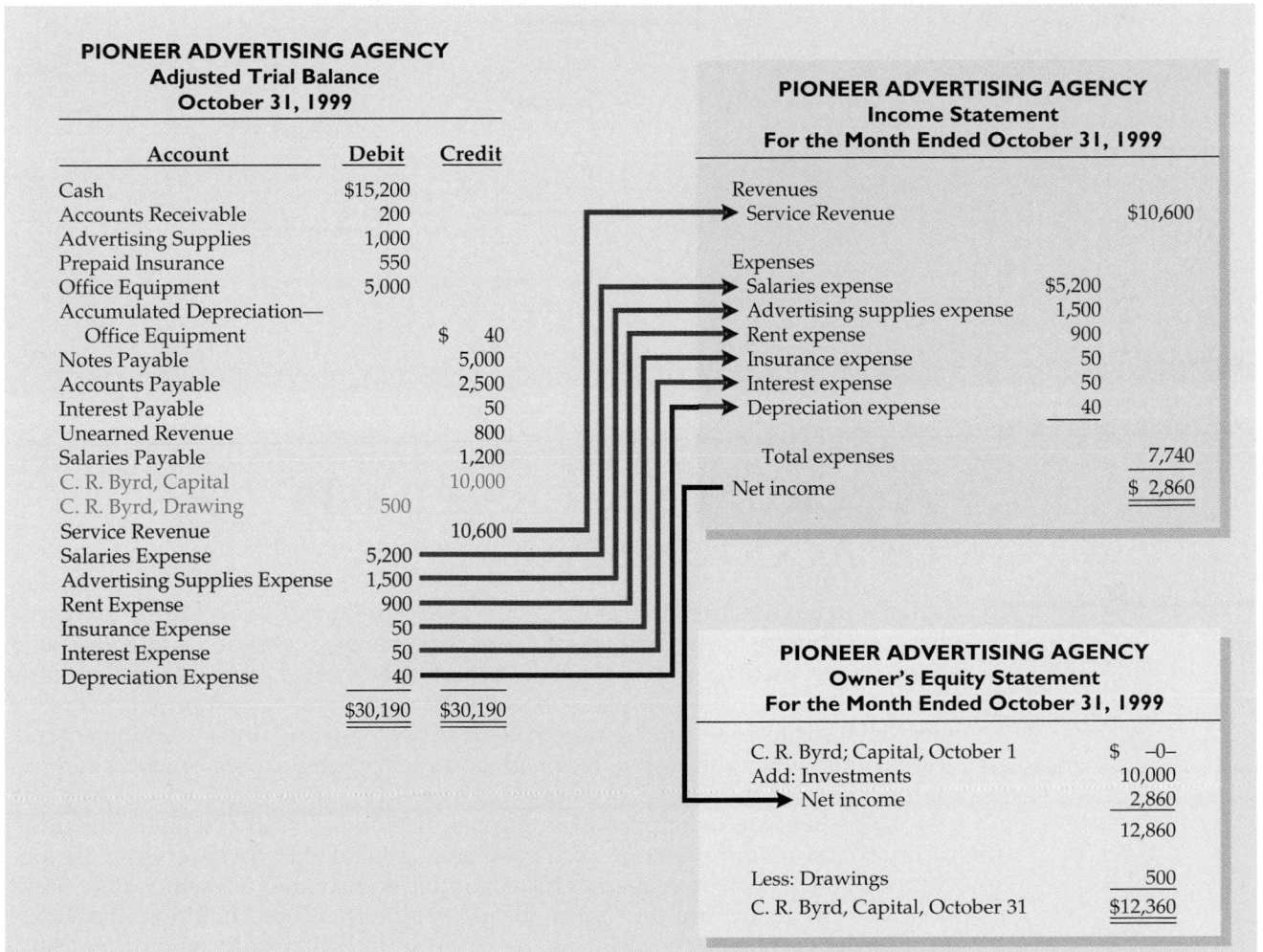

**PIONEER ADVERTISING AGENCY**
**Adjusted Trial Balance**
**October 31, 1999**

| Account | Debit | Credit |
|---|---|---|
| Cash | $15,200 | |
| Accounts Receivable | 200 | |
| Advertising Supplies | 1,000 | |
| Prepaid Insurance | 550 | |
| Office Equipment | 5,000 | |
| Accumulated Depreciation— Office Equipment | | $ 40 |
| Notes Payable | | 5,000 |
| Accounts Payable | | 2,500 |
| Interest Payable | | 50 |
| Unearned Revenue | | 800 |
| Salaries Payable | | 1,200 |
| C. R. Byrd, Capital | | 10,000 |
| C. R. Byrd, Drawing | 500 | |
| Service Revenue | | 10,600 |
| Salaries Expense | 5,200 | |
| Advertising Supplies Expense | 1,500 | |
| Rent Expense | 900 | |
| Insurance Expense | 50 | |
| Interest Expense | 50 | |
| Depreciation Expense | 40 | |
| | $30,190 | $30,190 |

**PIONEER ADVERTISING AGENCY**
**Income Statement**
**For the Month Ended October 31, 1999**

| Revenues | | |
|---|---|---|
| Service Revenue | | $10,600 |
| Expenses | | |
| Salaries expense | $5,200 | |
| Advertising supplies expense | 1,500 | |
| Rent expense | 900 | |
| Insurance expense | 50 | |
| Interest expense | 50 | |
| Depreciation expense | 40 | |
| Total expenses | | 7,740 |
| Net income | | $ 2,860 |

**PIONEER ADVERTISING AGENCY**
**Owner's Equity Statement**
**For the Month Ended October 31, 1999**

| C. R. Byrd, Capital, October 1 | $ –0– |
|---|---|
| Add: Investments | 10,000 |
| Net income | 2,860 |
| | 12,860 |
| Less: Drawings | 500 |
| C. R. Byrd, Capital, October 31 | $12,360 |

| PIONEER ADVERTISING AGENCY<br>Adjusted Trial Balance<br>October 31, 1999 | | |
| --- | --- | --- |
| **Account** | **Debit** | **Credit** |
| Cash | $15,200 | |
| Accounts Receivable | 200 | |
| Advertising Supplies | 1,000 | |
| Prepaid Insurance | 550 | |
| Office Equipment | 5,000 | |
| Accumulated Depreciation—<br>    Office Equipment | | $    40 |
| Notes Payable | | 5,000 |
| Accounts Payable | | 2,500 |
| Interest Payable | | 50 |
| Unearned Revenue | | 800 |
| Salaries Payable | | 1,200 |
| C. R. Byrd, Capital | | 10,000 |
| C. R. Byrd, Drawing | 500 | |
| Service Revenue | | 10,600 |
| Salaries Expense | 5,200 | |
| Advertising Supplies Expense | 1,500 | |
| Rent Expense | 900 | |
| Insurance Expense | 50 | |
| Interest Expense | 50 | |
| Depreciation Expense | 40 | |
| | $30,190 | $30,190 |

| PIONEER ADVERTISING AGENCY<br>Balance Sheet<br>October 31, 1999 | | |
| --- | --- | --- |
| **Assets** | | |
| Cash | | $15,200 |
| Accounts receivable | | 200 |
| Advertising supplies | | 1,000 |
| Prepaid insurance | | 550 |
| Office equipment | $5,000 | |
| Less: Accumulated depreciation | 40 | 4,960 |
| Total assets | | $21,910 |
| **Liabilities and Owner's Equity** | | |
| Liabilities | | |
| Notes payable | | $ 5,000 |
| Accounts payable | | 2,500 |
| Interest payable | | 50 |
| Unearned revenue | | 800 |
| Salaries payable | | 1,200 |
| Total liabilities | | 9,550 |
| Owner's equity | | |
| C. R. Byrd, Capital | | 12,360 |
| Total liabilities and<br>    owner's equity | | $21,910 |

Capital Balance at Oct. 31
from Owner's Equity
Statement in Illustration 3-19

**ILLUSTRATION 3-20**

*Preparation of the balance sheet from the adjusted trial balance*

# ACCRUAL VS. CASH BASIS OF ACCOUNTING

**8**

STUDY

OBJECTIVE

Explain the accrual basis of accounting.

What you have learned in this chapter is the accrual basis of accounting. Accrual basis accounting means that transactions that change a company's financial statements are recorded **in the periods in which the events occur**, rather than in the periods in which the company receives or pays cash. For example, using the accrual basis to determine net income means recognizing revenues when earned rather than when the cash is received, and recognizing expenses when incurred rather than when paid. Information presented on an accrual basis reveals relationships likely to be important in predicting future results. To illustrate, under accrual accounting, revenues are generally recognized when services are performed so they can be related to the economic environment in which they occur. Trends in revenues are thus more meaningful for decision-making purposes.

Under cash basis accounting, revenue is recorded only when the cash is received, and an expense is recorded only when cash is paid. As a result, the cash basis of accounting often leads to misleading financial statements. For example, it fails to record revenue which has been earned but for which the cash has not been received, violating the revenue recognition principle. In addition, expenses are also not matched with earned revenues and therefore the matching principle is not followed. Therefore, **the cash basis of accounting is not in accordance with generally accepted accounting principles.**

**INTERNATIONAL NOTE**

Although different accounting standards are often used in other major industrialized countries, the accrual basis of accounting is followed by all these countries.

Although most companies use the accrual basis of accounting, some small companies use the cash basis of accounting. The cash basis of accounting is justified by these businesses because they often have few receivables and payables. Accountants are sometimes asked to convert cash basis records to the accrual basis. As you might expect, extensive adjusting entries are required for this task.

## BEFORE YOU GO ON . . .

### Review It

1. What is the purpose of an adjusted trial balance?
2. How is an adjusted trial balance prepared?
3. What are the differences between the cash and accrual bases of accounting?

## A LOOK BACK AT OUR FEATURE STORY

Refer to the opening story about Arizona State University, and answer the following questions.

1. What are the purposes of adjusting entries?
2. Why should Arizona State be concerned about the period in which revenue is recognized?
3. What adjusting entries should be made for tuition revenue and supplies expense at the end of the summer session?
4. What other types of adjusting entries do you believe Arizona State University might make?

*Solution:*

1. Adjusting entries are necessary to make the financial statements complete and accurate. Adjusting entries are made to record revenues in the period in which they are earned and to recognize expenses in the period in which they are incurred. Therefore, adjustments ensure that the revenue recognition and matching principles are followed.
2. As a not-for-profit institution Arizona State University must operate within its state appropriations and its own budget. It must know what revenues are attributable to each operating/accounting period. Assignment of revenues to the proper operating periods (namely, in the period earned) is necessary in order to make operating/accounting periods (years) comparable.
3. ASU probably used Unearned Tuition Revenue because tuition is generally received before the semester begins. The adjusting entry is debit Unearned Tuition Revenue and credit Tuition Revenue. When supplies were purchased, ASU probably debited Supplies. The adjusting entry is a credit to Supplies and a debit to Supplies Expense.
4. (a) Accrued expenses: rent, salaries, utilities, interest.
   (b) Accrued revenues: unpaid tuition, lab fees, interest earned.
   (c) Prepaid expenses: insurance, depreciation.
   (d) Unearned revenues: tuition, lab fees, theatre tickets, athletic tickets.

THE
NAVIGATOR

## DEMONSTRATION PROBLEM

Terry Thomas opens the Green Thumb Lawn Care Company on April 1. At April 30, the trial balance shows the following balances for selected accounts:

|                   |          |
|-------------------|----------|
| Prepaid Insurance | $ 3,600  |
| Equipment         | 28,000   |
| Notes Payable     | 20,000   |
| Unearned Revenue  | 4,200    |
| Service Revenue   | 1,800    |

Analysis reveals the following additional data pertaining to these accounts:

1. Prepaid insurance is the cost of a two-year insurance policy, effective April 1.
2. Depreciation on the equipment is $500 per month.
3. The note payable is dated April 1. It is a six-month, 12% note.
4. Seven customers paid for the company's six months' lawn service package of $600 beginning in April. These customers were serviced in April.
5. Lawn services rendered other customers but not billed at April 30 totaled $1,500.

*Instructions*

Prepare the adjusting entries for the month of April. Show computations.

## SOLUTION TO DEMONSTRATION PROBLEM

### GENERAL JOURNAL    J2

**PROBLEM-SOLVING STRATEGIES**

1. Note that adjustments are being made for one month.
2. Make computations carefully.
3. Select account titles carefully.
4. Make sure debits are made first and credits are indented.
5. Check that debits equal credits for each entry.

| Date | Account Titles and Explanation | Ref. | Debit | Credit |
|------|-------------------------------|------|-------|--------|
| | Adjusting Entries | | | |
| Apr. 30 | Insurance Expense | | 150 | |
| |     Prepaid Insurance | | | 150 |
| |     (To record insurance expired: $3,600 ÷ 24 = $150 per month) | | | |
| 30 | Depreciation Expense | | 500 | |
| |     Accumulated Depreciation—Equipment | | | 500 |
| |     (To record monthly depreciation) | | | |
| 30 | Interest Expense | | 200 | |
| |     Interest Payable | | | 200 |
| |     (To record interest on notes payable: $20,000 × 12% × 1/12 = $200) | | | |
| 30 | Unearned Revenue | | 700 | |
| |     Service Revenue | | | 700 |
| |     (To record service revenue: $600 ÷ 6 = $100; $100 per month × 7 = $700) | | | |
| 30 | Accounts Receivable | | 1,500 | |
| |     Service Revenue | | | 1,500 |
| |     (To record revenue for services provided) | | | |

THE NAVIGATOR

# SUMMARY OF STUDY OBJECTIVES

**1. *Explain the time period assumption.*** The time period assumption assumes that the economic life of a business can be divided into artificial time periods.

**2. *Distinguish between the revenue recognition principle and the matching principle.*** The revenue recognition principle dictates that revenue be recognized in the accounting period in which it is earned. The matching principle dictates that expenses be recognized when they make their contribution to revenues.

**3. *Explain why adjusting entries are needed.*** Adjusting entries are made at the end of an accounting period. They ensure that revenues are recorded in the period in which they are earned and that expenses are recognized in the period in which they are incurred.

**4. *Identify the major types of adjusting entries.*** The major types of adjusting entries are prepaid expenses, unearned revenues, accrued revenues, and accrued expenses.

**5. *Prepare adjusting entries for prepayments.*** Prepayments are either prepaid expenses or unearned revenues. Adjusting entries for prepayments are required at the statement date to record the portion of the prepayment that represents the expense incurred or the revenue earned in the current accounting period.

**6. *Prepare adjusting entries for accruals.*** Accruals are either accrued revenues or accrued expenses. Adjusting entries for accruals are required to record revenues earned and expenses incurred in the current accounting period that have not been recognized through daily entries.

**7.** *Describe the nature and purpose of an adjusted trial balance.* An adjusted trial balance is a trial balance that shows the balances of all accounts, including those that have been adjusted, at the end of an accounting period. The purpose of an adjusted trial balance is to show the effects of all financial events that have occurred during the accounting period.

**8.** *Explain the accrual basis of accounting.* Accrual basis accounting means that events that change a company's financial statements are recorded in the periods in which the events occur, rather than in the periods in which the company receives or pays cash.

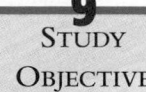
THE
NAVIGATOR

# GLOSSARY

**Accrual basis of accounting** Accounting basis in which transactions that change a company's financial statements are recorded in the periods in which the events occur, rather than in the periods in which the company receives or pays cash. (p. 112).

**Accrued expenses** Expenses incurred but not yet paid in cash or recorded. (p. 104).

**Accrued revenues** Revenues earned but not yet received in cash or recorded. (p. 103).

**Adjusted trial balance** A list of accounts and their balances after all adjustments have been made. (p. 110).

**Adjusting entries** Entries made at the end of an accounting period to ensure that the revenue recognition and matching principles are followed. (p. 94).

**Book value** The difference between the cost of a depreciable asset and its related accumulated depreciation. (p. 100).

**Calendar year** An accounting period that extends from January 1 to December 31. (p. 93).

**Cash basis accounting** Accounting basis in which revenue is recorded only when cash is received and an expense is recorded only when cash is paid. (p. 112).

**Contra asset account** An account that is offset against an asset account on the balance sheet. (p. 100).

**Depreciation** The process of allocating the cost of an asset to expense over its useful life in a rational and systematic manner. (p. 99).

**Fiscal year** An accounting period that is one year in length. (p. 93).

**Interim periods** Monthly or quarterly accounting time periods. (p. 93).

**Matching principle** The principle that efforts (expenses) be matched with accomplishments (revenues). (p. 94).

**Prepaid expenses** Expenses paid in cash and recorded as assets before they are used or consumed. (p. 97).

**Revenue recognition principle** The principle that revenue be recognized in the accounting period in which it is earned. (p. 93).

**Time period assumption** An assumption that the economic life of a business can be divided into artificial time periods. (p. 93).

**Unearned revenues** Cash received and recorded as liabilities before revenue is earned. (p. 101).

**Useful life** The length of service of a productive facility. (p. 99).

# APPENDIX ALTERNATIVE TREATMENT OF PREPAID EXPENSES AND UNEARNED REVENUES

In our discussion of adjusting entries for prepaid expenses and unearned revenues, we illustrated transactions for which the initial entries were made to balance sheet accounts. That is, in the case of prepaid expenses, the prepayment was debited to an asset account, and in the case of unearned revenue, the cash received was credited to a liability account. Some businesses use an alternative treatment: (1) At the time an expense is prepaid, it is debited to an expense account; (2) at the time of a receipt for future services, it is credited to a revenue account. The circumstances that justify such entries and the different adjusting entries that may be required are described below. The alternative treatment of prepaid expenses and unearned revenues has the same effect on the financial statements as the procedures described in the chapter.

**9**
STUDY
OBJECTIVE

Prepare adjusting entries for the alternative treatment of prepayments.

# PREPAID EXPENSES

Prepaid expenses become expired costs either through the passage of time, as in the case of insurance, or through consumption, as in the case of advertising supplies. If, at the time of purchase, the company expects to consume the supplies before the next financial statement date, **it may be more convenient initially to debit (increase) an expense account rather than an asset account**. Assume, for example, that Pioneer Advertising expects that all of the supplies purchased on October 5 will be used before October 31. A debit of $2,500 to Advertising Supplies Expense rather than to the asset account, Advertising Supplies, on October 5 will eliminate the need for an adjusting entry on October 31, if all the supplies are used. At October 31, the Advertising Supplies Expense account will show a balance of $2,500, which is equal to the cost of supplies used between October 5 and October 31.

Assume, however, that the company does not use all the supplies, and an inventory of $1,000 of advertising supplies remains on October 31. What then? Obviously, in such a case an adjusting entry is needed. Prior to adjustment, the expense account, Advertising Supplies Expense, is overstated $1,000, and the asset account, Advertising Supplies, is understated $1,000. Thus the following adjusting entry is made:

| A | = | L | + | OE |
|---|---|---|---|---|
| +1,000 | | | | +1,000 |

| Oct. 31 | Advertising Supplies | 1,000 | |
|---|---|---|---|
| | Advertising Supplies Expense | | 1,000 |
| | (To record supplies inventory) | | |

After posting the adjusting entry, the accounts show:

*Prepaid expenses accounts after adjustment*

| Advertising Supplies | | Advertising Supplies Expense | |
|---|---|---|---|
| 10/31 **Adj.** 1,000 | | 10/5 2,500 | 10/31 **Adj.** 1,000 |
| | | 10/31 **Bal.** 1,500 | |

After adjustment, the asset account, Advertising Supplies, shows a balance of $1,000, which is equal to the cost of supplies on hand at October 31. In addition, Advertising Supplies Expense shows a balance of $1,500, which is equal to the cost of supplies used between October 5 and October 31. If the adjusting entry is not made, expenses will be overstated and net income will be understated by $1,000 in the October income statement. Moreover, both assets and owner's equity will be understated by $1,000 on the October 31 balance sheet.

A comparative summary of the entries and accounts for advertising supplies is shown in Illustration 3A-2.

*Adjustment approaches— a comparison*

| | Prepayment Initially Debited to Asset Account (per chapter) | | | Prepayment Initially Debited to Expense Account (per appendix) | | |
|---|---|---|---|---|---|---|
| Oct. 5 | Advertising Supplies | 2,500 | | Oct. 5 | Advertising Supplies | |
| | Accounts Payable | | 2,500 | | Expense | 2,500 |
| | | | | | Accounts Payable | 2,500 |
| Oct. 31 | Advertising Supplies | | | Oct. 31 | Advertising Supplies | 1,000 |
| | Expense | 1,500 | | | Advertising Supplies | |
| | Advertising Supplies | | 1,500 | | Expense | 1,000 |

After posting the entries, the accounts appear as follows:

| (per chapter) Advertising Supplies | | | (per appendix) Advertising Supplies | | |
|---|---|---|---|---|---|
| 10/5 | 2,500 | 10/31 **Adj.** 1,500 | 10/31 **Adj.** 1,000 | | |
| 10/31 **Bal.** 1,000 | | | | | |
| Advertising Supplies Expense | | | Advertising Supplies Expense | | |
| 10/31 **Adj.** 1,500 | | | 10/5 | 2,500 | 10/31 **Adj.** 1,000 |
| | | | 10/31 **Bal.** 1,500 | | |

Note that the account balances under each alternative are the same at October 31; that is, Advertising Supplies $1,000, and Advertising Supplies Expense $1,500.

# UNEARNED REVENUES

Unearned revenues become earned either through the passage of time, as in the case of unearned rent, or through rendering the service, as in the case of unearned fees. Like prepaid expenses, a revenue account may be credited when cash is received for future services and a different adjusting entry may be necessary.

To illustrate, assume that when Pioneer Advertising received $1,200 for future services on October 2 the services were expected to be performed before October 31.[3] In such a case, Service Revenue is credited. If revenue is in fact earned before October 31, no adjustment is needed. However, if, at the statement date, $800 of the services have not been performed, an adjusting entry is required. Prior to adjustment, the revenue account, Service Revenue, is overstated $800, and the liability account, Unearned Revenue, is understated $800. Thus, the following adjusting entry is made:

| Oct. 31 | Service Revenue | 800 | |
| |     Unearned Revenue | | 800 |
| |       (To record unearned revenue) | | |

| A | = | L | + | OE |
|---|---|---|---|---|
| | | +800 | | −800 |

After posting the adjusting entry, the accounts show:

| Unearned Revenue | | Service Revenue | | |
|---|---|---|---|---|
| | 10/31 **Adj.** 800 | 10/31 **Adj.** 800 | 10/2 | 1,200 |
| | | | 10/31 **Bal.** | 400 |

---

[3]This example focuses only on the alternative treatment of unearned revenues. In the interest of simplicity, the entries to Service Revenue pertaining to the immediate earning of revenue ($10,000) and the adjusting entry for accrued revenue ($200) have been ignored.

The liability account, Unearned Revenue, shows a balance of $800, which is equal to the services that will be rendered in the future. In addition, the balance in Service Revenue equals the services rendered in October. If the adjusting entry is not made, both revenues and net income will be overstated by $800 in the October income statement. Moreover, liabilities will be understated by $800, and owner's equity will be overstated by $800 on the October 31 balance sheet.

A comparative summary of the entries and accounts for service revenue earned and unearned is presented in Illustration 3A-5:

**ILLUSTRATION 3A-5**

*Adjustment approaches—a comparison*

| | Unearned Revenue Initially Credited to Liability Account (per chapter) | | | | Unearned Revenue Initially Credited to Revenue Account (per appendix) | |
|---|---|---|---|---|---|---|
| Oct. 2 | Cash | 1,200 | | Oct. 2 | Cash | 1,200 |
| | Unearned Revenue | 1,200 | | | Service Revenue | 1,200 |
| Oct. 31 | Unearned Revenue | 400 | | Oct. 31 | Service Revenue | 800 |
| | Service Revenue | 400 | | | Unearned Revenue | 800 |

After posting the entries, the accounts will show:

**ILLUSTRATION 3A-6**

*Comparison of accounts*

| | (per chapter) Unearned Revenue | | | (per appendix) Unearned Revenue | |
|---|---|---|---|---|---|
| **10/31 Adj.**  400 | 10/2  1,200 | | | | **10/31 Adj.**  800 |
| | 10/31 Bal.  800 | | | | |

| | Service Revenue | | | Service Revenue | |
|---|---|---|---|---|---|
| | 10/31 **Adj.**  400 | | 10/31 **Adj.**  800 | 10/2  1,200 | |
| | | | | 10/31 Bal.  400 | |

Note that the balances in the accounts are the same under the two alternatives: Unearned Revenue $800, and Service Revenue $400.

# SUMMARY OF ADDITIONAL ADJUSTMENT RELATIONSHIPS

The use of alternative adjusting entries requires additions to the summary of basic relationships presented earlier in Illustration 3-15. The additions are shown in color in Illustration 3A-7.

Alternative adjusting entries do not apply to accrued revenues and accrued expenses because **no entries occur before these types of adjusting entries are made**. Hence, the summary data shown in Illustration 3-15 for these two types of adjustments remains unchanged.

| Type of Adjustment | Reason for Adjustment | Account Balances before Adjustment | Adjusting Entry |
|---|---|---|---|
| 1. Prepaid Expenses | (a) Prepaid expenses initially recorded in asset accounts have been used. | Assets overstated Expenses understated | Dr. Expenses Cr. Assets |
| | **(b) Prepaid expenses initially recorded in expense accounts have not been used.** | **Assets understated Expenses overstated** | **Dr. Assets Cr. Expenses** |
| 2. Unearned Revenues | (a) Unearned revenues initially recorded in liability accounts have been earned. | Liabilities overstated Revenues understated | Dr. Liabilities Cr. Revenues |
| | **(b) Unearned revenues initially recorded in revenue accounts have not been earned.** | **Liabilities understated Revenues overstated** | **Dr. Revenues Cr. Liabilities** |

# SUMMARY OF STUDY OBJECTIVE FOR APPENDIX

**9. *Prepare adjusting entries for the alternative treatment of prepayments.*** When prepayments are initially recorded in expense and revenue accounts, these accounts are overstated prior to adjustment. The adjusting entries for prepaid expenses are a debit to an asset account and a credit to an expense account. Adjusting entries for unearned revenues are a debit to a revenue account and a credit to a liability account.

***Note:** All asterisked Questions, Exercises, and Problems relate to material in the appendix to the chapter.

# SELF-STUDY QUESTIONS
· · · · · · · · · · · · · · · · · · · · · · · · · · · · · · · · · · · · · · · · · · · · · · · · · · · · · · · · · · · · · · · ·

Answers are at the end of the chapter.

(SO 1) 1. The time period assumption states that:
  a. revenue should be recognized in the accounting period in which it is earned.
  b. expenses should be matched with revenues.
  c. the economic life of a business can be divided into artificial time periods.
  d. the fiscal year should correspond with the calendar year.

(SO 2) 2. The principle which dictates that efforts (expenses) be matched with accomplishments (revenues) is the:
  a. matching principle.
  b. cost principle.
  c. periodicity principle.
  d. revenue recognition principle.

(SO 3) 3. Adjusting entries are made to ensure that:
  a. expenses are recognized in the period in which they are incurred.
  b. revenues are recorded in the period in which they are earned.

  c. balance sheet and income statement accounts have correct balances at the end of an accounting period.
  d. all of the above.

4. Each of the following is a major type (or category) of (SO 4) adjusting entries *except*:
  a. prepaid expenses.
  b. accrued revenues.
  c. accrued expenses.
  d. earned revenues.

5. The trial balance shows Supplies $1,350 and Supplies (SO 5) Expense $0. If $600 of supplies are on hand at the end of the period, the adjusting entry is:
  a. Supplies                    600
          Supplies Expense                    600
  b. Supplies                    750
          Supplies Expense                    750
  c. Supplies Expense           750
          Supplies                            750
  d. Supplies Expense           600
          Supplies                            600

(SO 5) 6. Adjustments for unearned revenues:
  a. decrease liabilities and increase revenues.
  b. have an assets and revenues account relationship.
  c. increase assets and increase revenues.
  d. decrease revenues and decrease assets.

(SO 6) 7. Adjustments for accrued revenues:
  a. have a liabilities and revenues account relationship.
  b. have an assets and revenues account relationship.
  c. decrease assets and revenues.
  d. decrease liabilities and increase revenues.

(SO 6) 8. Kathy Siska earned a salary of $400 for the last week of September. She will be paid on October 1. The adjusting entry for Kathy's employer at September 30 is:
  a. No entry is required

  b. Salaries Expense            | 400 |
      Salaries Payable      |     | 400

  c. Salaries Expense            | 400 |
      Cash                  |     | 400

  d. Salaries Payable           | 400 |
      Cash                  |     | 400

(SO 7) 9. Which of the following statements is *incorrect* concerning the adjusted trial balance?
  a. An adjusted trial balance proves the equality of the total debit balances and the total credit balances in the ledger after all adjustments are made.
  b. The adjusted trial balance provides the primary basis for the preparation of financial statements.

  c. The adjusted trial balance lists the account balances segregated by assets and liabilities.
  d. The adjusted trial balance is prepared after the adjusting entries have been journalized and posted.

10. One of the following statements about the accrual basis (SO 8) of accounting is *false*. That statement is:
  a. Events that change a company's financial statements are recorded in the periods in which the events occur.
  b. Revenue is recognized in the period in which it is earned.
  c. This basis is in accord with generally accepted accounting principles.
  d. Revenue is recorded only when cash is received, and expense is recorded only when cash is paid.

*11. The trial balance shows Supplies $0 and Supplies Ex- (SO 9) pense $1,500. If $800 of supplies are on hand at the end of the period, the adjusting entry is:
  a. debit Supplies $800 and credit Supplies Expense $800.
  b. debit Supplies Expense $800 and credit Supplies $800.
  c. debit Supplies $700 and credit Supplies Expense $700.
  d. debit Supplies Expense $700 and credit Supplies $700.

# QUESTIONS

1. (a) How does the time period assumption affect an accountant's analysis of business transactions?
   (b) Explain the terms *fiscal year*, *calendar year*, and *interim periods*.

2. Identify and state two generally accepted accounting principles that relate to adjusting the accounts.

3. Bon Barone, a lawyer, accepts a legal engagement in March, performs the work in April, and is paid in May. If Barone's law firm prepares monthly financial statements, when should it recognize revenue from this engagement? Why?

4. In completing the engagement in (3) above, Barone incurs $4,500 of expenses in March, which are paid in April. How much expense should be deducted from revenues in the month the revenue is recognized? Why?

5. "Adjusting entries are required by the cost principle of accounting." Do you agree? Explain.

6. Why may a trial balance not contain up-to-date and complete financial information?

7. Distinguish between the two categories of adjusting entries and identify the types of adjustments applicable to each category.

8. What is the debit/credit effect of a prepaid expense adjusting entry?

9. "Depreciation is a process of valuation that results in the reporting of the fair market value of the asset." Do you agree? Explain.

10. Explain the differences between depreciation expense and accumulated depreciation.

11. Shen Company purchased equipment for $15,000. By the current balance sheet date, $7,000 had been depreciated. Indicate the balance sheet presentation of the data.

12. What is the debit/credit effect of an unearned revenue adjusting entry?

13. A company fails to recognize revenue earned but not yet received. Which of the following accounts are involved in the adjusting entry: (a) asset, (b) liability, (c) revenue, or (d) expense? For the accounts selected, indicate whether they would be debited or credited in the entry.

14. A company fails to recognize an expense incurred but not paid. Indicate which of the following accounts is debited and which is credited in the adjusting entry: (a) asset, (b) liability, (c) revenue, or (d) expense.

15. A company makes an accrued revenue adjusting entry for $800 and an accrued expense adjusting entry for $600. How much was net income understated prior to these entries? Explain.

16. On January 9, a company pays $5,000 for salaries of which $2,000 was reported as Salaries Payable on December 31. Give the entry to record the payment.

17. For each of the following items before adjustment, indicate the type of adjusting entry (prepaid expense, unearned revenue, accrued revenue, and accrued expense) that is needed to correct the misstatement. If an item could result in more than one type of adjusting entry, indicate each of the types.
   (a) Assets are understated.
   (b) Liabilities are overstated.
   (c) Liabilities are understated.
   (d) Expenses are understated.
   (e) Assets are overstated.
   (f) Revenue is understated.

18. One-half of the adjusting entry is given below. Indicate the account title for the other half of the entry.

   (a) Salaries Expense is debited.
   (b) Depreciation Expense is debited.
   (c) Interest Payable is credited.
   (d) Supplies is credited.
   (e) Accounts Receivable is debited.
   (f) Unearned Service Revenue is debited.

19. "An adjusting entry may affect more than one balance sheet or income statement account." Do you agree? Why or why not?

20. Why is it possible to prepare financial statements directly from an adjusted trial balance?

21. Why do accrual basis financial statements provide more useful information than cash basis statements?

*22. The Alpha Company debits Supplies Expense for all purchases of supplies and credits Rent Revenue for all advanced rentals. For each type of adjustment, give the adjusting entry.

# BRIEF EXERCISES

**BE3–1** The ledger of the Hilo Company includes the following accounts. Explain why each account may require adjustment.

a. Prepaid Insurance    c. Unearned Revenue
b. Depreciation Expense   d. Interest Payable

*Indicate why adjusting entries are needed.*
*(SO 3)*

**BE3–2** The Reno Company accumulates the following adjustment data at December 31. Indicate (a) the type of adjustment (prepaid expense, accrued revenues and so on), and (b) the accounts before adjustment (overstated or understated).

1. Supplies of $600 are on hand.
2. Services provided but unbilled total $900.
3. Interest of $200 has accumulated on a note payable.
4. Rent collected in advance totaling $800 has been earned.

*Identify the major types of adjusting entries.*
*(SO 4)*

**BE3–3** The Spahn Advertising Company's trial balance at December 31 shows Advertising Supplies $8,700 and Advertising Supplies Expense $0. On December 31, there are $1,500 of supplies on hand. Prepare the adjusting entry at December 31 and, using T accounts, enter the balances in the accounts, post the adjusting entry, and indicate the adjusted balance in each account.

*Prepare adjusting entry for supplies.*
*(SO 5)*

**BE3–4** At the end of its first year, the trial balance of Tabor Company shows Equipment $25,000 and zero balances in Accumulated Depreciation—Equipment and Depreciation Expense. Depreciation for the year is estimated to be $4,000. Prepare the adjusting entry for depreciation at December 31, post the adjustments to T accounts, and indicate the balance sheet presentation of the equipment at December 31.

*Prepare adjusting entries for depreciation.*
*(SO 5)*

**BE3–5** On July 1, 1999, Blair Co. pays $18,000 to Hindi Insurance Co. for a three-year insurance contract. Both companies have fiscal years ending December 31. For Blair Co. journalize and post the entry on July 1 and the adjusting entry on December 31.

*Prepare adjusting entries for prepaid expense.*
*(SO 5)*
*Prepare adjusting entry for unearned revenue.*
*(SO 5)*

**BE3–6** Using the data in BE3–5, journalize and post the entry on July 1 and the adjusting entry on December 31 for Hindi Insurance Co. Hindi uses the accounts Unearned Insurance Revenue and Insurance Revenue.

**BE3–7** The bookkeeper for DeVoe Company asks you to prepare the following accrued adjusting entries at December 31.

1. Interest on notes payable of $300 is accrued.
2. Services provided but unbilled total $1,400.
3. Salaries earned by employees of $900 have not been recorded.

Use the following account titles: Service Revenue, Accounts Receivable, Interest Expense, Interest Payable, Salaries Expense, and Salaries Payable.

*Prepare adjusting entries for accruals.*
*(SO 6)*

**BE3–8** The trial balance of Wilson Company includes the following balance sheet accounts. Identify the accounts that require adjustment. For each account that requires adjustment, in-

*Analyze accounts in an adjusted trial balance.*
*(SO 7)*

dicate (a) the type of adjusting entry (prepaid expenses, unearned revenues, accrued revenues, and accrued expenses) and (b) the related account in the adjusting entry.

| | |
|---|---|
| Accounts Receivable | Notes Payable |
| Prepaid Insurance | Interest Payable |
| Equipment | Unearned Service Revenue |
| Accumulated Depreciation—Equipment | |

*Prepare an income statement from an adjusted trial balance.*
*(SO 7)*

**BE3–9**   The adjusted trial balance of Klar Company at December 31, 1999, includes the following accounts: S. Klar, Capital $15,600; S. Klar, Drawing $6,000; Service Revenue $38,400; Salaries Expense $13,000; Insurance Expense $2,000; Rent Expense $4,000; Supplies Expense $1,500; and Depreciation Expense $1,000. Prepare an income statement for the year.

*Prepare an owner's equity statement from an adjusted trial balance.*
*(SO 7)*
*Prepare adjusting entries under alternative treatment of prepayments.*
*(SO 9)*

**BE3–10**   Partial adjusted trial balance data for Klar Company is presented in BE3–9. The balance in S. Klar, Capital is the balance as of January 1. Prepare an owner's equity statement for the year assuming net income is $17,000 for the year.

**\*BE3–11**   Phelps Company records all prepayments in income statement accounts. At April 30, the trial balance shows Supplies Expense $2,800, Service Revenue $9,200, and zero balances in related balance sheet accounts. Prepare the adjusting entries at April 30 assuming (a) $1,500 of supplies on hand and (b) $800 of service revenue should be reported as unearned.

# EXERCISES

*Identify types of adjustments and account relationships.*
*(SO 4, 5, 6)*

**E3–1**   The McLain Company accumulates the following adjustment data at December 31.

1. Services provided but unbilled total $600.
2. Store supplies of $300 have been used.
3. Utility expenses of $225 are unpaid.
4. Unearned revenue of $260 has been earned.
5. Salaries of $800 are unpaid.
6. Prepaid insurance totaling $350 has expired.

**Instructions**
For each of the above items indicate:

(a) The type of adjustment (prepaid expense, unearned revenue, accrued revenue, or accrued expense).
(b) The accounts before adjustment (overstatement or understatement).

*Prepare adjusting entries from selected account data.*
*(SO 5, 6, 7)*

**E3–2**   The ledger of Duggan Rental Agency on March 31 of the current year includes the following selected accounts before adjusting entries have been prepared.

| | Debit | Credit |
|---|---|---|
| Prepaid Insurance | $ 3,600 | |
| Supplies | 2,800 | |
| Equipment | 25,000 | |
| Accumulated | | |
|    Depreciation—Equipment | | $ 8,400 |
| Notes Payable | | 20,000 |
| Unearned Rent Revenue | | 9,300 |
| Rent Revenue | | 60,000 |
| Interest Expense | –0– | |
| Wage Expense | 14,000 | |

An analysis of the accounts shows the following:

1. The equipment depreciates $250 per month.
2. One-third of the unearned rent was earned during the quarter.
3. Interest of $500 is accrued on the notes payable.
4. Supplies on hand total $850.
5. Insurance expires at the rate of $300 per month.

**Instructions**
Prepare the adjusting entries at March 31, assuming that adjusting entries are made quarterly. Additional accounts are: Depreciation Expense, Insurance Expense, Interest Payable, and Supplies Expense.

**E3–3**  Karen Weller, D.D.S., opened a dental practice on January 1, 1999. During the first month of operations the following transactions occurred.

*Prepare adjusting entries.*
*(SO 5, 6, 7)*

1. Performed services for patients who had dental plan insurance. At January 31, $750 of such services was earned but not yet billed to the insurance companies.
2. Utility expenses incurred but not paid prior to January 31 totaled $520.
3. Purchased dental equipment on January 1 for $80,000, paying $20,000 in cash and signing a $60,000, three-year-note payable. The equipment depreciates $400 per month. Interest is $500 per month.
4. Purchased a one-year malpractice insurance policy on January 1 for $12,000.
5. Purchased $1,600 of dental supplies. On January 31, determined that $500 of supplies were on hand.

**Instructions**

Prepare the adjusting entries on January 31. Account titles are: Accumulated Depreciation—Dental Equipment, Depreciation Expense, Service Revenue, Accounts Receivable, Insurance Expense, Interest Expense, Interest Payable, Prepaid Insurance, Supplies, Supplies Expense, Utilities Expense, and Utilities Payable.

**E3–4**  The trial balance for Pioneer Advertising Agency is shown in Illustration 3-3, p. 96. In lieu of the adjusting entries shown in the text at October 31, assume the following adjustment data:

*Prepare adjusting entries.*
*(SO 5, 6, 7)*

1. Advertising supplies on hand at October 31 total $1,400.
2. Expired insurance for the month is $100.
3. Depreciation for the month is $50.   ~~$700~~
4. Unearned revenue in October totals $600.
5. Services provided but unbilled at October 31 are $300.
6. Interest accrued at October 31 is $70.
7. Accrued salaries at October 31 are $1,500.

**Instructions**

Prepare the adjusting entries for the items above.

**E3–5**  The income statement of Ranier Co. for the month of July shows net income of $1,400 based on Service Revenue $5,500, Wages Expense $2,300, Supplies Expense $1,200, and Utilities Expense $600. In reviewing the statement, you discover the following:

*Prepare correct income statement.*
*(SO 2, 5, 6, 7)*

1. Insurance expired during July of $300 was omitted.
2. Supplies expense includes $500 of supplies that are still on hand at July 31.
3. Depreciation on equipment of $150 was omitted.
4. Accrued but unpaid wages at July 31 of $300 were not included.
5. Services provided but unrecorded totaled $900.

**Instructions**

Prepare a correct income statement for July.

**E3–6**  A partial adjusted trial balance of Piper Company at January 31, 1999, shows the following:

*Analyze adjusted data.*
*(SO 2, 4, 5, 6, 7)*

### PIPER COMPANY
### Adjusted Trial Balance
### January 31, 1999

|  | Debit | Credit |
|---|---|---|
| Supplies | $ 700 | |
| Prepaid Insurance | 2,400 | |
| Salaries Payable | | 800 |
| Unearned Revenue | | 750 |
| Supplies Expense | 950 | |
| Insurance Expense | 400 | |
| Salaries Expense | 1,800 | |
| Service Revenue | | 2,000 |

**Instructions**

Answer the following questions, assuming the year begins January 1:

(a) If the amount in Supplies Expense is the January 31 adjusting entry, and $850 of supplies was purchased in January, what was the balance in Supplies on January 1?

(b) If the amount in Insurance Expense is the January 31 adjusting entry, and the original insurance premium was for one year, what was the total premium and when was the policy purchased?

(c) If $2,500 of salaries was paid in January, what was the balance in Salaries Payable at December 31, 1998?

(d) If $1,600 was received in January for services performed in January, what was the balance in Unearned Revenue at December 31, 1998?

*Journalize basic transactions and adjusting entries.*
*(SO 5, 6, 7)*

**E3–7**   Selected accounts of Felipe Company are shown below:

**Supplies Expense**

| | | |
|---|---|---|
| 7/31 | 500 | |

**Supplies**

| | | | | |
|---|---|---|---|---|
| 7/1 | Bal. | 1,100 | 7/31 | 500 |
| 7/10 | | 200 | | |

**Salaries Payable**

| | | |
|---|---|---|
| | 7/31 | 1,200 |

**Accounts Receivable**

| | |
|---|---|
| 7/31 | 500 |

**Unearned Revenue**

| | | | | | |
|---|---|---|---|---|---|
| 7/31 | 900 | 7/1 | Bal. | 1,500 | |
| | | 7/20 | | 700 | |

**Salaries Expense**

| | |
|---|---|
| 7/15 | 1,200 |
| 7/31 | 1,200 |

**Service Revenue**

| | | |
|---|---|---|
| | 7/14 | 3,000 |
| | 7/31 | 900 |
| | 7/31 | 500 |

**Instructions**

After analyzing the accounts, journalize (a) the July transactions and (b) the adjusting entries that were made on July 31. (*Hint:* July transactions were for cash.)

*Prepare adjusting entries from analysis of trial balances.*
*(SO 5, 6, 7)*

**E3–8**   The trial balances before and after adjustment for Lund Company at the end of its fiscal year are presented below.

**LUND COMPANY**
**Trial Balance**
**August 31, 1999**

| | Before Adjustment | | After Adjustment | |
|---|---|---|---|---|
| | Dr. | Cr. | Dr. | Cr. |
| Cash | $10,400 | | $10,400 | |
| Accounts Receivable | 8,800 | | 9,400 | |
| Office Supplies | 2,300 | | 700 | |
| Prepaid Insurance | 4,000 | | 2,500 | |
| Office Equipment | 14,000 | | 14,000 | |
| Accumulated Depreciation—Office Equipment | | $ 3,600 | | $ 4,800 |
| Accounts Payable | | 5,800 | | 5,800 |
| Salaries Payable | | –0– | | 1,100 |
| Unearned Rent Revenue | | 1,500 | | 700 |
| R. Roni, Capital | | 15,600 | | 15,600 |
| Service Revenue | | 34,000 | | 34,600 |
| Rent Revenue | | 11,000 | | 11,800 |
| Salaries Expense | 17,000 | | 18,100 | |
| Office Supplies Expense | –0– | | 1,600 | |
| Rent Expense | 15,000 | | 15,000 | |
| Insurance Expense | –0– | | 1,500 | |
| Depreciation Expense | –0– | | 1,200 | |
| | $71,500 | $71,500 | $74,400 | $74,400 |

*Instructions*
Prepare the adjusting entries that were made.

**E3–9**  The adjusted trial balance for the Lund Company is given in E3–8.

*Prepare financial statements from adjusted trial balance. (SO 5, 6, 7)*

*Instructions*
Prepare the income and owner's equity statements for the year and the balance sheet at August 31.

**E3–10**  On numerous occasions proposals have surfaced to put the federal government on the accrual basis of accounting. This is no small issue because if this basis were used, it would mean that billions in unrecorded liabilities would have to be booked and the federal deficit would increase substantially.

*Distinguish between cash and accrual basis of accounting. (SO 8)*

*Instructions* ▭▭▭▭▭▶
(a) What is the difference between accrual basis accounting and cash basis accounting?
(b) Comment on why politicians prefer a cash basis accounting system over an accrual basis system.
(c) Write a letter to your senator explaining why you think the federal government should adopt the accrual basis of accounting.

**\*E3–11**  At the Harmony Company, prepayments are debited to expense when paid and unearned revenues are credited to revenue when received. During January of the current year, the following transactions occurred:

*Journalize transactions and adjusting entries using appendix. (SO 9)*

Jan.  2  Paid $2,400 for fire insurance protection for the year.
   10  Paid $1,700 for supplies.
   15  Received $5,100 for services to be performed in the future.

On January 31, it is determined that $1,500 of the services fees have been earned and that there are $800 of supplies on hand.

*Instructions*
(a) Journalize and post the January transactions. (Use T accounts.)
(b) Journalize and post the adjusting entries at January 31.
(c) Determine the ending balance in each of the accounts.

# PROBLEMS: SET A
••••••••••••••••••••••••••••••••••••••••••••••••••••

**P3–1A**  The trial balance before adjustment of Midwest Tours at the end of its first month of operations is presented below:

*Prepare adjusting entries, post, and prepare an adjusted trial balance. (SO 5, 6, 7)*

## MIDWEST TOURS
### Trial Balance
### June 30, 1999

|  | Debit | Credit |
|---|---|---|
| Cash | $  3,000 | |
| Prepaid Insurance | 7,800 | |
| Office Equipment | 1,800 | |
| Buses | 140,000 | |
| Notes Payable | | $ 62,000 |
| Unearned Tour Revenue | | 15,000 |
| Alan Kinsley, Capital | | 70,000 |
| Tour Revenue | | 15,900 |
| Salaries Expense | 8,400 | |
| Advertising Expense | 800 | |
| Gas and Oil Expense | 1,100 | |
| | $162,900 | $162,900 |

Other data:

1. The insurance policy has a one-year term beginning June 1, 1999.
2. The monthly depreciation is $50 on office equipment and $2,000 on buses.
3. Interest of $700 accrues on the notes payable each month.
4. Deposits of $1,500 each were received for advanced tour reservations from 10 school groups. At June 30, four of these deposits have been earned.
5. Bus drivers are paid a combined total of $400 per day. At June 30, 3 days' salaries are unpaid.
6. A senior citizen's organization that had not made an advance deposit took a Canyon tour on June 30 for $1,200. This group was not billed for the services rendered until July 3.

**Instructions**

(a) Journalize the adjusting entries at June 30, 1999.
(b) Prepare a ledger using the three-column form of account. Enter the trial balance amounts and post the adjusting entries. (Use J2 as the posting reference.)
(c) Prepare an adjusted trial balance at June 30, 1999.

*Prepare adjusting entries, adjusted trial balance, and financial statements.*
*(SO 5, 6, 7)*

**P3–2A**  The Super Motel opened for business on May 1, 1999. Its trial balance before adjustment on May 31 is as follows:

### SUPER MOTEL
### Trial Balance
### May 31, 1999

|                       | Debit      | Credit     |
|-----------------------|-----------:|-----------:|
| Cash                  | $  2,500   |            |
| Prepaid Insurance     | 1,800      |            |
| Supplies              | 1,900      |            |
| Land                  | 15,000     |            |
| Lodge                 | 70,000     |            |
| Furniture             | 16,800     |            |
| Accounts Payable      |            | $  4,700   |
| Unearned Rent Revenue |            | 3,600      |
| Mortgage Payable      |            | 35,000     |
| Sara Sutton, Capital  |            | 60,000     |
| Rent Revenue          |            | 9,200      |
| Salaries Expense      | 3,000      |            |
| Utilities Expense     | 1,000      |            |
| Advertising Expense   | 500        |            |
|                       | $112,500   | $112,500   |

Other data:

1. Insurance expires at the rate of $200 per month.
2. An inventory of supplies shows $1,200 of unused supplies on May 31.
3. Annual depreciation is $3,600 on the lodge and $3,000 on furniture.
4. The mortgage interest rate is 12%. (The mortgage was taken out on May 1.)
5. Unearned rent of $1,500 has been earned.
6. Salaries of $300 are accrued and unpaid at May 31.

**Instructions**

(a) Journalize the adjusting entries on May 31.
(b) Prepare a ledger using the three-column form of account. Enter the trial balance amounts and post the adjusting entries. (Use J1 as the posting reference.)
(c) Prepare an adjusted trial balance on May 31.
(d) Prepare an income statement and an owner's equity statement for the month of May and a balance sheet at May 31.

*Prepare adjusting entries and financial statements.*
*(SO 5, 6, 7)*

**P3–3A**  The Irabu Co. was organized on July 1, 1999. Quarterly financial statements are prepared. The unadjusted and adjusted trial balances as of September 30 are shown below.

**IRABU CO.**
**Trial Balance**
**September 30, 1999**

| | Unadjusted | | Adjusted | |
|---|---|---|---|---|
| | Dr. | Cr. | Dr. | Cr. |
| Cash | $ 6,700 | | $ 6,700 | |
| Accounts Receivable | 400 | | 1,000 | |
| Prepaid Rent | 1,500 | | 900 | |
| Supplies | 1,200 | | 1,000 | |
| Equipment | 15,000 | | 15,000 | |
| Accumulated Depreciation—Equipment | | | | $   350 |
| Notes Payable | | $ 5,000 | | 5,000 |
| Accounts Payable | | 1,510 | | 1,510 |
| Salaries Payable | | | | 400 |
| Interest Payable | | | | 50 |
| Unearned Rent Revenue | | 900 | | 600 |
| Yosuke Irabu, Capital | | 14,000 | | 14,000 |
| Yosuke Irabu, Drawing | 600 | | 600 | |
| Commission Revenue | | 14,000 | | 14,600 |
| Rent Revenue | | 400 | | 700 |
| Salaries Expense | 9,000 | | 9,400 | |
| Rent Expense | 900 | | 1,500 | |
| Depreciation Expense | | | 350 | |
| Supplies Expense | | | 200 | |
| Utilities Expense | 510 | | 510 | |
| Interest Expense | | | 50 | |
| | $35,810 | $35,810 | $37,210 | $37,210 |

**Instructions**

(a) Journalize the adjusting entries that were made.

(b) Prepare an income statement and an owner's equity statement for the 3 months ending September 30 and a balance sheet at September 30.

(c) If the note bears interest at 12%, how many months has it been outstanding?

**P3–4A**   A review of the ledger of Davis Company at December 31, 1999, produces the following data pertaining to the preparation of annual adjusting entries:

*Prepare adjusting entries.*
*(SO 5, 6)*

1. Prepaid Insurance $12,300. The company has separate insurance policies on its buildings and its motor vehicles. Policy B4564 on the building was purchased on July 1, 1998, for $9,000. The policy has a term of 3 years. Policy A2958 on the vehicles was purchased on January 1, 1999, for $4,800. This policy has a term of 2 years.

2. Unearned Subscription Revenue $49,000. The company began selling magazine subscriptions in 1999 on an annual basis. The selling price of a subscription is $50. A review of subscription contracts reveals the following:

| Subscription Date | Number of Subscriptions |
|---|---|
| October 1 | 200 |
| November 1 | 300 |
| December 1 | 480 |
| | 980 |

3. Notes Payable, $40,000. This balance consists of a note for 6 months at an annual interest rate of 9%, dated September 1.

4. Salaries Payable $0. There are eight salaried employees. Salaries are paid every Friday for the current week. Five employees receive a salary of $600 each per week, and three employees earn $700 each per week. December 31 is a Wednesday. Employees do not work weekends. All employees worked the last 3 days of December.

**Instructions**

Prepare the adjusting entries at December 31, 1999.

*Journalize transactions and follow through accounting cycle to preparation of financial statements.*
(SO 5, 6, 7)

**P3–5A**  On November 1, 1999, the account balances of Delino Equipment Repair were as follows:

| No. | Debits | | No. | Credits | |
|---|---|---|---|---|---|
| 101 | Cash | $ 2,790 | 154 | Accumulated Depreciation | $   500 |
| 112 | Accounts Receivable | 2,510 | 201 | Accounts Payable | 2,100 |
| 126 | Supplies | 1,000 | 209 | Unearned Service Revenue | 400 |
| 153 | Store Equipment | 10,000 | 212 | Salaries Payable | 500 |
| | | | 301 | P. Delino, Capital | 12,800 |
| | | $16,300 | | | $16,300 |

During November the following summary transactions were completed.

Nov.  8   Paid $1,100 for salaries due employees, of which $600 is for November.
10   Received $1,200 cash from customers on account.
12   Received $1,400 cash for services performed in November.
15   Purchased store equipment on account $3,000.
17   Purchased supplies on account $1,500.
20   Paid creditors on account $2,500.
22   Paid November rent $300.
25   Paid salaries $1,000.
27   Performed services on account and billed customers for services rendered $900.
29   Received $550 from customers for future service.

Adjustment data consist of:

1. Supplies on hand $1,600.
2. Accrued salaries payable $500.
3. Depreciation for the month is $120.
4. Unearned service revenue of $300 is earned.

*Instructions*
(a) Enter the November 1 balances in the ledger accounts.
(b) Journalize the November transactions.
(c) Post to the ledger accounts. Use J1 for posting reference and No. 407 Service Revenue, No. 615 Depreciation Expense, No. 631 Supplies Expense, No. 726 Salaries Expense, and No. 729 Rent Expense.
(d) Prepare a trial balance at November 30.
(e) Journalize and post adjusting entries.
(f) Prepare an adjusted trial balance.
(g) Prepare an income statement and an owner's equity statement for November and a balance sheet at November 30.

*Prepare adjusting entries, adjusted trial balance, and financial statements using appendix.*
(SO 5, 6, 7, 9)

**\*P3–6A**  Cordero Graphics Company was organized on January 1, 1999, by Jill Batke. At the end of the first 6 months of operations, the trial balance contained the following accounts:

| Debits | | Credits | |
|---|---|---|---|
| Cash | $  9,500 | Notes Payable | $ 17,000 |
| Accounts Receivable | 14,000 | Accounts Payable | 9,000 |
| Equipment | 45,000 | Jill Batke, Capital | 25,000 |
| Insurance Expense | 1,800 | Graphic Revenue | 52,100 |
| Salaries Expense | 30,000 | Consulting Revenue | 5,000 |
| Supplies Expense | 2,700 | | |
| Advertising Expense | 1,900 | | |
| Rent Expense | 1,500 | | |
| Utilities Expense | 1,700 | | |
| | $108,100 | | $108,100 |

Analysis reveals the following additional data:

1. The $2,700 balance in Supplies Expense represents supplies purchased in January. At June 30, there was $1,500 of supplies on hand.

2. The note payable was issued on February 1. It is a 12%, 6-month note.
3. The balance in Insurance Expense is the premium on a one-year policy, dated March 1, 1999.
4. Consulting fees are credited to revenue when received. At June 30, consulting fees of $1,000 are unearned.
5. Graphic revenue earned but unbilled at June 30 totals $2,000.
6. Depreciation is $2,000 per year.

*Instructions*
(a) Journalize the adjusting entries at June 30. (Assume adjustments are recorded every 6 months.)
(b) Prepare an adjusted trial balance.
(c) Prepare an income statement and owner's equity statement for the 6 months ended June 30 and a balance sheet at June 30.

# PROBLEMS: SET B

**P3–1B**  The Orosco Security Service began operations on January 1, 1999. At the end of the first year of operations, the trial balance before adjustment shows the following:

*Prepare adjusting entries, post, and prepare an adjusted trial balance.*
*(SO 5, 6, 7)*

## OROSCO SECURITY SERVICE
### Trial Balance
### December 31, 1999

|  | Debit | Credit |
|---|---|---|
| Cash | $ 12,400 |  |
| Accounts Receivable | 3,200 |  |
| Prepaid Insurance | 3,600 |  |
| Automobiles | 58,000 |  |
| Notes Payable |  | $ 45,000 |
| Unearned Revenue |  | 2,500 |
| C. Orosco, Capital |  | 18,000 |
| Service Revenue |  | 84,000 |
| Salaries Expense | 57,000 |  |
| Repair Expense | 6,000 |  |
| Gas and Oil Expense | 9,300 |  |
|  | $149,500 | $149,500 |

Other data:

1. Services provided but unbilled $2,500 at December 31.
2. Insurance coverage began on January 1 under a 2-year policy.
3. Automobile depreciation is $15,000 for the year.
4. Interest of $5,400 accrued on notes payable for the year.
5. $1,000 of the unearned fees has been earned.
6. Drivers' salaries total $500 per day. At December 31, 3 days' salaries are unpaid.
7. Repairs to automobiles of $650 have been incurred, but bills have not been received prior to December 31. (Use Accounts Payable.)

*Instructions*
(a) Journalize the annual adjusting entries at December 31, 1999.
(b) Prepare a ledger using the three-column account form. Enter the trial balance amounts and post the adjusting entries. (Use J15 as the posting reference.)
(c) Prepare an adjusted trial balance at December 31, 1999.

**P3–2B**  The Spring River Resort opened for business on June 1 with eight air-conditioned units. Its trial balance before adjustment on August 31 is as follows:

*Prepare adjusting entries, adjusted trial balance, and financial statements.*
*(SO 5, 6, 7)*

### SPRING RIVER RESORT
### Trial Balance
### August 31, 1999

|  | Debit | Credit |
|---|---|---|
| Cash | $ 19,600 |  |
| Prepaid Insurance | 5,400 |  |
| Supplies | 3,300 |  |
| Land | 25,000 |  |
| Cottages | 125,000 |  |
| Furniture | 26,000 |  |
| Accounts Payable |  | $  6,500 |
| Unearned Rent Revenue |  | 6,800 |
| Mortgage Payable |  | 80,000 |
| P. Villone, Capital |  | 100,000 |
| P. Villone, Drawing | 5,000 |  |
| Rent Revenue |  | 80,000 |
| Salaries Expense | 51,000 |  |
| Utilities Expense | 9,400 |  |
| Repair Expense | 3,600 |  |
|  | $273,300 | $273,300 |

Other data:

1. Insurance expires at the rate of $300 per month.
2. An inventory count on August 31 shows $900 of supplies on hand.
3. Annual depreciation is $4,800 on cottages and $2,400 on furniture.
4. Unearned rent of $5,000 was earned prior to August 31.
5. Salaries of $400 were unpaid at August 31.
6. Rentals of $800 were due from tenants at August 31. (Use Accounts Receivable.)
7. The mortgage interest rate is 12% per year. (The mortgage was taken out on August 1.)

*Instructions*
(a) Journalize the adjusting entries on August 31 for the 3-month period June 1–August 31.
(b) Prepare a ledger using the three-column form of account. Enter the trial balance amounts and post the adjusting entries. (Use J1 as the posting reference.)
(c) Prepare an adjusted trial balance on August 31.
(d) Prepare an income statement and an owner's equity statement for the 3 months ending August 31 and a balance sheet as of August 31.

*Prepare adjusting entries and financial statements.*
*(SO 5, 6, 7)*

**P3–3B**  The Yount Advertising Agency was founded by Thomas Grant in January of 1995. Presented below are both the adjusted and unadjusted trial balances as of December 31, 1999.

### YOUNT ADVERTISING AGENCY
### Trial Balance
### December 31, 1999

|  | Unadjusted | | Adjusted | |
|---|---|---|---|---|
|  | Dr. | Cr. | Dr. | Cr. |
| Cash | $ 11,000 |  | $ 11,000 |  |
| Accounts Receivable | 20,000 |  | 21,500 |  |
| Art Supplies | 8,400 |  | 5,000 |  |
| Prepaid Insurance | 3,350 |  | 2,500 |  |
| Printing Equipment | 60,000 |  | 60,000 |  |
| Accumulated Depreciation |  | $ 28,000 |  | $ 35,000 |
| Accounts Payable |  | 5,000 |  | 5,000 |
| Interest Payable |  | 0 |  | 150 |
| Notes Payable |  | 5,000 |  | 5,000 |
| Unearned Advertising Revenue |  | 7,000 |  | 5,600 |

| | Unadjusted | | Adjusted | |
| --- | --- | --- | --- | --- |
| | Dr. | Cr. | Dr. | Cr. |
| Salaries Payable | | 0 | | 1,300 |
| R. Yount, Capital | | 25,500 | | 25,500 |
| R. Yount, Drawing | 12,000 | | 12,000 | |
| Advertising Revenue | | 58,600 | | 61,500 |
| Salaries Expense | 10,000 | | 11,300 | |
| Insurance Expense | | | 850 | |
| Interest Expense | 350 | | 500 | |
| Depreciation Expense | | | 7,000 | |
| Art Supplies Expense | | | 3,400 | |
| Rent Expense | 4,000 | | 4,000 | |
| | $129,100 | $129,100 | $139,050 | $139,050 |

**Instructions**
(a) Journalize the annual adjusting entries that were made.
(b) Prepare an income statement and a statement of owner's equity for the year ending December 31, 1999, and a balance sheet at December 31.
(c) Answer the following questions:
   (1) If the note has been outstanding 3 months, what is the annual interest rate on that note?
   (2) If the company paid $13,500 in salaries in 1999, what was the balance in Salaries Payable on December 31, 1998?

**P3–4B**   A review of the ledger of Oklahoma Company at December 31, 1999, produces the following data pertaining to the preparation of annual adjusting entries.

*Prepare adjusting entries.*
*(SO 5, 6)*

1. Salaries Payable $0. There are eight salaried employees. Salaries are paid every Friday for the current week. Five employees receive a salary of $700 each per week, and three employees earn $500 each per week. December 31 is a Tuesday. Employees do not work weekends. All employees worked the last 2 days of December.
2. Unearned Rent Revenue $369,000. The company began subleasing office space in its new building on November 1. Each tenant is required to make a $5,000 security deposit that is not refundable until occupancy is terminated. At December 31, the company had the following rental contracts that are paid in full for the entire term of the lease.

| Date | Term (in months) | Monthly Rent | Number of Leases |
| --- | --- | --- | --- |
| Nov. 1 | 6 | $4,000 | 5 |
| Dec. 1 | 6 | $8,500 | 4 |

3. Prepaid Advertising $13,200. This balance consists of payments on two advertising contracts. The contracts provide for monthly advertising in two trade magazines. The terms of the contracts are as follows:

| Contract | Date | Amount | Number of Magazine Issues |
| --- | --- | --- | --- |
| A650 | May 1 | $6,000 | 12 |
| B974 | Oct. 1 | 7,200 | 24 |

The first advertisement runs in the month in which the contract is signed.
4. Notes Payable $80,000. This balance consists of a note for one year at an annual interest rate of 12%, dated June 1.

*Journalize transactions and follow through accounting cycle to preparation of financial statements.*
*(SO 5, 6, 7)*

**Instructions**
Prepare the adjusting entries at December 31, 1999. (Show all computations.)

**P3–5B**   On September 1, 1999, the account balances of Silva Equipment Repair were as follows:

| No. | Debits | | No. | Credits | |
|---|---|---|---|---|---|
| 101 | Cash | $ 4,880 | 154 | Accumulated Depreciation | $ 1,500 |
| 112 | Accounts Receivable | 3,520 | 201 | Accounts Payable | 3,400 |
| 126 | Supplies | 1,000 | 209 | Unearned Service Revenue | 400 |
| 153 | Store Equipment | 15,000 | 212 | Salaries Payable | 500 |
| | | | 301 | J. Silva, Capital | 18,600 |
| | | $24,400 | | | $24,400 |

During September the following summary transactions were completed.

Sept. 8 Paid $1,100 for salaries due employees, of which $600 is for September.
   10 Received $1,200 cash from customers on account.
   12 Received $3,400 cash for services performed in September.
   15 Purchased store equipment on account $3,000.
   17 Purchased supplies on account $1,500.
   20 Paid creditors $4,500 on account.
   22 Paid September rent $500.
   25 Paid salaries $1,050.
   27 Performed services on account and billed customers for services rendered $700.
   29 Received $650 from customers for future service.

Adjustment data consist of:

1. Supplies on hand $1,800.
2. Accrued salaries payable $400.
3. Depreciation is $200 per month.
4. Unearned service revenue of $350 is earned.

*Instructions*
(a) Enter the September 1 balances in the ledger accounts.
(b) Journalize the September transactions.
(c) Post to the ledger accounts. Use J1 for posting reference and No. 407 Service Revenue, No. 615 Depreciation Expense, No. 631 Supplies Expense, No. 726 Salaries Expense, and No. 729 Rent Expense.
(d) Prepare a trial balance at September 30.
(e) Journalize and post adjusting entries.
(f) Prepare an adjusted trial balance.
(g) Prepare an income statement and an owner's equity statement for September and a balance sheet at September 30.

# BROADENING YOUR PERSPECTIVE

# FINANCIAL REPORTING AND ANALYSIS

### FINANCIAL REPORTING PROBLEM: Kellogg Company

**BYP3–1** The financial statements of Kellogg's are presented in Appendix A at the end of this textbook.

*Instructions*
(a) Using the consolidated financial statements and related information, identify items that may result in adjusting entries for prepayments.
(b) Using the consolidated financial statements and related information, identify items that may result in adjusting entries for accruals.
(c) Using the Selected Financial Data section, what has been the trend since 1990 for depreciation and amortization expense and for advertising expense?

## COMPARATIVE ANALYSIS PROBLEM: Kellogg Company vs. General Mills

**BYP3–2**  Kellogg's financial statements are presented in Appendix A; General Mills's financial statements are presented in Appendix B.

**Instructions**
Based on information contained in these financial statements, determine the following for each company:

(a)  Net increase (decrease) in property, plant, and equipment from 1996 to 1997.
(b)  Increase (decrease) in selling, general, and administrative expenses from 1996 to 1997.
(c)  Increase (decrease) in accounts payable from 1996 to 1997.
(d)  Increase (decrease) in net income from 1996 to 1997.
(e)  Increase (decrease) in cash and cash equivalents from 1996 to 1997.

## RESEARCH ASSIGNMENT

**BYP3–3**  The Enterprise Standard Industrial Classification (SIC) coding scheme, a published classification of firms into separate industries, is commonly used in practice. SIC codes permit identification of company activities on three levels of detail. Two-digit codes designate a "major group," three-digit codes designate an "industry group," while four-digit codes identify a specific "industry."

**Instructions**
At your library, find the *Standard Industrial Classification Manual* (published by the U.S. Government's Office of Management and Budget in 1987) to answer the following questions:

(a)  On what basis are SIC codes assigned to companies?
(b)  Identify the major group/industry group/industry represented by the following codes: 12, 271, 3571, 7033, 75, and 872.
(c)  Identify the SIC code for the following industries:
  1.  Golfing equipment—manufacturing
  2.  Worm farms
  3.  Felt tip markers—manufacturing
  4.  Household appliance stores, electric, or gas—retail
  5.  Advertising agencies
(d)  You are interested in examining several companies in the passenger airline industry. Determine the appropriate two-, three-, and four-digit SIC codes. Use *Wards Business Directory of U.S. Private and Public Companies (Vol. 5)* to compile a list of the five largest parent companies (by total sales) in the industry. Note: If Wards is not available, alternative sources include *Standard & Poor's Register of Corporations, Directors, and Executives*, *Standard & Poor's Industry Surveys*, and the Dun & Bradstreet *Million Dollar Directory*.

## INTERPRETING FINANCIAL STATEMENTS: Smith's Food and Drug Centers, Inc.

**BYP3–4**  Smith's Food and Drug Centers, Inc. is a supermarket and drug store chain that operates 137 stores in the Intermountain and Southwestern regions of the United States. Smith's competes using a strategy of providing one-stop shopping for customers. This requires large inventories and frequent restocking of inventories. To reduce these costs, Smith's owns and operates its own warehouse and distribution facilities. The Current Liabilities section of the company's balance sheet included the following (dollar amounts are in thousands):

| SMITH'S FOOD AND DRUG CO. Balance Sheet (partial) | |
| --- | --- |
| Trade accounts payable | $235,843 |
| Accrued sales and other taxes | 44,379 |
| Accrued payroll and related benefits | 84,083 |

*Instructions*

(a) Why does the company have accrued payroll and related benefits? Does this mean that the company is behind in paying its employees? Explain.

(b) The company has state-of-the-art scanners at most of its registers. Even at older stores, each cash register computes daily totals for both sales and sales taxes. Why then does the company have accrued sales taxes?

### REAL-WORLD FOCUS: Laser Recording Systems Incorporated

**BYP3–5   Laser Recording Systems,** founded in 1981, produces laser disks for use in the home market. Sales since 1985 have increased approximately 15 percent per year. The following is an excerpt from Laser Recording Systems' financial statements (all dollars in thousands):

---

**LASER RECORDING SYSTEMS**
**Management Discussion**

---

Accrued liabilities increased to $1,642 at January 31, from $138 at the end of the previous fiscal year. Compensation and related accruals increased $195 due primarily to increases in accruals for severance, vacation, commissions, and relocation expenses. Accrued professional services increased by $137 primarily as a result of legal expenses related to several outstanding contractual disputes. Other expense increased $35, of which $18 was for interest payable.

*Instructions*

(a) Can you tell from the discussion whether Laser Recording has prepaid its legal expenses and is now making an adjustment to the asset account Prepaid Legal Expenses, or whether the company is handling the legal expense via an accrued expense adjustment?

(b) Identify each of the adjustments Laser Recording is discussing as one of the four types of possible adjustments discussed in the chapter. How is net income ultimately affected by each of the adjustments?

(c) What journal entry did Laser Recording make to record the accrued interest?

# CRITICAL THINKING

### GROUP DECISION CASE

**BYP3–6**   The Happy Travel Court was organized on April 1, 1998, by Nancy Fox. Nancy is a good manager but a poor accountant. From the trial balance prepared by a part-time bookkeeper, Nancy prepared the following income statement for the quarter that ended March 31, 1999.

**HAPPY TRAVEL COURT**
**Income Statement**
**For the Quarter Ended March 31, 1999**

| | | |
|---|---:|---:|
| Revenues | | |
| Travel court rental revenue | | $95,000 |
| Operating expenses | | |
| Advertising | $ 5,200 | |
| Wages | 29,800 | |
| Utilities | 900 | |
| Depreciation | 800 | |
| Repairs | 4,000 | |
| Total operating expenses | | 40,700 |
| Net income | | $54,300 |

Nancy knew that something was wrong with the statement because net income had never exceeded $20,000 in any one quarter. Knowing that you are an experienced accountant, she asks you to review the income statement and other data.

You first look at the trial balance. In addition to the account balances reported above in the income statement, the ledger contains the following additional selected balances at March 31, 1999:

| | |
|---|---|
| Supplies | $ 5,200 |
| Prepaid Insurance | 7,200 |
| Notes Payable | 12,000 |

You then make inquiries and discover the following:

1. Travel court rental fees include advanced rentals for summer month occupancy $30,000.
2. There were $1,300 of supplies on hand at March 31.
3. Prepaid insurance resulted from the payment of a one-year policy on January 1, 1999.
4. The mail on April 1, 1999, brought the following bills: advertising for week of March 24, $110; repairs made March 10, $260; and utilities, $180.
5. There are four employees who receive wages totaling $350 per day. At March 31, 2 days' wages have been incurred but not paid.
6. The note payable is a 3-month, 10% note dated January 1, 1999.

*Instructions*
With the class divided into groups, answer the following:

(a) Prepare a correct income statement for the quarter ended March 31, 1999.
(b) Explain to Nancy the generally accepted accounting principles that she did not recognize in preparing her income statement and their effect on her results.

## COMMUNICATION ACTIVITY

**BYP3–7**   In reviewing the accounts of the Marylee Co. at the end of the year, you discover that adjusting entries have not been made.

*Instructions*
Write a memorandum to Mary Lee Virgil, the owner of Marylee Co., that explains the following: the nature and purpose of adjusting entries, why adjusting entries are needed, and the types of adjusting entries that may be made.

## ETHICS CASE

**BYP3–8**   Die Hard Company is a pesticide manufacturer. Its sales declined greatly this year due to the passage of legislation outlawing the sale of several of Die Hard's chemical pesticides. During the coming year, Die Hard will have environmentally safe and competitive replacement chemicals to replace these discontinued products. Sales in the next year are expected to greatly exceed any prior year's. The decline in sales and profits appears to be a one-year aberration. But even so, the company president believes that a large dip in current year's profits could cause a significant drop in the market price of Die Hard's stock and make it a takeover target.

To avoid this possibility, the company president urges Becky Freeman, controller, in making this period's year-end adjusting entries to accrue every possible revenue and to defer as many expenses as possible. The president says to Becky, "We need the revenues this year, and next year can easily absorb expenses deferred from this year. We can't let our stock price be hammered down!" Becky didn't get around to recording the adjusting entries until January 17, but she dated the entries December 31 as if they were recorded then. Becky also made every effort to comply with the president's request.

*Instructions*
(a) Who are the stakeholders in this situation?
(b) What are the ethical considerations of (1) the president's request and (2) Becky's dating the adjusting entries December 31?
(c) Can Becky accrue revenues and defer expenses and still be ethical?

# SURFING THE NET

**BYP3–9**   A wealth of accounting-related information is available via the Internet. For example the Rutgers Accounting Web (http://www.rutgers.edu/accounting/raw.htm) offers access to a great variety of sources.

*Instructions*
Once in the Rutgers Accounting Web, click on "Accounting Resources" in the left margin, or click on "RAW's Features." (*Note:* Once on this page, you may have to click on the "text only" box to access the available information.)

   (a) List the categories of information available through the "Accounting Resources on the Internet" page.

   (b) Select any one of these categories and briefly describe the types of information available.

---

*Answers to Self-Study Questions*
1. c    2. a    3. d    4. d    5. c    6. a    7. b    8. b    9. c    10. d    11. a

---

*Answer to Kellogg Review It Question 4, p. 102*
1997 depreciation and amortization expense is $287.3 million; 1996 depreciation and amortization expense is $251.5 million.

**Remember to go back to the Navigator box on the chapter-opening page and check off your completed work.**

**Before studying this chapter you should know or, if necessary, review:**

a. How to apply the revenue recognition and matching principles. (Ch. 3, pp. 93–94)

b. How to make adjusting entries. (Ch. 3, pp. 94–108)

c. How to prepare an adjusted trial balance. (Ch. 3, p. 110)

d. How to prepare a balance sheet, income statement, and owner's equity statement. (Ch. 3, pp. 110–112)

THE NAVIGATOR

## FEATURE STORY

# A Little Knowledge Brings a Lot of Profits

Employee training in financial accounting has paid off for Jack Stack at SRC Corporation in Woodridge, Illinois, which rebuilds engines. President and owner of SRC, he was really concerned when his company lost $61,000 on sales of $16 million. He decided that the "only way to turn things around was to get employees to think like owners." But how to do it? He decided to "teach anyone who moved a broom or operated a grinder everything a bank lender would know. That way they would really understand how each nickel saved could make a difference."

Therefore, SRC spent $300,000 on financial accounting training for its employees. Each week the company stopped its operations for half an hour while its 800 employees broke into small groups to study the latest financial statements. "At first it wasn't easy for everyone to understand the numbers," concedes employee Craig Highbarger, "but we've been over the different figures enough times now, if you hand any one of us a financial statement and leave out a few numbers, we can fill them in." Employees now understand how much it costs to copy a document or turn on a light.

Has it made a difference? Recently SRC earned $6 million on sales of $100 million. As a result of this turnaround, SRC handed out $1.4 million in bonuses to its employees, who are now wealthier in both cash and knowledge.

THE NAVIGATOR

# CHAPTER 4

### THE NAVIGATOR ✔

- Understand *Concepts for Review* ☐
- Read *Feature Story* ☐
- Scan *Study Objectives* ☐
- Read *Preview* ☐
- Read text and answer *Before You Go On*
  p. 146 ☐ p. 156 ☐ p. 162 ☐
- Work *Demonstration Problem* ☐
- Review *Summary of Study Objectives* ☐
- Answer *Self-Study Questions* ☐
- Complete assignments ☐

# COMPLETION OF THE ACCOUNTING CYCLE

## STUDY OBJECTIVES

**After studying this chapter, you should be able to:**

1. *Prepare a work sheet.*
2. *Explain the process of closing the books.*
3. *Describe the content and purpose of a post-closing trial balance.*
4. *State the required steps in the accounting cycle.*
5. *Explain the approaches to preparing correcting entries.*
6. *Identify the sections of a classified balance sheet.*

THE NAVIGATOR

s was true at SRC Corporation, financial statements can help employees understand what is happening in the business. In Chapter 3, we prepared financial statements directly from the adjusted trial balance. However, with so many details involved in the end-of-period accounting procedures, it is easy to make errors. Locating and correcting errors can cost much time and effort. One way to minimize errors in the records and to simplify the end-of-period procedures is to use a work sheet.

In this chapter we will explain the role of the work sheet in accounting as well as the remaining steps in the accounting cycle, most especially, the closing process, again using Pioneer Advertising Agency as an example. Then we will consider (1) correcting entries and (2) classified balance sheets. The content and organization of the chapter are as follows:

# USING A WORK SHEET

**1**
STUDY
OBJECTIVE
........................................
Prepare a work sheet.

A work sheet is a multiple-column form that may be used in the adjustment process and in preparing financial statements. As its name suggests, the work sheet is a working tool or a supplementary device. **A work sheet is not a permanent accounting record;** it is neither a journal nor a part of the general ledger. The work sheet is merely a device used to make it easier to prepare adjusting entries and the financial statements. In small companies with relatively few accounts and adjustments, a work sheet may not be needed. In large companies with numerous accounts and many adjustments, it is almost indispensable.

The basic form of a work sheet and the procedure (5 steps) for preparing a work sheet are shown in Illustration 4-1. Each of the steps in preparing the work sheet must be performed in the prescribed sequence.

**ILLUSTRATION 4-1**

*Form and procedure for a work sheet*

| Account Titles | Work Sheet | | | | | | | | | |
|---|---|---|---|---|---|---|---|---|---|---|
| | Trial Balance | | Adjustments | | Adjusted Trial Balance | | Income Statement | | Balance Sheet | |
| | Dr. | Cr. | Dr. | Cr. | Dr. | Cr. | Dr. | Cr. | Dr. | Cr. |

| 1 | 2 | 3 | 4 |
|---|---|---|---|
| Prepare a trial balance on the work sheet | Enter adjustment data | Enter adjusted balances | Extend adjusted balances to appropriate statement columns |

5
Total the statement columns, compute net income (or net loss), and complete work sheet

**The use of a work sheet is optional.** When a work sheet is used, financial statements are prepared from the work sheet. The adjustments are entered in the work sheet columns and are then journalized and posted after the financial statements have been prepared. Thus, management and other interested parties can receive the financial statements at an earlier date than without a work sheet.

## Steps in Preparing a Work Sheet

We will use the October 31 trial balance and adjustment data of Pioneer Advertising in Chapter 3 to illustrate the preparation of a work sheet. Each step of the process is described below and demonstrated in Illustrations 4-2 and 4-3A, B, C, and D following page 143.

**Step 1.   Prepare a Trial Balance on the Work Sheet.**   The account title space and trial balance columns are used to prepare a trial balance. The data for the trial balance come directly from the ledger accounts. The trial balance for Pioneer Advertising Agency is entered in the trial balance columns of the work sheet as shown in Illustration 4-2.

**Step 2.   Enter the Adjustments in the Adjustment Columns.   Turn over the first transparency, Illustration 4-3A.** When a work sheet is used, all adjustments are entered in the adjustment columns. In entering the adjustments, applicable trial balance accounts should be used. If additional accounts are needed, they should be inserted on the lines immediately below the trial balance totals. Each adjustment is indexed and keyed to facilitate the journalizing of the adjusting entry in the general journal. **It is important to recognize that the adjustments are not journalized until after the work sheet is completed and the financial statements have been prepared.**

The adjustments for Pioneer Advertising Agency are the same as the adjustments illustrated on page 108. They are keyed in the adjustment columns of the work sheet as follows:

(a) An additional account, Advertising Supplies Expense, is debited $1,500 for the cost of supplies used, and Advertising Supplies is credited $1,500.

(b) An additional account, Insurance Expense, is debited $50 for the insurance that has expired, and Prepaid Insurance is credited $50.

(c) Two additional accounts are needed. Depreciation Expense is debited $40 for the month's depreciation, and Accumulated Depreciation—Office Equipment is credited $40.

(d) Unearned Revenue is debited $400 for services provided, and Service Revenue is credited $400.

(e) An additional account, Accounts Receivable, is debited $200 for services provided but not billed, and Service Revenue is credited $200.

(f) Two additional accounts are needed. Interest Expense is debited $50 for accrued interest, and Interest Payable is credited $50.

(g) Salaries Expense is debited $1,200 for accrued salaries, and an additional account, Salaries Payable, is credited $1,200.

Note in the illustration that after all the adjustments have been entered, the adjustment columns are totaled and the equality of the column totals is proved.

**Step 3.   Enter Adjusted Balances in the Adjusted Trial Balance Columns.   Turn over the second transparency, Illustration 4-3B.** The adjusted balance of an account is obtained by combining the amounts entered in the first four columns of the work sheet for each account. For example, the Prepaid Insurance account in the trial balance columns has a $600 debit balance. When this is combined with the $50 credit in the adjustment columns, the result is a $550 debit balance recorded in the adjusted trial balance columns. **For each account on the work sheet, the amount in the adjusted trial balance columns is equal to the account balance that will appear in the ledger after the adjusting entries have been journalized and posted.** The balances in these columns are the same as those in the adjusted trial balance in Illustration 3-18 on page 110.

## TECHNOLOGY IN ACTION

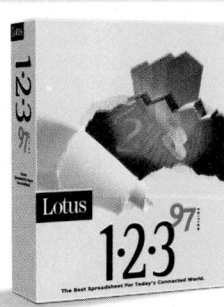

The work sheet can be computerized using an electronic spreadsheet program. The LOTUS 1–2–3 supplement for this textbook is one of the most popular versions of such spreadsheet packages. With a program like LOTUS 1–2–3, you can produce any type of work sheet (accounting or otherwise) that you could produce with paper and pencil on a columnar pad. The tremendous advantage of an electronic work sheet over the paper and pencil version is the ability to change selected data. When data are changed, the computer updates the balance of your computations instantly. More specific applications of electronic spreadsheets will be noted as we proceed.

After the balances of all accounts have been entered in the adjusted trial balance columns, the columns are totaled and their equality is proved. The agreement of the column totals facilitates the completion of the work sheet. If these columns are not in agreement, the statement columns will not balance and the financial statements will be incorrect.

**Step 4.   Extend Adjusted Trial Balance Amounts to Appropriate Financial Statement Columns.   Turn over the third transparency, Illustration 4-3C.** This step involves the extension of adjusted trial balance amounts to the last four columns of the work sheet. Balance sheet accounts such as Cash and Notes Payable are entered in the balance sheet debit and credit columns, respectively. The balance in accumulated depreciation is extended to the balance sheet credit column. This results because accumulated depreciation is a contra-asset account with a credit balance.

Because the work sheet does not have columns for the owner's equity statement, the balance in owner's capital is extended to the balance sheet credit column. In addition, the balance in owner's drawing is extended to the balance sheet debit column because it is an owner's equity account with a debit balance. The expense and revenue accounts such as Salaries Expense and Service Revenue are entered in the appropriate income statement columns. These extensions are shown in Illustration 4-3C.

**Step 5.    Total the Statement Columns, Compute the Net Income (or Net Loss), and Complete the Work Sheet.    Turn over the fourth transparency, Illustration 4-3D.** Each of the statement columns must be totaled. The net income or loss for the period is then found by computing the difference between the totals of the two income statement columns. If total credits exceed total debits, net income has resulted. In such a case, as shown in Illustration 4-3D, the words "net income" are inserted in the account title space. The amount then is entered in the income statement debit column and the balance sheet credit column. **The debit amount balances the income statement columns and the credit amount balances the balance sheet columns.** In addition, the credit in the balance sheet column indicates the increase in owner's equity resulting from net income. Conversely, if total debits in the income statement columns exceed total credits, a net loss has occurred. The amount of the net loss is entered in the income statement credit column and the balance sheet debit column.

After the net income or net loss has been entered, new column totals are determined. The totals shown in the debit and credit income statement columns will be identical. The totals shown in the debit and credit balance sheet columns will also be identical. If either the income statement columns or the balance sheet columns are not equal after the net income or net loss has been entered, an error has been made in completing the work sheet. The completed work sheet for Pioneer Advertising Agency is shown in Illustration 4-3D.

## Preparing Financial Statements from a Work Sheet

After a work sheet has been completed, the statement columns contain all the data that are required for the preparation of financial statements. The income statement is prepared from the income statement columns, and the balance sheet and owner's equity statement are prepared from the balance sheet columns. The financial statements prepared from the work sheet for Pioneer Advertising Agency are shown in Illustration 4-4. At this point, adjusting entries have not been journalized and posted. Therefore, the ledger does not support all financial statement amounts.

The amount shown for owner's capital on the work sheet is the account balance **before considering drawings and net income (or loss).** When there have been no additional investments of capital by the owner during the period, this amount is the balance at the beginning of the period.

Using a work sheet, financial statements can be prepared before adjusting entries are journalized and posted. **However, the completed work sheet is not a substitute for formal financial statements.** Data in the financial statement columns are not properly arranged for statement purposes. Moreover, as noted above, the financial statement presentation for some accounts differs from their statement columns on the work sheet. **A work sheet is essentially a working tool of the accountant and is not distributed to management and other parties.**

**HELPFUL HINT**
Every adjusted trial balance amount must be extended to one of the four statement columns. Debit amounts go to debit columns and credit amounts go to credit columns.

**HELPFUL HINT**
All pairs of columns must balance for a work sheet to be complete.

(Note: Text continues on page 146, following acetate overlays.)

ILLUSTRATION 4-2

*Preparing a trial balance*

**PIONEER ADVERTISING AGENCY**
**Work Sheet**
**For the Month Ended October 31, 1999**

| Account Titles | Trial Balance Dr. | Trial Balance Cr. | Adjustments Dr. | Adjustments Cr. | Adjusted Trial Balance Dr. | Adjusted Trial Balance Cr. | Income Statement Dr. | Income Statement Cr. | Balance Sheet Dr. | Balance Sheet Cr. |
|---|---|---|---|---|---|---|---|---|---|---|
| Cash | 15,200 | | | | | | | | | |
| Advertising Supplies | 2,500 | | | | | | | | | |
| Prepaid Insurance | 600 | | | | | | | | | |
| Office Equipment | 5,000 | | | | | | | | | |
| Notes Payable | | 5,000 | | | | | | | | |
| Accounts Payable | | 2,500 | | | | | | | | |
| Unearned Revenue | | 1,200 | | | | | | | | |
| C. R. Byrd, Capital | | 10,000 | | | | | | | | |
| C. R. Byrd, Drawing | 500 | | | | | | | | | |
| Service Revenue | | 10,000 | | | | | | | | |
| Salaries Expense | 4,000 | | | | | | | | | |
| Rent Expense | 900 | | | | | | | | | |
| Totals | 28,700 | 28,700 | | | | | | | | |

Include all accounts with balances from ledger.

Trial balance amounts are taken directly from ledger accounts.

ILLUSTRATION 4-4

*Financial statements from a work sheet*

**PIONEER ADVERTISING AGENCY**
**Income Statement**
**For the Month Ended October 31, 1999**

| | | |
|---|---:|---:|
| Revenues | | |
| Service revenue | | $10,600 |
| | | |
| Expenses | | |
| Salaries expense | $5,200 | |
| Advertising supplies expense | 1,500 | |
| Rent expense | 900 | |
| Insurance expense | 50 | |
| Interest expense | 50 | |
| Depreciation expense | 40 | |
| | | |
| Total expenses | | 7,740 |
| Net income | | $ 2,860 |

**PIONEER ADVERTISING AGENCY**
**Owner's Equity Statement**
**For the Month Ended October 31, 1999**

| | | |
|---|---:|---:|
| C. R. Byrd, Capital, October 1 | | $ –0– |
| Add: Investments | $10,000 | |
| Net income | 2,860 | 12,860 |
| | | 12,860 |
| Less: Drawings | | 500 |
| C. R. Byrd, Capital, October 31 | | $12,360 |

**PIONEER ADVERTISING AGENCY**
**Balance Sheet**
**October 31, 1999**

**Assets**

| | | |
|---|---:|---:|
| Cash | | $15,200 |
| Accounts receivable | | 200 |
| Advertising supplies | | 1,000 |
| Prepaid insurance | | 550 |
| Office equipment | $5,000 | |
| Less: Accumulated depreciation | 40 | 4,960 |
| Total assets | | $21,910 |

**Liabilities and Owner's Equity**

| | |
|---|---:|
| Liabilities | |
| Notes payable | $ 5,000 |
| Accounts payable | 2,500 |
| Interest payable | 50 |
| Unearned revenue | 800 |
| Salaries payable | 1,200 |
| Total liabilities | 9,550 |
| Owner's equity | |
| C. R. Byrd, Capital | 12,360 |
| Total liabilities and owner's equity | $21,910 |

## Preparing Adjusting Entries from a Work Sheet

**A work sheet is not a journal, and it cannot be used as a basis for posting to ledger accounts.** To adjust the accounts, it is necessary to journalize and post the adjustments to the ledger. **The adjusting entries are prepared from the adjustment columns of the work sheet.** The reference letters in the adjustment columns and the explanation of the adjustments that appear at the bottom of the work sheet help identify entries. However, writing the explanation to the adjustments at the bottom of the work sheet is not required. As indicated previously, the journalizing and posting of adjusting entries **follows** the preparation of financial statements when a work sheet is used. The adjusting entries on October 31 for Pioneer Advertising Agency are the same as those shown in Illustration 3-16 (page 108).

## BEFORE YOU GO ON . . .

### Review It

1. What are the five steps in preparing a work sheet?
2. How is net income or net loss shown in a work sheet?
3. How does a work sheet relate to preparing financial statements and adjusting entries?

### Do It

Melany Newby is preparing a work sheet. Explain to Melany how the following adjusted trial balance accounts should be extended to the financial statement columns of the work sheet: Cash; Accumulated Depreciation; Accounts Payable; R. Kerr, Drawing; Service Revenue; and Salaries Expense.

*Reasoning:* Asset and liability balances are extended to the balance sheet debit and credit columns, respectively, except for accumulated depreciation which is extended to the balance sheet credit column. The drawing account is extended to the balance sheet debit column. Expenses are extended to the income statement debit column. Revenue accounts are extended to the income statement credit column.

*Solution:*
Income statement debit column—Salaries Expense
Income statement credit column—Service Revenue
Balance sheet debit column—Cash; R. Kerr, Drawing
Balance sheet credit column—Accumulated Depreciation; Accounts Payable

As indicated in the Technology in Action box on page 142, the work sheet is an ideal application for electronic spreadsheet software like Microsoft Excel and LOTUS 1–2–3.

THE NAVIGATOR

*Related exercise material:* BE4–1, BE4–2, BE4–3, E4–1, E4–2, E4–4, and E4–5.

# CLOSING THE BOOKS

**2**
STUDY
OBJECTIVE

Explain the process of closing the books.

In closing the books, it is necessary to distinguish between temporary and permanent accounts. Temporary or nominal accounts relate only to a given accounting period. They include all income statement accounts and owner's drawing. All temporary accounts are closed. In contrast, permanent or real accounts relate to one or more future accounting periods. They consist of all balance sheet accounts including owner's capital. Permanent accounts are not closed. Instead, their balances are carried forward into the next accounting period. Illustration 4-5 identifies the accounts in each category.

**ILLUSTRATION 4-5**

*Temporary versus permanent accounts*

| TEMPORARY (NOMINAL) These accounts are closed | PERMANENT (REAL) These accounts are not closed |
|---|---|
| All revenue accounts | All asset accounts |
| All expense accounts | All liability accounts |
| Owner's drawing | Owner's capital account |

**HELPFUL HINT**
A contra asset account, such as accumulated depreciation, is a real account also.

## Preparing Closing Entries

At the end of the accounting period, the temporary account balances are transferred to the permanent owner's equity account, owner's capital, through the preparation of closing entries.[1] Closing entries formally recognize in the ledger the transfer of net income or net loss and owner's drawing to owner's capital as shown in the owner's equity statement. **These entries also produce a zero balance in each temporary account so it can be used to accumulate data in the next accounting period separate from the data of prior periods.** Permanent accounts are not closed.

**Journalizing and posting closing entries is a required step in the accounting cycle.** (See Illustration 4–12 on page 154.) This step is performed after financial statements have been prepared. In contrast to the steps in the cycle that you have already studied, closing entries are generally journalized and posted **only at the end of a company's annual accounting period**. This practice facilitates the preparation of annual financial statements because all temporary accounts will contain data for the entire year.

In preparing closing entries, each income statement account could be closed directly to owner's capital. However, to do so would result in excessive detail in the permanent owner's capital account. Accordingly, the revenue and expense accounts are closed to another temporary account, Income Summary, and only the net income or net loss is transferred from this account to owner's capital.

**Closing entries are journalized in the general journal.** A center caption entitled Closing Entries may be inserted in the journal between the last adjusting entry and the first closing entry to identify these entries. Then the closing entries are posted to the ledger accounts. Closing entries may be prepared directly from the adjusted balances in the ledger, from the income statement and balance sheet columns of the work sheet, or from the income and owner's equity statements. Separate closing entries could be prepared for each nominal account, but the following four entries accomplish the desired result more efficiently:

1. Debit each revenue account for its balance and credit Income Summary for total revenues.
2. Debit Income Summary for total expenses and credit each expense account for its balance.
3. Debit Income Summary and credit owner's capital for the amount of net income.

---

[1]Closing entries for a partnership and for a corporation are explained in Chapters 13 and 14, respectively.

**4.** Debit owner's capital for the balance in the owner's drawing account and credit owner's drawing for the same amount.

The four entries are referenced in the diagram of the closing process shown in Illustration 4-6 and in the journal entries in Illustration 4-7. The posting of closing entries is shown in Illustration 4-8.

| (Individual) Expenses | | (Individual) Revenues |
|---|---|---|

**Income Summary**

**Owner's Capital**

Owner's Capital is a permanent account; all other accounts are temporary accounts.

**Owner's Drawing**

**Key:**
1. Close revenues to income summary.
2. Close expenses to income summary.
3. Close income summary to owner's capital.
4. Close owner's drawing to owner's capital.

**ILLUSTRATION 4-6**

*Diagram of closing process—proprietorship*

If there were a net loss because expenses exceeded revenues, entry 3 in Illustration 4-6 would be reversed: Credit Income Summary and debit Owner's Capital.

## ACCOUNTING IN ACTION
### Business Insight

Until Sam Walton had opened twenty Wal-Mart stores, he used what he called the "ESP method" of closing the books. ESP was a pretty basic method: If the books didn't balance, Walton calculated the amount by which they were off and entered that amount under the heading ESP—which stood for "Error Some Place." As Walton noted, "It really sped things along when it came time to close those books."

*Source:* Sam Walton, *Made in America* (New York: Doubleday Publishing Company, 1992), p. 53.

### Closing Entries Illustrated

As explained above, closing entries are generally prepared only at the end of a company's annual accounting period. However, to illustrate the journalizing and posting of closing entries, we will assume that Pioneer Advertising Agency closes its books monthly. The closing entries at October 31 are shown in Illustration 4-7.

**ILLUSTRATION 4-7**
*Closing entries journalized*

| Date | Account Titles and Explanation | Ref. | Debit | Credit |
|---|---|---|---|---|
| | GENERAL JOURNAL | | | J3 |
| | Closing Entries | | | |
| | (1) | | | |
| 1999 | | | | |
| Oct. 31 | Service Revenue | 50 | 10,600 | |
| | Income Summary | 49 | | 10,600 |
| | (To close revenue account) | | | |
| | (2) | | | |
| 31 | Income Summary | 49 | 7,740 | |
| | Salaries Expense | 60 | | 5,200 |
| | Advertising Supplies Expense | 61 | | 1,500 |
| | Rent Expense | 62 | | 900 |
| | Insurance Expense | 63 | | 50 |
| | Interest Expense | 64 | | 50 |
| | Depreciation Expense | 65 | | 40 |
| | (To close expense accounts) | | | |
| | (3) | | | |
| 31 | Income Summary | 49 | 2,860 | |
| | C. R. Byrd, Capital | 40 | | 2,860 |
| | (To close net income to capital) | | | |
| | (4) | | | |
| 31 | C. R. Byrd, Capital | 40 | 500 | |
| | C. R. Byrd, Drawing | 41 | | 500 |
| | (To close drawings to capital) | | | |

**HELPFUL HINT**
Income Summary is a very descriptive title: total revenues are closed to Income Summary, total expenses are closed to Income Summary, and the balance in the Income Summary is a net income or net loss.

Note that the amounts for Income Summary in entries (1) and (2) are the totals of the income statement credit and debit columns, respectively, in the work sheet.

A couple of cautions in preparing closing entries: (1) Avoid unintentionally doubling the revenue and expense balances rather than zeroing them. (2) Do not close owner's drawing through the Income Summary account. **Owner's drawing is not an expense, and it is not a factor in determining net income.**

## Posting Closing Entries

The posting of the closing entries and the ruling of the accounts are shown in Illustration 4-8. Note that all temporary accounts have zero balances after posting the closing entries. In addition, you should realize that the balance in Owner's Capital represents the total equity of the owner at the end of the accounting period. This balance is shown on the balance sheet and is the ending capital reported on the owner's equity statement, as shown in Illustration 4-4 on page 145. **The Income Summary account is used only in closing.** No entries are journalized and posted to this account during the year.

As part of the closing process, the **temporary accounts** (revenues, expenses, and owner's drawing) in T-account form are totaled, balanced, and double ruled as shown in Illustration 4-8. The **permanent accounts** (assets, liabilities, and

**HELPFUL HINT**
The balance in Income Summary before it is closed must equal the net income or net loss for the period.

**ILLUSTRATION 4-8**

*Posting of closing entries*

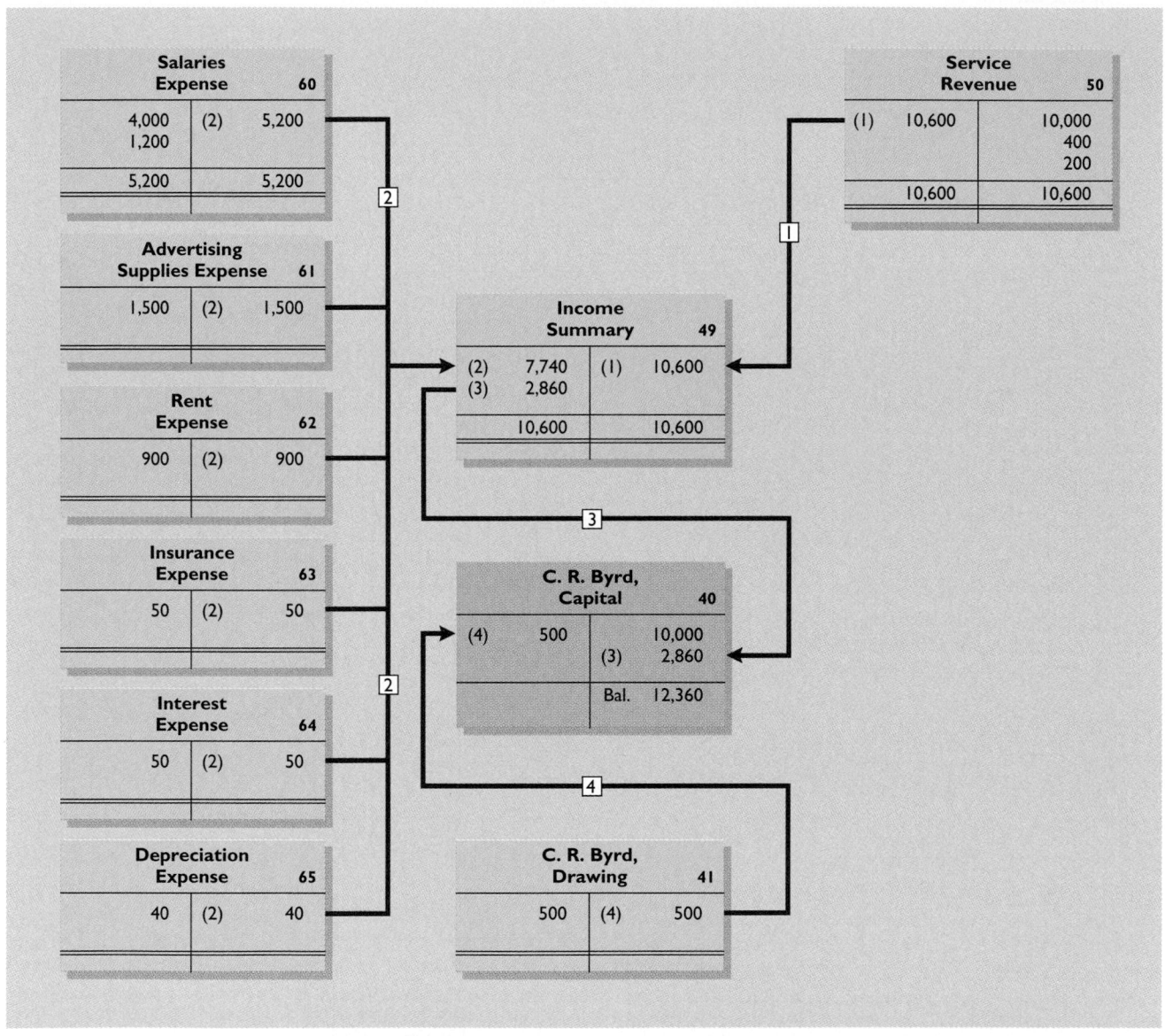

owner's capital) are not closed: A single rule is drawn beneath the current period entries, and the account balance carried forward to the next period is entered below the single rule. (For example, see C. R. Byrd, Capital.)

## Preparing a Post–Closing Trial Balance

**3**

STUDY

OBJECTIVE

········································

Describe the content and purpose of a post-closing trial balance.

After all closing entries have been journalized and posted, another trial balance, called a post-closing trial balance, is prepared from the ledger. A post-closing trial balance is a list of permanent accounts and their balances after closing entries have been journalized and posted. **The purpose of this trial balance is to prove the equality of the permanent account balances that are carried forward into the next accounting period.** Since all temporary accounts will have zero balances, **the post-closing trial balance will contain only permanent—balance sheet—accounts.**

The procedure for preparing a post-closing trial balance again consists entirely of listing the accounts and their balances. These balances are the same as those reported in the company's balance sheet in Illustration 4-4. The post-closing trial balance for Pioneer Advertising Agency is shown in Illustration 4-9.

**ILLUSTRATION 4-9**
*Post-closing trial balance*

| PIONEER ADVERTISING AGENCY<br>Post-Closing Trial Balance<br>October 31, 1999 | | |
|---|---|---|
| | **Debit** | **Credit** |
| Cash | $15,200 | |
| Accounts Receivable | 200 | |
| Advertising Supplies | 1,000 | |
| Prepaid Insurance | 550 | |
| Office Equipment | 5,000 | |
| Accumulated Depreciation—Office Equipment | | $    40 |
| Notes Payable | | 5,000 |
| Accounts Payable | | 2,500 |
| Interest Payable | | 50 |
| Unearned Revenue | | 800 |
| Salaries Payable | | 1,200 |
| C. R. Byrd, Capital | | 12,360 |
| | $21,950 | $21,950 |

**HELPFUL HINT**
Will total debits in a post-closing trial balance equal total assets on the balance sheet? Answer: No. Accumulated depreciation is deducted from assets on the balance sheet but added to the credit balance total in a post-closing trial balance.

The post-closing trial balance is prepared from the permanent accounts in the ledger. The permanent accounts of Pioneer Advertising are shown in the general ledger in Illustration 4-10. Remember that the balance of each permanent account is computed after every posting. Therefore, no additional work on these accounts is needed as part of the closing process. The remaining accounts in the general ledger are temporary accounts (shown in Illustration 4-11 on page 153). After the closing entries are posted, each temporary account has a zero balance. These accounts are double-ruled to finalize the closing process.

A post-closing trial balance provides evidence that the journalizing and posting of closing entries has been properly completed. In addition, it shows that the accounting equation is in balance at the end of the accounting period. However, as in the case of the trial balance, it does not prove that all transactions have been recorded or that the ledger is correct. For example, the post-closing trial balance will balance if a transaction is not journalized and posted or if a transaction is journalized and posted twice.

# SUMMARY OF THE ACCOUNTING CYCLE

The steps in the accounting cycle are shown graphically in Illustration 4-12. From the graphic you can see that the cycle begins with the analysis of business transactions and ends with the preparation of a post-closing trial balance. The steps in the cycle are performed in sequence and are repeated in each accounting period.

Steps 1–3 may occur daily during the accounting period, as explained in Chapter 2. Steps 4–7 are performed on a periodic basis, such as monthly, quarterly, or annually. Steps 8 and 9, closing entries, and a post-closing trial balance, are usually prepared only at the end of a company's **annual** accounting period.

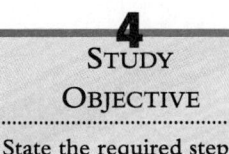

**4**
**STUDY**
**OBJECTIVE**

State the required steps in the accounting cycle.

**ILLUSTRATION 4-10**

*General ledger, permanent accounts*

## (Permanent Accounts Only)

### GENERAL LEDGER

**Cash**     **No. 1**

| Date | Explanation | Ref. | Debit | Credit | Balance |
|---|---|---|---|---|---|
| 1999 | | | | | |
| Oct. 1 | | J1 | 10,000 | | 10,000 |
| 2 | | J1 | 1,200 | | 11,200 |
| 3 | | J1 | | 900 | 10,300 |
| 4 | | J1 | | 600 | 9,700 |
| 20 | | J1 | | 500 | 9,200 |
| 26 | | J1 | | 4,000 | 5,200 |
| 31 | | J1 | 10,000 | | 15,200 |

**Accounts Receivable**     **No. 6**

| Date | Explanation | Ref. | Debit | Credit | Balance |
|---|---|---|---|---|---|
| 1999 | | | | | |
| Oct. 31 | Adj. entry | J2 | 200 | | 200 |

**Advertising Supplies**     **No. 8**

| Date | Explanation | Ref. | Debit | Credit | Balance |
|---|---|---|---|---|---|
| 1999 | | | | | |
| Oct. 5 | | J1 | 2,500 | | 2,500 |
| 31 | Adj. entry | J2 | | 1,500 | 1,000 |

**Prepaid Insurance**     **No. 10**

| Date | Explanation | Ref. | Debit | Credit | Balance |
|---|---|---|---|---|---|
| 1999 | | | | | |
| Oct. 4 | | J1 | 600 | | 600 |
| 31 | Adj. entry | J2 | | 50 | 550 |

**Office Equipment**     **No. 15**

| Date | Explanation | Ref. | Debit | Credit | Balance |
|---|---|---|---|---|---|
| 1999 | | | | | |
| Oct. 1 | | J1 | 5,000 | | 5,000 |

**Accumulated Depreciation—Office Equipment**     **No. 16**

| Date | Explanation | Ref. | Debit | Credit | Balance |
|---|---|---|---|---|---|
| 1999 | | | | | |
| Oct. 31 | Adj. entry | J2 | | 40 | 40 |

**Notes Payable**     **No. 25**

| Date | Explanation | Ref. | Debit | Credit | Balance |
|---|---|---|---|---|---|
| 1999 | | | | | |
| Oct. 1 | | J1 | | 5,000 | 5,000 |

**Accounts Payable**     **No. 26**

| Date | Explanation | Ref. | Debit | Credit | Balance |
|---|---|---|---|---|---|
| 1999 | | | | | |
| Oct. 5 | | J1 | | 2,500 | 2,500 |

**Interest Payable**     **No. 27**

| Date | Explanation | Ref. | Debit | Credit | Balance |
|---|---|---|---|---|---|
| 1999 | | | | | |
| Oct. 31 | Adj. entry | J2 | | 50 | 50 |

**Unearned Revenue**     **No. 28**

| Date | Explanation | Ref. | Debit | Credit | Balance |
|---|---|---|---|---|---|
| 1999 | | | | | |
| Oct. 2 | | J1 | | 1,200 | 1,200 |
| 31 | Adj. entry | J2 | 400 | | 800 |

**Salaries Payable**     **No. 29**

| Date | Explanation | Ref. | Debit | Credit | Balance |
|---|---|---|---|---|---|
| 1999 | | | | | |
| Oct. 31 | Adj. entry | J2 | | 1,200 | 1,200 |

**C. R. Byrd, Capital**     **No. 40**

| Date | Explanation | Ref. | Debit | Credit | Balance |
|---|---|---|---|---|---|
| 1999 | | | | | |
| Oct. 1 | | J1 | | 10,000 | 10,000 |
| 31 | Closing entry | J3 | | 2,860 | 12,860 |
| 31 | Closing entry | J3 | 500 | | 12,360 |

*Note:* The permanent accounts for Pioneer Advertising Agency are shown here; the temporary accounts are shown in Illustration 4-11. Both permanent and temporary accounts are part of the general ledger; they are segregated here to aid in learning.

ILLUSTRATION 4-11

*General ledger, temporary accounts*

## (Temporary Accounts Only)

### GENERAL LEDGER

#### C. R. Byrd, Drawing — No. 41

| Date | Explanation | Ref. | Debit | Credit | Balance |
|------|-------------|------|-------|--------|---------|
| 1999 | | | | | |
| Oct. 20 | | J1 | 500 | | 500 |
| 31 | Closing entry | J3 | | 500 | –0– |

#### Income Summary — No. 49

| Date | Explanation | Ref. | Debit | Credit | Balance |
|------|-------------|------|-------|--------|---------|
| 1999 | | | | | |
| Oct. 31 | Closing entry | J3 | | 10,600 | 10,600 |
| 31 | Closing entry | J3 | 7,740 | | 2,860 |
| 31 | Closing entry | J3 | 2,860 | | –0– |

#### Service Revenue — No. 50

| Date | Explanation | Ref. | Debit | Credit | Balance |
|------|-------------|------|-------|--------|---------|
| 1999 | | | | | |
| Oct. 31 | | J1 | | 10,000 | 10,000 |
| 31 | Adj. entry | J2 | | 400 | 10,400 |
| 31 | Adj. entry | J2 | | 200 | 10,600 |
| 31 | Closing entry | J3 | 10,600 | | –0– |

#### Salaries Expense — No. 60

| Date | Explanation | Ref. | Debit | Credit | Balance |
|------|-------------|------|-------|--------|---------|
| 1999 | | | | | |
| Oct. 26 | | J1 | 4,000 | | 4,000 |
| 31 | Adj. entry | J2 | 1,200 | | 5,200 |
| 31 | Closing entry | J3 | | 5,200 | –0– |

#### Advertising Supplies Expense — No. 61

| Date | Explanation | Ref. | Debit | Credit | Balance |
|------|-------------|------|-------|--------|---------|
| 1999 | | | | | |
| Oct. 31 | Adj. entry | J2 | 1,500 | | 1,500 |
| 31 | Closing entry | J3 | | 1,500 | –0– |

#### Rent Expense — No. 62

| Date | Explanation | Ref. | Debit | Credit | Balance |
|------|-------------|------|-------|--------|---------|
| 1999 | | | | | |
| Oct. 3 | | J1 | 900 | | 900 |
| 31 | Closing entry | J3 | | 900 | –0– |

#### Insurance Expense — No. 63

| Date | Explanation | Ref. | Debit | Credit | Balance |
|------|-------------|------|-------|--------|---------|
| 1999 | | | | | |
| Oct. 31 | Adj. entry | J2 | 50 | | 50 |
| 31 | Closing entry | J3 | | 50 | –0– |

#### Interest Expense — No. 64

| Date | Explanation | Ref. | Debit | Credit | Balance |
|------|-------------|------|-------|--------|---------|
| 1999 | | | | | |
| Oct. 31 | Adj. entry | J2 | 50 | | 50 |
| 31 | Closing entry | J3 | | 50 | –0– |

#### Depreciation Expense — No. 65

| Date | Explanation | Ref. | Debit | Credit | Balance |
|------|-------------|------|-------|--------|---------|
| 1999 | | | | | |
| Oct. 31 | Adj. entry | J2 | 40 | | 40 |
| 31 | Closing entry | J3 | | 40 | –0– |

*Note:* The temporary accounts for Pioneer Advertising Agency are shown here; the permanent accounts are shown in Illustration 4-10. Both permanent and temporary accounts are part of the general ledger; they are segregated here to aid in learning.

**ILLUSTRATION 4-12**

*Steps in the accounting cycle*

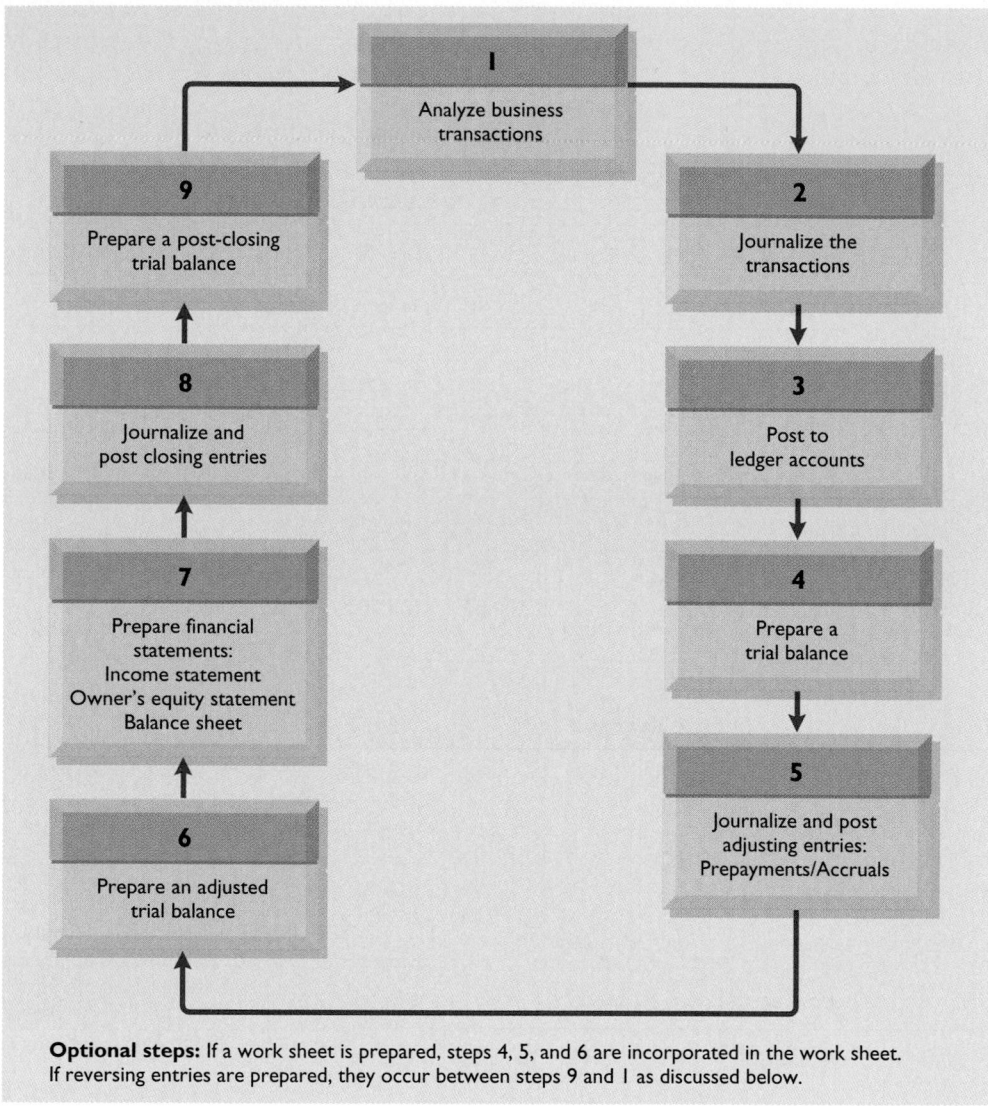

**Optional steps:** If a work sheet is prepared, steps 4, 5, and 6 are incorporated in the work sheet. If reversing entries are prepared, they occur between steps 9 and 1 as discussed below.

There are also two optional steps in the accounting cycle. As you have seen, a work sheet may be used in preparing adjusting entries and financial statements. In addition, reversing entries may be used as explained in the following section.

## Reversing Entries—An Optional Step

Some accountants prefer to reverse certain adjusting entries at the beginning of a new accounting period. A reversing entry is made at the beginning of the next accounting period and is the exact opposite of the adjusting entry made in the previous period. **The preparation of reversing entries is an optional bookkeeping procedure that is not a required step in the accounting cycle.** Accordingly, we have chosen to cover this topic in an appendix at the end of the chapter.

## Correcting Entries—An Avoidable Step

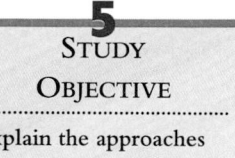

If the accounting records are free of errors, no correcting entries are necessary. Unfortunately, errors may occur in the recording process. Errors should be corrected **as soon as they are discovered** by journalizing and posting correcting entries. You should recognize several significant differences between correcting entries and adjusting entries. First, adjusting entries are an integral part of the accounting cycle, whereas correcting entries are unnecessary if the records are free of errors. Second, **adjustments are journalized and posted only at the end of an accounting period; in contrast, correcting entries are made whenever an error is discovered**. Finally, adjusting entries always affect at least one balance sheet account and one income statement account. In contrast, correcting entries may involve any combination of accounts in need of correction. Correcting entries must be posted before closing entries.

To determine the correcting entry, it is useful to compare the incorrect entry with the correct entry. Doing so helps identify the accounts and amounts that should—and should not—be corrected. After comparison, a correcting entry is made to correct the accounts. This approach is illustrated in the following two cases.

**Case 1.**  On May 10, a $50 cash collection on account from a customer is journalized and posted as a debit to Cash $50 and a credit to Service Revenue $50. The error is discovered on May 20, when the customer pays the remaining balance in full.

| Incorrect Entry (May 10) | | | Correct Entry (May 10) | | |
|---|---|---|---|---|---|
| Cash | 50 | | Cash | 50 | |
|     Service Revenue | | 50 |     Accounts Receivable | | 50 |

A comparison of the incorrect entry with the correct entry reveals that the debit to Cash $50 is correct. However, the $50 credit to Service Revenue should have been credited to Accounts Receivable. As a result, both Service Revenue and Accounts Receivable are overstated in the ledger. The following correcting entry is required:

| | Correcting Entry | | |
|---|---|---|---|
| May 20 | Service Revenue | 50 | |
| |     Accounts Receivable | | 50 |
| |     (To correct entry of May 10) | | |

**Case 2.**  On May 18, office equipment costing $450 is purchased on account. The transaction is journalized and posted as a debit to Delivery Equipment $45, and a credit to Accounts Payable $45. The error is discovered on June 3, when the monthly statement for May is received from the creditor.

| Incorrect Entry (May 18) | | | Correct Entry (May 18) | | |
|---|---|---|---|---|---|
| Delivery Equipment | 45 | | Office Equipment | 450 | |
|     Accounts Payable | | 45 |     Accounts Payable | | 450 |

A comparison of the two entries shows that three accounts are incorrect. Delivery Equipment is overstated $45; Office Equipment is understated $450; and Accounts Payable is understated $405. The correcting entry is:

| | Correcting Entry | | |
|---|---|---|---|
| June 3 | Office Equipment | 450 | |
| |     Delivery Equipment | | 45 |
| |     Accounts Payable | | 405 |
| |     (To correct May 18 entry) | | |

**ETHICS NOTE**

Citicorp once reported a correcting entry reducing reported revenue by $23 million, while firing 11 employees. Citicorp officials did not specify why the employees had apparently intentionally inflated the revenue figures, although it was noted that their bonuses were tied to their unit's performance.

**ILLUSTRATION 4-13**

*Comparison of entries*

**ILLUSTRATION 4-14**

*Correcting entry*

| A | = | L | + | OE |
|---|---|---|---|---|
| −50 | | | | −50 |

**ILLUSTRATION 4-15**

*Comparison of entries*

**ILLUSTRATION 4-16**

*Correcting entry*

| A | = | L | + | OE |
|---|---|---|---|---|
| +450 | | | | |
| −45 | | +405 | | |

Instead of preparing a correcting entry, **it is possible to reverse the incorrect entry and then prepare the correct entry.** This approach will result in more entries and postings than a correcting entry, but it will accomplish the desired result.

# ACCOUNTING IN ACTION
## Business Insight

Yale Express, a short-haul trucking firm, turned over much of its cargo to local truckers for delivery completion. Yale collected the entire delivery charge and, when billed by the local trucker, remitted payment for the final phase to the local trucker. Yale used a cutoff period of 20 days into the next accounting period in making its adjusting entries for accrued liabilities. That is, it waited 20 days to receive the local truckers' bills to determine the amount of the unpaid but incurred delivery charges as of the balance sheet date.

On the other hand, Republic Carloading, a nationwide, long-distance freight forwarder, frequently did not receive transportation bills from truckers to whom it passed on cargo until months after the year-end. In making its year-end adjusting entries, Republic waited for months in order to include all of these outstanding transportation bills.

When Yale Express merged with Republic Carloading, Yale's vice president employed the 20-day cutoff procedure for both firms. As a result, millions of dollars of Republic's accrued transportation bills went unrecorded. When the erroneous procedure was detected and correcting entries were made, these and other errors changed a reported profit of $1.14 million into a loss of $1.88 million!

# BEFORE YOU GO ON . . .
## Review It

1. How do permanent accounts differ from temporary accounts?
2. What four different types of entries are required in closing the books?
3. What is the content and purpose of a post-closing trial balance?
4. What are the required and optional steps in the accounting cycle?

## Do It

The work sheet for Hancock Company shows the following in the financial statement columns: R. Hancock, Drawing $15,000, R. Hancock, Capital $42,000, and net income $18,000. Prepare the closing entries at December 31 that affect owner's capital.

*Reasoning:* Closing entries are made in sequence. The first two entries close revenues and expenses. The remaining two entries close net income and owner's drawing to owner's capital.

*Solution:*

| | | | |
|---|---|---|---|
| Dec. 31 | Income Summary | 18,000 | |
| |     R. Hancock, Capital | | 18,000 |
| |       (To close net income to capital) | | |
| 31 | R. Hancock, Capital | 15,000 | |
| |     R. Hancock, Drawing | | 15,000 |
| |       (To close drawings to capital) | | |

*Related exercise material:* BE4–4, BE4–5, BE4–6, E4–3, E4–6, and E4–8.

# CLASSIFIED BALANCE SHEET

The financial statements illustrated up to this point were purposely kept simple. We classified items as assets, liabilities, and owner's equity in the balance sheet, and as revenues and expenses in the income statement. **Financial statements, however, become more useful to management, creditors, and potential investors when the elements are classified into significant subgroups.** In the remainder of this chapter we will introduce you to the primary balance sheet classifications. The classified income statement is presented in Chapter 5. The classified financial statements are what Jack Stack, the president of SRC Corporation, gave to his employees to understand what was happening in the business.

**6**
STUDY
OBJECTIVE
........................................
Identify the sections of a classified balance sheet.

## Standard Classifications

A classified balance sheet usually contains these standard classifications:

| Assets | Liabilities and Owner's Equity |
| --- | --- |
| Current Assets | Current Liabilities |
| Long-Term Investments | Long-Term Liabilities |
| Property, Plant, and Equipment | Owner's (Stockholders') Equity |
| Intangible Assets | |

**ILLUSTRATION 4-17**
*Standard balance sheet classifications*

These sections help the financial statement user to determine such matters as (1) the availability of assets to meet debts as they come due and (2) the claims of short- and long-term creditors on total assets. A classified balance sheet also makes it easier to compare companies in the same industry, such as GM, Ford, and Chrysler in the automobile industry. Each of the sections is explained below, except for owner's equity, which has already been discussed.

A complete set of specimen financial statements for Kellogg Company is shown in Appendix A at the back of the book.

### Current Assets

Current assets are cash and other resources that are reasonably expected to be realized in cash or sold or consumed in the business within one year of the balance sheet date or the company's operating cycle, whichever is longer. For example, accounts receivable are included in current assets because they will be realized in cash through collection within one year. In contrast, a prepayment such as supplies is a current asset because of its expected use or consumption in the business within one year.

The operating cycle of a company is the average time that is required to go from cash to cash in producing revenues. The term "cycle" suggests a circular flow, which in this case, starts and ends with cash. For example, in municipal transit companies, the operating cycle would tend to be very short since services are rendered entirely on a cash basis. On the other hand, the operating cycle in public utility companies is longer: they bill customers for services rendered and the collection period may extend for several months. Most companies have operating cycles of less than one year. More will be said about operating cycles in later chapters.

In a service enterprise, it is customary to recognize four types of current assets: (1) cash, (2) marketable securities such as U.S. government bonds held as a temporary (short-term) investment, (3) receivables (notes receivable, accounts

**INTERNATIONAL NOTE**
Other countries use a different format for the balance sheet. In Great Britain, for example, property, plant, and equipment are reported first on the balance sheet; assets and liabilities are netted and grouped into net current and net total assets.

receivable, and interest receivable), and (4) prepaid expenses (insurance and supplies). **These items are listed in the order of liquidity,** that is, in the order in which they are expected to be converted into cash. This arrangement is illustrated below in the presentation of UAL, Inc. (United Airlines).

**ILLUSTRATION 4-18**

*Current asset section*

**UNITED AIRLINES**

**UAL, INC. (UNITED AIRLINES)**
**Balance Sheet (partial)**
**(in thousands)**

| Current assets | |
| --- | --- |
| Cash | $ 52,368 |
| Marketable securities | 389,862 |
| Receivables | 721,479 |
| Aircraft fuel, spare parts, and supplies | 178,840 |
| Prepaid expenses | 83,662 |
| Total current assets | $1,426,211 |

A company's current assets are important in assessing the company's short-term debt-paying ability, as explained later in the chapter.

## Long-Term Investments

**HELPFUL HINT**

Long-term investments are investments made by the business—they are not investments by the owner in the business. Investments by the owner in the business are reported as part of owner's equity or stockholders' equity (see p. 160).

Like current assets, **long-term investments** are resources that can be realized in cash. However, the conversion into cash is not expected within one year or the operating cycle, whichever is longer. In addition, long-term investments are not intended for use or consumption within the business. This category, often just called "investments," normally includes stocks and bonds of other corporations. Deluxe Corporation reported the following in its balance sheet:

**ILLUSTRATION 4-19**

*Long-term investment section*

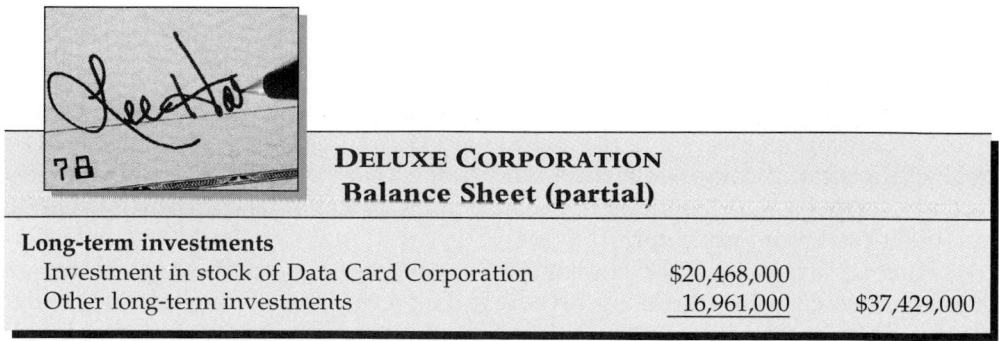

**DELUXE CORPORATION**
**Balance Sheet (partial)**

| Long-term investments | | |
| --- | --- | --- |
| Investment in stock of Data Card Corporation | $20,468,000 | |
| Other long-term investments | 16,961,000 | $37,429,000 |

## Property, Plant, and Equipment

**ALTERNATIVE TERMINOLOGY**

Property, plant, and equipment are sometimes referred to as *plant assets* or *fixed assets.*

**Property, plant, and equipment** are tangible resources of a relatively permanent nature that are used in the business and not intended for sale. This category includes land, buildings, machinery and equipment, delivery equipment, and furniture and fixtures. Assets subject to depreciation should be reported at cost less accumulated depreciation. This practice is illustrated in the following presentation of Delta Air Lines:

**ILLUSTRATION 4-20**

*Property, plant, and equipment section*

### DELTA AIR LINES, INC.
### Balance Sheet (partial)
### (in millions)

| Property, plant, and equipment | | | |
|---|---|---|---|
| Flight equipment | $9,619 | | |
| Less: Accumulated depreciation | 3,510 | $6,109 | |
| Ground property and equipment | 3,032 | | |
| Less: Accumulated depreciation | 1,758 | 1,274 | $7,383 |

## Intangible Assets

Intangible assets are noncurrent resources that do not have physical substance. Intangible assets are recorded at cost, and this cost is expensed over the useful life of the intangible asset. Intangible assets include patents, copyrights, and trademarks or trade names that give the holder **exclusive right** of use for a specified period of time. Their value to a company is generally derived from the rights or privileges granted by governmental authority.

In its balance sheet, Brunswick Corporation reported:

**ILLUSTRATION 4-21**

*Intangible assets section*

### BRUNSWICK CORPORATION
### Balance Sheet (partial)

| Intangible assets | |
|---|---|
| Patents, trademarks, and other intangibles | $10,460,000 |

## Current Liabilities

Listed first in the liabilities and owner's equity section of the balance sheet are current liabilities. Current liabilities are obligations that are reasonably expected to be paid from existing current assets or through the creation of other current liabilities. As in the case of current assets, the time period for payment is one year or the operating cycle, whichever is longer. Current liabilities include (1) debts related to the operating cycle, such as accounts payable and wages and salaries payable, and (2) other short-term debts, such as bank loans payable, interest payable, taxes payable, and current maturities of long-term obligations (payments to be made within the next year on long-term obligations).

The arrangement of items within the current liabilities section has evolved through custom rather than from a prescribed rule. Notes payable is usually listed first, followed by accounts payable. Other items are then listed in any order. The current liability section adapted from the balance sheet of UAL, Inc. (United Airlines) is as follows:

**ILLUSTRATION 4-22**

*Current liabilities section*

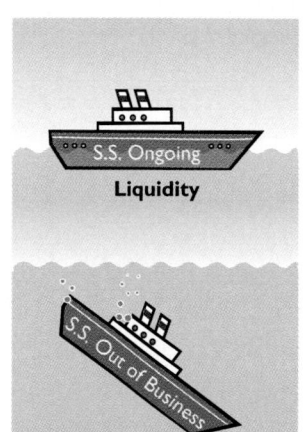

**Liquidity**

**Illiquidity**

| *UNITED AIRLINES* UAL, INC. (UNITED AIRLINES)<br>Balance Sheet (partial)<br>(in thousands) | |
|---|---:|
| **Current liabilities** | |
| Notes payable | $ 297,518 |
| Accounts payable | 382,967 |
| Current maturities of long-term obligations | 81,525 |
| Unearned ticket revenue | 432,979 |
| Salaries and wages payable | 435,622 |
| Taxes payable | 80,390 |
| Other current liabilities | 240,652 |
| Total current liabilities | $1,951,653 |

Users of financial statements look closely at the relationship between current assets and current liabilities. This relationship is important in evaluating a company's **liquidity**—its ability to pay obligations that are expected to become due within the next year or operating cycle. When current assets exceed current liabilities at the balance sheet date, the likelihood for paying the liabilities is favorable. When the reverse is true, short-term creditors may not be paid, and the company may ultimately be forced into bankruptcy.

### Long-Term Liabilities

**ALTERNATIVE TERMINLOGY**

Long-term liabilities are also called *long-term debt* or *noncurrent liabilities*.

Obligations expected to be paid after one year or an operating cycle, whichever is longer, are classified as **long-term liabilities (or long-term debt)**. Liabilities in this category include bonds payable, mortgages payable, long-term notes payable, lease liabilities, and obligations under employee pension plans. Many companies report long-term debt maturing after one year as a single amount in the balance sheet and show the details of the debt in the notes that accompany the financial statements. Others list the various sources of long-term liabilities. In its balance sheet, Consolidated Freightways, Inc. reported:

| *CF CONSOLIDATED FREIGHTWAYS* CONSOLIDATED FREIGHTWAYS, INC.<br>Balance Sheet (partial)<br>(in thousands) | |
|---|---:|
| **Long-term liabilities** | |
| Bank notes payable | $10,000 |
| Mortgage payable | 2,900 |
| Bonds payable | 53,422 |
| Other long-term debt | 9,597 |
| Total long-term liabilities | $75,919 |

**ILLUSTRATION 4-23**

*Long-term liabilities section*

### Owner's Equity

The content of the owner's equity section varies with the form of business organization. In a proprietorship, there is one capital account. In a partnership, there is a capital account for each partner. For a corporation, owners' equity is divided into two accounts—Capital Stock and Retained Earnings. Investments of assets in the business by the stockholders are recorded by debiting an asset account and crediting the Capital Stock account. Income retained for use in the business is recorded in the Retained Earnings account. These two accounts are combined and reported as **stockholders' equity** on the balance sheet. (We'll learn more about these corporation accounts in later chapters.)

In its balance sheet, Dell Computer Corporation reported its owners' (stockholders') equity section in 1997 as follows:

ILLUSTRATION 4-24
*Stockholders' equity section*

| **DELL COMPUTER CORPORATION**<br>**(in millions)** | |
| --- | --- |
| **Stockholders' equity:** | |
| Common stock 173,047,420 shares | $195 |
| Retained earnings | 611 |
| Total stockholders' equity | $806 |

## Classified Balance Sheet Illustrated

An unclassified balance sheet of Pioneer Advertising Agency was presented in Illustration 3-20 on page 112. Using the same adjusted trial balance accounts for Pioneer at October 31, 1999, we can prepare the classified balance sheet shown in Illustration 4-25. For illustrative purposes, we have assumed that $1,000 of the notes payable is due currently and $4,000 is long-term.

The balance sheet is most often presented in **report form**, as in Illustration 4-25, with the assets shown above the liabilities and owner's equity. The balance sheet may also be presented in **account form** with the assets section placed on the left and the liabilities and owner's equity sections on the right.

ILLUSTRATION 4-25
*Classified balance sheet in report form*

| **PIONEER ADVERTISING AGENCY**<br>**Balance Sheet**<br>**October 31, 1999** | | |
| --- | --- | --- |
| **Assets** | | |
| Current assets | | |
| Cash | | $15,200 |
| Accounts receivable | | 200 |
| Advertising supplies | | 1,000 |
| Prepaid insurance | | 550 |
| Total current assets | | 16,950 |
| Property, plant, and equipment | | |
| Office equipment | $5,000 | |
| Less: Accumulated depreciation | 40 | 4,960 |
| Total assets | | $21,910 |
| **Liabilities and Owner's Equity** | | |
| Current liabilities | | |
| Notes payable | | $ 1,000 |
| Accounts payable | | 2,500 |
| Interest payable | | 50 |
| Unearned revenue | | 800 |
| Salaries payable | | 1,200 |
| Total current liabilities | | 5,550 |
| Long-term liabilities | | |
| Notes payable | | 4,000 |
| Total liabilities | | 9,550 |
| Owner's equity | | |
| C. R. Byrd, Capital | | 12,360 |
| Total liabilities and owner's equity | | $21,910 |

# BEFORE YOU GO ON . . .

## Review It

1. What are the major sections in a classified balance sheet?
2. Using the Kellogg Company annual report, determine its current liabilities at December 31, 1997, and December 31, 1996. Were current liabilities higher or lower than current assets in these two years? The answers to this question is provided on page 185.
3. What is the difference between the report form and the account form of the classified balance sheet?

## A LOOK BACK AT OUR FEATURE STORY

Refer to the opening story about SRC Corporation, and answer the following questions:

1. hat is the lesson of the SRC story and Jack Stack's innovations?
2. How did Craig Highbarger's knowledge of financial statements, especially the income statement, contribute to his effectiveness as an employee?

*Solution:*

1. If you give employees equity in the company and provide them with the training and the information to understand the financial consequences of their decisions and actions, they will act more responsibly and make a greater contribution to the sales and income of the company. In other words, they begin to think like owners.
2. By understanding the income statement, he now recognizes the impact of revenues and expenses in arriving at net income—as well as how they affect his bonus.

THE NAVIGATOR

# DEMONSTRATION PROBLEM

At the end of its first month of operations, the Watson Answering Service has the following unadjusted trial balance:

### WATSON ANSWERING SERVICE
### August 31, 1999
### Trial Balance

|  | Debit | Credit |
|---|---|---|
| Cash | $ 5,400 | |
| Accounts Receivable | 2,800 | |
| Prepaid Insurance | 2,400 | |
| Supplies | 1,300 | |
| Equipment | 60,000 | |
| Notes Payable | | $40,000 |
| Accounts Payable | | 2,400 |
| Ray Watson, Capital | | 30,000 |
| Ray Watson, Drawing | 1,000 | |
| Service Revenue | | 4,900 |
| Salaries Expense | 3,200 | |
| Utilities Expense | 800 | |
| Advertising Expense | 400 | |
| | $77,300 | $77,300 |

**PROBLEM-SOLVING STRATEGIES**

1. In completing the work sheet, be sure to (a) key the adjustments, (b) extend adjusted balances to the correct statement columns, and (c) enter net income (or net loss) in the proper columns.
2. In preparing a classified balance sheet, know the contents of each of the sections.
3. In journalizing closing entries, remember that there are only four entries and that owner's drawing is closed to owner's capital.

Other data consist of the following:

1. Insurance expires at the rate of $200 per month.
2. There are $1,000 of supplies on hand at August 31.
3. Monthly depreciation is $900 on the equipment.
4. Interest of $500 has accrued during August on the notes payable.

*Instructions*

(a) Prepare a work sheet.
(b) Prepare a classified balance sheet assuming $35,000 of the notes payable are long-term.
(c) Journalize the closing entries.

# SOLUTION TO DEMONSTRATION PROBLEM

(a)

**WATSON ANSWERING SERVICE**
**Work Sheet**
**For the Month Ended August 31, 1999**

| Account Titles | Trial Balance Dr. | Trial Balance Cr. | Adjustments Dr. | Adjustments Cr. | Adjusted Trial Balance Dr. | Adjusted Trial Balance Cr. | Income Statement Dr. | Income Statement Cr. | Balance Sheet Dr. | Balance Sheet Cr. |
|---|---|---|---|---|---|---|---|---|---|---|
| Cash | 5,400 | | | | 5,400 | | | | 5,400 | |
| Accounts Receivable | 2,800 | | | | 2,800 | | | | 2,800 | |
| Prepaid Insurance | 2,400 | | | (a) 200 | 2,200 | | | | 2,200 | |
| Supplies | 1,300 | | | (b) 300 | 1,000 | | | | 1,000 | |
| Equipment | 60,000 | | | | 60,000 | | | | 60,000 | |
| Notes Payable | | 40,000 | | | | 40,000 | | | | 40,000 |
| Accounts Payable | | 2,400 | | | | 2,400 | | | | 2,400 |
| Ray Watson, Capital | | 30,000 | | | | 30,000 | | | | 30,000 |
| Ray Watson, Drawing | 1,000 | | | | 1,000 | | | | 1,000 | |
| Service Revenue | | 4,900 | | | | 4,900 | | 4,900 | | |
| Salaries Expense | 3,200 | | | | 3,200 | | 3,200 | | | |
| Utilities Expense | 800 | | | | 800 | | 800 | | | |
| Advertising Expense | 400 | | | | 400 | | 400 | | | |
| Totals | 77,300 | 77,300 | | | | | | | | |
| Insurance Expense | | | (a) 200 | | 200 | | 200 | | | |
| Supplies Expense | | | (b) 300 | | 300 | | 300 | | | |
| Depreciation Expense | | | (c) 900 | | 900 | | 900 | | | |
| Accumulated Depreciation— Equipment | | | | (c) 900 | | 900 | | | | 900 |
| Interest Expense | | | (d) 500 | | 500 | | 500 | | | |
| Interest Payable | | | | (d) 500 | | 500 | | | | 500 |
| Totals | | | 1,900 | 1,900 | 78,700 | 78,700 | 6,300 | 4,900 | 72,400 | 73,800 |
| Net Loss | | | | | | | | 1,400 | 1,400 | |
| Totals | | | | | | | 6,300 | 6,300 | 73,800 | 73,800 |

Explanation: (a) Insurance expired, (b) Supplies used, (c) Depreciation expensed, (d) Interest accrued.

(b)

**WATSON ANSWERING SERVICE**
**Balance Sheet**
**August 31, 1999**

**Assets**

| | | |
|---|---|---|
| Current assets | | |
| Cash | | $ 5,400 |
| Accounts receivable | | 2,800 |
| Prepaid insurance | | 2,200 |
| Supplies | | 1,000 |
| Total current assets | | 11,400 |
| Property, plant, and equipment | | |
| Equipment | $60,000 | |
| Less: Accumulated depreciation—equipment | 900 | 59,100 |
| Total assets | | $70,500 |

**Liabilities and Owner's Equity**

| | | |
|---|---:|---:|
| Current liabilities | | |
| Notes payable | | $ 5,000 |
| Accounts payable | | 2,400 |
| Interest payable | | 500 |
| Total current liabilities | | 7,900 |
| Long-term liabilities | | |
| Notes payable | | 35,000 |
| Total liabilities | | 42,900 |
| Owner's equity | | |
| Ray Watson, Capital | | 27,600* |
| Total liabilities and owner's equity | | $70,500 |

*Ray Watson, Capital, $30,000 less drawings $1,000 and net loss $1,400.

(c)

| | | | |
|---|---|---:|---:|
| Aug. 31 | Service Revenue | 4,900 | |
| |    Income Summary | | 4,900 |
| |     (To close revenue account) | | |
| 31 | Income Summary | 6,300 | |
| |    Salaries Expense | | 3,200 |
| |    Depreciation Expense | | 900 |
| |    Utilities Expense | | 800 |
| |    Interest Expense | | 500 |
| |    Advertising Expense | | 400 |
| |    Supplies Expense | | 300 |
| |    Insurance Expense | | 200 |
| |     (To close expense accounts) | | |
| 31 | Ray Watson, Capital | 1,400 | |
| |    Income Summary | | 1,400 |
| |     (To close net loss to capital) | | |
| 31 | Ray Watson, Capital | 1,000 | |
| |    Ray Watson, Drawing | | 1,000 |
| |     (To close drawings to capital) | | |

THE NAVIGATOR

# SUMMARY OF STUDY OBJECTIVES

**1. Prepare a work sheet.** The steps in preparing a work sheet are: (a) prepare a trial balance on the work sheet, (b) enter the adjustments in the adjustment columns, (c) enter adjusted balances in the adjusted trial balance columns, (d) extend adjusted trial balance amounts to appropriate financial statement columns, and (e) total the statement columns, compute net income (or net loss), and complete the work sheet.

**2. Explain the process of closing the books.** Closing the books occurs at the end of an accounting period. The process is to journalize and post closing entries and then rule and balance all accounts. In closing the books, separate entries are made to close revenues and expenses to Income Summary, Income Summary to owner's capital, and owner's drawings to owner's capital. Only temporary accounts are closed.

**3. Describe the content and purpose of a post-closing trial balance.** A post-closing trial balance contains the balances in permanent accounts that are carried forward to the next accounting period. The purpose of this trial balance is to prove the equality of these balances.

**4. State the required steps in the accounting cycle.** The required steps in the accounting cycle are: (a) analyze business transactions, (b) journalize the transactions, (c) post to ledger accounts, (d) prepare a trial balance, (e) journalize and post adjusting entries, (f) prepare an adjusted trial balance, (g) prepare financial statements, (h) journalize and post closing entries, and (i) prepare a post-closing trial balance.

**5. Explain the approaches to preparing correcting entries.** One approach for determining the correcting entry is to compare the incorrect entry with the correct entry. After comparison, a correcting entry is made to correct the accounts. An alternative to a correcting entry is to reverse the incorrect entry and then prepare the correct entry.

6. *Identify the sections of a classified balance sheet.* In a classified balance sheet, assets are classified as current assets; long-term investments; property, plant, and equipment; or intangibles. Liabilities are classified as either current or long-term. There is also an owner's equity section, which varies with the form of business organization.

# GLOSSARY

**Classified balance sheet**   A balance sheet that contains a number of standard classifications or sections. (p. 157).

**Closing entries**   Entries at the end of an accounting period to transfer the balances of temporary accounts to a permanent owner's equity account, owner's capital. (p. 147).

**Correcting entries**   Entries to correct errors made in recording transactions. (p. 154).

**Current assets**   Cash and other resources that are reasonably expected to be realized in cash or sold or consumed in the business within one year or the operating cycle, whichever is longer. (p. 157).

**Current liabilities**   Obligations reasonably expected to be paid from existing current assets or through the creation of other current liabilities within the next year or operating cycle, whichever is longer. (p. 159).

**Income Summary**   A temporary account used in closing revenue and expense accounts. (p. 147).

**Intangible assets**   Noncurrent resources that do not have physical substance. (p. 159).

**Liquidity**   The ability of a company to pay obligations that are expected to become due within the next year or operating cycle. (p. 160).

**Long-term investments**   Resources not expected to be realized in cash within the next year or operating cycle. (p. 158).

**Long-term liabilities (Long-term debt)**   Obligations expected to be paid after one year. (p. 160).

**Operating cycle**   The average time required to go from cash to cash in producing revenues. (p. 157).

**Permanent (real) accounts**   Balance sheet accounts whose balances are carried forward to the next accounting period. (p. 146).

**Post-closing trial balance**   A list of permanent accounts and their balances after closing entries have been journalized and posted. (p. 150).

**Property, plant, and equipment**   Assets of a relatively permanent nature that are being used in the business and not intended for resale. (p. 158).

**Reversing entry**   An entry at the beginning of the next accounting period that is the exact opposite of the adjusting entry made in the previous period. (p. 154).

**Stockholders' equity**   The ownership claim of shareholders on total assets. It is to a corporation what owner's equity is to a proprietorship. (p. 160).

**Temporary (nominal) accounts**   Revenue, expense, and drawing accounts whose balances are transferred to owner's capital at the end of an accounting period. (p. 146).

**Work sheet**   A multiple-column form that may be used in the adjustment process and in preparing financial statements. (p. 140).

# APPENDIX  REVERSING ENTRIES

After the financial statements are prepared and the books are closed, it is often helpful to reverse some of the adjusting entries before recording the regular transactions of the next period. Such entries are called reversing entries. **A reversing entry is made at the beginning of the next accounting period and is the exact opposite of the adjusting entry made in the previous period.** The recording of reversing entries is an **optional** step in the accounting cycle.

**7**
STUDY
OBJECTIVE
Prepare reversing entries.

The purpose of reversing entries is to simplify the recording of a subsequent transaction related to an adjusting entry. In Chapter 3, you may recall, the payment of salaries after an adjusting entry resulted in two debits: one to Salaries Payable and the other to Salaries Expense. With reversing entries, the entire subsequent payment can be debited to Salaries Expense. **The use of reversing entries does not change the amounts reported in the financial statements. It does, however, simplify the recording of subsequent transactions.**

# ILLUSTRATION OF REVERSING ENTRIES

Reversing entries are most often used to reverse two types of adjusting entries: accrued revenues and accrued expenses. They are seldom made for prepaid expenses and unearned revenues. To illustrate the optional use of reversing entries for accrued expenses, we will use the salaries expense transactions for Pioneer Advertising Agency. The transaction and adjustment data are as follows:

1. October 26 (initial salary entry): $4,000 of salaries earned between October 15 and October 26 are paid.
2. October 31 (adjusting entry): Salaries earned between October 29 and October 31 are $1,200. These will be paid in the November 9 payroll.
3. November 9 (subsequent salary entry): Salaries paid are $4,000. Of this amount, $1,200 applied to accrued wages payable and $2,800 was earned between November 1 and November 9.

**ILLUSTRATION 4A-1**

*Comparative entries—not reversing vs. reversing*

The comparative entries with and without reversing entries are shown in Illustration 4A-1.

| When Reversing Entries Are Not Used (per chapter) | | | | When Reversing Entries Are Used (per appendix) | | | |
|---|---|---|---|---|---|---|---|
| **Initial Salary Entry** | | | | **Initial Salary Entry** | | | |
| Oct. 26 | Salaries Expense | 4,000 | | Oct. 26 | Salaries Expense | 4,000 | |
| | Cash | | 4,000 | | Cash | | 4,000 |
| **Adjusting Entry** | | | | **Adjusting Entry** | | | |
| Oct. 31 | Salaries Expense | 1,200 | | Oct. 31 | **Salaries Expense** | 1,200 | |
| | Salaries Payable | | 1,200 | | **Salaries Payable** | | 1,200 |
| **Closing Entry** | | | | **Closing Entry** | | | |
| Oct. 31 | Income Summary | 5,200 | | Oct. 31 | **Income Summary** | 5,200 | |
| | Salaries Expense | | 5,200 | | **Salaries Expense** | | 5,200 |
| **Reversing Entry** | | | | **Reversing Entry** | | | |
| Nov. 1 | No reversing entry is made. | | | Nov. 1 | **Salaries Payable** | 1,200 | |
| | | | | | **Salaries Expense** | | 1,200 |
| **Subsequent Salary Entry** | | | | **Subsequent Salary Entry** | | | |
| Nov. 9 | Salaries Payable | 1,200 | | Nov. 9 | **Salaries Expense** | 4,000 | |
| | Salaries Expense | 2,800 | | | **Cash** | | 4,000 |
| | Cash | | 4,000 | | | | |

The comparative entries show that the first three entries are the same whether or not reversing entries are used. The last two entries, however, are different. The November 1 **reversing entry** eliminates the $1,200 balance in Salaries Payable that was created by the October 31 adjusting entry. The reversing entry also creates a $1,200 credit balance in the Salaries Expense account. As you know, it is unusual for an expense account to have a credit balance. The balance is correct in this instance, though, because it anticipates that the entire amount of the first salary payment in the new accounting period will be debited to Salaries Expense. This debit will eliminate the credit balance, and the resulting debit balance in the expense account will equal the salaries expense incurred in the new accounting period ($2,800 in this example).

# TECHNOLOGY IN ACTION

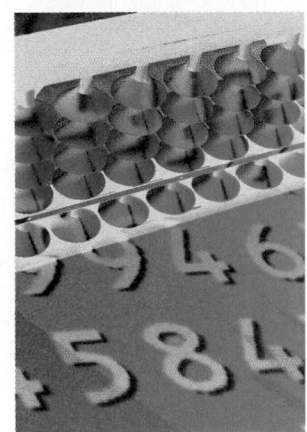

Using reversing entries in a computerized accounting system is more efficient than in a manual system. The reversing entry saves writing a program to locate the amount accrued from the preceding period and making the more complicated entry in the current period. That is, the computer does not have to be programmed to determine whether any accrued items exist.

When reversing entries are made, all cash payments of expenses can be debited to the expense account. This means that on November 9 (and every payday) Salaries Expense can be debited for the amount paid without regard to the existence of any accrued salaries payable. Being able to make the same entry each time simplifies the recording process. Note that when reversing entries are used, the recording of subsequent transactions is simplified because they can be recorded as if the related adjusting entry had never been made.

The posting of the entries with reversing entries is shown in Illustration 4A-2.

| Salaries Expense | | | | | Salaries Payable | | | |
|---|---|---|---|---|---|---|---|---|
| 10/26 Paid | 4,000 | 10/31 Closing | 5,200 | 11/1 **Reversing** | **1,200** | 10/31 Adjusting | 1,200 |
| 31 Adjusting | 1,200 | | | | | | |
| | 5,200 | | 5,200 | | | | |
| 11/9 Paid | 4,000 | 11/1 **Reversing** | **1,200** | | | | |

**ILLUSTRATION 4A-2**
*Postings with reversing entries*

Reversing entries may also be made for accrued revenue adjusting entries. For Pioneer Advertising, the adjusting entry was: Accounts Receivable (Dr.) $200 and Service Revenue (Cr.) $200. Thus, the reversing entry on November 1 is:

| Nov. 1 | Service Revenue | 200 | |
|---|---|---|---|
| | Accounts Receivable | | 200 |
| | (To reverse October 31 adjusting entry) | | |

| A | = | L | + | OE |
|---|---|---|---|---|
| −200 | | | | −200 |

When the accrued fees are collected, Cash is debited and Service Revenue is credited.

# SUMMARY OF STUDY OBJECTIVE FOR APPENDIX

**7. Prepare reversing entries.** Reversing entries are the direct opposite of the adjusting entry made in the preceding period. They are made at the beginning of a new accounting period to simplify the recording of later transactions related to the adjusting entry. In most cases, only accrued adjusting entries are reversed.

*Note: All asterisked Questions, Exercises, and Problems relate to material in the appendix to the chapter.

# SELF-STUDY QUESTIONS

Answers are at the end of the chapter.

(SO 1) 1. Which of the following statements is *incorrect* concerning the work sheet?
   a. The work sheet is essentially a working tool of the accountant.
   b. The work sheet is distributed to management and other interested parties.
   c. The work sheet cannot be used as a basis for posting to ledger accounts.
   d. Financial statements can be prepared directly from the work sheet before journalizing and posting the adjusting entries.

(SO 1) 2. In a work sheet, net income is entered in the following columns:
   a. income statement (Dr) and balance sheet (Dr).
   b. income statement (Cr) and balance sheet (Dr).
   c. income statement (Dr) and balance sheet (Cr).
   d. income statement (Cr) and balance sheet (Cr).

(SO 2) 3. An account that will have a zero balance after closing entries have been journalized and posted is:
   a. Service Revenue.
   b. Advertising Supplies.
   c. Prepaid Insurance.
   d. Accumulated Depreciation.

(SO 2) 4. When a net loss has occurred, Income Summary is:
   a. debited and owner's capital is credited.
   b. credited and owner's capital is debited.
   c. debited and owner's drawing is credited.
   d. credited and owner's drawing is debited.

(SO 2) 5. The closing process involves separate entries to close (1) expenses, (2) drawings, (3) revenues and (4) income summary. The correct sequencing of the entries is:
   a. (4), (3), (2), (1)
   b. (1), (2), (3), (4)
   c. (3), (1), (4), (2)
   d. (3), (2), (1), (4)

(SO 3) 6. Which types of accounts will appear in the post-closing trial balance?
   a. Permanent (real) accounts.
   b. Temporary (nominal) accounts.
   c. Accounts shown in the income statement columns of a work sheet.
   d. None of the above.

7. All of the following are required steps in the accounting (SO 4) cycle *except*:
   a. journalizing and posting closing entries.
   b. preparing financial statements.
   c. journalizing the transactions.
   d. preparing a work sheet.

8. Cash of $100 received at the time the service was ren- (SO 5) dered was journalized and posted as a debit to Cash $100 and a credit to Accounts Receivable $100. Assuming the incorrect entry is not reversed, the correcting entry is:
   a. debit Service Revenue $100 and credit Accounts Receivable $100.
   b. debit Accounts Receivable $100 and credit Service Revenue $100.
   c. debit Cash $100 and credit Service Revenue $100.
   d. debit Accounts Receivable $100 and credit Cash $100.

9. In a classified balance sheet, assets are usually classified (SO 6) using the following categories:
   a. current assets; long-term assets; property, plant, and equipment; and intangible assets.
   b. current assets; long-term investments; property, plant, and equipment; and other assets.
   c. current assets; long-term investments; tangible assets; and intangible assets.
   d. current assets; long-term investments; property, plant, and equipment; and intangible assets.

10. Current assets are listed: (SO 6)
   a. by liquidity.
   b. by importance.
   c. by longevity.
   d. alphabetically.

*11. On December 31, Salerno Company correctly made an (SO 7) adjusting entry to recognize $2,000 of accrued salaries payable. On January 8 of the next year, total salaries of $3,400 were paid. Assuming the correct reversing entry was made on January 1, the entry on January 8 will result in a credit to Cash $3,400, and the following debit(s):
   a. Salaries Payable $1,400 and Salaries Expense $2,000.
   b. Salaries Payable $2,000 and Salaries Expense $1,400.
   c. Salaries Expense $3,400.
   d. Salaries Payable $3,400.

THE
NAVIGATOR

# QUESTIONS

1. "A work sheet is a permanent accounting record and its use is required in the accounting cycle." Do you agree? Explain.

2. Explain the purpose of the work sheet.

3. What is the relationship, if any, between the amount shown in the adjusted trial balance column for an account and that account's ledger balance?

4. If a company's revenues are $125,000 and its expenses are $113,000, in which financial statement columns of the work sheet will the net income of $12,000 appear? When expenses exceed revenues, in which columns will the difference appear?

5. Why is it necessary to prepare formal financial statements when all of the data are in the statement columns of the work sheet?

6. Identify the account(s) debited and credited in each of the four closing entries, assuming the company has net income for the year.

7. Describe the nature of the Income Summary account and identify the types of summary data that may be posted to this account.

8. What are the content and purpose of a post-closing trial balance?

9. Which of the following accounts would not appear in the post-closing trial balance? Interest Payable; Equipment; Depreciation Expense; Kathy Ho, Drawing; Unearned Revenue; Accumulated Depreciation—Equipment; and Service Revenue.

10. Distinguish between a reversing entry and an adjusting entry. Are reversing entries required?

11. Indicate, in the sequence in which they are made, the three required steps in the accounting cycle that involve journalizing.

12. Identify, in the sequence in which they are prepared, the three trial balances that are often used to report financial information about a company.

13. How do correcting entries differ from adjusting entries?

14. What standard classifications are used in preparing a classified balance sheet?

15. What is meant by the term "operating cycle"?

16. Define current assets. What basis is used for arranging individual items within the current asset section?

17. Distinguish between long-term investments and property, plant, and equipment.

18. How do current liabilities differ from long-term liabilities?

19. (a) What is the term used to describe the owner's equity section of a corporation? (b) Identify the two owner's equity accounts in a corporation and indicate the purpose of each.

20. How does a report form balance sheet differ from an account form balance sheet?

*21. David Biel Company prepares reversing entries. If the adjusting entry for interest payable is reversed, what type of an account balance, if any, will there be in Interest Payable and Interest Expense after the reversing entry is posted?

*22. At December 31, accrued salaries payable totaled $4,500. On January 10, total salaries of $8,000 are paid. (a) Assume that reversing entries are made at January 1. Give the January 10 entry and indicate the Salaries Expense account balance after the entry is posted. (b) Repeat part (a) assuming reversing entries are not made.

# BRIEF EXERCISES

**BE4-1** The steps in using a work sheet are presented in random order below. List the steps in the proper order.

_____ Prepare a trial balance on the work sheet.
_____ Enter adjusted balances.
_____ Extend adjusted balances to appropriate statement columns.
_____ Total the statement columns, compute net income (loss), and complete the work sheet.
_____ Enter adjustment data.

*List the steps in preparing a work sheet.*
*(SO 1)*

**BE4-2** The ledger of Warren Company includes the following unadjusted balances: Prepaid Insurance $4,000, Service Revenue $58,000, and Salaries Expense $25,000. Adjusting entries are required for (a) expired insurance $1,600, (b) services provided $900, but unbilled and uncollected, and (c) accrued salaries payable $800. Enter the unadjusted balances and adjustments into a work sheet and complete the work sheet for all accounts. Note: You will need to add the following accounts: Accounts Receivable, Salaries Payable, and Insurance Expense.

*Prepare partial work sheet.*
*(SO 1)*

**BE4-3** The following selected accounts appear in the adjusted trial balance columns of the work sheet for the Falcetto Company: Accumulated Depreciation; Depreciation Expense;

*Identify work sheet columns for selected accounts.*
*(SO 1)*

L. Falcetto, Capital; L. Falcetto, Drawing; Service Revenue; Supplies; and Accounts Payable. Indicate the financial statement column (income statement Dr., balance sheet Cr., etc.) to which each balance should be extended.

*Prepare closing entries from ledger balances.*
*(SO 2)*

**BE4-4**   The ledger of the Perkins Company contains the following balances: R. Perkins, Capital $30,000; R. Perkins, Drawing $2,000; Service Revenue $45,000; Salaries Expense $26,000; and Supplies Expense $4,000. Prepare the closing entries at December 31.

*Post closing entries and rule and balance T accounts.*
*(SO 2)*

**BE4-5**   Using the data in BE4-4, enter the balances in T accounts, post the closing entries, and rule and balance the accounts.

*Journalize and post closing entries using the three-column form of account.*
*(SO 2)*

**BE4-6**   The income statement for Community Golf Club for the month ending July 31 shows Green Fee Revenue $14,000, Salaries Expense $6,200, Maintenance Expense $2,500, and Net Income $7,300. Prepare the entries to close the revenue and expense accounts. Post the entries to the revenue and expense accounts and complete the closing process for these accounts using the three-column form of account.

*Identify post-closing trial balance accounts.*
*(SO 3)*

**BE4-7**   Using the data in BE4-3, identify the accounts that would be included in a post-closing trial balance.

*List the required steps in the accounting cycle in sequence.*
*(SO 4)*

**BE4-8**   The steps in the accounting cycle are listed in random order below. List the steps in proper sequence, assuming no work sheet is prepared.

_4_ Prepare a trial balance.
_2_ Journalize the transactions.
_8_ Journalize and post closing entries.
_7_ Prepare financial statements.
_5_ Journalize and post adjusting entries.
_3_ Post to ledger accounts.
_9_ Prepare a post-closing trial balance.
_6_ Prepare an adjusted trial balance.
_1_ Analyze business transactions.

*Prepare correcting entries.*
*(SO 5)*

**BE4-9**   At Ruhly Company, the following errors were discovered after the transactions had been journalized and posted. Prepare the correcting entries.

1. A collection on account from a customer for $780 was recorded as a debit to Cash $780 and a credit to Service Revenue $780.
2. The purchase of store supplies on account for $1,630 was recorded as a debit to Store Supplies $1,360 and a credit to Accounts Payable $1,360.

*Prepare the current asset section of a balance sheet.*
*(SO 6)*

**BE4-10**   The balance sheet debit column of the work sheet for Rueben Company includes the following accounts: Accounts Receivable $14,500; Prepaid Insurance $3,600; Cash $18,400; Supplies $5,200, and Marketable Securities $8,200. Prepare the current asset section of the balance sheet listing the accounts in proper sequence.

*Prepare reversing entries.*
*(SO 7)*

*BE4-11**   At October 31, Julia Company made an accrued expense adjusting entry of $600 for salaries. Prepare the reversing entry on November 1 and indicate the balances in Salaries Payable and Salaries Expense after posting the reversing entry.

# EXERCISES

*Complete work sheet.*
*(SO 1)*

**E4-1**   The adjusted trial balance columns of the work sheet for Jose Navarro Company are as follows:

**JOSE NAVARRO COMPANY**
**Work Sheet (partial)**
**For the Month Ended April 30, 1999**

| Account Titles | Adjusted Trial Balance Dr. | Adjusted Trial Balance Cr. | Income Statement Dr. | Income Statement Cr. | Balance Sheet Dr. | Balance Sheet Cr. |
|---|---|---|---|---|---|---|
| Cash | 17,052 | | | | | |
| Accounts Receivable | 7,840 | | | | | |

| Account Titles | Adjusted Trial Balance | | Income Statement | | Balance Sheet | |
|---|---|---|---|---|---|---|
| | Dr. | Cr. | Dr. | Cr. | Dr. | Cr. |
| Prepaid Rent | 2,280 | | | | | |
| Equipment | 23,050 | | | | | |
| Accumulated Depreciation | | 4,921 | | | | |
| Notes Payable | | 5,700 | | | | |
| Accounts Payable | | 5,972 | | | | |
| J. Navarro, Capital | | 33,960 | | | | |
| J. Navarro, Drawing | 3,650 | | | | | |
| Service Revenue | | 12,590 | | | | |
| Salaries Expense | 7,840 | | | | | |
| Rent Expense | 760 | | | | | |
| Depreciation Expense | 671 | | | | | |
| Interest Expense | 57 | | | | | |
| Interest Payable | | 57 | | | | |
| Totals | 63,200 | 63,200 | | | | |

**Instructions**
Complete the work sheet.

**E4–2**  Work sheet data for the Jose Navarro Company are presented in E4–1. The owner did not make any additional investments in the business in April.

*Prepare financial statements from work sheet.*
*(SO 1, 6)*

**Instructions**
Prepare an income statement, an owner's equity statement, and a classified balance sheet.

**E4–3**  Work sheet data for the Jose Navarro Company are presented in E4–1.

*Journalize and post closing entries and prepare a post-closing trial balance.*
*(SO 2, 3)*

**Instructions**
(a) Journalize the closing entries at April 30.
(b) Post the closing entries to Income Summary and J. Navarro, Capital. Use T accounts.
(c) Prepare a post-closing trial balance at April 30.

**E4–4**  The adjustments columns of the work sheet for Goodyear Company are shown below.

*Prepare adjusting entries from a work sheet and extend balances to work sheet columns.*
*(SO 1)*

| Account Titles | Adjustments | |
|---|---|---|
| | Debit | Credit |
| Accounts Receivable | 800 | |
| Prepaid Insurance | | 400 |
| Accumulated Depreciation | | 1,000 |
| Salaries Payable | | 500 |
| Service Revenue | | 800 |
| Salaries Expense | 500 | |
| Insurance Expense | 400 | |
| Depreciation Expense | 1,000 | |
| | 2,700 | 2,700 |

**Instructions**
(a) Prepare the adjusting entries.
(b) Assuming the adjusted trial balance amount for each account is normal, indicate the financial statement column to which each balance should be extended.

*Derive adjusting entries from work sheet data.*
*(SO 1)*

**E4–5**   Selected work sheet data for Marinita Company are presented below.

| Account Titles | Trial Balance | | Adjusted Trial Balance | |
| --- | --- | --- | --- | --- |
| | Dr. | Cr. | Dr. | Cr. |
| Accounts Receivable | ? | | 34,000 | |
| Prepaid Insurance | 24,000 | | 18,000 | |
| Supplies | 9,000 | | ? | |
| Accumulated Depreciation | | 12,000 | | ? |
| Salaries Payable | | ? | | 6,000 |
| Service Revenue | | 90,000 | | 95,000 |
| Insurance Expense | | | ? | |
| Depreciation Expense | | | 10,000 | |
| Supplies Expense | | | 4,000 | |
| Salaries Expense | ? | | 49,000 | |

**Instructions**
(a) Fill in the missing amounts.
(b) Prepare the adjusting entries that were made.

*Journalize and post closing entries and prepare a post-closing trial balance.*
*(SO 2, 3)*

**E4–6**   The adjusted trial balance of Rafael Company at the end of its fiscal year is:

**RAFAEL COMPANY**
**Adjusted Trial Balance**
**July 31, 1999**

| No. | Account Titles | Debits | Credits |
| --- | --- | --- | --- |
| 101 | Cash | $ 11,940 | |
| 112 | Accounts Receivable | 8,780 | |
| 157 | Equipment | 15,900 | |
| 167 | Accumulated Depreciation | | $  5,400 |
| 201 | Accounts Payable | | 4,220 |
| 208 | Unearned Rent Revenue | | 1,800 |
| 301 | S. Rafael, Capital | | 45,200 |
| 306 | S. Rafael, Drawing | 14,000 | |
| 404 | Commission Revenue | | 65,100 |
| 429 | Rent Revenue | | 6,500 |
| 711 | Depreciation Expense | 4,000 | |
| 720 | Salaries Expense | 58,700 | |
| 732 | Utilities Expense | 14,900 | |
| | | $128,220 | $128,220 |

**Instructions**
(a) Prepare the closing entries using page J15.
(b) Post to S. Rafael, Capital and No. 350 Income Summary accounts. (Use the three-column form.)
(c) Prepare a post-closing trial balance at July 31.

**E4–7**   The adjusted trial balance for Rafael Company is presented in E4–6.

*Prepare financial statements.*
*(SO 6)*

**Instructions**
(a) Prepare an income statement and an owner's equity statement for the year. Rafael did not make any capital investments during the year.
(b) Prepare a classified balance sheet at July 31.

*Prepare closing entries and an owner's equity statement.*
*(SO 2)*

**E4–8**   Selected accounts for Comfort Zone Salon are presented below. All June 30 postings are from closing entries.

| Salaries Expense | | | | Service Revenue | | | | L. Pappas, Capital | | | |
| --- | --- | --- | --- | --- | --- | --- | --- | --- | --- | --- | --- |
| 6/10 | 3,200 | 6/30 | 8,800 | 6/30 | 15,600 | 6/15 | 7,200 | 6/30 | 2,500 | 6/1 | 12,000 |
| 6/28 | 5,600 | | | | | 6/24 | 8,400 | | | 6/30 | 1,800 |
| | | | | | | | | | | Bal. | 11,300 |

| Supplies Expense | | | Rent Expense | | | L. Pappas, Drawing | | |
|---|---|---|---|---|---|---|---|---|
| 6/12  800 | 6/30  1,500 | | 6/1  3,500 | 6/30  3,500 | | 6/13  1,000 | 6/30  2,500 | |
| 6/24  700 | | | | | | 6/25  1,500 | | |

### Instructions

(a) Prepare the closing entries that were made.

(b) Post the closing entries to Income Summary.

**E4–9**  The Kumar Company has an inexperienced accountant. During the first 2 weeks on the job, the following errors were made in journalizing transactions. All entries were posted as made.

*Prepare correcting entries.*
*(SO 5)*

1. A payment on account to a creditor of $630 was debited to Accounts Payable $360 and credited to Cash $360.
2. The purchase of supplies on account for $600 was debited to Equipment $60 and credited to Accounts Payable $60.
3. A $400 withdrawal of cash for P. Kumar's personal use was debited to Salaries Expense $400 and credited to Cash $400.

### Instructions

Prepare the correcting entries.

**E4–10**  The adjusted trial balance for Bel-Air's Bowling Alley at December 31, 1999, contains the following accounts.

*Prepare a classified balance sheet.*
*(SO 6)*

| Debits | | Credits | |
|---|---|---|---|
| Building | $123,800 | T. Henkel, Capital | $110,000 |
| Accounts Receivable | 14,520 | Accumulated Depreciation—Building | 45,600 |
| Prepaid Insurance | 4,680 | Accounts Payable | 13,480 |
| Cash | 20,840 | Mortgage Payable | 93,600 |
| Equipment | 62,400 | Accumulated Depreciation—Equipment | 18,720 |
| Land | 61,200 | Interest Payable | 2,600 |
| Insurance Expense | 780 | Bowling Revenues | 14,180 |
| Depreciation Expense | 7,360 | | $298,180 |
| Interest Expense | 2,600 | | |
| | $298,180 | | |

### Instructions

(a) Prepare a classified balance sheet; assume that $13,600 of the mortgage payable will be paid in 2000.

(b) ▭▭▭▶ Comment on the liquidity of the company.

**\*E4–11**  On December 31, the adjusted trial balance of Garrett Employment Agency shows the following selected data:

*Prepare closing and reversing entries.*
*(SO 2, 4, 7)*

| Accounts Receivable | $4,000 | Commission Revenue | $96,000 |
|---|---|---|---|
| Interest Expense | 7,800 | Interest Payable | 2,000 |

Analysis shows that adjusting entries were made to (a) accrue $4,000 of commission revenue and (b) accrue $2,000 interest expense.

### Instructions

(a) Prepare the closing entries for the temporary accounts at December 31.

(b) Prepare the reversing entries on January 1.

(c) Post the entries in (a) and (b). Rule and balance the accounts. (Use T accounts.)

(d) Prepare the entries to record (1) the collection of the accrued commissions on January 10 and (2) the payment of all interest due ($2,700) on January 15.

(e) Post the entries in (d) to the temporary accounts.

# PROBLEMS: SET A

*Prepare a work sheet, financial statements, and adjusting and closing entries.*
(SO 1, 2, 3, 6)

**P4–1A**   The trial balance columns of the work sheet for Spellman Roofing at March 31, 1999, are as follows:

### SPELLMAN ROOFING
### Work Sheet
### For the Month Ended March 31, 1999

| Account Titles | Trial Balance Dr. | Trial Balance Cr. |
|---|---|---|
| Cash | $ 2,700 | |
| Accounts Receivable | 1,600 | |
| Roofing Supplies | 1,100 | |
| Equipment | 6,000 | |
| Accumulated Depreciation—Equipment | | $ 1,200 |
| Accounts Payable | | 1,100 |
| Unearned Revenue | | 300 |
| A. Spellman, Capital | | 7,000 |
| A. Spellman, Drawing | 600 | |
| Service Revenue | | 3,000 |
| Salaries Expense | 500 | |
| Miscellaneous Expense | 100 | |
| | $12,600 | $12,600 |

Other data:

1. A physical count reveals only $320 of roofing supplies on hand.
2. Depreciation for March is $200.
3. Unearned revenue amounted to $200 after adjustment on March 31.
4. Accrued salaries are $400.

*Instructions*
(a) Enter the trial balance on a work sheet and complete the work sheet.
(b) Prepare an income statement and owner's equity statement for the month of March and classified balance sheet at March 31. A. Spellman did not make any additional investments in the business in March.
(c) Journalize the adjusting entries from the adjustments columns of the work sheet.
(d) Journalize the closing entries from the financial statement columns of the work sheet.

*Complete work sheet and prepare financial statements, closing entries, and post-closing trial balance.*
(SO 1, 2, 3, 6)

**P4–2A**   The adjusted trial balance columns of the work sheet for Perez Company, owned by Jose Perez, are as follows:

### PEREZ COMPANY
### Work Sheet
### For the Year Ended December 31, 1999

| Account No. | Account Titles | Adjusted Trial Balance Dr. | Adjusted Trial Balance Cr. |
|---|---|---|---|
| 101 | Cash | 16,600 | |
| 112 | Accounts Receivable | 15,400 | |
| 126 | Supplies | 1,500 | |
| 130 | Prepaid Insurance | 2,800 | |
| 151 | Office Equipment | 34,000 | |
| 152 | Accumulated Depreciation—Office Equipment | | 8,000 |
| 200 | Notes Payable | | 16,000 |
| 201 | Accounts Payable | | 6,000 |
| 212 | Salaries Payable | | 3,000 |
| 230 | Interest Payable | | 500 |

| Account No. | Account Titles | Adjusted Trial Balance Dr. | Adjusted Trial Balance Cr. |
|---|---|---|---|
| 301 | J. Perez, Capital | | 25,000 |
| 306 | J. Perez, Drawing | 10,000 | |
| 400 | Service Revenue | | 88,000 |
| 610 | Advertising Expense | 12,000 | |
| 631 | Supplies Expense | 5,700 | |
| 711 | Depreciation Expense | 4,000 | |
| 722 | Insurance Expense | 5,000 | |
| 726 | Salaries Expense | 39,000 | |
| 905 | Interest Expense | 500 | |
| | | 146,500 | 146,500 |

*Instructions*

(a) Complete the work sheet by extending the balances to the financial statement columns.

(b) Prepare an income statement, owner's equity statement, and a classified balance sheet. (Note: $10,000 of the notes payable become due in 2000.) J. Perez did not make any additional investments in the business during the year.

(c) Prepare the closing entries. Use J14 for the journal page.

(d) Post the closing entries and rule and balance the accounts. Use the three-column form of account. Income Summary is No. 350.

(e) Prepare a post-closing trial balance.

**P4–3A**  The completed financial statement columns of the work sheet for Strug Company are shown below.

*Prepare financial statements, closing entries, and post-closing trial balance.*
*(SO 1, 2, 3, 6)*

## STRUG COMPANY
## Work Sheet
### For the Year Ended December 31, 1999

| Account No. | Account Titles | Income Statement Dr. | Income Statement Cr. | Balance Sheet Dr. | Balance Sheet Cr. |
|---|---|---|---|---|---|
| 101 | Cash | | | 13,600 | |
| 112 | Accounts Receivable | | | 13,500 | |
| 130 | Prepaid Insurance | | | 3,500 | |
| 157 | Equipment | | | 26,000 | |
| 167 | Accumulated Depreciation | | | | 5,600 |
| 201 | Accounts Payable | | | | 11,300 |
| 212 | Salaries Payable | | | | 3,000 |
| 301 | K. Strug, Capital | | | | 36,000 |
| 306 | K. Strug, Drawing | | | 12,000 | |
| 400 | Service Revenue | | 56,000 | | |
| 622 | Repair Expense | 1,800 | | | |
| 711 | Depreciation Expense | 2,600 | | | |
| 722 | Insurance Expense | 2,200 | | | |
| 726 | Salaries Expense | 35,000 | | | |
| 732 | Utilities Expense | 1,700 | | | |
| | Totals | 43,300 | 56,000 | 68,600 | 55,900 |
| | Net Income | 12,700 | | | 12,700 |
| | | 56,000 | 56,000 | 68,600 | 68,600 |

*Instructions*

(a) Prepare an income statement, owner's equity statement, and a classified balance sheet.

(b) Prepare the closing entries.

(c) Post the closing entries and rule and balance the accounts. Use T accounts. Income Summary is No. 350.

(d) Prepare a post-closing trial balance.

*Complete work sheet and prepare classified balance sheet, entries, and post-closing trial balance.*
*(SO 1, 2, 3, 6)*

**P4–4A**  Logan Management Services began business on January 1, 1999, with a capital investment of $120,000. The company manages condominiums for owners (Service Revenue) and rents space in its own office building (Rent Revenue). The trial and adjusted trial balance columns of the work sheet at the end of the first year are as follows:

### LOGAN MANAGEMENT SERVICES
### Work Sheet
### For the Year Ended December 31, 1999

| Account Titles | Trial Balance Dr. | Trial Balance Cr. | Adjusted Trial Balance Dr. | Adjusted Trial Balance Cr. |
|---|---|---|---|---|
| Cash | 12,500 | | 12,500 | |
| Accounts Receivable | 23,600 | | 23,600 | |
| Prepaid Insurance | 3,100 | | 1,600 | |
| Land | 56,000 | | 56,000 | |
| Building | 106,000 | | 106,000 | |
| Equipment | 48,000 | | 48,000 | |
| Accounts Payable | | 10,400 | | 10,400 |
| Unearned Rent Revenue | | 4,000 | | 1,800 |
| Mortgage Payable | | 100,000 | | 100,000 |
| M. Logan, Capital | | 120,000 | | 120,000 |
| M. Logan, Drawing | 20,000 | | 20,000 | |
| Service Revenue | | 75,600 | | 75,600 |
| Rent Revenue | | 24,000 | | 26,200 |
| Salaries Expense | 32,000 | | 32,000 | |
| Advertising Expense | 17,000 | | 17,000 | |
| Utilities Expense | 15,800 | | 15,800 | |
| Totals | 334,000 | 334,000 | | |
| Insurance Expense | | | 1,500 | |
| Depreciation Expense—Building | | | 2,500 | |
| Accumulated Depreciation—Building | | | | 2,500 |
| Depreciation Expense—Equipment | | | 3,900 | |
| Accumulated Depreciation—Equipment | | | | 3,900 |
| Interest Expense | | | 10,000 | |
| Interest Payable | | | | 10,000 |
| Totals | | | 350,400 | 350,400 |

**Instructions**
(a) Prepare a complete work sheet.
(b) Prepare a classified balance sheet. (Note: $10,000 of the mortgage payable is due for payment next year.)
(c) Journalize the adjusting entries.
(d) Journalize the closing entries.
(e) Prepare a post-closing trial balance.

*Complete all steps in accounting cycle.*
*(SO 1, 2, 3, 4, 6)*

**P4–5A**  Jill Marsh opened Jill's Window Washing on July 1, 1999. During July the following transactions were completed.

July  1  Marsh invested $9,000 cash in the business.
    1  Purchased used truck for $6,000, paying $3,000 cash and the balance on account.
    3  Purchased cleaning supplies for $900 on account.
    5  Paid $1,200 cash on one-year insurance policy effective July 1.
   12  Billed customers $2,500 for cleaning services.
   18  Paid $1,000 cash on amount owed on truck and $500 on amount owed on cleaning supplies.

20  Paid $1,200 cash for employee salaries.
21  Collected $1,400 cash from customers billed on July 12.
25  Billed customers $2,000 for cleaning services.
31  Paid gas and oil for month on truck $200.
31  Withdrew $600 cash for personal use.

The chart of accounts for Jill's Window Washing contains the following accounts: No. 101 Cash, No. 112 Accounts Receivable, No. 128 Cleaning Supplies, No. 130 Prepaid Insurance, No. 157 Equipment, No. 158 Accumulated Depreciation—Equipment, No. 201 Accounts Payable, No. 212 Salaries Payable, No. 301 Jill Marsh, Capital, No. 306 Jill Marsh, Drawing, No. 350 Income Summary, No. 400 Service Revenue, No. 633 Gas & Oil Expense, No. 634 Cleaning Supplies Expense, No. 711 Depreciation Expense, No. 722 Insurance Expense, No. 726 Salaries Expense.

*Instructions*
(a) Journalize and post the July transactions. Use page J1 for the journal and the three-column form of account.
(b) Prepare a trial balance at July 31 on a work sheet.
(c) Enter the following adjustments on the work sheet and complete the work sheet.
   (1) Services provided but unbilled and uncollected at July 31 were $1,100.
   (2) Depreciation on equipment for the month was $200.
   (3) One-twelfth of the insurance expired.
   (4) An inventory count shows $600 of cleaning supplies on hand at July 31.
   (5) Accrued but unpaid employee salaries were $400.
(d) Prepare the income statement and owner's equity statement for July and a classified balance sheet at July 31.
(e) Journalize and post adjusting entries. Use page J2 for the journal.
(f) Journalize and post closing entries and complete the closing process. Use page J3 for the journal.
(g) Prepare a post-closing trial balance at July 31.

**P4–6A**  Jenny Denton, CPA, was retained by Everlast TV Repair to prepare financial statements for April 1999. Denton accumulated all the ledger balances per Everlast's records and found the following:

*Analyze errors and prepare correcting entries.*
*(SO 5)*

**EVERLAST TV REPAIR**
**Trial Balance**
**April 30, 1999**

|  | Debit | Credit |
|---|---|---|
| Cash | $ 5,100 |  |
| Accounts Receivable | 3,200 |  |
| Supplies | 800 |  |
| Equipment | 10,600 |  |
| Accumulated Depreciation |  | $ 1,350 |
| Accounts Payable |  | 2,100 |
| Salaries Payable |  | 500 |
| Unearned Revenue |  | 890 |
| S. Morris, Capital |  | 13,900 |
| Service Revenue |  | 5,450 |
| Salaries Expense | 3,300 |  |
| Advertising Expense | 400 |  |
| Miscellaneous Expense | 290 |  |
| Depreciation Expense | 500 |  |
|  | $24,190 | $24,190 |

Jenny Denton reviewed the records and found the following errors:

1. Cash received from a customer on account was recorded as $750 instead of $570.
2. A payment of $30 for advertising expense was entered as a debit to Miscellaneous Expense $30 and a credit to Cash $30.

3. The first salary payment this month was for $1,900, which included $500 of salaries payable on March 31. The payment was recorded as a debit to Salaries Expense $1,900 and a credit to Cash $1,900. (No reversing entries were made on April 1.)
4. The purchase, on account, of a typewriter costing $340 was recorded as a debit to Supplies and a credit to Accounts Payable for $340.
5. A cash payment of repair expense on equipment for $86 was recorded as a debit to Equipment $68 and a credit to Cash $68.

### Instructions

(a) Prepare an analysis of each error showing (1) the incorrect entry, (2) the correct entry, and (3) the correcting entry. Items 4 and 5 occurred on April 30, 1999.
(b) Prepare a correct trial balance.

# PROBLEMS: SET B

•••••••••••••••••••••••••••••••••••••••••••••••••••••••••••••••••••••••••••••••••

*Prepare work sheet, financial statements, and adjusting and closing entries.*
*(SO 1, 2, 3, 6)*

**P4–1B**   S. Columbo began operations as a private investigator on January 1, 1999. The trial balance columns of the work sheet for Columbo P.I. at March 31 are as follows:

**COLUMBO P.I.**
**Work Sheet**
**For the Quarter Ended March 31, 1999**

| Account Titles | Trial Balance Dr. | Trial Balance Cr. |
|---|---|---|
| Cash | $12,400 | |
| Accounts Receivable | 5,620 | |
| Supplies | 1,050 | |
| Prepaid Insurance | 2,400 | |
| Equipment | 30,000 | |
| Notes Payable | | $10,000 |
| Accounts Payable | | 12,350 |
| S. Columbo, Capital | | 20,000 |
| S. Columbo, Drawing | 600 | |
| Service Revenue | | 13,620 |
| Salaries Expense | 1,200 | |
| Travel Expense | 1,300 | |
| Rent Expense | 1,200 | |
| Miscellaneous Expense | 200 | |
| | $55,970 | $55,970 |

Other data:

1. Supplies on hand total $750.
2. Depreciation is $400 per quarter.
3. Interest accrued on 6-month note payable, issued January 1, $300.
4. Insurance expires at the rate of $150 per month.
5. Services provided but unbilled at March 31 total $750.

### Instructions

(a) Enter the trial balance on a work sheet and complete the work sheet.
(b) Prepare an income statement and owner's equity statement for the quarter and a classified balance sheet at March 31. S. Columbo did not make any additional investments in the business during the quarter ended March 31, 1999.
(c) Journalize the adjusting entries from the adjustments columns of the work sheet.
(d) Journalize the closing entries from the financial statement columns of the work sheet.

**P4–2B**  The adjusted trial balance columns of the work sheet for Oslo Company is as follows:

*Complete work sheet and prepare financial statements, closing entries, and post-closing trial balance.*
(SO 1, 2, 3, 6)

## OSLO COMPANY
### Work Sheet
### For the Year Ended December 31, 1999

| Account No. | Account Titles | Adjusted Trial Balance Dr. | Adjusted Trial Balance Cr. |
|---|---|---|---|
| 101 | Cash | 22,800 | |
| 112 | Accounts Receivable | 15,400 | |
| 126 | Supplies | 2,300 | |
| 130 | Prepaid Insurance | 4,800 | |
| 151 | Office Equipment | 44,000 | |
| 152 | Accumulated Depreciation—Office Equipment | | 18,000 |
| 200 | Notes Payable | | 20,000 |
| 201 | Accounts Payable | | 8,000 |
| 212 | Salaries Payable | | 3,000 |
| 230 | Interest Payable | | 1,000 |
| 301 | S. Oslo, Capital | | 36,000 |
| 306 | S. Oslo, Drawing | 12,000 | |
| 400 | Service Revenue | | 79,000 |
| 610 | Advertising Expense | 12,000 | |
| 631 | Supplies Expense | 3,700 | |
| 711 | Depreciation Expense | 6,000 | |
| 722 | Insurance Expense | 4,000 | |
| 726 | Salaries Expense | 37,000 | |
| 905 | Interest Expense | 1,000 | |
| | | 165,000 | 165,000 |

*Instructions*

(a)  Complete the work sheet by extending the balances to the financial statement columns.

(b)  Prepare an income statement, owner's equity statement, and a classified balance sheet. $10,000 of the notes payable become due in 2000. S. Oslo did not make any additional investments in the business during 1999.

(c)  Prepare the closing entries. Use J14 for the journal page.

(d)  Post the closing entries and rule and balance the accounts. Use the three-column form of account. Income Summary is No. 350.

(e)  Prepare a post-closing trial balance.

**P4–3B**  The completed financial statement columns of the work sheet for Sierra Company are shown below.

*Prepare financial statements, closing entries, and post-closing trial balance.*
(SO 1, 2, 3, 6)

## SIERRA COMPANY
### Work Sheet
### For the Year Ended December 31, 1999

| Account No. | Account Titles | Income Statement Dr. | Income Statement Cr. | Balance Sheet Dr. | Balance Sheet Cr. |
|---|---|---|---|---|---|
| 101 | Cash | | | 8,200 | |
| 112 | Accounts Receivable | | | 7,500 | |
| 130 | Prepaid Insurance | | | 1,800 | |
| 157 | Equipment | | | 28,000 | |
| 167 | Accumulated Depreciation | | | | 8,600 |
| 201 | Accounts Payable | | | | 12,000 |
| 212 | Salaries Payable | | | | 3,000 |
| 301 | M. Sierra, Capital | | | | 34,000 |
| 306 | M. Sierra, Drawing | | | 7,200 | |

| Account No. | Account Titles | Income Statement Dr. | Income Statement Cr. | Balance Sheet Dr. | Balance Sheet Cr. |
|---|---|---|---|---|---|
| 400 | Service Revenue | | 42,000 | | |
| 622 | Repair Expense | 3,200 | | | |
| 711 | Depreciation Expense | 2,800 | | | |
| 722 | Insurance Expense | 1,200 | | | |
| 726 | Salaries Expense | 36,000 | | | |
| 732 | Utilities Expense | 3,700 | | | |
| | Totals | 46,900 | 42,000 | 52,700 | 57,600 |
| | Net Loss | | 4,900 | 4,900 | |
| | | 46,900 | 46,900 | 57,600 | 57,600 |

*Instructions*
(a) Prepare an income statement, owner's equity statement, and a classified balance sheet. M. Sierra made an additional investment in the business of $4,000 during 1999.
(b) Prepare the closing entries.
(c) Post the closing entries and rule and balance the accounts. Use T accounts. Income Summary is No. 350.
(d) Prepare a post-closing trial balance.

**P4–4B**   Waterworld Amusement Park has a fiscal year ending on September 30. Selected data from the September 30 work sheet are presented below:

*Complete work sheet and prepare classified balance sheet, entries, and post-closing trial balance.*
*(SO 1, 2, 3, 6)*

## WATERWORLD AMUSEMENT PARK
### Work Sheet
### For the Year Ended September 30, 1999

| | Trial Balance Dr. | Trial Balance Cr. | Adjusted Trial Balance Dr. | Adjusted Trial Balance Cr. |
|---|---|---|---|---|
| Cash | 37,400 | | 37,400 | |
| Supplies | 18,600 | | 1,200 | |
| Prepaid Insurance | 31,900 | | 3,900 | |
| Land | 80,000 | | 80,000 | |
| Equipment | 120,000 | | 120,000 | |
| Accumulated Depreciation | | 36,200 | | 43,000 |
| Accounts Payable | | 14,600 | | 14,600 |
| Unearned Admissions Revenue | | 2,700 | | 1,700 |
| Mortgage Payable | | 50,000 | | 50,000 |
| N. Y. Berge, Capital | | 109,700 | | 109,700 |
| N. Y. Berge, Drawing | 14,000 | | 14,000 | |
| Admissions Revenue | | 278,500 | | 279,500 |
| Salaries Expense | 109,000 | | 109,000 | |
| Repair Expense | 30,500 | | 30,500 | |
| Advertising Expense | 9,400 | | 9,400 | |
| Utilities Expense | 16,900 | | 16,900 | |
| Property Taxes Expense | 18,000 | | 21,000 | |
| Interest Expense | 6,000 | | 12,000 | |
| Totals | 491,700 | 491,700 | | |
| Insurance Expense | | | 28,000 | |
| Supplies Expense | | | 17,400 | |
| Interest Payable | | | | 6,000 |
| Depreciation Expense | | | 6,800 | |
| Property Taxes Payable | | | | 3,000 |
| Totals | | | 507,500 | 507,500 |

*Instructions*
(a) Prepare a complete work sheet.
(b) Prepare a classified balance sheet. (Note: $10,000 of the mortgage payable is due for payment in the next fiscal year.)
(c) Journalize the adjusting entries using the work sheet as a basis.
(d) Journalize the closing entries using the work sheet as a basis.
(e) Prepare a post-closing trial balance.

**P4–5B**   Anna Khan opened Anna's Carpet Cleaners on March 1. During March, the following transactions were completed.

*Complete all steps in accounting cycle.*
*(SO 1, 2, 3, 4, 6)*

Mar.  1   Invested $10,000 cash in the business.
      1   Purchased used truck for $6,000, paying $4,000 cash and the balance on account.
      3   Purchased cleaning supplies for $1,200 on account.
      5   Paid $1,800 cash on one-year insurance policy effective March 1.
     14   Billed customers $2,800 for cleaning services.
     18   Paid $1,500 cash on amount owed on truck and $500 on amount owed on cleaning supplies.
     20   Paid $1,500 cash for employee salaries.
     21   Collected $1,600 cash from customers billed on March 14.
     28   Billed customers $3,500 for cleaning services.
     31   Paid gas and oil for month on truck $200.
     31   Withdrew $900 cash for personal use.

The chart of accounts for Anna's Carpet Cleaners contains the following accounts: No. 101 Cash, No. 112 Accounts Receivable, No. 128 Cleaning Supplies, No. 130 Prepaid Insurance, No. 157 Equipment, No. 158 Accumulated Depreciation—Equipment, No. 201 Accounts Payable, No. 212 Salaries Payable, No. 301 A. Khan, Capital, No. 306 A. Khan, Drawing, No. 350 Income Summary, No. 400 Service Revenue, No. 633 Gas & Oil Expense, No. 634 Cleaning Supplies Expense, No. 711 Depreciation Expense, No. 722 Insurance Expense, No. 726 Salaries Expense.

*Instructions*
(a) Journalize and post the March transactions. Use page J1 for the journal and the three-column form of account.
(b) Prepare a trial balance at March 31 on a work sheet.
(c) Enter the following adjustments on the work sheet and complete the work sheet.
    (1) Earned but unbilled revenue at March 31 was $600.
    (2) Depreciation on equipment for the month was $250.
    (3) One-twelfth of the insurance expired.
    (4) An inventory count shows $400 of cleaning supplies on hand at March 31.
    (5) Accrued but unpaid employee salaries were $500.
(d) Prepare the income statement and owner's equity statement for March and a classified balance sheet at March 31.
(e) Journalize and post adjusting entries. Use page J2 for the journal.
(f) Journalize and post closing entries and complete the closing process. Use page J3 for the journal.
(g) Prepare a post-closing trial balance at March 31.

## BROADENING YOUR PERSPECTIVE

# FINANCIAL REPORTING AND ANALYSIS

### FINANCIAL REPORTING PROBLEM: Kellogg Company

**BYP4–1**   The financial statements of Kellogg Company are presented in Appendix A at the end of this textbook.

*Instructions*
Answer the following questions using the Consolidated Balance Sheet and the Notes to Consolidated Financial Statements section.

  (a)   What were Kellogg's total current assets at December 31, 1997, and 1996?
  (b)   Are assets that Kellogg included under current assets listed in proper order? Explain.
  (c)   How are Kellogg's assets classified?
  (d)   What are "cash equivalents"?
  (e)   What were Kellogg's total current liabilities at December 31, 1997, and 1996?

### COMPARATIVE ANALYSIS PROBLEM: Kellogg Company vs. General Mills

**BYP4–2**   Kellogg's financial statements are presented in Appendix A; General Mills's financial statements are presented in Appendix B.

*Instructions*

  (a)   Based on the information contained in these financial statements, determine each of the following for Kellogg at December 31, 1997 and for General Mills at May 25, 1997:
     1.   Total current assets.
     2.   Net amount of property, plant, and equipment (land, buildings, and equipment).
     3.   Total current liabilities.
     4.   Total stockholders' (shareholders') equity.
  (b)   What conclusions concerning the companies' respective financial positions can be drawn from these data?

### RESEARCH ASSIGNMENT

**BYP4–3**   The March 1995 issue of *Management Review* includes an article by Barbara Ettorre, entitled "How Motorola Closes Its Books in Two Days."

*Instructions*
Read the article and answer the following questions.

  (a)   How often does Motorola close its books? How long did the process used to take?
  (b)   What was the major change Motorola initiated to shorten the closing process?
  (c)   What incentive does Motorola offer to ensure accurate and timely information?
  (d)   In a given year, how many journal entry lines does Motorola process?
  (e)   Provide an example of an external force that prevents Motorola from closing faster than a day-and-a-half.
  (f)   According to Motorola's corporate vice president and controller, how do external financial statement users perceive companies that release information early?

### INTERPRETING FINANCIAL STATEMENTS: Case Corporation

**BYP4–4**   Case Corporation, based in Racine, Wisconsin, manufactures farm tractors, farm equipment, and light- and medium-sized construction equipment. The company's products are distributed through both independent and company-owned distributing companies, which are located throughout the world. Case Corporation's partial income statement is shown on the next page.

### CASE CORPORATION
### Income Statement (partial)
### (in millions)

| | |
|---|---:|
| Revenues | |
| Net sales | $ 5,796 |
| Interest income and other | 228 |
| | 6,024 |
| Costs and expenses | |
| Cost of goods sold | 4,447 |
| Selling, general, and administrative | 570 |
| Research, development, and engineering | 196 |
| Interest expense | 170 |
| Other, net | 47 |
| | 5,430 |
| Income from operations before taxes | $   594 |

The internal audit staff identified the following items that require adjustments:
1. Depreciation on the administrative offices of $13 million needs to be recorded.
2. A physical inventory determined that $1 million in office supplies had been used during the year.
3. $4 million in salaries have been earned but not recorded, and half this amount is for the salaries of the engineering staff; the other half is for the administrative staff.
4. $3 million in annual insurance premiums were prepaid on May 1.
5. $7 million in prepaid rent has expired at year-end.
6. Cost of goods sold of $2 million was recorded in error as interest expense.

Assume that the partial income statement above was prepared before all adjusting entries had been made.

*Instructions*
(a) Make the adjusting journal entries required. Use standard account titles with prepayments having been recorded as assets.
(b) Which of the entries is not a routine adjusting entry? Explain your answer.
(c) For each of the accounts in these adjusting entries that will be posted to Case's general ledger, tell which item on the income statement will be increased or decreased.
(d) Recast the partial income statement based on the adjusting entries prepared.

## REAL-WORLD FOCUS: Bethlehem Corporation

**BYP4–5**   Located in Easton, Pennsylvania, **Bethlehem Corporation** was established in 1856. Today it offers contract services for industrial products, rebuilding and remanufacturing industrial and military equipment per customer specifications and designs. The company also manufactures and sells a line of equipment used in the chemical, environmental, and food industries.

Bethlehem Corporation had a net loss for the year of $239,251. One reason for the loss is that Bethlehem established an accrual to provide for expenses and costs associated with certain legal proceedings against Bethlehem.

*Instructions*
(a) Indicate how the net loss would be shown in Bethlehem's work sheet.
(b) Where in the general ledger would you expect to find the two accounts related to the accrual for expenses and costs associated with legal proceedings?
(c) Identify the financial statement columns to which the balances of the two accounts in part (b) would be extended on the work sheet.

# CRITICAL THINKING

## GROUP DECISION CASE

**BYP4–6**   Cleanfast Janitorial Service was started 2 years ago by Pat Hardy. Because business has been exceptionally good, Pat decided on July 1, 1999, to expand operations by acquiring an additional truck and hiring two more assistants. To finance the expansion, Pat obtained on July 1, 1999, a $25,000, 10% bank loan, payable $10,000 on July 1, 2000, and the balance on July 1, 2001. The terms of the loan require the borrower to have $10,000 more current assets than current liabilities at December 31, 1999. If these terms are not met, the bank loan will be refinanced at 15% interest. At December 31, 1999, the accountant for Cleanfast Janitorial Service Inc. prepared the following balance sheet:

**CLEANFAST JANITORIAL SERVICE**
**Balance Sheet**
**December 31, 1999**

**Assets**

| | | |
|---|---:|---:|
| Current assets | | |
| Cash | | $ 6,500 |
| Accounts receivable | | 9,000 |
| Janitorial supplies | | 5,200 |
| Prepaid insurance | | 4,800 |
| Total current assets | | 25,500 |
| Property, plant, and equipment | | |
| Cleaning equipment (net) | $22,000 | |
| Delivery trucks (net) | 34,000 | 56,000 |
| Total assets | | $81,500 |

**Liabilities and Owner's Equity**

| | |
|---|---:|
| Current liabilities | |
| Notes payable | $10,000 |
| Accounts payable | 2,500 |
| Total current liabilities | 12,500 |
| Long-term liability | |
| Notes payable | 15,000 |
| Total liabilities | 27,500 |
| Owner's equity | |
| Pat Hardy, capital | 54,000 |
| Total liabilities and owner's equity | $81,500 |

Pat presented the balance sheet to the bank's loan office on January 2, 2000, confident that the company had met the terms of the loan. The loan officer was not impressed. She said, "We need financial statements audited by a CPA." A CPA was hired and immediately realized that the balance sheet had been prepared from a trial balance and not from an adjusted trial balance. The adjustment data at the balance sheet date consisted of the following:

1. Earned but unbilled janitorial services were $3,000.
2. Janitorial supplies on hand were $3,500.
3. Prepaid insurance was a 3-year policy dated January 1, 1999.
4. December expenses incurred but unpaid at December 31, $300.
5. Interest on the bank loan was not recorded.
6. The amounts for plant assets were net of accumulated depreciation of $4,000 for cleaning equipment and $5,000 for delivery trucks as of January 1, 1999. Depreciation for 1999 was $2,000 for cleaning equipment and $5,000 for delivery trucks.

*Instructions*

With the class divided into groups, answer the following:

(a) Prepare a correct balance sheet.
(b) Were the terms of the bank loan met? Explain.

## COMMUNICATION ACTIVITY

**BYP4–7**   The accounting cycle is important in understanding the accounting process.

*Instructions*

Write a memorandum to your instructor which lists the steps of the accounting cycle in the order in which they should be completed. Complete your memorandum with a paragraph that explains the optional steps in the cycle.

## ETHICS CASE

**BYP4–8**   As the controller of Magnus Perfume Company, you discover a misstatement that overstated net income in the prior year's financial statements. The misleading financial statements appear in the company's annual report which was issued to banks and other creditors less than a month ago. After much thought about the consequences of telling the president, David Rudman, about this misstatement, you gather your courage to inform him. David says, "Hey! What they don't know won't hurt them. But, just so we set the record straight, we'll adjust this year's financial statements for last year's misstatement. We can absorb that misstatement better in this year than in last year anyway! Just don't make such a mistake again."

*Instructions*

(a) Who are the stakeholders in this situation?
(b) What are the ethical issues in this situation?
(c) What would you do as a controller in this situation?

# SURFING THE NET

**BYP4–9**   Numerous companies have established home pages on the Internet, e.g., Boston Beer Company (http://www.samadams.com), Ford Motor Company (http://www.ford.com), and Kodak (http://www.kodak.com). You may have noticed company Internet addresses in television commercials or magazine advertisements.

*Instructions*

Examine the home pages of any two companies and answer the following questions.

(a) What type of information is available?
(b) Is any accounting-related information presented?
(c) Would you describe the home page as informative, promotional, or both? Why?

---

*Answers to Self-Study Questions*

1. b   2. c   3. a   4. b   5. c   6. a   7. d   8. b   9. d   10. a   11. c

---

*Answers to Kellogg Review It Question 2, p. 162*

Current liabilities in 1997 were $1,657.3 million and current liabilities in 1996 were $2,199.0 million. In both 1997 and 1996, current liabilities were greater than current assets.

 **Remember to go back to the Navigator box on the chapter-opening page and check off your completed work.**

## CONCEPTS FOR REVIEW

**Before studying this chapter, you should know or, if necessary, review:**

a. How to prepare a work sheet. (Ch. 4, pp. 141–43)
b. How to close revenue, expense, and drawing accounts. (Ch. 4, pp. 146–50)
c. The steps in the accounting cycle. (Ch. 4, p. 154)

THE
NAVIGATOR

## FEATURE STORY

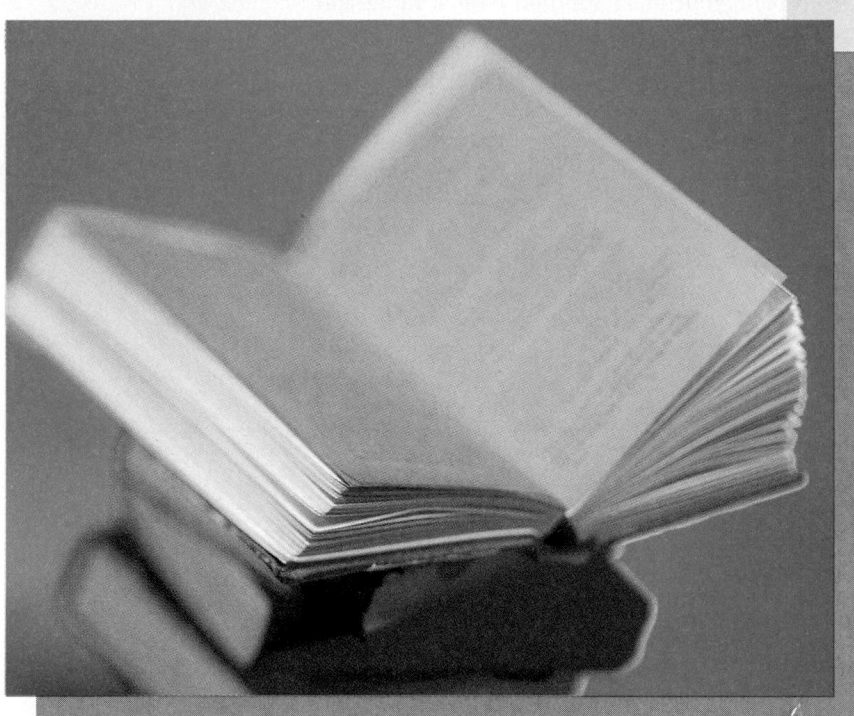

# Dropped Courses Produce Bookstore Headaches

Larry Martin is in charge of ordering textbooks for the Washington State University bookstore in Pullman,

Washington. The bookstore sells about $4 million in textbooks each year. The average inventory at any point in time is 2,500 titles.

Mr. Martin's big challenge is to order enough books to satisfy demand—but not to order too many. For example, say a course historically has sold 75 books; he'll order 85 to

be on the safe side. The reason: if he orders short, he'll have to order additional books by second-day air express—which is expensive and cuts into profits. However, if Martin orders too many, the publisher won't accept for return more than 20% of his original order.

Of course, returns occur all the time, especially when students drop courses during the first week of class. If the returned books are in "new and resalable" condition, the publisher will accept the return of such books and issue Martin a credit memo.

Washington State University starts its fall term before Labor Day. The busy book selling and return period lasts three to four weeks. Therefore, Martin waits until the end of September to take the inventory and determine his returns. That count verifies the accuracy of his computerized perpetual inventory accounting system. At that point, he is ready to order more books.

THE
NAVIGATOR

# CHAPTER 5

**THE NAVIGATOR** ✔

- Understand *Concepts for Review* ☐
- Read *Feature Story* ☐
- Scan *Study Objectives* ☐
- Read *Preview* ☐
- Read text and answer *Before You Go On*
  p. 196 ☐  p. 201 ☐  p. 207 ☐  p. 210 ☐
- Work *Demonstration Problem* ☐
- Review *Summary of Study Objectives* ☐
- Answer *Self-Study Questions* ☐
- Complete assignments ☐

# ACCOUNTING FOR MERCHANDISING OPERATIONS

## STUDY OBJECTIVES

**After studying this chapter, you should be able to:**

1. *Identify the differences between a service enterprise and a merchandising company.*
2. *Explain the entries for purchases under a perpetual inventory system.*
3. *Explain the entries for sales revenues under a perpetual inventory system.*
4. *Explain the computation and importance of gross profit.*
5. *Identify the features of the income statement for a merchandising company.*
6. *Explain the steps in the accounting cycle for a merchandising company.*
7. *Distinguish between a multiple-step and a single-step income statement.*

THE NAVIGATOR

*A*s indicated in the opening story, Washington State University Bookstore earns a profit by selling goods to customers rather than performing services. Merchandising companies that purchase and sell directly to consumers—such as Kmart, Washington State Bookstore, Safeway, and Toys "R" Us—are called **retailers**. In contrast, merchandising companies that sell to retailers are known as **wholesalers**. For example, retailer Walgreens might buy goods from wholesaler McKesson & Robbins; Office Depot might buy office supplies from wholesaler United Stationers.

The steps in the accounting cycle for a merchandising company are the same as the steps for a service enterprise. However, merchandising companies use additional accounts and entries which are required in recording merchandising transactions. The content and organization of this chapter are as follows:

THE NAVIGATOR

# MERCHANDISING OPERATIONS

**1**

STUDY

OBJECTIVE

Identify the differences between a service enterprise and a merchandising company.

Measuring net income for a merchandising company is conceptually the same as for a service enterprise. That is, net income (or loss) results from the matching of expenses with revenues. In a merchandising company, the primary source of revenues is the sale of merchandise, often referred to as sales revenue or sales. Unlike expenses for a service company, expenses for a merchandising company are divided into two categories: (1) the cost of goods sold and (2) operating expenses.

The cost of goods sold is the total cost of merchandise sold during the period. This expense is directly related to the revenue recognized from the sale of the goods. Sales revenue less cost of goods sold is called gross profit on sales. For example, when a calculator costing $15 is sold for $25, the gross profit is $10. Merchandising companies report gross profit on sales in the income statement.

After gross profit is calculated, operating expenses are deducted to determine net income (or loss). Operating expenses are expenses incurred in the process of earning sales revenue. Examples of operating expenses are sales salaries, advertising expense, and insurance expense. The operating expenses of a merchandising company include many of the expenses found in a service enterprise.

The income measurement process for a merchandiser may be diagrammed as shown in Illustration 5-1. The items in the three blue boxes are peculiar to a merchandising company; they are not used by a service company.

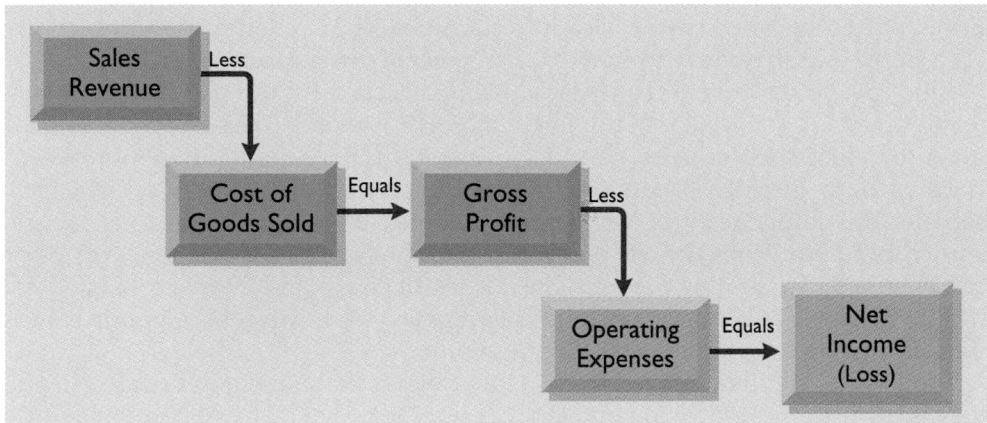

**ILLUSTRATION 5-1**

*Income measurement process for a merchandising company*

## Operating Cycles

While measuring income for a merchandising company is conceptually the same as for a service company, their operating cycles differ, as shown in Illustration 5-2. The operating cycle of a merchandising company ordinarily is longer than

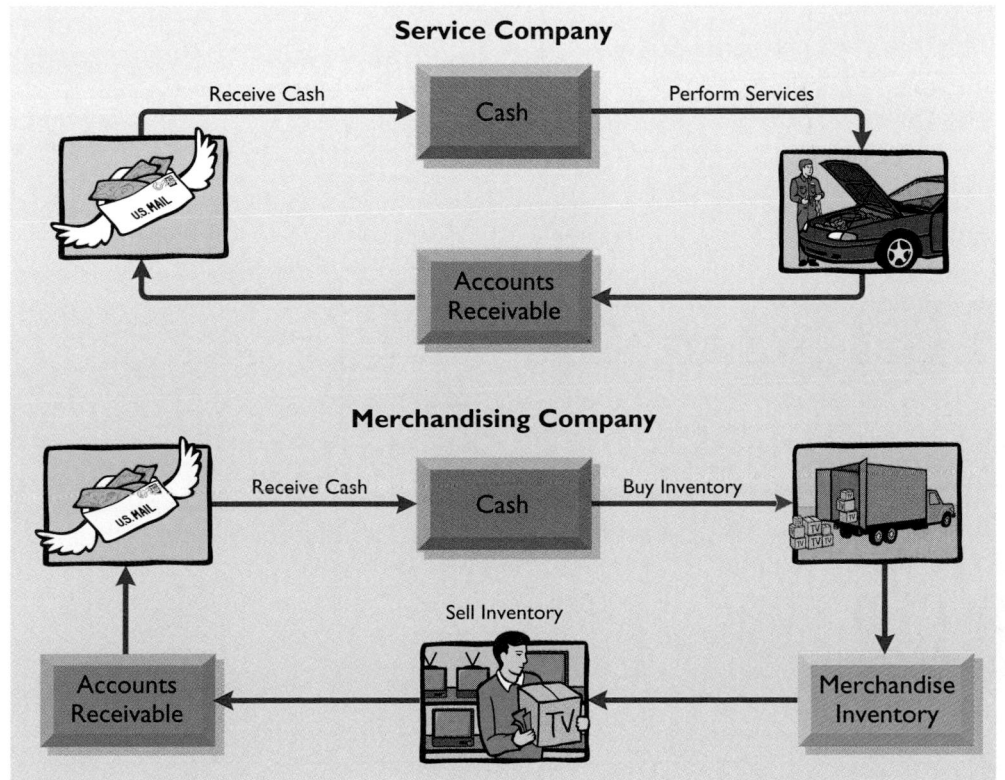

**ILLUSTRATION 5-2**

*Operating cycles for a service company and a merchandising company*

that of a service company. The purchase of merchandise inventory and its eventual sale lengthens the cycle. Note that the added asset account for a merchandising company is an **inventory** account (usually entitled Merchandise Inventory). Merchandise inventory is reported as a current asset on the balance sheet.

## Inventory Systems

Either of two systems may be used in accounting for merchandising transactions: (1) a **perpetual inventory system** or (2) a **periodic inventory system**.

In a perpetual inventory system, detailed records of the cost of each inventory purchase and sale are maintained and continuously (perpetually) show the inventory that should be on hand for every item. A perpetual inventory keeps track of both **quantities and costs**. For example, a Ford dealership will have separate inventory records for each automobile, truck, and van on its lot and showroom floor. With the use of bar codes and optical scanners, a grocery store can keep a daily running record of every box of cereal and every jar of jelly that it buys and sells. **Under a perpetual inventory system the cost of goods sold is determined and recorded each time a sale occurs.**

In a periodic inventory system, no attempt is made to keep detailed inventory records of the goods on hand throughout the period. **The cost of goods sold is determined only at the end of the accounting period when a physical inventory count is taken to determine the cost of goods on hand.**

To determine the cost of goods sold under a periodic inventory system, it is necessary to (1) record purchases of merchandise, (2) determine the cost of goods purchased, and (3) determine the cost of goods on hand at the beginning and end of the accounting period.

Illustration 5-3 graphically compares the sequence of activities and the timing of the cost of goods sold computation under the two inventory systems.

**ILLUSTRATION 5-3**

*Comparing perpetual to periodic inventory*

Some businesses employ the periodic system because they can control merchandise and manage day-to-day operations without detailed inventory records. In addition, perpetual systems are in many cases more expensive.

Under a perpetual inventory system, inventory shrinkage and lost or stolen goods are more readily determined. Also, reorder decisions are more accurately made under a perpetual system because exact inventory levels are known constantly. Because the perpetual inventory system is growing in popularity, we illustrate it in this chapter. The periodic system is described in Chapter 9.

# MERCHANDISING TRANSACTIONS

Recording merchandising transactions requires the analysis of purchases and sales of merchandise. Related to both purchases and sales are returns and allowances, discounts, and transportation costs.

## Recording Purchases

Purchases may be made for cash or on account (credit). Purchases are normally recorded when the goods are received from the supplier. Every purchase should be supported by business documents that provide written evidence of the transaction. Cash purchases should be supported by canceled checks or cash register receipts indicating the items purchased and amounts paid. Credit purchases should be supported by an **invoice**, like the one shown in Illustration 5-4, that indicates the items purchased and the total purchase price. An invoice is a document prepared by the seller that shows the relevant information about a sale. From the seller's perspective this document is a sales invoice, and from the buyer's perspective it is a purchase invoice.

Illustration 5-4 shows a sales invoice prepared by Highpoint Electronic to document a sale to Chelsea Video. Chelsea Video will use this as a purchase invoice to document the purchase from Highpoint. Chelsea will make the following entry to record the purchase of merchandise from Highpoint:

> **2**
> STUDY
> OBJECTIVE
> ..........................
> Explain the entries for purchases under a perpetual inventory system.

| May 4 | Merchandise Inventory | 3,800 | |
|---|---|---|---|
| | Accounts Payable | | 3,800 |
| | (To record goods purchased on account, terms 2/10, n/30, from Highpoint Electronic) | | |

| A | = | L | + | OE |
|---|---|---|---|---|
| +3,800 | | +3,800 | | |

Under the perpetual inventory system, purchases of merchandise for sale are recorded in the Merchandise Inventory account. Thus, Larry Martin, as manager of the Washington State University Bookstore, would **debit Merchandise Inventory for books purchased for resale to students**. However, not all purchases are debited to Merchandise Inventory. Purchases of assets acquired for use and not for resale, such as supplies, equipment, and similar items, should be **debited to specific asset accounts rather than to Merchandise Inventory**. For example, Larry Martin would debit Supplies for the supplies he buys to make shelf signs and labels that identify which books are for which courses.

### Purchase Returns and Allowances

A purchaser may be dissatisfied with the merchandise received because the goods are damaged or defective, of inferior quality, or not in accord with the purchaser's specifications. In such cases, the purchaser may return the goods to

**ILLUSTRATION 5-4**

*Invoice*

**HELPFUL HINT**

To better understand the contents of this invoice, identify the:
(1) Seller.
(2) Invoice date.
(3) Purchaser.
(4) Salesperson.
(5) Credit terms.
(6) Freight terms.
(7) Goods sold:
　　Catalogue no.
　　Description.
　　Quantity.
　　Price per unit.
(8) Total invoice amount.

---

**INVOICE NO. 731**

## HIGHPOINT ELECTRONIC
### 27 CIRCLE DRIVE
### HARDING, MICHIGAN 48281

| S O L D  T O | | |
|---|---|---|
| Firm Name | Chelsea Video | |
| Attention of | James Hoover, Purchasing Agent | |
| Address | 125 Main Street | |
| Chelsea | Illinois | 60915 |
| City | State | Zip |

| Date 5/4/99 | Salesperson Malone | Terms 2/10, n/30 | Freight FOB Sh.Pt. | | |
|---|---|---|---|---|---|
| Catalogue No. | Description | | Quantity | Price | Amount |
| X572Y9820 | Printed Circuit Board-prototype | | 1 | 2,300 | $2,300 |
| A2547Z45 | Production Model Circuits | | 5 | 300 | 1,500 |

| **IMPORTANT:** ALL RETURNS MUST BE MADE WITHIN 10 DAYS | **TOTAL** | **$3,800** |
|---|---|---|

---

the supplier for credit if the sale was made on credit, or for a cash refund if the purchase was originally for cash. This transaction is known as a **purchase return**. Alternatively, the purchaser may choose to keep the merchandise if the supplier is willing to grant an allowance (deduction) from the purchase price. This transaction is known as a **purchase allowance**.

The purchaser initiates the request for a reduction of the balance due through the issuance of a debit memorandum. A debit memorandum is a document issued by a purchaser to inform a supplier that a debit has been made to the supplier's account on the purchaser's books. The original copy of the memorandum is sent to the supplier and one copy is retained by the purchaser. The information contained in a debit memorandum is shown in Illustration 5-5; it relates to the sales invoice shown in Illustration 5-4.

The entry by Chelsea Video for the merchandise returned to Highpoint Electronic on May 8 is:

| A | = | L | + | OE |
|---|---|---|---|---|
| −300 | | −300 | | |

| May 8 | Accounts Payable | 300 | |
|---|---|---|---|
| | 　Merchandise Inventory | | 300 |
| | 　(To record return of inoperable goods received from Highpoint Electronic, DM No. 126) | | |

**ILLUSTRATION 5-5**

*Debit memorandum*

DEBIT-DM126

## CHELSEA VIDEO
### 125 MAIN STREET
### CHELSEA, IL 60915

**Purchased From:**

Firm Name ___Highpoint Electronic___

Attention of ___Susan Malone, Sales Representative___

Address ___27 Circle Drive___

| Harding | MI | 48281 |
|---|---|---|
| City | State | Zip |

| Date 5/8/99 | Salesperson Malone | Invoice No. 731 | Invoice Date 5/4/99 | Approved Reid |
|---|---|---|---|---|

| Catalogue No. | Description | Quantity | Price | Amount |
|---|---|---|---|---|
| A2547Z45 | Production Model Circuits (Inoperative) | 1 | 300 | $300 |

Cash Refund ☐   Debit Account ☒   Other ☐

Because Merchandise Inventory was debited when the goods were received, Merchandise Inventory is credited when the goods are returned.

## Purchase Discounts

The credit terms of a purchase on account may permit the purchaser to claim a cash discount for the prompt payment of a balance due. The purchaser calls this cash discount a purchase discount. This incentive offers advantages to both parties: The purchaser saves money, and the supplier is able to convert the accounts receivable into cash earlier.

The **credit terms** specify the amount and time period for the cash discount. They also indicate the length of time in which the purchaser is expected to pay the full invoice price. In the sales invoice in Illustration 5-4, credit terms are 2/10, n/30, which is read "two-ten, net thirty." This means that a 2% cash discount may be taken on the invoice price (less any returns or allowances) if payment is made within 10 days of the invoice date (the **discount period**); otherwise, the invoice price less any returns or allowances is due 30 days from the invoice date. Alternatively, the discount period may extend to a specified number of days following the month in which the sale occurs. For example, 1/10 EOM (end-of-month) means that a 1% discount is available if the invoice is paid within the first 10 days of the next month.

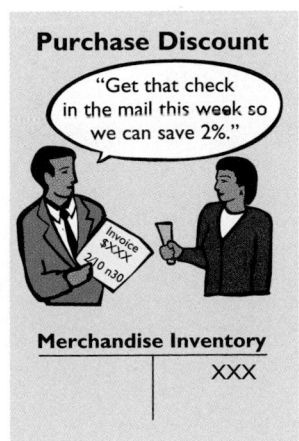

**Purchase Discount**

"Get that check in the mail this week so we can save 2%."

**Merchandise Inventory**

XXX

**HELPFUL HINT**
Assume goods were sold on June 1, terms 1/10, net 30. Question: What is the due date for taking the discount? Answer: June 11. Question: If the terms were 2/10 EOM, what is the due date for taking the discount? Answer: July 10.

When the supplier elects not to offer a cash discount for prompt payment, credit terms will specify only the maximum time period for paying the balance due. For example, the time period may be stated as n/30, n/60, or n/10 EOM.

When an invoice is paid within the discount period, the amount of the discount is credited to Merchandise Inventory. To illustrate, assume Chelsea Video pays the balance due of $3,500 (gross invoice price of $3,800 less purchase returns and allowances of $300) on May 14, the last day of the discount period. The cash discount is $70 ($3,500 × 2%), and the amount of cash paid by Chelsea Video is $3,430 ($3,500 − $70). The entry to record the May 14 payment by Chelsea Video is as follows:

| A | = | L | + | OE |
|---|---|---|---|---|
| −3,430 | | −3,500 | | |
| −70 | | | | |

| May 14 | Accounts Payable | 3,500 | |
| |     Cash | | 3,430 |
| |     Merchandise Inventory | | 70 |
| |     (To record payment within discount period) | | |

If Chelsea Video had failed to take the discount and full payment is made on June 3, Chelsea would have made the following entry:

| A | = | L | + | OE |
|---|---|---|---|---|
| −3,500 | | −3,500 | | |

| June 3 | Accounts Payable | 3,500 | |
| |     Cash | | 3,500 |
| |     (To record payment with no discount taken) | | |

## ACCOUNTING IN ACTION
### Business Insight

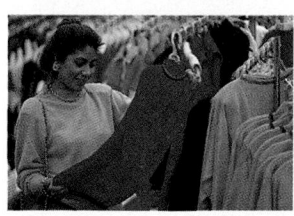

In the early 1990s, Sears wielded its retail clout by telling its suppliers that, rather than pay its obligations in the standard 30-day period, it would now pay in 60 days. This practice is often adopted by firms that are experiencing financial distress from a shortage of cash. A Sears spokesperson insisted, however, that Sears did not have cash problems, but, rather, was simply utilizing "vendor-financed inventory methods to improve its return on investment." Supplier trade groups criticized Sears' policy, and pointed out that consumers would be the ultimate victims, because the financing costs would eventually be passed on to them.

**HELPFUL HINT**
So as not to miss purchase discounts, unpaid invoices should be filed (electronically or manually) by due dates. This procedure helps the purchaser remember the discount date, prevents early payment of bills, and maximizes the time that cash can be used for other purposes.

A buyer usually should take all available discounts. For example, if Chelsea Video takes the discount, it pays $3,430 instead of $3,500, thus saving $70. If it does not take the discount and invests the $3,430 in a bank savings account for 20 days (30 − 10) at 10% interest, it will earn only $19.06 in interest.[1] The savings obtained by taking the discount is computed as follows:

---

[1]If Chelsea Video does not pay at the end of 10 days, it has the use of $3,430 for an additional 20 days at a cost (lost discount) of $70. For the 20-day period, the interest rate on the $3,430 is effectively 2.04% ($70 ÷ $3,430). Interest rates are generally expressed on an annualized basis of 360 days; thus Highpoint Electronic's discount terms are equivalent to 36.72% (360/20 × 2.04%). In view of this high interest rate, it would be better for Chelsea Video to take the discount.

| Discount of 2% on $3,500 | $70.00 |
| Interest received on $3,430 | |
| (for 20 days at 10%) | 19.06 |
| **Savings by taking the discount** | **$50.94** |

**ILLUSTRATION 5-6**

*Savings obtained by taking purchase discount*

## Freight Costs

The sales agreement should indicate whether the seller or the buyer is to pay the cost of transporting the goods to the buyer's place of business. When a common carrier such as a railroad, trucking company, or airline is used, the transportation company prepares a freight bill (often called a bill of lading) in accordance with the sales agreement. Freight terms are expressed as either **FOB shipping point** or **FOB destination**. The letters FOB mean **free on board**. Thus, FOB shipping point means that goods are placed free on board the carrier by the seller, and the buyer pays the freight costs. Conversely, FOB destination means that the goods are placed free on board to the buyer's place of business, and the seller pays the freight. For example, the sales invoice in Illustration 5-4 on page 192 indicates that freight is FOB shipping point. Thus, the buyer (Chelsea Video) pays the freight charges.

When the purchaser directly incurs the freight costs, the account Merchandise Inventory is debited. For example, if upon delivery of the goods on May 6, Chelsea Video pays Acme Freight Company $150 for freight charges, the entry on Chelsea's books is:

**HELPFUL HINT**
Freight terms may be stated by location. A Chicago seller may use "FOB Chicago" for FOB shipping point and the buyer's city for FOB destination.

| May 6 | Merchandise Inventory | 150 | |
| | Cash | | 150 |
| | (To record payment of freight, terms FOB | | |
| | shipping point) | | |

| A | = | L | + | OE |
| +150 | | | | |
| −150 | | | | |

In contrast, **freight costs incurred by the seller on outgoing merchandise are an operating expense to the seller**. These costs are debited to Freight-out or Delivery Expense. For example, if the freight terms on invoice no. 731 in Illustration 5-4 had specified FOB destination and Highpoint Electronic paid the $150 freight charges, the entry by Highpoint would be:

**HELPFUL HINT**
The freight cost under the terms FOB shipping point and paid by Chelsea does not enter into the computation of the discount shown above.

| May 4 | Freight-out (Delivery Expense) | 150 | |
| | Cash | | 150 |
| | (To record payment of freight on goods | | |
| | sold FOB destination) | | |

| A | = | L | + | OE |
| −150 | | | | −150 |

When the freight charges are paid by the seller, the seller will usually establish a higher invoice price for the goods, to cover the expense of shipping.

## Alternative Accounting for Returns and Allowances, Discounts, and Freight Costs

A business manager may want to keep detailed records of returns and allowances, discounts, and freight costs related to purchases of merchandise. For example, if management wishes to know the amount saved through cash discounts on purchases of merchandise, the amount of discounts taken can be accumulated in a separate Purchase Discounts account. Or, if management wishes to keep track of the purchase returns and allowances due to defective, inferior quality, or damaged goods, a special account, Purchase Returns and Allowances, may be credited to serve as a running record of such transactions. And, Freight-in could be debited for transportation costs on purchased merchandise. In order to report Merchandise Inventory at total cost in the financial statements, these separate accounts may be combined with the amount in Merchandise Inventory as follows:

| | | |
|---|---:|---:|
| Merchandise Inventory | | $XXXX |
| **Less: Purchase Returns and Allowances** | $XXX | |
| Purchase Discounts | XXX | XXX |
| Net purchases of merchandise inventory | | XXXX |
| **Add: Freight-in** | | XXX |
| Total cost of merchandise inventory | | $XXXX |

# BEFORE YOU GO ON . . .

## Review It

1. How do the components used in measuring net income in a merchandising company differ from those in a service enterprise?
2. In what ways is a perpetual inventory system different from a periodic inventory system?
3. What entries are made to record purchases of inventory, purchase returns and allowances, purchase discounts, and freight-in under a perpetual inventory system?
4. What is an alternative method of accounting for purchase returns and allowances, discounts, and freight costs?

THE NAVIGATOR

# Recording Sales

**3**
STUDY
OBJECTIVE
.................
Explain the entries for sales revenues under a perpetual inventory system.

Sales revenues, like service revenues, are recorded when earned. This is in accordance with the revenue recognition principle. Typically, sales revenues are earned when the goods are transferred from the seller to the buyer. At this point, the sales transaction is completed and the sales price is established.

Sales may be made on credit or for cash. Every sales transaction should be supported by a **business document** that provides written evidence of the sale. **Cash register tapes** provide evidence of cash sales. A sales invoice, like the one shown in Illustration 5-4, provides support for a credit sale. The original copy of the invoice goes to the customer, and a copy is kept by the seller for use in recording the sale. The invoice shows the date of sale, customer name, total sales price, and other relevant information.

For cash sales, the Cash account is debited and the Sales account is credited; and, under the perpetual inventory system, the **cost of the merchandise sold** and the **reduction in merchandise inventory** are also recorded. Therefore, two entries are made for each sale, one at the selling price of the goods and the other at the cost of the goods sold. For example, assume that on May 4 Highpoint Electronic has cash sales of $2,200 from merchandise having a cost of $1,400. The entries to record the day's cash sales are as follows:

| A | = | L | + | OE |
|---|---|---|---|---|
| +2,200 | | | | +2,200 |

| | | | | |
|---|---|---|---:|---:|
| May 4 | Cash | | 2,200 | |
| | Sales | | | 2,220 |
| | (To record daily cash sales) | | | |

| A | = | L | + | OE |
|---|---|---|---|---|
| −1,400 | | | | −1,400 |

| | | | | |
|---|---|---|---:|---:|
| 4 | Cost of Goods Sold | | 1,400 | |
| | Merchandise Inventory | | | 1,400 |
| | (To record cost of merchandise sold for cash) | | | |

For credit sales, Accounts Receivable is debited and Sales is credited; and, Cost of Goods Sold is debited and Merchandise Inventory is credited. In this way, under a perpetual inventory system, the Merchandise Inventory account will show at all times the amount of inventory that should be on hand. To illustrate a credit sales transaction, Highpoint Electronic's sales of $3,800 per invoice No. 731 (Illustration 5-4) of May 4 to Chelsea Video would be recorded as follows (assume the merchandise cost Highpoint $2,400):

**ALTERNATIVE TERMINOLOGY**
Credit sales are sometimes referred to as *charge sales* or *sales on account*.

| May 4 | Accounts Receivable | 3,800 | |
| | Sales | | 3,800 |
| | (To record credit sale to Chelsea Video per invoice #731) | | |
| 4 | Cost of Goods Sold | 2,400 | |
| | Merchandise Inventory | | 2,400 |
| | (To record cost of merchandise sold on invoice #731 to Chelsea Video) | | |

| A | = | L | + | OE |
|---|---|---|---|---|
| +3,800 | | | | +3,800 |

| A | = | L | + | OE |
|---|---|---|---|---|
| −2,400 | | | | −2,400 |

Merchandising companies may use more than one sales account. For example, Highpoint Electronic may decide to keep separate sales accounts for its sales of television sets, videocassette recorders, and microwave ovens. Because sales are the principal source of revenue for a merchandising company, the amount and trend of sales are of critical importance. For example, an increase in sales from the preceding year signifies a growing business and often leads to higher net income. A decrease in sales may suggest an unfavorable trend, and, therefore, lower future earnings.

**HELPFUL HINT**
The Sales account is credited only for sales of goods held for resale. Sales of assets not held for resale, such as equipment or land, are credited directly to the asset account.

# ACCOUNTING IN ACTION
## Ethics Insight

Inventory losses can be substantial. Shoplifting is a big crime in the United States, with a cost of more than $18 billion annually, or 5% of retail sales, not including thefts by store employees. Shoplifting losses have led to the demise of many companies. For example, Dayton-Hudson closed its landmark store in downtown Detroit, in part, because of excessive shoplifting losses. Many department stores are trying to reduce shoplifting losses by use of electronic tags on merchandise and by continuous surveillance of customers on closed circuit television.

## Sales Returns and Allowances

A purchase return and allowance on the purchaser's books is recorded as a **sales return and allowance** on the books of the seller. To grant the customer a sales return or allowance, the seller normally prepares a credit memorandum. This document informs a customer that a credit has been made to the customer's account receivable for a sales return or allowance. The information contained in a credit memorandum is similar to the information found in the debit memorandum in Illustration 5-5 (p. 193). The original copy of the credit memorandum is sent to the customer, and a copy is kept by the seller as evidence of the transaction. Highpoint's entries to record a credit memorandum for returned goods involve (1) a debit to Sales Returns and Allowances and a credit to Accounts Receivable at the $300 selling price, and (2) a debit to Merchandise Inventory (assume a $140 cost) and a credit to Cost of Goods Sold as follows:

**ETHICS NOTE**
Large retailers of electronics often have generous return policies, allowing returns for any reason within the first 30 days. Unfortunately, unscrupulous customers will "buy" video cameras or large stereos for special events such as weddings, use them, and then return them after the event. The retailer suffers a loss because they must then sell the item as returned merchandise.

| | | | | |
|---|---|---|---|---|
| A | = L | + | OE | |
| −300 | | | −300 | |

| May 8 | Sales Returns and Allowances | 300 | |
|---|---|---|---|
| | Accounts Receivable | | 300 |
| | (To record return of inoperable goods delivered to Chelsea Video, per credit memorandum) | | |

| | | | | |
|---|---|---|---|---|
| A | = L | + | OE | |
| +140 | | | +140 | |

| 8 | Merchandise Inventory | 140 | |
|---|---|---|---|
| | Cost of Goods Sold | | 140 |
| | (To record cost of goods returned per credit memorandum) | | |

When a sales allowance for damaged goods is granted on a **credit sale**, no entry to inventory and cost of goods sold is necessary because the supplier receives no returned goods from the customer. As shown in the first entry above, the supplier debits Sales Returns and Allowances and credits Accounts Receivable for the damaged goods allowance.

When goods are returned or an allowance is made on a **cash sale**, the supplier normally provides a cash refund and debits Sales Returns and Allowances and credits Cash. If the supplier **receives returned merchandise** in good condition, a second entry is made debiting Merchandise Inventory and crediting Cost of Goods Sold at cost. If the supplier grants an allowance and the **merchandise is not returned**, no entry affecting inventory and cost of goods sold is necessary by the supplier.

Sales Returns and Allowances is a contra revenue account to Sales with a normal debit balance. A contra account is used, instead of debiting Sales, to disclose the amount of sales returns and allowances in the accounts and in the income statement because disclosure of this information is important to management. Excessive returns and allowances suggest inferior merchandise, inefficiencies in filling orders, errors in billing customers, and mistakes in delivery or shipment of the goods. Moreover, a debit directly to Sales would obscure the relative importance of sales returns and allowances as a percentage of sales and could distort comparisons between total sales in different accounting periods.

# ACCOUNTING IN ACTION
## Business Insight

 How high is too high? Returns can become so high that it is questionable whether sales revenue should have been recognized in the first place. An example of high returns is Florafax International Inc., a floral supply company, which was alleged to ship its product without customer authorization on 10 holiday occasions, including 8,562 shipments of its product to customers for Mother's Day and 6,575 for Secretary's Day. The return rate on these shipments went as high as 69% of sales. As one employee noted: "Products went out the front door and came in the back door."

An offshoot of high returns is "channel stuffing." In channel stuffing, the seller "sells" its product by providing substantial inducements to buy. Although this helps the seller's revenue in the short run, the long term can be devastating when the merchandise bought remains on the purchasers' shelves for a long period of time.

## Sales Discounts

As mentioned in our discussion of purchase transactions, the seller may offer the customer a cash discount, called by the seller a sales discount, for the prompt payment of the balance due. Like a purchase discount, a sales discount is based on the invoice price less returns and allowances, if any. Sales Discounts is debited for the cash discounts that are taken. The entry by Highpoint to record the cash receipt on May 14 from Chelsea Video within the discount period is as follows:

| May 14 | Cash | 3,430 | |
| | Sales Discounts | 70 | |
| |    Accounts Receivable | | 3,500 |
| |    (To record collection within 2/10, n/30 | | |
| |    discount period from Chelsea Video) | | |

| A | = | L | + | OE |
|---|---|---|---|---|
| +3,430 | | | | −70 |
| −3,500 | | | | |

Like Sales Returns and Allowances, Sales Discounts is a **contra revenue account** to Sales. Its normal balance is a debit. This account is used, instead of debiting sales, to accumulate the amount of cash discounts taken by customers. If the discount is not taken, Highpoint Electronic debits Cash for $3,500 and credits Accounts Receivable for $3,500 at the date of the collection.

## Statement Presentation of Sales

As contra revenue accounts, sales returns and allowances and sales discounts are deducted from sales in the income statement to arrive at net sales. The sales revenues section of the income statement based on assumed data for Highpoint Electronic is as follows:

**Sales Discount**

"That's right, pay within 10 days and you'll get a 2% discount."

Sales Discounts

XXX

| HIGHPOINT ELECTRONIC | | |
|---|---|---|
| **Income Statement (partial)** | | |
| **Sales revenues** | | |
| Sales | | $480,000 |
|   Less: Sales returns and allowances | $12,000 | |
|        Sales discounts | 8,000 | 20,000 |
|   Net sales | | **$460,000** |

**ILLUSTRATION 5-7**

*Statement presentation of sales revenues section*

This presentation discloses the significant aspects of the company's principal revenue producing activities.

# MEASURING NET INCOME
## Gross Profit

From Illustration 5-1, you learned that cost of goods sold is deducted from sales revenue to determine **gross profit**. Sales revenue used for this computation is **net sales** (which takes into account sales returns and allowances and sales discounts). On the basis of the sales data presented in Illustration 5-7 (net sales of $460,000) and the cost of goods sold, accumulated under the perpetual inventory system (assume a balance of $316,000), the gross profit for Highpoint Electronic is $144,000, computed as follows:

**4**

STUDY

OBJECTIVE

Explain the computation and importance of gross profit.

**ILLUSTRATION 5-8**

*Computation of gross profit*

| Net sales | $460,000 |
|---|---|
| Cost of goods sold | 316,000 |
| **Gross profit** | **$144,000** |

**ALTERNATIVE TERMINOLOGY**

Gross profit is sometimes referred to as *merchandising profit* or *gross margin*.

A company's gross profit may also be expressed as a percentage by dividing the amount of gross profit by net sales. For Highpoint Electronic the gross profit rate is 31.3% ($144,000 ÷ $460,000). The gross profit rate is generally considered to be more useful than the gross profit amount because it expresses a more meaningful (qualitative) relationship between net sales and gross profit. For example, a gross profit of $1,000,000 may be impressive. But, if it is the result of a gross profit rate of only 7%, it is not so impressive. The gross profit rate tells how many cents of each sales dollar go to gross profit.

Gross profit represents the **merchandising profit** of a company. It is not a measure of the overall profitability of a company, because operating expenses have not been deducted. Nevertheless, the amount and trend of gross profit is closely watched by management and other interested parties. Comparisons of current gross profit with amounts reported in past periods, and comparisons of gross profit rates of competitors and with industry averages provide information about the effectiveness of a company's purchasing function and the soundness of its pricing policies.

## ACCOUNTING IN ACTION
### Business Insight

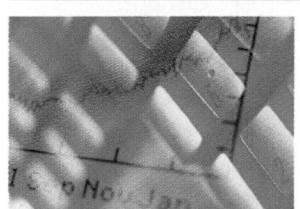

In a recent year, J.C. Penney Company reported a gross profit rate of 31%; Kmart, 24%; and Wal-Mart, 20%. Gross profit is critical. "If you don't have someone monitoring it," says one business consultant, "you are asking for instant death." A decline should trigger a search for the cause. The drop could be due to an increase in cost of goods sold or a decrease in sales revenue, either of which needs prompt attention. The change may be temporary and easily reversed, or it may signal the beginning of a bad trend.

## Operating Expenses

Operating expenses are the third component in measuring net income for a merchandising company. As indicated earlier, these expenses are similar in merchandising and service enterprises. At Highpoint Electronic, operating expenses were $114,000. The firm's net income is determined by subtracting operating expenses from gross profit. Thus, net income is $30,000 as shown below:

**ILLUSTRATION 5-9**

*Operating expenses in computing net income*

| | |
|---|---|
| Gross profit | $144,000 |
| **Operating expenses** | **114,000** |
| Net income | $ 30,000 |

The net income amount is the "bottom line" of a company's income statement.

**5**
**STUDY OBJECTIVE**

Identify the features of the income statement for a merchandising company.

## Income Statement

The income statement for retailers and wholesalers contains three features not found in the income statement of a service enterprise. These features are: (1) a sales revenue section, (2) a cost of goods sold section, and (3) gross profit. Using assumed data for specific operating expenses, the income statement for Highpoint Electronic, is shown in Illustration 5-10.

**ILLUSTRATION 5-10**

*Income statement for a merchandising company*

**HIGHPOINT ELECTRONIC**
**Income Statement**
**For the Year Ended December 31, 1999**

| | | |
|---|---:|---:|
| **Sales revenues** | | |
| Sales | | $480,000 |
| Less: Sales returns and allowances | $ 12,000 | |
|       Sales discounts | 8,000 | 20,000 |
| Net sales | | 460,000 |
| **Cost of goods sold** | | 316,000 |
| **Gross profit** | | 144,000 |
| **Operating expenses** | | |
| Store salaries expense | 45,000 | |
| Rent expense | 19,000 | |
| Utilities expense | 17,000 | |
| Advertising expense | 16,000 | |
| Depreciation expense—store equipment | 8,000 | |
| Freight-out | 7,000 | |
| Insurance expense | 2,000 | |
|      Total operating expenses | | 114,000 |
| **Net income** | | $ 30,000 |

# BEFORE YOU GO ON . . .

## Review It

1. What entries are made to record sales, sales returns and allowances, and sales discounts?
2. How are sales and contra revenue accounts reported in the income statement?
3. What is the significance of gross profit?
4. Determine Kellogg Company's gross profit rate for 1997 and 1996. Indicate whether it increased or decreased from 1996 to 1997. The answer to this question is provided on page 229.

# COMPLETING THE ACCOUNTING CYCLE

Up to this point, we have been primarily concerned with measuring net income in a merchandising company. We have also illustrated the basic entries in recording transactions relating to purchases and sales in a perpetual inventory system. Now it is time to consider the remaining steps in the accounting cycle that were identified in Chapter 4.

    Each of the required steps in the cycle applies to a merchandising company. Again, a work sheet is an optional step. To illustrate the steps in the cycle, we will assume that Highpoint Electronic uses a work sheet.

**6**
STUDY
OBJECTIVE
....................................
Explain the steps in the accounting cycle for a merchandising company.

## Using a Work Sheet

As indicated in Chapter 4, a work sheet enables financial statements to be prepared before the adjusting entries are journalized and posted. The steps in preparing a work sheet for a merchandising company are the same as they are for

ILLUSTRATION 5-11

*Work sheet for merchandising company*

a service enterprise (see pp. 141–143). The work sheet for Highpoint Electronic is shown in Illustration 5-11. The unique accounts for a merchandising company, using a perpetual inventory system, are shown in capital letters in red.

### HIGHPOINT ELECTRONIC
### Work Sheet
### For the Year Ended December 31, 1999

| | Trial Balance Dr. | Trial Balance Cr. | Adjustments Dr. | Adjustments Cr. | Adjusted Trial Balance Dr. | Adjusted Trial Balance Cr. | Income Statement Dr. | Income Statement Cr. | Balance Sheet Dr. | Balance Sheet Cr. |
|---|---|---|---|---|---|---|---|---|---|---|
| Cash | 9,500 | | | | 9,500 | | | | 9,500 | |
| Accounts Receivable | 16,100 | | | | 16,100 | | | | 16,100 | |
| MERCHANDISE INVENTORY | 40,000 | | | | 40,000 | | | | 40,000 | |
| Prepaid Insurance | 3,800 | | | (a) 2,000 | 1,800 | | | | 1,800 | |
| Store Equipment | 80,000 | | | | 80,000 | | | | 80,000 | |
| Accumulated Depreciation | | 16,000 | | (b) 8,000 | | 24,000 | | | | 24,000 |
| Accounts Payable | | 20,400 | | | | 20,400 | | | | 20,400 |
| R.A. Lamb, Capital | | 83,000 | | | | 83,000 | | | | 83,000 |
| R.A. Lamb, Drawing | 15,000 | | | | 15,000 | | | | 15,000 | |
| SALES | | 480,000 | | | | 480,000 | | 480,000 | | |
| SALES RETURNS AND ALLOWANCES | 12,000 | | | | 12,000 | | 12,000 | | | |
| SALES DISCOUNTS | 8,000 | | | | 8,000 | | 8,000 | | | |
| COST OF GOODS SOLD | 316,000 | | | | 316,000 | | 316,000 | | | |
| Freight-out | 7,000 | | | | 7,000 | | 7,000 | | | |
| Advertising Expense | 16,000 | | | | 16,000 | | 16,000 | | | |
| Rent Expense | 19,000 | | | | 19,000 | | 19,000 | | | |
| Store Salaries Expense | 40,000 | | (c) 5,000 | | 45,000 | | 45,000 | | | |
| Utilities Expense | 17,000 | | | | 17,000 | | 17,000 | | | |
| Totals | 599,400 | 599,400 | | | | | | | | |
| Insurance Expense | | | (a) 2,000 | | 2,000 | | 2,000 | | | |
| Depreciation Expense | | | (b) 8,000 | | 8,000 | | 8,000 | | | |
| Salaries Payable | | | | (c) 5,000 | | 5,000 | | | | 5,000 |
| Totals | | | 15,000 | 15,000 | 612,400 | 612,400 | 450,000 | 480,000 | 162,400 | 132,400 |
| Net Income | | | | | | | 30,000 | | | 30,000 |
| Totals | | | | | | | 480,000 | 480,000 | 162,400 | 162,400 |

Key: (a) Insurance expired, (b) Depreciation expensed, (c) Salaries accrued.

### Trial Balance Columns

Data for the trial balance are obtained from the ledger balances of Highpoint Electronic at December 31. The amount shown for Merchandise Inventory, $40,000, is the year-end inventory amount which results from the application of a perpetual inventory system.

### Adjustments Columns

A merchandising company generally has the same types of adjustments as a service company. As you see in the work sheet, adjustments (a), (b), and (c) are for insurance, depreciation, and salaries. These adjustments were also required for Pioneer Advertising Agency, as illustrated in Chapters 3 and 4.

After all adjustment data are entered on the work sheet, the equality of the adjustment column totals is established. The balances in all accounts are then extended to the adjusted trial balance columns.

## Adjusted Trial Balance

The adjusted trial balance shows the balance of all accounts after adjustment at the end of the accounting period.

## Income Statement Columns

The accounts and balances that affect the income statement are transferred from the adjusted trial balance columns to the income statement columns. For Highpoint Electronic, Sales of $480,000 is shown in the credit column whereas the contra revenue accounts, Sales Returns and Allowances of $12,000 and Sales Discounts of $8,000, are shown in the debit column. Thus, the difference of $460,000 is the net sales shown on the income statement (Illustration 5-10).

Finally, all the credits in the income statement column should be totaled and compared to the total of all the debits in the income statement column. If the credits exceed the debits, then the company has net income. In Highpoint Electronic's case there was net income of $30,000. Conversely if the debits exceed the credits, the company would report a net loss.

## Balance Sheet Columns

The major difference between the balance sheets of a service company and a merchandising company is inventory. For Highpoint Electronic, the ending inventory amount of $40,000 is shown in the balance sheet debit column. Note also that the information to prepare the owner's equity statement is also found in these columns. That is, the capital account of R. A. Lamb is $83,000. The drawings for R. A. Lamb are $15,000. Net income results when the total of the debit column exceeds the total of the credit column in the balance sheet columns of the work sheet. Conversely, a net loss results when the total of the credits exceeds the total of the debit balances.

## Preparing Financial Statements

As is true in a service enterprise, financial statements for a merchandising company are prepared from the financial statement columns of the work sheet. The income statement for Highpoint Electronic has already been illustrated (see Illustration 5-10).

The owner's equity statement is as follows:

**ILLUSTRATION 5-12**

*Owner's equity statement*

### HIGHPOINT ELECTRONIC
### Owner's Equity Statement
### For the Year Ended December 31, 1999

| | |
|---|---|
| R. A. Lamb, Capital, January 1 | $ 83,000 |
| Add: Net income | 30,000 |
| | 113,000 |
| Less: Drawings | 15,000 |
| R. A. Lamb, Capital, December 31 | $ 98,000 |

The classified balance sheet, then, is as follows:

**ILLUSTRATION 5-13**

*Classified balance sheet*

### HIGHPOINT ELECTRONIC
### Balance Sheet
### December 31, 1999

#### Assets

| | | |
|---|---:|---:|
| Current assets | | |
| Cash | | $ 9,500 |
| Accounts receivable | | 16,100 |
| **Merchandise inventory** | | **40,000** |
| Prepaid insurance | | 1,800 |
| Total current assets | | 67,400 |
| Property, plant, and equipment | | |
| Store equipment | $80,000 | |
| Less: Accumulated depreciation—store equipment | 24,000 | 56,000 |
| Total assets | | $123,400 |

#### Liabilities and Owner's Equity

| | |
|---|---:|
| Current liabilities | |
| Accounts payable | $ 20,400 |
| Salaries payable | 5,000 |
| Total current liabilities | 25,400 |
| Owner's equity | |
| R.A. Lamb, Capital | 98,000 |
| Total liabilities and owner's equity | $123,400 |

In the balance sheet, merchandise inventory is reported as a current asset immediately below accounts receivable. Recall that items are listed under current assets in the order of liquidity. Merchandise inventory is less liquid than accounts receivable because the goods must first be sold and then collection must be made from the customer.

## ACCOUNTING IN ACTION
### Ethics Insight

Phar Mor was one of the largest and fastest growing retail dry goods and pharmacy chains in the United States until a massive fraud was discovered by the company's auditors, Coopers and Lybrand. Dry goods were Phar Mor's business, but some of its executives had a taste for "raisin cookies." Schemers in Phar Mor's executive suite kept two sets of records, an official ledger that they sometimes manipulated with false entries, and another, nicknamed the "cookies," where they kept track of the false entries, called "raisins." They would refer to their ledger domain as "putting raisins in the cookies."

Based on reports in *The Wall Street Journal*, the assets of the company were overstated by more than $400 million, or about one-third of Phar Mor's gross revenue. Most of this overstatement pertained to fake or overvalued merchandise inventories at various store locations, and was perpetrated by the company's top financial managers.

## Adjusting and Closing Entries

Adjusting entries are journalized from the adjustment columns of the work sheet. Because the journalizing and posting of the entries are the same as they are for a service enterprise, they are not illustrated here.

For a merchandising company, like a service enterprise, all accounts that affect the determination of net income are closed to Income Summary. Data for the preparation of closing entries may be obtained from the income statement columns of the work sheet. In journalizing, all debit column amounts are credited, and all credit column amounts are debited, as shown below for Highpoint Electronic. Cost of goods sold is a new account that must be closed to Income Summary.

| Dec. 31 | Sales | 480,000 | |
| |     Income Summary | | 480,000 |
| |       (To close income statement accounts with | | |
| |        credit balances) | | |
| | | | |
| 31 | Income Summary | 450,000 | |
| |     Sales Returns and Allowances | | 12,000 |
| |     Sales Discounts | | 8,000 |
| |     Cost of Goods Sold | | 316,000 |
| |     Store Salaries Expense | | 45,000 |
| |     Rent Expense | | 19,000 |
| |     Freight-out | | 7,000 |
| |     Advertising Expense | | 16,000 |
| |     Utilities Expense | | 17,000 |
| |     Depreciation Expense | | 8,000 |
| |     Insurance Expense | | 2,000 |
| |       (To close income statement accounts with | | |
| |        debit balances) | | |
| | | | |
| 31 | Income Summary | 30,000 | |
| |     R.A. Lamb, Capital | | 30,000 |
| |       (To close net income to capital) | | |
| | | | |
| 31 | R.A. Lamb, Capital | 15,000 | |
| |     R. A. Lamb, Drawing | | 15,000 |
| |       (To close drawings to capital) | | |

**HELPFUL HINT**
The easiest way to prepare the first two closing entries is to identify the temporary accounts by their balances and then prepare one entry for the credits and one for the debits.

After the closing entries are posted, all temporary accounts have zero balances. In addition, R.A. Lamb, Capital has a credit balance of $98,000: beginning balance + net income — drawings ($83,000 + $30,000 − $15,000).

## Preparing the Post–Closing Trial Balance

After the closing entries are posted, the post-closing trial balance is prepared. The only new account in the post-closing trial balance is Merchandise Inventory. The post-closing trial balance for Highpoint Electronic at December 31, 1999, is shown in Illustration 5-14.

**ILLUSTRATION 5-14**

*Post-closing trial balance*

**HIGHPOINT ELECTRONIC**
**Post-Closing Trial Balance**
**December 31, 1999**

| | Debit | Credit |
|---|---|---|
| Cash | $ 9,500 | |
| Accounts receivable | 16,100 | |
| **Merchandise inventory** | **40,000** | |
| Prepaid insurance | 1,800 | |
| Store equipment | 80,000 | |
| Accumulated depreciation | | $ 24,000 |
| Accounts payable | | 20,400 |
| Salaries payable | | 5,000 |
| R.A. Lamb, Capital | | 98,000 |
| | $147,400 | $147,400 |

## Summary of Merchandising Entries

The entries for the merchandising accounts using a perpetual inventory system are summarized in Illustration 5-15.

**ILLUSTRATION 5-15**

*Daily recurring and closing entries*

| Transactions | Daily Recurring Entries | Dr. | Cr. |
|---|---|---|---|
| Selling merchandise to customers | Cash or Accounts Receivable | XX | |
| | Sales | | XX |
| | Cost of Goods Sold | XX | |
| | Merchandise Inventory | | XX |
| Granting sales returns or allowances to customers | Sales Returns and Allowances | XX | |
| | Cash or Accounts Receivable | | XX |
| | Merchandise Inventory | XX | |
| | Cost of Goods Sold | | XX |
| Paying freight costs on sales; FOB destination | Freight-out | XX | |
| | Cash | | XX |
| Receiving payment from customers within discount period | Cash | XX | |
| | Sales Discounts | XX | |
| | Accounts Receivable | | XX |
| Purchasing merchandise for resale | Merchandise Inventory | XX | |
| | Cash or Accounts Payable | | XX |
| Paying freight costs on merchandise purchased; FOB shipping point | Merchandise Inventory | XX | |
| | Cash | | XX |
| Receiving purchase returns or allowances from suppliers | Cash or Accounts Payable | XX | |
| | Merchandise Inventory | | XX |
| Paying suppliers within discount period | Accounts Payable | XX | |
| | Merchandise Inventory | | XX |
| | Cash | | XX |
| **Events** | **Closing Entries** | | |
| Closing accounts with credit balances | Sales | XX | |
| | Income Summary | | XX |
| Closing accounts with debit balances | Income Summary | XX | |
| | Sales Returns and Allowances | | XX |
| | Sales Discounts | | XX |
| | Cost of Goods Sold | | XX |
| | Freight-out | | XX |
| | Expenses | | XX |

# BEFORE YOU GO ON . . .

## Review It

1. How does a work sheet for a merchandising company differ from a work sheet for a service company? In what ways is the work sheet similar for a merchandising company and a service company?
2. In what columns of the work sheet will (a) merchandise inventory and (b) cost of goods sold be shown?
3. What merchandising account(s) will appear in the post-closing trial balance?

## Do It

The trial balance of Revere Clothing Company at December 31 shows Merchandise Inventory $25,000, Sales $162,400, Sales Returns and Allowances $4,800, Sales Discounts $3,600, Cost of Goods Sold $110,000, Rental Revenue $6,000, Freight-out $1,800, Rent Expense $8,800, and Salaries and Wages Expense $22,000. Prepare the closing entries for the above accounts.

*Reasoning:* The first closing entry for a merchandising company closes temporary accounts with credit balances to Income Summary. The second closing entry closes temporary accounts with debit balances to Income Summary.

*Solution:* The two closing entries are:

| | | | |
|---|---|---:|---:|
| Dec. 31 | Sales | 162,400 | |
| | Rental Revenue | 6,000 | |
| |    Income Summary | | 168,400 |
| |      (To close accounts with credit balances) | | |
| | | | |
| Dec. 31 | Income Summary | 151,000 | |
| |    Cost of Goods Sold | | 110,000 |
| |    Sales Returns and Allowances | | 4,800 |
| |    Sales Discounts | | 3,600 |
| |    Freight-out | | 1,800 |
| |    Rent Expense | | 8,800 |
| |    Salaries and Wages Expense | | 22,000 |
| |      (To close accounts with debit balances) | | |

*Related exercise material:* BE5–7, E5–5, and E5–6.

THE
NAVIGATOR

# FORMS OF INCOME STATEMENTS

Two forms of the income statement are widely used by merchandising companies. These income statements are explained below.

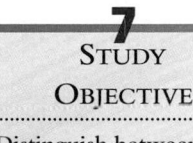

7
STUDY
OBJECTIVE

Distinguish between a multiple-step and a single-step income statement.

## Multiple-Step Income Statement

The **multiple-step income statement** is so named because it shows the numerous steps in determining net income (or net loss). The Highpoint Electronic income statement in Illustration 5-10 is an example. It shows two steps: (1) cost of goods sold was subtracted from net sales, and (2) operating expenses were deducted from gross profit. These steps pertain to the company's principal operating activities. A multiple-step statement provides users with more information about a company's income performance by distinguishing between **operating** and **non-operating activities**. The statement also highlights intermediate components of income and shows subgroupings of expenses.

## Nonoperating Activities

**Nonoperating activities** consist of (1) revenues and expenses that result from secondary or auxiliary operations and (2) gains and losses that are unrelated to the company's operations. The results of nonoperating activities are shown in two sections: Other revenues and gains and Other expenses and losses. For a merchandising company, these sections will typically include the following items:

**ILLUSTRATION 5-16**

*Items reported in nonoperating sections*

| Other Revenues and Gains | Other Expenses and Losses |
|---|---|
| Interest revenue from notes receivable and marketable securities | Interest expense on notes and loans payable |
| Dividend revenue from investments in capital stock | Casualty losses from recurring causes such as vandalism and accidents |
| Rent revenue from subleasing a portion of the store | Loss from the sale or abandonment of property, plant, and equipment |
| Gain from the sale of property, plant, and equipment | Loss from strikes by employees and suppliers |

The nonoperating sections are reported in the income statement immediately after the sections that pertain to the company's primary operating activities. These sections are shown in Illustration 5-17 using assumed data for Highpoint Electronic.

**ILLUSTRATION 5-17**

*Multiple-step income statement—nonoperating sections and subgroupings of operating expenses*

**HIGHPOINT ELECTRONIC**
**Income Statement**
**For the Year Ended December 31, 1999**

| | | | |
|---|---:|---:|---:|
| Sales revenues | | | |
| Sales | | | $480,000 |
| Less: Sales returns and allowances | | $ 12,000 | |
| Sales discounts | | 8,000 | 20,000 |
| Net sales | | | 460,000 |
| Cost of goods sold | | | 316,000 |
| Gross profit | | | 144,000 |
| Operating expenses | | | |
| **Selling expenses** | | | |
| Store salaries expense | $ 45,000 | | |
| Advertising expense | 16,000 | | |
| Depreciation expense—store equipment | 8,000 | | |
| Freight-out | 7,000 | | |
| Total selling expenses | | 76,000 | |
| **Administrative expenses** | | | |
| Rent expense | 19,000 | | |
| Utilities expense | 17,000 | | |
| Insurance expense | 2,000 | | |
| Total administrative expenses | | 38,000 | |
| Total operating expenses | | | 114,000 |
| Income from operations | | | 30,000 |
| Other revenues and gains | | | |
| Interest revenue | 3,000 | | |
| Gain on sale of equipment | 600 | 3,600 | |
| Other expenses and losses | | | |
| Interest expense | 1,800 | | |
| Casualty loss from vandalism | 200 | 2,000 | 1,600 |
| Net income | | | $ 31,600 |

When the two nonoperating sections are included, the label Income from operations (or Operating income) precedes them. It clearly identifies the results of the company's normal operations. Income from operations is determined by subtracting cost of goods sold and operating expenses from net sales.

Observe that the results of the two nonoperating sections are netted. The difference is added to or subtracted from income from operations to determine net income. Finally, within the nonoperating sections, items are generally reported at the net amount. Thus, if a company received a $2,500 insurance settlement on vandalism losses of $2,700, the loss is reported at $200. It is not uncommon for companies to combine these two nonoperating sections into a single "Other Revenues and Expenses" section.

**HELPFUL HINT**
Operating income relates to the sale of primary goods in the ordinary course of business.

# ACCOUNTING IN ACTION
## Business Insight

The distinction between operating and nonoperating activities is crucial to many external users of financial data. The reason is that operating income is viewed as sustainable and therefore long-term, and nonoperating is viewed as nonrecurring and therefore short-term. For example, it was reported that a large cinema chain in North America was selling some of its assets and counting the gains as part of operating income. As a result, operating losses were being offset by these gains. Because of unfavorable press reaction to this practice, the company revised its financial statements. By not counting its nonrecurring items as part of operating income, its first quarter results changed from $24.9 million operating income to a $22.6 million loss. Although the net income figure didn't change, investors were able to see that income was derived from selling assets rather than from selling movie tickets. Thus, with this new information, investors were able to make a more informed decision about the company's earnings.

## Subgrouping of Operating Expenses

In larger companies, operating expenses are often subdivided into selling expenses and administrative expenses, as illustrated in the income statement in Illustration 5-17. Selling expenses are those associated with making sales. They include sales promotional expenses as well as expenses of completing the sale, such as delivery and shipping expenses. Administrative expenses (sometimes called general expenses) relate to general operating activities such as personnel management, accounting, and store security.

When subgroupings are made, some expenses may have to be prorated, e.g., 70% to selling and 30% to administrative expenses. For example, if a store building is used for both selling and general functions, building expenses such as depreciation, utilities, and property taxes will need to be allocated.

Any reasonable classification of expenses that serves to inform those who use the statement is satisfactory. For example, the present tendency in statements prepared for management is to present in considerable detail expense data grouped along lines of responsibility.

**ETHICS NOTE**
How would *you* account for this expense? At the end of a celebratory lunch the employees of a sales department each gave the manager $10, and the manager paid the bill with his charge card. During the next week you notice that the manager reported the full amount of the lunch bill on his expense report (and requested reimbursement). When this question was posed to the CEO of Intel, he suggested that an appropriate action would be to report the problem anonymously to the internal audit staff for investigation.

## Single-Step Income Statement

Another format for income statement presentation is the single-step income statement. The statement is so named because only one step, subtracting total expenses from total revenues, is required in determining net income (or net loss).

In a single-step statement, all data are classified under two categories: (1) **Revenues**, which includes both operating revenues and other revenues and gains, or (2) **Expenses**, which includes cost of goods sold, operating expenses, and other expenses and losses. A condensed single-step statement for Highpoint Electronic is illustrated in Illustration 5-18.

ILLUSTRATION 5-18

*Single-step income statement*

| HIGHPOINT ELECTRONIC<br>Income Statement<br>For the Year Ended December 31, 1999 | | |
|---|---:|---:|
| **Revenues** | | |
| Net sales | | $460,000 |
| Interest revenue | | 3,000 |
| Gain on sale of equipment | | 600 |
| Total revenues | | 463,600 |
| **Expenses** | | |
| Cost of goods sold | $316,000 | |
| Selling expenses | 76,000 | |
| Administrative expenses | 38,000 | |
| Interest expense | 1,800 | |
| Casualty loss from vandalism | 200 | |
| Total expenses | | 432,000 |
| Net income | | $ 31,600 |

There are two primary reasons for using the single-step form: (1) A company does not realize any type of profit or income until total revenues exceed total expenses, so it makes sense to divide the statement into these two categories. (2) The form is simpler and easier to read than the multiple-step form. For homework problems, the single-step form of income statement should be used only when it is specifically requested.

# BEFORE YOU GO ON . . .

## Review It

1. What are nonoperating activities and how are they reported in the income statement?
2. How does a single-step income statement differ from a multiple-step income statement?

## A LOOK BACK AT OUR FEATURE STORY

Refer to the opening story about the Washington State University bookstore, and answer the following questions:

1. What entry, if any, would the WSU bookstore make when ordering books? When books are received? When returning books? When allowing the students to return books? When purchasing used books from students?
2. How often is it necessary for Larry Martin to take a physical inventory? Why is it necessary to take an inventory? For the inventory taken in September, does Larry need both quantities and costs? Explain.

*Solution*

1. No entry is made at the time books are ordered. Probably an open purchase order file or memo record is maintained for keeping track of open (unfilled) purchase orders. When books are received, the bookstore would record the purchases at invoice cost as follows:

| | | |
|---|---:|---:|
| Merchandise Inventory | XX | |
| Accounts Payable | | XX |
| (To record goods purchased on account) | | |

When books are returned to the publisher, the WSU bookstore would prepare a debit memo from which the following entry is made:

| Accounts Payable | XX | |
| Merchandise Inventory | | XX |
| (To record books returned to publisher) | | |

When the bookstore gives a refund for a returned book (not a used book purchase), the following entry would be made at the book's selling price:

| Sales Returns and Allowances | XX | |
| Cash | | XX |
| (To record payment to customer for returned book) | | |

And the following entry would be made at the book's cost :

| Merchandise Inventory | XX | |
| Cost of Goods Sold | | XX |
| (To record cost of book returned) | | |

When used books are bought from students, the bookstore would record the following entry:

| Inventory of Used Books | XX | |
| Cash | | XX |
| (To record purchase of used goods) | | |

2. Larry Martin waits about 4 weeks after the school term, when the busy book selling and return period ends, to take a physical inventory of books. He does that each school term. In addition Larry takes a physical inventory when the financial statements are prepared at least once a year.

It is necessary for Larry to take accurate inventory counts in order to ensure the accuracy of the perpetual inventory records. He needs accurate records to make good ordering and return decisions. Accurate ordering coupled with efficient return practices is a must for profitable bookstore operations.

Larry uses the September inventory balances for ordering books. Thus, only quantities—not costs—are needed by Larry.

THE
NAVIGATOR

## DEMONSTRATION PROBLEM

The adjusted trial balance columns of the work sheet for the year ended December 31, 1999, for Dykstra Company are as follows:

| Debit | | Credit | |
|---|---|---|---|
| Cash | $ 14,500 | Accumulated Depreciation | $ 18,000 |
| Accounts Receivable | 11,100 | Notes Payable | 25,000 |
| Merchandise Inventory | 29,000 | Accounts Payable | 10,600 |
| Prepaid Insurance | 2,500 | Gene Dykstra, Capital | 81,000 |
| Store Equipment | 95,000 | Sales | 536,800 |
| Gene Dykstra, Drawing | 12,000 | Interest Revenue | 2,500 |
| Sales Returns and Allowances | 6,700 | | $673,900 |
| Sales Discounts | 5,000 | | |
| Cost of Goods Sold | 363,400 | | |
| Freight-out | 7,600 | | |
| Advertising Expense | 12,000 | | |
| Store Salaries Expense | 56,000 | | |
| Utilities Expense | 18,000 | | |
| Rent Expense | 24,000 | | |
| Depreciation Expense | 9,000 | | |
| Insurance Expense | 4,500 | | |
| Interest Expense | 3,600 | | |
| | $673,900 | | |

*Instructions*

(a) Enter the adjusted trial balance data on a work sheet. Complete the work sheet.

(b) Prepare an income statement assuming Dykstra Company does not use subgroupings for operating expenses.

**PROBLEM-SOLVING STRATEGIES**

1. Make sure in the adjusted trial balance that debits and credits are equal before transferring amounts to the income statement and balance sheet columns.

2. Transfer all amounts in the adjusted trial balance to either the income statement or balance sheet columns.

3. The net income or net loss is the reconciling item in both the income statement and the balance sheet columns.

## SOLUTION TO DEMONSTRATION PROBLEM

(a)
### DYKSTRA COMPANY
### Work Sheet
### For the Year Ended December 31, 1999

| Account Titles | Adjusted Trial Balance | | Income Statement | | Balance Sheet | |
|---|---|---|---|---|---|---|
| | Dr. | Cr. | Dr. | Cr. | Dr. | Cr. |
| Cash | 14,500 | | | | 14,500 | |
| Accounts Receivable | 11,100 | | | | 11,100 | |
| Merchandise Inventory | 29,000 | | | | 29,000 | |
| Prepaid Insurance | 2,500 | | | | 2,500 | |
| Store Equipment | 95,000 | | | | 95,000 | |
| Accumulated Depreciation | | 18,000 | | | | 18,000 |
| Notes Payable | | 25,000 | | | | 25,000 |
| Accounts Payable | | 10,600 | | | | 10,600 |
| Gene Dykstra, Capital | | 81,000 | | | | 81,000 |
| Gene Dykstra, Drawing | 12,000 | | | | 12,000 | |
| Sales | | 536,800 | | 536,800 | | |
| Sales Returns and Allowances | 6,700 | | 6,700 | | | |
| Sales Discounts | 5,000 | | 5,000 | | | |
| Cost of Goods Sold | 363,400 | | 363,400 | | | |
| Freight-out | 7,600 | | 7,600 | | | |
| Advertising Expense | 12,000 | | 12,000 | | | |
| Store Salaries Expense | 56,000 | | 56,000 | | | |
| Utilities Expense | 18,000 | | 18,000 | | | |
| Rent Expense | 24,000 | | 24,000 | | | |
| Depreciation Expense | 9,000 | | 9,000 | | | |
| Insurance Expense | 4,500 | | 4,500 | | | |
| Interest Expense | 3,600 | | 3,600 | | | |
| Interest Revenue | | 2,500 | | 2,500 | | |
| Totals | 673,900 | 673,900 | 509,800 | 539,300 | 164,100 | 134,600 |
| Net Income | | | 29,500 | | | 29,500 |
| Totals | | | 539,300 | 539,300 | 164,100 | 164,100 |

**PROBLEM-SOLVING STRATEGIES**

1. In preparing the income statement, remember that the key components are net sales, cost of goods sold, gross profit, total operating expenses, and net income (loss). These components are reported in the right-hand column of the income statement.

2. Nonoperating items follow income from operations.

(b)
### DYKSTRA COMPANY
### Income Statement
### For the Year Ended December 31, 1999

| | | |
|---|---|---|
| Sales revenues | | |
| Sales | | $536,800 |
| Less: Sales returns and allowances | $ 6,700 | |
| Sales discounts | 5,000 | 11,700 |
| Net sales | | 525,100 |
| Cost of goods sold | | 363,400 |
| Gross profit | | 161,700 |
| Operating expenses | | |
| Store salaries expense | 56,000 | |
| Rent expense | 24,000 | |
| Utilities expense | 18,000 | |
| Advertising expense | 12,000 | |

| Account Titles | Adjusted Trial Balance | | Income Statement | | Balance Sheet | |
|---|---|---|---|---|---|---|
| | Dr. | Cr. | Dr. | Cr. | Dr. | Cr. |
| Depreciation expense | | | | | 9,000 | |
| Freight-out | | | | | 7,600 | |
| Insurance expense | | | | | 4,500 | |
| Total operating expenses | | | | | | 131,100 |
| Income from operations | | | | | | 30,600 |
| Other revenues and gains | | | | | | |
| Interest revenue | | | | | 2,500 | |
| Other expenses and losses | | | | | | |
| Interest expense | | | | | 3,600 | 1,100 |
| Net income | | | | | | $ 29,500 |

THE NAVIGATOR

# SUMMARY OF STUDY OBJECTIVES

**1.** *Identify the differences between a service enterprise and a merchandising company.* Because of the presence of inventory, a merchandising company has sales revenue, cost of goods sold, and gross profit. To account for inventory, a merchandising company must choose between a perpetual inventory system and a periodic inventory system.

**2.** *Explain the entries for purchases under a perpetual inventory system.* The Merchandise Inventory account is debited for all purchases of merchandise, for freight-in and other costs, and it is credited for purchase discounts and purchase returns and allowances.

**3.** *Explain the entries for sales revenues under a perpetual inventory system.* When inventory is sold, Accounts Receivable (or Cash) is debited and Sales is credited for the **selling price** of the merchandise. At the same time, Cost of Goods Sold is debited and Merchandise Inventory is credited for the **cost** of the inventory items sold.

**4.** *Explain the computation and importance of gross profit.* Gross profit is computed by subtracting cost of goods sold from net sales. Gross profit represents the merchandising profit of a company, and the amount and trend of gross profit is closely watched by management and other interested parties.

**5.** *Identify the features of the income statement for a merchandising company.* The income statement for a merchandising company contains three sections: sales revenues, cost of goods sold, and operating expenses.

**6.** *Explain the steps in the accounting cycle for a merchandising company.* Each of the required steps in the accounting cycle for a service enterprise applies to a merchandising company. A work sheet is again an optional step.

**7.** *Distinguish between a multiple-step and a single-step income statement.* A multiple-step income statement shows numerous steps in determining net income including nonoperating sections. In a single-step income statement all data are classified under two categories, revenues or expenses, and net income is determined by one step.

THE NAVIGATOR

# GLOSSARY
•••••••••••••••••••••••••••••••••••••••••••••••••••••••••••••••••••••••••••••••••••••••••

**Administrative expenses** Expenses relating to general operating activities such as personnel management, accounting, and store security. (p. 209).

**Contra revenue account** An account that is offset against a revenue account on the income statement. (p. 198).

**Cost of goods sold** The total cost of merchandise sold during the period. (p. 188).

**Credit memorandum** A document issued by a seller to inform a customer that a credit has been made to the customer's account receivable for a sales return or allowance. (p. 197).

**Debit memorandum** A document issued by a buyer to inform a seller that a debit has been made to the seller's account because of unsatisfactory merchandise. (p. 192).

**FOB destination** Freight terms indicating that the goods will be placed free on board at the buyer's place of business, and the seller pays the freight costs. (p. 195).

**FOB shipping point** Freight terms indicating that goods are placed free on board the carrier by the seller, and the buyer pays the freight costs. (p. 195).

**Gross profit** The excess of net sales over the cost of goods sold. (p. 188).

**Income from operations** Income from a company's principal operating activity determined by subtracting cost of goods sold and operating expenses from net sales. (p. 209).

**Invoice** A document that provides support for a credit purchase. (p. 191).

**Multiple-step income statement** An income statement that shows numerous steps in determining net income (or net loss). (p. 207).

**Net sales** Sales less sales returns and allowances and sales discounts. (p. 199).

**Operating expenses** Expenses incurred in the process of earning sales revenues that are deducted from gross profit in the income statement. (p. 188).

**Other expenses and losses** A nonoperating section of the income statement that shows expenses from auxiliary operations and losses unrelated to the company's operations. (p. 208).

**Other revenues and gains** A nonoperating section of the income statement that shows revenues from auxiliary operations and gains unrelated to the company's operations. (p. 208).

**Periodic inventory system** An inventory system in which detailed records are not maintained throughout the accounting period and the cost of goods sold is determined only at the end of an accounting period. (p. 190).

**Perpetual inventory system** A detailed inventory system in which the cost of each inventory item is maintained throughout the accounting period and the records continuously show the inventory that should be on hand. (p. 190).

**Purchase discount** A cash discount claimed by a buyer for prompt payment of a balance due. (p. 193).

**Sales discount** A reduction given by a seller for prompt payment of a credit sale. (p. 198).

**Sales invoice** A document that provides support for credit sales. (p. 196).

**Sales revenue (sales)** Primary source of revenue in a merchandising company. (p. 188).

**Selling expenses** Expenses associated with the making of sales. (p. 209).

**Single-step income statement** An income statement that shows only one step in determining net income (or net loss). (p. 209).

# SELF-STUDY QUESTIONS

Answers are at the end of the chapter.

(SO 1) 1. Gross profit will result if:
   a. operating expenses are less than net income.
   b. sales revenues are greater than operating expenses.
   c. sales revenues are greater than cost of goods sold.
   d. operating expenses are greater than cost of goods sold.

(SO 2) 2. Under a perpetual inventory system, when goods are purchased for resale by a company:
   a. purchases on account are debited to Merchandise Inventory.
   b. purchases on account are debited to Purchases.
   c. purchase returns are debited to Purchase Returns and Allowances.
   d. freight costs are debited to Freight-out.

(SO 3) 3. The sales accounts that normally have a debit balance are:
   a. Sales Discounts.
   b. Sales Returns and Allowances.
   c. both (a) and (b).
   d. neither (a) nor (b).

(SO 3) 4. A credit sale of $750 is made on June 13, terms 2/10, net/30, on which a return of $50 is granted on June 16. The amount received as payment in full on June 23 is:
   a. $700.
   b. $686.
   c. $685.
   d. $650.

5. Which of the following accounts will normally appear (SO 3) in the ledger of a merchandising company that uses a perpetual inventory system?
   a. Purchases.
   b. Freight-in.
   c. Cost of Goods Sold.
   d. Purchase Discounts.

6. If sales revenues are $400,000, cost of goods sold is (SO 4) $310,000, and operating expenses are $60,000, the gross profit is:
   a. $30,000.
   b. $90,000.
   c. $340,000.
   d. $400,000.

7. The multiple-step income statement for a merchandis- (SO 5) ing company shows each of the following features *except*:
   a. gross profit.
   b. cost of goods sold.
   c. a sales revenue section.
   d. investing activities section.

8. In a work sheet, Merchandise Inventory is shown in the (SO 6) following columns:
   a. Adjusted trial balance debit and balance sheet debit.
   b. Income statement debit and balance sheet debit.
   c. Income statement credit and balance sheet debit.
   d. Income statement credit and adjusted trial balance debit.

(SO 7)  9.  In a single-step income statement:
a. gross profit is reported.
b. cost of goods sold is not reported.
c. sales revenues and other revenues and gains are reported in the revenues section of the income statement.
d. operating income is separately reported.

10. Which of the following appears on both a single-step (SO 7) and multiple-step income statement?
a. sales.
b. gross profit.
c. income from operations.
d. cost of goods sold.

# QUESTIONS

1. (a) "The steps in the accounting cycle for a merchandising company are different from the accounting cycle for a service enterprise." Do you agree or disagree? (b) Is the measurement of net income in a merchandising company conceptually the same as in a service enterprise? Explain.

2. (a) How do the components of revenues and expenses differ between a merchandising company and a service enterprise? (b) Explain the income measurement process in a merchandising company.

3. How does income measurement differ between a merchandising company and a service company?

4. When is cost of goods sold determined in a perpetual inventory system?

5. Distinguish between FOB shipping point and FOB destination. Identify the freight terms that will result in a debit to Merchandise Inventory by the purchaser and a debit to Freight-out by the seller.

6. Explain the meaning of the credit terms 2/10, n/30.

7. Goods costing $2,000 are purchased on account on July 15 with credit terms of 2/10, n/30. On July 18 a $100 credit memo is received from the supplier for damaged goods. Give the journal entry on July 24 to record payment of the balance due within the discount period using a perpetual inventory system.

8. Patty Loveless believes revenues from credit sales may be earned before they are collected in cash. Do you agree? Explain.

9. (a) What is the primary source document for recording (1) cash sales, (2) credit sales, and (3) sales returns and allowances? (b) Using XXs for amounts, give the journal entry for each of the transactions in part (a).

10. A credit sale is made on July 10 for $800, terms 2/10, n/30. On July 12, $100 of goods are returned for credit. Give the journal entry on July 19 to record the receipt of the balance due within the discount period.

11. Randy Travis Co. has sales revenue of $110,000, cost of goods sold of $70,000, and operating expenses of $20,000. What is its gross profit?

12. Lionel Richie Company reports net sales of $800,000, gross profit of $580,000, and net income of $200,000. What are its operating expenses?

13. Identify the distinguishing features of an income statement for a merchandising company.

14. Indicate the columns of the work sheet in which (a) merchandise inventory, and (b) cost of goods sold will be shown.

15. Why is the normal operating cycle for a merchandising company likely to be longer than for a service company?

16. Prepare the closing entries for the Sales account, assuming a balance of $200,000 and the Cost of Goods Sold account which has a $120,000 balance.

17. What merchandising account(s) will appear in the post-closing trial balance?

18. Identify the sections of a multiple-step income statement that relate to (a) operating activities, and (b) nonoperating activities.

19. Distinguish between the types of functional groupings of operating expenses. What problem is created by these groupings?

20. How does the single-step form of income statement differ from the multiple-step form?

# BRIEF EXERCISES

**BE5–1**  Presented below are the components in Nacho Cano Company's income statement. Determine the missing amounts.

*Compute missing amounts in determining net income.*
*(SO 1)*

|  | Sales | Cost of Goods Sold | Gross Profit | Operating Expenses | Net Income |
|---|---|---|---|---|---|
| (a) | $75,000 | ? | $33,500 | ? | $10,800 |
| (b) | $108,000 | $70,000 | ? | ? | 29,500 |
| (c) | ? | $71,900 | $99,600 | $39,500 | ? |

*Journalize perpetual inventory entries.*
*(SO 2, 3)*

**BE5–2**   Chico Company buys merchandise on account from Cesar Company. The selling price of the goods is $800, and the cost of the goods is $600. Both companies use perpetual inventory systems. Journalize the transaction on the books of both companies.

*Journalize sales transactions.*
*(SO 3)*

**BE5–3**   Prepare the journal entries to record the following transactions on Ednita Company's books using a perpetual inventory system.

(a) On March 2, Ednita Company sold $800,000 of merchandise to Nazario Company, terms 2/10, n/30. The cost of the merchandise sold was $600,000.

(b) On March 6, Nazario Company returned $120,000 of the merchandise purchased on March 2 because it was defective. The cost of the returned merchandise was $90,000.

(c) On March 12, Ednita Company received the balance due from Nazario Company.

*Journalize purchases transactions.*
*(SO 2)*

**BE5–4**   From the information in BE5–3, prepare the journal entries to record these transactions on Nazario Company's books under a perpetual inventory system.

*Prepare sales revenues section of income statement.*
*(SO 3)*

**BE5–5**   Matt Damon Company provides the following information for the month ended October 31, 1999: Sales on credit $280,000, Cash sales $100,000, Sales discounts $5,000, Sales returns and allowances $20,000. Prepare the sales revenues section of the income statement based on this information.

*Identify work sheet columns for selecting accounts.*
*(SO 6)*

**BE5–6**   Presented below is the format of the work sheet presented in the chapter.

| Trial Balance | | Adjustments | | Adjusted Trial Balance | | Income Statement | | Balance Sheet | |
|---|---|---|---|---|---|---|---|---|---|
| Dr. | Cr. | Dr. | Cr. | Dr. | Cr. | Dr. | Cr. | Dr. | Cr. |

Indicate where the following items will appear on the work sheet: (a) Cash, (b) Merchandise Inventory, (c) Sales, (d) Cost of goods sold.
*Example:*
    Cash: Trial balance debit column; Adjusted trial balance debit column; and Balance sheet debit column.

*Prepare closing entries for merchandise accounts.*
*(SO 6)*

**BE5–7**   Cajon Company has the following merchandise account balances: Sales $180,000, Sales Discounts $2,000, Cost of Goods Sold $100,000, and Merchandise Inventory $40,000. Prepare the entries to record the closing of these items to Income Summary.

*Contrast presentation in multiple-step and single-step income statements.*
*(SO 7)*

**BE5–8**   ▰▰▰▱▷  Explain where each of the following items would appear on (1) a multiple-step income statement and on (2) a single-step income statement: (a) gain on sale of equipment, (b) casualty loss from vandalism, and (c) cost of goods sold.

*Compute net sales, gross profit, and income from operations.*
*(SO 3, 4, 7)*

**BE5–9**   Assume Bayou Company has the following account balances: Sales $500,000, Sales Returns and Allowances $15,000, Cost of Goods Sold $340,000, Selling Expenses $70,000, and Administrative Expenses $40,000. Compute (a) net sales, (b) gross profit, and (c) income from operations.

# EXERCISES

*Journalize purchases transactions.*
*(SO 2)*

**E5–1**   Information related to Esplande Co. is presented below.

1. On April 5, purchased merchandise from Dumaine Company for $16,000 terms 2/10, net/30, FOB shipping point.
2. On April 6 paid freight costs of $900 on merchandise purchased from Dumaine.
3. On April 7, purchased equipment on account for $26,000.
4. On April 8, returned damaged merchandise to Dumaine Company and was granted a $3,000 allowance.
5. On April 15 paid the amount due to Dumaine Company in full.

*Instructions*

(a) Prepare the journal entries to record these transactions on the books of Esplande Co. under a perpetual inventory system.

(b) Assume that Esplande Co. paid the balance due to Dumaine Company on May 4 instead of April 15. Prepare the journal entry to record this payment.

**E5–2**   On September 1, College Office Supply had an inventory of 30 deluxe pocket calculators at a cost of $20 each. The company uses a perpetual inventory system. During September, the following transactions occurred.

*Journalize perpetual inventory entries.*
(SO 2, 3)

Sept.  6   Purchased 80 calculators at $19 each from Digital Co. for cash.
    9   Paid freight of $80 on calculators purchased from Digital Co.
  10   Returned 2 calculators to Digital Co. for $40 credit because they did not meet specifications.
  12   Sold 26 calculators costing $20 (including freight-in) for $30 each to Campus Book Store, terms, n/30.
  14   Granted credit of $30 to Campus Book Store for the return of one calculator that was not ordered.
  20   Sold 30 calculators costing $20 for $30 each to Varsity Card Shop, terms, n/30.

**Instructions**
Journalize the September transactions.

**E5–3**   On June 10, Arcadian Company purchased $6,000 of merchandise from R. Duvall Company FOB shipping point, terms 2/10, n/30. Arcadian pays the freight costs of $300 on June 11. Damaged goods totaling $300 are returned to R. Duvall for credit on June 12. On June 19, Arcadian pays R. Duvall Company in full, less the purchase discount. Both companies use a perpetual inventory system.

*Prepare purchase and sale entries and closing entries.*
(SO 2, 3)

**Instructions**
(a) Prepare separate entries for each transaction on the books of Arcadian Company.
(b) Prepare separate entries for each transaction for Duvall Company. The merchandise purchased by Arcadian on June 10 had cost Duvall $3,000.

**E5–4**   Presented below are transactions related to S. Pippen Company.

*Journalize sales transactions.*
(SO 3)

1. On December 3, S. Pippen Company sold $480,000 of merchandise to D. Rodman Co., terms 2/10, n/30, FOB shipping point. The cost of the merchandise sold was $320,000.
2. On December 8, D. Rodman Co. was granted an allowance of $20,000 for merchandise purchased on December 3.
3. On December 13, S. Pippen Company received the balance due from D. Rodman Co.

**Instructions**
(a) Prepare the journal entries to record these transactions on the books of S. Pippen Company using a perpetual inventory system.
(b) Assume that S. Pippen Company received the balance due from D. Rodman Co. on January 2 of the following year instead of December 13. Prepare the journal entry to record the receipt of payment on January 2.

**E5–5**   The adjusted trial balance of Lopez Company shows the following data pertaining to sales at the end of its fiscal year October 31, 1999: Sales $800,000, Freight-out $12,000, Sales Returns and Allowances $24,000, and Sales Discounts $15,000.

*Prepare sales revenues section and closing entries.*
(SO 3, 5, 6)

**Instructions**
(a) Prepare the sales revenues section of the income statement.
(b) Prepare separate closing entries for (1) sales, and (2) the contra accounts to sales.

**E5–6**   Presented is information related to Gonzales Co. for the month of January 1999.

*Prepare closing entries.*
(SO 6)

| | | | |
|---|---|---|---|
| Cost of Goods Sold | 208,000 | Salary expense | 61,000 |
| Freight-out | 7,000 | Sales discounts | 8,000 |
| Insurance expense | 12,000 | Sales returns and allowances | 13,000 |
| Rent expense | 20,000 | Sales | 350,000 |

**Instructions**
Prepare the necessary closing entries.

**E5–7**   Presented below are selected accounts for Alvarez Company as reported in the work sheet at the end of May 1999.

*Complete work sheet.*
(SO 6)

| Accounts | Adjusted Trial Balance | | Income Statement | | Balance Sheet | |
|---|---|---|---|---|---|---|
| | Dr. | Cr. | Dr. | Cr. | Dr. | Cr. |
| Cash | 9,000 | | | | | |
| Merchandise Inventory | 80,000 | | | | | |
| Sales | | 450,000 | | | | |
| Sales Returns and Allowances | 10,000 | | | | | |
| Sales Discounts | 5,000 | | | | | |
| Cost of Goods Sold | 250,000 | | | | | |

**Instructions**

Complete the work sheet by extending amounts reported in the adjusted trial balance to the appropriate columns in the work sheet. Do not total individual columns.

*Prepare multiple-step and single-step income statements.*
*(SO 7)*

**E5–8**  In its income statement for the year ended December 31, 1999, Acevedo Company reported the following condensed data:

| | | | |
|---|---|---|---|
| Administrative expenses | $435,000 | Selling expenses | $ 690,000 |
| Cost of goods sold | 989,000 | Loss on sale of equipment | 10,000 |
| Interest expense | 70,000 | Net sales | 2,350,000 |
| Interest revenue | 45,000 | | |

**Instructions**

(a) Prepare a multiple-step income statement.
(b) Prepare a single-step income statement.

*Prepare correcting entries for sales and purchases.*
*(SO 2, 3)*

**E5–9**  An inexperienced accountant for Salvador Company made the following errors in recording merchandising transactions:

1. A $150 refund to a customer for faulty merchandise was debited to Sales $150 and credited to Cash $150.
2. A $200 credit purchase of supplies was debited to Merchandise Inventory $200 and credited to Cash $200.
3. An $80 sales discount was debited to Sales.
4. A cash payment of $30 for freight on merchandise purchases was debited to Freight-out $300 and credited to Cash $300.

**Instructions**

Prepare separate correcting entries for each error, assuming that the incorrect entry is not reversed. (Omit explanations.)

*Compute missing amounts.*
*(SO 3, 4, 5)*

**E5–10**  Presented below is financial information for two different companies:

| | Alatorre Company | Eduardo Company |
|---|---|---|
| Sales | $90,000 | (d) |
| Sales returns | (a) | $ 5,000 |
| Net sales | 81,000 | 95,000 |
| Cost of goods sold | 56,000 | (e) |
| Gross profit | (b) | 38,000 |
| Operating expenses | 15,000 | (f) |
| Net income | (c) | 15,000 |

**Instructions**

Determine the missing amounts.

# PROBLEMS: SET A

*Journalize, post, and prepare partial income statement.*
*(SO 2, 3, 4, 5)*

**P5–1A**  Carlos Hardware Store completed the following merchandising transactions in the month of May. At the beginning of May, the ledger of Carlos showed Cash of $5,000 and J. Carlos, Capital of $5,000.

May  1  Purchased merchandise on account from Depot Wholesale Supply $6,000, terms 2/10, n/30.

2  Sold merchandise on account $4,500, terms 2/10, n/30. The cost of the merchandise sold was $3,000.

5  Received credit from Depot Wholesale Supply for merchandise returned $200.

9  Received collections in full, less discounts, from customers billed on sales of $4,500 on May 2.

10  Paid Depot Wholesale Supply in full, less discount.

11  Purchased supplies for cash $900.

12  Purchased merchandise for cash $2,400.

15  Received refund for poor quality merchandise from supplier on cash purchase $230.

17  Purchased merchandise from Harlow Distributors $1,900, FOB shipping point, terms 2/10, n/30.

19  Paid freight on May 17 purchase $250.

24  Sold merchandise for cash $6,200. The merchandise sold had a cost of $4,340.

25  Purchased merchandise from Horicon Inc. $1,000, FOB destination, terms 2/10, n/30.

27  Paid Harlow Distributors in full, less discount.

29  Made refunds to cash customers for defective merchandise $100. The returned merchandise had a cost of $70.

31  Sold merchandise on account $1,600, terms n/30. The cost of the merchandise sold was $1,120.

Carlos Hardware's chart of accounts includes the following: No. 101 Cash, No. 112 Accounts Receivable, No. 120 Merchandise Inventory, No. 126 Supplies, No. 201 Accounts Payable, No. 301 J. Carlos Capital, No. 401 Sales, No. 412 Sales Returns and Allowances, No. 414 Sales Discounts, No. 505 Cost of Goods Sold.

### Instructions

(a) Journalize the transactions using a perpetual inventory system.

(b) Enter the beginning cash and capital balances and post the transactions. (Use J1 for the journal reference.)

(c) Prepare an income statement through gross profit for the month of May 1999.

**P5–2A**  Presented below are selected transactions for the Anna Mossity Company during September of the current year. Anna Mossity Company uses the perpetual inventory system.

*Journalize entries under a perpetual inventory system. (SO 2,3)*

Sept.  2  Purchased delivery equipment on account for $28,000.

4  Purchased merchandise on account from Carol Ling Company at a cost of $50,000, terms FOB shipping point, 2/10, n/30.

5  Paid freight charges of $2,000 on merchandise purchased from Carol Ling Company on September 4.

5  Returned damaged goods costing $7,000 received from Carol Ling Company on September 4.

6  Sold merchandise to Sal A. Mander Company costing $15,000 on account for $21,000, terms 1/10, n/30.

14  Paid Carol Ling balance due related to September 4 transaction.

15  Purchased supplies costing $4,000 for cash.

16  Received balance due from Sal A. Mander Company.

18  Purchased merchandise for cash $6,000.

22  Sold to Wayne E. Weather Company on account for $28,000 inventory costing $20,000, terms 1/10, n/30.

### Instructions

Journalize the September transactions.

*Complete accounting cycle beginning with a work sheet. (SO 5, 6, 7)*

**P5–3A**  The trial balance of Monty Zuma Wholesale Company contained the following accounts at December 31, the end of the company's fiscal year:

### MONTY ZUMA WHOLESALE COMPANY
### Trial Balance
### December 31, 1999

|  | Debit | Credit |
|---|---|---|
| Cash | $    23,400 |  |
| Accounts Receivable | 37,600 |  |
| Merchandise Inventory | 90,000 |  |
| Land | 92,000 |  |
| Buildings | 197,000 |  |
| Accumulated Depreciation—Buildings |  | $    54,000 |
| Equipment | 83,500 |  |
| Accumulated Depreciation—Equipment |  | 42,400 |
| Notes Payable |  | 50,000 |
| Accounts Payable |  | 37,500 |
| M. Zuma, Capital |  | 267,800 |
| M. Zuma, Drawing | 10,000 |  |
| Sales |  | 902,100 |
| Sales Discounts | 4,600 |  |
| Cost of Goods Sold | 709,900 |  |
| Salaries Expense | 69,800 |  |
| Utilities Expense | 19,400 |  |
| Repair Expense | 5,900 |  |
| Gas and Oil Expense | 7,200 |  |
| Insurance Expense | 3,500 |  |
|  | $1,353,800 | $1,353,800 |

Adjustment data:

1. Depreciation is $10,000 on buildings and $9,000 on equipment. (Both are administrative expenses.)
2. Interest of $7,000 is due and unpaid on notes payable at December 31.

Other data:

1. Salaries are 80% selling and 20% administrative.
2. Utilities expense, repair expense, and insurance expense are 100% administrative.
3. $15,000 of the notes payable are payable next year.
4. Gas and oil expense is a selling expense.

**Instructions**

(a) Enter the trial balance on a work sheet and complete the work sheet.
(b) Prepare a multiple-step income statement and owner's equity statement for the year, and a classified balance sheet at December 31, 1999.
(c) Journalize the adjusting entries.
(d) Journalize the closing entries
(e) Prepare a post-closing trial balance.

*Prepare financial statements and adjusting and closing entries.*
(SO 5, 6, 7)

**P5–4A**  Rowbuck Department Store is located in midtown Metropolis. During the past several years, net income has been declining because of suburban shopping centers. At the end of the company's fiscal year on November 30, 1999, the following accounts appeared in two of its trial balances:

|  | Unadjusted | Adjusted |
|---|---|---|
| Accounts Payable | $ 47,310 | $ 47,310 |
| Accounts Receivable | 11,770 | 11,770 |
| Accumulated Depreciation—Delivery Equipment | 15,680 | 19,680 |
| Accumulated Depreciation—Store Equipment | 32,300 | 41,800 |
| Cash | 8,000 | 8,000 |
| N. Rowbuck, Capital | 84,200 | 84,200 |
| Cost of Goods Sold | 633,220 | 633,220 |

|  | Unadjusted | Adjusted |
|---|---|---|
| Delivery Expense | 8,200 | 8,200 |
| Delivery Equipment | 57,000 | 57,000 |
| Depreciation Expense—Delivery Equipment |  | 4,000 |
| Depreciation Expense—Store Equipment |  | 9,500 |
| N. Rowbuck, Drawing | 12,000 | 12,000 |
| Insurance Expense |  | 9,000 |
| Interest Expense | 8,000 | 8,000 |
| Interest Revenue | 5,000 | 5,000 |
| Merchandise Inventory | 36,200 | 36,200 |
| Notes Payable | 46,000 | 46,000 |
| Prepaid Insurance | 13,500 | 4,500 |
| Property Tax Expense |  | 3,500 |
| Property Taxes Payable |  | 3,500 |
| Rent Expense | 19,000 | 19,000 |
| Salaries Expense | 120,000 | 120,000 |
| Sales | 850,000 | 850,000 |
| Sales Commissions Expense | 8,000 | 14,000 |
| Sales Commissions Payable |  | 6,000 |
| Sales Returns and Allowances | 10,000 | 10,000 |
| Store Equipment | 125,000 | 125,000 |
| Utilities Expense | 10,600 | 10,600 |

Analysis reveals the following additional data:

1. Salaries expense is 70% selling and 30% administrative.
2. Insurance expense is 50% selling and 50% administrative.
3. Rent expense, utilities expense, and property tax expense are administrative expenses.
4. Notes payable are due in 2002.

**Instructions**
(a) Prepare a multiple-step income statement, an owner's equity statement, and a classified balance sheet.
(b) Journalize the adjusting entries that were made.
(c) Journalize the closing entries that are necessary.

**P5–5A**  Chi Chi Garcia, a former professional golf star, operates Chi Chi's Pro Shop at Bay Golf Course. At the beginning of the current season on April 1, the ledger of Chi Chi's Pro Shop showed Cash $2,500, Merchandise Inventory $3,500, and C. C. Garcia, Capital $6,000. The following transactions were completed during April.

*Journalize, post, and prepare a trial balance.*
*(SO 2, 3, 6)*

Apr. 5   Purchased golf bags, clubs, and balls on account from Balata Co. $1,600, FOB shipping point, terms 2/10, n/60.
     7   Paid freight on Balata purchase $80.
     9   Received credit from Balata Co. for merchandise returned $100.
    10   Sold merchandise on account to members $900, terms n/30. The merchandise sold had a cost of $630.
    12   Purchased golf shoes, sweaters, and other accessories on account from Titleist Sportswear $660, terms 1/10, n/30.
    14   Paid Balata Co. in full.
    17   Received credit from Titleist Sportswear for merchandise returned $60.
    20   Made sales on account to members $700, terms n/30. The cost of the merchandise sold was $490.
    21   Paid Titleist Sportswear in full.
    27   Granted an allowance to members for clothing that did not fit properly $30.
    30   Received payments on account from members $1,100.

The chart of accounts for the pro shop includes the following: No. 101 Cash, No. 112 Accounts Receivable, No. 120 Merchandise Inventory, No. 201 Accounts Payable, No. 301 C. C. Garcia, Capital, No. 401 Sales, No. 412 Sales Returns and Allowances, No. 505 Cost of Goods Sold.

*Instructions*

(a) Journalize the April transactions using a perpetual inventory system.
(b) Enter the beginning balances in the ledger accounts and post the April transactions. (Use J1 for the journal reference.)
(c) Prepare a trial balance on April 30, 1999.

# PROBLEMS: SET B

*Journalize, post, and prepare a partial income statement.*
*(SO 2, 3, 4, 5)*

**P5–1B**  The Maggie Zine Distributing Company completed the following merchandising transactions in the month of April. At the beginning of April, the ledger of Maggie Zine showed Cash of $9,000 and M. Zine, Capital of $9,000.

Apr.  2   Purchased merchandise on account from Ken Tuckee Supply Co. $5,900, terms 2/10, n/30.
       4   Sold merchandise on account $5,000, FOB destination, terms 2/10, n/30. The cost of the merchandise sold was $4,000.
       5   Paid $200 freight on April 4 sale.
       6   Received credit from Ken Tuckee Supply Co. for merchandise returned $300.
      11   Paid Ken Tuckee Supply Co. in full, less discount.
      13   Received collections in full, less discounts, from customers billed on April 4.
      14   Purchased merchandise for cash $4,400.
      16   Received refund from supplier on cash purchase of April 14, $500.
      18   Purchased merchandise from Ida Hoe Distributors $4,200, FOB shipping point, terms 2/10, n/30.
      20   Paid freight on April 18 purchase $100.
      23   Sold merchandise for cash $6,400. The merchandise sold had a cost of $5,120.
      26   Purchased merchandise for cash $2,300.
      27   Paid Ida Hoe Distributors in full, less discount.
      29   Made refunds to cash customers for defective merchandise $90. The returned merchandise had a cost of $70.
      30   Sold merchandise on account $3,700, terms n/30. The cost of the merchandise sold was $3,000.

Maggie Zine Company's chart of accounts includes the following: No. 101 Cash, No. 112 Accounts Receivable, No. 120 Merchandise Inventory, No. 201 Accounts Payable, No. 301 M. Zine, Capital, No. 401 Sales, No. 412 Sales Returns and Allowances, No. 414 Sales Discounts, No. 505 Cost of Goods Sold, and No. 644 Freight-out.

*Instructions*

(a) Journalize the transactions using a perpetual inventory system.
(b) Enter the beginning cash and capital balances, and post the transactions. (Use J1 for the journal reference.)
(c) Prepare the income statement through gross profit for the month of April 1999.

*Journalize transactions under a perpetual inventory system.*
*(SO 2, 3)*

**P5–2B**  Tom E. Hawk Auto Sales uses a perpetual inventory system. On April 1, the new car inventory records show total inventory of $144,000 consisting of the following:

| Model | Units | Unit Cost |
|---|---|---|
| Custom Sedans | 4 | $15,000 |
| Convertibles | 3 | 16,000 |
| Recreational Vans | 2 | 18,000 |

During April, the following purchases and sales were made on account.

April  5   Purchased three custom sedans for $15,000 each.
       7   Sold two custom sedans for $18,200 each.
      13   Purchased two recreational vans for $18,000 each.
      17   Sold one custom sedan for $18,500.

20   Purchased two convertibles for $16,000 each.
22   Returned one convertible purchased on April 20 for $16,000 credit.
24   Sold three recreational vans for $24,000 each.
28   Sold one convertible for $21,000.

*Instructions*
Journalize the transactions using a perpetual inventory system.

**P5–3B**   The trial balance of Cal A. Fornia Fashion Center contained the following accounts at November 30, the end of the company's fiscal year.

*Complete accounting cycle beginning with a work sheet.*
*(SO 5, 6, 7)*

### CAL A. FORNIA FASHION CENTER
### Trial Balance
### November 30, 1999

|  | Debit | Credit |
|---|---|---|
| Cash | $ 26,700 |  |
| Accounts Receivable | 33,700 |  |
| Merchandise Inventory | 45,000 |  |
| Store Supplies | 5,500 |  |
| Store Equipment | 85,000 |  |
| Accumulated Depreciation—Store Equipment |  | $ 18,000 |
| Delivery Equipment | 48,000 |  |
| Accumulated Depreciation—Delivery Equipment |  | 6,000 |
| Notes Payable |  | 51,000 |
| Accounts Payable |  | 48,500 |
| C. A. Fornia, Capital |  | 110,000 |
| C. A. Fornia, Drawing | 12,000 |  |
| Sales |  | 757,200 |
| Sales Returns and Allowances | 4,200 |  |
| Cost of Goods Sold | 497,400 |  |
| Salaries Expense | 140,000 |  |
| Advertising Expense | 26,400 |  |
| Utilities Expense | 14,000 |  |
| Repair Expense | 12,100 |  |
| Delivery Expense | 16,700 |  |
| Rent Expense | 24,000 |  |
|  | $990,700 | $990,700 |

Adjustment data:

1. Store supplies on hand totaled $3,500.
2. Depreciation is $9,000 on the store equipment and $7,000 on the delivery equipment.
3. Interest of $11,000 is accrued on notes payable at November 30.

Other data:

1. Salaries expense is 70% selling and 30% administrative.
2. Rent expense and utilities expense are 80% selling and 20% administrative.
3. $30,000 of notes payable are due for payment next year.
4. Repair expense is 100% administrative.

*Instructions*
(a) Enter the trial balance on a work sheet and complete the work sheet.
(b) Prepare a multiple-step income statement and owner's equity statement for the year and a classified balance sheet as of November 30, 1999.
(c) Journalize the adjusting entries.
(d) Journalize the closing entries.
(e) Prepare a post-closing trial balance.

**P5–4B**   The Al Falfa Department Store is located near the Village shopping mall. At the end of the company's fiscal year on December 31, 1999, the following accounts appeared in two of its trial balances.

*Prepare financial statements and adjusting and closing entries.*
*(SO 5, 6, 7)*

|  | Unadjusted | Adjusted |
|---|---|---|
| Accounts Payable | $ 79,300 | $ 79,300 |
| Accounts Receivable | 50,300 | 50,300 |
| Accumulated Depreciation—Building | 42,100 | 52,500 |
| Accumulated Depreciation—Equipment | 29,600 | 42,900 |
| Building | 190,000 | 190,000 |
| Cash | 23,000 | 23,000 |
| L. Markan, Capital | 176,600 | 176,600 |
| Cost of Goods Sold | 412,700 | 412,700 |
| Depreciation Expense—Building |  | 10,400 |
| Depreciation Expense—Equipment |  | 13,300 |
| L. Markan, Drawing | 28,000 | 28,000 |
| Equipment | 110,000 | 110,000 |
| Insurance Expense |  | 7,200 |
| Interest Expense | 3,000 | 11,000 |
| Interest Payable |  | 8,000 |
| Interest Revenue | 4,000 | 4,000 |
| Merchandise Inventory | 75,000 | 75,000 |
| Mortgage Payable | 80,000 | 80,000 |
| Office Salaries Expense | 32,000 | 32,000 |
| Prepaid Insurance | 9,600 | 2,400 |
| Property Taxes Expense |  | 4,800 |
| Property Taxes Payable |  | 4,800 |
| Sales Salaries Expense | 76,000 | 76,000 |
| Sales | 628,000 | 628,000 |
| Sales Commissions Expense | 11,000 | 14,500 |
| Sales Commissions Payable |  | 3,500 |
| Sales Returns and Allowances | 8,000 | 8,000 |
| Utilities Expense | 11,000 | 11,000 |

Analysis reveals the following additional data:

1. Insurance expense and utilities expense are 60% selling and 40% administrative.
2. $20,000 of the mortgage payable is due for payment next year.
3. Depreciation on the building and property tax expense are administrative expenses; depreciation on the equipment is a selling expense.

**Instructions**
(a) Prepare a multiple-step income statement, an owner's equity statement, and a classi-fied balance sheet.
(b) Journalize the adjusting entries that were made.
(c) Journalize the closing entries that are necessary.

*Journalize, post, and prepare a trial balance.*
*(SO 2, 3, 6)*

**P5–5B**  Bobby Jo Evans, a former professional tennis star, operates B.J.'s Tennis Shop at the Jackson Lake Resort. At the beginning of the current season, the ledger of B.J.'s Tennis Shop showed Cash $2,500, Merchandise Inventory $1,700, and B. J. Evans, Capital $4,200. The fol-lowing transactions were completed during April:

Apr.  4  Purchased racquets and balls from Sampras Co. $640 FOB shipping point, terms 3/10, n/30.
      6  Paid freight on Sampras's purchase $40.
      8  Sold merchandise to members $900, terms n/30. The merchandise sold had a cost of $600.
     10  Received credit of $40 from Sampras Co. for a damaged racquet that was returned.
     11  Purchased tennis shoes from Niki Sports for cash, $300.
     13  Paid Sampras Co. in full.
     14  Purchased tennis shirts and shorts from Martina's Sportswear $700, FOB shipping point, terms 2/10, n/60.
     15  Received cash refund of $50 from Niki Sports for damaged merchandise that was returned.

17   Paid freight on Martina's Sportswear purchase $30.
18   Sold merchandise to members, $800, terms n/30. The cost of the merchandise sold was $530.
20   Received $500 in cash from members in settlement of their accounts.
21   Paid Martina's Sportswear in full.
27   Granted an allowance of $30 to members for tennis clothing that did not fit properly.
30   Received cash payments on account from members, $500.

The chart of accounts for the tennis shop includes the following: No. 101 Cash, No. 112 Accounts Receivable, No. 120 Merchandise Inventory, No. 201 Accounts Payable, No. 301 B. J. Evans, Capital, No. 401 Sales, No. 412 Sales Returns and Allowances, No. 505 Cost of Goods Sold.

*Instructions*
(a) Journalize the April transactions using a perpetual inventory system.
(b) Enter the beginning balances in the ledger accounts and post the April transactions. (Use J1 for the journal reference.)
(c) Prepare a trial balance on April 30, 1999.

## BROADENING YOUR PERSPECTIVE

# FINANCIAL REPORTING AND ANALYSIS

### FINANCIAL REPORTING PROBLEM: Kellogg Company

**BYP5–1**   The financial statements of Kellogg Company are presented in Appendix A at the end of this textbook.

*Instructions*
Answer the following questions using the Consolidated Statement of Earnings.

(a) What was the percentage change in (1) sales and in (2) net income from 1995 to 1996 and from 1996 to 1997?
(b) What was Kellogg's gross profit rate in 1995, 1996, and 1997?
(c) What was Kellogg's percentage of net income to net sales in 1995, 1996, and 1997? Comment on any trend in this percentage.

### COMPARATIVE ANALYSIS PROBLEM: Kellogg Company vs. General Mills

**BYP5–2**   Kellogg's financial statements are presented in Appendix A; General Mills's financial statements are presented in Appendix B.

*Instructions*
(a) Based on the information contained in these financial statements, determine each of the following for each company:
(1) Gross profit for 1997.
(2) Gross profit rate for 1997.
(3) Operating income for 1997.
(4) Percent change in operating income from 1996 to 1997.
(b) What conclusions concerning the relative profitability of the two companies can be drawn from these data?

### RESEARCH ASSIGNMENT

**BYP5–3**   The April 1996 issue of the *Journal of Accountancy* includes an article by Dennis R. Beresford, L. Todd Johnson, and Cheri L. Reither, entitled "Is a Second Income Statement Needed?"

*Instructions*

Read the article and answer the following questions:

(a) On what basis would the "second income statement" be prepared? Briefly describe this basis.

(b) Why is there a perceived need for a second income statement?

(c) Identify three alternatives for reporting the proposed measure of income.

## INTERPRETING FINANCIAL STATEMENTS: McDonnell Douglas

**BYP5–4**   Before being purchased by Boeing Co. in 1997, McDonnell Douglas, based in St. Louis, Missouri, described itself in its Annual Report as the world's largest builder of fighter and military transport aircraft, the third largest commercial aircraft maker, and a leading producer of helicopters, missiles, and satellite launch vehicles. The company's strategy for future growth might have been described as "cautiously aggressive," because it aggressively competed in markets in which it believed that it had a competitive advantage, while it evaluated other markets carefully, and then expanded its product line or divested, depending upon whether it believed that it could remain or become a leading competitor.

A recent pre-merger McDonnell Douglas income statement is reproduced below. Dollar amounts are in millions.

### McDONNELL DOUGLAS
### Income Statement (partial)

| | |
|---|---:|
| Revenues | $13,176 |
| Costs and expenses: | |
|     Cost of products, services, and rentals | 11,026 |
|     General and administrative expenses | 684 |
|     Research and development | 297 |
|     Interest expense | 249 |
|       Total costs and expenses | 12,256 |
| Earnings before income taxes | 920 |
| Income taxes | 322 |
| Net earnings | $    598 |

*Instructions*

(a) What account name appears to represent McDonnell Douglas's cost of goods sold account? Why do you think that company chose the account name that it did? Using that account as cost of goods sold, what is gross profit?

(b) The income statement shown is in summary form. This means that each account title listed is a summary of several other accounts. For example, the Revenue account includes such things as Commercial Aircraft Revenue, Defense Contract Revenue, and so forth, as well as any offsetting accounts such as Sales Discounts. Indicate in which summary account from the income statement the following merchandising accounts would be located:

1. Sales returns and allowances.

2. Freight-in.

3. Merchandise inventory increases and decreases.

4. Sales discounts.

(c) The company was evaluating a divisional plant that would build satellite launch vehicles. The product line consisted of a single vehicle, which was the only one of its kind, but competitors had built vehicles that could launch smaller satellites. The company was confident that it could produce an expanded product line, which would include both larger and smaller vehicles than the one currently made. The two choices being evaluated were: First, spend approximately $17 million in research and development to expand the product line. This cost would be considered an expense immediately. Revenue of about $100 million would be generated each year, beginning two years after development; it would continue at least five years, but possibly more. Second, sell the assets of the existing business to a competitor. This would generate a gain of $315 million next year.

If the choice had been made at the end of this year, how would net income be affected under each alternative? How would gross profit change? Which alternative would you have recommended? Give reasons for your answer.

## REAL-WORLD FOCUS: A.L. Laboratories

BYP5–5  **A.L. Laboratories** is headquartered in Ft. Lee, N.J., and also has operations in Scandinavia and Indonesia. The company develops and produces generic pharmaceuticals, specializing in both over-the-counter and prescription creams and ointments, aerosol inhalants, and liquids such as cough syrups. A significant share of its income is also derived from the development and distribution of animal health products such as food additives for poultry. The company was founded in 1975 and today has over 2,700 employees.

Gross profit at A.L. Laboratories declined in both dollars and as a percentage of revenues. The decline was attributed to lower sales volume, customer credits associated with product recalls, inventory disposals, and the impact of higher inventory costs. In addition to the above, the gross profit percentage declined as a result of lower production volumes.

### Instructions
(a) What account is affected when A.L. Laboratories has a product recall?
(b) What factors caused gross profit to decline?
(c) What factors could cause this company to have to dispose of inventory?

# CRITICAL THINKING
......................................................................................................................................

## GROUP DECISION CASE

BYP5–6  Three years ago, Kathy Webb and her brother-in-law John Utley opened FedCo Department Store. For the first 2 years, business was good, but the following condensed income results for 1998 were disappointing.

### FEDCO DEPARTMENT STORE
### Income Statement
### For the Year Ended December 31, 1998

| | | |
|---|---:|---:|
| Net sales | | $700,000 |
| Cost of goods sold | | 546,000 |
| Gross profit | | 154,000 |
| Operating expenses | | |
| Selling expenses | $100,000 | |
| Administrative expenses | 25,000 | 125,000 |
| Net income | | $ 29,000 |

Kathy believes the problem lies in the relatively low gross profit rate (gross profit divided by net sales) of 22%. John believes the problem is that operating expenses are too high.

Kathy thinks the gross profit rate can be improved by making both of the following changes: (1) Increase average selling prices by 17%; this increase is expected to lower sales volume so that total sales will increase only 6%. (2) Buy merchandise in larger quantities and take all purchase discounts; these changes are expected to increase the gross profit rate by 3%. Kathy does not anticipate that these changes will have any effect on operating expenses.

John thinks expenses can be cut by making both of the following changes: (1) Cut 1998 sales salaries of $60,000 in half and give sales personnel a commission of 2% of net sales. (2) Reduce store deliveries to one day per week rather than twice a week; this change will reduce 1998 delivery expenses of $30,000 by 40%. John feels that these changes will not have any effect on net sales.

Kathy and John come to you for help in deciding the best way to improve net income.

*Instructions*

With the class divided into groups, answer the following:

(a) Prepare a condensed income statement for 1999 assuming (1) Kathy's changes are implemented and (2) John's ideas are adopted.
(b) What is your recommendation to Kathy and John?
(c) Prepare a condensed income statement for 1999 assuming both sets of proposed changes are made.

## COMMUNICATION ACTIVITY

**BYP5–7**   The following situation is in chronological order:

1. Dexter decides to buy a surfboard.
2. He calls Surfing USA Co. to inquire about their surfboards.
3. Two days later he requests Surfing USA Co. to make him a surfboard.
4. Three days later, Surfing USA Co. sends him a purchase order to fill out.
5. He sends back the purchase order.
6. Surfing USA Co. receives the completed purchase order.
7. Surfing USA Co. completes the surfboard.
8. Dexter picks up the surfboard.
9. Surfing USA Co. bills Dexter.
10. Surfing USA Co. receives payment from Dexter.

*Instructions*

In a memo to the president of Surfing USA Co., explain the following:

(a) When should Surfing USA Co. record the sale?
(b) Suppose that with his purchase order, Dexter is required to make a down payment. Would that change your answer?

## ETHICS CASE

**BYP5–8**   Rita Pelzer was just hired as the assistant treasurer of Yorkshire Stores, a specialty chain store company consisting of nine retail stores concentrated in one metropolitan area. Among other things, the payment of all invoices is centralized in one of the departments Rita will manage. Her primary responsibility is to maintain the company's high credit rating by paying all bills when due and to take advantage of all cash discounts. Jamie Caterino, the former assistant treasurer who has been promoted to treasurer, is training Rita in her new duties. He instructs Rita that she is to continue the practice of preparing all checks "net of discount" and dating the checks the last day of the discount period. "But," Jamie continues, "we always hold the checks at least four days beyond the discount period before mailing them. That way we get another four days of interest on our money. Most of our creditors need our business and don't complain. And, if they scream about our missing the discount period, we blame it on the mail room or the post office. We've only lost one discount out of every hundred we take that way. I think everybody does it. By the way, welcome to our team!"

*Instructions*

(a) What are the ethical considerations in this case?
(b) Who are the stakeholders that are harmed or benefitted in this situation?
(c) Should Rita continue the practice started by Jamie? Does she have any choice?

# SURFING THE NET

**BYP5–9**   No financial decision maker should ever rely solely on the financial information reported in the annual report to make decisions. It is important to keep abreast of financial news. This activity demonstrates how to search for financial news on the Web.

**Address:** http://biz.yahoo.com

**Steps:**
1. Choose **Company**.
2. Type in either Kellogg Company or General Mills, Inc.

3. Choose **News**.
4. Select an article that sounds interesting to you.

*Instructions*

(a) What was the source of the article? (For example, Reuters, Businesswire, Prnewswire.)

(b) Pretend that you are a personal financial planner and that one of your clients owns stock in the company. Write a brief memo to your client summarizing the article and explaining the implications of the article for their investment.

---

*Answers to Self-Study Questions*

1. c    2. a    3. c    4. b    5. c    6. b    7. d    8. a    9. c    10. d

---

*Answer to Kellogg Review It Question 4, p. 201*

The 1997 gross profit rate is 52.1% ($3,560 ÷ $6,830.1) and the 1996 gross profit rate is 53.2% ($3,553.7 ÷ $6,676.6). The rate therefore decreased by 1.1% from 1996 to 1997. All this information was provided in the Kellogg Company's management discussion and analysis section. It also could be computed from the income statement presented.

**Remember to go back to the Navigator box on the chapter-opening page and check off your completed work.**

**Before studying this chapter, you should know or, if necessary, review:**

a. How to perform each of the steps in the accounting cycle.
   (Ch. 4, pp. 151–156)

b. How to record transactions for a merchandising company.
   (Ch. 5, pp. 188–199)

c. How to prepare financial statements for a merchandising company.
   (Ch. 5, pp. 200–204)

THE NAVIGATOR

## FEATURE STORY

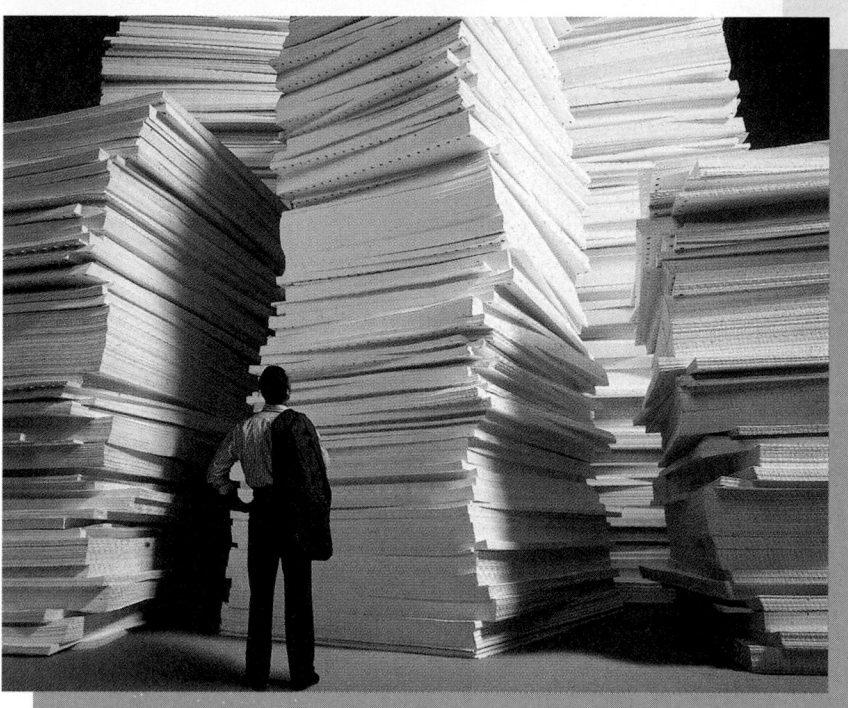

# Accidents Happen

How organized are you financially? Take a short quiz.

- Is your wallet jammed full of gas station receipts from places you don't remember ever going?
- Is your wallet such a mess that it is often faster to fish for money in the crack of your car seat than to dig around in your wallet?
- Was Michael Jordan playing high school basketball the last time you balanced your checkbook?
- Have you ever been tempted to burn down your house so you don't have to look for the receipts

and records that you need to fill out your tax returns?

If you think it is hard to keep track of the many transactions that make up *your* life, imagine what it is like for a major corporation like Fidelity Investments, which as the largest mutual fund management firm in the world, manages more than $400 billion of investments. Millions of individuals have the bulk of their life savings invested in mutual funds. If you were one of them, you might be just slightly displeased if, when you called to find out your balance, the representative said, "You know, I kind of remember

someone with a name like yours sending us some money—now what did we do with that?"

To ensure the accuracy of your balance and the security of your funds, Fidelity Investments, like all other companies large and small, relies on a sophisticated accounting information system. That's not to say that Fidelity or anybody else is error-free. In fact, if you've ever really messed up your checkbook register, you may take some comfort from one accountant's mistake at Fidelity Investments. The accountant failed to include a minus sign while doing a calculation, making what was actually a $1.3 billion loss look like a $1.3 billion gain! Fortunately, like most accounting errors, it was detected before any real harm was done.

No one expects that kind of mistake at a firm like Fidelity, which has sophisticated computer systems and top investment managers. In explaining the mistake to shareholders, a spokesperson wrote: "Some people have asked how, in this age of technology, such a mistake could be made. While many of our processes are computerized, accounting systems are complex and dictate that some steps must be handled manually by our managers and accountants, and people can make mistakes."

THE NAVIGATOR

*On the World Wide Web*
http://www.fidelity.com

# CHAPTER 6

**THE NAVIGATOR** ✔

- Understand *Concepts for Review*  ☐
- Read *Feature Story*  ☐
- Scan *Study Objectives*  ☐
- Read *Preview*  ☐
- Read text and answer *Before You Go On*
  p. 237 ☐  p. 250 ☐  p. 255 ☐
- Work *Demonstration Problem*  ☐
- Review *Summary of Study Objectives*  ☐
- Answer *Self-Study Questions*  ☐
- Complete assignments  ☐

# ACCOUNTING INFORMATION SYSTEMS

## STUDY OBJECTIVES

**After studying this chapter, you should be able to:**

1. *Identify the basic principles of accounting information systems.*
2. *Explain the major phases involved in the development of an accounting system.*
3. *Describe the nature and purpose of a subsidiary ledger.*
4. *Explain how special journals are used in journalizing.*
5. *Indicate how a columnar journal is posted.*
6. *Distinguish between computer hardware and accounting software and the principal methods of data processing.*
7. *Identify the key points in comparing manual and electronic accounting systems.*

THE NAVIGATOR

*A*s you see from the opening story, a reliable information system is a necessity for any company. Whether you use pen, pencil, or computers in maintaining accounting records, certain principles and procedures apply. The purpose of this chapter is to explain and illustrate these features. The content and organization of this chapter are as follows:

THE
NAVIGATOR

# SECTION 1 BASIC CONCEPTS

The system of collecting and processing transaction data and disseminating financial information to interested parties is known as the accounting information system. It includes each of the steps in the accounting cycle that you have studied in earlier chapters, the documents that provide evidence of the transactions and events, and the records, trial balances, work sheets, and financial statements that result. An accounting information system may be either manual or electronic.

# PRINCIPLES OF ACCOUNTING INFORMATION SYSTEMS

1
STUDY
OBJECTIVE

Identify the basic principles of accounting information systems.

To have an efficient and effective accounting information system (hereafter referred to simply as the accounting system), certain basic principles must be followed. These principles are: (1) cost awareness, (2) usefulness, and (3) flexibility, as shown in Illustration 6-1.

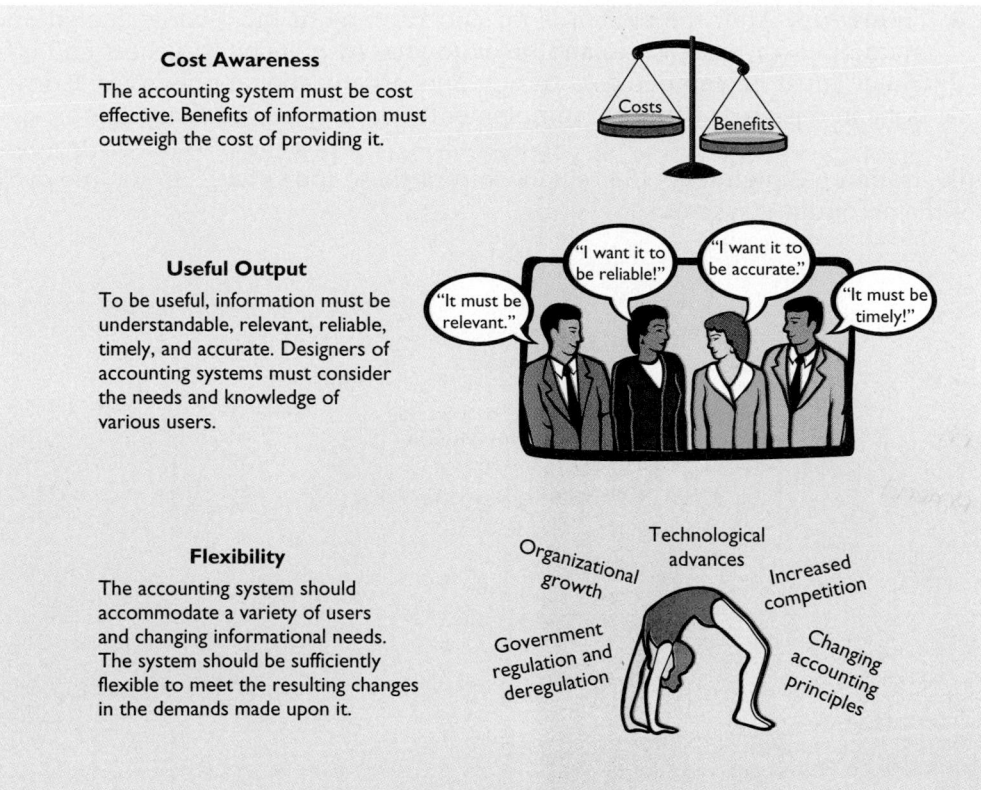

**ILLUSTRATION 6-1**

*Principles of an efficient and effective accounting information system*

If the accounting system is cost effective, provides useful output, and has the flexibility to meet future needs, it can provide a valuable service and make a major contribution to both individual and organizational goals.

# DEVELOPING AN ACCOUNTING SYSTEM

Good accounting systems do not just happen. They are carefully planned, designed, installed, managed, and refined. Generally, developing an accounting system involves the following four phases:

1. **Analysis.** The starting point of analysis is to determine the information needs of internal and external users. Once this is established, the system analyst proceeds to identify the sources of the information and the records and procedures for collecting and reporting the data. If an existing system is being analyzed, its strengths and weaknesses must be identified.

2. **Design.** For a new system, forms and documents must be designed; methods and procedures selected from alternatives; job descriptions prepared; controls integrated; reports formatted; and equipment selected. Redesigning an existing system may involve only minor changes, a complete overhaul, or replacement of a manual system by a computerized system.

3. **Implementation.** Implementation of either new or revised systems requires that documents, procedures, reports, and processing equipment must be installed and made operational. Personnel must be hired, trained, and closely supervised through a start-up or transition period.

**2**

STUDY OBJECTIVE

Explain the major phases involved in the development of an accounting system.

4. **Follow-up.** After the system is up and running, it must be evaluated and monitored for weaknesses and breakdowns. Also, its effectiveness and efficiency must be compared to design and organizational objectives. Corrections in design or changes in implementation may be necessary.

Illustration 6-2 highlights the relationship of these four phases in the life cycle of the accounting system.

**ILLUSTRATION 6-2**

*Phases in the development of an accounting system*

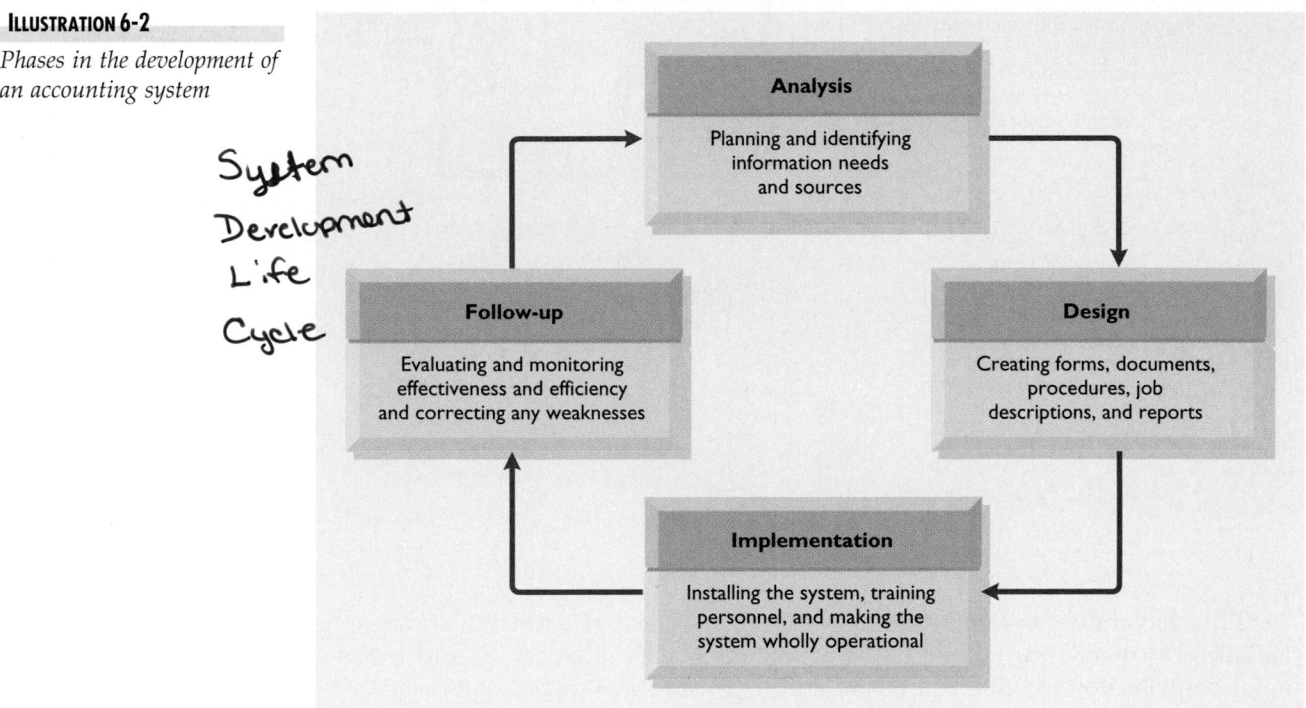

These phases, which represent the life cycle of an accounting system, suggest that few systems remain the same forever. As experience and knowledge are obtained, and as technological and organizational changes occur, the accounting system may also have to grow and change.

The accounting system in the first five chapters is satisfactory in a company where the volume of transactions is extremely low. However, in most companies, it is necessary to add additional ledgers and journals to the accounting system to record transaction data efficiently.

# SECTION 2    MANUAL ACCOUNTING SYSTEMS

In a manual accounting system, each of the steps in the accounting cycle is performed by hand. For example, each accounting transaction is entered manually in the journal and posted manually to the ledger. To obtain ledger account balances and to prepare a trial balance and financial statements, additional manual computations must be made. In this section, therefore, we discuss how the manual processing system can be more efficiently used to process accounting data.

At this point you might be wondering, "Why cover manual accounting systems if the real world uses computerized systems?" First, small businesses still abound. Most of them begin operations with manual (or even "shoe box") accounting systems and convert to computerized systems as the business grows. Second, to understand what computerized accounting systems do, you need to understand how manual accounting systems work.

# SUBSIDIARY LEDGERS

Imagine a business that has several thousand charge (credit) customers and shows the transactions with these customers in only one account—Accounts Receivable—in the general ledger. It would be virtually impossible to determine the balance owed by an individual customer at any specific time. Similarly, the amount payable to one creditor would be difficult to locate quickly from a single Accounts Payable account in the general ledger.

To provide such information, companies use subsidiary ledgers to keep track of individual balances. A subsidiary ledger is a group of accounts with a common characteristic (for example, all customer accounts—that is, accounts receivable). The subsidiary ledger frees the general ledger from the details of individual balances. A subsidiary ledger is an addition to, and an expansion of, the general ledger.

Two common subsidiary ledgers are:

1. The accounts receivable (or customers') ledger which accumulates transaction data with individual customers.
2. The accounts payable (or creditors') ledger which maintains transaction data with individual creditors.

In each of these subsidiary ledgers, individual accounts are usually arranged in alphabetical order.

The detailed data shown in a subsidiary ledger are summarized in a general ledger account. The accounts for the two ledgers above are Accounts Receivable and Accounts Payable, respectively. The general ledger account that summarizes subsidiary ledger data is called a control account. **Each general ledger control account balance must equal the composite balance of the individual accounts in the related subsidiary ledger at the end of an accounting period.** An overview of the relationship of subsidiary ledgers to the general ledger is shown in Illustration 6-3, with the general ledger control accounts and subsidiary ledger accounts in green color.

**3**
STUDY
OBJECTIVE
Describe the nature and purpose of a subsidiary ledger.

**ILLUSTRATION 6-3**

*Relationship of general ledgers and subsidiary accounts*

Note that cash and owner's capital in this illustration are not control accounts.

## Illustration

An example of a control account and subsidiary ledger for Larson Enterprises is provided in Illustration 6-4. The explanation column in these accounts is not shown in this and subsequent illustrations due to space considerations.

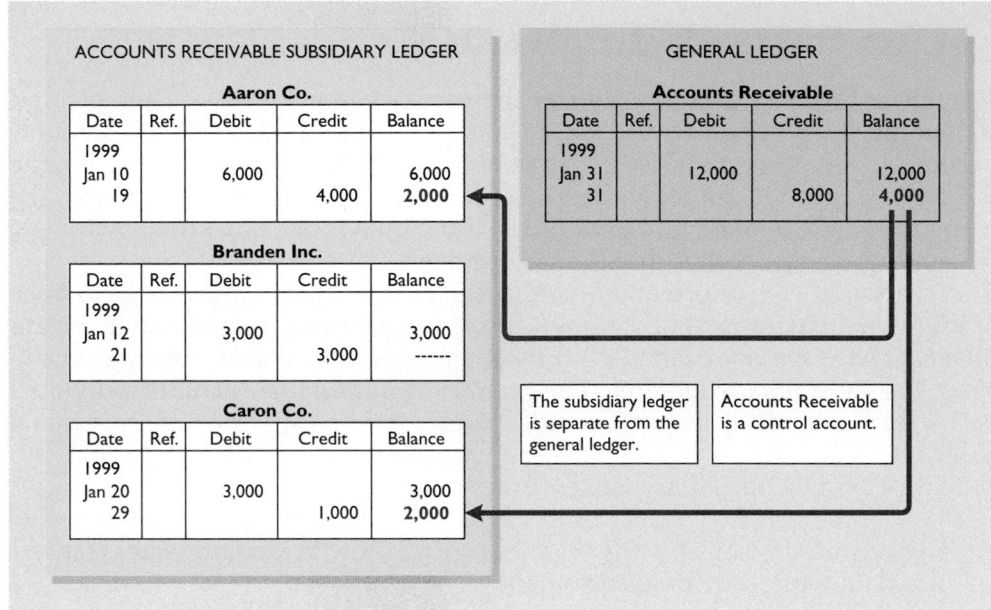

The example is based on the following transactions:

| Credit Sales | | | Collections on Account | | |
|---|---|---|---|---|---|
| Jan. 10 | Aaron Co. | $ 6,000 | Jan. 19 | Aaron Co. | $ 4,000 |
| 12 | Branden Inc. | 3,000 | 21 | Branden Inc. | 3,000 |
| 20 | Caron Co. | 3,000 | 29 | Caron Co. | 1,000 |
| | | $12,000 | | | $ 8,000 |

The total debits and credits in Accounts Receivable in the general ledger are reconcilable to the detailed debits and credits in the subsidiary accounts. In addition, the balance of $4,000 in the accounts receivable control account agrees with the total of the balances in the individual accounts (Aaron Co. $2,000 + Branden Inc. $0 + Caron Co. $2,000) in the subsidiary ledger.

As shown, postings are made monthly to the control accounts in the general ledger so that monthly financial statements may be prepared. Postings to the individual accounts in the subsidiary ledger are made daily. The rationale for posting daily is to ensure that current account information can be used as a basis for monitoring credit limits, billing customers, and answering inquiries from customers about their account balances.

## Advantages of Subsidiary Ledgers

The advantages of using subsidiary ledgers are that they:

1. **Show transactions affecting one customer or one creditor in a single account**, thus providing necessary up-to-date information on specific account balances.

2. **Free the general ledger of excessive details**. As a result, a trial balance of the general ledger does not contain vast numbers of individual account balances.

3. **Help locate errors in individual accounts** by reducing the number of accounts combined in one ledger and by using controlling accounts.

4. **Make possible a division of labor** in posting by having one employee post to the general ledger and someone else post to the subsidiary ledgers.

## TECHNOLOGY IN ACTION

 Rather than relying on customer or creditor names in a subsidiary ledger, a computer system expands the account number of the control account in a pre-specified manner. For example, if accounts receivable was numbered 10010, the first account in the accounts receivable subsidiary ledger might be numbered 10010-0001. Most systems allow inquiries about specific accounts in the subsidiary ledger (by account number) or about the control account. With the latter, the system would automatically total all the subsidiary accounts whenever an inquiry to the control account was made.

## BEFORE YOU GO ON . . .

### Review It

1. What are the basic principles to be followed in designing and developing an efficient and effective accounting information system?
2. What are the major phases in the development of an accounting information system?
3. What is a subsidiary ledger, and what purpose does it serve?

### Do It

Presented below is information related to Sims Company for its first month of operations. Identify the balances that appear in the accounts payable subsidiary ledger and the Accounts Payable balance that appears in the general ledger at the end of January.

| Credit Purchases | | | Cash Paid | | |
|---|---|---|---|---|---|
| Jan 5 | Devon Co. | $11,000 | Jan 9 | Devon Co. | $7,000 |
| Jan 11 | Shelby Co. | 7,000 | Jan 14 | Shelby Co. | 2,000 |
| Jan 22 | Taylor Co. | 14,000 | Jan 27 | Taylor Co. | 9,000 |

*Reasoning:* Note that only one account appears in the general ledger, but the detail related to this account is shown in the subsidiary ledger.

*Solution:* Subsidiary ledger balances: Devon Co. $4,000 ($11,000 − $7,000); Shelby Co. $5,000 ($7,000 − $2,000); Taylor Co. $5,000 ($14,000 − $9,000). General ledger Accounts Payable balance $14,000 ($32,000 − $18,000).

*Related exercise material:* BE6–3, BE6–4, E6–1, E6–2, E6–3, E6–4, E6–5, and E6–9.

THE
NAVIGATOR

## SPECIAL JOURNALS

So far you have learned to journalize transactions in a two-column general journal and post these entries individually to the general ledger. This procedure is satisfactory in only the very smallest companies. To expedite journalizing and posting transactions, most companies use special journals **in addition to the general journal**.

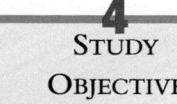

**4**
STUDY
OBJECTIVE
..................
Explain how special journals are used in journalizing.

A **special journal** is used to record similar types of transactions, such as all sales of merchandise on account, or all cash receipts. The types of special journals used depend largely on the types of transactions that occur frequently in a business enterprise. Most merchandising enterprises use the journals shown in Illustration 6-6 to record transactions daily:

**ILLUSTRATION 6-6**

*Use of special journals and the general journal*

If a transaction cannot be recorded in a special journal, it is recorded in the general journal. For example, if you had special journals only for the four types of transactions listed above, purchase returns and allowances or sales returns and allowances would be recorded in the general journal. Similarly, **correcting, adjusting, and closing entries are recorded in the general journal**. Other types of special journals may be used in some situations. For example, when purchase returns and allowances or sales returns and allowances are frequent, special journals may be used to record these transactions.

Special journals **permit greater division of labor** because several individuals can record entries in different journals at the same time. For example, one employee may be responsible for journalizing all cash receipts, and another for journalizing credit sales. In addition, the use of special journals **reduces the time necessary to complete the posting process**. When special journals are used, monthly postings to some accounts may be substituted for daily postings, as will be illustrated later in the chapter.

## Sales Journal

The **sales journal** is used to record sales of merchandise on account. Cash sales of merchandise are entered in the cash receipts journal. Credit sales of assets other than merchandise are entered in the general journal.

### Journalizing Credit Sales

Karns Wholesale Supply uses a **perpetual inventory** system. Under a perpetual inventory system, each entry in the sales journal results in one entry **at selling price**—a debit to Accounts Receivable (a control account) and a credit of equal amount to Sales—and another entry **at cost**—a debit to Cost of Goods Sold and a credit of equal amount to Merchandise Inventory (a control account). A sales journal with two amount columns can accommodate a sales transaction recognizing both selling price and cost using only one line. Assuming that Karns Wholesale Supply has the following credit sales transactions (per sales invoices 101–107), its two-column sales journal is shown in Illustration 6-7.

ILLUSTRATION 6-7

*Journalizing the sales journal—perpetual inventory system*

| | | | | | |
|---|---|---|---|---|---|
| **Karns Wholesale Supply** | | | | | |
| SALES JOURNAL | | | | | **S1** |
| Date | Account Debited | Invoice No. | Ref. | Accts. Receivable Dr. Sales Cr. | Cost of Goods Sold Dr. Merchandise Inventory Cr. |
| 1999 | | | | | |
| May 3 | Abbot Sisters | 101 | | 10,600 | 6,360 |
| 7 | Babson Co. | 102 | | 11,350 | 7,370 |
| 14 | Carson Bros. | 103 | | 7,800 | 5,070 |
| 19 | Deli Co. | 104 | | 9,300 | 6,510 |
| 21 | Abbot Sisters | 105 | | 15,400 | 10,780 |
| 24 | Deli Co. | 106 | | 21,210 | 15,900 |
| 27 | Babson Co. | 107 | | 14,570 | 10,200 |
| | | | | 90,230 | 62,190 |

The reference (Ref.) column is not used in journalizing. It is used in posting the sales journal, as explained in the next section. Also, note that, unlike the general journal, an explanation is not required for each entry in a special journal. Finally, note that each invoice is prenumbered to ensure that all invoices are journalized.

## Posting the Sales Journal

Postings from the sales journal are made **daily to the individual accounts receivable** in the subsidiary ledger and **monthly to the general ledger**, as shown in Illustration 6-8.

A check mark (√) is inserted in the reference posting column to indicate that the daily posting to the customer's account has been made. A check mark (√) is used in this illustration because the subsidiary ledger accounts are not numbered. At the end of the month, the column totals of the sales journal are posted to the general ledger—as a debit of $90,230 to Accounts Receivable (account No. 4), a credit of $90,230 to Sales (account No. 60), a debit of $62,190 to Cost of Goods Sold (account No. 75), and a credit of $62,190 to Merchandise Inventory (account No. 6). The insertion of the respective account numbers below the column total indicates that the postings have been made. In both the general ledger and subsidiary ledger accounts, the reference **S1** indicates that the posting came from page 1 of the sales journal.

## Proving the Ledgers

To prove the ledgers it is necessary to determine that (1) the total of the general ledger debit balances equals the total of the general ledger credit balances and (2) the sum of the subsidiary ledger balances equals the balance in the control accounts. The proof of the postings from the sales journal to the general ledger and the accounts receivable subsidiary ledger is shown in Illustration 6-9.

## Advantages of the Sales Journal

The use of a special journal to record sales on account has a number of advantages. First, the one-line entry for each sales transaction **saves time**, because it is not necessary to write out the four account titles for each transaction. Second, only totals, rather than individual entries, are posted to the general ledger, thus **saving posting time and reducing the possibilities of errors in posting**. Finally,

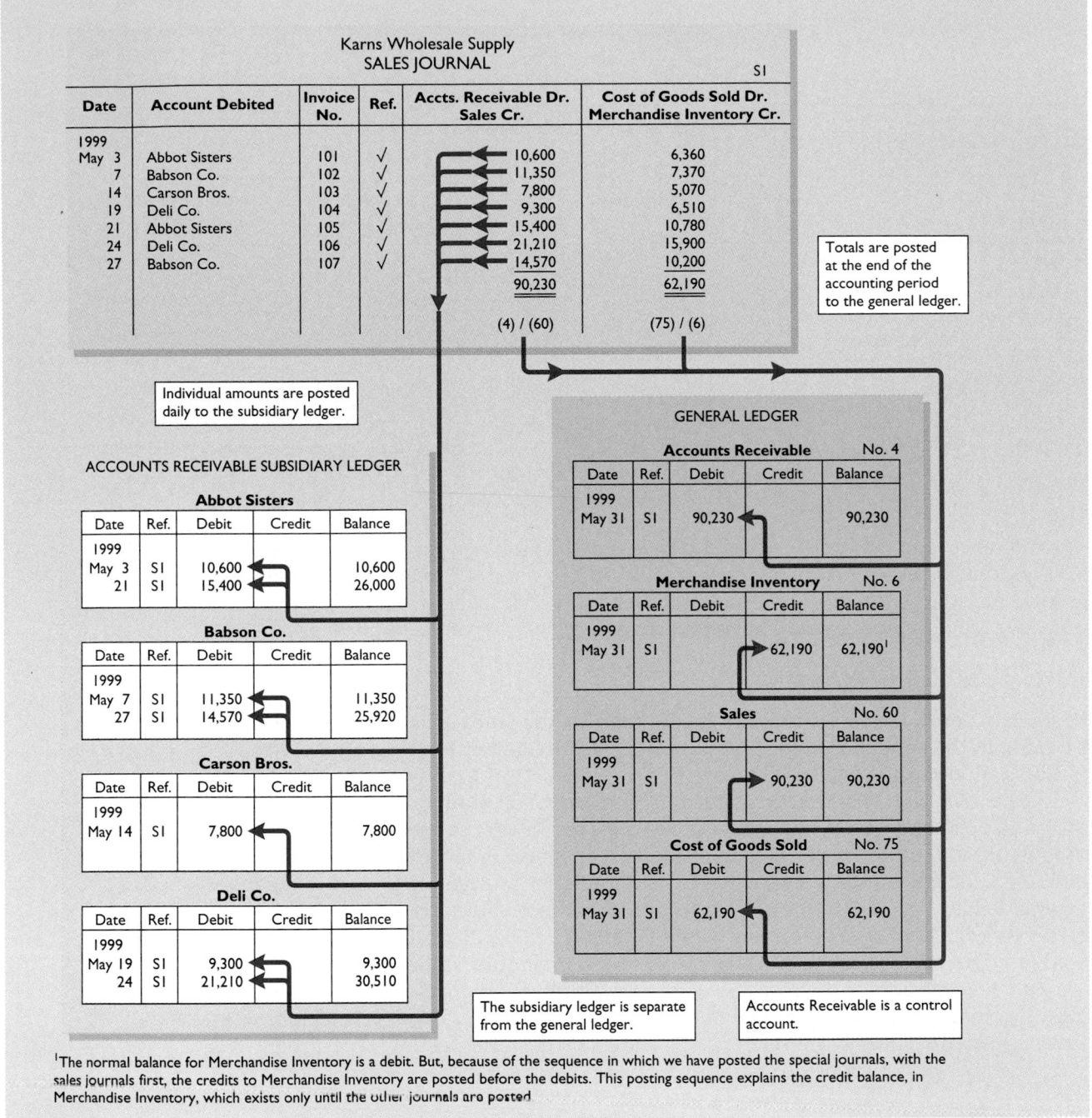

ILLUSTRATION 6-8

*Posting the sales journal*

a division of labor results, because one individual can take responsibility for the sales journal.

## Cash Receipts Journal

All receipts of cash are recorded in the cash receipts journal. The most common types of cash receipts are cash sales of merchandise and collections of accounts receivable. Many other possibilities exist, however, such as receipt of money from bank loans and cash proceeds from disposals of equipment, buildings, or land. A one- or two-column cash receipts journal is not sufficient to accommodate all possible cash receipt transactions. Therefore, a multiple-column cash receipts journal is used.

**ILLUSTRATION 6-9**

*Proving the equality of the postings from the sales journal*

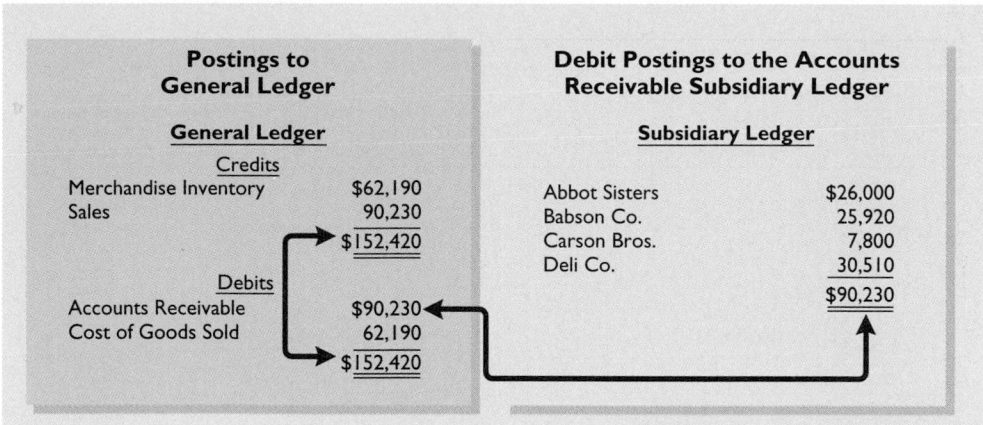

Generally, a cash receipts journal includes debit columns for cash and sales discounts and credit columns for accounts receivable, sales, and "other" accounts. The other accounts category is used when the cash receipt does not involve a cash sale or a collection of accounts receivable. Under a perpetual inventory system, each sales entry is accompanied by another entry that debits Cost of Goods Sold and credits Merchandise Inventory for the cost of the merchandise sold. This entry may be recorded separately. A six-column cash receipts journal that accommodates both entries is shown in Illustration 6-10. When a special journal has more than one account column it is referred to as a columnar journal.

Additional credit columns may be used if they significantly reduce postings to a specific account. For example, the cash receipts of a loan company, such as Household International, include thousands of collections from customers. These collections are credited to Loans Receivable and Interest Revenue. A significant saving in posting would result from using separate credit columns for Loans Receivable and Interest Revenue, rather than using the other accounts credit column for these amounts. In contrast, a retailer that has only one interest collection a month would not find it useful to have a separate column for interest revenue.

## Journalizing Cash Receipts Transactions

To illustrate the journalizing of cash receipts transactions, we will continue with the transactions of Karns Wholesale Supply during the month of May. Collections from customers relate to the entries recorded in the sales journal in Illustration 6-7. The entries in the cash receipts journal are based on the following cash receipts transactions:

May  1  D. A. Karns makes an investment of $5,000 in the business.
     7  Cash sales of merchandise total $1,900 (cost, $1,240).
   10  A check for $10,388 is received from Abbot Sisters in payment of invoice No. 101 for $10,600 less a 2% discount.
   12  Cash sales of merchandise total $2,600 (cost, $1,690).
   17  A check for $11,123 is received from Babson Co. in payment of invoice No. 102 for $11,350 less a 2% discount.
   22  Cash is received by signing a note for $6,000.
   23  A check for $7,644 is received from Carson Bros. in full for invoice No. 103 for $7,800 less a 2% discount.
   28  A check for $9,114 is received from Deli Co. in full for invoice No. 104 for $9,300 less a 2% discount.

Further information about the columns in the cash receipts journal (see Illustration 6-10) is as follows:

**ILLUSTRATION 6-10**

*Journalizing and posting the cash receipts journal*

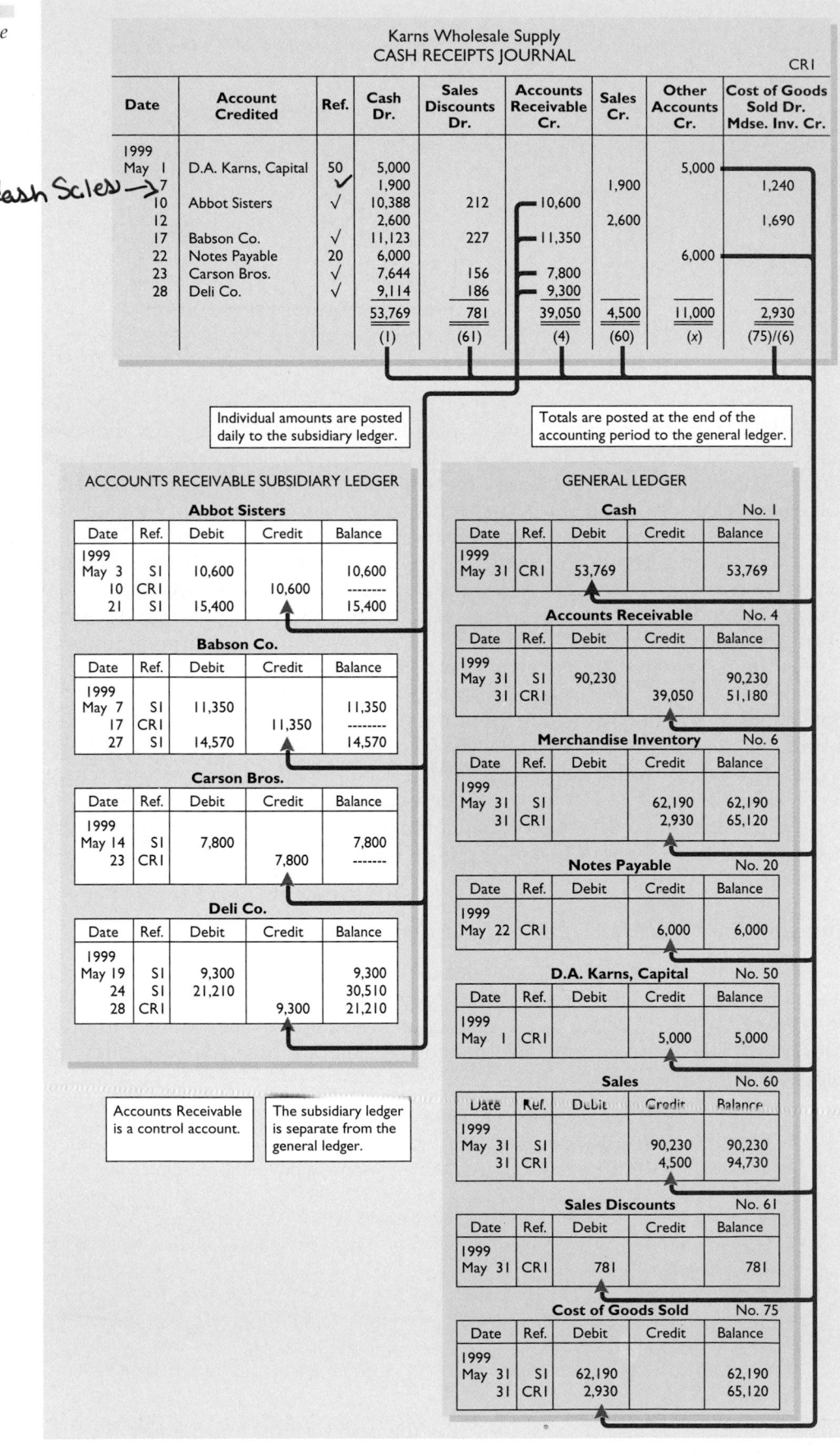

**Debit Columns:**

1. **Cash.** The amount of cash actually received in each transaction is entered in this column; the column total indicates the total cash receipts for the month.
2. **Sales Discounts.** The Sales Discounts column is included so that it is not necessary to enter sales discount items in the general journal. As a result, the collection of an account receivable within the discount period is expressed on one line in the appropriate columns of the cash receipts journal.

**Credit Columns:**

3. **Accounts Receivable.** The Accounts Receivable column is used to record cash collections on account. The amount entered in this column is the amount to be credited to the individual customer's account.
4. **Sales.** The Sales column records all cash sales of merchandise. Cash sales of plant assets, for example, are not reported in this column.
5. **Other Accounts.** The Other Accounts column, often referred to as the **sundry accounts column**, is used whenever the credit is other than to Accounts Receivable or Sales. For example, in the first entry, $5,000 is entered as a credit to D. A. Karns, Capital.

**Debit and Credit Column:**

6. **Cost of Goods Sold and Merchandise Inventory.** This column records debits to Cost of Goods Sold and credits to Merchandise Inventory.

In a columnar journal, as in a single-column journal, generally only one line is needed for each entry. There must be equal debit and credit amounts for each line. When the collection from Abbot Sisters on May 10 is journalized, for example, three amounts are indicated. Note also that the Account Credited column is used to identify both general ledger and subsidiary ledger account titles. The former is illustrated in the May 1 entry for Karns's investment; the latter is illustrated in the May 10 entry for the collection in full from Abbot Sisters.

When the journalizing of a columnar journal has been completed, the amount columns are totaled, and the totals are balanced to prove the equality of debits and credits. The proof of the equality of Karns's cash receipts journal is as follows:

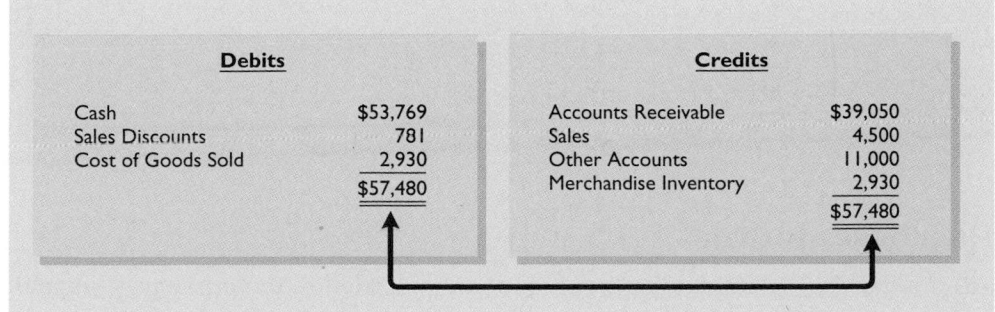

| Debits | | Credits | |
|---|---|---|---|
| Cash | $53,769 | Accounts Receivable | $39,050 |
| Sales Discounts | 781 | Sales | 4,500 |
| Cost of Goods Sold | 2,930 | Other Accounts | 11,000 |
| | $57,480 | Merchandise Inventory | 2,930 |
| | | | $57,480 |

**ILLUSTRATION 6-11**

*Proving the equality of the cash receipts journal*

Totaling the columns of a journal and proving the equality of the totals is called **footing** and **cross-footing** a journal.

## Posting the Cash Receipts Journal

Posting a columnar journal involves the following procedures.

**5**
STUDY
OBJECTIVE

Indicate how a columnar
journal is posted.

1. All column totals except the total for the Other Accounts column are posted **once at the end of the month** to the account title or titles specified in the column heading, such as Cash or Accounts Receivable. Account numbers are entered below the column totals to show that they have been posted.
2. The total of the Other Accounts column is not posted. Instead, the **individual amounts comprising the total are posted separately** to the general ledger accounts specified in the Accounts Credited column. See, for example, the credit posting to D. A. Karns, Capital. The symbol (X) is inserted below the total to this column to indicate that the amount has not been posted.
3. The individual amounts in a column, posted in total to a control account (Accounts Receivable, in this case), are posted **daily to the subsidiary ledger** account specified in the Account Credited column. See, for example, the credit posting of $10,600 to Abbot Sisters.

Therefore, cash is posted to account No. 1, accounts receivable to account No. 4, merchandise inventory to account No. 6, sales to account No. 60, sales discounts to account No. 61, and cost of goods sold to account No. 75. The symbol **CR** is used in the ledgers to identify postings from the cash receipts journal.

## Proving the Ledgers

After the posting of the cash receipts journal is completed, it is necessary to prove the ledgers. As shown in Illustration 6-12, the general ledger totals are in agreement and the sum of the subsidiary ledger balances equals the control account balance.

**ILLUSTRATION 6-12**

*Proving the ledgers after posting the sales and the cash receipts journals*

## Purchases Journal

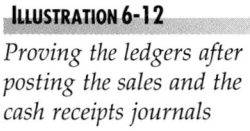

**HELPFUL HINT**
A single-column purchases journal needs only to be footed to prove the equality of debits and credits.

All purchases of merchandise on account are recorded in the **purchases journal**. Each entry in this journal results in a debit to Merchandise Inventory and a credit to Accounts Payable. When a one-column purchases journal is used, other types of purchases on account and cash purchases cannot be journalized in it. For example, credit purchases of equipment or supplies must be recorded in the general journal, and all cash purchases are entered in the cash payments journal. As illustrated later, where credit purchases for items other than merchandise are numerous, the purchases journal is often expanded to a multi-column format. The single-column purchases journal for Karns Wholesale Supply is shown in Illustration 6-13.

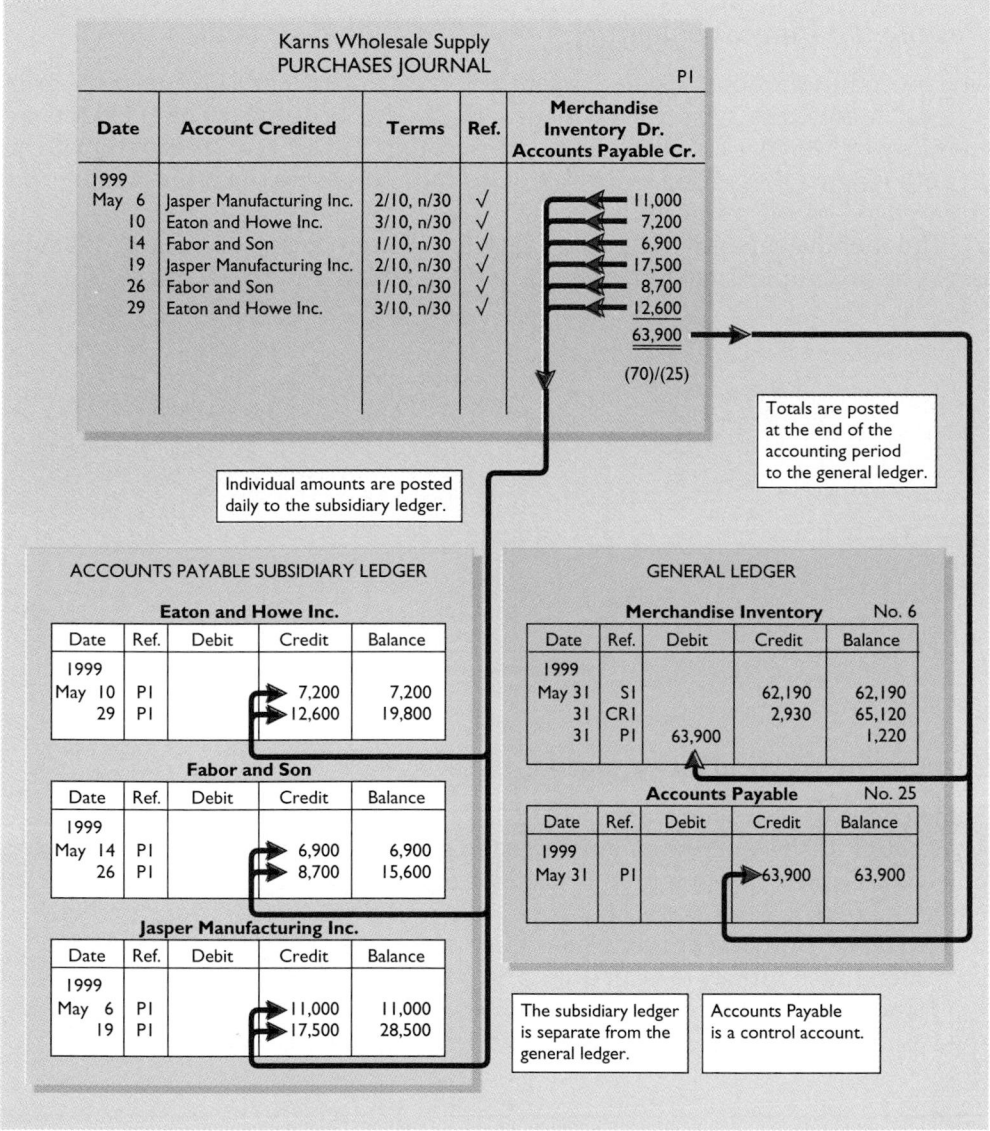

**ILLUSTRATION 6-13**

*Journalizing and posting the purchases journal*

## Journalizing Credit Purchases of Merchandise

Entries in the purchases journal are made from purchase invoices. The journalizing procedure is similar to the procedures for a single-column sales journal. In contrast to the sales journal, the purchases journal may not have an invoice number column, because invoices received from different suppliers will not be in numerical sequence. To assure that all purchase invoices are recorded, however, some companies consecutively number each invoice upon receipt and then provide for an internal document number column in the purchases journal.

The entries for Karns Wholesale Supply are based on the following assumed purchases on credit transactions:

| Date | Supplier | Amount | Date | Supplier | Amount |
|------|----------|--------|------|----------|--------|
| 5/6 | Jasper Manufacturing Inc. | $11,000 | 5/19 | Jasper Manufacturing Inc. | $17,500 |
| 5/10 | Eaton and Howe, Inc. | 7,200 | 5/26 | Fabor and Son | 8,700 |
| 5/14 | Fabor and Son | 6,900 | 5/29 | Eaton and Howe, Inc. | 12,600 |

## Posting the Purchases Journal

The procedures for posting the purchases journal are similar to those for the sales journal. In this case, postings are made **daily** to the **accounts payable ledger** and **monthly** to Merchandise Inventory and Accounts Payable in the general ledger. In both ledgers, P1 is used in the reference column to show that the postings are from page 1 of the purchases journal.

Proof of the equality of the postings from the purchases journal to both ledgers in this example is shown by the following tabulation:

## Expanding the Purchases Journal

Some companies expand the purchases journal to include all types of purchases on account. Instead of one column for merchandise inventory and accounts payable, a multiple-column format is used. The multiple-column format usually includes a credit column for accounts payable and debit columns for purchases of merchandise, purchases of office supplies, purchases of store supplies, and other accounts. Illustration 6-16 is an example of a multiple-column purchases journal for Hanover Co. The posting procedures are similar to those used for posting the cash receipts journal illustrated earlier.

### Hanover Co.
### PURCHASES JOURNAL                                                                 P1

| Date | Account Credited | Ref. | Accounts Payable Cr. | Merchandise Inventory Dr. | Office Supplies Dr. | Store Supplies Dr. | Other Accounts Dr. Account | Other Accounts Dr. Ref. | Other Accounts Dr. Amount |
|------|------------------|------|----------------------|---------------------------|---------------------|--------------------|----------------------------|-------------------------|---------------------------|
| 1999 | | | | | | | | | |
| June 1 | Signe Audio | ✓ | 2,000 | | 2,000 | | | | |
| 3 | Wright Co. | ✓ | 1,500 | 1,500 | | | | | |
| 5 | Orange Tree Co. | ✓ | 2,600 | | | | Equipment | 18 | 2,600 |
| 30 | Sue's Business Forms | ✓ | 800 | | | 800 | | | |
| | | | 56,600 | 43,000 | 7,500 | 1,200 | | | 4,900 |

# Cash Payments Journal

All disbursements of cash are entered in a cash payments journal. Entries in this journal are made from prenumbered checks. Because cash payments may be made for a variety of purposes, the cash payments journal has multiple columns. A four-column journal is shown in Illustration 6-17.

**ALTERNATIVE TERMINOLOGY**

The cash payments journal is sometimes called the *cash disbursements journal*.

**ILLUSTRATION 6-17**

*Journalizing and posting the cash payments journal*

**Karns Wholesale Supply**
**CASH PAYMENTS JOURNAL**                                    CP1

| Date | Ck. No. | Account Debited | Ref. | Other Accounts Dr. | Accounts Payable Dr. | Merchandise Inventory Cr. | Cash Cr. |
|------|---------|-----------------|------|--------------------|-----------------------|----------------------------|----------|
| 1999 | | | | | | | |
| May 1 | 101 | Prepaid Insurance | 10 | 1,200 | | | 1,200 |
| 3 | 102 | Mdse. Inventory | 6 | 100 | | | 100 |
| 8 | 103 | Mdse. Inventory | 6 | 4,400 | | | 4,400 |
| 10 | 104 | Jasper Manuf. Inc. | ✓ | | 11,000 | 220 | 10,780 |
| 19 | 105 | Eaton & Howe Inc. | ✓ | | 7,200 | 216 | 6,984 |
| 23 | 106 | Fabor and Son | ✓ | | 6,900 | 69 | 6,831 |
| 28 | 107 | Jasper Manuf. Inc. | ✓ | | 17,500 | 350 | 17,150 |
| 30 | 108 | D.A. Karns, Drawing | 51 | 500 | | | 500 |
| | | | | 6,200 | 42,600 | 855 | 47,945 |
| | | | | (x) | (25) | (6) | (1) |

Individual amounts are posted daily to the subsidiary ledger.

Totals are posted at the end of the accounting period to the general ledger.

**ACCOUNTS PAYABLE SUBSIDIARY LEDGER**

**Eaton and Howe Inc.**

| Date | Ref. | Debit | Credit | Balance |
|------|------|-------|--------|---------|
| 1999 | | | | |
| May 10 | P1 | | 7,200 | 7,200 |
| 19 | CP1 | 7,200 | | ------- |
| 29 | P1 | | 12,600 | 12,600 |

**Fabor and Son**

| Date | Ref. | Debit | Credit | Balance |
|------|------|-------|--------|---------|
| 1999 | | | | |
| May 14 | P1 | | 6,900 | 6,900 |
| 23 | CP1 | 6,900 | | ------- |
| 26 | P1 | | 8,700 | 8,700 |

**Jasper Manufacturing Inc.**

| Date | Ref. | Debit | Credit | Balance |
|------|------|-------|--------|---------|
| 1999 | | | | |
| May 6 | P1 | | 11,000 | 11,000 |
| 10 | CP1 | 11,000 | | -------- |
| 19 | P1 | | 17,500 | 17,500 |
| 28 | CP1 | 17,500 | | -------- |

Accounts Payable is a control account.

The subsidiary ledger is separate from the general ledger.

**GENERAL LEDGER**

**Cash**                                                No. 1

| Date | Ref. | Debit | Credit | Balance |
|------|------|-------|--------|---------|
| 1999 | | | | |
| May 31 | CR1 | 53,769 | | 53,769 |
| 31 | CP1 | | 47,945 | 5,824 |

**Accounts Payable**                                    No. 25

| Date | Ref. | Debit | Credit | Balance |
|------|------|-------|--------|---------|
| 1999 | | | | |
| May 31 | P1 | | 63,900 | 63,900 |
| 31 | CP1 | 42,600 | | 21,300 |

**Prepaid Insurance**                                   No. 10

| Date | Ref. | Debit | Credit | Balance |
|------|------|-------|--------|---------|
| 1999 | | | | |
| May 1 | CP1 | 1,200 | | 1,200 |

**D.A. Karns, Drawing**                                 No. 51

| Date | Ref. | Debit | Credit | Balance |
|------|------|-------|--------|---------|
| 1999 | | | | |
| May 30 | CP1 | 500 | | 500 |

**Merchandise Inventory**                               No. 6

| Date | Ref. | Debit | Credit | Balance |
|------|------|-------|--------|---------|
| 1999 | | | | |
| May 3 | CP1 | 100 | | 100 |
| 8 | CP1 | 4,400 | | 4,500 |
| 31 | S1 | | 62,190 | 57,690 |
| 31 | CR1 | | 2,930 | 60,620 |
| 31 | P | 63,900 | | 3,280 |
| 31 | CP1 | | 855 | 2,425 |

## Journalizing Cash Payments Transactions

The procedures for journalizing transactions in this journal are similar to those described earlier for journalizing transactions in the cash receipts journal. For example, each transaction is entered on one line, and for each line there must be equal debit and credit amounts. The entries in the cash payments journal shown in Illustration 6-17 are based on the following transactions for Karns Wholesale Supply:

May   1   Check No. 101 for $1,200 issued for the annual premium on a fire insurance policy.
     3   Check No. 102 for $100 issued in payment of freight when terms were FOB shipping point.
     8   Check No. 103 for $4,400 issued for the purchase of merchandise.
   10   Check No. 104 for $10,780 sent to Jasper Manufacturing Inc. in payment of May 6 invoice for $11,000 less a 2% discount.
   19   Check No. 105 for $6,984 mailed to Eaton and Howe, Inc. in payment of May 10 invoice for $7,200 less a 3% discount.
   23   Check No. 106 for $6,831 sent to Fabor and Son in payment of May 14 invoice for $6,900 less a 1% discount.
   28   Check No. 107 for $17,150 sent to Jasper Manufacturing Inc. in payment of May 19 invoice for $17,500 less a 2% discount.
   30   Check No. 108 for $500 issued to D. A. Karns as a cash withdrawal for personal use.

Note that whenever an amount is entered in the Other Accounts column, a specific general ledger account must be identified in the Accounts Debited column. The entries for check Nos. 101, 102, and 103 illustrate this situation. Similarly, a subsidiary account must be identified in the Account Debited column whenever an amount is entered in the Accounts Payable column, as, for example, the entry for check No. 104.

When the journalizing of the cash payments journal has been completed, the amount columns are totaled. The totals are then balanced to prove the equality of debits and credits.

## Posting the Cash Payments Journal

The procedures for posting the cash payments journal are similar to those for posting the cash receipts journal. Specifically, the amounts recorded in the Accounts Payable column are posted individually to the subsidiary ledger and in total to the control account. Merchandise Inventory and Cash are posted only in total at the end of the month. When a transaction is recorded in the Other Accounts column, it is posted individually to the appropriate account(s) affected. No totals are posted for this column.

The posting of the cash payments journal is shown in Illustration 6-17. Note that the symbol **CP** is used as the posting reference for this journal. After postings from the journals are completed, the equality of the debit and credit balances in the general ledger should be determined. In addition, the control account balances should agree with the subsidiary ledger total balance. The agreement of these balances is shown in Illustration 6-18.

# Effects of Special Journals on General Journal

Special journals for sales, purchases, and cash substantially reduce the number of entries that are made in the general journal. **Only transactions that cannot be entered in a special journal are recorded in the general journal.** For example,

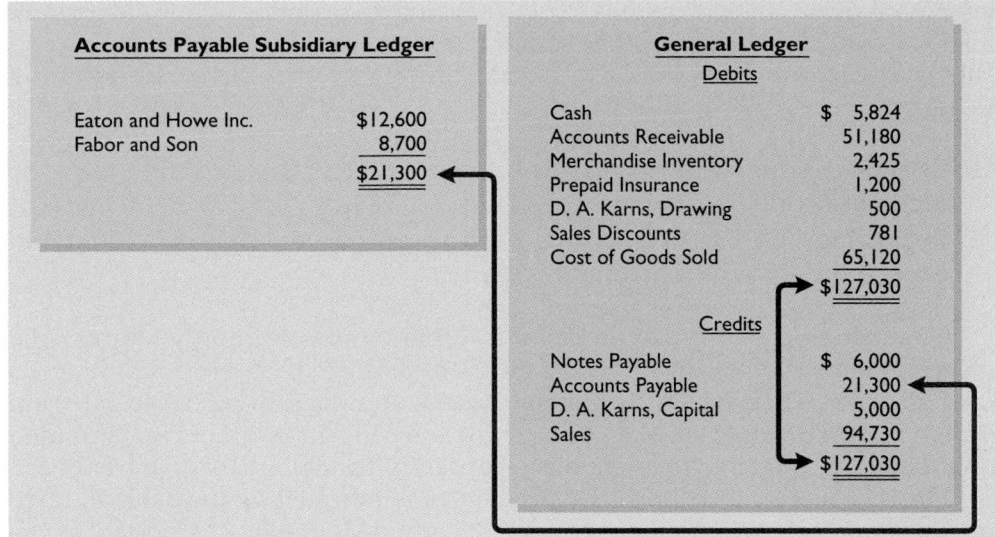

ILLUSTRATION 6-18

*Proving the ledgers after postings from the sales, cash receipts, purchases, and cash payments journals*

the general journal may be used to record such transactions as granting of credit to a customer for a sales return or allowance, granting of credit from a supplier for purchases returned, acceptance of a note receivable from a customer, and purchase of equipment by issuing a note payable. In addition, correcting, adjusting, and closing entries are made in the general journal.

The general journal has columns for date, account titles and explanation, reference, and debit and credit amounts. When control and subsidiary accounts

ILLUSTRATION 6-19

*Journalizing and posting the general journal*

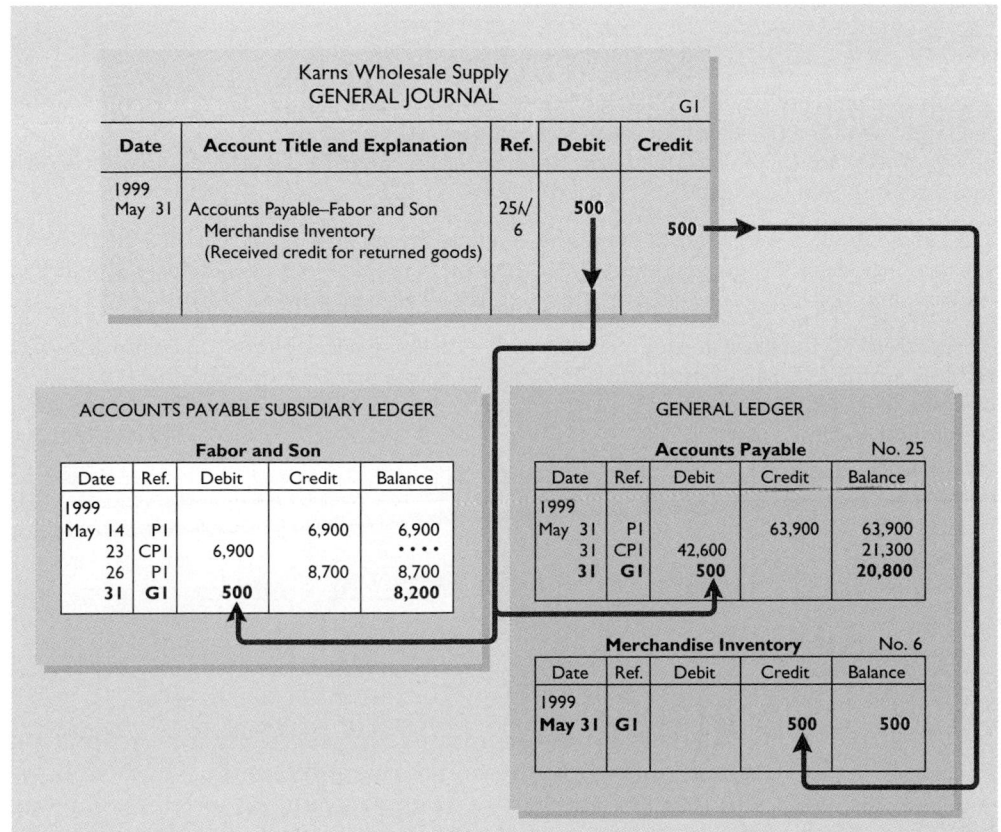

are not involved, the procedures for journalizing and posting of transactions are identical with those described in earlier chapters. However, when control and subsidiary accounts are involved, two modifications of earlier procedures are required:

1.  In **journalizing**, both the control and the subsidiary accounts must be identified.
2.  In **posting**, there must be a **dual posting**: once to the control account and once to the subsidiary account.

To illustrate, assume that on May 31, Karns Wholesale Supply returns $500 of merchandise for credit to Fabor and Son because of an error in filling its May 26 order. The entry in the general journal and the posting of the entry are shown in Illustration 6-19. Note that if cash is received instead of credit granted on this return, then the transaction is recorded in the cash receipts journal.

Observe in the journal that two accounts are indicated for the debit and two postings are indicated in the reference column. One amount is posted to the control account and the other to the creditor's account in the subsidiary ledger.

## BEFORE YOU GO ON . . .

### Review It

1.  What types of special journals are usually used to record transactions? Why are special journals used?
2.  Explain how transactions recorded in the sales journal and the cash receipts journal are posted.
3.  Indicate the types of transactions that are recorded in the general journal when special journals are used.

### Do It

The Vilas Company has the following selected transactions: (1) purchase of equipment for cash, (2) cash sale, (3) sales returns and allowances, (4) withdrawal of cash for proprietor's personal use, and (5) sale of merchandise on account. Identify the journals in which each transaction should be entered.

*Reasoning:* It is necessary to know the content of each special journal and the effect of special journals on the general journal. For example, the sales journal contains only sales on account, and the cash payments journal is used for all cash payments.

*Solution:* (1) Purchase of equipment for cash—cash payments journal. (2) Cash sale—cash receipts journal. (3) Sales return and allowance—general journal. (4) Withdrawal of cash for proprietor's personal use—cash payments journal. (5) Sale of merchandise on account—sales journal.

*Related exercise material:* BE6–5, BE6–6, E6–1, E6–4, E6–5, E6–6, E6–7, and E6–8.

# SECTION 3   ELECTRONIC ACCOUNTING SYSTEMS

An **electronic accounting system** uses computers in processing transaction data and in disseminating accounting information to interested parties. In the following sections, we briefly describe the hardware and accounting software that may be used in such systems, and then we explain and illustrate two common data processing methods.

## ACCOUNTING IN ACTION
### Business Insight

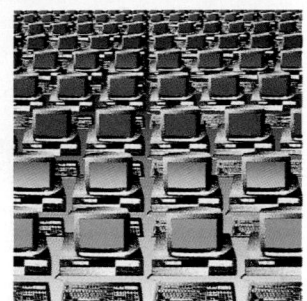

The growth of computers has been phenomenal. The first experimental computers were developed in the 1940s, and primitive computers were used in business in the early 1950s. The first serious business applications for computers were put into use in the mid-1960s. From the time of their invention in the 1940s up to 1980, there were approximately one million computer systems of all kinds. By the middle of the 1990s, it is estimated that *250 million* personal computers (PCs) alone were in use.

# COMPUTER HARDWARE

Computers can be divided into three classes, by size: mainframes, minicomputers, and microcomputers. **Mainframes** are large, powerful, very expensive computers that are used by major corporations to process huge volumes of transactions. Mainframes are able to serve many users and perform different processing functions at one time. **Minicomputers** are less powerful and not as expensive as mainframes. They can perform different tasks for several users at a time. The **microcomputer** is commonly referred to as a personal computer (PC). It has speed and power (though generally less than minicomputers), and it is very affordable. In many companies, each employee has his or her own PC.

Computer hardware is the physical equipment associated with a computerized accounting system. The basic hardware configuration consists of the central processing unit (CPU) and peripheral devices. The **central processing unit (CPU)** is composed of three parts:

1. The **control unit**, which directs and coordinates the entire system, including the entry and removal of information from storage.
2. The **internal storage unit**, or computer memory, which stores the program instructions and the data to be processed.
3. The **arithmetic-logic unit**, which performs mathematical computations (addition, subtraction, multiplication, division) and certain logical operations (such as comparisons).

Common types of computer hardware are shown in Illustration 6-20.

**6**
STUDY
OBJECTIVE
..................................
Distinguish between computer hardware and accounting software and the principal methods of data processing.

**ILLUSTRATION 6-20**

*Computer hardware*

**Central Processing Unit (CPU)**
Control unit
Computer memory
Arithmetic-logic unit

**Peripheral Equipment**
Keyboard
Mouse
Magnetic disk / tape drive
CD-ROM
Display screen
Printer

CPU
Monitor
Printer
Keyboard
Mouse

A computer linked with one or more other computers and running with a common software package is called a **network**. A computer network may be as small as two computers in the same dormitory room. In contrast, the Internet is a worldwide network, with a hookup of millions of computers.

## ACCOUNTING IN ACTION
### Ethics Insight

The Internet is our new frontier—a digital Wild West, with its own forms of lawlessness. By some estimates, roughly $2 billion worth of software was stolen from "the Net" in a recent year. In one year, for example, an international software piracy ring stole 140,000 telephone credit card numbers and sold them to computer hackers who used them to make $140 million worth of long-distance phone calls. As commerce expands on the Internet, such thievery is not likely to stop. Digital socialism rules the Net, not copyright capitalism.

*Source: Newsweek*, November 14, 1994, pp. 46–47.

## ACCOUNTING SOFTWARE

**International Note**

It has recently been noted that, in an unusual turning of the tables, some companies in countries such as Brazil that were slow to adopt computer systems early on are often now more advanced than U.S. corporations. The reason: The systems they are buying today are far more sophisticated than many systems that U.S. corporations bought years ago and continue to use.

**Accounting software** consists of programs that relate to specific parts of the accounting process. For example, there are programs for the general ledger and each subsidiary ledger, and there are programs for performing the steps in the accounting cycle such as journalizing, posting, and preparing a trial balance. In addition, there is software for business functions such as billing customers, preparing the payroll, and budgeting.

Accounting software can be purchased "off the shelf," or it can be custom-made by individual companies and users. For maximum efficiency, related programs are generally used together. For example, a program for paying creditors would be used with programs for journalizing the payments and maintaining both the general ledger and the accounts payable subsidiary ledger. When programs are used together, the company is said to be using **integrated accounting software**.

## TECHNOLOGY IN ACTION

For PCs, several leading off-the-shelf accounting software packages are Peachtree's **Complete Accounting**®, Intuit's **Quick Books**®, M-USA's **Pacioli 2000**®, Solomon's **III and IV for Windows**, and DAC Easy's **Accounting and Payroll**®. DAC Easy offers, among other products, accounts receivable, accounts payable, management information, and inventory programs.

## DATA PROCESSING METHODS

The term **data processing methods** refers to how data are entered into and processed by a computer. That is, it includes *both* data entry *and* the processing of the data once entered into the system. Two widely used data processing methods are batch processing and on-line processing.

# Batch Processing

In **batch processing**, data are accumulated by classes of transactions and are periodically entered into the computer and processed in batches. A batch may include such transaction classes as credit sales, collections on account, or cash payments to creditors.

As shown in Illustration 6-21, transaction data are entered into the computer and coded by batch as they occur. At specified intervals—such as daily or weekly—the coded transactions are sorted (transferred) on computer transaction files that are the equivalent of special journals in a manual system. Next, the transaction files are used to update the master files (the general ledger and subsidiary ledger accounts). This step is similar to posting in a manual system.

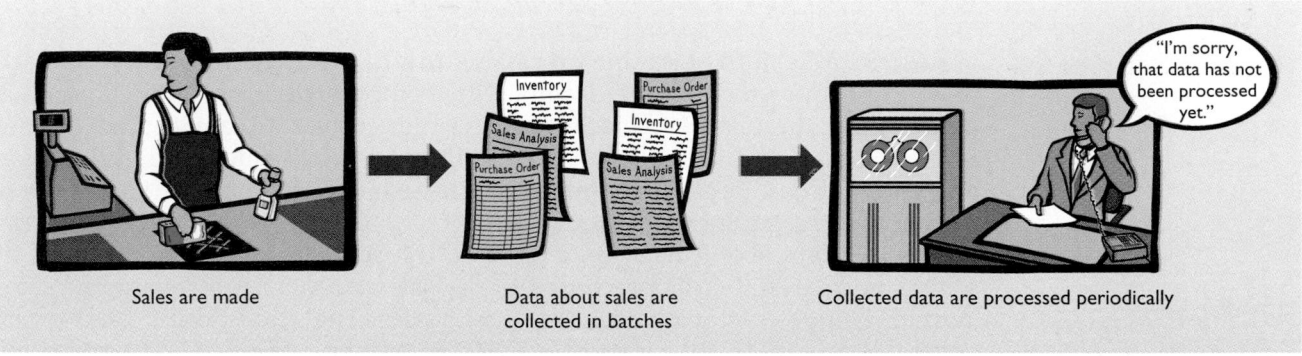

Sales are made          Data about sales are          Collected data are processed periodically
                        collected in batches

**ILLUSTRATION 6-21**

*Batch processing*

Batch processing is an efficient method because similar transactions are processed together. The principal disadvantage of batch processing is that files may not always contain up-to-date information. For such files as subsidiary ledgers for accounts receivable and accounts payable, lack of current information could be, at the least, an annoyance.

## ACCOUNTING IN ACTION
### Business Insight

Under a system called *electronic data interchange (EDI)*, a company's computer can use dial-up communication lines to communicate electronically with other businesses. Recently, EDI was being used in the accounting systems of about 75% of the Fortune 100 companies and 39% of the Fortune 500. For example, computers at over 3,000 suppliers to Chrysler accept purchase orders transmitted by computers from assembly plants, and in turn electronically invoice Chrysler's computers for parts shipped. Wal-Mart, which operates the largest EDI program in the retail industry, processes about 75% of its payments to suppliers using EDI.

# On-line Processing

In **on-line processing**, files are updated as data entry takes place. In addition, a transaction log (or tape) is produced that shows a chronological record of all transactions. This processing method is used in airline and hotel reservation systems, among others.

A common accounting application of on-line processing is found in many retail stores, where electronic cash registers are connected directly with the central processing unit of the store's computer. An example of on-line processing in a grocery store is shown in Illustration 6-22.

Data about the sale are scanned into the cash register/computer.

General and subsidiary ledgers are updated for sales and inventory.

Reports and other documents are generated.

**ILLUSTRATION 6-22**

*On-line processing*

A critical feature of on-line processing is a **bar code identification** for each product. In our grocery store example, the computerized accounting system is activated by the cashier, who moves the product over a scanner. The scanner reads the product being sold and the selling price and enters the information directly into the CPU. At the same time, the cash register shows the same information on a screen for the customer.[2]

As the data about the sale are entered into the computer, the total sale at selling price and at cost is recorded in the sales journal. In this case, the sales journal includes both cash and credit card sales. The sale is also posted to the general ledger and filed for sales analysis. In addition, the system immediately updates the inventory records. As illustrated, the system can also print out a purchase order when an inventory item reaches a programmed reorder point, and it can generate inventory reports.

## TECHNOLOGY IN ACTION

Data processing professionals use the acronym GIGO—garbage-in, garbage-out—to indicate that a computer system is only as good as the data it receives. Data entry is the garbage-in stage of the acronym. Garbage-in is not automated, garbage-out is. The real trick—and the expensive part—of both manual and automated systems (either micros, minis, or mainframes) is to get what we might call DIIO, that is, data-in, information-out.

## COMPARING MANUAL AND ELECTRONIC SYSTEMS

STUDY

OBJECTIVE

**7**

Identify the key points in comparing manual and electronic accounting systems.

Despite the tremendous capabilities of computers, one should not conclude that electronic systems are always better. As with any choice, the costs and benefits of each alternative should be weighed before the choice is made. The following

---

[2]When a product does not have an attached bar code, the cashier must "punch in" the code number and price using the keyboard on the register.

key points should be considered when evaluating and comparing manual and electronic systems.

**ILLUSTRATION 6-23**

*Comparison of manual versus electronic systems*

| Key Points | Manual Systems | Electronic Systems |
|---|---|---|
| **Costs** | Bookkeepers' salaries. Costs of manual record keeping. | Computer operators' salaries. Costs of computer hardware and software. Usually requires fewer employees than manual systems. |
| **Processing Speed** | Fewer delays due to breakdowns or power outages. | Faster. |
| **Errors** | People can get fatigued, bored, or can be incompetent, so errors are normal. | Generally more accurate, although errors in data entry or hardware failure may occur. |
| **Report Generation** | Reports have to be separately and manually prepared. | Reports can be quickly prepared once data are entered. |

# BEFORE YOU GO ON . . .

## Review It

1. Identify the components of computer hardware.
2. Distinguish between batch and on-line processing.
3. What are the advantages of using a computerized system to record business transactions?

## A LOOK BACK AT OUR FEATURE STORY

Refer to the opening story about Fidelity Investments, and answer the following questions:

1. How could a highly sophisticated and computerized firm like Fidelity Investments make an embarrassing $1.3 billion accounting error?
2. What is causing many small businesses to switch to computer bookkeeping systems?
3. Is it likely that in the future some businesses will continue to use manual systems?

*Solution:*

1. Although Fidelity Investments is highly computerized, some financial information, like the computation of some gains and losses, is generated manually. When people perform such tasks, they occasionally make errors.
2. As discussed in the chapter, more and more small businesses are switching to computerized systems because computers are becoming cheaper, faster, and more reliable, and software is becoming increasingly user-friendly. Furthermore, since a business may have already purchased computers for other parts of its business, it makes sense to employ them for record keeping as well.
3. While the percentage of businesses using manual systems will likely decline, it will probably always make sense for certain businesses to use manual systems. For many start-up businesses, or businesses with few transactions, the advantages of installing a computerized system do not appear to outweigh the costs.

THE NAVIGATOR

# DEMONSTRATION PROBLEM

Celine Dion Company uses a six-column cash receipts journal with columns for Cash (Dr.), Sales Discounts (Dr.), Accounts Receivable (Cr.), Sales (Cr.), Other Accounts (Cr.) and Cost of Goods Sold (Dr.) and Merchandise Inventory (Cr.). Cash receipts transactions for the month of July 1999 are as follows:

**PROBLEM-SOLVING STRATEGIES**

1. All cash receipts are recorded in the cash receipts journal.

2. The "account credited" indicate items posted individually to the subsidiary ledger or general ledger.

3. Cash sales are recorded in the cash receipts journal—not in the sales journal.

4. The total debits must equal the total credits.

July 3   Cash sales total $5,800 (cost, $3,480).

5   A check for $6,370 is received from the Jeltz Company in payment of invoice dated June 26 for $6,500 terms 2/10, n/30.

9   An additional investment of $5,000 in cash is made in the business by Celine Dion, the proprietor.

10   Cash sales total $12,519 (cost, $7,511).

12   A check for $7,275 is received from R. Eliot & Co. in payment of a $7,500 invoice dated July 3, terms 3/10, n/30.

15   A customer advance of $700 cash is received for future sales.

20   Cash sales total $15,472 (cost, $9,283).

22   A check for $5,880 is received from Beck Company in payment of $6,000 invoice dated July 13, terms 2/10, n/30.

29   Cash sales total $17,660 (cost, $10,596).

31   Cash of $200 is received on interest earned for July.

*Instructions*

(a)  Journalize the transactions in the cash receipts journal.

(b)  Contrast the posting of the Accounts Receivable and Other Accounts columns.

# SOLUTION TO DEMONSTRATION PROBLEM

(a)                                    **Celine Dion Company**
                                        **CASH RECEIPTS JOURNAL**                                          **CR1**

| Date | Account Credited | Ref. | Cash Dr. | Sales Discounts Dr. | Accounts Receivable Cr. | Sales Cr. | Other Accounts Cr. | Cost of Goods Sold Dr. Mdse. Inv. Cr. |
|------|------------------|------|----------|---------------------|-------------------------|-----------|--------------------|-----------------------------------------|
| 1999 |                  |      |          |                     |                         |           |                    |                                         |
| 7/3  |                  |      | 5,800    |                     |                         | 5,800     |                    | 3,480                                   |
| 5    | Jeltz Company    |      | 6,370    | 130                 | 6,500                   |           |                    |                                         |
| 9    | Celine Dion, Capital |  | 5,000    |                     |                         |           | 5,000              |                                         |
| 10   |                  |      | 12,519   |                     |                         | 12,519    |                    | 7,511                                   |
| 12   | R. Eliot & Co.   |      | 7,275    | 225                 | 7,500                   |           |                    |                                         |
| 15   | Unearned Revenues |     | 700      |                     |                         |           | 700                |                                         |
| 20   |                  |      | 15,472   |                     |                         | 15,472    |                    | 9,283                                   |
| 22   | Beck Company     |      | 5,880    | 120                 | 6,000                   |           |                    |                                         |
| 29   |                  |      | 17,660   |                     |                         | 17,660    |                    | 10,596                                  |
| 31   | Interest Revenue |      | 200      |                     |                         |           | 200                |                                         |
|      |                  |      | 76,876   | 475                 | 20,000                  | 51,451    | 5,900              | 30,870                                  |

(b) The Accounts Receivable column is posted as a credit to Accounts Receivable. The individual amounts are credited to the customers' accounts identified in the Account Credited column, which are maintained in the accounts receivable subsidiary ledger.

The amounts in the Other Accounts Column are only posted individually. They are credited to the account titles identified in the Account Credited column.

## SUMMARY OF STUDY OBJECTIVES

**1. *Identify the basic principles of accounting information systems.*** The basic principles in developing an accounting information system are cost awareness, useful output, and flexibility.

**2. *Explain the major phases involved in the development of an accounting system.*** The major phases in the development of an accounting system are analysis, design, implementation, and follow-up.

**3. *Describe the nature and purpose of a subsidiary ledger.*** A subsidiary ledger is a group of accounts with a common characteristic. It facilitates the recording process by freeing the general ledger from details of individual balances.

**4. *Explain how special journals are used in journalizing.*** A special journal is used to group similar types of transactions. In a special journal, generally only one line is used to record a complete transaction.

**5. *Indicate how a columnar journal is posted.*** In posting a columnar journal:
(a) all column totals except for the Other Accounts column are posted once at the end of the month to the account title specified in the column heading.

(b) the total of the Other Accounts column is not posted. Instead, the individual amounts comprising the total are posted separately to the general ledger accounts specified in the Account Credited column.

(c) the individual amounts in a column posted in total to a control account are posted daily to the subsidiary ledger accounts specified in the Account Credited column.

**6. *Distinguish between computer hardware and accounting software and the principal methods of data processing.*** Computer hardware is the physical equipment associated with a computerized accounting system. Accounting software consists of programs that relate to specific parts of the accounting process. The principal methods of data processing are batch processing and on-line processing.

**7. *Identify the key points in comparing manual and electronic accounting systems.*** The key points in comparing manual and electronic accounting systems are (a) dollar costs, (b) processing speed, (c) processing errors, and (d) report generation.

THE NAVIGATOR

# GLOSSARY

**Accounting information system** A system that involves collecting and processing transaction data, and disseminating financial information to interested parties. (p. 232).

**Accounting software** Programs that relate to specific parts of the accounting process. (p. 252).

**Accounts payable (creditors') ledger** A subsidiary ledger that contains accounts with individual creditors. (p. 235).

**Accounts receivable (customers') ledger** A subsidiary ledger that contains individual customer accounts. (p. 235).

**Batch processing** A method in which data are accumulated by classes of transactions and are entered into the computer and processed in batches. (p. 253).

**Cash payments journal** A special journal used to record all cash paid. (p. 247).

**Cash receipts journal** A special journal used to record all cash received. (p. 240).

**Columnar journal** A special journal with more than one column. (p. 241).

**Computer hardware** The physical equipment associated with an electronic accounting system. (p. 251).

**Control account** An account in the general ledger that controls a subsidiary ledger. (p. 235).

**Electronic accounting system** A system that uses computers in processing transaction data and in disseminating accounting information to interested parties. (p. 250).

**Manual accounting system** A system in which each of the steps in the accounting cycle is performed by hand. (p. 234).

**On-line processing** A method in which files are updated concurrently with data entry. (p. 253).

**Purchases journal** A special journal used to record all purchases of merchandise on account. (p. 244).

**Sales journal** A special journal used to record all sales of merchandise on account. (p. 238).

**Special journal** A journal that is used to record similar types of transactions such as all credit sales. (p. 238).

**Subsidiary ledger** A group of accounts with a common characteristic. (p. 235).

# SELF-STUDY QUESTIONS

Answers are at the end of the chapter.

(SO 1)  1. The basic principles of an accounting information system include all of the following *except:*
a. cost awareness.
b. flexibility.
c. useful output.
d. periodicity.

(SO 2)  2. Which of the following is *not* a major phase in the development of an accounting information system?
a. Design.
b. Responsiveness.
c. Implementation.
d. Follow-up.

(SO 3)  3. Which of the following is *incorrect* concerning subsidiary ledgers?
a. The purchases ledger is a common subsidiary ledger for creditor accounts.
b. The accounts receivable ledger is a subsidiary ledger.
c. A subsidiary ledger is a group of accounts with a common characteristic.
d. An advantage of the subsidiary ledger is that it permits a division of labor in posting.

(SO 4)  4. A sales journal will be used for:

|   | Credit Sales | Cash Sales | Sales Discounts |
|---|---|---|---|
| a. | no | yes | yes |
| b. | yes | no | yes |
| c. | yes | no | no |
| d. | yes | yes | no |

(SO 5)  5. Which of the following statements is correct?
a. The sales discount column is included in the cash receipts journal.
b. The purchases journal records all purchases of merchandise whether for cash or on account.
c. The cash receipts journal records sales on account.
d. Merchandise returned by the buyer is recorded by the seller in the purchases journal.

(SO 5)  6. Which of the following is *incorrect* concerning the posting of the cash receipts journal?
a. The total of the Other Accounts column is not posted.
b. All column totals except the total for the Other Accounts column are posted once at the end of the month to the account title(s) specified in the column heading.
c. The total of all columns are posted daily to the accounts specified in the column heading.
d. The individual amounts in a column posted in total to a control account are posted daily to the subsidiary ledger account specified in the Accounts Credited column.

(SO 5)  7. Postings from the purchases journal to the subsidiary ledger are generally made:
a. yearly.
b. monthly.
c. weekly.
d. daily.

(SO 4)  8. Which statement is *incorrect* regarding the general journal?
a. Only transactions that cannot be entered in a special journal are recorded in the general journal.
b. Dual postings are always required in the general journal.
c. The general journal may be used to record acceptance of a note receivable for an accounts receivable.
d. Correcting, adjusting, and closing entries are made in the general journal.

(SO 6)  9. Computer hardware consists of the:
a. central processing unit.
b. accounting software.
c. peripheral equipment.
d. Both (a) and (c).

(SO 7)  10. Which of the following is *not* a key point in evaluating and comparing manual and electronic systems?
a. Cost considerations and processing speed.
b. Processing errors and responsiveness.
c. Posting general journals and special journals.
d. Report generation.

THE NAVIGATOR

# QUESTIONS

1. (a) What is an accounting information system? (b) "An accounting information system applies only to a manual system." Do you agree? Explain.

2. Certain principles should be followed in the development of an accounting information system. Identify and explain each of the principles.

3. Chandler Company is considering changing its accounting system for its accounts receivable billing procedure. At present, the procedure is performed manually by three clerks. A consultant has recommended that a new computer and related software be purchased for $1,000,000. What basic principle of designing and developing an effective accounting system might be violated by this proposal?

4. There are four phases in the life cycle of an accounting system. Identify and briefly explain each phase.

5. What are the advantages of using subsidiary ledgers?

6. (a) When are postings normally made to (1) the subsidiary accounts and (2) the general ledger control accounts? (b) Describe the relationship between a control account and a subsidiary ledger.

7. Identify and explain the four specific journals discussed in the chapter. List an advantage of using each of these journals rather than using only a general journal.

8. Oliva Company uses special journals. A sale made on account to C. Morton for $435 was recorded in a single-column sales journal. A few days later, Morton returns $70 worth of merchandise for credit. Where should Oliva Company record the sales return? Why?

9. A $500 purchase of merchandise on account from Monico Company was properly recorded in the purchases journal. When posted, however, the amount recorded in the subsidiary ledger was $50. How might this error be discovered?

10. Why would special journals used in different businesses not be identical in format? Can you think of a business that would maintain a cash receipts journal but not include a column for accounts receivable?

11. The cash and the accounts receivable columns in the cash receipts journal were mistakenly overadded by $4,000 at the end of the month. (a) Will the customers' ledger agree with the Accounts Receivable control account? (b) Assuming no other errors, will the trial balance totals be equal?

12. One column total of a special journal is posted at month end to only two general ledger accounts. One of these two accounts is Accounts Receivable. What is the name of this special journal? What is the other general ledger account to which that same month-end total is posted?

13. In what journal would the following transactions be recorded? (Assume that a two-column sales journal and a single-column purchases journal are used.)

(a) Recording of depreciation expense for the year.
(b) Gave credit to a customer for merchandise purchased on credit and returned.
(c) Sales of merchandise for cash.
(d) Sales of merchandise on account.
(e) Collection of cash on account from a customer.
(f) Purchase of office supplies on account.

14. In what journal would the following transactions be recorded? (Assume that a two-column sales journal and a single-column purchases journal are used.)
(a) Cash received from signing a note payable.
(b) Investment of cash by the owner of the business.
(c) Closing of the expense accounts at the end of the year.
(d) Purchase of merchandise on account.
(e) Received credit for merchandise purchased and returned to supplier.
(f) Payment of cash on account due a supplier.

15. What transactions might be included in a multiple-column purchases journal that would not be included in a single-column purchases journal?

16. Give an example of a transaction in the general journal that causes an entry to be posted twice (i.e., to two accounts), one in the general ledger, the other in the subsidiary ledger. Does this affect the debit/credit equality of the general ledger?

17. Give some examples of appropriate general journal transactions for an organization using special journals.

18. (a) Identify and explain the units that comprise the central processing unit (CPU). (b) What types of equipment are considered to be peripheral?

19. (a) What is accounting software? (b) What is integrated computer software?

20. Identify and distinguish between the two widely used methods of data processing in an electronic system.

21. What are the key points to be considered in evaluating and comparing manual and electronic systems?

# BRIEF EXERCISES

**BE6–1**   Indicate whether each of the following statements is true or false.

1. When designing an accounting system, we need to think about the needs and knowledge of both the top management and various other users.
2. When the environment changes as a result of technological advances, increased competition, or government regulation, an accounting system does not have to be sufficiently flexible to meet the changes in order to save money.
3. In developing an accounting system, cost is relevant. The system must be cost effective; that is, the benefits obtained from the information disseminated must outweigh the cost of providing it.

*Identify basic principles of accounting information system development.*
*(SO 1)*

**BE6–2**   The development of an accounting system involves four phases: analysis, design, implementation, and follow-up. Identify the statement that best describes each of these four phases.

*Identify major phases in accounting system development.*
*(SO 2)*

1. Determining internal and external information needs, identifying information sources and the needs for controls, and studying alternatives.

2. Evaluation and monitoring of effectiveness and efficiency, and correction of weaknesses, implementation, and design.
3. Creation of forms and documents, selection of procedures, and preparation of job descriptions.
4. Implementing new or revised documents, procedures, reports, and processing equipment; hiring and training personnel through a start-up or transition period.

*Identify subsidiary ledger balances.*
*(SO 3)*

**BE6–3**   Presented below is information related to Bryan Company for its first month of operations. Identify the balances that appear in the accounts receivable subsidiary ledger and the accounts receivable balance that appears in the general ledger at the end of January.

| | Credit Sales | | | Cash Collections | |
|---|---|---|---|---|---|
| Jan. 7 | Ace Co. | $9,000 | Jan. 17 | Ace Co. | $7,000 |
| 15 | Bono Co. | $6,000 | 24 | Bono Co. | $5,000 |
| 23 | Carr Co. | $9,000 | 29 | Carr Co. | $9,000 |

*Identify subsidiary ledger accounts.*
*(SO 3)*

**BE6–4**   Identify in what ledger (general or subsidiary) each of the following accounts is shown.

1. Rent Expense           3. Notes Payable
2. Accounts Receivable—Olsen   4. Accounts Payable—Kyle

*Identify special journals.*
*(SO 4)*

**BE6–5**   Identify the journal in which each of the following transactions is recorded.

1. Cash sales                4. Credit sales
2. Owner withdrawal of cash   5. Purchase of merchandise on account
3. Cash purchase of land      6. Receipt of cash for services performed

*Identify entries to cash receipts journal.*
*(SO 4)*

**BE6–6**   Indicate whether each of the following debits and credits is included in the cash receipts journal. (Use "Yes" or "No" to answer this question.)

1. Debit to Sales                  3. Credit to Accounts Receivable
2. Credit to Merchandise Inventory   4. Debit to Accounts Payable

*Indicate postings to cash receipts journal.*
*(SO 5)*

**BE6–7**   Starr Computer Components Inc. uses a columnar cash receipts journal. Indicate which column(s) is/are posted only in total, only daily, or both in total and daily.

1. Accounts Receivable    3. Cash
2. Sales Discounts        4. Other Accounts

*Identify transactions for special journals.*
*(SO 4)*

**BE6–8**   Coffey Co. uses special journals and a general journal. Identify the journal in which each of the following transactions is recorded.

1. Purchased equipment on account.
2. Purchased merchandise on account.
3. Paid utility expense in cash.
4. Sold merchandise on account.

*Identify transactions for special journals.*
*(SO 4)*

**BE6–9**   Identify the special journal(s) in which the following column headings appear.

1. Sales Discounts Dr.          4. Sales Cr.
2. Accounts Receivable Cr.      5. Merchandise Inventory Dr.
3. Cash Dr.

*Prepare a flowchart of the on-line processing method.*
*(SO 6)*

**BE6–10**   (a) Prepare a flowchart of the on-line processing method in an electronic accounting system. (b) Explain the manual system equivalent of this method of data processing.

# EXERCISES

* * * * * * * * * * * * * * * * * * * * * * * * * * * * * * * * * * * * * * * * * * * * *

*Determine control account balances and explain posting of special journals.*
*(SO 3, 5)*

**E6–1**   Valdes Company uses both special journals and a general journal as described in this chapter. On June 30, after all monthly postings had been completed, the Accounts Receivable controlling account in the general ledger had a debit balance of $350,000 and the Accounts Payable controlling account had a credit balance of $87,000.

The July transactions recorded in the special journals are summarized below. No entries affecting accounts receivable and accounts payable were recorded in the general journal for July.

Sales journal                 Total sales, $161,400
Purchases journal             Total purchases, $54,360
Cash receipts journal         Accounts receivable column total, $135,000
Cash payments journal         Accounts payable column total, $47,500

**Instructions**
(a) What is the balance of the Accounts Receivable control account after the monthly postings on July 31?
(b) What is the balance of the Accounts Payable control account after the monthly postings on July 31?
(c) To what account(s) is the column total of $161,400 in the sales journal posted?
(d) To what account(s) is the accounts receivable column total of $135,000 in the cash receipts journal posted?

**E6–2**   Presented below is the subsidiary accounts receivable account of Rico Perez.

*Explain postings to subsidiary ledger.*
*(SO 3)*

| Date | Ref. | Debit | Credit | Balance |
|------|------|-------|--------|---------|
| 1999 | | | | |
| Sept.  2 | S31 | 61,000 | | 61,000 |
| 9 | G4 | | 12,000 | 49,000 |
| 27 | CR8 | | 49,000 | — |

**Instructions**

Write a memo that explains each transaction.

**E6–3**   On September 1 the balance of the Accounts Receivable controlling account in the general ledger of Cremer Company was $10,960. The customers' subsidiary ledger contained account balances as follows: Alou, $1,440; Farr, $2,640; Keaton, $2,060; Skiles, $4,820. At the end of September the various journals contained the following information:

*Post various journals to control and subsidiary accounts.*
*(SO 3, 5)*

**Sales journal:** Sales to Skiles, $800; to Alou, $1,350; to George, $1,030; to Keaton, $1,100.

**Cash receipts journal:** Cash received from Keaton, $1,310; from Skiles, $2,300; from George, $410; from Farr, $1,800; from Alou, $1,240.

**General journal:** An allowance is granted to Skiles, $220.

**Instructions**
(a) Set up control and subsidiary accounts and enter the beginning balances. Do not construct the journals.
(b) Post the various journals. Post the items as individual items or as totals, whichever would be the appropriate procedure. (No sales discounts given.)
(c) Prepare a list of customers and prove the agreement of the controlling account with the subsidiary ledger at September 30, 1999.

**E6–4**   Harris Company uses special journals and a general journal. The following transactions occurred during September 1999.

*Record transactions in sales and purchases journal.*
*(SO 3, 4)*

Sept.  2   Sold merchandise on account to F. Vina, invoice no. 101, $500, terms n/30. The cost of the merchandise sold was $300.
     10   Purchased merchandise on account from F. Kotsch $600, terms 2/10, n/30.
     12   Purchased office equipment on account from J. Wells, $6,500.
     21   Sold merchandise on account to J. Rich, invoice no. 102 for $800, terms 2/10, n/30. The cost of the merchandise sold was $480.
     25   Purchased merchandise on account from M. Watt $900, terms n/30.
     27   Sold merchandise to R. Cowan for $700 cash. The cost of the merchandise sold was $420.

**Instructions**
(a) Draw a sales journal (see Illustration 6-8) and a single-column purchase journal (see Illustration 6-13). (Use page 1 for each journal.)
(b) Record the transaction(s) for September that should be journalized in the sales journal and the purchases journal.

*Record transactions in cash receipts and cash payments journal.*
*(SO 3, 4)*

**E6–5** Briggs Co. uses special journals and a general journal. The following transactions occurred during May 1999.

May  1  J. Briggs invested $62,000 cash in the business.
   2  Sold merchandise to L. Bean for $6,000 cash. The cost of the merchandise sold was $4,200.
   3  Purchased merchandise for $9,000 from R. L. Sanchez using check no. 101.
   14  Paid salary to F. Sparks $700 by issuing check no. 102.
   16  Sold merchandise on account to B. Ready for $900, terms n/30. The cost of the merchandise sold was $630.
   22  A check of $9,000 is received from M. Lane in full for invoice 101; no discount given.

**Instructions**

(a) Draw a multiple-column cash receipts journal (see Illustration 6-10) and a multiple-column cash payments journal (see Illustration 6-17). (Use page 1 for each journal.)

(b) Record the transaction(s) for May that should be journalized in the cash receipts journal and cash payments journal.

*Explain journalizing in cash journals.*
*(SO 4)*

**E6–6** Abbott Company uses the columnar cash journals illustrated in the textbook. In April, the following selected cash transactions occurred:

1. Made a refund to a customer for the return of damaged goods.
2. Received collection from customer within the 3% discount period.
3. Purchased merchandise for cash.
4. Paid a creditor within the 3% discount period.
5. Received collection from customer after the 3% discount period had expired.
6. Paid freight on merchandise purchased.
7. Paid cash for office equipment.
8. Received cash refund from supplier for merchandise returned.
9. Withdrew cash for personal use of owner.
10. Made cash sales.

**Instructions**

Indicate (a) the journal, and (b) the columns in the journal that should be used in recording each transaction.

*Journalize transactions in general journal and post.*
*(SO 3, 4)*

**E6–7** Warner Company has the following selected transactions during March:

Mar.  2  Purchased equipment costing $5,000 from Pena Company on account.
   5  Received credit memorandum for $300 from Simon Company for merchandise damaged in shipment to Warner.
   7  Issued a credit memorandum for $400 to Farr Company for merchandise the customer returned. The returned merchandise had a cost of $260.

Warner Company uses a one-column purchases journal, a sales journal, the columnar cash journals used in the text, and a general journal.

**Instructions**

(a) Journalize the transactions in the general journal.

(b) █████▶ In a brief memo to the president of Warner Company, explain the postings to the control and subsidiary accounts.

*Indicate journalizing in special journals.*
*(SO 4)*

**E6–8** Below are some typical transactions incurred by Littlejohn Company.

1. Payment of creditors on account.
2. Return of merchandise sold for credit.
3. Collection on account from customers.
4. Sold land for cash.
5. Sale of merchandise on account.
6. Sale of merchandise for cash.
7. Received credit for merchandise purchased on credit.
8. Sales discount taken on goods sold.
9. Payment of employee wages.
10. Close income summary to owner's capital.
11. Depreciation on building.
12. Purchase of office supplies for cash.
13. Purchase of merchandise on account.

**Instructions**

For each transaction, indicate whether it would normally be recorded in a cash receipts journal, cash payments journal, sales journal, single-column purchases journal, or general journal.

**E6–9**  The general ledger of the Torres Company contained the following Accounts Payable control account (in T-account form). Also shown is the related subsidiary ledger.

*Explain posting to control account and subsidiary ledger.*
*(SO 3, 5)*

### GENERAL LEDGER

**Accounts Payable**

| | | | | | | | |
|---|---|---|---|---|---|---|---|
| Feb. 15 | General Journal | 1,400 | Feb. 1 | Balance | 26,025 |
| 28 | ? | ? | 5 | General Journal | 265 |
| | | | 11 | General Journal | 550 |
| | | | 28 | Purchases | 13,700 |
| | | | Feb. 28 | Balance | 9,640 |

### ACCOUNTS PAYABLE LEDGER

**Sealy**

| Feb. 28 | Bal. | 4,600 |
|---|---|---|

**Wolcott**

| Feb. 28 | Bal. | ? |
|---|---|---|

**Gates**

| Feb. 28 | Bal. | 2,000 |
|---|---|---|

*Instructions*
(a) Indicate the missing posting reference and amount in the control account and the missing ending balance in the subsidiary ledger.
(b) Indicate the amounts in the control account that were dual-posted (i.e., posted to the control account and the subsidiary accounts).

**E6–10**  Selected accounts from the ledgers of Moyer Company at July 31 showed the following:

*Prepare purchases and general journals.*
*(SO 3, 4)*

### GENERAL LEDGER

**Store Equipment**                No. 153

| Date | Explanation | Ref. | Debit | Credit | Balance |
|---|---|---|---|---|---|
| July 1 | | G1 | 3,600 | | 3,600 |

**Merchandise Inventory**                No. 120

| Date | Explanation | Ref. | Debit | Credit | Balance |
|---|---|---|---|---|---|
| July 15 | | G1 | 400 | | 400 |
| 18 | | G1 | | 100 | 300 |
| 25 | | G1 | | 200 | 100 |
| 31 | | P1 | 8,400 | | 8,500 |

**Accounts Payable**                No. 201

| Date | Explanation | Ref. | Debit | Credit | Balance |
|---|---|---|---|---|---|
| July 1 | | G1 | | 3,600 | 3,600 |
| 15 | | G1 | | 400 | 4,000 |
| 18 | | G1 | 100 | | 3,900 |
| 25 | | G1 | 200 | | 3,700 |
| 31 | | P1 | | 8,400 | 12,100 |

### ACCOUNTS PAYABLE LEDGER

**Alcott Equipment Co.**

| Date | Explanation | Ref. | Debit | Credit | Balance |
|---|---|---|---|---|---|
| July 1 | | G1 | | 3,600 | 3,600 |

**Delco Co.**

| Date | Explanation | Ref. | Debit | Credit | Balance |
|---|---|---|---|---|---|
| July 14 | | P1 | | 1,100 | 1,100 |
| 25 | | G1 | 200 | | 900 |

**Bradley Co.**

| Date | Explanation | Ref. | Debit | Credit | Balance |
|---|---|---|---|---|---|
| July 3 | | P1 | | 2,000 | 2,000 |
| 20 | | P1 | | 700 | 2,700 |

**Erick Co.**

| Date | Explanation | Ref. | Debit | Credit | Balance |
|---|---|---|---|---|---|
| July 12 | | P1 | | 500 | 500 |
| 21 | | P1 | | 600 | 1,100 |

**Costo Materials**

| Date | Explanation | Ref. | Debit | Credit | Balance |
|---|---|---|---|---|---|
| July 17 | | P1 | | 1,400 | 1,400 |
| 18 | | G1 | 100 | | 1,300 |
| 29 | | P1 | | 2,100 | 3,400 |

**Gaetti Transit**

| Date | Explanation | Ref. | Debit | Credit | Balance |
|---|---|---|---|---|---|
| July 15 | | G1 | | 400 | 400 |

**Instructions**

From the data prepare:

(a) the single-column purchases journal for July.

(b) the general journal entries for July.

*Determine correct posting amount to control account.*
*(SO 5)*

**E6–11** Yan Products uses both special journals and a general journal as described in this chapter. Yan also posts customers' accounts in the accounts receivable subsidiary ledger. The postings for the most recent month are included in the subsidiary T accounts below.

**Edmonds**

| | | |
|---|---|---|
| Bal. | 340 | 250 |
| | 180 | |

**Roemer**

| | | |
|---|---|---|
| Bal. | 150 | 150 |
| | 290 | |

**Schulz**

| | | |
|---|---|---|
| Bal. | –0– | 145 |
| | 145 | |

**Park**

| | | |
|---|---|---|
| Bal. | 120 | 120 |
| | 190 | |
| | 170 | |

**Instructions**

Determine the correct amount of the end-of-month posting from the sales journal to the Accounts Receivable controlling account.

# PROBLEMS: SET A

*Journalize transactions in cash receipts journal and post to control account and subsidiary ledger.*
*(SO 3, 4, 5)*

**P6–1A** Koslo Company's chart of accounts includes the following selected accounts:

| | |
|---|---|
| 101 Cash | 401 Sales |
| 112 Accounts Receivable | 414 Sales Discounts |
| 120 Merchandise Inventory | 505 Cost of Goods Sold |
| 301 T. Koslo, Capital | |

On June 1 the accounts receivable ledger of the Koslo Company showed the following balances: Bell & Son, $2,500; Ellis Co., $1,900; Gant Bros., $1,600; and Mejia Co., $1,000. The June transactions involving the receipt of cash were as follows:

June 1  The owner, T. Koslo, invested additional cash in the business, $9,000.

3  Received check in full from Mejia Co. less 2% cash discount.

6  Received check in full from Ellis Co. less 2% cash discount.

7  Made cash sales of merchandise totaling $6,135. The cost of the merchandise sold was $4,090.

9  Received check in full from Bell & Son less 2% cash discount.

11  Received cash refund from a supplier for damaged merchandise, $200.

15  Made cash sales of merchandise totaling $5,250. The cost of the merchandise sold was $3,500.

20  Received check in full from Gant Bros., $1,600.

**Instructions**

(a) Journalize the transactions above in a six-column cash receipts journal with columns for Cash Dr.; Sales Discounts Dr.; Accounts Receivable Cr.; Sales Cr.; Other Accounts Cr; and Cost of Goods Sold Dr./Merchandise Inventory Cr. Foot and crossfoot the journal.

(b) Insert the beginning balances in the Accounts Receivable control and subsidiary accounts and post the June transactions to these accounts.

(c) Prove the agreement of the control account and subsidiary account balances.

**P6–2A**   Cline Company's chart of accounts includes the following selected accounts:

*Journalize transactions in cash payments journal and post to the general and subsidiary ledger.*
*(SO 3, 4, 5)*

| | |
|---|---|
| 101 Cash | 157 Equipment |
| 120 Merchandise Inventory | 201 Accounts Payable |
| 130 Prepaid Insurance | 306 B. Cline, Drawing |

On November 1 the accounts payable ledger of the Cline Company showed the following balances: S. Haley & Co., $3,750; C. King, $2,350; W. Ortega, $1,000; and Welch Bros., $1,900. The November transactions involving the payment of cash were as follows:

Nov.  1  Purchased merchandise, check no. 11, $900.
   3  Purchased store equipment, check no. 12, $1,650.
   5  Paid Welch Bros. balance due of $1,900, less 1% discount, check no. 13, $1,881.
   11  Purchased merchandise, check no. 14, $2,000.
   15  Paid W. Ortega balance due of $1,000, less 3% discount, check no. 15, $970.
   16  B. Cline, the owner, withdraws $500 cash for own use, check no. 16.
   19  Paid C. King in full for invoice no. 1245, $1,300 less 2% discount, check no. 17, $1,274.
   25  Paid premium due on one year insurance policy, check no. 18, $3,000.
   30  Paid S. Haley & Co. in full for invoice no. 832, $2,250, check no. 19.

*Instructions*

(a) Journalize the transctions above in a four-column cash payments journal with columns for Other Accounts Dr.; Accounts Payable Dr.; Merchandise Inventory Cr.; and Cash Cr. Foot and crossfoot the journal.

(b) Insert the beginning balances in the Accounts Payable control and subsidiary accounts and post the November transactions to these accounts.

(c) Prove the agreement of the control account and the subsidiary account balances.

**P6–3A**   The chart of accounts of Pagnozzi Company includes the following selected accounts:

*Journalize transactions in multicolumn purchases journal and post to the general and subsidiary ledgers.*
*(SO 3, 4, 5)*

| | |
|---|---|
| 112 Accounts Receivable | 401 Sales |
| 120 Merchandise Inventory | 412 Sales Returns and Allowances |
| 126 Supplies | 505 Cost of Goods Sold |
| 157 Equipment | 610 Advertising Expense |
| 201 Accounts Payable | |

In May the following selected transactions were completed. All purchases and sales were on account except as indicated. The cost of all merchandise sold was 70% of the sales price.

May  2  Purchased merchandise from Vena Company, $9,000.
   3  Received freight bill from Abel Freight on Vena purchase, $400.
   5  Sales were made to Potts Company, $1,600; Hogan Bros., $2,700; and Nance Company, $1,500.
   8  Purchased merchandise from Gore Company, $8,000 and Deleon Company, $8,700.
   10  Received credit on merchandise returned to Deleon Company, $500.
   15  Purchased supplies from Eaton Supply, $900.
   16  Purchased merchandise from Vena Company, $4,500; and Gore Company, $6,000.
   17  Returned supplies to Eaton Supply, receiving credit, $100. (*Hint:* Credit Supplies.)
   18  Received freight bills on May 16 purchases from Abel Freight, $500.
   20  Returned merchandise to Vena Company receiving credit, $300.
   23  Made sales to Hogan Bros., $2,400; and Nance Company, $2,200.
   25  Received bill for advertising from Beck Advertising, $900.
   26  Granted allowance to Nance Company for merchandise damaged in shipment, $200.
   28  Purchased equipment from Eaton Supply, $250.

*Instructions*

(a) Journalize the transactions above in a purchases journal, a sales journal, and a general journal. The purchases journal should have the following column headings: Date, Accounts Credited (Debited), Ref., Other Accounts Dr., Merchandise Inventory Dr., and Accounts Payable Cr.

(b) Post to both the general and subsidiary ledger accounts. (Assume that all accounts have zero beginning balances.)

(c) Prove the agreement of the control and subsidiary accounts.

*Journalize transactions in special journals.*
*(SO 3, 4, 5)*

**P6–4A**   Selected accounts from the chart of accounts of Santos Company are shown below.

| | |
|---|---|
| 101 Cash | 201 Accounts Payable |
| 112 Accounts Receivable | 401 Sales |
| 120 Merchandise Inventory | 414 Sales Discounts |
| 126 Supplies | 505 Cost of Goods Sold |
| 140 Land | 610 Advertising Expense |
| 145 Buildings | |

The cost of all merchandise sold was 60% of the sales price. During October, Santos Company completed the following transactions:

Oct.  2   Purchased merchandise on account from Ming Company, $17,500.
4   Sold merchandise on account to Pinka Co., $8,000. Invoice no. 204; terms 2/10, n/30.
5   Purchased supplies for cash, $80.
7   Made cash sales for the week totaling $9,160.
9   Paid in full the amount owed the Ming Company less a 2% discount.
10   Purchased merchandise on account from Quayle Corp., $4,200.
12   Received payment from Pinka Co. for invoice no. 204.
13   Issued a debit memorandum to Quayle Corp. and returned $250 worth of damaged goods.
14   Made cash sales for the week totaling $8,180.
16   Sold a parcel of land for $27,000 cash, the land's book value.
17   Sold merchandise on account to C. Baden & Co., $5,350, invoice no. 205, terms 2/10, n/30.
18   Purchased merchandise for cash, $2,125.
21   Made cash sales for the week totaling $8,465.
23   Paid in full the amount owed the Quayle Corp. for the goods kept (no discount).
25   Purchased supplies on account from Flott Co., $260.
25   Sold merchandise on account to Gregg Corp., $5,220, invoice no. 206, terms 2/10, n/30.
25   Received payment from C. Baden & Co. for invoice no. 205.
26   Purchased for cash a small parcel of land and a building on the land to use as a storage facility. The total cost of $35,000 was allocated $21,000 to the land and $14,000 to the building.
27   Purchased merchandise on account from Singer Co., $8,500.
28   Made cash sales for the week totaling $8,540.
30   Purchased merchandise on account from Ming Company, $14,000.
30   Paid advertising bill for the month from the Gazette, $400.
30   Sold merchandise on account to C. Baden & Co., $4,600. Invoice no. 207; terms 2/10, n/30.

Santos Company uses the following journals:

1. Sales journal.
2. Single-column purchases journal.
3. Cash receipts journal with columns for Cash Dr.; Sales Discounts Dr.; Accounts Receivable Cr.; Sales Cr.; Other Accounts Cr.; and Cost of Goods Sold Dr./Merchandise Inventory Cr.
4. Cash payments journal with columns for Other Accounts Dr.; Accounts Payable Dr.; Merchandise Inventory, Cr.; and Cash Cr.
5. General journal.

*Instructions*

Using the selected accounts provided:

(a) Record, in the appropriate journals, the October transactions.

(b) Foot and crossfoot all special journals.

(c) Show how postings would be made by placing ledger account numbers and check marks as needed in the journals. (Actual posting to ledger accounts is not required.)

*Journalize in purchase and cash payments journals, post, prepare a trial balance, prove control to subsidiary, prepare adjusting entries, and prepare an adjusted trial balance.*
(SO 3, 4, 5)

**P6–5A**   Presented below are the sales and cash receipts journals for Tino Co. for its first month of operations.

**SALES JOURNAL**                                                             S1

| Date | Account Debited | Ref. | Accounts Receivable Dr. Sales Cr. | Cost of Goods Sold Dr. Merchandise Inventory Cr. |
|---|---|---|---|---|
| Feb.  3 | D. Alco | | 5,000 | 3,300 |
| 9 | P. Barber | | 6,500 | 4,290 |
| 12 | D. Casey | | 8,000 | 5,280 |
| 26 | K. Dennis | | 6,000 | 3,960 |
| | | | 25,500 | 16,830 |

**CASH RECEIPTS JOURNAL**                                                      CR1

| Date | Account Credited | Ref. | Cash Dr. | Sales Discounts Dr. | Accounts Receivable Cr. | Sales Cr. | Other Accounts Cr. | Cost of Goods Sold Dr. Merchandise Inventory Cr. |
|---|---|---|---|---|---|---|---|---|
| Feb.  1 | J. Tino, Capital | | 30,000 | | | | 30,000 | |
| 2 | | | 6,500 | | | 6,500 | | 4,290 |
| 13 | D. Alco | | 4,950 | 50 | 5,000 | | | |
| 18 | Merchandise Inventory | | 150 | | | | 150 | |
| 26 | P. Barber | | 6,500 | | 6,500 | | | |
| | | | 48,100 | 50 | 11,500 | 6,500 | 30,150 | 4,290 |

In addition, the following transactions have not been journalized for February 1999.

Feb.  2   Purchased merchandise on account from J. Carsen for $3,000, terms 1/10, n/30.

7   Purchased merchandise on account from K. Cooper for $30,000, terms 1/10, n/30.

9   Paid cash of $1,000 for purchase of supplies.

12   Paid $2,970 to J. Carsen in payment for $3,000 invoice, less 1% discount.

15   Purchased equipment for $8,000 cash.

16   Purchased merchandise on account from M. Kim, $2,400, terms 2/10, n/30.

17   Paid $29,700 to K. Cooper in payment of $30,000 invoice, less 1% discount.

20   Withdrew cash of $1,100 from business for personal use.

21   Purchased merchandise on account from G. Azar for $6,500, terms 1/10, n/30.

28   Paid $2,400 to M. Kim in payment of $2,400 invoice.

*Instructions*

(a) Open the following accounts in the general ledger.

| | |
|---|---|
| 101 Cash | 301 J. Tino, Capital |
| 112 Accounts Receivable | 306 J. Tino, Drawing |
| 120 Merchandise Inventory | 401 Sales |
| 126 Supplies | 414 Sales Discounts |
| 157 Equipment | 505 Cost of Goods Sold |
| 158 Accumulated Depreciation—Equipment | 631 Supplies Expense |
| 201 Accounts Payable | 711 Depreciation Expense |

(b) Journalize the transactions that have not been journalized in a one-column purchases journal, and the cash payments journal (see Illustration 6-17).

(c) Post to the accounts receivable and accounts payable subsidiary ledgers. Follow the sequence of transactions as shown in the problem.

(d) Post the individual entries and totals to the general ledger.

(e) Prepare a trial balance at February 28, 1999.

(f) Determine that the subsidiary ledgers agree with the control accounts in the general ledger.

(g) The following adjustments at the end of February are necessary.

1. A count of supplies indicates that $300 is still on hand.
2. Depreciation on equipment for February is $200.

Prepare the adjusting entries and then post the adjusting entries to the general ledger.

(h) Prepare an adjusted trial balance.

*Journalize in special journals, post, and prepare a trial balance.*

(SO 3, 4, 5)

**P6–6A** The post-closing trial balance for Gonzalez Co. is as follows:

### GONZALES CO.
### Post-Closing Trial Balance
### December 31, 1999

|  | Debit | Credit |
|---|---|---|
| Cash | $ 39,500 |  |
| Accounts Receivable | 15,000 |  |
| Notes Receivable | 45,000 |  |
| Merchandise Inventory | 23,000 |  |
| Equipment | 6,450 |  |
| Accumulated Depreciation—Equipment |  | $ 1,500 |
| Accounts Payable |  | 43,000 |
| L. Gonzales, Capital |  | 84,450 |
|  | $128,950 | $128,950 |

The subsidiary ledgers contain the following information: (1) accounts receivable—P. Naab $2,500; K. Hoyt $7,500; A. Deitz $5,000; (2) accounts payable—D. Kraft $10,000; W. Henrie $18,000; and J. Fanning $15,000. The cost of all merchandise sold was 65% of the sales price.

The transactions for January 2000 are as follows:

Jan.  3  Sell merchandise to C. Hernandez, $3,000, terms 2/10, n/30.
  5  Purchase merchandise from D. Greer, $2,500, terms 2/10, n/30.
  7  Receive a check from A. Deitz, $3,500.
  11  Pay freight on merchandise purchased, $300.
  12  Pay rent of $1,000 for January.
  13  Receive payment in full from C. Hernandez.
  14  Post all entries to the subsidiary ledgers. Issue a credit memo to acknowledge receipt of damaged merchandise of $700 returned by P. Naab.
  15  Send J. Fanning a check for $14,850 in full payment of account, discount, $150.
  17  Purchase merchandise from B. Masoni, $1,600, terms 2/10, n/30.
  18  Pay sales salaries of $2,800 and office salaries, $1,500.
  20  Give W. Henrie a 60-day note for $18,000 in full payment of account payable.
  23  Total cash sales amount to $8,600.
  24  Post all entries to the subsidiary ledgers. Sell merchandise on account to K. Hoyt, $7,700, terms 1/10, n/30.
  27  Send D. Greer a check for $950.
  29  Receive payment on a note of $40,000 from L. Danza.
  30  Return merchandise of $500 to B. Masoni for credit. Post all journals to the subsidiary ledger.

*Instructions*

(a) Open general and subsidiary ledger accounts for the following:

| 101 Cash | 157 Equipment |
|---|---|
| 112 Accounts Receivable | 158 Accumulated Depreciation—Equipment |
| 115 Notes Receivable | 200 Notes Payable |
| 120 Merchandise Inventory | 201 Accounts Payable |

| | | | |
|---|---|---|---|
| 301 | L. Gonzalez, Capital | 505 | Cost of Goods Sold |
| 401 | Sales | 726 | Sales Salaries Expense |
| 412 | Sales Returns and Allowances | 727 | Office Salaries Expense |
| 414 | Sales Discounts | 729 | Rent Expense |

(b) Record the January transactions in a sales journal, a single-column purchases journal, a cash receipts journal (see Illustration 6-10), a cash payments journal (see Illustration 6-17), and a general journal.
(c) Post the appropriate amounts to the general ledger.
(d) Prepare a trial balance at January 31, 2000.
(e) Determine whether the subsidiary ledgers agree with controlling accounts in the general ledger.

# PROBLEMS: SET B

**P6–1B**  Morrow Company's chart of accounts includes the following selected accounts:

*Journalize transactions in cash receipts journal and post to control account and subsidiary ledger.*
*(SO 3, 4, 5)*

| | | | |
|---|---|---|---|
| 101 | Cash | 401 | Sales |
| 112 | Accounts Receivable | 414 | Sales Discounts |
| 120 | Merchandise Inventory | 505 | Cost of Goods Sold |
| 301 | T. Morrow, Capital | | |

On April 1 the accounts receivable ledger of Morrow Company showed the following balances: Horner, $1,550; Kile, $1,200; Nicci Co., $2,900; and Starr, $1,600. The April transactions involving the receipt of cash were as follows:

Apr.  1  The owner, T. Morrow, invested additional cash in the business, $6,000.
      4  Received check for payment of account from Starr less 2% cash discount.
      5  Received check for $620 in payment of invoice no. 307 from Nicci Co.
      8  Made cash sales of merchandise totaling $7,245. The cost of the merchandise sold was $4,347.
   10  Received check for $800 in payment of invoice no. 309 from Horner.
   11  Received cash refund from a supplier for damaged merchandise, $550.
   23  Received check for $1,600 in payment of invoice no. 310 from Nicci Co.
   29  Received check for payment of account from Kile.

*Instructions*
(a) Journalize the transactions above in a six-column cash receipts journal with columns for Cash Dr.; Sales Discounts Dr.; Accounts Receivable Cr.; Sales Cr.; Other Accounts Cr., and Cost of Goods Sold Dr./Merchandise Inventory Cr. Foot and crossfoot the journal.
(b) Insert the beginning balances in the Accounts Receivable control and subsidiary accounts and post the April transactions to these accounts.
(c) Prove the agreement of the control account and subsidiary account balances.

**P6–2B**  Norton Company's chart of accounts includes the following selected accounts:

*Journalize transactions in cash payments journal and post to control account and subsidiary ledger.*
*(SO 3, 4, 5)*

| | | | |
|---|---|---|---|
| 101 | Cash | 201 | Accounts Payable |
| 120 | Merchandise Inventory | 306 | R. Norton, Drawing |
| 130 | Prepaid Insurance | 505 | Cost of Goods Sold |
| 157 | Equipment | | |

On October 1 the accounts payable ledger of Norton Company showed the following balances: Heston Company, $1,600; Menke & Sons, $2,500; Ogle Co., $1,400; and Paige Company, $3,700. The October transactions involving the payment of cash were as follows:

Oct.  1  Purchased merchandise, check no. 63, $700.
      3  Purchased equipment, check no. 64, $800.
      5  Paid Heston Company balance due of $1,600, less 2% discount, check no. 65, $1,568.
   10  Purchased merchandise, check no. 66, $2,250.
   15  Paid Ogle Co. balance due of $1,400, check no. 67.

16  R. Norton, the owner, pays his personal insurance premium of $400, check no. 68.

19  Paid Menke & Sons in full for invoice no. 610, $1,400 less 2% cash discount, check no. 69, $1,372.

29  Paid Paige Company in full for invoice no. 264, $2,500, check no. 70.

**Instructions**

(a) Journalize the transactions above in a four-column cash payments journal with columns for Other Accounts Dr.; Accounts Payable Dr.; Merchandise Inventory Dr.; and Cash Cr. Foot and crossfoot the journal.

(b) Insert the beginning balances in the Accounts Payable control and subsidiary accounts and post the October transactions to these accounts.

(c) Prove the agreement of the control account and the subsidiary account balances.

*Journalize transactions in multi-column purchases journal and post to the general and subsidiary ledgers.*
*(SO 3, 4, 5)*

**P6–3B**  The chart of accounts of Cruz Company includes the following selected accounts:

| | |
|---|---|
| 112 Accounts Receivable | 401 Sales |
| 120 Merchandise Inventory | 412 Sales Returns and Allowances |
| 126 Supplies | 505 Cost of Goods Sold |
| 157 Equipment | 610 Advertising Expense |
| 201 Accounts Payable | |

In July the following selected transactions were completed. All purchases and sales were on account. The cost of all merchandise sold was 70% of the sales price.

July  1  Purchased merchandise from DeVito Company, $7,000.

2  Received freight bill from Carlin Shipping on DeVito purchase, $400.

3  Made sales to Laird Company, $1,300; and Flood Bros., $1,900.

5  Purchased merchandise from Granger Company, $3,200.

8  Received credit on merchandise returned to Granger Company, $300.

13  Purchased store supplies from Beyer Supply, $720.

15  Purchased merchandise from DeVito Company, $3,600; and Reeble Company, $2,800.

16  Made sales to Marquez Company, $3,450; and Flood Bros., $1,570.

18  Received bill for advertising from Meyer's Advertisements, $600.

21  Sales were made to Laird Company, $310; and Resch Company, $2,200.

22  Granted allowance to Laird Company for merchandise damaged in shipment, $40.

24  Purchased merchandise from Granger Company, $3,000.

26  Purchased equipment from Beyer Supply, $600.

28  Received freight bill from Carlin Shipping on Granger purchase of July 24, $380.

30  Sales were made to Marquez Company, $4,900.

**Instructions**

(a) Journalize the transactions above in a purchases journal, a sales journal, and a general journal. The purchases journal should have the following column headings: Date, Accounts Credited (Debited), Ref., Other Accounts Dr., Merchandise Inventory Dr., and Accounts Payable Cr.

(b) Post to both the general and subsidiary ledger accounts. (Assume that all accounts have zero beginning balances.)

(c) Prove the agreement of the control and subsidiary accounts.

*Journalize transactions in special journals.*
*(SO 3, 4, 5)*

**P6–4B**  Selected accounts from the chart of accounts of Shell Company are shown below.

| | |
|---|---|
| 101 Cash | 401 Sales |
| 112 Accounts Receivable | 412 Sales Returns and Allowances |
| 120 Merchandise Inventory | 414 Sales Discounts |
| 126 Supplies | 505 Cost of Goods Sold |
| 157 Equipment | 726 Salaries Expense |
| 201 Accounts Payable | |

The cost of all merchandise sold was 60% of the sales price. During January, Shell completed the following transactions:

Jan.  3  Purchased merchandise on account from Blue Co., $9,900.
      4  Purchased supplies for cash, $80.
      4  Sold merchandise on account to Grimm, $7,250, invoice no. 371, terms 1/10, n/30.
      5  Issued a debit memorandum to Blue Co. and returned $300 worth of damaged goods.
      6  Made cash sales for the week totaling $3,150.
      8  Purchased merchandise on account from Fritz Co., $4,500.
      9  Sold merchandise on account to Mai Corp., $5,600, invoice no. 372, terms 1/10, n/30.
     11  Purchased merchandise on account from Hatch Co., $3,700.
     13  Paid in full the Blue Co. on account less a 2% discount.
     13  Made cash sales for the week totaling $5,340.
     15  Received payment from Mai Corp. for invoice no. 372.
     15  Paid semi-monthly salaries of $14,300 to employees.
     17  Received payment from Grimm for invoice no. 371.
     17  Sold merchandise on account to Engel Co., $1,200, invoice no. 373, terms 1/10, n/30.
     19  Purchased equipment on account from Jaeger Corp., $5,500.
     20  Cash sales for the week totaled $3,200.
     20  Paid in full the Fritz Co. on account less a 2% discount.
     23  Purchased merchandise on account from Blue Co., $7,800.
     24  Purchased merchandise on account from Rankin Corp., $4,690.
     27  Made cash sales for the week totaling $3,730.
     30  Received payment from Engel Co. for invoice no. 373.
     31  Paid semi-monthly salaries of $13,200 to employees.
     31  Sold merchandise on account to Grimm, $9,330, invoice no. 374, terms 1/10, n/30.

Shell Company uses the following journals:

1.  Sales journal.
2.  Single-column purchases journal.
3.  Cash receipts journal with columns for Cash Dr.; Sales Discounts Dr.; Accounts Receivable Cr.; Sales Cr.; Other Accounts Cr.; and Cost of Goods Sold Dr./Merchandise Inventory Cr.
4.  Cash payments journal with columns for Other Accounts Dr.; Accounts Payable Dr.; Merchandise Inventory Cr.; and Cash Cr.
5.  General journal.

*Instructions*
Using the selected accounts provided:

(a)  Record, in the appropriate journal noted, the January transactions.
(b)  Foot and crossfoot all special journals.
(c)  Show how postings would be made by placing ledger account numbers and check-marks as needed in the journals. (Actual posting to ledger accounts is not required.)

**P6–5B**  Presented below are the purchases and cash payments journal for Weber Co. for its first month of operations.

*Journalize in sales and cash receipts journals, post, prepare a trial balance, prove control to subsidiary, prepare adjusting entries, and prepare an adjusted trial balance.*
*(SO 3, 4, 5)*

### PURCHASES JOURNAL                                    P1

| Date | | Account Credited | Ref. | Merchandise Inventory Dr. Accounts Payable Cr. |
|------|---|------------------|------|------------------------------------------------|
| July | 4 | P. Coley | | 6,800 |
| | 5 | S. Farr | | 7,500 |
| | 11 | B. Goltra | | 3,720 |
| | 13 | C. Hunt | | 15,300 |
| | 20 | R. Jenks | | 8,800 |
| | | | | 42,120 |

## CASH PAYMENTS JOURNAL                                                          CP1

| Date | Account Debited | Ref. | Other Accounts Dr. | Accounts Payable Dr. | Merchandise Inventory Cr. | Cash Cr. |
|------|-----------------|------|--------------------|----------------------|---------------------------|----------|
| July  4 | Store Supplies | | 600 | | | 600 |
| 10 | S. Farr | | | 7,500 | 75 | 7,425 |
| 11 | Prepaid Rent | | 6,000 | | | 6,000 |
| 15 | P. Coley | | | 6,800 | | 6,800 |
| 19 | Weber, Drawing | | 2,500 | | | 2,500 |
| 21 | C. Hunt | | | 15,300 | 153 | 15,147 |
| | | | 9,100 | 29,600 | 228 | 38,472 |

In addition, the following transactions have not been journalized for July. The cost of all merchandise sold was 65% of the sales price.

July  1  The founder, M. Weber, invests $80,000 in cash.
  6  Sell merchandise on account to Lantz Co., $5,400 terms 1/10, n/30.
  7  Make cash sales totaling $4,000.
  8  Sell merchandise on account to J. Wenger, $3,600, terms, 1/10, n/30.
  10  Sell merchandise on account to G. Linton, $4,900, terms 1/10, n/30.
  13  Receive payment in full from J. Wenger.
  16  Receive payment in full from G. Linton.
  20  Receive payment in full from Lantz Co.
  21  Sell merchandise on account to A. Kear, $3,000, terms, 1/10, n/30.
  29  Return damaged goods to P. Coley and received cash refund of $450.

*Instructions*
(a) Open the following accounts in the general ledger.

| | |
|---|---|
| 101  Cash | 306  Weber, Drawing |
| 112  Accounts Receivable | 401  Sales |
| 120  Merchandise Inventory | 412  Sales Returns and Allowances |
| 127  Store Supplies | 414  Sales Discounts |
| 131  Prepaid Rent | 505  Cost of Goods Sold |
| 201  Accounts Payable | 631  Supplies Expense |
| 301  Weber, Capital | 729  Rent Expense |

(b) Journalize the transactions that have not been journalized in the sales journal, the cash receipts journal (see Illustration 6-10), and the general journal.
(c) Post to the accounts receivable and accounts payable subsidiary ledgers. Follow the sequence of transactions as shown in the problem.
(d) Post the individual entries and totals to the general ledger.
(e) Prepare a trial balance at July 31, 1999.
(f) Determine whether the subsidiary ledgers agree with the controlling accounts in the general ledger.
(g) The following adjustments at the end of July are necessary.
   1.  A count of supplies indicates that $140 is still on hand.
   2.  Recognize rent expense for July, $500.
   Prepare the necessary entries in the general journal. Post the entries to the general ledger.
(h) Prepare an adjusted trial balance at July 31, 1999.

## BROADENING YOUR PERSPECTIVE

# FINANCIAL REPORTING AND ANALYSIS
••••••••••••••••••••••••••••••••••••••••••••••••••••••••••••••••••••••••••••••••••••••••••••••••••••

## FINANCIAL REPORTING PROBLEM—A MINI PRACTICE SET

**BYP6–1**   (The working papers that accompany this textbook are needed in order to work this mini practice set.)

Stone Co. uses both an accounts receivable and an accounts payable subsidiary ledger. Balances related to both the general ledger and the subsidiary ledger for Stone are indicated in the working papers. Presented below are a series of transactions for Stone Co. for the month of January. Credit sales terms are 2/10, n/30. The cost of all merchandise sold was 60% of the sales price.

Jan.   3   Sell merchandise on credit to B. Sargent $3,200, invoice No. 510, and to J. Eaton $1,800, invoice No. 511.

  5   Purchase merchandise from S. Walden $3,000 and D. Landell $2,200, terms n/30.

  7   Receive checks from S. Lowell, $4,000 and B. Jaggar $2,000 after discount period has lapsed.

  8   Pay freight on merchandise purchased $180.

  9   Send checks to S. Lee for $9,000 less 2% cash discount and D. Nordin for $11,000 less 1% cash discount.

  9   Issue credit memo for $300 to J. Eaton for merchandise returned.

  10   Summary daily cash sales total $15,500.

  11   Sell merchandise on credit to R. Dansig $1,300, invoice No. 512, and to S. Lowell $900, invoice No. 513.

  12   Pay rent of $1,000 for January.

  13   Receive payment in full from B. Sargent and J. Eaton less cash discounts.

  15   Withdraw $800 cash by M. Stone for personal use.

  15   Post all entries to the subsidiary ledgers.

  16   Purchase merchandise from D. Nordin $16,000, terms 1/10, n/30; S. Lee $14,200, terms 2/10, n/30; and S. Walden $1,500, terms n/30.

  17   Pay $400 cash for office supplies.

  18   Return $200 of merchandise to S. Lee and receive credit.

  20   Summary daily cash sales total $17,500.

  21   Issue $15,000 note to R. Mannon in payment of balance due.

  21   Receive payment in full from S. Lowell less cash discount.

  22   Sell merchandise on credit to B. Sargent $1,700, invoice No. 514 and to R. Dansig $800, invoice No. 515.

  22   Post all entries to the subsidiary ledger.

  23   Send checks to D. Nordin and S. Lee in full payment less cash discounts.

  25   Sell merchandise on credit to B. Jaggar $3,500, invoice No. 516 and to J. Eaton $6,100, invoice No. 517.

  27   Purchase merchandise from D. Nordin $14,500, terms 1/10, n/30; D. Landell $1,200, terms n/30; and S. Walden $2,800, terms n/30.

  27   Post all entries to the subsidiary ledger.

  28   Pay $200 cash for office supplies.

  31   Summary daily cash sales total $21,300.

  31   Pay sales salaries $4,300 and office salaries $2,600.

*Instructions*

(a) Record the January transactions in a sales journal, a single-column purchases journal, a cash receipts journal as shown on page 242, a cash payments journal as shown on page 247, and a two-column general journal.

(b) Post the journals to the general ledger.

(c) Prepare a trial balance at January 31, 1999, in the trial balance columns of the work sheet. Complete the work sheet using the following additional information.
  (1) Office supplies at January 31 total $500.
  (2) Insurance coverage expires on October 31, 1999.
  (3) Annual depreciation on the equipment is $1,500.
  (4) Interest of $60 has accrued on the note payable.
(d) Prepare a multiple-step income statement and an owner's equity statement for January and a classified balance sheet at the end of January.
(e) Prepare and post adjusting and closing entries.
(f) Prepare a post-closing trial balance and determine whether the subsidiary ledgers agree with the controlling accounts in the general ledger.

## REAL-WORLD FOCUS: Alco Standard Corporation

**BYP6–2**    **Alco Standard Corporation's** operations are divided into two business groups: Alco Office Products and Unisource. Alco Office Products sells, leases, and rents various electronic office machines; Unisource markets and distributes papers primarily for office use. The company owns or leases facilities in 49 states and 9 foreign countries.

The president of Alco wrote the following in his letter in a recent annual report:

---

### ALCO STANDARD CORPORATION
### President's Letter to Stockholders

The creation of Unisource allows us to pursue strategies that are practical only on a unified basis. Our efforts to upgrade information technology, for example, will now be directed to building a common system throughout North America. This unified approach will give us online electronic link suppliers, cutting order entry costs and improving inventory management. As a result, we will be able to improve service to customers with more timely and more accurate order fulfillment, faster inquiry response and enhanced technical support.

---

*Instructions*
(a) When a company computerizes customer order entry, what equivalent special journal type must be programmed into such an electronic system?
(b) When a company computerizes inventory management (which involves more timely ordering of new merchandise), what special journal type must be programmed into such an electronic system?

# CRITICAL THINKING
..................................................................................................................

## GROUP DECISION CASE

**BYP6–3**    Davis & Ruiz is a wholesaler of small appliances and parts. Davis & Ruiz is operated by two owners, Phil Davis and Tony Ruiz. In addition, the company has one employee, a repair specialist, who is on a fixed salary. Revenues are earned through the sale of appliances to retailers (approximately 75% of total revenues), appliance parts to do-it-yourselfers (10%), and the repair of appliances brought to the store (15%). Appliance sales are made on both a credit and cash basis. Customers are billed on prenumbered sales invoices. Credit terms are always net/30 days. All parts sales and repair work are cash only.

Merchandise is purchased on account from the manufacturers of both the appliances and the parts. Practically all suppliers offer cash discounts for prompt payments, and it is company policy to take all discounts. Most cash payments are made by check. Checks are most frequently issued to suppliers, to trucking companies for freight on merchandise purchases, and to newspapers, radio, and TV stations for advertising. All advertising bills are paid as received. Phil and Tony each make a monthly drawing in cash for personal living expenses. The salaried repairman is paid twice monthly.

Davis & Ruiz currently has a manual accounting system. However, the business is growing and some consideration is being given to an electronic accounting system.

*Instructions*

With the class divided into groups, answer the following:

(a) Identify the special journals that Davis & Ruiz should have in its manual system. List the column headings appropriate for each of the special journals.

(b) What control and subsidiary accounts should be included in Davis & Ruiz's manual system? Why?

(c) Identify for Phil and Tony the key points they should consider in deciding whether to install an electronic system.

## COMMUNICATION ACTIVITY

**BYP6–4**    Sue Marsh, a classmate, has a part-time bookkeeping job. She is concerned about the inefficiencies in journalizing and posting transactions. Raul Hindi is the owner of the company where Sue works. In response to numerous complaints from Sue and others, Raul hired two additional bookkeepers a month ago. However, the inefficiencies have continued at an even higher rate. The accounting information system for the company has only a general journal and a general ledger. Raul refuses to install an electronic accounting system.

*Instructions*

Now that Sue is an expert in manual accounting information systems, she decides to send a letter to Raul Hindi explaining (1) why the additional personnel did not help and (2) what changes should be made to improve the efficiency of the accounting department. Write the letter that you think Sue should send.

## ETHICS CASE

**BYP6–5**    Tyler Products Company operates three divisions, each with its own manufacturing plant and marketing/sales force. The corporate headquarters and central accounting office are in Tyler with the plants in Freeport, Rockport, and Bayport, all within 50 miles of Tyler. Corporate management treats each division as an independent profit center and encourages competition among them. They each have similar but different product lines. As a competitive incentive, bonuses are awarded each year to the employees of the fastest growing and most profitable division.

Don Henke is the manager of Tyler's centralized computer accounting operation that keyboards the sales transactions and maintains the accounts receivable for all three divisions. Don came up in the accounting ranks from the Bayport division where his wife, several relatives, and many friends still work.

As sales documents are keyboarded into the computer, the originating division is identified by code. Most sales documents (95%) are coded, but some (5%) are not coded or are coded incorrectly. As the manager, Don has instructed the keyboard operators to assign the Bayport code to all uncoded and incorrectly coded sales documents. This is done he says, "in order to expedite processing and to keep the computer files current since they are updated daily." All receivables and cash collections for all three divisions are handled by Tyler as one subsidiary accounts receivable ledger.

*Instructions*

(a) Who are the stakeholders in this situation?

(b) What are the ethical issues in this case?

(c) How might the system be improved to prevent this situation?

# SURFING THE NET

· · · · · · · · · · · · · · · · · · · · · · · · · · · · · · · · · · · · · · · · · · · · · · · · · · · · · · · · · · · · · · · · · · · · · · · · · · · · · · · · · · · · · · ·

**BYP6–6**    Great Plains Dynamics is one of the leading accounting software packages. Information related to this package is found at its web site.

**Address:** http://www.gps.com/dynamics

**Steps:**
1. Go to the site shown above.
2. Choose **Product Details** then choose **General Ledger.** Perform instruction (a) below.
3. Choose **Product Details** then choose **Payables Management.** Perform instruction (b) below.
4. Choose **Product Details** then choose **Receivables Management.** Perform instruction (c) below.

*Instructions*

(a) What are three key features of the general ledger module highlighted by the company?
(b) What are three key features of the payables management module highlighted by the company?
(c) What are three key features of the receivables management module highlighted by the company?

---

*Answers to Self-Study Questions*
1. d    2. b    3. a    4. c    5. a    6. c    7. d    8. b    9. d    10. c

**Remember to go back to the Navigator box on the chapter-opening page and check off your completed work.**

**Before studying this chapter, you should know or, if necessary, review:**

a. How cash transactions are journalized in special journals.
   (Ch. 6, pp. 240–244, 247–248)
b. How postings are made to the cash account from special journals.
   (Ch. 6, pp. 240–244, 247–248)
c. The phases in developing an accounting system. (Ch. 6, pp. 233–234)

## FEATURE STORY

# No Free Lunch

At Columbia University, thousands of dollars in cash changes hands between students and dining facility cashiers. Making sure that all of the money received by cashiers gets to where it's supposed to go requires various control measures. In accounting, these measures are called internal control.

One control measure used in the cafeteria at Columbia is that the register tape that records the sale and the amount of cash received must reconcile with the amount of cash in the cash drawer at the end of the day. "We see if there are significant overages or shortages at the end of each day for each register," says Susan McLaughlin, director of Columbia's dining facilities. Do cash differences happen very often? "No, because the cashier knows that if there are repeated or significant shortages, disciplinary action will be taken," she says. "There should not be a variance of more than $5, either over or under, at any given time— or else it indicates poor cash handling."

If a student buying a meal at a register sees that a sale isn't rung up or if the student doesn't get a receipt, there is a possibility that the cashier is stealing. "We know that taking the receipt is an annoyance," says Ms. McLaughlin, "but issuing receipts is an absolutely mandatory control for us."

# CHAPTER 7

**THE NAVIGATOR** ✔

- Understand *Concepts for Review* ☐
- Read *Feature Story* ☐
- Scan *Study Objectives* ☐
- Read *Preview* ☐
- Read text and answer *Before You Go On*
  p. 286 ☐  p. 294 ☐  p. 303 ☐  p. 304 ☐
- Work *Demonstration Problem* ☐
- Review *Summary of Study Objectives* ☐
- Answer *Self-Study Questions* ☐
- Complete assignments ☐

# INTERNAL CONTROL AND CASH

## STUDY OBJECTIVES

**After studying this chapter, you should be able to:**

1. *Define internal control.*
2. *Identify the principles of internal control.*
3. *Explain the applications of internal control principles to cash receipts.*
4. *Describe the applications of internal control principles to cash disbursements.*
5. *Explain the operation of a petty cash fund.*
6. *Indicate the control features of a bank account.*
7. *Prepare a bank reconciliation.*
8. *Explain the reporting of cash.*

THE
NAVIGATOR

*A*s the story about the dining facilities at Columbia University indicates, control of cash is important. Similarly, controls are needed to safeguard other types of assets. For example, Columbia University undoubtedly has controls to prevent the theft of food served in the cafeteria and controls to prevent the theft of computer equipment and supplies from its computer laboratories.

In this chapter, we explain the essential features of an internal control system and then describe how those controls apply to cash. The applications include some controls with which you may be already familiar. Toward the end of the chapter, we describe the use of a bank and explain how cash is reported on the balance sheet. The content and organization of Chapter 7 are as follows:

THE NAVIGATOR

## INTERNAL CONTROL

STUDY OBJECTIVE

Define internal control.

Could there be dishonest employees in the business that you own or manage? Unfortunately, the answer sometimes is Yes. For example, the financial press recently reported the following:

A bookkeeper in a small company diverted $750,000 of bill payments to a personal bank account over a 3-year period.

A shipping clerk with 28 years of service shipped $125,000 of merchandise to himself.

A computer operator embezzled $21 million from Wells Fargo Bank over a 2-year period.

A church treasurer "borrowed" $150,000 of church funds to finance a friend's business dealings.

These situations emphasize the need for a good system of internal control.

**Internal control** consists of the plan of organization and all the related methods and measures adopted within a business to:

*Policies that*

1. **Safeguard its assets** from employee theft, robbery, and unauthorized use.
2. **Enhance the accuracy and reliability of its accounting records** by reducing the risk of **errors** (unintentional mistakes) and **irregularities** (intentional mistakes and misrepresentations) in the accounting process.

Under the Foreign Corrupt Practices Act of 1977, all major U.S. corporations are required to maintain an adequate system of internal control. Companies that fail to comply are subject to fines, and company officers may be imprisoned. Also, the National Commission on Fraudulent Financial Reporting concluded that all companies whose stock is publicly traded should maintain internal controls that can provide reasonable assurance that fraudulent financial reporting will be prevented or subject to early detection.[1]

**INTERNATIONAL NOTE**

U.S. companies also adopt model business codes that guide their international operations to provide for a safe and healthy workplace, avoid child and forced labor, abstain from bribes, and follow sound environmental practices.

## TECHNOLOGY IN ACTION

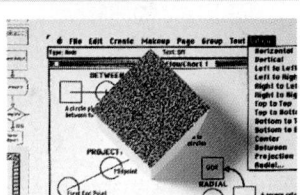

Good internal control must be designed into computerized systems. The starting point is usually flow charts that graphically depict each component of a firm's operations. The assembled flow charts serve as the basis for writing detailed programs. An example of flow charting is given in this chapter. When attempts to automate or improve accounting systems fail, it is often due to the absence of such well-documented procedures.

## Principles of Internal Control

To safeguard its assets and enhance the accuracy and reliability of its accounting records, a company follows specific control principles. Of course, internal control measures vary with the size and nature of the business and with management's control philosophy. However, the six principles listed in Illustration 7-1 apply to most enterprises. Each principle is explained in the following sections.

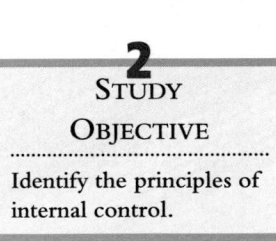

**2**
STUDY
OBJECTIVE
............................................
Identify the principles of internal control.

**ILLUSTRATION 7-1**
*Principles of internal control*

---

[1]Report of the National Commission on Fraudulent Financial Reporting, October 1987, p. 11.

It's your shift now. I'm turning in my cash drawer and heading home.

**Transfer of cash drawers**

## Establishment of Responsibility

An essential characteristic of internal control is the assignment of responsibility to specific individuals. **Control is most effective when only one person is responsible for a given task.** To illustrate, assume that the cash on hand at the end of the day in a Safeway supermarket is $10 short of the cash rung up on the cash register. If only one person has operated the register, responsibility for the shortage can be assessed quickly. However, if two or more individuals have worked the register, it may be impossible to determine who is responsible for the error unless each person is assigned a separate cash drawer and register key. The principle of establishing responsibility was followed by Columbia University's dining services (in the opening story) by assigning a cashier to a cash register and keeping each cashier's cash drawer separate from others.

Establishing responsibility includes the authorization and approval of transactions. For example, the vice president of sales should have the authority to establish policies for making credit sales. The policies ordinarily will require written credit department approval of credit sales.

## Segregation of Duties

This principle (also identified as separation of functions or division of work) is indispensable in a system of internal control. There are two common applications of this principle:

1. The responsibility for related activities should be assigned to different individuals.
2. The responsibility for establishing the accountability (keeping the records) for an asset should be separate from the physical custody of that asset.

**The rationale for segregation of duties is that the work of one employee should, without a duplication of effort, provide a reliable basis for evaluating the work of another employee.**

**Related Activities.**    Related activities that should be assigned to different individuals arise in both the purchasing and selling areas. **When one individual is responsible for all of the related activities, the potential for errors and irregularities is increased.** Related purchasing activities include ordering the merchandise, receiving the goods, and paying (or authorizing payment) for the merchandise. In purchasing, for example, orders could be placed with friends or with suppliers who give kickbacks. Similarly, only a cursory count and inspection could be made upon receiving the goods, which could lead to errors and poor quality merchandise. In addition, payment might be authorized without a careful review of the invoice, or even worse, fictitious invoices might be approved for payment. When the responsibility for ordering, receiving, and paying are assigned to different individuals or departments, the risk of such abuses is minimized.

Similarly, related sales activities should be assigned to different individuals. Related selling activities include making a sale, shipping (or delivering) the goods to the customer, billing the customer, and receiving payment. When one person is responsible for related sales transactions, a salesperson could make sales at unauthorized prices to increase sales commissions; a shipping clerk could ship goods to himself, as indicated at the beginning of the chapter; a billing clerk could understate the amount billed for sales made to friends and relatives. These abuses are reduced when salespersons make the sale, shipping department employees ship the goods on the basis of the sales order, and billing department employees prepare the sales invoice after comparing the sales order with the report of goods shipped.

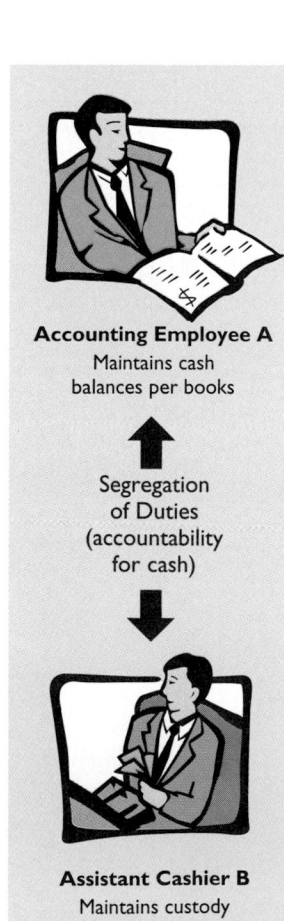

**Accounting Employee A**
Maintains cash balances per books

Segregation of Duties (accountability for cash)

**Assistant Cashier B**
Maintains custody of cash on hand

**Accountability for Assets.**   If accounting is to provide a valid basis of accountability for an asset, the accountant should have neither physical custody of the asset nor access to it. Moreover, the custodian of the asset should not maintain or have access to the accounting records. **When one employee maintains the record of the asset that should be on hand, and a different employee has physical custody of the asset, the custodian of the asset is not likely to convert the asset to personal use.** The separation of accounting responsibility from the custody of assets is especially important for cash and inventories because these assets are very vulnerable to unauthorized use or misappropriation.

# ACCOUNTING IN ACTION
### International Insight

Recently Sumitomo Corporation became the fifth Japanese company to announce a huge loss, this time $1.8 billion, due to a single copper trader. Some are blaming Japanese culture because it encourages group harmony over confrontation and thus may contribute to poor internal controls. For example good controls require that both parties to a copper trade send a confirmation slip to management to verify all trades. In Japan the counterparty to the trade often sends the confirmation slip to the trader, who then forwards it to management. Thus, it is possible for the trader to change the confirmation slip. An unethical trader could create fictitious trades to hide losses for an extended period of time or to conceal trades that are larger than allowed limits.

*Source:* Sheryl Wudunn, "Big New Loss Makes Japan Look Inward," *New York Times*, June 17, 1996, P. D1.

## *Documentation Procedures*

Documents provide evidence that transactions and events have occurred. In the Columbia University cafeteria, the cash register tape was the university's documentation for the sale and the amount of cash received. Similarly, the shipping document indicates that the goods have been shipped, and the sales invoice indicates that the customer has been billed for the goods. By adding signatures (or initials) to the documents, the individual(s) responsible for the transaction or event can be identified. Documentation of transactions should be made when the transaction occurs. Documentation of events, such as those leading to adjusting entries, is generally developed when the adjustments are made.

Several procedures should be established for documents. First, whenever possible, **documents should be prenumbered and all documents should be accounted for.** Prenumbering helps to prevent a transaction from being recorded more than once, or conversely, to prevent the transactions from not being recorded. Second, documents that are **source documents for accounting entries should be promptly forwarded to the accounting department to help ensure timely recording of the transaction and event.** Thus, this control measure contributes directly to the accuracy and reliability of the accounting records.

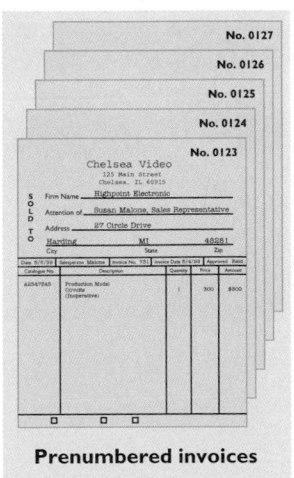

**Prenumbered invoices**

**HELPFUL HINT**
An important corollary to prenumbering is that voided documents be kept until all documents are accounted for.

## *Physical, Mechanical, and Electronic Controls*

Use of physical, mechanical, and electronic controls is essential. Physical controls relate primarily to the safeguarding of assets. Mechanical and electronic controls safeguard assets and enhance the accuracy and reliability of the accounting records. Examples of these controls are shown in Illustration 7-2.

**ILLUSTRATION 7-2**

*Physical, mechanical, and electronic controls*

### Physical Controls

Safes, vaults, and safety deposit boxes for cash and business papers

Locked warehouses and storage cabinets for inventories and records

Computer facilities with pass key access

### Mechanical and Electronic Controls

Alarms to prevent break-ins

Television monitors and garment sensors to deter theft

Time clocks for recording time worked

# ACCOUNTING IN ACTION
## Business Insight

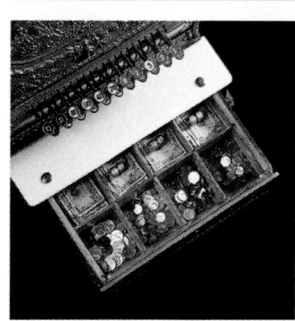

John Patterson, a young Ohio merchant, couldn't understand why his retail business didn't show a profit. There were lots of customers, but the money just seemed to disappear. Patterson suspected pilferage and sloppy bookkeeping by store clerks. Frustrated, he placed an order with a Dayton, Ohio, company for two rudimentary cash registers. A year later, Patterson's store was in the black.

"What is a good thing for this little store is a good thing for every retail store in the world," he observed. A few months later, in 1884, John Patterson and his brother, Frank, bought the tiny cash register maker for $6,500. The word around Dayton was that the Patterson boys got stung.

In the following 37 years, John Patterson built National Cash Register Co. into a corporate giant. Patterson died in 1922, the year in which NCR sold its two millionth cash register.

*Source: The Wall Street Journal, January 28, 1989.*

### Independent Internal Verification

Most systems of internal control provide for independent internal verification. This principle involves the review, comparison, and reconciliation of data prepared by one or several employees. To obtain maximum benefit from independent internal verification:

1. The verification should be made periodically or on a surprise basis.
2. The verification should be done by an employee who is independent of the personnel responsible for the information.
3. Discrepancies and exceptions should be reported to a management level that can take appropriate corrective action.

Independent internal verification is especially useful in comparing recorded accountability with existing assets. The reconciliation of the cash register tape with the cash in the register in the Columbia University dining facility is an example of this internal control principle. Another common example is the reconciliation by an independent person of the cash balance per books with the cash balance per bank. The relationship between this principle and the segregation of duties principle is shown graphically in Illustration 7-3.

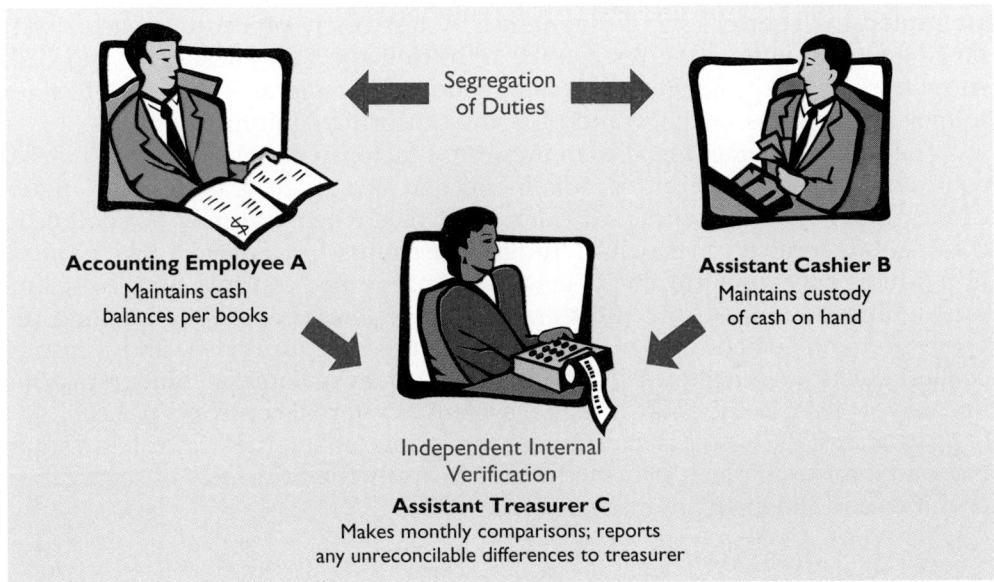

**ILLUSTRATION 7-3**

*Comparison of segregation of duties principle with independent internal verification principle*

In large companies, independent internal verification is often assigned to internal auditors. **Internal auditors** are employees of the company who evaluate on a continuous basis the effectiveness of the company's system of internal control. They periodically review the activities of departments and individuals to determine whether prescribed internal controls are being followed and to make recommendations for improvement. The importance of this function is illustrated by the number of internal auditors employed by companies. In a recent year, AT&T had 350 internal auditors, Exxon had 395, and IBM had 142.

## Other Controls

Other control measures include the following:

1. **Bonding of employees who handle cash.** Bonding involves obtaining insurance protection against misappropriation of assets by dishonest employees. This measure contributes to the safeguarding of cash in two ways: First, the insurance company carefully screens all individuals before adding them to the policy and may reject risky applicants. Second, bonded employees know that the insurance company will vigorously prosecute all offenders.
2. **Rotating employees' duties and requiring employees to take vacations.** These measures are designed to deter employees from attempting any thefts since they will not be able to permanently conceal their improper actions. Many bank embezzlements, for example, have been discovered when the perpetrator has been on vacation or assigned to a new position.

## Limitations of Internal Control

A company's system of internal control is generally designed to provide reasonable assurance that assets are properly safeguarded and that the accounting records are reliable. **The concept of reasonable assurance rests on the premise that the costs of establishing control procedures should not exceed their expected benefit.** To illustrate, consider shoplifting losses in retail stores. Such losses could be completely eliminated by having a security guard stop and search customers as they leave the store. Store managers have concluded, however, that the negative effects of adopting such a procedure cannot be justified. Instead, stores have attempted to "control" shoplifting losses by less costly procedures such as: (1) posting signs saying, "We reserve the right to inspect all packages," and "All shoplifters will be prosecuted," (2) using hidden TV cameras and store detectives to monitor customer activity, and (3) using sensoring equipment at exits.

The **human element** is also an important factor in every system of internal control. A good system can become ineffective as a result of employee fatigue, carelessness, or indifference. For example, a receiving clerk may not bother to count goods received or may just "fudge" the counts. Occasionally, two or more individuals may work together to get around prescribed controls. Such **collusion** can significantly impair the effectiveness of a system, because it eliminates the protection anticipated from segregation of duties. If a supervisor and a cashier collaborate to understate cash receipts, the system of internal control may be negated (at least in the short run). No system of internal control is perfect.

The size of the business may impose limitations on internal control. In a small company, for example, it may be difficult to apply the principles of segregation of duties and independent internal verification.

## TECHNOLOGY IN ACTION

 Unfortunately, computer-related frauds have become a major concern. The average computer fraud loss is $650,000, compared with an average loss of only $19,000 resulting from other types of white-collar crime.

Computer fraud can be perpetrated almost invisibly and done with electronic speed. Psychologically, stealing with impersonal computer tools can seem far less criminal. Therefore, the moral threshold to commit computer fraud is far lower than fraud involving person-to-person contact.

Preventing and detecting computer fraud represents a major challenge. One of the best ways for a company to minimize the likelihood of computer fraud is to have a good system of internal control that allows the benefits of computerization to be gained without opening the possibility for rampant fraud.

## BEFORE YOU GO ON . . .

### Review It

1. What are the two primary objectives of internal control?
2. Identify and describe the principles of internal control.
3. What are the limitations of internal control?

### Do It

Li Song owns a small retail store. Li wants to establish good internal control procedures but is confused about the difference between segregation of duties and independent internal verification. Explain the differences to Li.

*Reasoning:* In order to help Li, you need to thoroughly understand each principle. From this knowledge, and a study of Illustration 7-3, it should be possible to explain the differences between the two principles.

*Solution:* Segregation of duties pertains to the assignment of responsibility so that the work of one employee will permit the evaluation of the work of another employee. Segregation of duties occurs daily in executing and recording transactions. In contrast, independent internal verification involves reviewing, comparing, and reconciling data prepared by one or several employees. Independent internal verification occurs after the fact, as in the case of reconciling cash register totals at the end of the day with cash on hand.

*Related exercise material: BE7-1, BE7-2, E7-1, E7-2, and E7-3.*

# CASH CONTROLS

Just as cash is the beginning of a company's operating cycle, it is usually the starting point for a company's system of internal control. Cash is the one asset that is readily convertible into any other type of asset; it is easily concealed and transported; and it is highly desired. Because of these characteristics, **cash is the asset most susceptible to improper diversion and use**. Moreover, because of the large volume of cash transactions, numerous errors may occur in executing and recording cash transactions. To safeguard cash and to assure the accuracy of the accounting records for cash, effective internal control over cash is imperative.

Cash consists of coins, currency (paper money), checks, money orders, and money on hand or on deposit in a bank or similar depository. The general rule is that if the bank will accept it for deposit, it is cash. Items such as postage stamps and postdated checks (checks payable in the future) are not cash. Stamps are a prepaid expense; the postdated checks are accounts receivable. The application of internal control principles to cash receipts and cash disbursements is explained in the following sections.

## Internal Control over Cash Receipts

Cash receipts may result from a variety of sources: cash sales; collections on account from customers; the receipt of interest, rents, and dividends; investments by owners; bank loans; and proceeds from the sale of noncurrent assets. The internal control principles explained earlier apply to cash receipts transactions as shown in Illustration 7-4.

As might be expected, companies vary considerably in how they apply these principles. To illustrate internal control over cash receipts, we will examine control measures for a retail store with both over-the-counter and mail receipts.

**3**
STUDY
OBJECTIVE

Explain the applications of internal control principles to cash receipts.

### Over-the-Counter Receipts

Control of over-the-counter receipts in retail businesses is centered on cash registers that are visible to customers. In supermarkets and variety stores such as Kmart, cash registers are placed in check-out lines near the exit(s). In Sears, Roebuck & Co. and J. C. Penney stores each department has its own cash register. When a cash sale occurs, the sale is "rung up" on a cash register **with the amount clearly visible to the customer**. This measure prevents the cashier from ringing up a lower amount and pocketing the difference. The customer receives an itemized cash register receipt slip and is expected to count the change received. A cash register tape, which is locked into the register until removed by a supervisor or manager, accumulates the daily transactions and totals. When the tape is removed, the supervisor compares the total with the amount of cash in the register. It should show all registered receipts accounted for. The supervisor's findings

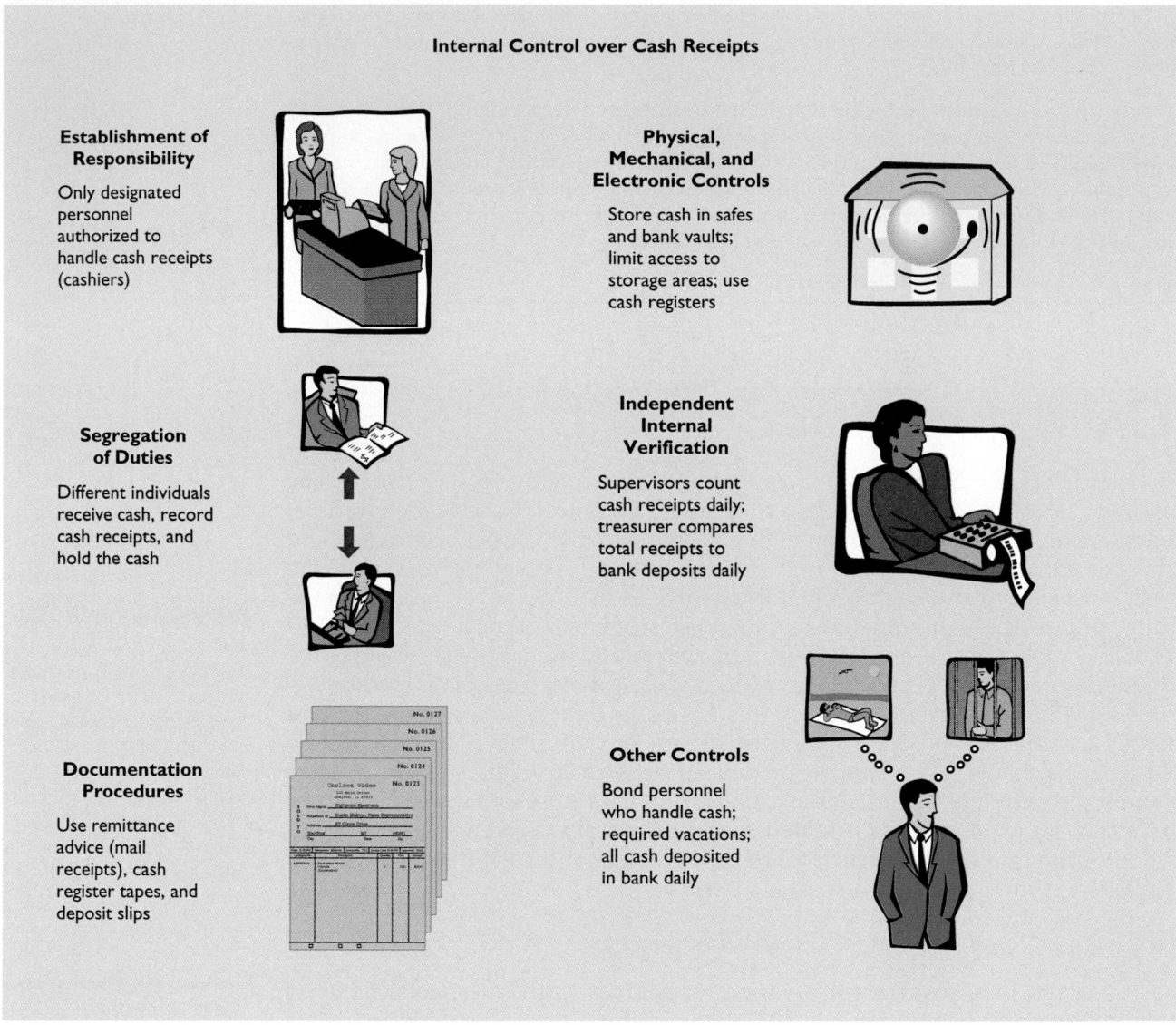

**Internal Control over Cash Receipts**

**Establishment of Responsibility**

Only designated personnel authorized to handle cash receipts (cashiers)

**Physical, Mechanical, and Electronic Controls**

Store cash in safes and bank vaults; limit access to storage areas; use cash registers

**Segregation of Duties**

Different individuals receive cash, record cash receipts, and hold the cash

**Independent Internal Verification**

Supervisors count cash receipts daily; treasurer compares total receipts to bank deposits daily

**Documentation Procedures**

Use remittance advice (mail receipts), cash register tapes, and deposit slips

**Other Controls**

Bond personnel who handle cash; required vacations; all cash deposited in bank daily

**ILLUSTRATION 7-4**

*Application of internal control principles to cash receipts*

are reported on a cash count sheet that is signed by both the cashier and supervisor. The cash count sheet used by Alrite Food Mart is shown in Illustration 7-5.

The count sheets, register tapes, and cash are then given to the head cashier. This individual prepares a daily cash summary showing the total cash received and the amount from each source, such as cash sales and collections on account. The head cashier sends one copy of the summary to the accounting department for entry into the cash receipts journal. The other copy goes to the treasurer's office for subsequent comparison with the daily bank deposit. Next, the head cashier prepares a deposit slip (see Illustration 7-9 on page 296) and makes the bank deposit. The total amount deposited should be equal to the total receipts on the daily cash summary. This will assure that all receipts have been placed in the custody of the bank. In accepting the bank deposit, the bank stamps (authenticates) the duplicate deposit slip and sends it to the company treasurer, who makes the comparison with the daily cash summary. The foregoing measures for cash sales are graphically presented in Illustration 7-6. The activities of the sales department are shown separate from those of the cashier's department to indicate the segregation of duties in handling cash.

**ILLUSTRATION 7-5**

*Cash count sheet*

| Store No. ___8___ | Date March 8, 1999 |
|---|---|
| 1. Opening cash balance | $ 50.00 |
| 2. Cash sales per tape (attached) | 6,956.20 |
| 3. Total cash to be accounted for | 7,006.20 |
| 4. Cash on hand (see list) | 6,996.10 |
| 5. Cash (short) or over | $ (10.10) |
| 6. Ending cash balance | $ 50.00 |
| 7. Cash for deposit (Line 4 – Line 6) | $6,946.10 |

Cashier *J. Cruse*　　　Supervisor *M. Braun*

**ILLUSTRATION 7-6**

*Executing over-the-counter cash sales*

**Store Sales Departments**

Cashiers ring up sales on registers

Supervisor reads register totals

Supervisor makes cash counts

Supervisor prepares cash count sheets

Cash / Count sheets / Register tapes

**Cashier's Department**

Cash / Count sheets / Register tapes

Prepare daily cash summary

Smith Company
123 Cherry Lane
Anytown, Montana

6489 00032 385700991

Prepare deposit slip

Deposit slip　1 / Cash

Deposit slip　2 / Daily Cash Summary　2 / Daily Cash Summary　1

To bank
(for deposit)

To treasurer
(for verification)

To accounting
(for recording)

**HELPFUL HINT**
Flowcharts enhance the understanding of the flow of documents, the processing steps, and the internal control procedures.

### Mail Receipts

Because of your experience as an individual customer, you may be more familiar with over-the-counter receipts than with mail receipts. However, mail receipts resulting from billings and credit sales are by far the most common way cash is received by the greatest variety of businesses. Think, for example, of the number of checks received through the mail daily by a national retailer such as Land's End or L.L. Bean.

All mail receipts should be received in the presence of two mail clerks. These receipts are generally in the form of checks or money orders and frequently are accompanied by a remittance advice stating the purpose of the check. Each check should be promptly endorsed "For Deposit Only" by use of a company stamp. This **restrictive endorsement** reduces the likelihood that the check will be diverted to personal use because banks will not give an individual any cash under this type of endorsement.

A list of the checks received each day should be prepared in duplicate showing the name of the issuer of the check, the purpose of the payment, and the amount of the check. Each mail clerk should sign the list to establish responsibility for the data. The original copy of the list, along with the checks and remittance advices, are then sent to the cashier's department, where they are added to over-the-counter receipts (if any) in preparing the daily cash summary and in making the daily bank deposit. In addition, a copy of the list is sent to the treasurer's office for comparison with the total mail receipts shown on the daily cash summary, to assure that all mail receipts have been included.

## Internal Control over Cash Disbursements

**STUDY**
**OBJECTIVE**

Describe the applications of internal control principles to cash disbursements.

Cash may be disbursed for a variety of reasons, such as to pay expenses and liabilities, or to purchase assets. **Generally, internal control over cash disbursements is more effective when payments are made by check, rather than by cash, except for incidental amounts that are paid out of petty cash.**[2] Payment by check generally occurs only after specified control procedures have been followed. In addition, the "paid" check provides proof of payment. Principles of internal control apply to cash disbursements as shown in Illustration 7-7 on the next page.

### Voucher System

Most medium and large companies use a voucher system as part of their internal control over cash disbursements. A voucher system is an extensive network of approvals by authorized individuals acting independently to ensure that all disbursements by check are proper.

The system begins with the authorization to incur the cost or expense and ends with the issuance of a check for the liability incurred. A voucher is an authorization form prepared for each expenditure in a voucher system. Vouchers are required for all types of cash disbursements except those from petty cash. The voucher is prepared in the accounts payable department.

The starting point in preparing a voucher is to fill in the appropriate information about the liability on the face of the voucher from the vendor's invoice. Then, the voucher must be recorded (in the journal called a **voucher register**) and filed according to the date on which it is to be paid. A check is sent on that

---

[2]The operation of a petty cash fund is explained on pages 292–94.

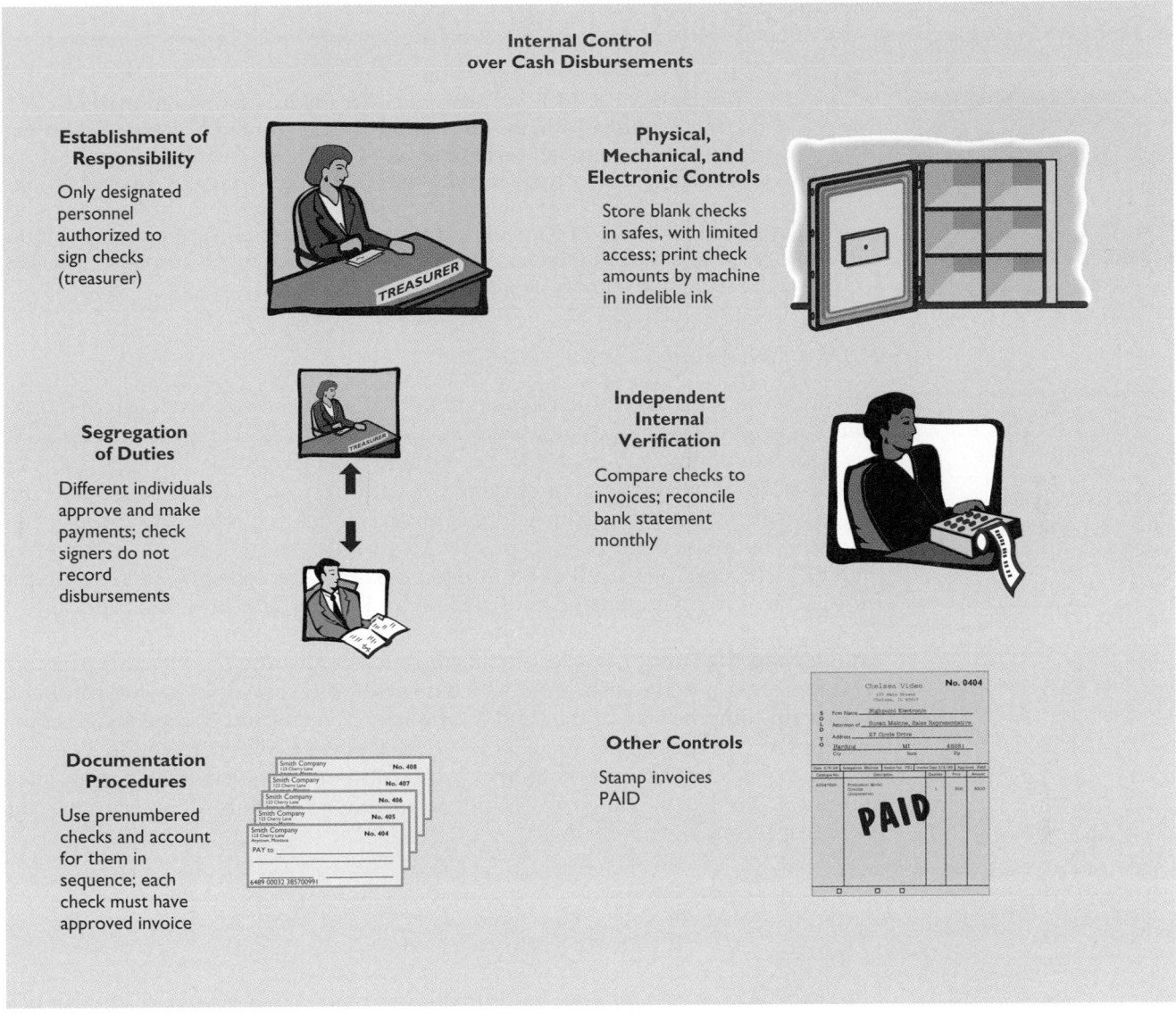

**Internal Control over Cash Disbursements**

**Establishment of Responsibility**

Only designated personnel authorized to sign checks (treasurer)

**Physical, Mechanical, and Electronic Controls**

Store blank checks in safes, with limited access; print check amounts by machine in indelible ink

**Segregation of Duties**

Different individuals approve and make payments; check signers do not record disbursements

**Independent Internal Verification**

Compare checks to invoices; reconcile bank statement monthly

**Documentation Procedures**

Use prenumbered checks and account for them in sequence; each check must have approved invoice

**Other Controls**

Stamp invoices PAID

**ILLUSTRATION 7-7**

*Application of internal control principles to cash disbursements*

date, the voucher is stamped "paid," and the paid voucher is sent to the accounting department for recording (in a journal called the **check register**).

## Electronic Funds Transfer (EFT) System

To account for and control cash is an expensive and time-consuming process. For example, it was estimated recently that the cost to process a check through a bank system ranges from $0.55 to $1.00 and is increasing. It is not surprising, therefore, that new approaches are being developed to transfer funds among parties without the use of paper (deposit tickets, checks, etc.). Such a procedure is called an **electronic funds transfer (EFT)**. EFT is a disbursement system that uses wire, telephone, telegraph, or computer to transfer cash from one location to another. Use of EFT is quite common. For example, the authors receive no formal payroll checks from their universities, which simply send magnetic tapes to the appropriate banks for deposit. Regular payments such as those for house, car, or utilities are frequently made by EFT.

# TECHNOLOGY IN ACTION

The development of EFT will continue. Already it is estimated that over 80% of the total volume of bank transactions in the United States is performed using EFT. The computer technology is available to create a "checkless" society. The only major barriers appear to be the individual's concern for privacy and protection and certain legislative constraints. It should be noted that numerous safeguards have been built into EFT systems. However, the possibility of errors and fraud still exists because only a limited number of individuals are involved in the transfers, which may prevent appropriate segregation of duties.

## Petty Cash Fund

**5**

STUDY
OBJECTIVE
..................................................
Explain the operation of
a petty cash fund.

As you learned earlier in the chapter, better internal control over cash disbursements is possible when payments are made by check. However, using checks to pay such small amounts as those for postage due, employee lunches, and taxi fares is both impractical and a nuisance. A common way of handling such payments, while maintaining satisfactory control, is to use a petty cash fund. A petty cash fund is a cash fund used to pay relatively small amounts. The operation of a petty cash fund, often called an **imprest system**, involves (1) establishing the fund, (2) making payments from the fund, and (3) replenishing the fund.[3]

**Establishing the Fund.** Two essential steps in establishing a petty cash fund are (1) appointing a petty cash custodian who will be responsible for the fund and (2) determining the size of the fund. Ordinarily, the amount is expected to cover anticipated disbursements for a 3- to 4-week period. When the fund is established, a check payable to the petty cash custodian is issued for the stipulated amount. If the Laird Company decides to establish a $100 fund on March 1, the entry in general journal form is:

| A = L + OE |
|---|
| + 100 |
| − 100 |

| Mar. 1 | Petty Cash | 100 | |
|---|---|---|---|
| | Cash | | 100 |
| | (To establish a petty cash fund) | | |

The check is then cashed and the proceeds are placed in a locked petty cash box or drawer. Most petty cash funds are established on a fixed amount basis. Moreover, no additional entries will be made to the Petty Cash account unless the stipulated amount of the fund is changed. For example, if Laird Company decides on July 1 to increase the size of the fund to $250, it would debit Petty Cash $150 and credit Cash $150.

**Making Payments from the Fund.** The custodian of the petty cash fund has the authority to make payments from the fund that conform to prescribed management policies. Usually, management limits the size of expenditures that may be made and does not permit use of the fund for certain types of transactions (such as making short-term loans to employees). Each payment from the fund must be documented on a prenumbered petty cash receipt (or petty cash voucher), as shown in Illustration 7-8. Note that the signatures of both the custodian and the individual receiving payment are required on the receipt. If other supporting documents such as a freight bill or invoice are available, they should be attached to the petty cash receipt.

---

[3]The term "imprest" means an advance of money for a designated purpose.

**ILLUSTRATION 7-8**

*Petty cash receipt*

No. 7                    W. A. LAIRD COMPANY
                        Petty Cash Receipt

                                            Date___3/6/99___

Paid to___Acme Express Agency___    Amount___$18.00___

For___Collect Express Charges___

CHARGE TO_____Freight-in_____

Approved                            Received Payment

___L. A. Bird___ Custodian          ___R. Meins___

The receipts are kept in the petty cash box until the fund is replenished. As a result, the sum of the petty cash receipts and money in the fund should equal the established total at all times. This means that surprise counts can be made at any time by an independent person, such as an internal auditor, to determine whether the fund is being maintained intact.

No accounting entry is made to record a payment at the time it is made from petty cash. It is considered to be both inexpedient and unnecessary to do so. Instead, the accounting effects of each payment are recognized when the fund is replenished.

**Replenishing the Fund.**    When the money in the petty cash fund reaches a minimum level, the fund is replenished. The request for reimbursement is initiated by the petty cash custodian. This individual prepares a schedule (or summary) of the payments that have been made and sends the schedule, supported by petty cash receipts and other documentation, to the treasurer's office. The receipts and supporting documents are examined in the treasurer's office to verify that they were proper payments from the fund. The treasurer then approves the request and a check is prepared to restore the fund to its established amount. At the same time, all supporting documentation is stamped "paid" so that it cannot be submitted again for payment.

To illustrate, assume that on March 15 the petty cash custodian requests a check for $87. The fund contains $13 cash and petty cash receipts for postage $44, freight-out $38, and miscellaneous expenses $5. The entry, in general journal form, to record the check is:

| Mar. 15 | Postage Expense | 44 | |
| | Freight-out | 38 | |
| | Miscellaneous Expense | 5 | |
| |     Cash | | 87 |
| |       (To replenish petty cash fund) | | |

| A | = | L | + | OE |
|---|---|---|---|---|
| −87 | | | | −44 |
| | | | | −38 |
| | | | | −5 |

Note that the Petty Cash account is not affected by the reimbursement entry. Replenishment changes the composition of the fund by replacing the petty cash receipts with cash, but it does not change the balance in the fund.

It may be necessary in replenishing a petty cash fund to recognize a cash shortage or overage. This results when the cash plus receipts in the petty cash box do not equal the established amount of the petty cash fund. To illustrate, assume in the example above that the custodian had only $12 in cash in the fund

**HELPFUL HINT**
Cash over and short situations result from mathematical errors or from failure to keep accurate records.

plus the receipts as listed. The request for reimbursement would, therefore, have been for $88, and the following entry would be made:

| A | = | L | + | OE |
|---|---|---|---|---|
| −88 | | | | −44 |
| | | | | −38 |
| | | | | −5 |
| | | | | −1 |

| | | | | |
|---|---|---|---|---|
| Mar. 15 | Postage Expense | | 44 | |
| | Freight-out | | 38 | |
| | Miscellaneous Expense | | 5 | |
| | Cash Over and Short | | 1 | |
| |    Cash | | | 88 |
| |     (To replenish petty cash fund) | | | |

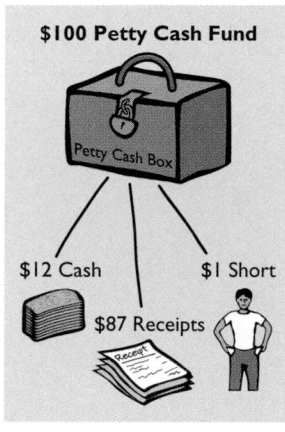

**$100 Petty Cash Fund**

Petty Cash Box

$12 Cash     $1 Short

$87 Receipts

Conversely, if the custodian had $14 in cash, the reimbursement request would have been for $86 and Cash Over and Short would have been credited for $1. A debit balance in Cash Over and Short is reported in the income statement as miscellaneous expense; a credit balance is reported as miscellaneous revenue. Cash Over and Short is closed to Income Summary at the end of the year.

A petty cash fund should be replenished at the end of the accounting period regardless of the cash in the fund. Replenishment at this time is necessary in order to recognize the effects of the petty cash payments on the financial statements.

Internal control over a petty cash fund is strengthened by (1) having a supervisor make surprise counts of the fund to ascertain whether the paid vouchers and fund cash equal the imprest amount and (2) canceling or mutilating the paid vouchers so they cannot be resubmitted for reimbursement.

# Before You Go On . . .

## Review It

1. How do the principles of internal control apply to cash receipts?
2. How do the principles of internal control apply to cash disbursements?
3. When are entries required in a petty cash system?

## Do It

L. R. Cortez is concerned about the control over cash receipts in his fast-food restaurant, Big Cheese. The restaurant has two cash registers. At no time do more than two employees take customer orders and ring up sales. Work shifts for employees range from 4 to 8 hours. Cortez asks your help in installing a good system of internal control over cash receipts.

*Reasoning:* Cortez needs to understand the principles of internal control, especially the principles of establishing responsibility, the use of electronic controls, and independent internal verification. Using this knowledge, an effective system of control over cash receipts can be designed and implemented.

*Solution:* Cortez should assign a cash register to each employee at the start of each work shift, with register totals set at zero. Each employee should be instructed to use only the assigned register and to ring up all sales. At the end of each work shift, Cortez or a supervisor/manager should total the register and make a cash count to see whether all cash is accounted for.

THE NAVIGATOR

*Related exercise material: BE7–3 and E7–2.*

# Use of a Bank

**The use of a bank contributes significantly to good internal control over cash.** A company can safeguard its cash by using a bank as a depository and clearing house for checks received and checks written. Use of a bank minimizes the amount of currency that must be kept on hand. In addition, the use of a bank facilitates the control of cash because a double record is maintained of all bank transactions—one by the business and the other by the bank. The asset account, Cash, maintained by the depositor is the reciprocal of the bank's liability account for each depositor. It should be possible to **reconcile these accounts** (make them agree) at any time.

Opening a bank checking account is a relatively simple procedure. Typically, the bank makes a credit check on the new customer and the depositor is required to sign a **signature card**. The card should contain the signatures of each person authorized to sign checks on the account. The signature card is used by bank employees to validate signatures on the checks.

As soon as possible after an account is opened, the bank will provide the depositor with a book of serially numbered checks and deposit slips imprinted with the depositor's name and address. Each check and deposit slip is imprinted with both a bank and a depositor identification number in magnetic ink to permit computer processing of the transaction.

Many companies have more than one bank account. For efficiency of operations and better control, national retailers like Wal-Mart Stores and Kmart may have regional bank accounts. Similarly, a company such as Exxon with more than 150,000 employees may have a payroll bank account, as well as one or more general bank accounts. In addition, a company may maintain several bank accounts in order to have more than one source for obtaining short-term loans when needed.

## Making Bank Deposits

Bank deposits should be made by an authorized employee, such as the head cashier. Each deposit must be documented by a deposit slip (ticket), as shown in Illustration 7-9.

**ILLUSTRATION 7-9**

*Deposit slip*

**6**

STUDY
OBJECTIVE

Indicate the control features of a bank account.

Deposit slips are prepared in duplicate. The original is retained by the bank; the duplicate, machine stamped by the bank to establish its authenticity, is retained by the depositor.

## Writing Checks

A **check** is a written order signed by the depositor directing the bank to pay a specified sum of money to a designated recipient. Thus, there are three parties to a check: the **maker** (or drawer) who issues the check, the **bank** (or payer) on which the check is drawn, and the **payee** to whom the check is payable. A check is a negotiable instrument that can be transferred to another party by endorsement. Each check should be accompanied by an explanation of its purposes. In many businesses, this is done by attaching a remittance advice to the check, as shown in Illustration 7-10.

**ILLUSTRATION 7-10**

*Check with remittance advice*

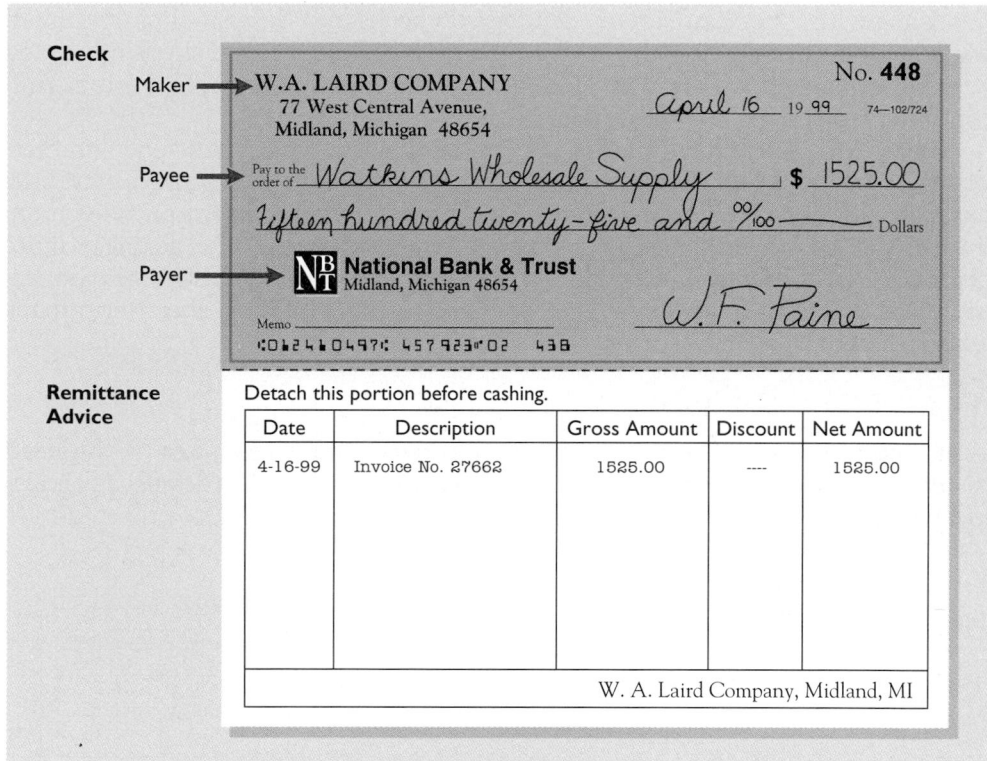

For both individuals and businesses, it is important to know the balance in the checking account at all times. To keep the balance current, each deposit and check should be entered on running balance memorandum forms provided by the bank or on the check stubs contained in the checkbook.

## TECHNOLOGY IN ACTION

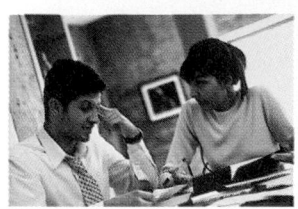

The first big consumer business on the information highway is shaping up as a set of financial household chores: balancing the checkbook, paying bills, and saving for retirement. Many U.S. banks now offer electronic home banking. For customers, the new capabilities mean more convenient service, more up-to-date information about their finances, and more control over their money. Nearly half-a-million households now do a substantial amount of their money management electronically from home, and this number is expected to increase significantly in the near future.

# Bank Statements

Each month, the depositor receives a bank statement from the bank. A **bank statement** shows the depositor's bank transactions and balances. For example, the statement, like the one in Illustration 7-11, shows (1) checks paid and other debits that reduce the balance in the depositor's account, (2) deposits and other credits that increase the balance in the depositor's account, and (3) the account balance after each day's transactions.

**ILLUSTRATION 7-11**

*Bank statement*

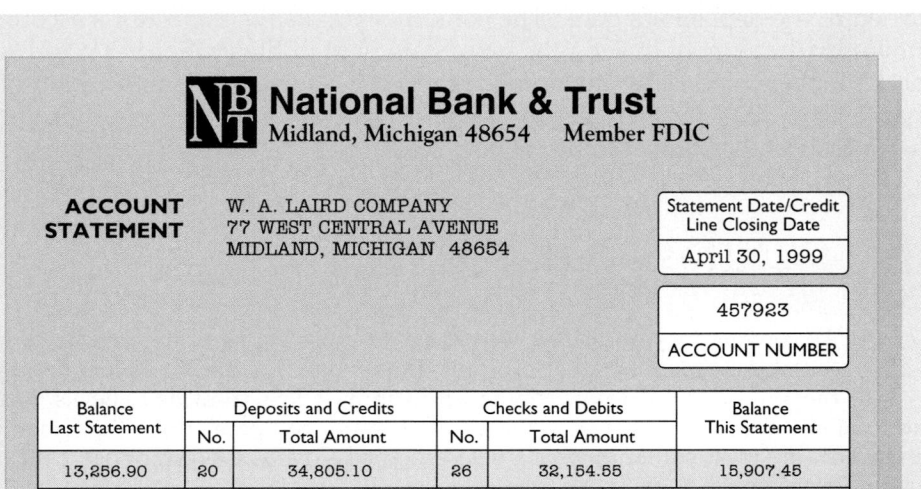

Most banks offer depositors the option of receiving "paid" checks with their bank statements. For those who decline, the bank keeps a record of each check on microfilm. Irrespective of the depositor's choice, all "paid" checks are listed in numerical sequence on the bank statement along with the date the check was paid and its amount. Upon paying a check, the bank stamps the check "paid"; a paid check is sometimes referred to as a **canceled** check. In addition, the bank includes with the bank statement memoranda explaining other debits and credits made by the bank to the depositor's account.

## Debit Memorandum

Banks charge a monthly fee for the use of their services. Often the fee is charged only when the average monthly balance in a checking account falls below a specified amount. The fee, called a bank service charge, is often identified on the bank statement by a code symbol such as SC. A debit memorandum explaining the charge is included with the bank statement. Separate debit memoranda may also be issued for other bank services such as the cost of printing checks, issuing traveler's checks, and wiring funds to other locations. The symbol DM is often used for such charges.

A debit memorandum is used by the bank when a previously deposited customer's check "bounces" because of insufficient funds. In such a case, the check is marked NSF (not sufficient funds) by the customer's bank and is returned to the depositor's bank. The bank then debits the depositor's account, as shown by the symbol NSF on the bank statement in Illustration 7-11, and sends the NSF check and debit memorandum to the depositor as notification of the charge. The NSF check creates an account receivable for the depositor and reduces cash in the bank account.

## ACCOUNTING IN ACTION
### Business Insight

As copying machines have become ever more sophisticated, check counterfeiting has flourished. For example, in just one quarter of a recent fiscal year, the Woolworth Corporation had a $5 million loss from bad checks. Most of the total occurred in the Foot Locker division of the company, a spokesperson said. In the U.S. business community as a whole, some $10 billion worth of bad checks are written every year.

Checkmate Electronic Inc. thinks it has at least a partial answer to this problem. It makes electronic devices that read the magnetic ink used to print account and routing numbers on checks. By identifying the magnetic frequencies as well as the precise shape and size of the numbers, the machine can determine if a check is a fake. Checkmate has a machine small enough to be installed beside cash registers, and it is now in use by such retailers as J.C. Penney, Neiman-Marcus, and Pier 1 Imports.

*Source: The Wall Street Journal, March 31, 1994, p. C2; and Business Week, May 23, 1994, p. 9.*

### Credit Memorandum

A depositor may ask the bank to collect its notes receivable. In such a case, the bank will credit the depositor's account for the cash proceeds of the note, as illustrated on the bank statement by the symbol CM. It will issue a credit memorandum which is sent with the statement to explain the entry. Many banks also offer interest on checking accounts. The interest earned may be indicated on the bank statement by the symbol CM or INT.

## Reconciling the Bank Account

**7**
STUDY
OBJECTIVE
......................
Prepare a bank
reconciliation.

Because the bank and the depositor maintain independent records of the depositor's checking account, you might assume that the respective balances will always agree. In fact, the two balances are seldom the same at any given time, and it is necessary to make the balance per books agree with the balance per bank—a process called **reconciling the bank account**. The lack of agreement between the two balances is due to:

1. **Time lags** that prevent one of the parties from recording the transaction in the same period.
2. **Errors** by either party in recording transactions.

Time lags occur frequently. For example, several days may elapse between the time a check is mailed to a payee and the date the check is paid by the bank.

# ACCOUNTING IN ACTION
## Ethics Insight

Some firms have used time lags to their advantage. For example, E. F. Hutton managers at one time overdrew their accounts by astronomical amounts—on some days the overdrafts totaled $1 billion—creating interest-free loans they could invest. The loans lasted as long as it took for the covering checks to be collected. Although not technically illegal at the time, Hutton's actions were wrong because it did not have bank permission to do so.

Similarly, when the depositor uses the bank's night depository to make its deposits, there will be a difference of at least one day between the time the receipts are recorded by the depositor and the time they are recorded by the bank. A time lag also occurs whenever the bank mails a debit or credit memorandum to the depositor.

The incidence of errors depends on the effectiveness of the internal controls maintained by the depositor and the bank. Bank errors are infrequent. However, either party could inadvertently record a $450 check as $45 or $540. In addition, the bank might mistakenly charge a check drawn by C. D. Berg to the account of C. D. Burg.

# TECHNOLOGY IN ACTION

A malfunctioning computer software program doubled all withdrawals and transfers made at Chemical Bank automatic teller machines (ATMs) in New York state for about 12 hours. The printed record of transactions spit out by the ATM was accurate, but the computerized posting of the transactions was automatically doubled. The bank corrected all errors, which in the aggregate may have been $15 million.

*Source: Denver Post, February 19, 1994.*

## Reconciliation Procedure

**To obtain maximum benefit from a bank reconciliation, the reconciliation should be prepared by an employee who has no other responsibilities pertaining to cash.** When the internal control principle of independent internal verification is not followed in preparing the reconciliation, cash embezzlements may escape unnoticed. For example, a cashier who prepares the reconciliation can embezzle cash and conceal the embezzlement by misstating the reconciliation. Thus, the bank accounts would reconcile and the embezzlement would not be detected.

In reconciling the bank account, it is customary to reconcile the balance per books and balance per bank to their adjusted (correct or true) cash balances. The reconciliation schedule is divided into two sections, as shown in Illustration 7-12. The starting point in preparing the reconciliation is to enter the balance per bank statement and balance per books on the schedule. The following steps should reveal all the reconciling items that cause the difference between the two balances.

1. Compare the individual deposits on the bank statement with deposits in transit from the preceding bank reconciliation and with the deposits per company records or copies of duplicate deposit slips. Deposits recorded by the depositor that have not been recorded by the bank represent deposits in transit and are added to the balance per bank.

2. Compare the paid checks shown on the bank statement or the paid checks returned with the bank statement with (a) checks outstanding from the preceding bank reconciliation and (b) checks issued by the company as recorded in the cash payments journal. Issued checks recorded by the company that have not been paid by the bank represent outstanding checks that are deducted from the balance per the bank.

3. Note any **errors** discovered in the foregoing steps and list them in the appropriate section of the reconciliation schedule. For example, if a paid check correctly written by the company for $195 was mistakenly recorded by the company for $159, the error of $36 is deducted from the balance per books. All errors made by the depositor are reconciling items in determining the adjusted cash balance per books. In contrast, all errors made by the bank are reconciling items in determining the adjusted cash balance per the bank.

4. Trace **bank memoranda** to the depositor's records. Any unrecorded memoranda should be listed in the appropriate section of the reconciliation schedule. For example, a $5 debit memorandum for bank service charges is deducted from the balance per books, and $32 of interest earned is added to the balance per books.

**ILLUSTRATION 7-12**

*Bank reconciliation procedures*

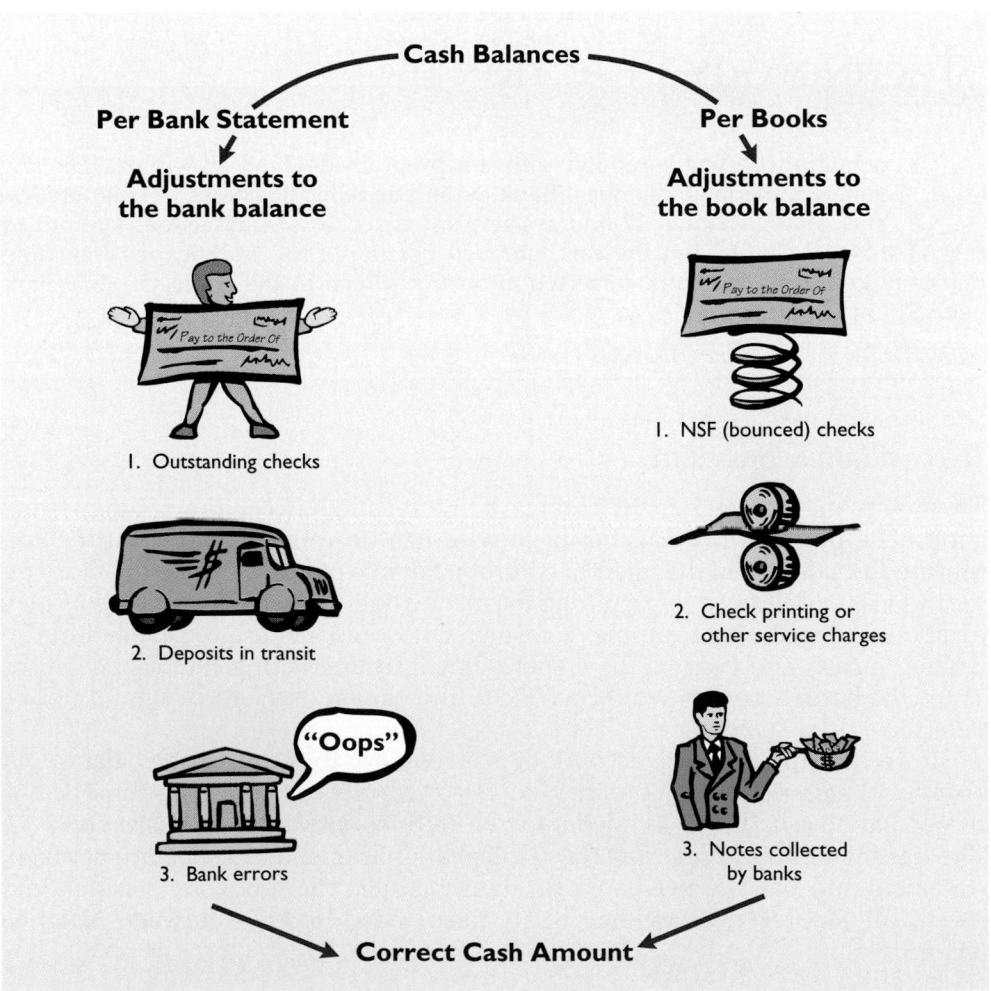

**Cash Balances**

**Per Bank Statement**

**Adjustments to the bank balance**

1. Outstanding checks

2. Deposits in transit

3. Bank errors

"Oops"

**Per Books**

**Adjustments to the book balance**

1. NSF (bounced) checks

2. Check printing or other service charges

3. Notes collected by banks

**Correct Cash Amount**

## Bank Reconciliation Illustrated

The bank statement for the Laird Company is shown in Illustration 7-11. It shows a balance per bank of $15,907.45 on April 30, 1999. On this date the balance of cash per books is $11,589.45. From the foregoing steps, the following reconciling items are determined.

1. **Deposits in transit:** April 30 deposit (received by bank on May 1).    $2,201.40

2. **Outstanding checks:** No. 453 $3,000.00; No. 457 $1,401.30; No. 460 $1,502.70.    5,904.00

3. **Errors:** Check No. 443 was correctly written by Laird for $1,226.00 and was correctly paid by the bank. However, it was recorded for $1,262.00 by Laird Company.    36.00

4. **Bank memoranda:**
   a. Debit—NSF check from J. R. Baron for $425.60    425.60
   b. Debit—Printing company checks charge, $30.00    30.00
   c. Credit—Collection of note receivable for $1,000 plus interest earned $50, less bank collection fee $15.00    1,035.00

**HELPFUL HINT**
Note in the bank statement that checks No. 459 and 461 have been paid but check No. 460 is not listed. Thus, this check is outstanding. If a complete bank statement were provided, checks No. 453 and 457 would also not be listed. The amounts for these three checks are obtained from the company's cash payments records.

The bank reconciliation is shown in Illustration 7-13.

**ILLUSTRATION 7-13**
*Bank reconciliation*

| LAIRD COMPANY<br>Bank Reconciliation<br>April 30, 1999 | | |
|---|---:|---:|
| Cash balance per bank statement | | $15,907.45 |
| Add: Deposits in transit | | 2,201.40 |
| | | 18,108.85 |
| Less: Outstanding checks | | |
| No. 453 | $3,000.00 | |
| No. 457 | 1,401.30 | |
| No. 460 | 1,502.70 | 5,904.00 |
| Adjusted cash balance per bank | | $12,204.85 |
| Cash balance per books | | $11,589.45 |
| Add: Collection of note receivable, $1,000 plus interest | | |
|      earned $50, less collection fee $15 | $1,035.00 | |
|      Error in recording check No. 443 | 36.00 | 1,071.00 |
| | | 12,660.45 |
| Less: NSF check | 425.60 | |
|      Bank service charge | 30.00 | 455.60 |
| Adjusted cash balance per books | | $12,204.85 |

**ALTERNATIVE TERMINOLOGY**
The terms *adjusted balance, true cash balance,* and *correct cash balance* may be used interchangeably.

## Entries from Bank Reconciliation

Each reconciling item in determining the **adjusted cash balance per books** should be recorded by the depositor. **If these items are not journalized and posted, the Cash account will not show the correct balance.** The entries for the Laird Company on April 30 are as follows:

**Collection of Note Receivable.** This entry involves four accounts. Assuming that the interest of $50 has not been accrued and the collection fee is charged to Miscellaneous Expense, the entry is:

**HELPFUL HINT**
The entries that follow are adjusting entries. In prior chapters, Cash was an account that did not require adjustment because a bank reconciliation had not been explained.

| A | = | L | + | OE |
|---|---|---|---|---|
| +1,035 | | | | −15 |
| −1,000 | | | | +50 |

| Apr. 30 | Cash | 1,035.00 | |
|---|---|---|---|
| | Miscellaneous Expense | 15.00 | |
| |    Notes Receivable | | 1,000.00 |
| |    Interest Revenue | | 50.00 |
| |       (To record collection of notes receivable | | |
| |       by bank) | | |

**Book Error.**   An examination of the cash disbursements journal shows that check No. 443 was a payment on account to Andrea Company, a supplier. The correcting entry is:

| A | = | L | + | OE |
|---|---|---|---|---|
| +36 | | +36 | | |

| Apr. 30 | Cash | 36.00 | |
|---|---|---|---|
| |    Accounts Payable—Andrea Company | | 36.00 |
| |       (To correct error in recording check | | |
| |       No. 443) | | |

**NSF Check.**   As indicated earlier, an NSF check becomes an accounts receivable to the depositor. The entry is:

| A | = | L | + | OE |
|---|---|---|---|---|
| +425.60 | | | | |
| −425.60 | | | | |

| Apr. 30 | Accounts Receivable—J. R. Baron | 425.60 | |
|---|---|---|---|
| |    Cash | | 425.60 |
| |       (To record NSF check) | | |

**Bank Service Charges.**   Check printing charges (DM) and other bank service charges (SC) are debited to Miscellaneous Expense because they are usually nominal in amount. The entry is:

| A | = | L | + | OE |
|---|---|---|---|---|
| −30 | | | | −30 |

| Apr. 30 | Miscellaneous Expense | 30.00 | |
|---|---|---|---|
| |    Cash | | 30.00 |
| |       (To record charge for printing company | | |
| |       checks) | | |

The foregoing entries could also be combined into one compound entry. After the entries are posted, the cash account will show the following:

**ILLUSTRATION 7-14**

*Adjusted balance in cash account*

| Cash | | | | |
|---|---|---|---|---|
| Apr. 30 Bal. | 11,589.45 | Apr. 30 | | 425.60 |
| 30 | 1,035.00 | 30 | | 30.00 |
| 30 | 36.00 | | | |
| Apr. 30 Bal. | 12,204.85 | | | |

The adjusted cash balance in the ledger should agree with the adjusted cash balance per books in the bank reconciliation in Illustration 7-13.

What entries does the bank make? If any bank errors are discovered in preparing the reconciliation, the bank should be notified so it can make the necessary corrections on its records. The bank does not make any entries for deposits in transit or outstanding checks. Only when these items reach the bank will the bank record these items.

# BEFORE YOU GO ON . . .

## Review It

1. Why is it necessary to reconcile a bank account?
2. What steps are involved in the reconciliation procedure?
3. What information is included in a bank reconciliation?

## Do It

Sally Kist owns Linen Kist Fabrics. Sally asks you to explain how the following reconciling items should be treated in reconciling the bank account at December 31: (1) a debit memorandum for an NSF check, (2) a credit memorandum for a note collected by the bank, (3) outstanding checks, and (4) a deposit in transit.

*Reasoning:* Sally needs to understand that one cause of a reconciling item is time lags. Items (1) and (2) are reconciling items because Linen Kist Fabrics has not yet recorded the memoranda. Items (3) and (4) are reconciling items because the bank has not recorded the transactions.

*Solution:* In reconciling the bank account, the reconciling items are treated as follows:

NSF check: Deducted from balance per books.
Collection of note: Added to balance per books.
Outstanding checks: Deducted from balance per bank.
Deposit in transit: Added to balance per bank.

*Related exercise material:* BE7–6, BE7–7, BE7–8, BE7–9, E7–7, E7–8, E7–9, and E7–10.

THE NAVIGATOR

# REPORTING CASH

Cash on hand, cash in banks, and petty cash are often combined and reported simply as **Cash**. Because it is the most liquid asset owned by a company, cash is listed first in the current asset section of the balance sheet. Some companies use the designation "cash and cash equivalents" in reporting cash as illustrated by the following:

**8**
STUDY
OBJECTIVE
Explain the reporting of cash.

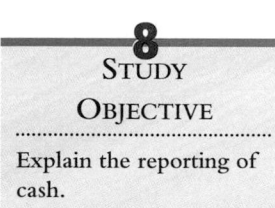

**ILLUSTRATION 7-15**

*Presentation of cash and cash equivalents*

| **EASTMAN KODAK COMPANY** Balance Sheets (partial) | | |
|---|---|---|
| | 1997 | 1996 |
| Current assets (in millions) | | |
| Cash and cash equivalents | $728 | $1,777 |

Cash equivalents are highly liquid investments, with maturities of 3 months or less when purchased, that can be converted into a specific amount of cash. They include money market funds, money market savings certificates, bank certificates of deposit, and U.S. Treasury bills and notes.

A company may have cash that is restricted for a special purpose. Examples include a payroll bank account for paying salaries and wages, and plant expansion fund cash for financing new construction. If the restricted cash is expected to be used within the next year, the amount should be reported as a current asset.

However, when this is not the case, the restricted funds should be reported as a noncurrent asset. Since a payroll bank account will be used as early as the next payday for employees, it is reported as a current asset. In contrast, unless the new construction will begin within the next year, plant expansion fund cash is classified as a noncurrent asset.

In making loans to depositors, it is common for banks to require the borrowers to maintain minimum cash balances. These minimum balances, called **compensating balances**, provide the bank with support for the loans. Compensating balances are a restriction on the use of cash that may affect a company's liquidity. Accordingly, compensating balances should be disclosed in the financial statements.

# BEFORE YOU GO ON . . .

## Review It

1. What is generally reported as cash on a company's balance sheet?
2. What is meant by cash equivalents and compensating balances?
3. At what amount does Kellogg Company report cash and cash equivalents in its 1997 consolidated balance sheet? The answer to this question is provided on page 322.

## A LOOK BACK AT OUR FEATURE STORY

Refer to the opening story about Columbia University, and answer the following questions:

1. Does Susan McLaughlin have a valid basis for establishing responsibility for overages or shortages? Why or why not?
2. What internal control principles are applicable to reconciling cash register tapes and the amount of cash in the cash drawer at the end of the day?
3. What internal control principle is involved in seeing that a student gets a cash register receipt when buying a meal? How does this requirement contribute to good internal control?
4. Do you think the cashiers are, or should be, bonded?

*Solution*

1. Establishing responsibility for overages or shortages is made only at the end of the day. This will provide a valid basis for evaluation only if one person worked the register for the entire day. If more than one person works the register during the day, the single count will not provide a valid basis for establishing who is responsible for the overage or shortage.
2. Applicable internal control principles are: (a) Segregation of duties—the cashier(s) should not be involved in performing the reconciliation. (b) Documentation procedures—the cash register tape provides the documentation for total receipts for the day. (c) Independent internal verification—a supervisor should perform the reconciliation.
3. The internal control principle of documentation procedures is involved. The control does not reside in the receipt itself. For example, there will not be any subsequent reconciliation of cash register receipts with cash at the end of the day. The control is forcing the cashier to ring up each sale so that a receipt is produced. Each receipt is recorded on the cash register tape. At the end of the day, the tape is used in determining overages or shortages.
4. If the dining facility has nonstudent employees who work as cashiers, they may be bonded. However, if students work part-time as cashiers, it is doubtful that they are bonded. From the employer's standpoint, bonding is protection against major embezzlements. The risk of this occurring with student help is relatively low.

THE NAVIGATOR

# DEMONSTRATION PROBLEM

Trillo Company's bank statement for May 1999 shows the following data:

| | | | |
|---|---|---|---|
| Balance 5/1 | $12,650 | Balance 5/31 | $14,280 |
| Debit memorandum: | | Credit memorandum: | |
| NSF check | $175 | Collection of note receivable | $505 |

The cash balance per books at May 31 is $13,319. Your review of the data reveals the following:

1. The NSF check was from Hup Co., a customer.
2. The note collected by the bank was a $500, three-month, 12% note. The bank charged a $10 collection fee. No interest has been accrued.
3. Outstanding checks at May 31 total $2,410.
4. Deposits in transit at May 31 total $1,752.
5. A Trillo Company check for $352 dated May 10 cleared the bank on May 25. This check, which was a payment on account, was journalized for $325.

**Instructions**

(a) Prepare a bank reconciliation at May 31.
(b) Journalize the entries required by the reconciliation.

## SOLUTION TO DEMONSTRATION PROBLEM

(a)

**TRILLO COMPANY**
**Bank Reconciliation**
**May 31, 1999**

| | | |
|---|---|---|
| Cash balance per bank statement | | $14,280 |
| Add: Deposits in transit | | 1,752 |
| | | 16,032 |
| Less: Outstanding checks | | 2,410 |
| Adjusted cash balance per bank | | $13,622 |
| Cash balance per books | | $13,319 |
| Add: Collection of note receivable $500, plus $15 interest less collection fee $10 | | 505 |
| | | 13,824 |
| Less: NSF check | $175 | |
| Error in recording check | 27 | 202 |
| Adjusted cash balance per books | | $13,622 |

(b)

| | | | |
|---|---|---|---|
| May 31 | Cash | 505 | |
| | Miscellaneous Expense | 10 | |
| | Notes Receivable | | 500 |
| | Interest Revenue | | 15 |
| | (To record collection of note by bank) | | |
| 31 | Accounts Receivable—Hup Co. | 175 | |
| | Cash | | 175 |
| | (To record NSF check from Hup Co.) | | |
| 31 | Accounts Payable | 27 | |
| | Cash | | 27 |
| | (To correct error in recording check) | | |

**PROBLEM-SOLVING STRATEGIES**

1. Follow the four steps used in reconciling items (p. 300).
2. Work carefully to minimize mathematical errors in the reconciliation.
3. All entries are based on reconciling items per books.
4. Make sure the cash ledger balance after posting the reconciling entries agrees with the adjusted cash balance per books.

THE NAVIGATOR

# Summary of Study Objectives

**1. Define internal control.** Internal control is the plan of organization and related methods and procedures adopted within a business to safeguard its assets and to enhance the accuracy and reliability of its accounting records.

**2. Identify the principles of internal control.** The principles of internal control are: establishment of responsibility; segregation of duties; documentation procedures; physical, mechanical, and electronic controls; independent internal verification; and other controls.

**3. Explain the applications of internal control principles to cash receipts.** Internal controls over cash receipts include: (a) designating only personnel such as cashiers to handle cash; (b) assigning the duties of receiving cash, recording cash, and custody of cash to different individuals; (c) obtaining remittance advices for mail receipts, cash register tapes for over-the-counter receipts, and deposit slips for bank deposits; (d) using company safes and bank vaults to store cash with access limited to authorized personnel, and using cash registers in executing over-the-counter receipts; (e) making independent daily counts of register receipts and daily comparisons of total receipts with total deposits; and (f) bonding personnel that handle cash and requiring them to take vacations.

**4. Describe the applications of internal control principles to cash disbursements.** Internal controls over cash disbursements include: (a) having only specified individuals such as the treasurer authorized to sign checks; (b) assigning the duties of approving items for payment, paying the items, and recording the payment to different individuals; (c) using prenumbered checks and accounting for all checks, with each check supported by an approved invoice; (d) storing blank checks in a safe or vault with access restricted to authorized personnel, and using a checkwriter to imprint amounts on checks; (e) comparing each check with the approved invoice before issuing the check, and making monthly reconciliations of bank and book balances; and (f) after payment, stamping each approved invoice "paid."

**5. Explain the operation of a petty cash fund.** In operating a petty cash fund, it is necessary to establish the fund, make payments from the fund, and replenish the fund.

**6. Indicate the control features of a bank account.** A bank account contributes to good internal control by providing physical controls for the storage of cash, minimizing the amount of currency that must be kept on hand, and creating a double record of a depositor's bank transactions.

**7. Prepare a bank reconciliation.** In reconciling the bank account, it is customary to reconcile the balance per books and balance per bank to their adjusted balances. The steps in determining the reconciling items are to ascertain deposits in transit, outstanding checks, errors by the depositor or the bank, and unrecorded bank memoranda.

**8. Explain the reporting of cash.** Cash is listed first in the current assets section of the balance sheet. In some cases, cash is reported together with cash equivalents. Cash restricted for a special purpose is reported separately as a current asset or as a noncurrent asset depending on when the cash is expected to be used.

THE NAVIGATOR

# GLOSSARY

**Bank service charge** A fee charged by a bank for the use of its services. (p. 298).

**Bank statement** A statement received monthly from the bank that shows the depositor's bank transactions and balances. (p. 297).

**Cash** Resources that consist of coins, currency, checks, money orders, and money on hand or on deposit in a bank or similar depository. (p. 287).

**Cash equivalents** Highly liquid investments, with maturities of three months or less when purchased, that can be converted to a specific amount of cash. (p. 303).

**Check** A written order signed by the depositor directing the bank to pay a specified sum of money to a designated recipient. (p. 295).

**Compensating balances** Minimum cash balances required by a bank in support of bank loans. (p. 304).

**Deposits in transit** Deposits recorded by the depositor that have not been recorded by the bank. (p. 300).

**Electronic funds transfer (EFT)** A disbursement system that uses wire, telephone, telegraph, or computer to transfer cash from one location to another. (p. 291).

**Internal auditors** Company employees who evaluate on a continuous basis the effectiveness of the company's system of internal control. (p. 285).

**Internal control** The plan of organization and all the related methods and measures adopted within a business to safeguard its assets and enhance the accuracy and reliability of its accounting records. (p. 280).

**NSF check** A check that is not paid by a bank because of insufficient funds in a customer's bank account. (p. 298).

**Outstanding checks** Checks issued and recorded by a company that have not been paid by the bank. (p. 300).

**Petty cash fund** A cash fund used to pay relatively small amounts. (p. 292).

**Voucher** An authorization form prepared for each payment by check in a voucher system. (p. 290).

**Voucher system** An extensive network of approvals by authorized individuals acting independently to ensure that all disbursements by check are proper. (p. 290).

# SELF-STUDY QUESTIONS

Answers are at the end of the chapter.

(SO 1) 1. Internal control is used in a business to enhance the accuracy and reliability of its accounting records and to:
   a. safeguard its assets.
   b. prevent fraud.
   c. produce correct financial statements.
   d. deter employee dishonesty.

(SO 2) 2. The principles of internal control do not include:
   a. establishment of responsibility.
   b. documentation procedures.
   c. management responsibility.
   d. independent internal verification.

(SO 2) 3. Physical controls do *not* include:
   a. safes and vaults to store cash.
   b. independent bank reconciliations.
   c. locked warehouses for inventories.
   d. bank safety deposit boxes for important papers.

(SO 3) 4. Which of the following items in a cash drawer at November 30 is *not* cash?
   a. Money orders.
   b. Coins and currency.
   c. A customer check dated December 1.
   d. A customer check dated November 28.

(SO 3) 5. Permitting only designated personnel such as cashiers to handle cash receipts is an application of the principle of:
   a. segregation of duties.
   b. establishment of responsibility.
   c. independent check.
   d. other controls.

(SO 4) 6. The use of prenumbered checks in disbursing cash is an application of the principle of:
   a. establishment of responsibility.
   b. segregation of duties.
   c. physical, mechanical, and electronic controls.
   d. documentation procedures.

7. A check is written to replenish a $100 petty cash fund (SO 5) when the fund contains receipts of $94 and $3 in cash. In recording the check,
   a. Cash Over and Short should be debited for $3.
   b. Petty Cash should be debited for $94.
   c. Cash should be credited for $94.
   d. Petty Cash should be credited for $3.

8. The control features of a bank account do *not* include:
   a. having bank auditors verify the correctness of the (SO 6) bank balance per books.
   b. minimizing the amount of cash that must be kept on hand.
   c. providing a double record of all bank transactions.
   d. safeguarding cash by using a bank as a depository.

9. In a bank reconciliation, deposits in transit are:
   a. deducted from the book balance. (SO 7)
   b. added to the book balance
   c. added to the bank balance.
   d. deducted from the bank balance.

10. The reconciling item in a bank reconciliation that will result in an adjusting entry by the depositor is: (SO 7)
   a. outstanding checks.
   b. deposit in transit.
   c. a bank error.
   d. bank service charges.

11. The statement that correctly describes the reporting of cash is: (SO 8)
   a. Cash cannot be combined with cash equivalents.
   b. Restricted cash funds may be combined with Cash.
   c. Cash is listed first in the current asset section.
   d. Restricted cash funds cannot be reported as a current asset.

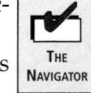

# QUESTIONS

1. "Internal control is concerned only with enhancing the accuracy of the accounting records." Do you agree? Explain.

2. What principles of internal control apply to most business enterprises?

3. In the corner grocery store, all sales clerks make change out of one cash register drawer. Is this a violation of internal control? Why?

4. W. Mozart is reviewing the principle of segregation of duties. What are the two common applications of this principle?

5. How do documentation procedures contribute to good internal control?

6. What internal control objectives are met by physical, mechanical, and electronic controls?

7. (a) Explain the control principle of independent internal verification. (b) What practices are important in applying this principle?

8. The management of Cobo Company asks you, as the company accountant, to explain (a) the concept of reasonable assurance in internal control and (b) the importance of the human factor in internal control.

9. Fauji Fertilizer Co. owns the following assets at the balance sheet date:

| | |
|---|---:|
| Cash in bank-savings account | $ 6,000 |
| Cash on hand | 850 |
| Cash refund due from the IRS | 1,000 |
| Checking account balance | 12,000 |
| Postdated checks | 500 |

What amount should be reported as cash in the balance sheet?

10. What principle(s) of internal control is (are) involved in making daily cash counts of over-the-counter receipts?

11. Metro Department Stores has just installed new electronic cash registers in its stores. How do cash registers improve internal control over cash receipts?

12. In Bangkok Wholesale Company, two mail clerks open all mail receipts. How does this strengthen internal control?

13. "To have maximum effective internal control over cash disbursements, all payments should be made by check." Is this true? Explain.

14. Mardi Gras Company's internal controls over cash disbursements provide for the treasurer to sign checks imprinted by a checkwriter after comparing the check with the approved invoice. Identify the internal control principles that are present in these controls.

15. How do the principles of (a) physical, mechanical, and electronic controls and (b) other controls apply to cash disbursements?

16. (a) What is a voucher system? (b) What principles of internal control apply to a voucher system?

17. What is the essential feature of an electronic funds transfer (EFT) procedure?

18. (a) Identify the three activities that pertain to a petty cash fund, and indicate an internal control principle that is applicable to each activity. (b) When are journal entries required in the operation of a petty cash fund?

19. "The use of a bank contributes significantly to good internal control over cash." Is this true? Why?

20. Lou Reid is confused about the lack of agreement between the cash balance per books and the balance per the bank. Explain the causes for the lack of agreement to Lou, and give an example of each cause.

21. What are the four steps involved in finding differences between the balance per books and balance per banks?

22. Anne Warin asks your help concerning an NSF check. Explain to Anne (a) what an NSF check is, (b) how it is treated in a bank reconciliation, and (c) whether it will require an adjusting entry per bank.

23. (a) "Cash equivalents are the same as cash." Do you agree? Explain. (b) How should restricted cash funds be reported on the balance sheet?

# BRIEF EXERCISES

*Explain the importance of internal control.*
*(SO 1)*

**BE7–1** Sarah McLachlan is the new owner of Galaxy Parking. She has heard about internal control but is not clear about its importance for her business. Explain to Sarah the two purposes of internal control and give her one application of each purpose for Galaxy Parking.

*Identify internal control principles.*
*(SO 2)*

**BE7–2** The internal control procedures in The Wallflowers Company provide that:

(a) Employees who have physical custody of assets do not have access to the accounting records.

(b) Each month the assets on hand are compared to the accounting records by an internal auditor.

(c) A prenumbered shipping document is prepared for each shipment of goods to customers.

Identify the principles of internal control that are being followed.

*Identify the internal control principles applicable to cash receipts.*
*(SO 3)*

**BE7–3** Fresno Company has the following internal control procedures over cash receipts. Identify the internal control principle that is applicable to each procedure.

1. All over-the-counter receipts are registered on cash registers.
2. All cashiers are bonded.
3. Daily cash counts are made by cashier department supervisors.
4. The duties of receiving cash, recording cash, and custody of cash are assigned to different individuals.
5. Only cashiers may operate cash registers.

*Identify the internal control principle applicable to cash disbursements.*
*(SO 4)*

**BE7–4** Romez Company has the following internal control procedures over cash disbursements. Identify the internal control principle that is applicable to each procedure.

1. Company checks are prenumbered.
2. The bank statement is reconciled monthly by an internal auditor.

3. Blank checks are stored in a safe in the treasurer's office.
4. Only the treasurer or assistant treasurer may sign checks.
5. Check signers are not allowed to record cash disbursement transactions.

**BE7–5**  On March 20, Grandy's petty cash fund of $100 is replenished when the fund contains $9 in cash and receipts for postage $52, freight-out $26, and travel expense $10. Prepare the journal entry to record the replenishment of the petty cash fund.

*Prepare entry to replenish a petty cash fund.*
*(SO 5)*

**BE7–6**  Olga C. Boad is uncertain about the control features of a bank account. Explain the control benefits of (a) a signature card, (b) a check, and (c) a bank statement.

*Identify the control features of a bank account.*
*(SO 6)*

**BE7–7**  The following reconciling items are applicable to the bank reconciliation for Cindy Crawford Company: (1) outstanding checks, (2) bank debit memorandum for service charge, (3) bank credit memorandum for collecting a note for the depositor, (4) deposit in transit. Indicate how each item should be shown on a bank reconciliation.

*Indicate location of reconciling items in a bank reconciliation.*
*(SO 7)*

**BE7–8**  Using the data in BE7–7, indicate (a) the items that will result in an adjustment to the depositor's records and (b) why the other items do not require adjustment.

*Identify reconciling items that require adjusting entries.*
*(SO 7)*

**BE7–9**  At July 31, Murphy Company has the following bank information: cash balance per bank, $7,920, outstanding checks $762, deposits in transit $1,700, and a bank service charge $20. Determine the adjusted cash balance per bank at July 31.

*Prepare partial bank reconciliation.*
*(SO 7)*

**BE7–10**  At August 31, Rolex Company has a cash balance per books of $9,500 and the following additional data from the bank statement: charge for printing Rolex Company checks $35, interest earned on checking account balance $40, and outstanding checks $800. Determine the adjusted cash balance per books at August 31.

*Prepare partial bank reconciliation.*
*(SO 7)*

**BE7–11**  Dupre Company has the following cash balances: Cash in Bank $15,742, Payroll Bank Account $6,000, and Plant Expansion Fund Cash $25,000. Explain how each balance should be reported on the balance sheet.

*Explain the statement presentation of cash balances.*
*(SO 8)*

# EXERCISES
........................................................................

**E7–1**  Fern Galenti is the owner of Galenti's Pizza. Galenti's is operated strictly on a carryout basis. Customers pick up their orders at a counter where a clerk exchanges the pizza for cash. While at the counter, the customer can see other employees making the pizzas and the large ovens in which the pizzas are baked.

*Identify the principles of internal control.*
*(SO 2)*

**Instructions**
Identify the six principles of internal control and give an example of each principle that you might observe when picking up your pizza. (Note: It may not be possible to observe all the principles.)

**E7–2**  The following control procedures are used in the Seymor Company for over-the-counter cash receipts.

*List internal control weaknesses over cash receipts and suggest improvements.*
*(SO 2, 3)*

1. To minimize the risk of robbery, cash in excess of $100 is stored in an unlocked attaché case in the stock room until it is deposited in the bank.
2. All over-the-counter receipts are registered by three clerks who use a cash register with a single cash drawer.
3. The company accountant makes the bank deposit and then records the day's receipts.
4. At the end of each day, the total receipts are counted by the cashier on duty and reconciled to the cash register total.
5. Cashiers are experienced; thus they are not bonded.

**Instructions**
(a) For each procedure, explain the weakness in internal control and identify the control principle that is violated.
(b) For each weakness, suggest a change in procedure that will result in good internal control.

**E7–3**  The following control procedures are used in Hilga's Botique Shoppe for cash disbursements.

*List internal control weaknesses over cash disbursements and suggest improvements.*
*(SO 2, 4)*

1. The company accountant prepares the bank reconciliation and reports any discrepancies to the owner.

2. The store manager personally approves all payments before signing and issuing checks.
3. Each week, Hilga leaves 100 company checks in an unmarked envelope on a shelf behind the cash register.
4. After payment, bills are "filed" in a paid invoice folder.
5. The company checks are unnumbered.

**Instructions**

(a) For each procedure, explain the weakness in internal control and identify the internal control principle that is violated.
(b) For each weakness, suggest a change in the procedure that will result in good internal control.

*Identify internal control weaknesses for cash disbursements and make recommendations for improvement.*
*(SO 4)*

**E7–4**   At Vermont Company, checks are not prenumbered because both the purchasing agent and the treasurer are authorized to issue checks. Each signer has access to unissued checks kept in an unlocked file cabinet. The purchasing agent pays all bills pertaining to goods purchased for resale. Prior to payment, the purchasing agent determines that the goods have been received and verifies the mathematical accuracy of the vendor's invoice. After payment, the invoice is filed by vendor, and the purchasing agent records the payment in the cash disbursements journal. The treasurer pays all other bills following approval by authorized employees. After payment, the treasurer stamps all bills PAID, files them by payment date, and records the checks in the cash disbursements journal. Vermont Company maintains one checking account that is reconciled by the treasurer.

**Instructions**

(a) List the weaknesses in internal control over cash disbursements.
(b) ▉▉▆═══▷ Write a memo to your boss indicating your recommendations for improvement.

*Prepare journal entries for a petty cash fund.*
*(SO 5)*

**E7–5**   Acura Company uses an imprest petty cash system. The fund was established on March 1 with a balance of $100. During March the following petty cash receipts were found in the petty cash box:

| Date | Receipt No. | For | Amount |
|------|------|------|------|
| 3/5 | 1 | Stamp Inventory | $35 |
| 7 | 2 | Freight-out | 19 |
| 9 | 3 | Miscellaneous Expense | 12 |
| 11 | 4 | Travel Expense | 24 |
| 14 | 5 | Miscellaneous Expense | 5 |

The fund was replenished on March 15 when the fund contained $2 in cash. On March 20, the amount in the fund was increased to $150.

**Instructions**

Journalize the entries in March that pertain to the operation of the petty cash fund.

*Prepare bank reconciliation and adjusting entries.*
*(SO 7)*

**E7–6**   Alana Davis is unable to reconcile the bank balance at January 31. Alana's reconciliation is as follows:

| | |
|------|------|
| Cash balance per bank | $3,660.20 |
| Add: NSF check | 430.00 |
| Less: Bank service charge | 25.00 |
| Adjusted balance per bank | $4,065.20 |
| Cash balance per books | $3,875.20 |
| Less: Deposits in transit | 490.00 |
| Add: Outstanding checks | 730.00 |
| Adjusted balance per books | $4,115.20 |

**Instructions**

(a) Prepare a correct bank reconciliation.
(b) Journalize the entries required by the reconciliation.

**E7–7** On April 30, the bank reconciliation of Bossa Nova Company shows three outstanding checks: No. 254 $650, No. 255 $720, and No. 257 $410. The May bank statement and the May cash payments journal show the following:

*Determine outstanding checks.*
*(SO 7)*

| Bank Statement | | | Cash Payments Journal | | |
| --- | --- | --- | --- | --- | --- |
| Checks Paid | | | Checks Issued | | |
| Date | Check No. | Amount | Date | Check No. | Amount |
| 5/4 | 254 | 650 | 5/2 | 258 | 159 |
| 5/2 | 257 | 410 | 5/5 | 259 | 275 |
| 5/17 | 258 | 159 | 5/10 | 260 | 925 |
| 5/12 | 259 | 275 | 5/15 | 261 | 500 |
| 5/20 | 261 | 500 | 5/22 | 262 | 750 |
| 5/29 | 263 | 480 | 5/24 | 263 | 480 |
| 5/30 | 262 | 750 | 5/29 | 264 | 360 |

**Instructions**
Using step 2 in the reconciliation procedure, list the outstanding checks at May 31.

**E7–8** The following information pertains to Cody Camera Company.

*Prepare bank reconciliation and adjusting entries.*
*(SO 7)*

1. Cash balance per bank, July 31, $7,263.
2. July bank service charge not recorded by the depositor $15.
3. Cash balance per books, July 31, $7,190.
4. Deposits in transit, July 31, $1,700.
5. Bank collected $1,000 note for Cody in July, plus interest $36 less fee $20. The collection has not been recorded by Cody, and no interest has been accrued.
6. Outstanding checks, July 31, $772.

**Instructions**
(a) Prepare a bank reconciliation at July 31.
(b) Journalize the adjusting entries at July 31 on the books of Cody Company.

**E7–9** The information below relates to the Cash account in the ledger of Mawmeg Company.

*Prepare bank reconciliation and adjusting entries.*
*(SO 7)*

Balance September 1—$17,150; Cash deposited—$64,000.
Balance September 30—$17,404; Checks written—$63,746.

The September bank statement shows a balance of $16,422 on September 30 and the following memorandum:

| Credits | | Debits | |
| --- | --- | --- | --- |
| Collection of $1,800 note plus interest $30 | $1,830 | NSF check: J. Hower | $410 |
| Interest earned on checking account | $45 | Safety deposit box rent | $30 |

At September 30, deposits in transit were $4,800 and outstanding checks totaled $2,383.

**Instructions**
(a) Prepare the bank reconciliation at September 30.
(b) Prepare the adjusting entries at September 30, assuming (1) the NSF check was from a customer on account, and (2) no interest had been accrued on the note.

**E7–10** The cash records of Chi Chi Company show the following:

*Compute deposits in transit and outstanding checks for two bank reconciliations.*
*(SO 7)*

1. The June 30 bank reconciliation indicated that deposits in transit total $750. During July the general ledger account Cash shows deposits of $15,750, but the bank statement indicates that only $15,600 in deposits were received during the month.
2. The June 30 bank reconciliation also reported outstanding checks of $920. During the month of July, Chi Chi Company books show that $17,200 of checks were issued, yet the bank statement showed that $16,400 of checks cleared the bank in July.
3. In September, deposits per the bank statement totaled $26,700, deposits per books were $25,400, and deposits in transit at September 30 were $2,400.
4. In September, cash disbursements per books were $23,700, checks clearing the bank were $24,000, and outstanding checks at September 30 were $2,100.

There were no bank debit or credit memoranda, and no errors were made by either the bank or Chi Chi Company.

*Instructions*
Answer the following questions:

    (a)  In situation (1), what were the deposits in transit at July 31?
    (b)  In situation (2), what were the outstanding checks at July 31?
    (c)  In situation (3), what were the deposits in transit at August 31?
    (d)  In situation (4), what were the outstanding checks at August 31?

# PROBLEMS: SET A

*Identify internal control weaknesses over cash receipts.*
*(SO 2, 3)*

**P7–1A**  Burlington Theater is located in the Burlington Mall. A cashier's booth is located near the entrance to the theater. Two cashiers are employed. One works from 1–5 P.M., the other from 5–9 P.M. Each cashier is bonded. The cashiers receive cash from customers and operate a machine that ejects serially numbered tickets. The rolls of tickets are inserted and locked into the machine by the theater manager at the beginning of each cashier's shift.

After purchasing a ticket, the customer takes the ticket to a doorperson stationed at the entrance of the theater lobby some 60 feet from the cashier's booth. The doorperson tears the ticket in half, admits the customer, and returns the ticket stub to the customer. The other half of the ticket is dropped into a locked box by the doorperson.

At the end of each cashier's shift, the theater manager removes the ticket rolls from the machine and makes a cash count. The cash count sheet is initialed by the cashier. At the end of the day, the manager deposits the receipts in total in a bank night deposit vault located in the mall. In addition, the manager sends copies of the deposit slip and the initialed cash count sheets to the theater company treasurer for verification and to the company's accounting department. Receipts from the first shift are stored in a safe located in the manager's office.

*Instructions*
    (a)  Identify the internal control principles and their application to the cash receipts transactions of the Burlington Theater.
    (b)  If the doorperson and cashier decide to collaborate to misappropriate cash, what actions might they take?

*Journalize and post petty cash fund transactions.*
*(SO 5)*

**P7–2A**  ABM Company maintains a petty cash fund for small expenditures. The following transactions occurred over a 2-month period:

July  1   Established petty cash fund by writing a check on Metro Bank for $200.
     15   Replenished the petty cash fund by writing a check for $194.30. On this date the fund consisted of $5.70 in cash and the following petty cash receipts: Freight-out $94.00, postage expense $42.40, entertainment expense $46.60, and miscellaneous expense $10.70.
     31   Replenished the petty cash fund by writing a check for $192.00. At this date, the fund consisted of $8.00 in cash and the following petty cash receipts: Freight-out $82.10, charitable contributions expense $30.00, postage expense $47.80, and miscellaneous expense $32.10.

Aug. 15   Replenished the petty cash fund by writing a check for $188.00. On this date, the fund consisted of $12.00 in cash and the following petty cash receipts: Freight-out $74.40, entertainment expense $43.00, postage expense $33.00, and miscellaneous expense $38.00.
     16   Increased the amount of the petty cash fund to $400 by writing a check for $200.
     31   Replenished petty cash fund by writing a check for $283.00. On this date, the fund consisted of $117 in cash and the following petty cash receipts: Postage expense $145.00, entertainment expense $90.60, and freight-out $45.40.

*Instructions*
    (a)  Journalize the petty cash transactions.
    (b)  Post to the Petty Cash account.
    (c)  What internal control features exist in a petty cash fund?

**P7–3A**  On July 31, 1999, Long Company had a cash balance per books of $5,815.30. The statement from First State Bank on that date showed a balance of $7,075.80. A comparison of the bank statement with the cash account revealed the following facts:

*Prepare a bank reconciliation and adjusting entries.*
*(SO 7)*

1. The bank service charge for July was $25.
2. The bank collected a note receivable of $1,200 for Long Company on July 15, plus $48 of interest. The bank made a $10 charge for the collection. Long has not accrued any interest on the note.
3. The July 31 receipts of $1,819.60 were not included in the bank deposits for July. These receipts were deposited by the company in a night deposit vault on July 31.
4. Company check No. 2480 issued to J. Brokaw, a creditor, for $492 that cleared the bank in July was incorrectly entered in the cash payments journal on July 10 for $429.
5. Checks outstanding on July 31 totaled $2,480.10.
6. On July 31, the bank statement showed an NSF charge of $550 for a check received by the company from R. Close, a customer, on account.

*Instructions*
(a)  Prepare the bank reconciliation as of July 31.
(b)  Prepare the necessary adjusting entries at July 31.

**P7–4A**  The bank portion of the bank reconciliation for Zurich Company at October 31, 1999, was as follows:

*Prepare a bank reconciliation and adjusting entries from detailed data.*
*(SO 7)*

**ZURICH COMPANY**
**Bank Reconciliation**
**October 31, 1999**

| | | |
|---|---|---:|
| Cash balance per bank | | $12,367.90 |
| Add: Deposits in transit | | 1,530.20 |
| | | 13,898.10 |
| Less: Outstanding checks | | |
| Check Number | Check Amount | |
| 2451 | $1,260.40 | |
| 2470 | 720.10 | |
| 2471 | 844.50 | |
| 2472 | 426.80 | |
| 2474 | 1,050.00 | 4,301.80 |
| Adjusted cash balance per bank | | $ 9,596.30 |

The adjusted cash balance per bank agreed with the cash balance per books at October 31.
The November bank statement showed the following checks and deposits:

**Bank Statement**

| | Checks | | | Deposits | |
|---|---|---|---|---|---|
| Date | Number | Amount | Date | | Amount |
| 11-1 | 2470 | $   720.10 | 11-1 | | $ 1,530.20 |
| 11-2 | 2471 | 844.50 | 11-4 | | 1,211.60 |
| 11-5 | 2474 | 1,050.00 | 11-8 | | 990.10 |
| 11-4 | 2475 | 1,640.70 | 11-13 | | 2,575.00 |
| 11-8 | 2476 | 2,830.00 | 11-18 | | 1,472.70 |
| 11-10 | 2477 | 600.00 | 11-21 | | 2,945.00 |
| 11-15 | 2479 | 1,750.00 | 11-25 | | 2,567.30 |
| 11-18 | 2480 | 1,330.00 | 11-28 | | 1,650.00 |
| 11-27 | 2481 | 695.40 | 11-30 | | 1,186.00 |
| 11-30 | 2483 | 575.50 | Total | | $16,127.90 |
| 11-29 | 2486 | 900.00 | | | |
| | Total | $12,936.20 | | | |

The cash records per books for November showed the following:

| Cash Payments Journal | | | | | | Cash Receipts Journal | |
|---|---|---|---|---|---|---|---|
| Date | Number | Amount | Date | Number | Amount | Date | Amount |
| 11-1 | 2475 | $1,640.70 | 11-20 | 2483 | $  575.50 | 11-3 | $ 1,211.60 |
| 11-2 | 2476 | 2,830.00 | 11-22 | 2484 | 829.50 | 11-7 | 990.10 |
| 11-2 | 2477 | 600.00 | 11-23 | 2485 | 974.80 | 11-12 | 2,575.00 |
| 11-4 | 2478 | 538.20 | 11-24 | 2486 | 900.00 | 11-17 | 1,472.70 |
| 11-8 | 2479 | 1,570.00 | 11-29 | 2487 | 398.00 | 11-20 | 2,954.00 |
| 11-10 | 2480 | 1,330.00 | 11-30 | 2488 | 800.00 | 11-24 | 2,567.30 |
| 11-15 | 2481 | 695.40 | Total | | $14,294.10 | 11-27 | 1,650.00 |
| 11-18 | 2482 | 612.00 | | | | 11-29 | 1,186.00 |
| | | | | | | 11-30 | 1,225.00 |
| | | | | | | Total | $15,831.70 |

The bank statement contained two bank memoranda:

1.  A credit of $1,905.00 for the collection of an $1,800 note for Zurich Company plus interest of $120 and less a collection fee of $15. Zurich Company has not accrued any interest on the note.
2.  A debit for the printing of additional company checks, $50.00.

At November 30 the cash balance per books was $11,133.90, and the cash balance per the bank statement was $17,414.60. The bank did not make any errors, but two errors were made by Zurich Company.

*Instructions*
(a)  Using the four steps in the reconciliation procedure described on page 300, prepare a bank reconciliation at November 30.
(b)  Prepare the adjusting entries based on the reconciliation. (*Hint:* The correction of any errors pertaining to recording checks should be made to Accounts Payable. The correction of any errors relating to recording cash receipts should be made to Accounts Receivable.)

*Prepare a bank reconciliation and adjusting entries. (SO 7)*

**P7–5A**   Melo Company's bank statement from First National Bank at August 31, 1999, shows the following information:

| | | | | |
|---|---|---|---|---|
| Balance, August 1 | $17,400 | Bank credit memorandum: | | |
| August deposits | 72,000 | Collection of note | | |
| Checks cleared in August | 68,660 | receivable plus $90 | | |
| Balance, August 31 | 24,850 | interest | $4,090 | |
| | | Interest earned | 45 | |
| | | Bank debit memorandum | | |
| | | Safety deposit box rent | 25 | |

A summary of the Cash account in the ledger for August shows: Balance, August 1, $16,900; receipts $77,000; disbursements $73,570; and balance, August 31, $20,330. Analysis reveals that the only reconciling items on the July 31 bank reconciliation were a deposit in transit for $4,000 and outstanding checks of $4,500. The deposit in transit was the first deposit recorded by the bank in August. In addition, you determine that there were two errors involving company checks drawn in August: (1) a check for $400 to a creditor on account that cleared the bank in August was journalized and posted for $420, and (2) a salary check to an employee for $275 was recorded by the bank for $285.

*Instructions*
(a)  Prepare a bank reconciliation at August 31.
(b)  Journalize the adjusting entries to be made by Melo Company at August 31. Assume the interest on the note has been accrued by the company.

*Prepare comprehensive bank reconciliation with theft and internal control deficiencies. (SO 2, 3, 4, 7)*

**P7–6A**   Giant Company is a very profitable small business. It has not, however, given much consideration to internal control. For example, in an attempt to keep clerical and office expenses to a minimum, the company has combined the jobs of cashier and bookkeeper. As a result, K. Kilgora handles all cash receipts, keeps the accounting records, and prepares the monthly bank reconciliations.

The balance per the bank statement on October 31, 1999, was $18,180. Outstanding checks were: No. 62 for $126.75, No. 183 for $150, No. 284 for $253.25, No. 862 for $190.71, No. 863 for $226.80, and No. 864 for $165.28. Included with the statement was a credit memorandum of $400 indicating the collection of a note receivable for the Giant Company by the bank on October 25. This memorandum has not been recorded by Giant Company.

The company's ledger showed one cash account with a balance of $21,892.72. The balance included undeposited cash on hand. Because of the lack of internal controls, Kilgora took for personal use all of the undeposited receipts in excess of $3,795.51. He then prepared the following bank reconciliation in an effort to conceal his theft of cash.

### BANK RECONCILIATION

| | | |
|---|---:|---:|
| Cash balance per books, October 31 | | $21,892.72 |
| Add: Outstanding checks | | |
| No. 862 | $190.71 | |
| No. 863 | 226.80 | |
| No. 864 | 165.28 | 482.79 |
| | | 22,375.51 |
| Less: Undeposited receipts | | 3,795.51 |
| Unadjusted balance per bank, October 31 | | 18,580.00 |
| Less: Bank credit memorandum | | 400.00 |
| Cash balance per bank statement, October 31 | | $18,180.00 |

**Instructions**
(a) Prepare a correct bank reconciliation. (*Hint:* Deduct the amount of the theft from the adjusted balance per books.)
(b) Indicate the three ways that Kilgora attempted to conceal the theft and the dollar amount pertaining to each method.
(c) What principles of internal control were violated in this case?

# PROBLEMS: SET B

**P7–1B** Talley Office Supply Company recently changed its system of internal control over cash disbursements. The system includes the following features.

Instead of being unnumbered and manually prepared, all checks must now be pre-numbered and written by using the new checkwriter purchased by the company. Before a check can be issued, each invoice must have the approval of Lois Bedient, the purchasing agent, and Sara Power, the receiving department supervisor. Checks must be signed by either Amy Rochford, the treasurer, or Joel Reid, the assistant treasurer. Before signing a check, the signer is expected to compare the amounts of the check with the amounts on the invoice.

After signing a check, the signer stamps the invoice PAID and inserts within the stamp, the date, check number, and amount of the check. The "paid" invoice is then sent to the accounting department for recording.

Blank checks are stored in a safe in the treasurer's office. The combination to the safe is known only by the treasurer and assistant treasurer. Each month, the bank statement is reconciled with the bank balance per books by the assistant chief accountant.

*Identify internal control principles over cash disbursements.*
*(SO 2, 4)*

**Instructions**
Identify the internal control principles and their application to cash disbursements of Talley Office Supply Company.

**P7–2B** Vickers Company maintains a petty cash fund for small expenditures. The following transactions occurred over a 2-month period:

July 1 Established petty cash fund by writing a check on Metro Bank for $200.
　 15 Replenished the petty cash fund by writing a check for $195.00. On this date the fund consisted of $5.00 in cash and the following petty cash receipts: Freight-out

*Journalize and post petty cash fund transactions.*
*(SO 5)*

$94.00, postage expense $42.40, entertainment expense $46.60, and miscellaneous expense $11.90.

    31    Replenished the petty cash fund by writing a check for $192.00. At this date, the fund consisted of $8.00 in cash and the following petty cash receipts: Freight-out $82.10, charitable contributions expense $40.00, postage expense $27.80, and miscellaneous expense $42.10.

Aug. 15    Replenished the petty cash fund by writing a check for $187.00. On this date, the fund consisted of $13.00 in cash and the following petty cash receipts: Freight-out $74.60, entertainment expense $43.00, postage expense $33.00, and miscellaneous expense $37.00.

    16    Increased the amount of the petty cash fund to $400 by writing a check for $200.

    31    Replenished petty cash fund by writing a check for $283.00. On this date, the fund consisted of $117 in cash and the following petty cash receipts: Postage expense $140.00, travel expense $95.60, and freight-out $46.40.

**Instructions**

(a) Journalize the petty cash transactions.

(b) Post to the Petty Cash account.

(c) What internal control features exist in a petty cash fund?

*Prepare a bank reconciliation and adjusting entries.*
*(SO 7)*

**P7–3B**    On May 31, 1999, Maris Company had a cash balance per books of $6,781.50. The bank statement from Community Bank on that date showed a balance of $6,804.60. A comparison of the statement with the cash account revealed the following facts:

1. The statement included a debit memo of $40 for the printing of additional company checks.
2. Cash sales of $836.15 on May 12 were deposited in the bank. The cash receipts journal entry and the deposit slip were incorrectly made for $846.15. The bank credited Maris Company for the correct amount.
3. Outstanding checks at May 31 totaled $276.25, and deposits in transit were $936.15.
4. On May 18, the company issued check No. 1181 for $685 to M. Helms, on account. The check, which cleared the bank in May, was incorrectly journalized and posted by Maris Company for $658.
5. A $2,000 note receivable was collected by the bank for Maris Company on May 31 plus $80 interest. The bank charged a collection fee of $20. No interest has been accrued on the note.
6. Included with the cancelled checks was a check issued by Teller Company to P. Jonet for $600 that was incorrectly charged to Maris Company by the bank.
7. On May 31, the bank statement showed an NSF charge of $700 for a check issued by W. Hoad, a customer, to Maris Company on account.

**Instructions**

(a) Prepare the bank reconciliation at May 31, 1999.

(b) Prepare the necessary adjusting entries for Maris Company at May 31, 1999.

*Prepare a bank reconciliation and adjusting entries from detailed data.*
*(SO 7)*

**P7–4B**    The bank portion of the bank reconciliation for Kona Company at November 30, 1999, was as follows:

**KONA COMPANY**
**Bank Reconciliation**
**November 30, 1999**

| | | |
|---|---|--:|
| Cash balance per bank | | $14,367.90 |
| Add: Deposits in transit | | 2,530.20 |
| | | 16,898.10 |
| Less: Outstanding checks | | |

| Check Number | Check Amount | |
|:---:|:---:|--:|
| 3451 | $2,260.40 | |
| 3470 | 720.10 | |
| 3471 | 844.50 | |
| 3472 | 1,426.80 | |
| 3474 | 1,050.00 | 6,301.80 |

| | |
|---|--:|
| Adjusted cash balance per bank | $10,596.30 |

The adjusted cash balance per bank agreed with the cash balance per books at November 30.

The December bank statement showed the following checks and deposits:

| Bank Statement | | | | |
|---|---|---|---|---|
| **Checks** | | | **Deposits** | |
| Date | Number | Amount | Date | Amount |
| 12-1 | 3451 | $ 2,260.40 | 12-1 | $ 2,530.20 |
| 12-2 | 3471 | 844.50 | 12-4 | 1,211.60 |
| 12-7 | 3472 | 1,426.80 | 12-8 | 2,365.10 |
| 12-4 | 3475 | 1,640.70 | 12-16 | 2,672.70 |
| 12-8 | 3476 | 1,300.00 | 12-21 | 2,945.00 |
| 12-10 | 3477 | 2,130.00 | 12-26 | 2,567.30 |
| 12-15 | 3479 | 3,080.00 | 12-29 | 2,836.00 |
| 12-27 | 3480 | 600.00 | 12-30 | 1,025.00 |
| 12-30 | 3482 | 475.50 | Total | $18,152.90 |
| 12-29 | 3483 | 1,140.00 | | |
| 12-31 | 3485 | 540.80 | | |
| | Total | $15,438.70 | | |

The cash records per books for December showed the following:

| Cash Payments Journal | | | | | | Cash Receipts Journal | |
|---|---|---|---|---|---|---|---|
| Date | Number | Amount | Date | Number | Amount | Date | Amount |
| 12-1 | 3475 | $1,640.70 | 12-20 | 3482 | $ 475.50 | 12-3 | $ 1,211.60 |
| 12-2 | 3476 | 1,300.00 | 12-22 | 3483 | 1,140.00 | 12-7 | 2,365.10 |
| 12-2 | 3477 | 2,130.00 | 12-23 | 3484 | 832.00 | 12-15 | 2,672.70 |
| 12-4 | 3478 | 538.20 | 12-24 | 3485 | 450.80 | 12-20 | 2,954.00 |
| 12-8 | 3479 | 3,080.00 | 12-30 | 3486 | 1,389.50 | 12-25 | 2,567.30 |
| 12-10 | 3480 | 600.00 | Total | | $14,384.10 | 12-28 | 2,836.00 |
| 12-17 | 3481 | 807.40 | | | | 12-30 | 1,025.00 |
| | | | | | | 12-31 | 1,190.40 |
| | | | | | | Total | $16,822.10 |

The bank statement contained two memoranda:

1. A credit of $3,145 for the collection of a $3,000 note for Kona Company plus interest of $160 and less a collection fee of $15.00. Kona Company has not accrued any interest on the note.
2. A debit of $547.10 for an NSF check written by D. Lu, a customer. At December 31, the check had not been redeposited in the bank.

At December 31 the cash balance per books was $13,034.30, and the cash balance per the bank statement was $19,680.00. The bank did not make any errors, but two errors were made by Kona Company.

**Instructions**
(a) Using the four steps in the reconciliation procedure, prepare a bank reconciliation at December 31.
(b) Prepare the adjusting entries based on the reconciliation. (*Hint:* The correction of any errors pertaining to recording checks should be made to Accounts Payable. The correction of any errors relating to recording cash receipts should be made to Accounts Receivable.)

**P7–5B**  Aluminum Company maintains a checking account at the Port City Bank. At July 31, selected data from the ledger balance and the bank statement are as follows:

*Prepare a bank reconciliation and adjusting entries.*
(SO 7)

|  | Cash in Bank | |
|---|---|---|
|  | Per Books | Per Bank |
| Balance, July 1 | $17,600 | $19,200 |
| July receipts | 82,000 | |
| July credits | | 80,070 |
| July disbursements | 76,900 | |
| July debits | | 74,740 |
| Balance, July 31 | $22,700 | $24,530 |

Analysis of the bank data reveals that the credits consist of $79,000 of July deposits and a credit memorandum of $1,070 for the collection of a $1,000 note plus interest revenue of $70. The July debits per bank consist of checks cleared, $74,700 and a debit memorandum of $40 for printing additional company checks.

You also discover the following errors involving July checks: (1) a check for $230 to a creditor on account that cleared the bank in July was journalized and posted as $320, and (2) a salary check to an employee for $255 was recorded by the bank for $155.

The June 30 bank reconciliation contained only two reconciling items: deposits in transit $5,000 and outstanding checks of $6,600.

*Instructions*
(a) Prepare a bank reconciliation at July 31.
(b) Journalize the adjusting entries to be made by Aluminum Company at July 31, 1999. Assume that the interest on the note has been accrued.

# BROADENING YOUR PERSPECTIVE

# FINANCIAL REPORTING AND ANALYSIS
...........................................................................................................

### FINANCIAL REPORTING PROBLEM: Kellogg Company

BYP7–1   The financial statements of Kellogg Company are presented in Appendix A at the end of this textbook.

*Instructions*
(a) What comments, if any, are made about cash in the report of the independent auditors?
(b) What data about cash and cash equivalents are shown in the consolidated balance sheet (statement of financial condition)?
(c) What activities are identified in the consolidated statement of cash flows as being responsible for the changes in cash during 1997?
(d) How are cash equivalents defined under the Notes to Consolidated Financial Statements?

### COMPARATIVE ANALYSIS PROBLEM: Kellogg Company vs. General Mills

BYP7–2   Kellogg's financial statements are presented in Appendix A; General Mills's financial statements are presented in Appendix B.

*Instructions*
(a) Based on the information contained in these financial statements, determine each of the following for each company:
  1. Cash and cash equivalents balance at December 31, 1997, for Kellogg, and May 25, 1997, for General Mills.
  2. Increase (decrease) in cash and cash equivalents from 1996 to 1997.
  3. Cash provided by operating activities during 1997 (from Statement of Cash Flows).
(b) What conclusions concerning the management of cash can be drawn from these data?

## RESEARCH ASSIGNMENT

BYP7–3 The "Fortune 500" issue of *Fortune* magazine can serve as a useful reference. This annual issue of *Fortune*, generally appearing in late April or early May, contains a great deal of information regarding the largest U.S. industrial and service companies.

### Instructions
Examine the most recent edition and answer the following questions.

(a) Identify the three largest U.S. corporations in terms of revenues, profits, assets, market value, and employees.

(b) Identify the largest corporation headquartered (or operating, if needed) in your state (by total revenue). How does this corporation rank in terms of revenues, profits, assets, market value, and number of employees?

## INTERPRETING FINANCIAL STATEMENTS: Microsoft, Inc. and Oracle

BYP7–4 Microsoft is the leading developer of software in the world. To continue to be successful Microsoft must generate new products. Generating new products requires significant amounts of cash. Shown below is the current assets section of Microsoft's June 30, 1995, balance sheet and excerpts from a footnote describing the first item listed in the balance sheet, "cash and short-term investments." Below Microsoft is the current asset section of Oracle, another major software developer. (All dollar amounts are in millions.)

**Microsoft**

### MICROSOFT, INC.
### Balance Sheets (partial)
### As of June 30

| | 1994 | 1995 |
|---|---|---|
| Current assets | | |
| Cash and short-term investments (see Note 1) | $3,614 | $4,750 |
| Accounts receivable—net of allowances of $92 and $139 | 475 | 581 |
| Inventories | 102 | 88 |
| Other | 121 | 201 |
| Total current assets | $4,312 | $5,620 |
| Total current liabilities | $ 913 | $1,347 |

| Note 1: | 1994 | 1995 |
|---|---|---|
| Cash and equivalents | $1,477 | $1,962 |
| Short-term investments | 2,137 | 2,788 |
| Cash and short-term investments | $3,614 | $4,750 |

**ORACLE**

### ORACLE
### Balance Sheets (partial)
### As of May 31

| | 1994 | 1995 |
|---|---|---|
| Current assets | | |
| Cash and cash equivalents | $ 409 | $ 480 |
| Short-term cash investments | 60 | 106 |
| Receivables | 516 | 846 |
| Other current assets | 95 | 185 |
| Total current assets | $1,080 | $1,617 |
| Current liabilities | $ 682 | $1,055 |

*Instructions*

    (a) What is the definition of a cash equivalent? Give some examples of cash equivalents. How do cash equivalents differ from other types of short-term investments?

    (b) Comment on Microsoft's presentation of cash in its balance sheet.

    (c) What problems might this presentation of cash pose for a user of Microsoft's financial statements?

    (d) Compare the liquidity of Microsoft and Oracle for 1995.

    (e) Is it possible to have too many liquid assets?

## REAL-WORLD FOCUS: Alternative Distributor Corp.

**BYP7–5    Alternative Distributor Corp.,** a distributor of groceries and related products, is headquartered in Medford, Massachusetts. It was founded in 1980 and today has seven employees, with a total sales of $7 million.

    During its audit, the Alternative Distributor Corp. was advised that previously existing internal controls necessary for the company to develop reliable financial statements were inadequate. The audit report stated that the current system of accounting for sales, receivables, and cash receipts constituted a material weakness.

    Among other items, the report focused on non-timely deposit of cash receipts, exposing Alternative Distributor to potential loss or misappropriation; excessive past due accounts receivable due to lack of collection efforts; disregard of advantages offered by vendors for prompt payment of invoices; absence of appropriate segregation of duties by personnel consistent with appropriate control objectives; inadequate procedures for applying accounting principles; lack of qualified management personnel; lack of supervision by an outside board of directors; and overall poor record keeping.

*Instructions*

Identify the principles of internal control violated by Alternative Distributor Corp.

# CRITICAL THINKING

## GROUP DECISION CASE

**BYP7–6**    The board of trustees of a local church is concerned about the internal accounting controls pertaining to the offering collections made at weekly services. The trustees ask you to serve on a three-person audit team with the internal auditor of the university and a CPA who has just joined the church.

    At a meeting of the audit team and the board of trustees you learn the following:

    1. The church's board of trustees has delegated responsibility for the financial management and audit of the financial records to the finance committee. This group prepares the annual budget and approves major disbursements but is not involved in collections or record keeping. No audit has been made in recent years because the same trusted employee has kept church records and served as financial secretary for 15 years. The church does not carry any fidelity insurance.

    2. The collection at the weekly service is taken by a team of ushers who volunteer to serve one month. The ushers take the collection plates to a basement office at the rear of the church. They hand their plates to the head usher and return to the church service. After all plates have been turned in, the head usher counts the cash received. The head usher then places the cash in the church safe along with a notation of the amount counted. The head usher volunteers to serve for 3 months.

    3. The next morning the financial secretary opens the safe and recounts the collection. The secretary withholds $150–$200 in cash, depending on the cash expenditures expected for the week, and deposits the remainder of the collections in the bank. To facilitate the deposit, church members who contribute by check are asked to make their checks payable to "cash."

4. Each month, the financial secretary reconciles the bank statement and submits a copy of the reconciliation to the board of trustees. The reconciliations have rarely contained any bank errors and have never shown any errors per books.

*Instructions*

With the class divided into groups, answer the following:

(a) Indicate the weaknesses in internal accounting control over the handling of collections.

(b) List the improvements in internal control procedures that you plan to make at the next meeting of the audit team for (1) the ushers, (2) the head usher, (3) the financial secretary, and (4) the finance committee.

(c) What church policies should be changed to improve internal control?

## COMMUNICATION ACTIVITY

**BYP7–7**  As a new auditor for the CPA firm of Kennedy, Maison, and Davis you have been assigned to review the internal controls over mail cash receipts of Emerik Company. Your review reveals the following: Checks are promptly endorsed "For Deposit Only," but no list of the checks is prepared by the person opening the mail. The mail is opened either by the cashier or by the employee who maintains the accounts receivable records. Mail receipts are deposited in the bank weekly by the cashier.

*Instructions*

Write a letter to L. S. Croix, owner of the Emerik Company, explaining the weaknesses in internal control and your recommendations for improving the system.

## ETHICS CASE

**BYP7–8**  You are the assistant controller in charge of general ledger accounting at Bad Water Bottling Company. Your company has a large loan from an insurance company. The loan agreement requires that the company's cash account balance be maintained at $200,000 or more as reported monthly. At June 30 the cash balance is $80,000, which you report to Marais Thompson, the financial vice president. Marais excitedly instructs you to keep the cash receipts book open for one additional day for purposes of the June 30 report to the insurance company. Marais says, "If we don't get that cash balance over $200,000, we'll default on our loan agreement. They could close us down, put us all out of our jobs!" Marais continues, "I talked to Grochum Distributors (one of Bad Water's largest customers) this morning and they said they sent us a check for $150,000 yesterday. We should receive it tomorrow. If we include just that one check in our cash balance, we'll be in the clear. It's in the mail!"

*Instructions*

(a) Who will suffer negative effects if you do not comply with Marais Thompson's instructions? Who will suffer if you do comply?

(b) What are the ethical considerations in this case?

(c) What alternatives do you have?

# SURFING THE NET

**BYP7–9**  All organizations should have systems of internal control. Universities are no exception. This site discusses the basics of internal control in a university setting.

**Address:** http://www.bc.edu/bc_org/fvp/ia/ic/intro.html

**Steps:** Go the site shown above.

*Instructions*

The front page of this site provides links to pages that answer six critical questions. Use these links to answer the following questions:

www.wiley.com/college/weygandt

(a) In a university setting who has responsibility for evaluating the adequacy of the system of internal control?
(b) What do reconciliations ensure in the university setting? Who should review the reconciliation?
(c) What are some examples of physical controls?
(d) What are two ways to accomplish inventory counts?

---

*Answers to Self-Study Questions*
1. a    2. c    3. b    4. c    5. b    6. d    7. a    8. a    9. c    10. d    11. c

---

*Answer to Kellogg Review It Question 3, p. 304*
Kellogg reports cash and cash equivalents on its balance sheet for 1997 of $173.2 million.

**Remember to go back to the Navigator box on the chapter-opening page and check off your completed work.**

**Before studying this chapter, you should know or, if necessary, review:**

a. How to record sales transactions. (Ch. 5, pp. 196–199)
b. Why adjusting entries are made. (Ch. 3, pp. 94–95)
c. How to compute interest. (Ch. 3, pp. 104–105)

THE
NAVIGATOR

## FEATURE STORY

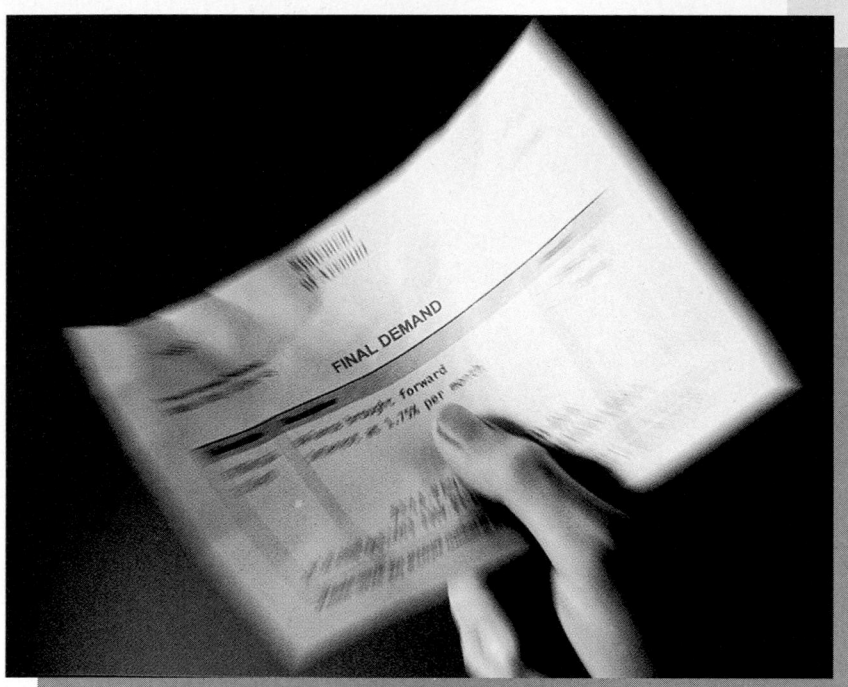

# How Long Should the Check *Be* in the Mail?

Take a look at your campus newspaper. Read the advertisements—the nearby pizza parlor, a local clothing merchant, maybe a review course for the Law School Admission Test. In many cases these advertisers set up accounts with the campus paper and pay their bills 30 days after the ad runs. The paper keeps track of these accounts and bills them on a timely basis.

For more than 70 years, the North Carolina State University newspaper, the *Technician*, has published stories by student writers and run ads by local merchants. "Eighty-five percent of our $400,000 annual operating budget comes from advertising," says Tim Ellington, General Manager—a graduate of NC State. "The rest comes from student fees."

Ellington says that the paper requires prepayment from new advertising accounts. After a trial period, the advertiser will be granted a 30-day payment period. From time to time, however, advertisers don't pay on time. "When it comes to bill paying time, our bill often gets put on the bottom of the pile," says Ellington. "If they are going to anger somebody, they'll anger us before they do a supplier."

The newspaper follows a series of steps in trying to collect late accounts: Once a bill is 30 days past due, the advertiser is sent a letter that says, nicely, "If you haven't sent your payment, please do." At 45 days, the letter isn't as nice: "If we don't receive payment in 30 days, then we could pursue it through small claims court." At 75 days, the newspaper files a small claims suit.

THE
NAVIGATOR

# CHAPTER 8

**THE NAVIGATOR** ✔

- Understand *Concepts for Review* ☐
- Read *Feature Story* ☐
- Scan *Study Objectives* ☐
- Read *Preview* ☐
- Read text and answer *Before You Go On*
  p. 337 ☐  p. 342 ☐  p. 345 ☐
- Work *Demonstration Problem* ☐
- Review *Summary of Study Objectives* ☐
- Answer *Self-Study Questions* ☐
- Complete assignments ☐

# ACCOUNTING FOR RECEIVABLES

## STUDY OBJECTIVES

**After studying this chapter, you should be able to:**

1. *Identify the different types of receivables.*
2. *Explain how accounts receivable are recognized in the accounts.*
3. *Distinguish between the methods and bases used to value accounts receivable.*
4. *Describe the entries to record the disposition of accounts receivable.*
5. *Compute the maturity date of, and interest on, notes receivable.*
6. *Explain how notes receivable are recognized in the accounts.*
7. *Describe how notes receivable are valued.*
8. *Describe the entries to record the disposition of notes receivable.*
9. *Explain the statement presentation and analysis of receivables.*

THE NAVIGATOR

*A*s you read this chapter, you will learn what journal entries the *Technician* makes when it sells its ad space, when it collects the cash for those sales, and when it writes off an uncollectible account. The types of entries the *Technician* makes are typical of most businesses, because our economy depends heavily on the use of credit, which takes the form of accounts and notes receivable. The content and organization of this chapter are as follows:

**ACCOUNTING FOR RECEIVABLES**

| Accounts Receivable | Notes Receivable | Statement Presentation and Analysis |
|---|---|---|
| • Types of receivables | • Determining maturity date | • Presentation |
| • Recognizing accounts receivable | • Computing interest | • Analysis |
| • Valuing accounts receivable | • Recognizing notes receivable | |
| • Disposing of accounts receivable | • Valuing notes receivable | |
| | • Disposing of notes receivable | |

THE NAVIGATOR

# ACCOUNTS RECEIVABLE

## Types of Receivables

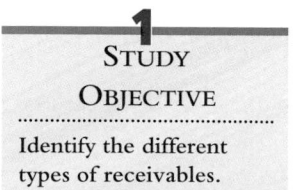

**1**

STUDY OBJECTIVE

Identify the different types of receivables.

The term "receivables" refers to amounts due from individuals and other companies. Receivables are claims that are expected to be collected in cash. Receivables are frequently classified as (1) accounts, (2) notes, and (3) other.

**Accounts receivable** are amounts owed by customers on account. They result from the sale of goods and services. These receivables generally are expected to be collected within 30 to 60 days. They are the most significant type of claim held by a company.

**Notes receivable** represent claims for which formal instruments of credit are issued as evidence of the debt. The credit instrument normally requires the debtor to pay interest and extends for time periods of 60–90 days or longer. Notes and accounts receivable that result from sales transactions are often called **trade receivables**

**Other receivables** include nontrade receivables such as interest receivable, loans to company officers, advances to employees, and income taxes refundable. These are unusual; therefore, they are generally classified and reported as separate items in the balance sheet.

The three primary accounting problems associated with accounts receivable are:

1. **Recognizing** accounts receivable.
2. **Valuing** accounts receivable.
3. **Disposing of** accounts receivable.

## Recognizing Accounts Receivable

Recognizing accounts receivable is relatively straightforward. In Chapter 5 we saw how accounts receivable are affected by the sale of merchandise. To illustrate, assume that Jordache Co. on July 1, 1999, sells merchandise on account to Polo Company for $1,000 terms 2/10, n/30. On July 5, merchandise worth $100 is returned to Jordache Co. On July 11, payment is received from Polo Company for the balance due. The journal entries to record these transactions on the books of Jordache Co. are as follows:

| July 1 | Accounts Receivable—Polo Company | 1,000 | |
| | Sales | | 1,000 |
| | (To record sales on account) | | |
| | | | |
| July 5 | Sales Returns and Allowances | 100 | |
| | Accounts Receivable—Polo Company | | 100 |
| | (To record merchandise returned) | | |
| | | | |
| July 11 | Cash ($900 − $18) | 882 | |
| | Sales Discounts ($900 × .02) | 18 | |
| | Accounts Receivable—Polo Company | | 900 |
| | (To record collection of accounts receivable) | | |

| A | = | L | + | OE |
|---|---|---|---|---|
| + 1,000 | | | | + 1,000 |

| A | = | L | + | OE |
|---|---|---|---|---|
| − 100 | | | | − 100 |

| A | = | L | + | OE |
|---|---|---|---|---|
| + 882 | | | | − 18 |
| − 900 | | | | |

The opportunity to receive a cash discount usually occurs when a manufacturer sells to a wholesaler or a wholesaler sells to a retailer. A discount is given in these situations either to encourage prompt payment or for competitive reasons.

On the other hand, retailers rarely grant cash discounts to customers. For example, we would be surprised if you ever received a cash discount in purchasing goods from any well-known retailer, such as Kmart, Sears, Wal-Mart, and so on. In these situations, most sales are either cash or credit card sales. In fact, when you use a retailer's credit card (J. C. Penney or Sears, for example), instead of giving a discount, the retailer charges interest on the balance due if not paid within a specified period (usually 25–30 days).

To illustrate, assume that you charge on your J. C. Penney account an outfit that costs $300. J. C. Penney will make the following entry at the date of sale:

| | Accounts Receivable | 300 | |
| | Sales | | 300 |
| | (To record sale of merchandise) | | |

| A | = | L | + | OE |
|---|---|---|---|---|
| + 300 | | | | + 300 |

J. C. Penney will then send you a monthly statement of this transaction and any others that have occurred during the month. If you fail to pay in full within 30 days, J. C. Penney adds an interest (financing) charge to the balance due. Although interest rates vary from state to state and from time to time (depending

**ETHICS NOTE**

Receivables from employees and officers of a company are reported in the financial statements. The reason: Sometimes those assets are valued inappropriately or are not based on an "arm's length" transaction.

**2**
**STUDY**
**OBJECTIVE**

Explain how accounts receivable are recognized in the accounts.

**HELPFUL HINT**

These entries are the same as those described in Chapter 5. For simplicity, inventory and cost of goods sold are omitted from this set of journal entries.

in part on federal monetary policy), a common rate for retailers is 18% per year or 1.5% per month.

When financing charges are added, the seller recognizes interest revenue. Assuming that you owe $300 at the end of the month, and J. C. Penney charges 1.5% per month on the balance due, the adjusting entry to record interest revenue of $4.50 ($300 × 1.5%) is as follows:

| A | = | L | + | OE |
|---|---|---|---|---|
| +4.50 | | | | +4.50 |

| | | |
|---|---|---|
| Accounts Receivable | 4.50 | |
|    Interest Revenue | | 4.50 |
|      (To record interest on amount due) | | |

Interest revenue is often substantial for many retailers.

## ACCOUNTING IN ACTION
### Business Insight

Interest rates on most credit cards are quite high, averaging approximately 18.8%. As a result, consumers are often looking for companies that charge lower rates. But be careful—some companies offer lower interest rates but have eliminated the standard 25-day grace period before finance charges are incurred. Other companies encourage consumers to get more in debt by advertising that only a $1 minimum payment is due on a $1,000 account balance! They, of course, earn more interest! Chase Manhattan Corp. markets a credit card that allows cardholders to skip a payment twice a year. However, the outstanding balance continues to incur interest. Other credit card companies calculate finance charges initially on two-month, rather than one-month averages, a practice which often translates into higher interest charges. In short, read the fine print.

## Valuing Accounts Receivable

**3**
STUDY
OBJECTIVE
·····································
Distinguish between the methods and bases used to value accounts receivable.

Once receivables are recorded in the accounts, the next question is: How should these receivables be reported on the balance sheet? Determining the amount to report as an asset is important because some receivables will become uncollectible. To ensure that receivables are not overstated on the balance sheet, they are stated at their cash (net) realizable value. **Cash (net) realizable value** is the net amount expected to be received in cash. The cash realizable value excludes amounts that the company estimates it will not be able to collect. Receivables are therefore reduced by estimated uncollectible receivables on the balance sheet.

The income statement also is affected by the amount of uncollectibles. An expense for estimated uncollectibles is recorded to make certain that expenses are not understated and are matched with related sales revenue. This expense is reported as **bad debts expense** on the income statement.

### Uncollectible Accounts Receivable

Although each customer must satisfy the credit requirements of the seller before the credit sale is approved, inevitably some accounts receivable become uncollectible. For example, a company may experience a decline in sales because of a downturn in the economy, and as a result, the wholesaler may be unable to collect its accounts receivable from the retailer. Similarly, individuals may be laid off from their jobs or be faced with unexpected hospital bills.

In accounting, credit losses are debited to Bad Debts Expense (or Uncollectible Accounts Expense). Such losses are considered a normal and necessary risk of doing business on a credit basis. In fact, from a management point of view, a reasonable amount of uncollectible accounts is evidence of a sound credit policy.

When bad debts are abnormally low, the company may be losing profitable business by following a credit policy that is too strict. Of course, abnormally high bad debts indicate a credit policy that is too lenient.

Two methods are used in accounting for uncollectible accounts: (1) the allowance method and (2) the direct write-off method. Each of these methods is explained in the following sections.

**Allowance Method.**    The allowance method is required for financial reporting purposes when bad debts are material in amount. Its essential features are:

1. Uncollectible accounts are estimated and the expense for the uncollectible accounts is matched against sales in the same accounting period in which the sales occurred.
2. Estimated uncollectibles are debited to Bad Debts Expense and credited to Allowance for Doubtful Accounts through an adjusting entry at the end of each period.
3. Actual uncollectibles are debited to Allowance for Doubtful Accounts and credited to Accounts Receivable at the time the specific account is written off.

*Recording Estimated Uncollectibles.*    To illustrate the allowance method, assume that Hampson Furniture has credit sales of $1,200,000 in 1998, of which $200,000 remain uncollected at December 31. The credit manager estimates that $12,000 of these sales will prove uncollectible. The adjusting entry to record the estimated uncollectibles is:

| | | | |
|---|---|---|---|
| Dec. 31 | Bad Debts Expense | 12,000 | |
| | Allowance for Doubtful Accounts | | 12,000 |
| | (To record estimate of uncollectible accounts) | | |

| A | = | L | + | OE |
|---|---|---|---|---|
| −12,000 | | | | −12,000 |

Bad Debts Expense is reported in the income statement as an operating expense (usually as a selling expense). Thus, the estimated uncollectibles are **matched** with sales in 1998 because the expense is recorded in the same year the sales are made.

Allowance for Doubtful Accounts is a contra asset account that shows the claims on customers that are expected to become uncollectible in the future. A contra account is used instead of a direct credit to Accounts Receivable because we do not know which customers will not pay. The credit balance in this account will absorb the specific write-offs when they occur. **Allowance for Doubtful Accounts is not closed at the end of the fiscal year.** It is deducted from Accounts Receivable in the current asset section of the balance sheet as follows:

**HAMPSON FURNITURE**
**Balance Sheet (partial)**

| | | |
|---|---|---|
| Current assets | | |
| Cash | | $ 14,800 |
| **Accounts receivable** | $200,000 | |
| **Less: Allowance for doubtful accounts** | 12,000 | 188,000 |
| Merchandise inventory | | 310,000 |
| Prepaid expense | | 25,000 |
| Total current assets | | $537,800 |

The amount of $188,000 represents the expected **cash realizable value** of the accounts receivable at the statement date.

***Recording the Write-off of an Uncollectible Account.*** Companies use various methods of collecting past-due accounts, such as the sequence of letters, calls, and legal action described by Tim Ellington of the NCSU *Technician* in the opening story. When all means of collecting a past-due account have been exhausted and collection appears impossible, the account should be written off. To prevent premature write-offs, each write-off should be formally approved in writing by authorized management personnel.

Assume, for example, that the vice president of finance of Hampson Furniture authorizes the write-off of the $500 balance owed by R. A. Ware on March 1, 1999. The entry to record the write-off is:

| A | = | L | + | OE |
|---|---|---|---|---|
| +500 | | | | |
| −500 | | | | |

| | | | | |
|---|---|---|---|---|
| Mar. 1 | Allowance for Doubtful Accounts | | 500 | |
| | Accounts Receivable—R. A. Ware | | | 500 |
| | (Write-off of R. A. Ware account) | | | |

Bad Debts Expense is not debited when the write-off occurs. **Under the allowance method, every bad debt write-off is debited to the allowance account and not to Bad Debts Expense.** A debit to Bad Debts Expense would be incorrect, because the expense is recognized when the adjusting entry is made for estimated bad debts. After posting, the general ledger accounts will show:

**ILLUSTRATION 8-2**

*General ledger balances after write-off*

| Accounts Receivable | | | | | Allowance for Doubtful Accounts | | | | |
|---|---|---|---|---|---|---|---|---|---|
| 1/1/99 | Bal. | 200,000 | 3/1/99 | 500 | 3/1/99 | 500 | 1/1/99 | Bal. | 12,000 |
| 3/1/99 | Bal. | 199,500 | | | | | 3/1/99 | | 11,500 |

A write-off affects only balance sheet accounts. The write-off of the account reduces both Accounts Receivable and the Allowance for Doubtful Accounts. Cash realizable value in the balance sheet, therefore, remains the same as illustrated below.

**ILLUSTRATION 8-3**

*Cash realizable value comparison*

| | Before Write-off | After Write-off |
|---|---|---|
| Accounts receivable | $200,000 | $199,500 |
| Allowance for doubtful accounts | 12,000 | 11,500 |
| Cash realizable value | $188,000 | $188,000 |

***Recovery of an Uncollectible Account.*** Occasionally, a company collects from a customer after the account has been written off as uncollectible. Two entries are required to record the recovery of a bad debt: (1) The entry made in writing off the account is reversed to reinstate the customer's account. (2) The collection is journalized in the usual manner. To illustrate, assume that on July 1, R. A. Ware pays the $500 amount that had been written off on March 1. The entries are:

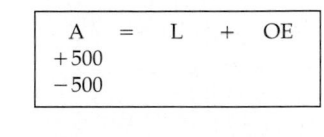

|  | (1) |  |  |
|---|---|---|---|
| July   1 | Accounts Receivable—R. A. Ware | 500 |  |
|  | Allowance for Doubtful Accounts |  | 500 |
|  | (To reverse write-off of R. A. Ware account) |  |  |

| A | = | L | + | OE |
|---|---|---|---|---|
| + 500 |  |  |  |  |
| − 500 |  |  |  |  |

|  | (2) |  |  |
|---|---|---|---|
| 1 | Cash | 500 |  |
|  | Accounts Receivable—R. A. Ware |  | 500 |
|  | (To record collection from R. A. Ware) |  |  |

| A | = | L | + | OE |
|---|---|---|---|---|
| + 500 |  |  |  |  |
| − 500 |  |  |  |  |

Note that the recovery of a bad debt, like the write-off of a bad debt, affects only balance sheet accounts. The net effect of the two entries above is a debit to Cash and a credit to Allowance for Doubtful Accounts for $500. Accounts Receivable is debited and the Allowance for Doubtful Accounts is credited for two reasons: First, the company made an error in judgment when it wrote off the account receivable. Second, R. A. Ware did pay, and therefore the Accounts Receivable account in the general ledger and Ware's account in the subsidiary accounts receivable ledger should show this collection for possible future credit purposes.

**HELPFUL HINT**
Like the write-off, a recovery does not involve the income statement.

**Bases Used for Allowance Method.**    To simplify the preceding explanation, the amount of the expected uncollectibles was given. However, in "real life" companies must estimate that amount if they use the allowance method. Two bases are used to determine this amount: **(1) percentage of sales**, and **(2) percentage of receivables**. Both bases are generally accepted in accounting. The choice is a management decision. It depends on the relative emphasis that management wishes to give to expenses and revenues on the one hand or to cash realizable value of the accounts receivable on the other. The choice is whether to emphasize income statement or balance sheet relationships. Illustration 8-4 compares the two bases.

**ILLUSTRATION 8-4**

*Comparison of bases of estimating uncollectibles*

The percentage of sales basis results in a better matching of expenses with revenues—an income statement viewpoint. In contrast, the percentage of receivables basis produces the better estimate of cash realizable value—a balance sheet viewpoint. Under both bases, it is necessary to determine the company's past experience with bad debt losses.

*Percentage of Sales.*    In the percentage of sales basis, management establishes a percentage relationship between the amount of credit sales and expected losses from uncollectible accounts. The percentage is based on past experience and anticipated credit policy.

The percentage is usually applied to either total credit sales or net credit sales of the current year. To illustrate, assume that Gonzalez Company elects to use the percentage of sales basis and concludes that 1% of net credit sales will become uncollectible. If net credit sales for 1999 are $800,000, the estimated bad debts expense is $8,000 (1% × $800,000). The adjusting entry is:

| A | = | L | + | OE |
|---|---|---|---|---|
| −8,000 | | | | −8,000 |

| Dec. 31 | Bad Debts Expense | 8,000 | |
|---|---|---|---|
| | Allowance for Doubtful Accounts | | 8,000 |
| | (To record estimated bad debts for year) | | |

After the adjusting entry is posted, assuming the allowance account already has a credit balance of $1,723, the accounts of Gonzalez Company will show:

**ILLUSTRATION 8-5**

*Bad debts accounts after posting*

| Bad Debts Expense | | Allowance for Doubtful Accounts | |
|---|---|---|---|
| 12/31  Adj.  **8,000** | | Bal.                          1,723 | |
| | | 12/31   Adj.   **8,000** | |
| | | Bal.                          9,723 | |

**This basis of estimating uncollectibles emphasizes the matching of expenses with revenues.** As a result, Bad Debts Expense will show a direct percentage relationship to the sales base on which it is computed. **When the adjusting entry is made, the existing balance in the Allowance for Doubtful Accounts is disregarded**. The adjusted balance in this account should result in a reasonable approximation of the realizable value of the receivables. If actual write-offs differ significantly from the amount estimated, the percentage for future years should be modified.

***Percentage of Receivables.***   Under the percentage of receivables basis, management establishes a percentage relationship between the amount of receivables and expected losses from uncollectible accounts. A schedule (often called an **aging schedule**) is prepared, in which customer balances are classified by the length of time they have been unpaid. Because of its emphasis on time, the analysis is often called aging the accounts receivable.

## TECHNOLOGY IN ACTION

The aging schedule is another example of output that can be obtained from a computerized accounts receivable system. Manually, preparation of this schedule is an onerous and time-consuming task. However, the schedule can be done in minutes on computer systems.

After the accounts are aged, the expected bad debt losses are determined by applying percentages based on past experience to the totals of each category. The longer a receivable is past due, the less likely it is to be collected. As a result, the estimated percentage of uncollectible debts increases as the number of days past due increases. An aging schedule for Dart Company is shown in Illustration 8-6. Note the increasing percentages from 2% to 40%.

**ILLUSTRATION 8-6**
*Aging schedule*

| Customer | Total | Not Yet Due | Number of Days Past Due | | | |
|---|---|---|---|---|---|---|
| | | | 1–30 | 31–60 | 61–90 | Over 90 |
| T. E. Adert | $   600 | | $  300 | | $  200 | $  100 |
| R. C. Bortz | 300 | $   300 | | | | |
| B. A. Carl | 450 | | 200 | $  250 | | |
| O. L. Diker | 700 | 500 | | | 200 | |
| T. O. Ebbet | 600 | | | 300 | | 300 |
| Others | 36,950 | 26,200 | 5,200 | 2,450 | 1,600 | 1,500 |
| | $39,600 | $27,000 | $5,700 | $3,000 | $2,000 | $1,900 |
| Estimated Percentage Uncollectible | | 2% | 4% | 10% | 20% | 40% |
| Total Estimated Bad Debts | **$ 2,228** | $  540 | $  228 | $  300 | $  400 | $  760 |

**HELPFUL HINT**
The higher percentages are used for the older categories because the longer an account is past due, the more susceptible it is to being uncollectible.

Total uncollectibles for Dart Company ($2,228) represent the amount of existing customer claims expected to become uncollectible in the future. Thus, this amount represents the **required balance** in Allowance for Doubtful Accounts at the balance sheet date. Accordingly, **the amount of the bad debt adjusting entry is the difference between the required balance and the existing balance in the allowance account**. If the trial balance shows Allowance for Doubtful Accounts with a credit balance of $528, an adjusting entry for $1,700 ($2,228 − $528) is necessary, as shown below:

| Dec. 31 | Bad Debts Expense | 1,700 | |
|---|---|---|---|
| | Allowance for Doubtful Accounts | | 1,700 |
| | (To adjust allowance account to total estimated uncollectibles) | | |

| A | = | L | + | OE |
|---|---|---|---|---|
| −1,700 | | | | −1,700 |

After the adjusting entry is posted, the accounts of the Dart Company will show:

**ILLUSTRATION 8-7**
*Bad debt accounts after posting*

| **Bad Debts Expense** | | **Allowance for Doubtful Accounts** | |
|---|---|---|---|
| 12/31  Adj.  **1,700** | | Bal.                                  528 | |
| | | 12/31   Adj.   **1,700** | |
| | | Bal.                              2,228 | |

Occasionally the allowance account will have a **debit balance** prior to adjustment, because write-offs during the year have exceeded previous provisions for bad debts. In such a case **the debit balance is added to the required balance** when the adjusting entry is made. Thus, if there had been a $500 debit balance in the allowance account before adjustment, the adjusting entry would have been for $2,728 ($2,228 + $500) to arrive at a credit balance of $2,228.

The percentage of receivables method will normally result in the better approximation of cash realizable value. This method, however, will not result in the better matching of expenses with revenues if some customers' accounts are more than one year past due. In such a case, bad debts expense for the current period would include amounts applicable to the sales of a prior period.

**Direct Write-off Method.**    Under the direct write-off method, bad debt losses are not estimated and no allowance account is used. When an account is determined to be uncollectible, the loss is charged to Bad Debts Expense. Assume, for example, that Warden Co. writes off M. E. Doran's $200 balance as uncollectible on December 12. The entry is:

| | | | |
|---|---|---|---|
| Dec. 12 | Bad Debts Expense | 200 | |
| | Accounts Receivable—M. E. Doran | | 200 |
| | (To record write-off of M. E. Doran account) | | |

| | | | | |
|---|---|---|---|---|
| A | = | L | + | OE |
| − 200 | | | | − 200 |

When this method is used, bad debts expense will show only actual losses from uncollectibles. Accounts receivable will be reported at its gross amount.

Under the direct write-off method, bad debts expense is often recorded in a period different from the period in which the revenue was recorded. Thus, no attempt is made to match bad debts expense to sales revenues in the income statement or to show the cash realizable value of the accounts receivable in the balance sheet. **Consequently, unless bad debt losses are insignificant, the direct write-off method is not acceptable for financial reporting purposes.** The direct write-off method is, however, used for tax purposes. The Internal Revenue Service allows a tax deduction for uncollectible accounts only when specific accounts receivable are deemed uncollectible.

## Disposing of Accounts Receivable

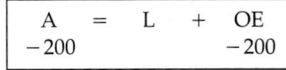

**STUDY OBJECTIVE**

Describe the entries to record the disposition of accounts receivable.

HELPFUL HINT

Two common expressions apply here:
1. Time is money; i.e., waiting for the normal collection process costs money.
2. A bird in the hand is worth two in the bush; i.e., getting the cash now is better than getting it later.

In the normal course of events, accounts receivable are collected in cash and removed from the books. However, as credit sales and receivables have grown in size and significance, the "normal course of events" has changed. In order to accelerate the receipt of cash from receivables, companies frequently sell the receivables to another company for cash, thereby shortening the cash-to-cash operating cycle.

There are several reasons for the sale of receivables. **First, for competitive reasons, sellers** (retailers, wholesalers, and manufacturers) **often must provide financing to purchasers of their goods.** For example, in the sale of durable goods, such as automobiles, trucks, industrial and farm equipment, computers, and appliances, a majority of the sales are on a credit basis. Many major companies in these industries have therefore created companies that accept responsibility for accounts receivable financing. General Motors has General Motors Acceptance Corp. (GMAC), Sears has Sears Roebuck Acceptance Corp. (SRAC), Ford has Ford Motor Credit Corp. (FMCC), and Chrysler has Chrysler Finance Corporation (CFC). These companies are referred to as captive finance companies because they are wholly owned by the company making the product. The purpose of captive financing companies is to encourage the sale of their product by assuring financing to buyers.

**Second, receivables may be sold because they may be the only reasonable source of cash.** When money is tight, companies may not be able to borrow money in the usual credit markets. If money is available, the cost of borrowing may be prohibitive. A final reason for selling receivables is that **billing and collection are often time consuming and costly.** As a result, it is often easier for a retailer to sell the receivable to another party with expertise in billing and collection matters. Credit card companies such as MasterCard, VISA, American Express, and Diners Club specialize in billing and collecting accounts receivable.

# ACCOUNTING IN ACTION
## Business Insight

You don't have to go far to find an example of the sale of receivables for competitive reasons. Most local car dealers simply do not have the financial resources to finance the sale of cars, because most loans today are quite large in relationship to the cost of the car. Recently, the percentage of the price financed by the Big Three automobile manufacturers in the United States was 93% of the selling price of the automobile. In addition, the average length of the loan was 53.5 months, compared to 35 months a decade ago. It is no wonder, therefore, that a captive finance subsidiary like General Motors Acceptance Corporation, if it were a bank, would rank among the largest banks in the world in total assets.

## Sale of Receivables

A common sale of receivables is a sale to a factor. A **factor** is a finance company or bank that buys receivables from businesses for a fee and then collects the payments directly from the customers. Factoring was traditionally associated with the textiles, apparel, footwear, furniture, and home furnishing industries. It has now spread to many other types of businesses and is a multibillion dollar business. For example, Sears, Roebuck and Co. recently sold $14.8 billion of customer accounts receivable.

Factoring arrangements vary widely, but typically the factor (purchaser of the receivables) charges a commission. It ranges from 1% to 3% of the amount of receivables purchased. To illustrate, assume that Hendredon Furniture factors $600,000 of receivables to Federal Factors, Inc. Federal Factors assesses a service charge of 2% of the amount of receivables sold. The journal entry to record the sale by Hendredon Furniture is as follows:

**HELPFUL HINT** The seller can usually earn more than the commission by (1) taking advantage of 2–3% purchase discounts, (2) investing in short-term securities, or (3) reinvesting the money in productive assets.

| | | |
|---|---|---|
| Cash | 588,000 | |
| Service Charge Expense (2% × $600,000) | 12,000 | |
|     Accounts Receivable | | 600,000 |
|     (To record the sale of accounts receivable) | | |

| A | = | L | + | OE |
|---|---|---|---|---|
| +588,000 | | | | −12,000 |
| −600,000 | | | | |

If the company usually sells its receivables, the service charge expense incurred by Hendredon Furniture is recorded as selling expense. If receivables are sold infrequently, this amount may be reported in the Other Expenses and Losses section of the income statement.

# ACCOUNTING IN ACTION
## Business Insight

"They're the devil in disguise," is how CEO Barry Weinstein described factors. Unable to raise capital from bankers or outside investors, Weinstein turned to factoring receivables. The arrangement was pricey: the factor charged interest of 5% a month, to a maximum of 13% of the total invoice, on any uncollected invoices that were factored. The deal became an endless cycle. Soon Weinstein was factoring all new invoices to get the cash to pay the interest on the older factored invoices.

*Source: Inc., July 1994, p. 97.*

## Credit Card Sales

Approximately 1 billion credit cards were estimated to be in use recently—more than three credit cards for every man, woman, and child in this country. A com-

**HELPFUL HINT**
Having millions of cards in use translates to more sales with zero bad debts. Both are powerful reasons for a retailer to accept national credit cards.

mon type of credit card is a national credit card such as VISA, MasterCard, and American Express. Three parties are involved when national credit cards are used in making retail sales: (1) the credit card issuer, who is independent of the retailer, (2) the retailer, and (3) the customer. A retailer's acceptance of a national credit card is another form of selling (factoring) the receivable.

The major advantages of these national credit cards to the retailer are shown in Illustration 8-8. In exchange for these advantages, the retailer pays the credit card issuer a fee of 2–6% of the invoice price for its services.

**ILLUSTRATION 8-8**

*Advantages of credit cards to the retailer*

**VISA and MasterCard Sales.**    Sales resulting from the use of VISA and MasterCard are considered cash sales by the retailer. These cards are issued by banks. Upon receipt of credit card sales slips from a retailer, the bank immediately adds the amount to the seller's bank balance. These credit card sales slips are therefore recorded in the same manner as checks deposited from a cash sale. Banks generally charge a fee of 2–4% of the credit card sales slips for this service. To illustrate, Anita Ferreri purchases a number of compact discs for her restaurant from Karen Kerr Music Co. for $1,000 using her VISA First Bank Card. The service fee that First Bank charges is 3%. The entry to record this transaction by Karen Kerr Music is as follows:

| A | = | L | + | OE |
|---|---|---|---|---|
| +970 | | | | −30 |
| | | | | +1,000 |

| | | |
|---|---|---|
| Cash | 970 | |
| Service Charge Expense | 30 | |
| Sales | | 1,000 |
| (To record Visa credit card sales) | | |

# ACCOUNTING IN ACTION
## Business Insight

Many *are* leaving home without it! Despite long-standing advertisements that urge customers not to leave home without it, more than two million users have cut up their AmEx (American Express) cards and gone in search of better bargains in credit cards. In response, AmEx has staked its future on a new set of twelve different types of credit cards. All offer revolving credit at rates comparable to AmEx's principal rivals, Visa and MasterCard. The U.S. market is saturated with 1 *billion* cards issued by 6,500 companies. Competition is fierce because the pool of potential new customers is shrinking at the same time America's plastic habit is growing. The industry average for bad debt losses on credit cards is 5%.

*Source: Time,* September 12, 1994, p. 60.

**American Express Sales.**    Sales using American Express cards are reported as credit sales, not cash sales. Conversion into cash does not occur until American Express remits the net amount to the seller. To illustrate, assume that Four Seasons restaurant accepts an American Express card for a $300 bill. The entry for the sale by Four Seasons (assuming a 5% fee) is:

| | | |
|---|---|---|
| Accounts Receivable—American Express | 285 | |
| Service Charge Expense | 15 | |
| Sales | | 300 |
| (To record American Express credit card sales) | | |

| A | = | L | + | OE |
|---|---|---|---|---|
| + 285 | | | | − 15 |
| | | | | + 300 |

Thus American Express will subsequently pay the restaurant $285 which the restaurant will record as follows:

| | | |
|---|---|---|
| Cash | 285 | |
| Accounts Receivable—American Express | | 285 |
| (To record redemption of credit card billings) | | |

| A | = | L | + | OE |
|---|---|---|---|---|
| + 285 | | | | |
| − 285 | | | | |

Service Charge Expense is reported as a selling expense in the income statement by the restaurant.

# BEFORE YOU GO ON . . .

## Review It

1. How are accounts receivable recognized in the accounts?
2. What are the essential features of the allowance method?
3. Explain the difference between the percentage of sales and the percentage of receivables methods.
4. Why do companies sell their receivables?
5. What is the journal entry when a company sells its receivables to a factor?
6. What factors indicate that Kellogg Company has limited its risks related to concentrations of credit? (*Hint:* See "Credit Risk Concentration" paragraph of Note 11 in Kellogg's 1997 Annual Report.) The answer to this question is provided on page 362.

## Do It

Peter M. Dell Wholesalers Co. has been expanding faster than it can raise capital and, according to its local banker, the company has reached its debt ceiling. Dell's customers are slow in paying (60–90 days), but its suppliers (creditors) are demanding 30-day payment. Dell has a cash flow problem.

Dell needs to raise $120,000 in cash to safely cover next Friday's employee payroll. Dell's present balance of outstanding receivables totals $750,000. What might Dell do to alleviate this cash crunch? Record the entry that Dell would make when it raises the needed cash.

*Reasoning:* One source of immediate cash at a competitive cost is the sale of receivables to a factor. Rather than waiting until it can collect receivables, Dell may raise immediate cash by selling its receivables. The last thing Dell (or any employer) wants to do is miss a payroll.

*Solution:* Assuming that Dell Co. factors $125,000 of its accounts receivable at a 1% service charge, the following entry would be made:

| | | |
|---|---:|---:|
| Cash | 123,750 | |
| Service Charge Expense | 1,250 | |
|     Accounts Receivable | | 125,000 |
|       (To record sale of receivables to factor) | | |

*Related exercise material:* BE8–9 and E8–5.

THE NAVIGATOR

# NOTES RECEIVABLE

Credit may also be granted in exchange for a formal credit instrument known as a promissory note. A **promissory note** is a written promise to pay a specified amount of money on demand or at a definite time. Promissory notes may be used (1) when individuals and companies lend or borrow money, (2) when the amount of the transaction and the credit period exceed normal limits, and (3) in settlement of accounts receivable.

In a promissory note, the party making the promise to pay is called the **maker**; the party to whom payment is to be made is called the **payee**. The payee may be specifically identified by name or may be designated simply as the bearer of the note. In the note shown in Illustration 8-9, Brent Company is the maker and Wilma Company is the payee. To the Wilma Company, the promissory note is a note receivable; to the Brent Company, the note is a note payable.

Notes receivable give the holder a stronger legal claim to assets than accounts receivable. Like accounts receivable, notes receivable can be readily sold to another party. Promissory notes are negotiable instruments (as are checks), which means that they can be transferred to another party by endorsement.

**ILLUSTRATION 8-9**

*Promissory note*

**HELPFUL HINT**

Who are the two key parties to a note, and what entry does each party make when the note is issued?
Answer:
1. The maker, Brent Company, credits Notes Payable.
2. The payee, Wilma Company, debits Notes Receivable.

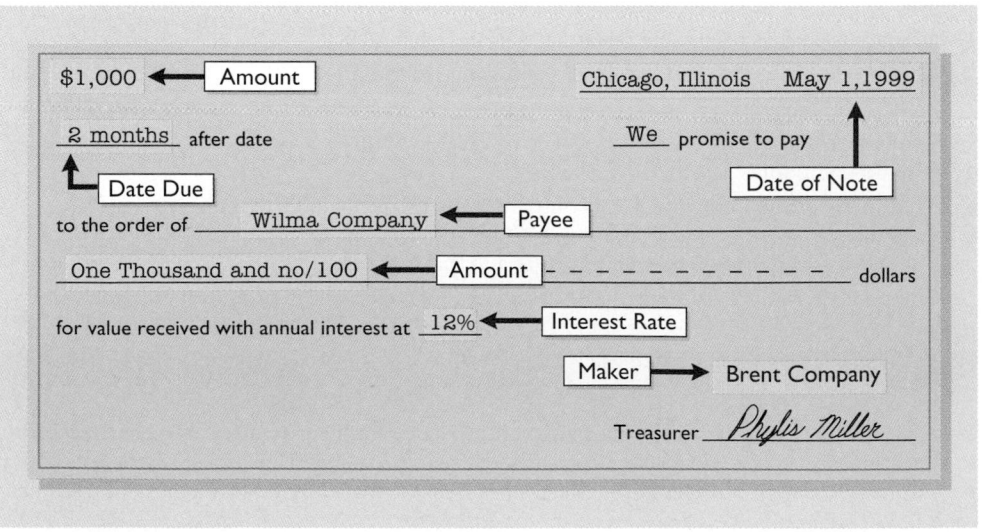

Notes receivable are frequently accepted from customers who need to extend the payment of an outstanding account receivable and are often required from high-risk customers. In some industries (e.g., the pleasure and sport boat industry) all credit sales are supported by notes. The majority of notes, however, originate from lending transactions. The basic issues in accounting for notes receivable are the same as those for accounts receivable.

1. **Recognizing** notes receivable.
2. **Valuing** notes receivable.
3. **Disposing of** notes receivable.

On the following pages, we will look at each of these issues. Before we do, though, we need to consider two issues that did not apply to accounts receivable: the maturity date and the computation of interest.

## Determining the Maturity Date

When the life of a note is expressed in terms of months, the due date is found by counting the months from the date of issue. For example, the maturity date of a 3-month note dated May 1 is August 1. A note drawn on the last day of a month matures on the last day of a subsequent month; that is, a July 31 note due in 2 months matures on September 30. When the due date is stated in terms of days, it is necessary to count the exact number of days to determine the maturity date. In counting, **the date the note is issued is omitted but the due date is included.** For example, the maturity date of a 60-day note dated July 17 is September 15, computed as follows:

**5**
STUDY
OBJECTIVE
..................................................
Compute the maturity date of, and interest on, notes receivable.

| | | |
|---|---|---|
| Term of note | | 60 |
| July (31 – 17) | 14 | |
| August | 31 | 45 |
| **Maturity date, September** | | 15 |

**ILLUSTRATION 8-10**

*Computation of maturity date*

The due date (maturity date) of a promissory note may be stated in one of three ways, as shown in Illustration 8-11.

**ILLUSTRATION 8-11**

*Maturity date of different notes*

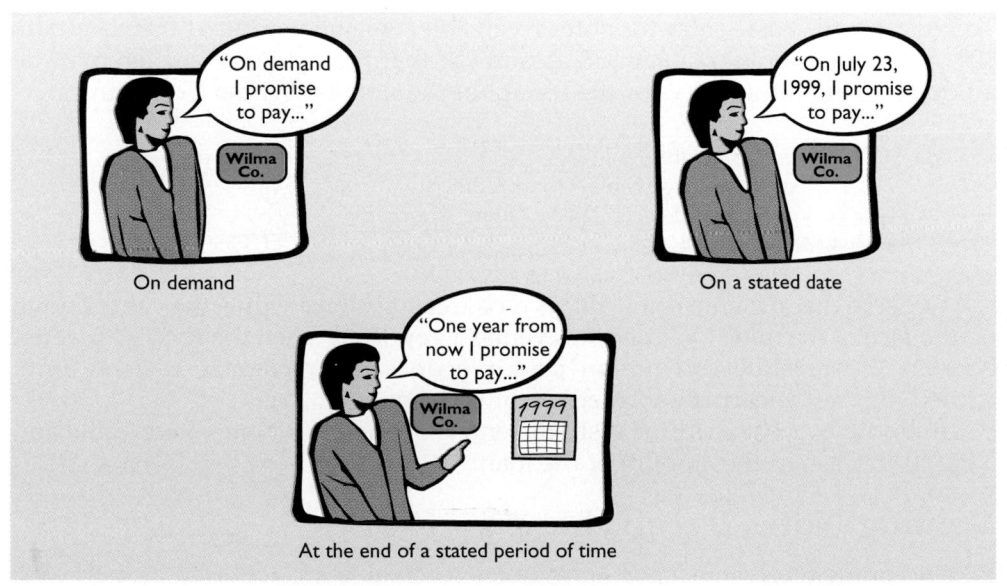

On demand

On a stated date

At the end of a stated period of time

## Computing Interest

As indicated in Chapter 3, the basic formula for computing interest on an interest-bearing note is:

ILLUSTRATION 8-12

*Formula for computing interest*

HELPFUL HINT

The interest rate specified is the *annual* rate.

The interest rate specified on the note is an **annual** rate of interest. The time factor in the computation above expresses the fraction of a year that the note is outstanding. When the maturity date is stated in days, the time factor is frequently the number of days divided by 360. When the due date is stated in months, the time factor is the number of months divided by 12. The computation of interest is shown in Illustration 8-13.

ILLUSTRATION 8-13

*Computation of interest*

| Terms of Note | Interest Computation |
| --- | --- |
| | Face × Rate × Time = Interest |
| $ 730, 18%, 120 days | $ 730 × 18% × 120/360 = $ 43.80 |
| $1,000, 15%, 6 months | $1,000 × 15% × 6/12 = $ 75.00 |
| $2,000, 12%, 1 year | $2,000 × 12% × 1/1 = $240.00 |

There are many different ways to calculate interest. For example, the computation above assumed the total days to be used for the year are 360. Many financial institutions use 365 days to compute interest. It is more profitable, though, to use 360 days because the holder of the note receives more interest than if 365 days are used. For homework problems, assume 360 days.

**6**

STUDY

OBJECTIVE

Explain how notes receivable are recognized in the accounts.

## Recognizing Notes Receivable

To illustrate the basic entry for notes receivable, we will use the $1,000, 2-month, 12% promissory note on page 338. Assuming that the note was written to settle an open account, the entry for the receipt of the note by Wilma Company is:

A   =   L   +   OE
+1,000
−1,000

| May 1 | Notes Receivable | 1,000 | |
| | Accounts Receivable—Brent Company | | 1,000 |
| | (To record acceptance of Brent Company note) | | |

Observe that the note receivable is recorded at its **face value**, the value shown on the face of the note. No interest revenue is reported when the note is accepted because the revenue recognition principle does not recognize revenue until earned. Interest is earned (accrued) as time passes.

If a note is exchanged for cash, the entry is a debit to Notes Receivable and a credit to Cash in the amount of the loan.

## Valuing Notes Receivable

Like accounts receivable, short-term notes receivable are reported at their **cash (net) realizable value**. The notes receivable allowance account is Allowance for

Doubtful Accounts. Valuing short-term notes receivable is the same as valuing accounts receivable. The computations and estimations involved in determining cash realizable value and in recording the proper amount of bad debt expense and related allowance are similar.

Long-term notes receivable, however, pose additional estimation problems. As an example, we need only look at the problems a number of large U.S. banks are having in collecting their receivables. Loans to less-developed countries are particularly worrisome. Developing countries need loans for development but often find repayment difficult. U.S. loans (notes) to less-developed countries at one time totaled approximately $135 billion. In Brazil alone, Citibank at one time had loans equivalent to 80% of its stockholders' equity; Chemical Bank had 77% of its equity lent out in Mexico. Determining the proper allowance is understandably difficult for these types of long-term receivables.

**7**
STUDY
OBJECTIVE
..............................
Describe how notes
receivable are valued.

## ACCOUNTING IN ACTION

### International Insight

Varied plans have been proposed to solve the international debt problem. These plans range from encouraging more lending to reducing or forgiving the debt. At one time, this debt burden to banks worldwide exceeded $1.3 trillion. (As an aside, a trillion is a lot of money—enough money to give every man, woman, and child in the world approximately $250 each.) Why were these loans made in the first place? The reasons are numerous, but the three major ones are: (1) to provide stability to these governments and thereby increase trade, (2) the belief that governments would never default on payment, and (3) the desire by banks to increase their income by lending to these countries.

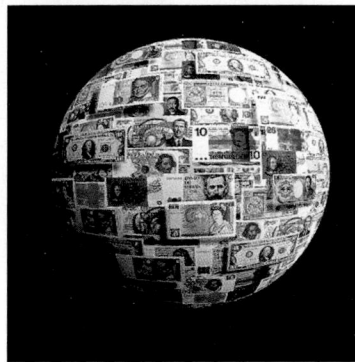

## Disposing of Notes Receivable

Notes may be held to their maturity date, at which time the face value plus accrued interest is due. In some situations, the maker of the note defaults and appropriate adjustment must be made. In other situations, similar to accounts receivable, the holder of the note speeds up the conversion to cash by selling the receivables. The entries for honoring and dishonoring notes are illustrated below.

**8**
STUDY
OBJECTIVE
..............................
Describe the entries to
record the disposition of
notes receivable.

### Honor of Notes Receivable

A note is **honored** when it is paid in full at its maturity date. For each interest-bearing note, the amount due at maturity is the face value of the note plus interest for the length of time specified on the note.

To illustrate, assume that Betty Co. lends Wayne Higley Inc. $10,000 on June 1, accepting a 4-month, 9% interest note. In this situation, interest is $300 ($10,000 × 9% × 4/12); the amount due, the maturity value, is $10,300. To obtain payment, Betty Co. (the payee) must present the note either to Wayne Higley Inc. (the maker) or to the maker's duly appointed agent, such as a bank. Assuming that Betty Co. presents the note to Wayne Higley Inc. on October 1, the maturity date, the entry by Betty Co. to record the collection is:

| Oct. 1 | Cash | 10,300 | |
|---|---|---|---|
| | Notes Receivable | | 10,000 |
| | Interest Revenue | | 300 |
| | (To record collection of Higley Inc. note) | | |

| A | = | L | + | OE |
|---|---|---|---|---|
| + 10,300 | | | | + 300 |
| − 10,000 | | | | |

If Betty Co. prepares financial statements as of September 30, it would be necessary to accrue interest. In this case, the adjusting entry by Betty Co. would be for 4 months, or $300, as shown at the top of the next page.

| A | = | L | + | OE |
|---|---|---|---|---|
| +300 | | | | +300 |

| Sept. 30 | Interest Receivable | 300 | |
| | Interest Revenue | | 300 |
| | (To accrue 4 months' interest) | | |

When interest has been accrued, it is necessary to credit Interest Receivable at maturity. The entry by Betty Co. to record the honoring of the Wayne Higley Inc. note on October 1 is:

| A | = | L | + | OE |
|---|---|---|---|---|
| +10,300 | | | | |
| −10,000 | | | | |
| −300 | | | | |

| Oct. 1 | Cash | 10,300 | |
| | Notes Receivable | | 10,000 |
| | Interest Receivable | | 300 |
| | (To record collection of note at maturity) | | |

In this case, Interest Receivable is credited because the receivable was established in the adjusting entry.

## Dishonor of Notes Receivable

A **dishonored note** is a note that is not paid in full at maturity. A dishonored note receivable is no longer negotiable. However, the payee still has a claim against the maker of the note. Therefore the Notes Receivable account is usually transferred to an Account Receivable.

To illustrate, assume that Wayne Higley Inc. on October 1 indicates that it cannot pay at the present time. The entry to record the dishonor of the note depends on whether eventual collection is expected. If Betty Co. expects eventual collection, the amount due (face value and interest) on the note is debited to Accounts Receivable. Betty Co. would make the following entry at the time the note is dishonored (assuming no previous accrual of interest):

| A | = | L | + | OE |
|---|---|---|---|---|
| +10,300 | | | | +300 |
| −10,000 | | | | |

| Oct. 1 | Accounts Receivable | 10,300 | |
| | Notes Receivable | | 10,000 |
| | Interest Revenue | | 300 |
| | (To record the dishonor of the note) | | |

If there is no hope of collection, the face value of the note should be written off by debiting the Allowance for Doubtful Accounts. No interest revenue would be recorded because collection will not occur.

## Sale of Notes Receivable

The accounting for the sales of notes receivable is recorded in a manner similar to the sale of accounts receivable. The accounting entries for the sale of notes receivable are left for a more advanced course.

# BEFORE YOU GO ON . . .

## Review It

1. What is the basic formula for computing interest?
2. At what value are notes receivable reported on the balance sheet?
3. Explain the difference between honoring and dishonoring a note receivable.

## Do It

Gambit Stores accepts from Leonard Co. a $3,400, 90-day, 12% note dated May 10 in settlement of Leonard's overdue open account. What is the maturity date of the note? What is the entry made by Gambit at the maturity date, assuming Leonard pays the note and interest in full at that time?

*Reasoning:* When the due date is stated in terms of days, it is necessary to count the exact number of days to determine the maturity date. In counting, the date the note is issued is omitted, but the due date is included. The entry to record interest at maturity in this solution assumes that no interest is accrued on this note.

*Solution:* The maturity date is August 8, computed as follows:

| | | |
|---|---|---|
| Term of note: | | 90 days |
| May (31 − 10) | 21 | |
| June | 30 | |
| July | 31 | 82 |
| Maturity date, August | | 8 |

The interest payable at maturity date is $102, computed as follows:

$$\text{Face} \times \text{Rate} \times \text{Time} = \text{Interest}$$
$$\$3,400 \times 12\% \times 90/360 = \$102$$

The entry recorded by Gambit Stores at the maturity date is:

| | | |
|---|---|---|
| Cash | 3,502 | |
|    Notes Receivable | | 3,400 |
|    Interest Revenue | | 102 |
|    (To record collection of Leonard note) | | |

*Related exercise material:* BE8–8, BE8–10, E8–8, and E8–9.

## ACCOUNTING IN ACTION
### Business Insight

Give the man credit. Like most of us, John Galbreath receives piles of unsolicited, "preapproved" credit card applications in the mail. Galbreath doesn't just toss them out, though. In April he filled out a credit card application on which he stated he was 97 years old and had no income, no telephone, and no Social Security number. In a space inviting him to let the credit card company pay off his other credit card balances, Galbreath said he owed money to the Mafia.

Back came a credit card and a letter welcoming John to the fold with a $1,500 credit limit. Galbreath had requested the card under a false name, John C. Reath, an alias under which he had received two other credit cards—earning exemplary credit. John C. Reath might be a bit "long in the tooth," but it seems he paid his bills on time.

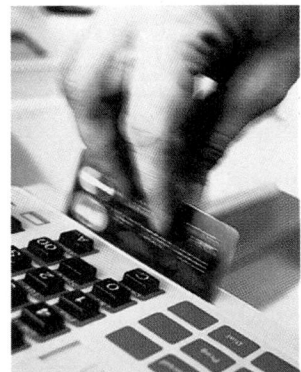

Source: "Forbes Informer," edited by Kate Bohner Lewis, *Forbes*, August 14, 1995, p. 19. Reprinted by permission of FORBES Magazine © Forbes Inc., 1995

# STATEMENT PRESENTATION AND ANALYSIS

## Presentation

Each of the major types of receivables should be identified in the balance sheet or in the notes to the financial statements. Short-term receivables are reported within the current asset section of the balance sheet below temporary investments. Temporary investments appear before short-term receivables, because these investments are more liquid, or nearer to cash. Both the gross amount of receivables and the allowance for doubtful accounts should be reported. Illus-

**9**
STUDY
OBJECTIVE

Explain the statement presentation and analysis of receivables.

tration 8-14 shows the current asset presentation of receivables for Kellogg Company, at December 31, 1997.

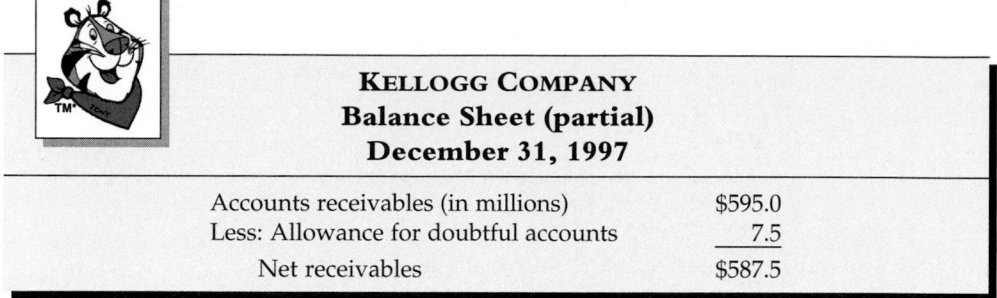

**KELLOGG COMPANY**
**Balance Sheet (partial)**
**December 31, 1997**

| | |
|---|---|
| Accounts receivables (in millions) | $595.0 |
| Less: Allowance for doubtful accounts | 7.5 |
| Net receivables | $587.5 |

In a multiple-step income statement, Bad Debts Expense and Service Charge Expense are reported as selling expenses in the Operating Expenses section. Interest Revenue is shown under Other Revenues and Gains in the nonoperating section of the income statement.

## Analysis

Financial ratios are frequently computed to evaluate the liquidity of a company's accounts receivable. The ratio used to assess the liquidity of the receivables is the accounts receivables turnover ratio. This ratio measures the number of times, on average, accounts receivable are collected during the period. The accounts receivable turnover ratio is computed by dividing net credit sales (net sales less cash sales) by the average net accounts receivable during the year. Unless seasonal factors are significant, average net accounts receivable outstanding can be computed from the beginning and ending balance of the net accounts receivable.

For example, in 1997 Kellogg had net sales of $6,830.1 million for the year and a beginning net accounts receivable balance of $592.3 million. Assuming that Kellogg's sales were all on credit, its accounts receivable turnover ratio is computed as follows:

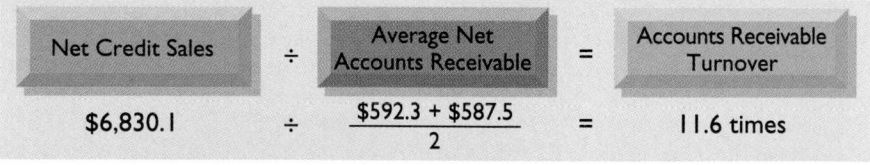

| Net Credit Sales | ÷ | Average Net Accounts Receivable | = | Accounts Receivable Turnover |
|---|---|---|---|---|
| $6,830.1 | ÷ | $\dfrac{\$592.3 + \$587.5}{2}$ | = | 11.6 times |

The result indicates an accounts receivable turnover ratio of 11.6 times per year. The higher the turnover ratio the more liquid the company's receivables.

Another variant of the accounts receivable turnover ratio that makes the liquidity even more evident is the conversion of it into an average collection period in terms of days. This is done by dividing the turnover ratio into 365 days. For example, Kellogg's turnover of 11.6 times is divided into 365 days, as follows, to obtain approximately 31.5 days:

| Days in Year | ÷ | Accounts Receivable Turnover | = | Average Collection Period in Days |
|---|---|---|---|---|
| 365 days | ÷ | 11.6 times | = | 31.5 days |

This means that Kellogg's average collection period for accounts receivable is 31.5 days. The average collection period is frequently used to assess the effectiveness of a company's credit and collection policies. The general rule is that the collection period should not greatly exceed the credit term period (i.e., the time allowed for payment).

# BEFORE YOU GO ON . . .

## Review It

1. Explain where accounts and notes receivable are reported on the balance sheet.
2. Where are bad debts expense, service charge expense, and interest revenue reported on the multiple-step income statement?

## A LOOK BACK AT OUR FEATURE STORY

Refer back to the story about the North Carolina State University newspaper at the beginning of the chapter, and answer the following questions:

1. If you had sold advertising space to a tardy paying client, how would you persuade them to pay?
2. At what point would you recommend that the newspaper write off uncollectible receivables?
3. Indicate the accounts to be debited and credited for each of the following transactions of the newspaper: (a) ad space is sold on account; (b) ad space is sold and prepaid; (c) cash is collected on account; (d) the ad is run for the advertiser who prepaid; (e) an uncollectible account is written off.

*Solution:*

1. The collection process used by the newspaper: a friendly letter at the end of 30 days, a less-than-friendly letter at the end of 45 days, and the filing of a suit in small claims court at the end of 75 days. In addition, a tactful, persuasive telephone call might be added to the attempts to collect.
2. An unpaid receivable should be written off when it is determined that it is uncollectible. Past experience with small unpaid ad bills will usually dictate the appropriate point at which bills are deemed uncollectible. With the limited information given in this case, the write-off would seem proper at the conclusion of an unsuccessful court claim.
3. (a) Debit Accounts Receivable, credit Advertising Revenue.
   (b) Debit Cash, credit Unearned Advertising Revenue.
   (c) Debit Cash, credit Accounts Receivable.
   (d) Debit Unearned Advertising Revenue, credit Advertising Revenue.
   (e) Debit Allowance for Doubtful Accounts, credit Accounts Receivable.

THE
NAVIGATOR

# DEMONSTRATION PROBLEM

Presented below are selected transactions related to Falcetto Company.

Mar.  1  Sold $20,000 of merchandise to Potter Company, terms 2/10, n/30.

     11  Received payment in full from Potter Company for balance due.

     12  Accepted Juno Company's $20,000 6-month, 12% note for balance due.

     13  Made Falcetto Company credit card sales for $13,200.

     15  Made American Express credit sales totaling $6,700. A 5% service fee is charged by American Express.

     30  Received payment in full from American Express Company less the 5% service charge.

Apr. 11    Sold accounts receivable of $8,000 to Harcot Factor. Harcot Factor assesses a service charge of 2% of the amount of receivables sold.

13    Received collections of $8,200 on Falcetto Company credit card sales and added finance charges of 1.5% to the remaining balances.

May 10    Wrote off as uncollectible $16,000 of accounts receivable. Falcetto uses the percentage of sales basis to estimate bad debts.

June 30    Credit sales for the first six months total $2,000,000 and the bad debt percentage is 1% of credit sales. At June 30, the balance in the allowance account is $3,500.

July 16    One of the accounts receivable written off in May pays the amount due, $4,000, in full.

*Instructions*

Prepare the journal entries for the transactions.

## SOLUTION TO DEMONSTRATION PROBLEM

**PROBLEM-SOLVING STRATEGIES**

1. Accounts receivable are generally recorded at invoice price.
2. Sales returns and allowances and cash discounts reduce the amount received on accounts receivable.
3. When accounts receivable are sold, a service charge expense is incurred by the seller.
4. Bad debts expense is an adjusting entry.
5. Percentage of sales basis ignores any balance in the allowance account. Percentage of receivables basis does not ignore this balance.
6. Write-offs of accounts receivable affect only balance sheet accounts.

| Date | Account | Debit | Credit |
|---|---|---|---|
| Mar. 1 | Accounts Receivable—Potter | 20,000 | |
| |     Sales | | 20,000 |
| |       (To record sales on account) | | |
| Mar. 11 | Cash | 19,600 | |
| | Sales Discounts (2% × $20,000) | 400 | |
| |     Accounts Receivable—Potter | | 20,000 |
| |       (To record collection of accounts receivable) | | |
| Mar. 12 | Notes Receivable | 20,000 | |
| |     Accounts Receivable—Juno | | 20,000 |
| |       (To record acceptance of Juno Company note) | | |
| Mar. 13 | Accounts Receivable | 13,200 | |
| |     Sales | | 13,200 |
| |       (To record company credit card sales) | | |
| Mar. 15 | Accounts Receivable—American Express | 6,365 | |
| | Service Charge Expense (5% × $6,700) | 335 | |
| |     Sales | | 6,700 |
| |       (To record credit card sales) | | |
| Mar. 30 | Cash | 6,365 | |
| |     Accounts Receivable—American Express | | 6,365 |
| |       (To record redemption of credit card billings) | | |
| Apr. 11 | Cash | 7,840 | |
| | Service Charge Expense (2% × $8,000) | 160 | |
| |     Accounts Receivable | | 8,000 |
| |       (To record sale of receivables to factor) | | |
| Apr. 13 | Cash | 8,200 | |
| |     Accounts Receivable | | 8,200 |
| |       (To record collection of accounts receivable) | | |
| | Accounts Receivable [($13,200 − $8,200) × 1.5%] | 75 | |
| |     Interest Revenue | | 75 |
| |       (To record interest on amount due) | | |

| May 10 | Allowance for Doubtful Accounts | 16,000 | |
| |     Accounts Receivable | | 16,000 |
| |     (To record write-off of accounts receivable) | | |
| June 30 | Bad Debts Expense ($2,000,000 × 1%) | 20,000 | |
| |     Allowance for Doubtful Accounts | | 20,000 |
| |     (To record estimate of uncollectible accounts) | | |
| July 16 | Accounts Receivable | 4,000 | |
| |     Allowance for Doubtful Accounts | | 4,000 |
| |     (To reverse write-off of accounts receivable) | | |
| | Cash | 4,000 | |
| |     Accounts Receivable | | 4,000 |
| |     (To record collection of accounts receivable) | | |

THE NAVIGATOR

# SUMMARY OF STUDY OBJECTIVES

**1. Identify the different types of receivables.** Receivables are frequently classified as (1) accounts, (2) notes, and (3) other. Accounts receivable are amounts owed by customers on account. Notes receivable represent claims that are evidenced by formal instruments of credit. Other receivables include nontrade receivables such as interest receivable, loans to company officers, advances to employees, and income taxes refundable.

**2. Explain how accounts receivable are recognized in the accounts.** Accounts receivable are recorded at invoice price. They are reduced by Sales Returns and Allowances. Cash discounts reduce the amount received on accounts receivable. When interest is charged on a past due receivable, this interest is added to the accounts receivable balance and is recognized as interest revenue.

**3. Distinguish between the methods and bases used to value accounts receivable.** There are two methods of accounting for uncollectible accounts: (1) the allowance method and (2) the direct write-off method. Either the percentage of sales or the percentage of receivables basis may be used to estimate uncollectible accounts using the allowance method. The percentage of sales basis emphasizes the matching principle. The percentage of receivables basis emphasizes the cash realizable value of the accounts receivable. An aging schedule is frequently used with this basis.

**4. Describe the entries to record the disposition of accounts receivable.** When an account receivable is collected, Accounts Receivable is credited. When an account receivable is sold, a service charge expense is charged which reduces the amount collected.

**5. Compute the maturity date of, and interest on, notes receivable.** The maturity date of a note must be computed unless the due date is specified or the note is payable on demand. For a note stated in months, the maturity date is found by counting the months from the date of issue. For a note stated in days, the number of days is counted, omitting the issue date and counting the due date. The formula for computing interest is face value × interest rate × time.

**6. Explain how notes receivable are recognized in the accounts.** Notes receivable are recorded at face value. In some cases, it is necessary to accrue interest prior to maturity. In this case, Interest Receivable is debited and Interest Revenue is credited.

**7. Describe how notes receivable are valued.** Like accounts receivable, notes receivable are reported at their cash (net) realizable value. The notes receivable allowance account is the Allowance for Doubtful Accounts. The computation and estimations involved in valuing notes receivables at cash realizable value, and in recording the proper amount of bad debt expense and related allowance are similar to accounts receivable.

**8. Describe the entries to record the disposition of notes receivable.** Notes can be held to maturity, at which time the face value plus accrued interest is due and the note is removed from the accounts. However, in many cases, similar to accounts receivable, the holder of the note speeds up the conversion by selling the receivable to another party. In some situations, the maker of the note dishonors the note (defaults), and the note is written off.

**9. Explain the statement presentation and analysis of receivables.** Each major type of receivable should be identified in the balance sheet or in the notes to the financial statements. Short-term receivables are considered current assets. The gross amount of receivables and allowance for doubtful accounts should be reported. Bad debts and service charge expenses are reported in the multiple-step income statement as operating (selling) expenses, and interest revenue is shown as other revenues and gains in the nonoperating section of the statement. Accounts receivables may be evaluated for liquidity by computing a turnover ratio and an average collection period.

THE NAVIGATOR

# GLOSSARY

**Accounts receivable turnover ratio**   A measure of the liquidity of accounts receivable, computed by dividing net credit sales by average net accounts receivable. (p. 344).

**Aging of accounts receivable**   The analysis of customer balances by the length of time they have been unpaid. (p. 332).

**Average collection period**   The average amount of time that a receivable is outstanding, calculated by dividing 365 days by the receivables turnover ratio. (p. 344).

**Cash (net) realizable value**   The net amount expected to be received in cash. (p. 328).

**Dishonored note**   A note that is not paid in full at maturity. (p. 342).

**Factor**   A finance company or bank that buys receivables from businesses for a fee and then collects the payments directly from the customers. (p. 335).

**Maker**   The party in a promissory note who is making the promise to pay. (p. 338).

**Payee**   The party to whom payment of a promissory note is to be made. (p. 338).

**Percentage of receivables basis**   Management establishes a percentage relationship between the amount of receivables and the expected losses from uncollectible accounts. (p. 332).

**Percentage of sales basis**   Management establishes a percentage relationship between the amount of credit sales and expected losses from uncollectible accounts. (p. 331).

**Promissory note**   A written promise to pay a specified amount of money on demand or at a definite time. (p. 338).

**Trade receivables**   Notes and accounts receivable that result from sales transactions. (p. 326).

# SELF-STUDY QUESTIONS

Answers are at the end of the chapter.

(SO 2)  1. Remmers Company on June 15 sells merchandise on account to Tucci Co. for $1,000 terms 2/10, n/30. On June 20, Tucci Co. returns merchandise worth $300 to Remmers Company. On June 24, payment is received from Tucci Co. for the balance due. What is the amount of cash received?
   a. $700.
   b. $680.
   c. $686.
   d. None of the above.

(SO 3)  2. Which of the following approaches for bad debts is best described as a balance sheet method?
   a. Percentage of receivables basis.
   b. Direct write-off method.
   c. Percentage of sales basis.
   d. Both a and b.

(SO 3)  3. Net sales for the month are $800,000 and bad debts are expected to be 1.5% of net sales. The company uses the percentage of sales basis. If the Allowance for Doubtful Accounts has a credit balance of $15,000 before adjustment, what is the balance after adjustment?
   a. $15,000.
   b. $27,000.
   c. $23,000.
   d. $31,000.

(SO 3)  4. In 1999, Roland Carlson Company had net credit sales of $750,000. On January 1, 1999, Allowance for Doubtful Accounts had a credit balance of $18,000. During 1999, $30,000 of uncollectible accounts receivable were written off. Past experience indicates that 3% of net credit

sales become uncollectible. What should be the adjusted balance of Allowance for Doubtful Accounts at December 31, 1999?
   a. $10,050.
   b. $10,500.
   c. $22,500.
   d. $40,500.

(SO 3)  5. An analysis and aging of the accounts receivable of Machiavelli Company at December 31 reveals the following data:

| | |
|---|---|
| Accounts Receivable | $800,000 |
| Allowance for Doubtful Accounts per books before adjustment | 50,000 |
| Amounts expected to become uncollectible | 65,000 |

The cash realizable value of the accounts receivable at December 31, after adjustment, is:
   a. $685,000.
   b. $750,000.
   c. $800,000.
   d. $735,000.

(SO 6)  6. One of the following statements about promissory notes is incorrect. The *incorrect* statement is:
   a. The party making the promise to pay is called the maker.
   b. The party to whom payment is to be made is called the payee.
   c. A promissory note is not a negotiable instrument.
   d. A promissory note is more liquid than an accounts receivable.

(SO 4)    7. Which of the following statements about VISA credit card sales is *incorrect*?
   a. The credit card issuer makes the credit investigation of the customer.
   b. The retailer is not involved in the collection process.
   c. Two parties are involved.
   d. The retailer receives cash more quickly than it would from individual customers on account.

(SO 4)    8. Morgan Retailers accepted $50,000 of Citibank VISA credit card charges for merchandise sold on July 1. Citibank charges 4% for its credit card use. The entry to record this transaction by Morgan Retailers will include a credit to Sales of $50,000 and a debit(s) to:

|   |   |   |
|---|---|---|
| a. | Cash | $48,000 |
|    | and Service Charge Expense | $2,000 |
| b. | Accounts Receivable | $48,000 |
|    | and Service Charge Expense | $2,000 |
| c. | Cash | $50,000 |
| d. | Accounts Receivable | $50,000 |

(SO 6)    9. Bickner Co. accepts a $1,000, 3-month, 12% promissory note in settlement of an account with Streisand Co. The entry to record this transaction is as follows:

|   |   |   |   |
|---|---|---|---|
| a. | Notes Receivable | 1,030 | |
|    | Accounts Receivable | | 1,030 |
| b. | Notes Receivable | 1,000 | |
|    | Accounts Receivable | | 1,000 |
| c. | Notes Receivable | 1,000 | |
|    | Sales | | 1,000 |
| d. | Notes Receivable | 1,020 | |
|    | Accounts Receivable | | 1,020 |

(SO 8)    10. Schlicht Co. holds Osgrove Inc.'s $10,000, 120-day, 9% note. The entry made by Schlicht Co. when the note is collected, assuming no interest has been accrued, is

|   |   |   |   |
|---|---|---|---|
| a. | Cash | 10,300 | |
|    | Notes Receivable | | 10,300 |
| b. | Cash | 10,000 | |
|    | Notes Receivable | | 10,000 |
| c. | Accounts Receivable | 10,300 | |
|    | Notes Receivable | | 10,000 |
|    | Interest Revenue | | 300 |
| d. | Cash | 10,300 | |
|    | Notes Receivable | | 10,000 |
|    | Interest Revenue | | 300 |

THE NAVIGATOR

# QUESTIONS

1. What is the difference between an account receivable and a note receivable?

2. What are some common types of receivables other than accounts receivable or notes receivable?

3. Texaco Oil Company issues its own credit cards. Assume that Texaco charges you $40 on an unpaid balance. Prepare the journal entry that Texaco makes to record this revenue.

4. What are the essential features of the allowance method of accounting for bad debts?

5. Dorothy Fleming cannot understand why cash realizable value does not decrease when an uncollectible account is written off under the allowance method. Clarify this point for Dorothy Fleming.

6. Distinguish between the two bases that may be used in estimating uncollectible accounts.

7. Kosinsky Company has a credit balance of $3,500 in Allowance for Doubtful Accounts. The estimated bad debts expense under the percentage of sales basis is $4,100, and the total estimated uncollectibles under the percentage of receivables basis is $5,800. Prepare the adjusting entry under each basis.

8. How are bad debts accounted for under the direct write-off method? What are the disadvantages of this method?

9. Elbe Company accepts both its own credit cards and national credit cards. What are the advantages of accepting both types of cards?

10. An article recently appeared in *The Wall Street Journal* indicating that companies are selling their receivables at a record rate. Why are companies selling their receivables?

11. Southern Textiles decides to sell $800,000 of its accounts receivable to First Central Factors Inc. First Central Factors assesses a service charge of 2% of the amount of receivables sold. Prepare the journal entry that Southern Textiles makes to record this sale.

12. Your roommate is uncertain about the advantages of a promissory note. Compare the advantages of a note receivable with those of an accounts receivable.

13. How may the maturity date of a promissory note be stated?

14. Indicate the maturity date of each of the following promissory notes:

| Date of Note | Terms |
|---|---|
| (a) March 13 | one year after date of note |
| (b) May 4 | 3 months after date |
| (c) June 20 | 30 days after date |
| (d) July 1 | 60 days after date |

15. Compute the missing amounts for each of the following notes:

|  | Principal | Annual Interest Rate | Time | Total Interest |
| --- | --- | --- | --- | --- |
| (a) | ? | 9% | 120 days | $   450 |
| (b) | $30,000 | 10% | 3 years | ? |
| (c) | $60,000 | ? | 5 months | $3,000 |
| (d) | $50,000 | 11% | ? | $1,375 |

16. In determining interest revenue, some financial institutions use 365 days per year whereas others use 360 days. Why might a financial institution use 360 days?

17. Nick Coffin Company dishonors a note at maturity. What actions by Coffin may occur with the dishonoring of the note?

18. Paula Company has accounts receivable and notes receivable. How should the receivables be reported on the balance sheet?

19. If the accounts receivables turnover ratio is 7.15 and average net receivables during the period are $210,000, what is the amount of net credit sales for the period?

# BRIEF EXERCISES

*Identify different types of receivables.*
*(SO 1)*

**BE8–1**   Presented below are three receivable transactions. Indicate whether these receivables are reported as accounts receivable, notes receivable, or other receivables on a balance sheet.

1. Sold merchandise on account for $60,000 to a customer.
2. Received a promissory note of $57,000 for services performed.
3. Advanced $10,000 to an employee.

*Record basic accounts receivable transactions.*
*(SO 2)*

**BE8–2**   Record the following transactions on the books of Jose Co.

1. On July 1, Jose Co. sold merchandise on account to Cambridge Inc. for $15,000, terms 2/10, n/30.
2. On July 8, Cambridge Inc. returned merchandise worth $3,800 to Jose Co.
3. On July 11, Cambridge Inc. paid for the merchandise.

*Prepare entries for allowance method and classifications.*
*(SO 3, 9)*

**BE8–3**   During its first year of operations, Alvarado Company had credit sales of $3,000,000, of which $600,000 remained uncollected at year-end. The credit manager estimates that $30,000 of these receivables will become uncollectible. (a) Prepare the journal entry to record the estimated uncollectibles. (b) Prepare the current asset section of the balance sheet for Alvarado Company, assuming that in addition to the receivables it has cash of $90,000, merchandise inventory of $130,000, and prepaid expenses of $13,000.

*Prepare entries for write-off and determine cash realizable value.*
*(SO 3)*

**BE8–4**   At the end of 1999, Delacruz Co. has accounts receivable of $700,000 and an allowance for doubtful accounts of $54,000. On January 24, 2000, it is learned that the company's receivable from Hutley Inc. is not collectible and therefore management authorizes a write-off of $6,000. (a) Prepare the journal entry to record the write-off. (b) What is the cash realizable value of the accounts receivable (1) before the write-off and (2) after the write-off?

*Prepare entries for collection of bad debt write-off.*
*(SO 3)*

**BE8–5**   Assume the same information as BE8–4 and that on March 4, 2000, Delacruz Co. receives payment of $6,000 in full from Hutley Inc. Prepare the journal entries to record this transaction.

*Prepare entry using percentage of sales method.*
*(SO 3)*

**BE8–6**   Einhause Co. elects to use the percentage of sales basis in 1999 to record bad debts expense and concludes that 2% of net credit sales will become uncollectible. Sales are $800,000 for 1999, sales returns and allowances are $50,000, and the allowance for doubtful accounts has a credit balance of $12,000. Prepare the adjusting entry to record bad debts expense in 1999.

*Prepare entry using percentage of receivables method.*
*(SO 3)*

**BE8–7**   Grolesky Co. uses the percentage of accounts receivable basis to record bad debt expense, and concludes that 1% of accounts receivable will become uncollectible. Accounts receivable are $400,000 at the end of the year, and the allowance for doubtful accounts has a credit balance of $3,000. (a) Prepare the adjusting journal entry to record bad debt expense for the year. (b) If the allowance for doubtful accounts had a debit balance of $800 instead of credit balance of $3,000, determine the amount to be reported for bad debt expense.

**BE8–8** Presented below are three promissory notes. Determine the missing amounts.

*Compute maturity date and interest on note.*
*(SO 5)*

| Date of Note | Terms | Maturity Date | Principal | Annual Interest Rate | Total Interest |
|---|---|---|---|---|---|
| (a) April 1 | 60 days | ? | $900,000 | 9% | ? |
| (b) July 2 | 30 days | ? | 90,000 | ? | $600 |
| (c) March 7 | 6 months | ? | 60,000 | 12% | ? |

**BE8–9** Presented below are the following transactions.

*Prepare entries to dispose of accounts receivable.*
*(SO 4)*

1. Castle Restaurant accepted a Visa card in payment of a $100 lunch bill. The bank charges a 3% fee. What entry should Castle make?
2. Mayfield Company sold its accounts receivable of $80,000. What entry should Mayfield make, given a service charge of 3% on the amount of receivables sold?

**BE8–10** On January 10, 1999, Raja Co. sold merchandise on account to Dewey Yeager for $9,000, n/30. On February 9, Dewey Yeager gave Raja Co. a 10% promissory note in settlement of this account. Prepare the journal entry to record the sale and the settlement of the accounts receivable.

*Prepare entry for notes receivable exchanged for account receivable.*
*(SO 6)*

**BE8–11** The financial statements of Minnesota Mining and Manufacturing Company (3M) report net sales of $9.4 billion. Accounts receivable are $1.6 billion at the beginning of the year and $1.4 billion at the end of the year. Compute 3M's receivable's turnover ratio. Compute 3M's average collection period for accounts receivable in days.

*Compute ratios to analyze receivables.*
*(SO 9)*

# EXERCISES

**E8–1** Presented below are two independent situations that occurred during the year.

*Journalize entries for recognizing accounts receivable.*
*(SO 2)*

1. On January 6, Herzog Co. sells merchandise on account to Watson Inc. for $3,000, terms 2/10, n/30. On January 16, Watson pays the amount due. Prepare the entries on Herzog's books to record the sale and related collection.
2. On January 10, Diane Leto uses her Salizar Co. credit card to purchase merchandise from Salizar Co. for $11,000. On February 10, Leto is billed for the amount due of $11,000. On February 12, Leto pays $6,000 on the balance due. On March 10, Leto is billed for the amount due, including interest at 2% per month on the unpaid balance as of February 12. Prepare the entries on Salizar Co.'s books related to the transactions that occurred on January 10, February 12, and March 10.

**E8–2** The ledger of the Kadlec Company at the end of the current year shows Accounts Receivable $90,000, Sales $840,000, and Sales Returns and Allowances $40,000.

*Journalize entries to record allowance for doubtful accounts using two different bases.*
*(SO 3)*

**Instructions**

(a) If Allowance for Doubtful Accounts has a credit balance of $800 in the trial balance, journalize the adjusting entry at December 31, assuming bad debts are expected to be (1) 1% of net sales, and (2) 10% of accounts receivable.

(b) If Allowance for Doubtful Accounts has a debit balance of $500 in the trial balance, journalize the adjusting entry at December 31, assuming bad debts are expected to be (1) .75% of net sales and (2) 8% of accounts receivable.

**E8–3** Garcia Company has accounts receivable of $92,500 at March 31. An analysis of the accounts shows the following:

*Determine bad debts expense and prepare the adjusting entry for bad debts expense.*
*(SO 3)*

| Month of Sale | Balance, March 31 |
|---|---|
| March | $65,000 |
| February | 12,600 |
| December and January | 8,500 |
| November and October | 6,400 |
| | $92,500 |

Credit terms are 2/10, n/30. At March 31, there is a $1,600 credit balance in Allowance for Doubtful Accounts prior to adjustment. The company uses the percentage of receivables basis for estimating uncollectible accounts. The company's estimate of bad debts is as follows:

| Age of Accounts | Estimated Percentage Uncollectible |
|---|---|
| 1–30 days past due | 2.0% |
| 30–60 days past due | 5.0% |
| 60–90 days past due | 30.0% |
| Over 90 days | 50.0% |

### Instructions

(a) Determine the total estimated uncollectibles.

(b) Prepare the adjusting entry at March 31 to record bad debts expense.

*Journalize percentage of sales basis, write-off, recovery.*
*(SO 3)*

**E8–4**  On December 31, 1999, Jana Co. estimates that 2% of its net sales of $400,000 will become uncollectible and records this amount as an addition to Allowance for Doubtful Accounts. On May 11, 2000, Jana Co. determined that Bob Knight's account was uncollectible and wrote off $900. On June 12, 2000, Knight paid the amount previously written off.

### Instructions

Prepare the journal entries on December 31, 1999, May 11, 2000, and June 12, 2000.

*Journalize entries for the sale of accounts receivable.*
*(SO 4)*

**E8–5**  Presented below are two independent situations:

1. On March 3, Dennis Stoia Appliances sells $800,000 of its receivables to Potter Factors Inc. Potter Factors Inc. assesses a finance charge of 3% of the amount of receivables sold. Prepare the entry on Dennis Stoia Appliances' books to record the sale of the receivables.

2. On May 10, Monee Company sold merchandise for $4,000 and accepted the customer's First Business Bank MasterCard. At the end of the day, the First Business Bank MasterCard receipts were deposited in the company's bank account. First Business Bank charges a 4% service charge for credit card sales. Prepare the entry on Monee Company's books to record the sale of merchandise.

*Journalize entries for credit card sales.*
*(SO 4)*

**E8–6**  Presented below are two independent situations that occurred during the year.

1. On April 2, Elaine Stahl uses her J. C. Penney credit card to purchase merchandise from a J. C. Penney store for $1,300. On May 1, Stahl is billed for the $1,300 amount due. Stahl pays $800 on the balance due on May 3. On June 1, Stahl receives a bill for the amount due, including interest at 1.0% per month on the unpaid balance as of May 3. Prepare the entries on J. C. Penney Co.'s books related to the transactions that occurred on April 2, May 3, and June 1.

2. On July 4, Robyn's Restaurant accepts an American Express card for a $300 dinner bill. American Express charges a 4% service fee. On July 10, American Express pays Robyn $288. Prepare the entries on Robyn's books related to the transactions.

*Journalize credit card sales and indicate the statement presentation of financing charges and service charge expense.*
*(SO 4)*

**E8–7**  Sapaniak Stores accepts both its own and national credit cards. During the year the following selected summary transactions occurred.

Jan. 15  Made Sapaniak credit card sales totaling $15,000. (There were no balances prior to 1y15.)

20  Made American Express credit card sales (service charge fee, 5%) totaling $2,600.

30  Received payment in full from American Express less a 5% service charge.

Feb. 10  Collected $12,000 on Sapaniak credit card sales.

15  Added finance charges of 1.5% to Sapaniak credit card balance.

### Instructions

(a) Journalize the transactions for Sapaniak Stores.

(b) Indicate the statement presentation of the financing charges and the credit card service expense for Sapaniak Stores.

*Journalize entries for notes receivable transactions.*
*(SO 5, 6)*

**E8–8**  Marv Tice Supply Co. has the following transactions related to notes receivable during the last 2 months of the year.

Nov. 1   Loaned $18,000 cash to Sheila Skinner on a 1-year, 10% note.

Dec. 11   Sold goods to Lucinda Higdon, Inc., receiving a $3,600, 90-day, 12% note.

   16   Received a $4,000, 6-month, 12% note on account from Deanna Prentice.

   31   Accrued interest revenue on all notes receivable.

**Instructions**
Journalize the transactions for Marv Tice Supply Co.

**E8–9**   Record the following transactions for the Plano Molding Co. in the general journal:

*Journalize entries for notes receivable.*
*(SO 5, 6)*

1999

May 1   Received a $9,000, 1-year, 10% note on account from John Lewis.

Dec. 31   Accrued interest on the Lewis note.

Dec. 31   Closed the interest revenue account.

2000

May 1   Received principal plus interest on the Lewis note. (No interest has been accrued in 2000.)

**E8–10**   On May 2, Cynthia Taylor Company lends $6,000 to Nancy Barnes Inc., issuing a 6-month, 10% note. At the maturity date, November 2, Barnes indicates that it cannot pay.

*Journalize entries for dishonor of notes receivable.*
*(SO 5, 8)*

**Instructions**
(a) Prepare the entry to record the dishonor of the note, assuming that Taylor Company expects collection will occur.
(b) Prepare the entry to record the dishonor of the note, assuming that Taylor Company does not expect collection in the future.

# PROBLEMS: SET A

**P8–1A**   At December 31, 1999, Mike Muzzillo Imports reported the following information on its balance sheet:

*Prepare journal entries related to bad debt expense.*
*(SO 2, 3)*

| | |
|---|---|
| Accounts receivable | $1,000,000 |
| Less: Allowance for doubtful accounts | 60,000 |

During 2000, the company had the following transactions related to receivables.

| | |
|---|---|
| 1. Sales on account | $2,600,000 |
| 2. Sales returns and allowances | 40,000 |
| 3. Collections of accounts receivable | 2,300,000 |
| 4. Write-offs of accounts receivable deemed uncollectible | 65,000 |
| 5. Recovery of bad debts previously written off as uncollectible | 25,000 |

**Instructions**
(a) Prepare the journal entries to record each of these five transactions. Assume that no cash discounts were taken on the collections of accounts receivable.
(b) Enter the January 1, 2000, balances in Accounts Receivable and Allowance for Doubtful Accounts, post the entries to the two accounts (use T accounts), and determine the balances.
(c) Prepare the journal entry to record bad debts expense for 2000, assuming that an aging of accounts receivable indicates that estimated bad debts are $70,000.
(d) Compute the accounts receivable turnover ratio for the year 2000.

**P8–2A**   Information related to Tisinai Company for 1999 is summarized below:

*Compute bad debts amounts.*
*(SO 3)*

| | |
|---|---|
| Total credit sales | $1,500,000 |
| Accounts receivable at December 31 | 600,000 |
| Bad debts written off | 24,000 |

**Instructions**
(a) What amount of bad debts expense will Tisinai Company report if it uses the direct write-off method of accounting for bad debts?

(b) Assume that Tisinai Company decides to estimate its bad debts expense to be 3% of credit sales. What amount of bad debts expense will Tisinai Company record if Allowance for Doubtful Accounts has a credit balance of $3,000?

(c) Assume that Tisinai Company decides to estimate its bad debts expense based on 5% of accounts receivable. What amount of bad debts expense will Tisinai Company record if Allowance for Doubtful Accounts balance has a credit balance of $4,000?

(d) Assume the same facts as in (c), except that there is a $2,000 debit balance in Allowance for Doubtful Accounts. What amount of bad debts expense will Tisinai record?

(e) ▭▭▭▷ What is the weakness of the direct write-off method of reporting bad debts expense?

*Journalize entries to record transactions related to bad debts.*
*(SO 2, 3)*

**P8–3A**    Presented below is an aging schedule for Chris Cain Company.

| Customer | Total | Not Yet Due | Number of Days Past Due | | | |
| --- | --- | --- | --- | --- | --- | --- |
| | | | 1–30 | 31–60 | 61–90 | Over 90 |
| Sandy Freewalt | $ 20,000 | | $ 9,000 | $11,000 | | |
| Joni Schnabel | 30,000 | $ 30,000 | | | | |
| Kay Nelson | 50,000 | 15,000 | 5,000 | | $30,000 | |
| Ken Mason | 38,000 | | | | | $38,000 |
| Others | 120,000 | 92,000 | 15,000 | 13,000 | | |
| | $258,000 | $137,000 | $29,000 | $24,000 | $30,000 | $38,000 |
| Estimated Percentage Uncollectible | | | 3% | 6% | 12% | 24% | 50% |
| Total Estimated Bad Debts | $ 34,930 | $  4,110 | $ 1,740 | $ 2,880 | $ 7,200 | $19,000 |

At December 31, 1999, the unadjusted balance in Allowance for Doubtful Accounts is a credit of $10,000.

*Instructions*

(a) Journalize and post the adjusting entry for bad debts at December 31, 1999.

(b) Journalize and post to the allowance account the following events and transactions in the year 2000:
   (1) March 1, an $800 customer balance originating in 1999 is judged uncollectible.
   (2) May 1, a check for $800 is received from the customer whose account was written off as uncollectible on March 1.

(c) Journalize the adjusting entry for bad debts on December 31, 2000, assuming that the unadjusted balance in Allowance for Doubtful Accounts is a debit of $1,100 and the aging schedule indicates that total estimated bad debts will be $29,100.

*Journalize entries to record transactions related to bad debts.*
*(SO 3)*

**P8–4A**    At December 31, 1999, the trial balance of John Gleason Company contained the following amounts before adjustment:

| | Debits | Credits |
| --- | --- | --- |
| Accounts Receivable | $350,000 | |
| Allowance for Doubtful Accounts | | $  1,500 |
| Sales | | 875,000 |

*Instructions*

(a) Prepare the adjusting entry at December 31, 1999, to record bad debt expense under each of the following independent assumptions:
   (1) An aging schedule indicates that $16,750 of accounts receivable will be uncollectible.
   (2) It is estimated that 2% of sales will be uncollectible.

(b) Repeat part (a) assuming that instead of a credit balance there is a $1,500 debit balance in the Allowance for Doubtful Accounts.

(c) During the next month, January 2000, a $4,500 account receivable is written off as uncollectible. Prepare the journal entry to record the write-off.

(d) Repeat part (c) assuming that John Gleason Company uses the direct write-off method instead of the allowance method in accounting for uncollectible accounts receivable.

(e) ▮▮▭▭▷ What are the advantages of using the allowance method in accounting for uncollectible accounts as compared to the direct write-off method?

**P8–5A** Connie Kolzow Co. closes its books monthly. On June 30, selected ledger account balances are:

*Prepare entries for various note receivable transactions.*
*(SO 2, 4, 5, 8, 9)*

| | |
|---|---|
| Notes Receivable | $20,800 |
| Interest Receivable | $132.80 |

Notes Receivable include the following:

| Date | Maker | Face | Term | Interest |
|------|-------|------|------|----------|
| May 21 | Don Inc. | $6,000 | 60 days | 12% |
| May 25 | John Co. | 4,800 | 60 days | 11% |
| June 30 | Pete Corp. | 10,000 | 6 months | 9% |

During July, the following transactions were completed.

July 5   Made sales of $6,200 on Connie Kolzow Co. credit cards.

  14   Made sales of $700 on VISA credit cards. The credit card service charge is 3%.

  16   Added $415 to Connie Kolzow Co. charge customer balances for finance charges on unpaid balances.

  20   Received payment in full from Don Inc. on the amount due.

  25   Received notice that John Co. note has been dishonored. (Assume that John Co. is expected to pay in the future.)

**Instructions**

(a) Journalize the July transactions and the July 31 adjusting entry for accrued interest receivable. (Interest is computed using 360 days.)

(b) Enter the balances at July 1 in the receivable accounts and post the entries to all of the receivable accounts.

(c) Show the balance sheet presentation of the receivable accounts at July 31.

**P8–6A** On January 1, 1999, Judy Elam Company had Accounts Receivable $54,200 and Allowance for Doubtful Accounts $4,700. Judy Elam Company prepares financial statements annually. During the year the following selected transactions occurred.

*Prepare entries for various receivables transactions.*
*(SO 2, 4, 5, 6, 7, 8)*

Jan. 5   Sold $6,000 of merchandise to Garth Brooks Company, terms n/30.

Feb. 2   Accepted a $6,000, 4-month, 12% promissory note from Garth Brooks Company for balance due.

  12   Sold $7,800 of merchandise to Lynn Easton Company and accepted Easton's $7,800, 2-month, 10% note for the balance due.

  26   Sold $4,000 of merchandise to Mathias Co., terms n/10.

Apr. 5   Accepted a $4,000, 3-month, 8% note from Mathias Co. for balance due.

  12   Collected Lynne Easton Company note in full.

June 2   Collected Garth Brooks Company note in full.

July 5   Mathias Co. dishonors its note of April 5. It is expected that Mathias will eventually pay the amount owed.

  15   Sold $3,000 of merchandise to John Ross Co. and accepted Ross's $3,000, 3-month, 12% note for the amount due.

Oct. 15   John Ross Co. note was dishonored. John Ross Co. is bankrupt, and there is no hope of future settlement.

**Instructions**
Journalize the transactions.

# PROBLEMS: SET B

*Prepare journal entries related to bad debts expense.*
*(SO 2, 3, 4)*

**P8–1B**   At December 31, 1999, Cellular Ten Co. reported the following information on its balance sheet.

| | |
|---|---|
| Accounts receivable | $960,000 |
| Less: Allowance for doubtful accounts | 70,000 |

During 2000, the company had the following transactions related to receivables.

| | |
|---|---|
| 1. Sales on account | $3,200,000 |
| 2. Sales returns and allowances | 50,000 |
| 3. Collections of accounts receivable | 2,800,000 |
| 4. Write-offs of accounts receivable deemed uncollectible | 90,000 |
| 5. Recovery of bad debts previously written off as uncollectible | 25,000 |

**Instructions**
- (a) Prepare the journal entries to record each of these five transactions. Assume that no cash discounts were taken on the collections of accounts receivable.
- (b) Enter the January 1, 2000, balances in Accounts Receivable and Allowance for Doubtful Accounts, post the entries to the two accounts (use T accounts), and determine the balances.
- (c) Prepare the journal entry to record bad debts expense for 2000, assuming that an aging of accounts receivable indicates that expected bad debts are $100,000.
- (d) Compute the accounts receivable turnover ratio for 2000.

*Compute bad debts amounts.*
*(SO 3)*

**P8–2B**   Information related to Sue Hohenberger Company for 1999 is summarized below:

| | |
|---|---|
| Total credit sales | $2,000,000 |
| Accounts receivable at December 31 | 800,000 |
| Bad debts written off | 36,000 |

**Instructions**
- (a) What amount of bad debts expense will Hohenberger Company report if it uses the direct write-off method of accounting for bad debts?
- (b) Assume that Hohenberger Company decides to estimate its bad debts expense to be 3% of credit sales. What amount of bad debts expense will Hohenberger Company record if it has an Allowance for Doubtful Accounts credit balance of $4,000?
- (c) Assume that Hohenberger Company decides to estimate its bad debts expense based on 6% of accounts receivable. What amount of bad debts expense will Hohenberger Company record if it has an Allowance for Doubtful Accounts credit balance of $3,000?
- (d) Assume the same facts as in (c), except that there is a $3,000 debit balance in Allowance for Doubtful Accounts. What amount of bad debts expense will Hohenberger record?
- (e) What is the weakness of the direct write-off method of reporting bad debts expense?

*Journalize entries to record transactions related to bad debts.*
*(SO 2, 3)*

**P8–3B**   Presented below is an aging schedule for Sandy Hake Company.

| Customer | Total | Not Yet Due | Number of Days Past Due | | | |
|---|---|---|---|---|---|---|
| | | | 1–30 | 31–60 | 61–90 | Over 90 |
| Ruth Benson | $ 22,000 | | $10,000 | $12,000 | | |
| Jean Ripper | 40,000 | $ 40,000 | | | | |
| Mary Ann Bilek | 57,000 | 16,000 | 6,000 | | $35,000 | |
| Sherri Freeland | 34,000 | | | | | $34,000 |
| Others | 126,000 | 96,000 | 16,000 | 14,000 | | |
| | $279,000 | $152,000 | $32,000 | $26,000 | $35,000 | $34,000 |
| Estimated Percentage Uncollectible | | 4% | 7% | 13% | 25% | 50% |
| Total Estimated Bad Debts | $ 37,450 | $ 6,080 | $ 2,240 | $ 3,380 | $ 8,750 | $17,000 |

At December 31, 1999, the unadjusted balance in Allowance for Doubtful Accounts is a credit of $12,000.

*Instructions*

(a) Journalize and post the adjusting entry for bad debts at December 31, 1999.
(b) Journalize and post to the allowance account the following events and transactions in the year 2000:
   (1) March 31, an $800 customer balance originating in 1999 is judged uncollectible.
   (2) May 31, a check for $800 is received from the customer whose account was written off as uncollectible on March 31.
(c) Journalize the adjusting entry for bad debts on December 31, 2000, assuming that the unadjusted balance in Allowance for Doubtful Accounts is a debit of $800 and the aging schedule indicates that total estimated bad debts will be $30,300.

**P8–4B** At December 31, 1999, the trial balance of Lexington Company contained the following amounts before adjustment:

*Journalize entries to record transactions related to bad debts.*
*(SO 3)*

|  | Debits | Credits |
|---|---|---|
| Accounts Receivable | $400,000 | |
| Allowance for Doubtful Accounts | | $ 1,000 |
| Sales | | 950,000 |

*Instructions*

(a) Based on the information given, which method of accounting for bad debts is Lexington Company using—the direct write-off method or the allowance method? How can you tell?
(b) Prepare the adjusting entry at December 31, 1999, for bad debt expense under each of the following independent assumptions:
   (1) An aging schedule indicates that $11,750 of accounts receivable will be uncollectible.
   (2) It is estimated that 1% of sales will be uncollectible.
(c) Repeat part (b) assuming that instead of a credit balance there is a $1,000 debit balance in the Allowance of Doubtful Accounts.
(d) During the next month, January 2000, a $5,000 account receivable is written off as uncollectible. Prepare the journal entry to record the write-off.
(e) Repeat part (d) assuming that Lexington uses the direct write-off method instead of the allowance method in accounting for uncollectible accounts receivable.
(f) ▦▭▭▭▭▷ What type of account is the allowance for doubtful accounts? How does it affect how accounts receivable is reported on the balance sheet at the end of the accounting period?

**P8–5B** Cheryl French Company closes its books monthly. On September 30, selected ledger account balances are:

*Prepare entries for various note receivable transactions.*
*(SO 2, 4, 5, 8, 9)*

| | |
|---|---|
| Notes Receivable | $23,200 |
| Interest Receivable | $182.40 |

Notes Receivable include the following:

| Date | Maker | Face | Term | Interest |
|---|---|---|---|---|
| Aug. 16 | Valaitis Co. | $ 8,000 | 60 days | 12% |
| Aug. 25 | Jenelle Co. | 5,200 | 60 days | 12% |
| Sept. 30 | Grumieaux Corp. | 12,000 | 6 months | 9% |

Interest is computed using a 360-day year. During October, the following transactions were completed.

Oct.  7  Made sales of $6,900 on Cheryl French credit cards.
    12  Made sales of $750 on VISA credit cards. The credit card service charge is 4%.
    15  Added $485 to Cheryl French charge customer balance for finance charges on unpaid balances.
    15  Received payment in full from Valaitis Co. on the amount due.
    24  Received notice that Jenelle note has been dishonored. (Assume that Jenelle is expected to pay in future.)

*Instructions*

(a) Journalize the October transactions and the October 31 adjusting entry for accrued interest receivable.

(b) Enter the balances at October 1 in the receivable accounts and post the entries to all of the receivable accounts.

(c) Show the balance sheet presentation of the receivable accounts at October 31.

*Prepare entries for various receivable transactions.*
*(SO 2, 4, 5, 6, 7, 8)*

**P8–6B**   On January 1, 1999, Paul Gleason Company had Accounts Receivable $146,000, Notes Receivable $15,000, and Allowance for Doubtful Accounts $13,200. The note receivable is from the Linda Johnson Company. It is a 4-month, 12% note dated December 31, 1998. Paul Gleason Company prepares financial statements annually. During the year the following selected transactions occurred.

Jan.  5   Sold $16,000 of merchandise to George Company, terms n/15.

   20   Accepted George Company's $16,000, 3-month, 9% note for balance due.

Feb. 18   Sold $8,000 of merchandise to Swaim Company and accepted Swaim's $8,000, 6-month, 10% note for the amount due.

Apr. 20   Collected George Company note in full.

   30   Received payment in full from Linda Johnson Company on the amount due.

May 25   Accepted Avery Inc.'s $6,000, 3-month, 8% note in settlement of a past-due balance on account.

Aug. 18   Received payment in full from Swaim Company on note due.

   25   The Avery Inc. note was dishonored. Avery Inc. is not bankrupt and future payment is anticipated.

Sept. 1   Sold $10,000 of merchandise to Jose Trevino Company and accepted a $10,000, 6-month, 10% note for the amount due.

**Instructions**
Journalize the transactions.

# BROADENING YOUR PERSPECTIVE

# FINANCIAL REPORTING AND ANALYSIS

### FINANCIAL REPORTING PROBLEM: SCH Company

**BYP8–1**   SCH Company sells office equipment and supplies to many organizations in the city and surrounding area on contract terms of 2/10, n/30. In the past, over 75% of the credit customers have taken advantage of the discount by paying within 10 days of the invoice date.

The number of customers taking the full 30 days to pay has increased within the last year. Current indications are that less than 60% of the customers are now taking the discount. Bad debts as a percentage of gross credit sales have risen from the 1.5% provided in past years to about 4% in the current year.

The controller has responded to a request from the Finance Committee for more information on the collections of accounts receivable with the report reproduced below.

**SCH COMPANY**
**Accounts Receivable Collections**
**May 31, 1999**

The fact that some credit accounts will prove uncollectible is normal. Annual bad debt write-offs have been 1.5% of gross credit sales over the past five years. During the last fiscal year, this percentage increased to slightly less than 4%. The current Accounts Receivable balance is $1,400,000. The condition of this balance in terms of age and probability of collection is as follows:

| Proportion of Total | Age Categories | Probability of Collection |
|---|---|---|
| 66% | not yet due | 99% |
| 16% | less than 30 days past due | 96½% |
| 9% | 30 to 60 days past due | 95% |
| 5% | 61 to 120 days past due | 91% |
| 2½% | 121 to 180 days past due | 75% |
| 1½% | over 180 days past due | 30% |

The Allowance for Doubtful Accounts had a credit balance of $29,500 on June 1, 1998. SCH has provided for a monthly bad debts expense accrual during the current fiscal year based on the assumption that 4% of gross credit sales will be uncollectible. Total gross credit sales for the 1998–99 fiscal year amounted to $2,800,000. Write-offs of bad accounts during the year totaled $96,000.

*Instructions*

(a) Prepare an accounts receivable aging schedule for SCH Company using the age categories identified in the controller's report to the Finance Committee showing:
   1. The amount of accounts receivable outstanding for each age category and in total.
   2. The estimated amount that is uncollectible for each category and in total.

(b) Compute the amount of the year-end adjustment necessary to bring Allowance for Doubtful Accounts to the balance indicated by the age analysis. Then prepare the necessary journal entry to adjust the accounting records.

(c) In a recessionary environment with tight credit and high interest rates:
   1. Identify steps SCH Company might consider to improve the accounts receivable situation.
   2. Then evaluate each step identified in terms of the risks and costs involved.

## COMPARATIVE ANALYSIS PROBLEM: Kellogg Company vs. General Mills

**BYP8–2**  Kellogg's financial statements are presented in Appendix A; General Mills's financial statements are presented in Appendix B.

*Instructions*

(a) Based on the information contained in these financial statements, compute the following 1997 ratios for each company:
   1. Accounts receivable turnover ratio.
   2. Average collection period for receivables.

(b) What conclusions concerning the management of accounts receivable can be drawn from these data?

## RESEARCH ASSIGNMENT

**BYP8–3**  The May 6, 1996, issue of *Forbes* magazine includes an article by Matthew Schifrin and Howard Rudnitsky, entitled "Rx for Receivables."

*Instructions*

Read the article and answer the following questions:

(a) Why has the pharmacy business moved from a cash-based business to a receivables-based business?

(b) What is the economic motivation for pharmacies to sell their receivables?

(c) What is the economic motivation for the Pharmacy Fund to purchase the receivables?

## INTERPRETING FINANCIAL STATEMENTS: Sears Roebuck & Co.

**BYP8–4**  Sears is one of the world's largest retailers. It is also a huge provider of credit through its Sears credit card. Revenue generated from credit operations was $4.4 billion in 1996. The rate of interest Sears earns on outstanding receivables varies from 10 to 21 percent in the United States to up to 28 percent in Canada. Managing these receivables is critical to the performance of the corporation. One aspect of receivables management is that in some instances, to acquire cash when needed, the company will sell its receivables. At December 31, 1996 Sears had sold $6.33 billion of its receivables.

The following information was available in Sears 1996 financial statements (in millions of dollars).

|  | 1996 | 1995 | 1994 |
|---|---|---|---|
| Accounts receivable (gross) | $22,371 | $20,949 | $19,033 |
| Allowance for doubtful accounts | 808 | 843 | 832 |
| Merchandise sales | 33,812 | 31,035 | 29,451 |
| Credit revenues | 4,424 | 3,890 | 3,574 |
| Bad debts expense | 1,136 | 826 | 698 |

*Instructions*
 (a) Discuss whether the sale of receivables by Sears represents a significant portion of its receivables. Why might they have sold these receivables? As an investor, what concerns might you have about these sales?
 (b) Calculate and discuss the accounts receivable turnover ratio and average collection period for Sears for 1996 and 1995.
 (c) Do you think Sears provided credit as a revenue-generating activity, or as a convenience for its customers?
 (d) Compute the ratio of Bad Debt Expense to Merchandise sales for 1996 and 1995. Did this ratio improve or get worse? What considerations should Sears make in deciding whether it wants to have liberal or conservative policies?

## REAL-WORLD FOCUS: Art World Industries, Inc.

**BYP8-5   Art World Industries, Inc.** was incorporated in 1986 in Delaware, though it is located in Los Angeles. The company employs 25 people to print, publish, and sell limited edition graphics and reproductive prints in the wholesale market.

The operating expenses for the fiscal year for Art World Industries, Inc., include bad debts expense of $6,715.50. The balance sheet shows an allowance for doubtful accounts of $175,477. The allowance was set up against certain Japanese accounts receivable which average over one year in age. The Japanese acknowledge the amount due, but with the slow economy in Japan lack the resources to pay at this time.

*Instructions*
 (a) Which basis for estimating uncollectible accounts does Art World Industries use?
 (b) When Art World makes its adjusting entry to record bad debts expense must it consider a previous existing balance in the Allowance for Doubtful Accounts?
 (c) Explain the difference between the percentage of sales and percentage of receivables methods. In applying either of these methods, based on Art World's disclosure above, what important factor would you have to consider in arriving at appropriate percentages to apply?

# CRITICAL THINKING

## GROUP DECISION CASE

**BYP8-6** Linda and Gene Shumway own Somonauk Fashions. From its inception Somonauk Fashions has sold merchandise on either a cash or credit basis, but no credit cards have been accepted. During the past several months, the Shumways have begun to question their sales policies. First, they have lost some sales because of refusing to accept credit cards. Second, representatives of two metropolitan banks have been persuasive in convincing them to accept their national credit cards. One bank, City National Bank, has stated that (1) its credit card fee is 4%, and (2) it pays the retailer 96 cents on each $1 of sales within 3 days of receiving the credit card billings.

The Shumways decide that they should determine the cost of carrying their own credit sales. From the accounting records of the past three years they accumulate the following data:

|                                        | 1999      | 1998      | 1997      |
|----------------------------------------|-----------|-----------|-----------|
| Net credit sales                       | $500,000  | $600,000  | $400,000  |
| Collection agency fees for slow paying |           |           |           |
| customers                              | 2,450     | 2,500     | 2,400     |
| Salary of part-time accounts receivable clerk | 3,800 | 3,800  | 3,800     |

Credit and collection expenses as a percentage of net credit sales: uncollectible accounts 1.6%, billing and mailing costs 0.5%, and credit investigation fee on new customers 0.15%.

Linda and Gene also determine that the average accounts receivable balance outstanding during the year is 5% of net credit sales. The Shumways estimate that they could earn an average of 10% annually on cash invested in other business opportunities.

### Instructions

With the class divided into groups, answer the following:

(a) Prepare a tabulation showing for each year total credit and collection expenses in dollars and as a percentage of net credit sales.

(b) Determine the net credit and collection expense in dollars and as a percentage of sales after considering the revenue not earned from other investment opportunities. (Note: The income lost on the cash held by the bank for 3 days is considered to be immaterial.)

(c) Discuss both the financial and nonfinancial factors that are relevant to the decision.

## COMMUNICATION ACTIVITY

**BYP8–7**   Jackie Henning, a friend of yours who knows little about accounting, asks you to help make sense of a discussion she overheard at work about changes her employer wants to make in accounting for uncollectible accounts. Specifically, she asks you to explain the differences between the percentage of sales, percentage of receivables, and the direct write-off methods for uncollectible accounts.

### Instructions

In a letter of one page (or less), explain to Jackie the three methods of accounting for uncollectibles. Be sure to discuss differences among these methods.

## ETHICS CASE

**BYP8–8**   Jacket Co. is a subsidiary of Suit Corp. The controller believes that the yearly allowance for doubtful accounts for Jacket Co. should be 2% of net credit sales. The president of Jacket Co., nervous that the parent company might expect the subsidiary to sustain its 10% growth rate, suggests that the controller increase the allowance for doubtful accounts to 4%. The president thinks that the lower net income, which reflects a 6% growth rate, will be a more sustainable rate for Jacket Co.

### Instructions

(a) Who are the stakeholders in this case?

(b) Does the president's request pose an ethical dilemma for the controller?

(c) Should the controller be concerned with Jacket Co.'s growth rate in estimating the allowance? Explain your answer.

# SURFING THE NET

**BYP8–9**   The Security Exchange Act of 1934 requires any firm that is listed on one of the national exchanges to file annual reports (form 10-K), financial statements, and quarterly reports (form 10-Q) with the SEC. This exercise demonstrates how to search and access available SEC filings through the Internet.

**Address:** http://biz.yahoo.com (May use SEC address instead.)

**Steps:**
1. Choose **Company.**
2. Type in a company's name, or use index to find a company name.
3. Choose **SEC Filings.**

*Instructions*
Answer the following questions:
(a) Which SEC filings were available for the company you selected?
(b) In the company's annual report, what was one key point discussed in the "Management's Discussion and Analysis of Results of Operations and Financial Condition"?
(c) What was the net income for the period selected?

---

*Answers to Self-Study Questions*
1. c    2. a    3. b    4. b    5. d    6. c    7. c    8. a    9. b    10. d

---

*Answer to Kellogg Review It Question 6, p. 337*
Concentrations of credit risk with respect to accounts receivable are limited due to (1) the large number of customers, (2) generally short payment terms, and (3) their dispersion across geographic areas.

**Remember to go back to the Navigator box on the chapter-opening page and check off your completed work.**

**Before studying this chapter, you should know or, if necessary, review:**

a. The cost principle (Ch. 1, p. 11) and matching principle of accounting. (Ch. 3, p. 94)

b. How to record purchases, sales, and cost of goods sold under a perpetual inventory system. (Ch. 5, pp. 191–199)

c. How to prepare financial statements for a merchandising company. (Ch. 5, pp. 199–201)

## FEATURE STORY

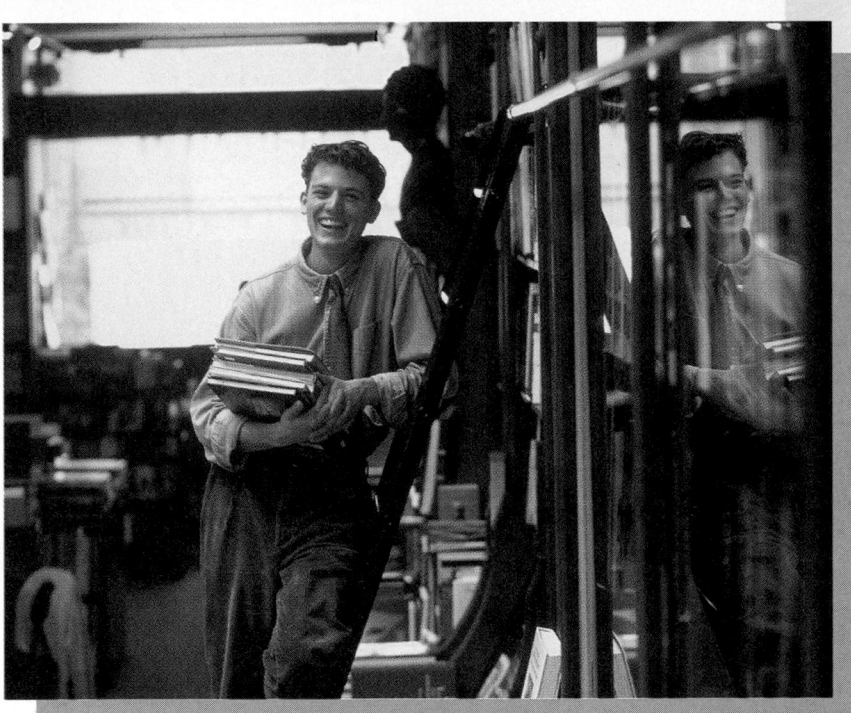

# Keeping the Books on the Books

If you go to a large college or university, chances are that your bookstore or student union has state-of-the-art computer technology for tracking inventories. In an instant, the clerk at the check-out stand "whooshes" your purchases over a scanning machine that automatically rings up the price and deducts the item from inventory.

Not all schools have such state-of-the-art technology. Some bookstores are even small enough that the person managing it can take a "mom-and-pop corner grocery" approach. One such bookstore is at Erie Community College in Buffalo, New York, which produces annual sales of $500,000 per year. Instead of using "point-of-sale" computer technology, the bookstore uses an old-fashioned cash register. The inventory of textbooks, notebooks, art supplies, and so on is counted every month by Joel Damiani, manager. Because the quantity of inventory is relatively small, Damiani, or his two assistants, can specifically identify each item when sold. A larger bookstore would have too much inventory to use that approach; instead, they would use inventory costing methods that do not specifically match the cost of inventory to the actual sale of goods.

Damiani is candid, too, about some problems at his store. For one thing, the accounting records were in disarray when he took the job. "They told me it was going to be a challenge," he says. "And I like challenges." His challenges have included working with the school's accountant to produce a monthly balance sheet and income statement for the bookstore and making sure he has enough inventory of books and supplies on hand for the start of classes. "Sometimes, students say we're not quick enough."

# CHAPTER 9

# INVENTORIES

## THE NAVIGATOR ✔

- Understand *Concepts for Review*  ☐
- Read *Feature Story*  ☐
- Scan *Study Objectives*  ☐
- Read *Preview*  ☐
- Read text and answer *Before You Go On*
  *p. 370* ☐ *p. 376* ☐ *p. 385* ☐ *p. 390* ☐
- Work *Demonstration Problem*  ☐
- Review *Summary of Study Objectives*  ☐
- Answer *Self-Study Questions*  ☐
- Complete assignments  ☐

## STUDY OBJECTIVES

**After studying this chapter, you should be able to:**

1. Describe the steps in determining inventory quantities.
2. Prepare the entries for purchases and sales of inventory under a periodic inventory system.
3. Determine cost of goods sold under a periodic inventory system.
4. Identify the unique features of the income statement for a merchandising company using a periodic inventory system.
5. Explain the basis of accounting for inventories and describe the inventory cost flow methods.
6. Explain the financial statement and tax effects of each of the inventory cost flow methods.
7. Explain the lower of cost or market basis of accounting for inventories.
8. Indicate the effects of inventory errors on the financial statements.
9. Compute and interpret the inventory turnover ratio.

THE NAVIGATOR

*A*s indicated in the opening story about the bookstore at Erie Community College, accounting for inventory can be time-consuming and complex. In this chapter we will explain the procedures for determining inventory quantities and the methods used in determining the cost of inventory on hand at the balance sheet date. In addition, we will discuss differences in perpetual and periodic inventory systems, and the effects of inventory errors on a company's financial statements. The content and organization of this chapter are as follows:

**INVENTORIES**

| **Inventory Basics** | **Periodic Inventory System** | **Inventory Costing** | **Lower of Cost or Market** | **Inventory Errors** | **Statement Presentation and Analysis** |
|---|---|---|---|---|---|
| • Classifications<br>• Determining inventory quantities<br>• Inventory accounting systems | • Recording transactions<br>• Comparison of perpetual and periodic<br>• Cost of goods sold<br>• Income statement presentation | • Actual inventory costs<br>• Assumed inventory costs<br>• Financial statement effects<br>• Consistent use | | • Income statement effects<br>• Balance sheet effects | |

THE NAVIGATOR

# INVENTORY BASICS

In our economy, inventories are an important barometer of business activity. The U.S. Commerce Department, for example, publishes monthly combined inventory data for retailers, wholesalers, and manufacturers. The amount of inventories and the time required to sell the goods on hand are two indicators that are closely watched. During downturns in the economy, there is an initial buildup of inventories, as the length of time needed to sell existing quantities increases. The reverse effects are generally associated with an upturn in business activity. A delicate balance must be maintained between too little inventory and too much. A merchandiser or manufacturer with too little inventory to meet demand will have dissatisfied customers and sales personnel. One with too much inventory will be burdened with unnecessary carrying costs.

Inventories affect both the balance sheet and the income statement. In the **balance sheet** of merchandising companies, inventory is frequently the most significant current asset. Of course, its amount and relative importance can vary, even for enterprises in the same industry. For example, Wal-Mart reported inventory of $14 billion, representing 90% of total current assets, whereas for the same period, J.C. Penney Company reported $3.9 billion of inventory, representing 41% of total current assets. In the **income statement**, inventory is vital in determining the results of operations for a particular period. Moreover, gross profit (net sales less cost of goods sold) is closely watched by management, owners, and other interested parties (as explained in Chapter 5).

## Classifying Inventory

How a company classifies its inventory depends on whether the firm is a merchandiser or a manufacturer. In a **merchandising enterprise**, inventory consists of many different items. For example, in a grocery store, canned goods, dairy products, meats, and produce are just a few of the inventory items on hand. These items have two common characteristics: (1) they are owned by the company, and (2) they are in a form ready for sale to customers in the ordinary course of business. Thus, only one inventory classification, **merchandise inventory**, is needed to describe the many different items that make up the total inventory.

In a **manufacturing enterprise**, inventories are also owned by the company, but some goods may not yet be ready for sale. As a result, inventory is usually classified into three categories: finished goods, work in process, and raw materials. For example, General Motors classifies automobiles completed and ready for sale as **finished goods**. The automobiles on the assembly line in various stages of production are classified as **work in process**. The steel, glass, upholstery, and other components that are on hand waiting to be used in the production of automobiles are identified as **raw materials**.

**HELPFUL HINT**

Regardless of the classification, all inventories are reported under Current Assets on the balance sheet.

The accounting principles and concepts discussed in this chapter apply to inventory classifications of both merchandising and manufacturing companies. In this chapter we will focus on merchandise inventory.

## Determining Inventory Quantities

Many businesses take a physical inventory count on the last day of the year. Businesses using the periodic inventory system are required to take an end-of-the-period physical inventory to determine the inventory on hand at the balance sheet date and to compute cost of goods sold. Even businesses using a perpetual inventory system must take a physical inventory at some time during the year.

Determining inventory quantities consists of two steps: (1) taking a physical inventory of goods on hand, and (2) determining the ownership of goods.

**1**

STUDY
OBJECTIVE
················································
Describe the steps in determining inventory quantities.

### *Taking a Physical Inventory*

Taking a physical inventory involves actually counting, weighing, or measuring each kind of inventory on hand. In many companies, taking an inventory is a formidable task. Retailers, such as Kmart, True Value Hardware, or your favorite music store have thousands of different inventory items. An inventory count is generally more accurate when goods are not being sold or received during the counting. Consequently, companies often "take inventory" when the business is closed or when business is slow. Many retailers, for example, close early on a chosen day in January—after the holiday sales and returns—to count their inventory.

To minimize errors in taking the inventory, a company should adopt the following procedures to adhere to **internal control** principles that safeguard inventory:

1. The counting should be done by employees who do not have custodial responsibility for the inventory. (Segregation of duties)
2. Each counter should establish the authenticity of each inventory item, e.g., each box does contain a 25-inch television set, and each storage tank does contain gasoline. (Establishment of responsibility)

3. There should be a second count by another employee. (Independent internal verification)

4. Prenumbered inventory tags should be used, and all inventory tags should be accounted for. (Documentation procedures)

5. A designated supervisor should ascertain at the conclusion of the count that all inventory items are tagged and that no items have more than one tag. (Independent internal verification)

After the physical inventory is taken, the quantity of each kind of inventory is listed on **inventory summary sheets**. To assure the accuracy of the summary sheets, the listing should be verified by a second employee or supervisor. Subsequently, unit costs will be applied to the quantities in order to determine a total cost of the inventory—which is the topic of later sections.[1]

## ACCOUNTING IN ACTION
### Business Insight

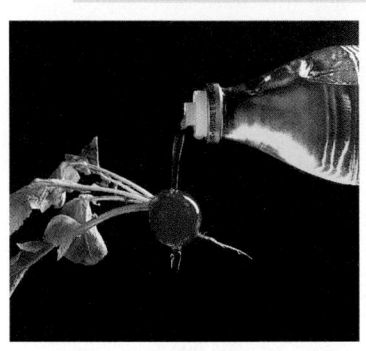

Failure to observe the foregoing internal control procedures contributed to the Great Salad Oil Swindle. In this case, management intentionally overstated its salad oil inventory, which was stored in large holding tanks. Three procedures contributed to overstating the oil inventory: (1) Water added to the bottom of the holding tanks caused the oil to float to the top. Inventory-taking crews who viewed the holding tanks from the top observed only salad oil, when, in fact, as much as 37 out of 40 feet of many of the holding tanks contained water. (2) The company's inventory records listed more holding tanks than it actually had. The company repainted numbers on the tanks after inventory crews examined them, so the crews counted the same tanks twice. (3) Underground pipes pumped oil from one holding tank to another during the inventory taking; therefore, the same salad oil was counted more than once. Although the salad oil swindle was unusual, it demonstrates the complexities involved in assuring that inventory is properly counted.

### Determining Ownership of Goods

Before we can begin to calculate the cost of inventory, we need to consider the ownership of goods: specifically, we need to be sure that we have not included in the inventory any goods that do not belong to the company.

**Goods in Transit.**    Goods are considered to be **in transit** when they are in the hands of a public carrier, such as a railroad, trucking, or airline company at the statement date. Goods in transit should be included in the inventory of the party that has legal title to the goods. Legal title is determined by the terms of sale, as shown in Illustration 9-1 and described below:

1. When the terms are **FOB (free on board) shipping point**, ownership of the goods passes to the buyer when the public carrier accepts the goods from the seller.

2. When the terms are **FOB destination**, legal title to the goods remains with the seller until the goods reach the buyer.

**HELPFUL HINT**
AMICO Co.'s goods in transit at December 31 consist of sales made (1) FOB destination and (2) FOB shipping point, and purchases made (3) FOB destination and (4) FOB shipping point. Which items should be included in AMICO's inventory at December 31? Answer: Items (1) and (4).

---

[1]To arrive at an estimate of the cost of inventory when a physical inventory cannot be taken (the inventory is destroyed) or when it is inconvenient (during interim periods), estimating methods are applied. These methods (gross profit method and retail inventory method) are discussed in Appendix 9A.

**ILLUSTRATION 9-1**

*Terms of sale*

Significant errors may occur in determining inventory quantities if goods in transit at the statement date are ignored. Assume, for example, that Hargrove Company has 20,000 units of inventory on hand on December 31 and the following goods in transit: (1) **sales** of 1,500 units shipped December 31 FOB destination, and (2) **purchases** of 2,500 units shipped FOB shipping point by the seller on December 31. Hargrove has legal title to both the units sold and the units purchased. Consequently, inventory quantities would be understated by 4,000 units (1,500 + 2,500) if units in transit are ignored.

# TECHNOLOGY IN ACTION

Many companies have invested large amounts of time and money in automated inventory systems. One of the most sophisticated is Federal Express' Digitally Assisted Dispatch System (DADS). This system uses hand-held "SuperTrackers" to transmit data about the packages and documents to the firm's computer system. Based on bar codes, the system allows the firm to know where any package is at any time to prevent losses and to fulfill the firm's delivery commitments. More recently, FedEx's newly developed software enables customers to track shipments on their own PCs.

**Consigned Goods.**   In some lines of business, it is customary to acquire merchandise on consignment. Under a consignment arrangement, the holder of the goods (called the *consignee*) does not own the goods. Ownership remains with the shipper of the goods (called the *consignor*) until the goods are actually sold to a customer. Because consigned goods are not owned by the consignee, they should not be included in the consignee's physical inventory count. Conversely, the consignor should include merchandise held by the consignee as part of its inventory.

## Inventory Accounting Systems

One of two basic systems of accounting for inventories may be used: **(1) the perpetual inventory system, or (2) the periodic inventory system.** Chapter 5 of this textbook discussed and illustrated the characteristics of the perpetual inventory system. This chapter discusses and illustrates the periodic inventory system and provides a comparison of it with the perpetual inventory system; Appendix B to this chapter continues coverage of the perpetual inventory system.

Some businesses find it either unnecessary or uneconomical to invest in a computerized perpetual inventory system that maintains up-to-date records of merchandise on hand and cost of goods sold. Many small merchandising business managers especially still feel a perpetual inventory system costs more than it is worth. These managers can control merchandise and manage day-to-day operations without detailed inventory records. They use a periodic inventory system.

## BEFORE YOU GO ON . . .

### Review It

1. What steps are involved in determining inventory quantities?
2. How is ownership determined for goods in transit at the balance sheet date?
3. Who has title to consigned goods?
4. Name two basic systems of accounting for inventories.

### Do It

Hasbeen Company completed its inventory count, arriving at a total value for inventory of $200,000. You have been informed of the information listed below. Discuss how this information affects the reported cost of inventory.

1. Goods held on consignment for Falls Co., costing $15,000, were included in the inventory.
2. Purchased goods of $10,000 which were in transit (terms: FOB shipping point) were not included in the count.
3. Sold inventory with a cost of $12,000 which was in transit (terms: FOB shipping point) was not included in the count.

*Reasoning:* For goods in transit, ownership is determined by the freight terms. For consigned goods, ownership rests with the consignor until the goods are sold by the consignee.

*Solution:* The goods held on consignment of $15,000 should be deducted from the inventory count. The goods of $10,000 purchased FOB shipping point should be added to the inventory count. Sold goods of $12,000 which were in transit FOB shipping point should not be included in the ending inventory.

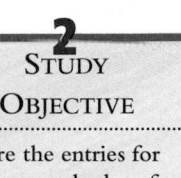

THE NAVIGATOR

*Related exercise material:* BE9-4, E9-1, E9-4

## PERIODIC INVENTORY SYSTEM

**STUDY OBJECTIVE 2**

Prepare the entries for purchases and sales of inventory under a periodic inventory system.

In a periodic inventory system, revenues from the sale of merchandise are recorded when sales are made in the same way as in a perpetual system. But, no attempt is made on the date of sale to record the cost of the merchandise sold. Instead, a physical inventory count is taken at the end of the period to determine (1) the cost of the merchandise then on hand and (2) the cost of the goods sold during the period. And, under a periodic system, purchases of merchandise are recorded in a Purchases account rather than a Merchandise Inventory account. Also, under a periodic system, it is customary to record purchase returns and allowances, purchase discounts, and freight-in on purchases in separate accounts so that the accumulated amounts for each are known.

### Recording Transactions

To illustrate the recording of merchandise transactions under a periodic inventory system, we will use the purchase/sale transactions between Highpoint Electronic and Chelsea Video discussed in Chapter 5.

# Recording Purchases of Merchandise

On the basis of the sales invoice (Illustration 5-4) shown on page 192 and receipt of the merchandise ordered from Highpoint Electronic, Chelsea Video records the $3,800 purchase as follows:

| May 4 | Purchases | 3,800 | |
|---|---|---|---|
| | Accounts Payable | | 3,800 |
| | (To record goods purchased on account, terms 2/10, n/30) | | |

| A | = | L | + | OE |
|---|---|---|---|---|
| | | +3,800 | | −3,800 |

Purchases is a temporary account whose normal balance is a debit.

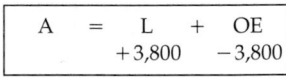
**HELPFUL HINT**
Be careful not to fall into the trap of debiting purchases of equipment or supplies to Purchases.

## Purchase Returns and Allowances

Because $300 of merchandise received from Highpoint Electronic is inoperable, Chelsea Video returns the goods, issues the debit memorandum (Illustration 5-5) shown on page 193, and prepares the following entry to recognize the purchase return:

| May 8 | Accounts Payable | 300 | |
|---|---|---|---|
| | Purchase Returns and Allowances | | 300 |
| | (To record return of inoperable goods purchased from Highpoint Electronic) | | |

| A | = | L | + | OE |
|---|---|---|---|---|
| | | −300 | | +300 |

Purchases Returns and Allowances is a temporary account whose normal balance is a credit.

## Freight Costs

When the purchaser directly incurs the freight costs, the account Freight-in (or Transportation-in) is debited. For example, if upon delivery of the goods on May 6, Chelsea pays Acme Freight Company $150 for freight charges on its purchase from Highpoint Electronic, the entry on Chelsea's books is:

| May 9 | Freight-in (Transportation-in) | 150 | |
|---|---|---|---|
| | Cash | | 150 |
| | (To record payment of freight, terms FOB shipping point) | | |

| A | = | L | + | OE |
|---|---|---|---|---|
| −150 | | | | −150 |

Like Purchases, Freight-in is a temporary account whose normal balance is a debit. **Freight-in is part of cost of goods purchased.** The reason is that cost of goods purchased should include any freight charges necessary to bring the goods to the purchaser. Freight costs are not subject to a purchase discount. Purchase discounts apply on the invoice cost of the merchandise.

## Purchase Discounts

On May 14 Chelsea Video pays the balance due on account to Highpoint Electronic taking the 2% cash discount allowed by Highpoint for payment within 10 days. The payment and discount are recorded by Chelsea Video as follows:

| A | = | L | + | OE |
|---|---|---|---|---|
| −3,430 | | −3,500 | | +70 |

| May 14 | Accounts Payable | 3,500 | |
|---|---|---|---|
| | Purchase Discounts | | 70 |
| | Cash | | 3,430 |
| | (To record payment to Highpoint Electronic within the discount period) | | |

Purchase Discounts is a temporary account whose normal balance is a credit.

## Recording Sales of Merchandise

The sale of $3,800 of merchandise to Chelsea Video on May 4 (sales invoice No. 731, Illustration 5-4) is recorded by the seller, Highpoint Electronic, as follows:

| A | = | L | + | OE |
|---|---|---|---|---|
| +3,800 | | | | +3,800 |

| May 4 | Accounts Receivable | 3,800 | |
|---|---|---|---|
| | Sales | | 3,800 |
| | (To record credit sales per invoice #731 to Chelsea Video) | | |

### Sales Returns and Allowances

Based on the debit memorandum (Illustration 5-5, page 193) received from Chelsea Video on May 8 for returned goods, Highpoint Electronic records the $300 sales return as follows:

| A | = | L | + | OE |
|---|---|---|---|---|
| −300 | | | | −300 |

| May 8 | Sales Returns and Allowances | 300 | |
|---|---|---|---|
| | Accounts Receivable | | 300 |
| | (To record return of goods from Chelsea Video) | | |

### Sales Discounts

On May 15, Highpoint Electronic receives payment of $3,430 on account from Chelsea Video. Highpoint honors the 2% cash discount and records the payment of Chelsea's account receivable in full as follows:

| A | = | L | + | OE |
|---|---|---|---|---|
| +3,430 | | | | −70 |
| −3,500 | | | | |

| May 15 | Cash | 3,430 | |
|---|---|---|---|
| | Sales Discounts | 70 | |
| | Accounts Receivable | | 3,500 |
| | (To record collection from Chelsea Video within 2/10, n/30 discount period) | | |

## Comparison of Entries—Perpetual vs. Periodic

The periodic inventory system entries above are shown in Illustration 9-2 on page 373 next to those that were illustrated in Chapter 5 (pages 191–199) under the perpetual inventory system for both Highpoint Electronic and Chelsea Video.

## Cost of Goods Sold

**3**
STUDY
OBJECTIVE
••••••••••••••••••••••••••••••••
Determine cost of goods sold under a periodic inventory system.

As noted from the entries in Illustration 9-2, under a periodic inventory system, a running account of the changes in inventory is not recorded as either purchases or sales transactions occur. Neither the daily amount of inventory of merchandise on hand is known nor is the cost of goods sold. To determine the cost of goods sold under a periodic inventory system, it is necessary to (1) record purchases of merchandise (as shown above), (2) determine the cost of goods purchased, and (3) determine the cost of goods on hand at the beginning and end of the accounting period. The cost of goods on hand must be determined by a physical inventory count and application of the cost to the items counted in the inventory.

| | Transaction | Perpetual Inventory System | | Periodic Inventory System | |
|---|---|---|---|---|---|
| May 4 | Purchase of merchandise on credit. | Merchandise Inventory 3,800<br>　Accounts Payable | 3,800 | Purchases 3,800<br>　Accounts Payable | 3,800 |
| May 8 | Purchase returns and allowances. | Accounts Payable 300<br>　Merchandise Inventory | 300 | Accounts Payable 300<br>　Purchase Returns<br>　and Allowances | 300 |
| May 9 | Freight costs on purchases. | Merchandise Inventory 150<br>　Cash | 150 | Freight-in 150<br>　Cash | 150 |
| May 14 | Payment on account with a discount. | Accounts Payable 3,500<br>　Cash<br>　Merchandise Inventory | 3,430<br>70 | Accounts Payable 3,500<br>　Cash<br>　Purchase Discounts | 3,430<br>70 |

**Entries on Chelsea Video's Books** *(handwritten annotation: "→ differences" / "both")*

| | Transaction | Perpetual Inventory System | | Periodic Inventory System | |
|---|---|---|---|---|---|
| May 4 | Sale of merchandise on credit. | Accounts Receivable 3,800<br>　Sales | 3,800 | Accounts Receivable 3,800<br>　Sales | 3,800 |
| | | Cost of Goods Sold 2,400<br>　Merchandise Inventory | 2,400 | No entry for cost of goods sold | |
| May 8 | Return of merchandise sold. | Sales Returns and<br>Allowances 300<br>　Accounts Receivable | 300 | Sales Returns and<br>Allowances 300<br>　Accounts Receivable | 300 |
| | | Merchandise Inventory 140<br>　Cost of Goods Sold | 140 | No entry | |
| May 15 | Cash received on account with a discount. | Cash 3,430<br>Sales Discounts 70<br>　Accounts Receivable | 3,500 | Cash 3,430<br>Sales Discounts 70<br>　Accounts Receivable | 3,500 |

**Entries on Highpoint Electronic's Books**

**ILLUSTRATION 9-2**

*Comparison of journal entries under perpetual and periodic inventory systems*

## Determining Cost of Goods Purchased

We used four accounts to record the purchase of inventory under a periodic inventory system. These accounts are:

**ILLUSTRATION 9-3**

*Normal balances: cost of goods purchased accounts*

| Account | Normal Balance |
|---|---|
| Purchases | Debit |
| Purchase Returns and Allowances | Credit |
| Purchase Discounts | Credit |
| Freight-in | Debit |

All of these accounts are temporary accounts because they are used to determine the cost of goods sold which is an expense disclosed on the income statement. Therefore, the balances in these accounts must be reduced to zero at the end of each accounting period so that information about cost of goods sold can be accumulated in the next accounting period. The procedure for determining the cost of goods purchased is as follows:

1. The accounts with credit balances (Purchase Returns and Allowances and Purchase Discounts) are subtracted from Purchases to produce net purchases.
2. Freight-in is then added to net purchases to produce cost of goods purchased.

To illustrate, assume that Highpoint Electronic shows the following balances for the accounts above: Purchases $325,000; Purchase Returns and Allowances $10,400; Purchase Discounts $6,800; and Freight-in $12,200. Net purchases and cost of goods purchased are $307,800 and $320,000, respectively, as computed in Illustration 9-4:

**ILLUSTRATION 9-4**

*Computation of net purchases and cost of goods purchased*

|  |  |  |  |
|---|---|---:|---:|
| Purchases |  |  | $325,000 |
| (1) Less: Purchase returns and allowances |  | $10,400 |  |
| Purchase discounts |  | 6,800 | 17,200 |
| **Net purchases** |  |  | **307,800** |
| (2) Add: Freight-in |  |  | 12,200 |
| **Cost of goods purchased** |  |  | **$320,000** |

## Determining Cost of Goods on Hand

To **determine the cost of inventory on hand, it is necessary to take a physical inventory**. As explained earlier in this chapter, taking a physical inventory involves:

1. Counting the units on hand for each item of inventory.
2. Applying unit costs to the total units on hand for each item of inventory.
3. Aggregating the costs for each item of inventory to determine the total cost of goods on hand.

A physical inventory should be taken at or near the balance sheet date. To improve the accuracy of the count, many businesses suspend operations while inventory is being taken.

The account Merchandise Inventory is used to record the cost of inventory on hand at the balance sheet date. This amount becomes the beginning inventory for the next accounting period. For Highpoint Electronic, the balance in Merchandise Inventory at December 31, 1998, is $36,000. This amount is also the January 1, 1999, balance in Merchandise Inventory. During 1999, **no entries are made to Merchandise Inventory**. At December 31, 1999, entries are made to eliminate the beginning inventory and to record the ending inventory, which we will assume is $40,000.

## Computing Cost of Goods Sold

We have now reached the point where we can compute cost of goods sold. Doing so involves two steps:

**ALTERNATIVE TERMINOLOGY**

Some use the term *cost of sales* instead of *cost of goods sold.*

1. Add the cost of goods purchased to the cost of goods on hand at the beginning of the period (beginning inventory) to obtain the cost of goods available for sale.
2. Subtract the cost of goods on hand at the end of the period (ending inventory) from the cost of goods available for sale to arrive at the cost of goods sold.

For Highpoint Electronic the cost of goods available for sale and the cost of goods sold are $356,000 and $316,000, respectively, as shown below.

**ILLUSTRATION 9-5**

*Computation of cost of goods available for sale and cost of goods sold*

|  | | |
|---|---|---|
| Beginning inventory | $ 36,000 | |
| (1) Add: Cost of goods purchased | 320,000 | |
| **Cost of goods available for sale** | **356,000** | |
| (2) Less: Ending inventory | 40,000 | |
| **Cost of goods sold** | **$316,000** | |

Gross profit, operating expenses, and net income are computed and reported in a periodic inventory system in the same manner as under a perpetual inventory system as shown in Illustration 9-6. (See also Chapter 5, Illustration 5-17.)

## Income Statement Presentation

As under a perpetual inventory system, the income statement for retailers and wholesalers under a periodic inventory system contains three features not found in the income statement of a service enterprise. These features are: (1) a sales

**4**
**STUDY**
**OBJECTIVE**

Identify the unique features of the income statement for a merchandising company using a periodic inventory system.

### HIGHPOINT ELECTRONIC
### Income Statement
### For the Year Ended December 31, 1999

| | | | | |
|---|---|---|---|---|
| **Sales revenues** | | | | |
| Sales | | | | $480,000 |
| Less: Sales returns and allowances | | | $ 12,000 | |
| Sales discounts | | | 8,000 | 20,000 |
| Net sales | | | | 460,000 |
| **Cost of goods sold** | | | | |
| Inventory, January 1 | | | 36,000 | |
| Purchases | | $325,000 | | |
| Less: Purchases returns and allowances | $10,400 | | | |
| Purchase discounts | 6,800 | 17,200 | | |
| Net purchases | | 307,800 | | |
| Add: Freight-in | | 12,200 | | |
| Cost of goods purchased | | | 320,000 | |
| Cost of goods available for sale | | | 356,000 | |
| Inventory, December 31 | | | 40,000 | |
| Cost of goods sold | | | | 316,000 |
| **Gross profit** | | | | 144,000 |
| **Operating expenses** | | | | |
| Store salaries expense | | | 45,000 | |
| Rent expense | | | 19,000 | |
| Utilities expense | | | 17,000 | |
| Advertising expense | | | 16,000 | |
| Depreciation expense—store equipment | | | 8,000 | |
| Freight-out | | | 7,000 | |
| Insurance expense | | | 2,000 | |
| Total operating expenses | | | | 114,000 |
| **Net income** | | | | $ 30,000 |

**HELPFUL HINT**
The far right column identifies the major subdivisions of the income statement. The next column identifies the primary items comprising cost of goods sold of $316,000 and operating expenses of $114,000; in addition, contra revenue items of $20,000 are reported. The third column explains cost of goods purchased of $320,000. The fourth column reports contra purchase items of $17,200.

**ILLUSTRATION 9-6**

*Income statement for a merchandising company using a periodic inventory system*

**ALTERNATIVE TERMINOLOGY**
Gross profit is sometimes referred to as *merchandising profit* or *gross margin*.

revenue section, (2) a cost of goods sold section, and (3) gross profit. But, under a periodic inventory system, the cost of goods sold section generally will contain more detail. Using assumed data for specific operating expenses, the income statement for Highpoint Electronic using a periodic inventory system is shown in Illustration 9-6. Whether the periodic or the perpetual inventory system is used, merchandise inventory is reported at the same amount in the current asset section.

# BEFORE YOU GO ON . . .

## Review It

1. Identify the three steps in determining cost of goods sold.
2. What accounts are used in determining the cost of goods purchased?
3. What is included in cost of goods available for sale?

## Do It

Aerosmith Company's accounting records show the following at year-end: Purchase Discounts $3,400; Freight-in $6,100; Sales $240,000; Purchases $162,500; Beginning Inventory $18,000; Ending Inventory $20,000; Sales Discounts $10,000; Purchase Returns $5,200; and Operating Expenses $57,000. Compute the following amounts for Aerosmith Company: net sales, cost of goods purchased, cost of goods sold, gross profit, and net income.

*Reasoning:* To compute the required amounts, it is important to know the relationships in measuring net income for a merchandising company. For example, it is necessary to know the difference between the following: sales and net sales, goods available for sale and cost of goods sold, and gross profit and net income.

*Solution:*
Net sales: $240,000 − $10,000 = $230,000.
Cost of goods purchased: $162,500 − $5,200 − $3,400 + $6,100 = $160,000.
Cost of goods sold: $18,000 + $160,000 − $20,000 = $158,000.
Gross profit: $230,000 − $158,000 = $72,000.
Net income: $72,000 − $57,000 = $15,000.

*Related exercise material:* BE9-2, BE9-3, E9-2, E9-3

THE
NAVIGATOR

# INVENTORY COSTING UNDER A PERIODIC INVENTORY SYSTEM

**5**
STUDY
OBJECTIVE

Explain the basis of accounting for inventories and describe the inventory cost flow methods.

All expenditures necessary to acquire the goods and to make them ready for sale are included as inventoriable costs. Inventoriable costs may be regarded as a pool of costs that consists of two elements: (1) the cost of the beginning inventory and (2) the cost of goods purchased during the year. The sum of these two elements equals the cost of goods available for sale. Conceptually, the costs of the purchasing, receiving, and warehousing departments (whose efforts make the goods available for sale) should also be included in inventoriable costs. However, because of the practical difficulties in allocating these costs to inventory, they are generally accounted for as **operating expenses** in the period in which they are incurred.

Inventoriable costs are allocated to ending inventory and to cost of goods sold. Under a periodic inventory system, the allocation is made at the end of the accounting period. First, the costs assignable to the ending inventory are determined. Second, the cost of the ending inventory is subtracted from the cost of goods available for sale to determine the cost of goods sold. Cost of goods sold is then deducted from sales revenues in accordance with the matching principle.

To illustrate, assume that General Suppliers has a cost of goods available for sale of $120,000, based on a beginning inventory of $20,000 and cost of goods purchased of $100,000. The physical inventory indicates that 5,000 units are on hand. The costs applicable to the units are $3.00 per unit. The allocation of the pool of costs is shown in Illustration 9-7. As shown, the $120,000 of goods available for sale are allocated $15,000 to ending inventory and $105,000 to cost of goods sold.

**HELPFUL HINT**
Under a perpetual inventory system, described in Chapter 5, the allocation is continuously recognized as purchases and sales are made.

**ILLUSTRATION 9-7**
*Allocation (matching) of pool of costs*

| Pool of Costs | | |
|---|---|---|
| **Cost of Goods Available for Sale** | | |
| Beginning inventory | $ 20,000 | |
| Cost of goods purchased | 100,000 | |
| Cost of goods available for sale | **$120,000** | |

| Step 1 | | | Step 2 | |
|---|---|---|---|---|
| **Ending Inventory** | | | **Cost of Goods Sold** | |
| Units | Unit Cost | Total Cost | Cost of goods available for sale | $120,000 |
| | | | Less: Ending inventory | 15,000 |
| 5,000 | $3.00 | **$15,000** | Cost of goods sold | **$105,000** |

# Using Actual Physical Flow Costing—Specific Identification

Costing of the inventory is complicated because the units on hand for a specific item of inventory may have been purchased at different prices. For example, in a period of rising prices, a company may experience several increases in the cost of identical goods within a given year. Alternatively, unit costs may decline. Under such circumstances, how should the different unit costs in the cost of goods available for sale be allocated between the ending inventory and cost of goods sold?

One answer is to use specific identification of the units purchased. This method tracks the **actual physical flow** of the goods. **Each item of inventory is marked, tagged, or coded with its "specific" unit cost.** Items still in inventory at the end of the year are specifically costed to arrive at the total cost of the ending inventory. Assume, for example, that Southland Music Company purchases three 46-inch television sets at costs of $700, $750, and $800, respectively. During the year, two sets are sold at $1,200 each. At December 31, the company determines that the $750 set is still on hand. Accordingly, the ending inventory is $750 and the cost of goods sold is $1,500 ($700 + $800). This is shown graphically in Illustration 9-8.

**HELPFUL HINT**
What gross profit will Southland Music report? Answer: $900 (Sales $2,400 − CGS $1,500).

Specific identification is possible when a company sells a limited variety of high-unit cost items that can be clearly identified from the time of purchase through the time of sale. Examples of such companies are automobile dealerships (cars, trucks, and vans), music stores (pianos and organs), and antique shops (tables and cabinets). Although the bookstore at Erie Community College uses specific identification, it is somewhat unusual to do so for that type of business.

**ILLUSTRATION 9-8**

*Specific identification*

Ordinarily, however, the identity of goods purchased at a specific cost is lost between the date of purchase and the date of sale. For example, drug, grocery, and hardware stores sell thousands of relatively low unit-cost items of inventory. These items are often indistinguishable from one another, making it impossible or impractical to track each item's cost.

When feasible, specific identification seems to be the ideal method of allocating cost of goods available for sale. Under this method, the ending inventory is reported at actual cost and the actual cost of goods sold is matched against sales revenue. This method, however, may enable management to manipulate net income. For example, assume that a music store has three identical Steinway grand pianos that were purchased at different costs. When selling one piano, management could maximize its net income by selecting the piano with the lowest cost to match with revenues. Alternatively, it could minimize net income by selecting the highest-cost piano.

## Using Assumed Cost Flow Methods— FIFO, LIFO, and Average Cost

Because specific identification is often impractical, other cost flow methods are allowed. These differ from specific identification in that they assume flows of costs that may be unrelated to the physical flow of goods. For this reason we call them **assumed cost flow methods** or **cost flow assumptions**. They are:

1. First-in, first-out (FIFO).
2. Last-in, first-out (LIFO).
3. Average cost.

**INTERNATIONAL NOTE**

A survey of accounting standards in 21 major industrial countries found that all three methods were permissible. In Ireland and the U.K., LIFO is permitted only in extreme circumstances.

**There is no accounting requirement that the cost flow assumption be consistent with the physical movement of the goods.** The selection of the appropriate cost flow assumption (method) is made by management. The management of companies in the same industry may reach different conclusions as to the most appropriate method.

To illustrate these three inventory cost flow methods, we will assume that Bow Valley Electronics uses a **periodic inventory system** and has the information shown in Illustration 9-9 for its Z202 Astro condenser.

### First-in, First-out (FIFO)

The FIFO method assumes that the **earliest goods** purchased are the first to be sold. FIFO often parallels the actual physical flow of merchandise because it

ILLUSTRATION 9-9

*Inventoriable units and costs*

## BOW VALLEY ELECTRONICS
## Z202 Astro Condensers

| Date | Explanation | Units | Unit Cost | Total Cost |
|------|-------------|-------|-----------|------------|
| 1/1 | Beginning inventory | 100 | $10 | $ 1,000 |
| 4/15 | Purchase | 200 | 11 | 2,200 |
| 8/24 | Purchase | 300 | 12 | 3,600 |
| 11/27 | Purchase | 400 | 13 | 5,200 |
| | Total | 1,000 | | $12,000 |

During the year, 550 units were sold and 450 units are on hand at December 31.

generally is good business practice to sell the oldest units first. Under the FIFO method, therefore, the **costs** of the earliest goods purchased are the first to be recognized as cost of goods sold. The allocation of the cost of goods available for sale at Bow Valley Electronics under FIFO is shown in Illustrations 9-10 and 9-ll.

ILLUSTRATION 9-10

*Allocation of costs—FIFO method*

### Pool of Costs
### Cost of Goods Available for Sale

| Date | Explanation | Units | Unit Cost | Total Cost |
|------|-------------|-------|-----------|------------|
| 1/1 | Beginning inventory | 100 | $10 | $ 1,000 |
| 4/15 | Purchase | 200 | 11 | 2,200 |
| 8/24 | Purchase | 300 | 12 | 3,600 |
| 11/27 | Purchase | 400 | 13 | 5,200 |
| | Total | 1,000 | | $12,000 |

**Step 1**
**Ending Inventory**

| Date | Units | Unit Cost | Total Cost |
|------|-------|-----------|------------|
| 11/27 | 400 | $13 | $5,200 |
| 8/24 | 50 | 12 | 600 |
| Total | 450 | | $5,800 |

**Step 2**
**Cost of Goods Sold**

| | |
|---|---|
| Cost of goods available for sale | $12,000 |
| Less: Ending inventory | 5,800 |
| Cost of goods sold | $ 6,200 |

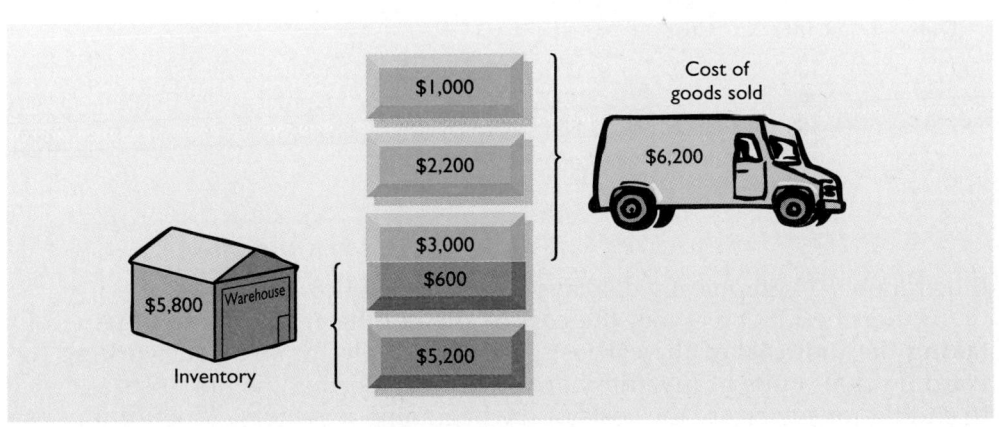

Note that the ending inventory is based on the latest units purchased. That is, **the cost of the ending inventory is obtained by taking the unit cost of the most recent purchase and working backward until all units of inventory have been costed**.

We can verify the accuracy of the cost of goods sold by recognizing that the **first units acquired are the first units sold**. The computations for the 550 units sold are shown in Illustration 9-12.

**ILLUSTRATION 9-12**

*Proof of cost of goods sold*

| Date | Units | | Unit Cost | | Total Cost |
|------|-------|---|-----------|---|-----------|
| 1/1 | 100 | × | $10 | = | $1,000 |
| 4/15 | 200 | × | 11 | = | 2,200 |
| 8/24 | 250 | × | 12 | = | 3,000 |
| Total | 550 | | | | $6,200 |

### Last-in, First-out (LIFO)

The LIFO method assumes that the **latest goods** purchased are the first to be sold. LIFO seldom coincides with the actual physical flow of inventory. Under the LIFO method, the **costs** of the latest goods purchased are the first to be recognized as cost of goods sold. The allocation of the cost of goods available for sale at Bow Valley Electronics under LIFO is shown in Illustration 9-13.

**ILLUSTRATION 9-13**

*Allocation of costs—LIFO method*

**Pool of Costs**

**Cost of Goods Available for Sale**

| Date | Explanation | Units | Unit Cost | Total Cost |
|------|-------------|-------|-----------|-----------|
| 1/1 | Beginning inventory | 100 | $10 | $ 1,000 |
| 4/15 | Purchase | 200 | 11 | 2,200 |
| 8/24 | Purchase | 300 | 12 | 3,600 |
| 11/27 | Purchase | 400 | 13 | 5,200 |
| | Total | 1,000 | | $12,000 |

| Step 1 | | | | Step 2 | |
|--------|--|--|--|--------|--|
| **Ending Inventory** | | | | **Cost of Goods Sold** | |

| Date | Units | Unit Cost | Total Cost | | |
|------|-------|-----------|-----------|---|---|
| 1/1 | 100 | $10 | $1,000 | Cost of goods available for sale | $12,000 |
| 4/15 | 200 | 11 | 2,200 | Less: Ending inventory | 5,000 |
| 8/24 | 150 | 12 | 1,800 | Cost of goods sold | $ 7,000 |
| Total | 450 | | $5,000 | | |

**HELPFUL HINT**
The costs allocated to ending inventory ($5,000) plus the costs allocated to CGS ($7,000) must equal CGAS ($12,000).

Illustration 9-14 graphically displays the LIFO cost flow.

Under the LIFO method, **the cost of the ending inventory is obtained by taking the unit cost of the earliest goods available for sale and working forward until all units of inventory are costed**. As a result, the first costs assigned to ending inventory are the costs of the beginning inventory. Proof of the costs allocated to cost of goods sold is shown in Illustration 9-15.

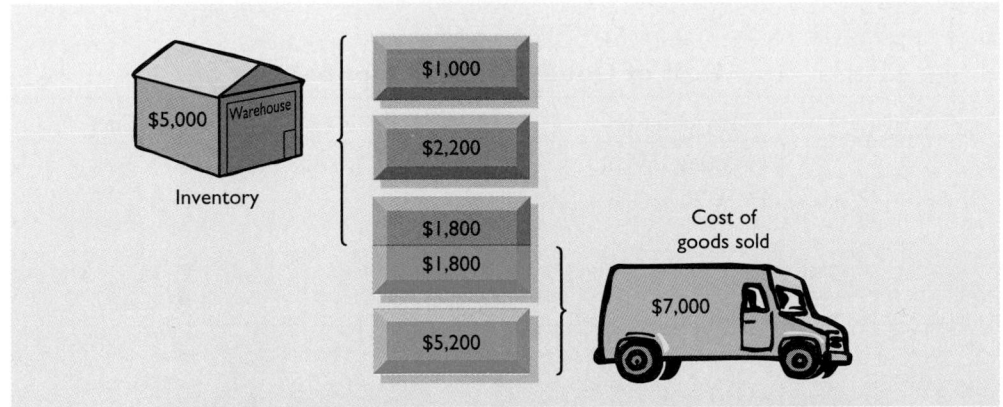

**ILLUSTRATION 9-14**

*LIFO—Last costs in are first costs out in computing cost of goods sold*

| Date | Units | | Unit Cost | | Total Cost |
|------|-------|---|-----------|---|-----------|
| 11/27 | 400 | × | $13 | = | $5,200 |
| 8/24 | 150 | × | 12 | = | 1,800 |
| Total | 550 | | | | $7,000 |

**ILLUSTRATION 9-15**

*Proof of cost of goods sold*

Note that the cost of the **last** goods in are the **first** to be assigned to cost of goods sold. Under a periodic inventory system, which we are using here, **all goods purchased during the period are assumed to be available for the first sale, regardless of the date of purchase**.

## Average Cost

The **average cost method** assumes that the goods available for sale have the same (average) cost per unit; generally they are homogeneous. Under this method, the allocation of the cost of goods available for sale is made on the basis of the **weighted average unit cost** incurred. The formula and a sample computation of the weighted average unit cost are:

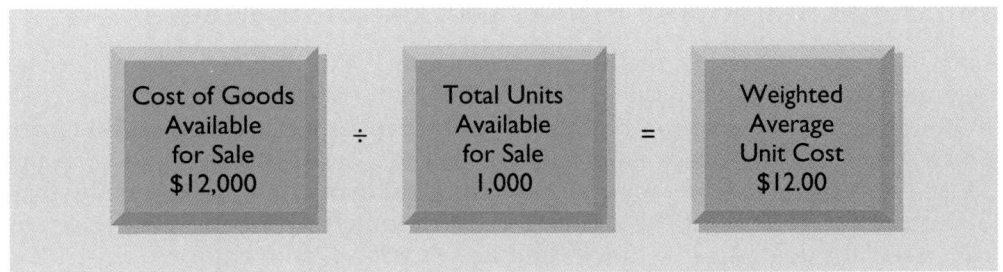

**ILLUSTRATION 9-16**

*Formula for weighted average unit cost*

The weighted average unit cost is then applied to the units on hand to determine the cost of the ending inventory. The allocation of the cost of goods available for sale at Bow Valley Electronics using average cost is shown in Illustrations 9-17 and 9-18.

We can verify the cost of goods sold data presented in Illustration 9-17 under this method by multiplying the units sold by the weighted average unit cost (550 × $12 = $6,600). Note that this method does not use the average of the unit costs. That average is $11.50 ($10 + $11 + $12 + $13 = $46; $46 ÷ 4). The average cost method instead uses the average **weighted** by the quantities purchased at each unit cost.

**ILLUSTRATION 9-17**

*Allocation of costs—average cost method*

### Pool of Costs
### Cost of Goods Available for Sale

| Date | Explanation | Units | Unit Cost | Total Cost |
|------|-------------|-------|-----------|-----------|
| 1/1 | Beginning inventory | 100 | $10 | $ 1,000 |
| 4/15 | Purchase | 200 | 11 | 2,200 |
| 8/24 | Purchase | 300 | 12 | 3,600 |
| 11/27 | Purchase | 400 | 13 | 5,200 |
| | Total | 1,000 | | $12,000 |

|  Step 1  |  Step 2  |
|----------|----------|
| **Ending Inventory** | **Cost of Goods Sold** |

$12,000  ÷  1,000  =  $12.00

|  | Units | Unit Cost | Total Cost |
|--|-------|-----------|-----------|
|  | 450 | × $12.00 | = **$5,400** |

| Cost of goods available for sale | $12,000 |
|----------------------------------|---------|
| Less: Ending inventory | 5,400 |
| Cost of goods sold | **$ 6,600** |

**ILLUSTRATION 9-18**

*Average cost—The average cost of the goods available for sale during the period is the cost used to compute cost of goods sold*

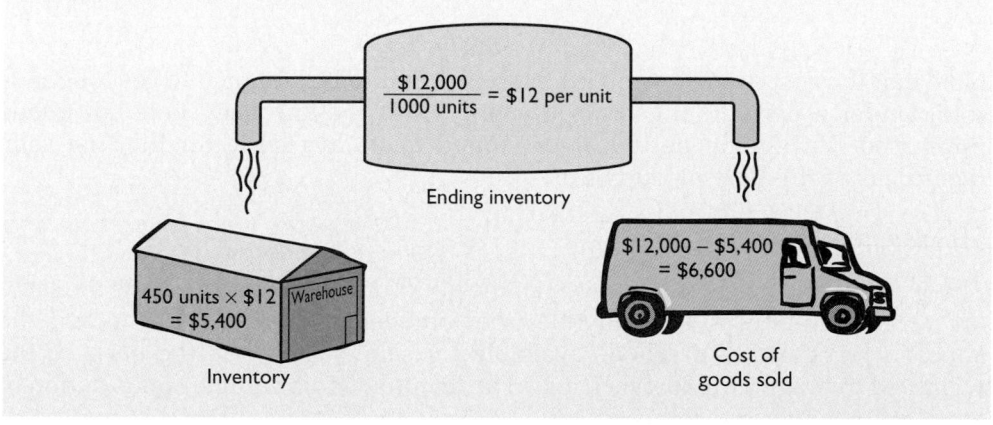

**6**
STUDY
OBJECTIVE

Explain the financial statement and tax effects of each of the inventory cost flow methods.

**ILLUSTRATION 9-19**

*Use of cost flow methods in major U.S. companies*

## Financial Statement Effects of Cost Flow Methods

Each of the three cost flow methods is acceptable. For example, Black and Decker Manufacturing Company and Wendy's International currently use the FIFO method of inventory costing. Campbell Soup Company, Krogers, and Walgreen Drugs use LIFO for part or all of their inventory. Bristol-Myers-Squibb Co. and Motorola, Inc. use the average cost method. A company may also use more than one cost flow method at the same time. Del Monte Corporation, for example, uses LIFO for domestic inventories and FIFO for foreign inventories. Illustration 9-19 shows the use of the three cost flow methods in the 600 largest companies in the U.S. The reasons why companies adopt different inventory cost flow methods are varied, but they usually involve one of the following factors:

1. Income statement effects
2. Balance sheet effects
3. Tax effects

### Income Statement Effects

To understand why companies might choose a particular cost flow method, let's examine the effects of the different flow assumptions on the financial statements of Bow Valley Electronics. The condensed income statements in Illustration 9-20 assume that Bow Valley sold its 550 units for $11,500, its operating expenses were $2,000, and its income tax rate is 30%.

ILLUSTRATION 9-20

*Comparative effects of cost flow methods*

| BOW VALLEY ELECTRONICS<br>Condensed Income Statements | | | |
|---|---|---|---|
| | FIFO | LIFO | Average Cost |
| Sales | $11,500 | $11,500 | $11,500 |
| Beginning inventory | 1,000 | 1,000 | 1,000 |
| Purchases | 11,000 | 11,000 | 11,000 |
| Cost of goods available for sale | 12,000 | 12,000 | 12,000 |
| Ending inventory | 5,800 | 5,000 | 5,400 |
| Cost of goods sold | 6,200 | 7,000 | 6,600 |
| Gross profit | 5,300 | 4,500 | 4,900 |
| Operating expenses | 2,000 | 2,000 | 2,000 |
| Income before income taxes[2] | 3,300 | 2,500 | 2,900 |
| Income tax expense (30%) | 990 | 750 | 870 |
| Net income | $ 2,310 | $ 1,750 | $ 2,030 |

Although the cost of goods available for sale ($12,000) is the same under each of the three inventory cost flow methods, both the ending inventories and cost of goods sold are different. This difference is due to the unit costs that are allocated to cost of goods sold and to ending inventory. Each dollar of difference in ending inventory results in a corresponding dollar difference in income before income taxes. For Bow Valley, there is an $800 difference between FIFO and LIFO. In a period of inflation, FIFO produced a higher net income because the lower unit costs of the first units purchased are matched against revenues. In a period of rising prices (as is the case here), FIFO reports the highest net income ($2,310) and LIFO the lowest ($1,750); average cost falls in the middle ($2,030). If prices are falling, the results from the use of FIFO and LIFO are reversed. FIFO will report the lowest net income and LIFO the highest. To management, higher net income is an advantage: it causes external users to view the company more favorably. In addition, if management bonuses are based on net income, FIFO will provide the basis for higher bonuses.

Some argue that the use of LIFO in a period of inflation enables the company to avoid reporting **paper or phantom profit** as economic gain. To illustrate, assume that Kralik Company buys 200 XR492s at $20 per unit on January 10 and 200 more on December 31 at $24 each. During the year, 200 units are sold at $30 each. The results under FIFO and LIFO are shown in Illustration 9-21.

ILLUSTRATION 9-21

*Income statement effects compared*

| | FIFO | | LIFO | |
|---|---|---|---|---|
| Sales (200 × $30) | $6,000 | | $6,000 | |
| **Cost of goods sold** | 4,000 | (200 × $20) | 4,800 | (200 × $24) |
| Gross profit | $2,000 | | $1,200 | |

---

[2]It is assumed that Bow Valley is a corporation, and corporations are required to pay income taxes.

Under LIFO, the company has recovered the current replacement cost ($4,800) of the units sold. Thus, the gross profit in economic terms is real. However, under FIFO, the company has recovered only the January 10 cost ($4,000). To replace the units sold, it must reinvest $800 (200 × $4) of the gross profit. Thus, $800 of the gross profit is said to be phantom or illusory. As a result, reported net income is also overstated in real terms.

### Balance Sheet Effects

A major advantage of the FIFO method is that in a period of inflation, the costs allocated to ending inventory will approximate their current cost. For example, for Bow Valley, 400 of the 450 units in the ending inventory are costed at the November 27 unit cost of $13.

Conversely, a major shortcoming of the LIFO method is that in a period of inflation, the costs allocated to ending inventory may be significantly understated in terms of current cost. This is true for Bow Valley, where the cost of the ending inventory includes the $10 unit cost of the beginning inventory. The understatement becomes greater over prolonged periods of inflation if the inventory includes goods purchased in one or more prior accounting periods.

### Tax Effects

We have seen that both inventory on the balance sheet and net income on the income statement are higher when FIFO is used in a period of inflation. Yet, many companies have switched to LIFO. The reason is that LIFO results in the lowest income taxes (because of lower net income) during times of rising prices. For example, at Bow Valley Electronics, income taxes are $750 under LIFO, compared to $990 under FIFO. The tax saving of $240 makes more cash available for use in the business.

## ACCOUNTING IN ACTION
### Business Insight

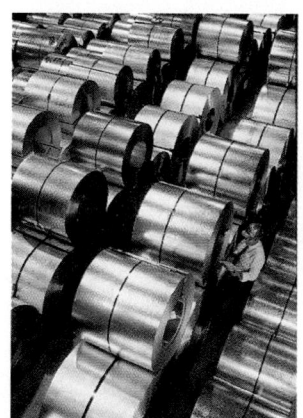

Most small firms use the FIFO method. But fears of rising inflation often cause many firms to switch to LIFO. For example, Chicago Heights Steel Co. in Illinois boosted cash "by 5% to 10% by lowering income taxes" when it switched to LIFO. Electronic games distributor Atlas Distributing Inc., Chicago, considered a switch "because the costs of our games, made in Japan, are rising 15% a year," says Joseph Serpico, treasurer. When inflation heats up, "the number of companies electing LIFO will rise dramatically," says William Spiro of BDO Seidman, New York.

## Using Inventory Cost Flow Methods Consistently

Whatever cost flow method a company chooses, it should be used consistently from one accounting period to another. Consistent application enhances the comparability of financial statements over successive time periods. In contrast, using the FIFO method in one year and the LIFO method in the next year would make it difficult to compare the net incomes of the two years.

Although consistent application is preferred, it does not mean that a company may *never* change its method of inventory costing. When a company adopts a different method, the change and its effects on net income should be disclosed in the financial statements. A typical disclosure is shown in Illustration 9-22, using information from recent financial statements of the Quaker Oats Company.

**QUAKER OATS COMPANY**
**Notes to the Financial Statements**

**ILLUSTRATION 9-22**

*Disclosure of change in cost flow method*

**Note 1**   Effective July 1, the Company adopted the LIFO cost flow assumption for valuing the majority of U.S. Grocery Products inventories. The Company believes that the use of the LIFO method better matches current costs with current revenues. The effect of this change on the current year was to decrease net income by $16.0 million.

# ACCOUNTING IN ACTION
## International Insight

U.S. companies typically choose between LIFO and FIFO. Many choose LIFO because it reduces inventory profits and taxes. However, the international community recently considered rules that would ban LIFO entirely and force companies to use FIFO. This proposal was defeated, but the issue will not go away.

The issue is sensitive. As John Wulff, controller for Union Carbide noted, "We were in support of the international effort up until the proposal to eliminate LIFO." Wulff says that if Union Carbide had been suddenly forced to switch from LIFO to FIFO, its reported $632 million pretax income would have jumped by $300 million. That would have increased Carbide's income tax bill by as much as $120 million. Given this, do you believe that accounting principles and rules should be the same around the world?

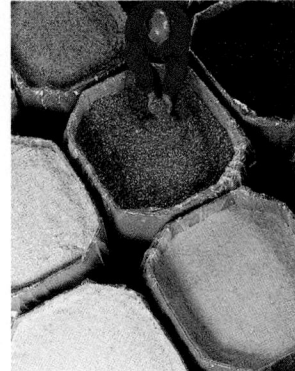

# BEFORE YOU GO ON . . .
## Review It

1. How do the cost and matching principles apply to inventoriable costs?
2. How are the three assumed cost flow methods applied in allocating inventoriable costs?
3. What factors should be considered by management in selecting an inventory cost flow method?
4. Which inventory cost flow method produces (a) the highest net income in a period of rising prices, and (b) the lowest income taxes?
5. What amount is reported by Kellogg Company in its 1997 Annual Report as inventories at December 31, 1997? Which inventory cost flow method does Kellogg Company use? The answer to this question is provided on p. 416.

## Do It

The accounting records of Shumway Ag Implement show the following data:

|  |  |
|---|---|
| Beginning inventory | 4,000 units at $3 |
| Purchases | 6,000 units at $4 |
| Sales | 5,000 units at $12 |

Determine the cost of goods sold during the period under a periodic inventory system using (a) the FIFO method, (b) the LIFO method, and (c) the average cost method.

*Reasoning:* Because the units of inventory on hand and available for sale may have been purchased at different prices, a systematic method must be adopted to allocate the costs between the goods sold and the goods on hand (ending inventory).

*Solution:*

(a) FIFO:   (4,000 @ $3) + (1,000 @ $4) = $12,000 + $4,000 = $16,000.

(b) LIFO:   5,000 @ $4 = $20,000.

(c) Average cost: [(4,000 @ $3) + (6,000 @ $4)] ÷ 10,000 = ($12,000 + $24,000) ÷ 10,000 = $3.60 per unit; 5,000 @ $3.60 = $18,000.

*Related exercise material:* BE9-6, BE9-7, E9-5, E9-6, E9-7.

THE NAVIGATOR

# VALUING INVENTORY AT THE LOWER OF COST OR MARKET (LCM)

**7**
STUDY
OBJECTIVE

Explain the lower of cost
or market basis
of accounting for
inventories.

When the value of inventory is lower than its cost, the inventory is written down to its market value. This is accomplished by valuing the inventory at the lower of cost or market (LCM) in the period in which the price decline occurs. LCM is an example of the accounting concept of conservatism. **Conservatism** means that when choosing among accounting alternatives, the best choice is to select the method that is least likely to overstate assets and net income.

Under the LCM basis, market is defined as current replacement cost, not selling price. For a merchandising company, market is the cost of purchasing the same goods at the present time from the usual suppliers in the usual quantities. Current replacement cost is used because a decline in the replacement cost of an item usually leads to a decline in the selling price of the item.

The lower of cost or market basis may be applied to individual items of inventory, major categories of inventory, or total inventory. For example, assume that Len's TV has the following lines of merchandise with costs and market values as indicated. LCM produces the following three results:

**ILLUSTRATION 9-23**

*Alternative lower of cost or
market results*

|  | Cost | Market | Lower of Cost or Market by: Individual Items | Lower of Cost or Market by: Major Categories | Lower of Cost or Market by: Total Inventory |
|---|---|---|---|---|---|
| Television sets |  |  |  |  |  |
| Consoles | $ 60,000 | $ 55,000 | $ 55,000 |  |  |
| Portables | 45,000 | 52,000 | 45,000 |  |  |
| Total | 105,000 | 107,000 |  | $105,000 |  |
| Video equipment |  |  |  |  |  |
| Recorders | 48,000 | 45,000 | 45,000 |  |  |
| Movies | 15,000 | 14,000 | 14,000 |  |  |
| Total | 63,000 | 59,000 |  | 59,000 |  |
| Total inventory | $168,000 | $166,000 | $159,000 | $164,000 | $166,000 |

The amount entered in the individual items column is the lower of the cost or market amount for **each item**. For the major categories column, the amount is the lower of the total cost or total market for **each category**. Finally, the amount for the total inventory column is the lower of the cost or market for the **entire inventory**. The common practice is to use individual items in determining the LCM valuation. This approach gives the most conservative valuation for balance sheet purposes and also the lowest net income. LCM should be applied consistently from period to period.

LCM is applied to the items in inventory after one of the costing methods (specific identification, FIFO, LIFO, or average cost) has been applied to determine cost.

**8**
STUDY
OBJECTIVE

Indicate the effects of
inventory errors on the
financial statements.

# INVENTORY ERRORS

Unfortunately, errors occasionally occur in taking or costing inventory. In some cases, errors are caused by failure to count or price the inventory correctly. In other cases, errors occur because proper recognition is not given to the transfer of legal title to goods that are in transit. When errors occur, they affect both the income statement and the balance sheet.

## Income Statement Effects

Remember that both the beginning and ending inventories are used to determine cost of goods sold in a periodic system. The ending inventory of one period automatically becomes the beginning inventory of the next period. Inventory errors affect the determination of cost of goods sold and net income.

The effects on cost of goods sold can be determined by entering the incorrect data in the following formula and then substituting the correct data.

**ILLUSTRATION 9-24**

*Formula for cost of goods sold*

**ETHICS NOTE**

Inventory fraud includes pricing inventory at amounts in excess of their actual value, or claiming to have inventory when no inventory exists. Inventory fraud is usually done to overstate ending inventory, and so understate cost of goods sold and create higher income.

If beginning inventory is understated, cost of goods sold will be understated. On the other hand, an understatement of ending inventory will overstate cost of goods sold. The effects of inventory errors on the current year's income statement are shown in Illustration 9-25.

| Inventory Error | Cost of Goods Sold | Net Income |
|---|---|---|
| Understate beginning inventory | Understated | Overstated |
| Overstate beginning inventory | Overstated | Understated |
| Understate ending inventory | Overstated | Understated |
| Overstate ending inventory | Understated | Overstated |

**ILLUSTRATION 9-25**

*Effects of inventory errors on current year's income statement*

An error in ending inventory of the current period will have a **reverse effect on net income of the next accounting period**. This is shown in Illustration 9-26 on the next page. Note that the understatement of ending inventory in 1999 results in an understatement of beginning inventory in 2000 and an overstatement of net income in 2000.

Over the 2 years, total net income is correct because the errors offset one another. Notice that total income using incorrect data is $35,000 ($22,000 + $13,000), which is the same as the total income of $35,000 ($25,000 + $10,000) using correct data. Also note in this example that an error in the beginning inventory does not result in a corresponding error in the ending inventory for that period. The correctness of the ending inventory depends entirely on the accuracy of taking and costing the inventory at the balance sheet date.

## Balance Sheet Effects

The effect of ending inventory errors on the balance sheet can be determined by using the basic accounting equation: assets equal liabilities plus owner's

**Condensed Income Statement**

| | 1999 | | | | 2000 | | | |
|---|---|---|---|---|---|---|---|---|
| | Incorrect | | Correct | | Incorrect | | Correct | |
| Sales | | $80,000 | | $80,000 | | $90,000 | | $90,000 |
| Beginning inventory | $20,000 | | $20,000 | | **$12,000** | | **$15,000** | |
| Cost of goods purchased | 40,000 | | 40,000 | | 68,000 | | 68,000 | |
| Cost of goods available for sale | 60,000 | | 60,000 | | 80,000 | | 83,000 | |
| Ending inventory | **12,000** | | **15,000** | | 23,000 | | 23,000 | |
| Cost of goods sold | | 48,000 | | 45,000 | | 57,000 | | 60,000 |
| Gross profit | | 32,000 | | 35,000 | | 33,000 | | 30,000 |
| Operating expenses | | 10,000 | | 10,000 | | 20,000 | | 20,000 |
| Net income | | $22,000 | | $25,000 | | $13,000 | | $10,000 |

($3,000)
Net income
understated

$3,000
Net income
overstated

Total income for
2 years correct

**ILLUSTRATION 9-26**

*Effects of inventory errors on 2 years' income statements*

equity. Errors in the ending inventory have the following effects on these components:

**ILLUSTRATION 9-27**

*Ending inventory error— balance sheet effects*

| Ending Inventory Error | Assets | Liabilities | Owner's Equity |
|---|---|---|---|
| Overstated | Overstated | None | Overstated |
| Understated | Understated | None | Understated |

The effect of an error in ending inventory on the subsequent period was shown in Illustration 9-26. Recall that if the error is not corrected, total net income for the two periods would be correct. Thus, total owner's equity reported on the balance sheet at the end of 2000 will also be correct.

# STATEMENT PRESENTATION AND ANALYSIS

As indicated in an earlier chapter, inventory is classified as a current asset after receivables in the balance sheet, and cost of goods sold is subtracted from sales in a multiple-step income statement. In addition, there should be disclosure of (1) the major inventory classifications, (2) the basis of accounting (cost or lower of cost or market), and (3) the costing method (FIFO, LIFO, or average).

Kellogg Company, for example, in its December 31, 1997, balance sheet reported inventory of $434,300,000 under current assets. The accompanying notes to the financial statements, as shown in Illustration 9-28, disclosed the following information:

**KELLOGG COMPANY**
**Notes to the Financial Statements**

Note 1. Accounting Policies
Inventories
Inventories are valued at the lower of cost (principally average) or market.

**ILLUSTRATION 9-28**

*Inventory disclosures by Kellogg Company*

As indicated in this brief note, Kellogg Company values its inventories at the lower of cost or market using the average cost method to apply costs to inventory and cost of goods sold.

The amount of inventory carried by a company has significant economic consequences. And, inventory management is a double-edged sword that requires constant attention. On the one hand, management wants to have a great variety and quantity on hand so customers have the greatest selection and inventory items are always in stock. But, such an inventory policy may incur excessive carrying costs (e.g., investment, storage, insurance, taxes, obsolescence, and damage). On the other hand, low inventory levels lead to stockouts, lost sales, and disgruntled customers. Common ratios used in the management and evaluation of inventory levels are inventory turnover and a related measure, average days to sell the inventory.

The **inventory turnover ratio** measures the number of times on average the inventory is sold during the period. Its purpose is to measure the liquidity of the inventory. The inventory turnover is computed by dividing cost of goods sold by the average inventory during the period. Unless seasonal factors are significant, average inventory can be computed from the beginning and ending inventory balances. For example, Kellogg Company reported in its 1997 Annual Report a beginning inventory of $424,900,000, and cost of goods sold for the year 1997 of $3,270,100,000; its inventory turnover formula and computation are shown below:

**9**
**STUDY**
**OBJECTIVE**
................................
Compute and interpret the inventory turnover ratio.

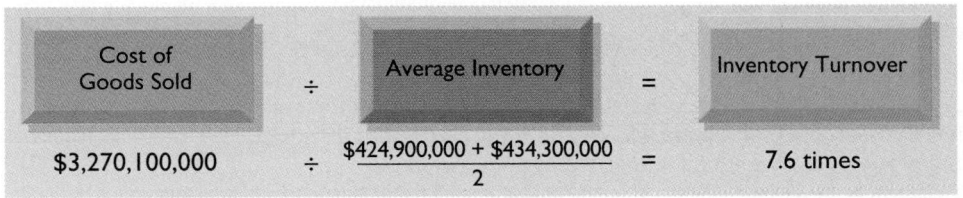

$$\text{Cost of Goods Sold} \div \text{Average Inventory} = \text{Inventory Turnover}$$

$$\$3,270,100,000 \div \frac{\$424,900,000 + \$434,300,000}{2} = 7.6 \text{ times}$$

**ILLUSTRATION 9-29**

*Inventory turnover formula and computation for Kellogg Company*

A variant of the inventory turnover ratio is the **average days to sell inventory**. For example, the inventory turnover for Kellogg Company of 7.6 times divided into 365 is approximately 48 days. There are typical levels of inventory in every industry. However, companies that are able to keep their inventory at lower levels and higher turnovers and still satisfy customer needs are the most successful.

## BEFORE YOU GO ON . . .

### Review It

1. Why is it appropriate to report inventories at the lower of cost or market?
2. How do inventory errors affect financial statements?
3. What does the inventory turnover ratio reveal?

## A LOOK BACK AT OUR FEATURE STORY

Refer to the opening story concerning the bookstore at Erie Community College, and answer the following questions.
1. Why might a small bookstore use specific identification to determine inventory?
2. If the inventory is overstated at the end of the month, what effect does this error have on the balance sheet and the income statement?

*Solution:*

1. A small bookstore, as opposed to a large bookstore, might use specific identification because of:
   a. A smaller number of any one book in inventory.
   b. Fewer different books in inventory.
   c. The familiarity of the owner/manager (who handles sales) with the books being sold.
2. An end-of-month, inventory overstatement will result in overstated inventory in the balance sheet along with overstated stockholders' equity, due to overstated net income on the income statement. Cost of goods sold will be understated on the income statement. The next month's income statement will have overstated beginning inventory and understated net income.

THE
NAVIGATOR

## DEMONSTRATION PROBLEM

Gerald D. Englehart Company has the following inventory, purchases, and sales data for the month of March:

| Inventory, March 1 | 200 units @ $4.00 | $ 800 |
|---|---|---|
| Purchases: | | |
| March 10 | 500 units @ $4.50 | 2,250 |
| March 20 | 400 units @ $4.75 | 1,900 |
| March 30 | 300 units @ $5.00 | 1,500 |
| Sales: | | |
| March 15 | 500 units | |
| March 25 | 400 units | |

The physical inventory count on March 31 shows 500 units on hand.

### PROBLEM-SOLVING STRATEGIES

1. For FIFO, the latest costs are allocated to inventory.
2. For LIFO, the earliest costs are allocated to inventory.
3. For average costs, use a weighted average for periodic.
4. Remember, the costs allocated to cost of goods sold can be proved.
5. Total purchases are the same under all three cost flow methods.

*Instructions*

Under a **periodic inventory system**, determine the cost of inventory on hand at March 31 and the cost of goods sold for March under the (a) first-in, first-out (FIFO) method, (b) last-in, first-out (LIFO) method, and (c) average cost method.

### SOLUTION TO DEMONSTRATION PROBLEM

The cost of goods available for sale is $6,450:

| Inventory | 200 units @ $4.00 | $ 800 |
|---|---|---|
| Purchases: | | |
| March 10 | 500 units @ $4.50 | 2,250 |
| March 20 | 400 units @ $4.75 | 1,900 |
| March 30 | 300 units @ $5.00 | 1,500 |
| Total cost of goods available for sale | | $6,450 |

Under a **periodic inventory system**, the cost of goods sold under each cost flow method is as follows:

### FIFO Method

Ending Inventory:

| Date | Units | Unit Cost | Total Cost | |
|---|---|---|---|---|
| March 30 | 300 | $5.00 | $1,500 | |
| March 20 | 200 | 4.75 | 950 | $2,450 |

Cost of goods sold: $6,450 − $2,450 =                                              $4,000

### LIFO Method

Ending Inventory:

| Date | Units | Unit Cost | Total Cost | |
|---|---|---|---|---|
| March 1 | 200 | $4.00 | $ 800 | |
| March 10 | 300 | 4.50 | 1,350 | $2,150 |

Cost of goods sold: $6,450 − $2,150 =                                              $4,300

### Weighted Average Cost Method

Weighted average unit cost: $6,450 ÷ 1,400 = $4.607
Ending inventory: 500 × $4.607 =                                              $2,303.50

Cost of goods sold: $6,450 − $2,303.50 =                                       $4,146.50

THE NAVIGATOR

# SUMMARY OF STUDY OBJECTIVES

**1. Describe the steps in determining inventory quantities.** The steps in determining inventory quantities are (1) taking a physical inventory of goods on hand and (2) determining the ownership of goods in transit.

**2. Prepare the entries for purchases and sales of inventory under a periodic inventory system.** In recording purchases, entries are required for (a) cash and credit purchases, (b) purchase returns and allowances, (c) purchase discounts, and (d) freight costs. In recording sales, entries are required for (a) cash and credit sales, (b) sales returns and allowances, and (c) sales discounts.

**3. Determine cost of goods sold under a periodic inventory system.** The steps in determining cost of goods sold are (a) recording the purchase of merchandise, (b) determining the cost of goods purchased, and (c) determining the cost of goods on hand at the beginning and end of the accounting period.

**4. Identify the unique features of the income statement for a merchandising company using a periodic inventory system.** The income statement for a merchandising company contains three sections: sales revenue, cost of goods sold, and operating expenses. The cost of goods sold section under a periodic inventory system generally shows more detail by reporting beginning and ending inventory, net purchases, and total goods available for sale.

**5. Explain the basis of accounting for inventories and describe the inventory cost flow methods.** The primary basis of accounting for inventories is cost. Cost includes all expenditures necessary to acquire goods and place them in condition ready for sale. Inventoriable costs include (1) cost of beginning inventory and (2) the cost of goods purchased. The inventory cost flow methods are: specific identification, FIFO, LIFO, and average cost.

**6. Explain the financial statement and tax effects of each of the inventory cost flow methods.** The cost of goods available for sale may be allocated to cost of goods sold and ending inventory by specific identification or by a method based on an assumed cost flow. These methods have different effects on financial statements during periods of changing prices. When prices are rising, the first-in, first-out method (FIFO) results in lower cost of goods sold and higher net income than the average and the last-in, first-out (LIFO) methods. LIFO results in the lowest income taxes (because of lower net income). The reverse is true when prices are falling. In the balance sheet, FIFO results in an ending inventory that is closest to current value, whereas the inventory under LIFO is the farthest from current value.

**7. Explain the lower of cost or market basis of accounting for inventories.** The lower of cost or market basis (LCM) is used when the current replacement cost (market) is less than cost. Under LCM, the loss is recognized in the period in which the price decline occurs. LCM may be applied to individual inventory items, major categories of inventory, or to total inventory.

**8.** *Indicate the effects of inventory errors on the financial statements.* In the income statement of the current year: (a) an error in beginning inventory will have a reverse effect on net income (overstatement of inventory results in understatement of net income) and (b) an error in ending inventory will have a similar effect on net income (overstatement of inventory results in overstatement of net income). If ending inventory errors are not corrected in the following period, their effect on net income for that period is reversed, and total net income for the two years will be correct. In the balance sheet, ending inventory errors will have the same effect on total assets and total stockholders' equity and no effect on liabilities.

**9.** *Compute and interpret the inventory turnover ratio.* The inventory turnover ratio is calculated as cost of goods sold divided by average inventory. It can be converted to average days in inventory by dividing 365 days by the inventory turnover ratio. A higher turnover ratio or lower average days in inventory suggests that management is trying to keep inventory levels low relative to its sales level.

THE NAVIGATOR

# GLOSSARY

**Average cost method**   An inventory costing method that assumes that the goods available for sale have the same (average) cost per unit; generally they are homogeneous. (p. 381).

**Consigned goods**   Goods shipped by a consignor, who retains ownership, to another party called the consignee. (p. 369).

**Cost of goods available for sale**   The sum of the beginning merchandise inventory plus the cost of goods purchased. (p. 374).

**Cost of goods purchased**   The sum of net purchases plus freight-in. (p. 374).

**Cost of goods sold**   The total cost of merchandise sold during the period, determined by subtracting ending inventory from the cost of goods available for sale. (p. 374).

**Current replacement cost**   The amount that would be paid at the present time to acquire an identical item. (p. 386).

**First-in, first-out method (FIFO)**   An inventory costing method that assumes that the costs of the earliest goods acquired are the first to be recognized as cost of goods sold. (p. 378).

**Inventoriable costs**   The pool of costs that consists of two elements: (1) the cost of the beginning inventory and (2) the cost of goods purchased during the period. (p. 376).

**Inventory turnover ratio**   A ratio that measures the number of times on average the inventory is sold during the period. It is computed by dividing cost of goods sold by the average inventory during the period. (p. 389).

**Last-in, first-out method (LIFO)**   An inventory costing method that assumes that the costs of the latest units purchased are the first to be allocated to cost of goods sold. (p. 380).

**Lower of cost or market basis (LCM) (inventories)**   A method of valuing inventory that recognizes the decline in the value when the current purchase price (market) is less than cost. (p. 386).

**Net purchases**   Purchases less purchase returns and allowances and purchase discounts. (p. 374).

**Periodic inventory system**   An inventory system in which inventoriable costs are allocated to ending inventory and cost of goods sold at the end of the period. Cost of goods sold is computed at the end of the period by subtracting the ending inventory (costs are assigned to a physical count of items on hand) from the cost of goods available for sale. (p. 370).

**Specific identification method**   An actual physical flow costing method in which items still in inventory are specifically costed to arrive at the total cost of the ending inventory. (p. 377).

# APPENDIX 9A   ESTIMATING INVENTORIES

**10**
STUDY
OBJECTIVE

Describe the two methods of estimating inventories.

We have assumed throughout the chapter that a company would be able to do a physical count of its inventory. But what if it cannot, as in the example of the lumber inventory destroyed by fire? In that case, we would use an estimate.

Two circumstances explain the reasons for estimating rather than counting inventories. First, management may want monthly or quarterly financial statements but a physical inventory is taken only annually. Second, a casualty such as fire, flood, or earthquake may make it impossible to take a physical inventory. The need for estimating inventories is associated primarily with a periodic inventory system because of the absence of detailed inventory records.

There are two widely used methods of estimating inventories: (1) the gross profit method and (2) the retail inventory method.

# GROSS PROFIT METHOD

The gross profit method estimates the cost of ending inventory by applying a gross profit rate to net sales. It is used in preparing monthly financial statements under a periodic system when physical inventories are not taken. This method is a relatively simple but effective estimation technique. Accountants, auditors, and managers frequently use the gross profit method to test the reasonableness of the ending inventory amount. This method will detect large errors. To use this method, a company needs to know its net sales, cost of goods available for sale, and gross profit rate. The company then uses the gross profit rate to estimate its gross profit for the accounting period. The formulas for using the gross profit method are given in Illustration 9A-1.

ILLUSTRATION 9A-1

*Gross profit method formulas*

To illustrate, assume that Williams Company wishes to prepare an income statement for the month of January, when its records show net sales $200,000; beginning inventory $40,000; and cost of goods purchased $120,000. In the preceding year, the company realized a 30% gross profit rate, and it expects to earn the same rate this year. Given these facts and assumptions, the estimated cost of the ending inventory at January 31 under the gross profit method is $20,000, computed as follows:

ILLUSTRATION 9A-2

*Example of gross profit method*

| Step 1: | |
|---|---|
| Net sales | $200,000 |
| Less: Estimated gross profit (30% × $200,000) | 60,000 |
| **Estimated cost of goods sold** | **$140,000** |
| | |
| Step 2: | |
| Beginning inventory | $ 40,000 |
| Cost of goods purchased | 120,000 |
| Cost of goods available for sale | 160,000 |
| Less: Estimated cost of goods sold | 140,000 |
| **Estimated cost of ending inventory** | **$ 20,000** |

The gross profit method is based on the assumption that the rate of gross profit will remain constant from one year to the next. It may not remain constant, though, because of a change either in merchandising policies or in market conditions. In such cases, the rate of the prior period should be adjusted to reflect current operating conditions. In some cases, a more accurate estimate may be obtained by applying this method on a department or product-line basis.

The gross profit method should not be used in preparing a company's financial statements at the end of the year. These statements should be based on a physical inventory count.

# RETAIL INVENTORY METHOD

A retail store such as Kmart, Ace Hardware, or Wal-Mart has thousands of different types of merchandise at low unit costs. In such cases the application of unit costs to inventory quantities is difficult and time-consuming. An alternative is to use the retail inventory method to estimate the cost of inventory. In most retail concerns, a relationship between cost and sales price can be established. Under the retail inventory method, the cost to retail percentage is then applied to the ending inventory at retail prices to determine inventory at cost.

To use the retail inventory method, a company must maintain records that show both the cost and retail value of the goods available for sale. Under the retail inventory method, the estimated cost of the ending inventory is derived from the formulas presented in Illustration 9A-3.

**ILLUSTRATION 9A-3**

*Retail inventory method formulas*

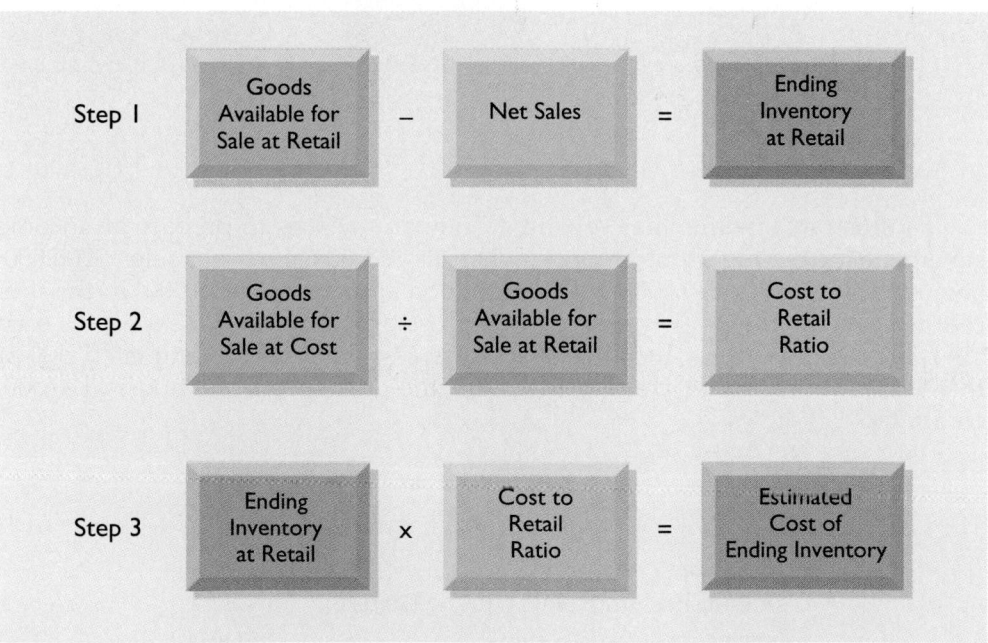

The logic of the retail method can be demonstrated by using unit cost data. Assume that 10 units purchased at $7.00 each are marked to sell for $10 per unit. Thus, the cost to retail ratio is 70% ($70 ÷ $100). If 4 units remain unsold, their retail value is $40 and their cost is $28 ($40 × 70%), which agrees with the total cost of goods on hand on a per unit basis (4 × $7).

The application of the retail method based on the accounting records and supplementary data for Lacy Co. is shown in Illustration 9A-4. Note that it is not necessary to take a physical inventory to determine the estimated cost of goods on hand at any given time.

|  | At Cost | At Retail |
|---|---|---|
| Beginning inventory | $14,000 | $ 21,500 |
| Goods purchased | 61,000 | 78,500 |
| Goods available for sale | $75,000 | 100,000 |
| Net sales | | 70,000 |
| **(1) Ending inventory at retail** | | **$ 30,000** |
| **(2) Cost to retail ratio = ($75,000 ÷ $100,000) = 75%** | | |
| **(3) Estimated cost of ending inventory = ($30,000 × 75%)** | **$22,500** | |

**ILLUSTRATION 9A-4**

*Example of retail inventory method*

The retail inventory method also facilitates taking a physical inventory at the end of year. With this method, the goods on hand can be valued at the prices marked on the merchandise. The cost to retail ratio is then applied to the goods actually on hand at retail to determine the ending inventory at cost.

The major disadvantage of the retail method is that it is an averaging technique. It may produce an incorrect inventory valuation if the mix of the ending inventory is not representative of the mix in the goods available for sale. Assume, for example, that the cost to retail ratio of 75% in the Lacy Co. consists of equal proportions of inventory items that have cost to retail ratios of 70%, 75%, and 80%, respectively. If the ending inventory contains only items with a 70% ratio, an incorrect inventory cost will result. This problem can be minimized by applying the retail method on a departmental or product-line basis.

**HELPFUL HINT**
In determining inventory at retail, selling prices on the units are used, and tracing actual unit costs to invoices is unnecessary.

# SUMMARY OF STUDY OBJECTIVE FOR APPENDIX 9A

**10. *Describe the two methods of estimating inventories.*** The two methods of estimating inventories are the gross profit method and the retail inventory method. Under the gross profit method, a gross profit rate is applied to net sales to determine estimated cost of goods sold. Estimated cost of goods sold is then subtracted from cost of goods available for sale to determine the estimated cost of the ending inventory. Under the retail inventory method, a cost to retail ratio is computed by dividing the cost of goods available for sale by the retail value of the goods available for sale. This ratio is then applied to the ending inventory at retail to determine the estimated cost of the ending inventory.

# GLOSSARY FOR APPENDIX 9A
• • • • • • • • • • • • • • • • • • • • • • • • • • • • • • • • • • • • • • • • • • • • • • • • • • • • • • •

**Gross profit method**   A method for estimating the cost of the ending inventory by applying a gross profit rate to net sales. (p. 393).

**Retail inventory method**   A method used to estimate the cost of the ending inventory by applying a cost to retail ratio to the ending inventory at retail. (p. 394).

# APPENDIX 9B INVENTORY COST FLOW METHODS IN PERPETUAL INVENTORY SYSTEMS

**11**
STUDY
OBJECTIVE

Apply the inventory cost flow methods to perpetual inventory records.

Each of the inventory cost flow methods described in the chapter for a periodic inventory system may be used in a perpetual inventory system. To illustrate the application of the three assumed cost flow methods (FIFO, LIFO, and average cost), we will use the data shown below and in this chapter for Bow Valley Electronics' product Z202 Astro Condenser.

**BOW VALLEY ELECTRONICS**
**Z202 Astro Condensers**

| Date | Explanation | Units | Unit Cost | Total Cost | Balance in Units |
|------|-------------|-------|-----------|------------|------------------|
| 1/1 | Beginning inventory | 100 | $10 | $1,000 | 100 |
| 4/15 | Purchases | 200 | 11 | 2,200 | 300 |
| 8/24 | Purchases | 300 | 12 | 3,600 | 600 |
| 9/10 | Sales | 550 | | | 50 |
| 11/27 | Purchases | 400 | 13 | 5,200 | 450 |
| | | | | $12,000 | |

**ILLUSTRATION 9B-1**

*Inventoriable units and costs*

## FIRST-IN, FIRST-OUT (FIFO)

Under FIFO, the cost of the earliest goods on hand prior to each sale is charged to cost of goods sold. Therefore, the cost of goods sold on September 10 consists of the units on hand January 1 and the units purchased April 15 and August 24. The inventory on a FIFO method perpetual system is shown in Illustration 9B-2.

**ILLUSTRATION 9B-2**

*Perpetual system—FIFO*

| Date | Purchases | Sales | Balance |
|------|-----------|-------|---------|
| January 1 | | | (100 @ $10)  $1,000 |
| April 15 | (200 @ $11)  $2,200 | | (100 @ $10) }  $3,200 (200 @ $11) |
| August 24 | (300 @ $12)  $3,600 | | (100 @ $10) (200 @ $11) } $6,800 (300 @ $12) |
| September 10 | | (100 @ $10) (200 @ $11) (250 @ $12) | (50 @ $12)  $ 600 |
| | | $6,200 | |
| November 27 | (400 @ $13)  $5,200 | | (50 @ $12) } $5,800 (400 @ $13) |

The ending inventory in this situation is $5,800 and the cost of goods sold is $6,200 [(100 @ $10) + (200 @ $11) + (250 @ $12)].

The results under FIFO in a perpetual system are the **same as in a periodic system** (see Illustration 9-10 on page 379 where, similarly, the ending inventory is $5,800 and cost of goods sold is $6,200). Regardless of the system, the first costs in are the costs assigned to cost of goods sold.

# LAST-IN, FIRST-OUT (LIFO)

Under the LIFO method using a perpetual system, the cost of the most recent purchase prior to sale is allocated to the units sold. Therefore, the cost of the goods sold on September 10 consists of all the units from the August 24 and April 15 purchases and 50 of the units in beginning inventory. The ending inventory on a LIFO method is computed in Illustration 9B-3.

| Date | Purchases | Sales | Balance |
|------|-----------|-------|---------|
| January 1 | | | (100 @ $10)   $1,000 |
| April 15 | (200 @ $11)   $2,200 | | (100 @ $10) ⎫<br>(200 @ $11) ⎬ $3,200 |
| August 24 | (300 @ $12)   $3,600 | | (100 @ $10) ⎫<br>(200 @ $11) ⎬ $6,800<br>(300 @ $12) ⎭ |
| September 10 | | (300 @ $12)<br>(200 @ $11)<br>(50 @ $10)<br>‾‾‾‾‾‾‾‾<br>$6,300 | (50 @ $10)   $   500 |
| November 27 | (400 @ $13)   $5,200 | | (50 @ $10) ⎫<br>(400 @ $13) ⎬ $5,700 |

**ILLUSTRATION 9B-3**

*Perpetual system—LIFO*

The use of LIFO in a perpetual system will usually produce cost allocations that differ from using LIFO in a periodic system. In a perpetual system, the latest units incurred prior to each sale are allocated to cost of goods sold. In contrast, in a periodic system, the latest units incurred during the period are allocated to cost of goods sold. Thus, when a purchase is made after the last sale, the LIFO periodic system will apply this purchase to the previous sale. See Illustration 9-15 on page 381 where the proof shows the 400 units @ $13 purchased on November 27 applied to the sale of 550 units on September 10.

As shown above under the LIFO perpetual system, the 400 units @ $13 purchased on November 27 are all applied to the ending inventory.

The ending inventory in this LIFO perpetual illustration is $5,700 and cost of goods sold is $6,300 as compared to the LIFO periodic illustration where the ending inventory is $5,000 and cost of goods sold is $7,000.

# AVERAGE COST

The average cost method in a perpetual inventory system is called the **moving average method**. Under this method a new average is computed **after each purchase**. The average cost is computed by dividing the cost of goods available for sale by the units on hand. The average cost is then applied to: (1) the units sold, to determine the cost of goods sold, and (2) the remaining units on hand, to determine the ending inventory amount. The application of the average cost method by Bow Valley Electronics is shown in Illustration 9B-4.

ILLUSTRATION 9B-4

*Perpetual system—average cost method*

| Date | Purchases | | Sales | | Balance | |
|------|-----------|---|-------|---|---------|---|
| January 1 | | | | | (100 @ $10) | $1,000 |
| April 15 | (200 @ $11) | $2,200 | | | (300 @ $10.667) | $3,200 |
| August 24 | (300 @ $12) | $3,600 | | | (600 @ $11.333) | $6,800 |
| September 10 | | | (550 @ $11.333) | ($6,233) | (50 @ $11.333) | $ 567 |
| November 27 | (400 @ $13) | $5,200 | | | (450 @ $12.816) | $5,767 |

As indicated above, **a new average is computed each time a purchase is made**. On April 15, after 200 units are purchased for $2,200, a total of 300 units costing $3,200 ($1,000 + $2,200) are on hand. The average unit cost is $10.667 ($3,200 ÷ 300). On August 24, after 300 units are purchased for $3,600, a total of 600 units costing $6,800 ($1,000 + $2,200 + $3,600) are on hand at an average cost per unit of $11.333 ($6,800 ÷ 600). This unit cost of $11.333 is used in costing sales until another purchase is made, when a new unit cost is computed. Accordingly, the unit cost of the 550 units sold on September 10 is $11.333, and the total cost of goods sold is $6,233. On November 27, following the purchase of 400 units for $5,200, there are 450 units on hand costing $5,767 ($567 + $5,200) with a new average cost of $12.816 ($5,767 ÷ 450).

This moving average cost under the perpetual inventory system should be compared to Illustration 9-17 on page 382 showing the weighted average method under a periodic inventory system.

# DEMONSTRATION PROBLEM

The Demonstration Problem on page 390 showed cost of goods sold computations under a periodic inventory system. Now let's assume that Gerald D. Englehart Company uses a perpetual inventory system and has the same inventory, purchases, and sales data for the month of March as shown earlier:

|  | | | |
|--|--|--|--|
| Inventory, March 1 | | 200 units @ $4.00 | $ 800 |
| Purchases: | | | |
| | March 10 | 500 units @ $4.50 | 2,250 |
| | March 20 | 400 units @ $4.75 | 1,900 |
| | March 30 | 300 units @ $5.00 | 1,500 |
| Sales: | | | |
| | March 15 | 500 units | |
| | March 25 | 400 units | |

The physical inventory count on March 31 shows 500 units on hand.

## PROBLEM-SOLVING STRATEGIES

1. For FIFO, the latest costs are allocated to inventory.

2. For LIFO, the earliest costs are allocated to inventory.

3. For average costs, use a weighted average for periodic and a moving average for perpetual.

4. Remember, the costs allocated to cost of goods sold can be proved.

5. Total purchases are the same under all three cost flow methods.

*Instructions*

Under a **perpetual inventory system**, determine the cost of inventory on hand at March 31 and the cost of goods sold for March under the (a) first-in, first-out (FIFO) method, (b) last-in, first-out (LIFO) method, and (c) average cost method.

## SOLUTION TO DEMONSTRATION PROBLEM

The cost of goods available for sale is $6,450:

|  | | | |
|--|--|--|--|
| Inventory | | 200 units @ $4.00 | $ 800 |
| Purchases: | | | |
| | March 10 | 500 units @ $4.50 | 2,250 |
| | March 20 | 400 units @ $4.75 | 1,900 |
| | March 30 | 300 units @ $5.00 | 1,500 |
| Total cost of goods available for sale | | | $6,450 |

Under a **perpetual inventory system**, the cost of goods sold under each cost flow method is as follows:

### FIFO Method

| Date | Purchases | | Sales | Balance | |
|------|-----------|---|-------|---------|---|
| March 1 | | | | (200 @ $4.00) | $ 800 |
| March 10 | (500 @ $4.50) | $2,250 | | (200 @ $4.00) (500 @ $4.50) } | $3,050 |
| March 15 | | | (200 @ $4.00) (300 @ $4.50) — $2,150 | (200 @ $4.50) | $ 900 |
| March 20 | (400 @ $4.75) | $1,900 | | (200 @ $4.50) (400 @ $4.75) } | $2,800 |
| March 25 | | | (200 @ $4.50) (200 @ $4.75) — $1,850 | (200 @ $4.75) | $ 950 |
| March 30 | (300 @ $5.00) | $1,500 | | (200 @ $4.75) (300 @ $5.00) } | $2,450 |

Ending inventory, $2,450. Cost of goods sold: $6,450 − $2,450 = $4,000

### LIFO Method

| Date | Purchases | | Sales | | Balance | |
|------|-----------|---|-------|---|---------|---|
| March 1 | | | | | (200 @ $4.00) | $ 800 |
| March 10 | (500 @ $4.50) | $2,250 | | | (200 @ $4.00) (500 @ $4.50) } | $3,050 |
| March 15 | | | (500 @ $4.50) | $2,250 | (200 @ $4.00) | $ 800 |
| March 20 | (400 @ $4.75) | $1,900 | | | (200 @ $4.00) (200 @ $4.75) } | $2,700 |
| March 25 | | | (400 @ $4.75) | $1,900 | (200 @ $4.00) | $ 800 |
| March 30 | (300 @ $5.00) | $1,500 | | | (200 @ $4.00) (300 @ $5.00) } | $2,300 |

Ending inventory, $2,300. Cost of goods sold: $6,450 − $2,300 = $4,150

### Moving Average Cost Method

| Date | Purchases | | Sales | | Balance | |
|------|-----------|---|-------|---|---------|---|
| March 1 | | | | | (200 @ $4.00) | $ 800 |
| March 10 | (500 @ $4.50) | $2,250 | | | (700 @ $4.357) | $3,050 |
| March 15 | | | (500 @ $4.357) | $2,179 | (200 @ $4.357) | $ 871 |
| March 20 | (400 @ $4.75) | $1,900 | | | (600 @ $4.618) | $2,771 |
| March 25 | | | (400 @ $4.618) | $1,847 | (200 @ $4.618) | $ 924 |
| March 30 | (300 @ $5.00) | $1,500 | | | (500 @ $4.848) | $2,424 |

Ending inventory, $2,424. Cost of goods sold: $6,450 − $2,424 = $4,026

# SUMMARY OF STUDY OBJECTIVE FOR APPENDIX 9B

**11. *Apply the inventory cost flow methods to perpetual inventory records.*** Under FIFO, the cost of the earliest goods on hand prior to each sale is charged to cost of goods sold. Under LIFO, the cost of the most recent purchase prior to sale is charged to cost of goods sold. Under the average cost method, a new average cost is computed after each purchase.

*Note: All asterisked Questions, Exercises, and Problems relate to material in the appendixes to the chapter.

# SELF-STUDY QUESTIONS

Answers are at the end of the chapter.

(SO 2) 1. When goods are purchased for resale by a company using a periodic inventory system:
   a. purchases on account are debited to Merchandise Inventory.
   b. purchases on account are debited to Purchases.
   c. purchase returns are debited to Purchase Returns and Allowances.
   d. freight costs are debited to Purchases.

(SO 3) 2. In determining cost of goods sold:
   a. purchases discounts are deducted from net purchases.
   b. freight-out is added to net purchases.
   c. purchase returns and allowances are deducted from net purchases.
   d. freight-in is added to net purchases.

(SO 3) 3. If beginning inventory is $60,000, cost of goods purchased is $380,000, and ending inventory is $50,000, cost of goods sold is:
   a. $390,000.     c. $330,000.
   b. $370,000.     d. $420,000.

(SO 1) 4. Which of the following should *not* be included in the physical inventory of a company?
   a. Goods held on consignment from another company.
   b. Goods shipped on consignment to another company.
   c. Goods in transit from another company shipped FOB shipping point.
   d. None of the above.

(SO 5) 5. Inventoriable costs consist of two elements: beginning inventory and
   a. ending inventory.
   b. cost of goods purchased.
   c. cost of goods sold.
   d. cost of goods available for sale.

(SO 5) 6. Electrolux Company has the following:

| | Units | Unit Cost |
|---|---|---|
| Inventory, Jan. 1 | 8,000 | $11 |
| Purchase, June 19 | 13,000 | 12 |
| Purchase, Nov. 8 | 5,000 | 13 |

If 9,000 units are on hand at December 31, the cost of the ending inventory under FIFO is:
   a. $99,000.     c. $113,000.
   b. $108,000.     d. $117,000.

(SO 5) 7. Using the data in (6) above, the cost of the ending inventory under LIFO is:
   a. $113,000.     c. $99,000.
   b. $108,000.     d. $100,000.

8. In periods of rising prices, LIFO will produce: (SO 6)
   a. higher net income than FIFO.
   b. the same net income as FIFO.
   c. lower net income than FIFO.
   d. higher net income than average costing.

9. Factors that affect the selection of an inventory costing (SO 6) method do *not* include:
   a. tax effects.
   b. balance sheet effects.
   c. income statement effects.
   d. perpetual vs. periodic inventory system.

10. The lower of cost or market basis may be applied to: (SO 7)
   a. categories of inventories.
   b. individual items of inventories.
   c. total inventory.
   d. all of the above.

*11. Volvo Company has sales of $150,000 and cost of goods (SO 9) available for sale of $135,000. If the gross profit rate is 30%, the estimated cost of the ending inventory under the gross profit method is:
   a. $15,000.
   b. $30,000.
   c. $45,000.
   d. $75,000.

12. Peugeot Company's ending inventory is understated (SO 8) $4,000. The effects of this error on the current year's cost of goods sold and net income, respectively, are:
   a. understated, overstated.
   b. overstated, understated.
   c. overstated, overstated.
   d. understated, understated.

13. Which of these would cause the inventory turnover ratio (SO 9) to increase the most?
   a. Increasing the amount of inventory on hand.
   b. Keeping the amount of inventory on hand constant but increasing sales.
   c. Keeping the amount of inventory on hand constant but decreasing sales.
   d. Decreasing the amount of inventory on hand and increasing sales.

*14. In a perpetual inventory system, (SO 10)
   a. LIFO cost of goods sold will be the same as in a periodic inventory system.
   b. average costs are based entirely on unit cost averages.
   c. a new average is computed under the average cost method after each sale.
   d. FIFO cost of goods sold will be the same as in a periodic inventory system.

THE NAVIGATOR

# QUESTIONS

1. Goods costing $1,700 are purchased on account on July 15 with credit terms of 2/10, n/30. On July 18 a $200 credit memo is received from the supplier for damaged goods. Give the journal entry on July 24 to record payment of the balance due within the discount period.

2. Identify the accounts that are added to or deducted from purchases to determine the cost of goods purchased. For each account, indicate (a) whether it is added or deducted and (b) its normal balance.

3. In the following separate mini cases, using a periodic inventory system, identify the item(s) designated by letter.
   (a) Purchases − X − Y = Net purchases.
   (b) Cost of goods purchased − Net purchases = X.
   (c) Beginning inventory + X = Cost of goods available for sale.
   (d) Cost of goods available for sale − Cost of goods sold = X.

4. "The key to successful business operations is effective inventory management." Do you agree? Explain.

5. An item must possess two characteristics to be classified as inventory by a merchandiser. What are these two characteristics?

6. Your friend Tom Wetzel has been hired to help take the physical inventory in Hitachi Hardware Store. Explain to Tom Wetzel what this job will entail.

7. (a) Janine Company ships merchandise to Laura Company on December 30. The merchandise reaches the buyer on January 6. Indicate the terms of sale that will result in the goods being included in (1) Janine's December 31 inventory, and (2) Laura's December 31 inventory.
   (b) Under what circumstances should Janine Company include consigned goods in its inventory?

8. Mary Ann's Hat Shop received a shipment of hats for which it paid the wholesaler $2,940. The price of the hats was $3,000, but Mary Ann's was given a $60 cash discount and required to pay freight charges of $80. In addition, Mary Ann's paid $130 to cover the travel expenses of an employee who negotiated the purchase of the hats. What amount will Mary Ann record for inventory? Why?

9. What is the primary basis of accounting for inventories? What is the major objective in accounting for inventories? What accounting principles are involved here?

10. Identify the distinguishing features of an income statement for a merchandising company.

11. Roland Carlson believes that the allocation of inventoriable costs should be based on the actual physical flow of the goods. Explain to Roland why this may be both impractical and inappropriate.

12. What is a major advantage and a major disadvantage of the specific identification method of inventory costing?

13. "The selection of an inventory cost flow method is a decision made by accountants." Do you agree? Explain. Once a method has been selected, what accounting requirement applies?

14. Which assumed inventory cost flow method:
   (a) usually parallels the actual physical flow of merchandise?
   (b) assumes that goods available for sale during an accounting period are homogeneous?
   (c) assumes that the latest units purchased are the first to be sold?

15. In a period of rising prices, the inventory reported in Jim Groat Company's balance sheet is close to the current cost of the inventory, whereas Greg Hanson Company's inventory is considerably below its current cost. Identify the inventory cost flow method being used by each company. Which company has probably been reporting the higher gross profit?

16. Char Lewis Company has been using the FIFO cost flow method during a prolonged period of inflation. During the same time period, Char Lewis has been paying out all of its net income as dividends. What adverse effects may result from this policy?

17. Bob Thebeau is studying for the next accounting midterm examination. What should Bob know about (a) departing from the cost basis of accounting for inventories and (b) the meaning of "market" in the lower of cost or market method?

18. John Hohenberger Music Center has 5 CD players on hand at the balance sheet date that cost $400 each. The current replacement cost is $320 per unit. Under the lower of cost or market basis of accounting for inventories, what value should be reported for the CD players on the balance sheet? Why?

19. What methods may be used under the lower of cost or market basis of accounting for inventories? Which method will produce the lowest inventory value?

20. Elaine Stahl Company discovers in 1999 that its ending inventory at December 31, 1998, was $5,000 understated. What effect will this error have on (a) 1998 net income, (b) 1999 net income, and (c) the combined net income for the 2 years?

21. Maureen & Nathan Company's balance sheet shows Inventories $162,800. What additional disclosures should be made?

22. Under what circumstances might the inventory turnover ratio be too high; that is, what possible negative consequences might occur?

*23. When is it necessary to estimate inventories?

*24. Both the gross profit method and the retail inventory method are based on averages. For each method, indicate the average used, how it is determined, and how it is applied.

*25. Jana Kingston Company has net sales of $400,000 and cost of goods available for sale of $300,000. If the gross profit rate is 30%, what is the estimated cost of the ending inventory? Show computations.

*26. John Ross Shoe Shop had goods available for sale in 1999 with a retail price of $120,000. The cost of these goods was $84,000. If sales during the period were $90,000, what is the ending inventory at cost using the retail inventory method?

*27. "When perpetual inventory records are kept, the results under the FIFO and LIFO methods are the same as they would be in a periodic inventory system." Do you agree? Explain.

*28. How does the average method of inventory costing differ between a perpetual inventory system and a periodic inventory system?

# BRIEF EXERCISES

*Journalize purchases transactions.*
*(SO 2)*

**BE9–1**  Prepare the journal entries to record the following transactions on Svenska Company's books using a periodic inventory system.

(a) On March 2, Svenska Company purchased $900,000 of merchandise from Sing Tao Company, terms 2/10, n/30.
(b) On March 6, Svenska Company returned $130,000 of the merchandise purchased on March 2 because it was defective.
(c) On March 12, Svenska Company paid the balance due to Sing Tao Company.

*Compute net purchases and cost of goods purchased.*
*(SO 3)*

**BE9–2**  Assume that Shinhan Company uses a periodic inventory system and has the following account balances: Purchases $440,000, Purchase Returns and Allowances $11,000, Purchase Discounts $8,000, and Freight-in $16,000. Determine (a) net purchases and (b) cost of goods purchased.

*Compute cost of goods sold and gross profit.*
*(SO 3)*

**BE9–3**  Assume the same information as in BE9–2, and also that Shinhan Company has beginning inventory of $60,000, ending inventory of $90,000, and net sales of $650,000. Determine the amounts to be reported for cost of goods sold and gross profit.

*Identify items to be included in taking a physical inventory.*
*(SO 1)*

**BE9–4**  Oriental Press Company identifies the following items for possible inclusion in the taking of a physical inventory. Indicate whether each item should be included or excluded from the inventory taking.

1. Goods shipped on consignment by Oriental Press to another company.
2. Goods in transit from a supplier shipped FOB destination.
3. Goods sold but being held for customer pickup.
4. Goods held on consignment from another company.

*Identify the components of inventoriable costs.*
*(SO 5)*

**BE9–5**  The ledger of Norway Company includes the following items: (1) Freight-in, (2) Purchase Returns and Allowances, (3) Purchases, (4) Sales Discounts, (5) Purchase Discounts. Identify which items are included in inventoriable costs.

*Compute ending inventory using FIFO and LIFO.*
*(SO 5)*

**BE9–6**  In its first month of operations, Finlandia Company made three purchases of merchandise in the following sequence: (1) 300 units at $6, (2) 400 units at $7, and (3) 300 units at $8. Assuming there are 400 units on hand, compute the cost of the ending inventory under the (1) FIFO method and (2) LIFO method. Finlandia uses a periodic inventory system.

*Compute the ending inventory using average costs.*
*(SO 5)*

**BE9–7**  Data for Finlandia Company are presented in BE9–6. Compute the cost of the ending inventory under the average cost method, assuming there are 400 units on hand.

*Determine the LCM valuation using inventory categories.*
*(SO 7)*

**BE9–8**  Germania Appliance Center accumulates the following cost and market data at December 31:

| Inventory Categories | Cost Data | Market Data |
| --- | --- | --- |
| Cameras | $12,000 | $10,200 |
| Camcorders | 9,000 | 9,700 |
| VCRs | 14,000 | 12,800 |

Compute the lower of cost or market valuation using categories.

*Compute inventory turnover ratio and days in inventory.*
*(SO 9)*

**BE9–9**  At December 31, 1999, the following information was available for Aurora Company: ending inventory $80,000; beginning inventory $60,000; cost of goods sold $210,000; and sales revenue $280,000. Calculate the inventory turnover ratio and days in inventory for Aurora Company.

**BE9–10** Italy Company reports net income of $90,000 in 1999. However, ending inventory was understated $7,000. What is the correct net income for 1999? What effect, if any, will this error have on total assets as reported in the balance sheet at December 31, 1999?

*Determine correct income statement amounts.*
*(SO 8)*

***BE9–11** At May 31, Poland Company has net sales of $300,000 and cost of goods available for sale of $230,000. Compute the estimated cost of the ending inventory assuming the gross profit rate is 40%.

*Apply the gross profit method.*
*(SO 10)*

***BE9–12** On June 30, French Fabrics has the following data pertaining to the retail inventory method: Goods available for sale: at cost $35,000, at retail $50,000; net sales $30,000, and ending inventory at retail $20,000. Compute the estimated cost of the ending inventory using the retail inventory method.

*Apply the retail inventory method.*
*(SO 10)*

***BE9–13** Spain Department Store uses a perpetual inventory system. Data for product E2–D2 include the following purchases:

*Apply cost flow methods to records.*
*(SO 11)*

| Date | Number of Units | Unit Price |
|------|----------------|------------|
| May 7 | 50 | $10 |
| July 28 | 30 | 15 |

On June 1 Spain sold 30 units, and on August 27, 33 more units. Prepare the perpetual inventory card for the above transactions using (1) FIFO, (2) LIFO, and (3) average cost.

# EXERCISES

**E9–1** Presented below is the following information related to Brazil Co.

*Journalize purchases transactions.*
*(SO 2)*

1. On April 5, purchased merchandise from Chile Company for $18,000 terms 2/10, net/30, FOB shipping point.
2. On April 6, paid freight costs of $800 on merchandise purchased from Chile.
3. On April 7, purchased equipment on account for $26,000.
4. On April 8, returned damaged merchandise to Chile Company and was granted a $3,000 allowance.
5. On April 15, paid the amount due to Chile Company in full.

**Instructions**
(a) Prepare the journal entries to record these transactions on the books of Brazil Co. using a periodic inventory system.
(b) Assume that Brazil Co. paid the balance due to Chile Company on May 4 instead of April 15. Prepare the journal entry to record this payment.

**E9–2** The trial balance of Colombia Company at the end of its fiscal year, August 31, 1999, includes the following accounts: Merchandise Inventory $17,200, Purchases $142,400, Sales $190,000, Freight-in $4,000, Sales Returns and Allowances $3,000, Freight-out $1,000, and Purchase Returns and Allowances $2,000. The ending (August 31, 1999) merchandise inventory is $27,000.

*Prepare cost of goods sold section.*
*(SO 3)*

**Instructions**
Prepare a cost of goods sold section for the year ending August 31 (periodic inventory).

**E9–3** Presented is information related to Mexico Co. for the month of January 1999.

*Prepare an income statement.*
*(SO 4)*

| | | | |
|---|---|---|---|
| Freight-in | $10,000 | Rent expense | 19,000 |
| Freight-out | 5,000 | Salary expense | 61,000 |
| Insurance expense | 12,000 | Sales discounts | 8,000 |
| Purchases | 200,000 | Sales returns and allowances | 13,000 |
| Purchase discounts | 3,000 | Sales | 312,000 |
| Purchase returns and allowances | 6,000 | | |

Beginning merchandise inventory was $42,000 and ending inventory was $63,000.

*Instructions*

Prepare an income statement using the format presented on page 375. Operating expenses should not be segregated into selling and administrative expenses.

*Determine the correct inventory amount.*
*(SO 1)*

**E9–4** Yorkville Bank and Trust is considering giving Canada Company a loan. Before doing so, they decide that further discussions with Canada's accountant may be desirable. One area of particular concern is the inventory account, which has a year-end balance of $295,000. Discussions with the accountant reveal the following:

1. Canada sold goods costing $38,000 to Moghul Company FOB shipping point on December 28. The goods are not expected to arrive in India until January 12. The goods were not included in the physical inventory because they were not in the warehouse.
2. The physical count of the inventory did not include goods costing $95,000 that were shipped to Canada FOB destination on December 27, and were still in transit at year-end.
3. Canada received goods costing $25,000 on January 2. The goods were shipped FOB shipping point on December 26 by Cellar Co. The goods were not included in the physical count.
4. Canada sold goods costing $40,000 to Sterling of Mexico FOB destination on December 30. The goods were received in Mexico on January 8. They were not included in Canada's physical inventory.
5. Canada received goods costing $44,000 on January 2 that were shipped FOB destination on December 29. The shipment was a rush order that was supposed to arrive December 31. This purchase was included in the ending inventory of $297,000.

*Instructions*

Determine the correct inventory amount on December 31.

*Compute inventory and cost of goods sold using FIFO and LIFO.*
*(SO 5)*

**E9–5** Egypt Co. uses a periodic inventory system. Its records show the following for the month of May, in which 78 units were sold.

|  |  | Units | Unit Cost | Total Cost |
|---|---|---|---|---|
| May 1 | Inventory | 30 | $ 8 | $240 |
| 15 | Purchases | 25 | 10 | 250 |
| 24 | Purchases | 35 | 13 | 455 |
|  | Totals | 90 |  | $945 |

*Instructions*

Compute the ending inventory at May 31 using the FIFO and LIFO methods. Prove the amount allocated to cost of goods sold under each method.

*Compute inventory and cost of goods sold using FIFO and LIFO.*
*(SO 5, 6)*

**E9–6** In June, Luxemburg Company reports the following for the month of June.

|  |  | Units | Unit Cost | Total Cost |
|---|---|---|---|---|
| June 1 | Inventory | 200 | $5 | $1,000 |
| 12 | Purchases | 300 | 6 | 1,800 |
| 23 | Purchases | 500 | 7 | 3,500 |
| 30 | Inventory | 180 |  |  |

*Instructions*

(a) Compute the cost of the ending inventory and the cost of goods sold under (1) FIFO and (2) LIFO.
(b) Which costing method gives the higher ending inventory? Why?
(c) Which method results in the higher cost of goods sold? Why?

*Compute inventory and cost of goods sold using average costs.*
*(SO 5, 6)*

**E9–7** Inventory data for Luxemburg Company are presented in E9–6.

*Instructions*

(a) Compute the cost of the ending inventory and the cost of goods sold using the average cost method.
(b) Will the results in (a) be higher or lower than the results under (1) FIFO and (2) LIFO?
(c) Why is the average unit cost not $6?

**E9–8** China Camera Shop uses the lower of cost or market basis for its inventory. The following data are available at December 31:

*Determine ending inventory under lower of cost or market inventory method.*
*(SO 7)*

| Item | Units | Unit Cost | Market |
|---|---|---|---|
| Cameras | | | |
| Minolta | 5 | $170 | $160 |
| Canon | 7 | 150 | 152 |
| Light Meters | | | |
| Vivitar | 12 | 125 | 110 |
| Kodak | 10 | 115 | 135 |

**Instructions**
Determine the amount of the ending inventory by applying the lower of cost or market basis to (a) individual items, (b) inventory categories, and (c) the total inventory.

**E9–9** Korea Hardware reported cost of goods sold as follows:

*Determine effects of inventory errors.*
*(SO 8)*

| | 1999 | 2000 |
|---|---|---|
| Beginning inventory | $ 20,000 | $ 30,000 |
| Cost of goods purchased | 150,000 | 175,000 |
| Cost of goods available for sale | 170,000 | 205,000 |
| Ending inventory | 30,000 | 35,000 |
| Cost of goods sold | $140,000 | $170,000 |

Korea made two errors: (1) 1999 ending inventory was overstated $4,000 and (2) 2000 ending inventory was understated $3,000.

**Instructions**
Compute the correct cost of goods sold for each year.

**E9–10** Zurich Watch Company reported the following income statement data for a 2-year period.

*Prepare correct income statements.*
*(SO 8)*

| | 1999 | 2000 |
|---|---|---|
| Sales | $210,000 | $250,000 |
| Cost of goods sold | | |
| Beginning inventory | 32,000 | 40,000 |
| Cost of goods purchased | 173,000 | 202,000 |
| Cost of goods available for sale | 205,000 | 242,000 |
| Ending inventory | 40,000 | 52,000 |
| Cost of goods sold | 165,000 | 190,000 |
| Gross profit | $ 45,000 | $ 60,000 |

Zurich uses a periodic inventory system. The inventories at January 1, 1999, and December 31, 2000, are correct. However, the ending inventory at December 31, 1999, was overstated $6,000.

**Instructions**
(a) Prepare correct income statement data for the 2 years.
(b) What is the cumulative effect of the inventory error on total gross profit for the 2 years?
(c) ▣▤▤▷ Explain in a letter to the president of Zurich Company what has happened—i.e., the nature of the error and its effect on the financial statements.

**E9–11** This information is available for Linda Wasisko Corporation for 1997, 1998, and 1999:

*Compute inventory turnover ratio, days in inventory, and gross profit rate.*
*(SO 9, 10)*

| | 1997 | 1998 | 1999 |
|---|---|---|---|
| Beginning inventory | $ 200,000 | $ 300,000 | $ 400,000 |
| Ending inventory | 300,000 | 400,000 | 500,000 |
| Cost of goods sold | 900,000 | 1,120,000 | 1,250,000 |
| Sales | 1,200,000 | 1,600,000 | 1,900,000 |

*Determine merchandise lost
using the gross profit method
of estimating inventory.*
(SO 10)

*Determine ending inventory at
cost using retail method.*
(SO 10)

*Apply cost flow methods to
perpetual records.*
(SO 11)

*Journalize, post, and prepare
trial balance and partial
income statement.*
(SO 2, 3, 4)

**Instructions**

Calculate the inventory turnover ratio, days in inventory, and gross profit rate (from Chapter 5) for Linda Wasisko Corporation for 1997, 1998, 1999. Comment on any trends.

**\*E9–12**  The inventory of DeBeers Company was destroyed by fire on March 1. From an examination of the accounting records, the following data for the first 2 months of the year are obtained: Sales $51,000, Sales Returns and Allowances $1,000, Purchases $28,200, Freight-in $1,200, and Purchase Returns and Allowances $1,400.

**Instructions**

Determine the merchandise lost by fire, assuming:

(a)  A beginning inventory of $20,000 and a gross profit rate of 30% on net sales.
(b)  A beginning inventory of $25,000 and a gross profit rate of 25% on net sales.

**\*E9–13**  Swiss Shoe Store uses the retail inventory method for its two departments: Women's Shoes and Men's Shoes. The following information for each department is obtained:

| Item | Women's Department | Men's Department |
|---|---|---|
| Beginning inventory at cost | $ 32,000 | $ 46,450 |
| Cost of goods purchased at cost | 148,000 | 137,300 |
| Net sales | 187,000 | 195,000 |
| Beginning inventory at retail | 45,000 | 60,000 |
| Cost of goods purchased at retail | 182,000 | 185,000 |

**Instructions**

Compute the estimated cost of the ending inventory for each department under the retail inventory method.

**\*E9–14**  Morocco Appliance uses a perpetual inventory system. For its model B47 television sets, the January 1 inventory was four sets at $600 each. During January, the following purchase was made: Jan. 10, 6 units at $640 each. That month, the company had the following sales: Jan. 8, 2 units and Jan. 15, 4 units.

**Instructions**

Compute the ending inventory under (1) FIFO, (2) LIFO, and (3) average cost.

# PROBLEMS: SET A

**P9–1A**  Chi Chi Lopez, a former professional golf star, operates Chi Chi's Pro Shop at Bay Golf Course. At the beginning of the current season on April 1, 1999, the ledger of Chi Chi's Pro Shop showed Cash $2,500, Merchandise Inventory $3,500, and Capital $6,000. The following transactions were completed during April.

Apr.  5  Purchased golf bags, clubs, and balls on account from Balata Co. $1,600, FOB shipping point, terms 2/10, n/60.
     7  Paid freight on Balata purchase $80.
     9  Received credit from Balata Co. for merchandise returned $100.
    10  Sold merchandise on account to members $900, terms n/30.
    12  Purchased golf shoes, sweaters, and other accessories on account from Arrow Sportswear $660, terms 1/10, n/30.
    14  Paid Balata Co. in full.
    17  Received credit from Arrow Sportswear for merchandise returned $60.
    20  Made sales on account to members $700, terms n/30.
    21  Paid Arrow Sportswear in full.
    27  Granted credit to members for clothing that did not fit $30.
    30  Made cash sales $600.
    30  Received payments on account from members $1,100.

The chart of accounts for the pro shop includes the following: No. 101 Cash, No. 112 Accounts Receivable, No. 120 Merchandise Inventory, No. 201 Accounts Payable, No. 301 Capital, No. 401 Sales, No. 412 Sales Returns and Allowances, No. 510 Purchases, No. 512 Purchase Returns and Allowances, No. 514 Purchase Discounts, No. 516 Freight-in.

## Instructions

(a) Journalize the April transactions using a periodic inventory system.
(b) Enter the beginning balances in the ledger accounts and post the April transactions. (Use J1 for the journal reference.)
(c) Prepare a trial balance on April 30, 1999.
(d) Prepare an income statement through gross profit, assuming merchandise inventory on hand at April 30 is $4,200.

**P9–2A**  Asian Department Store is located in midtown Metropolis. During the past several years, net income has been declining because of suburban shopping centers. At the end of the company's fiscal year on November 30, 1999, the following accounts appeared in its adjusted trial balance:

*Prepare an income statement.*
*(SO 3, 4)*

| | |
|---|---:|
| Accounts Payable | $ 35,310 |
| Accounts Receivable | 11,770 |
| Accumulated Depreciation—Delivery Equipment | 19,680 |
| Accumulated Depreciation—Store Equipment | 41,800 |
| Cash | 8,000 |
| Delivery Expense | 8,200 |
| Delivery Equipment | 57,000 |
| Depreciation Expense—Delivery Equipment | 4,000 |
| Depreciation Expense—Store Equipment | 9,500 |
| Freight-in | 5,060 |
| Common Stock | 70,000 |
| Retained Earnings | 17,200 |
| Dividends | 12,000 |
| Insurance Expense | 9,000 |
| Merchandise Inventory | 34,360 |
| Notes Payable | 46,000 |
| Prepaid Insurance | 4,500 |
| Property Tax Expense | 3,500 |
| Purchases | 640,000 |
| Purchase Discounts | 7,000 |
| Purchase Returns and Allowances | 3,000 |
| Rent Expense | 19,000 |
| Salaries Expense | 120,000 |
| Sales | 860,000 |
| Sales Commissions Expense | 12,000 |
| Sales Commissions Payable | 8,000 |
| Sales Returns and Allowances | 10,000 |
| Store Equipment | 125,000 |
| Property Taxes Payable | 3,500 |
| Utilities Expense | 10,600 |

Analysis reveals the following additional data:

1. Salaries expense is 70% selling and 30% administrative.
2. Insurance expense is 50% selling and 50% administrative.
3. Merchandise inventory at November 30, 1999, is $36,200.
4. Rent expense, utilities expense, and property tax expense are administrative expenses.

## Instructions

Prepare an income statement for the year ended November 30, 1999.

**P9–3A**  Europe Company had a beginning inventory on January 1 of 100 units of Product WD-44 at a cost of $20 per unit. During the year, the following purchases were made.

*Determine cost of goods sold and ending inventory, using FIFO, LIFO, and average cost with analysis.*
*(SO 5, 6)*

| | | | | |
|---|---|---|---|---|
| Mar. 15 | 300 units at $24 | Sept. 4 | 300 units at $28 |
| July 20 | 200 units at  25 | Dec.  2 | 100 units at  30 |

850 units were sold. Europe Company uses a periodic inventory system.

## Instructions

(a) Determine the cost of goods available for sale.
(b) Determine (1) the ending inventory, and (2) the cost of goods sold under each of the

assumed cost flow methods (FIFO, LIFO, and average). Prove the accuracy of the cost of goods sold under the FIFO and LIFO methods.
(c) Which cost flow method results in (1) the highest inventory amount for the balance sheet and (2) the highest cost of goods sold for the income statement?

*Compute ending inventory, prepare income statements, and answer questions using FIFO and LIFO.*
*(SO 5, 6)*

**P9–4A** The management of African Co. asks your help in determining the comparative effects of the FIFO and LIFO inventory cost flow methods. For 1999, the accounting records show the following data:

| | |
|---|---|
| Inventory, January 1 (10,000 units) | $ 35,000 |
| Cost of 110,000 units purchased | 460,000 |
| Selling price of 95,000 units sold | 665,000 |
| Operating expenses | 120,000 |

Units purchased consisted of 40,000 units at $4.00 on May 10; 50,000 units at $4.20 on August 15; and 20,000 units at $4.50 on November 20. Income taxes are 28%.

*Instructions*
(a) Prepare comparative condensed income statements for 1999 under FIFO and LIFO. (Show computations of ending inventory.)
(b) ▉▉▉▉▊➤ Answer the following questions for management in the form of a business letter:
  (1) Which inventory cost flow method produces the most meaningful inventory amount for the balance sheet? Why?
  (2) Which inventory cost flow method produces the most meaningful net income? Why?
  (3) Which inventory cost flow method is most likely to approximate actual physical flow of the goods? Why?
  (4) How much additional cash will be available for management under LIFO than under FIFO? Why?
  (5) How much of the gross profit under FIFO is illusionary in comparison with the gross profit under LIFO?

*Compute gross profit rate and inventory loss using gross profit method.*
*(SO 10)*

**\*P9–5A** Australia Company lost all of its inventory in a fire on December 26, 1999. The accounting records showed the following gross profit data for November and December.

| | November | December (to 12/26) |
|---|---|---|
| Net sales | $400,000 | $300,000 |
| Beginning inventory | 22,100 | 29,100 |
| Purchases | 314,975 | 236,000 |
| Purchase returns and allowances | 11,800 | 5,000 |
| Purchase discounts | 8,577 | 6,000 |
| Freight-in | 4,402 | 3,700 |
| Ending inventory | 29,100 | ? |

Australia is fully insured for fire losses but must prepare a report for the insurance company.

*Instructions*
(a) Compute the gross profit rate for November.
(b) Using the gross profit rate for November, determine the estimated cost of the inventory lost in the fire.

*Compute ending inventory using retail method.*
*(SO 10)*

**\*P9–6A** French's Book Store uses the retail inventory method to estimate its monthly ending inventories. The following information is available for two of its departments at October 31, 1999.

| | Hardcovers | | Paperbacks | |
|---|---|---|---|---|
| | Cost | Retail | Cost | Retail |
| Beginning inventory | $ 260,000 | $ 400,000 | $ 65,000 | $ 90,000 |
| Purchases | 1,180,000 | 1,800,000 | 266,000 | 380,000 |
| Freight-in | 5,000 | | 2,000 | |
| Purchase discounts | 15,000 | | 4,000 | |
| Net sales | | 1,810,000 | | 363,000 |

At December 31, French's Book Store takes a physical inventory at retail. The actual retail values of the inventories in each department are: Hardcovers $400,000 and Paperbacks $100,000.

*Instructions*

(a) Determine the estimated cost of the ending inventory for each department at **October 31**, 1999, using the retail inventory method.

(b) Compute the ending inventory at cost for each department at **December 31**, assuming the cost to retail ratios for the year are 65% for hardcovers and 70% for paperbacks.

*P9–7A    Save-Mart Center began operations on July 1. It uses a perpetual inventory system. During July the company had the following purchases and sales:

*Determine ending inventory under a perpetual inventory system.*
*(SO 11)*

| Date | Purchases | | Sales Units |
|---|---|---|---|
| | Units | Unit Cost | |
| July  1 | 5 | $90 | |
| July  6 | | | 3 |
| July 11 | 4 | $99 | |
| July 14 | | | 3 |
| July 21 | 3 | $106 | |
| July 27 | | | 4 |

*Instructions*

(a) Determine the ending inventory under a perpetual inventory system using (1) FIFO, (2) average cost, and (3) LIFO.

(b) Which costing method produces the highest ending inventory valuation?

# PROBLEMS: SET B
••••••••••••••••••••••••••••••••••••••••••••••••••

P9–1B    Billy Jean Evert, a former professional tennis star, operates B.J.'s Tennis Shop at the Jackson Lake Resort. At the beginning of the current season, the ledger of B.J.'s Tennis Shop showed Cash $2,500, Merchandise Inventory $1,700, and Capital $4,200. The following transactions were completed during April:

*Journalize, post, and prepare a trial balance and partial income statement.*
*(SO 2, 3, 4)*

Apr.  4   Purchased racquets and balls from Robert Co. $640 FOB shipping point, terms 3/10, n/30.

  6   Paid freight on Robert purchase $40.

  8   Sold merchandise to members $900, terms n/30.

 10   Received credit of $40 from Robert Co. for a damaged racquet that was returned.

 11   Purchased tennis shoes from Niki Sports for cash, $300.

 13   Paid Robert Co. in full.

 14   Purchased tennis shirts and shorts from Martina's Sportswear $700, FOB shipping point, terms 2/10, n/60.

 15   Received cash refund of $50 from Niki Sports for damaged merchandise that was returned.

 17   Paid freight on Martina's Sportswear purchase $30.

 18   Sold merchandise to members, $800, terms n/30.

 20   Received $500 in cash from members in settlement of their accounts.

 21   Paid Martina's Sportswear in full.

 27   Granted credit of $30 to members for tennis clothing that did not fit.

 30   Sold merchandise to members $900, terms n/30.

 30   Received cash payments on account from members, $500.

The chart of accounts for the tennis shop includes the following: No. 101 Cash, No. 112 Accounts Receivable, No. 120 Merchandise Inventory, No. 201 Accounts Payable, No. 301 Capital, No. 401 Sales, No. 412 Sales Returns and Allowances, No. 510 Purchases, No. 512 Purchase Returns and Allowances, No. 514 Purchase Discounts, No. 516 Freight-in.

*Instructions*
  (a) Journalize the April transactions using a periodic inventory system.
  (b) Enter the beginning balances in the ledger accounts and post the April transactions. (Use J1 for the journal reference.)
  (c) Prepare a trial balance on April 30, 1999.
  (d) Prepare an income statement through gross profit, assuming merchandise inventory on hand at April 30 is $1,800.

*Prepare an income statement.*
*(SO 3, 4)*

**P9–2B**  Austrian Department Store is located near the Village shopping mall. At the end of the company's fiscal year on December 31, 1999, the following accounts appeared in its adjusted trial balance:

| | |
|---|---:|
| Accounts Payable | $ 89,300 |
| Accounts Receivable | 50,300 |
| Accumulated Depreciation—Building | 52,500 |
| Accumulated Depreciation—Equipment | 42,900 |
| Building | 190,000 |
| Cash | 23,000 |
| Depreciation Expense—Building | 10,400 |
| Depreciation Expense—Equipment | 13,300 |
| Equipment | 110,000 |
| Freight-in | 3,600 |
| Insurance Expense | 7,200 |
| Merchandise Inventory | 40,500 |
| Mortgage Payable | 80,000 |
| Office Salaries Expense | 32,000 |
| Prepaid Insurance | 2,400 |
| Property Taxes Payable | 4,300 |
| Purchases | 462,000 |
| Purchase Discounts | 12,000 |
| Purchase Returns and Allowances | 6,400 |
| Sales Salaries Expense | 74,000 |
| Sales | 618,000 |
| Sales Commissions Expense | 14,500 |
| Sales Commissions Payable | 4,000 |
| Sales Returns and Allowances | 8,000 |
| Capital | 177,600 |
| Drawings | 28,000 |
| Property Taxes Expense | 4,800 |
| Utilities Expense | 11,000 |

Analysis reveals the following additional data:

  1. Merchandise inventory on December 31, 1999, is $75,000.
  2. Insurance expense and utilities expense are 60% selling and 40% administrative.
  3. Depreciation on the building and property tax expense are administrative expenses; depreciation on the equipment is a selling expense.

*Instructions*
Prepare an income statement for the year ended December 31, 1999.

*Determine cost of goods sold and ending inventory, using FIFO, LIFO, and average cost.*
*(SO 5, 6)*

**P9–3B**  Russia Company had a beginning inventory of 400 units of Product USSR at a cost of $8.00 per unit. During the year, purchases were:

| | | | | | |
|---|---|---|---|---|---|
| Feb. | 20 | 700 units at $9.00 | Aug. | 12 | 300 units at $11.00 |
| May | 5 | 500 units at $10.00 | Dec. | 8 | 100 units at $12.00 |

Russia Company uses a periodic inventory system. Sales totaled 1,550 units.

*Instructions*
  (a) Determine the cost of goods available for sale.
  (b) Determine (1) the ending inventory, and (2) the cost of goods sold under each of the assumed cost flow methods (FIFO, LIFO, and average). Prove the accuracy of the cost of goods sold under the FIFO and LIFO methods.
  (c) Which cost flow method results in (1) the lowest inventory amount for the balance sheet, and (2) the lowest cost of goods sold for the income statement?

**P9–4B** The management of India Co. is reevaluating the appropriateness of using its present inventory cost flow method, which is average cost. They request your help in determining the results of operations for 1999 if either the FIFO method or the LIFO method had been used. For 1999, the accounting records show the following data:

*Compute ending inventory, prepare income statements, and answer questions using FIFO and LIFO.*
*(SO 5, 6)*

| Inventories | | Purchases and Sales | |
|---|---|---|---|
| Beginning (15,000 units) | $34,000 | Total net sales (225,000 units) | $865,000 |
| Ending (20,000 units) | | Total cost of goods purchased (230,000 units) | 578,500 |

Purchases were made quarterly as follows:

| Quarter | Units | Unit Cost | Total Cost |
|---|---|---|---|
| 1 | 60,000 | $2.30 | $138,000 |
| 2 | 50,000 | 2.50 | 125,000 |
| 3 | 50,000 | 2.60 | 130,000 |
| 4 | 70,000 | 2.65 | 185,500 |
| | 230,000 | | $578,500 |

Operating expenses were $147,000, and the company's income tax rate is 32%.

**Instructions**
(a) Prepare comparative condensed income statements for 1999 under FIFO and LIFO. (Show computations of ending inventory.)
(b) ▭▭▭▭▷ Answer the following questions for management:
   (1) Which cost flow method (FIFO or LIFO) produces the more meaningful inventory amount for the balance sheet? Why?
   (2) Which cost flow method (FIFO or LIFO) produces the more meaningful net income? Why?
   (3) Which cost flow method (FIFO or LIFO) is more likely to approximate actual physical flow of the goods? Why?
   (4) How much additional cash will be available for management under LIFO than under FIFO? Why?
   (5) Will gross profit under the average cost method be higher or lower than (a) FIFO and (b) LIFO? (*Note:* It is not necessary to quantify your answer.)

**\*P9–5B** Tibet Company lost 80% of its inventory in a fire on March 25, 1999. The accounting records showed the following gross profit data for February and March.

*Estimate inventory loss using gross profit method.*
*(SO 10)*

| | February | March (to 3/25) |
|---|---|---|
| Net sales | $270,000 | $260,000 |
| Net purchases | 200,800 | 191,000 |
| Freight-in | 2,900 | 4,000 |
| Beginning inventory | 16,500 | 20,400 |
| Ending inventory | 20,400 | ? |

Tibet Company is fully insured for fire losses but must prepare a report for the insurance company.

**Instructions**
(a) Compute the gross profit rate for the month of February.
(b) Using the gross profit rate for February, determine both the estimated total inventory and inventory lost in the fire in March.

**\*P9–6B** Japanese Department Store uses the retail inventory method to estimate its monthly ending inventories. The following information is available for two of its departments at August 31, 1999.

*Compute ending inventory and cost of inventory lost using retail method.*
*(SO 10)*

| | Sporting Goods | | Jewelry and Cosmetics | |
|---|---|---|---|---|
| | Cost | Retail | Cost | Retail |
| Net sales | | $1,020,000 | | $1,160,000 |
| Purchases | $670,000 | 1,066,000 | $733,000 | 1,158,000 |
| Purchase returns | (26,000) | (40,000) | (12,000) | (20,000) |
| Purchase discounts | (15,360) | — | (9,440) | — |
| Freight-in | 6,000 | — | 8,000 | — |
| Beginning inventory | 47,360 | 74,000 | 36,440 | 62,000 |

At December 31, Japanese Department Store takes a physical inventory at retail. The actual retail values of the inventories in each department are: Sporting Goods $75,000, and Jewelry and Cosmetics $44,000.

**Instructions**

(a) Determine the estimated cost of the ending inventory for each department on August 31, 1999, using the retail inventory method.

(b) Compute the ending inventory at cost for each department at December 31, assuming the cost-to-retail ratios are 60% for Sporting Goods and 65% for Jewelry and Cosmetics.

*Prepare subsidiary ledger records under a perpetual inventory system.*
*(SO 11)*

**\*P9–7B**   The Family Home Appliance Mart begins operations on May 1. It uses a perpetual inventory system. During May the company had the following purchases and sales for its Model 25 Sureshot camera.

| | Purchases | | Sales |
|---|---|---|---|
| Date | Units | Unit Cost | Units |
| May  1 | 7 | $150 | |
| 4 | | | 5 |
| 8 | 8 | $170 | |
| 12 | | | 5 |
| 15 | 5 | $180 | |
| 20 | | | 4 |
| 25 | | | 3 |

**Instructions**

(a) Determine the ending inventory under a perpetual inventory system using (1) FIFO, (2) average cost, and (3) LIFO.

(b) Which costing method produces (1) the highest ending inventory valuation and (2) the lowest ending inventory valuation?

# BROADENING YOUR PERSPECTIVE

# FINANCIAL REPORTING AND ANALYSIS

**FINANCIAL REPORTING PROBLEM: Kellogg Company**

**BYP9–1**   The notes that accompany a company's financial statements provide informative details that would clutter the amounts and descriptions presented in the statements. Refer to the financial statements of Kellogg Company and the Notes to Consolidated Financial Statements in Appendix A.

**Instructions**

Answer the following questions. Complete the requirements in millions of dollars, as shown in Kellogg's annual report.

(a) What did Kellogg report for the amount of inventories in its Consolidated Balance Sheet at December 31, 1997? December 31, 1996?

(b) Compute the dollar amount of change and the percentage change in inventories between 1996 and 1997. Compute inventory as a percentage of current assets for 1997.

(c) How does Kellogg value its inventories? Which inventory cost flow method does Kellogg use?

(d) What is the cost of sales (cost of goods sold) reported by Kellogg for 1997, 1996, and 1995? Compute the percentage of cost of sales to net sales in 1997.

## COMPARATIVE ANALYSIS PROBLEM: Kellogg Company vs. General Mills

**BYP9–2**  Kellogg's financial statements are presented in Appendix A; General Mills's financial statements are presented in Appendix B.

*Instructions*

(a) Based on the information contained in these financial statements, compute the following 1997 ratios for each company:
1. Inventory turnover ratio
2. Average days to sell inventory

(b) What conclusions concerning the management of the inventory can be drawn from these data?

## RESEARCH ASSIGNMENT

**BYP9–3**  The September 23, 1994, edition of *The Wall Street Journal* includes an article entitled "CompUSA Auctions Notebook Computers Through Bulk Sale."

*Instructions*

Read the article and answer the following inventory-related questions.

(a) At what amount did CompUSA estimate the retail value of the computers? What was the estimate made by one of the bidders?

(b) What was wrong with the computers?

(c) What were the rules of the auction as specified by CompUSA?

(d) CompUSA had just recorded a $3 million inventory writedown in the preceding quarter. Based on the information in the article, does it appear that additional writedowns were called for?

## INTERPRETING FINANCIAL STATEMENTS: Nike and Reebok

**BYP9–4**  Nike and Reebok compete head-to-head in the sport shoe and sport apparel business. For both companies, inventory is a significant portion of their total assets. The following information was taken from each company's financial statements and notes to those financial statements.

### NIKE, INC.

**Inventory note**

Inventories are stated at the lower of cost or market. Cost is determined using the last-in, first-out (LIFO) method for substantially all U.S. inventories. Non-U.S. inventories are valued on a first-in, first-out (FIFO) basis.

Inventories by major classification are as follows (in thousands):

|  | May 31 | |
|---|---|---|
|  | **1997** | **1996** |
| Finished goods | $1,248,401 | $ 874,700 |
| Work-in-process | 50,245 | 28,940 |
| Raw materials | 39,994 | 27,511 |

Other information for Nike:

|  | May 31 | |
|---|---|---|
|  | **1997** | **1996** |
| Inventory | $1,338,640 | $ 931,151 |
| Cost of goods sold | 5,502,993 | 3,906,746 |

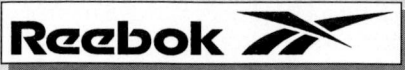

### REEBOK INTERNATIONAL, LTD.

**Inventory note**
Inventory, substantially all finished goods, is recorded at the lower of cost (first-in, first-out method) or market.

Other information for Reebok (in thousands):

| | December 31 | |
| --- | --- | --- |
| | 1996 | 1995 |
| Inventory | $ 544,522 | $ 635,012 |
| Cost of goods sold | 2,144,422 | 2,114,084 |

*Instructions*
Address each of the following questions which deal with how these two companies manage their inventory.

(a) What problems of inventory management face Nike and Reebok in the international sport apparel industry?

(b) What inventory cost flow assumptions does each company use? Why might Nike use a different approach for U.S. operations versus international operations? What are the implications of their respective cost flow assumptions for their financial statements?

(c) Nike provides more detail regarding the nature of its inventory (e.g., raw materials, work-in-process, and finished goods) than does Reebok. How might this additional information be useful in evaluating Nike?

(d) Calculate and interpret the inventory turnover ratio and average days to sell inventory for each company. Comment on how the use of different inventory methods by the two companies impacts your ability to compare their ratios.

## REAL-WORLD FOCUS: General Motors Corporation

**BYP9–5   General Motors** is the largest producer of automobiles in the world, as well as the world's biggest industrial enterprise. After stumbling in the early 1990s, GM has enacted numerous cost-cutting measures, including downsizing and renegotiating contracts with suppliers. In addition, it has shifted more of its resources to the hot-selling truck market.

The annual report of General Motors Corporation disclosed the following information about its accounting for inventories:

### GENERAL MOTORS CORPORATION
### Notes to the Financial Statements

**Note 5.   Inventories**
Major Classes of Inventories (in millions)

| | December 31 | |
| --- | --- | --- |
| | 1995 | 1994 |
| Productive material, work in process, and supplies | $ 6,570.4 | $5,478.3 |
| Finished product, service parts, etc. | 4,959.1 | 4,649.5 |
| Total | $11,529.5 | $10,127.8 |
| Memo: Increase in LIFO inventories if valued at FIFO | $ 2,424.4 | $2,535.9 |

Inventories are stated generally at cost, which is not in excess of market. The cost of substantially all U.S. inventories other than the inventories of Saturn Corporation (Saturn) and Hughes is determined by the last-in, first-out (LIFO) method. The cost of non-U.S., Saturn, and Hughes inventories is determined generally by the first-in, first-out (FIFO) or average cost methods.

*Instructions*
(a) What is meant by "inventories are stated generally at cost, which is not in excess of market"?
(b) The company uses LIFO for most of its inventory. What impact does this have on reported ending inventory if prices are increasing?
(c) General Motors uses different inventory methods for different types of inventory. Why might it do this?

# CRITICAL THINKING

## GROUP DECISION CASE

**BYP9–6**  On April 10, 1998, fire damaged the office and warehouse of Gibson Company. Most of the accounting records were destroyed but the following account balances were determined as of March 31, 1998: Merchandise Inventory, January 1, 1998, $80,000; Sales (January 1–March 31, 1998), $150,000; Purchases (January 1–March 31, 1998), $84,000.

The company's fiscal year ends on December 31, and it uses a periodic inventory system.

From an analysis of the April bank statement you discover cancelled checks of $4,200 during the period April 1–10 for cash purchases. Deposits during the same period totaled $18,500 of which 60% were collections on accounts receivable and the balance was cash sales.

Correspondence with the company's principal suppliers revealed $12,400 of purchases on account from April 1 to April 10 of which $1,800 was for merchandise in transit on April 10 that was shipped FOB destination.

Correspondence with the company's principal customers produced acknowledgments of credit sales totaling $28,000 from April 1 to April 10. It was estimated that $4,600 of credit sales will never be acknowledged or recovered from customers.

Gibson Company reached an agreement with the insurance company that its fire-loss claim should be based on the average of the gross profit rates for the preceding 2 years. The financial statements for 1996 and 1997 showed the following data:

|  | 1997 | 1996 |
|---|---|---|
| Net sales | $600,000 | $480,000 |
| Cost of goods purchased | 416,000 | 356,000 |
| Beginning inventory | 60,000 | 40,000 |
| Ending inventory | 80,000 | 60,000 |

Inventory with a cost of $19,000 was salvaged from the fire.

*Instructions*
With the class divided into groups, answer the following:
(a) Determine the balances in (1) Sales and (2) Purchases at April 10.
*(b) Determine the average profit rate for the years 1996 and 1997. (*Hint:* Find the gross profit rate for each year and divide the sum by 2.)
*(c) Determine the inventory loss as a result of the fire, using the gross profit method.

## COMMUNICATION ACTIVITY

**BYP9–7**  You are the controller of Small Toys Inc. Joe Paisley, the president, recently mentioned to you that he found an error in the 1998 financial statements which he believes has corrected itself. He determined, in discussions with the Purchasing Department, that 1998 ending inventory was overstated by $1 million. Joe says that the 1999 ending inventory is correct, thus he assumes that 1999 income is correct. Joe says to you, "What happened has happened—there's no point in worrying about it anymore."

*Instructions*
You conclude that Joe is incorrect. Write a brief, tactful memo to Joe, clarifying the situation.

## ETHICS CASE

**BYP9–8**  Lonergan Wholesale Corp. uses the LIFO method of inventory costing. In the current year, profit at Lonergan is running unusually high. The corporate tax rate is also high this year, but it is scheduled to decline significantly next year. In an effort to lower current year's net income and to take advantage of the changing income tax rate, the president of Lonergan Wholesale instructs the plant accountant to recommend to the purchasing department a large purchase of inventory for delivery 3 days before the end of the year. The price of the inventory to be purchased has doubled during the year and the purchase will represent a major portion of the ending inventory value.

*Instructions*
 (a) What is the effect of this transaction on this year's and next year's income statement and income tax expense? Why?
 (b) If Lonergan Wholesale had been using the FIFO method of inventory costing, would the president give the same directive?
 (c) Should the plant accountant order the inventory purchase to lower income? What are the ethical implications of this order?

# SURFING THE NET

**BYP9–9**  A company's annual report usually will identify the inventory method used. Knowing that, you can analyze the effects of the inventory method on the income statement and balance sheet.

**Address:** http://www.cisco.com

**Steps:**
 1. From Cisco System's homepage, use the **quick search**, type annual report.
 2. Choose **Search**.
 3. Choose **Cisco System Annual Report**.
 4. Choose **Financial Review**.
 5. Use the financial statements and relating notes to the financial statements to answer the questions below.

*Instructions*
Answer the following questions:
 (a) At Cisco's fiscal year-end, what was the net inventory on the balance sheet?
 (b) How has this changed from the previous fiscal year-end?
 (c) How much of the inventory was finished goods?
 (d) What inventory method do they use?

---

*Answers to Self-Study Questions*
1. b    2. d    3. a    4. a    5. b    6. c    7. d    8. c    9. d    10. d    *11. b
12. b    13. d    *14. d

---

*Answer to Kellogg Review It Question 5, p. 385.*
Kellogg Company reported inventories of $434,300,000 at December 31, 1997. Kellogg reports in Note 1—Accounting Policies that it uses the **average cost method** in applying product costs to inventories and cost of goods sold.

**Remember to go back to the Navigator box on the chapter-opening page and check off your completed work.**

**Before studying this chapter, you should know or, if necessary, review:**

a. The time period assumption. (Ch. 3, pp. 92–93)
b. The cost principle. (Ch. 1, p. 11) and the matching principle. (Ch. 3, pp. 93–94)
c. What is depreciation? (Ch. 3, p. 99)
d. How to make adjustments for depreciation. (Ch. 3, pp. 99–100)

THE NAVIGATOR

## FEATURE STORY

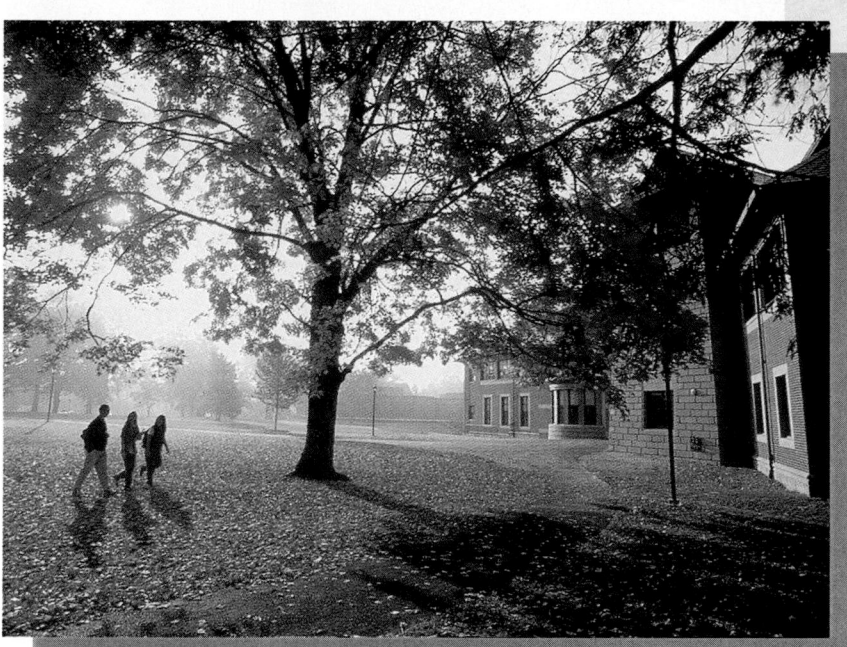

# On the Books, Your Classroom May Be Worthless

Take a stroll around your campus. Some of those buildings were built before you were born. How much do you think they cost to build? Are they depreciating? Are they appreciating?

These questions are not merely academic. It costs millions of dollars to construct, maintain, and sometimes demolish these campus buildings. Where does the money come from? Partly your tuition, perhaps tax dollars, perhaps from contributions of wealthy alumni, or from long-term borrowing. How these dollars are allocated can depend upon a reasonable estimate of a building's condition, its remaining life—

and of course, how much it would cost to replace (its replacement cost).

At Westbrook College in Portland, Maine, Ms. Betty-Ann Doucette, the school's controller, recently researched the age of certain buildings on campus. The reason: a recent Financial Accounting Standards Board rule mandates that private colleges report fixed assets and depreciate them. Ms. Doucette found that some of the college's buildings go back to the nineteenth century. In order to value each building, she tried to find original construction costs and periodic renovations costs, as well as current replacement costs.

"For example, the building I'm in, Goddard Hall, was built in the early part of this century," says Ms. Doucette. "It's now being depreciated over 40 years, and because it's over eighty years old, I show it as fully depreciated." If it is fully depreciated, does that mean it has a zero value? "On the books it says it does," she says. Of course, that doesn't mean it's worthless. An asset can have a zero value on the books yet have a substantial market value.

THE NAVIGATOR

# CHAPTER 10

# PLANT ASSETS, NATURAL RESOURCES, AND INTANGIBLE ASSETS

**THE NAVIGATOR** ✔

- Understand *Concepts for Review*  ☐
- Read *Feature Story*  ☐
- Scan *Study Objectives*  ☐
- Read *Preview*  ☐
- Read text and answer *Before You Go On*
  p. 425 ☐  p. 437 ☐  p. 440 ☐  p. 447 ☐
- Work *Demonstration Problems*  ☐
- Review *Summary of Study Objectives*  ☐
- Answer *Self-Study Questions*  ☐
- Complete assignments  ☐

## STUDY OBJECTIVES

**After studying this chapter, you should be able to:**

1. Describe the application of the cost principle to plant assets.
2. Explain the concept of depreciation.
3. Compute periodic depreciation using different methods.
4. Describe the procedure for revising periodic depreciation.
5. Distinguish between revenue and capital expenditures and explain the entries for these expenditures.
6. Explain how to account for the disposal of a plant asset through retirement, sale, or exchange.
7. Identify the basic accounting issues related to natural resources.
8. Contrast the accounting for intangible assets with the accounting for plant assets.
9. Indicate how plant assets, natural resources, and intangible assets are reported and analyzed.

THE NAVIGATOR

$A$s you can see, the accounting for campus buildings at Westbrook College is complex. In this chapter, we explain the application of the cost principle of accounting to buildings like those at Westbrook, as well as to natural resources and intangible assets such as Westbrook's school logo. We also describe the methods that may be used to allocate an asset's cost over its useful life. In addition, the accounting for expenditures incurred during the useful life of assets is discussed. The content and organization of this chapter are as follows:

# SECTION 1  PLANT ASSETS

Plant assets are tangible resources that are used in the operations of the business and are not intended for sale to customers. They are also called **property, plant, and equipment; plant and equipment;** or **fixed assets**. These assets are generally long-lived and are expected to provide services to the company for a number of years. Except for land, plant assets decline in service potential over their useful lives.

Many companies have substantial investments in plant assets. In public utility companies, for example, net plant assets (plant assets less accumulated depreciation) often represent more than 70% of total assets. Recently net plant assets were 75% of Citizens Utilities' total assets and 72% of Northern Illinois Gas Company's (NICOR). In other types of companies the percentages of plant assets to total assets were:

**ILLUSTRATION 10-1**

*Percentages of plant assets to total assets*

| | | | |
|---|---|---|---|
| McDonald's | 86% | Delta Airlines | 82% |
| Marriott Corporation | 63% | General Motors Corporation | 37% |
| Caterpillar | 26% | Wal-Mart | 44% |

In the income statement, the relationship of depreciation expense and maintenance expense to total operating expenses was 10.4% for Consolidated Edison, 9.6% for Delta Airlines, and 6.2% for General Motors.

Plant assets are often subdivided into four classes:

1. **Land**, such as a building site.
2. **Land improvements**, such as driveways, parking lots, fences, and underground sprinkler systems.
3. **Buildings**, such as stores, offices, factories, and warehouses.
4. **Equipment**, such as store check-out counters, cash registers, coolers, office furniture, factory machinery, and delivery equipment.

Like the purchase of a home by an individual, the acquisition of plant assets is an important decision for a business enterprise. It is also important for a business enterprise to (1) keep the asset in good operating condition, (2) replace worn-out or outdated facilities, and (3) expand its productive resources as needed. The decline of rail travel in the United States can be traced in part to the failure of railroad companies to meet the first two conditions. Conversely, the growth of air travel in this country can be attributed in part to the general willingness of airline companies to observe these essential conditions.

# DETERMINING THE COST OF PLANT ASSETS

Plant assets are recorded at cost in accordance with the **cost principle** of accounting. Thus the buildings at Westbrook College are recorded at cost. Cost consists of all expenditures necessary to acquire the asset and make it ready for its intended use. For example, the purchase price, freight costs paid by the purchaser, and installation costs are all considered part of the cost of factory machinery.

Cost is measured by the cash paid in a cash transaction or by the **cash equivalent price** paid when noncash assets are used in payment. **The cash equivalent price is equal to the fair market value of the asset given up or the fair market value of the asset received, whichever is more clearly determinable.** Once cost is established, it becomes the basis of accounting for the plant asset over its useful life. Current market or replacement values are not used after acquisition. The application of the cost principle to each of the major classes of plant assets is explained in the following sections.

## Land

The cost of land includes (1) the cash purchase price, (2) closing costs such as title and attorney's fees, (3) real estate brokers' commissions, and (4) accrued property taxes and other liens on the land assumed by the purchaser. For example, if the cash price is $50,000 and the purchaser agrees to pay accrued taxes of $5,000, the cost of the land is $55,000.

**1**
**STUDY**
**OBJECTIVE**

Describe the application of the cost principle to plant assets.

**INTERNATIONAL NOTE**

The United Kingdom (UK) is more flexible regarding asset valuation. Most companies in the UK make occasional revaluations to fair value when they believe this information is more relevant. Other examples of countries that permit revaluations are Switzerland and the Netherlands.

All necessary costs incurred in making land **ready for its intended use** are debited to the Land account. When vacant land is acquired, these costs include expenditures for clearing, draining, filling, and grading. Sometimes the land has a building on it that must be removed to make the site suitable for construction of a new building. In this case, all demolition and removal costs less any proceeds from salvaged materials are chargeable to the Land account. To illustrate, assume that Hayes Manufacturing Company acquires real estate at a cash cost of $100,000. The property contains an old warehouse that is razed at a net cost of $6,000 ($7,500 in costs less $1,500 proceeds from salvaged materials). Additional expenditures consist of the attorney's fee, $1,000, and the real estate broker's commission, $8,000. Given these factors, the cost of the land is $115,000, computed as follows:

**ILLUSTRATION 10-2**

*Computation of cost of land*

| Land | |
|---|---|
| Cash price of property | $100,000 |
| Net removal cost of warehouse | 6,000 |
| Attorney's fee | 1,000 |
| Real estate broker's commission | 8,000 |
| **Cost of land** | **$115,000** |

In recording the acquisition, Land is debited for $115,000 and Cash is credited for $115,000.

## Land Improvements

The cost of land improvements includes all expenditures necessary to make the improvements ready for their intended use. For example, the cost of a new company parking lot will include the amount paid for paving, fencing, and lighting. These improvements have limited useful lives and their maintenance and replacement are the responsibility of the company. Thus, these costs are debited to Land Improvements and are depreciated over the useful lives of the improvements.

## Buildings

All necessary expenditures relating to the purchase or construction of a building are charged to the Buildings account. When a building is purchased, such costs include the **purchase price, closing costs (attorney's fees, title insurance, etc.), and real estate broker's commission**. Costs to make the building ready for its intended use consist of **expenditures for remodeling rooms and offices and replacing or repairing the roof, floors, electrical wiring, and plumbing**.

When a new building is constructed, such as a new science building by Westbrook College, cost consists of the contract price plus payments made by the owner for architects' fees, building permits, and excavation costs. In addition, interest costs incurred to finance the project are included in the cost of the asset when a significant period of time is required to get the asset ready for use. In these circumstances, interest costs are considered as necessary as materials and labor. The inclusion of interest costs in the cost of a constructed building is **limited to the construction period**. When construction has been completed, subsequent interest payments on funds borrowed to finance the construction are debited to Interest Expense.

# Equipment

The cost of equipment consists of the **cash purchase price, sales taxes, freight charges, and insurance during transit paid by the purchaser**. It also includes **expenditures required in assembling, installing, and testing the unit**. However, motor vehicle licenses and accident insurance on company trucks and cars are expensed as incurred, because they represent annual recurring expenditures and do not benefit future periods.

To illustrate, assume that the Lenard Company purchases a delivery truck at a cash price of $22,000. Related expenditures consist of sales taxes $1,320, painting and lettering $500, motor vehicle license $80, and a 3-year accident insurance policy $1,600. The cost of the delivery truck is $23,820, computed as follows:

**HELPFUL HINT**
Two criteria apply in determining cost here: (1) the frequency of the cost—one-time or recurring, and (2) the benefit period—life of asset or one year.

| Delivery Truck | |
|---|---|
| Cash price | $22,000 |
| Sales taxes | 1,320 |
| Painting and lettering | 500 |
| Cost of delivery truck | $23,820 |

**ILLUSTRATION 10-3**

*Computation of cost of delivery truck*

The motor vehicle license is expensed when incurred and the insurance policy is a prepaid asset. Thus, the summary entry to record the purchase of the truck and related expenditures is:

| | | |
|---|---|---|
| Delivery Truck | 23,820 | |
| License Expense | 80 | |
| Prepaid Insurance | 1,600 | |
|     Cash | | 25,500 |
|     (To record purchase of delivery truck and related expenditures) | | |

| A | = | L | + | OE |
|---|---|---|---|---|
| +23,820 | | | | −80 |
| +1,600 | | | | |
| −25,500 | | | | |

For another example, assume the Merten Company purchases factory machinery at a cash price of $50,000. Related expenditures consist of sales taxes $3,000, insurance during shipping $500, and installation and testing $1,000. The cost of the factory machinery is $54,500 computed as follows:

| Factory Machinery | |
|---|---|
| Cash price | $50,000 |
| Sales taxes | 3,000 |
| Insurance during shipping | 500 |
| Installation and testing | 1,000 |
| Cost of factory machinery | $54,500 |

**ILLUSTRATION 10-4**

*Computation of cost of factory machinery*

The summary entry to record the purchase and related expenditures is:

| | | |
|---|---|---|
| Factory Machinery | 54,500 | |
|     Cash | | 54,500 |
|     (To record purchase of factory machine) | | |

| A | = | L | + | OE |
|---|---|---|---|---|
| +54,500 | | | | |
| −54,500 | | | | |

**ILLUSTRATION 10-5**

*Depreciation as an allocation concept*

# DEPRECIATION

As explained in Chapter 3, **depreciation is the process of allocating to expense the cost of a plant asset over its useful (service) life in a rational and systematic manner.** Cost allocation is designed to provide for the proper matching of expenses with revenues in accordance with the matching principle (see Illustration 10-5).

**HELPFUL HINT**
Remember that depreciation is the process of allocating cost over the useful life of an asset. It is not a measure of value.

**HELPFUL HINT**
Land does not depreciate because it does not wear out.

**Depreciation is a process of cost allocation, not a process of asset valuation.** Accountants make no attempt to measure the change in an asset's market value during ownership, because plant assets are not held for resale. Thus, the **book value** (cost less accumulated depreciation) of a plant asset may differ significantly from its market value. This is why Goddard Hall, in the opening story, can have zero book value and still have substantial market value.

Depreciation applies to three classes of plant assets: land improvements, buildings, and equipment. Each of these classes is considered to be a **depreciable asset,** because the usefulness to the company and revenue-producing ability of each class will decline over the asset's useful life. Depreciation does not apply to land because its usefulness and revenue-producing ability generally remain intact as long as the asset is owned. In fact, in many cases, the usefulness of land is greater over time because of the scarcity of good land sites. Thus, **land is not a depreciable asset**.

During a depreciable asset's useful life its revenue-producing ability will decline because of **wear and tear.** A delivery truck that has been driven 100,000 miles will be less useful to a company than one driven only 800 miles. Similarly, trucks and planes exposed to snow and salt will deteriorate faster than equipment that is not exposed to these elements.

A decline in revenue-producing ability may also occur because of **obsolescence**. Obsolescence is the process of becoming out of date before the asset physically wears out. The rerouting of major airlines from Chicago's Midway Airport to Chicago-O'Hare International Airport because Midway's runways were too short for jumbo jets is an example. Likewise, diesel train engines made coal-burning locomotives obsolete, and municipal buses sent streetcars to the scrap heap.

**Recognition of depreciation does not result in the accumulation of cash for the replacement of the asset.** The balance in Accumulated Depreciation represents the total cost that has been charged to expense; it is not a cash fund.

## Factors in Computing Depreciation

Three factors affect the computation of depreciation, as shown in Illustration 10-6.

1. **Cost.** Considerations affecting the cost of a depreciable asset have been explained earlier in this chapter. You will recall that plant assets are recorded at cost, in accordance with the cost principle of accounting.

**ILLUSTRATION 10-6**
*Three factors in computing depreciation*

**Cost:** all expenditures necessary to acquire the asset and make it ready for intended use

**Useful life:** estimate of the expected life based on need for repair, service life, and vulnerability to obsolescence

**Salvage value:** estimate of the asset's value at the end of its useful life

**HELPFUL HINT**
Depreciation expense is reported on the income statement, and accumulated depreciation is reported as a deduction from plant assets on the balance sheet.

2. **Useful life.** Useful life is an estimate of the expected productive life, also called service life, of the asset. Useful life may be expressed in terms of time, units of activity such as machine hours, or in units of output. Like salvage value, useful life is an estimate. In making the estimate, management should consider such factors as the intended use of the asset, its expected repair and maintenance policies, and its vulnerability to obsolescence. The company's past experience with similar assets is often helpful in deciding on expected useful life.

3. **Salvage value.** Salvage value is an estimate of the asset's value at the end of its useful life. The value may be based on the asset's worth as scrap or salvage or on its expected trade-in value. Salvage value is an estimate. In making the estimate, management should consider how it plans to dispose of the asset and its experience with similar assets.

**ALTERNATIVE TERMINOLOGY**
Another term sometimes used for salvage value is *residual value.*

## ACCOUNTING IN ACTION
### Business Insight

Not all companies use the same useful life for assets. Compare the useful lives used by the Big Three automakers, for example: At one time General Motors depreciated its machinery over 10 years, compared to Ford's 12 years and Chrysler's 11 years. GM also depreciated its buildings over 28 years while Ford used 30 years and Chrysler used 26 years. General Motors also depreciated its dies and equipment used to manufacture car bodies about twice as fast as Ford and three times as fast as Chrysler. Now GM has changed and aligned itself with its principal competitors by applying more liberal depreciation policies that have increased annual income. Should companies in the same industry be required to use the same useful life for the same type of assets?

## BEFORE YOU GO ON . . .
### Review It

1. What are plant assets? What are the major classes of plant assets? How is the cost principle applied to accounting for plant assets?
2. What is the relationship, if any, of depreciation to (a) cost allocation, (b) asset valuation, and (c) cash accumulation?
3. Explain the factors that affect the computation of depreciation.
4. Where does Kellogg report the detail about its "Property, net" of $2,773.3 million? What classifications and amounts does Kellogg report in the details of its "Property, net" for 1997? The answer to this question is provided on page 467.

**Do It**

Assume that a delivery truck is purchased for $15,000 cash, plus sales taxes of $900 and delivery costs to the dealer of $500. The buyer also pays $200 for painting and lettering, $600 for an annual insurance policy, and $80 for a motor vehicle license. Explain how each of these costs would be accounted for.

*Reasoning:* The cost principle applies to all expenditures made in order to get delivery equipment ready for its intended use. The principle does not apply to operating costs incurred during the useful life of the equipment, such as gas and oil, motor tune-ups, and insurance.

*Solution:* The first four payments ($15,000, $900, $500, and $200) are considered to be expenditures necessary to make the truck ready for its intended use. Thus, the cost of the truck is $16,600. The payments for insurance and the license are considered to be operating expenses incurred during the useful life of the asset.

*Related exercise material:* BE10–1, BE10–2, E10–1, and E10–2.

# Depreciation Methods

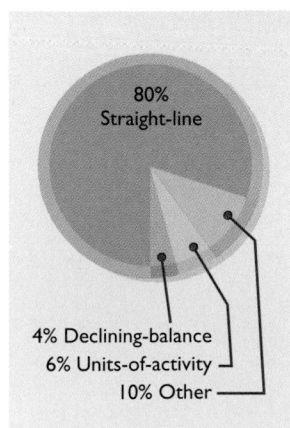

**3**

STUDY
OBJECTIVE

Compute periodic depreciation using different methods.

Depreciation is generally computed using one of the following methods:

1. Straight-line
2. Units-of-activity
3. Declining-balance

Like the inventory methods discussed in Chapter 9, each method is acceptable under generally accepted accounting principles. Management selects the method or methods it believes to be appropriate in the circumstances. The objective is to select the method that best measures the asset's contribution to revenue over its useful life. Once a method is chosen, it should be applied consistently over the useful life of the asset. Consistency enhances the comparability of financial statements.

To facilitate the comparison of the three depreciation methods, we will base all computations on the following data applicable to a small delivery truck purchased by Barb's Florists on January 1, 1999:

**ILLUSTRATION 10-7**

*Delivery truck data*

| | |
|---|---|
| Cost | $13,000 |
| Expected salvage value | $ 1,000 |
| Estimated useful life in years | 5 |
| Estimated useful life in miles | 100,000 |

Depreciation affects the balance sheet through accumulated depreciation and the income statement through depreciation expense. Illustration 10-8 shows the use of the different depreciation methods in 600 of the largest companies in the United States.

## Straight-Line

Under the **straight-line method**, depreciation is the same for each year of the asset's useful life. It is measured solely by the passage of time. In order to compute depreciation expense, it is necessary to determine depreciable cost. **Depreciable cost** is the cost of the asset less its salvage value. It is the total amount subject to depreciation. Depreciable cost is then divided by the asset's useful life to determine depreciation expense. The formula and computation of depreciation expense in the first year for Barb's Florists are shown in Illustration 10-9.

**ILLUSTRATION 10-8**

*Use of depreciation methods*

80%
Straight-line

4% Declining-balance
6% Units-of-activity
10% Other

**ILLUSTRATION 10-9**

*Formula for straight-line method*

Alternatively, we also can compute an annual rate at which the delivery truck is being depreciated. In this case, the rate is 20% (100% ÷ 5 years). When an annual rate is used under the straight-line method, the percentage rate is applied to the depreciable cost of the asset, as shown in the following **depreciation schedule**:

| | BARB'S FLORISTS | | | | |
|---|---|---|---|---|---|
| | Computation | | Annual | End of Year | |
| Year | Depreciable Cost | × Depreciation Rate = | Depreciation Expense | Accumulated Depreciation | Book Value |
| 1999 | $12,000 | 20% | $2,400 | $ 2,400 | $10,600* |
| 2000 | 12,000 | 20 | 2,400 | 4,800 | 8,200 |
| 2001 | 12,000 | 20 | 2,400 | 7,200 | 5,800 |
| 2002 | 12,000 | 20 | 2,400 | 9,600 | 3,400 |
| 2003 | 12,000 | 20 | 2,400 | 12,000 | 1,000 |

*($13,000 − $2,400).

**ILLUSTRATION 10-10**

*Straight-line depreciation schedule*

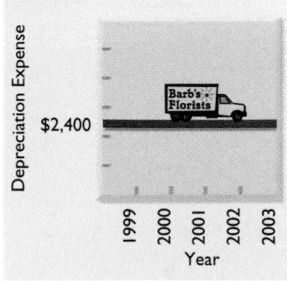

Note that the depreciation expense of $2,400 is the same each year, and that the book value at the end of the useful life is equal to the estimated $1,000 salvage value.

What happens when an asset is purchased **during** the year, rather than on January 1, as in our example? In that case, it is necessary to **prorate the annual depreciation** for the proportion of time used. If Barb's Florists had purchased the delivery truck on April 1, 1999, the depreciation for 1999 would be $1,800 ($12,000 × 20% × 9/12 of a year).

The straight-line method predominates in practice, as shown in Illustration 10-8. For example, such large companies as Campbell Soup, Marriott Corporation, and General Mills use the straight-line method. It is simple to apply, and it matches expenses with revenues appropriately when the use of the asset is reasonably uniform throughout the service life. In the opening story, Westbrook College is probably using the straight-line method of depreciation for its buildings.

## Units-of-Activity

Under the **units-of-activity method**, instead of expressing the life as a time period, useful life is expressed in terms of the total units of production or use expected from the asset. The units-of-activity method is ideally suited to factory machinery: production can be measured in terms of units of output or in terms of machine hours used in operating the machinery. It is also possible to use this method for such items as delivery equipment (miles driven) and airplanes (hours in use). The units-of-activity method is generally not suitable for such assets as buildings or furniture, because depreciation for these assets is more a function of time than of use.

To use this method, the total units of activity for the entire useful life are estimated, the amount is divided into depreciable cost to determine the depreciation cost per unit. The depreciation cost per unit is then applied to the units of activity during the year to determine the annual depreciation. To illustrate, assume that the delivery truck of Barb's Florists is driven 15,000 miles in the first year. The formula and computation of depreciation expense in the first year are:

**ILLUSTRATION 10-11**

*Formula for units-of-activity method*

The depreciation schedule, using assumed mileage data, is as follows:

**ILLUSTRATION 10-12**

*Units-of-activity depreciation schedule*

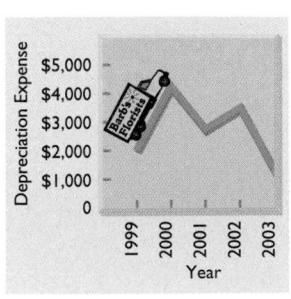

| | | | | | |
|---|---|---|---|---|---|
| **BARB'S FLORISTS** | | | | | |
| | Computation | | Annual | End of Year | |
| Year | Units of Activity | × Depreciation Cost/Unit = | Depreciation Expense | Accumulated Depreciation | Book Value |
| 1999 | 15,000 | $.12 | **$1,800** | $ 1,800 | $11,200* |
| 2000 | 30,000 | .12 | **3,600** | 5,400 | 7,600 |
| 2001 | 20,000 | .12 | **2,400** | 7,800 | 5,200 |
| 2002 | 25,000 | .12 | **3,000** | 10,800 | 2,200 |
| 2003 | 10,000 | .12 | **1,200** | 12,000 | **1,000** |

*($13,000 − $1,800).

The units-of-activity method is not nearly as popular as the straight-line method (see Illustration 10-8), primarily because it is often difficult to make a reasonable estimate of total activity. However, this method is used by some very large companies, such as Standard Oil Company of California and Boise Cascade Corporation. When the productivity of the asset varies significantly from one period to another, the units-of-activity method results in the best matching of expenses with revenues. This method is easy to apply when assets are purchased during the year. In such a case, the productivity of the asset for the partial year is used in computing the depreciation.

## Declining-Balance

The **declining-balance method** produces a decreasing annual depreciation expense over the useful life of the asset. The method is so named because the computation of periodic depreciation is based on a **declining book value** (cost less accumulated depreciation) of the asset. Annual depreciation expense is computed by multiplying the book value at the beginning of the year by the declining-balance depreciation rate. **The depreciation rate remains constant from year to year, but the book value to which the rate is applied declines each year.**

Book value for the first year is the cost of the asset, because the balance in accumulated depreciation at the beginning of the asset's useful life is zero. In subsequent years, book value is the difference between cost and accumulated depreciation at the beginning of the year. **Unlike the other depreciation methods, salvage value is ignored in determining the amount to which the declining balance rate is applied.** Salvage value, however, does limit the total depreciation that can be taken. Depreciation stops when the asset's book value equals expected salvage value.

A common declining-balance rate is double the straight-line rate. As a result, the method is often referred to as the **double-declining-balance method**. If Barb's Florists uses the double-declining-balance method, the depreciation rate is 40% (2 × the straight-line rate of 20%). The formula and computation of depreciation for the first year on the delivery truck are:

**HELPFUL HINT**
Book value is variable and the depreciation rate is constant for this method.

**ILLUSTRATION 10-13**
*Formula for declining-balance method*

The depreciation schedule under this method is as follows:

**ILLUSTRATION 10-14**
*Double-declining-balance depreciation schedule*

### BARB'S FLORISTS

| | Computation | | Annual | End of Year | |
| Year | Book Value Beginning of Year | × Depreciation Rate | = Depreciation Expense | Accumulated Depreciation | Book Value |
|---|---|---|---|---|---|
| 1999 | $13,000 | 40% | $5,200 | $ 5,200 | $7,800 |
| 2000 | 7,800 | 40 | 3,120 | 8,320 | 4,680 |
| 2001 | 4,680 | 40 | 1,872 | 10,192 | 2,808 |
| 2002 | 2,808 | 40 | 1,123 | 11,315 | 1,685 |
| 2003 | 1,685 | 40 | 685* | 12,000 | 1,000 |

*Computation of $674 ($1,685 × 40%) is adjusted to $685 in order for book value to equal salvage value.

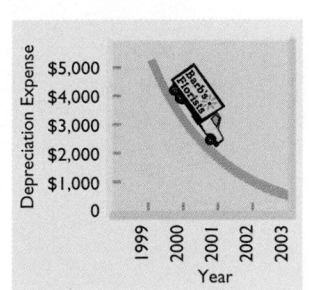

You can see that the delivery equipment is 69% depreciated ($8,320 ÷ $12,000) at the end of the second year. Under the straight-line method it would be depreciated 40% ($4,800 ÷ $12,000) at that time. Because the declining-balance method produces higher depreciation expense in the early years than in the later years, it is considered an accelerated-depreciation method. The declining-balance method is compatible with the matching principle. The higher depreciation expense in early years is matched with the higher benefits received in these years. Conversely, lower depreciation expense is recognized in later years when the asset's contribution to revenue is less. Also, some assets lose usefulness rapidly because of obsolescence. In these cases, the declining-balance method provides a more appropriate depreciation amount.

When an asset is purchased during the year, it is necessary to prorate the declining-balance depreciation in the first year on a time basis. For example, if Barb's Florists had purchased the delivery equipment on April 1, 1999, depreciation for 1999 would become $3,900 ($13,000 × 40% × 9/12). The book value for computing depreciation in 2000 then becomes $9,100 ($13,000 − $3,900), and the 2000 depreciation is $3,640 ($9,100 × 40%).

# ACCOUNTING IN ACTION
## Business Insight

Why does Gingiss Formal Wear have 70 depreciation accounts and use the units-of-activity method for its tuxedos? The reason is that Gingiss wants to track wear and tear on each of its 16,000 dinner jackets individually. So each tuxedo has a bar code, like a box of cereal at the supermarket. When a tux is rented, a clerk runs its code across an electronic scanner. At year-end, the computer adds up the total rentals for each of 15 styles, then divides by expected total use to compute the rate. For instance, on one dolphin-gray tux, Gingiss expects a life of 30 rentals. In a recent year the tux was rented 13 times. So depreciation that period was 43% (13 ÷ 30) of the total cost.

## Comparison of Methods

A comparison of annual and total depreciation expense under each of the three methods is shown for Barb's Florists in Illustration 10-15.

**ILLUSTRATION 10-15**

*Comparison of depreciation methods*

| Year | Straight-Line | Units-of-Activity | Declining-Balance |
|------|--------------|-------------------|-------------------|
| 1999 | $ 2,400 | $ 1,800 | $ 5,200 |
| 2000 | 2,400 | 3,600 | 3,120 |
| 2001 | 2,400 | 2,400 | 1,872 |
| 2002 | 2,400 | 3,000 | 1,123 |
| 2003 | 2,400 | 1,200 | 685 |
| | **$12,000** | **$12,000** | **$12,000** |

Observe that periodic depreciation varies considerably among the methods, but total depreciation is the same for the 5-year period. Each method is acceptable in accounting, because each recognizes the decline in service potential of the asset in a rational and systematic manner. The depreciation expense pattern under each method is presented graphically in Illustration 10-16.

**ILLUSTRATION 10-16**

*Patterns of depreciation*

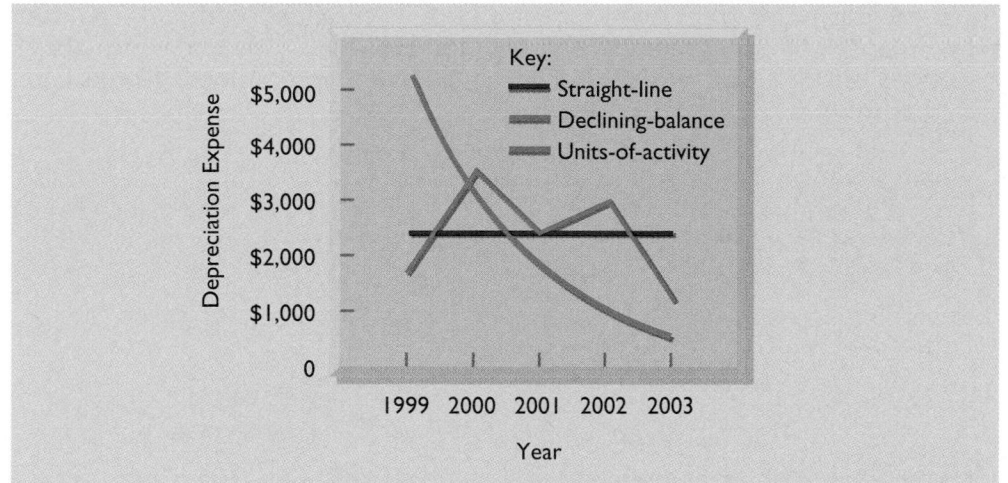

## Depreciation and Income Taxes

The Internal Revenue Service (IRS) allows corporate taxpayers to deduct depreciation expense when computing taxable income. However, the IRS does not require the taxpayer to use the same depreciation method on the tax return that is used in preparing financial statements. Consequently, many corporations use straight-line in their financial statements to maximize net income, and at the same time, a special accelerated-depreciation method is generally used on their tax returns to minimize their income taxes. Taxpayers must use on their tax returns either the straight-line method or a special accelerated-depreciation method called **Modified Accelerated Cost Recovery System** (MACRS).

**INTERNATIONAL NOTE**

In Germany, tax laws have a strong influence on financial accounting. Depreciation expense determined by the tax code must also be used for preparing financial statements.

## TECHNOLOGY IN ACTION

Software packages to account for plant assets exist for both large and small computer systems. Even the least sophisticated packages can maintain a control and subsidiary ledger for plant assets and make the necessary depreciation computations and adjusting entries. Many packages also maintain separate depreciation schedules for both financial statement and income tax purposes, with reconciliations made for any differences.

## Revising Periodic Depreciation

Depreciation is one example of the estimation procedures that are part of the accounting process. Annual depreciation expense should be reviewed periodically by management. If wear and tear or obsolescence indicate that annual depreciation is inadequate or excessive, a change in the amount should be made.

When a change in an estimate is required, the change is made in **current and future years but not to prior periods**. Thus, (1) there is no correction of previously recorded depreciation expense, and (2) depreciation expense for current and future years is revised. The rationale—continual restatement of prior periods would adversely affect the reader's confidence in financial statements.

To determine the new annual depreciation expense, we compute the asset's depreciable cost at the time of the revision and allocate it to the remaining useful life. To illustrate, assume that Barb's Florists decides on January 1, 2002, to extend

**4**

STUDY
OBJECTIVE
·····································
Describe the procedure
for revising periodic
depreciation.

the useful life of the truck one year because of its excellent condition. The company has used the straight-line method to depreciate the asset to date, and book value is $5,800 ($13,000 − $7,200). The new annual depreciation is $1,600, computed as follows:

**ILLUSTRATION 10-17**

*Revised depreciation computation*

| | | |
|---|---|---|
| Book value, 1/1/02 | $5,800 | |
| Less: Salvage value | 1,000 | |
| Depreciable cost | $4,800 | |
| Remaining useful life | 3 years | (2002–2004) |
| Revised annual depreciation ($4,800 ÷ 3) | $1,600 | |

**HELPFUL HINT**

Use a step-by-step approach: (1) determine new depreciable cost; (2) divide by remaining useful life.

On January 1, 2002, or at any other time, Barb's Florists makes no entry for the change in estimate. On December 31, 2002, during the preparation of adjusting entries, it would record depreciation expense of $1,600. Significant changes in estimates must be described in the financial statements.

# EXPENDITURES DURING USEFUL LIFE

**5**

**STUDY OBJECTIVE**

Distinguish between revenue and capital expenditures and explain the entries for these expenditures.

During the useful life of a plant asset a company may incur costs for ordinary repairs, additions, and improvements. **Ordinary repairs** are expenditures to maintain the operating efficiency and expected productive life of the unit. They usually are fairly small amounts that occur frequently throughout the asset's service life. Motor tune-ups and oil changes, the painting of buildings, and the replacing of worn-out gears on factory machinery are examples. They are debited to Repair (or Maintenance) Expense as incurred. Because they are immediately charged against revenues as an expense, these costs are often referred to as **revenue expenditures**

**Additions and improvements** are costs incurred to increase the operating efficiency, productive capacity, or expected useful life of the plant asset. These expenditures are usually material in amount and occur infrequently during the period of ownership. Expenditures for additions and improvements increase the company's investment in productive facilities and are generally debited to the plant asset affected. Accordingly, they are often referred to as **capital expenditures**. Most major U.S. corporations disclose the amount of their annual capital expenditures. In a recent year, both IBM and General Motors reported capital expenditures slightly in excess of $6 billion. The accounting for capital expenditures varies depending on the nature of the expenditure.

# PLANT ASSET DISPOSALS

**6**

**STUDY OBJECTIVE**

Explain how to account for the disposal of a plant asset through retirement, sale, or exchange.

Plant assets of various types may be disposed of in three ways, as shown in Illustration 10-18. Whatever the method of disposal, at the time of disposal it is necessary to determine the book value of the plant asset. The book value is the difference between the cost of the plant asset and the accumulated depreciation to date. If the disposal occurs at any time during the year, depreciation for the fraction of the year to the date of disposal must be recorded. The book value is then eliminated by debiting Accumulated Depreciation for the total depreciation to the date of disposal and crediting the asset account for the cost of the asset.

In this section we will examine the accounting for each of the three methods of plant asset disposal.

**Retirement**
Equipment is scrapped or discarded.

**Sale**
Equipment is sold to another party.

**Exchange**
Existing equipment is traded for new equipment.

**ILLUSTRATION 10-18**

*Methods of plant asset disposal*

## Retirement of Plant Assets

To illustrate the accounting for a retirement of plant assets, assume that Hobart Enterprises retires its computer printers, which cost $32,000. The accumulated depreciation on these printers is also $32,000; the equipment, therefore, is fully depreciated (zero book value). The entry to record this retirement is as follows:

| | | |
|---|---|---|
| Accumulated Depreciation—Printing Equipment | 32,000 | |
| Printing Equipment | | 32,000 |
| (To record retirement of fully depreciated equipment) | | |

| A | = | L | + | OE |
|---|---|---|---|---|
| + 32,000 | | | | |
| − 32,000 | | | | |

What happens if a fully depreciated plant asset is still useful to the company? In this case, the plant asset and the related accumulated depreciation continue to be reported on the balance sheet without further depreciation or adjustment until the asset is retired. Reporting the asset and related accumulated depreciation on the balance sheet informs the reader of the financial statements that the asset is still being used by the company. However, once an asset is fully depreciated, even if it is still being used, no additional depreciation should be taken. In no situation can the accumulated depreciation on the plant asset exceed its cost.

**HELPFUL HINT**
When a plant asset is disposed of, all amounts related to the asset must be removed from the accounts. This includes the original cost in the asset account and the total depreciation to date in the accumulated depreciation account.

If a plant asset is retired before it is fully depreciated, and no scrap or salvage value is received, a loss on disposal occurs. For example, assume that Sunset Company discards delivery equipment that cost $18,000 and has accumulated depreciation of $14,000 at the date of retirement. The entry is as follows:

| | | |
|---|---|---|
| Accumulated Depreciation—Delivery Equipment | 14,000 | |
| Loss on Disposal | 4,000 | |
| Delivery Equipment | | 18,000 |
| (To record retirement of delivery equipment at a loss) | | |

| A | = | L | + | OE |
|---|---|---|---|---|
| + 14,000 | | | | − 4,000 |
| − 18,000 | | | | |

The loss on disposal is reported in the Other Expenses and Losses section of the income statement.

## Sale of Plant Assets

In a disposal by sale, the book value of the asset is compared with the proceeds received from the sale. **If the proceeds of the sale exceed the book value of the plant asset, a gain on disposal occurs. If the proceeds of the sale are less than the book value of the plant asset sold, a loss on disposal occurs.**

Only by coincidence will the book value and the fair market value of the asset be the same at the time the asset is sold. Gains and losses on sales of plant assets are, therefore, quite common. As an example, Delta Airlines, Inc. reported a $94,343,000 gain on the sale of five Boeing B-727-200 aircraft and five Lockheed L-1011-1 aircraft.

## Gain on Disposal

To illustrate a gain, assume that on July 1, 1999, Wright Company sells office furniture for $16,000 cash. The office furniture originally cost $60,000 and as of January 1, 1999, had accumulated depreciation of $41,000. Depreciation for the first 6 months of 1999 is $8,000. The entry to record depreciation expense and update accumulated depreciation to July 1 is as follows:

| A | = | L | + | OE |
|---|---|---|---|---|
| −8,000 | | | | −8,000 |

| July 1 | Depreciation Expense | 8,000 | |
|---|---|---|---|
| |     Accumulated Depreciation—Office Furniture | | 8,000 |
| |     (To record depreciation expense for the first | | |
| |     six months of 1999) | | |

After the accumulated depreciation balance is updated, a gain on disposal of $5,000 is computed:

**ILLUSTRATION 10-19**

*Computation of gain on disposal*

| Cost of office furniture | | $60,000 |
|---|---|---|
| Less: Accumulated depreciation ($41,000 + $8,000) | | 49,000 |
| Book value at date of disposal | | 11,000 |
| Proceeds from sale | | 16,000 |
| Gain on disposal | | $ 5,000 |

The entry to record the sale and the gain on disposal is as follows:

| A | = | L | + | OE |
|---|---|---|---|---|
| +16,000 | | | | +5,000 |
| +49,000 | | | | |
| −60,000 | | | | |

| July 1 | Cash | 16,000 | |
|---|---|---|---|
| | Accumulated Depreciation—Office Furniture | 49,000 | |
| |     Office Furniture | | 60,000 |
| |     Gain on Disposal | | 5,000 |
| |     (To record sale of office furniture at a gain) | | |

The gain on disposal is reported in the Other Revenues and Gains section of the income statement.

## Loss on Disposal

Assume that instead of selling the office furniture for $16,000, Wright sells it for $9,000. In this case, a loss of $2,000 is computed:

**ILLUSTRATION 10-20**

*Computation of loss on disposal*

| Cost of office furniture | | $60,000 |
|---|---|---|
| Less: Accumulated depreciation | | 49,000 |
| Book value at date of disposal | | 11,000 |
| Proceeds from sale | | 9,000 |
| Loss on disposal | | $ 2,000 |

The entry to record the sale and the loss on disposal is as follows:

| July 1 | Cash | 9,000 | | | A | = | L | + | OE |
|---|---|---|---|---|---|---|---|---|---|
| | Accumulated Depreciation—Office Furniture | 49,000 | | | +9,000 | | | | −2,000 |
| | Loss on Disposal | 2,000 | | | +49,000 | | | | |
| |    Office Furniture | | 60,000 | | −60,000 | | | | |
| |      (To record sale of office furniture at a loss) | | | | | | | | |

The loss on disposal is reported in the Other Expenses and Losses section of the income statement.

# Exchange of Plant Assets

Plant assets may also be disposed of through exchange. Exchanges can be for either similar or dissimilar assets. Because exchanges of similar assets are more common, they are discussed here.

An exchange of similar assets involves assets of the same type. This occurs, for example, when old delivery equipment is exchanged for new delivery equipment or when old office furniture is exchanged for new office furniture. In an exchange of similar assets, the new asset performs the **same function** as the old asset.

In exchanges of similar plant assets, it is necessary to determine (1) the cost of the asset acquired and (2) the gain or loss on the asset given up. Because a noncash asset is given up in the exchange, cost is equal to the **cash equivalent price** paid. Cost, therefore, is the fair market value of the asset given up plus the cash paid. The gain or loss on disposal is the **difference between the fair market value and the book value of the asset given up**. These determinations and the resulting accounting entries are explained and illustrated below.

## *Loss Treatment*

When a loss occurs on the exchange of similar assets, it is recognized immediately. To illustrate the accounting for a loss, assume that Roland Company exchanged old office equipment for similar new office equipment. The book value of the old office equipment is $26,000 (cost $70,000 less accumulated depreciation $44,000), its fair market value is $10,000, and cash of $81,000 is paid. The cost of the new office equipment, $91,000, is computed as follows:

| | |
|---|---|
| Fair market value of old office equipment | $10,000 |
| Cash | 81,000 |
| **Cost of new office equipment** | **$91,000** |

**ILLUSTRATION 10-21**

*Computation of cost of new office equipment*

Through this exchange, a loss on disposal of $16,000 is incurred. A loss results when the book value is greater than the fair market value of the asset given up. The computation is as follows:

| | |
|---|---|
| Book value of old office equipment ($70,000 − $44,000) | $26,000 |
| Fair market value of old office equipment | 10,000 |
| **Loss on disposal** | **$16,000** |

**ILLUSTRATION 10-22**

*Computation of loss on disposal*

In recording an exchange at a loss it is necessary to (1) eliminate the book value of the asset given up, (2) record the cost of the asset acquired, and (3) recognize the loss on disposal. The entry for the Roland Company is as follows:

| A | = | L | + | OE |
|---|---|---|---|---|
| +91,000 | | | | −16,000 |
| +44,000 | | | | |
| −70,000 | | | | |
| −81,000 | | | | |

| | | |
|---|---|---|
| Office Equipment (new) | 91,000 | |
| Accumulated Depreciation—Office Equipment (old) | 44,000 | |
| Loss on Disposal | 16,000 | |
|     Office Equipment (old) | | 70,000 |
|     Cash | | 81,000 |
|         (To record exchange of old office equipment for similar new equipment) | | |

## Gain Treatment

When a gain occurs on the exchange of similar assets, it is not recognized immediately. Instead, the gain is deferred by reducing the cost basis of the new asset. Thus, in determining the cost of the asset acquired, it is necessary to compute the **cost before deferral of the gain** and then the **cost after deferral of the gain**.

To illustrate the accounting for similar assets, assume that Mark's Express Delivery decides to exchange its old delivery equipment plus cash of $3,000 for new delivery equipment. At this time, the book value of the old delivery equipment is $12,000 (cost $40,000 less accumulated depreciation $28,000). In addition, it is determined that the fair market value of the old delivery equipment is $19,000.

The cost of the new asset received (before deferral of the gain) is equal to the **fair market value of the old asset exchanged plus any cash or other consideration given up**. The cost of the new delivery equipment (before deferral of the gain) is $22,000, computed as follows:

**HELPFUL HINT**

Gains on the exchange of similar assets are not recognized because the earnings process is not considered completed. Losses, however, are recognized, to be conservative.

**ILLUSTRATION 10-23**

*Cost of new equipment (before deferral of gain)*

| | |
|---|---|
| Fair market value of old delivery equipment | $19,000 |
| Cash | 3,000 |
| **Cost of new delivery equipment (before deferral of gain)** | **$22,000** |

A gain results when the fair market value is greater than the book value of the asset given up. For Mark's Express, there is a gain of $7,000, computed as follows, on the disposal:

**ILLUSTRATION 10-24**

*Computation of gain on disposal*

| | |
|---|---|
| Fair market value of old delivery equipment | $19,000 |
| Book value of old delivery equipment ($40,000 − $28,000) | 12,000 |
| **Gain on disposal** | **$ 7,000** |

The $7,000 gain on disposal is then offset against the $22,000 cost of the new delivery equipment. The result is a $15,000 cost of the new delivery equipment, after deferral of the gain, as shown in Illustration 10-25.

**ILLUSTRATION 10-25**

*Cost of new equipment (after deferral of gain)*

| | |
|---|---|
| Cost of new delivery equipment (before deferral of gain) | $22,000 |
| Less: Gain on disposal | 7,000 |
| **Cost of new delivery equipment (after deferral of gain)** | **$15,000** |

The entry to record the exchange is as follows:

| | | | | | A | = | L | + | OE |
|---|---|---|---|---|---|---|---|---|---|
| Delivery Equipment (new) | 15,000 | | | | +15,000 | | | | |
| Accumulated Depreciation—Delivery Equipment (old) | 28,000 | | | | +28,000 | | | | |
|    Delivery Equipment (old) | | 40,000 | | | −40,000 | | | | |
|    Cash | | 3,000 | | | −3,000 | | | | |
|      (To record exchange of old delivery equipment for similar new delivery equipment) | | | | | | | | | |

This entry does not eliminate the gain; it just postpones or defers it to future periods. The deferred gain of $7,000 reduces the $22,000 cost to $15,000. As a result, net income in future periods increases because depreciation expense on the newly acquired delivery equipment is less by $7,000.

Summarizing, the rules for accounting for exchanges of similar assets are as follows:

| Type of Event | Recognition |
|---|---|
| Loss | Recognize immediately by debiting Loss on Disposal |
| Gain | Defer and reduce cost of new asset |

**ILLUSTRATION 10-26**

*Accounting rules for plant exchanges*

# BEFORE YOU GO ON . . .

## Review It

1. What are the formulas for computing annual depreciation under each of the depreciation methods?
2. How do the methods differ in terms of their effects on annual depreciation over the useful life of the asset?
3. Are revisions of periodic depreciation made to prior periods? Explain.
4. How does a capital expenditure differ from a revenue expenditure?
5. What is the proper accounting for the retirement and sale of plant assets?
6. What is the proper accounting for the exchange of similar plant assets?

## Do It

Overland Trucking has an old truck that cost $30,000, has accumulated depreciation of $16,000, and a fair value of $17,000. It has a choice of either selling the truck for cash of $17,000 or exchanging the old truck and $3,000 cash for a new truck. What is the entry that Overland Trucking would record under each option?

*Reasoning:* Gains and losses on the sale or exchange of plant assets are determined by the difference between the book value and the fair value of the company's asset. Gains on the exchange of similar assets are deferred.

*Solution:*
Sale of truck for cash:

| | | |
|---|---|---|
| Cash | 17,000 | |
| Accumulated Depreciation—Truck (old) | 16,000 | |
|    Truck (old) | | 30,000 |
|    Gain on Disposal [$17,000 − ($30,000 − $16,000)] | | 3,000 |
|      (To record sale of truck at a gain) | | |

Exchange of old truck and cash for new truck:

| | | |
|---|---:|---:|
| Truck (new)* | 17,000 | |
| Accumulated Depreciation—Truck (old) | 16,000 | |
|     Truck (old) | | 30,000 |
|     Cash | | 3,000 |
|       (To record exchange of old truck for similar new truck) | | |

*($20,000 − $3,000)

If the old truck is exchanged for the new truck, the $3,000 gain is deferred, and the recorded cost of the new truck is reduced by $3,000.

*Related exercise material:* BE10–8, BE10–9, BE10–10, BE10–11, E10–6, E10–7, E10–8, and E10–9.

# SECTION 2 NATURAL RESOURCES

**Natural resources** consist of standing timber and underground deposits of oil, gas, and minerals. Such resources include the much-publicized offshore oil deposits of major petroleum companies and the oil deposits for which the Alaskan pipeline was built. These long-lived productive assets have two distinguishing characteristics: (1) they are physically extracted in operations (such as mining, cutting, or pumping), and (2) they are replaceable only by an act of nature. Because of these characteristics, natural resources are frequently called **wasting assets.**

**HELPFUL HINT**
On a balance sheet, natural resources may be described as Timberlands, Mineral Deposits, Oil Reserves, and so on.

# ACQUISITION COST

**7**
**STUDY OBJECTIVE**

Identify the basic accounting issues related to natural resources.

The acquisition cost of a natural resource is the cash or cash equivalent price necessary to acquire the resource and prepare it for its intended use. For an already discovered resource, such as an existing coal mine, cost is the price paid for the property.

Determining acquisition cost becomes a problem when exploration is involved. For example, some argue that the costs of unsuccessful exploration as well as successful exploration should be capitalized. They believe that, using an oil well as an example, the cost of drilling the dry holes is a cost that is needed to find the commercially profitable wells. As a result, both successful and unsuccessful explorations are capitalized, and the costs are written off to expense over the useful life of the successful wells. This method is often referred to as the **full-cost approach**.

Others disagree, arguing that the costs of only successful projects should be capitalized and unsuccessful projects should be expensed. They maintain that if only one of ten exploratory wells becomes commercially viable, it is inappropriate to assign the costs of the nine unsuccessful wells to the cost of the successful well. This method is referred to as the **successful efforts approach**. At present, both approaches are used in accounting for natural resources. For example, such companies as American Petrofina, DuPont, Callahan Mining, and Copperweld use full costing, whereas Texaco, Mobil, and Gulf use successful efforts.

## ACCOUNTING IN ACTION
### Business Insight

Should both full cost and successful efforts be permitted in accounting? Views are particularly strong on this subject. As one financial expert, commenting on the full-cost method, noted: "It lets them call a dry hole an asset, and as far as I am concerned, any company that uses full-cost accounting is guilty until proven innocent." On the other hand, companies using the full-cost method argue that "it enables us to undertake risky exploration projects without having sharp swings in reported earnings." Or as one writer noted: "Forcing companies to use successful efforts accounting would retard domestic oil and gas exploration and imperil national security." The debate raises some interesting questions: Does the choice of accounting method actually affect a company's exploration activities? If it does, should accounting be concerned with national security, or should it "tell it like it is"?

# DEPLETION

The process of allocating the cost of natural resources to expense in a rational and systematic manner over the resource's useful life is called depletion. **The units-of-activity method is generally used to compute depletion, because periodic depletion generally is a function of the units extracted during the year.** Under this method, the total cost of the natural resource minus salvage value, if any, is divided by the number of units estimated to be in the resource. The result is a depletion cost per unit of product. The depletion cost per unit is then multiplied by the number of units extracted and sold, to compute the depletion expense. The formula is as follows:

**ILLUSTRATION 10-27**

*Formula to compute depletion expense*

**HELPFUL HINT.**
The computation for depletion is similar to the computation for depreciation using the units-of-activity method of depreciation.

To illustrate, assume that the Lane Coal Company invests $5 million in a mine estimated to have 10 million tons of coal and no salvage value. In the first year, 800,000 tons of coal are extracted and sold. Using the formulas above, the computations are as follows:

$$\$5,000,000 \div 10,000,000 = \$.50 \text{ depletion cost per ton}$$

$$\$.50 \times 800,000 = \$400,000 \text{ depletion expense}$$

The entry to record depletion expense for the first year of operation is as follows:

| A | = | L | + | OE |
|---|---|---|---|---|
| −400,000 | | | | −400,000 |

| Dec. 31 | Depletion Expense | 400,000 | |
|---|---|---|---|
| |     Accumulated Depletion | | 400,000 |
| |     (To record depletion expense on coal | | |
| |     deposits) | | |

**HELPFUL HINT**

Natural resources are generally reported as part of Property, Plant, and Equipment on the balance sheet.

The account Depletion Expense is reported as a part of the cost of producing the product. Accumulated Depletion, a contra asset account similar to accumulated depreciation, is deducted from the cost of the natural resource in the balance sheet as follows:

**ILLUSTRATION 10-28**

*Statement presentation of accumulated depletion*

| LANE COAL COMPANY<br>Balance Sheet (partial) | | |
|---|---|---|
| Coal mine | $5,000,000 | |
| Less: Accumulated depletion | 400,000 | $4,600,000 |

However, in many companies an Accumulated Depletion account is not used, and the amount of depletion is credited directly to the natural resource account.

Sometimes, natural resources extracted in one accounting period will not be sold until a later period. In this case, depletion is not expensed until the resource is sold. The amount not sold is reported in the Current Asset section as inventory.

# BEFORE YOU GO ON . . .

## Review It

1. What is the difference between the full-cost and successful efforts methods in accounting for natural resources?
2. How is depletion expense computed?

## Do It

Explain the method used in computing depletion and show the computation, assuming Hard Rock Mining Corporation invests $12 million in a mine estimated to have 10 million tons of ore and a $2 million salvage value. In the first year 40,000 tons of ore are mined and sold.

*Reasoning:* There are many similarities between depreciation and depletion. In computing depletion expense, the units-of-activity method is generally used.

*Solution:* Under the units-of-activity method, a depletion cost per unit is determined by dividing total cost minus salvage value by the total estimated units. The computation is as follows:

$$(\$12,000,000 - \$2,000,000) \div 10,000,000 = \$1 \text{ depletion cost per ton}$$

The cost per unit is then multiplied by the number of units extracted and sold to determine depletion expense. Depletion expense for Hard Rock is $40,000 ($1 × 40,000).

*Related exercise material:* BE10–12, BE10–13, and E10–10.

THE NAVIGATOR

# SECTION 3    INTANGIBLE ASSETS

**Intangible assets** are rights, privileges, and competitive advantages that result from the ownership of long-lived assets that do not possess physical substance. Evidence of intangibles may exist in the form of contracts, licenses, and other documents. Intangibles may arise from:

1. Government grants such as patents, copyrights, franchises, trademarks, and trade names.
2. Acquisition of another business in which the purchase price includes a payment for goodwill.
3. Private monopolistic arrangements arising from contractual agreements, such as franchises and leases.

Some widely known intangibles are the patents of Polaroid, the franchises of McDonald's, the trade name of Col. Sander's Kentucky Fried Chicken, and the trademark 3M of Minnesota Mining and Manufacturing Company.

# ACCOUNTING FOR INTANGIBLE ASSETS

In general, accounting for intangible assets parallels the accounting for plant assets. That is, **intangible assets are recorded at cost**, and this cost is expensed **over the useful life of the intangible asset in a rational and systematic manner**. At disposal, the book value of the intangible asset is eliminated, and a gain or loss, if any, is recorded.

There are, however, differences between accounting for intangible assets and accounting for plant assets. First, the term used to describe the allocation of the cost of an intangible asset to expense is **amortization**, rather than depreciation. To record amortization of an intangible, an amortization expense is debited and the specific intangible asset is credited. An alternative is to credit an accumulated amortization account, similar to accumulated depreciation. Most companies, however, choose simply to reduce the cost of the intangible asset.

There is also a difference in determining cost. For plant assets, cost includes both the purchase price of an asset and the costs incurred by a company in designing and constructing the plant asset. In contrast, cost for an intangible asset includes only the purchase price. Costs incurred in developing an intangible asset are expensed as incurred.

A third difference is that **the amortization period of an intangible asset cannot be longer than 40 years**. For example, even if the useful life of an intangible asset is 60 years, it must be written off over 40 years. Conversely, if the useful life is less than 40 years, the useful life is used. This rule ensures that all intangibles, especially those with indeterminable lives, will be written off in a reasonable period of time.

Intangible assets are typically amortized on a straight-line basis. The widespread use of this method adds comparability in accounting for intangible assets.

**8**

STUDY OBJECTIVE

Contrast the accounting for intangible assets with the accounting for plant assets.

## Patents

A **patent** is an exclusive right issued by the United States Patent Office that enables the recipient to manufacture, sell, or otherwise control an invention for a period of 17 years from the date of the grant. A patent is nonrenewable, but the legal life of a patent may be extended beyond its original term by obtaining new patents for improvements and other changes in the basic design.

**The initial cost of a patent is the cash or cash equivalent price paid to acquire the patent.** It should be noted that the saying, "A patent is only as good as the money you're prepared to spend defending it," is very true. Most patents are subject to some type of litigation by competitors. A well-known example is the patent infringement suit won by Polaroid against Eastman Kodak in protecting its patent on instant cameras. If the owner incurs legal costs in successfully defending the patent in an infringement suit, such costs are considered necessary to establish the validity of the patent. Thus, **they are added to the Patent account and amortized over the remaining life of the patent.**

**The cost of a patent should be amortized over its 17-year legal life or its useful life, whichever is shorter.** In determining useful life, obsolescence, inadequacy, and other factors should be considered; these may cause a patent to become economically ineffective before the end of its legal life. To illustrate the computation of patent expense, assume that National Labs purchases a patent at a cost of $60,000. If the useful life of the patent is 8 years, the annual amortization expense is $7,500 ($60,000 ÷ 8). The entry to record the annual amortization is:

| A = L + OE | Dec. 31 | Patent Expense | 7,500 | |
|---|---|---|---|---|
| −7,500     −7,500 | | Patents | | 7,500 |
| | | (To record patent amortization) | | |

Patent Expense is classified as an **operating expense** in the income statement.

## Copyrights

Copyrights are granted by the federal government, giving the owner the exclusive right to reproduce and sell an artistic or published work. Copyrights extend for the life of the creator plus 50 years. The cost of the copyright consists of the **cost of acquiring and defending it**. The cost may be only the $10 fee paid to the U.S. Copyright office, or it may amount to a great deal more if a copyright infringement suit is involved.

The useful life of a copyright generally is significantly shorter than its legal life. Similar to other intangible assets, the maximum write-off is 40 years. However, because of the difficulties of determining the period over which benefits are to be received, copyrights usually are amortized over a relatively short period of time.

## ACCOUNTING IN ACTION
### International Insight

One of the significant new items copyrighted today is computer software. Lotus 1-2-3, Windows 98, and WordPerfect are some examples. These intangible assets—copyrights, in this case—are one of the most valuable assets of these corporations. To illustrate how important copyrights are, consider that in China only $1 million in computer software was sold in two recent years because China had no copyright law to discourage software piracy. Now an agreement has been reached with the Chinese that will provide protection against unlicensed copying of software. As one software maker observed, "If copyrights are protected, the value of the computer-software market in China will skyrocket."

## Trademarks and Trade Names

A trademark or trade name is a word, phrase, jingle, or symbol that distinguishes or identifies a particular enterprise or product. Trade names like Wheaties, Trivial Pursuit, Sunkist, Kleenex, Windows, Coca-Cola, Big Mac, and Cadillac create immediate product identification and generally enhance the sale of the product. The creator or original user may obtain exclusive legal right to the trademark or trade name by registering it with the U.S. Patent Office. Such registration provides 20 years' protection and may be renewed indefinitely as long as the trademark or trade name is in use.

If the trademark or trade name is purchased, the cost is the purchase price. If it is developed by the enterprise itself, the cost includes attorney's fees, registration fees, design costs, successful legal defense costs, and other expenditures directly related to securing it.

As with other intangibles, the cost of trademarks and trade names must be amortized over the shorter of its useful life or 40 years. Because of the uncertainty involved in estimating the useful life, the cost is frequently amortized over a much shorter period.

## Franchises and Licenses

When you drive down the street in your Trans-Am purchased from a General Motors dealer, fill up your tank at the corner Standard Oil station, eat lunch at Wendy's, and vacation at a Club Med resort, you are dealing with franchises. A franchise is a contractual arrangement under which the franchisor grants the franchisee the right to sell certain products, to render specific services, or to use certain trademarks or trade names, usually within a designated geographical area.

Another type of franchise is that entered into between a governmental body (commonly municipalities) and a business enterprise. This type of franchise permits the enterprise to use public property in performing its services. Examples are the use of city streets for a bus line or taxi service, use of public land for telephone and electric lines, and the use of airwaves for radio or TV broadcasting. Such operating rights are referred to as licenses.

Franchises and licenses may be granted for a definite period of time, an indefinite period, or perpetual. **When costs can be identified with the acquisition of the franchise or license, an intangible asset should be recognized.** In the case of a limited life, the cost of a franchise (or license) should be amortized as operating expense over the useful life. If the life is indefinite or perpetual, the cost may be amortized over a reasonable period not to exceed 40 years. Annual payments made under a franchise agreement should be recorded as **operating expenses** in the period in which they are incurred.

**ETHICS NOTE**

A pharmaceutical company was growing rapidly by buying unwanted drug licensing rights. These licensing rights, reported as intangible assets, represented over 70% of the company's total assets. The company experienced a 50% drop in value when the market realized the rights were being amortized over 40 years. If a more reasonable life had been used to amortize the rights, the company's reported profits would, instead, have been huge losses.

## ACCOUNTING IN ACTION
### Business Insight

King World's most valuable asset is the right to license television shows such as "Wheel of Fortune," "Jeopardy," "The Oprah Winfrey Show," and "Inside Edition." Almost 90% of its $396.4 million in a recent year came from the fees associated with the rights to license agreements on these intangible assets.

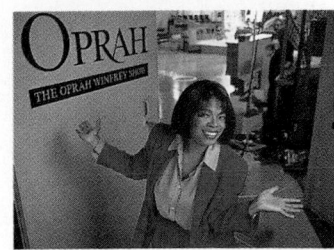

## Goodwill

Usually, the largest intangible asset that appears on a company's balance sheet is goodwill. Goodwill is the value of all favorable attributes that relate to a business enterprise. These include exceptional management, desirable location, good customer relations, skilled employees, high-quality products, fair pricing policies, and harmonious relations with labor unions. Some view goodwill as expected earnings in excess of normal earnings. Goodwill is, therefore, unusual: unlike other assets such as investments, plant assets, and other intangibles that can be sold individually in the marketplace, goodwill can be identified only with the business as a whole.

If goodwill can be identified only with the business as a whole, how can it be determined? Certainly, many of the factors above (exceptional management, desirable location, and so on) are present in many business enterprises. However, to determine the amount of goodwill in these types of situations would be too difficult and very subjective. In other words, to recognize goodwill without an exchange transaction would lead to subjective valuations that do not contribute to the reliability of financial statements. **Therefore, goodwill is recorded only when there is an exchange transaction that involves the purchase of an entire business. When an entire business is purchased, goodwill is the excess of cost over the fair market value of the net assets (assets less liabilities) acquired.**

In recording the purchase of a business, the net assets are shown at their fair market values, goodwill is recorded at its cost, and cash is credited for the purchase price. Subsequently, goodwill is written off over its useful life, not to exceed 40 years. The amortization entry generally results in a debit to Goodwill Expense and a credit to Goodwill. Goodwill is reported in the balance sheet under Intangible Assets.

## ACCOUNTING IN ACTION
### International Insight

Does the amortization requirement for goodwill create a disadvantage for U.S. companies? British companies, for example, do not have to amortize goodwill against earnings. Rather, they bypass the income statement completely and charge goodwill directly to stockholders' equity. For example, Pillsbury was purchased by Grand Met, a British firm. Many complained that U.S. companies were reluctant to bid for Pillsbury because it would mean that they would have to record a large amount of goodwill, which would substantially depress income in the future. What should be done when accounting practices are different among countries and perhaps give one country a competitive edge?

# RESEARCH AND DEVELOPMENT COSTS

Research and development costs are not intangible costs, but because these expenditures may lead to patents and copyrights, they are discussed in this section. Many companies spend considerable sums of money on research and development in an ongoing effort to develop new products or processes. For example, in a recent year IBM spent over $2.5 billion on research and development, an amount greater than the total expenditure budget of some state governments.

Research and development costs present accounting problems: (1) it is sometimes difficult to assign the costs to specific projects, and (2) there are uncertainties in identifying the extent and timing of future benefits. As a result, research and development costs are **usually recorded as an expense when incurred**, whether the research and development is successful or not.

To illustrate, assume that Laser Scanner Company spent $3 million on research and development. These research and development costs resulted in the development of two highly successful patents. The R&D costs, however, cannot be included in the cost of the patent. Rather, they are recorded as an expense when incurred.

Many disagree with this accounting approach. They argue that to expense these costs leads to understated assets and net income. Others, however, argue that capitalizing these costs will lead only to highly speculative assets on the balance sheet. Who is right is difficult to determine. The controversy, however, illustrates how difficult it is to establish proper guidelines for financial reporting.

# STATEMENT PRESENTATION AND ANALYSIS

## Presentation

Usually plant assets and natural resources are combined under Property, Plant, and Equipment, and intangibles are shown separately under Intangible Assets. Either within the balance sheet or in the notes, there should be disclosure of the balances of the major classes of assets, such as land, buildings, and equipment, and accumulated depreciation by major classes or in total. In addition, the depreciation and amortization methods used should be described and the amount of depreciation and amortization expense for the period disclosed.

The financial statement presentation of property, plant, and equipment by Kellogg Company in its 1997 balance sheet is quite brief, as shown in Illustration 10-29.

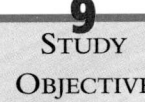

**9**
STUDY
OBJECTIVE
Indicate how plant assets, natural resources, and intangible assets are reported and analyzed.

| KELLOGG COMPANY Balance Sheet (partial) December 31 (in millions) | | |
|---|---|---|
| | 1997 | 1996 |
| Property, net | $2,773.3 | $2,932.9 |
| Other assets | 636.6 | 588.5 |

**ILLUSTRATION 10-29**

*Kellogg's presentation of property, plant, and equipment, and intangible assets*

The notes to Kellogg's financial statements present greater details, namely, that "Other assets" contains goodwill of $194.7 million and other intangibles of $191.2 million.

A more comprehensive presentation of property, plant, and equipment is excerpted from the balance sheet of Owens-Illinois and shown in Illustration 10-30. The notes to the financial statements of Owens-Illinois identify the major classes of property, plant, and equipment. They also indicate that depreciation is by the straight-line method, depletion is by the units-of-activity method, and amortization is by the straight-line method.

| OWENS-ILLINOIS, INC.<br>Balance Sheet (partial)<br>(in millions of dollars) | | | |
| --- | --- | --- | --- |
| Property, plant, and equipment | | | |
| Timberlands, at cost, less accumulated depletion | | $ 95.4 | |
| Buildings and equipment, at cost | $2,207.1 | | |
| Less: Accumulated depreciation | 1,229.0 | 978.1 | |
| Total property, plant, and equipment | | | $1,073.5 |
| Intangibles | | | |
| Patents | | | 410.0 |
| Total | | | $1,483.5 |

## Analysis

Because the original cost ($4,980.6 million), the accumulated depreciation ($2,207.3 million), and the current period's depreciation expense for property, plant, and equipment ($287.3 million), are reported in the notes to Kellogg's 1997 financial statements, it is possible to analyze the lives and ages of these assets (especially for companies, like Kellogg, that use the straight-line method of depreciation). A measure of the average life and the average age of these assets can be computed using the following formulas and the data above from Kellogg Company:

**ILLUSTRATION 10-31**

*Average life and average age formulas and computations*

These averages are only rough estimates and possess all the weaknesses of averages. The actual lives of the individual assets that are contained in these averages range from 3 years (tools and office machines) to 35 years (buildings). However, the usefulness of these averages may come from a comparison with averages of other companies in the same industry.

The turnover of assets may be used in analyzing the productivity of a company's assets. That is, the asset turnover ratio is computed to measure how efficiently a company uses its assets to generate sales. This ratio is computed by dividing net sales by average total assets for the period, as shown in the formula in Illustration 10-32. (Kellogg's net sales for 1997 are $6,830.1 million, and total ending assets are $4,877.6 million and beginning are $5,050.0 million.)

**ILLUSTRATION 10-32**

*Asset turnover formula and computation*

| Net Sales | ÷ | Average Total Assets | = | Asset Turnover Ratio |
|---|---|---|---|---|
| $6,830.1 | ÷ | $\dfrac{\$4,877.6 + \$5,050.0}{2}$ | = | 1.376 times |

This ratio shows the dollars of sales produced for each dollar invested in average total assets. If a company is using its assets efficiently, each dollar of assets will create a high amount of sales. This ratio varies greatly among different industries—from those that are asset intensive (utility) to those that are not (services).

# BEFORE YOU GO ON . . .

## Review It

1. What are the main differences between accounting for intangible assets and plant assets?
2. Identify the major types of intangibles and the proper accounting for them.
3. Explain the accounting for research and development costs.
4. What ratios may be computed to analyze property, plant, and equipment?

## A LOOK BACK AT OUR FEATURE STORY

Refer back to the opening story about Westbrook College, and answer the following questions:

1. Why should Westbrook College depreciate its buildings?
2. How can Westbrook College have a building with a zero book value yet a substantial market value?
3. Give some examples of intangibles other than a trademark that you might find on your college campus.
4. Give some examples of company or product trademarks or trade names. Are trade names and trademarks reported on a company's balance sheet? Explain.

*Solution*

1. Westbrook College should depreciate its buildings because depreciation is necessary in order to allocate the cost of the buildings to the periods in which they are used.
2. A building can have a zero book value if it has no salvage value and it is fully depreciated—that is, if it has been used for a period longer than its expected life. Because depreciation is used to allocate cost rather than to reflect actual value, it is not at all unlikely that a building could have a low or zero book value, but a positive market value.
3. Examples of other intangibles that might be found on a college campus are franchise of a bookstore chain, license to operate a radio station, patents developed by professors, and a permit to operate a bus service.
4. Typical company or product trade names are:
   Clothes—Gap, Gitano, Dockers, Calvin Klein, Chaus, Guess.
   Perfume—Passion, Ruffles, Chanel No. 5, Diamonds.
   Cars—TransAm, Nova, Prelude, Coupe DeVille, Eclipse.
   Shoes—Nike, Florsheim, L.A. Gear, Adidas.
   Breakfast cereals—Cheerios, Wheaties, Frosted Mini-Wheats, Rice Krispies.

Trade names and trademarks are reported on a balance sheet if there is a cost attached to them. If the trade name or trademark is purchased, the cost is the purchase price. If it is developed by the enterprise, the cost includes attorney's fees, registration fees, design costs, successful legal defense costs, and other expenditures directly related to securing the trade name or trademark.

THE NAVIGATOR

# DEMONSTRATION PROBLEM

DuPage Company purchases a factory machine at a cost of $18,000 on January 1, 1999. The machine is expected to have a salvage value of $2,000 at the end of its 4-year useful life.

During its useful life, the machine is expected to be used 160,000 hours. Actual annual hourly use was: Year 1, 40,000; Year 2, 60,000; Year 3, 35,000; and Year 4, 25,000.

*Instructions*

Prepare depreciation schedules for the following methods: (a) the straight-line, (b) units-of-activity, and (c) declining-balance using double the straight-line rate.

## SOLUTION TO DEMONSTRATION PROBLEM

(a)

**PROBLEM-SOLVING STRATEGIES**

1. Under the straight-line method, the depreciation rate is applied to depreciable cost.

2. Under the units-of-activity method, depreciation cost per unit is computed by dividing depreciable cost by total units of activity.

3. Under the declining-balance method, the depreciation rate is applied to **book value** at the beginning of the year.

### Straight-Line Method

| Year | Depreciable Cost | × | Depreciation Rate | = | Annual Depreciation Expense | Accumulated Depreciation | Book Value |
|------|------------------|---|-------------------|---|------------------------------|--------------------------|------------|
| | | | | | | *End of Year* | |
| 1999 | $16,000 | | 25% | | $4,000 | $ 4,000 | $14,000* |
| 2000 | 16,000 | | 25% | | 4,000 | 8,000 | 10,000 |
| 2001 | 16,000 | | 25% | | 4,000 | 12,000 | 6,000 |
| 2002 | 16,000 | | 25% | | 4,000 | 16,000 | 2,000 |

*$18,000 − $4,000.

(b)

### Units-of-Activity Method

| Year | Units of Activity | × | Depreciation Cost/Unit | = | Annual Depreciation Expense | Accumulated Depreciation | Book Value |
|------|-------------------|---|------------------------|---|------------------------------|--------------------------|------------|
| | *Computation* | | | | | *End of Year* | |
| 1999 | 40,000 | | $.10 | | $4,000 | $ 4,000 | $14,000 |
| 2000 | 60,000 | | .10 | | 6,000 | 10,000 | 8,000 |
| 2001 | 35,000 | | .10 | | 3,500 | 13,500 | 4,500 |
| 2002 | 25,000 | | .10 | | 2,500 | 16,000 | 2,000 |

(c)

### Declining-Balance Method

| Year | Book Value Beginning of Year | × | Depreciation Rate | = | Annual Depreciation Expense | Accumulated Depreciation | Book Value |
|------|------------------------------|---|-------------------|---|------------------------------|--------------------------|------------|
| | | | | | | *End of Year* | |
| 1999 | $18,000 | | 50% | | $9,000 | $ 9,000 | $9,000 |
| 2000 | 9,000 | | 50% | | 4,500 | 13,500 | 4,500 |
| 2001 | 4,500 | | 50% | | 2,250 | 15,750 | 2,250 |
| 2002 | 2,250 | | 50% | | 250* | 16,000 | 2,000 |

*Adjusted to $250 because ending book value should not be less than expected salvage value.

THE NAVIGATOR

# DEMONSTRATION PROBLEM

On January 1, 1997, the Skyline Limousine Co. purchased a limousine at an acquisition cost of $28,000. The vehicle has been depreciated by the straight-line method using a 4-year service life and a $4,000 salvage value. The company's fiscal year ends on December 31.

### Instructions

Prepare the journal entry or entries to record the disposal of the limousine assuming that it was:

(1) Retired and scrapped with no salvage value on January 1, 2001.

(2) Sold for $5,000 on July 1, 2000.

(3) Traded in on a new limousine on January 1, 2000. The fair market value of the old vehicle was $9,000 and $22,000 was paid in cash.

(4) Traded in on a new limousine on January 1, 2000. The fair market value of the old vehicle was $11,000 and $2,000 was paid in cash.

## SOLUTION TO DEMONSTRATION PROBLEM

| | | | | |
|---|---|---|---:|---:|
| (1) | 1/1/01 | Accumulated Depreciation—Limousine | 24,000 | |
| | | Loss on Disposal | 4,000 | |
| | |     Limousine | | 28,000 |
| | |     (To record retirement of limousine) | | |
| (2) | 7/1/00 | Depreciation Expense | 3,000 | |
| | |     Accumulated Depreciation—Limousine | | 3,000 |
| | |     (To record depreciation to date of disposal) | | |
| | | Cash | 5,000 | |
| | | Accumulated Depreciation—Limousine | 21,000 | |
| | | Loss on Disposal | 2,000 | |
| | |     Limousine | | 28,000 |
| | |     (To record sale of limousine) | | |
| (3) | 1/1/00 | Limousine (new) | 31,000 | |
| | | Accumulated Depreciation—Limousine | 18,000 | |
| | | Loss on Disposal | 1,000 | |
| | |     Limousine | | 28,000 |
| | |     Cash | | 22,000 |
| | |     (To record exchange of limousines) | | |
| (4) | 1/1/00 | Limousine (new)* | 12,000 | |
| | | Accumulated Depreciation—Limousine (old) | 18,000 | |
| | |     Limousine (old) | | 28,000 |
| | |     Cash | | 2,000 |
| | |     (To record exchange of limousines) | | |
| | | *($11,000 + $2,000 − $1,000) | | |

**PROBLEM-SOLVING STRATEGIES**

1. At the time of disposal, determine the book value of the asset.

2. Recognize any gain or loss from disposal of the asset.

3. Remove the book value of the asset from the records by debiting Accumulated Depreciation for the total depreciation to date of disposal and crediting the asset account for the cost of the asset.

THE NAVIGATOR

# SUMMARY OF STUDY OBJECTIVES

**1. Describe the application of the cost principle to plant assets.** The cost of plant assets includes all expenditures necessary to acquire the asset and make it ready for its intended use. Cost is measured by the cash or cash equivalent price paid.

**2. Explain the concept of depreciation.** Depreciation is the process of allocating to expense the cost of a plant asset over its useful (service) life in a rational and systematic manner. Depreciation is not a process of valuation, and it is not a process that results in an accumulation of cash. Depreciation is caused by wear and tear and by obsolescence.

**3. Compute periodic depreciation using different methods.** There are three depreciation methods:

| Method | Effect on Annual Depreciation | Formula |
|---|---|---|
| Straight-line | Constant amount | Depreciable cost ÷ useful life (in years) |
| Units-of-activity | Varying amount | Depreciation cost per unit × units of activity during the year |
| Declining-balance | Decreasing amount | Book value at beginning of year × declining-balance rate |

**4. Describe the procedure for revising periodic depreciation.** Revisions of periodic depreciation are made in present and future periods, not retroactively. The new annual depreciation is determined by dividing the depreciable cost at the time of the revision by the remaining useful life.

**5. Distinguish between revenue and capital expenditures and explain the entries for these expenditures.** Revenue expenditures are incurred to maintain the operating efficiency and expected productive life of the asset. These expenditures are debited to Repair Expense as incurred. Capital expenditures increase the operating efficiency, productive capacity, or expected useful life of the asset. These expenditures are generally debited to the plant asset affected.

**6. Explain how to account for the disposal of a plant asset through retirement, sale, or exchange.** The accounting for disposal of a plant asset through retirement or sale is as follows:
(a) Eliminate the book value of the plant asset at the date of disposal.
(b) Record cash proceeds, if any.
(c) Account for the difference between the book value and the cash proceeds as a gain or loss on disposal.

In accounting for exchanges of similar assets:
(a) Eliminate the book value of the old asset at the date of the exchange.

(b) Record the acquisition cost of the new asset.
(c) Account for the loss or gain, if any, on the old asset.
  1. If a loss, recognize it immediately.
  2. If a gain, defer and reduce the cost of the new asset.

**7. Identify the basic accounting issues related to natural resources.** The basic accounting issues related to natural resources are whether exploration costs on unsuccessful explorations should be capitalized or expensed. Under the full-cost approach, both successful and unsuccessful explorations are capitalized and the costs amortized to expense over the useful life of the successful efforts. The other approach is to capitalize only the costs of successful explorations. This is referred to as the successful efforts approach.

**8. Contrast the accounting for intangible assets with the accounting for plant assets.** The accounting for intangible assets and plant assets is much the same. One difference is that the term used to describe the write-off of an intangible asset is amortization, rather than depreciation. In addition, the amortization of the intangible asset cannot be longer than 40 years. The straight-line method is normally used for amortizing intangible assets.

**9. Indicate how plant assets, natural resources, and intangible assets are reported and analyzed.** Usually plant assets and natural resources are combined under Property, Plant, and Equipment; intangibles are shown separately under Intangible Assets. Either within the balance sheet or in the notes, the balances of the major classes of assets, such as land, buildings, and equipment, and accumulated depreciation by major classes or in total should be disclosed. Also, the depreciation and amortization methods used should be described, and the amount of depreciation and amortization expense for the period should be disclosed. Assets may be analyzed to measure average life, average age, and asset turnover.

# GLOSSARY

•••••••••••••••••••••••••••••••••••••••••••••••••••••••••••••••••••••••••••••••••••••••

**Accelerated-depreciation method**   A depreciation method that produces higher depreciation expense in the early years than in the later years. (p. 430).

**Additions and improvements**   Costs incurred to increase the operating efficiency, productive capacity, or expected useful life of a plant asset. (p. 432).

**Amortization**   The allocation of the cost of an intangible asset to expense over its useful life in a systematic and rational manner. (p. 441).

**Asset turnover ratio**   A measure of how efficiently a company uses its assets to generate sales, calculated as net sales divided by average assets. (p. 446).

**Average age of plant assets**   A comparative measure of the age of a company's plant assets, calculated as accumulated depreciation divided by depreciation expense. (p. 446).

**Average life of plant assets**   A comparative measure of a company's plant assets, calculated as cost of plant assets divided by depreciation expense. (p. 446).

**Capital expenditures**   Expenditures that increase the company's investment in productive facilities. (p. 432).

**Cash equivalent price**   An amount equal to the fair market value of the asset given up or the fair market value of the asset received, whichever is more clearly determinable. (p. 421).

**Copyright**   An exclusive right granted by the federal government allowing the owner to reproduce and sell an artistic or published work. (p. 442).

**Declining-balance method**   A depreciation method that applies a constant rate to the declining book value of the asset and produces a decreasing annual depreciation expense over the useful life of the asset. (p. 429).

**Depletion**   The process of allocating the cost of a natural resource to expense in a rational and systematic manner over the resources's useful life. (p. 439).

**Depreciable cost**   The cost of a plant asset less its salvage value. (p. 426).

**Franchise (license)**   A contractual arrangement under which the franchisor grants the franchisee the right to sell certain products, to render specific services, or to use certain trademarks or trade names, usually within a designated geographical area. (p. 443).

**Full-cost approach**   Method in which both successful and unsuccessful exploration costs are included in the cost of a natural resource and the costs are written off to expense over the useful life of the successful wells. (p. 438).

**Goodwill**   The value of all favorable attributes that relate to a business enterprise. (p. 444).

**Intangible assets**   Rights, privileges, and competitive advantages that result from the ownership of long-lived assets that do not possess physical substance. (p. 441).

**Licenses**   Operating rights to use public property, granted by a governmental agency to a business enterprise. (p. 443).

**Natural resources**   Assets that consist of standing timber and underground deposits of oil, gas, and minerals. Also called *wasting assets*. (p. 438).

**Ordinary repairs**   Expenditures to maintain the operating efficiency and expected productive life of the unit. (p. 432).

**Patent**   An exclusive right issued by the U.S. Patent Office that enables the recipient to manufacture, sell, or otherwise control an invention for a period of 17 years from the date of the grant. (p. 441).

**Plant assets**   Tangible resources that are used in the operations of the business and are not intended for sale to customers. (p. 420).

**Research and development costs**   Expenditures that may lead to patents, copyrights, new processes, and products. (p. 444).

**Revenue expenditures**   Expenditures that are immediately charged against revenues as an expense. (p. 432).

**Straight-line method**   A method in which periodic depreciation is the same for each year of the asset's useful life. (p. 426).

**Successful efforts approach**   Method in which only the costs of successful exploration are included in the cost of a natural resource. (p. 438).

**Trademark (trade name)**   A word, phrase, jingle, or symbol that distinguishes or identifies a particular enterprise or product. (p. 443).

**Units-of-activity method**   A depreciation method in which useful life is expressed in terms of the total units of production or use expected from the asset. (p. 428).

# SELF-STUDY QUESTIONS

Answers are at the end of the chapter.

(SO 1)   1. Erin Danielle Company purchased equipment and the following costs were incurred:

| | |
|---|---|
| Cash price | $24,000 |
| Sales taxes | 1,200 |
| Insurance during transit | 200 |
| Installation and testing | 400 |
| Total costs | $25,800 |

What amount should be recorded as the cost of the equipment?
a. $24,000.
b. $25,200.
c. $25,400.
d. $25,800.

(SO 2)   2. Depreciation is a process of:
a. valuation.
b. cost allocation.
c. cash accumulation.
d. appraisal.

(SO 3)   3. Micah Bartlett Company purchased equipment on January 1, 1998, at a total invoice cost of $400,000. The equipment has an estimated salvage value of $10,000 and an estimated useful life of 5 years. The amount of accumulated depreciation at December 31, 1999, if the straight-line method of depreciation is used, is:
a. $80,000.
b. $160,000.
c. $78,000.
d. $156,000.

(SO 3)   4. Ann Torbert purchased a truck for $11,000 on January 1, 1998. The truck will have an estimated salvage value of $1,000 at the end of 5 years. Using the units-of-activity method, the balance in accumulated depreciation at December 31, 1999, can be computed by the following formula:
a. ($11,000 ÷ Total estimated activity) × Units of activity for 1999.
b. ($10,000 ÷ Total estimated activity) × Units of activity for 1999.
c. ($11,000 ÷ Total estimated activity) × Units of activity for 1998 and 1999.
d. ($10,000 ÷ Total estimated activity) × Units of activity for 1998 and 1999.

(SO 4)   5. When there is a change in estimated depreciation:
a. previous depreciation should be corrected.
b. current and future years' depreciation should be revised.
c. only future years' depreciation should be revised.
d. None of the above.

(SO 5)  6. Additions to plant assets are:
  a. revenue expenditures.
  b. debited to a Repair Expense account.
  c. debited to a Purchases account.
  d. capital expenditures.

(SO 6)  7. Schopenhauer Company exchanged an old machine, with a book value of $39,000 and a fair market value of $35,000, and paid $10,000 cash for a similar new machine. At what amount should the machine acquired in the exchange be recorded on the books of Schopenhauer?
  a. $45,000.
  b. $46,000.
  c. $49,000.
  d. $50,000.

(SO 6)  8. In exchanges of similar assets:
  a. neither gains nor losses are recognized immediately.
  b. gains, but not losses, are recognized immediately.
  c. losses, but not gains, are recognized immediately.
  d. both gains and losses are recognized immediately.

(SO 7)  9. Maggie Sharrer Company expects to extract 20 million tons of coal from a mine that cost $12 million. If no salvage value is expected, and 2 million tons are mined and sold in the first year, the entry to record depletion will include a:

  a. debit to Accumulated Depletion of $2,000,000.
  b. credit to Depletion Expense of $1,200,000.
  c. debit to Depletion Expense of $1,200,000.
  d. credit to Accumulated Depletion of $2,000,000.

(SO 8, 9) 10. Martha Beyerlein Company incurred $150,000 of research and development costs in its laboratory to develop a patent granted on January 2, 1999. On July 31, 1999, Beyerlein paid $35,000 for legal fees in a successful defense of the patent. The total amount debited to Patents through July 31, 1999, should be:
  a. $150,000.
  b. $35,000.
  c. $185,000.
  d. some other amount.

(SO 9) 11. Indicate which of the following statements is *true*.
  a. Since intangible assets lack physical substance they need be disclosed only in the notes to the financial statements.
  b. Goodwill should be reported as a contra-account in the Stockholder's Equity section.
  c. Totals of major classes of assets can be shown in the balance sheet, with asset details disclosed in the notes to the financial statements.
  d. Intangible assets are typically combined with plant assets and natural resources and then shown in the Property, Plant, and Equipment section.

THE NAVIGATOR

# QUESTIONS

1. Phil Collins is uncertain about the applicability of the cost principle to plant assets. Explain the principle to Phil.

2. How is cost for a plant asset measured in (a) a cash transaction, and (b) a noncash transaction?

3. Winans Company acquires the land and building owned by Corrs Company. What types of costs may be incurred to make the asset ready for its intended use if Winans Company wants to use (a) only the land, and (b) both the land and the building?

4. In a recent newspaper release, the president of Smashing Pumpkins Company asserted that something has to be done about depreciation. The president said, "Depreciation does not come close to accumulating the cash needed to replace the asset at the end of its useful life." What is your response to the president?

5. Michael is studying for the next accounting examination. He asks your help on two questions: (a) What is salvage value? (b) Is salvage value used in determining depreciable cost under each depreciation method? Answer Michael's questions.

6. Contrast the straight-line method and the units-of-activity method as to (a) useful life, and (b) the pattern of periodic depreciation over useful life.

7. Contrast the effects of the three depreciation methods on annual depreciation expense.

8. In the fourth year of an asset's 5-year useful life, the company decides that the asset will have a 6-year service life. How should the revision of depreciation be recorded? Why?

9. Distinguish between revenue expenditures and capital expenditures during useful life.

10. How is a gain or loss on the sale of a plant asset computed?

11. Bimini Corporation owns a machine that is fully depreciated but is still being used. How should Bimini account for this asset and report it in the financial statements?

12. When similar assets are exchanged, how is the gain or loss on disposal computed?

13. Batman Refrigeration Company trades in an old machine on a new model when the fair market value of the old machine is greater than its book value. Should Batman recognize a gain on disposal? If the fair market value of the old machine is less than its book value, should Batmam recognize a loss on disposal?

14. Moon Company experienced a gain on disposal when exchanging similar machines. In accordance with generally accepted accounting principles, the gain was not recognized. How will Moon's future financial statements be affected by not recognizing the gain?

15. What are natural resources, and what are their distinguishing characteristics?

16. Van Amos and Benedict Arnold are arguing about the full-cost approach and the successful efforts approach. Amos says that the full-cost approach will provide a greater reported asset value, while Arnold says that the successful efforts approach would. Who is correct?

17. What are the similarities and differences between the terms depreciation, depletion, and amortization?

18. Mitra Company hires an accounting intern who says that intangible assets should always be amortized over their legal lives. Is the intern correct? Explain.

19. Goodwill has been defined as the value of all favorable attributes that relate to a business enterprise. What types of attributes could result in goodwill?

20. Clint Eastwood, a business major, is working on a case problem for one of his classes. In this case problem, the company needs to raise cash to market a new product it developed. Jack Gleason, an engineering major, takes one look at the company's balance sheet and says, "This company has an awful lot of goodwill. Why don't you recommend that they sell some of it to raise cash?" How should Clint respond to Jack?

21. Under what conditions is goodwill recorded?

22. Often research and development costs provide companies with benefits that last a number of years. (For example, these costs can lead to the development of a patent that will increase the company's income for many years.) However, generally accepted accounting principles require that such costs be recorded as an expense when incurred. Why?

23. McDonald's Corporation reports total average assets of $14.5 billion and net sales of $9.8 billion. What is the company's asset turnover ratio?

24. Morgan Corporation and Fairchild Corporation both operate in the same industry. Morgan uses the straight-line method to account for depreciation, whereas Fairchild uses an accelerated method. Explain what complications might arise in trying to compare the results of these two companies.

25. Lucille Corporation uses straight-line depreciation for financial reporting purposes but an accelerated method for tax purposes. Is it acceptable to use different methods for the two purposes? What is Lucille Corporation's motivation for doing this?

26. You are comparing two companies in the same industry. You have determined that Betty Corp. depreciates its plant assets over a 40-year life, whereas Veronica Corp. depreciates its plant assets over a 20-year life. Discuss the implications this has for comparing the results of the two companies.

27. Pizner Company is doing significant work to revitalize its warehouses. It is not sure whether it should capitalize these costs or expense them. What are the implications for current year net income and future net income of expensing verses capitalizing these costs?

# BRIEF EXERCISES

**BE10–1**  The following expenditures were incurred by JFK Company in purchasing land. Cash price $40,000, accrued taxes $3,000, attorneys' fees $2,500, real estate broker's commission $2,000, and clearing and grading $3,500. What is the cost of the land?

*Determine the cost of land.*
*(SO 1)*

**BE10–2**  Housman Company incurs the following expenditures in purchasing a truck: cash price $20,000, accident insurance $2,000, sales taxes $900, motor vehicle license $100, and painting and lettering $400. What is the cost of the truck?

*Determine the cost of a truck.*
*(SO 1)*

**BE10–3**  Graig Ehlo Company acquires a delivery truck at a cost of $26,000. The truck is expected to have a salvage value of $2,000 at the end of its 4-year useful life. Compute annual depreciation for the first and second years using the straight-line method.

*Compute straight-line depreciation.*
*(SO 3)*

**BE10–4**  Olympic Company purchased land and a building on January 1, 1999. Management's best estimate of the value of the land was $100,000 and of the building $200,000, but management told the accounting department to record the land at $250,000 and the building at $50,000. The building is being depreciated on a straight-line basis over 20 years with no salvage value. Why do you suppose management requested this accounting treatment? Is it ethical?

*Compute depreciation and evaluate treatment.*
*(SO 3)*

**BE10–5**  Depreciation information for Graig Ehlo Company is given in BE10–3. Assuming the declining-balance depreciation rate is double the straight-line rate, compute annual depreciation for the first and second years under the declining-balance method.

*Compute declining-balance depreciation.*
*(SO 3)*

**BE10–6**  Spud Webb Taxi Service uses the units-of-activity method in computing depreciation on its taxicabs. Each cab is expected to be driven 120,000 miles. Taxi No. 10 cost $36,500 and is expected to have a salvage value of $500. Taxi No. 10 is driven 30,000 miles in Year 1 and 20,000 miles in Year 2. Compute the depreciation for each year.

*Compute depreciation using the units-of-activity method.*
*(SO 3)*

*Compute revised depreciation.*
*(SO 4)*
**BE10–7**  On January 1, 1999, the Wilkins Company ledger shows Equipment $32,000 and Accumulated Depreciation $9,000. The depreciation resulted from using the straight-line method with a useful life of 10 years and salvage value of $2,000. On this date, the company concludes that the equipment has a remaining useful life of only 4 years with the same salvage value. Compute the revised annual depreciation.

*Prepare entries for disposal by retirement.*
*(SO 6)*
**BE10–8**  Prepare journal entries to record the following:

    (a)  Arna Company retires its delivery equipment, which cost $41,000. Accumulated depreciation is also $41,000 on this delivery equipment. No salvage value is received.

    (b)  Assume the same information as (a), except that accumulated depreciation for Arna Company is $38,000, instead of $41,000.

*Prepare entries for disposal by sale.*
*(SO 6)*
**BE10–9**  Garrison Company sells office equipment on September 30, 1999, for $20,000 cash. The office equipment originally cost $72,000 and as of January 1, 1999, had accumulated depreciation of $42,000. Depreciation for the first 9 months of 1999 is $6,250. Prepare the journal entries to (a) update depreciation to September 30, 1999, and (b) record the sale of the equipment.

*Prepare entry for disposal by exchange.*
*(SO 6)*
**BE10–10**  Keillor Company exchanges old delivery equipment for similar new delivery equipment. The book value of the old delivery equipment is $31,000 (cost $61,000 less accumulated depreciation $30,000), its fair market value is $19,000, and cash of $5,000 is paid. Prepare the entry to record the exchange.

*Prepare entry for disposal by exchange.*
*(SO 6)*
**BE10–11**  Assume the same information as BE10–10, except that the fair market value of the old delivery equipment is $42,000. Prepare the entry to record the exchange.

*Prepare depletion expense entry and balance sheet presentation for natural resources.*
*(SO 7)*
**BE10–12**  Adamson Mining Co. purchased for $7 million a mine which is estimated to have 28 million tons of ore and no salvage value. In the first year, 6 million tons of ore are extracted and sold. (a) Prepare the journal entry to record depletion expense for the first year. (b) Show how this mine is reported on the balance sheet at the end of the first year.

*Prepare patent expense entry and balance sheet presentation for intangibles.*
*(SO 8)*
**BE10–13**  Fayne Company purchases a patent for $160,000 on January 2, 1999. Its estimated useful life is 10 years. (a) Prepare the journal entry to record patent expense for the first year. (b) Show how this patent is reported on the balance sheet at the end of the first year.

*Classify long-lived assets on balance sheet.*
*(SO 9)*
**BE10–14**  Information related to plant assets, natural resources and intangibles at the end of 1999 for Riddler Company is as follows: buildings $900,000; accumulated depreciation—buildings $650,000; goodwill $410,000; coal mine $200,000; accumulated depletion—coal mine $108,000. Prepare a partial balance sheet of Riddler Company for these items.

*Analyze long-lived assets.*
*(SO 9)*
**BE10–15**  In its 1996 annual report McDonald's Corporation reported beginning total assets of $15.4 billion; ending total assets of $17.4 billion; property, plant, and equipment (at cost) of $19.1 billion; accumulated depreciation of $4.8 billion; depreciation expense of $673.4 million; and net sales of $10.7 billion. (a) Compute the average life of McDonald's property, plant, and equipment. (b) Compute the average age of McDonald's property, plant, and equipment. (c) Compute McDonald's asset turnover ratio.

# EXERCISES

*Determine cost of plant acquisitions.*
*(SO 1)*
**E10–1**  The following expenditures relating to plant assets were made by Salvador Company during the first 2 months of 1999.

    1. Paid $5,000 of accrued taxes at time plant site was acquired.

    2. Paid $200 insurance to cover possible accident loss on new factory machinery while the machinery was in transit.

    3. Paid $850 sales taxes on new delivery truck.

    4. Paid $17,500 for parking lots and driveways on new plant site.

    5. Paid $250 to have company name and advertising slogan painted on new delivery truck.

    6. Paid $8,000 for installation of new factory machinery.

    7. Paid $900 for one-year accident insurance policy on new delivery truck.

    8. Paid $75 motor vehicle license fee on the new truck.

*Instructions*
  (a) ▭▭▭▷ Explain the application of the cost principle in determining the acquisition cost of plant assets.
  (b) List the numbers of the foregoing transactions, and opposite each indicate the account title to which each expenditure should be debited.

**E10–2** On March 1, 1999, Neil Young Company acquired real estate, on which it planned to construct a small office building, by paying $90,000 in cash. An old warehouse on the property was razed at a cost of $6,600; the salvaged materials were sold for $1,700. Additional expenditures before construction began included $1,100 attorney's fee for work concerning the land purchase, $4,000 real estate broker's fee, $7,800 architect's fee, and $14,000 to put in driveways and a parking lot.

*Determine acquisition costs on land.*
*(SO 1)*

*Instructions*
  (a) Determine the amount to be reported as the cost of the land.
  (b) For each cost not used in part (a), indicate the account to be debited.

**E10–3** Galactic Bus Lines uses the units-of-activity method in depreciating its buses. One bus was purchased on January 1, 1999, at a cost of $108,000. Over its 4-year useful life, the bus is expected to be driven 100,000 miles. Salvage value is expected to be $8,000.

*Compute depreciation under units-of-activity method.*
*(SO 3)*

*Instructions*
  (a) Compute the depreciation cost per unit.
  (b) Prepare a depreciation schedule assuming actual mileage was: 1999, 26,000; 2000, 32,000; 2001, 25,000; and 2002, 17,000.

**E10–4** Tory Amos Company purchased a new machine on October 1, 1999, at a cost of $96,000. The company estimated that the machine will have a salvage value of $12,000. The machine is expected to be used for 70,000 working hours during its 5-year life.

*Determine depreciation for partial periods.*
*(SO 3)*

*Instructions*
Compute the depreciation expense under the following methods for the year indicated: (a) straight-line for 1999, (b) units-of-activity for 1999, assuming machine usage was 1,700 hours, and (c) declining-balance using double the straight-line rate for 1999 and 2000.

**E10–5** Bill Simpson, the new controller of the Bellingham Company, has reviewed the expected useful lives and salvage values of selected depreciable assets at the beginning of 1999. His findings are as follows:

*Compute revised annual depreciation.*
*(SO 3, 4)*

| Type of Asset | Date Acquired | Cost | Accumulated Depreciation 1/1/99 | Useful Life in Years Old | Proposed | Salvage Value Old | Proposed |
|---|---|---|---|---|---|---|---|
| Building | 1/1/93 | $800,000 | $114,000 | 40 | 50 | $40,000 | $48,000 |
| Warehouse | 1/1/96 | 100,000 | 11,400 | 25 | 20 | 5,000 | 3,600 |

All assets are depreciated by the straight-line method. Bellingham Company uses a calendar year in preparing annual financial statements. After discussion, management has agreed to accept Bill's proposed changes.

*Instructions*
  (a) Compute the revised annual depreciation on each asset in 1999. (Show computations.)
  (b) Prepare the entry (or entries) to record depreciation on the building in 1999.

**E10–6** Presented below are selected transactions at Chen Company for 1999.

*Journalize entries for disposal of plant assets.*
*(SO 6)*

Jan.  1  Retired a piece of machinery that was purchased on January 1, 1989. The machine cost $62,000 on that date, and had a useful life of 10 years with no salvage value.

June 30  Sold a computer that was purchased on January 1, 1996. The computer cost $35,000, and had a useful life of 7 years with no salvage value. The computer was sold for $25,000.

Dec. 31  Discarded a delivery truck that was purchased on January 1, 1995. The truck cost $27,000 and was depreciated based on a 6-year useful life with a $3,000 salvage value.

*Journalize entries for exchange of similar assets.*
*(SO 6)*

**Instructions**
Journalize all entries required on the above dates, including entries to update depreciation, where applicable, on assets disposed of. Chen Company uses straight-line depreciation. (Assume depreciation is up to date as of December 31, 1998.)

**E10–7**    Presented below are two independent transactions:

1. White Cloud Co. exchanged trucks (cost $64,000 less $22,000 accumulated depreciation) plus cash of $17,000 for new trucks. The old trucks had a fair market value of $38,000. Prepare the entry to record the exchange of similar assets by White Cloud Co.
2. Nelle Inc. trades its used machine (cost $10,000 less $4,000 accumulated depreciation) for a new machine. In addition to exchanging the old machine (which had a fair market value of $9,000), Nelle also paid cash of $2,000.

*Journalize entries for the exchange of similar plant assets.*
*(SO 6)*

**Instructions**
Prepare the entry to record the exchange of similar assets by Nelle Inc.

**E10–8**    Wind Company exchanges similar equipment with the Earth Company. Also Sun Company exchanges similar equipment with Moon Company. The following information pertains to these two exchanges:

|  | Wind Co. | Sun Co. |
|---|---|---|
| Equipment (cost) | $28,000 | $22,000 |
| Accumulated depreciation | 20,000 | 5,000 |
| Fair market value of equipment | 12,000 | 14,000 |
| Cash paid | 2,000 | –0– |

**Instructions**
Prepare the journal entries to record the exchange on the books of Wind Company and Sun Company.

*Journalize entries for the exchange of similar plant assets.*
*(SO 6)*

**E10–9**    Peru's Delivery Company and Brazil's Express Delivery exchanged similar delivery trucks on January 1, 1999. Peru's truck cost $20,000, had accumulated depreciation of $13,000, and has a fair market value of $3,000. Brazil's truck cost $10,000, had accumulated depreciation of $8,000, and has a fair market value of $3,000.

**Instructions**
(a) Journalize the exchange for Peru's Delivery Company.
(b) Journalize the exchange for Brazil's Express Delivery.

*Journalize entries for natural resources depletion.*
*(SO 7)*

**E10–10**    On July 1, 1999, Reggie Inc. invested $360,000 in a mine estimated to have 800,000 tons of ore of uniform grade. During the last 6 months of 1999, 100,000 tons of ore were mined and sold.

**Instructions**
(a) Prepare the journal entry to record depletion expense.
(b) Assume that the 100,000 tons of ore were mined, but only 80,000 units were sold. How are the costs applicable to the 20,000 unsold units reported?

*Prepare adjusting entries for amortization.*
*(SO 8)*

**E10–11**    The following are selected 1999 transactions of McGillis Corporation.

Jan. 1    Purchased a small company and recorded goodwill of $140,000. The goodwill has a useful life of 55 years.

May 1    Purchased a patent with an estimated useful life of 5 years and a legal life of 17 years for $30,000.

**Instructions**
Prepare all adjusting entries at December 31 to record amortization required by the events above.

*Prepare entries to set up appropriate accounts for different intangibles; amortize intangible assets.*
*(SO 8)*

**E10–12**    Vail Company, organized in 1999, has the following transactions related to intangible assets.

| | | |
|---|---|---|
| 1/2/99 | Purchased patent (7-year life) | $420,000 |
| 4/1/99 | Goodwill purchased (indefinite life) | 360,000 |
| 7/1/99 | 10-year franchise; expiration date 7/1/2009 | 450,000 |
| 9/1/99 | Research and development costs | 185,000 |

## Instructions

Prepare the necessary entries to record these intangibles. All costs incurred were for cash. Make the entries as of December 31, 1999, recording any necessary amortization and reflecting all balances accurately as of that date.

**E10–13**  During 1998 Kettle Corporation reported net sales of $2,500,000, net income of $1,500,000, and depreciation expense of $150,000. Its balance sheet reported total assets of $1,400,000, plant assets of $800,000, and accumulated depreciation on plant assets of $300,000.

*Calculate average useful life, average age of plant assets, and asset turnover ratio.*
*(SO 9)*

## Instructions

Calculate (a) average useful life of plant assets, (b) average age of plant assets, and (c) asset turnover ratio.

# PROBLEMS: SET A

**P10–1A**  Superior Company was organized on January 1. During the first year of operations, the following plant asset expenditures and receipts were recorded in random order.

*Determine acquisition costs of land and building.*
*(SO 1)*

### Debits

| | |
|---|---|
| 1. Cost of real estate purchased as a plant site (land $100,000 and building $25,000) | $125,000 |
| 2. Installation cost of fences around property | 4,000 |
| 3. Cost of demolishing building to make land suitable for construction of new building | 13,000 |
| 4. Excavation costs for new building | 20,000 |
| 5. Accrued real estate taxes paid at time of purchase of real estate | 2,000 |
| 6. Cost of parking lots and driveways | 12,000 |
| 7. Architect's fees on building plans | 10,000 |
| 8. Real estate taxes paid for the current year on land | 3,000 |
| 9. Full payment to building contractor | 500,000 |
| | $689,000 |

### Credits

| | |
|---|---|
| 10. Proceeds from salvage of demolished building | $ 2,500 |

## Instructions

Analyze the foregoing transactions using the following tabular arrangement. Insert the number of each transaction in the Item space and insert the amounts in the appropriate columns. For amounts entered in the Other Accounts column also indicate the account title.

| Item | Land | Building | Other Accounts |
|---|---|---|---|

**P10–2A**  In recent years, Erie Company has purchased three machines. Because of heavy turnover in the accounting department, a different accountant was in charge of selecting the depreciation method for each machine, and various methods have been selected. Information concerning the machines is summarized below:

*Compute depreciation under different methods.*
*(SO 3)*

| Machine | Acquired | Cost | Salvage Value | Useful Life in Years | Depreciation Method |
|---|---|---|---|---|---|
| 1 | 1/1/96 | $ 96,000 | $ 6,000 | 10 | Straight-line |
| 2 | 1/1/97 | 80,000 | 10,000 | 8 | Declining-balance |
| 3 | 11/1/99 | 78,000 | 6,000 | 6 | Units-of-activity |

For the declining-balance method, Erie Company uses the double-declining rate. For the units-of-activity method, total machine hours are expected to be 24,000. Actual hours of use in the first 3 years were: 1999, 4,000; 2000, 4,500; and 2001, 5,000.

*Instructions*

(a) Compute the amount of accumulated depreciation on each machine at December 31, 1999.

(b) If machine 2 was purchased on April 1 instead of January 1, what is the depreciation expense for this machine in (1) 1997 and (2) 1998?

*Compute depreciation under different methods.*
*(SO 3)*

**P10–3A**   On January 1, 1999, Rose Company purchased the following two machines for use in its production process:

Machine A:  The cash price of this machine was $30,000. Related expenditures included: sales tax $1,800, shipping costs $175, insurance during shipping $75, installation and testing costs $50, and $90 of oil and lubricants to be used with the machinery during its first year of operation. Rose estimates that the useful life of the machine is 4 years with a $5,000 salvage value remaining at the end of that time period.

Machine B:  The recorded cost of this machine was $60,000. Rose estimates that the useful life of the machine is 4 years with a $5,000 salvage value remaining at the end of that time period.

*Instructions*

(a) Prepare the following for Machine A:

  (1)  The journal entry to record its purchase on January 1, 1999.

  (2)  The journal entry to record annual depreciation at December 31, 1999 assuming the straight-line method of depreciation is used.

(b) Calculate the amount of depreciation expense that Rose should record for Machine B each year of its useful life assuming:

  (1)  Rose uses the straight-line method of depreciation.

  (2)  Rose uses the declining-balance method. The rate used is twice the straight-line rate.

  (3)  Rose uses the units-of-activity method and estimates that the useful life of the machine is 27,500 units. Actual usage is as follows: 1999, 9,000 units; 2000, 7,500 units; 2001, 6,000 units; 2002, 5,000 units.

(c) Which method used to calculate depreciation on Machine B reports the lowest amount of depreciation expense in year 1 (1999)? The lowest amount in year 4 (2002)? The lowest total amount over the 4-year period?

*Journalize a series of equipment transactions related to purchase, sale, retirement, and depreciation.*
*(SO 6, 9)*

**P10–4A**   At December 31, 1999, Wallace Company reported the following as plant assets:

| | | |
|---|---:|---:|
| Land | | $ 3,000,000 |
| Buildings | $26,500,000 | |
| Less: Accumulated depreciation—buildings | 12,100,000 | 14,400,000 |
| Equipment | 40,000,000 | |
| Less: Accumulated depreciation—equipment | 5,000,000 | 35,000,000 |
| Total plant assets | | $52,400,000 |

During 2000, the following selected cash transactions occurred:

April 1   Purchased land for $2,200,000.

May 1   Sold equipment that cost $600,000 when purchased on January 1, 1996. The equipment was sold for $360,000.

June 1   Sold land purchased on June 1, 1990 for $1,800,000. The land cost $500,000.

July 1   Purchased equipment for $1,400,000.

Dec. 31   Retired equipment that cost $500,000 when purchased on December 31, 1990. No salvage value was received.

*Instructions*

(a) Journalize the above transactions. Wallace uses straight-line depreciation for buildings and equipment. The buildings are estimated to have a 40-year useful life and no salvage value; the equipment is estimated to have a 10-year useful life and no salvage value. Update depreciation on assets disposed of at the time of sale or retirement.

(b) Record adjusting entries for depreciation for 2000.

(c) Prepare the plant asset section of Wallace's balance sheet at December 31, 2000.

*Record disposals.*
*(SO 6)*

**P10–5A**   Ghani Co. has delivery equipment that cost $50,000 and that has been depreciated $20,000. Record the disposal under the following assumptions:

(a) It was scrapped as having no value.
(b) It was sold for $31,000.
(c) It was sold for $18,000.
(d) It was exchanged for similar delivery equipment. The old delivery equipment has a fair market value of $12,000 and $32,000 was paid.
(e) It was exchanged for similar delivery equipment. The old delivery equipment has a fair market value of $35,000 and $9,000 was paid.

**P10–6A**  The intangible assets section of El-Gazzar Company at December 31, 1999, is presented below:

| | |
|---|---|
| Patent ($60,000 cost less $6,000 amortization) | $54,000 |
| Copyright ($36,000 cost less $14,400 amortization) | 21,600 |
| Total | $75,600 |

*Prepare entries to record transactions related to acquisition and amortization of intangibles; prepare the intangible assets section. (SO 8, 9)*

The patent was acquired in January 1999 and has a useful life of 10 years. The copyright was acquired in January 1996 and also has a useful life of 10 years. The following cash transactions may have affected intangible assets during 2000:

Jan. 2   Paid $18,000 legal costs to successfully defend the patent against infringement by another company.
Jan.–June   Developed a new product incurring $140,000 in research and development costs. A patent was granted for the product on July 1, and its useful life is equal to its legal life.
Sept. 1   Paid $60,000 to a quarterback to appear in commercials advertising the company's products. The commercials will air in September and October.
Oct. 1   Acquired a copyright for $80,000. The copyright has a useful life of 50 years.

**Instructions**
(a) Prepare journal entries to record the transactions above.
(b) Prepare journal entries to record the 2000 amortization expense for intangible assets.
(c) Prepare the intangible assets section of the balance sheet at December 31, 2000.
(d) ▭▭▭▶ Prepare the note to the financials on El-Gazzar's intangibles as of December 31, 2000.

**P10–7A**  Due to rapid turnover in the accounting department, a number of transactions involving intangible assets were improperly recorded by Baird Company in 1999.

1. Baird developed a new manufacturing process, incurring research and development costs of $85,000. The company also purchased a patent for $37,400. In early January, Baird capitalized $122,400 as the cost of the patents. Patent amortization expense of $7,200 was recorded based on a 17-year useful life.
2. On July 1, 1999, Baird purchased a small company and as a result acquired goodwill of $60,000. Baird recorded a half-year's amortization in 1999, based on a 50-year life ($600 amortization).

*Prepare entries to correct errors made in recording and amortizing intangible assets. (SO 8)*

**Instructions**
Prepare all journal entries necessary to correct any errors made during 1999. Assume the books have not yet been closed for 1999.

**P10–8A**  Croix Corporation and Rye Corporation, two corporations of roughly the same size, are both involved in the manufacture of canoes and sea kayaks. Each company depreciates its plant assets using the straight-line apprroach. An investigation of their financial statements reveals this information:

*Calculate and comment on average age, average useful life of plant assets, and asset turnover ratio. (SO 9)*

| | Croix Corp. | Rye Corp. |
|---|---|---|
| Net income | $ 400,000 | $ 600,000 |
| Sales | 1,400,000 | 1,200,000 |
| Total assets | 2,000,000 | 1,500,000 |
| Plant assets | 1,500,000 | 800,000 |
| Accumulated depreciation | 300,000 | 625,000 |
| Depreciation expense | 75,000 | 25,000 |
| Intangible assets (goodwill) | 300,000 | 0 |
| Amortization expense | 60,000 | 0 |

*Instructions*
(a) For each company, calculate these values:
  (1) Average age of plant assets.
  (2) Average useful life.
  (3) Asset turnover ratio.
(b) ▰▰▰▶ Based on your calculations in part (a), comment on the relative effectiveness of the two companies in using their assets to generate sales and produce net income. What factors complicate your ability to compare the two companies?

# PROBLEMS: SET B

*Determine acquisition costs of land and building.*
*(SO 1)*

**P10–1B** Bob Duran Company was organized on January 1. During the first year of operations, the following plant asset expenditures and receipts were recorded in random order.

**Debits**

| | |
|---|---:|
| 1. Cost of real estate purchased as a plant site (land $100,000 and building $45,000) | $145,000 |
| 2. Accrued real estate taxes paid at time of purchase of real estate | 2,000 |
| 3. Cost of demolishing building to make land suitable for construction of new building | 12,000 |
| 4. Cost of filling and grading the land | 4,000 |
| 5. Excavation costs for new building | 20,000 |
| 6. Architect's fees on building plans | 10,000 |
| 7. Full payment to building contractor | 600,000 |
| 8. Cost of parking lots and driveways | 14,000 |
| 9. Real estate taxes paid for the current year on land | 5,000 |
| | $812,000 |

**Credits**

| | |
|---|---:|
| 10. Proceeds for salvage of demolished building | $ 3,500 |

*Instructions*
Analyze the foregoing transactions using the following tabular arrangement. Insert the number of each transaction in the Item space and insert the amounts in the appropriate columns. For amounts entered in the Other Accounts column, also indicate the account titles.

| Item | Land | Building | Other Accounts |
|---|---|---|---|

*Compute depreciation under different methods.*
*(SO 3)*

**P10–2B** In recent years, Lakeshore Transportation purchased three used buses. Because of frequent turnover in the accounting department, a different accountant selected the depreciation method for each bus, and various methods have been selected. Information concerning the buses is summarized below:

| Bus | Acquired | Cost | Salvage Value | Useful Life in Years | Depreciation Method |
|---|---|---|---|---|---|
| 1 | 1/1/97 | $ 86,000 | $ 6,000 | 5 | Straight-line |
| 2 | 1/1/97 | 140,000 | 10,000 | 4 | Declining-balance |
| 3 | 1/1/98 | 80,000 | 8,000 | 5 | Units-of-activity |

For the declining balance method, Lakeshore Transportation uses the double-declining rate. For the units-of-activity method, total miles are expected to be 120,000. Actual miles of use in the first 3 years were: 1998, 24,000; 1999, 34,000; and 2000, 30,000.

*Instructions*
(a) Compute the amount of accumulated depreciation on each bus at December 31, 1999.
(b) If Bus No. 2 was purchased on April 1 instead of January 1, what is the depreciation expense for this bus in (1) 1997 and (2) 1998?

**P10–3B**   On January 1, 1999, Axel Company purchased the following two machines for use in its production process:

*Compute depreciation under different methods.*
*(SO 3)*

Machine A: The cash price of this machine was $25,000. Related expenditures included: sales tax $1,500, shipping costs $150, insurance during shipping $80, installation and testing costs $70, and $100 of oil and lubricants to be used with the machinery during its first year of operations. Axel estimates that the useful life of the machine is 5 years with a $5,000 salvage value remaining at the end of that time period. Assume that the straight-line method of depreciation is used.

Machine B: The recorded cost of this machine was $50,000. Axel estimates that the useful life of the machine is 4 years with a $5,000 salvage value remaining at the end of that time period.

*Instructions*
(a) Prepare the following for Machine A:
    (1) The journal entry to record its purchase on January 1, 1999.
    (2) The journal entry to record annual depreciation at December 31, 1999.
(b) Calculate the amount of depreciation expense that Axel should record for Machine B each year of its useful life assuming:
    (1) Axel uses the straight-line method of depreciation.
    (2) Axel uses the declining-balance method. The rate used is twice the straight-line rate.
    (3) Axel uses the units-of-activity method and estimates that the useful life of the machine is 125,000 units. Actual usage is as follows: 1999, 45,000 units; 2000, 35,000 units; 2001, 25,000 units; 2002, 20,000 units.
(c) Which method used to calculate depreciation on Machine B reports the highest amount of depreciation expense in year 1 (1999)? The highest amount in year 4 (2002)? The highest total amount over the 4-year period?

**P10–4B**   At December 31, 1999, Los Alamos Company reported the following as plant assets:

*Journalize a series of equipment transactions related to purchase, sale, retirement, and depreciation.*
*(SO 6, 9)*

| | | |
|---|---:|---:|
| Land | | $ 4,000,000 |
| Buildings | $28,500,000 | |
| Less: Accumulated depreciation—buildings | 12,100,000 | 16,400,000 |
| Equipment | 48,000,000 | |
| Less: Accumulated depreciation—equipment | 5,000,000 | 43,000,000 |
| Total plant assets | | $63,400,000 |

During 2000, the following selected cash transactions occurred:

April 1   Purchased land for $2,630,000.
May 1    Sold equipment that cost $600,000 when purchased on January 1, 1996. The equipment was sold for $350,000.
June 1   Sold land purchased on June 1, 1990, for $1,800,000. The land cost $200,000.
July 1   Purchased equipment for $1,000,000.
Dec. 31  Retired equipment that cost $500,000 when purchased on December 31, 1990. No salvage value was received.

*Instructions*
(a) Journalize the above transactions. Los Alamos uses straight-line depreciation for buildings and equipment. The buildings are estimated to have a 40-year life and no salvage value; the equipment is estimated to have a 10-year useful life and no salvage value. Update depreciation on assets disposed of at the time of sale or retirement.
(b) Record adjusting entries for depreciation for 2000.
(c) Prepare the plant assets section of Los Alamos's balance sheet at December 31, 2000.

**P10–5B**   Chon Co. has office furniture that cost $80,000 and that has been depreciated $48,000. Record the disposal under the following assumptions:

*Record disposals.*
*(SO 6)*

(a) It was scrapped as having no value.
(b) It was sold for $21,000.
(c) It was sold for $61,000.
(d) It was exchanged for similar office furniture. The old office furniture has a fair market value of $46,000 and $8,000 was paid.

(e) It was exchanged for similar office furniture. The old office furniture has a fair market value of $25,000 and $29,000 was paid.

*Prepare entries to record transactions related to acquisition and amortization of intangibles; prepare the intangible assets section.*
*(SO 8, 9)*

**P10–6B**   The intangible assets section of De Paul Company at December 31, 1999, is presented below:

| | |
|---|---:|
| Patent ($70,000 cost less $7,000 amortization) | $63,000 |
| Copyright ($48,000 cost less $19,200 amortization) | 28,800 |
| Total | $91,800 |

The patent was acquired in January 1999 and has a useful life of 10 years. The copyright was acquired in January 1996 and also has a useful life of 10 years. The following cash transactions may have affected intangible assets during 2000:

Jan. 2   Paid $18,000 legal costs to successfully defend the patent against infringement by another company.

Jan.–June   Developed a new product incurring $140,000 in research and development costs. A patent was granted for the product on July 1, and its useful life is equal to its legal life.

Sept. 1   Paid $80,000 to an extremely large defensive lineman to appear in commercials advertising the company's products. The commercials will air in September and October.

Oct. 1   Acquired a copyright for $160,000. The copyright has a useful life of 50 years.

*Instructions*
(a) Prepare journal entries to record the transactions above.
(b) Prepare journal entries to record the 2000 amortization expense.
(c) Prepare the intangible assets section of the balance sheet at December 31, 2000.

*Prepare entries to correct for errors made in recording and amortizing intangible assets.*
*(SO 8)*

**P10–7B**   Due to rapid turnover in the accounting department, a number of transactions involving intangible assets were improperly recorded by the Coker Company in 1999.

1. Coker developed a new manufacturing process, incurring research and development costs of $153,000. The company also purchased a patent for $39,100. In early January, Coker capitalized $192,100 as the cost of the patents. Patent amortization expense of $11,300 was recorded based on a 17-year useful life.

2. On July 1, 1999, Coker purchased a small company and as a result acquired goodwill of $76,000. Coker recorded a half-year's amortization in 1999, based on a 50-year life ($760 amortization).

*Instructions*
Prepare all journal entries necessary to correct any errors made during 1999. Assume the books have not yet been closed for 1999.

*Calculate and comment on average age, average useful life of plant assets, and asset turnover ratio.*
*(SO 9)*

**P10–8B**   Reggie Company and Newman Corporation, two corporations of roughly the same size, are both involved in the manufacture of in-line skates. Each company depreciates its plant assets using the straight-line approach. An investigation of their financial statements reveals the information:

| | Reggie Co. | Newman Corp. |
|---|---:|---:|
| Net income | $ 800,000 | $1,000,000 |
| Sales | 1,600,000 | 1,300,000 |
| Total assets | 2,500,000 | 1,700,000 |
| Plant assets | 1,800,000 | 1,000,000 |
| Accumulated depreciation | 500,000 | 825,000 |
| Depreciation expense | 120,000 | 31,250 |
| Intangible assets (goodwill) | 300,000 | 0 |
| Amortization expense | 60,000 | 0 |

*Instructions*
(a) For each company, calculate these values:
   (1) Average age of plant assets.
   (2) Average useful life.
   (3) Asset turnover ratio.

(b) ▣▥▤▻ Based on your calculations in part (a), comment on the relative effectiveness of the two companies in using their assets to generate sales and produce net income. What factors complicate your ability to compare the two companies?

## BROADENING YOUR PERSPECTIVE

# FINANCIAL REPORTING AND ANALYSIS

## FINANCIAL REPORTING AND ANALYSIS: Kellogg Company

**BYP10–1** The financial statements and the Notes to Consolidated Financial Statements of Kellogg Company are presented in Appendix A.

*Instructions*
Refer to Kellogg's financial statements and answer the following questions:

(a) What was the total cost and book value of property, plant, and equipment at December 31, 1997?
(b) What method or methods of depreciation are used by Kellogg for financial reporting purposes?
(c) What was the amount of depreciation and amortization expense for each of the three years 1995–1997?
(d) Using the Statement of Cash Flows, what is the amount of additions to properties in 1997 and 1996?
(e) Where does Kellogg disclose its intangible assets, and what are the classifications and amounts of its intangibles at December 31, 1997?
(f) In December 1996, Kellogg acquired Lender's Bagel's business for $466 million in cash. Name the three components and the amounts of the intangible assets included in the acquisition price. What useful life is used to amortize these intangibles?
(g) What was the amount of research and development expenses Kellogg had in 1997?

## COMPARATIVE ANALYSIS PROBLEM: Kellogg Company vs. General Mills

**BYP10–2** Kellogg's financial statements are presented in Appendix A; General Mills's financial statements are presented in Appendix B.

*Instructions*
(a) The cost of General Mills's plant assets was $2,571.6 and its accumulated depreciation was $1,292.2. Based on the information contained in these financial statements, compute the following 1997 ratios for each company (use "depreciation and amortization expense" amount for both companies):
   1. Average life of plant assets.
   2. Average age of plant assets.
   3. Asset turnover ratio.
(b) What conclusions concerning the management of assets can be drawn from these data?

## RESEARCH ASSIGNMENT

**BYP10–3** The December 18, 1995, issue of *Forbes* includes an article by Rita Koselka, entitled "Tall Story."

*Instructions*
Read the article and answer the following questions:

(a) What is the biggest expense in running a video rental store?
(b) Over how long a period does Hollywood Entertainment Corp. depreciate its video tapes? How did the author arrive at this figure?

(c) The author asserts that, once a store is fully stocked, depreciation expense should be approximately equal to the cost of new tapes. Calculate and compare the ratio of depreciation expense to new purchases for Hollywood and Blockbuster.

(d) If Hollywood can open a new store for $400,000 or buy an existing store for $1.2 million, why might investors value Hollywood at an average of $3 million per store?

## INTERPRETING FINANCIAL STATEMENTS
### Boeing and McDonnell Douglas

**BYP10–4**  Boeing and McDonnell Douglas were two leaders in the manufacture of aircraft. In 1996 Boeing announced intentions to acquire McDonnell Douglas and create one huge corporation. Its competitors, primarily Airbus of Europe, were very concerned that they would not be able to compete with such a huge rival. In addition, customers are concerned that this will reduce the number of suppliers to a point where Boeing would be able to dictate prices. Provided below are figures taken from the financial statements of Boeing and McDonnell Douglas which allow a comparison of the operations of the two corporations prior to their merger.

| (in millions of dollars) | Boeing | McDonnell Douglas |
|---|---|---|
| Total revenue | $19,515 | $14,322 |
| Net income (loss) | 393 | (416) |
| Total assets | 22,098 | 10,466 |
| Land | 404 | 91 |
| Buildings and fixtures | 5,791 | 1,647 |
| Machinery and equipment | 7,251 | 2,161 |
| Total property, plant, and equipment (at cost) | 13,744 | 3,899 |
| Accumulated depreciation | 7,288 | 2,541 |
| Depreciation expense | 976 | 196 |

*Instructions*
(a) Which company had older assets?
(b) Which company used a longer average estimated useful life for its assets?
(c) Based on the total asset turnover ratio, which company used its assets more effectively to generate sales?
(d) Besides an increase in size, what other factors might have motivated this merger?

### Merck and Johnson & Johnson

**BYP10–5**  Merck Co., Inc. and Johnson & Johnson are two leading producers of health care products. Each has considerable assets, as well as expending considerable funds each year toward the development of new products. The development of a new health care product is often very expensive, and risky. New products frequently must undergo considerable testing before approval for distribution to the public. For example, it took Johnson & Johnson 4 years and $200 million to develop its 1-DAY ACUVUE contact lenses. Below are some basic data compiled from the financial statements of these two companies.

| (all dollars in millions) | Johnson & Johnson | Merck |
|---|---|---|
| Total assets | $15,668 | $21,857 |
| Total revenue | 15,734 | 14,970 |
| Net income | 2,006 | 2,997 |
| Research and development expense | 1,278 | 1,230 |
| Intangible assets | 2,403 | 7,212 |

*Instructions*
(a) What kinds of intangible assets might a health care products company have? Does the composition of these intangibles matter to investors—that is, would it be perceived differently if all of Merck's intangibles were goodwill, than if all of its intangibles were patents?
(b) By employing the asset turnover ratio, determine which company is using its assets more effectively. (*Note*: The previous year's total assets were $19,928 million for Merck and $12,242 million for Johnson & Johnson.)

(c) Suppose the president of Merck has come to you for advice. He has noted that by eliminating research and development expenditures the company could have reported $1.3 billion more in net income in the current year. He is frustrated because much of the research never results in a product, or the products take years to develop. He says shareholders are eager for higher returns, so he is considering eliminating research and development expenditures for at least a couple of years. What would you advise?

(d) The notes to Merck's financial statements indicate that Merck has goodwill of $4.1 billion. Where does recorded goodwill come from? Is it necessarily a good thing to have a lot of goodwill on your books?

## REAL-WORLD FOCUS: Clark Equipment Company

**BYP10–6    Clark Equipment Company** was originally formed in 1902 as a general manufacturing company. During its history it has specialized in the manufacture of drills, gears, towing tractors, lift trucks, and truck transmissions. At the time of the example presented below, Clark operated throughout the U.S. and Europe in the design, manufacture, and sale of skid steer loaders and mini-excavators, golf carts and utility vehicles, axles and transmissions for off-highway vehicles, and asphalt paving equipment. In 1995, Ingersoll-Rand Company acquired Clark and combined its operating units with existing I-R businesses.

The following information relates to the plant assets of Clark Equipment:

### CLARK EQUIPMENT COMPANY
### Balance Sheet (partial)
### (in millions)

|  | Previous Year | Current Year |
| --- | --- | --- |
| Land | $ 7.4 | $ 13.2 |
| Land improvements | 5.9 | 8.8 |
| Buildings | 77.3 | 126.0 |
| Machinery and equipment | 398.4 | 451.7 |
| Totals | 489.0 | 599.7 |
| Accumulated depreciation | 272.8 | 315.9 |
| Total plant assets | $216.2 | $283.8 |

*Instructions*

(a) What type of costs would Clark Equipment capitalize in the land category of plant assets?

(b) Cite several possible types of land improvements that Clark Equipment might have made.

(c) What is the book value of Clark Equipment's plant assets?

# CRITICAL THINKING

## GROUP DECISION CASE

**BYP10–7**   Fresno Company and Auburn Company are two proprietorships that are similar in many respects except that Fresno Company uses the straight-line method and Auburn Company uses the declining-balance method at double the straight-line rate. On January 2, 1997, both companies acquired the following depreciable assets.

| Asset | Cost | Salvage Value | Useful Life |
|---|---|---|---|
| Building | $320,000 | $20,000 | 40 years |
| Equipment | 110,000 | 10,000 | 10 years |

Including the appropriate depreciation charges, annual net income for the companies in the years 1997, 1998, and 1999 and total income for the 3 years were as follows:

|  | 1997 | 1998 | 1999 | Total |
|---|---|---|---|---|
| Fresno Company | $84,000 | $88,400 | $90,000 | $262,400 |
| Auburn Company | 68,000 | 76,000 | 85,000 | 229,000 |

At December 31, 1999, the balance sheets of the two companies are similar except that Auburn Company has more cash than Fresno Company.

Mary Flaherty is interested in buying one of the companies, and she comes to you for advice.

*Instructions*

With the class divided into groups, answer the following:

(a) Determine the annual and total depreciation recorded by each company during the 3 years.

(b) Assuming that Auburn Company also uses the straight-line method of depreciation instead of the declining-balance method as in (a), prepare comparative income data for the 3 years.

(c) Which company should Mrs. Flaherty buy? Why?

## COMMUNICATION ACTIVITY

**BYP10–8**    The following was published with the financial statements to American Exploration Company:

---

### AMERICAN EXPLORATION COMPANY
### Notes to the Financial Statements

**Property, Plant, and Equipment**—The Company accounts for its oil and gas exploration and production activities using the successful efforts method of accounting. Under this method, acquisition costs for proved and unproved properties are capitalized when incurred. . . . The costs of drilling exploratory wells are capitalized pending determination of whether each well has discovered proved reserves. If proved reserves are not discovered, such drilling costs are charged to expense. . . . Depletion of the cost of producing oil and gas properties is computed on the units-of-activity method.

---

*Instructions*

Write a brief memo to your instructor discussing American Exploration Company's note regarding property, plant, and equipment. Your memo should address what is meant by the "successful efforts method" and "units-of-activity method."

## ETHICS CASE

**BYP10–9**    Finney Container Company is suffering declining sales of its principal product, nonbiodegradeable plastic cartons. The president, Philip Shapeero, instructs his controller, Sharon Fetters, to lengthen asset lives to reduce depreciation expense. A processing line of automated plastic extruding equipment, purchased for $2.7 million in January 1999 was originally estimated to have a useful life of 8 years and a salvage value of $300,000. Depreciation has been recorded for 2 years on that basis. Philip wants the estimated life changed to 12 years total, and the straight-line method continued. Sharon is hesitant to make the change, believing it is unethical to increase net income in this manner. Philip says, "Hey, the life is only an estimate, and I've heard that our competition uses a 12-year life on their production equipment."

*Instructions*

(a) Who are the stakeholders in this situation?

(b) Is the change in asset life unethical or simply a good business practice by an astute president?

(c) What is the effect of Philip Shapeero's proposed change on income before taxes in the year of change?

# SURFING THE NET

**BYP10–10**   A company's annual report identifies the amount of its plant assets and the depreciation method used.

**Address:** http://www.reportgallery.com

**Steps:**

1. From Report Gallery Homepage, choose **Viewing Library.**
2. Select a particular company.
3. Choose **Annual Report.**
4. Follow instructions below.

*Instructions*

Answer the following questions:

(a) What is the name of the company?

(b) What is the Internet address of the annual report?

(c) At fiscal year-end, what is the net amount of its plant assets?

(d) What is the accumulated depreciation?

(e) Which method of depreciation does the company use?

---

*Answers to Self-Study Questions*

1. d     2. b     3. d     4. d     5. b     6. d     7. a     8. c     9. c     10. b     11. c

---

*Answer to Kellogg Review It Question 4, p. 425.*

Kellogg reports the detail about its "Property, net" in Note 14 "Supplemental financial statement data." The classifications and amounts constituting the detail for "Property, net" are reported by Kellogg as (in millions) land $49; buildings $1,213.8; machinery and equipment $3,434.7; construction in progress $283.1; and accumulated depreciation $2,207.3.

**Remember to go back to the Navigator box on the chapter-opening page and check off your completed work.**

Before studying this chapter, you should know or, if necessary, review:

a.  The importance of liquidity in evaluating the financial position of a company. (Ch. 4, p. 160)
b.  How to make adjusting entries related to unearned revenue (Ch. 3, pp. 101–102) and accrued expenses. (Ch. 3, pp. 104–107)
c.  The principles of internal control. (Ch. 7, p. 281)

THE NAVIGATOR

## FEATURE STORY

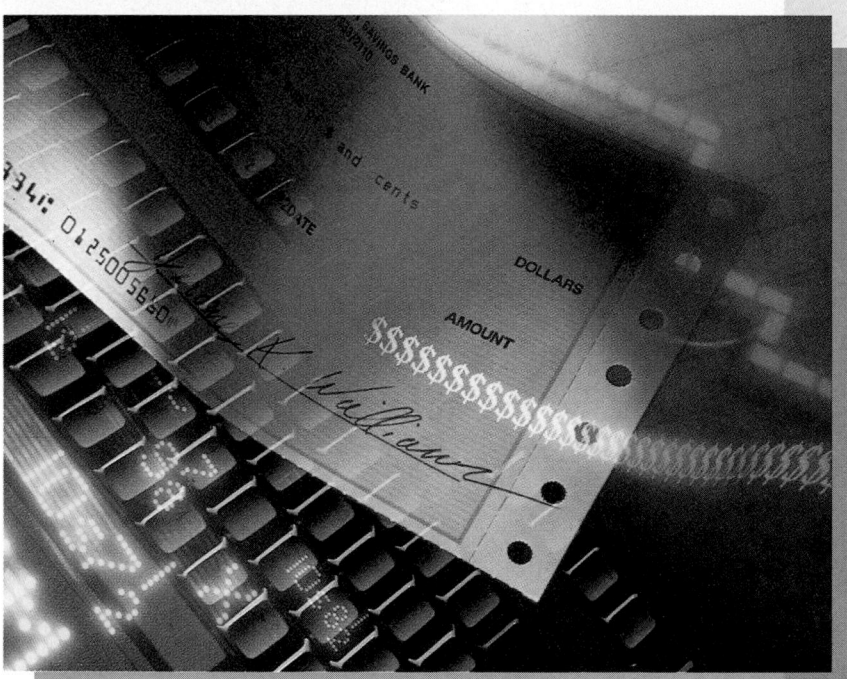

# No Computer? Your Paycheck May Be Late

When it comes to payroll, colleges are very much like the "real world." There's a payroll supervisor, a few clerks, a giant computer, reams of computer printouts—and, of course, paychecks.

Mrs. Dianna Webb is the payroll supervisor at Casper College in Cas-

per, Wyoming, a school with 6,000 students and 550 people on the payroll. "I take out tax deductions, credit union contributions, contributions to tax-sheltered annuities, United Way donations, and even garnishments when an employee has been ordered by a court to pay a debt. Wyoming has no state income tax, so that's one deduction I don't have to worry about."

The payroll staff consists of just Mrs. Webb and the computer. Their job: To process monthly checks for

the faculty, administrators, and students and semi-monthly checks for staff. What if she didn't have a computer? "I doubt I'd be able to pay as many people," she laughs.

Just as in any other business, Dianna Webb keeps timecards for all hourly employees. The faculty and administrators—salaried employees—are on the honor system to work the required number of hours, but even their pay has to be authorized.

The computer provides Dianna Webb with many useful reports: The main report shows the payroll in alphabetical order, listing gross pay, tax deductions, other payroll deductions, and net pay. She also gets a report that lists year-to-date totals. "In May, faculty members get paid the balance on their contracts, so I need to know those year-to-date totals."

Student employees provide one extra wrinkle: They don't have Social Security (FICA) taxes withheld during the school year. The reason: Federal regulations consider students who work for the college and are enrolled and attend classes to be exempt from Social Security and Medicare taxes. For work done during the summer months, though, Social Security taxes are withheld.

THE NAVIGATOR

# CHAPTER 11

# CURRENT LIABILITIES AND PAYROLL ACCOUNTING

**THE NAVIGATOR** ✔

- Understand *Concepts for Review* ☐
- Read *Feature Story* ☐
- Scan *Study Objectives* ☐
- Read *Preview* ☐
- Read text and answer *Before You Go On*
  p. 478 ☐ p. 489 ☐ p. 492 ☐ p. 495 ☐
- Work *Demonstration Problems* ☐
- Review *Summary of Study Objectives* ☐
- Answer *Self-Study Questions* ☐
- Complete assignments ☐

## STUDY OBJECTIVES

**After studying this chapter, you should be able to:**

1. *Explain a current liability and identify the major types of current liabilities.*
2. *Describe the accounting for notes payable.*
3. *Explain the accounting for other current liabilities.*
4. *Explain the methods for the financial statement presentation and analysis of current liabilities.*
5. *Describe the accounting and disclosure requirements for contingent liabilities.*
6. *Discuss the objectives of internal control for payroll.*
7. *Compute and record the payroll for a pay period.*
8. *Describe and record employer payroll taxes.*
9. *Identify additional fringe benefits associated with employee compensation.*

THE NAVIGATOR

469

Whether it be a college like Casper College, a pizza parlor like Pizza Hut, a public accounting firm like Arthur Andersen & Co., or a large multinational company like IBM, all enterprises have liabilities for payroll. In addition, they also have many other types of liabilities. Examples are the purchase of supplies on account, the borrowing of money on a bank loan, and the obligation to pay interest. Liabilities are classified as current or long-term on the balance sheet. We will explain current liabilities in this chapter and long-term liabilities in Chapter 16. The content and organization of this chapter are as follows:

THE
NAVIGATOR

# ACCOUNTING FOR CURRENT LIABILITIES

**1**

STUDY
OBJECTIVE

Explain a current liability
and identify the major
types of current
liabilities.

As explained in Chapter 4, a **current liability** is a debt that can reasonably be expected to be paid (1) from existing current assets or through the creation of other current liabilities, and (2) within one year or the operating cycle, whichever is longer. Debts that do not meet both criteria are classified as long-term liabilities. In most companies, current liabilities are paid within one year out of current assets, rather than through the creation of other liabilities.

Companies must carefully monitor the relationship of current liabilities to current assets. This relationship is critical in evaluating a company's liquidity, or short-term debt paying ability. A company that has more current liabilities than current assets is usually the subject of some concern because the company may not be able to meet its current obligations when they become due.

Current liabilities include notes payable, accounts payable, unearned revenues, and accrued liabilities such as taxes, salaries and wages, and interest payable. The entries for accounts payable and adjusting entries for some current liabilities have been explained in previous chapters. Other types of current liabilities that are frequently encountered in practice are discussed in the following sections.

**HELPFUL HINT**
The current liability section gives creditors a good idea of what obligations are coming due.

## Notes Payable

Obligations in the form of written promissory notes are recorded as notes payable. Notes payable are often used instead of accounts payable. Doing so gives the lender written documentation of the obligation in case legal remedies are needed to collect the debt. Notes payable usually require the borrower to pay interest and frequently are issued to meet short-term financing needs.

Notes are issued for varying periods. **Those due for payment within one year of the balance sheet date are usually classified as current liabilities.** Most notes are interest bearing. To illustrate the accounting for notes payable, assume that First National Bank agrees to lend $100,000 on March 1, 1999, if Cole Williams Co. signs a $100,000, 12%, 4-month note. With an interest-bearing promissory note, the amount of assets received upon issuance of the note generally equals the note's face value. Cole Williams Co. therefore will receive $100,000 cash and will make the following journal entry:

**2
STUDY
OBJECTIVE**
Describe the accounting for notes payable.

| Mar. 1 | Cash | 100,000 | |
| | Notes Payable | | 100,000 |
| | (To record issuance of 12%, 4-month note to First National Bank) | | |

| A | = | L | + | OE |
|---|---|---|---|---|
| + 100,000 | | + 100,000 | | |

Interest accrues over the life of the note and must be recorded periodically. If Cole Williams Co. prepares financial statements semiannually, an adjusting entry is required to recognize interest expense and interest payable of $4,000 ($100,000 × 12% × 4/12) at June 30. The formula for computing interest and its application to Cole Williams Co. are shown in Illustration 11-1.

**ILLUSTRATION 11-1**
*Formula for computing interest*

The adjusting entry is:

| June 30 | Interest Expense | 4,000 | |
| | Interest Payable | | 4,000 |
| | (To accrue interest for 4 months on First National Bank note) | | |

| A | = | L | + | OE |
|---|---|---|---|---|
| | | + 4,000 | | − 4,000 |

In the June 30 financial statements, the current liability section of the balance sheet will show notes payable $100,000 and interest payable $4,000. In addition, interest expense of $4,000 will be reported under Other Expenses and Losses in the income statement. If Cole Williams Co. prepared financial statements monthly, the adjusting entry at the end of each month would have been $1,000 ($100,000 × 12% × 1/12).

At maturity (July 1), Cole Williams Co. must pay the face value of the note ($100,000) plus $4,000 interest ($100,000 × 12% × 4/12). The entry to record payment of the note and accrued interest is as follows:

| A | = | L | + OE |
|---|---|---|---|
| − 104,000 | | − 100,000 | |
| | | − 4,000 | |

| | | | | |
|---|---|---|---|---|
| July 1 | Notes Payable | | 100,000 | |
| | Interest Payable | | 4,000 | |
| |    Cash | | | 104,000 |
| |    (To record payment of First National Bank | | | |
| |    interest-bearing note and accrued interest at | | | |
| |    maturity) | | | |

**STUDY OBJECTIVE**

····································

Explain the accounting for other current liabilities.

## Sales Taxes Payable

As consumers, we are well aware that many of the products we purchase at retail stores are subject to sales taxes. The tax is expressed as a stated percentage of the sales price. The retailer (or selling company) collects the tax from the customer when the sale occurs, and periodically (usually monthly) remits the collections to the state's department of revenue.

Under most state sales tax laws, the amount of the sale and the amount of the sales tax collected must be rung up separately on the cash register. (Gasoline sales are a major exception.) The cash register readings are then used to credit Sales and Sales Taxes Payable. For example, assuming that the March 25 cash register readings for Cooley Grocery show sales of $10,000 and sales taxes of $600 (sales tax rate of 6%), the entry is:

| A | = | L | + OE |
|---|---|---|---|
| + 10,600 | | + 600 | + 10,000 |

| | | | | |
|---|---|---|---|---|
| Mar. 25 | Cash | | 10,600 | |
| |    Sales | | | 10,000 |
| |    Sales Taxes Payable | | | 600 |
| |    (To record daily sales and sales taxes) | | | |

When the taxes are remitted to the taxing agency, Sales Taxes Payable is debited and Cash is credited. The company does not report sales taxes as an expense; it simply forwards the amount paid by the customer to the government. Thus, Cooley Grocery serves only as a **collection agent** for the taxing authority.

## ACCOUNTING IN ACTION
### Business Insight

Sales taxes do not apply exclusively to retail companies. They also apply to manufacturing companies, service companies, and public utilities, and the extent of the taxes is increasing. There are now over 9,000 state and local sales taxes. "Compliance is becoming much more complex as states expand their sales taxes," says an American Telephone and Telegraph (AT&T) tax attorney. They are also becoming more costly. AT&T employs a staff just to file the company's sales tax returns and handle the sales tax audits.

When sales taxes are not rung up separately on the cash register, total receipts are divided by 100% plus the sales tax percentage to determine sales. To illustrate, assume in the above example that Cooley Grocery "rings up" total receipts, which are $10,600. Because the amount received from the sale is equal to the sales price 100% plus 6% of sales, or 1.06 times the sales total, we can compute sales as follows:

$$\$10,600 \div 1.06 = \$10,000$$

Thus, the sales tax amount of $600 is found either by (1) subtracting sales from total receipts ($10,600 − $10,000) or (2) multiplying sales by the sales tax rate ($10,000 × 6%).

## Unearned Revenues

A magazine publisher such as Sports Illustrated may receive a customer's check when magazines are ordered, and an airline company, such as American Airlines, often receives cash when it sells tickets for future flights. How do these companies account for unearned revenues that are received before goods are delivered or services are rendered?

1. When the advance is received, Cash is debited, and a current liability account identifying the source of the unearned revenue is credited.
2. When the revenue is earned, the unearned revenue account is debited, and an earned revenue account is credited.

To illustrate, assume that Superior University sells 10,000 season football tickets at $50 each for its five-game home schedule. The entry for the sales of season tickets is:

| Aug. 6 | Cash | 500,000 | |
| | Unearned Football Ticket Revenue | | 500,000 |
| | (To record sale of 10,000 season tickets) | | |

| A | = | L | + OE |
| +500,000 | | +500,000 | |

As each game is completed, the following entry is made:

| Sept. 7 | Unearned Football Ticket Revenue | 100,000 | |
| | Football Ticket Revenue | | 100,000 |
| | (To record football ticket revenues earned) | | |

| A | = | L | + OE |
| | | −100,000 | +100,000 |

Unearned Football Ticket Revenue is, therefore, unearned revenue and is reported as a current liability in the balance sheet. As revenue is earned, a transfer from unearned revenue to earned revenue occurs. Unearned revenue is material for some companies: In the airline industry, for example, tickets sold for future flights represent almost 50% of total current liabilities. At United Air Lines, unearned ticket revenue is the largest current liability, recently amounting to over $1 billion.

Illustration 11-2 shows specific unearned and earned revenue accounts used in selected types of businesses.

| Type of Business | Account Title | |
| | Unearned Revenue | Earned Revenue |
| --- | --- | --- |
| Airline | Unearned Passenger Ticket Revenue | Passenger Revenue |
| Magazine publisher | Unearned Subscription Revenue | Subscription Revenue |
| Hotel | Unearned Rental Revenue | Rental Revenue |

**ILLUSTRATION 11-2**

*Unearned and earned revenue accounts*

## Current Maturities of Long-Term Debt

Companies often have a portion of long-term debt that comes due in the current year. For example, assume that Wendy Construction issues a 5-year interest-bearing $25,000 note on January 1, 1999. This note specifies that each January 1, starting January 1, 2000, $5,000 of the note should be paid. When financial statements are prepared on December 31, 1999, $5,000 should be reported as a current liability and $20,000 as a long-term liability. Current maturities of long-term debt are often identified on the balance sheet as **long-term debt due within one year**.

It is not necessary to prepare an adjusting entry to recognize the current maturity of long-term debt. The proper statement classification of each balance sheet account is recognized when the balance sheet is prepared.

## Statement Presentation and Analysis

### Presentation

**4**

STUDY
OBJECTIVE

Explain the methods for the financial statement presentation and analysis of current liabilities.

As indicated in Chapter 4, current liabilities are the first category under liabilities on the balance sheet. Each of the principal types of current liabilities is listed separately within the category. In addition, the terms of notes payable and other pertinent information concerning the individual items are disclosed in the notes to the financial statements.

Current liabilities are seldom listed in the order of maturity because of the varying maturity dates that may exist for specific obligations such as notes payable. A more common, and entirely satisfactory, method of presenting current liabilities is to list them by **order of magnitude**, with the largest obligations first. Many companies, as a matter of custom, show notes payable and accounts payable first, regardless of amount. The following adapted excerpt from the balance sheet of Kellogg Company illustrates this practice.

**ILLUSTRATION 11-3**

*Balance sheet presentation of current liabilities*

| **KELLOGG COMPANY**<br>**Balance Sheet**<br>**December 31, 1997**<br>**(in millions)** | |
| --- | --- |
| **Assets** | |
| Current assets | $1,467.7 |
| Property, plant, and equipment (net) | 2,773.3 |
| Identifiable intangible assets and goodwill | 636.6 |
| Total assets | $4,877.6 |
| **Liabilities and Stockholders' Equity** | |
| Current liabilities | |
| Current maturities of long-term debt | $   211.2 |
| Notes payable | 368.6 |
| Accounts payable | 328.0 |
| Other current liabilities | 749.5 |
| Total current liabilities | 1,657.3 |
| Noncurrent liabilities | 2,222.8 |
| Shareholders' equity | 997.5 |
| Total liabilities and shareholders' equity | $4,877.6 |

**HELPFUL HINT**

For another example of a current liability section refer to the General Mills balance sheet in Appendix B.

### Analysis

Classifying assets and liabilities into current and noncurrent allows a company's liquidity to be analyzed and evaluated. Liquidity refers to the ability of a company to pay its maturing obligations and meet unexpected needs for cash. The relationship of current assets and current liabilities is critical in analyzing liquidity. This relationship is expressed as a dollar amount called working capital and as a ratio called the current ratio.

The excess of current assets over current liabilities is working capital. The formula for the computation of Kellogg's working capital is shown in Illustration 11-4 (dollar amounts in millions).

ILLUSTRATION 11-4
*Working capital formula and computation*

As an absolute dollar amount, working capital is limited in its informational value. For example $1 million of working capital may be far more than needed for a small company but be inadequate for a large corporation. And, $1 million of working capital may be adequate for a company at one time but be inadequate at another time. The current ratio permits us to compare the liquidity of different sized companies and of a single company at different times. The current ratio is current assets divided by current liabilities. The formula for this ratio is illustrated below, along with its computation using Kellogg's current asset and current liability data:

ILLUSTRATION 11-5
*Current ratio and computation*

Historically, a ratio of 2:1 was considered to be the standard for a good credit rating. In recent years, however, many healthy companies have maintained ratios well below 2:1. This is exemplified by Kellogg, which is considered a healthy company even though its current ratio is below 1:1.

# CONTINGENT LIABILITIES

With notes payable, interest payable, accounts payable, and sales taxes payable, we know that an obligation exists to make payment. But suppose that your company is currently involved in a dispute with the Internal Revenue Service (IRS) over the amount of its income tax liability. Do you have to report the disputed amount on the balance sheet as a liability? Or suppose your company is the defendant in a lawsuit in which an adverse decision might result in bankruptcy. How should this major contingency be reported? The answers to these questions are difficult, because these liabilities are dependent—contingent—upon some future event. In other words, a contingent liability is a potential liability that may become an actual liability in the future.

How, then, should contingent liabilities be reported? Guidelines have been adopted that are helpful in resolving these problems. The guidelines require that:

1. If the contingency is **probable**—if it is likely to occur—**and** the amount can be **reasonably estimated**, the liability should be recorded in the accounts.

**5**
STUDY
OBJECTIVE

Describe the accounting and disclosure requirements for contingent liabilities.

**HELPFUL HINT**
Another example of a contingency is toxic waste cleanup costs. Some expect that insurance will cover these costs, but insurance companies are arguing that general liability policies were never meant to cover this type of situation.

2. If the contingency is only **reasonably possible**—if it could happen—then it need be disclosed only in the notes accompanying the financial statements.

3. If the contingency is **remote**—if it is unlikely to occur—it need not be recorded or disclosed.

## ACCOUNTING IN ACTION
### Business Insight

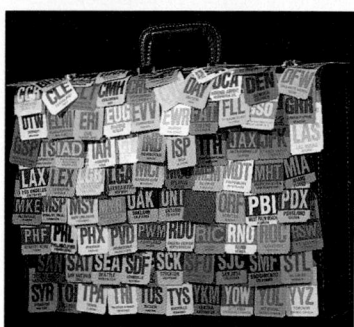

Contingent liabilities abound in the real world. Consider the following: Manville Corp. filed bankruptcy when it was hit by billions of dollars in asbestos product liability claims. Companies having multiple toxic waste sites are faced with cleanup costs that average $10 to $30 million and can reach as high as $500 million depending on the type of waste. For life and health insurance companies and their stockholders, the cost of AIDS is like an iceberg—everybody wonders how big it really is and what damage it might do in the future; according to the U.S. Centers for Disease Control treatment costs could be $8 billion to $16 billion. And frequent-flyer programs are so popular that airlines at one time owed participants more than 3 million round-trip domestic tickets. That's enough to fly at least 5.4 billion miles—free for the passengers but at what future cost to the airlines?

## Recording a Contingent Liability

**INTERNATIONAL NOTE**

International accounting standards basically use criteria similar to those in the U.S. in determining how to account for contingencies.

Product warranties are a good example of a contingent liability that should be recorded in the accounts. Warranty contracts result in future costs that may be incurred in replacing defective units or repairing malfunctioning units without charge to the customer for a specified period after the product is sold. Generally, a manufacturer, such as Black & Decker, knows that some warranty costs will be incurred. Moreover, on the basis of prior experience with the product (or similar products), the company usually can make a reasonable estimate of the anticipated cost of servicing (honoring) the contract.

The accounting for warranty costs is based on the matching principle. To comply with this principle, **the estimated cost of honoring product warranty contracts should be recognized as an expense in the period in which the sale occurs**. To illustrate, assume that in 1999 Denson Manufacturing Company sells 10,000 washers and dryers at an average price of $600 each. The selling price includes a one-year warranty on parts. It is expected that 500 units (5%) will be defective and that warranty repair costs will average $80 per unit. In the year of sale, warranty contracts are honored on 300 units at a total cost of $24,000.

At December 31, it is necessary to accrue the estimated warranty costs on the 1999 sales. The computation is as follows:

**ILLUSTRATION 11-6**

*Computation of estimated product warranty liability*

| | |
|---|---|
| Number of units sold | 10,000 |
| Estimated rate of defective units | × 5% |
| Total estimated defective units | 500 |
| Average warranty repair cost | × $80 |
| **Estimated product warranty liability** | **$40,000** |

The adjusting entry, therefore, is:

| A | = | L | + | OE |
|---|---|---|---|---|
| | | +40,000 | | −40,000 |

| Dec. 31 | Warranty Expense | 40,000 | |
|---|---|---|---|
| |    Estimated Warranty Liability | | 40,000 |
| |      (To accrue estimated warranty costs) | | |

The entry to record repair costs incurred in 1999 to honor warranty contracts on 1999 sales is shown in summary form below:

| | | | |
|---|---|---|---|
| Jan. 1– Dec. 31 | Estimated Warranty Liability | 24,000 | |
| | Repair Parts | | 24,000 |
| | (To record honoring of 300 warranty contracts on 1999 sales) | | |

| A | = | L | + | OE |
|---|---|---|---|---|
| − 24,000 | | − 24,000 | | |

Warranty expense of $40,000 is reported under selling expenses in the income statement, and estimated warranty liability of $16,000 ($40,000 − $24,000) is classified as a current liability on the balance sheet.

In the following year, all expenses incurred in honoring warranty contracts on 1999 sales should be debited to Estimated Warranty Liability. To illustrate, assume that 20 defective units are replaced in January 2000, at an average cost of $80 in parts and labor. The summary entry for the month of January is:

| | | | |
|---|---|---|---|
| Jan. 31 | Estimated Warranty Liability | 1,600 | |
| | Repair Parts | | 1,600 |
| | (To record honoring of 20 warranty contracts on 1997 sales) | | |

| A | = | L | + | OE |
|---|---|---|---|---|
| − 1,600 | | − 1,600 | | |

## Disclosure of Contingent Liabilities

When it is probable that a contingent liability will be incurred but the amount cannot be reasonably estimated, or when the contingent liability is only reasonably possible, only disclosure of the contingency is required. Examples of contingencies that may require disclosure are pending or threatened lawsuits and assessment of additional income taxes pending an IRS audit of the tax return.

The disclosure should identify the nature of the item, and if known, the amount of the contingency and the expected outcome of the future event. Disclosure is usually accomplished through a note to the financial statements, as illustrated by the following:

**USAIR**
**Notes to the Financial Statements**

**Legal Proceedings**
The Company and various subsidiaries have been named as defendants in various suits and proceedings which involve, among other things, environmental concerns about noise and air pollution and employment matters. These suits and proceedings are in various stages of litigation, and the status of the law with respect to several of the issues involved is unsettled. For these reasons the outcome of these suits and proceedings is difficult to predict. In the Company's opinion, however, the disposition of these matters is not likely to have a material adverse effect on its financial condition.

**ILLUSTRATION 11-7**
*Disclosure of contingent liability*

## BEFORE YOU GO ON . . .

### Review It

1. What are the two criteria for classifying a debt as a current liability?
2. Identify three liabilities classified as current by Kellogg. The answer to this question is provided on page 512.
3. What entries are made for an interest-bearing note payable?
4. How are sales taxes recorded by a retailer? Identify three unearned revenues.
5. What are the accounting guidelines for contingent liabilities?
6. How may the liquidity of a company be analyzed?

### Do It

You and several classmates are studying for the next accounting examination. They ask you to answer the following questions: (1) How is the sales tax amount determined when the cash register total includes sales taxes? (2) When should a contingency be recorded in the accounts?

*Reasoning:* To answer the first question, you must remove the sales taxes from the total sales. To answer the second question, you need to know the criteria for recording and disclosing contingent liabilities.

*Solution:*

(1) First, divide the total proceeds by 100% plus the sales tax percentage to find the sales amount; second, subtract the sales amount from the total proceeds to determine the sales taxes.

(2) A contingency should be recorded when it is *probable* that a liability will be incurred *and* the amount can be *reasonably* estimated.

THE NAVIGATOR

*Related exercise material:* BE11–3, BE11–4, BE11–5, E11–2, E11–3, E11–4, and E11–5.

# PAYROLL ACCOUNTING

Payroll and related fringe benefits often constitute a substantial percentage of current liabilities. In addition, employee compensation is often the most significant expense that a company incurs. For example, General Motors recently reported total employees of 516,000 and labor costs of $31.3 billion. Add to labor costs such fringe benefits as health insurance, life insurance, disability insurance, and so on, and you can see why proper accounting and control of payroll are so important.

It should be emphasized that payroll accounting involves more than paying employees' wages. Companies are required by law to maintain payroll records for each employee, file and pay payroll taxes, and comply with numerous state and federal tax laws applicable to employee compensation. Accounting for payroll has become much more complex as a result of these regulations.

The term "payroll" pertains to all salaries and wages paid to employees. Managerial, administrative, and sales personnel are generally paid salaries, which are often expressed in terms of a specified amount per month or per year rather than an hourly rate. For example, in the opening story the faculty and administrative personnel at Casper College are paid salaries. In contrast, store clerks, factory employees, and manual laborers are normally paid wages, which are based on a rate per hour or on a piecework basis (such as per unit of product). Frequently, the terms "salaries" and "wages" are used interchangeably.

The term "payroll" does not extend to payments made for personal service by professionals such as certified public accountants, attorneys, and architects. Such professionals are independent contractors, and payments to them are called **fees**, rather than salaries or wages. This distinction is important because government regulations relating to the payment and reporting of payroll taxes apply only to employees.

## Internal Control

Internal control was introduced in Chapter 7. As applied to payrolls, the objectives of internal control are (1) to safeguard company assets against unauthorized payments of payrolls and (2) to assure the accuracy and reliability of the accounting records pertaining to payrolls.

Unfortunately, irregularities often result if internal control is lax. Overstating hours, using unauthorized pay rates, adding fictitious employees to the payroll, continuing terminated employees on the payroll, and distributing duplicate payroll checks are all methods of stealing from a company. Moreover, inaccurate records will result in incorrect paychecks, financial statements, and payroll tax returns.

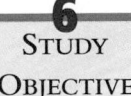

**6**
STUDY
OBJECTIVE
..............................
Discuss the objectives of internal control for payroll.

## TECHNOLOGY IN ACTION

A Senate hearing revealed that the U.S. Army spent $8 million on unauthorized pay, including payments to deserters and "ghost" soldiers. The underlying cause was a computer system so lax that it was possible to create new pay records and destroy old ones without leaving an audit trail.

Payroll activities involve four functions: hiring employees, timekeeping, preparing the payroll, and paying the payroll. For an internal control system to work effectively, these four functions should be assigned to different departments or individuals. To illustrate these functions in more detail, we will examine the case of Academy Company and one of its employees, Michael Jordan.

### Hiring Employees

Posting job openings, screening and interviewing applicants, and hiring employees are responsibilities of the personnel department. From a control standpoint, the personnel department provides significant documentation and authorization. When an employee is hired, the personnel department prepares an authorization form like the one used by Academy Company for Michael Jordan shown in Illustration 11-8.

The authorization form is sent to the payroll department, where it is used to place the new employee on the payroll. A chief concern of the personnel department is ensuring the accuracy of this form. The reason is quite simple: one of the most common types of payroll frauds is adding fictitious employees to the payroll.

The personnel department is also responsible for authorizing (1) changes in pay rates during employment and (2) terminations of employment. In each instance, the authorization should be in writing, and a copy of the change in status should be sent to the payroll department. Note in Illustration 11-8 that Jordan received a pay increase of $2 per hour.

**Hiring Employees**

Personnel

Personnel department documents and authorizes employment.

**ILLUSTRATION 11-8**

*Personnel authorization form*

### ACADEMY COMPANY

Employee Name _____ Jordan, _____ Michael _____        Starting Date _____ 9/01/95 _____
                       LAST              FIRST         MI

Classification _____ Skilled-Level 10 _____             Social Security No. _____ 329-36-9547 _____

Department _____ Shipping _____                          Division _____ Entertainment _____

| | | |
|---|---|---|
| **NEW HIRE** | Classification _____ Clerk _____  Salary Grade _____ Level 10 _____  Trans. from Temp. ☐ <br> Rate $ _____ 10.00 _____ per _____ hour _____  Bonus _____ N/A _____  Non-exempt ☒ Exempt ☐ | |
| **RATE CHANGE** | New Rate $ _____ 12.00 _____  Effective Date _____ 9/1/97 _____ <br> Present Rate $ _____ 10.00 _____ <br> Merit ☒ Promotion ☐ Decrease ☐  Other _____ <br> Previous Increase Date _____ None _____  Amount $ _____ per _____ Type _____ | |
| **SEPARATION** | Resignation ☐ Discharge ☐ Retirement ☐  Reason _____ <br> <br> Leave of absence ☐ From _____ to _____ Type _____ <br> Last Day Worked _____ | |
| **APPROVALS** | *BEW*  9/1/97 <br> BRANCH OR DEPT. MANAGER  DATE | *EMW*  9-1-97 <br> DIVISION V.P.  DATE <br> *James E. Speer* <br> PERSONNEL DEPARTMENT |

**Timekeeping**

Supervisors monitor hours worked through time cards and time reports.

## Timekeeping

Another area in which internal control is important is timekeeping. Hourly employees are usually required to record time worked by "punching" a time clock. The time of arrival and departure are automatically recorded by the employee when he or she inserts a time card into the clock. The time card for Michael Jordan is shown in Illustration 11-9.

In large companies, time clock procedures are often monitored by a supervisor or security guard to make sure an employee punches only one card. At the end of the pay period, the employee's supervisor is required to approve the hours shown by signing the time card. When overtime hours are involved, approval by a supervisor is usually mandatory to guard against unauthorized overtime. The approved time card is then sent to the payroll department. For salaried employees, a manually prepared weekly or monthly time report kept by a supervisor may be used to record time worked.

**Preparing the Payroll**

Two (or more) employees verify payroll amounts; supervisor approves.

## Preparing the Payroll

The payroll is prepared in the payroll department on the basis of two sources of input: (1) personnel department authorizations and (2) approved time cards. Because of the numerous calculations involved in determining gross wages and payroll deductions, it is customary for a second payroll department employee, working independently, to verify all amounts, and a payroll department supervisor then approves the payroll. The payroll department is also responsible for preparing (but not signing) payroll checks, maintaining payroll records, and preparing payroll tax returns.

**ILLUSTRATION 11-9**

*Time card*

| PAY PERIOD ENDING | | |
|---|---|---|
| No. 17 | | 1/14/99 |

NAME Michael Jordan

| EXTRA TIME | | | REGULAR TIME | |
|---|---|---|---|---|
| | | 1st Day | A.M. IN | 8:58 |
| | | | NOON OUT | 12:00 |
| | | | IN | 1:00 |
| | | | P.M. OUT | 5:01 |
| | | 2nd Day | A.M. IN | 9:00 |
| | | | NOON OUT | 11:59 |
| | | | IN | 12:59 |
| | | | P.M. OUT | 5:00 |
| | THIS | 3rd Day | A.M. IN | 8:59 |
| | | | NOON OUT | 12:01 |
| | SIDE | | IN | 1:01 |
| | | | P.M. OUT | 5:00 |
| 5:00 | | 4th Day | A.M. IN | 9:00 |
| 9:00 | | | NOON OUT | 12:00 |
| | OUT | | IN | 1:00 |
| | | | P.M. OUT | 5:00 |
| | | 5th Day | A.M. IN | 8:57 |
| | | | NOON OUT | 11:58 |
| | | | IN | 1:00 |
| | | | P.M. OUT | 5:01 |
| | | 6th Day | A.M. IN | 8:00 |
| | | | NOON OUT | 1:00 |
| | | | IN | |
| | | | P.M. OUT | |
| | | 7th Day | A.M. IN | |
| | | | NOON OUT | |
| | | | IN | |
| | | | P.M. OUT | |
| TOTAL 4 | | | TOTAL | 40 |

## Paying the Payroll

The payroll is paid by the treasurer's department. **Payment by check minimizes the risk of loss from theft, and the endorsed check provides proof of payment.** For good internal control, payroll checks should be prenumbered, and all checks should be accounted for. All checks must be signed by the treasurer (or a designated agent), and their distribution to employees should be controlled by the treasurer's department. Checks may be distributed by the treasurer or paymaster.

If the payroll is paid in currency, it is customary to have a second person count the cash in each pay envelope and for the paymaster to obtain a signed receipt from the employee upon payment. Thus, if alleged discrepancies arise, adequate safeguards have been established to protect each party involved.

**Paying the Payroll**

Treasurer signs and distributes checks.

## Determining the Payroll

Determining the payroll involves computing (1) gross earnings, (2) payroll deductions, and (3) net pay.

### Gross Earnings

Gross earnings are the total compensation earned by an employee. There are three major types of gross earnings: wages, salaries, and bonuses.

Total **wages** for an employee are determined by multiplying the hours worked by the hourly rate of pay. In addition to the hourly pay rate, most companies are required by law to pay hourly workers a minimum of one and one-half times the regular hourly rate for overtime work in excess of 8 hours per day

**7**

STUDY
OBJECTIVE
......................................
Compute and record the payroll for a pay period.

or 40 hours per week. For example, companies involved in interstate commerce are required by the Federal Fair Labor Standards Act to pay one and one-half times the regular wage rate. In addition, many employers pay overtime rates for work done at night, on weekends, and on holidays. The computation of Michael Jordan's gross earnings (total wages) for the 44 hours shown on his time card for the weekly pay period ending January 14 is as follows:

**ILLUSTRATION 11-10**

*Computation of total wages*

| Type of Pay | Hours | × | Rate | = | Gross Earnings |
|---|---|---|---|---|---|
| Regular | 40 | × | $12.00 | = | $480.00 |
| Overtime | 4 | × | 18.00 | = | 72.00 |
| **Total wages** | | | | | **$552.00** |

This computation assumes that Jordan receives one and one-half times his regular hourly rate ($12.00 × 1.5) for his overtime hours. Union contracts often require that overtime rates be as much as twice the regular rates.

The **salary** for an employee is generally based on a monthly or yearly rate rather than on an hourly basis. These rates are then applied ratably to the payroll periods used by the company. Most executive and administrative positions are salaried. The Federal Fair Labor Standards Act does not require overtime pay for such positions. In the Casper College example at the beginning of the chapter, overtime is not given to either faculty or administrative personnel.

Many companies have bonus agreements for management personnel and other employees. For example, a recent survey indicated that over 94% of the largest manufacturing companies in the United States provide annual bonuses to their key executives. Bonus arrangements may be based on such factors as increased sales or net income. Bonuses may be paid in cash and/or by granting executives and employees the opportunity to acquire shares of stock in the company at favorable prices (called stock option plans). Bonuses have become very lucrative, as companies attempt to retain the services of key executives—so lucrative, in fact, that they have come under intense public scrutiny.

**ETHICS NOTE**

Bonuses often reward outstanding individual performance; however, a successful corporation also needs considerable teamwork. A challenge is to motivate individuals while preventing an unethical team member from taking another's idea for his or her own advantage.

# ACCOUNTING IN ACTION
## Business Insight

In a recent year Amoco Corporation employees received shares of the company's stock equal to 3.5% of their salaries as a result of the company's strong total return to shareholders in the previous year. Amoco's performance plan awards shares to employees when the return to shareholders meets or exceeds the average of seven major oil companies. Amoco's return of 18.8% was the second highest of the group of competitors.

## Payroll Deductions

As anyone who has received a paycheck knows, gross earnings are usually very different from the amount actually received. The difference is attributable to payroll deductions. Payroll deductions do not result in payroll tax expense to the employer. The employer serves only as a collection agency, and it subsequently transfers the deductions to the government and designated recipients. Payroll deductions may be mandatory or voluntary. The former are required by law and consist of FICA taxes and income taxes. The latter are at the option of the employee. Illustration 11-11 summarizes the types of payroll deductions.

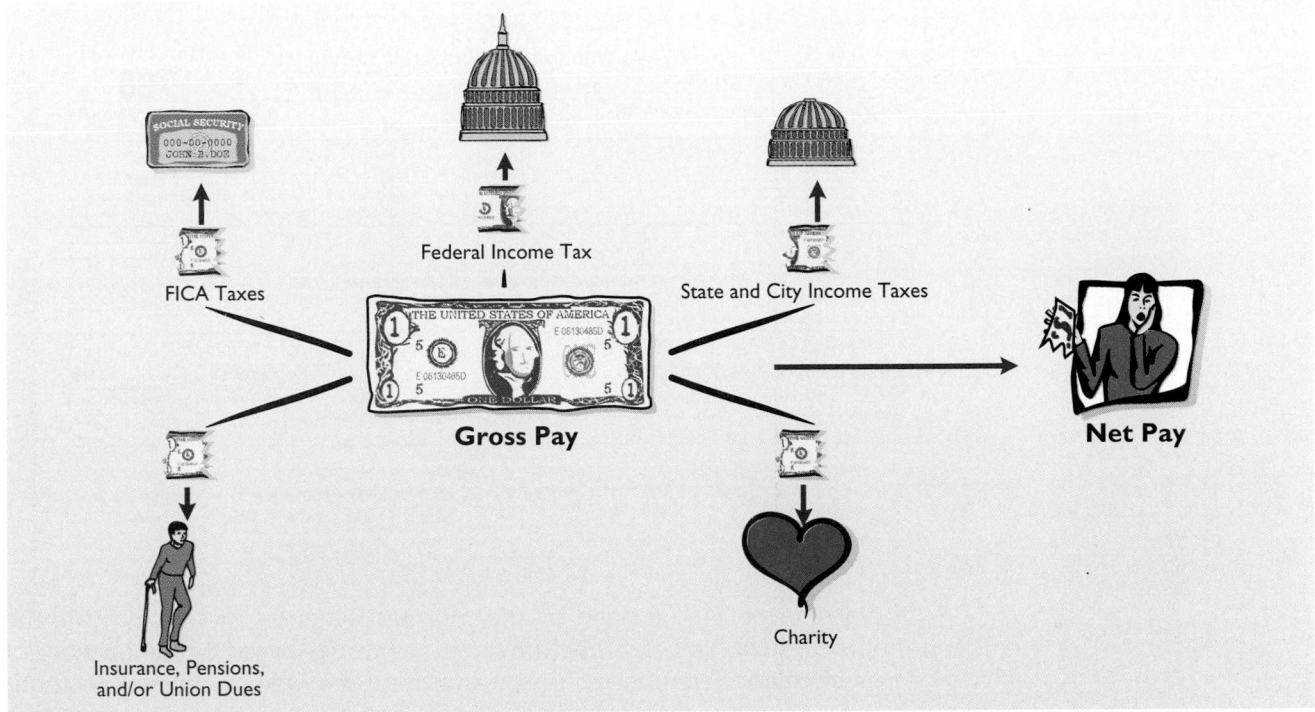

FICA Taxes

Federal Income Tax

State and City Income Taxes

Gross Pay

Charity

Insurance, Pensions, and/or Union Dues

Net Pay

**ILLUSTRATION 11-11**

*Payroll deductions*

**FICA Taxes.** In 1937 Congress enacted the Federal Insurance Contribution Act (FICA). **FICA taxes are designed to provide workers with supplemental retirement, employment disability, and medical benefits.** In 1965, benefits were expanded to include Medicare for individuals over 65 years of age. The benefits are financed by a tax levied on employees' earnings. FICA taxes are commonly referred to as **Social Security taxes**.

The tax rate and the tax base for FICA taxes are set by Congress, and they are changed intermittently. When FICA taxes were first imposed, the rate was 1% on the first $3,000 of gross earnings, or a maximum of $30 per year. The rate and base have changed dramatically since that time! In 1998, that rate was 7.65% (6.2% Social Security and 1.45% Medicare) on the first $68,400 of gross earnings for each employee, or a maximum of $5,232.60.[1] For purpose of illustration in this chapter, we will assume a rate of 8% on the first $65,000 of gross earnings, or a maximum of $5,200. Using the 8% rate, the FICA withholding for Jordan for the weekly pay period ending January 14 is $44.16 ($552 × 8%).

**Income Taxes.** Under the United States pay-as-you-go system of federal income taxes, employers are required to withhold income taxes from employees each pay period. The amount to be withheld is determined by three variables: (1) the employee's gross earnings; (2) the number of allowances claimed by the employee for herself or himself, his or her spouse, and other dependents; and (3) the length of the pay period. **To indicate to the Internal Revenue Service the number of allowances claimed, the employee must complete an Employee's Withholding Allowance Certificate (Form W-4).** As shown in Illustration 11-12, Michael Jordan claims two allowances on his W-4.

---

[1]The Medicare provision also includes a tax of 1.45% on gross earnings in excess of $68,400. In the interest of simplification, our end-of-chapter assignment material ignores this 1.45% charge. We assume zero withholdings on gross earnings above $65,000.

**ILLUSTRATION 11-12**

*W-4 form*

| Form **W-4** | **Employee's Withholding Allowance Certificate** | OMB No. 1545-0010 |
|---|---|---|

Department of the Treasury Internal Revenue Service ► For Privacy Act and Paperwork Reduction Act Notice, see page 2.

**1998**

| 1 Type or print your first name and middle initial | Last name | 2 Your social security number |
|---|---|---|
| Michael | Jordan | 329-36-9547 |

Home address (number and street or rural route)
2345 Mifflin Ave.

**3** ☐ Single ☒ Married ☐ Married, but withhold at higher Single rate.
**Note:** *If married, but legally separated, or spouse is a nonresident alien, check the Single box.*

City or town, State, and ZIP code
Hampton, MI 48292

**4** If your last name differs from that on your social security card, check here and call 1-800-772-1213 for a new card . . . . . . ► ☐

5 Total number of allowances you are claiming (from line H above or from the worksheet on page 2 if they apply) . . . **5** 2
6 Additional amount, if any, you want withheld from each paycheck . . . . . . . . . . **6** $
7 I claim exemption from withholding for 1998, and I certify that I meet BOTH of the following conditions for exemption:
• Last year I had a right to a refund of ALL Federal income tax withheld because I had NO tax liability AND
• This year I expect a refund of ALL Federal income tax withheld because I expect to have NO tax liability.
If you meet both conditions, enter "Exempt" here . . . . . . . . . ► **7**

Under penalties of perjury, I certify that I am entitled to the number of withholding allowances claimed on this certificate or entitled to claim exempt status.

Employee's signature ►  *Michael Jordan*     Date ►  September 1   , 19 99

| 8 Employer's name and address (Employer: Complete 8 and 10 only if sending to the IRS) | 9 Office code (optional) | 10 Employer identification number |
|---|---|---|

Cat. No. 102200

Withholding tables furnished by the Internal Revenue Service indicate the amount of income tax to be withheld from gross wages based on the number of allowances claimed. Separate tables are provided for weekly, biweekly, semimonthly, and monthly pay periods. The portion of the withholding tax table for Michael Jordan (assuming he earns $552 per week) is shown in Illustration 11-13. As indicated in the table, for a weekly salary of $552 with two allowances, the income tax to be withheld is $49.

**ILLUSTRATION 11-13**

*Withholding tax table*

**MARRIED** Persons — **WEEKLY** Payroll Period
(For Wages Paid in 1998)

| If the wages are – | | And the number of withholding allowances claimed is – | | | | | | | | | | |
|---|---|---|---|---|---|---|---|---|---|---|---|---|
| At least | But less than | 0 | 1 | 2 | 3 | 4 | 5 | 6 | 7 | 8 | 9 | 10 |
| | | The amount of income tax to be withheld is – | | | | | | | | | | |
| 490 | 500 | 56 | 48 | 40 | 32 | 24 | 17 | 9 | 1 | 0 | 0 | 0 |
| 500 | 510 | 57 | 49 | 42 | 34 | 26 | 18 | 10 | 3 | 0 | 0 | 0 |
| 510 | 520 | 59 | 51 | 43 | 35 | 27 | 20 | 12 | 4 | 0 | 0 | 0 |
| 520 | 530 | 60 | 52 | 45 | 37 | 29 | 21 | 13 | 6 | 0 | 0 | 0 |
| 530 | 540 | 62 | 54 | 46 | 38 | 30 | 23 | 15 | 7 | 0 | 0 | 0 |
| 540 | 550 | 63 | 55 | 48 | 40 | 32 | 24 | 16 | 9 | 1 | 0 | 0 |
| 550 | 560 | 65 | 57 | **49** | 41 | 33 | 26 | 18 | 10 | 2 | 0 | 0 |
| 560 | 570 | 66 | 58 | 51 | 43 | 35 | 27 | 19 | 12 | 4 | 0 | 0 |
| 570 | 580 | 68 | 60 | 52 | 44 | 36 | 29 | 21 | 13 | 5 | 0 | 0 |
| 580 | 590 | 69 | 61 | 54 | 46 | 38 | 30 | 22 | 15 | 7 | 0 | 0 |
| 590 | 600 | 71 | 63 | 55 | 47 | 39 | 32 | 24 | 16 | 8 | 1 | 0 |
| 600 | 610 | 72 | 64 | 57 | 49 | 41 | 33 | 25 | 18 | 10 | 2 | 0 |
| 610 | 620 | 74 | 66 | 58 | 50 | 42 | 35 | 27 | 19 | 11 | 4 | 0 |
| 620 | 630 | 75 | 67 | 60 | 52 | 44 | 36 | 28 | 21 | 13 | 5 | 0 |
| 630 | 640 | 77 | 69 | 61 | 53 | 45 | 38 | 30 | 22 | 14 | 7 | 0 |
| 640 | 650 | 78 | 70 | 63 | 55 | 47 | 39 | 31 | 24 | 16 | 8 | 0 |
| 650 | 660 | 80 | 72 | 64 | 56 | 48 | 41 | 33 | 25 | 17 | 10 | 2 |
| 660 | 670 | 81 | 73 | 66 | 58 | 50 | 42 | 34 | 27 | 19 | 11 | 3 |
| 670 | 680 | 83 | 75 | 67 | 59 | 51 | 44 | 36 | 28 | 20 | 13 | 5 |
| 680 | 690 | 84 | 76 | 69 | 61 | 53 | 45 | 37 | 30 | 22 | 14 | 6 |

Most states and some cities also require employers to withhold income taxes from the earnings of employees. As a general rule, the amounts to be withheld are determined by applying a percentage specified in the state revenue code to the amount withheld for the federal income tax or to the employee's earnings. For the sake of simplicity, we have assumed that Jordan's wages are subject to state income taxes of 2%, or $11.04 (2% $\times$ $552).

There is no limit on the amount of gross earnings subject to income tax withholdings. In fact, the higher the earnings, the higher the amount of taxes withheld.

**Other Deductions.** Employees may voluntarily authorize withholdings for charitable, retirement, and other purposes. All voluntary deductions from gross earnings should be authorized in writing by the employee. The authorization(s) may be made individually or as part of a group plan. Deductions for charitable organizations, such as the United Fund, or for financial arrangements, such as U.S. savings bonds and repayment of loans from company credit unions are made individually. In contrast, deductions for union dues, health and life insurance, and pension plans are often made on a group basis. For purpose of illustration, we will assume that Jordan has voluntary deductions of $10 for the United Fund and $5 for union dues.

## Net Pay

**ALTERNATIVE TERMINOLOGY**
Net pay is also called *take-home pay.*

Net pay is determined by subtracting payroll deductions from gross earnings. For Michael Jordan, net pay for the pay period is $432.80, computed as follows:

**ILLUSTRATION 11-14**
*Computation of net pay*

| | | |
|---|---:|---:|
| Gross earnings | | $552.00 |
| Payroll deductions: | | |
| FICA taxes | $44.16 | |
| Federal income taxes | 49.00 | |
| State income taxes | 11.04 | |
| United Fund | 10.00 | |
| Union dues | 5.00 | 119.20 |
| **Net pay** | | **$432.80** |

Assuming that Michael Jordan's wages for each week during the year are $552, total wages for the year are $28,704 (52 $\times$ $552). Thus, all of Jordan's wages are subject to FICA tax during the year. However, if an employee's wages are $1,350 per week, or $70,200 for the year, only the first $65,000 is subject to FICA taxes. In such case, the maximum FICA withholdings would be $5,200 ($65,000 $\times$ 8%).

# Recording the Payroll

Recording the payroll involves maintaining payroll department records, recognizing payroll expenses and liabilities, and recording payment of the payroll.

## Maintaining Payroll Department Records

To comply with state and federal laws, an employer must keep a cumulative record of each employee's gross earnings, deductions, and net pay during the year. The record that provides this information and other essential data is the **employee earnings record**. Michael Jordan's employee earnings record is shown in Illustration 11-15.

**ILLUSTRATION 11-15**

*Employee earnings record*

### ACADEMY COMPANY
### Employee Earnings Record
### For the Year 1999

| Name | Michael Jordan | Address | 2345 Mifflin Ave. |
|---|---|---|---|
| Social Security Number | 329-36-9547 | | Hampton, Michigan 48292 |
| Date of Birth | December 24, 1962 | Telephone | 555-238-9051 |
| Date Employed | September 1, 1995 | Date Employment Ended | |
| Sex | Male | Exemptions | 2 |
| Single _____ | Married ___X___ | | |

| 1999 Period Ending | Total Hours | Gross Earnings | | | | Deductions | | | | | | Payment | |
|---|---|---|---|---|---|---|---|---|---|---|---|---|---|
| | | Regular | Overtime | Total | Cumulative | FICA | Fed. Inc. Tax | State Inc. Tax | United Fund | Union Dues | Total | Net Amount | Check No. |
| 1/7 | 42 | 480.00 | 36.00 | 516.00 | 516.00 | 41.28 | 43.00 | 10.32 | 10.00 | 5.00 | 109.60 | 406.40 | 974 |
| 1/14 | 44 | 480.00 | 72.00 | 552.00 | 1,068.00 | 44.16 | 49.00 | 11.04 | 10.00 | 5.00 | 119.20 | 432.80 | 1028 |
| 1/21 | 43 | 480.00 | 54.00 | 534.00 | 1,602.00 | 42.72 | 46.00 | 10.68 | 10.00 | 5.00 | 114.40 | 419.60 | 1077 |
| 1/28 | 42 | 480.00 | 36.00 | 516.00 | 2,118.00 | 41.28 | 43.00 | 10.32 | 10.00 | 5.00 | 109.60 | 406.40 | 1133 |
| Jan. Total | | 1,920.00 | 198.00 | 2,118.00 | | 169.44 | 181.00 | 42.36 | 40.00 | 20.00 | 452.80 | 1,665.20 | |

A separate earnings record is kept for each employee, and it is updated after each pay period. The cumulative payroll data on the earnings record are used by the employer in (1) determining when an employee has earned the maximum earnings subject to FICA taxes, (2) filing state and federal payroll tax returns (as explained later in the chapter), and (3) providing each employee with a statement of gross earnings and tax withholdings for the year, as shown in Illustration 11-19 on page 492. In the opening story about Casper College, Dianna Webb's report that lists the year-to-date totals is the employee earnings record.

In addition to employee earnings records, many companies find it useful to prepare a **payroll register** to accumulate the gross earnings, deductions, and net pay by employee for each pay period. It provides the documentation for preparing a paycheck for each employee. The payroll register is presented in Illustration 11-16, with the data for Michael Jordan shown in the wages section. In this example, Academy Company's total payroll is $17,210, as shown in the gross pay column.

Note that this record is a listing of each employee's payroll data for the pay period. In some companies, a payroll register is a journal or book of original entry, and postings are made directly to ledger accounts from the register. In other companies, the payroll register is a memorandum record that provides the data for a general journal entry and subsequent posting to the ledger accounts. In the Academy Company situation, the latter procedure is followed. The main payroll report provided by the computer at Casper College is the payroll register.

**ILLUSTRATION 11-16**

*Payroll register*

### ACADEMY COMPANY
### Payroll Register
### For the Week Ending January 14, 1999

| | | Earnings | | | Deductions | | | | | | Paid | | Accounts Debited | |
|---|---|---|---|---|---|---|---|---|---|---|---|---|---|---|
| Employee | Total Hours | Regular | Over-time | Gross | FICA | Federal Income Tax | State Income Tax | United Fund | Union Dues | Total | Net Pay | Check No. | Office Salaries Expense | Wages Expense |
| Office Salaries | | | | | | | | | | | | | | |
| Arnold, Patricia | 40 | 580.00 | | 580.00 | 46.40 | 61.00 | 11.60 | 15.00 | | 134.00 | 446.00 | 998 | 580.00 | |
| Canton, Matthew | 40 | 590.00 | | 590.00 | 47.20 | 63.00 | 11.80 | 20.00 | | 142.00 | 448.00 | 999 | 590.00 | |
| Mueller, William | 40 | 530.00 | | 530.00 | 42.40 | 54.00 | 10.60 | 11.00 | | 118.00 | 412.0 | 1000 | 530.00 | |
| Subtotal | | 5,200.00 | | 5,200.00 | 416.00 | 1,090.00 | 104.00 | 120.00 | | 1,730.00 | 3,470.00 | | 5,200.00 | |
| Wages | | | | | | | | | | | | | | |
| Bennett, Robin | 42 | 480.00 | 36.00 | 516.00 | 41.28 | 43.00 | 10.32 | 18.00 | 5.00 | 117.60 | 398.40 | 1025 | | 516.00 |
| Jordan, Michael | 44 | 480.00 | 72.00 | 552.00 | 44.16 | 49.00 | 11.04 | 10.00 | 5.00 | 119.20 | 432.80 | 1028 | | 552.00 |
| Milroy, Lee | 43 | 480.00 | 54.00 | 534.00 | 42.72 | 46.00 | 10.68 | 10.00 | 5.00 | 114.40 | 419.60 | 1029 | | 534.00 |
| Subtotal | | 11,000.00 | 1,010.00 | 12,010.00 | 960.80 | 2,400.00 | 240.20 | 301.50 | 115.00 | 4,017.50 | 7,992.50 | | | 12,010.00 |
| Total | | 16,200.00 | 1,010.00 | 17,210.00 | 1,376.80 | 3,490.00 | 344.20 | 421.50 | 115.00 | 5,747.50 | 11,462.50 | | 5,200.00 | 12,010.00 |

## Recognizing Payroll Expenses and Liabilities

From the payroll register in Illustration 11-16, a journal entry is made to record the payroll. For the week ending January 14 the entry is:

| Jan. 14 | Office Salaries Expense ⎱ Gross pay | 5,200.00 | |
|---|---|---|---|
| | Wages Expense ⎰ | 12,010.00 | |
| | FICA Taxes Payable | | 1,376.80 |
| | Federal Income Taxes Payable | | 3,490.00 |
| | State Income Taxes Payable | | 344.20 |
| | United Fund Payable | | 421.50 |
| | Union Dues Payable | | 115.00 |
| | Salaries and Wages Payable — net pay | | 11,462.50 |
| | (To record payroll for the week ending January 14) | | |

| A | = | L | + | OE |
|---|---|---|---|---|
| | | + 1,376.80 | | − 5,200.00 |
| | | + 3,490.00 | | − 12,010.00 |
| | | + 344.20 | | |
| | | + 421.50 | | |
| | | + 115.00 | | |
| | | + 11,462.50 | | |

Specific liability accounts are credited for the mandatory and voluntary deductions made during the pay period. In the example, debits to Office Salaries and Wages Expense are used for gross earnings because office workers are on a salary and other employees are paid on an hourly rate. In other cases, there may be additional debits such as Store Salaries and Sales Salaries. The amount credited to Salaries and Wages Payable is the sum of the individual checks the employees will receive.

## Recording Payment of the Payroll

Payment by check is made either from the employer's regular bank account or a payroll bank account. Each check is usually accompanied by a detachable **state-**

ment of earnings document that shows the employee's gross earnings, payroll deductions, and net pay. The Academy Company uses its regular bank account for payroll checks. The check and statement of earnings for Michael Jordan are shown in Illustration 11-17.

**ILLUSTRATION 11-17**

*Check and statement of earnings*

**HELPFUL HINT**
Do any of the income tax liabilities result in payroll tax expense for the employer? Answer: No, the employer is acting only as a collection agent for the government.

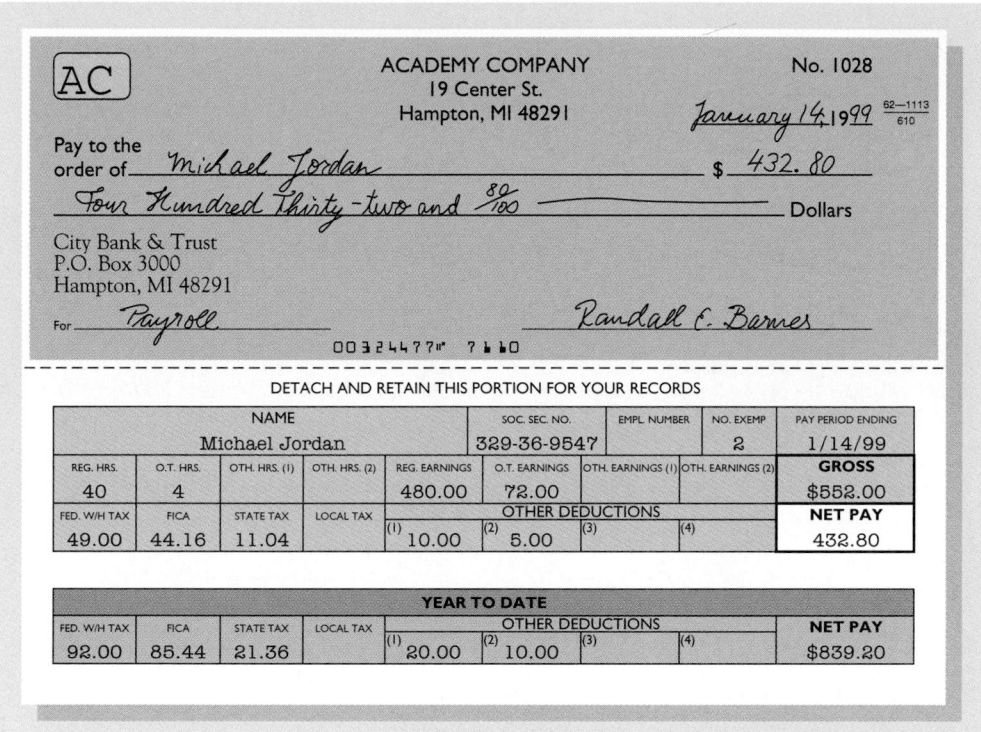

| NAME | | | | | SOC. SEC. NO. | | EMPL. NUMBER | NO. EXEMP | PAY PERIOD ENDING |
|------|---|---|---|---|------------|---|---|---|---|
| Michael Jordan | | | | | 329-36-9547 | | | 2 | 1/14/99 |
| REG. HRS. | O.T. HRS. | OTH. HRS. (1) | OTH. HRS. (2) | REG. EARNINGS | O.T. EARNINGS | OTH. EARNINGS (1) | OTH. EARNINGS (2) | | **GROSS** |
| 40 | 4 | | | 480.00 | 72.00 | | | | $552.00 |
| FED. W/H TAX | FICA | STATE TAX | LOCAL TAX | OTHER DEDUCTIONS | | | | | **NET PAY** |
| 49.00 | 44.16 | 11.04 | | (1) 10.00 | (2) 5.00 | (3) | (4) | | 432.80 |

| YEAR TO DATE | | | | | | | | |
|------|---|---|---|---|---|---|---|---|
| FED. W/H TAX | FICA | STATE TAX | LOCAL TAX | OTHER DEDUCTIONS | | | | **NET PAY** |
| 92.00 | 85.44 | 21.36 | | (1) 20.00 | (2) 10.00 | (3) | (4) | $839.20 |

Following payment of the payroll, the check numbers are entered in the payroll register. The entry to record payment of the payroll for Academy Company is as follows:

| A | = | L | + OE |
|---|---|---|------|
| − 11,462.50 | | − 11,462.50 | |

| Jan. 14 | Salaries and Wages Payable | 11,462.50 | |
|---------|---------------------------|-----------|-----------|
| | Cash | | 11,462.50 |
| | (To record payment of payroll) | | |

When currency is used in payment, one check is prepared for the net pay. The check is then cashed, and the coins and currency are inserted in individual pay envelopes for disbursement to individual employees.

## TECHNOLOGY IN ACTION

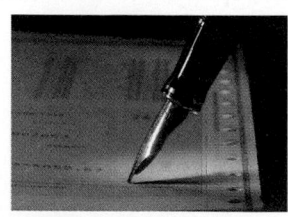

In addition to supplying the entry to record the payroll, the output for a computerized payroll system would include (1) payroll checks, (2) a payroll check register sorted by check and department, and (3) updated employee earnings records which become the source for monthly, quarterly, and annual reporting of wages to taxing agencies.

# BEFORE YOU GO ON . . .

## Review It

1. Identify two internal control procedures that are applicable to each payroll function.
2. What are the primary sources of gross earnings?
3. What payroll deductions are (a) mandatory and (b) voluntary?
4. What account titles are used in recording a payroll, assuming only mandatory payroll deductions are involved?

## Do It

Your cousin Stan is establishing a house-cleaning business and will have a number of employees working for him. From his prior work experience, he is aware that documentation procedures are an important part of internal control. However, he is confused about the difference between an employee earnings record and a payroll register. He asks you to explain the principal differences, because he wants to be sure that he sets up the proper payroll procedures.

*Reasoning:* You may need to review the material on payroll department records and study Illustrations 11-15 and 11-16 in order to identify and explain the differences for Stan.

*Solution:* An employee earnings record is kept for *each* employee. It shows gross earnings, payroll deductions, and net pay for each pay period. It provides cumulative payroll data for that employee. In contrast, a payroll register is a listing of *all* employees' gross earnings, payroll deductions, and net pay for each pay period. It is the documentation for preparing paychecks and for recording the payroll. Of course, Stan will need to keep both documents.

*Related exercise material:* BE11–7, BE11–8, BE11–9, E11–8, E11–9, E11–10, and E11–11.

THE
NAVIGATOR

# Employer Payroll Taxes

Payroll tax expense for businesses and educational institutions, like Casper College, results from three taxes **levied on employers** by governmental agencies. These taxes are: FICA, federal unemployment tax, and state unemployment tax. Each of these taxes plus such items as paid vacations and pensions are collectively referred to as "fringe benefits." As indicated earlier, the cost of fringe benefits in many companies is substantial.

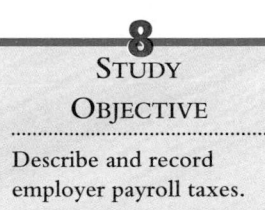

**8**
STUDY
OBJECTIVE
..............................................
Describe and record
employer payroll taxes.

## FICA Taxes

We have seen that each employee must pay FICA taxes. The employer must match each employee's FICA contribution. The matching contribution results in **payroll tax expense** to the employer. The employer's tax is subject to the same rate and maximum earnings applicable to the employee. The account, FICA Taxes Payable, is used for both the employee's and the employer's FICA contributions. For the January 14 payroll, Academy Company's FICA tax is $1,376.80 ($17,210.00 × 8%).

## Federal Unemployment Taxes

The Federal Unemployment Tax Act (FUTA) is another feature of the federal social security program. **Federal unemployment taxes** provide benefits for a limited period of time to employees who lose their jobs through no fault of their own. Under provisions of the Act, the employer is required to pay a tax of 6.2%

**HELPFUL HINT**
FICA taxes are paid both by the employer and employee. Federal unemployment taxes and (in most states) the state unemployment taxes are borne entirely by the employer.

on the first $7,000 of gross wages paid to each employee during a calendar year. The law, however, allows the employer a maximum credit of 5.4% on the federal rate for contributions to state unemployment taxes. Because of this provision, state unemployment tax laws generally provide for a 5.4% rate, and the effective federal unemployment tax rate becomes 0.8% (6.2% − 5.4%). This tax is borne **entirely by the employer**; there is no deduction or withholding from employees. The account Federal Unemployment Taxes Payable is used to recognize this liability. The federal unemployment tax for Academy Company for the January 14 payroll is $137.68 ($17,210.00 × 0.8%).

## State Unemployment Taxes

All states have unemployment compensation programs under state unemployment tax acts (SUTA). Like federal unemployment taxes, state unemployment taxes provide benefits to employees who lose their jobs. These taxes are levied on employers.[2] The basic rate is usually 5.4% on the first $7,000 of wages paid to an employee during the year. The basic rate is adjusted according to the employer's experience rating: Companies with a history of unstable employment may pay more than the basic rate. Companies with a history of stable employment may pay less than 5.4%. Regardless of the rate paid, the credit on the federal unemployment tax is still 5.4%. The account State Unemployment Taxes Payable is used for this liability. The state unemployment tax for Academy Company for the January 14 payroll is $929.34 ($17,210.00 × 5.4%). Illustration 11-18 summarizes the types of employer payroll taxes.

**ILLUSTRATION 11-18**

*Employer payroll taxes*

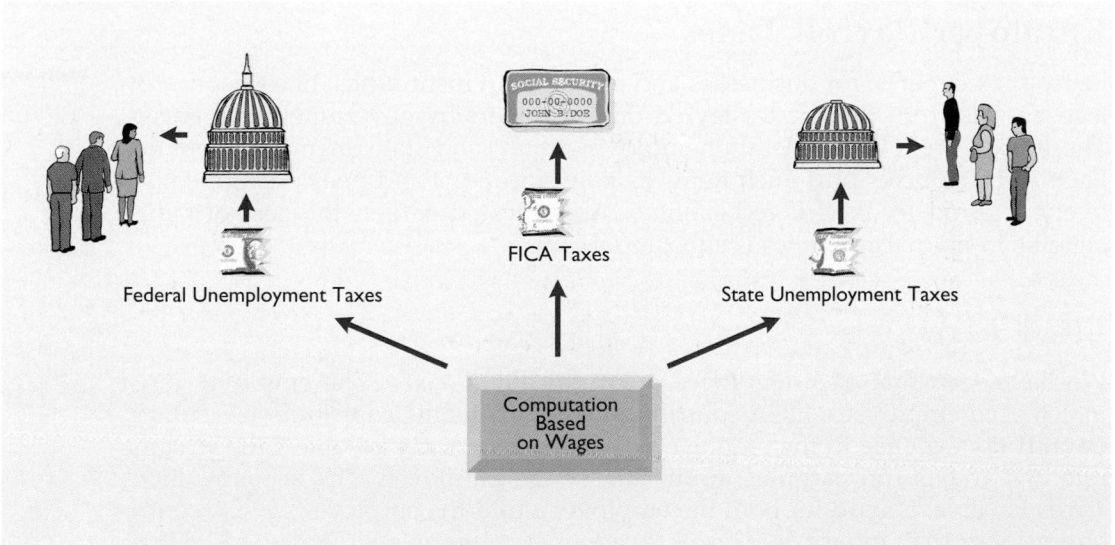

## Recording Employer Payroll Taxes

Employer payroll taxes are usually recorded at the same time the payroll is journalized. The entire amount of gross pay ($17,210.00) shown in the payroll register in Illustration 11-16 is subject to each of the three taxes mentioned above. Ac-

---

[2]In a few states, the employee is also required to make a contribution. In this textbook, including the homework, we will assume that the tax is only on the employer.

cordingly, the entry to record the payroll tax expense associated with the January 14 payroll is:

| Jan. 14 | Payroll Tax Expense | 2,443.82 | |
|---|---|---|---|
| | FICA Taxes Payable | | 1,376.80 |
| | Federal Unemployment Taxes Payable | | 137.68 |
| | State Unemployment Taxes Payable | | 929.34 |
| | (To record employer's payroll taxes on January 14 payroll) | | |

| A | = | L | + | OE |
|---|---|---|---|---|
| | | +1,376.80 | | −2,443.82 |
| | | + 137.68 | | |
| | | + 929.34 | | |

Separate liability accounts are used instead of a single credit to Payroll Taxes Payable, because these liabilities are payable to different taxing authorities at different dates. The liability accounts are classified as current liabilities since they will be paid within the next year. Payroll Tax Expense is classified on the income statement as an operating expense.

## Filing and Remitting Payroll Taxes

Preparation of payroll tax returns is the responsibility of the payroll department; payment of the taxes is made by the treasurer's department. Much of the information for the returns is obtained from employee earnings records.

For purposes of reporting and remitting, FICA taxes and federal income taxes withheld are combined. **The taxes must be reported quarterly**, no later than one month following the close of each quarter. The remitting requirements depend on the amount of taxes withheld and the length of the pay period. Remittances are made through deposits in either a Federal Reserve Bank or an authorized commercial bank.

## ACCOUNTING IN ACTION
### Business Insight

The owner of a newly restored Victorian hotel, nestled in a small Massachusetts town, skipped payment of withholding taxes for three quarters because of cash flow problems. Before long, he received a call from the IRS. After months of haggling, the hotel owner was told that unless he paid the $70,000 owed, the IRS would be forced to liquidate the hotel, the land, and dozens of antiques in the inn, which had taken him and his wife years to acquire.

As this story indicates, cash-hungry small businesses are often tempted to skip or delay paying withholding taxes. Increasingly, federal and state agencies are cracking down on such cheaters. Penalties for late or nonpayment can be devastating: Fines are levied at the rate of 5% of taxes owed for *each month* a payroll tax isn't filed. And in cases where nothing is paid, penalties of 100% can be applied, with interest added, to the unpaid balance. Under the 100% penalty, the government can padlock the doors, seize assets, and hold the officers or certain other employees personally responsible for the penalties.

What happened to the Massachusetts hotel owner? He's now working on a repayment plan, rather than lose his years of hard work.

Federal unemployment taxes are generally filed and remitted **annually** on or before January 31 of the subsequent year. Earlier payments are required, however, when the tax exceeds a specified amount. State unemployment taxes usually must be filed and paid by the **end of the month following each quarter**. When payroll taxes are paid, payroll liability accounts are debited and cash is credited.

The employer is also required to provide each employee with a Wage and Tax Statement (Form W-2) by January 31 following the end of a calendar year.

This statement shows gross earnings, FICA taxes withheld, and income taxes withheld for the year. The required W-2 form for Michael Jordan, using assumed annual data, is shown in Illustration 11-19.

**ILLUSTRATION 11-19**

*W-2 form*

| Form **W-2 Wage and Tax Statement** | | | |
|---|---|---|---|
| **1** Control number | | OMB No. 1545-0008 | |

| **2** Employer's name, address and ZIP code | **3** Employer's identification number | | **4** Employer's State number |
|---|---|---|---|
| Academy Company<br>19 Center St.<br>Hampton, MI 48291 | 36-2167852 | | |

| **5** Stat. employee | Deceased | Legal rep. | 942 emp. | Subtotal | Void |
|---|---|---|---|---|---|
| ☐ | ☐ | ☐ | ☐ | ☐ | ☐ |

| **6** Allocated tips | **7** Advance EIC payment |
|---|---|

| **8** Employee's social security number | **9** Federal income tax withheld | **10** Wages, tips, other compensation | **11** Social security tax withheld |
|---|---|---|---|
| 329-36-9547 | $2,248.00 | $26,300.00 | $2,104.00 |

| **12** Employee's name, address, and ZIP code | **13** Social security wages | **14** Social security tips |
|---|---|---|
| | $26,300.00 | |

| **16** |
|---|

Michael Jordan
2345 Mifflin Ave.
Hampton, MI 48292

| **17** State income tax | **18** State wages, tips, etc. | **19** Name of State |
|---|---|---|
| $526.00 | | Michigan |

| **20** Local income tax | **21** Local wages, tips, etc. | **22** Name of locality |
|---|---|---|

The employer must send a copy of each employee's Wage and Tax Statement to the Social Security Administration. This agency subsequently furnishes the Internal Revenue Service with the income data required.

# BEFORE YOU GO ON . . .

## Review It

1. What payroll taxes are levied on employers?
2. What accounts are involved in accruing employer payroll taxes?

## Do It

In January, the payroll supervisor determines that gross earnings in Halo Company are $70,000. All earnings are subject to 8% FICA taxes, 5.4% state unemployment taxes, and 0.8% federal unemployment taxes. You are asked to record the employer's payroll taxes.

*Reasoning:* In recording the taxes, you should remember that (1) the total expense can be debited to one account and (2) separate accounts are required for each of the three liabilities.

*Solution:* The entry to record the employer's payroll taxes is:

| | | |
|---|---|---|
| Payroll Tax Expense | 9,940 | |
|    FICA Taxes Payable ($70,000 × 8%) | | 5,600 |
|    Federal Unemployment Taxes Payable ($70,000 × 0.8%) | | 560 |
|    State Unemployment Taxes Payable ($70,000 × 5.4%) | | 3,780 |
|    (To record employer's payroll taxes on January<br>   payroll) | | |

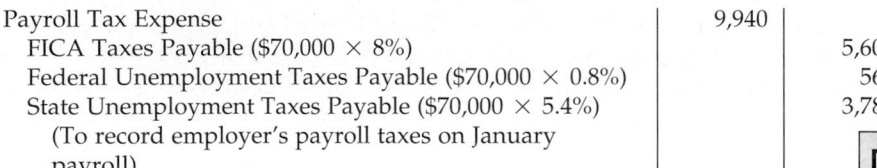

THE NAVIGATOR

*Related exercise material: BE11–10, E11–10, and E11–12.*

# Additional Fringe Benefits

**9**
STUDY
OBJECTIVE
................................................
Identify additional fringe
benefits associated with
employee compensation.

In addition to the three payroll tax fringe benefits, employers incur other substantial fringe benefit costs. Two of the most important are paid absences and postretirement benefits.

## Paid Absences

Employees often have rights to receive compensation for future absences when certain conditions of employment are met. The compensation may pertain to paid vacations, sick pay benefits, and paid holidays. When the payment of such compensation is **probable** and the amount can be **reasonably estimated**, a liability should be accrued for paid future absences. When the amount cannot be reasonably estimated, the potential liability should be disclosed. Ordinarily, vacation pay is the only paid absence that is accrued; the other types of paid absences are only disclosed.[3]

To illustrate, assume that Academy Company employees are entitled to one day's vacation for each month worked. If thirty employees earn an average of $110 per day in a given month, the accrual for vacation benefits in one month is $3,300. The liability is recognized at the end of the month by the following adjusting entry:

| Jan. 31 | Vacation Benefits Expense | 3,300 | |
| | Vacation Benefits Payable | | 3,300 |
| | (To accrue vacation benefits expense) | | |

| A | = | L | + | OE |
|---|---|---|---|---|
| | | +3,300 | | −3,300 |

This accrual is required by the matching principle. Vacation Benefits Expense is reported as an operating expense in the income statement, and Vacation Benefits Payable is reported as a current liability in the balance sheet. When vacation benefits are paid, Vacation Benefits Payable is debited and Cash is credited. For example if the above benefits for ten employees are paid in July, the entry is:

| July 31 | Vacation Benefits Payable | 1,100 | |
| | Cash | | 1,100 |
| | (To record payment of vacation benefits) | | |

| A | = | L | + | OE |
|---|---|---|---|---|
| −1,100 | | −1,100 | | |

The magnitude of unpaid absences has gained employers' attention. Consider the case of an assistant superintendent of schools who worked for around 20 years and rarely took a vacation or sick day. A month or so before she retired, the school district discovered that she was due nearly $30,000 in accrued benefits. Yet the liability was never accrued.

## Postretirement Benefits

Postretirement benefits consist of benefits provided by employers to retired employees for (1) health care and life insurance and (2) pensions. For many years the accounting for postretirement benefits was on a cash basis. However, both types of postretirement benefits are now accounted for on the accrual basis.

**Postretirement Health Care and Life Insurance Benefits.** Providing medical and related health care benefits for retirees—at one time an inexpensive and highly effective way of generating employee goodwill—has turned into one of corporate America's most worrisome financial problems. Runaway medical costs, early

---

[3]The typical U.S. company provides an average of 12 days of paid vacations for its employees, at an average cost of 5% of gross earnings.

retirement, and increased longevity are sending the liability for retiree health plans through the roof.

Many companies began offering retiree health care coverage in the form of Medicare supplements in the 1960s. Almost all plans operated on a pay-as-you-go basis—the companies simply paid for the bills as they came in, rather than setting aside funds to meet the cost of future benefits. These plans were accounted for on the cash basis rather than the accrual basis. However, the FASB concluded that shareholders and creditors should know the amount of the employer's obligations. As a result, employers must now use the **accrual basis** in accounting for postretirement health care and life insurance benefits.

# ACCOUNTING IN ACTION
## Business Insight

The battle over fringe benefits is increasing in intensity as benefits outpace wages and salaries. Growing faster than pay, benefits equaled 38% of wages and salaries in a recent year. While vacations and other forms of paid leave still take the biggest bite of the benefits pie, medical costs are the fastest-growing item.

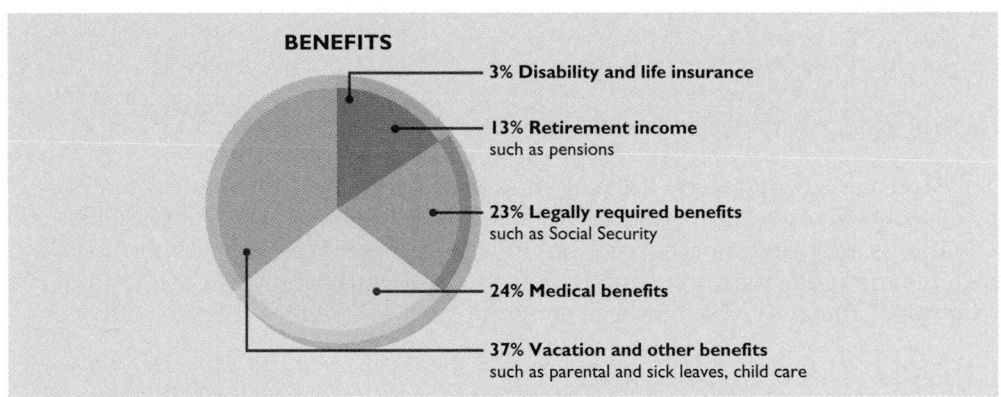

**BENEFITS**

- 3% Disability and life insurance
- 13% Retirement income such as pensions
- 23% Legally required benefits such as Social Security
- 24% Medical benefits
- 37% Vacation and other benefits such as parental and sick leaves, child care

**HELPFUL HINT**
With more than $4 trillion in assets overall, both public and private pension funds comprise over one-fifth of the total financial assets in the United States today—and these figures are growing.

**ILLUSTRATION 11-20**

*Parties in a pension plan*

**Pension Plans.** A **pension plan** is an agreement whereby an employer provides benefits (payments) to employees after they retire. Over 50 million workers currently participate in pension plans in the United States. The need for proper administration of and good accounting for pension plans becomes apparent when one appreciates the size of existing pension funds. Most pension plans are subject to the provisions of ERISA (Employee Retirement Income Security Act), a law enacted to curb abuses in the administration and funding of such plans.

Three parties are generally involved in a pension plan. The **employer** (company) sponsors the pension plan. The **plan administrator** receives the contributions from the employer, invests the pension assets, and makes the benefit payments to the **pension recipients** (retired employees). Illustration 11-20 shows the three distinct parties involved in a pension plan and indicates the flow of cash among them.

An employer-financed pension is part of the employees' compensation. The provisions of ERISA establish the minimum contribution that a company must make each year toward employee pensions. The company records the pension costs as an expense while the employees are working because that is when the company receives benefits from the employees' services. Generally the pension expense is reported as an operating expense in the company's income statement. Frequently, the amount contributed by the company to the pension plan is different from the amount of the pension expense. A **liability** is recognized when the pension expense to date is **more than** the company's contributions to date; an **asset** is recognized when the pension expense to date is **less than** the company's contributions to date. Further consideration of the accounting for pension plans is left for more advanced courses.

## BEFORE YOU GO ON . . .

### Review It

1. What accounts are involved in accruing and paying vacation benefits?
2. What basis should be used in accounting for postretirement benefits?

## A LOOK BACK AT OUR FEATURE STORY

Refer back to the story about Casper College at the beginning of the chapter, and answer the following questions:

1. In addition to taxes withheld from employees, what employer payroll taxes are remitted by Casper College to governmental agencies?
2. For each of the four payroll functions, give examples of internal control procedures used by Casper College.

*Solution:*

1. In addition to the amounts withheld for FICA and federal income taxes, Casper College must match the FICA taxes withheld from employees and must pay federal and state unemployment taxes.
2. *Hiring:* Contracts are issued to faculty and administrative personnel, and their pay must be approved.

   *Timekeeping:* Timecards are used for hourly employees.

   *Preparing the payroll:* Deductions from gross earnings for each employee are documented. For example, there must be a W-4 form for withholding federal income taxes. The computer prepares useful reports that include maintaining a payroll record for each employee.

   *Paying the payroll:* Although these procedures are not explicitly stated, the payroll checks generated by the computer would be signed by the school's chief financial officer, and paychecks would be distributed directly to employees.

THE
NAVIGATOR

## DEMONSTRATION PROBLEM

Indiana Jones Company had the following selected transactions:

Feb. 1  Signs a $50,000 6-month 9%-interest-bearing note payable to CitiBank receiving $50,000 in cash.

10  Cash register sales total $43,200 which includes an 8% sales tax.

28  The payroll for the month consists of Sales Salaries $32,000 and Office Salaries $18,000. All wages are subject to 8% FICA taxes. A total of $8,900 federal income taxes are withheld. The salaries are paid on March 1.

Feb 28 The following adjustment data are developed:

1. Interest expense of $375 has been incurred on the note.
2. Employer payroll taxes include 8% FICA taxes, a 5.4% state unemployment tax, and a 0.8% federal unemployment tax.
3. Some sales were made under warranty. Of the units sold under warranty, 350 are expected to become defective. Repair costs are estimated to be $40 per unit.

*Instructions*

(a) Journalize the February transactions.
(b) Journalize the adjusting entries at February 28.

## SOLUTION TO DEMONSTRATION PROBLEM

(a) Feb.  1 | Cash | 50,000 |
| Notes Payable | | 50,000 |
| (Issued 6-month 9%-interest-bearing note to CitiBank) | | |

10 | Cash | 43,200 |
| Sales ($43,200 ÷ 1.08) | | 40,000 |
| Sales Taxes Payable ($40,000 × 8%) | | 3,200 |
| (To record sales and sales taxes payable) | | |

28 | Sales Salaries Expense | 32,000 |
| Office Salaries Expense | 18,000 |
| FICA Taxes Payable (8% × $50,000) | | 4,000 |
| Federal Income Taxes Payable | | 8,900 |
| Salaries Payable | | 37,100 |
| (To record February salaries) | | |

(b) Feb. 28 | Interest Expense | 375 |
| Interest Payable | | 375 |
| (To record accrued interest for February) | | |

28 | Payroll Tax Expense | 7,100 |
| FICA Taxes Payable | | 4,000 |
| Federal Unemployment Taxes Payable | | 400 |
| (0.8% × $50,000) | | |
| State Unemployment Taxes Payable | | 2,700 |
| (5.4% × $50,000) | | |
| (To record employer's payroll taxes on February payroll) | | |

28 | Warranty Expense (350 × $40) | 14,000 |
| Estimated Warranty Liability | | 14,000 |
| (To record estimated product warranty liability) | | |

THE NAVIGATOR

# SUMMARY OF STUDY OBJECTIVES

**1. *Explain a current liability and identify the major types of current liabilities.*** A current liability is a debt that can reasonably be expected to be paid (1) from existing current assets or through the creation of other current liabilities, and (2) within one year or the operating cycle, whichever is longer. The major types of current liabilities are notes payable, accounts payable, sales taxes payable, unearned revenues, and accrued liabilities such as taxes, salaries and wages, and interest payable.

**2. *Describe the accounting for notes payable.*** When a promissory note is interest-bearing, the amount of assets received upon the issuance of the note is generally equal to the face value of the note, and interest expense is accrued over the life of the note. At maturity, the amount paid is equal to the face value of the note plus accrued interest.

**3. *Explain the accounting for other current liabilities.*** Sales taxes payable are recorded at the time the related sales occur. The company serves as a collection agent for the taxing authority. Sales taxes are not an expense to the company. Unearned revenues are initially recorded in an unearned revenue account. As the revenue is earned, a transfer from unearned revenue to earned revenue occurs. The current maturities of long-term debt should be reported as a current liability in the balance sheet.

**4. *Explain the methods for the financial statement presentation and analysis of current liabilities.*** The nature and amount of each current liability should be reported in the balance sheet or in schedules in the notes accompanying the statements. The liquidity of a company may be analyzed by computing working capital and the current ratio.

**5. *Describe the accounting and disclosure requirements for contingent liabilities.*** If it is probable (likely to occur) that the contingency will happen and the amount is reasonably estimable, the liability should be recorded in the accounts. However, if it is only reasonably possible (it could happen), then it need be disclosed only in the notes to the financial statements. If the possibility that the contingency will happen is remote (unlikely to occur), it need not be recorded or disclosed.

**6. *Discuss the objectives of internal control for payroll.*** The objectives of internal control for payroll are (1) to safeguard company assets against unauthorized payments of payrolls, and (2) to assure the accuracy and reliability of the accounting records pertaining to payrolls.

**7. *Compute and record the payroll for a pay period.*** The computation of the payroll involves gross earnings, payroll deductions, and net pay. In recording the payroll, salaries (or wages) expense is debited for gross earnings, individual tax and other liability accounts are credited for payroll deductions, and salaries (wages) payable is credited for net pay. When the payroll is paid, Salaries and Wages Payable is debited, and Cash is credited.

**8. *Describe and record employer payroll taxes.*** Employer payroll taxes consist of FICA, federal unemployment taxes, and state unemployment taxes. The taxes are usually accrued at the time the payroll is recorded by debiting Payroll Tax Expense and crediting separate liability accounts for each type of tax.

**9. *Identify additional fringe benefits associated with employee compensation.*** Additional fringe benefits associated with wages are paid absences (paid vacations, sick pay benefits, and paid holidays), and postretirement benefits (health care and life insurance and pensions). Both types of benefits should be accounted for on the accrual basis.

# GLOSSARY

**Bonus** Compensation to management personnel and other employees, based on factors such as increased sales or the amount of net income. (p. 482)

**Contingent liability** A potential liability that may become an actual liability in the future. (p. 475)

**Current ratio** A measure of a company's liquidity, computed as current assets divided by current liabilities. (p. 475)

**Employee earnings record** A cumulative record of each employee's gross earnings, deductions, and net pay during the year. (p. 486)

**Employee's Withholding Allowance Certificate (Form W-4)** An Internal Revenue Service form on which the employee indicates the number of allowances claimed for withholding federal income taxes. (p. 483)

**Federal unemployment taxes** Taxes imposed on the employer that provide benefits for a limited time period to employees who lose their jobs through no fault of their own. (p. 489)

**FICA taxes** Taxes designed to provide workers with supplemental retirement, employment disability, and medical benefits. (p. 483)

**Gross earnings** Total compensation earned by an employee. (p. 481)

**Net pay** Gross earnings less payroll deductions. (p. 485)

**Payroll deductions** Deductions from gross earnings to determine the amount of a paycheck. (p. 482)

**Payroll register** A payroll record that accumulates the gross earnings, deductions, and net pay by employee for each pay period. (p. 486)

**Pension plan** An agreement whereby an employer provides benefits to employees after they retire. (p. 494)

**Postretirement benefits** Payments by employers to retired employees for health care, life insurance, and pensions. (p. 493)

**Salaries** Employee pay that is based on a fixed amount rather than an hourly rate. (p. 478)

**Statement of earnings** A document attached to a paycheck that indicates the employee's gross earnings, payroll deductions, and net pay. (p. 488)

**State unemployment taxes** Taxes imposed on the employer that provide benefits to employees who lose their jobs. (p. 490)

**Wage and Tax Statement (Form W-2)** A form showing gross earnings, FICA taxes withheld, and income taxes withheld which is prepared annually by an employer for each employee. (p. 491)

**Wages** Amounts paid to employees based on a rate per hour or on a piece-work basis. (p. 478)

**Working capital** A measure of a company's liquidity, computed as the excess of current assets over current liabilities. (p. 475)

# SELF-STUDY QUESTIONS

Answers are at the end of the chapter.

**(SO 1)** 1. The time period for classifying a liability as current is one year or the operating cycle, whichever is:
   a. longer.
   b. shorter.
   c. probable.
   d. possible.

**(SO 1)** 2. To be classified as a current liability, a debt must be expected to be paid:
   a. out of existing current assets.
   b. by creating other current liabilities.
   c. within two years.
   d. both (a) and (b).

**(SO 2)** 3. Julie Gilbert Company borrows $88,500 on September 1, 1999, from the Sandwich State Bank by signing an $88,500 12%, one-year note. What is the accrued interest at December 31, 1999?
   a. $2,655.
   b. $3,540.
   c. $4,425.
   d. $10,620.

**(SO 3)** 4. Reeves Company has total proceeds from sales of $4,515. If the proceeds include sales taxes of 5%, the amount to be credited to Sales is:
   a. $4,000.
   b. $4,300.
   c. $4,289.25.
   d. No correct answer given.

**(SO 4)** 5. Working capital is calculated as:
   a. current assets minus current liabilities.
   b. total assets minus total liabilities.
   c. long-term liabilities minus current liabilities.
   d. both (b) and (c).

**(SO 5)** 6. A contingent liability should be recorded in the accounts when:
   a. It is probable the contingency will happen but the amount cannot be reasonably estimated.

   b. It is reasonably possible the contingency will happen and the amount can be reasonably estimated.
   c. It is probable the contingency will happen and the amount can be reasonably estimated.
   d. It is reasonably possible the contingency will happen but the amount cannot be reasonably estimated.

**(SO 5)** 7. At December 31, Hanes Company prepares an adjusting entry for a product warranty contract. Which of the following accounts is/are included in the entry?
   a. Miscellaneous Expense.
   b. Estimated Warranty Liability.
   c. Repair Parts/Wages Payable.
   d. Both (a) and (b).

**(SO 6)** 8. The department that should pay the payroll is the:
   a. timekeeping department.
   b. personnel department.
   c. payroll department.
   d. treasurer's department.

**(SO 7)** 9. J. Barr earns $14 per hour for a 40-hour week and $21 per hour for any overtime work. If Barr works 45 hours in a week, gross earnings are:
   a. $560.
   b. $630.
   c. $650.
   d. $665.

**(SO 8)** 10. Employer payroll taxes do not include:
   a. federal unemployment taxes.
   b. state unemployment taxes.
   c. federal income taxes.
   d. FICA taxes.

**(SO 9)** 11. Which of the following is *not* an additional fringe benefit?
   a. Postretirement pensions.
   b. Paid absences.
   c. Paid vacations.
   d. Salaries.

# QUESTIONS

1. Rubin Ely believes a current liability is a debt that can be expected to be paid in one year. Is Rubin correct? Explain.

2. Mesa Verde Company obtains $25,000 in cash by signing a 9%, 6-month $25,000 note payable to First Bank on July 1. Mesa Verde's fiscal year ends on September 30. What information should be reported for the note payable in the annual financial statements?

3. (a) Your roommate says, "Sales taxes are reported as an expense in the income statement." Do you agree? Explain.

(b) Planet Hollywood has cash proceeds from sales of $10,400. This amount includes $400 of sales taxes. Give the entry to record the proceeds.

4. Colorado State sold 10,000 season football tickets at $80 each for its five-game home schedule. What entries should be made (a) when the tickets were sold and (b) after each game?

5. What is liquidity? What are two measures of liquidity?

6. What is a contingent liability? Give an example of a contingent liability that is usually recorded in the accounts.

7. Under what circumstances is a contingent liability disclosed only in the notes to the financial statements? Under what circumstances is a contingent liability not recorded in the accounts nor disclosed in the notes to the financial statements?

8. You are a newly hired accountant with Goh Company. On your first day, the controller asks you to identify the main internal control objectives related to payroll accounting. How would you respond?

9. What are the four functions associated with payroll activities?

10. What is the difference between gross pay and net pay? Which amount should a company record as wages or salaries expense?

11. Which payroll tax is levied on both employers and employees?

12. Are the federal and state income taxes withheld from employee paychecks a payroll tax expense for the employer? Explain your answer.

13. What do the following acronyms stand for: FICA, FUTA, and SUTA?

14. What information is shown on a W-4 statement? A W-2 statement?

15. Distinguish between the two types of payroll deductions and give examples of each.

16. What are the primary uses of the employee earnings record?

17. (a) Identify the three types of employer payroll taxes. (b) How are tax liability accounts and payroll tax expense classified in the financial statements?

18. Identify three additional types of fringe benefits associated with employees' compensation.

19. Often during job interviews, the candidate asks the potential employer about the firm's paid absences policy. What are paid absences? How are they accounted for?

20. What are two types of postretirement benefits? During what years does the FASB advocate expensing the employer's costs of these postretirement benefits?

21. What basis of accounting for the employer's cost of postretirement health care and life insurance benefits has been used by most companies, and what basis does the FASB now require? Explain the basic difference between these methods in accounting for postretirement benefit costs.

22. Identify the three parties in a pension plan. What role does each party have in the plan?

# BRIEF EXERCISES

**BE11–1**   Toledo Company has the following obligations at December 31: (a) a note payable for $100,000 due in 2 years, (b) a 10-year mortgage payable of $300,000 payable in ten $30,000 annual payments, (c) interest payable of $15,000 on the mortgage, and (d) accounts payable of $60,000. For each obligation, indicate whether it should be classified as a current liability. (Assume an operating cycle of less than one year.)

*Identify whether obligations are current liabilities.*
*(SO 1)*

**BE11–2**   Chi Ho Company borrows $80,000 on July 1 from the bank by signing an $80,000 10%, one-year note payable. Prepare the journal entries to record (a) the proceeds of the note and (b) accrued interest at December 31, assuming adjusting entries are made only at the end of the year.

*Prepare entries for an interest-bearing note payable.*
*(SO 2)*

**BE11–3**   Hobbes Auto Supply does not segregate sales and sales taxes at the time of sale. The register total for March 16 is $8,925. All sales are subject to a 5% sales tax. Compute sales taxes payable and make the entry to record sales taxes payable and sales.

*Compute and record sales taxes payable.*
*(SO 3)*

**BE11–4**   Western Michigan University sells 4,000 season basketball tickets at $60 each for its 12-game home schedule. Give the entry to record (a) the sale of the season tickets and (b) the revenue earned by playing the first home game.

*Prepare entries for unearned revenues.*
*(SO 3)*

**BE11–5**   Motorola's 1995 financial statements contain the following selected data (in millions):

*Analyze liquidity.*
*(SO 4)*

| | |
|---|---|
| Current assets | $10,510 |
| Total assets | 22,801 |
| Current liabilities | 7,791 |
| Total liabilities | 11,753 |

Compute the following ratios:

(a) Working capital
(b) Current ratio

**BE11–6**   On December 1, Kearns Company introduces a new product that includes a one-year warranty on parts. In December 1,000 units are sold. Management believes that 5% of the units will be defective and that the average warranty costs will be $60 per unit. Prepare the adjusting entry at December 31 to accrue the estimated warranty cost.

*Prepare adjusting entry for warranty costs.*
*(SO 5)*

*Identify payroll functions.*
*(SO 6)*

**BE11–7**    Marmon Company has the following payroll procedures:

1. Supervisor approves overtime work.
2. The personnel department prepares hiring authorization forms for new hires.
3. A second payroll department employee verifies payroll calculations.
4. The treasurer's department pays employees.

Identify the payroll function to which each procedure pertains.

*Compute gross earnings and net pay.*
*(SO 7)*

**BE11–8**    Ellen Monroe's regular hourly wage rate is $14, and she receives an hourly rate of $21 for work in excess of 40 hours. During a January pay period, Ellen works 45 hours. Ellen's federal income tax withholding is $70, and she has no voluntary deductions. Compute Ellen Monroe's gross earnings and net pay for the pay period.

*Record a payroll and the payment of wages.*
*(SO 7)*

**BE11–9**    Data for Ellen Monroe are presented in BE11–8. Prepare the journal entries to record (a) Ellen's pay for the period and (b) the payment of Ellen's wages. Use January 15 for the end of the pay period and the payment date.

*Record employer payroll taxes.*
*(SO 8)*

**BE11–10**    In January, gross earnings in the Poh Company totaled $55,000. All earnings are subject to 8% FICA taxes, 5.4% state unemployment taxes, and 0.8% federal unemployment taxes. Prepare the entry to record January payroll tax expense.

*Record estimated vacation benefits.*
*(SO 9)*

**BE11–11**    At Drexel Company employees are entitled to one day's vacation for each month worked. In January, 50 employees worked the full month. Record the vacation pay liability for January assuming the average daily pay for each employee is $140.

# EXERCISES

............................................................................................

*Prepare entries for interest-bearing notes.*
*(SO 2)*

**E11–1**    On June 1 Norfolk Company borrows $60,000 from First Bank on a 6-month, $60,000, 12% note.

**Instructions**

(a) Prepare the entry on June 1.
(b) Prepare the adjusting entry on June 30.
(c) Prepare the entry at maturity (December 1), assuming monthly adjusting entries have been made through November 30.
(d) What was the total financing cost (interest expense)?

*Journalize sales and related taxes.*
*(SO 3)*

**E11–2**    In providing accounting services to small businesses, you encounter the following situations pertaining to cash sales:

1. Jardine Company rings up sales and sales taxes separately on its cash register. On April 10, the register totals are sales $25,000 and sales taxes $2,000.
2. Lim Company does not segregate sales and sales taxes. Its register total for April 15 is $14,840, which includes a 6% sales tax.

**Instructions**

Prepare the entry to record the sales transactions and related taxes for each client.

*Journalize unearned subscription revenue.*
*(SO 3)*

**E11–3**    Redlands Company publishes a monthly sports magazine, *Fishing Preview*. Subscriptions to the magazine cost $30 per year. During November 1999, Redlands sells 6,000 subscriptions beginning with the December issue. Redlands prepares financial statements quarterly and recognizes subscription revenue earned at the end of the quarter. The company uses the accounts Unearned Subscription Revenue and Subscription Revenue.

**Instructions**

(a) Prepare the entry in November for the receipt of the subscriptions.
(b) Prepare the adjusting entry at December 31, 1999, to record subscription revenue earned in December of 1999.
(c) Prepare the adjusting entry at March 31, 2000, to record subscription revenue earned in the first quarter of 2000.

*Record estimated liability and expense for warranties.*
*(SO 5)*

**E11–4**    Sangsoo Company sells automatic can openers under a 75-day warranty for defective merchandise. Based on past experience, Sangsoo estimates that 3% of the units sold will become defective during the warranty period. Management estimates that the average cost of replacing or repairing a defective unit is $15. The units sold and units defective that occurred during the last 2 months of 1999 are as follows:

| Month | Units Sold | Units Defective Prior to December 31 |
|---|---|---|
| November | 30,000 | 600 |
| December | 32,000 | 400 |

**Instructions**

(a) Determine the estimated warranty liability at December 31 for the units sold in November and December.

(b) Prepare the journal entries to record the estimated liability for warranties and the costs (assume actual costs of $15,000) incurred in honoring 1,000 warranty claims.

(c) Give the entry to record the honoring of 400 warranty contracts in January at an average cost of $15.

**E11–5** Lieberman Company has the following liability accounts after posting adjusting entries: Accounts Payable $66,000, Unearned Ticket Revenue $24,000, Estimated Warranty Liability $18,000, Interest Payable $12,000, Mortgage Payable $120,000, Notes Payable $80,000, and Sales Taxes Payable $10,000. Assume the company's operating cycle is less than one year, ticket revenue will be earned within 1 year, warranty costs are expected to be incurred within 1 year, and the notes mature in 3 years.

*Prepare the current liability section of the balance sheet. (SO 1, 2, 3, 4, 5)*

**Instructions**

(a) Prepare the current liability section of the balance sheet, assuming $30,000 of the mortgage is payable next year.

(b) Comment on Lieberman Company's liquidity, assuming total current assets are $300,000.

**E11–6** McDonald's 1995 financial statements contained the following selected data (in millions):

*Calculate liquidity ratios; discuss impact of unrecorded obligations on liquidity and solvency. (SO 4)*

| | | | |
|---|---|---|---|
| Current assets ✓ | $   955.8 | Interest expense | $   340.2 |
| Total assets | 15,414.6 | Income taxes | 741.8 |
| Current liabilities | 1,794.9 | Net income | 1,427.3 |
| Total liabilities | 7,553.3 | | |
| Cash ✓ | 334.8 | | |
| Accounts receivable ✓ | 377.3 | | |
| Notes receivable | 36.3 | | |

**Instructions**

Compute these values:

1. Working capital
2. Current ratio

**E11–7** The following financial data were reported by Minnesota Mining and Manufacturing (3M) for 1997 and 1996 ($ in millions):

*Calculate current ratios and working capital before and after paying accounts payable. (SO 4)*

| MINNESOTA MINING AND MANUFACTURING Balance Sheets (partial) | | |
|---|---|---|
| | **1997** | **1996** |
| Current assets | | |
| Cash and cash equivalents | $  230 | $  583 |
| Other securities | 247 | 161 |
| Accounts receivable, net | 2,434 | 2,504 |
| Inventories | 2,399 | 2,264 |
| Other current assets | 858 | 974 |
| Total current assets | $6,168 | $6,486 |
| Current liabilities | $3,983 | $3,606 |

*Compute net pay and record pay for one employee.*
*(SO 7)*

**Instructions**
(a) Calculate the current ratio and working capital for 3M for 1997 and 1996.
(b) Suppose that at the end of 1997 3M management used $500 million cash to pay off $500 million of accounts payable. How would its current ratio and working capital have changed?

**E11–8**   Karen Ortega's regular hourly wage rate is $16.00, and she receives a wage of 1½ times the regular hourly rate for work in excess of 40 hours. During a March weekly pay period Karen worked 42 hours. Her gross earnings prior to the current week were $19,000. Karen is married and claims three withholding allowances. Her only voluntary deduction is for group hospitalization insurance at $10.00 per week.

**Instructions**
(a) Compute the following amounts for Karen's wages for the current week.
   1. Gross earnings.
   2. FICA taxes. (Assume an 8% rate on maximum of $65,000.)
   3. Federal income taxes withheld. (Use the withholding table in the text, page 484.)
   4. State income taxes withheld. (Assume a 2.0% rate.)
   5. Net pay.
(b) Record Karen's pay, assuming she is an office computer operator.

*Compute maximum FICA deductions.*
*(SO 7)*

**E11–9**   Employee earnings records for Kokomo Company reveal the following gross earnings for four employees through the pay period of December 15.

|  |  |  |  |
|---|---|---|---|
| K. Ostman | $63,500 | B. Sailors | $64,300 |
| C. Leggett | $64,600 | R. Ryan | $65,000 |

For the pay period ending December 31, each employee's gross earnings is $1,000. The FICA tax rate is 8% on gross earnings of $65,000.

**Instructions**
Compute the FICA withholdings that should be made for each employee for the December 31 pay period. (Show computations.)

*Prepare payroll register and record payroll and payroll tax expense.*
*(SO 7, 8)*

**E11–10**   Egypt Company has the following data for the weekly payroll ending January 31.

| Employee | M | T | W | T | F | S | Hourly Rate | Federal Income Tax Withholding | Health Insurance |
|---|---|---|---|---|---|---|---|---|---|
| S. Rude | 8 | 8 | 9 | 8 | 10 | 3 | $10 | $34 | $10 |
| N. Siena | 8 | 8 | 8 | 8 | 8 | 2 | 12 | 37 | 15 |
| V. Ruble | 9 | 10 | 8 | 8 | 9 | 0 | 12 | 58 | 15 |

Employees are paid 1½ times the regular hourly rate for all hours worked in excess of 40 hours per week. FICA taxes are 8% on the first $65,000 of gross earnings. Egypt Company is subject to 5.4% state unemployment taxes and 0.8% federal unemployment taxes on the first $7,000 of gross earnings.

**Instructions**
(a) Prepare the payroll register for the weekly payroll.
(b) Prepare the journal entry to record the payroll and Egypt's payroll tax expense.

*Compute missing payroll amounts and record payroll.*
*(SO 7)*

**E11–11**   Selected data from a February payroll register for Mira Stice Company are presented below with some amounts intentionally omitted.

| Gross earnings: |  |  |  |
|---|---|---|---|
| Regular | $8,900 | State income taxes | $ (3) |
| Overtime | (1) | Union dues | 100 |
| Total | (2) | Total deductions | (4) |
| Deductions: |  | Net pay | $7,760 |
| FICA taxes | $ 800 | Accounts debited: |  |
| Federal income taxes | 1,140 | Warehouse wages | (5) |
|  |  | Store wages | $4,000 |

FICA taxes are 8% and state income taxes are 2% of gross earnings.

**Instructions**
(a) Fill in the missing amounts.
(b) Journalize the February payroll and the payment of the payroll.

**E11–12** According to a payroll register summary of Strickland Company, the amount of employees' gross pay in December was $800,000, of which $60,000 was not subject to FICA tax and $760,000 was not subject to state and federal unemployment taxes.

*Determine employer's payroll taxes and record payroll tax expense.*
*(SO 8)*

**Instructions**
(a) Determine the employer's payroll tax expense for the month, using the following rates: FICA, 8%; state unemployment, 5.4%; federal unemployment, 0.8%.
(b) Prepare the journal entry to record December payroll tax expense.

**E11–13** Austin Company has two fringe benefit plans for its employees:

*Prepare adjusting entries for fringe benefits.*
*(SO 9)*

1. It grants employees 2 days' vacation for each month worked. Ten employees worked the entire month of March at an average daily wage of $100 per employee.
2. In its pension plan the company recognizes 10% of gross earnings as an expense. Gross earnings in March were $30,000. No contribution has been made to the pension fund.

**Instructions**
Prepare the adjusting entries at March 31.

# PROBLEMS: SET A

**P11–1A** On January 1, 1999, the ledger of Calcutta Company contains the following liability accounts.

*Prepare current liability entries, adjusting entries, and current liability section.*
*(SO 1, 2, 3, 4, 5)*

| | |
|---|---|
| Accounts Payable | $42,500 |
| Sales Taxes Payable | 5,600 |
| Unearned Service Revenue | 15,000 |

During January the following selected transactions occurred:

Jan. 1 Borrowed $15,000 in cash from Midland Bank on a 4-month, 12%, $15,000 note.
  5 Sold merchandise for cash totaling $7,800 which includes 4% sales taxes.
  12 Provided services for customers who had made advance payments of $8,000. (Credit Service Revenue.)
  14 Paid state treasurer's department for sales taxes collected in December 1998 $5,600.
  20 Sold 500 units of a new product on credit at $52 per unit, plus 4% sales tax. This new product is subject to a 1-year warranty.
  25 Sold merchandise for cash totaling $11,440, which includes 4% sales taxes.

**Instructions**
(a) Journalize the January transactions.
(b) Journalize the adjusting entries at January 31 for (1) the outstanding note payable, and (2) estimated warranty liability, assuming warranty costs are expected to equal 8% of sales of the new product.
(c) Prepare the current liability section of the balance sheet at January 31, 1999. Assume no change in Accounts Payable.

**P11–2A** Villanova Drug Store has four employees who are paid on an hourly basis plus time-and-one-half for all hours worked in excess of 40 a week. Payroll data for the week ended February 15, 1999, are presented below:

*Prepare payroll register and payroll entries.*
*(SO 7, 8)*

| Employees | Hours Worked | Hourly Rate | Federal Income Tax Withholdings | United Fund |
|---|---|---|---|---|
| O. Stratton | 39 | $13.00 | $ ? | $ –0– |
| E. Muse | 42 | 12.00 | ? | 5.00 |
| A. Horton | 44 | 12.00 | 58 | 7.50 |
| F. Lupino | 46 | 12.00 | 33 | 5.00 |

Stratton and Muse are married. They claim 2 and 4 withholding allowances, respectively. The following tax rates are applicable: FICA 8%, state income taxes 3%, state unemployment taxes 5.4%, and federal unemployment 0.8%. The first three employees are sales clerks (store wages expense), and the other employee performs administrative duties (office wages expense).

*Instructions*

(a) Prepare a payroll register for the weekly payroll. (Use the wage-bracket withholding table in the text for federal income tax withholdings.)

(b) Journalize the payroll on February 15, 1999, and the accrual of employer payroll taxes.

(c) Journalize the payment of the payroll on February 16, 1999.

(d) Journalize the deposit in a federal reserve bank on February 28, 1999, of the FICA and federal income taxes payable to the government.

*Identify internal control weaknesses and make recommendations for improvement.*
*(SO 6)*

**P11–3A** The payroll procedures used by three different companies are described below:

1. In Sanchez Company each employee is required to mark the hours worked on a clock card. At the end of each pay period, the employee must have this clock card approved by the department manager. The approved card is then given to the payroll department by the employee. Subsequently, the treasurer's department pays the employee by check.

2. In Moscove Company clock cards and time clocks are used. At the end of each pay period, the department manager initials the cards, indicates the rates of pay, and sends them to payroll. A payroll register is prepared from the cards by the payroll department. Cash equal to the total net pay in each department is given to the department manager, who pays the employees in cash.

3. In Dominion Company employees are required to record hours worked on clock cards by "punching" a time clock. At the end of each pay period, the clock cards are collected by the department manager. The manager prepares a payroll register in duplicate and forwards the original to payroll. In payroll, the summaries are checked for mathematical accuracy and a payroll supervisor pays each employee by check.

*Instructions*

(a)  Indicate the weakness(es) in internal control in each company.

(b) For each weakness, describe the control procedure(s) that will provide effective internal control. Use the following format for your answer:

| (a) Weaknesses | (b) Recommended Procedures |
| --- | --- |

*Journalize payroll transactions and adjusting entries.*
*(SO 7, 8, 9)*

**P11–4A** The following payroll liability accounts are included in the ledger of Carlos Costa Company on January 1, 1999:

| | |
| --- | --- |
| FICA Taxes Payable | $ 662.20 |
| Federal Income Taxes Payable | 954.60 |
| State Income Taxes Payable | 102.15 |
| Federal Unemployment Taxes Payable | 2,400.00 |
| State Unemployment Taxes Payable | 1,954.40 |
| Union Dues Payable | 250.00 |
| U.S. Savings Bonds Payable | 350.00 |

In January, the following transactions occurred:

Jan. 10  Sent check for $250.00 to union treasurer for union dues.

12  Deposited check for $1,616.80 in Federal Reserve Bank for FICA taxes and federal income taxes withheld.

15  Purchased U.S. Savings Bonds for employees by writing check for $350.00.

17  Paid state income taxes withheld from employees.

20  Paid federal and state unemployment taxes.

31  Completed monthly payroll register, which shows office salaries $14,600, store wages $27,400, FICA taxes withheld $3,360, federal income taxes payable $1,654, state income taxes payable $360, union dues payable $400, United Fund contributions payable $1,688, and net pay $34,538.

31  Prepared payroll checks for the net pay and distributed checks to employees.

At January 31, the company also makes the following accruals pertaining to employee compensation:

1. Employer payroll taxes: FICA taxes (8%), state unemployment taxes (5.4%), and federal unemployment taxes (0.8%).

2. Vacation pay: 4% of gross earnings.

**Instructions**

(a) Journalize the January transactions.

(b) Journalize the adjustments pertaining to employee compensation at January 31.

**P11–5A**   For the year ended December 31, 1999, San Juan Electric Company reports the following summary payroll data:

*Prepare entries for payroll and payroll taxes, and prepare W-2 data.*
*(SO 7, 8, 9)*

| | |
|---|---:|
| Gross earnings: | |
| Administrative salaries | $180,000 |
| Electricians' wages | 370,000 |
| Total | $550,000 |
| | |
| Deductions: | |
| FICA taxes | $ 39,600 |
| Federal income taxes withheld | 168,000 |
| State income taxes withheld (2.6%) | 14,300 |
| United Fund contributions payable | 27,500 |
| Hospital insurance premiums | 17,200 |
| Total | $266,600 |

San Juan Company's payroll taxes are: FICA 8%, state unemployment 2.5% (due to a stable employment record), and 0.8% federal unemployment. Gross earnings subject to (1) FICA taxes total $495,000, and (2) unemployment taxes total $400,000.

**Instructions**

(a) Prepare a summary journal entry at December 31 for the full year's payroll.

(b) Journalize the adjusting entry at December 31 to record the employer's payroll taxes.

(c) The W-2 Wage and Tax Statement requires the following dollar data:

| Wages, Tips, Other Compensation | Federal Income Tax Withheld | State Income Tax Withheld | FICA Wages | FICA Tax Withheld |
|---|---|---|---|---|
| | | | | |

Complete the required data for the following employees:

| Employee | Gross Earnings | Federal Income Tax Withheld |
|---|---|---|
| R. Cheng | $60,000 | $27,500 |
| D. Craig | 25,000 | 10,200 |

**P11–6A**   The following are selected transactions of Zimmer Company. Zimmer prepares financial statements *quarterly*.

*Journalize and post note transactions and show balance sheet presentation.*
*(SO 2)*

Jan.  2   Purchased merchandise on account from Alicea Company, $18,000, terms 2/10, n/30.

Feb.  1   Issued a 10%, 2-month, $18,000 note to Alicea in payment of account.

Mar. 31   Accrued interest for 2 months on Alicea note.

Apr.  1   Paid face value and interest on Alicea note.

July  1   Purchased equipment from Vincent Equipment paying $11,000 in cash and signing a 10%, 3-month, $24,000 note.

Sept. 30   Accrued interest for 3 months on Vincent note.

Oct.  1   Paid face value and interest on Vincent note.

Dec.  1   Borrowed $10,000 from the Otago Bank by issuing a 3-month, 12%-interest-bearing note with a face value of $10,000.

Dec. 31   Recognized interest expense for 1 month on Otago Bank note.

**Instructions**

(a) Prepare journal entries for the above transactions and events.

(b) Post to the accounts, Notes Payable, Interest Payable, and Interest Expense.

(c) Show the balance sheet presentation of notes payable at December 31.

(d) What is total interest expense for the year?

# PROBLEMS: SET B

•••••••••••••••••••••••••••••••••••••••••••••••••••••••••••••••••••••••••••••

*Prepare current liability entries, adjusting entries, and current liability section.*
*(SO 1, 2, 3, 4, 5)*

**P11–1B**   On January 1, 1999, the ledger of El Paso Company contains the following liability accounts:

|                            |          |
| -------------------------- | -------- |
| Accounts Payable           | $52,000  |
| Sales Taxes Payable        | 7,500    |
| Unearned Service Revenue   | 16,000   |

During January the following selected transactions occurred:

Jan.  5   Sold merchandise for cash totaling $16,632, which includes 8% sales taxes.
  12   Provided services for customers who had made advance payments of $9,000. (Credit Service Revenue)
  14   Paid state revenue department for sales taxes collected in December 1998 ($7,500).
  20   Sold 500 units of a new product on credit at $50 per unit, plus 8% sales tax. This new product is subject to a 1-year warranty.
  21   Borrowed $18,000 from Midland Bank on a 3-month, 10%, $18,000 note.
  25   Sold merchandise for cash totaling $11,340, which includes 8% sales taxes.

*Instructions*
(a) Journalize the January transactions.
(b) Journalize the adjusting entries at January 31 for (1) the outstanding notes payable, and (2) estimated warranty liability, assuming warranty costs are expected to equal 8% of sales of the new product. (*Hint*: Use one-third of a month for the Midland Bank note.)
(c) Prepare the current liability section of the balance sheet at January 31, 1999. Assume no change in accounts payable.

*Prepare payroll register and payroll entries.*
*(SO 7, 8)*

**P11–2B**   UCLA Hardware has four employees who are paid on an hourly basis plus time-and-one-half for all hours worked in excess of 40 a week. Payroll data for the week ended March 15, 1999, are presented below:

| Employee  | Hours Worked | Hourly Rate | Federal Income Tax Withholdings | United Fund |
| --------- | ------------ | ----------- | ------------------------------- | ----------- |
| J. Sanders | 40 | $14.00 | $? | $5.00 |
| S. Black   | 42 | 13.00  | ?  | 5.00 |
| D. Torres  | 44 | 13.00  | 42 | 8.00 |
| K. Kim     | 46 | 13.00  | 48 | 5.00 |

Sanders and Black are married. They claim 0 and 4 withholding allowances, respectively. The following tax rates are applicable: FICA 8%, state income taxes 3%, state unemployment taxes 5.4%, and federal unemployment 0.8%. The first three employees are sales clerks (store wages expense) and the other employee performs administrative duties (office wages expense).

*Instructions*
(a) Prepare a payroll register for the weekly payroll. (Use the wage bracket withholding table in the text for federal income tax withholdings.)
(b) Journalize the payroll on March 15, 1999, and the accrual of employer payroll taxes.
(c) Journalize the payment of the payroll on March 16, 1999.
(d) Journalize the deposit in a federal reserve bank on March 31, 1999, of the FICA and federal income taxes payable to the government.

*Identify internal control weaknesses and make recommendations for improvement.*
*(SO 6)*

**P11–3B**   Selected payroll procedures of Merced Sotera Company are described below:

1. Department managers interview applicants and on the basis of the interview either hire or reject the applicants. When an applicant is hired, the applicant fills out a W-4 form (Employer's Withholding Exemption Certificate). One copy of the form is sent to the personnel department and one copy is sent to the payroll department as notice that the individual has been hired. On the copy of the W-4 sent to payroll, the managers manually indicate the hourly pay rate for the new hire.
2. The payroll checks are manually signed by the chief accountant and given to the de-

partment managers for distribution to employees in their department. The managers are responsible for seeing that any absent employees receive their checks.

3.  There are two clerks in the payroll department. The payroll is divided alphabetically with one clerk having employees A to L and the other employees M to Z. Each clerk computes the gross earnings, deductions, and net pay for employees in the section and posts the data to the employee earning records.

**Instructions**

(a) ▯▯▯▯▯⯈  Indicate the weaknesses in internal control.
(b) ▯▯▯▯▯⯈  For each weakness, describe the control procedures that will provide effective internal control. Use the following format for your answer:

| (a) Weaknesses | (b) Recommended Procedures |
| --- | --- |
|  |  |

**P11–4B**  The following payroll liability accounts are included in the ledger of Amora Company on January 1, 1999:

*Journalize payroll transactions and adjusting entries.*
*(SO 7, 8, 9)*

| | |
| --- | --- |
| FICA Taxes Payable | $  760.00 |
| Federal Income Taxes Payable | 954.60 |
| State Income Taxes Payable | 108.95 |
| Federal Unemployment Taxes Payable | 288.95 |
| State Unemployment Taxes Payable | 1,954.40 |
| Union Dues Payable | 870.00 |
| U.S. Savings Bonds Payable | 360.00 |

In January, the following transactions occurred:

Jan. 10   Sent check for $870.00 to union treasurer for union dues.
    12   Deposited check for $1,714.60 in Federal Reserve Bank for FICA taxes and federal income taxes withheld.
    15   Purchased U.S. Savings Bonds for employees by writing check for $360.00.
    17   Paid state income taxes withheld from employees.
    20   Paid federal and state unemployment taxes.
    31   Completed monthly payroll register, which shows office salaries $14,600, store wages $28,400, FICA taxes withheld $3,440, federal income taxes payable $1,684, state income taxes payable $360, union dues payable $400, United Fund contributions payable $1,888, and net pay $35,228.
    31   Prepared payroll checks for the net pay and distributed checks to employees.

At January 31, the company also makes the following accrued adjustments pertaining to employee compensation:

1.  Employer payroll taxes: FICA taxes (8%), federal unemployment taxes (0.8%), and state unemployment taxes (5.4%).
2.  Vacation pay: 4% of gross earnings.

**Instructions**

(a)  Journalize the January transactions.
(b)  Journalize the adjustments pertaining to employee compensation at January 31.

**P11–5B**  For the year ended December 31, 1999, McMaster Electrical Repair Company reports the following summary payroll data:

*Prepare entries for payroll and payroll taxes and prepare W-2 data.*
*(SO 7, 8, 9)*

| Gross earnings: | |
| --- | --- |
| Administrative salaries | $180,000 |
| Electricians' wages | 470,000 |
| Total | $650,000 |

| Deductions: | |
| --- | --- |
| FICA taxes | $  46,000 |
| Federal income taxes withheld | 188,000 |
| State income taxes withheld (2.6%) | 16,900 |
| United Fund contributions payable | 32,500 |
| Hospital insurance premiums | 20,300 |
| Total | $303,700 |

McMaster Company's payroll taxes are: FICA 8%, state unemployment 2.5% (due to a stable employment record), and 0.8% federal unemployment. Gross earnings subject to (1) FICA taxes total $575,000; and (2) unemployment taxes total $450,000.

*Instructions*
  (a)  Prepare a summary journal entry at December 31 for the full year's payroll.
  (b)  Journalize the adjusting entry at December 31 to record the employer's payroll taxes.
  (c)  The W-2 Wage and Tax Statement requires the following dollar data:

| Wages, Tips, Other Compensation | Federal Income Tax Withheld | State Income Tax Withheld | FICA Wages | FICA Tax Withheld |
|---|---|---|---|---|

Complete the required data for the following employees:

| Employee | Gross Earnings | Federal Income Tax Withheld |
|---|---|---|
| J. Walker | $59,000 | $28,500 |
| I. Zimmer | 28,000 | 10,800 |

# BROADENING YOUR PERSPECTIVE

# FINANCIAL REPORTING AND ANALYSIS

## FINANCIAL REPORTING PROBLEM: Kellogg Company

**BYP11-1**  The financial statements of Kellogg Company and the Notes to Consolidated Financial Statements appear in Appendix A.

*Instructions*
Refer to Kellogg's financial statements and answer the following questions about current and contingent liabilities and payroll costs:

  (a)  What were Kellogg's total current liabilities at December 31, 1997? What was the increase/decrease in Kellogg's total current liabilities from the prior year?
  (b)  How much were the "current maturities of long-term debt" at December 31, 1997?
  (c)  What were the components of total current liabilities on December 31, 1997 (other than "current maturities of long-term debt" already discussed in b above)?

## COMPARATIVE ANALYSIS PROBLEM: Kellogg Company vs. General Mills

**BYP11-2**  Kellogg's financial statements are presented in Appendix A; General Mills's financial statements are presented in Appendix B.

*Instructions*
  (a)  At December 31, 1997, what was Kellogg's largest current liability account? What was its total current liabilities? At May 25, 1997, what was General Mills's largest current liability account? What was its total current liabilities?
  (b)  Based on information contained in those financial statements, compute the following 1997 values for each company:
   (1)  Working capital
   (2)  Current ratio
  (c)  What conclusions concerning the relative liquidity of these companies can be drawn from these data?

## RESEARCH ASSIGNMENT

**BYP11-3**  The December 1995 issue of *Management Accounting* includes a reprint of an article by Glenn Cheney entitled "It's Not Easy Being Green But Top Companies Are Trying."

*Instructions*

Read the article and answer the following questions.

(a) What portion of the Fortune 500 companies disclose their position on the environment? What type of information is included in these disclosures?

(b) How can companies save money by "being green"?

(c) What is the "take-back" principle"?

(d) What is the role of public accountants in this area?

## INTERPRETING FINANCIAL STATEMENTS: Northland Cranberries

**BYP11–4**  Despite being a publicly traded company only since 1987, Northland Cranberries of Wisconsin Rapids, Wisconsin, is the world's largest cranberry grower. It has engaged in an aggressive growth strategy, and as a consequence, the company has taken on significant amounts of both short-term and long-term debt. The following information is taken from recent annual reports of the company.

|  | 1995 | 1994 |
|---|---|---|
| Current assets | $  6,745,759 | $ 5,598,054 |
| Total assets | 107,744,751 | 83,074,339 |
| Current liabilities | 10,168,685 | 4,484,687 |
| Total liabilities | 73,118,204 | 49,948,787 |
| Stockholders' equity | 34,626,547 | 33,125,552 |
| Net sales | 21,783,966 | 18,051,355 |
| Cost of goods sold | 13,057,275 | 8,751,220 |
| Interest expense | 3,654,006 | 2,393,792 |
| Income tax expense | 1,051,000 | 1,917,000 |
| Net income | 1,581,707 | 2,942,954 |

*Instructions*

(a) Evaluate the company's liquidity by calculating and analyzing working capital and the current ratio.

(b) The following discussion of the company's liquidity was provided by the company in the Management Discussion and Analysis section of the company's 1995 annual report. Comment on whether you agree with management's statements, and what might be done to remedy the situation.

### NORTHLAND CRANBERRIES
### Management Discussion and Analysis

The lower comparative current ratio at March 31, 1995, was due to $3 million of short-term borrowing then outstanding which was incurred to fund the Company's September 1994 Yellow River Marsh acquisitions. As a result of the extreme seasonality of its business, the Company does not believe that its current ratio or its underlying stated working capital at its March 31, 1995, fiscal year end is a meaningful indication of the Company's liquidity. As of March 31 of each fiscal year, the Company has historically carried no significant amounts of inventories and by such date all of the Company's accounts receivable from its crop sold for processing under the supply agreements have been paid in cash, with the resulting cash received from such payments used to reduce indebtedness. The Company utilizes its revolving bank credit facility, together with cash generated from operations, to fund its working capital requirements throughout its growing season.

**REAL-WORLD FOCUS: Capitol American Financial Corporation**

BYP11–5   Formed in 1970, **Capitol American Financial Corporation** is licensed throughout most of the United States, Puerto Rico, and the U.S. Virgin Islands. The company's 285 employees develop, underwrite, market, and distribute individual supplemental health and accidental insurance. A primary product line is cancer insurance. Presented below is a note to the financial statements of Capitol American Financial Corporation:

---

### CAPITOL AMERICAN FINANCIAL CORPORATION
#### Notes to the Financial Statements

The Company is the subject of an employment tax examination by the Internal Revenue Service ("IRS") with respect to the treatment of its agents as independent contractors rather than employees for financial reporting and tax purposes for 1987 and 1988. The IRS has proposed for 1987 and 1988 an increase in the tax liability of the Company in the aggregate amount of approximately $6.1 million, including approximately $1.5 million in penalties, for assessment of Federal Insurance Contributions Act ("FICA") taxes, federal unemployment compensation taxes and federal income taxes on wages not withheld by the Company. Management believes, based in part on the opinion of legal counsel, that the Company's treatment of its agents as independent contractors rather than employees is correct for federal tax purposes and that the Company should prevail. Accordingly, no liability or loss that could result upon adverse resolution of this matter has been recognized in the Company's consolidated financial statements. If the Company does not prevail, it can be expected that the Company would be assessed similar, but generally increasing, amounts for the years 1989 through 1992 (representing a total potential liability to the Company, including penalties, of approximately $28.1 million, for 1987 through 1992), and also for 1993 and future years unless the Company changes certain of its practices regarding the treatment of its agents. In addition, an adverse resolution of this matter could also be expected to have an adverse effect on the Company with respect to certain state and local taxes.

---

*Instructions*
  (a)  How is the company's net income affected by hiring work to be done by independent contractors rather than employees?
  (b)  If Capitol American Financial Corporation loses the lawsuit, which accounts will have been understated by using the independent contractor arrangement?
  (c)  What assessment has the Corporation made with respect to the likelihood and estimatability of this contingent liability?

# CRITICAL THINKING

## GROUP DECISION CASE

BYP11–6   Sauk Processing Company provides word-processing services for clients and students in a university community. The work for clients is fairly steady throughout the year, but the work for students peaks significantly in December and May as a result of term papers, research project reports, and dissertations.

Two years ago, the company attempted to meet the peak demand by hiring part-time help. However, this led to numerous errors and considerable customer dissatisfaction. A year ago, the company hired four experienced employees on a permanent basis instead of using part-time help. This proved to be much better in terms of productivity and customer satisfaction. However, it has caused an increase in annual payroll costs and a significant decline in annual net income.

Recently, Tammy Berg, a sales representative of Harrington Services Inc., has made a proposal to the company. Under the plan, Harrington Services will provide up to four experienced workers at a daily rate of $105 per person for an 8-hour workday. Harrington workers are not available on an hourly basis. Sauk Processing would have to pay only the daily rate for the workers used.

The owner of Sauk Processing, Martha Bell, asks you, as the company's accountant, to prepare a report on the expenses that are pertinent to the decision. If the Harrington plan is adopted, Martha will terminate the employment of two permanent employees who are each earning an average annual salary of $30,000. The remaining permanent employees each earn an annual income of $30,000. Sauk Processing pays 8% FICA taxes, 0.8% Federal Unemployment Taxes, and 5.4% State Unemployment Taxes. The unemployment taxes apply to only the first $7,000 of gross earnings. In addition, Sauk Processing pays $40 per month for each employee for medical and dental insurance.

Martha indicates that if the Harrington Services plan is accepted, her needs for workers will be as follows:

| Months | Number | Working Days per Month |
|---|---|---|
| January–March | 2 | 20 |
| April–May | 3 | 25 |
| June–October | 2 | 18 |
| November–December | 3 | 23 |

### Instructions

With the class divided into groups, answer the following:
  (a) Prepare a report showing the comparative payroll expense of continuing to employ permanent workers compared to adopting the Harrington Services Inc. plan.
  (b) What other factors should Martha consider before finalizing her decision?

## COMMUNICATION ACTIVITY

**BYP11–7**   Tim Harp, president of the Low Cloud Company, has recently hired a number of additional employees. He recognizes that additional payroll taxes will be due as a result of this hiring, and that the company will serve as the collection agent for other taxes.

### Instructions

In a memorandum to Tim Harp, explain each of the taxes, and identify the taxes that result in payroll tax expense to the employer.

## ETHICS CASE

**BYP11–8**   Harry Smith owns and manages Harry's Restaurant, a 24-hour restaurant near the city's medical complex. Harry employs nine full-time employees and sixteen part-time employees. He pays all of the full-time employees by check, the amounts of which are determined by Harry's public accountant, Pam Web. Harry pays all of his part-time employees in currency that he computes and withdraws directly from his cash register. Pam has repeatedly urged Harry to pay all employees by check. But as Harry has told his competitor and friend, Steve Hill, who owns the Greasy Diner, "First of all, my part-time employees prefer the currency over a check, and secondly I don't withhold or pay any taxes or workmen's compensation insurance on those wages because they go totally unrecorded and unnoticed."

### Instructions

  (a) Who are the stakeholders in this situation?
  (b) What are the legal and ethical considerations regarding Harry's handling of his payroll?
  (c) Pam Web is aware of Harry's payment of the part-time payroll in currency. What are her ethical responsibilities in this case?
  (d) What internal control principle is violated in this payroll process?

# SURFING THE NET

**BYP11–9**  The Internal Revenue Service provides considerable information over the Internet. The following demonstrates how useful one of its sites is in answering payroll tax questions faced by employers.

**Address:** http://www.irs.ustreas.gov/prod/forms_pubs/index.html

**Steps:**
1. Go to the site shown above.
2. Choose **Publications Online**.
3. Choose **Circular E, Employer's Tax Guide**.

*Instructions*
Answer each of the following questions:

(a) How does the government define "employees"?
(b) What are the special rules for Social Security and Medicare regarding children who are employed by their parents?
(c) How can an employee obtain a Social Security card if he or she doesn't have one?
(d) Must employees report tips received from customers to their employer? If so, what is the process?
(e) Where should the employer deposit Social Security taxes withheld or contributed?

*Answers to Self-Study Questions*
1. a    2. d    3. b    4. b    5. a    6. c    7. b    8. d    9. d    10. c    11. d

*Answer to Kellogg Review It Question 2, p. 478*
Under the heading of current liabilities Kellogg has listed current maturities of long-term debt, notes payable, and accounts payable.

**Remember to go back to the Navigator box on the chapter-opening page and check off your completed work.**

**Before studying this chapter, you should know or, if necessary, review:**

a. The two organizations primarily responsible for setting accounting standards. (Ch. 1, pp. 10–11)

b. The monetary unit assumption, the economic entity assumption, and the time period assumption. (Chs. 1 and 3, pp. 10, 11, 92–93)

c. The cost principle, the revenue recognition principle, and the matching principle. (Chs. 1 and 3, pp. 11, 93–94)

THE NAVIGATOR

## FEATURE STORY

# Timing Is Everything

A few simple truths:

Truth 1: Net income = Revenues − Expenses

Truth 2: In general, more net income is better than less.

Truth 3: To increase net income you must increase reported revenue or decrease reported expense.

Truth 4: Timing is everything.

So far you have learned some nice orderly rules about how to keep track of corporate transactions. Guess what? It isn't that nice and neat. In fact, it is often difficult to determine in what period some revenues and expenses should be reported. There are rules that give guidance, but occasionally these rules are overlooked, misinterpreted, or even intentionally ignored. Consider the following examples:

• Media Vision Technology Inc., a maker of sound and animation equipment for computers, was accused of operating a "phantom" warehouse to hide inventory for returned products already recorded as sales.

• Policy Management Systems Corp., which makes insurance software, said that it reported some sales before contracts were signed or products delivered.

• Penguin USA, a book publisher, said that it understated expenses in some years because it failed to report expenses for discounts given to customers for paying early.

In each case, accrual accounting concepts were violated. That is, revenues or expenses were not recorded in the proper period, which had a substantial impact on reported income.

Why might management want to report revenues or expenses in the wrong period? One *Wall Street Journal* article states that high-tech firms have intense pressure to report higher earnings every year. If actual perfomance falls short of expectations, management might be tempted to bend the rules. An accounting expert suggests that investors and auditors should be suspicious of sharp increases in monthly sales at the end of each quarter or big jumps in fourth-quarter sales. Such events don't always mean management is cheating, but they are certainly worth investigating.

Source: Lee Burton, "Tech Concerns Fudge Figures to Buoy Stocks," *The Wall Street Journal*, May 19, 1994, p. B1.

THE NAVIGATOR

# CHAPTER **12**

# ACCOUNTING PRINCIPLES

**THE NAVIGATOR** ✔

- Understand *Concepts for Review* ☐
- Read *Feature Story* ☐
- Scan *Study Objectives* ☐
- Read *Preview* ☐
- Read text and answer *Before You Go On*
  p. 520 ☐ p. 532 ☐
- Work *Demonstration Problems* ☐
- Review *Summary of Study Objectives* ☐
- Answer *Self-Study Questions* ☐
- Complete assignments ☐

## STUDY OBJECTIVES

**After studying this chapter, you should be able to:**

1. *Explain the meaning of generally accepted accounting principles and identify the key items of the conceptual framework.*
2. *Describe the basic objectives of financial reporting.*
3. *Discuss the qualitative characteristics of accounting information and elements of financial statements.*
4. *Identify the basic assumptions used by accountants.*
5. *Identify the basic principles of accounting.*
6. *Identify the two constraints in accounting.*
7. *Explain the accounting principles used in international operations.*

THE NAVIGATOR

*A*s indicated in the opening story, it is important that general guidelines be available to resolve accounting issues. Without these basic guidelines, each enterprise would have to develop its own set of accounting practices. If this happened, we would have to become familiar with every company's peculiar accounting and reporting rules in order to understand their financial statements. Thus, it would be difficult, if not impossible, to compare the financial statements of different companies.

This chapter explores the basic accounting principles followed in developing specific accounting guidelines. The content and organization of the chapter are as follows:

THE
NAVIGATOR

# THE CONCEPTUAL FRAMEWORK OF ACCOUNTING

**1**
STUDY
OBJECTIVE

Explain the meaning of generally accepted accounting principles and identify the key items of the conceptual framework.

The accounting profession has established a set of standards and rules that are recognized as a general guide for financial reporting purposes. This recognized set of standards is called generally accepted accounting principles (GAAP). "Generally accepted" means that these principles must have "substantial authoritative support." Such support usually comes from two standard-setting bodies: the Financial Accounting Standards Board (FASB) and the Securities and Exchange Commission (SEC).[1]

Since the early 1970s the business and governmental communities have given the FASB the responsibility for developing accounting principles in this country.

---

[1]The SEC is an agency of the U.S. government that was established in 1933 to administer laws and regulations relating to the exchange of securities and the publication of financial information by U.S. businesses. The agency has the authority to mandate generally accepted accounting principles for companies under its jurisdiction. However, throughout its history, the SEC has been willing to accept the principles set forth by the FASB and similar bodies.

This job is an ongoing process in which accounting principles change to reflect changes in the business environment and in the needs of users of accounting information.

Prior to the establishment of the FASB, accounting principles were developed on a problem-by-problem basis. Thus, rule-making bodies developed and issued accounting rules and methods to solve specific problems. Critics charged that the problem-by-problem approach led to inconsistent rules and practices over time. Unfortunately, no clearly developed conceptual framework of accounting existed for the accounting rule makers to refer to in solving problems.

In response to these criticisms, the FASB developed a conceptual framework to serve as the basis for resolving accounting and reporting problems. The FASB spent considerable time and effort on this project. The Board views its conceptual framework as "... a constitution, a coherent system of interrelated objectives and fundamentals."[2]

The FASB's conceptual framework consists of the following four items:

1. Objectives of financial reporting.
2. Qualitative characteristics of accounting information.
3. Elements of financial statements.
4. Operating guidelines (assumptions, principles, and constraints).

We will discuss each of these items on the following pages.

## ACCOUNTING IN ACTION

### International Insight

You should recognize that different political and cultural influences affect the accounting that occurs in foreign countries. For example, in Sweden, accounting is considered an instrument to be used to shape fiscal policy. In Europe generally, more emphasis is given to social reporting (more information on employment statistics, health of workers, and so on) because employees and their labor organizations are strong and demand that type of information from management.

## Objectives of Financial Reporting

In developing the conceptual framework, the FASB concluded that the first level of study was to determine the objectives of financial reporting. Determining these objectives required answers to such basic questions as: Who uses financial statements? Why? What information do they need? How knowledgeable about business and accounting are the users of financial statements? How should financial information be reported so that it is best understood?

In answering these questions, the FASB concluded that the objectives of financial reporting are to provide information that:

1. Is useful to those making investment and credit decisions.
2. Is helpful in assessing future cash flows.
3. Identifies the economic resources (assets), the claims to those resources (liabilities), and the changes in those resources and claims.

**2**
STUDY
OBJECTIVE
..............................
Describe the basic objectives of financial reporting.

[2]"Conceptual Framework for Financial Accounting and Reporting: Elements of Financial Statements and Their Measurement," *FASB Discussion Memorandum* (Stamford, Conn.: 1976), p. 1.

The FASB then undertook to describe the characteristics that make accounting information useful.

## Qualitative Characteristics of Accounting Information

**3**
STUDY
OBJECTIVE

Discuss the qualitative characteristics of accounting information and elements of financial statements.

How does a company like Microsoft decide on the amount of financial information to disclose? In what format should its financial information be presented? How should assets, liabilities, revenues, and expenses be measured? **The FASB concluded that the overriding criterion by which such accounting choices should be judged is decision usefulness.** The accounting practice selected or the policy adopted should be the one that generates the most useful financial information for making a decision. To be useful, information should possess the following qualitative characteristics: relevance, reliability, comparability, and consistency.

### Relevance

Accounting information is relevant if it makes a difference in a decision. Relevant information has either predictive or feedback value or both. **Predictive value** helps users forecast future events. For example, when Exxon issues financial statements, the information in the statements is considered relevant because it provides a basis for forecasting (predicting) future earnings. **Feedback value** confirms or corrects prior expectations. When Exxon issues financial statements, in addition to helping predict future events, it confirms or corrects prior expectations about the financial health of the company.

In addition, for accounting information to be relevant it must be **timely**. That is, it must be available to decision makers before it loses its capacity to influence decisions. If Exxon reported its financial information only every 5 years, the information would have limited usefulness for decision-making purposes.

### Reliability

Reliability of information means that the information is free of error and bias; it can be depended on. To be reliable, accounting information must be **verifiable**—we must be able to prove that it is free of error and bias. The information must be a **faithful representation** of what it purports to be—it must be factual. If Sears, Roebuck's income statement reports sales of $100 billion when it had sales of $51 billion, then the statement is not a faithful representation. Finally, accounting information must be **neutral**—it cannot be selected, prepared, or presented to favor one set of interested users over another. To ensure reliability, certified public accountants audit financial statements, just as the Internal Revenue Service audits tax returns for the same purpose.

### Comparability and Consistency

Accounting information about an enterprise is most useful when it can be compared with accounting information about other enterprises. Comparability results when different companies use the same accounting principles. For example, Sears, Roebuck, Montgomery Ward, and J.C. Penney all use the cost principle in reporting plant assets on the balance sheet. Moreover, each company uses the revenue recognition and matching principles in determining its net income.

Conceptually, comparability should also extend to the methods used by companies in complying with an accounting principle. Accounting methods include the FIFO and LIFO methods of inventory costing, and various depreciation methods. At this point, comparability of methods is not required, even for companies in the same industry. Thus, Ford, General Motors, and Chrysler may use different inventory costing and depreciation methods in their financial statements. The

HELPFUL HINT
What makes accounting information relevant? Answer: Relevant accounting information provides feedback, serves as a basis for predictions, and is timely (current).

HELPFUL HINT
What makes accounting information reliable? Answer: Reliable accounting information is free of error and bias, is factual, verifiable, and neutral.

only accounting requirement is that each company **must disclose** the accounting methods used. From the disclosures, the external user can determine whether the financial information is comparable.

Consistency means that a company uses the same accounting principles and methods from year to year. Thus, if a company selects FIFO as the inventory costing method in the first year of operations, it is expected to continue to use FIFO in succeeding years. When financial information has been reported on a consistent basis, the financial statements permit meaningful analysis of trends within a company.

A company can change to a new method of accounting if management can justify that the new method results in more meaningful financial information. In the year in which the change occurs, the change must be disclosed in the notes to the financial statements so that users of the financial statements are aware of the lack of consistency.

# ACCOUNTING IN ACTION
## Business Insight

There is an old story that professors often tell students about a company looking for an accountant. The company approached the first accountant and asked: "What do you believe our net income will be this year?" The accountant said $4 million dollars. The company asked the second accountant the same question, and the answer was "What would you like it to be?" Guess who got the job? The reason we tell the story here is that, because accounting principles offer flexibility, it is important that a consistent treatment be provided from period to period. Otherwise it would be very difficult to interpret financial statements. Perhaps *no* alternative methods should be permitted in accounting. What do you think?

The qualitative characteristics of accounting information are summarized in Illustration 12-1.

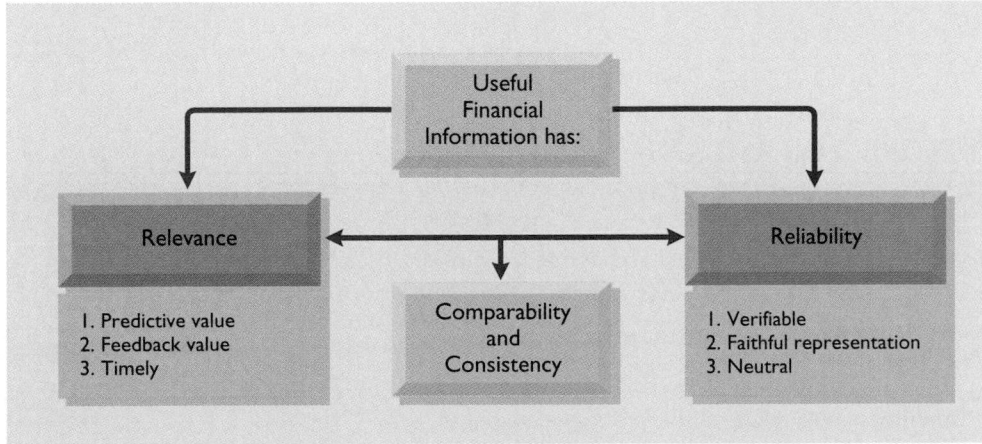

**ILLUSTRATION 12-1**

*Qualitative characteristics of accounting information*

## Elements of Financial Statements

An important part of an accounting conceptual framework is a set of definitions that describe the basic terms used in accounting. The FASB refers to this set of definitions as the elements of financial statements. They include such terms as assets, liabilities, equity, revenues, and expenses.

Because these elements are so important, it is imperative that they be precisely defined and universally understood and applied. Finding the appropriate definition for many of these elements is not easy. For example, how should an asset be defined? Should the value of a company's employees be reported as an asset on a balance sheet? Should the death of the company's president be reported as a loss? A good set of definitions should provide answers to these types of questions. Because you have already encountered most of these definitions in earlier chapters, they are not repeated here.

## Operating Guidelines

The objectives of financial statements, the qualitative characteristics of accounting information, and the elements of financial statements are very broad. However, because practicing accountants and standard-setting bodies must solve practical problems, more detailed guidelines are needed. In its conceptual framework, the FASB recognized the need for operating guidelines. We have chosen to classify these guidelines as assumptions, principles, and constraints. These guidelines are well-established and accepted in accounting.

**Assumptions** provide a foundation for the accounting process. **Principles** are specific rules that indicate how economic events should be reported in the accounting process. **Constraints** on the accounting process allow for a relaxation of the principles under certain circumstances. Illustration 12-2 provides a roadmap of the operating guidelines of accounting. These guidelines are discussed in more detail in the following sections.

**ILLUSTRATION 12-2**

*The operating guidelines of accounting*

| Assumptions | Principles | Constraints |
|---|---|---|
| Monetary unit | Revenue recognition | Materiality |
| Economic entity | Matching | Conservatism |
| Time period | Full disclosure | |
| Going concern | Cost | |

## BEFORE YOU GO ON . . .

### Review It

1. What are generally accepted accounting principles?
2. What is stated about generally accepted accounting principles in the Report of Independent Accountants for Kellogg? The answer to this question appears on page 547.
3. What are the basic objectives of financial information?
4. What are the qualitative characteristics that make accounting information useful? Identify two elements of the financial statements.

THE NAVIGATOR

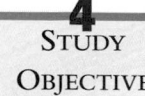

**4**
STUDY OBJECTIVE

Identify the basic assumptions used by accountants.

# ASSUMPTIONS

As noted above, assumptions provide a foundation for the accounting process. You have already studied three of the major assumptions in preceding chapters—the monetary unit, economic entity, and time period assumptions. The fourth is called the going concern assumption.

## Monetary Unit Assumption

The monetary unit assumption states that only transaction data capable of being expressed in terms of money should be included in the accounting records of the economic entity. For example, the value of a company president is not reported in a company's financial records because it cannot be expressed easily in dollars.

An important corollary to the monetary unit assumption is the added assumption that the unit of measure remains sufficiently constant over time. This point will be discussed in more detail later in this chapter.

## Economic Entity Assumption

The economic entity assumption states that economic events can be identified with a particular unit of accountability. For example, it is assumed that the activities of IBM can be distinguished from those of other computer companies such as Apple, Compaq, and Hewlett-Packard.

## Time Period Assumption

The time period assumption states that the economic life of a business can be divided into artificial time periods. Thus, it is assumed that the activities of business enterprises such as General Electric, America Online, Exxon, or any enterprise can be subdivided into months, quarters, or a year for meaningful financial reporting purposes.

## Going Concern Assumption

The going concern assumption assumes that the enterprise will continue in operation long enough to carry out its existing objectives. Experience indicates that, in spite of numerous business failures, companies have a fairly high continuance rate, and it has proved useful to adopt a going concern assumption for accounting purposes.

The accounting implications of adopting this assumption are critical. If a going concern assumption is not used, then plant assets should be stated at their liquidation value (selling price less cost of disposal)—not at their cost. As a result, depreciation and amortization of these assets would not be needed. Each period these assets would simply be reported at their liquidation value. Also, without this assumption, the current–noncurrent classification of assets and liabilities would have little significance. Labeling anything as fixed or long-term would be difficult to justify.

Acceptance of the going concern assumption gives credibility to the cost principle. If, instead, liquidation were assumed, assets would be better stated at liquidation value than at cost. Only when liquidation appears imminent is the going concern assumption inapplicable.

These basic accounting assumptions are illustrated graphically in Illustration 12-3 on the next page.

> **INTERNATIONAL NOTE**
>
> In an action that sent shock waves through the French business community, the CEO of Alcatel-Alsthom was taken into custody for an apparent violation of the economic entity assumption. Allegedly, the executive improperly used company funds to install an expensive security system in his home.

> **HELPFUL HINT**
>
> (1) Which accounting assumption assumes that an enterprise will remain in business long enough to recover the cost of its assets? (2) Which accounting assumption is justification for the cost principle? Answers: (1) and (2) Going concern assumption.

# PRINCIPLES

On the basis of these fundamental assumptions of accounting, the accounting profession has developed principles that dictate how transactions and other economic events should be recorded and reported. In earlier chapters we discussed the cost principle (Chapter 1) and the revenue recognition and matching principles (Chapter 3). We now examine a number of reporting issues related to

**5**
STUDY
OBJECTIVE

Identify the basic principles of accounting.

## Economic Entity

Ford

Chrysler

GM

Economic events can be identified with a particular unit of accountability.

## Monetary Unit

| Measure of employee satisfaction | Salaries paid |
| Total number of employees | Percent of international employees |

$ Acct. Records -Salaries paid

Only transaction data capable of being expressed in terms of money should be included in the accounting records of the economic entity.

## Time Period

1995                2005

1997  1999  2001  2003

Start of business

QTR QTR QTR QTR
 1    2    3    4
J FMAMJ JASOND

End of business

The economic life of a business can be divided into artificial time periods.

## Going Concern

Now                    Future

The enterprise will continue in operation long enough to carry out its existing objectives.

**ILLUSTRATION 12-3**

*Assumptions used in accounting*

these principles. In addition, another principle, the full disclosure principle, is discussed.

# Revenue Recognition Principle

The revenue recognition principle dictates that revenue should be recognized in the accounting period in which it is earned. Applying this general principle in practice, however, can be difficult. For example, it was reported that Automatic Inc. was improperly recognizing revenue on goods that had not been shipped to customers. Similarly, many questioned the revenue recognition practices of financial institutions, which until recently recorded a large portion of their fees for granting a loan as revenue immediately rather than spreading those fees over the life of the loan.

When a sale is involved, revenue is recognized at the point of sale. The **sales basis** involves an exchange transaction between the seller and buyer, and the sales price provides an objective measure of the amount of revenue realized. There are, however, two exceptions to the sales basis for revenue recognition that have become generally accepted.

## Percentage-of-Completion Method

In long-term construction contracts, recognition of revenue is usually required before the contract is completed. For example, assume that Warrior Construction Co. had a contract to build a dam for the U.S. Department of the Interior for $400 million. Construction is estimated to take 3 years (starting in 1997) at a construction cost of $360 million. If Warrior applies the point-of-sale basis, it will report no revenues and no profit in the first two years. But, in 1999 when completion and sale take place, Warrior will report $400 million in revenues, costs of $360 million, and the entire profit of $40 million. Was Warrior really producing no revenues and earning no profit in 1997 and 1998? Obviously not. The earning process is considered substantially completed at various stages and therefore revenue should be recognized as construction progresses.

In recognizing revenue, Warrior can apply the **percentage-of-completion method**. This method recognizes revenue and income over the life of a long-term project on the basis of reasonable estimates of the project's progress toward completion. Progress toward completion is measured by comparing the costs incurred in a year to the total estimated costs for the entire project. That percentage is multiplied by the total revenue for the project; the result is then recognized as revenue for the period. The formulas for this method are as follows:

**HELPFUL HINT**
For long-term construction contracts, it is appropriate to use the percentage-of-completion method of revenue recognition because the critical event in the earning process is making progress toward completion. The ultimate sale and selling price are assured by the contract.

**ILLUSTRATION 12-4**

*Formula to recognize revenue in the percentage-of-completion method*

The costs incurred in the current period are then subtracted from the revenue recognized during the current period to arrive at the gross profit.

Let's look at an illustration of the percentage-of-completion method. Assume that Warrior Construction Co. incurs costs of $54 million in 1997, $180 million in 1998, and $126 million in 1999 on the dam project. The portion of the $400 million of revenue recognized in each of the 3 years is shown in Illustration 12-5.

**ILLUSTRATION 12-5**

*Revenue recognized— percentage-of-completion method*

| Year | Costs Incurred (Current Period) | ÷ | Total Estimated Cost | = | Percent Complete (Current Period) | × | Total Revenue | = | Revenue Recognized (Current Period) |
|---|---|---|---|---|---|---|---|---|---|
| 1997 | $ 54,000,000 | | $360,000,000 | | 15% | | $400,000,000 | | $ 60,000,000 |
| 1998 | 180,000,000 | | 360,000,000 | | 50% | | 400,000,000 | | 200,000,000 |
| 1999 | 126,000,000 | | Balance required to complete the contract | | | | | | 140,000,000 |
| Totals | $360,000,000 | | | | | | | | $400,000,000 |

Note that no estimate is made of the percentage of work completed during the final period. In the final period, all remaining revenue is recognized. In this example, the company's cost estimates have been very accurate; the costs incurred in the third year were 35% of the total estimated cost ($126,000 ÷ $360,000). The gross profit recognized each period is as follows:

ILLUSTRATION 12-6

*Gross profit recognized—percentage-of-completion method*

| Year | Revenue Recognized (Current Period) | − | Actual Cost Incurred (Current Period) | = | Gross Profit Recognized (Current Period) |
|------|------|---|------|---|------|
| 1997 | $ 60,000,000 | | $ 54,000,000 | | $ 6,000,000 |
| 1998 | 200,000,000 | | 180,000,000 | | 20,000,000 |
| 1999 | 140,000,000 | | 126,000,000 | | 14,000,000 |
| Totals | $400,000,000 | | $360,000,000 | | $40,000,000 |

Application of the percentage-of-completion method involves some subjectivity. As a result, there is the possibility of error in determining the amount of revenue recognized and net income reported. Yet to wait until completion would seriously distort each period's financial statements. Naturally, **if it is not possible to obtain dependable estimates of costs and progress, then the revenue should be recognized at the completion date** and not by the percentage-of-completion method.

### Installment Method

Another basis for revenue recognition is the receipt of cash. The cash basis is generally used only when it is difficult to determine the revenue amount at the time of a credit sale because collection is so uncertain. One popular approach to the recognition of revenue using the cash basis is the installment method.

Under the installment method, each cash collection from a customer consists of (1) a partial recovery of the cost of the goods sold, and (2) partial gross profit from the sale. For example, if the gross profit rate at date of sale is 40%, each subsequent receipt consists of 60% recovery of cost of goods sold and 40% gross profit. The formula to recognize gross profit is as follows:

**ILLUSTRATION 12-7**

*Gross profit formula—installment method*

To illustrate, assume that an Iowa farm machinery dealer in the first year of operations had installment sales of $600,000 and a cost of goods sold on installment of $420,000. Total gross profit is, therefore, $180,000 ($600,000 − $420,000), and the gross profit percentage is 30% ($180,000 ÷ $600,000). The collections on the installment sales were as follows: First year, $280,000 (down payment plus monthly payments); second year, $200,000; and, third year, $120,000. The collections of cash and recognition of the gross profit are summarized in Illustration 12-8 (interest charges are ignored in this illustration):

**ILLUSTRATION 12-8**

*Gross profit recognized—installment method*

| Year | Cash Collected | × | Gross Profit Percentage | = | Gross Profit Recognized |
|------|------|---|------|---|------|
| 1997 | $280,000 | | 30% | | $ 84,000 |
| 1998 | 200,000 | | 30% | | 60,000 |
| 1999 | 120,000 | | 30% | | 36,000 |
| Total | $600,000 | | | | $180,000 |

Under the installment method of accounting, gross profit is therefore recognized **in the period in which the cash is collected**.

As indicated earlier, use of the installment method is justified when the risk of not collecting an account receivable may be such that the sale is not sufficient evidence for revenue to be recognized.

## ACCOUNTING IN ACTION
### Business Insight

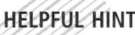

Datapoint Corp. encouraged its customers to load up with large shipments at the end of the year, allowing Datapoint to report these shipments as revenues, even though payment hadn't been collected. Unfortunately, some of the customers either went broke or quit before paying for the equipment received. As a result, the company had to record substantial bad debts or in some cases reverse previously recorded sales. If Datapoint had used the installment method, this revenue would not have been reported. As a result, revenue recognition practices that are cash-basis oriented, such as the installment method, are becoming more acceptable as it becomes difficult to tell when a sale is a sale.

## Matching Principle (Expense Recognition)

Expense recognition is traditionally tied to revenue recognition: "Let the expense follow the revenue." This practice is referred to as the matching principle: it dictates that expenses be matched with revenues in the period in which efforts are expended to generate revenues. Expenses are not recognized when cash is paid, or when the work is performed, or when the product is produced; they are recognized when the labor (service) or the product actually makes its contribution to revenue.

The problem is that it is sometimes difficult to determine the accounting period in which the expense contributed to the generation of revenues. Several approaches have therefore been devised for matching expenses and revenues on the income statement.

To understand these approaches, it is necessary to examine the nature of expenses. Costs that will generate revenues only in the current accounting period are expensed immediately. They are reported as operating expenses in the income statement. Examples include such costs as advertising, sales salaries, and repairs. These expenses are often called **expired costs**.

Costs that will generate revenues in future accounting periods are recognized as assets. Examples include merchandise inventory, prepaid expenses, and plant assets. These costs represent **unexpired costs**. Unexpired costs become expenses in two ways:

1. **Cost of goods sold.** Costs carried as merchandise inventory are expensed as cost of goods sold in the period when the sale occurs. Thus, there is a direct matching of expenses with revenues.
2. **Operating expenses.** Unexpired costs become operating expenses through use or consumption (as in the case of store supplies) or through the passage of time (as in the case of prepaid insurance and prepaid rent). The cost of plant assets and other long-lived productive resources is expensed through rational and systematic allocation methods which result in periodic depreciation and amortization. Operating expenses contribute to the revenues of the period but their association with revenues is less direct than for cost of goods sold.

These points about expense recognition are illustrated in Illustration 12-9.

**HELPFUL HINT**
Costs are the source of expenses. Costs become expenses when they are charged against revenue.

**ETHICS NOTE**
Many appear to do it, but few like to discuss it: it's earnings management, and it's a clear violation of the revenue recognition and matching principles. Banks sometimes time the sale of investments or the expensing of bad debts to accomplish earnings objectives. Prominent companies, such as GE, have been accused of matching one-time gains with one-time charge-offs so that current period earnings are not so high that they can't be surpassed next period.

ILLUSTRATION 12-9

*Expense recognition pattern*

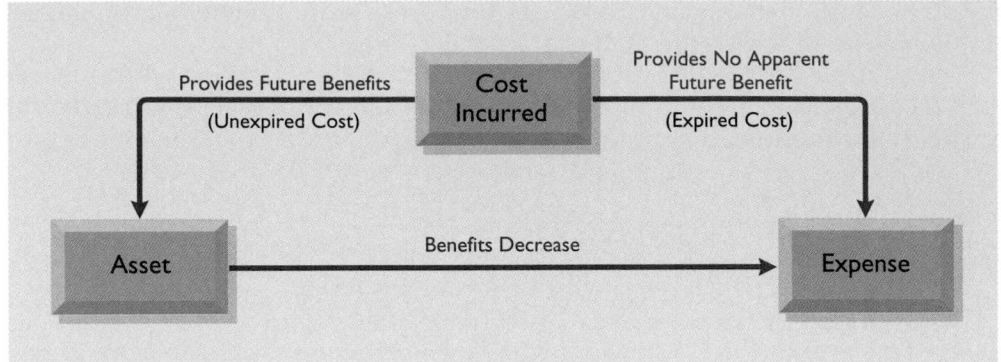

## ACCOUNTING IN ACTION
### Business Insight

Implementing expense recognition guidelines can be difficult. Consider, for example, Harold's Club (a gambling casino) in Reno, Nevada. How should it report expenses related to the payoff of its progressive slot machines? Progressive slot machines, which generally have no ceiling on their jackpots, are capable of providing a lucky winner with all the money that many losers had previously put in. Payoffs tend to be huge, but infrequent; at Harold's, the progressive slots pay off on average every 4½ months. The basic accounting question is: Can Harold's deduct the millions of dollars sitting in its progressive slot machines from the revenue recognized at the end of the accounting period? One might argue that no, you cannot deduct the money until the "winning handle pull." However, a winning handle pull might not occur for many months or even years. Although admittedly an estimate would have to be used, the better answer is to match these costs with the revenue recognized, assuming that an average 4½ months' payout is well documented. This example demonstrates that the matching principle can be difficult to apply in practice.

## Full Disclosure Principle

The **full disclosure principle** requires that circumstances and events that make a difference to financial statement users be disclosed. For example, most accountants would agree that Manville Corporation should have disclosed the 52,000 asbestos liability suits (totaling $2 billion) pending against it so that interested parties were made aware of this contingent loss. Similarly, it is generally agreed that companies should disclose the major provisions of employee pension plans and long-term lease contracts.

Compliance with the full disclosure principle occurs through the data contained in the financial statements and the information in the notes that accompany the statements. The first note in most cases is a **summary of significant accounting policies**. The summary includes, among others, the methods used by the company for inventory costing, depreciation of plant assets, and amortization of intangible assets.

Deciding how much disclosure is enough can be difficult. Accountants could disclose every financial event that occurs and every contingency that exists. However, accounting information must be condensed and combined to make it understandable. Providing additional information entails a cost, and the benefits of providing this information in some cases may be less than the costs. Many companies complain of an accounting standards overload. In addition, they object to requirements that force them to disclose confidential information. Determining where to draw the line on disclosure is not easy.

One thing is certain: financial statements were much simpler years ago, when many companies provided little additional information regarding the financial statements. In 1930, General Electric had no notes to the financial statements; today it has over 10 pages of notes! Why this change? A major reason is that the objectives of financial statements have changed. In the past, information was generally presented on what the business had done. Today the objectives of financial reporting are more future-oriented; accounting is trying to provide information that makes it possible to predict the amount, timing, and uncertainty of future cash flows.

## TECHNOLOGY IN ACTION

Some accountants are reconsidering the current means of financial reporting. These accountants propose a data base concept of financial reporting. In such a system, all the information from transactions would be stored in a computerized data base to be accessed by various user groups. The main benefit of such a system is the ability to tailor the information requested to the needs of each user.

What makes it controversial? Discussion currently revolves around access and aggregation issues. Questions such as "Who should be allowed to make inquiries of the system?" "What is the lowest/smallest level of information to be provided?" and "Will such a system necessarily improve on the current means of disclosure?" must be answered before such a system can be implemented on a large scale.

## Cost Principle

As you know, the cost principle dictates that assets are recorded at their cost. Cost is used because it is both relevant and reliable. Cost is **relevant** because it represents the price paid, the assets sacrificed, or the commitment made at date of acquisition. Cost is **reliable** because it is objectively measurable, factual, and verifiable. It is the result of an exchange transaction. Cost is the basis used in preparing financial statements.

The cost principle, however, has come under much criticism. It is criticized by some as irrelevant. Subsequent to acquisition, the argument goes, cost is not equivalent to market value or current value. For that matter, as the purchasing power of the dollar changes, so also does the meaning associated with the dollar that is used as the basis of measurement. Consider the classic story about the individual who went to sleep and woke up 10 years later. Hurrying to a telephone, he got through to his broker and asked what his formerly modest stock portfolio was worth. He was told that he was a multi-millionaire—his General Motors stock was worth $5 million and his AT&T stock was up to $10 million. Elated, he was about to inquire about his other holdings, when the telephone operator cut in with "Your time is up. Please deposit $100,000 for the next 3 minutes."[3]

This story demonstrates that prices can and do change over a period of time, and that one is not necessarily better off when they do. Although the numbers in the story are extreme, consider some more realistic data that compare prices

---

[3]Adapted from *Barron's*, January 28, 1980, p. 27.

in 1980 with what is expected in 1999, assuming average price increases of 6% and 12% per year.

**ILLUSTRATION 12-10**

*Example of changing prices*

**HELPFUL HINT**

Are you a winner or loser when you hold cash in a period of inflation? Answer: A loser, because the value of the cash declines as inflation climbs.

| | 1980 | 1999 | |
| --- | --- | --- | --- |
| **Assumed average price increase** | | **6%** | **12%** |
| Public college, yearly average cost | $ 3,350.00 | $ 10,135.76 | $ 28,852.75 |
| Average taxi ride, New York City (before tip) | 2.95 | 8.93 | 25.40 |
| Slice of pizza | .65 | 1.97 | 5.60 |
| First-class postage stamp | .15 | .45 | 1.29 |
| Run-of-the-mill suburban house, New York City | 150,000.00 | 453,840.00 | 1,291,914.00 |
| McDonald's milk shake | .75 | 2.27 | 6.46 |

Despite the inevitability of changing prices during a period of inflation, the accounting profession still follows the stable monetary unit assumption in preparing a company's primary financial statements. While admitting that some changes in prices do occur, the profession believes the unit of measure—the dollar—has remained sufficiently constant over time to provide meaningful financial information. If presented, the **disclosure of price-level adjusted data is in the form of supplemental information** that accompanies the financial statements.

The basic principles of accounting are summarized in Illustration 12-11.

**ILLUSTRATION 12-11**

*Basic principles used in accounting*

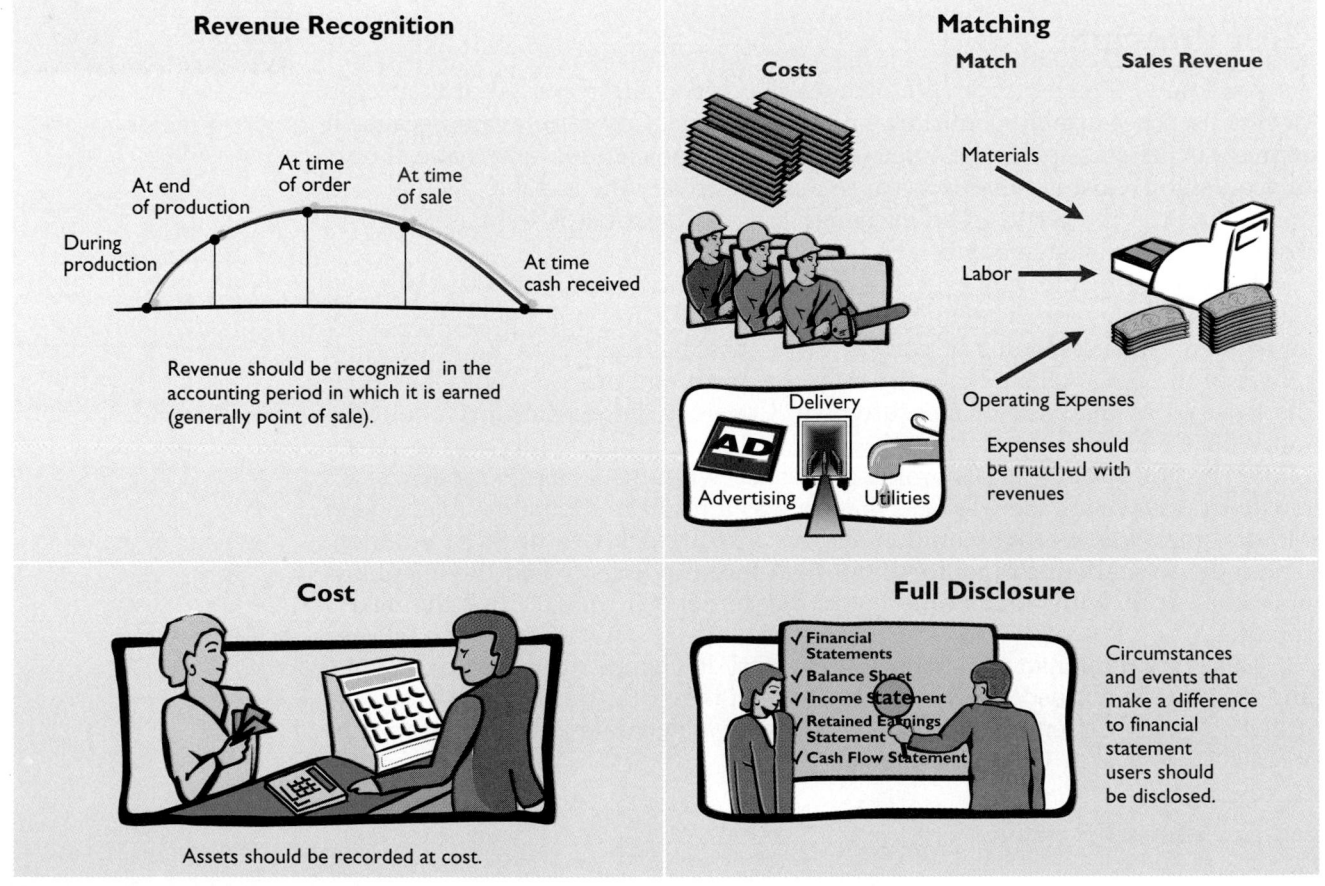

**Revenue Recognition**

At end of production

At time of order

At time of sale

During production

At time cash received

Revenue should be recognized in the accounting period in which it is earned (generally point of sale).

**Matching**

Costs    Match    Sales Revenue

Materials

Labor

Delivery

Advertising    Utilities

Operating Expenses

Expenses should be matched with revenues

**Cost**

Assets should be recorded at cost.

**Full Disclosure**

✓ Financial Statements
✓ Balance Sheet
✓ Income Statement
✓ Retained Earnings Statement
✓ Cash Flow Statement

Circumstances and events that make a difference to financial statement users should be disclosed.

# CONSTRAINTS IN ACCOUNTING

**Constraints** permit a company to modify generally accepted accounting principles without reducing the usefulness of the reported information. The constraints are materiality and conservatism.

**6**
STUDY
OBJECTIVE

Identify the two constraints in accounting.

## Materiality

**Materiality** relates to an item's impact on a firm's overall financial condition and operations. An item is material when it is likely to influence the decision of a reasonably prudent investor or creditor. It is immaterial if its inclusion or omission has no impact on a decision maker. In short, if the item does not make a difference, GAAP does not have to be followed. To determine the materiality of an amount—that is, to determine its financial significance, the accountant usually compares it with such items as total assets, total liabilities, and net income.

To illustrate how the constraint of materiality is applied, assume that Rodriguez Co. purchases a number of low-cost plant assets, such as wastepaper baskets. Although the proper accounting would appear to be to depreciate these wastepaper baskets over their useful life, they are usually expensed immediately. This practice is justified because these costs are considered immaterial. Establishing depreciation schedules for these assets is costly and time-consuming and will not make a material difference on total assets and net income. Other applications of the materiality constraint are the expensing of small tools or the expensing of any plant assets under a certain dollar amount.

## Conservatism

**Conservatism** in accounting means that when in doubt choose the method that will be least likely to overstate assets and income. It does **not** mean **understating** assets or income. Conservatism provides a guide in difficult situations, and the guide is a reasonable one: do not overstate assets and income.

A common application of the conservatism constraint is the use of the lower of cost or market method for inventories. As indicated in Chapter 9, inventories are reported at market value if market value is below cost. This practice results in a higher cost of goods sold and lower net income. In addition, inventory on the balance sheet is stated at a lower amount when market value is below cost. Other examples of conservatism in accounting are the use of the LIFO method for inventory valuation when prices are rising and the use of accelerated depreciation methods for plant assets. Both these methods result in lower asset carrying values and lower net income than alternative methods.

The two constraints are graphically depicted in Illustration 12-12.

**HELPFUL HINT**
In other words, if two methods are otherwise equally appropriate, choose the one that will least likely overstate assets and income.

| Materiality | Conservatism |
|---|---|
| For small amounts, GAAP does not have to be followed. | When in doubt, choose the solution that will be least likely to overstate assets and income. |

**ILLUSTRATION 12-12**

*Constraints in accounting*

## Summary of Conceptual Framework

As we have seen, the conceptual framework for developing sound reporting practices starts with a set of objectives for financial reporting and follows with the development of qualities that make information useful. In addition, elements of financial statements are defined. Operating guidelines in the form of assumptions and principles are then provided. The conceptual framework also recognizes that important constraints exist on the reporting environment. These points are illustrated graphically in Illustration 12-13:

**ILLUSTRATION 12-13**

*Conceptual framework*

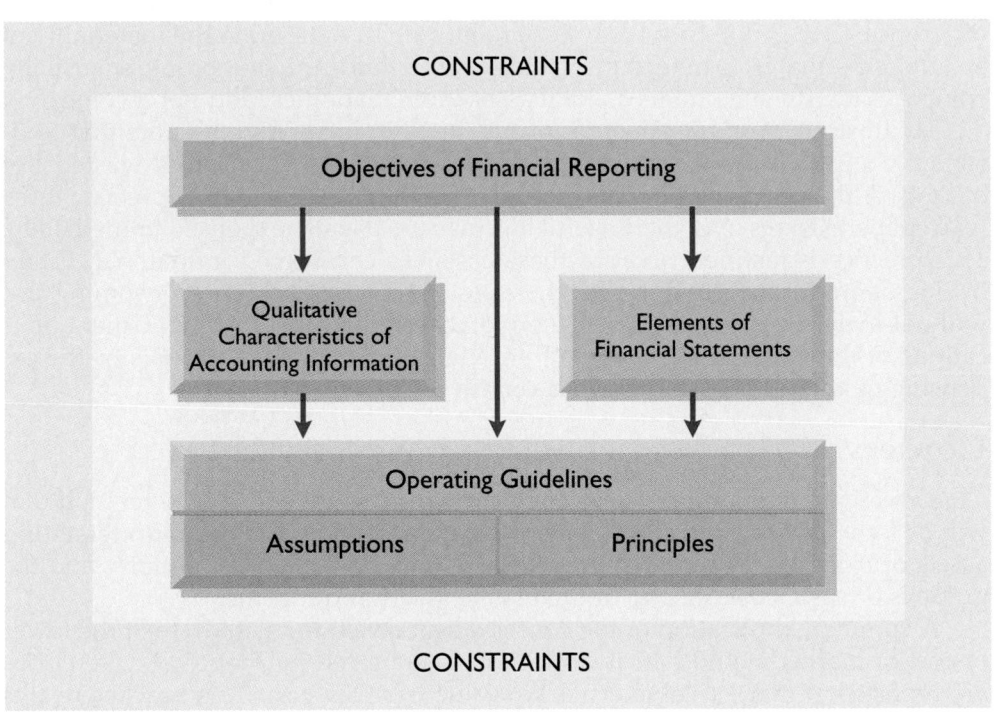

---

**7**
STUDY
OBJECTIVE

Explain the accounting principles used in international operations.

# INTERNATIONAL ACCOUNTING STANDARDS

World markets are becoming increasingly intertwined. Foreigners use American computers, eat American breakfast cereals, read American magazines, listen to American rock music, watch American movies and TV shows, and drink American soda. And, Americans drive Japanese cars, wear Italian shoes and Scottish woolens, drink Brazilian coffee and Indian tea, eat Swiss chocolate bars, sit on Danish furniture, and use Arabian oil. The tremendous variety and volume of both exported and imported goods indicates the extensive involvement of U.S. business in international trade. For many U.S. companies, the world is their market.

The following table illustrates the magnitude of foreign sales and type of product sold by U.S. companies.

| Company | Foreign Sales as a % of Total | Product |
|---|---|---|
| Reebok | 44.3 | Sport clothing |
| Coca-Cola | 67.0 | Beverages |
| Disney | 23.0 | Entertainment |
| E.I. duPont de Nemours | 42.1 | Specialty chemicals |
| General Electric | 27.7 | Diversified |
| Ford Motor | 32.7 | Motor vehicles and parts |
| Campbell Soup | 31.0 | Prepared foods |
| Sears, Roebuck & Co. | 8.9 | Retail and diversified |
| Phillip Morris | 53.8 | Tobacco, beverages, food products |
| RJR Nabisco | 37.0 | Tobacco, beverages, food products |

**ILLUSTRATION 12-14**

*Foreign sales and type of product*

Firms that conduct their operations in more than one country through subsidiaries, divisions, or branches in foreign countries are referred to as **multinational corporations**. The accounting for multinational corporations is complicated because foreign currencies are involved. These international transactions and operations must be translated into U.S. dollars.

## Differences in Standards

As the "world economy" is becoming globalized, many investment and credit decisions require the analysis and interpretation of foreign financial statements. Unfortunately, there is a lack of uniformity in accounting standards from country to country. This lack of uniformity is the result of different legal systems, different processes for developing accounting standards, different governmental requirements, and different economic environments.

## ACCOUNTING IN ACTION
### International Insight

Research and development costs are an example of different international accounting standards. Compare how four countries account for research and development:

| Country | Accounting Treatment |
|---|---|
| United States | Expenditures are expensed. |
| United Kingdom | Certain expenditures may be capitalized. |
| Germany | Expenditures are expensed. |
| Japan | Expenditures may be capitalized and amortized over 5 years. |

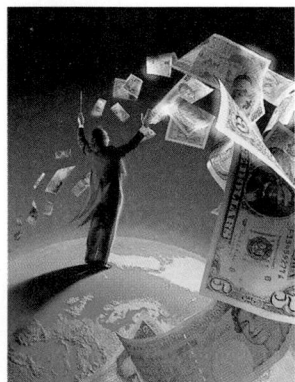

Thus, a research and development expenditure of $100 million is charged totally to expense in the current period in the United States and Germany. This expense could range from zero to $100 million in the United Kingdom and from $20 million to $100 million in Japan!

Do you believe that accounting principles should be comparable across countries?

## Uniformity in Standards

Efforts to obtain uniformity in international accounting practices are taking place. In 1973 the International Accounting Standards Committee (IASC) was formed by agreement of accounting organizations in the United States, the United Kingdom, Canada, Australia, France, Germany, Japan, Mexico, and the Netherlands. The purpose of the IASC is to formulate and publish international accounting standards and to promote their acceptance worldwide.

To date, numerous International Accounting Standards have been issued for IASC members to introduce to their respective countries. But, because the IASC has no enforcement powers, these standards are by no means universally applied. They are, however, generally followed by the large multinational companies that are audited by international public accounting firms. Thus, the foundation has been laid for considerable progress toward greater uniformity in international accounting.

## BEFORE YOU GO ON . . .

### Review It

1. What are the monetary unit assumption, the economic entity assumption, the time period assumption, and the going concern assumption?
2. What are the revenue recognition principle, the matching principle, the full disclosure principle, and the cost principle?
3. What are the materiality constraint and the conservatism constraint?
4. What is the purpose of the International Accounting Standards Committee?

## A LOOK BACK AT OUR FEATURE STORY

Refer back to the opening story, and answer the following questions:

1. Policy Management Systems Corp., which produces insurance software, said that it reported some sales before contracts were signed or product delivered. Is the concept of revenue recognition violated in this situation? Explain.
2. In addition, the story noted that Penguin USA failed to report certain expenses for discounts given to customers for paying early. Why might a company overstate revenue or understate expenses in the wrong period?

*Solution:*

1. The revenue recognition principle dictates that revenue should be recognized in the accounting period in which it is earned. When a sale of product is involved, revenue is generally recognized at the point of sale. Policy Management violated the revenue recognition principle because the sale had not yet occurred.
2. As indicated in the opening story, high-tech firms feel intense pressure to report higher earnings every year. If actual performance falls short of expectations, management might be tempted to bend the rules to prevent its stock price from falling. Although high-tech firms are particularly susceptible to earnings declines, many companies attempt to manage their net income from period to period, as Penguin USA appears to have done.

THE NAVIGATOR

## DEMONSTRATION PROBLEM

Carver Construction Company is under contract to build a condominium at a contract price of $2,000,000. The building will take 18 months to complete at an estimated cost of $1,400,000. Construction began in November 1998, and was finished in April 2000. Actual construction costs incurred in each year were: 1998, $140,000; 1999, $910,000; and 2000, $350,000.

*Instructions*
Compute the gross profit to be recognized in each year.

## SOLUTION TO DEMONSTRATION PROBLEM

| Year | Costs Incurred (Current Period) | ÷ Total Estimated Cost = | Percent Complete (Current Period) | × Total Revenue = | Revenue Recognized (Current Period) |
|---|---|---|---|---|---|
| 1998 | $ 140,000 | $1,400,000 | 10% | $2,000,000 | $ 200,000 |
| 1999 | 910,000 | 1,400,000 | 65% | 2,000,000 | 1,300,000 |
| 2000 | 350,000 | Balance to complete contract | | | 500,000 |
| | $1,400,000 | | | | $2,000,000 |

| Year | Revenue Recognized (Current Period) | − Actual Costs Incurred (Current Period) = | Gross Profit Recognized (Current Period) |
|---|---|---|---|
| 1998 | $ 200,000 | $ 140,000 | $ 60,000 |
| 1999 | 1,300,000 | 910,000 | 390,000 |
| 2000 | 500,000 | 350,000 | 150,000 |
| | $2,000,000 | $1,400,000 | $600,000 |

**PROBLEM-SOLVING STRATEGIES**

(1) Percent complete is determined by dividing costs incurred by total estimated costs.

(2) Percent complete is multiplied by contract price to find revenue recognized.

(3) Gross profit equals revenue recognized less actual costs incurred.

(4) Percentage-of-completion method recognizes revenue as the construction occurs—it is viewed as a series of sales.

## DEMONSTRATION PROBLEM

Valdes Inc. uses the installment method in accounting for its sales. During its first year of operations, it had installment sales of $900,000 and a cost of goods sold on installments of $600,000. The collections on installment sales were as follows: Year 1, $330,000; Year 2, $420,000; and Year 3, $150,000.

*Instructions*

Compute the amount of gross profit to be recognized each year.

**PROBLEM-SOLVING STRATEGIES**

(1) Installment method used when cash collection is uncertain.

(2) Must always find gross profit percentage.

(3) Gross profit recognized each period results from cash collected times gross profit percentage.

## SOLUTION TO DEMONSTRATION PROBLEM

| Year | Cash Collected | × | Gross Profit Percentage* | = | Gross Profit Recognized |
|---|---|---|---|---|---|
| 1 | $330,000 | | 33⅓% | | $110,000 |
| 2 | 420,000 | | 33⅓% | | 140,000 |
| 3 | 150,000 | | 33⅓% | | 50,000 |
| | $900,000 | | | | $300,000 |

*$900,000 − $600,000 = $300,000; $300,000 ÷ $900,000 = 33⅓%

## SUMMARY OF STUDY OBJECTIVES

**1. Explain the meaning of generally accepted accounting principles and identify the key items of the conceptual framework.** Generally accepted accounting principles are a set of rules and practices that are recognized as a general guide for financial reporting purposes. Generally accepted means that these principles must have "substantial authoritative support." The key items of the conceptual framework are: (1) objectives of financial reporting; (2) qualitative characteristics of accounting information; (3) elements of financial statements; and (4) operating guidelines (assumptions, principles, and constraints).

**2. Describe the basic objectives of financial reporting.** The basic objectives of financial reporting are to provide information that is (1) useful to those making investment and credit decisions; (2) helpful in assessing future cash flows; and (3) helpful in identifying economic resources (assets), the claims to those resources (liabilities), and the changes in those resources and claims.

**3. Discuss the qualitative characteristics of accounting information and elements of financial statements.** To be judged useful, information should possess the following qualitative characteristics: relevance, reliability, comparability, and consistency. The elements of financial statements are a set of definitions that can be used to describe the basic terms used in accounting.

**4. *Identify the basic assumptions used by accountants.*** The major assumptions are: monetary unit, economic entity, time period, and going concern.

**5. *Identify the basic principles of accounting.*** The major principles are revenue recognition, matching, full disclosure, and cost.

**6. *Identify the two constraints in accounting.*** The major constraints are materiality and conservatism.

**7. *Explain the accounting principles used in international operations.*** There are few recognized worldwide accounting standards. The International Accounting Standards Committee (IASC), of which the United States is a member, is making efforts to obtain conformity in international accounting practices.

# GLOSSARY

**Comparability** Ability to compare accounting information of different companies because they use the same accounting principles. (p. 518).

**Conceptual framework** A coherent system of interrelated objectives and fundamentals that can lead to consistent standards. (p. 517).

**Conservatism** The approach of choosing an accounting method when in doubt that will least likely overstate assets and net income. (p. 529).

**Consistency** Use of the same accounting principles and methods from year to year within a company. (p. 519).

**Cost principle** Accounting principle that assets should be recorded at their historical cost. (p. 527).

**Economic entity assumption** Accounting assumption that economic events can be identified with a particular unit of accountability. (p. 521).

**Elements of financial statements** Definitions of basic terms used in accounting. (p. 519).

**Full disclosure principle** Accounting principle that circumstances and events that make a difference to financial statement users should be disclosed. (p. 526).

**Generally accepted accounting principles (GAAP)** A set of rules and practices, having substantial authoritative support, that are recognized as a general guide for financial reporting purposes. (p. 516).

**Going concern assumption** The assumption that the enterprise will continue in operation long enough to carry out its existing objectives and commitments. (p. 521).

**Installment method** A method of recognizing revenue using the cash basis; each cash collection consists of a partial recovery of cost of goods sold and partial gross profit from the sale. (p. 524).

**International Accounting Standards Committee (IASC)** An accounting organization whose purpose is to formulate and publish international accounting standards and to promote their acceptance worldwide. (p. 531).

**Matching principle** Accounting principle that expenses should be matched with revenues in the period when efforts are expended to generate revenues. (p. 525).

**Materiality** The constraint of determining if an item is important enough to likely influence the decision of a reasonably prudent investor or creditor. (p. 529).

**Monetary unit assumption** Accounting assumption that only transaction data capable of being expressed in monetary terms should be included in accounting records. (p. 521).

**Percentage-of-completion method** Recognizes revenue and income on a construction project on the basis of costs incurred during the period to the total estimated costs for the entire project. (p. 523).

**Relevance** The quality of information that indicates the information makes a difference in a decision. (p. 518).

**Reliability** The quality of information that gives assurance that it is free of error and bias. (p. 518).

**Revenue recognition principle** Accounting principle that revenue should be recognized in the accounting period in which it is earned (generally at the point of sale). (p. 522).

**Time period assumption** Accounting assumption that the economic life of a business can be divided into artificial time periods. (p. 521).

# SELF-STUDY QUESTIONS

Answers are at the end of the chapter.

(SO 1) 1. Generally accepted accounting principles are:
   a. a set of standards and rules that are recognized as a general guide for financial reporting.
   b. usually established by the Internal Revenue Service.
   c. the guidelines used to resolve ethical dilemmas.
   d. fundamental truths that can be derived from the laws of nature.

(SO 2) 2. Which of the following is *not* an objective of financial reporting?
a. Provide information that is useful in investment and credit decisions.
b. Provide information about economic resources, claims to those resources, and changes in them.
c. Provide information that is useful in assessing future cash flows.
d. Provide information on the liquidation value of a business.

(SO 3) 3. The primary criterion by which accounting information can be judged is:
a. consistency.
b. predictive value.
c. decision-usefulness.
d. comparability.

(SO 3) 4. Verifiable is an ingredient of:

| | Reliability | Relevance |
|---|---|---|
| a. | Yes | Yes |
| b. | No | No |
| c. | Yes | No |
| d. | No | Yes |

(SO 4, 5, 6) 5. Valuing assets at their liquidation value rather than their cost is *inconsistent* with the:
a. time period assumption.
b. matching principle.
c. going concern assumption.
d. materiality constraint.

(SO 5) 6. Gonzalez's Construction Company began a long-term construction contract on January 1, 1999. The contract is expected to be completed in 2000 at a total cost of $20,000,000. Gonzalez's revenue for the project is $24,000,000. Gonzalez incurred contract costs of $4,000,000 in 1999. What gross profit should be recognized in 1999?
a. $800,000.
b. $1,000,000.
c. $2,000,000.
d. $4,000,000.

(SO 5) 7. Dunlop Company had installment sales of $1,000,000 in their first year of operations. The cost of goods sold on installment was $650,000, and Dunlop collected a total of $500,000 on the installment sales. Using the installment method, how much gross profit should be recognized in the first year?
a. $140,000.
b. $175,000.
c. $350,000.
d. $500,000.

(SO 5) 8. The full disclosure dictates that:
a. financial statements should disclose all assets at their cost.
b. financial statements should disclose only those events that can be measured in dollars.
c. financial statements should dislose all events and circumstances that would matter to users of financial statements.
d. financial statements should not be relied on unless an auditor has expressed an unqualified opinion on them.

(SO 6) 9. The accounting constraint that means that when in doubt the accountant should choose the method that will be least likely to overstate assets and income is called (the):
a. matching principle.
b. materiality.
c. conservatism.
d. monetary unit assumption.

(SO 7) 10. The organization that issues international accounting standards is the:
a. Financial Accounting Standards Board.
b. International Accounting Standards Committee.
c. International Auditing Standards Committee.
d. None of the above.

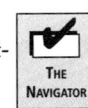

# QUESTIONS

1. (a) What are generally accepted accounting principles (GAAP)? (b) What bodies provide authoritative support for GAAP?

2. What elements comprise the FASB's conceptual framework?

3. (a) What are the objectives of financial reporting? (b) Identify the qualitative characteristics of accounting information.

4. Doug Evans, the president of Packer Company, is pleased. Packer substantially increased its net income in 1999 while keeping its unit inventory relatively the same. Tom Jones, chief accountant, cautions Evans, however. Jones says that since Packer changed from the LIFO to the FIFO method of inventory valuation, there is a consistency problem and it would be difficult to determine if Packer is better off. Is Jones correct? Why?

5. What is the distinction between comparability and consistency?

6. Why is it necessary for accountants to assume that an economic entity will remain a going concern?

7. When should revenue be recognized? Why has the date of sale been chosen as the point at which to recognize the revenue resulting from the entire producing and selling process?

8. Matson Construction Company has a $210 million contract to build a bridge. Its total estimated cost for the project is $170 million. Costs incurred in the first year of the project were $34 million. Matson appropriately uses the percentage-of-completion method. How much revenue and gross profit should Ryder recognize in the first year of the project?

9. Merchandise with a cost of $80,000 was sold during the year for $100,000. Cash collected for the year amounted to $45,000. How much gross profit should be recognized during the year if the company uses the installment method?

10. Distinguish between expired costs and unexpired costs.

11. (a) Where does the accountant disclose information about an entity's financial position, operations, and cash flows? (b) The full disclosure principle recognizes that the nature and amount of information included in financial reports reflect a series of judgmental trade-offs. What are the objectives of these trade-offs?

12. Sal Troia is the president of Better Books. He has no accounting background. Troia cannot understand why current cost is not used as the basis for accounting measurement and reporting. Explain what basis is used and why.

13. Describe the two constraints inherent in the presentation of accounting information.

14. Your roommate believes that international accounting standards are uniform throughout the world. Is your roommate correct? Explain.

15. What organization establishes international accounting standards?

# Brief exercises

•••••••••••••••••••••••••••••••••••••••••••••••••••••••••••••••••••••••••••••••••••••••••••••••••

*Identify generally accepted accounting principles.*
*(SO 1)*

**BE12–1**  Indicate whether each of the following statements is true or false.

1. ____ "*Generally accepted*" means that these principles must have "substantial authoritative support."
2. ____ GAAP is a set of rules and practices established by the accounting profession to serve as a general guide for financial reporting purposes.
3. ____ Substantial authoritative support for GAAP usually comes from two standard-setting bodies: the FASB and the IRS. *sec*

*Identify items included in conceptual framework.*
*(SO 1)*

**BE12–2**  Indicate which of the following items is(are) included in the FASB's conceptual framework. (Use "Yes" or "No" to answer this question.)

1. ____ Qualitative characteristics of accounting information.
2. ____ Analysis of financial statement ratios.
3. ____ Objectives of financial reporting.

*Identify objectives of financial reporting.*
*(SO 2)*

**BE12–3**  According to the FASB's conceptual framework, which of the following are objectives of financial reporting? (Use "Yes" or "No" to answer this question.)

1. ____ Provide information that identifies the economic resources (assets), the claims to those resources (liabilities), and the changes in those resources and claims.
2. ____ Provide information that is helpful in assessing past cash flows and stock prices.
3. ____ Provide information that is useful to those making investment and credit decisions.

*Identify qualitative characteristics.*
*(SO 3)*

**BE12–4**  Presented below is a chart of the qualitative characteristics of accounting information. Fill in the blanks from (a) to (e).

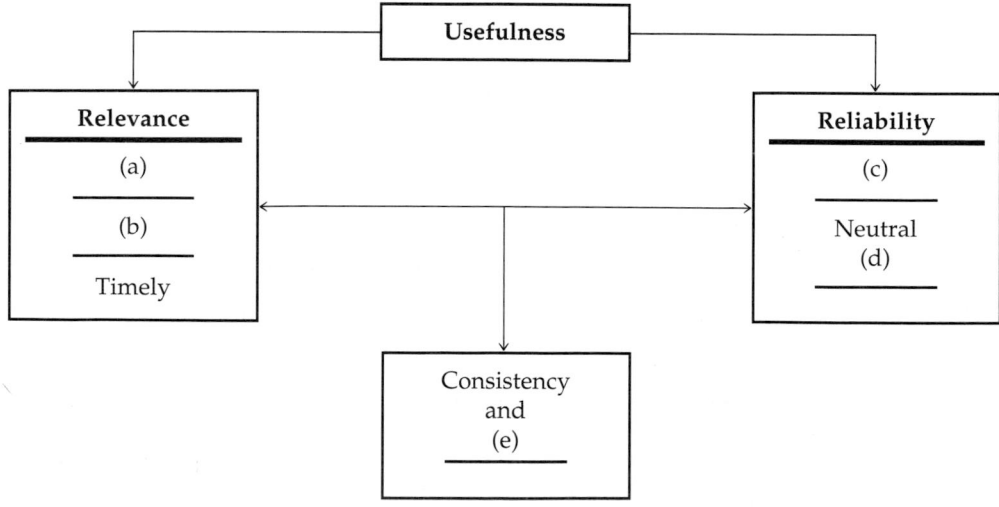

**BE12–5** Given the *qualitative characteristics* of accounting established by the FASB's conceptual framework, complete each of the following statements:

1. For information to be _____, it should have predictive or feedback value, and it must be presented on a timely basis.
2. _____ is the quality of information that gives assurance that it is free of error and bias; it can be depended on.
3. _____ means using the same accounting principles and methods from year to year within a company.

*Identify qualitative characteristics.*
*(SO 3)*

**BE12–6** Presented below is a set of qualitative characteristics of accounting information.

(a) Predictive value        (c) Verifiable
(b) Neutral                 (d) Timely

*Identify qualitative characteristics.*
*(SO 3)*

Match these qualitative characteristics to the following statements, using letters a through d.

1. _____ Accounting information must be proved to be free of error and bias.
2. _____ Accounting information must be available to decision makers before it loses its capacity to influence their decisions.
3. _____ Accounting information should help users make predictions about the outcome of past, present, and future events.
4. _____ Accounting information cannot be selected, prepared, or presented to favor one set of interested users over another.

**BE12–7** Presented below are four concepts discussed in this chapter.

(a) Time period assumption    (c) Full disclosure principle
(b) Cost principle            (d) Conservatism

*Identify operating guidelines.*
*(SO 4, 5, 6)*

Match these concepts to the following accounting practices. Each letter can be used only once.

1. _____ Preparing financial statements on an annual basis.
2. _____ Using the lower of cost or market method for inventory valuation.
3. _____ Recording inventory at its purchase price.
4. _____ Using notes and supplementary schedules in the financial statements.

**BE12–8** Won Construction Company is under contract to build a commercial building at a price of $3,600,000. Construction began in January 1998 and was finished in December 2000. Total estimated construction costs are $2,800,000. Actual construction costs incurred in each year were: 1998, $560,000; 1999, $1,820,000; 2000, $420,000. Compute the revenue to be recognized in each year using the *percentage-of-completion* method.

*Compute revenue—percentage-of-completion.*
*(SO 5)*

**BE12–9** Grasso Co. uses the installment method to determine its net income. During its first year of operations, it had installment sales of $800,000 and a cost of goods sold of $560,000. The collections on installment sales were as follows: Year 1, $360,000; Year 2, $440,000. Determine the gross profit recognized for Year 1 and 2.

*Compute gross profit—installment method.*
*(SO 5)*

**BE12–10** Wriston Company uses the following accounting practices:

1. The income statement shows paper clips expense of $10.
2. Revenue on installment sales is recognized at the time of sale.
3. Small tools are recorded as plant assets and depreciated.
4. Inventory is reported at cost when market value is lower.

Indicate the accounting constraint, if any, that has been violated by each practice.

*Identify the constraints that have been violated.*
*(SO 6)*

# EXERCISES
· · · · · · · · · · · · · · · · · · · · · · · · · · · · · · · · · · · · · · · · · · · · · · · · · · · · · · · · · ·

**E12–1** A number of accounting reporting situations are described below.

1. Taylor Company uses the direct write-off method of accounting for uncollectible accounts.
2. Morita Hospital Supply Corporation reports only current assets and current liabilities on its balance sheet. Property, plant, and equipment and bonds payable are reported as current assets and current liabilities, respectively. Liquidation of the company is unlikely.

*Identify the assumption, principle, or constraint that has been violated.*
*(SO 4, 5, 6)*

3. Allen Company is in its fifth year of operation and has yet to issue financial statements. (Do not use full disclosure principle.)
4. Casino Company has inventory on hand that cost $400,000. Casino reports inventory on its balance sheet at its current market value of $425,000.
5. Marla Downs, president of the Classic Music Company, bought a computer for her personal use. She paid for the computer by using company funds and debited the "computers" account.
6. Ruff Company recognizes revenue at the end of the production cycle, but before sale. The price of the product, as well as the amount that can be sold, is not certain.
7. In preparing its financial statements, Johnson Company omitted information concerning its method of accounting for inventories.

**Instructions**
For each of the above, list the assumption, principle, or constraint that has been violated, if any. List only one term for each case.

*Identify the assumption, principle, or constraint that has been violated and prepare correct entries.*
*(SO 4, 5, 6)*

**E12–2** Presented below are some business transactions that occurred during 1999 for Georgia Co.

(a) Equipment worth $80,000 was acquired at a cost of $64,000 from a company that had water damage in a flood. The following entry was made:

| | | |
|---|---|---|
| Equipment | 80,000 | |
| Cash | | 64,000 |
| Gain | | 16,000 |

(b) Merchandise inventory with a cost of $208,000 is reported at its market value of $260,000. The following entry was made:

| | | |
|---|---|---|
| Merchandise Inventory | 52,000 | |
| Gain | | 52,000 |

(c) An account receivable has been deemed to be a bad debt. The following entry was made:

| | | |
|---|---|---|
| Allowance for Doubtful Accounts | 10,000 | |
| Accounts Receivable | | 10,000 |

(d) The president of Georgia Co., George Warden, purchased a truck for personal use and charged it to his expense account. The following entry was made:

| | | |
|---|---|---|
| Travel Expense | 18,000 | |
| Cash | | 18,000 |

(e) An electric pencil sharpener costing $40 is being depreciated over 5 years. The following entry was made:

| | | |
|---|---|---|
| Depreciation Expense—Pencil Sharpener | 8 | |
| Accumulated Depreciation—Pencil Sharpener | | 8 |

**Instructions**
In each of the situations above, identify the assumption, principle, or constraint that has been violated, if any, and discuss the appropriateness of the journal entries. Give the correct journal entry, if necessary.

*Identify accounting assumptions, principles, and constraints to different situations.*
*(SO 4, 5, 6)*

**E12–3** Presented below are the assumptions, principles, and constraints discussed in this chapter:

(a) Economic entity assumption
(b) Going concern assumption
(c) Monetary unit assumption
(d) Time period assumption
(e) Cost principle

(f) Matching principle
(g) Full disclosure principle
(h) Revenue recognition principle
(i) Materiality
(j) Conservatism

**Instructions**
Identify by letter the accounting assumption, principle, or constraint that describes each situation below. Do not use a letter more than once.

1. Requires that the operational guidelines be followed for all significant items.
2. Separates financial information into time periods for reporting purpose.

3. Requires recognition of expenses in the same period as related revenues.
4. Indicates that market value changes subsequent to purchase are not recorded in the accounts.
5. Is the rationale for why plant assets are not reported at liquidation value. (Do not use historical cost principle.)
6. Indicates that personal and business record keeping should be separately maintained.
7. Ensures that all relevant financial information is reported.
8. Assumes that the dollar is the "measuring stick" used to report on financial performance.

**E12–4**   Consider the following transactions of Brown Group Company for 1999.

*Determine the amount of revenue to be recognized.*
*(SO 5)*

1. Leased office space to Patel Supplies for a 1-year period beginning September 1. The rent of $30,000 was paid in advance.
2. Sold a 6-month insurance policy to Oliva Corporation for $8,000 on March 1.
3. A sales order for merchandise costing $9,000 that had a sales price of $12,000 was received on December 28 from Weaver Company. The goods were shipped FOB shipping point on December 31, and Weaver received them on January 3, 2000.
4. Signed a long-term contract to construct a building at a total price of $1,600,000. Total estimated cost of construction is $1,200,000. During 1999, the company incurred $300,000 of costs and collected $330,000 in cash. The percentage-of-completion method is used to recognize revenue.
5. Merchandise inventory on hand at year-end amounted to $160,000. Brown Group expects to sell the inventory in 2000 for $190,000.

*Instructions*
For each item above, indicate the amount of revenue Brown Group should recognize in calendar year 1999. Explain.

**E12–5**   Fong Construction Company currently has one long-term construction project. The project has a contract price of $130,000,000 with total estimated costs of $100,000,000. Fong appropriately uses the percentage-of-completion method. After 2 years of construction, the following costs have been accumulated:

*Determine gross profit for construction projects.*
*(SO 5)*

| | |
|---|---|
| Actual cost incurred, Year 1 | $30,000,000 |
| Total estimated cost remaining after Year 1 | 70,000,000 |
| Actual cost incurred, Year 2 | 50,000,000 |
| Total estimated cost remaining after Year 2 | 20,000,000 |

*Instructions*
Determine the gross profit for each of the first 2 years of the construction contract.

**E12–6**   Quincy Company sold equipment for $300,000 in 1998. Collections on the sale were as follows: 1998, $70,000; 1999, $190,000; 2000, $40,000. Quincy's cost of goods sold is typically 70% of sales.

*Determine gross profit using installment sales and point-of-sale bases.*
*(SO 5)*

*Instructions*
(a) Determine Quincy's gross profit for 1998, 1999, and 2000, assuming that Quincy recognizes revenue under the installment method.
(b) Determine Quincy's gross profit for 1998, 1999, and 2000, assuming that Quincy recognizes revenue under the point-of-sale basis.

# PROBLEMS: SET A

**P12–1A**   Carson and McMann are accountants for Desktop Computers. They are having disagreements concerning the following transactions that occurred during the calendar year 1999.

*Analyze transactions to identify accounting principle or assumption violated and prepare correct entries.*
*(SO 4, 5)*

1. Desktop purchased equipment for $35,000 at a going-out-of-business sale. The equipment was worth $45,000. Carson believes that the following entry should be made:

| | | |
|---|---|---|
| Equipment | 45,000 | |
|     Cash | | 35,000 |
|     Gain | | 10,000 |

2. Land costing $60,000 was appraised at $90,000. Carson suggests the following journal entry:

| | | |
|---|---|---|
| Land | 30,000 | |
|     Gain on Appreciation of Land | | 30,000 |

3. Depreciation for the year was $18,000. Since net income is expected to be lower this year, Carson suggests deferring depreciation to a year when there is more net income.

4. Desktop bought a custom-made piece of equipment for $18,000. This equipment has a useful life of 6 years. Desktop depreciates equipment using the straight-line method. "Since the equipment is custom-made, it will have no resale value and, therefore, shouldn't be depreciated but instead expensed immediately," argues Carson. "Besides, it provides for lower net income."

5. Carson suggests that equipment should be reported on the balance sheet at its liquidation value, which is $15,000 less than its cost.

McMann disagrees with Carson on each of the above situations.

**Instructions**

For each transaction, indicate why McMann disagrees. Identify the accounting principle or assumption that Carson would be violating if his suggestions were used. Prepare the correct journal entry for each transaction, if any.

*Determine the appropriateness of journal entries in terms of generally accepted accounting principles or assumptions.*
*(SO 4, 5)*

**P12–2A**    Presented below are a number of business transactions that occurred during the current year for Jose, Inc.

1. Materials were purchased on March 31 for $65,000 and this amount was entered in the Materials account. On December 31, the materials would have cost $85,000, so the following entry was made:

| | | |
|---|---|---|
| Inventory | 20,000 | |
|     Gain on Inventories | | 20,000 |

2. An order for $30,000 has been received from a customer for products on hand. This order is to be shipped on January 9 next year. The following entry was made:

| | | |
|---|---|---|
| Accounts Receivable | 30,000 | |
|     Sales | | 30,000 |

3. The president of Jose, Inc. used his expense account to purchase a new Saab 9000 solely for personal use. The following entry was made:

| | | |
|---|---|---|
| Miscellaneous Expense | 34,000 | |
|     Cash | | 34,000 |

4. Because of a "flood sale," equipment obviously worth $230,000 was acquired at a cost of $150,000. The following entry was made:

| | | |
|---|---|---|
| Equipment | 230,000 | |
|     Cash | | 150,000 |
|     Gain on Purchase of Equipment | | 80,000 |

5. Because the general level of prices increased during the current year, Jose, Inc. determined that there was a $10,000 understatement of depreciation expense on its equipment and decided to record it in its accounts. The following entry was made:

| | | |
|---|---|---|
| Depreciation Expense | 10,000 | |
|     Accumulated Depreciation | | 10,000 |

**Instructions**

 In each of the situations above, discuss the appropriateness of the journal entries in terms of generally accepted accounting principles.

*Recognize gross profit using percentage-of-completion.*
*(SO 5)*

**P12–3A**    Rasheed Construction Company is involved in a long-term construction contract to build an office building at a total estimated cost of $30 million and contract price of $38 million. Additional information follows:

**Office Building**

| | Cash Collections | Actual Costs Incurred |
|---|---|---|
| 1998 | $ 7,000,000 | $ 4,500,000 |
| 1999 | 9,000,000 | 6,000,000 |
| 2000 | 12,500,000 | 12,000,000 |
| 2001 | 9,500,000 | 7,500,000 |

The project is completed in 2001, and all cash to be received from the contract has been received.

**Instructions**
Prepare a schedule to determine the gross profit in each year for the long-term construction contract using the percentage-of-completion method.

**P12–4A** Engram Construction sold apartments it had constructed to Fisher Management Company for $2.5 million. Engram's cost to construct the apartments was $1.5 million. Engram appropriately uses the installment method. Additional information follows:

*Recognize gross profit using the installment method.*
*(SO 5)*

**Cash Collected**

| 1998 | $ 800,000 |
|---|---|
| 1999 | 1,200,000 |
| 2000 | 500,000 |

(a) Determine the gross profit for each year using the installment method.
(b) Repeat (a) assuming the construction costs were $1.6 million.

**P12–5A** Presented below are the assumptions, principles, and constraints used in this chapter.

*Identify accounting assumptions, principles, and constraints.*
*(SO 4, 5, 6)*

(a) Economic entity assumption
(b) Going concern assumption
(c) Monetary unit assumption
(d) Time period assumption
(e) Full disclosure principle
(f) Revenue recognition principle
(g) Matching principle
(h) Cost principle
(i) Materiality
(j) Conservatism

Identify by letter the accounting assumption, principle, or constraint that describes each situation below. Do not use a letter more than once.

1. Market value changes subsequent to purchase are not recorded in the accounts. (Do not use the revenue recognition principle.)
2. Indicates that personal and business record keeping should be separately maintained.
3. Ensures that all relevant financial information is reported.
4. Lower of cost or market is used to value inventories.
5. Repair tools are expensed when purchased. These repair tools have a useful life of more than one accounting period. (Do not use conservatism.)
6. Allocates expenses to revenues in proper period.
7. Assumes that the dollar is the measuring stick used to report financial information.
8. Separates financial information into time periods for reporting purposes.

# PROBLEMS: SET B
••••••••••••••••••••••••••••••••••••••••••••••••••••••••••••

**P12–1B** Carlos and Dana are accountants for Arruza Printers. They are having disagreements concerning the following transactions that occurred during the year.

*Analyze transactions to identify accounting principle or assumption violated and prepare correct entries.*
*(SO 4, 5)*

1. Arruza purchased equipment at a fire sale for $21,000. The equipment was worth $26,000. Carlos believes that the following entry should be made:

| | | |
|---|---|---|
| Equipment | 26,000 | |
|     Cash | | 21,000 |
|     Gain | | 5,000 |

2. Carlos suggests that Arruza should carry equipment on the balance sheet at its liquidation value, which is $20,000 less than its cost.

3. Arruza rented office space for 1 year starting October 1, 1999. The total amount of $30,000 was paid in advance. Carlos believes that the following entry should be made on October 1:

| | | |
|---|---|---|
| Rent Expense | 30,000 | |
|     Cash | | 30,000 |

4. Land costing $41,000 was appraised at $49,000. Carlos suggests the following journal entry:

| | | |
|---|---|---|
| Land | 8,000 | |
|     Gain on Appreciation of Land | | 8,000 |

5. Arruza bought equipment for $40,000, including installation costs. The equipment has a useful life of 5 years. Arruza depreciates equipment using the straight-line method. "Since the equipment as installed into our system cannot be removed without considerable damage, it will have no resale value, and therefore should not be depreciated but instead expensed immediately," argues Carlos. "Besides, it lowers net income."

6. Depreciation for the year was $26,000. Since net income is expected to be lower this year, Carlos suggests deferring depreciation to a year when there is more net income.

Dana disagrees with Carlos on each of the situations above.

*Instructions*

For each transaction, indicate why Dana disagrees. Identify the accounting principle or assumption that Carlos would be violating if his suggestions were used. Prepare the correct journal entry for each transaction, if any.

*Determine the appropriateness of journal entries in terms of generally accepted accounting principles or assumptions. (SO 4, 5)*

**P12–2B**  Presented below are a number of business transactions that occurred during the current year for Quester, Inc.

1. The president of Quester, Inc., used his expense account to purchase a pre-owned Mercedes-Benz E420 solely for personal use. The following entry was made:

| | | |
|---|---|---|
| Miscellaneous Expense | 54,000 | |
|     Cash | | 54,000 |

2. Land was purchased on April 30 for $200,000 and this amount was entered in the Land account. On December 31, the land would have cost $230,000, so the following entry was made:

| | | |
|---|---|---|
| Land | 30,000 | |
|     Gain on Land | | 30,000 |

3. An order for $60,000 has been received from a customer for products on hand. This order is to be shipped on January 9 next year. The following entry was made:

| | | |
|---|---|---|
| Accounts Receivable | 60,000 | |
|     Sales | | 60,000 |

4. Because of a "flood sale," equipment obviously worth $300,000 was acquired at a cost of $250,000. The following entry was made:

| | | |
|---|---|---|
| Equipment | 300,000 | |
|     Cash | | 250,000 |
|     Gain on Purchase of Equipment | | 50,000 |

5. Because the general level of prices increased during the current year, Quester, Inc., determined that there was a $40,000 understatement of depreciation expense on its equipment and decided to record it in its accounts. The following entry was made:

| | | |
|---|---|---|
| Depreciation Expense | 40,000 | |
|     Accumulated Depreciation | | 40,000 |

*Instructions*

▥▥▤▤▷ In each of the situations above, discuss the appropriateness of the journal entries in terms of generally accepted accounting principles.

**P12–3B** Estafan Construction Company is involved in a long-term construction contract. Estafan contracted to build a shopping center with a total estimated cost of $20 million and contract price of $28 million. Additional information follows:

*Recognize gross profit using the percentage-of-completion method.*
*(SO 5)*

**Shopping Center**

| | Cash Collections | Actual Costs Incurred |
|---|---|---|
| 1998 | $ 4,500,000 | $3,000,000 |
| 1999 | 10,000,000 | 9,000,000 |
| 2000 | 7,000,000 | 5,000,000 |
| 2001 | 6,500,000 | 3,000,000 |

The project was completed in 2001, and all cash collections related to the contract have been received.

*Instructions*

Prepare a schedule to determine the gross profit for each year for the long-term construction contract, using the percentage-of-completion method.

**P12–4B** Donovan Inc. sold condominiums it had constructed to Ashbrook Management Company for $6 million. Donovan's cost to construct the condominiums was $4.2 million. Donovan appropriately uses the installment method. Additional information follows:

*Recognize gross profit using the installment method.*
*(SO 5)*

**Cash Collected**

| | |
|---|---|
| 1998 | $ 900,000 |
| 1999 | 3,800,000 |
| 2000 | 1,300,000 |

*Instructions*

(a) Prepare a schedule to determine the gross profit for each year using the installment method.

(b) Repeat (a) assuming construction costs were $4.5 million.

**P12–5B** Presented below are assumptions, principles, and constraints.

*Identify accounting assumptions, principles, and constraints.*
*(SO 4, 5, 6)*

(a) Economic entity assumption
(b) Going concern assumption
(c) Monetary unit assumption
(d) Time period assumption
(e) Full disclosure principle

(f) Revenue recognition principle
(g) Matching principle
(h) Cost principle
(i) Materiality
(j) Conservatism

*Instructions*

Identify by letter the accounting assumption, principle, or constraint that describes each situation below. Do not use a letter more than once.

1. Each entity is kept as a unit distinct from its owner or owners.
2. Reporting must be done at defined intervals.
3. Revenue is recorded at the point of sale.
4. When in doubt, it is better to understate rather than overstate net income.
5. All important information related to inventories is presented in the footnotes or in the financial statements.
6. Assets are not stated at their liquidation value. (Do not use the cost principle.)
7. The death of the president is not recorded in the accounts.
8. Pencil sharpeners are expensed when purchased.
9. An allowance for doubtful accounts is established. (Do not use conservatism.)

# BROADENING YOUR PERSPECTIVE

# FINANCIAL REPORTING AND ANALYSIS

........................................................................................

### FINANCIAL REPORTING PROBLEM

**BYP12–1**    Suzanne Wessels has successfully completed her first accounting course during the spring semester and is now working as a management trainee for First Arizona Bank during the summer. One of her fellow management trainees, Wade Greaton, is taking the same accounting course this summer and has been having a "lot of trouble." On the second examination, for example, Wade became confused about inventory valuation methods and completely missed all the points on a problem involving LIFO and FIFO.

Wade's instructor recently indicated that the third examination will probably have a number of essay questions dealing with accounting principle issues. Wade is quite concerned about the third examination for two reasons. First, he has never taken an accounting examination where essay answers were required. Second, Wade feels he has to do well on this examination to get an acceptable grade in the course.

Wade has therefore asked Suzanne to help him prepare for the next examination. She agrees, and suggests that Wade develop a set of possible questions on the accounting principles material that they might discuss.

*Instructions*

Answer the following questions that were developed by Wade.

   (a) What is a conceptual framework?
   (b) Why is there a need for a conceptual framework?
   (c) What are the objectives of financial reporting?
   (d) If you had to explain generally accepted accounting principles to a nonaccountant, what essential characteristics would you include in your explanation?
   (e) What are the qualitative characteristics of accounting? Explain each one.
   (f) Identify the basic assumptions used in accounting.
   (g) What are two major constraints involved in financial reporting? Explain both of them.

### RESEARCH ASSIGNMENT

**BYP12–2**    During the years 1978–85, the Financial Accounting Standards Board (FASB) issued six *Statements of Financial Accounting Concepts* (SFACs). From the library, obtain copies of SFAC No. 2 (*Qualitative Characteristics of Accounting Information*) and SFAC No. 3 (*Elements of Financial Statements of Business Enterprises*).

*Instructions*

Use these statements to answer the following questions:

   (a) Your textbook indicates that "an item is material when it is likely to influence the decision of a reasonably prudent investor or creditor." SFAC No. 2 identifies a number of examples in which specific quantitative guidelines are provided to accountants and auditors. Identify two of these examples. Do you think that materiality guidelines should be quantified? Why or why not?
   (b) SFAC No. 3 discusses the concept of "articulation" between financial statement elements. Briefly summarize the meaning of this term and how it relates to an entity's financial statements.

### REAL-WORLD FOCUS: Newcor Incorporated

**BYP12–3**    **Newcor Inc.** designs, manufactures, and sells specialty-purpose equipment and also manufactures and sells precision-machined parts and molded rubber and plastic products. The company previously had operating facilities in Belgium and Canada, both of which were sold. The company employs 747 employees and has roughly 2,000 shareholders.

The annual report of Newcor Inc. reports the following information in the president's letter to stockholders:

### NEWCOR INC.
### President's Letter to Stockholders

As indicated in last year's report, we were considering adoption of the percentage-of-completion method of accounting for long-term contracts. During the first quarter this year, we did adopt this method which has the effect of better matching revenues with work performed when compared to the completed-contract method of accounting that had previously been used to report financial results.

*Instructions*

(a) Which two accounting principles are discussed in Newcor's president's letter?
(b) Explain how the change in method will provide better matching of revenues with work performed.


# CRITICAL THINKING

## GROUP DECISION CASE

**BYP12–4**   Margo Industries has two operating divisions—Talley Construction Division and Shumway Securities Division. Both divisions maintain their own accounting system and method of revenue recognition.

**Talley Construction Division**
During the fiscal year ended November 30, 1999, Talley Construction Division had one construction project in process. A $30,000,000 contract for construction of a civic center was granted on June 19, 1999, and construction began on August 1, 1999. Estimated costs of completion at the contract date were $26,000,000 over a 2-year time period from the date of the contract. On November 30, 1999, construction costs of $8,000,000 had been incurred. The construction costs to complete the remainder of the project were reviewed on November 30, 1999, and were estimated to amount to only $16,000,000 because of an expected decline in raw materials costs. Revenue recognition is based upon a percentage-of-completion method.

**Shumway Securities Division**
Shumway Securities Division works through manufacturers' agents in various cities. Orders for alarm systems and down payments are forwarded from agents, and the division ships the goods f.o.b. factory directly to customers (usually police departments and security guard companies). Customers are billed directly for the balance due plus actual shipping costs. The firm received orders for $6,000,000 of goods during the fiscal year ended November 30, 1999. Down payments of $600,000 were received and goods with a selling price of $5,000,000 were billed and shipped. Actual freight costs of $100,000 were also billed. Commissions of 10% on product price are paid manufacturing agents after goods are shipped to customers. Such goods are warranted for 90 days after shipment, and warranty returns have been about 1% of sales. Revenue is recognized at the point of sale by this division.

*Instructions*
With the class divided into groups, answer the following:

(a) There are a variety of methods of revenue recognition. Define and describe each of the following methods of revenue recognition, and indicate whether each is in accordance with generally accepted accounting principles.
   1. Point of sale.
   2. Percentage-of-completion.
   3. Installment contract.
(b) Compute the revenue to be recognized in fiscal year 1999 for both operating divisions of Margo Industries in accordance with generally accepted accounting principles.

## COMMUNICATION ACTIVITY

**BYP12–5**  If you go on to advanced accounting courses, you'll study the differences between accounting in the business world and university accounting. You'll find that there's one major similarity: both depend heavily on the matching principle.

At Long Beach City College, a two-year community college with 30,000 students, most of the revenues come from the state of California and the federal government. As a condition of receiving these grants, "we must match expenses against revenues in the right fiscal year," says the school's accounting manager.

For example, the college receives federal funding under the Job Training Partnership Act. "We receive funding from the federal government, which allows us to offer classes to students for job preparation. The government specifies the grant periods, for instance, from July 1 to June 30. We therefore have to ensure that all transactions for that project are completed within that fiscal year." Another project is the amnesty program, the federal government's legalization of foreign nationals. Expenses to offset the grant money are mostly teaching salaries and instructional materials.

By year-end, the goal is to break even. Excess funds, if any, have to be returned. But program managers do not want a deficit, either, because these projects are accountable to the college administration and any overspending will come from the college's general fund.

### Instructions
Write a letter to your instructor covering the following points:

1. Why is the matching principle important in accounting for government grants?
2. Give some examples of grant or special programs to which the matching principle might be applied at your college or university.
3. What are some examples of costs that Long Beach Community College might properly charge to its grant or special programs?

## ETHICS CASE

**BYP12–6**  When the Financial Accounting Standards Board issues new standards, the required implementation date is usually 12 months or more from the date of issuance, with early implementation encouraged. Sarah Lane, accountant at Mintur Corporation, discusses with her financial vice president the need for early implementation of a recently issued standard that would result in a much fairer presentation of the company's financial condition and earnings. When the financial vice president determines that early implementation of the standard will adversely affect reported net income for the year, he strongly discourages Sarah from implementing the standard until it is required.

### Instructions
(a) Who are the stakeholders in this situation?
(b) What, if any, are the ethical considerations in this situation?
(c) What does Sarah have to gain by advocating early implementation? Who might be affected by the decision against early implementation?

# SURFING THE NET

**BYP12–7**  The Financial Accounting Standards Board (FASB) is a private organization established to improve accounting standards and financial reporting. The FASB conducts extensive research before issuing a "Statement of Financial Accounting Standards," which represents an authoritative expression of generally accepted accounting principles.

**Address:** http://www.rutgers.edu/accounting/raw/fasb/home.htm

**Steps:** Visit the homepage of the FASB

*Instructions*

Answer the following questions:

(a) What is the mission of the FASB?

(b) Using the table of contents, locate FASB Statement 128. What topic does Statement 128 address? What was the issue date?

---

*Answers to Self-Study Questions*

1. a    2. d    3. c    4. c    5. c    6. a    7. b    8. c    9. c    10. b

---

*Answer to Kellogg Review It Question 2, p. 520*

The Report of Independent Accountants indicates that the financial statements (balance sheet, income statement, shareholders' equity, and cash flows) are presented fairly, in accordance with generally accepted accounting principles.

 **Remember to go back to the Navigator box on the chapter-opening page and check off your completed work.**

**Before studying this chapter, you should know or, if necessary, review:**

a. The cost principle of accounting. (Ch. 1, p. 11)

b. The owner's equity statement. (Ch. 1, pp. 23–25)

c. How to make closing entries and prepare the post-closing trial balance. (Ch. 4, pp. 146–151)

d. The steps in the accounting cycle. (Ch. 4, p. 154)

e. The format of classified financial statements. (Ch. 4, pp. 157–161)

THE NAVIGATOR

## FEATURE STORY

# From Trials to Top Ten

Razor & Tie Music opened its doors in 1990 when Cliff Chenfield and Craig Balsam gave up the razors, ties, and six-figure salaries they had become accustomed to as New York lawyers to set up a partnership in Cliff's living room. In 1998 the label is at the forefront of marketing contemporary music—the only record company in the country that has achieved success by selling music both on television and in the stores. Razor & Tie's entertaining and ef-

fective TV commercials have yielded unprecedented sales for multi-artist music compilations, while its hot young retail label has been behind some of the most recent original, progressive releases.

Razor & Tie's first TV release, *Those Fabulous '70s* (100,000 copies sold), was followed by *Disco Fever* (over 300,000). These albums generated so much publicity that partners Cliff and Craig were guests on dozens of TV interview shows.

After restoring the respectability of the oft-maligned 1970s, the partners forged into the musical '80s with the same zeal that elicited suc-

cess with their first releases. In July 1993, Razor & Tie released *Totally '80s,* a collection of Top 10 singles from the 1980s that has sold over 450,000 units since its release. Featuring the tag line "The greatest hits from the decade when communism died and music videos were born," *Totally '80s* was the best-selling direct-response album in the country in 1993.

In 1995, Razor & Tie broke into the contemporary music world with *Living In The '90s,* the most successful record in the history of the company. Featuring a number of songs that were still recurrent hits on the radio at the time the package initially aired, *Living In The '90s* was a blockbuster, receiving Gold certification in less than nine months and rewriting the rules on direct-response albums. For the first time, contemporary music was available through an album offered only through direct-response spots.

How has Razor & Tie carved out such a sizable piece of the market? Through the complementary talents of the two partners. Their imagination and savvy, along with exciting new releases planned for the coming years, ensure Razor & Tie such continued growth that the partnership form of organization may be challenged to its limits.

THE NAVIGATOR

*On the World Wide Web*
www.razorandtie.com

# CHAPTER 13

# ACCOUNTING FOR PARTNERSHIPS

**THE NAVIGATOR** ✔

- Understand *Concepts for Review* ☐
- Read *Feature Story* ☐
- Scan *Study Objectives* ☐
- Read *Preview* ☐
- Read text and answer *Before You Go On*
  p. 554 ☐ p. 559 ☐ p. 568 ☐ p. 574 ☐
- Work *Demonstration Problems* ☐
- Review *Summary of Study Objectives* ☐
- Answer *Self-Study Questions* ☐
- Complete assignments ☐

## STUDY OBJECTIVES

**After studying this chapter, you should be able to:**

1. *Identify the characteristics of the partnership form of business organization.*
2. *Explain the accounting entries for the formation of a partnership.*
3. *Identify the bases for dividing net income or net loss.*
4. *Describe the form and content of partnership financial statements.*
5. *Explain the effects of the entries when a new partner is admitted.*
6. *Describe the effects of the entries when a partner withdraws from the firm.*
7. *Prepare the entries to record the liquidation of a partnership.*

THE NAVIGATOR

*I*t is not surprising that when Cliff Chenfield and Craig Balsam began Razor & Tie, they decided to use the partnership form of organization. Both saw the need for hands-on control of their product and its promotion. In this chapter, we will discuss reasons why the partnership form of organization is often selected and explain the major issues in accounting for partnerships. The content and organization of this chapter are as follows:

......................................................................

# PARTNERSHIP FORM OF ORGANIZATION

The Uniform Partnership Act provides the basic rules for the formation and operation of partnerships in more than 90% of the states. This act defines a **partnership** as "an association of two or more persons to carry on as co-owners of a business for profit." Partnerships are common in retail establishments and in small manufacturing companies. Similarly, if you enter a profession such as accounting, law, or medicine, you may find it desirable to form a partnership with other professionals in your field. Professional partnerships vary in size from a medical partnership of 3 to 5 doctors to 150 to 200 partners in a large law firm and more than 2,000 partners in an international accounting firm.

## Characteristics of Partnerships

**1**
STUDY
OBJECTIVE
..............................
Identify the
characteristics of the
partnership form of
business organization.

Partnerships are fairly easy to form. They can be formed by a verbal agreement, although partners who have not taken the next step—to put in writing the rights and obligations of the partners—have found that the characteristics of partnerships can sometimes lead to later difficulties.

The principal characteristics of the partnership form of business organization are shown in Illustration 13-1 and explained in the following sections.

**ILLUSTRATION 13-1**
*Partnership characteristics*

## Association of Individuals

The voluntary association of two or more individuals in a partnership may be based on as simple an act as a handshake. However, it is preferable to state the agreement in writing. Under the Uniform Partnership Act, a partnership is considered a legal entity for certain purposes. For instance, property (land, buildings, equipment) can be owned in the name of the partnership, and the firm can sue or be sued. **A partnership also represents an accounting entity for financial reporting purposes.** Thus, the purely personal assets, liabilities, and transactions of the partners are excluded from the accounting records of the partnership, just as they are in a proprietorship.

The net income of a partnership is not taxed as a separate entity. However, a partnership is required to file an information tax return showing partnership net income and each partner's share of net income. Each partner's share is taxable at personal tax rates, regardless of the amount of net income withdrawn from the business during the year.

## Mutual Agency

Mutual agency means that each partner acts on behalf of the partnership when engaging in partnership business. The act of any partner is binding on all other partners, even when partners act beyond the scope of their authority, so long as the act appears to be appropriate for the partnership. For example, a partner of a grocery store who purchases a delivery truck creates a binding contract in the name of the partnership, even if the partnership agreement denies this authority. On the other hand, if a partner in a law firm purchased a snowmobile for the partnership, such an act would not be binding on the partnership, because it is clearly outside the scope of partnership business.

**HELPFUL HINT**
Because of mutual agency, an individual should be extremely cautious in selecting partners.

## Limited Life

A partnership does not have unlimited life. A partnership may be ended voluntarily at any time through the acceptance of a new partner into the firm or the withdrawal of a partner. A partnership may be ended involuntarily by the death or incapacity of a partner. Thus the life of a partnership is indefinite. Partnership dissolution occurs whenever a partner withdraws or a new partner is admitted.

Dissolution of a partnership does not necessarily mean that the business ends. If the continuing partners agree, operations can continue without interruption by forming a new partnership.

### Unlimited Liability

Each partner is **personally and individually liable** for all partnership liabilities. Creditors' claims attach first to partnership assets and then to the personal resources of any partner, irrespective of that partner's equity in the partnership. To illustrate, assume that: (1) the Rowe-Sanchez partnership is terminated when the claims of company creditors exceed partnership assets by $30,000, and (2) L. Rowe's personal assets total $40,000 but B. Sanchez has no personal assets. Creditors can collect their total claims from Rowe regardless of Rowe's equity in the firm, even though Sanchez and Rowe may be equal partners. Rowe, in turn, has a legal claim on Sanchez, but this would be worthless under the conditions described.

Some states allow limited partnerships. In a limited partnership, one or more partners have unlimited liability and one or more partners have limited liability for the debts of the firm. The former are called general partners and the latter are called limited partners. The responsibility of limited partners for the debts of the partnership is limited to their investment in the firm. For the privilege of limited liability, the limited partner usually accepts less compensation than a general partner and exercises less influence in the affairs of the firm. This form of organization works well in large partnerships where the partners do not work together closely. In such cases, partners want some protection from liability caused by the acts of partners they may hardly know.

## ACCOUNTING IN ACTION
### Business Insight

The prestigious New York law firm of Kaye, Scholer, Fierman, Hays, & Handler, accused of withholding damaging information during a federal investigation of its client, Lincoln Savings & Loan, settled out of court for $41 million. The firm's liability insurance covered only $25 million of the total. Thus, its 109 partners had to pay the remaining $16 million out of their own pockets.

In a recent year, court damage awards in malpractice suits against U.S. accountants and attorneys was close to $1 billion.

### Co-Ownership of Property

Partnership assets are owned jointly by all the partners. If the partnership is terminated, the assets do not legally revert to the original contributor. Each partner has a claim on total assets equal to the balance in his or her respective capital account. This claim does not attach to specific assets that an individual partner contributed to the firm.

Similarly, if a partner invests a building in the partnership valued at $100,000 and the building is later sold at a gain of $20,000, that partner does not personally receive the entire gain. Partnership net income (or net loss) is also co-owned. **If the partnership contract does not specify to the contrary, all net income or net loss is shared equally by the partners.** As you will see later, however, partners may agree to unequal sharing of net income or net loss.

## Advantages and Disadvantages of Partnerships

Why do people choose to form partnerships? One major advantage of doing so is that the **skills and resources of two or more individuals can be combined.** For example, a large public accounting firm such as Ernst & Young must have combined expertise in auditing, taxation, and management consulting, not to mention specialists within each of these areas. In addition, a partnership does not have to contend with the "red tape" that a corporation must face. That is, a partnership is **easily formed and is relatively free from governmental regulations and restrictions**. Decisions can be made quickly on substantive matters affecting the firm, whereas in a corporation, formal meetings with the board of directors are often needed.

On the other hand, partnerships also have some major disadvantages: **mutual agency**, **limited life**, and **unlimited liability**. Unlimited liability is particularly troublesome to many individuals, because they may lose not only their initial investment but also their personal assets, if those assets are needed to pay partnership creditors. As a result, partnerships often find it difficult to obtain large amounts of investment capital. That is one reason why the largest business enterprises in the United States are corporations, not partnerships.

The advantages and disadvantages of the partnership form of business organization are summarized in Illustration 13-2.

| Advantages | Disadvantages |
| --- | --- |
| Combining skills and resources of two or more individuals | Mutual agency |
| Ease of formation | Limited life |
| Freedom from governmental regulations and restrictions | Unlimited liability |
| Ease of decision making | |

**ILLUSTRATION 13-2**

*Advantages and disadvantages of a partnership*

## ACCOUNTING IN ACTION
### Business Insight

With surprising speed, states are creating two new forms of business organizations that are being adopted by many small companies. Known as **limited liability companies (LLCs)** and **limited liability partnerships (LLPs),** they combine the advantages of partnerships and corporations by shielding owners from personal liability while taxing income at the individual level. The LLC structure is an option for many sole proprietorships as well.

## The Partnership Agreement

Ideally, the voluntary agreement of two or more individuals to form a partnership should be expressed in writing. This written contract is often referred to as the partnership agreement or **articles of co-partnership**. The partnership agreement contains such basic information as the name and principal location of the firm, the purpose of the business, and date of inception. In addition, different relationships that will exist among the partners should be specified, such as the following:

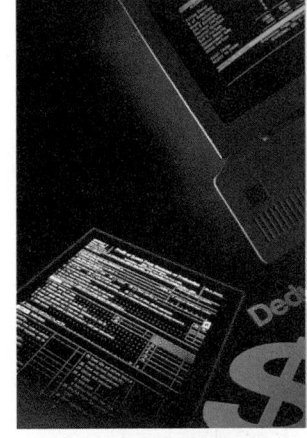

1. Names and capital contributions of partners.
2. Rights and duties of partners.
3. Basis for sharing net income or net loss.
4. Provision for withdrawals of assets.
5. Procedures for submitting disputes to arbitration.
6. Procedures for the withdrawal or addition of a partner.
7. Rights and duties of surviving partners in the event of a partner's death.

**ETHICS NOTE**

A well-developed partnership agreement reduces ethical conflict among partners because it specifies in clear and concise language the process by which ethical and legal problems will be resolved. This issue is especially significant when the partnership experiences financial distress.

The importance of a written contract cannot be overemphasized. The agreement should be drawn with care and should attempt to anticipate all possible situations, contingencies, and disagreements. The help of a lawyer is highly desirable in preparing the agreement. A poorly drawn contract may create friction among the partners and eventually cause the termination of the partnership.

# BEFORE YOU GO ON . . .

## Review It

1. What are the distinguishing characteristics of a partnership?
2. What are the principal advantages and disadvantages of a partnership? Why is Kellogg Company not a partnership? The answer to this question is provided on page 586.
3. What are the major items in a partnership agreement?

THE NAVIGATOR

# BASIC PARTNERSHIP ACCOUNTING

We now turn our attention to the basic accounting for partnerships. The major accounting issues relate to forming the partnership, dividing net income or net loss, and preparing financial statements.

## Forming a Partnership

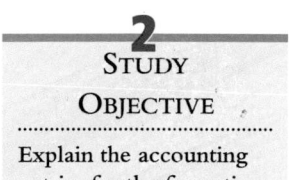

**2**
STUDY
OBJECTIVE

Explain the accounting entries for the formation of a partnership.

Each partner's initial investment in a partnership should be recorded at the **fair market value of the assets at the date of their transfer to the partnership.** The values assigned must be agreed to by all of the partners.

To illustrate, assume that A. Rolfe and T. Shea combine their proprietorships to start a partnership named U.S. Software. The firm will specialize in developing financial modeling software packages. Rolfe and Shea have the following assets prior to the formation of the partnership:

**ILLUSTRATION 13-3**

*Book and market values of assets invested*

|  | Book Value | | Market Value | |
|---|---|---|---|---|
|  | **A. Rolfe** | **T. Shea** | **A. Rolfe** | **T. Shea** |
| Cash | $ 8,000 | $ 9,000 | $ 8,000 | $ 9,000 |
| Office equipment | 5,000 | | 4,000 | |
| Accumulated depreciation | (2,000) | | | |
| Accounts receivable | | 4,000 | | 4,000 |
| Allowance for doubtful accounts | | (700) | | (1,000) |
|  | $11,000 | $12,300 | $12,000 | $12,000 |

The entries to record the investments are:

### Investment of A. Rolfe

| A = L + OE |
|---|
| +8,000      +12,000 |
| +4,000 |

| | | |
|---|---|---|
| Cash | 8,000 | |
| Office Equipment | 4,000 | |
|    A. Rolfe, Capital | | 12,000 |
|      (To record investment of Rolfe) | | |

### Investment of T. Shea

| A = L + OE |
|---|
| +9,000      +12,000 |
| +4,000 |
| −1,000 |

| | | |
|---|---|---|
| Cash | 9,000 | |
| Accounts Receivable | 4,000 | |
|    Allowance for Doubtful Accounts | | 1,000 |
|    T. Shea, Capital | | 12,000 |
|      (To record investment of Shea) | | |

Note that neither the original cost of the equipment ($5,000) nor its book value ($5,000 − $2,000) is recorded by the partnership. The equipment is recorded at its fair market value, $4,000. Since the equipment has not been used by the partnership, there can be no accumulated depreciation. In contrast, the gross claims on customers ($4,000) are carried forward to the partnership, and the allowance for doubtful accounts is adjusted to $1,000 to arrive at a cash (net) realizable value of $3,000. A partnership may start with an Allowance for Doubtful Accounts account, because this balance pertains to existing accounts receivable that are expected to be uncollectible in the future. In addition, this procedure maintains the control and subsidiary relationship between accounts receivable and the accounts receivable subsidiary ledger.

After the partnership has been formed, the accounting for transactions is similar to any other type of business organization. For example, all transactions with outside parties, such as the purchase or sale of merchandise inventory and the payment or receipt of cash, should be recorded in the same manner for a partnership as for a proprietorship.

The steps in the accounting cycle described in Chapter 4 for a proprietorship also apply to a partnership. For example, it is necessary to prepare a trial balance and to journalize and post adjusting entries. In addition, a work sheet may be used. There are minor differences in journalizing and posting closing entries and in preparing financial statements, as explained in the following sections. The differences occur because there is more than one owner in a partnership.

## Dividing Net Income or Net Loss

**Partnership net income or net loss is shared equally unless the partnership contract specifically indicates otherwise.** The same basis of division usually applies to both net income and net loss. As a result, it is customary to refer to the basis as the **income ratio**, the **income and loss ratio**, or the **profit and loss ratio**. Because of its wide acceptance, we will use the term income ratio to identify the basis for dividing both net income and net loss. A partner's share of net income or net loss is recognized in the accounts through closing entries.

**ALTERNATIVE TERMINOLOGY**
The *P&L ratio* terminology is frequently used in business.

### Closing Entries

As in the case of a proprietorship, four entries are required in preparing closing entries for a partnership. The entries are:

1. Debit each revenue account for its balance and credit Income Summary for total revenues.
2. Debit Income Summary for total expenses and credit each expense account for its balance.
3. Debit Income Summary for its balance and credit each partner's capital account for his or her share of net income. Conversely, credit Income Summary and debit each partner's capital account for his or her share of net loss.
4. Debit each partner's capital account for the balance in that partner's drawing account, and credit each partner's drawing account for the same amount.

The first two entries are the same as in a proprietorship. The last two entries are different because (1) there are two or more owners' capital and drawing accounts and (2) it is necessary to divide net income (or net loss) among the partners.

To illustrate the last two closing entries, we will assume that the AB Company has net income of $32,000 for 1999. The partners, L. Arbor and D. Barnett, share net income and net loss equally, and drawings for the year were Arbor $8,000 and Barnett $6,000. The last two closing entries are:

**ILLUSTRATION 13-4**

*Closing net income and drawing accounts*

| Dec. 31 | Income Summary | 32,000 | |
| | L. Arbor, Capital ($32,000 × 50%) | | 16,000 |
| | D. Barnett, Capital ($32,000 × 50%) | | 16,000 |
| | (To transfer net income to owners' capital accounts) | | |
| 31 | L. Arbor, Capital | 8,000 | |
| | D. Barnett, Capital | 6,000 | |
| | L. Arbor, Drawing | | 8,000 |
| | D. Barnett, Drawing | | 6,000 |
| | (To close drawing accounts to capital accounts) | | |

Assuming the beginning capital balance is $47,000 for Arbor and $36,000 for Barnett, the capital and drawing accounts will show the following after posting the closing entries:

**ILLUSTRATION 13-5**

*Partners' capital and drawing accounts after closing*

**L. Arbor, Capital**

| 12/31  Clos.  8,000 | 1/1    Bal.   47,000 |
| | 12/31  Clos.  16,000 |
| | 12/31  Bal.   55,000 |

**D. Barnett, Capital**

| 12/31  Clos.  6,000 | 1/1    Bal.   36,000 |
| | 12/31  Clos.  16,000 |
| | 12/31  Bal.   46,000 |

**L. Arbor, Drawing**

| 12/31  Bal.    8,000 | 12/31  Clos.  8,000 |

**D. Barnett, Drawing**

| 12/31  Bal.    6,000 | 12/31  Clos.  6,000 |

As in a proprietorship, the partners' capital accounts are permanent accounts; the partners' drawing accounts are temporary accounts. Normally, the capital accounts will have credit balances and the drawing accounts will have debit balances. Drawing accounts are debited when partners withdraw cash or other assets from the partnership for personal use. For example, the partnership agreement may permit each partner to withdraw cash monthly for personal living expenses.

## Income Ratios

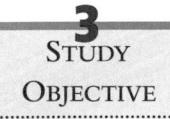

**3**

STUDY

OBJECTIVE

Identify the bases for dividing net income or net loss.

As indicated earlier, the partnership agreement should specify the basis for sharing net income or net loss. The following are typical of the ratios that may be used:

1. A fixed ratio, expressed as a proportion (6:4), a percentage (70% and 30%), or a fraction (2/3 and 1/3).
2. A ratio based either on capital balances at the beginning of the year or on average capital balances during the year.
3. Salaries to partners and the remainder on a fixed ratio.
4. Interest on partners' capitals and the remainder on a fixed ratio.
5. Salaries to partners, interest on partners' capitals, and the remainder on a fixed ratio.

The objective is to reach agreement on a basis that will equitably reflect the differences among partners in terms of their capital investment and service to the partnership.

A fixed ratio is easy to apply, and it may be an equitable basis in some circumstances. Assume, for example, that Hughes and Lane are partners. Each contributes the same amount of capital, but Hughes expects to work full-time in the partnership and Lane expects to work only half-time. Accordingly, the partners agree to a fixed ratio of 2/3 to Hughes and 1/3 to Lane.

**HELPFUL HINT**
Use one relationship for all; that is, proportion—3:1 percentage—75% & 25% fraction—¾ & ¼.

A ratio based on capital balances may be appropriate when the funds invested in the partnership are considered the critical factor. Capital balances may also be equitable when a manager is hired to run the business and the partners do not plan to take an active role in daily operations.

The three remaining ratios (3, 4, and 5) give specific recognition to differences that may exist among partners. These ratios provide salary allowances for time worked and interest allowances for capital invested. Then, any remaining net income or net loss is allocated on a fixed ratio. Some caution needs to be exercised in working with these types of income ratios. These ratios pertain exclusively to **the computations that are required in dividing net income or net loss.**

**Salaries to partners and interest on partners' capitals are not expenses of the partnership. Therefore, these items do not enter into the matching of expenses with revenues and the determination of net income or net loss.** For a partnership, as well as for other entities, salaries expense pertains to the cost of services performed by employees, and interest expense relates to the cost of borrowing money from creditors. Partners in their ownership capacity are not considered either **employees** or **creditors**. Thus, when the income ratio includes a salary allowance for partners, some partnership agreements permit the partner to make monthly withdrawals of cash based on their "salary." In such cases, the withdrawals are debited to the partner's drawing account.

## ACCOUNTING IN ACTION

### Business Insight

Partners in professional firms can and do make substantial incomes. For example, in one large international public accounting firm, the average earnings of all partners in a recent year was over $400,000, and the individual earnings of the five most highly compensated partners was over $1 million. Note, however, that the compensation of partners in most large partnerships differs in both form and substance from the compensation of a corporate executive. Partners are not guaranteed an annual salary. Compensation depends entirely on each year's operating results. Substantial investment is required of each partner. This capital is at risk for the partner's entire career—often 25–30 years—without an established return. Upon leaving, it is repayable without adjustment for inflation or appreciation in value.

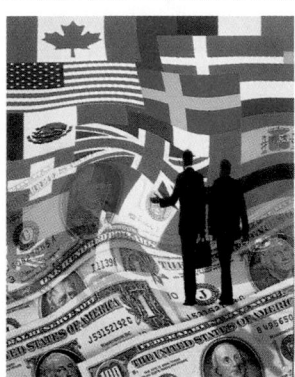

### Salaries, Interest, and Remainder on a Fixed Ratio

Under this income ratio (item 5 in the list above), the provisions for salaries and interest must be applied **before** the remainder is allocated on the specified fixed ratio. **This is true even if the provisions exceed net income or the partnership has suffered a net loss for the year.** Detailed information concerning the division of net income or net loss should be shown at the bottom of the income statement.

To illustrate this income ratio, assume that Sara King and Ray Lee are co-partners in the Kingslee Company. The partnership agreement provides for (1) salary allowances of $8,400 to King and $6,000 to Lee, (2) interest allowances of 10% on capital balances at the beginning of the year, and (3) the remainder equally. Capital balances on January 1 were King, $28,000, and Lee, $24,000. In 1999, partnership net income is $22,000. The division of net income is as follows:

**ILLUSTRATION 13-6**

*Income statement with division of net income*

**KINGSLEE COMPANY**
**Income Statement**
**For the Year Ended December 31, 1999**

| | Sara King | Ray Lee | Total |
|---|---|---|---|
| Sales | | | $200,000 |
| Net income | | | $ 22,000 |

**Division of Net Income**

| | Sara King | Ray Lee | Total |
|---|---|---|---|
| **Salary allowance** | $ 8,400 | $6,000 | $14,400 |
| **Interest allowance** | | | |
| Sara King ($28,000 × 10%) | 2,800 | | |
| Ray Lee ($24,000 × 10%) | | 2,400 | |
| Total interest | | | 5,200 |
| Total salaries and interest | 11,200 | 8,400 | 19,600 |
| **Remaining income, $2,400** | | | |
| ($22,000 − $19,600) | | | |
| Sara King ($2,400 × 50%) | 1,200 | | |
| Ray Lee ($2,400 × 50%) | | 1,200 | |
| Total remainder | | | 2,400 |
| **Total division** | $12,400 | $9,600 | $22,000 |

The entry to record the division of net income is:

| A | = | L | + | OE |
|---|---|---|---|---|
| | | | | − 22,000 |
| | | | | + 12,400 |
| | | | | + 9,600 |

| | | | |
|---|---|---|---|
| Dec. 31 | Income Summary | 22,000 | |
| | Sara King, Capital | | 12,400 |
| | Ray Lee, Capital | | 9,600 |
| | (To close net income to partners' capitals) | | |

To illustrate a situation in which the salary and interest allowances exceed net income, assume that net income in the Kingslee Company is only $18,000. In this case, the salary and interest allowances will create a deficiency of $1,600 ($19,600 − $18,000). Since the computations of the allowances are the same as those in the preceding example, we will begin the division of net income with total salaries and interest as follows:

**ILLUSTRATION 13-7**

*Division of net income—income deficiency*

| | Sara King | Ray Lee | Total |
|---|---|---|---|
| Total salaries and interest | $11,200 | $8,400 | $19,600 |
| **Remaining deficiency ($1,600)** | | | |
| ($18,000 − $19,600) | | | |
| Sara King ($1,600 × 50%) | (800) | | |
| Ray Lee ($1,600 × 50%) | | (800) | |
| Total remainder | | | (1,600) |
| **Total division** | $10,400 | $7,600 | $18,000 |

## Partnership Financial Statements

The financial statements of a partnership are similar to those of a proprietorship. The differences are related to the fact that a number of owners are involved in a partnership. The income statement for a partnership is identical to the income statement for a proprietorship except for the division of net income, as shown earlier.

The owners' equity statement for a partnership is called the **partners' capital statement**. Its function is to explain the changes in each partner's capital account and in total partnership capital during the year. As in a proprietorship, changes in capital may result from three causes: additional capital investment, drawings, and net income or net loss.

The partners' capital statement for the Kingslee Company shown below is based on the division of $22,000 of net income in Illustration 13-6. The statement includes assumed data for the additional investment and drawings.

**4**
STUDY
OBJECTIVE
..................................
Describe the form and content of partnership financial statements.

| KINGSLEE COMPANY Partners' Capital Statement For the Year Ended December 31, 1999 | | | |
| --- | --- | --- | --- |
| | Sara King | Ray Lee | Total |
| Capital, January 1 | $28,000 | $24,000 | $52,000 |
| Add: Additional investment | 2,000 | | 2,000 |
| Net income | 12,400 | 9,600 | 22,000 |
| | 42,400 | 33,600 | 76,000 |
| Less: Drawings | 7,000 | 5,000 | 12,000 |
| Capital, December 31 | $35,400 | $28,600 | $64,000 |

**ILLUSTRATION 13-8**
*Partners' capital statement*

**HELPFUL HINT**
As in a proprietorship, partners' capital may change due to (1) additional investment, (2) drawings, and (3) net income or loss.

The partners' capital statement is prepared from the income statement and the partners' capital and drawing accounts.

The balance sheet for a partnership is the same as for a proprietorship except in the owner's equity section. In a partnership, the capital balances of each partner are shown in the balance sheet. The owners' equity section for Kingslee Company would show the following:

| KINGSLEE COMPANY Balance Sheet (partial) December 31, 1999 | | |
| --- | --- | --- |
| Total liabilities (assumed amount) | | $115,000 |
| Owners' equity | | |
| Sara King, Capital | $35,400 | |
| Ray Lee, Capital | 28,600 | |
| Total owners' equity | | 64,000 |
| Total liabilities and owners' equity | | $179,000 |

**ILLUSTRATION 13-9**
*Owners' equity section of a partnership balance sheet*

# BEFORE YOU GO ON . . .

## Review It

1. How should a partner's initial investment of assets be valued?
2. What are the closing entries for a partnership?
3. What income ratios may be used in a partnership?
4. How do partnership financial statements differ from proprietorship financial statements?

**Do It**

LeMay Company reports net income of $57,000. The partnership agreement provides for salaries of $15,000 to L. Lee and $12,000 to R. May, with the remainder to be shared on a 60:40 basis, respectively. L. Lee asks your help to divide the net income between the partners and to prepare the closing entry.

*Reasoning:* Salaries to partners and interest on partners' capital are not expenses of the partnership. These items do not enter into the matching of expenses with revenues and the determination of net income or net loss. Therefore, after net income for LeMay is computed, salaries are deducted and then the income ratios are applied to the remainder. The closing entry for net income in a partnership is the same as in a proprietorship except that more than one capital account is credited.

*Solution:* The division of net income is as follows:

|  | L. Lee | R. May | Total |
|---|---|---|---|
| Salary allowance | $15,000 | $12,000 | $27,000 |
| Remaining income ($57,000 − $27,000) |  |  |  |
|    L. Lee (60% × $30,000) | 18,000 |  |  |
|    R. May (40% × $30,000) |  | 12,000 |  |
|      Total remaining income |  |  | 30,000 |
| Total division of income | $33,000 | $24,000 | $57,000 |

The closing entry for net income therefore is:

| | | |
|---|---|---|
| Income Summary | 57,000 | |
|    L. Lee, Capital | | 33,000 |
|    R. May, Capital | | 24,000 |
|    (To close net income to partners' capitals) | | |

*Related exercise material:* BE13–3, BE13–4, BE13–5, and E13–2.

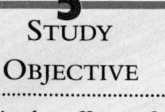
THE NAVIGATOR

# ADMISSION AND WITHDRAWAL OF PARTNERS

We have seen how the basic accounting for a partnership works. We now look at how to account for a common occurrence in partnerships—the addition or withdrawal of a partner.

## Admission of a Partner

**5**
STUDY
OBJECTIVE

Explain the effects of the entries when a new partner is admitted.

The admission of a new partner results in the **legal dissolution of the existing partnership** and **the beginning of a new partnership**. From an economic standpoint, however, the admission of a new partner (or partners) may be of minor significance in the continuity of the business. For example, in large public accounting or law firms, partners are admitted annually without any change in operating policies established by the continuing partners. **To recognize the economic effects, it is necessary only to open a capital account for each new partner.** The entries described and illustrated below are based on the assumption that the accounting records of the predecessor firm will continue to be used by the new partnership.

A new partner may be admitted either by (1) purchasing the interest of one or more existing partners or (2) investing assets in the partnership, as shown in Illustration 13-10. The former affects only the capital accounts of the partners who are parties to the transaction. The latter increases both net assets (total assets less total liabilities) and total capital of the partnership.

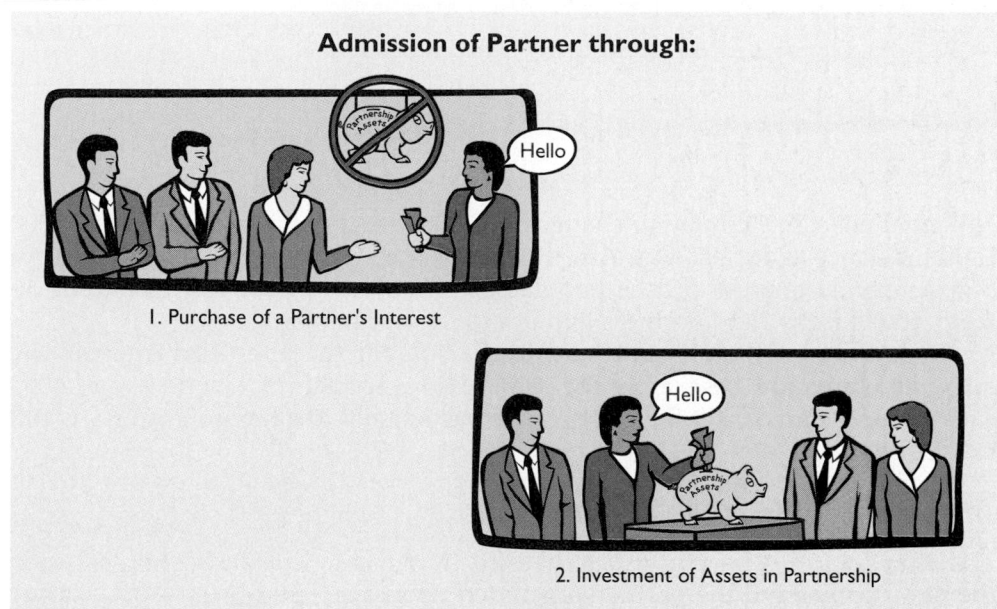

**Admission of Partner through:**

1. Purchase of a Partner's Interest

2. Investment of Assets in Partnership

**ILLUSTRATION 13-10**

*Procedures in adding partners*

## Purchase of a Partner's Interest

The admission of a partner by purchase of an interest in the firm is a personal transaction between one or more existing partners and the new partner. Each party acts as an individual separate from the partnership entity. The price paid is negotiated and determined by the individuals involved. It may be equal to or different from the capital equity acquired. The amount of the purchase price passes directly from the new partner to the partners who are giving up part or all of their ownership claims. Any money or other consideration exchanged is the personal property of the participants and **not** the property of the partnership. Upon purchase of an interest, the new partner acquires each selling partner's capital interest and income ratio. A partner does not have to obtain the approval of the other partners to sell his or her interest. However, the Uniform Partnership Act provides that the purchaser does not become a partner until he or she is accepted into the firm by the continuing partners.

**HELPFUL HINT**

In a purchase of an interest, the partnership is **not** a participant in the transaction. For example, no cash is contributed to the partnership.

Accounting for the purchase of an interest is straightforward. As far as the partnership is concerned, only the realignment of partners' capital is recorded. **Each partner's capital account is debited for the ownership claims that have been relinquished, and the new partner's capital account is credited with the capital equity purchased.** Total assets, total liabilities, and total capital remain unchanged, as do all individual asset and liability accounts.

To illustrate, assume that L. Carson agrees to pay $10,000 each to C. Ames and D. Barker for 33⅓% (one-third) of their interest in the Ames–Barker partnership. At the time of the admission of Carson, each partner has a $30,000 capital balance. Both partners, therefore, give up $10,000 of their capital equity. The entry to record the admission of Carson is:

| | | |
|---|---|---|
| C. Ames, Capital | 10,000 | |
| D. Barker, Capital | 10,000 | |
| L. Carson, Capital | | 20,000 |
| (To record admission of Carson by purchase) | | |

**ILLUSTRATION 13-11**

*Ledger balances after purchase of a partner's interest*

The effect of this entry on net assets and partners' capital is shown below:

| Net Assets | | C. Ames, Capital | | D. Barker, Capital | | L. Carson, Capital |
|---|---|---|---|---|---|---|
| 60,000 | | **10,000** | 30,000 | **10,000** | 30,000 | **20,000** |
| | | Bal. | 20,000 | Bal. | 20,000 | |

Note that net assets remain unchanged at $60,000 and each partner has a $20,000 capital balance. Note also that Ames and Barker continue as partners in the firm but the capital interest of each has changed. The cash paid by Carson goes directly to the individual partners and not to the partnership.

**Regardless of the amount paid by Carson for the one-third interest, the entry above would be exactly the same.** For example, if Carson pays $12,000 each to Ames and Barker for 33⅓% of the partnership, the foregoing entry is still made.

### Investment of Assets in a Partnership

The admission of a partner by an investment of assets is a transaction between the new partner and the partnership. Often referred to simply as **admission by investment**, the transaction **increases both the net assets and total capital of the partnership**. To illustrate, assume that instead of purchasing an interest, Carson invests $30,000 in cash in the Ames–Barker partnership for a 33⅓% capital interest. In such a case, the entry is:

| | | |
|---|---|---|
| Cash | 30,000 | |
| L. Carson, Capital | | 30,000 |
| (To record admission of Carson by investment) | | |

The effects of this transaction on the partnership accounts may be shown as follows:

**ILLUSTRATION 13-12**

*Ledger balances after investment of assets*

| Net Assets | | C. Ames, Capital | | D. Barker, Capital | | L. Carson, Capital |
|---|---|---|---|---|---|---|
| 60,000 | | | 30,000 | | 30,000 | **30,000** |
| **30,000** | | | | | | |
| Bal. | 90,000 | | | | | |

Note that both net assets and total capital have increased by $30,000.

Remember that Carson's one-third capital interest might not result in a one-third income ratio. Carson's income ratio should be specified in the new partnership agreement, and it may or may not be equal to the one-third capital interest.

The different effects of the purchase of an interest and admission by investment are shown in the comparison of the net assets and capital balances in Illustration 13-13.

| Purchase of an Interest | | Admission by Investment | |
|---|---:|---|---:|
| Net Assets | $60,000 | Net Assets | $90,000 |
| Capital | | Capital | |
| C. Ames | $20,000 | C. Ames | $30,000 |
| D. Barker | 20,000 | D. Barker | 30,000 |
| L. Carson | 20,000 | L. Carson | 30,000 |
| Total capital | $60,000 | Total capital | $90,000 |

**ILLUSTRATION 13-13**
*Comparison of purchase of an interest and admission by investment*

When an interest is purchased, the total net assets and total capital of the partnership do not change. However, when a partner is admitted by investment, both the total net assets and the total capital change.

In the case of admission by investment, further complications occur when the new partner's investment differs from the capital equity acquired. When those amounts are not the same, the difference is considered a bonus either to (1) the existing (old) partners or (2) the new partner.

**Bonus to Old Partners.**   The existing partners may be unwilling to admit a new partner without receiving a bonus for both personal and business reasons. In an established firm, existing partners may insist on a bonus as compensation for the work they have put into the company over the years. Two accounting-related factors underlie the business reason: First, total partners' capital equals the **book value** of the recorded net assets of the partnership. At the time the new partner is admitted, the fair market values of assets such as land and buildings may be higher than their book values. Second, when the partnership has been profitable, goodwill may exist. However, the goodwill will not be recorded or included in total partners' capital. In such cases the new partner is usually willing to pay the bonus to become a partner.

A bonus to old partners results when the new partner's capital credit on the date of admittance is less than his or her investment in the firm. The bonus results in **an increase in the capital balances of the old partners that is allocated to them on the basis of their income ratios before the admission of the new partner**.

To illustrate, assume that the Bart–Cohen partnership owned by Sam Bart and Tom Cohen has total capital of $120,000 when Lea Eden is admitted to the partnership. Lea acquires a 25% ownership (capital) interest by making a cash investment of $80,000 in the partnership. The procedure for determining Eden's capital credit and the bonus to the old partners is as follows:

**HELPFUL HINT**
(1) The debit to Cash is greater than the new partner's capital credit. (2) Credits to old partners' capitals are needed for equal debits and credits.

1. **Determine the total capital of the new partnership** by adding the new partner's investment to the total capital of the old partnership. In this case the total capital of the new firm is $200,000, computed as follows:

   | | |
   |---|---:|
   | Total capital of existing partnership | $120,000 |
   | Investment by new partner, Eden | 80,000 |
   | Total capital of new partnership | $200,000 |

2. **Determine the new partner's capital credit** by multiplying the total capital of the new partnership by the new partner's ownership interest. Eden's capital credit is $50,000 ($200,000 × 25%).

3. **Determine the amount of bonus** by subtracting the new partner's capital credit from the new partner's investment. The bonus in this case is $30,000 ($80,000 − $50,000).

4. **Allocate the bonus to the old partners on the basis of their income ratios.** Assuming the ratios are Bart, 60%, and Cohen, 40%, the allocation is: Bart, $18,000 ($30,000 × 60%) and Cohen, $12,000 ($30,000 × 40%).

The entry to record the admission of Eden is:

| A | = | L | + | OE |
|---|---|---|---|---|
| +80,000 | | | | +18,000 |
| | | | | +12,000 |
| | | | | +50,000 |

| | | |
|---|---|---|
| Cash | 80,000 | |
|    Sam Bart, Capital | | 18,000 |
|    Tom Cohen, Capital | | 12,000 |
|    Lea Eden, Capital | | 50,000 |
|      (To record admission of Eden and bonus to old partners) | | |

**Bonus to New Partner.** A bonus to a new partner results when the new partner's capital credit is greater than his or her investment of assets in the firm. This may occur when the new partner possesses resources or special attributes that are desired by the partnership. For example, when bank interest rates are high, the new partner may be able to supply cash that is urgently needed for expansion or to meet maturing debts. Alternatively, the new partner may be a recognized expert or authority in a relevant field. Thus, an engineering firm may be willing to give a world-renowned engineer a bonus to join the firm. Similarly, the partners of a restaurant may offer a bonus to a sports celebrity in order to add the athlete's name to the partnership name. A bonus to a new partner may also result when recorded book values on the partnership books are higher than their market values.

A bonus to a new partner results in a **decrease in the capital balances of the old partners based on their income ratios before the admission of the new partner**. To illustrate, assume that Lea Eden invests $20,000 in cash for a 25% ownership interest in the Bart–Cohen partnership. Using the procedures described in the preceding section, the computations for Eden's capital credit and the bonus are as follows:

**ILLUSTRATION 13-14**

*Computation of capital credit and bonus to new partner*

| | | |
|---|---|---|
| 1. Total capital of Bart–Cohen partnership | | $120,000 |
|    Investment by new partner, Eden | | 20,000 |
|    Total capital of new partnership | | $140,000 |
| 2. **Eden's capital credit** (25% × $140,000) | | **$ 35,000** |
| 3. **Bonus to Eden** ($35,000 − $20,000) | | **$ 15,000** |
| 4. Allocation of bonus: | | |
|    Bart ($15,000 × 60%) | $9,000 | |
|    Cohen ($15,000 × 40%) | 6,000 | $ 15,000 |

The entry to record the admission of Eden is as follows:

| A | = | L | + | OE |
|---|---|---|---|---|
| +20,000 | | | | − 9,000 |
| | | | | − 6,000 |
| | | | | +35,000 |

| | | |
|---|---|---|
| Cash | 20,000 | |
| Sam Bart, Capital | 9,000 | |
| Tom Cohen, Capital | 6,000 | |
|    Lea Eden, Capital | | 35,000 |
|      (To record Eden's admission and bonus) | | |

## Withdrawal of a Partner

Now let's look at the opposite situation—the withdrawal of a partner. A partner may withdraw from a partnership **voluntarily** by selling his or her equity in the firm or **involuntarily** by reaching mandatory retirement age or by dying. The withdrawal of a partner, like the admission of a partner, legally dissolves the partnership. The legal effects may be recognized in accounting for a withdrawal by dissolving the firm. However, it is customary to record only the economic effects. As indicated earlier, the partnership agreement should specify the terms of withdrawal. The withdrawal of a partner may be accomplished by (1) payment from partners' personal assets or (2) payment from partnership assets, as shown in Illustration 13-15. The former affects only the partners' capital accounts. The latter decreases total net assets and total capital of the partnership.

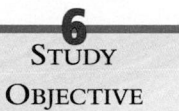

**6**
STUDY
OBJECTIVE
·········································
Describe the effects of the entries when a partner withdraws from the firm.

**Withdrawal of Partner through:**

1. Payment from Partners' Personal Assets

Bye

2. Payment from Partnership Assets

Bye

**ILLUSTRATION 13-15**

*Procedures in partnership withdrawal*

## Payment from Partners' Personal Assets

**The withdrawal of a partner when payment is made from partners' personal assets is the direct opposite of admitting a new partner who purchases a partner's interest.** Withdrawal by payment from partners' personal assets is a personal transaction between the partners. Payment to the retiring partner is made directly from the remaining partners' personal assets. **Partnership assets are not involved in any way, and total capital does not change.** Thus, the effect on the partnership is limited to a realignment of the partners' capital balances.

To illustrate, assume that Anne Morz, Mary Nead, and Jill Odom have capital balances of $25,000, $15,000, and $10,000, respectively, when Morz and Nead agree to buy out Odom's interest. Each of them agrees to pay Odom $8,000 in exchange for one-half of Odom's total interest of $10,000. The entry to record the withdrawal is:

| Jill Odom, Capital | 10,000 | |
|     Anne Morz, Capital | | 5,000 |
|     Mary Nead, Capital | | 5,000 |
|       (To record purchase of Odom's interest) | | |

The effect of this entry on the partnership accounts is shown below:

**HELPFUL HINT**
If each purchaser acquires one-fourth of Odom's total interest for $8,000 each, the debit becomes $5,000 and the credits $2,500.

| A | = | L | + | OE |
|---|---|---|---|---|
| | | | | − 10,000 |
| | | | | + 5,000 |
| | | | | + 5,000 |

**ILLUSTRATION 13-16**

*Ledger balances after payment from partners' personal assets*

| Net Assets | | Anne Morz, Capital | | Mary Nead, Capital | | Jill Odom, Capital | |
|---|---|---|---|---|---|---|---|
| 50,000 | | | 25,000 | | 15,000 | 10,000 | 10,000 |
| | | | 5,000 | | 5,000 | | |
| | | Bal. | 30,000 | Bal. | 20,000 | Bal. | −0− |

Note that net assets and total capital remain the same at $50,000. Note also that the $16,000 paid to Odom is not recorded. Odom's capital is debited only for $10,000, not for the $16,000 that she received. Similarly, both Morz and Nead credit their capital accounts for only $5,000, not the $8,000 they each paid. Morz and Nead will share net income or net loss equally unless they specifically indicate another income ratio in the partnership agreement.

## Payment from Partnership Assets

Using partnership assets to pay for a withdrawing partner's interest is the **reverse** of admitting a partner through the investment of assets in the partnership. Withdrawal by payment from partnership assets is a transaction that involves the partnership. **Both partnership net assets and total capital are decreased.**

Many partnership agreements provide that the amount paid should be based on the fair market value of the assets at the time of the partner's withdrawal. When this basis is required, some maintain that any differences between recorded asset balances and their fair market values should be (1) recorded by an adjusting entry and (2) allocated to all partners on the basis of their income ratios. This position has serious flaws, however. Recording the revaluations violates the cost principle, which requires that assets be stated at original cost. It also is a departure from the going-concern assumption, which assumes the entity will continue indefinitely. The terms of the partnership contract should not dictate the accounting for the event.

In accounting for a withdrawal by payment from partnership assets:

1. Asset revaluations should not be recorded.
2. Any difference between the amount paid and the withdrawing partner's capital balance should be considered a bonus to the retiring partner or a bonus to the remaining partners.

**Bonus to Retiring Partner.**    A bonus may be paid to a retiring partner when:

1. The fair market value of partnership assets is more than their book value,
2. There is unrecorded goodwill resulting from the partnership's superior earnings record, or
3. The remaining partners are anxious to remove the partner from the firm.

**The bonus is deducted from the remaining partners' capital balances on the basis of their income ratios at the time of the withdrawal.**

To illustrate, assume that the following capital balances exist in the RST partnership: Fred Roman $50,000, Dee Sand $30,000, and Betty Terk $20,000. The partners share income in the ratio of 3:2:1, respectively. Terk retires from the partnership and receives a cash payment of $25,000 from the firm. The procedure for determining the bonus to the retiring partner and the allocation of the bonus to the remaining partners is as follows:

1. **Determine the amount of the bonus** by subtracting the retiring partner's capital balance from the cash paid by the partnership. The bonus in this case is $5,000 ($25,000 − $20,000).
2. **Allocate the bonus to the remaining partners on the basis of their income ratios.** The ratios of Roman and Sand are 3:2. Thus, the allocation of the $5,000 bonus is: Roman $3,000 ($5,000 × 3/5) and Sand $2,000 ($5,000 × 2/5).

The entry to record the withdrawal of Terk is:

| | | |
|---|---|---|
| Betty Terk, Capital | 20,000 | |
| Fred Roman, Capital | 3,000 | |
| Dee Sand, Capital | 2,000 | |
| Cash | | 25,000 |
| (To record withdrawal of and bonus to Terk) | | |

The remaining partners, Roman and Sand, will recover the bonus given to Terk as the undervalued assets are sold or used in the partnership.

**Bonus to Remaining Partners.**   The retiring partner may give a bonus to the remaining partners when:

1. Recorded assets are overvalued,
2. The partnership has a poor earnings record, or
3. The partner is anxious to leave the partnership.

In such cases, the cash paid to the retiring partner will be less than the retiring partner's capital balance. **The bonus is allocated (credited) to the capital accounts of the remaining partners on the basis of their income ratios.**

To illustrate, assume that, instead of the example above, Terk is paid only $16,000 for her $20,000 equity upon withdrawing from the RST partnership. In such case:

1. The bonus to remaining partners is $4,000 ($20,000 − $16,000).
2. The allocation of the $4,000 bonus is: Roman $2,400 ($4,000 × 3/5) and Sand $1,600 ($4,000 × 2/5).

The entry to record the withdrawal is:

| | | |
|---|---|---|
| Betty Terk, Capital | 20,000 | |
| Fred Roman, Capital | | 2,400 |
| Dee Sand, Capital | | 1,600 |
| Cash | | 16,000 |
| (To record withdrawal of Terk and bonus to remaining partners) | | |

It is important to note that if Sand had withdrawn from the partnership, any bonus would be divided between Roman and Terk on the basis of their income ratio which is 3:1 or 75% and 25%.

## Death of a Partner

The death of a partner dissolves the partnership, but provision generally is made for the surviving partners to continue operations. When a partner dies, it usually is necessary to determine the partner's equity at the date of death. This is done by (1) determining the net income or loss for the year to date, (2) closing the books, and (3) preparing financial statements. The partnership agreement may also require an audit of the financial statements by independent auditors and a revaluation of assets by an independent appraisal firm.

The surviving partners may agree either to (1) purchase the deceased partner's equity from their personal assets or (2) use partnership assets to settle with the deceased partner's estate. In both instances, the entries to record the withdrawal of the partner are similar to those presented in previous illustrations.

To facilitate payment from partnership assets, some partnerships obtain life insurance policies on each partner with the partnership as the beneficiary. The proceeds from the insurance policy on the deceased partner are then used to settle with the estate.

# BEFORE YOU GO ON . . .

## Review It

1. How does the accounting for admission by purchase of an interest differ from admission by investing assets in the partnership?
2. Contrast the accounting effects of the withdrawal of a partner by payment from (a) personal assets and (b) partnership assets.

## Do It

Curly, Moe, and Larry have a partnership. Each partner has a $40,000 balance in his capital account. Record journal entries for each of the independent events listed below.

1. Curly, Moe, and Larry agree to admit Stan as a new one-quarter-interest partner. Stan pays $10,000 in cash directly to each partner.
2. Curly, Moe, and Larry agree to admit Stan as a new one-quarter-interest partner. Stan contributes $40,000 into the partnership.
3. Curly and Moe agree to let Larry withdraw from the partnership, and $30,000 of partnership cash is distributed to Larry. Curly and Moe share income and losses equally.
4. Curly and Moe agree to let Larry withdraw from the partnership. Each pays Larry $25,000 out of his personal assets. Curly and Moe share income and losses equally.

*Reasoning:* You need to understand that admission (withdrawal) by purchase (sale) of an interest is a personal transaction between one or more existing partners and the new (withdrawing) partner. In contrast, admission (withdrawal) by investment (distribution) of partnership assets is a transaction between the new (withdrawing) partner and the partnership.

*Solution:*

1.

| | | |
|---|---|---|
| Curly, Capital | 10,000 | |
| Moe, Capital | 10,000 | |
| Larry, Capital | 10,000 | |
|     Stan, Capital | | 30,000 |
|     (To record admission of Stan by purchase) | | |

2.

| | | |
|---|---|---|
| Cash | 40,000 | |
|     Stan, Capital | | 40,000 |
|     (To record admission of Stan by investment) | | |

3.

| | | |
|---|---|---|
| Larry, Capital | 40,000 | |
|     Cash | | 30,000 |
|     Curly, Capital | | 5,000 |
|     Moe, Capital | | 5,000 |
|     (To record withdrawal of Larry and bonus to remaining partners) | | |

4.

| | | |
|---|---|---|
| Larry, Capital | 40,000 | |
|     Curly, Capital | | 20,000 |
|     Moe, Capital | | 20,000 |
|     (To record purchase of Larry's interest) | | |

*Related exercise material:* BE13–6, BE13–7, BE13–8, BE13–9, E13–4, E13–5, E13–6, and E13–7.

THE
NAVIGATOR

# LIQUIDATION OF A PARTNERSHIP

The liquidation of a partnership terminates the business. It entails selling the assets of the firm, paying liabilities, and distributing any remaining assets to the partners. Liquidation may result from the sale of the business by mutual agreement of the partners, from the death of a partner, or from bankruptcy. In contrast to the dissolution of a partnership, partnership liquidation ends both the legal and economic life of the entity.

From an accounting standpoint, liquidation should be preceded by completing the accounting cycle for the partnership for the final operating period. This includes preparing adjusting entries and financial statements. It also involves preparing closing entries and a post-closing trial balance. Thus, only balance sheet accounts should be open as the liquidation process begins.

The liquidation process may occur at a specific point in time or it may occur over a period of time. In liquidation, the sale of noncash assets for cash is called **realization**, and the difference between book value and the cash proceeds is called the **gain or loss on realization**. To liquidate a partnership, it is necessary to:

1. Sell noncash assets for cash and recognize a gain or loss on realization.
2. Allocate gain/loss on realization to the partners based on their income ratios.
3. Pay partnership liabilities in cash.
4. Distribute remaining cash to partners on the basis of their capital balances.

**Each of the steps must be performed in sequence** because creditors must be paid **before** partners receive any cash distributions. Each step also must be recorded by an accounting entry.

When a partnership is liquidated, all partners may have credit balances in their capital accounts—a situation termed no capital deficiency; or at least one partner's capital account may have a debit balance—a situation termed a capital deficiency. To illustrate each of these conditions, assume that the Ace Company is liquidated when its ledger shows the following assets, liabilities, and owners' equity accounts:

| Assets | | Liabilities and Owners' Equity | |
|---|---|---|---|
| Cash | $ 5,000 | Notes payable | $15,000 |
| Accounts receivable | 15,000 | Accounts payable | 16,000 |
| Inventory | 18,000 | R. Arnet, Capital | 15,000 |
| Equipment | 35,000 | P. Carey, Capital | 17,800 |
| Accum. depr.—equipment | (8,000) | W. Eaton, Capital | 1,200 |
| | $65,000 | | $65,000 |

## No Capital Deficiency

The partners of Ace Company agree to liquidate the partnership on the following terms: (1) a cash sale of the noncash assets of the partnership to Jackson Enterprises for $75,000, and (2) payment of partnership liabilities by the partnership. The income ratios of the partners are 3:2:1, respectively. The steps in the liquidation process are as follows:

1. The noncash assets (accounts receivable, inventory, and equipment) are sold for $75,000. Since the book value of these assets is $60,000 ($15,000 +

---

**7**
**STUDY**
**OBJECTIVE**

Prepare the entries to record the liquidation of a partnership.

**HELPFUL HINT**
These steps are indispensable to correct homework and examination results.

**ILLUSTRATION 13-17**
*Account balances prior to liquidation*

$18,000 + $35,000 − $8,000), a gain of $15,000 is realized on the sale. The entry is:

**(1)**

| | | |
|---|---|---|
| Cash | 75,000 | |
| Accumulated Depreciation—Equipment | 8,000 | |
|     Accounts Receivable | | 15,000 |
|     Inventory | | 18,000 |
|     Equipment | | 35,000 |
|     Gain on Realization | | 15,000 |
|        (To record realization of noncash assets) | | |

```
A    =  L   +  OE
+75,000        +15,000
+ 8,000
−15,000
−18,000
−35,000
```

2. The gain on realization of $15,000 is allocated to the partners on their income ratios, which are 3:2:1. The entry is:

**(2)**

| | | |
|---|---|---|
| Gain on Realization | 15,000 | |
|     R. Arnet, Capital ($15,000 × 3/6) | | 7,500 |
|     P. Carey, Capital ($15,000 × 2/6) | | 5,000 |
|     W. Eaton, Capital ($15,000 × 1/6) | | 2,500 |
|        (To allocate gain to partners' capitals) | | |

```
A   =  L   +  OE
           −15,000
           + 7,500
           + 5,000
           + 2,500
```

3. Partnership liabilities consist of Notes Payable $15,000 and Accounts Payable $16,000. Creditors are paid in full by a cash payment of $31,000. The entry is:

**(3)**

| | | |
|---|---|---|
| Notes Payable | 15,000 | |
| Accounts Payable | 16,000 | |
|     Cash | | 31,000 |
|        (To record payment of partnership liabilities) | | |

```
A    =   L   +  OE
−31,000  −15,000
         −16,000
```

4. The remaining cash is distributed to the partners on the basis of **their capital balances**. After the entries in the first three steps are posted, all partnership accounts, including Gain on Realization, will have zero balances except for four accounts: Cash $49,000; R. Arnet, Capital $22,500; P. Carey, Capital $22,800; and W. Eaton, Capital $3,700, as shown below:

**ILLUSTRATION 13-18**

*Ledger balances before distribution of cash*

| Cash | | | | R. Arnet, Capital | | | P. Carey, Capital | | | W. Eaton, Capital | | |
|---|---|---|---|---|---|---|---|---|---|---|---|---|
| Bal. | 5,000 | (3) | 31,000 | | Bal. | 15,000 | | Bal. | 17,800 | | Bal. | 1,200 |
| (1) | 75,000 | | | | (2) | 7,500 | | (2) | 5,000 | | (2) | 2,500 |
| Bal. | 49,000 | | | | Bal. | 22,500 | | Bal. | 22,800 | | Bal. | 3,700 |

The entry to record the distribution of cash is as follows:

**(4)**

| | | |
|---|---|---|
| R. Arnet, Capital | 22,500 | |
| P. Carey, Capital | 22,800 | |
| W. Eaton, Capital | 3,700 | |
|     Cash | | 49,000 |
|        (To record distribution of cash to partners) | | |

```
A    =   L   +  OE
−49,000       −22,500
              −22,800
              − 3,700
```

After this entry is posted, all partnership accounts will have zero balances, as shown in Illustration 13-19.

| Cash | | | | | R. Arnet, Capital | | | | P. Carey, Capital | | | | W. Eaton, Capital | | |
|---|---|---|---|---|---|---|---|---|---|---|---|---|---|---|---|
| Bal. | 5,000 | (3) | 31,000 | (4) | 22,500 | Bal. | 15,000 | (4) | 22,800 | Bal. | 17,800 | (4) | 3,700 | Bal. | 1,200 |
| (1) | 75,000 | (4) | 49,000 | | | (2) | 7,500 | | | (2) | 5,000 | | | (2) | 2,500 |
| Bal. | –0– | | | | | Bal. | –0– | | | Bal. | –0– | | | Bal. | –0– |

ILLUSTRATION 13-19
*Ledger balances after distribution of cash*

A word of caution: **Cash should not be distributed to partners on the basis of their income-sharing ratios.** On this basis, for example, Arnet would receive three-sixths, or $24,500, which would produce an erroneous debit balance of $2,000. The income ratio is a proper basis for allocating net income or loss, **but it is not a proper basis for making the final distribution of cash to the partners.**

**HELPFUL HINT**

Zero balances after posting is a quick proof of the accuracy of the cash distribution entry.

## Schedule of Cash Payments

Some accountants prepare a cash payments schedule to determine the distribution of cash to the partners in the liquidation of a partnership. The **schedule of cash payments**, sometimes called a **safe cash payments schedule**, is organized around the basic accounting equation. The schedule for the Ace Company is shown in Illustration 13-20. The numbers in parentheses refer to the four required steps in the liquidation of a partnership. They also identify the accounting entries that must be made. The cash payments schedule is especially useful when the liquidation process extends over a period of time.

ILLUSTRATION 13-20
*Schedule of cash payments, no capital deficiency*

### ACE COMPANY
### Schedule of Cash Payments

| Item | | Cash | + | Noncash Assets | = | Liabilities | + | R. Arnet Capital | + | P. Carey Capital | + | W. Eaton Capital |
|---|---|---|---|---|---|---|---|---|---|---|---|---|
| Balances before liquidation | | 5,000 | + | 60,000 | = | 31,000 | + | 15,000 | + | 17,800 | + | 1,200 |
| Sales of noncash assets and allocation of gain | (1)&(2) | 75,000 | + | (60,000) | = | | | 7,500 | + | 5,000 | + | 2,500 |
| New balances | | 80,000 | + | –0– | = | 31,000 | + | 22,500 | + | 22,800 | + | 3,700 |
| Pay liabilities | (3) | (31,000) | | | = | (31,000) | | | | | | |
| New balances | | 49,000 | + | –0– | = | –0– | + | 22,500 | + | 22,800 | + | 3,700 |
| Cash distribution to partners | (4) | (49,000) | | | = | | | (22,500) | + | (22,800) | + | (3,700) |
| Final balances | | –0– | | –0– | | –0– | | –0– | | –0– | | –0– |

## Capital Deficiency

A capital deficiency may be caused by recurring net losses, excessive drawings before liquidation, or by losses from realization suffered during liquidation. To illustrate, assume that Ace Company is on the brink of bankruptcy. The partners decide to liquidate by having a "going-out-of-business" sale in which merchandise is sold at substantial discounts, and the equipment is sold at auction. Cash proceeds from these sales and collections from customers total only $42,000. Accordingly, the loss from liquidation is $18,000 ($60,000 − $42,000). The steps in the liquidation process are as follows:

**1.** The entry for the realization of noncash assets is:

(1)

| | | |
|---|---|---|
| Cash | 42,000 | |
| Accumulated Depreciation—Equipment | 8,000 | |
| Loss on Realization | 18,000 | |
|     Accounts Receivable | | 15,000 |
|     Inventory | | 18,000 |
|     Equipment | | 35,000 |
|       (To record realization of noncash assets) | | |

```
A      =   L   +   OE
+42,000              −18,000
+ 8,000
−15,000
−18,000
−35,000
```

**2.** The loss on realization is allocated to the partners on the basis of their income ratios. The entry is:

(2)

| | | |
|---|---|---|
| R. Arnet, Capital ($18,000 × 3/6) | 9,000 | |
| P. Carey, Capital ($18,000 × 2/6) | 6,000 | |
| W. Eaton, Capital ($18,000 × 1/6) | 3,000 | |
|     Loss on Realization | | 18,000 |
|       (To allocate loss on realization to partners) | | |

```
A   =   L   +   OE
              − 9,000
              − 6,000
              − 3,000
              +18,000
```

**3.** Partnership liabilities are paid. This entry is the same as in the previous example.

(3)

| | | |
|---|---|---|
| Notes Payable | 15,000 | |
| Accounts Payable | 16,000 | |
|     Cash | | 31,000 |
|       (To record payment of partnership liabilities) | | |

```
A       =   L      +   OE
−31,000   −15,000
          −16,000
```

**4.** After posting the three entries, two accounts will have debit balances—Cash, $16,000, and W. Eaton, Capital, $1,800—and two accounts will have credit balances—R. Arnet, Capital, $6,000, and P. Carey, Capital, $11,800, as shown below:

**ILLUSTRATION 13-21**

*Ledger balances before distribution of cash*

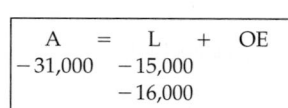

| Cash | | | | R. Arnet, Capital | | | | P. Carey, Capital | | | | W. Eaton, Capital | | | |
|---|---|---|---|---|---|---|---|---|---|---|---|---|---|---|---|
| Bal. | 5,000 | (3) | 31,000 | (2) | 9,000 | Bal. | 15,000 | (2) | 6,000 | Bal. | 17,800 | (2) | 3,000 | Bal. | 1,200 |
| (1) | 42,000 | | | | | | | | | | | | | | |
| Bal. | 16,000 | | | | | Bal. | 6,000 | | | Bal. | 11,800 | Bal. | 1,800 | | |

Eaton has a capital deficiency of $1,800. Eaton, therefore, owes the partnership $1,800, and Arnet and Carey have a legally enforceable claim against Eaton's personal assets. The distribution of cash is still made on the basis of capital balances. However, the amount will vary depending on how the deficiency is settled.

### Payment of Deficiency

If the partner with the capital deficiency pays the amount owed the partnership, the deficiency is eliminated. To illustrate, assume that Eaton pays $1,800 to the partnership. The entry is:

(a)

| | | |
|---|---|---|
| Cash | 1,800 | |
|     W. Eaton, Capital | | 1,800 |
|       (To record payment of capital deficiency by Eaton) | | |

```
A      =   L   +   OE
+1,800            +1,800
```

After posting this entry, account balances are as follows:

| Cash | | | | R. Arnet, Capital | | | | P. Carey, Capital | | | | W. Eaton, Capital | | | |
|---|---|---|---|---|---|---|---|---|---|---|---|---|---|---|---|
| Bal. | 5,000 | (3) | 31,000 | (2) | 9,000 | Bal. | 15,000 | (2) | 6,000 | Bal. | 17,800 | (2) | 3,000 | Bal. | 1,200 |
| (1) | 42,000 | | | | | | | | | | | | | (a) | 1,800 |
| (a) | 1,800 | | | | | Bal. | 6,000 | | | Bal. | 11,800 | | | | |
| | | | | | | | | | | | | | | Bal. | –0– |
| Bal. | 17,800 | | | | | | | | | | | | | | |

**ILLUSTRATION 13-22**

*Ledger balances after paying capital deficiency*

The cash balance of $17,800 is now equal to the credit balances in the capital accounts (Arnet $6,000 + Carey $11,800), and cash is distributed on the basis of these balances. The entry is:

| | | |
|---|---|---|
| R. Arnet, Capital | 6,000 | |
| P. Carey, Capital | 11,800 | |
| Cash | | 17,800 |
| (To record distribution of cash to the partners) | | |

| A | = | L | + | OE |
|---|---|---|---|---|
| –17,800 | | | | – 6,000 |
| | | | | –11,800 |

After this entry is posted, all accounts will have zero balances.

## Nonpayment of Deficiency

If a partner with a capital deficiency is unable to pay the amount owed to the partnership, the partners with credit balances must absorb the loss. The loss is allocated on the basis of the income ratios that exist between the partners with credit balances. The income ratios of Arnet and Carey are 3:2 or 3/5 and 2/5, respectively. Thus, the following entry is made to remove Eaton's capital deficiency:

| **(a)** | | |
|---|---|---|
| R. Arnet, Capital ($1,800 × 3/5) | 1,080 | |
| P. Carey, Capital ($1,800 × 2/5) | 720 | |
| W. Eaton, Capital | | 1,800 |
| (To record write-off of capital deficiency) | | |

| A | = | L | + | OE |
|---|---|---|---|---|
| | | | | –1,080 |
| | | | | – 720 |
| | | | | +1,800 |

**ILLUSTRATION 13-23**

*Ledger balances after non-payment of capital deficiency*

After posting this entry, the cash and capital accounts will have the following balances:

| Cash | | | | R. Arnet, Capital | | | | P. Carey, Capital | | | | W. Eaton, Capital | | | |
|---|---|---|---|---|---|---|---|---|---|---|---|---|---|---|---|
| Bal. | 5,000 | (3) | 31,000 | (2) | 9,000 | Bal. | 15,000 | (2) | 6,000 | Bal. | 17,800 | (2) | 3,000 | Bal. | 1,200 |
| (1) | 42,000 | | | (a) | 1,080 | | | (a) | 720 | | | | | (a) | 1,800 |
| Bal. | 16,000 | | | | | Bal. | 4,920 | | | Bal. | 11,080 | | | Bal. | –0– |

The cash balance of $16,000 now equals the sum of the credit balances in the capital accounts (Arnet $4,920 + Carey $11,080). The entry to record the distribution of cash is:

| | | |
|---|---|---|
| R. Arnet, Capital | 4,920 | |
| P. Carey, Capital | 11,080 | |
| Cash | | 16,000 |
| (To record distribution of cash to partners) | | |

| A | = | L | + | OE |
|---|---|---|---|---|
| –16,000 | | | | – 4,920 |
| | | | | –11,080 |

After this entry is posted, all accounts will have zero balances.

## BEFORE YOU GO ON . . .

### Review It

1. Identify the steps in liquidating a partnership.
2. What basis is used in making the final distribution of cash to the partners?

## A LOOK BACK AT OUR FEATURE STORY

Refer back to the opening story about Razor & Tie Music, and answer the following questions:

1. Speculate as to why Razor & Tie selected the partnership form of organization for its business.
2. What do you believe are the major items written into the partnership agreement for Razor & Tie?
3. How is net income or loss divided if the partnership is silent regarding the percentage allocation?

*Solution:*

1. Cliff Chenfield and Craig Balsam may have chosen to form a partnership, rather than a corporation, for a number of reasons. First, the partnership is much quicker and easier to form, with little of the red tape associated with a corporation. Second, the partnership form has distinct tax advantages relative to a corporation. Third, since the two partners knew each other well prior to beginning Razor & Tie, their concerns about the risk of unlimited liabilities that might be incurred due to inappropriate actions by the other partner are reduced.
2. A partnership agreement of Razor & Tie should specify the capital contributed by both partners, and the basis for sharing income and losses and for withdrawing funds from the partnership. In addition, it is good to specify a mechanism for resolving disputes, adding or removing a partner, or what to do in the event of the death of one of the partners. A well-written partnership agreement can significantly reduce conflicts as the firm grows.
3. In this case, income and losses are shared equally.

THE NAVIGATOR

## DEMONSTRATION PROBLEM

On January 1, 1999, the capital balances in Hollingsworth Company are Lois Holly $26,000, and Jim Worth $24,000. In 1999 the company reports net income of $30,000. The income ratio provides for salary allowances of $12,000 for Holly and $10,000 to Worth and the remainder equally. Neither partner had any drawings in 1999.

Assume that the following independent transactions occur on January 1, 2000:

1. Donna Reichenbacher purchases one-half of Holly's capital interest for $25,000.
2. Marsha Mears is admitted with a 25% capital interest by a cash investment of $40,000.
3. Stan Wells is admitted with a 35% capital interest by a cash investment of $40,000.

*Instructions*

(a) Prepare a schedule showing the distribution of net income in 1999.
(b) Journalize the division of 1999 net income to the partners.
(c) Journalize each of the independent transactions that occurred on January 1, 2000.

## SOLUTION TO DEMONSTRATION PROBLEM

(a) Net income                                                                        $30,000

### Division of Net Income

|  | Lois Holly | Jim Worth | Total |
|---|---|---|---|
| Salary allowance | $12,000 | $10,000 | $22,000 |
| Remaining income $8,000 | | | |
| ($30,000 − $22,000) | | | |
| Lois Holly ($8,000 × 50%) | 4,000 | | |
| Jim Worth ($8,000 × 50%) | | 4,000 | |
|   Total remainder | | | 8,000 |
| Total division | $16,000 | $14,000 | $30,000 |

(b) 

| 12/31/99 | Income Summary | 30,000 | |
|---|---|---|---|
| |   Lois Holly, Capital ($12,000 + $4,000) | | 16,000 |
| |   Jim Worth, Capital ($10,000 + $4,000) | | 14,000 |
| |     (To close net income to partners' capitals) | | |

(1)

(c)

| 1/1/00 | Lois Holly, Capital ($26,000 + $16,000) × ½) | 21,000 | |
|---|---|---|---|
| |   Donna Reichenbacher, Capital | | 21,000 |
| |     (To record purchase of one-half of Holly's | | |
| |     interest) | | |

(2)

| 1/1/00 | Cash | 40,000 | |
|---|---|---|---|
| |   Lois Holly, Capital | | 5,000 |
| |   Jim Worth, Capital | | 5,000 |
| |   Marsha Mears, Capital | | 30,000 |
| |     (To record admission of Mears and bonus to | | |
| |     old partners) | | |

Total capital after investment: $120,000
(Holly, $42,000, Worth $38,000, Mears
investment $40,000)

| Mears' capital credit (25% × $120,000) | | | $30,000 |
|---|---|---|---|

| Bonus to old partners ($40,000 − $30,000) | | | $10,000 |
|---|---|---|---|

Allocation of bonus:

| Holly ($10,000 × 50%) | $ 5,000 | |
|---|---|---|
| Worth ($10,000 × 50%) | 5,000 | $10,000 |

(3)

| 1/1/00 | Cash | 40,000 | |
|---|---|---|---|
| | Lois Holly, Capital | 1,000 | |
| | Jim Worth, Capital | 1,000 | |
| |   Stan Wells, Capital | | 42,000 |
| |     (To record Wells's admission and bonus) | | |

| Wells's capital credit (35% × $120,000) | | $42,000 |
|---|---|---|

| Bonus to Wells ($42,000 − $40,000) | | $ 2,000 |
|---|---|---|

Allocation of bonus:

| Holly ($2,000 × 50%) | $1,000 | |
|---|---|---|
| Worth ($2,000 × 50%) | 1,000 | $ 2,000 |

**PROBLEM-SOLVING STRATEGIES**

1. Journalizing the division of net income is a closing entry.

2. The entry for purchase of an interest involves only capital accounts.

3. The entry for admission by investment must have a debit to cash.

4. Allocation of a bonus occurs only in admission by investment.

THE NAVIGATOR

# Summary of Study Objectives

1. *Identify the characteristics of the partnership form of business organization.* The principal characteristics of a partnership are: (a) association of individuals, (b) mutual agency, (c) limited life, (d) unlimited liability, and (e) co-ownership of property.

2. *Explain the accounting entries for the formation of a partnership.* When a partnership is formed, each partner's initial investment should be recorded at the fair market value of the assets at the date of their transfer to the partnership.

3. *Identify the bases for dividing net income or net loss.* Net income or net loss is divided on the basis of the income ratio, which may be (a) a fixed ratio, (b) a ratio based on beginning or average capital balances, (c) salaries to partners and the remainder on a fixed ratio, (d) interest on partners' capitals and the remainder on a fixed ratio, and (e) salaries to partners, interest on partners' capitals, and the remainder on a fixed ratio.

4. *Describe the form and content of partnership financial statements.* The financial statements of a partnership are similar to those of a proprietorship. The principal differences are: (a) the division of net income is shown on the income statement, (b) the owners' equity statement is called a partners' capital statement, and (c) each partner's capital is reported on the balance sheet.

5. *Explain the effects of the entries when a new partner is admitted.* The entry to record the admittance of a new partner by purchase of a partner's interest affects only partners' capital accounts. The entries to record the admittance by investment of assets in the partnership (a) increase both net assets and total capital and (b) may result in recognition of a bonus to either the old partners or the new partner.

6. *Describe the effects of the entries when a partner withdraws from the firm.* The entry to record a withdrawal from the firm when payment is made from partners' personal assets only affects partners' capital accounts. The entry to record a withdrawal when payment is made from partnership assets (a) decreases net assets and total capital and (b) may result in recognizing a bonus either to the retiring partner or the remaining partners.

7. *Prepare the entries to record the liquidation of a partnership.* When a partnership is liquidated, it is necessary to record the (a) sale of noncash assets, (b) allocation of the gain or loss on realization, (c) payment of partnership liabilities, and (d) distribution of cash to the partners.

# Glossary

**Admission by investment**    Admission of a partner by investing assets in the partnership, in which both partnership net assets and total capital increase. (p. 562).

**Admission by purchase of an interest**    Admission of a partner in a personal transaction between one or more existing partners and the new partner, which does not change total partnership assets or total capital. (p. 561).

**Capital deficiency**    A debit balance in a partner's capital account after allocation of gain or loss. (p. 569).

**General partner**    A partner who has unlimited liability for the debts of the firm. (p. 552).

**Income ratio**    The basis for dividing both net income and net loss in a partnership. (p. 555).

**Limited partner**    A partner who has limited liability for the debts of the firm. (p. 552).

**Limited partnership**    A partnership in which one or more general partners have unlimited liability and one or more partners have limited liability for the obligations of the firm. (p. 552).

**No capital deficiency**    All partners have credit balances after allocation of gain or loss. (p. 569).

**Partners' capital statement**    The owners' equity statement for a partnership which shows the changes in each partner's capital balance and in total partnership capital during the year. (p. 559).

**Partnership**    An association of two or more persons to carry on as co-owners of a business for profit. (p. 550).

**Partnership agreement**    A contract expressing the voluntary agreement of two or more individuals in a partnership. (p. 553).

**Partnership dissolution**    A change in partners due to withdrawal or admission which does not necessarily terminate the business. (p. 551).

**Partnership liquidation**    An event that ends both the legal and economic life of a partnership. (p. 569).

**Schedule of cash payments**    A schedule showing the distribution of cash to the partners in the liquidation of a partnership. (p. 571).

**Withdrawal by payment from partners' personal assets**    Withdrawal of a partner in a personal transaction between partners, which does not change total partnership assets or total capital. (p. 565).

**Withdrawal by payment from partnership assets**    Withdrawal of a partner in a transaction involving the partnership which decreases both partnership net assets and total capital. (p. 566).

# SELF-STUDY QUESTIONS

Answers are at the end of the chapter.

(SO 1) 1. Which of the following is *not* a characteristic of a partnership?
   a. Taxable entity
   b. Co-ownership of property
   c. Mutual agency
   d. Limited life

(SO 1) 2. The advantages of a partnership do *not* include:
   a. ease of formation.
   b. unlimited liability.
   c. freedom from government regulation.
   d. ease of decision making.

(SO 2) 3. Upon formation of a partnership, each partner's initial investment of assets should be recorded at their:
   a. book values.
   b. cost.
   c. market values.
   d. appraised values.

(SO 3) 4. The XYZ Company reports net income of $60,000. If partners X, Y, and Z have an income ratio of 50%, 30%, and 20%, respectively, Z's share of the net income is:
   a. $30,000.
   b. $12,000.
   c. $18,000.
   d. No correct answer is given.

(SO 3) 5. Using the data in (4) above, what is Y's share of net income if the percentages are applicable after each partner receives a $10,000 salary allowance?
   a. $12,000
   b. $20,000
   c. $19,000
   d. $21,000

(SO 4) 6. Which of the following statements about partnership financial statements is true?
   a. Details of the distribution of net income are shown in the owners' equity statement.
   b. The distribution of net income is shown on the balance sheet.
   c. Only the total of all partner capital balances is shown in the balance sheet.
   d. The owners' equity statement is called the partners' capital statement.

(SO 5) 7. Maria Taxco purchases 50% of Louie Limb capital interest in the K & L partnership for $22,000. If the capital balances of Kim and Louie Limb are $40,000 and $30,000, respectively, Taxco's capital balance following the purchase is:
   a. $22,000.
   b. $35,000.
   c. $20,000.
   d. $15,000.

(SO 5) 8. Capital balances in the DEA partnership are D Capital $60,000, E Capital $50,000, and A Capital $40,000, and income ratios are 5:3:2, respectively. The DEAR partnership is formed by admitting R to the firm with a cash investment of $60,000 for a 25% capital interest. The bonus to be credited to A Capital in admitting R is:
   a. $10,000.
   b. $7,500.
   c. $3,750.
   d. $1,500.

(SO 6) 9. Capital balances in the TERM partnership are T Capital $50,000, E Capital $40,000, R Capital $30,000, and M Capital $20,000, and income ratios are 4:3:2:1, respectively. M withdraws from the firm following payment of $29,000 in cash from the partnership. E's capital balance after recording the withdrawal of M is:
   a. $36,000.
   b. $37,000.
   c. $38,000.
   d. $40,000.

(SO 7) 10. In the liquidation of a partnership it is necessary to (1) distribute cash to the partners, (2) sell noncash assets, (3) allocate any gain or loss on realization to the partners, and (4) pay liabilities. These steps should be performed in the following order:
   a. (2), (3), (4), (1).
   b. (2), (3), (1), (4).
   c. (3), (2), (1), (4).
   d. (3), (2), (4), (1).

# QUESTIONS

1. The characteristics of a partnership include the following: (a) association of individuals, (b) limited life, and (c) co-ownership of property. Explain each of these terms.

2. Vera Cruz is confused about the partnership characteristics of (a) mutual agency and (b) unlimited liability. Explain these two characteristics for Vera.

3. Swen Varberg and Egor Karlstad are considering a business venture. They ask you to explain the advantages and disadvantages of the partnership form of organization.

4. Ginny Brown and John Fleming form a partnership. Brown contributes land with a book value of $50,000 and a fair market value of $75,000. Brown also contrib-

utes equipment with a book value of $52,000 and a fair market value of $57,000. The partnership assumes a $20,000 mortgage on the land. What should be the balance in Brown's capital account upon formation of the partnership?

5. Roy Orbison, S. Innis, and David Bowie have a partnership called Depeche Mode. A dispute has arisen among the partners because Orbison has invested twice as much in assets as the other two partners and believes net income and net losses should be shared in accordance with the capital ratios. The partnership agreement does not specify the division of profits and losses. How will net income and net loss be divided?

6. Leon Redbone and Elvis Costello are discussing how income and losses should be divided in a partnership they plan to form. What factors should be considered in determining the division of net income or net loss?

7. Doreen Shaffer and Quincy Jones have capital balances of $40,000 and $80,000, respectively, in a partnership. The partnership agreement indicates that net income or net loss should be shared equally. If the net income for the partnership is $24,000, how should the net income be divided?

8. Robben Ford and Gregg Allman share net income and net loss equally. (a) Which account(s) is (are) debited and credited to record the division of net income between the partners? (b) If Robben Ford withdraws $30,000 in cash for personal use in lieu of salary, which account is debited and which is credited?

9. Partners Reba McEntire and B. Zander are provided salary allowances of $30,000 and $25,000, respectively. They divide the remainder of the partnership income in a ratio of 60:40. If partnership net income is $50,000, how much is allocated to McEntire and Zander?

10. Are the financial statements of a partnership similar to those of a proprietorship? Discuss.

11. Patty Loveless decides to pay Mark Waller $50,000 for a one-third interest in the partnership of Waller and Rose. What effect does this transaction have on partnership net assets?

12. Billy Joel decides to invest $25,000 in a partnership for a one-sixth capital interest. How much do the partnership's net assets increase? Does Joel also acquire a one-sixth income ratio through this investment?

13. Pia Zadora purchases Ramos's interest in the Morgan–Ramos partnership for $72,000. Assuming that Ramos has a $63,000 capital balance in the partnership, what journal entry is made by the partnership to record this transaction?

14. Won Jang has a $37,000 capital balance in a partnership. She sells her interest to Carla Cardosa for $45,000 cash. What entry is made by the partnership for this transaction?

15. Natalie Cole retires from the partnership of Suarez, Tanks, and Cole. She receives $89,000 of partnership assets in settlement of her capital balance of $77,000. Assuming that the income-sharing ratios are 5:3:2, respectively, how much of Cole's bonus is debited to Tanks' capital account?

16. Your roommate argues that partnership assets should be revalued in situations like those in question 15. Why is this generally not done?

17. How is a deceased partner's equity determined?

18. How does the liquidation of a partnership differ from the dissolution of a partnership?

19. Phil Collins and Herb Alpert are discussing the liquidation of a partnership. Phil maintains that all cash should be distributed to partners on the basis of their income ratios. Is he correct? Explain.

20. In continuing their discussion, Herb says that even in the case of a capital deficiency, all cash should still be distributed on the basis of capital balances. Is Herb correct? Explain.

21. Mike, Larry, and Joan have income ratios of 5:3:2 and capital balances of $34,000, $31,000, and $28,000, respectively. Noncash assets are sold at a gain. After creditors are paid, $119,000 of cash is available for distribution to the partners. How much cash should be paid to Larry?

22. Before the final distribution of cash, account balances are: Cash $25,000; B. Springsteen, Capital $19,000 (Cr.); M. Moss, Capital $12,000 (Cr.); and T. Zaret, Capital $6,000 (Dr.). Zaret is unable to pay any of the capital deficiency. If the income-sharing ratios are 5:3:2, respectively, how much cash should be paid to M. Moss?

# BRIEF EXERCISES

*Journalize entries in forming a partnership.*
*(SO 2)*

**BE13–1**  Elton John and Pablo Cruise decide to organize the ALL-Star partnership. Elton John invests $15,000 cash, and Cruise contributes $10,000 cash and equipment having a book value of $3,500. Prepare the entry to record Cruise's investment in the partnership, assuming the equipment has a fair market value of $6,000.

*Prepare portion of opening balance sheet for partnership.*
*(SO 2)*

**BE13–2**  C. Held and G. Kamp decide to merge their proprietorships into a partnership called HeldKamp Company. The balance sheet of Kamp Co. shows:

| Accounts receivable | $15,000 | |
|---|---|---|
| Less: Allowance for doubtful accounts | 1,200 | $13,800 |
| Equipment | 20,000 | |
| Less: Accumulated depreciation | 8,000 | 12,000 |

The partners agree that the net realizable value of the receivables is $12,500 and that the fair market value of the equipment is $10,000. Indicate how the four accounts should appear in the opening balance sheet of the partnership.

**BE13–3**   Fleetwood Mac Co. reports net income of $60,000. The income ratios are: Fleetwood 60% and Mac 40%. Indicate the division of net income to each partner and prepare the entry to distribute the net income.

*Journalize the division of net income using fixed income ratios.*
*(SO 3)*

**BE13–4**   MET Co. reports net income of $60,000. Partner salary allowances are M $20,000, E $5,000, and T $5,000. Indicate the division of net income to each partner, assuming the income ratio is 50:30:20, respectively.

*Compute division of net income with a salary allowance and fixed ratios.*
*(SO 3)*

**BE13–5**   Bill&Til Co. reports net income of $20,000. Interest allowances are Bill $6,000 and Til $5,000; salary allowances are Bill $15,000 and Til $10,000; the remainder is shared equally. Show the distribution of income on the income statement.

*Show division of net income when allowances exceed net income.*
*(SO 3)*

**BE13–6**   In ABC Co. capital balances are: Ali $30,000, Babson $25,000, and Curtis $20,000. The partners share income equally. Daniel is admitted to the firm by purchasing one-half of Curtis's interest for $15,000. Journalize the admission of Daniel to the partnership.

*Journalize admission by purchase of an interest.*
*(SO 5)*

**BE13–7**   In the EZ Co., capital balances are Evelynn $40,000 and Zane $30,000. The partners share income equally. Kerns is admitted to the firm with a 40% interest by an investment of cash of $42,000. Journalize the admission of Kerns.

*Journalize admission by investment.*
*(SO 5)*

**BE13–8**   Capital balances in DEB Co. are Ditka $40,000, Elbert $30,000, and Boyd $28,000. Ditka and Elbert each agree to pay Boyd $12,000 from their personal assets. Ditka and Elbert each receive 50% of Boyd's equity. The partners share income equally. Journalize the withdrawal of Boyd.

*Journalize withdrawal paid by personal assets.*
*(SO 6)*

**BE13–9**   Data pertaining to DEB Co. are presented in BE13–8. Instead of payment from personal assets, assume that Boyd receives $32,000 from partnership assets in withdrawing from the firm. Journalize the withdrawal of Boyd.

*Journalize withdrawal paid by partnership assets.*
*(SO 6)*

**BE13–10**   After liquidating noncash assets and paying creditors, account balances in the ARB Co. are Cash $19,000, A Capital (Cr.) $9,000, R Capital (Cr.) $7,000, and B Capital (Cr.) $3,000. The partners share income equally. Journalize the final distribution of cash to the partners.

*Journalize final cash distribution in liquidation.*
*(SO 7)*

# EXERCISES

••••••••••••••••••••••••••••••••••••••••••••••••••••••••••••••••••

**E13–1**   Kenny Rogers has owned and operated a proprietorship for several years. On January 1, he decides to terminate this business and become a partner in the firm of Payne and Rogers. Rogers's investment in the partnership consists of $15,000 in cash, and the following assets of the proprietorship: accounts receivable $14,000 less allowance for doubtful accounts of $2,000, and equipment $20,000 less accumulated depreciation of $4,000. It is agreed that the allowance for doubtful accounts should be $4,000 for the partnership, and the fair market value of the equipment is $17,000.

*Journalize entry for formation of a partnership.*
*(SO 2)*

**Instructions**
Journalize Rogers's admission to the firm of Payne and Rogers.

**E13–2**   B. Manilow and W. How have capital balances on January 1 of $50,000 and $40,000, respectively. The partnership income sharing agreement provides for (1) annual salaries of $14,000 for Manilow and $12,000 for How, (2) interest at 10% on beginning capital balances, and (3) remaining income or loss to be shared 70% by Manilow and 30% by How.

*Prepare schedule showing distribution of net income and closing entry.*
*(SO 3)*

**Instructions**
(a) Prepare a schedule showing the distribution of net income, assuming net income is
(1) $55,000 and (2) $30,000.
(b) Journalize the allocation of net income in each of the situations above.

**E13–3**   In Led Zeppelin Co., beginning capital balances on January 1, 1999, are Karen Ackers $20,000 and Chris Cross $18,000. During the year, drawings were Ackers $8,000 and Cross $3,000. Net income was $30,000, and the partners share income equally.

*Prepare partners' capital statement and partial balance sheet.*
*(SO 4)*

*Instructions*
  (a) Prepare the partners' capital statement for the year.
  (b) Prepare the owners' equity section of the balance sheet at December 31, 1999.

*Journalize admission of a new partner by purchase of an interest.*
*(SO 5)*

**E13–4**   T. Halo, K. Rose, and J. Lamp share income on a 5:3:2 basis. They have capital balances of $30,000, $26,000, and $18,000, respectively, when Tony Bennett is admitted to the partnership.

*Instructions*
Prepare the journal entry to record the admission of Tony Bennett under each of the following assumptions:

  1. Purchase of 50% of Halo's equity for $19,000.
  2. Purchase of 50% of Rose's equity for $10,000.
  3. Purchase of 33⅓% of Lamp's equity for $9,000.

*Journalize admission of a new partner by investment.*
*(SO 5)*

**E13–5**   Joe Keho and Mike McLain share income on a 6:4 basis. They have capital balances of $90,000 and $70,000, respectively, when Linda Ronstadt is admitted to the partnership.

*Instructions*
Prepare the journal entry to record the admission of Linda Ronstadt under each of the following assumptions:

  1. Investment of $100,000 cash for a 25% ownership interest with bonuses to the existing partners.
  2. Investment of $36,000 cash for a 25% ownership interest with a bonus to the new partner.

*Journalize withdrawal of a partner with payment from partners' personal assets.*
*(SO 6)*

**E13–6**   Mary Toshiba, Vera Miles, and Debra Noll have capital balances of $50,000, $30,000, and $22,000, respectively, and their income ratios are 5:3:2. Noll withdraws from the partnership under each of the following independent conditions:

  1. Toshiba and Miles agree to purchase Noll's equity by paying $15,000 each from their personal assets. Each purchaser receives 50% of Noll's equity.
  2. Miles agrees to purchase all of Noll's equity by paying $22,000 cash from her personal assets.
  3. Toshiba agrees to purchase all of Noll's equity by paying $26,000 cash from her personal assets.

*Instructions*
Journalize the withdrawal of Noll under each of the assumptions above.

*Journalize withdrawal of a partner with payment from partnership assets.*
*(SO 6)*

**E13–7**   Dale Nagel, Keith White, and Todd Rundgren have capital balances of $95,000, $75,000, and $60,000, respectively. They share income or loss on a 5:3:2 basis. White withdraws from the partnership under each of the following conditions:

  1. White is paid $82,000 in cash from partnership assets, and a bonus is granted to the retiring partner.
  2. White is paid $68,000 in cash from partnership assets, and bonuses are granted to the remaining partners.

*Instructions*
Journalize the withdrawal of White under each of the assumptions above.

*Prepare cash distribution schedule.*
*(SO 7)*

**E13–8**   The Pips Company at December 31 has cash $20,000, noncash assets $100,000, liabilities $55,000, and the following capital balances: Gladys $45,000 and Knight $20,000. The firm is liquidated, and $120,000 in cash is received for the noncash assets. Gladys and Knight income ratios are 60% and 40%, respectively.

*Instructions*
Prepare a cash distribution schedule.

*Journalize transactions in a liquidation.*
*(SO 7)*

**E13–9**   Data for The Pips partnership are presented in E13–8.

*Instructions*
Prepare the entries to record (1) the sale of noncash assets, (2) the allocation of the gain or loss on liquidation to the partners, (3) payment of creditors, and (4) distribution of cash to the partners.

*Journalize transactions with a capital deficiency.*
*(SO 7)*

**E13–10**   Prior to the distribution of cash to the partners, the accounts in the MEL Company are: Cash $30,000, M Capital (Cr.) $18,000, E Capital (Cr.) $15,000, and L Capital (Dr.) $3,000. The income ratios are 5:3:2, respectively.

## Instructions

(a) Prepare the entry to record (1) L's payment of $3,000 in cash to the partnership and (2) the distribution of cash to the partners with credit balances.

(b) Prepare the entry to record (1) the absorption of L's capital deficiency by the other partners and (2) the distribution of cash to the partners with credit balances.

# PROBLEMS: SET A

**P13–1A**  The post-closing trial balances of two proprietorships on January 1, 1999, are presented below.

*Prepare entries for formation of a partnership and a balance sheet.*
*(SO 2, 4)*

| | Roberta Company | | Flack Company | |
|---|---|---|---|---|
| | Dr. | Cr. | Dr. | Cr. |
| Cash | $ 6,500 | | $ 8,000 | |
| Accounts receivable | 15,000 | | 23,000 | |
| Allowance for doubtful accounts | | $ 2,500 | | $ 4,000 |
| Merchandise inventory | 28,000 | | 17,000 | |
| Equipment | 52,000 | | 30,000 | |
| Accumulated depreciation—equipment | | 24,000 | | 13,000 |
| Notes payable | | 20,000 | | |
| Accounts payable | | 25,000 | | 37,000 |
| Roberta, Capital | | 30,000 | | |
| Flack, Capital | | | | 24,000 |
| | $101,500 | $101,500 | $78,000 | $78,000 |

Roberta and Flack decide to form the Roberta Flack Company with the following agreed upon valuations for noncash assets:

| | Roberta Company | Flack Company |
|---|---|---|
| Accounts receivable | $15,000 | $23,000 |
| Allowance for doubtful accounts | 3,500 | 5,000 |
| Merchandise inventory | 32,000 | 21,000 |
| Equipment | 31,000 | 18,000 |

All cash will be transferred to the partnership, and the partnership will assume all the liabilities of the two proprietorships. Further, it is agreed that Roberta will invest $15,000 in cash, and Flack will invest $5,000 in cash.

## Instructions

(a) Prepare separate journal entries to record the transfer of each proprietorship's assets and liabilities to the partnership.

(b) Journalize the additional cash investment by each partner.

(c) Prepare a balance sheet for the partnership on January 1, 1999.

**P13–2A**  At the end of its first year of operations on December 31, 1999, the LMC Company's accounts show the following:

*Journalize divisions of net income and prepare a partners' capital statement.*
*(SO 3, 4)*

| Partner | Drawings | Capital |
|---|---|---|
| Lois Lang | $12,000 | $30,000 |
| Mary Mio | 9,000 | 20,000 |
| Kim Casey | 6,000 | 10,000 |

The capital balance represents each partner's initial capital investment. Therefore, net income or net loss for 1999 has not been closed to the partners' capital accounts.

## Instructions

(a) Journalize the entry to record the division of net income for 1999 under each of the following independent assumptions:

1.  Net income is $32,600, and income is shared 5:3:2.
2.  Net income is $30,000; Lang and Mio are given salary allowances of $13,000 and $8,000, respectively, and the remainder is shared equally.

3. Net income is $25,200; each partner is allowed interest of 10% on beginning capital balances; Lang is given a $15,000 salary allowance; and the remainder is shared equally.

(b) Prepare a schedule showing the division of net income under assumption (3) above.

(c) Prepare a partner's capital statement for the year under assumption (3) above.

*Journalize admission of a partner under different assumptions.*
*(SO 5)*

**P13–3A** At April 30, partners' capital balances in the ELM Company are: A. Eksjo $49,000, C. Ludvika $24,000, and W. Matt $17,000. The income sharing ratios are 3:2:1, respectively. On May 1, the ELMO Company is formed by admitting N. Ortiz to the firm as a partner.

*Instructions*

(a) Journalize the admission of Ortiz under each of the following independent assumptions:
   1. Ortiz purchases 50% of Matt's ownership interest by paying Matt $9,000 in cash.
   2. Ortiz purchases 50% of Ludvika's ownership interest by paying Ludvika $16,000 in cash.
   3. Ortiz invests $35,000 cash in the partnership for a 40% ownership interest that includes a bonus to the new partner.
   4. Ortiz invests $30,000 in the partnership for a 15% ownership interest and bonuses are given to the old partners.

(b) Matt's capital balance is $18,000 after admitting Ortiz to the partnership by investment. If Matt's ownership interest is 15% of total partnership capital, what was Ortiz's cash investment and the total bonus to the old partners?

*Journalize withdrawal of a partner under different assumptions.*
*(SO 6)*

**P13–4A** On December 31, the capital balances and income ratios in the ART Company are as follows:

| Partner | Capital Balance | Income Ratio |
| --- | --- | --- |
| E. Arhus | $70,000 | 60% |
| P. Ross | 30,000 | 30 |
| L. Tower | 20,000 | 10 |

*Instructions*

(a) Journalize the withdrawal of Tower under each of the following independent assumptions:
   1. Each of the remaining partners agrees to pay $12,000 in cash from personal funds to purchase Tower's ownership equity. Each receives 50% of Tower's equity.
   2. Ross agrees to purchase Tower's ownership interest for $18,000 in cash.
   3. From partnership assets, Tower is paid $29,000, which includes a bonus to the retiring partner.
   4. Tower is paid $17,000 from partnership assets, and bonuses to the remaining partners are recognized.

(b) If Ross's capital balance after Tower's withdrawal is $33,000, what was the total bonus to the remaining partners and the cash paid by the partnership to Tower?

*Prepare entries and schedule of cash payments in liquidation of a partnership.*
*(SO 7)*

**P13–5A** The partners in Inland Lakes Company decide to liquidate the firm when the balance sheet shows the following:

## INLAND LAKES COMPANY
### Balance Sheet
### April 30, 1999

| Assets | | Liabilities and Owners' Equity | |
| --- | --- | --- | --- |
| Cash | $24,000 | Notes payable | $14,000 |
| Accounts receivable | 18,000 | Accounts payable | 24,000 |
| Allowance for doubtful accounts | (1,000) | Wages payable | 2,000 |
| Merchandise inventory | 30,000 | T. E. Huron, Capital | 24,000 |
| Equipment | 17,000 | P. A. Erie, Capital | 12,800 |
| Accumulated depreciation—equip. | (8,000) | C. R. Lake, Capital | 3,200 |
| Total | $80,000 | Total | $80,000 |

The partners share income and loss 5:3:2. During the process of liquidation, the transactions below were completed in the following sequence:

1. A total of $48,000 was received from converting noncash assets into cash.
2. Liabilities were paid in full.
3. Cash was paid to the partners with credit balances.

*Instructions*
   (a) Prepare a cash distribution schedule.
   (b) Prepare the entries to record the transactions.
   (c) Post to the cash and capital accounts.

# PROBLEMS: SET B
••••••••••••••••••••••••••••••••••••••••••••••••••••••••••••••••••••••••

**P13–1B**  The post-closing trial balances of two proprietorships on January 1, 1999, are presented below.

*Prepare entries for formation of a partnership and a balance sheet.*
*(SO 2, 4)*

|  | Elvis Company | | Costello Company | |
|---|---|---|---|---|
|  | **Dr.** | **Cr.** | **Dr.** | **Cr.** |
| Cash | $ 13,000 | | $16,000 | |
| Accounts receivable | 17,500 | | 26,000 | |
| Allowance for doubtful accounts | | $ 3,000 | | $ 4,400 |
| Merchandise inventory | 26,500 | | 18,400 | |
| Equipment | 45,000 | | 28,000 | |
| Accumulated depreciation—equipment | | 24,000 | | 12,000 |
| Notes payable | | 20,000 | | 15,000 |
| Accounts payable | | 20,000 | | 31,000 |
| Elvis, Capital | | 35,000 | | |
| Costello, Capital | | | | 26,000 |
|  | $102,000 | $102,000 | $88,400 | $88,400 |

Elvis and Costello decide to form the Elvis Costello Company with the following agreed upon
valuations for noncash assets:

|  | Elvis Company | Costello Company |
|---|---|---|
| Accounts receivable | $17,500 | $26,000 |
| Allowance for doubtful accounts | 4,500 | 4,000 |
| Merchandise inventory | 30,000 | 20,000 |
| Equipment | 25,000 | 18,000 |

All cash will be transferred to the partnership, and the partnership will assume all the liabilities
of the two proprietorships. Further, it is agreed that Elvis will invest $20,000 in cash and
Costello will invest $9,000 in cash.

*Instructions*
   (a) Prepare separate journal entries to record the transfer of each proprietorship's assets
       and liabilities to the partnership.
   (b) Journalize the additional cash investment by each partner.
   (c) Prepare a balance sheet for the partnership on January 1, 1999.

**P13–2B**  At the end of its first year of operations on December 31, 1999, HRZ Company's
accounts show the following:

*Journalize divisions of net income and prepare a partners' capital statement.*
*(SO 3, 4)*

| Partner | Drawings | Capital |
|---|---|---|
| Sue Hidalgo | $23,000 | $45,000 |
| Tracey Rugen | 14,000 | 30,000 |
| Eileen Zak | 10,000 | 25,000 |

The capital balance represents each partner's initial capital investment; therefore, net income
or net loss for 1999 has not been closed to the partners' capital accounts.

*Instructions*
   (a) Journalize the entry to record the division of net income for the year 1999 under each
       of the following independent assumptions:

1. Net income is $28,000, and income is shared 6:3:1.
2. Net income is $34,000; Hidalgo and Rugen are given salary allowances of $18,000 and $10,000, respectively; and the remainder is shared equally.
3. Net income is $22,000; each partner is allowed interest of 10% on beginning capital balances; Hidalgo is given a $15,000 salary allowance; and the remainder is shared equally.

(b) Prepare a schedule showing the division of net income under assumption (3) above.

(c) Prepare a partners' capital statement for the year under assumption (3) above.

*Journalize admission of a partner under different assumptions.*
*(SO 5)*

**P13–3B**    At April 30, partners' capital balances in NSW Company are: A. Nolan $62,000, D. Spoda $36,000, and T. Wuhan $12,000. The income sharing ratios are 5:4:1, respectively. On May 1, the NSWO Company is formed by admitting M. Otton to the firm as a partner.

**Instructions**

(a) Journalize the admission of Otton under each of the following independent assumptions:
   1. Otton purchases 50% of Wuhan's ownership interest by paying Wuhan $16,000 in cash.
   2. Otton purchases 33⅓% of Spoda's ownership interest by paying Spoda $15,000 in cash.
   3. Otton invests $60,000 for a 30% ownership interest, and bonuses are given to the old partners.
   4. Otton invests $40,000 for a 32% ownership interest, which includes a bonus to the new partner.

(b) Spoda's capital balance is $30,000 after admitting Otton to the partnership by investment. If Spoda's ownership interest is 20% of total partnership capital, what was Otton's cash investment and the bonus to the new partner?

*Journalize withdrawal of a partner under different assumptions.*
*(SO 6)*

**P13–4B**    On December 31, the capital balances and income ratios in the BAG Company are as follows:

| Partner | Capital Balance | Income Ratio |
|---|---|---|
| R. Beano | $60,000 | 50% |
| D. Alman | 40,000 | 30% |
| P. Garth | 32,000 | 20% |

**Instructions**

(a) Journalize the withdrawal of Garth under each of the following assumptions:
   1. Each of the continuing partners agrees to pay $17,000 in cash from personal funds to purchase Garth's ownership equity. Each receives 50% of Garth's equity.
   2. Alman agrees to purchase Garth's ownership interest for $30,000 cash.
   3. Garth is paid $38,000 from partnership assets, which includes a bonus to the retiring partner.
   4. Garth is paid $28,000 from partnership assets, and bonuses to the remaining partners are recognized.

(b) If Alman's capital balance after Garth's withdrawal is $43,000, what was the total bonus to the remaining partners and the cash paid by the partnership to Garth?

*Prepare entries and schedules of cash payments with a capital deficiency in liquidation of a partnership.*
*(SO 7)*

**P13–5B**    The partners in the JRS Company decide to liquidate the firm when the balance sheet shows the following:

**JRS COMPANY**
**Balance Sheet**
**May 31, 1999**

| Assets | | Liabilities and Owners' Equity | |
|---|---|---|---|
| Cash | $ 27,500 | Notes payable | $ 13,500 |
| Accounts receivable | 24,000 | Accounts payable | 27,000 |
| Allowance for doubtful accounts | (1,000) | Wages payable | 3,800 |
| Merchandise inventory | 34,500 | M. Jagger, Capital | 35,000 |
| Equipment | 21,000 | K. Richards, Capital | 20,000 |
| Accumulated depreciation—equipment | (5,500) | R. Simka, Capital | 1,200 |
| Total | $100,500 | Total | $100,500 |

The partners share income and loss 5:3:2. During the process of liquidation, the following transactions were completed in the following sequence:

1. A total of $53,000 was received from converting noncash assets into cash.
2. Liabilities were paid in full.
3. Simka paid his capital deficiency.
4. Cash was paid to the partners with credit balances.

*Instructions*
(a) Prepare the entries to record the transactions.
(b) Post to the cash and capital accounts.
(c) Assume that Simka is unable to pay the capital deficiency.
    1. Prepare the entry to allocate Simka's debit balance to Jagger and Richards.
    2. Prepare the entry to record the final distribution of cash.

# BROADENING YOUR PERSPECTIVE

# CRITICAL THINKING
## GROUP DECISION CASE

**BYP13–1**   Dan Staffan and Donna Havasi, two professionals in the finance area, have worked for Advanced Leasing for a number of years. Advanced Leasing is a company that leases high-tech medical equipment to hospitals. Dan and Donna have decided that, with their financial expertise, they might start their own company to provide consulting services to individuals interested in leasing equipment. One form of organization they are considering is a partnership.

If they start a partnership, each individual plans to contribute $15,000 in cash. In addition, Dan has a used IBM microcomputer that originally cost $3,800, which he intends to invest in the partnership. The computer has a present market value of $1,800.

Although both Dan and Donna are financial wizards, they do not know a great deal about how a partnership operates. As a result, they have come to you for advice.

*Instructions*
With the class divided into groups, answer the following:
(a) What are the major disadvantages of starting a partnership?
(b) What type of document is needed for a partnership and what should this document contain?
(c) Both Dan and Donna plan to work full-time in the new partnership. Therefore they believe that net income or net loss should be shared equally. However, they are wondering how they can provide compensation to Dan Staffan for his additional investment of the microcomputer. What would you tell them?
(d) Dan is not sure how the computer equipment should be reported on his tax return. What would you tell him?
(e) As indicated above, Dan and Donna have worked together for a number of years. Dan's skills complement Donna's and vice versa. If one of them dies, it will be very difficult for the other to maintain the business, not to mention the difficulty of paying the deceased partner's estate for his or her partnership interest. What would you advise them to do?

## COMMUNICATION ACTIVITY

**BYP13–2**   You are an expert in the field of forming partnerships. Doug Stahl and Enid Halsingborg want to establish a partnership to start up "Enid's Pasta Shop," and they are going to meet with you to discuss their plans. Prior to the meeting you will send them a memo discussing the issues they need to consider before their visit.

*Instructions*
Write a memo in good form to be sent to Doug and Enid.

## ETHICS CASE

**BYP13–3**  Susan and Karen operate a beauty salon as partners who share profits and losses equally. The success of their business has exceeded their expectations and is operating quite profitably. Karen is anxious to maximize profits and schedules appointments from 8 a.m. to 6 p.m. daily, even sacrificing some lunch hours to accommodate regular customers. Susan schedules her appointments from 9 a.m. to 5 p.m. and takes long lunch hours. Susan regularly makes significantly larger withdrawals of cash than Karen does. But, she says, "Karen, you needn't worry, I never make a withdrawal without you knowing about it, so it is properly recorded in my drawing account and charged against my capital at the end of the year." Susan's withdrawals to date are double Karen's.

*Instructions*

(a) Who are the stakeholders in this situation?
(b) Identify the problems with Susan's actions and discuss the ethical considerations of her actions.
(c) How might the partnership agreement be revised to accommodate the differences in Susan's and Karen's work and withdrawal habits?

# SURFING THE NET

**BYP13–4**  This exercise is an introduction to the Big Six Accounting firms.

| Addresses: | | |
|---|---|---|
| | Arthur Andersen | http://www.arthurandersen.com/ |
| | Coopers & Lybrand | http://www.colybrand.com/ |
| | Deloitte & Touche | http://www.dttus.com/ |
| | Ernst & Young | http://www.ey.com/default.htm |
| | KPMG Peat Marwick | http://www.us.kpmg.com/ |
| | Price Waterhouse | http://www.pw.com/ |

**Steps:**

1. Select a firm that is of interest to you.
2. Go to the firm's homepage.

**Instructions**

Answer the following questions:

(a) Name two services provided by the firm.
(b) What is the firm's total annual revenue?
(c) How many clients does it service?
(d) How many people are employed by the firm?

---

*Answers to Self-Study Questions*

1. a    2. b    3. c    4. b    5. c    6. d    7. d    8. d    9. b    10. a

---

*Answer to Kellogg Review It Question 2, p. 554*

Mutual agency, limited life, unlimited liability, and co-ownership of property are major characteristics of a partnership. As a company becomes very large, it becomes difficult to remain as a partnership because of these factors. Unlimited liability is particularly troublesome because owners may lose not only their initial investment but also their personal assets, if those assets are needed to pay partnership creditors.

 **Remember to go back to the Navigator box on the chapter-opening page and check off your completed work.**

## CONCEPTS FOR REVIEW

**Before studying this chapter, you should know or, if necessary, review:**

a. The content of the owner's equity section of a balance sheet. (Ch. 4, pp. 160–161)

b. The content of the owner's equity section of the balance sheet for a proprietorship (Ch. 1, pp. 24–25) and for a partnership. (Ch. 13, p. 559)

c. How to prepare closing entries for a proprietorship (Ch. 4, pp. 146–149) and for a partnership. (Ch. 13, pp. 555–556)

THE NAVIGATOR

## FEATURE STORY

# "Have You Driven a Ford Lately?"

A company that has produced such renowned successes as the Model T and the Mustang, and such a dismal failure as the Edsel, would have some interesting tales to tell. Henry Ford was a defiant visionary from the day Ford Motor Company was formed in 1903. His goal from day one was to design a car he could mass-produce and sell at a price that was affordable to the masses. In short order he accomplished this goal, and by 1920 60 percent of all vehicles on American roads were Fords.

Henry Ford was intolerant of anything that stood between himself and success. In the early years Ford issued shares to the public in order to finance the company's exponential growth. In 1916 he decided that, to retain funds to finance expansion, the company would skip a dividend payment to its shareholders. The shareholders sued. Henry Ford's re-action was swift and direct: if the shareholders didn't see things his way, he would get rid of them. In 1919 the Ford family purchased 100 percent of the outstanding shares of Ford, eliminating any outside "interference." It was over 35 years before shares were again issued to the public.

Ford Motor Company has continued to evolve over the years while at the same time it sometimes has appeared to become even more like the company Henry Ford originally dreamed of. Today there are nearly a billion shares of publicly traded Ford stock outstanding, and the President and Chief Executive is not a member of the Ford family. However, the Ford family still retains a significant stake in Ford. In a move Henry Ford might have supported, top management recently decided to centralize decision making—that is, to have more key decisions made by top management, rather than by division managers. And, reminiscent of Henry Ford's most famous car, the company is attempting to make a "global car"—a mass-produced car that can be sold around the world with only minor changes.

THE NAVIGATOR

*On the World Wide Web*
http://www.ford.com

# CHAPTER 14

## THE NAVIGATOR ✔

- Understand *Concepts for Review* ☐
- Read *Feature Story* ☐
- Scan *Study Objectives* ☐
- Read *Preview* ☐
- Read text and answer *Before You Go On*
  p. 596 ☐  p. 600 ☐  p. 603 ☐  p. 607 ☐
  p. 614 ☐
- Work *Demonstration Problems* ☐
- Review *Summary of Study Objectives* ☐
- Answer *Self-Study Questions* ☐
- Complete assignments ☐

# CORPORATIONS: ORGANIZATION AND CAPITAL STOCK TRANSACTIONS

## STUDY OBJECTIVES

**After studying this chapter, you should be able to:**

1. *Identify and discuss the major characteristics of a corporation.*
2. *Differentiate between paid-in capital and retained earnings.*
3. *Record the issuance of common stock.*
4. *Explain the accounting for treasury stock.*
5. *Differentiate preferred stock from common stock.*
6. *Prepare a stockholders' equity section.*
7. *Compute book value per share.*

THE NAVIGATOR

C orporations like Ford Motor Company have substantial resources. In fact, the corporation is the dominant form of business organization in the United States in terms of dollar volume of sales, earnings, and employees. All of the 500 largest companies in the United States are corporations. In this chapter we will explain the essential features of a corporation and the accounting for a corporation's capital stock transactions. (In Chapter 15 we will look at other issues related to accounting for corporations.) The content and organization of this chapter are as follows:

# THE CORPORATE FORM OF ORGANIZATION

In 1819, Chief Justice John Marshall defined a corporation as "an artificial being, invisible, intangible, and existing only in contemplation of law." This definition has become the foundation for the prevailing legal interpretation that a corporation is an **entity separate and distinct from its owners**.

A corporation is created by law, and its continued existence depends upon the corporate statutes of the state in which it is incorporated. As a legal entity, a corporation has most of the rights and privileges of a person. The major exceptions relate to privileges that can be exercised only by a living person, such as the right to vote or to hold public office. Similarly, a corporation is subject to the same duties and responsibilities as a person, e.g., it must abide by the laws and it must pay taxes.

Corporations may be classified in a variety of ways. Two common bases are by purpose and by ownership. A corporation may be organized for the **purpose** of making a **profit**, or it may be **nonprofit**. Corporations for profit include such well-known companies as McDonald's, General Motors, Kellogg, and Apple

Computer. Nonprofit corporations are organized for charitable, medical, and educational purposes and include the Salvation Army, the American Cancer Society, and the Ford Foundation.

Classification by **ownership** distinguishes between publicly held and privately held corporations. A publicly held corporation may have thousands of stockholders, and its stock is regularly traded on a national securities market such as the New York Stock Exchange. Most of the largest U.S. corporations are publicly held. Examples of publicly held corporations are International Business Machines, Caterpillar Inc., and General Electric. In contrast, a privately held corporation, often referred to as a closely held corporation, usually has only a few stockholders, and does not offer its stock for sale to the general public. Privately held companies are generally much smaller than publicly held companies.

## Characteristics of a Corporation

A number of characteristics distinguish a corporation from proprietorships and partnerships. The most important of these characteristics are explained below.

### Separate Legal Existence

As an entity separate and distinct from its owners, the corporation acts under its own name rather than in the name of its stockholders. A corporation may buy, own, and sell property, borrow money, and enter into legally binding contracts in its own name. It may also sue or be sued, and it pays its own taxes.

In contrast to a partnership, in which the acts of the owners (partners) bind the partnership, the acts of the owners (stockholders) do not bind the corporation unless such owners are duly appointed agents of the corporation. For example, if you owned shares of Ford Motor Company stock, you would not have the right to purchase automobile parts for the company unless you were appointed as an agent of the corporation.

### Limited Liability of Stockholders

Since a corporation is a separate legal entity, creditors ordinarily have recourse only to corporate assets to satisfy their claims. The liability of stockholders is normally limited to their investment in the corporation, and creditors have no legal claim on the personal assets of the owners unless fraud has occurred. Thus, even in the event of bankruptcy of the corporation, stockholders' losses are generally limited to their capital investment in the corporation.

### Transferable Ownership Rights

Ownership of a corporation is shown in shares of capital stock, which are transferable units. Stockholders may dispose of part or all of their interest in a corporation simply by selling their stock. In contrast to the transfer of an ownership interest in a partnership, which requires the consent of each owner, the transfer of stock is entirely at the discretion of the stockholder. It does not require the approval of either the corporation or other stockholders. The transfer of ownership rights between stockholders normally has no effect on the operating activities of the corporation or on a corporation's assets, liabilities, and total ownership equity. That is, the enterprise does not participate in the transfer of these ownership rights after it issues the capital stock.

### Ability to Acquire Capital

It generally is relatively easy for a corporation to obtain capital through the issuance of stock. Buying stock in a corporation is often more attractive to an investor than investing in a partnership because a stockholder has limited liability and shares of stock are readily transferable. Moreover, many individuals

**1**
STUDY
OBJECTIVE
Identify and discuss the major characteristics of a corporation.

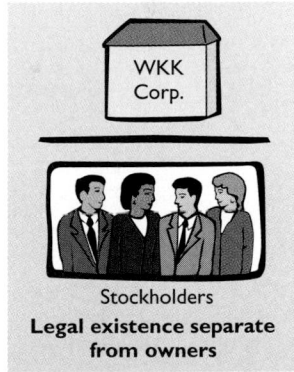
Legal existence separate from owners

Limited liability of stockholders

Transferable ownership rights

Ability to acquire capital

can become stockholders by investing small amounts of money. In sum, the ability of a successful corporation to obtain capital is virtually unlimited.

## Continuous Life

**Continuous life**

The life of a corporation is stated in its charter; it may be perpetual or it may be limited to a specific number of years. If it is limited, the period of existence can be extended through renewal of the charter. Since a corporation is a separate legal entity, the life of a corporation and its continuance as a going concern are not affected by the withdrawal, death, or incapacity of a stockholder, employee, or officer. As a result, a successful enterprise can have a continuous and perpetual life.

## Corporation Management

Although stockholders legally own the corporation, as in Ford Motor Company, they manage the corporation indirectly through a board of directors they elect. The board, in turn, formulates the operating policies for the company and selects officers, such as a president and one or more vice presidents, to execute policy and to perform daily management functions.

A typical organization chart showing the delegation of responsibility is shown in Illustration 14-1. The **president** is the chief executive officer with direct responsibility for managing the business. As the organization chart shows, the president delegates responsibility to other officers. The chief accounting officer is the **controller**. The controller's responsibilities include (1) maintaining the accounting records, (2) maintaining an adequate system of internal control, and (3) preparing financial statements, tax returns, and internal reports. The **treasurer** has custody of the corporation's funds and is responsible for maintaining the company's cash position.

**ILLUSTRATION 14-1**

*Corporation organization chart*

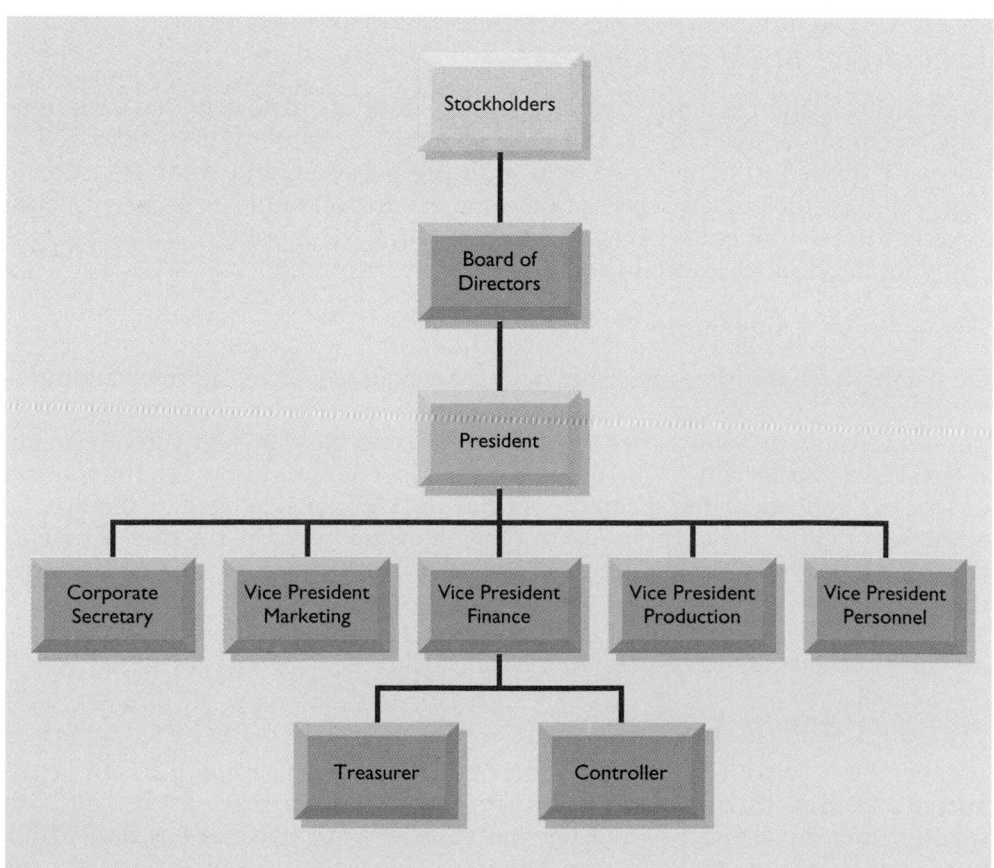

The organizational structure of a corporation enables a company to hire professional managers to run the business. On the other hand, the separation of ownership and management prevents owners from having an active role in managing the company, which some owners like to have.

# ACCOUNTING IN ACTION
### Business Insight

An interesting question is: Who runs a corporation—the stockholders or the board of directors? This issue has taken on increased importance because stockholders and boards of directors are often on the opposite sides of the fence these days when potential takeovers occur.

A classic example is the unfriendly takeover bid made by Paramount Communication Inc. for Time Inc. Paramount bid up Time's stock price substantially; many stockholders said sell—but Time's board of directors had other plans. They were in the process of trying to make a friendly deal with Warner Communications. Some stockholders said, "Let's vote on what we should do." But Time decided to proceed without a stockholders' vote, even though the board of directors knew the Warner deal would depress Time's stock price. They figured that many stockholders would prefer to accept the Paramount bid. The stockholders sued to overturn the deal with Warner Communications but lost. The judge wrote: "Corporation law does not operate on the theory that directors, in exercising their powers to manage the firm, are obligated to follow the wishes of a majority of stockholders. In fact, the directors, not the stockholders, are charged with the duty to manage the firm."

## Government Regulations

A corporation is subject to numerous state and federal regulations. For example, state laws usually prescribe the requirements for issuing stock, the distributions of earnings permitted to stockholders, and the effects of retiring stock, as well as other procedures and restrictions. Similarly, federal securities laws govern the sale of capital stock to the general public. Also, most publicly held corporations are required to make extensive disclosure of their financial affairs to the Securities and Exchange Commission through quarterly and annual reports. In addition, when a corporate stock is listed and traded on organized securities markets, the corporation must comply with the reporting requirements of these exchanges.

Government regulations are designed to protect the owners of the corporation. Unlike the owners of most proprietorships and partnerships, most stockholders do not participate in the day-to-day management of the company.

State laws       SEC laws

WKK
Corp.

Stock
exchange              Federal
requirements          regulations

**Goverment regulations**

## Additional Taxes

Neither proprietorships nor partnerships pay income taxes. The owner's share of these organizations' earnings is reported on his or her personal income tax return. Taxes are then paid by the individual on this amount. Corporations, on the other hand, must pay federal and state income taxes as a separate legal entity. These taxes are substantial: they can amount to as much as 40% of taxable income.

In addition, stockholders are required to pay taxes on cash dividends, which are pro rata distributions of net income. Thus, many argue that corporate income is **taxed twice (double taxation)**, once at the corporate level, and again at the individual level.

From the foregoing, we can identify the following advantages and disadvantages of a corporation compared to a proprietorship and partnership:

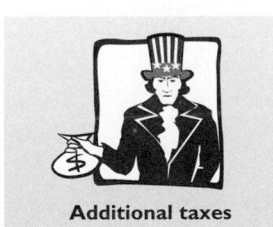

**Additional taxes**

**ILLUSTRATION 14-2**

*Advantages and disadvantages of a corporation*

| Advantages | Disadvantages |
|---|---|
| Separate legal existence | Corporation management—separation of ownership and management |
| Limited liability of stockholders | |
| Transferable ownership rights | Government regulations |
| Ability to acquire capital | Additional taxes |
| Continuous life | |
| Corporation management—professional managers | |

## Forming a Corporation

The initial step in the formation of a corporation is to file an application with the Secretary of State in the state in which incorporation is desired. The application contains the following types of information: (1) the name, purpose, and duration of the proposed corporation; (2) amounts, kinds, and number of shares of capital stock to be authorized; (3) the address of the corporation's principal office; (4) the names and addresses of the incorporators; and (5) the shares of stock to which each has subscribed.

After the incorporation fee is paid and the application approved, a charter is granted. The charter may be an approved copy of the application form or it may be a separate document containing the same basic data. The issuance of the charter, often referred to as the **articles of incorporation**, creates the corporation. Upon receipt of the charter, the corporation develops its by-laws. The by-laws establish the internal rules and procedures for conducting the affairs of the corporation and indicate the powers and relationships of the stockholders, directors, and officers of the enterprise.[1]

## ACCOUNTING IN ACTION

### Business Insight

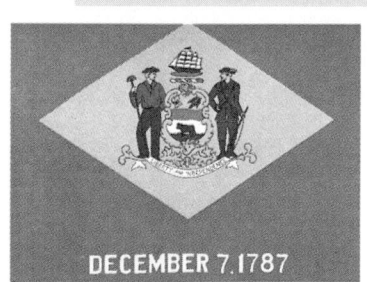

It is not necessary for a corporation to have an office in the state in which it incorporates. In fact, more than 50% of the Fortune 500 corporations are incorporated in Delaware. A primary reason is the Delaware courts' long-standing "business judgment rule." The rule provides that as long as directors exercise "due care" in the interests of stockholders, their actions will not be second-guessed by the courts. The rule has enabled directors to reject hostile takeover offers, even with hefty premiums, or to spurn takeovers simply because they did not want to sell the company. However, new interpretations are emerging. In a recent case, the state court ruled for the company that made a hostile takeover bid. On appeal, the Delaware Supreme Court ruled for the directors but gave the following guideline to the state courts: "Was the board's response reasonable in the light of the threat posed?"

Regardless of the number of states in which a corporation has operating divisions, it is incorporated in only one state. It is to the company's advantage to incorporate in a state whose laws are favorable to the corporate form of business organization. General Motors, for example, is incorporated in Delaware, whereas USX Corp. is a New Jersey corporation. In fact, many corporations choose to incorporate in states with rules favorable to existing management. For example, Gulf Oil changed its state of incorporation to Delaware to thwart possible un-

---

[1]Following approval by two-thirds of the stockholders, the by-laws become binding upon all stockholders, directors, and officers. Legally, a corporation is regulated first by the laws of the state, second by its charter, and third by its by-laws. Care must be exercised to ensure that the provisions of the by-laws are not in conflict with either state laws or the charter.

friendly takeovers. There, certain defensive tactics against takeovers can be approved by the board of directors alone, without a vote by shareholders.

Corporations engaged in interstate commerce must obtain a license from each state in which they do business. The license subjects the corporation's operating activities to the general corporation laws of the state. Costs incurred in the formation of a corporation are called organization costs. These costs include fees to underwriters for handling stock and bond issues, legal fees, state incorporation fees, and promotional expenditures involved in the organization of the business.

These organization costs are capitalized by debiting an intangible asset entitled Organization Costs. It may be argued that organization costs have an asset life equal to the life of the corporation. Many companies, however, **amortize these costs** over an arbitrary period of time, up to a maximum of 40 years. Because income tax regulations require the amortization of organization costs over a period of at least five years, some companies prefer to use the same period of amortization for accounting purposes. Determining the amount to be recorded when capital stock is used to pay for organization costs is explained later.

**INTERNATIONAL NOTE**

U.S. corporations are identified by *Inc.*, which stands for *incorporated*. In Italy the letters used are *SpA* (Societa per Azioni); in Sweden *AB* (Aktiebolag); in France *SA* (Sociedad Anonima); and in the Netherlands *NV* (Naamloze Vennootschap).

In the United Kingdom public limited corporations are identified by *PLC*, while private corporations are denoted by *LTD*. The parallel designations in Germany are *AG* for public corporations and *GmbH* for private corporations.

## Ownership Rights of Stockholders

When chartered, the corporation may begin selling ownership rights in the form of shares of stock. When a corporation has only one class of stock, it is identified as **common stock**. Each share of common stock gives the stockholder the ownership rights pictured in Illustration 14-3. The ownership rights of a share of stock are stated in the articles of incorporation or in the by-laws.

**Stockholders have the right:**

1. To vote in election of board of directors at annual meeting. To vote on actions that require stockholder approval.

2. To share the corporate earnings through receipt of dividends.

dividends

Before          New shares issued          After

14%                                        14%

3. To keep same percentage ownership when new shares of stock are issued (**preemptive right²**).

4. To share in assets upon liquidation, in proportion to their holdings. Called a **residual claim** because owners are paid with assets remaining after all claims have been paid.

GON Corp. Going out of business          Lenders          Stockholders

Creditors

**ILLUSTRATION 14-3**

*Ownership rights of stockholders*

---

²A number of companies have eliminated the preemptive right, because they believe it makes an unnecessary and cumbersome demand on management. For example, IBM, by stockholder approval, has dropped its preemptive right for stockholders.

## ACCOUNTING IN ACTION

### International Insight

In Japan, stockholders are considered to be far less important to a corporation than employees, customers, and suppliers. Stockholders are rarely asked to vote on an issue, and the notion of bending corporate policy to favor stockholders borders on the heretical in Japan. This attitude toward stockholders appears to be slowly changing, however, as influential Japanese are advocating listening to investors, raising the extremely low dividends paid by Japanese corporations, and improving disclosure of financial information.

Proof of stock ownership is evidenced by a printed or engraved form known as a **stock certificate**. As shown in Illustration 14-4, the face of the certificate shows the name of the corporation, the stockholder's name, the class and special features of the stock, the number of shares owned, and the signatures of duly authorized corporate officials. Certificates are prenumbered to facilitate their accountability; they may be issued for any quantity of shares.

**ILLUSTRATION 14-4**

*A stock certificate*

## BEFORE YOU GO ON . . .

### Review It

1. What are the advantages and disadvantages of a corporation compared to a proprietorship and a partnership?
2. Identify the principal steps in forming a corporation.
3. What rights are inherent in owning a share of stock in a corporation?

THE NAVIGATOR

## Stock Issue Considerations

In considering the issuance (or sale) of stock, a corporation must resolve a number of basic questions: How many shares should be authorized for sale? How should the stock be issued? At what price should the shares be issued? What value should be assigned to the stock? These questions are answered in the following sections.

## Authorized Stock

The amount of stock that a corporation is **authorized** to sell is indicated in its charter. The total amount of authorized stock at the time of incorporation normally anticipates both initial and subsequent capital needs of a company. As a result, the number of total shares authorized generally exceeds the number of shares initially sold. If all authorized stock is sold, a corporation must obtain consent of the state to amend its charter before it can issue additional shares.

**The authorization of capital stock does not result in a formal accounting entry, since the event has no immediate effect on either corporate assets or stockholders' equity.** However, disclosure of the number of shares of authorized stock is required in the stockholders' equity section. To determine the number of unissued shares that can be issued without amending the charter, the total shares issued are subtracted from the total authorized. For example, if Advanced Micro was authorized to sell 100,000 shares of common stock and issued 80,000 shares, 20,000 shares would remain unissued.

## Issuance of Stock

A corporation has the choice of issuing common stock **directly** to investors or **indirectly** through an investment banking firm (brokerage house) that specializes in bringing securities to the attention of prospective investors. Direct issue is typical in closely held companies, whereas indirect issue is customary for a publicly held corporation.

In an indirect issue, the investment banking firm may agree to **underwrite** the entire stock issue. Under this arrangement, the investment banker buys the stock from the corporation at a stipulated price and resells the shares to investors. The corporation avoids any risk of being unable to sell the shares, and it obtains immediate use of the cash received from the underwriter. The investment banking firm, in turn, assumes the risk of reselling the shares in return for an underwriting fee—the profits expected to be realized from a sales price to the public higher than the price paid to the corporation.[3] For example, Kolff Medical, maker of the Jarvik artificial heart, used an underwriter to help it issue common stock to the public. The underwriter charged a 6.6% underwriting fee on Kolff Medical's approximate $20 million public offering.

How does a corporation set the price for a new issue of stock? Among the factors to be considered are (1) the company's anticipated future earnings, (2) its expected dividend rate per share, (3) its current financial position, (4) the current state of the economy, and (5) the current state of the securities market. The calculation can be complex and is properly the subject of a finance course.

## Market Value of Stock

The stock of publicly held companies is traded on organized exchanges at dollar prices per share established by the interaction between buyers and sellers. In general, the prices set by the marketplace tend to follow the trend of a company's earnings and dividends. However, factors beyond a company's control, such as

**INTERNATIONAL NOTE**

U.S. and U.K. corporations raise most of their capital through millions of outside shareholders and bondholders. In contrast, companies in Germany, France, and Japan acquire financing from large banks or other institutions. Consequently, in the latter environment, shareholders are less important, and external reporting and auditing receive less emphasis.

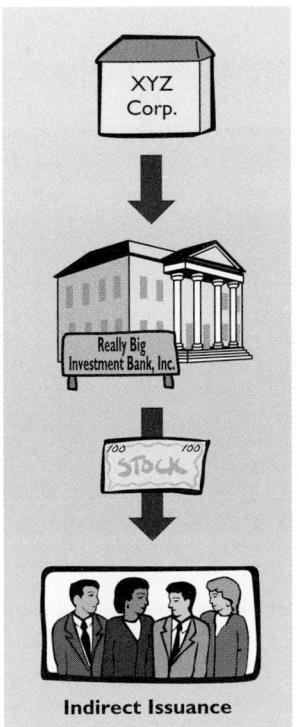

**Indirect Issuance**

---

[3]Alternatively, the investment banking firm may agree only to enter into a **best efforts** contract with the corporation. In such cases, the banker agrees to sell as many shares as possible at a specified price, and the corporation bears the risk of unsold stock. Under a best efforts arrangement, the banking firm is paid a fee or commission for its services.

the imposition of an oil embargo, changes in interest rates, and the outcome of a presidential election, may cause day-to-day fluctuations in market prices.

The volume of trading on national and international exchanges is heavy. Shares in excess of 600 million are often traded daily on the New York Stock Exchange alone. For each listed security the financial press reports the highs and lows of the stock during the year, the total volume of stock traded for a given day, the high and low price for the day, and the closing market price, with the net change for the day. A recent listing for Kellogg is shown below:

**ILLUSTRATION 14-5**

*Stock market price information*

| Stock | 52 Weeks | | Volume | High | Low | Close | Net Change |
|---|---|---|---|---|---|---|---|
| | High | Low | | | | | |
| Kellogg | 50½ | 34⅞ | 3303 | 41¼ | 40⁹⁄₁₆ | 41 | −⅛ |

These numbers indicate that Kellogg's high and low market prices for the last 52 weeks have been 50½ and 34⅞; the trading volume was 330,300 shares; the high, low, and closing prices for that date were 41¼, 40⁹⁄₁₆, and 41, respectively; and the net change for the day was a decrease of −⅛, or $.125 per share.

The trading of capital stock on securities exchanges involves the transfer of **already issued shares** from an existing stockholder to another investor. Consequently, these transactions have no impact on a corporation's stockholders' equity section.

# TECHNOLOGY IN ACTION

The giant, publicly held corporation could not exist without the organized stock markets, and the stock markets could not exist without massive computerization. Not too many years ago, the NYSE "ticker" would run behind, or trading would even be halted, when sales exceeded 30 million shares or so. Now, with sales sometimes in excess of 600 million shares, the NYSE and its companion exchanges throughout the country operate efficiently with computer technology. Technology has also made possible extended trading hours. An investor in New York, for example, can trade electronically at 3:30 A.M., which is the time in New York when the London Stock Exchange opens. Some predict that 24-hour-trading is not far off.

## Par and No-Par Value Stocks

**Par value stock** is capital stock that has been assigned a value per share in the corporate charter. The par value may be any amount selected by the corporation. Generally, the amount of par value is quite low, because states often levy a tax on the corporation based on par value. For example, International Business Machines has a par of $1.25, Ford Motor Company, $1 par, General Motors Corporation, $1.67, and PepsiCo has 1⅔ cents.

Par value is not indicative of the worth or market value of the stock. As indicated above, IBM has a par value of $1.25, but its recent market price was $120 per share. **The significance of par value is a legal matter.** Par value represents the legal capital per share that must be retained in the business for the protection of corporate creditors. That is, it is not available for withdrawal by stockholders. Thus, most states require the corporation to sell its shares at par or above.

**No-par value stock** is capital stock that has not been assigned a value in the corporate charter. No-par value stock is often issued because some confusion still exists concerning par value and fair market value. If shares have no par value, the questionable treatment of using par value as a basis for fair market value never arises. The major disadvantage of no-par stock is that some states levy a high tax on the shares issued.

No-par value stock is quite common today. For example, Procter & Gamble and North American Van Lines both have no-par stock. In many states the board of directors is permitted to assign a stated value to the no-par shares, which becomes the legal capital per share. The stated value of no-par stock may be changed at any time by action of the directors. Stated value, like par value, is not indicative of the market value of the stock. When there is no assigned stated value, the entire proceeds received upon issuance of the stock is considered to be legal capital.

The relationship of par and no-par value to legal capital is shown below.

| Stock | Legal Capital per Share |
| --- | --- |
| Par value $\longrightarrow$ | Par value |
| No-par value with stated value $\longrightarrow$ | Stated value |
| No-par value without stated value $\longrightarrow$ | Entire proceeds |

**ILLUSTRATION 14-6**

*Relationship of par and no-par value stock to legal capital*

As will be explained later, a common stock account is credited for the legal capital per share each time stock is issued.

## Corporate Capital

Owners' equity is identified as **stockholders' equity, shareholders' equity**, or **corporate capital**. The stockholders' equity section of a corporation's balance sheet consists of: (1) paid-in (contributed) capital, and (2) retained earnings (earned capital). The distinction between paid-in capital and retained earnings is important from both a legal and an economic point of view. Legally, dividends can be declared out of retained earnings in all states, but in many states dividends cannot be declared out of paid-in capital. Economically, management, stockholders, and others look to earnings for the continued existence and growth of the corporation.

**2**

STUDY
OBJECTIVE
..............................
Differentiate between paid-in capital and retained earnings.

### Paid-in Capital

Paid-in capital is the term used to describe the total amount of cash and other assets paid in to the corporation by stockholders in exchange for capital stock. As noted earlier, when a corporation has only one class of stock, it is identified as **common stock**.

### Retained Earnings

Retained earnings is net income retained in a corporation. Net income is recorded in Retained Earnings by a closing entry in which Income Summary is debited and Retained Earnings is credited. For example, assuming that net income for Delta Robotics in its first year of operations is $130,000, the closing entry is:

| | | |
| --- | --- | --- |
| Income Summary | 130,000 | |
|     Retained Earnings | | 130,000 |
|       (To close income summary and transfer net income to retained earnings) | | |

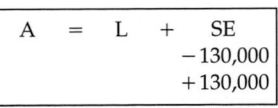

| A | = | L | + | SE |
| --- | --- | --- | --- | --- |
| | | | | −130,000 |
| | | | | +130,000 |

If Delta Robotics has a balance of $800,000 in Common Stock at the end of its first year, its stockholders' equity section is as follows:

**ILLUSTRATION 14-7**

*Stockholders' equity section*

| DELTA ROBOTICS | | |
|---|---|---|
| **Balance Sheet (partial)** | | |
| Stockholders' equity | | |
| **Paid-in capital** | | |
| Common stock | $800,000 | |
| **Retained earnings** | 130,000 | |
| Total stockholders' equity | | $930,000 |

The following illustration compares the owners' equity (stockholders' equity) accounts reported on a balance sheet for a proprietorship, a partnership, and a corporation.

**ILLUSTRATION 14-8**

*Comparison of owners' equity accounts*

# BEFORE YOU GO ON . . .

## Review It

1. Of what significance to a corporation is the amount of authorized stock?
2. What alternative approaches may a corporation use in issuing stock?
3. Distinguish between par value and fair market value.

## Do It

At the end of its first year of operation, Doral Corporation has $750,000 of common stock and net income of $122,000. Prepare (a) the closing entry for net income and (b) the stockholders' equity section at year-end.

*Reasoning:* Net income is recorded in Retained Earnings by a closing entry in which Income Summary is debited and Retained Earnings is credited. The stockholders' equity section consists of (1) paid-in capital and (2) retained earnings.

*Solution:*

| | | |
|---|---|---|
| (a) Income Summary | 122,000 | |
|     Retained Earnings | | 122,000 |
|       (To close income summary and transfer net income to retained earnings) | | |

| | | |
|---|---|---|
| (b) Stockholders' equity | | |
|     Paid-in capital | | |
|       Common stock | $750,000 | |
|     Retained earnings | 122,000 | |
|       Total stockholders' equity | | $872,000 |

*Related exercise material:* BE14–2, BE14–8, E14–5, and E14–9.

THE
NAVIGATOR

---

# ACCOUNTING FOR COMMON STOCK ISSUES

Let's now look at how to account for issues of common stock. The primary objectives in accounting for the issuance of common stock are to (1) identify the specific sources of paid-in capital and (2) maintain the distinction between paid-in capital and retained earnings. As shown below, **the issue of common stock affects only paid-in capital accounts.**

**3**
STUDY
OBJECTIVE
..............................
Record the issuance of common stock.

## Issuing Par Value Common Stock for Cash

As discussed earlier, par value does not indicate a stock's market value. Therefore, the cash proceeds from issuing par value stock may be equal to, greater than, or less than par value. When the issuance of common stock for cash is recorded, the par value of the shares is credited to Common Stock, and the portion of the proceeds that is above or below par value is recorded in a separate paid-in capital account.

To illustrate, assume that Hydro-Slide, Inc. issues 1,000 shares of $1 par value common stock at par for cash. The entry to record this transaction is:

| | | |
|---|---|---|
| Cash | 1,000 | |
|     Common Stock | | 1,000 |
|       (To record issuance of 1,000 shares of $1 par common stock at par) | | |

| A | = | L | + | SE |
|---|---|---|---|---|
| +1,000 | | | | +1,000 |

If Hydro-Slide, Inc., issues an additional 1,000 shares of the $1 par value common stock for cash at $5 per share, the entry is:

**ALTERNATIVE TERMINOLOGY**
Paid-in Capital in Excess of Par is also called *Premium on Stock.*

| | | |
|---|---|---|
| Cash | 5,000 | |
|     Common Stock | | 1,000 |
|     Paid-in Capital in Excess of Par Value | | 4,000 |
|       (To record issuance of 1,000 shares of common stock in excess of par) | | |

| A | = | L | + | SE |
|---|---|---|---|---|
| +5,000 | | | | +1,000 |
| | | | | +4,000 |

The total paid-in capital from these two transactions is $6,000, and the legal capital is $2,000. If Hydro-Slide, Inc. has retained earnings of $27,000, the stockholders' equity section is as follows:

| HYDRO-SLIDE, INC. Balance Sheet (partial) | | |
|---|---:|---:|
| Stockholders' equity | | |
| Paid-in capital | | |
| Common stock | | $ 2,000 |
| **Paid-in capital in excess of par value** | | **4,000** |
| Total paid-in capital | | 6,000 |
| Retained earnings | | 27,000 |
| Total stockholders' equity | | $33,000 |

When stock is issued for less than par value, the account Paid-in Capital in Excess of Par Value is debited, if a credit balance exists in this account. If a credit balance does not exist, then the amount less than par is debited to Retained Earnings. This situation occurs only rarely: The sale of common stock below par value is not permitted in most states, because stockholders may be held personally liable for the difference between the price paid upon original sale and par value.

## Issuing No-Par Common Stock for Cash

When no-par common stock has a stated value, the entries are similar to those illustrated for par value stock. The stated value represents legal capital and therefore is credited to Common Stock. In addition, when the selling price of no-par stock exceeds stated value, the excess is credited to Paid-in Capital in Excess of Stated Value. For example, assume that instead of $1 par value stock, Hydro-Slide, Inc. has $5 stated value no-par stock and that it issues 5,000 shares at $8 per share for cash. The entry is:

| A | = | L | + | SE |
|---|---|---|---|---|
| +40,000 | | | | +25,000 |
| | | | | +15,000 |

| Cash | 40,000 | |
|---|---:|---:|
| Common Stock | | 25,000 |
| Paid-in Capital in Excess of Stated Value | | 15,000 |
| (To record issue of 5,000 shares of $5 stated value no-par stock) | | |

Paid-in Capital in Excess of Stated Value is reported as part of paid-in capital in the stockholders' equity section.

When no-par stock does not have a stated value, the entire proceeds from the issue become legal capital and are credited to Common Stock. Thus, if Hydro-Slide does not assign a stated value to its no-par stock, the issuance of the 5,000 shares at $8 per share for cash is recorded as follows:

| A | = | L | + | SE |
|---|---|---|---|---|
| +40,000 | | | | +40,000 |

| Cash | 40,000 | |
|---|---:|---:|
| Common Stock | | 40,000 |
| (To record issue of 5,000 shares of no-par stock) | | |

The amount of legal capital for Hydro-Slide with a $5 stated value is $25,000; without a stated value, it is $40,000.

## Issuing Common Stock for Services or Noncash Assets

Stock may be issued for services (compensation to attorneys, consultants, and others) or for noncash assets (land, buildings, and equipment). In such cases, a question arises as to the cost that should be recognized in the exchange transaction. To comply with the **cost principle** in a noncash transaction, **cost is the cash equivalent price.** Thus, **cost is either the fair market value of the consideration given up or the fair market value of the consideration received,** whichever is more clearly determinable.

To illustrate, assume that the attorneys for The Jordan Company agree to accept 4,000 shares of $1 par value common stock in payment of their bill of $5,000 for services performed in helping the company to incorporate. At the time of the exchange, there is no established market price for the stock. In this case, the market value of the consideration received, $5,000, is more clearly evident. Accordingly, the entry is:

| | | | |
|---|---|---|---|
| Organization Costs | 5,000 | | |
|     Common Stock | | 4,000 | |
|     Paid-in Capital in Excess of Par Value | | 1,000 | |
|       (To record issuance of 4,000 shares of $1 par value | | | |
|       stock to attorneys) | | | |

| A | = | L | + | SE |
|---|---|---|---|---|
| +5,000 | | | | +4,000 |
| | | | | +1,000 |

As explained on page 595, organization costs are classified as an intangible asset in the balance sheet.

In contrast, assume that Athletic Research Inc. is a publicly held corporation whose $5 par value stock is actively traded at $8 per share. The company issues 10,000 shares of stock to acquire land recently advertised for sale at $90,000. On the basis of these facts the most clearly evident value is the market price of the consideration given, $80,000. Thus, the transaction is recorded as follows:

| | | | |
|---|---|---|---|
| Land | 80,000 | | |
|     Common Stock | | 50,000 | |
|     Paid-in Capital in Excess of Par Value | | 30,000 | |
|       (To record issuance of 10,000 shares of $5 par value | | | |
|       stock for land) | | | |

| A | = | L | + | SE |
|---|---|---|---|---|
| +80,000 | | | | +50,000 |
| | | | | +30,000 |

As illustrated in these examples, **the par value of the stock is never a factor in determining the cost of the assets received**. This is also true of the stated value of no-par stock.

# BEFORE YOU GO ON . . .

## Review It

1. Explain the accounting for par and no-par common stock issued for cash.
2. Explain the accounting for the issuance of stock for services or noncash assets.
3. What is the par or stated value per share of Kellogg's common stock? How many shares of common stock is Kellogg authorized to issue? How many shares are issued at December 31, 1997? The answers to these questions are provided on page 630.

## Do It

Cayman Corporation begins operations on March 1 by issuing 100,000 shares of $10 par value common stock for cash at $12 per share. On March 15, it issues 5,000 shares of common stock to attorneys in settlement of their bill of $50,000 for organization costs. Journalize the issuance of the shares assuming the stock is not publicly traded.

*Reasoning:* In issuing shares for cash, common stock is credited for par value per share and any additional proceeds are credited to a separate paid-in capital account. When stock is issued for services, the cash equivalent price should be used. In this case, this price is the value of the attorneys' services.

*Solution:*

| | | | |
|---|---|---|---|
| Mar. 1 | Cash | 1,200,000 | |
| |     Common Stock | | 1,000,000 |
| |     Paid-in Capital in Excess of Par Value | | 200,000 |
| |         (To record issuance of 100,000 shares at $12 per share) | | |
| | | | |
| Mar. 15 | Organization Costs | 50,000 | |
| |     Common Stock | | 50,000 |
| |         (To record issuance of 5,000 shares for attorneys' fees) | | |

*Related exercise material:* BE14–3, BE14–4, BE14–5, E14–1, E14–2, E14–3, E14–7, and E14–8.

# ACCOUNTING FOR TREASURY STOCK

**4**
STUDY
OBJECTIVE

Explain the accounting for treasury stock.

**HELPFUL HINT**
Treasury stock is so named because the company often holds the shares in its treasury for safekeeping.

Treasury stock is a corporation's own stock that has been issued, fully paid for, and reacquired by the corporation but not retired. A corporation may acquire treasury stock for the reasons listed below.

1. Reissue the shares to officers and employees under bonus and stock compensation plans.
2. Increase trading of the company's stock in the securities market in the hopes of enhancing its market value.
3. Have additional shares available for use in the acquisition of other companies.
4. Reduce the number of shares outstanding and thereby increase earnings per share.
5. Rid the company of disgruntled investors, perhaps to avoid a takeover, as illustrated in the Ford Motor Company opening story.

Many corporations have treasury stock. For example, one survey of 600 companies in the United States found that 62% have treasury stock.[4] Specifically, Campbell Soup Company recently reported 84 million treasury shares, The Coca-Cola Company 459.5 million, and McDonald's Corporation 135.7 million.

## Purchase of Treasury Stock

**The cost method is generally used in accounting for treasury stock.** This method derives its name from the fact that the Treasury Stock account is maintained at the cost of shares purchased. Under the cost method, **Treasury Stock is debited at the price paid to reacquire the shares, and the same amount is credited to Treasury Stock when the shares are sold.** To illustrate, assume that on January 1, 1999, the stockholders' equity section of Mead, Inc., has 100,000

---

[4]*Accounting Trends & Techniques 1997* (New York: American Institute of Certified Public Accountants).

# ACCOUNTING IN ACTION
## Business Insight

Both Nike and Reebok have repurchased many shares in recent years. During 1994 and 1995 Nike repurchased roughly 5 million of its shares—about 10% of those outstanding. Nike's stock price has soared since then. Thus, the stock repurchase worked out well for those investors who kept their shares. With fewer shares outstanding, the surge in Nike's profits dramatically increased the price of the remaining shares.

Reebok, in a bold (and some would say very risky) move in late 1996, brought back nearly a *third* of its shares. This decision was risky because the repurchase of shares dramatically reduced Reebok's available cash. In fact, the company borrowed significant funds to accomplish the repurchase. In a press release, management stated that it was repurchasing the shares because it believed that the stock was severely underpriced. The repurchase of so many shares was meant to signal management's belief in good future earnings. Skeptics, however, suggest that Reebok's management is repurchasing shares to make it less likely that the company will be taken over by a different company (in which case Reebok's top managers would likely lose their jobs). By depleting its cash Reebok is less likely to be acquired because acquiring companies like to purchase companies with large cash reserves so they can pay off debt used in the acquisition.

Reebok stockholders have not profited nearly as much as Nike stockholders did from the repurchase of shares, but that has been due primarily to a decline in Reebok's earnings in 1997.

shares of $5 par value common stock outstanding (all issued at par value) and Retained Earnings of $200,000.

The stockholders' equity section before purchase of treasury stock is as follows:

**ILLUSTRATION 14-10**

*Stockholders' equity with no treasury stock*

| MEAD, INC. Balance Sheet (partial) | |
|---|---:|
| Stockholders' equity | |
| Paid-in capital | |
| Common stock, $5 par value, 100,000 shares issued and outstanding | $500,000 |
| Retained earnings | 200,000 |
| Total stockholders' equity | $700,000 |

On February 1, 1999, Mead acquires 4,000 shares of its stock at $8 per share. The entry is:

| Feb. 1 | Treasury Stock | 32,000 | |
|---|---|---|---|
| | Cash | | 32,000 |
| | (To record purchase of 4,000 shares of treasury stock at $8 per share) | | |

| A | = | L | + | SE |
|---|---|---|---|---|
| −32,000 | | | | −32,000 |

Note that Treasury Stock is debited for the cost of the shares purchased. The original paid-in capital account, Common Stock, is not affected because the number of issued shares does not change. Treasury stock is deducted from total paid-in capital and retained earnings in the stockholders' equity section. Treasury Stock is a contra stockholders' equity account.

**HELPFUL HINT**
Treasury shares do not have dividend rights or voting rights.

The stockholders' equity section of Mead, Inc., after purchase of treasury stock is as follows:

**ILLUSTRATION 14-11**

*Stockholders' equity with treasury stock*

| MEAD, INC.<br>Balance Sheet (partial) | |
|---|---:|
| Stockholders' equity | |
| Paid-in capital | |
| Common stock, $5 par value, 100,000 shares issued and 96,000 shares outstanding | $500,000 |
| Retained earnings | 200,000 |
| Total paid-in capital and retained earnings | 700,000 |
| **Less: Treasury stock (4,000 shares)** | **32,000** |
| Total stockholders' equity | $668,000 |

Thus, the acquisition of treasury stock reduces stockholders' equity.

Both the number of shares issued (100,000) and the number in the treasury (4,000) are disclosed. The difference is the number of shares of stock outstanding (96,000). The term outstanding stock means the number of shares of issued stock that are being held by stockholders.

Some maintain that treasury stock should be reported as an asset because it can be sold for cash. Under this reasoning, unissued stock should also be shown as an asset, clearly an erroneous conclusion. Rather than being an asset, treasury stock reduces stockholder claims on corporate assets. This effect is correctly shown by reporting treasury stock as a deduction from total paid-in capital and retained earnings.

## Disposal of Treasury Stock

Treasury stock is usually sold or retired. The accounting for its sale is different when treasury stock is sold above cost than when it is sold below cost.

### Sale of Treasury Stock above Cost

If the selling price of the treasury shares is equal to cost, the sale of the shares is recorded by a debit to Cash and a credit to Treasury Stock. When the selling price of the shares is greater than cost, the difference is credited to Paid-in Capital from Treasury Stock. To illustrate, assume that 1,000 shares of treasury stock of Mead, Inc., previously acquired at $8 per share, are sold at $10 per share on July 1. The entry is as follows:

| A | = | L | + | SE |
|---|---|---|---|---|
| +10,000 | | | | +8,000 |
| | | | | +2,000 |

| July 1 | Cash | 10,000 | |
|---|---|---|---|
| | Treasury Stock | | 8,000 |
| | Paid-in Capital from Treasury Stock | | 2,000 |
| | (To record sale of 1,000 shares of treasury stock above cost) | | |

The $2,000 credit in the entry is **not** made to Gain on Sale of Treasury Stock for two reasons: (1) Gains on sales occur when assets are sold and treasury stock is not an asset. (2) A corporation does not realize a gain or suffer a loss from stock transactions with its own stockholders. Thus, paid-in capital arising from the sale of treasury stock should not be included in the measurement of net income. Paid-in Capital from Treasury Stock is listed separately on the balance sheet as a part of paid-in capital.

## Sale of Treasury Stock below Cost

When treasury stock is sold below its cost, the excess of cost over selling price is usually debited to Paid-in Capital from Treasury Stock. Thus, if Mead, Inc. sells an additional 800 shares of treasury stock on October 1 at $7 per share, the entry is as follows:

| Oct. 1 | Cash | 5,600 | |
| | Paid-in Capital from Treasury Stock | 800 | |
| |     Treasury Stock | | 6,400 |
| |       (To record sale of 800 shares of treasury | | |
| |       stock below cost) | | |

| A | = | L | + | SE |
|---|---|---|---|---|
| +5,600 | | | | − 800 |
| | | | | +6,400 |

Observe from the two sales entries that (1) Treasury Stock is credited at cost in each entry, (2) Paid-in Capital from Treasury Stock is used for the difference between the cost and resale price of the shares, and (3) the original paid-in capital account, Common Stock, again is not affected. **The sale of treasury stock increases both total assets and total stockholders' equity.**

After posting the foregoing entries, the treasury stock accounts will show the following balances on October 1:

| Treasury Stock | | | | Paid-in Capital from Treasury Stock | | | |
|---|---|---|---|---|---|---|---|
| Feb. 1 | 32,000 | July 1 | 8,000 | Oct. 1 | 800 | July 1 | 2,000 |
| | | Oct. 1 | 6,400 | | | | |
| | | | | | | Oct. 1 Bal. | 1,200 |
| Oct. 1 Bal. | 17,600 | | | | | | |

**ILLUSTRATION 14-12**
*Treasury stock accounts*

When the credit balance in Paid-in Capital from Treasury Stock is eliminated, any additional excess of cost over selling price is debited to Retained Earnings. To illustrate, assume that Mead, Inc., sells its remaining 2,200 shares at $7 per share on December 1. The excess of cost over selling price is $2,200 [2,200 × ($8 − $7)]. In this case, $1,200 of the excess is debited to Paid-in Capital from Treasury Stock, and the remainder is debited to Retained Earnings. The entry is:

| Dec. 1 | Cash | 15,400 | |
| | Paid-in Capital from Treasury Stock | 1,200 | |
| | Retained Earnings | 1,000 | |
| |     Treasury Stock | | 17,600 |
| |       (To record sale of 2,200 shares of treasury | | |
| |       stock at $7 per share) | | |

| A | = | L | + | SE |
|---|---|---|---|---|
| +15,400 | | | | − 1,200 |
| | | | | − 1,000 |
| | | | | +17,600 |

# BEFORE YOU GO ON . . .

## Review It

1. What is treasury stock, and why do companies acquire it?
2. How is treasury stock recorded?
3. Where is treasury stock reported in the financial statements? Does a company record gains and losses on treasury stock transactions? Explain.
4. How many shares of treasury stock did Kellogg have outstanding at December 31, 1996 and at December 31, 1997? Why the huge difference between 1996 and 1997? The answers to these questions are provided on page 630.

**Do It**

Santa Anita Inc. purchases 3,000 shares of its $50 par value common stock for $180,000 cash on July 1. The shares are to be held in the treasury until resold. On November 1, the corporation sells 1,000 shares of treasury stock for cash at $70 per share. Journalize the treasury stock transactions.

*Reasoning:* The purchase of treasury stock is recorded at cost. When treasury stock is sold, the excess of the selling price over cost is credited to Paid-in Capital from Treasury Stock.

*Solution:*

| July 1 | Treasury Stock | 180,000 | |
| |    Cash | | 180,000 |
| |      (To record the purchase of 3,000 shares at | | |
| |      $60 per share) | | |
| | | | |
| Nov. 1 | Cash | 70,000 | |
| |    Treasury Stock | | 60,000 |
| |    Paid-in Capital from Treasury Stock | | 10,000 |
| |      (To record the sale of 1,000 shares at $70 | | |
| |      per share) | | |

*Related exercise material:* BE14–6, E14–2, E14–4, E14–7, and E14–8.

THE NAVIGATOR

# PREFERRED STOCK

**5**
STUDY
OBJECTIVE

Differentiate preferred stock from common stock.

To appeal to a larger segment of potential investors, a corporation may issue a class of stock in addition to common stock, called preferred stock. **Preferred stock** has contractual provisions that give it a preference or priority over common stock in certain areas. Typically, preferred stockholders have a priority as to (1) dividends and (2) assets in the event of liquidation. However, they generally do not have voting rights.

Like common stock, preferred stock may be issued for cash or for noncash assets. The entries for these transactions are similar to the entries for common stock. When a corporation has more than one class of stock, each paid-in capital account title should identify the stock to which it relates (e.g., Preferred Stock, Common Stock, Paid-in Capital in Excess of Par Value—Preferred Stock, and Paid-in Capital in Excess of Par Value—Common Stock). Assume that Stine Corporation issues 10,000 shares of $10 par value preferred stock for $12 cash per share. The entry to record the issuance is:

| A = L + SE |
|---|
| + 120,000       + 100,000 |
|              + 20,000 |

| Cash | 120,000 | |
| | --- | --- |
|    Preferred Stock | | 100,000 |
|    Paid-in Capital in Excess of Par Value—Preferred Stock | | 20,000 |
|      (To record the issuance of 10,000 shares of $10 par | | |
|      value preferred stock) | | |

Preferred stock may have either a par value or no-par value. For example, Walgreen Drug Co. has $0.50 par value preferred and General Motors has three classes of no-par preferred stock, each with a stated value of $100. In the stockholders' equity section, preferred stock is shown first because of its dividend and liquidation preferences over common stock.

The discussion that follows reflects features associated with the issuance of preferred stock, including dividend preferences, liquidation preferences, convertibility, and callability.

## Dividend Preferences

As indicated before, **preferred stockholders have the right to share in the distribution of corporate income before common stockholders.** For example, if the dividend rate on preferred stock is $5 per share, common shareholders will not receive any dividends in the current year until preferred stockholders have received $5 per share. The first claim to dividends does not, however, guarantee dividends. Dividends depend on many factors, such as adequate retained earnings and availability of cash.

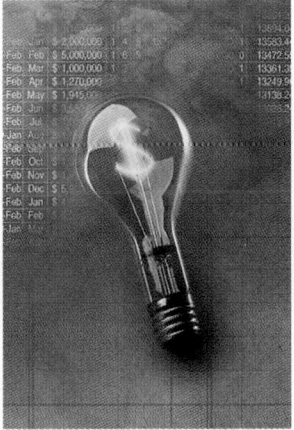

I hope there is some money left when it's my turn.

Preferred      Common
stockholders  stockholders

**Dividend Preference**

The per share dividend amount is stated as a percentage of the par value of preferred stock or as a specified amount. For example, the Crane Company specifies 3¾% dividend on its $100 par value preferred ($100 × 3¾% = $3.75 per share), whereas DuPont has both a $4.50 and a $3.50 series of no-par preferred stock.

### Cumulative Dividend

Preferred stock contracts often contain a cumulative dividend feature. This right means that preferred stockholders must be paid both current-year dividends and any unpaid prior-year dividends before common stockholders receive dividends. When preferred stock is cumulative, preferred dividends not declared in a given period are called **dividends in arrears**. To illustrate, assume that Scientific-Leasing has 5,000 shares of 7%, $100 par value cumulative preferred stock outstanding. The annual dividend is $35,000 (5,000 × $7 per share). If dividends are 2 years in arrears, preferred stockholders are entitled to receive the following dividends in the current year before any distribution is made to common stockholders:

| | |
|---|---|
| Dividends in arrears ($35,000 × 2) | $ 70,000 |
| Current-year dividends | 35,000 |
| **Total preferred dividends** | **$105,000** |

**ILLUSTRATION 14-13**

*Computation of total dividends to preferred stock*

## ACCOUNTING IN ACTION
### Business Insight

Dividends in arrears can extend for fairly long periods of time. Long Island Lighting Company's directors voted at one time to make up some $390 million in preferred dividends that had been in arrears since 1984 and to resume normal quarterly preferred payments. The announcement resulted from an agreement between the company and New York State to abandon a nuclear power plant in exchange for sizable rate increases over the next 10 years.

**Payment of a Cumulative Dividend**

Dividend in arrears

Current dividend

Preferred stockholders

**Dividends in arrears are not considered a liability. No obligation exists until a dividend is declared by the board of directors.** However, the amount of dividends in arrears should be disclosed in the notes to the financial statements. Doing so enables investors to assess the potential impact of this commitment on the corporation's financial position.

Dividends cannot be paid on common stock while any dividend on preferred stock is in arrears. The cumulative feature is often critical in investor acceptance of a preferred stock issue. When preferred stock is noncumulative, a dividend passed in any year is lost forever. Companies that are unable to meet their dividend obligations are not looked upon favorably by the investment community. As a financial officer noted in discussing one company's failure to pay its cumulative preferred dividend for a period of time, "Not meeting your obligations on something like that is a major black mark on your record." The accounting entries for preferred stock dividends are explained in Chapter 15.

## Liquidation Preference

Most preferred stocks have a preference on corporate assets if the corporation fails. This feature provides security for the preferred stockholder. The preference to assets may be for the par value of the shares or for a specified liquidating value. For example, Commonwealth Edison issued preferred stock that entitles the holders to receive $31.80 per share, plus accrued and unpaid dividends, in the event of involuntary liquidation. The liquidation preference is used in litigation pertaining to bankruptcy lawsuits involving the respective claims of creditors and preferred stockholders.

## Convertible Preferred Stock

The attractiveness of preferred stock as an investment is enhanced by adding a conversion privilege. Convertible preferred stock provides for the exchange of preferred stock into common stock at a specified ratio at the stockholder's option.

Convertible preferred stock is purchased by investors who want the greater security of a preferred stock, but who also desire the added option of conversion if the market value of the common stock increases significantly. To illustrate, assume that Ross Industries issues at par value 1,000 shares of $100 par value convertible preferred stock. One share of preferred is convertible into 10 shares of $5 par value common (current price $9 per share). At this point, it would not be advantageous for the holders of the preferred to convert, because they would exchange preferred stock worth $100,000 (1,000 × $100) for common stock worth $90,000 (10,000 × $9). However, if the price of the common stock were to increase above $10 per share, it usually would be advantageous for the preferred holders to convert.

In recording the conversion, it is customary to transfer the amount paid in on the preferred stock to appropriate common stock accounts. To illustrate, assume that the 1,000 shares of Ross Industries $100 par preferred issued at $105 are converted into 10,000 shares of common stock ($5 par) when the market values per share of the two classes of stock are $101 and $12, respectively. The entry to record the conversion is:

| A | = | L | + | SE |
|---|---|---|---|---|
| | | | | − 100,000 |
| | | | | − 5,000 |
| | | | | + 50,000 |
| | | | | + 55,000 |

| | | |
|---|---|---|
| Preferred Stock | 100,000 | |
| Paid-in Capital in Excess of Par Value—Preferred Stock | 5,000 | |
|     Common Stock | | 50,000 |
|     Paid-in Capital in Excess of Par Value—Common Stock | | 55,000 |
|       (To record conversion of 1,000 shares of preferred stock into 10,000 shares of $5 par value common stock) | | |

**The conversion of preferred stock does not result in either gain or loss to the corporation.** If the preferred stock was issued for more than its par value, the paid-in capital in excess of the par value on the preferred stock should be eliminated.

Note that the market values of the shares at the time of the transaction are not considered in recording the transaction. The reason is that the exchange of shares is made directly through the corporation and the corporation has not received any assets equal to fair market value.

## Callable Preferred Stock

Many preferred stocks are issued with a call feature. A callable preferred stock grants the issuing corporation the right to purchase the stock from stockholders at specified future dates and prices. The call feature offers some flexibility to a corporation by enabling it to eliminate this type of equity security when it is advantageous to do so. The **call (or redemption) price** is frequently slightly above the par or stated value of the shares. When preferred stock is callable, the call price tends to set a ceiling on the market price of the shares. Often shares that are callable are also convertible. Sometimes companies will call their preferred shares to induce investors to convert those preferred shares into common stock.

# STATEMENT PRESENTATION AND ANALYSIS

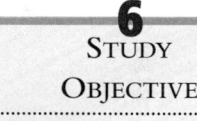

**6**
STUDY
OBJECTIVE

Prepare a stockholders' equity section.

In the stockholders' equity section of the balance sheet, paid-in capital and retained earnings are reported, and the specific sources of paid-in capital are identified.

Within paid-in capital, two classifications are recognized:

1. **Capital stock**, which consists of preferred and common stock. Preferred stock is shown before common stock because of its preferential rights. Information as to the par value, shares authorized, shares issued, and shares outstanding is reported for each class of stock.
2. **Additional paid-in capital**, which includes the excess of amounts paid in over par or stated value and paid-in capital from treasury stock.

**ALTERNATIVE TERMINOLOGY**
Paid-in capital is sometimes called *contributed capital.*

## Illustrations

The stockholders' equity section of Connally Inc. shown in Illustration 14-14 includes most of the accounts discussed in this chapter. The disclosures pertaining to Connally's common stock indicate that 400,000 shares are issued, 100,000 shares are unissued (500,000 authorized less 400,000 issued), and 390,000 shares are outstanding (400,000 issued less 10,000 shares in treasury).

In published annual reports, subclassifications within the stockholders' equity section are seldom presented. Moreover, the individual sources of additional paid-in capital are often combined and reported as a single amount as shown in Illustration 14-15.

In practice, the term "capital surplus" is sometimes used in place of additional paid-in capital and "earned surplus" in place of retained earnings. The use of the term "surplus" suggests that an excess amount of funds is available. Such is not necessarily the case, which is why **the term surplus should not be employed in accounting**. Unfortunately, a number of financial statements still include these terms.

**ILLUSTRATION 14-14**

*Stockholders' equity section*

### CONNALLY INC.
### Balance Sheet (partial)

| | | |
|---|---:|---:|
| Stockholders' equity | | |
| Paid-in capital | | |
| **Capital stock** | | |
| 9% preferred stock, $100 par value, callable at $120, cumulative, 10,000 shares authorized, 6,000 shares issued and outstanding | | $ 600,000 |
| Common stock, no par, $5 stated value, 500,000 shares authorized, 400,000 shares issued, and 390,000 outstanding | | 2,000,000 |
| Total capital stock | | 2,600,000 |
| **Additional paid-in capital** | | |
| In excess of par value—preferred stock | $ 30,000 | |
| In excess of stated value—common stock | 860,000 | |
| From treasury stock | 140,000 | |
| Total additional paid-in capital | | 1,030,000 |
| Total paid-in capital | | 3,630,000 |
| Retained earnings | | 1,058,000 |
| Total paid-in capital and retained earnings | | 4,688,000 |
| Less: Treasury stock—common (10,000 shares) (at cost) | | (80,000) |
| Total stockholders' equity | | $4,608,000 |

**ILLUSTRATION 14-15**

*Published stockholders' equity section*

### KNIGHT-RIDDER INC.
### Balance Sheet (partial)
### (in millions)

| | |
|---|---:|
| Stockholders' equity | |
| Preferred stock, $1.00 par value; shares authorized—2,000,000; shares issued—1,754,930 | $ 1,755 |
| Common stock, $.02½ par value; shares authorized—250,000,000; shares issued—81,597,631 | 1,700 |
| Additional paid-in capital | 911,572 |
| Retained earnings | 636,646 |
| Total stockholders' equity | $1,551,673 |

## Book Value—Another Per Share Amount

**7**

**STUDY OBJECTIVE**

Compute book value per share.

You have learned about a number of per share amounts in this chapter. Another per share amount of some importance is book value per share. This per share amount represents **the equity a common stockholder has in the net assets of the corporation** from owning one share of stock. Since the net assets of a corporation must be equal to total stockholders' equity, the formula for computing book value per share when a company has only one class of stock outstanding is:

**ILLUSTRATION 14-16**

*Book value per share formula*

Thus, if the Marlo Corporation has total stockholders' equity of $1,500,000 (Common Stock $1,000,000 and Retained Earnings $500,000) and 50,000 shares of common stock outstanding, book value per share is $30 ($1,500,000 ÷ 50,000).

When a company has both preferred and common stock, the computation of book value is more complex. Since preferred stockholders have a prior claim on net assets over common stockholders, their equity must be deducted from total stockholders' equity to determine the stockholders' equity that applies to the common stock. The computation of book value per share involves the following steps:

1. Compute the preferred stock equity. This equity is equal to the sum of the call price of preferred stock plus any cumulative dividends in arrears. If the preferred stock does not have a call price, the par value of the stock is used.
2. Determine the common stock equity by subtracting the preferred stock equity from total stockholders' equity.
3. Divide common stock equity by shares of common stock outstanding to determine book value per share.

## Illustration

We will use the stockholders' equity section of Connally Inc. shown in Illustration 14-14. Connally's preferred stock is callable at $120 per share and cumulative. Assume that dividends on Connally's preferred stock were in arrears for one year, $54,000 (6,000 × $9). The computation of preferred stock equity is:

| | |
|---|---:|
| Call price (6,000 shares × $120) | $720,000 |
| Dividends in arrears (6,000 shares × $9) | 54,000 |
| Preferred stock equity | $774,000 |

**ILLUSTRATION 14-17**

*Computation of preferred stock equity—Step 1*

The computation of book value is as follows:

| | |
|---|---:|
| Total stockholders' equity | $4,608,000 |
| Less: Preferred stock equity | 774,000 |
| Common stock equity | $3,834,000 |
| Shares of common stock outstanding | 390,000 |
| Book value per share ($3,834,000 ÷ 390,000) | $9.83 |

The call price of $120 was used instead of the par value of $100. Note also that the paid-in capital in excess of par value of preferred stock, $30,000, **is not assigned to the preferred stock equity**. Preferred stockholders ordinarily do not have a right to amounts paid-in in excess of par value. Accordingly, such amounts are assigned to the common stock equity in computing book value.

## Book Value versus Market Value

**Book value per share may not equal market value**. Book value is based on recorded costs; market value reflects the subjective judgment of thousands of stockholders and prospective investors about a company's potential for future earnings and dividends. Market value per share may exceed book value per share, but that fact does not necessarily mean that the stock is overpriced. The correlation between book value and the annual range of a company's market value per share is often remote, as indicated by the following recent data:

**ILLUSTRATION 14-19**

*Book and market values compared*

| Company | Book Value (year-end) | Market Range (for year) |
|---|---|---|
| Nike, Inc. | $10.63 | $47.87–$76.37 |
| Campbell Soup Company | $ 3.10 | $32.00–$52.81 |
| Motorola, Inc. | $22.21 | $54.00–$90.50 |
| Kellogg Company | $ 2.43 | $32.00–$50.38 |

Book value per share **is** useful in determining the trend of a stockholder's per share equity in a corporation. It is also significant in many contracts and in court cases where the rights of individual parties are based on cost information.

# BEFORE YOU GO ON . . .

### Review It

1. Identify the classifications within the paid-in capital section and the totals that are stated in the stockholders' equity section of a balance sheet.
2. What is the method for computing book value per share when there is (a) only one class of stock and (b) both preferred and common stock?

## A LOOK BACK AT OUR FEATURE STORY

Refer back to the opening story about Ford Motor Company, and answer the following questions.
1. Why did Henry Ford originally choose to form a corporation rather than a sole proprietorship?
2. Why did the Ford Motor Company repurchase all of its shares?
3. What advantages and disadvantages of being organized as a corporation are illustrated by Ford?

*Solution:*

1. Henry Ford wanted to take full advantage of mass-production. This would require large factories and many employees, which would in turn require considerable funds. The most efficient way to raise these funds was to issue stock.
2. Ford Motor Company initiated a massive treasury stock purchase when Henry Ford's vision was not consistent with the wishes of the shareholders.
3. The history of Ford Motor Company illustrates a number of the strengths and weaknesses of being formed as a corporation. Forming a corporation allowed for more efficient access to funds, and thus more rapid expansion. This was critical because, in the early 1900s, many companies were trying to build cars for the American market. However, by issuing shares, Henry Ford relinquished his control over the firm. This led to a collision in 1916 when the founder believed that it was in the company's best interest to retain funds in the firm rather than to pay dividends. To the extent that outside shareholders are not as well informed as a corporation's managers, the shareholders may force management to do things that hinder the firm's success.

THE
NAVIGATOR

# DEMONSTRATION PROBLEM

The Rolman Corporation is authorized to issue 1,000,000 shares of $5 par value common stock. In its first year, the company has the following stock transactions:

Jan. 10   Issued 400,000 shares of stock at $8 per share.

July 1   Issued 100,000 shares of stock for land. The land had an asking price of $900,000. The stock is currently selling on a national exchange at $8.25 per share.

Sept. 1   Purchased 10,000 shares of common stock for the treasury at $9.00 per share.

Dec. 1   Sold 4,000 shares of the treasury stock at $10 per share.

**Instructions**

(a) Journalize the transactions.
(b) Prepare the stockholders' equity section assuming the company had retained earnings of $200,000 at December 31.

# SOLUTION TO DEMONSTRATION PROBLEM

| | | | | |
|---|---|---|---:|---:|
| (a) Jan. 10 | Cash | | 3,200,000 | |
| | Common Stock | | | 2,000,000 |
| | Paid-in Capital in Excess of Par Value | | | 1,200,000 |
| | (To record issuance of 400,000 shares of $5 par value stock) | | | |
| July 1 | Land | | 825,000 | |
| | Common Stock | | | 500,000 |
| | Paid-in Capital in Excess of Par Value | | | 325,000 |
| | (To record issuance of 100,000 shares of $5 par value stock for land) | | | |
| Sept. 1 | Treasury Stock | | 90,000 | |
| | Cash | | | 90,000 |
| | (To record purchase of 10,000 shares of treasury stock at cost) | | | |
| Dec. 1 | Cash | | 40,000 | |
| | Treasury Stock | | | 36,000 |
| | Paid-in Capital from Treasury Stock | | | 4,000 |
| | (To record sale of 4,000 shares of treasury stock above cost) | | | |

**PROBLEM-SOLVING STRATEGIES**

1. When common stock has a par value, Common Stock is always credited for par value.

2. In a noncash transaction, fair market value should be used.

3. The Treasury Stock account is debited and credited at cost.

4. Differences between the cost and selling price of treasury stock are recorded in stockholders' equity accounts, not as gains or losses.

(b)

## ROLMAN CORPORATION
### Balance Sheet (partial)

| | | |
|---|---:|---:|
| Stockholders' equity | | |
| Paid-in capital | | |
| Capital stock | | |
| Common stock, $5 par value, 1,000,000 shares authorized, 500,000 shares issued, 494,000 shares outstanding | | $2,500,000 |
| Additional paid-in capital | | |
| In excess of par value | $1,525,000 | |
| From treasury stock | 4,000 | |
| Total additional paid-in capital | | 1,529,000 |
| Total paid-in capital | | 4,029,000 |
| Retained earnings | | 200,000 |
| Total paid-in capital and retained earnings | | 4,229,000 |
| Less: Treasury stock (6,000 shares) | | (54,000) |
| Total stockholders' equity | | $4,175,000 |

THE NAVIGATOR

# SUMMARY OF STUDY OBJECTIVES

**1. Identify and discuss the major characteristics of a corporation.** The major characteristics of a corporation are separate legal existence, limited liability of stockholders, transferable ownership rights, ability to acquire capital, continuous life, corporation management, government regulations, and additional taxes.

**2. Differentiate between paid-in capital and retained earnings.** Paid-in capital is the total amount paid in on capital stock. It is often referred to as contributed capital. Retained earnings is net income retained in a corporation. It is often referred to as earned capital.

**3. Record the issuance of common stock.** When the issuance of common stock for cash is recorded, the par value of the shares is credited to Common Stock and the portion of the proceeds that is above or below par value is recorded in a separate paid-in capital account. When no-par common stock has a stated value, the entries are similar to those for par value stock. When no-par does not have a stated value, the entire proceeds from the issue become legal capital and are credited to Common Stock.

**4. Explain the accounting for treasury stock.** The cost method is generally used in accounting for treasury stock. Under this approach, Treasury Stock is debited at the price paid to reacquire the shares, and the same amount is credited to Treasury Stock when the shares are sold. The difference between the sales price and cost is recorded in stockholders' equity accounts, not in income statement accounts.

**5. Differentiate preferred stock from common stock.** Preferred stock has contractual provisions that give it priority over common stock in certain areas. Typically, preferred stockholders have a preference as to (1) dividends and (2) assets in the event of liquidation. However, they usually do not have voting rights. In addition, preferred stock may be convertible and/or callable. A convertible preferred stock entitles the holder of the preferred stock to convert those shares to common stock in a specified ratio. The callable feature grants to the issuing corporation the right to purchase the stock from stockholders at specified future dates and prices.

**6. Prepare a stockholders' equity section.** In the stockholders' equity section, paid-in capital and retained earnings are reported and specific sources of paid-in capital are identified. Within paid-in capital, two classifications are shown: capital stock and additional paid-in capital. If a corporation has treasury stock, the cost of treasury stock is deducted from total paid-in capital and retained earnings to obtain total stockholders' equity.

**7. Compute book value per share.** Book value per share represents the equity a common stockholder has in the net assets of a corporation from owning one share of stock. When there is only common stock outstanding, the formula for computing book value is: Total Stockholders' Equity ÷ Number of Common Shares Outstanding = Book Value per Share.

THE NAVIGATOR

# GLOSSARY

**Authorized stock**   The amount of stock that a corporation is authorized to sell as indicated in its charter. (p. 597).

**Book value per share**   The equity a common stockholder has in the net assets of the corporation from owning one share of stock. (p. 612).

**By-laws**   The internal rules and procedures for conducting the affairs of a corporation. (p. 594).

**Callable preferred stock**   Preferred stock that grants the issuer the right to purchase the stock from stockholders at specified future dates and prices. (p. 611).

**Charter**   A document that creates a corporation. (p. 594).

**Convertible preferred stock**   Preferred stock that provides for the exchange of preferred stock into common stock at a specified ratio at the stockholder's option. (p. 610).

**Corporation**   A business organized as a legal entity separate and distinct from its owners under state corporation law. (p. 590).

**Cumulative dividend**   A feature of preferred stock entitling the stockholder to receive current and unpaid prior-year dividends before common stockholders receive any dividends. (p. 609).

**Legal capital**   The amount per share of stock that must be retained in the business for the protection of corporate creditors. (p. 598).

**No-par value stock**   Capital stock that has not been assigned a value in the corporate charter. (p. 598).

**Organization costs**   Costs incurred in the formation of a corporation. (p. 595).

**Outstanding stock**   Capital stock that has been issued and is being held by stockholders. (p. 606).

**Paid-in capital**   Total amount of cash and other assets paid in to the corporation by stockholders in exchange for capital stock. (p. 599).

**Par value stock**   Capital stock that has been assigned a value per share in the corporate charter. (p. 598).

**Preferred stock**   Capital stock that has contractual preferences over common stock in certain areas. (p. 608).

**Privately held corporation**   A corporation that has only a few stockholders and whose stock is not available for sale to the general public. (p. 591).

**Publicly held corporation**   A corporation that may have thousands of stockholders and whose stock is regularly traded on a national securities market. (p. 591).

**Retained earnings**   Net income retained in the corporation. (p. 599).

**Stated value**   The amount per share assigned by the board of directors to no-par stock that becomes legal capital per share. (p. 599).

**Treasury stock**   A corporation's own stock that has been issued, fully paid for, and reacquired by the corporation but not retired. (p. 604).

# SELF-STUDY QUESTIONS

Answers are at the end of the chapter.

(SO 1)   1. Which of the following is *not* a major advantage of a corporation?
   a. Separate legal existence.
   b. Continuous life.
   c. Government regulations.
   d. Transferable ownership rights.

(SO 1)   2. A major disadvantage of a corporation is:
   a. limited liability of stockholders.
   b. additional taxes.
   c. transferable ownership rights.
   d. none of the above.

(SO 2)   3. Which of the following statements is *false*?
   a. Ownership of common stock gives the owner a voting right.
   b. The stockholders' equity section begins with paid-in capital.

   c. The authorization of capital stock does not result in a formal accounting entry.
   d. Legal capital per share applies to par value stock but not to no-par value stock.

4. The account, Retained Earnings, is:   (SO 2)
   a. a subdivision of paid-in capital.
   b. net income retained in the corporation.
   c. reported as an expense in the income statement.
   d. closed to capital stock.

5. ABC Corporation issues 1,000 shares of $10 par value (SO 3) common stock at $12 per share. In recording the transaction, credits are made to:
   a. Common Stock $10,000 and Paid-in Capital in Excess of Stated Value, $2,000.
   b. Common Stock $12,000.
   c. Common Stock $10,000 and Paid-in Capital in Excess of Par Value $2,000.
   d. Common Stock $10,000 and Retained Earnings $2,000.

(SO 4) 6. XYZ, Inc., sells 100 shares of $5 par value treasury stock at $13 per share. If the cost of acquiring the shares was $10 per share, the entry for the sale should include credits to:
   a. Treasury Stock $1,000 and Paid-in Capital from Treasury Stock $300.
   b. Treasury Stock $500 and Paid-in Capital from Treasury Stock $800.
   c. Treasury Stock $1,000 and Retained Earnings $300.
   d. Treasury Stock $500 and Paid-in Capital in Excess of Par Value $800.

(SO 4) 7. In the stockholders' equity section, the cost of treasury stock is deducted from:
   a. Total paid-in capital and retained earnings.
   b. Retained earnings.
   c. Total stockholders' equity.
   d. Common stock in paid-in capital.

(SO 5) 8. Preferred stock may have priority over common stock *except* in:
   a. dividends.
   b. assets in the event of liquidation.
   c. conversion.
   d. voting.

(SO 6) 9. Which of the following is *not* reported under additional paid-in capital?
   a. Paid-in capital in excess of par value.
   b. Common stock.
   c. Paid-in capital in excess of stated value.
   d. Paid-in capital from treasury stock.

(SO 7) 10. The ledger of JFK, Inc., shows common stock, common treasury stock, and no preferred stock. For this company, the formula for computing book value per share is:
   a. Total paid-in capital and retained earnings divided by the number of shares of common stock issued.
   b. Common stock divided by the number of shares of common stock issued.
   c. Total stockholders' equity divided by the number of shares of common stock outstanding.
   d. Total stockholders' equity divided by the number of shares of common stock issued.

THE NAVIGATOR

# QUESTIONS

1. Vicky Gray, a student, asks your help in understanding the following characteristics of a corporation: (a) separate legal existence, (b) limited liability of stockholders, and (c) transferable ownership rights. Explain these characteristics to Vicky.

2. (a) Your friend Cesar Cedeno cannot understand how the characteristic of corporation management is both an advantage and a disadvantage. Clarify this problem for Cesar.
   (b) Identify and explain two other disadvantages of a corporation.

3. (a) The following terms pertain to the forming of a corporation: (1) charter, (2) by-laws, and (3) organization costs. Explain the terms.
   (b) Jim Henry believes a corporation must be incorporated in the state in which its headquarters office is located. Is Jim correct? Explain.

4. What are the basic ownership rights of common stockholders in the absence of restrictive provisions?

5. (a) What are the two principal components of stockholders' equity?
   (b) What is paid-in capital? Give three examples.

6. How do the financial statements for a corporation differ from the statements for a proprietorship?

7. The corporate charter of Leno Corporation allows the issuance of a maximum of 100,000 shares of common stock. During its first two years of operations, Leno sold 70,000 shares to shareholders and reacquired 7,000 of these shares. After these transactions, how many shares are authorized, issued, and outstanding?

8. Which is the better investment—common stock with a par value of $5 per share or common stock with a par value of $20 per share?

9. What factors help determine the market value of stock?

10. What effect does the issuance of stock at a price above par value have on the issuer's net income? Explain.

11. Why is common stock usually not issued at a price that is less than par value?

12. Land appraised at $80,000 is purchased by issuing 1,000 shares of $20 par value common stock. The market price of the shares at the time of the exchange, based on active trading in the securities market, is $95 per share. Should the land be recorded at $20,000, $80,000, or $95,000? Explain.

13. For what reasons might a company like IBM repurchase some of its stock (treasury stock)?

14. Wilton, Inc., purchases 1,000 shares of its own previously issued $5 par common stock for $12,000. Assuming the shares are held in the treasury, what effect does this transaction have on (a) net income, (b) total assets, (c) total paid-in capital, and (d) total stockholders' equity?

15. The treasury stock purchased in question 14, above, is resold by Wilton Inc., for $14,500. What effect does this transaction have on (a) net income, (b) total assets, (c) total paid-in capital, and (d) total stockholders' equity?

16. (a) What are the principal differences between common stock and preferred stock?
    (b) Preferred stock may be cumulative. Discuss this feature.
    (c) How are dividends in arrears presented in the financial statements?

17. A preferred stockholder exercises her right to convert her convertible preferred stock into common stock. What effect does this have on the corporation's (a) total assets, (b) total liabilities, and (c) total stockholders' equity?

18. What is the formula for computing book value per share when a corporation has only common stock?

19. MCE Inc.'s common stock has a par value of $1, a book value of $29, and a current market value of $15. Explain why these amounts are all different.

20. Indicate how each of the following accounts should be classified in the stockholders' equity section.
    (a) Common stock
    (b) Paid-in capital in excess of par value
    (c) Retained earnings
    (d) Treasury stock
    (e) Paid-in capital from treasury stock
    (f) Paid-in capital in excess of stated value
    (g) Preferred stock

# BRIEF EXERCISES

**BE14–1**  Tammy Barto is studying for her accounting midterm examination. Identify for Tammy the advantages and disadvantages of the corporate form of business organization.

*List the advantages and disadvantages of a corporation.*
*(SO 1)*

**BE14–2**  At December 31, Milton Corporation reports net income of $500,000. Prepare the entry to close net income.

*Prepare closing entries for a corporation.*
*(SO 2)*

**BE14–3**  On May 10, Alzado Corporation issues 1,000 shares of $10 par value common stock for cash at $15 per share. Journalize the issuance of the stock.

*Prepare entries for issuance of par value common stock.*
*(SO 3)*

**BE14–4**  On June 1, Eller Inc. issues 2,000 shares of no-par common stock at a cash price of $6 per share. Journalize the issuance of the shares assuming the stock has a stated value of $1 per share.

*Prepare entries for issuance of no-par value common stock.*
*(SO 3)*

**BE14–5**  Stein Inc.'s $10 par value common stock is actively traded at a market value of $15 per share. Stein issues 5,000 shares to purchase land advertised for sale at $80,000. Journalize the issuance of the stock in acquiring the land.

*Prepare entries for issuance of stock in a noncash transaction.*
*(SO 3)*

**BE14–6**  On July 1, Ale Corporation purchases 500 shares of its $5 par value common stock for the treasury at a cash price of $8 per share. On September 1, it sells 300 shares of the treasury stock for cash at $10 per share. Journalize the two treasury stock transactions.

*Prepare entries for treasury stock transactions.*
*(SO 4)*

**BE14–7**  Omar Inc. issues 5,000 shares of $100 par value preferred stock for cash at $110 per share. Journalize the issuance of the preferred stock.

*Prepare entries for issuance of preferred stock.*
*(SO 5)*

**BE14–8**  Brokaw Corporation has the following accounts at December 31: Common Stock, $10 par, 5,000 shares issued, $50,000; Paid-in Capital in Excess of Par Value $10,000; Retained Earnings $39,000; and Treasury Stock—Common, 500 shares, $7,000. Prepare the stockholders' equity section of the balance sheet.

*Prepare stockholders' equity section.*
*(SO 6)*

**BE14–9**  The balance sheet for Lott Inc. shows the following: total paid-in capital and retained earnings $860,000, total stockholders' equity $820,000, common stock issued 44,000 shares, and common stock outstanding 40,000 shares. Compute the book value per share.

*Compute book value per share.*
*(SO 7)*

# EXERCISES

**E14–1**  During its first year of operations, the Levy Corporation had the following transactions pertaining to its common stock.

*Journalize issuance of common stock.*
*(SO 3)*

Jan. 10   Issued 70,000 shares for cash at $5 per share.
July  1   Issued 30,000 shares for cash at $7 per share.

*Instructions*
(a) Journalize the transactions, assuming that the common stock has a par value of $5 per share.
(b) Journalize the transactions, assuming that the common stock is no-par with a stated value of $1 per share.

*Journalize issuance of common and preferred stock and purchase of treasury stock.*
*(SO 3, 4, 5)*

**E14–2** Alomar Co. had the following transactions during the current period:

Mar. 2 Issued 5,000 shares of $1 par value common stock to attorneys in payment of a bill for $25,000 for services rendered in helping the company to incorporate.

June 12 Issued 60,000 shares of $1 par value common stock for cash of $375,000.

July 11 Issued 1,000 shares of $100 par value preferred stock for cash at $108 per share.

Nov. 28 Purchased 2,000 shares of treasury stock for $80,000.

**Instructions**
Journalize the transactions.

*Journalize noncash common stock transactions.*
*(SO 3)*

**E14–3** As an auditor for the CPA firm of Barr and Hilo, you encounter the following situations in auditing different clients:

1. The Roth Corporation is a closely held corporation whose stock is not publicly traded. On December 5, the corporation acquired land by issuing 5,000 shares of its $20 par value common stock. The owners' asking price for the land was $120,000, and the fair market value of the land was $115,000.

2. The Weaks Corporation is a publicly held corporation whose common stock is traded on the securities markets. On June 1, it acquired land by issuing 20,000 shares of its $10 par value stock. At the time of the exchange, the land was advertised for sale at $250,000, and the stock was selling at $11 per share.

**Instructions**
Prepare the journal entries for each of the situations above.

*Journalize treasury stock transactions.*
*(SO 4)*

**E14–4** On January 1, 1999, the stockholders' equity section of the Mintz Corporation shows: Common stock ($5 par value) $1,500,000; Paid-in capital in excess of par value $1,000,000; and Retained earnings $1,200,000. During the year, the following treasury stock transactions occurred:

Mar. 1 Purchased 50,000 shares for cash at $15 per share.

July 1 Sold 10,000 treasury shares for cash at $16 per share.

Sept. 1 Sold 8,000 treasury shares for cash at $14 per share.

**Instructions**
(a) Journalize the treasury stock transactions.
(b) Restate the entry for September 1, assuming the treasury shares were sold at $11 per share.

*Journalize preferred stock transactions and indicate statement presentation.*
*(SO 5, 6)*

**E14–5** Tolan Corporation is authorized to issue both preferred and common stock. The par value of the preferred is $50. During the first year of operations, the company had the following events and transactions pertaining to its preferred stock:

Feb. 1 Issued 30,000 shares for cash at $51 per share.

July 1 Issued 10,000 shares for cash at $57 per share.

**Instructions**
(a) Journalize the transactions.
(b) Post to the stockholders' equity accounts.
(c) Indicate the statement presentation of the accounts.

*Journalize conversion of preferred stock.*
*(SO 5)*

**E14–6** Nolte Corporation has 10,000 shares of $100 par value preferred stock outstanding. Each share is convertible into 5 shares of $15 par value common stock. When the market values of the two classes of stock are $110 and $25, respectively, 2,000 shares of preferred stock are converted into common stock.

**Instructions**
(a) Journalize the conversion of the 2,000 shares.
(b) Repeat (a) assuming that market values at conversion are $105 and $25, respectively.
(c) Repeat (a) assuming each share is convertible into 8 shares of $10 par value common stock.

*Prepare correct entries for capital stock transactions.*
*(SO 3, 4, 5)*

**E14–7** Fernetti Corporation recently hired a new accountant with extensive experience in accounting for partnerships. Because of the pressure of the new job, the accountant was unable to review what he had learned earlier about corporation accounting. During the first month, the accountant made the following entries for the corporation's capital stock:

| | | | | |
|---|---|---|---:|---:|
| May 2 | Cash | | 120,000 | |
| | | Capital Stock | | 120,000 |
| | | (Issued 10,000 shares of $5 par value common stock at $12 per share) | | |
| 10 | Cash | | 600,000 | |
| | | Capital Stock | | 600,000 |
| | | (Issued 10,000 shares of $50 par value preferred stock at $60 per share) | | |
| 15 | Capital Stock | | 13,000 | |
| | | Cash | | 13,000 |
| | | (Purchased 1,000 shares of common stock for the treasury at $13 per share) | | |
| 31 | Cash | | 7,500 | |
| | | Capital Stock | | 2,500 |
| | | Gain on Sale of Stock | | 5,000 |
| | | (Sold 500 shares of treasury stock at $15 per share) | | |

**Instructions**

On the basis of the explanation for each entry, prepare the entry that should have been made for the capital stock transactions.

**E14–8**  The stockholders' equity section of Waters Corporation at December 31 is as follows:

*Answer questions about stockholders' equity section. (SO 3, 4, 5, 6)*

**WATERS CORPORATION**
**Balance Sheet (partial)**

| | |
|---|---:|
| Paid-in capital | |
| Preferred stock, cumulative, 10,000 shares authorized, 6,000 shares issued and outstanding | $ 600,000 |
| Common stock, no par, 750,000 shares authorized, 600,000 shares issued | 1,800,000 |
| Total paid-in capital | 2,400,000 |
| Retained earnings | 1,158,000 |
| Total paid-in capital and retained earnings | 3,558,000 |
| Less: Treasury stock (15,000 common shares) | (64,000) |
| Total stockholders' equity | $3,494,000 |

**Instructions**

From a review of the stockholders' equity section, as chief accountant, write a memo to the president of the company answering the following questions.

  (a)  How many shares of common stock are outstanding?
  (b)  Assuming there is a stated value, what is the stated value of the common stock?
  (c)  What is the par value of the preferred stock?
  (d)  If the annual dividend on preferred stock is $36,000, what is the dividend rate on preferred stock?
  (e)  If dividends of $72,000 were in arrears on preferred stock, what would be the balance reported for Retained Earnings?

**E14–9**  In a recent year, the stockholders' equity section of the Aluminum Company of America (Alcoa) showed the following (in alphabetical order): Additional (Paid-in) capital $680.5, Common stock $88.3, Preferred stock $66.0, and Retained earnings $3,750.2. All dollar data are in millions.

*Prepare a stockholders' equity section and compute book value. (SO 6, 7)*

    The preferred stock has 660,000 shares authorized with a par value of $100 and an annual $3.75 per share cumulative dividend preference. At December 31, all authorized preferred stock is issued and outstanding. There are 300 million shares of $1 par value common stock authorized of which 88.3 million are outstanding at December 31.

**Instructions**

  (a)  Prepare the stockholders' equity section, including disclosure of all relevant data.
  (b)  Compute the book value per share of common stock, assuming there are no preferred dividends in arrears. (Round to two decimals.)

*Classify stockholders' equity accounts.*
*(SO 6)*

**E14–10**   The ledger of Gomez Corporation contains the following accounts: Common Stock, Preferred Stock, Treasury Stock—Common, Paid-in Capital in Excess of Par Value—Preferred Stock, Paid-in Capital in Excess of Stated Value—Common Stock, Paid-in Capital from Treasury Stock, and Retained Earnings.

**Instructions**
Classify each account using the following tabular alignment:

| | Paid-in Capital | | | |
|---|---|---|---|---|
| | Capital | | Retained | |
| Account | Stock | Additional | Earnings | Other |

*Compute book value per share with preferred stock.*
*(SO 7)*

**E14–11**   At December 31, Leiter Corporation has total stockholders' equity of $4,000,000. Included in this total are Preferred stock $500,000 and Paid-in capital in excess of par value—Preferred stock $50,000. There are 10,000 shares of $50 par value 10% cumulative preferred stock outstanding. At year-end, 200,000 shares of common stock are outstanding.

**Instructions**
Compute the book value per share of common stock, under each of the following assumptions:

(a)  There are no preferred dividends in arrears, and the preferred stock does not have a call price.
(b)  Preferred dividends are one year in arrears, and the preferred stock has a call price of $60 per share.

# PROBLEMS: SET A

*Journalize stock transactions, post, and prepare paid-in capital section.*
*(SO 3, 5, 6)*

**P14–1A**   Brazil Corporation was organized on January 1, 1999. It is authorized to issue 20,000 shares of 6%, $50 par value preferred stock, and 500,000 shares of no-par common stock with a stated value of $1 per share. The following stock transactions were completed during the first year:

Jan. 10   Issued 100,000 shares of common stock for cash at $3 per share.
Mar.  1   Issued 10,000 shares of preferred stock for cash at $51 per share.
Apr.  1   Issued 25,000 shares of common stock for land. The asking price of the land was $90,000; the company's estimate of fair market value of the land was $85,000.
May   1   Issued 75,000 shares of common stock for cash at $4 per share.
Aug.  1   Issued 10,000 shares of common stock to attorneys in payment of their bill for $50,000 pertaining to services rendered in helping the company organize.
Sept. 1   Issued 5,000 shares of common stock for cash at $6 per share.
Nov.  1   Issued 2,000 shares of preferred stock for cash at $53 per share.

**Instructions**
(a)  Journalize the transactions.
(b)  Post to the stockholders' equity accounts. (Use J1 as the posting reference.)
(c)  Prepare the paid-in capital section of stockholders' equity at December 31, 1999.

*Journalize treasury stock transactions, post, and prepare stockholders' equity section.*
*(SO 4, 6)*

**P14–2A**   Santana Corporation had the following stockholders' equity accounts on January 1, 1999: Common Stock ($1 par) $400,000, Paid-in Capital in Excess of Par Value $500,000, and Retained Earnings $100,000. In 1999, the company had the following treasury stock transactions:

Mar. 1   Purchased 5,000 shares at $7 per share.
June 1   Sold 1,000 shares at $10 per share.
Sept. 1   Sold 2,000 shares at $9 per share.
Dec. 1   Sold 1,000 shares at $6 per share.

Santana Corporation uses the cost method of accounting for treasury stock. In 1999, the company reported net income of $50,000.

**Instructions**
(a)  Journalize the treasury stock transactions, and prepare the closing entry at December 31, 1999, for net income.

(b) Open accounts for (1) Paid-in Capital from Treasury Stock, (2) Treasury Stock, and (3) Retained Earnings. Post to these accounts using J12 as the posting reference.

(c) Prepare the stockholders' equity section for Santana Corporation at December 31, 1999.

**P14–3A**  The stockholders' equity accounts of Chung Corporation on January 1, 1999, were as follows:

*Journalize and post
transactions, prepare
stockholders' equity section,
and compute book value.*
(SO 2, 3, 4, 5, 6, 7)

| | |
|---|---:|
| Preferred Stock (10%, $100 par noncumulative, 5,000 shares authorized) | $ 300,000 |
| Common Stock ($5 stated value, 300,000 shares authorized) | 1,000,000 |
| Paid-in Capital in Excess of Par Value—Preferred Stock | 15,000 |
| Paid-in Capital in Excess of Stated Value—Common Stock | 400,000 |
| Retained Earnings | 488,000 |
| Treasury Stock—Common (5,000 shares) | 40,000 |

During 1999, the corporation had the following transactions and events pertaining to its stockholders' equity:

Feb.  1   Issued 4,000 shares of common stock for $25,000.
Mar. 20   Purchased 1,000 additional shares of common treasury stock at $8 per share.
June 14   Sold 4,000 shares of treasury stock—common for $34,000.
Sept.  3   Issued 2,000 shares of common stock for a patent valued at $13,000.
Dec. 31   Determined that net income for the year was $215,000.

*Instructions*
(a) Journalize the transactions and the closing entry for net income.
(b) Enter the beginning balances in the accounts and post the journal entries to the stockholders' equity accounts. (Use J1 as the posting reference.)
(c) Prepare a stockholders' equity section at December 31, 1999.
(d) Compute the book value per share of common stock at December 31, 1999, assuming the preferred stock does not have a call price.

**P14–4A**  Jackie Remmers Corporation is authorized to issue 10,000 shares of $100 par value, 10% convertible preferred stock and 200,000 shares of $5 par value common stock. On January 1, 1999, the ledger contained the following stockholders' equity balances:

*Journalize and post preferred
stock transactions and prepare
stockholders' equity section.*
(SO 2, 5, 6)

| | |
|---|---:|
| Preferred Stock (4,000 shares) | $400,000 |
| Paid-in Capital in Excess of Par Value—Preferred | 40,000 |
| Common Stock (70,000 shares) | 350,000 |
| Paid-in Capital in Excess of Par Value—Common | 700,000 |
| Retained Earnings | 300,000 |

During 1999, the following transactions occurred:

Feb. 1   Issued 1,000 shares of preferred stock for land having a fair market value of $125,000.

Mar. 1   Issued 1,000 shares of preferred stock for cash at $120 per share.

July 1   Holders of 2,000 shares of preferred stock purchased at $110 per share converted the shares into common stock. Each share of preferred was convertible into 10 shares of common stock. Market values were: preferred stock $122 and common stock $15.

Sept. 1   Issued 400 shares of preferred stock for a patent. The asking price of the patent was $60,000. Market values were: preferred stock $125 and patent, indeterminable.

Dec. 1   Holders of 1,000 shares of preferred stock purchased at $115 per share converted the shares into common stock. Each share of preferred was convertible into 10 shares of common stock. Market values were: preferred stock $125 and common stock $16.

Dec. 31   Net income for the year was $210,000. No dividends were declared.

*Instructions*
  (a) Journalize the transactions and the closing entry for net income.
  (b) Enter the beginning balances in the accounts and post the journal entries to the stock-holders' equity accounts. (Use J2 as the posting reference.)
  (c) Prepare a stockholders' equity section at December 31, 1999.

*Prepare stockholders' equity section and compute book value.*
*(SO 6, 7)*

**P14–5A**   The following stockholders' equity accounts arranged alphabetically are in the ledger of Ireland Corporation at December 31, 1999:

| | |
|---|---:|
| Common Stock ($10 stated value) | $1,500,000 |
| Paid-in Capital from Treasury Stock | 6,000 |
| Paid-in Capital in Excess of Stated Value—Common Stock | 900,000 |
| Paid-in Capital in Excess of Par Value—Preferred Stock | 280,000 |
| Preferred Stock (8%, $100 par, noncumulative) | 400,000 |
| Retained Earnings | 1,276,000 |
| Treasury Stock—Common (8,000 shares) | 88,000 |

*Instructions*
  (a) Prepare a stockholders' equity section at December 31, 1999.
  (b) Compute the book value per share of the common stock, assuming the preferred stock has a call price of $110 per share.

*Prepare entries for stock transactions and stockholders' equity section.*
*(SO 3, 4, 5, 6)*

**P14–6A**   Littell Corporation has been authorized to issue 20,000 shares of $100 par value, 10%, noncumulative preferred stock and 1,000,000 shares of no-par common stock. The corporation assigned a $2.50 stated value to the common stock. At December 31, 1999, the ledger contained the following balances pertaining to stockholders' equity:

| | |
|---|---:|
| Preferred Stock | $  120,000 |
| Paid-in Capital in Excess of Par Value—Preferred | 24,000 |
| Common Stock | 1,000,000 |
| Paid-in Capital in Excess of Stated Value—Common | 2,850,000 |
| Treasury Stock—Common (1,000 shares) | 10,000 |
| Paid-in Capital from Treasury Stock | 2,000 |
| Retained Earnings | 82,000 |

The preferred stock was issued for land having a fair market value of $144,000. All common stock issued was for cash. In November, 1,500 shares of common stock were purchased for the treasury at a per share cost of $10. In December, 500 shares of treasury stock were sold for $14 per share. No dividends were declared in 1999.

*Instructions*
  (a) Prepare the journal entries for the:
      (1) Issuance of preferred stock for land.
      (2) Issuance of common stock for cash.
      (3) Purchase of common treasury stock for cash.
      (4) Sale of treasury stock for cash.
  (b) Prepare the stockholders' equity section at December 31, 1999.

# PROBLEMS: SET B

*Journalize stock transactions, post, and prepare paid-in capital section.*
*(SO 3, 5, 6)*

**P14–1B**   The Wetland Corporation was organized on January 1, 1999. It is authorized to issue 10,000 shares of 8%, $100 par value preferred stock, and 500,000 shares of no-par common stock with a stated value of $2 per share. The following stock transactions were completed during the first year:

Jan. 10   Issued 80,000 shares of common stock for cash at $3 per share.
Mar.  1   Issued 5,000 shares of preferred stock for cash at $104 per share.
Apr.  1   Issued 24,000 shares of common stock for land. The asking price of the land was $90,000; the fair market value of the land was $80,000.

May   1   Issued 80,000 shares of common stock for cash at $4 per share.

Aug.   1   Issued 10,000 shares of common stock to attorneys in payment of their bill of $50,000 for services rendered in helping the company organize.

Sept.  1   Issued 10,000 shares of common stock for cash at $5 per share.

Nov.   1   Issued 1,000 shares of preferred stock for cash at $108 per share.

**Instructions**
(a) Journalize the transactions.
(b) Post to the stockholders' equity accounts. (Use J5 as the posting reference.)
(c) Prepare the paid-in capital section of stockholders' equity at December 31, 1999.

**P14–2B**   Ramos Corporation had the following stockholders' equity accounts on January 1, 1999: Common Stock ($5 par) $500,000, Paid-in Capital in Excess of Par Value $200,000, and Retained Earnings $100,000. In 1999, the company had the following treasury stock transactions:

*Journalize treasury stock transactions, post, and prepare stockholders' equity section.*
*(SO 4, 6)*

Mar. 1   Purchased 5,000 shares at $8 per share.

June 1   Sold 1,000 shares at $12 per share.

Sept. 1   Sold 2,000 shares at $10 per share.

Dec. 1   Sold 1,000 shares at $7 per share.

Ramos Corporation uses the cost method of accounting for treasury stock. In 1999, the company reported net income of $50,000.

**Instructions**
(a) Journalize the treasury stock transactions and prepare the closing entry at December 31, 1999, for net income.
(b) Open accounts for (1) Paid-in Capital from Treasury Stock, (2) Treasury Stock, and (3) Retained Earnings. Post to these accounts using J10 as the posting reference.
(c) Prepare the stockholders' equity section for Ramos Corporation at December 31, 1999.

**P14–3B**   The stockholders' equity accounts of the Capozza Corporation on January 1, 1999, were as follows:

*Journalize and post transactions, prepare stockholders' equity section, and compute book value.*
*(SO 2, 3, 4, 5, 6, 7)*

| Preferred Stock (12%, $50 par cumulative, 10,000 shares authorized) | $  400,000 |
|---|---|
| Common Stock ($1 stated value, 2,000,000 shares authorized) | 1,000,000 |
| Paid-in Capital in Excess of Par Value—Preferred Stock | 80,000 |
| Paid-in Capital in Excess of Stated Value—Common Stock | 1,400,000 |
| Retained Earnings | 1,816,000 |
| Treasury Stock—Common (10,000 shares) | 40,000 |

During 1999, the corporation had the following transactions and events pertaining to its stockholders' equity:

Feb.   1   Issued 20,000 shares of common stock for $100,000.

Apr.  14   Sold 6,000 shares of treasury stock—common for $28,000.

Sept.  3   Issued 5,000 shares of common stock for a patent valued at $25,000.

Nov.  10   Purchased 1,000 shares of common stock for the treasury at a cost of $6,000.

Dec.  31   Determined that net income for the year was $377,000.

The preferred stock has a call price of $55 per share and no dividends were declared during the year.

**Instructions**
(a) Journalize the transactions and the closing entry for net income.
(b) Enter the beginning balances in the accounts and post the journal entries to the stockholders' equity accounts. (Use J5 for the posting reference.)
(c) Prepare a stockholders' equity section at December 31, 1999, including the disclosure of the preferred dividends in arrears.
(d) Compute the book value per share of common stock at December 31, 1999. (Round to two decimals.)

*Journalize and post preferred stock transactions and prepare stockholders' equity section.*
(SO 2, 5, 6)

**P14–4B**   Shirley Denson Corporation is authorized to issue 10,000 shares of $100 par value, 10% convertible preferred stock and 125,000 shares of $5 par value common stock. On January 1, 1999, the ledger contained the following stockholders' equity balances:

| | |
|---|---|
| Preferred Stock (5,000 shares) | $500,000 |
| Paid-in Capital in Excess of Par Value—Preferred | 50,000 |
| Common Stock (70,000 shares) | 350,000 |
| Paid-in Capital in Excess of Par Value—Common | 700,000 |
| Retained Earnings | 300,000 |

During 1999, the following transactions occurred:

Feb. 1   Issued 1,000 shares of preferred stock for land having a fair market value of $125,000.

Mar. 1   Issued 1,000 shares of preferred stock for cash at $120 per share.

July 1   Holders of 2,000 shares of preferred stock purchased at $110 per share converted the shares into common stock. Each share of preferred was convertible into 8 shares of common stock. Market values were: preferred stock $122 and common stock $17.

Sept. 1   Issued 400 shares of preferred stock for a patent. The asking price of the patent was $60,000. Market values were: preferred stock $125 and patent indeterminable.

Dec. 1   Holders of 1,000 shares of preferred stock purchased at $120 per share converted the shares into common stock. Each share of preferred was convertible into 8 shares of common stock. Market values were: preferred stock $125 and common stock $16.

Dec. 31   Net income for the year was $260,000. No dividends were declared.

**Instructions**
(a) Journalize the transactions and the closing entry for net income.
(b) Enter the beginning balances in the accounts and post the journal entries to the stockholders' equity accounts. (Use J2 for the posting reference.)
(c) Prepare a stockholders' equity section at December 31, 1999.

*Prepare stockholders' equity section and compute book value.*
(SO 6, 7)

**P14–5B**   The following stockholders' equity accounts arranged alphabetically are in the ledger of Howitt Corporation at December 31, 1999:

| | |
|---|---|
| Common Stock ($5 stated value) | $2,500,000 |
| Paid-in Capital from Treasury Stock | 10,000 |
| Paid-in Capital in Excess of Stated Value—Common Stock | 1,500,000 |
| Paid-in Capital in Excess of Par Value—Preferred Stock | 692,000 |
| Preferred Stock (8%, $50 par, noncumulative) | 800,000 |
| Retained Earnings | 2,448,000 |
| Treasury Stock—Common (10,000 shares) | 130,000 |

**Instructions**
(a) Prepare a stockholders' equity section at December 31, 1999.
(b) Compute the book value per share of the common stock, assuming the preferred stock has a call price of $60 per share.

## BROADENING YOUR PERSPECTIVE

# FINANCIAL REPORTING AND ANALYSIS

### FINANCIAL REPORTING PROBLEM: Kellogg Company

**BYP14–1**   The stockholders' equity section for Kellogg Company is shown in Appendix A. You will also find data relative to this problem on other pages of the appendix.

*Instructions*
Answer the following questions.

   (a) What is the par or stated value per share of Kellogg's common stock?

   (b) What percentage of Kellogg's authorized common stock was issued at December 31, 1997? (Round to the nearest full percentage.)

   (c) How many shares of common stock were outstanding at December 31, 1997, and at December 31, 1996?

   (d) What was book value per share at December 31, 1997, and at December 31, 1996? (*Note:* The currency translation adjustment is part of stockholders' equity.)

   (e) What was the closing market price per share at December 31, 1997, as reported under Note 12?

   (f) What were the low and high quarterly cash dividends per share during the two-year period 1997 and 1996? What information concerning Kellogg's dividends is reported in the financial highlights section?

### COMPARATIVE ANALYSIS PROBLEM: Kellogg Company vs. General Mills

**BYP14–2**   Kellogg's financial statements are presented in Appendix A; General Mills's financial statements are presented in Appendix B.

*Instructions*

   (a) Based on the information contained in these financial statements, compute the 1997 book value per share for each company.

   (b) Compare the market value per share for each company to the book value per share at year-end 1997. The market value of General Mills's stock was $64.25 at year-end 1997.

   (c) Why are book value and market value per share different?

### RESEARCH ASSIGNMENT

**BYP14–3**   The September 4, 1995, issue of *Fortune* includes an article by Richard D. Hylton, entitled "Stock Buybacks Are Hot—Here's How You Can Cash In."

*Instructions*
Read the article and answer the following questions:

   (a) What was the total amount of announced intentions to repurchase shares of stock in 1994? What was this figure during the first six months of 1995?

   (b) The goal of many of these repurchase programs was to increase the price of the remaining outstanding shares. Identify the three factors that will determine the impact of repurchases on share price.

   (c) What did Microsoft do with the shares it repurchased? Why might it use repurchased shares for this purpose rather than issuing new shares?

## INTERPRETING FINANCIAL STATEMENTS: Kellogg Company

**BYP14-4**    In recent years Kellogg Company has taken numerous steps aimed at improving its profitability and earnings per share. Included in these steps was the lay-off of 2,000 employees, roughly 13% of Kellogg's workforce. In addition, in 1995, 1994, and 1993 the company repurchased 5,684,864, 6,194,500, and 9,487,508 of its own shares, and announced plans for significant additional repurchases in the coming year. During 1995, 1994, and 1993 amounts expended for share repurchases were $380 million, $327 million, and $548 million—nearly $1.3 billion over a three-year period. Total amounts expended for new property during this same period was $1.1 billion. Thus the company spent more money repurchasing stock than building the company. Also during this period the company issued $400 million in new debt. Presented below are some basic facts for Kellogg.

| (all dollars in millions) | 1995 | 1994 |
|---|---|---|
| Net sales | $7,003 | $6,562 |
| Net income | 490 | 705 |
| Common stock, $.25 par value | 78 | 78 |
| Capital in excess of par value | 105 | 69 |
| Retained earnings | 3,963 | 3,801 |
| Treasury stock, at cost | 2,361 | 1,981 |
| Preferred stock | 0 | 0 |
| Number of shares outstanding (in millions) | 217 | 222 |

### Instructions

(a)  What are some of the reasons that management purchases its own stock?

(b)  What was the approximate impact on earnings per share of the common stock repurchases during this three-year period? (That is, calculate earnings per share with the share repurchases and without the repurchases for 1995. Use the total repurchases during the three-year period—21,366,872 shares—rounded to 21 million.)

## REAL-WORLD FOCUS: Barrister Information Systems Corporation

**BYP14-5    Barrister Information Systems Corp.** develops, assembles, markets, and services computer systems and local area networks for law firms. Headquartered in Buffalo, N.Y., it has offices in 19 U.S. cities. The company has two classes of preferred stock—A and C—in addition to its common stock. The 1,300 shares of Series A preferred stock are nonvoting, have a 12% cumulative dividend, have liquidation preference rights over the Series C preferred stock and the common stock, and are callable by the company at any time for $1,000 per share plus cumulative unpaid dividends. Each share of Series A preferred stock is convertible into 500 shares of common stock. As of March 31, 1993, the cumulative unpaid dividends on the Series A preferred stock totaled $254,000.

### Instructions

(a)  Should the $254,000 in dividends not paid be reported as a liability on the balance sheet?

(b)  If the par value of the Class A preferred stock is $100 per share, what dollar amount in dividends can the shareholders expect annually on the Class A preferred stock?

# CRITICAL THINKING

## GROUP DECISION CASE

**BYP14-6**    The stockholders' meeting for McGwire Corporation has been in progress for some time. The chief financial officer for McGwire is presently reviewing the company's financial statements and is explaining the items that comprise the stockholders' equity section of the balance sheet for the current year. The stockholders' equity section of McGwire Corporation at December 31, 1999, is as follows:

### McGwire Corporation
### Balance Sheet (partial)
### December 31, 1999

| | | |
|---|---:|---:|
| Paid-in capital | | |
| Capital stock | | |
| Preferred stock, authorized 1,000,000 shares | | |
| cumulative, $100 par value, $8 per share, 6,000 | | |
| shares issued and outstanding | | $    600,000 |
| Common stock, authorized 5,000,000 shares, $1 par | | |
| value, 3,000,000 shares issued, and 2,700,000 | | |
| outstanding | | 3,000,000 |
| Total capital stock | | 3,600,000 |
| Additional paid-in capital | | |
| In excess of par value-preferred stock | $    50,000 | |
| In excess of par value-common stock | 25,000,000 | |
| Total additional paid-in capital | | 25,050,000 |
| Total paid-in capital | | 28,650,000 |
| Retained earnings | | 900,000 |
| Total paid-in capital and retained earnings | | 29,550,000 |
| Less: Common treasury stock (300,000 shares) | | 9,300,000 |
| Total stockholders' equity | | $20,250,000 |

A number of questions regarding the stockholders' equity section of McGwire Corporation's balance sheet have been raised at the meeting.

*Instructions*
With the class divided into groups, answer the following questions as if you were the chief financial officer for McGwire Corporation.

(a) "What does the cumulative provision related to the preferred stock mean?"
(b) "I thought the common stock was presently selling at $29.75, and yet the company has the stock stated at $1 per share. How can that be?"
(c) "Why is the company buying back its common stock? Furthermore, the treasury stock has a debit balance because it is subtracted from stockholders' equity. Why is treasury stock not reported as an asset if it has a debit balance?"
(d) "Why is it necessary to show additional paid-in capital? Why not just show common stock at the total amount paid in?"

## COMMUNICATION ACTIVITY

**BYP14–7**   Tony Baden, your uncle, is an inventor who has decided to incorporate. Uncle Tony knows that you are an accounting major at U.N.O. In a recent letter to you, he ends with the question, "I'm filling out a state incorporation application; can you tell me the difference in the following terms: (1) authorized stock, (2) issued stock, (3) outstanding stock, (4) preferred stock?"

*Instructions*
In a brief note, differentiate for Uncle Tony among the four different stock terms. Write the letter to be friendly, yet professional.

## ETHICS CASE

**BYP14–8**   The R & D division of Spencer Chemical Corp. has just developed a chemical for sterilizing the vicious Brazilian "killer bees" which are invading Mexico and the southern states of the United States. The president of Spencer is anxious to get the chemical on the market because Spencer's profits need a boost—his job is in jeopardy because of decreasing sales and profits. Spencer has an opportunity to sell this chemical in Central American countries, where the laws are much more relaxed than in the United States.

The director of Spencer's R & D division strongly recommends further testing in the laboratory for side effects of this chemical on other insects, birds, animals, plants, and even humans. He cautions the president, "We could be sued from all sides if the chemical has tragic side effects that we didn't even test for in the labs." The president answers, "We can't wait an additional year for your lab tests. We can avoid losses from such lawsuits by establishing a separate wholly owned corporation to shield Spencer Corp. from such lawsuits. We can't lose any more than our investment in the new corporation, and we'll invest just the patent covering this chemical. We'll reap the benefits if the chemical works and is safe, and avoid the losses from lawsuits if it's a disaster." The following week Spencer creates a new wholly owned corporation called Zarle Inc., sells the chemical patent to it for $10, and watches the spraying begin.

*Instructions*

(a) Who are the stakeholders in this situation?
(b) Are the president's motives and actions ethical?
(c) Can Spencer shield itself against losses of Zarle Inc.?

# SURFING THE NET

**BYP14–9** SEC filings of publicly-traded companies are available to view online.

**Address:** http://www.yahoo.com/i (or go to the Wiley home page)

**Steps:**
1. From the Yahoo homepage, choose **Stock Quotes.**
2. Enter stock symbol or use "Symbol Lookup."
3. Choose **Get Quotes.**

*Instructions*
Answer the following questions:

(a) What company did you select?
(b) What is its stock symbol?
(c) What was the stock's trading range today?
(d) What was the stock's trading range for the year?

---

*Answers to Self-Study Questions*
1. c    2. b    3. d    4. b    5. c    6. a    7. a    8. d    9. b    10. c

---

*Answers to Kellogg Review It Question 3, p. 603 and Question 4, p. 607.*
3. The par value of Kellogg's common stock is $0.25 per share. Kellogg is authorized to issue 500,000,000 shares of common stock. On December 31, 1997, 414,823,142 shares had been issued.
4. Treasury shares outstanding on December 31, 1996, at Kellogg Company were 101,876,325 and on December 31, 1997, were 4,143,124. The huge decrease was due to the retirement of 105.3 million shares during 1997 as disclosed in the stockholders' equity statement and in Note 1 on Accounting Principles (common stock split).

**Remember to go back to the Navigator box on the chapter-opening page and check off your completed work.**

**Before studying this chapter, you should know or, if necessary, review:**

a.  Why it is important to distinguish between paid-in capital and retained earnings. (Ch. 14, p. 599)

b.  The significance of legal capital in accounting for capital stock transactions. (Ch. 14, p. 598)

c.  The form and content of the stockholders' equity section of the balance sheet. (Ch. 14, pp. 611–12)

d.  The rights of cumulative preferred stockholders to dividends. (Ch. 14, pp. 609–10)

THE NAVIGATOR

## FEATURE STORY

# What's Cooking?

What major U.S. corporation got its start 25 years ago with a waffle iron? Hint: It doesn't sell food. Another hint: Swoosh. Another hint: "just do it." That's right, Nike. In 1971 Nike cofounder, Bill Bowerman, put a piece of rubber into a kitchen waffle iron, and the trademark waffle sole was born.

Nike was cofounded by Bowerman and Phil Knight, a member of Bowerman's University of Oregon track team. Each began in the shoe business independently during the

early 1960s. Bowerman got his start by making hand-crafted running shoes for his university track team. Knight, after completing graduate school, started a small business importing low-cost, high-quality shoes from Japan. In 1964 the two joined forces, each contributing $500, and formed Blue Ribbon Sports, a partnership. At first they marketed Japanese shoes. It wasn't until 1971 that the company began manufacturing its own line of shoes. With the new shoes came a new corporate name— Nike—the Greek goddess of victory. It is hard to imagine that the com-

pany that now boasts a stable full of world-class athletes as promoters at one time had part-time employees selling shoes out of car trunks at track meets.

By 1980 Nike was sufficiently established that it was able to issue its first stock to the public. In that same year it also created a stock ownership program for its employees, allowing them to share in the company's success. Since then Nike has enjoyed phenomenal growth, with 1997 sales reaching $9.2 billion—fully $2.7 billion over 1996 sales. Its dividend per share to shareholders has increased every year for the last 10 years.

Nike is not alone in its quest for the top of the sport shoe world. Reebok pushes Nike every step of the way. But recently Reebok stumbled. While Reebok shareholders watched their stock price slide, Nike shareholders watched their stock soar. Is the race over? Probably not. The shoe market is fickle, with new styles becoming popular almost daily. Reebok's unwillingness to give up the race was boldly stated in its recent ad campaign: "This is my planet." Whether one of these two giants does eventually take control of the planet remains to be seen. Meanwhile the shareholders sit anxiously in the stands as this Olympic-size drama unfolds.

THE NAVIGATOR

*On the World Wide Web*
http://www.nike.com
http://www.reebok.com

# CHAPTER 15

**THE NAVIGATOR** ✔

- ■ Understand *Concepts for Review*
- ■ Read *Feature Story*
- ■ Scan *Study Objectives*
- ■ Read *Preview*
- ■ Read text and answer *Before You Go On*
  p. 641 ⬜ p. 646 ⬜ p. 652 ⬜ p. 655 ⬜
- ■ Work *Demonstration Problems*
- ■ Review *Summary of Study Objectives*
- ■ Answer *Self-Study Questions*
- ■ Complete assignments

# CORPORATIONS: DIVIDENDS, RETAINED EARNINGS, AND INCOME REPORTING

## STUDY OBJECTIVES

**After studying this chapter, you should be able to:**

1. *Prepare the entries for cash dividends and stock dividends.*
2. *Identify the items that are reported in a retained earnings statement.*
3. *Prepare and analyze a comprehensive stockholders' equity section.*
4. *Describe the form and content of corporation income statements.*
5. *Indicate the statement presentation of material items not typical of regular operations.*
6. *Compute earnings per share.*

THE NAVIGATOR

*A*s indicated in the opening story, a corporation like Nike that is profitable often distributes substantial dividends. In addition, it often reinvests a portion of its earnings in the business. This chapter discusses dividends, retained earnings, corporation income statements, and earnings per share. The content and organization of the chapter are as follows:

THE NAVIGATOR

# DIVIDENDS

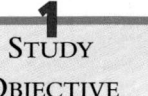

A dividend **is a distribution by a corporation to its stockholders on a pro rata (proportional) basis.** Potential buyers and sellers of a corporation's stock are very interested in a company's dividend policies and practices. Dividends can take four forms: cash, property, scrip (promissory note to pay cash), or (capital) stock. Cash dividends, which predominate in practice, and stock dividends, which are declared with some frequency, will be the focus of discussion in this chapter.

Dividends may be expressed as a percentage of the par or stated value of the stock or as a dollar amount per share. In the financial press, **dividends are generally reported quarterly as a dollar amount per share.** For example, Boeing Company's quarterly dividend rate is 28 cents a share, Ford Motor Company's is 38.5 cents, and Nike's is 9.5 cents.

## Cash Dividends

A cash dividend is a pro rata distribution of cash to stockholders. For a cash dividend to occur, a corporation must have:

1. **Retained earnings.** The legality of a cash dividend depends on the laws of the state in which the company is incorporated. In general, cash dividends

based on retained earnings are legal, and distributions based on common stock (legal capital) are illegal. Statutory provisions vary considerably with respect to cash dividends based on paid-in capital in excess of par or stated value. Many states permit such dividends. A dividend declared out of paid-in capital is termed a **liquidating dividend**, because the amount originally paid in by stockholders is being reduced or "liquidated."

2. **Adequate cash.** The legality of a dividend does not indicate a company's ability to pay a dividend. For example, a company such as Nike, with a cash balance of $445 million and retained earnings of $2,974 million, could legally declare a dividend of $2,974 million. However, if it attempted to pay the dividend, it would need to raise additional cash through the sale of other assets or through additional financing. It follows that before declaring a cash dividend, the board of directors must carefully consider both current and future demands on the company's cash resources. In some cases, current liabilities may make a cash dividend inappropriate; in other cases, a major plant expansion program may warrant only a relatively small dividend.

3. **Declared dividends.** The board of directors has full authority to determine the amount of income to be distributed in the form of a dividend and the amount to be retained in the business. Dividends do not accrue like interest on a note payable, and they are not a liability until declared.

The amount and timing of a dividend are important issues for management to consider. The payment of a large cash dividend could lead to liquidity problems for the enterprise. Conversely, a small dividend or a missed dividend may cause unhappiness among stockholders who expect to receive a reasonable cash payment from the company on a periodic basis. Many companies declare and pay cash dividends quarterly.

# ACCOUNTING IN ACTION
### Business Insight

In order to remain in business, companies must honor their interest payments to creditors, bankers, and bondholders. But the payment of dividends to stockholders is another matter. Many companies can survive, even thrive, without such payouts. In fact, managements might consider dividend payments unnecessary, even harmful to the company. Pay your creditors, by all means. But, fork over perfectly good cash to stockholders as dividends? "Why give money to those strangers?" is the response of one company president.

Investors must keep an eye on the company's dividend policy. For most companies, regular boosts in the face of irregular earnings can be a warning signal. So can the refusal of management to lower dividends when earnings fall or capital requirements rise. Companies with high dividends and rising debt may be borrowing money to pay shareholders. For investors who are seeking high returns on their stock investments, low dividends may mean high returns through market appreciation.

## Entries for Cash Dividends

Three dates are important in connection with dividends: (1) the declaration date, (2) the record date, and (3) the payment date. Normally, there is a time span of two to four weeks between each date. Accounting entries are required on two of the dates—the declaration date and the payment date.

On the **declaration date**, the board of directors formally declares (authorizes) the cash dividend and announces it to stockholders. The declaration of a cash dividend **commits the corporation to a binding legal obligation** that cannot be rescinded. Thus, an entry is required to recognize the decrease in retained earn-

**HELPFUL HINT**
What is the effect of the *declaration* of a cash dividend on (1) total stockholders' equity, (2) total liabilities, (3) total assets? Answer: (1) decrease, (2) increase, (3) no effect.

ings and the increase in the liability, Dividends Payable. To illustrate, assume that on December 1, 1999, the directors of Media General declare a 50¢ per share cash dividend on 100,000 shares of $10 par value common stock. The dividend is $50,000 (100,000 × 50¢), and the entry to record the declaration is:

**Declaration Date**

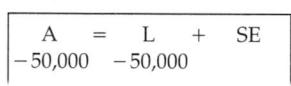

| Dec. 1 | Retained Earnings | 50,000 | |
| |     Dividends Payable | | 50,000 |
| |     (To record declaration of cash dividend) | | |

A   =   L   +   SE
     +50,000   −50,000

Dividends Payable is a current liability because it will normally be paid within the next several months. Instead of debiting Retained Earnings, the account Dividends may be debited. This account provides additional information in the ledger. For example, a company may have separate dividend accounts for each class of stock. When a dividend account is used, its balance is transferred to Retained Earnings at the end of the year by a closing entry. Consequently, the effect of the declaration is the same: retained earnings is decreased and a current liability is increased. For homework problems, you should use the Retained Earnings account for recording dividend declarations.

The **record date** marks the time when ownership of the outstanding shares is determined for dividend purposes. The stockholders' records maintained by the corporation supply this information. The time interval between the declaration date and the record date enables the corporation to update its stock ownership records. Between the declaration date and record date, the number of shares outstanding should remain the same. Thus, the purpose of the record date is to identify the persons or entities that will receive the dividend, not to determine the amount of the dividend liability. For Media General, the record date is December 22. No entry is required on this date because the corporation's liability recognized on the declaration date is unchanged:

**Record Date**

| Dec. 22 | | | |
| |     No entry necessary | | |

On the **payment date**, dividend checks are mailed to the stockholders and the payment of the dividend is recorded. Assuming that the payment date is January 20 for Media General, the entry on that date is:

**Payment Date**

| Jan. 20 | Dividends Payable | 50,000 | |
| |     Cash | | 50,000 |
| |     (To record payment of cash dividend) | | |

A   =   L   +   SE
−50,000   −50,000

Note that payment of the dividend reduces both current assets and current liabilities but has no effect on stockholders' equity. The cumulative effect of the **declaration and payment** of a cash dividend on a company's financial statements is to **decrease both stockholders' equity and total assets.** Illustration 15-1 summarizes the three important dates associated with dividends.

## Allocating Cash Dividends between Preferred and Common Stock

As explained in Chapter 14, preferred stock has priority over common stock in regard to dividends. That is, cash dividends must be paid to preferred stockholders before common stockholders are paid any dividends.

To illustrate, assume that IBR Inc. has 1,000 shares of 8%, $100 par value cumulative preferred stock and 50,000 shares of $10 par value common stock out-

**ILLUSTRATION 15-1**
*Key dividend dates*

standing at December 31, 1999. The dividend per share for preferred stock is $8 ($100 par value × 8%), and the required annual dividend for preferred stock is $8,000 (1,000 × $8). At December 31, 1999, the directors declare a $6,000 cash dividend. In this case, the entire dividend amount goes to preferred stockholders because of their dividend preference. The entry to record the declaration of the dividend is:

| Dec. 31 | Retained Earnings | 6,000 | |
| |   Dividends Payable | | 6,000 |
| |   (To record $6 per share cash dividend to preferred stockholders) | | |

| A | = | L | + | SE |
|---|---|---|---|---|
| | | +6,000 | | −6,000 |

Because of the cumulative feature, dividends of $2 per share are in arrears on preferred stock for 1999. These dividends must be paid to preferred stockholders before any future dividends can be paid to common stockholders. As explained in Chapter 14, dividends in arrears should be disclosed in the financial statements.

At December 31, 2000, IBR declares a $50,000 cash dividend. The allocation of the dividend to the two classes of stock is as follows:

| | | |
|---|---|---|
| Total dividend | | $50,000 |
| Allocated to preferred stock | | |
|   Dividends in arrears, 1999 (1,000 × $2) | $2,000 | |
|   2000 dividend (1,000 × $8) | 8,000 | 10,000 |
| Remainder allocated to common stock | | $40,000 |

**ILLUSTRATION 15-2**
*Allocating dividends to preferred and common stock*

The entry to record the declaration of the dividend is:

| Dec. 31 | Retained Earnings | 50,000 | |
| |   Dividends Payable | | 50,000 |
| |   (To record declaration of cash dividends of $10,000 to preferred stock and $40,000 to common stock) | | |

| A | = | L | + | SE |
|---|---|---|---|---|
| | | +50,000 | | −50,000 |

If the preferred stock were not cumulative, preferred stockholders would have received only $8,000 in dividends in 2000, and common stockholders would have received $42,000.

## Stock Dividends

A stock dividend is a pro rata distribution of the corporation's own stock to stockholders. Whereas a cash dividend is paid in cash, a stock dividend is paid in stock. **A stock dividend results in a decrease in retained earnings and an increase in paid-in capital.** Unlike a cash dividend, a stock dividend does not decrease total stockholders' equity or total assets.

To illustrate a stock dividend, assume that you have a 2% ownership interest in Cetus Inc. by virtue of owning 20 of its 1,000 shares of common stock. In a 10% stock dividend, 100 shares (1,000 × 10%) of stock would be issued. You would receive two shares (2% × 100), but your ownership interest would remain at 2% (22 ÷ 1,100). **You now own more shares of stock but your ownership interest has not changed.** Moreover, no cash is disbursed, and no liabilities have been assumed by the corporation. Illustration 15-3 shows the effect of a stock dividend.

**ILLUSTRATION 15-3**

*Effect of stock dividend*

**Before stock dividend          After stock dividend**

"I owned 40 shares before and I own 120 shares now, but I still own only ¼ of the company!"

Number of shares owned increases, but percentage of company owned remains the same.

What then are the purposes and benefits of a stock dividend? Corporations issue stock dividends generally for one or more of the following reasons:

1. To satisfy stockholders' dividend expectations without spending cash.
2. To increase the marketability of its stock by increasing the number of shares outstanding and thereby decreasing the market price per share. Decreasing the market price of the stock makes it easier for smaller investors to purchase the shares.
3. To emphasize that a portion of stockholders' equity has been permanently reinvested in the business and therefore is unavailable for cash dividends.

The size of the stock dividend and the value to be assigned to each dividend share are determined by the board of directors when the dividend is declared. The per share amount must be at least equal to the par or stated value in order to meet legal requirements.

The accounting profession distinguishes between a **small stock dividend** (less than 20–25% of the corporation's issued stock) and a **large stock dividend** (greater than 20–25%). It recommends that the directors assign the **fair market value per share** for small stock dividends. The recommendation is based on the assumption that a small stock dividend will have little effect on the market price of the shares previously outstanding. Thus, many stockholders consider small stock dividends to be distributions of earnings equal to the fair market value of the shares distributed. The amount to be assigned for a large stock dividend is not specified by the accounting profession. However, **par or stated value per share** is normally assigned. Small stock dividends predominate in practice. Thus, we will illustrate only the entries for small stock dividends.

## Entries for Stock Dividends

To illustrate the accounting for stock dividends, assume that Medland Corporation has a balance of $300,000 in retained earnings and declares a 10% stock dividend on its 50,000 shares of $10 par value common stock. The current fair market value of its stock is $15 per share. The number of shares to be issued is 5,000 (10% × 50,000) and the total amount to be debited to Retained Earnings is $75,000 (5,000 × $15). The entry to record this transaction at the declaration date is as follows:

| | | |
|---|---|---|
| Retained Earnings | 75,000 | |
|     Common Stock Dividends Distributable | | 50,000 |
|     Paid-in Capital in Excess of Par Value | | 25,000 |
|         (To record declaration of 10% stock dividend) | | |

$$A = L + SE$$
$$-75,000$$
$$+50,000$$
$$+25,000$$

Note that Retained Earnings is debited for the fair market value of the stock issued; Common Stock Dividends Distributable is credited for the par value of the dividend shares (5,000 × $10); and the excess over par (5,000 × $5) is credited to an additional paid-in capital account.

Common Stock Dividends Distributable is a stockholders' equity account; it is not a liability because assets will not be used to pay the dividend. If a balance sheet is prepared before the dividend shares are issued, the distributable account is reported in paid-in capital as an addition to common stock issued, as shown below:

| Paid-in capital | | |
|---|---|---|
|   Common stock | $500,000 | |
|   **Common stock dividends distributable** | **50,000** | **$550,000** |

**ILLUSTRATION 15-4**

*Statement presentation of common stock dividends distributable*

When the dividend shares are issued, Common Stock Dividends Distributable is debited and Common Stock is credited as follows:

| | | |
|---|---|---|
| Common Stock Dividends Distributable | 50,000 | |
|     Common Stock | | 50,000 |
|         (To record issuance of 5,000 shares in a stock dividend) | | |

$$A = L + SE$$
$$-50,000$$
$$+50,000$$

## Effects of Stock Dividends

How do stock dividends affect stockholders' equity? They **change the composition of stockholders' equity** because a portion of retained earnings is transferred to paid-in capital. However, **total stockholders' equity remains the same**. Stock dividends also have no effect on the par or stated value per share, but the number of shares outstanding increases and the book value per share decreases. These effects are shown for Medland Corporation in Illustration 15-5.

| | Before Dividend | After Dividend |
|---|---|---|
| Stockholders' equity | | |
| Paid-in capital | | |
| Common stock, $10 par | $500,000 | $550,000 |
| Paid-in capital in excess of par value | — | 25,000 |
| Total paid-in capital | 500,000 | 575,000 |
| Retained earnings | 300,000 | 225,000 |
| Total stockholders' equity | $800,000 | $800,000 |
| Outstanding shares | 50,000 | 55,000 |
| Book value per share | $ 16.00 | $ 14.55 |

In this example, total paid-in capital is increased by $75,000 and retained earnings is decreased by the same amount. Note also that total stockholders' equity remains unchanged at $800,000.

## Stock Splits

A stock split, like a stock dividend, involves the issuance of additional shares of stock to stockholders according to their percentage ownership. However, **a stock split results in a reduction in the par or stated value per share.** The purpose of a stock split is to increase the marketability of the stock by lowering its market value per share. This, in turn, makes it easier for the corporation to issue additional stock. The effect of a split on market value is generally inversely proportional to the size of the split. For example, after a recent 2-for-1 stock split, the market value of Nike's stock fell from $111 to approximately $55. Within one year it was trading above $100 again.

In a stock split, the number of shares is increased in the same proportion that par or stated value per share is decreased. For example, in a 2-for-1 split, one share of $10 par value stock is exchanged for two shares of $5 par value stock. **A stock split does not have any effect on total paid-in capital, retained earnings, and total stockholders' equity.** However, the number of shares outstanding increases and book value per share decreases. These effects are shown in Illustration 15-6 for Medland Corporation, assuming that it splits its 50,000 shares of common stock on a 2-for-1 basis.

**HELPFUL HINT**
A stock split changes the par value per share but does not affect any balances in stockholders' equity.

| | Before Stock Split | After Stock Split |
|---|---|---|
| Stockholders' equity | | |
| Paid-in capital | | |
| Common stock | $500,000 | $500,000 |
| Paid-in capital in excess of par value | –0– | –0– |
| Total paid-in capital | 500,000 | 500,000 |
| Retained earnings | 300,000 | 300,000 |
| Total stockholders' equity | $800,000 | $800,000 |
| Outstanding shares | 50,000 | 100,000 |
| Book value per share | $16.00 | $8.00 |

Because a stock split does not affect the balances in any stockholders' equity accounts, **it is not necessary to journalize a stock split**. Significant differences between stock splits and stock dividends are shown in Illustration 15-7:

| Item | Stock Split | Stock Dividend |
|------|-------------|----------------|
| Total paid-in capital | No change | Increase |
| Total retained earnings | No change | Decrease |
| Total par value (common stock) | No change | Increase |
| Par value per share | Decrease | No change |

**ILLUSTRATION 15-7**

*Differences between the effects of stock splits and stock dividends*

# ACCOUNTING IN ACTION
## Business Insight

A handful of U.S. companies have no intention of keeping their stock trading in a range accessible to mere mortals. These companies never split their stock, no matter how high their stock price gets. The king of these is investment company Berkshire Hathaway's Class A stock, which goes for a pricey $68,000—per share! The company's Class B stock is a relative bargain at roughly $2,300 per share. Other "premium" stocks are A.D. Makepeace at $9,000 and Mechanics Bank of Richmond, California, at $9,600.

# BEFORE YOU GO ON . . .
## Review It

1. What entries are made for cash dividends on (a) the declaration date, (b) the record date, and (c) the payment date?
2. Distinguish between a small and large stock dividend and indicate the basis for valuing each kind of dividend.
3. Contrast the effects of a small stock dividend and a 2 for 1 stock split on (a) stockholders' equity, (b) outstanding shares, and (c) book value per share.

## Do It

Due to 5 years of record earnings at Sing CD Corporation, the market price of its 500,000 shares of $2 par value common stock tripled from $15 per share to $45. During this period, paid-in capital remained the same at $2,000,000, but retained earnings increased from $1,500,000 to $10,000,000. President Joan Elbert is considering either (1) a 10% stock dividend or (2) a 2-for-1 stock split. She asks you to show the before and after effects of each option on (a) retained earnings and (b) book value per share.

*Reasoning:* A stock dividend decreases retained earnings and increases paid-in capital, but total stockholders' equity remains the same. Because additional shares of stock are issued in the dividend, book value per share is decreased. A stock split only changes par value per share and the number of shares outstanding. Thus, this event has no effect on the retained earnings balance, and it decreases book value per share.

*Solution:*

(a) (1) The stock dividend amount is $2,250,000 [(500,000 × 10%) × $45]. The new balance in retained earnings is $7,750,000 ($10,000,000 − $2,250,000).

(2) The retained earnings balance after the stock split is the same as it was before the split: $10,000,000.

(b) The book value effects are as follows:

|  | Original Balances | After Dividend | After Split |
|---|---|---|---|
| Paid-in capital | $ 2,000,000 | $ 4,250,000 | $ 2,000,000 |
| Retained earnings | 10,000,000 | 7,750,000 | 10,000,000 |
| Total stockholders' equity | $12,000,000 | $12,000,000 | $12,000,000 |
| Shares outstanding | 500,000 | 550,000 | 1,000,000 |
| Book value per share | $24 | $21.82 | $12 |

*Related exercise material:* BE15–2, BE15–3, E15–3, E15–4, E15–5, E15–6, and E15–7.

# RETAINED EARNINGS

**2**
STUDY
OBJECTIVE

Identify the items that are reported in a retained earnings statement.

**Retained earnings** is net income that is retained in the business. The balance in retained earnings is part of the stockholders' claim on the total assets of the corporation. It does not, however, represent a claim on any specific asset. Nor can the amount of retained earnings be associated with the balance of any asset account. For example, a $100,000 balance in retained earnings does not mean that there should be $100,000 in cash. The reason is that the cash resulting from the excess of revenues over expenses may have been used to purchase buildings, equipment, and other assets. Illustration 15-8 shows the relationship of cash to retained earnings in selected companies.

**ILLUSTRATION 15-8**

*Retained earnings and cash balances*

| | | (in millions) | |
|---|---|---|---|
| **Company** | | **Retained Earnings** | **Cash** |
| Walt Disney Co. | | $1,278 | $7,933 |
| Sears, Roebuck and Co. | | 3,330 | 660 |
| The Home Depot | | 146 | 2,173 |
| Netscape | | (2) | 88 |

When expenses exceed revenues, a **net loss** results. In contrast to net income, a net loss is debited to Retained Earnings in preparing closing entries. This is done even if a debit balance results in Retained Earnings. **Net losses are not debited to paid-in capital accounts.** To do so would destroy the distinction between paid-in and earned capital. A debit balance in retained earnings is identified as a **deficit** and is reported as a deduction in the stockholders' equity section, as shown below:

**ILLUSTRATION 15-9**

*Stockholders' equity with deficit*

| | |
|---|---|
| Stockholders' equity | |
| Paid-in capital | |
| Common stock | $800,000 |
| Retained earnings (deficit) | (50,000) |
| Total stockholders' equity | $750,000 |

# Retained Earnings Restrictions

The balance in retained earnings is generally available for dividend declarations. Some companies state this fact. For example, in the notes to its financial statements, Martin Lockheed Corporation states:

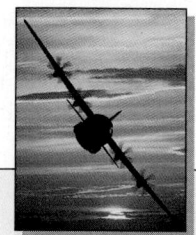

**MARTIN LOCKHEED CORPORATION**
**Notes to the Financial Statements**

At December 31, retained earnings were unrestricted and available for dividend payments.

**ILLUSTRATION 15-10**
*Disclosure of unrestricted retained earnings*

In some cases, however, there may be retained earnings restrictions that make a portion of the balance currently unavailable for dividends. Restrictions result from one or more of the following causes: legal, contractual, or voluntary.

1.  **Legal restrictions.** Many states require a corporation to restrict retained earnings for the cost of treasury stock purchased. The restriction serves to keep intact the corporation's legal capital that is temporarily being held as treasury stock. When the treasury stock is sold, the restriction is lifted.
2.  **Contractual restrictions.** Long-term debt contracts may impose a restriction on retained earnings as a condition for the loan. The restriction limits the use of corporate assets for the payment of dividends. Thus, it enhances the likelihood that the corporation will be able to meet required loan payments.
3.  **Voluntary restrictions.** The board of directors of a corporation may voluntarily create retained earnings restrictions for specific purposes. For example, the board may authorize a restriction for the purpose of future plant expansion. By reducing the amount of retained earnings available for dividends, more cash may be available for the planned expansion.

**Retained earnings restrictions** are generally disclosed in the notes to the financial statements. For example, Pratt & Lambert, a leading producer of architectural finishes (paint) has the following note in a recent financial statement:

**PRATT & LAMBERT**
**Notes to the Financial Statements**

**Note D:  Long-term Debt and Retained Earnings**  Loan agreements contain, among other covenants, a restriction on the payment of dividends, which limits future dividend payments to $20,565,000 plus 75% of future net income.

**ILLUSTRATION 15-11**
*Disclosure of restriction*

# Prior Period Adjustments

Suppose that after the books have been closed and the financial statements have been issued, a corporation discovers that a material error has been made in reporting net income of a prior year. How should this situation be recorded in the accounts and reported in the financial statements? The correction of an error in previously issued financial statements is known as a **prior period adjustment**. The correction is made directly to Retained Earnings because the effect of the error is now in this account; the net income for the prior period has been recorded in retained earnings through the journalizing and posting of closing entries.

To illustrate, assume that General Microwave discovers in 1999 that it understated depreciation expense in 1998 by $300,000 as a result of computational errors. These errors overstated net income for 1998, and the current balance in retained earnings is also overstated. The entry for the prior period adjustment, assuming all tax effects are ignored, is as follows:

| A | = | L | + | SE |
|---|---|---|---|----|
| − 300,000 | | | | − 300,000 |

| | | |
|---|---|---|
| Retained Earnings | 300,000 | |
|    Accumulated Depreciation | | 300,000 |
|      (To adjust for understatement of depreciation in a prior period) | | |

A debit to an income statement account in 1999 would be incorrect because the error pertains to a prior year.

Prior period adjustments are reported in the retained earnings statement.[1] They are added (or deducted) from the beginning retained earnings balance to show the adjusted beginning balance. Assuming General Microwave has a beginning balance of $800,000 in retained earnings, the prior period adjustment is reported as follows:

ILLUSTRATION 15-12

*Statement presentation of prior period adjustments*

| **GENERAL MICROWAVE** **Retained Earnings Statement (partial)** | |
|---|---|
| Balance, January 1, as reported | $800,000 |
| Correction for overstatement of net income in prior period (depreciation error) | 300,000 |
| Balance, January 1, as adjusted | $500,000 |

Reporting the correction in the current year's income statement would be incorrect because it applies to a prior year's income statement.

## Retained Earnings Statement

The **retained earnings statement** shows the changes in retained earnings during the year. The statement is prepared from the Retained Earnings account. Transactions and events that affect retained earnings are tabulated in account form as shown in Illustration 15-13.

ILLUSTRATION 15-13

*Debits and credits to retained earnings*

| Retained Earnings | |
|---|---|
| 1. Net loss | 1. Net income |
| 2. Prior period adjustments for overstatement of net income | 2. Prior period adjustments for understatement of net income |
| 3. Cash and stock dividends | |
| 4. Some disposals of treasury stock | |

---

[1]A complete retained earnings statement is shown in Illustration 15-14 on the next page.

As indicated, net income increases retained earnings, and a net loss decreases retained earnings. Prior period adjustments may either increase or decrease retained earnings, whereas both cash and stock dividends decrease retained earnings. The circumstances when treasury stock transactions decrease retained earnings are explained in Chapter 14. The retained earnings statement for Graber Inc., based on assumed data, is as follows:

ILLUSTRATION 15-14
*Retained earnings statement*

### GRABER INC.
### Retained Earnings Statement
### For the Year Ended December 31, 1999

| | | |
|---|---:|---:|
| Balance, January 1, as reported | | $1,050,000 |
| Correction for understatement of net income in prior period (inventory error) | | 50,000 |
| Balance, January 1, as adjusted | | 1,100,000 |
| Add: Net income | | 360,000 |
| | | 1,460,000 |
| Less: Cash dividends | $100,000 | |
| Stock dividends | 200,000 | 300,000 |
| Balance, December 31 | | $1,160,000 |

## Statement Presentation and Analysis

### Presentation

The stockholders' equity section of the balance sheet of Graber Inc. is presented in Illustration 15-15. Note that (1) Common Stock Dividends Distributable is shown under capital stock in paid-in capital, and (2) a retained earnings restriction is disclosed in the notes.

**3**
STUDY
OBJECTIVE
..........................................
Prepare and analyze a comprehensive stockholders' equity section.

ILLUSTRATION 15-15
*Comprehensive stockholders' equity section*

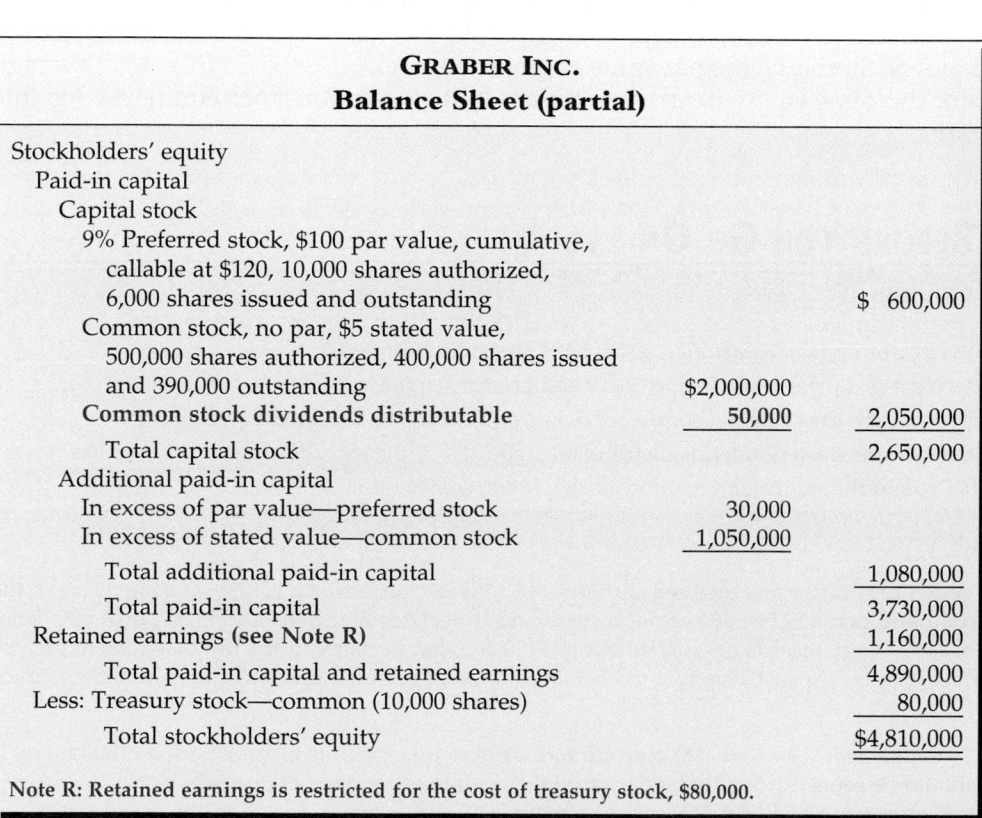

### GRABER INC.
### Balance Sheet (partial)

| | | |
|---|---:|---:|
| Stockholders' equity | | |
| Paid-in capital | | |
| Capital stock | | |
| 9% Preferred stock, $100 par value, cumulative, callable at $120, 10,000 shares authorized, 6,000 shares issued and outstanding | | $ 600,000 |
| Common stock, no par, $5 stated value, 500,000 shares authorized, 400,000 shares issued and 390,000 outstanding | $2,000,000 | |
| Common stock dividends distributable | 50,000 | 2,050,000 |
| Total capital stock | | 2,650,000 |
| Additional paid-in capital | | |
| In excess of par value—preferred stock | 30,000 | |
| In excess of stated value—common stock | 1,050,000 | |
| Total additional paid-in capital | | 1,080,000 |
| Total paid-in capital | | 3,730,000 |
| Retained earnings (see Note R) | | 1,160,000 |
| Total paid-in capital and retained earnings | | 4,890,000 |
| Less: Treasury stock—common (10,000 shares) | | 80,000 |
| Total stockholders' equity | | $4,810,000 |

**Note R: Retained earnings is restricted for the cost of treasury stock, $80,000.**

INTERNATIONAL NOTE

In Switzerland, there are no specific disclosure requirements for stockholders' equity. However, companies typically disclose separate categories of capital on the balance sheet.

Instead of presenting a detailed stockholders' equity section in the balance sheet and a retained earnings statement, many companies prepare a stockholders' equity statement. This statement shows the changes in each stockholders' equity account and in total stockholders' equity that have occurred during the year. An example of a stockholders' equity statement is illustrated in the appendix to this chapter and in Kellogg's financial statements in Appendix A.

### Analysis

A widely used ratio that measures profitability from the common stockholder's viewpoint is return on common stockholders' equity. This ratio shows how many dollars of net income were earned for each dollar invested by the owners. It is computed by dividing net income available to common stockholders (which is Net income − Preferred stock dividends) by average common stockholders' equity. For example, assuming that Kellogg's beginning-of-the-year and end-of-the-year common stockholders' equity were $1,282.4 and $997.5 million respectively, net income was $546.0 million, and no preferred stock was outstanding, the return on common stockholders' equity ratio is shown graphically and computed as follows:

**ILLUSTRATION 15-16**

*Return on common stockholders' equity ratio and computation*

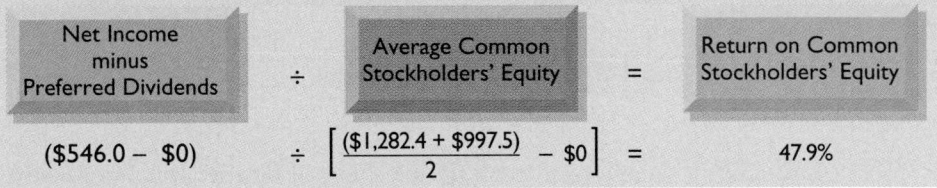

As shown above, if preferred stock is present, **preferred dividend** requirements are deducted from net income to compute income available to common stockholders. Similarly, the par value of preferred stock is deducted from total average stockholders' equity to arrive at the amount of common stock equity used in this ratio.

## BEFORE YOU GO ON . . .

### Review It

1. How are retained earnings restrictions generally reported?
2. What is a prior period adjustment and how is it reported?
3. What are the principal sources of debits and credits to Retained Earnings?
4. How are stock dividends distributable reported in the stockholders' equity section?
5 Explain the return on common stockholders' equity ratio.

### Do It

Vega Corporation has retained earnings of $5,130,000 on January 1, 1999. During the year, the company earns $2,000,000 of net income and it declares and pays a $250,000 cash dividend. In 1999, Vega records an adjustment of $180,000 that pertains to the understatement of 1998 depreciation expense due to a mathematical error. Prepare a retained earnings statement for 1999.

*Reasoning:* The $180,000 correction of 1998 depreciation is a prior period adjustment. It should be reported as a deduction from the beginning retained earnings balance. Net income is shown as an addition in the statement and dividends are deducted in the statement.

*Solution:*

| VEGA CORPORATION<br>Retained Earnings Statement<br>For the Year Ended December 31, 1999 | |
| --- | ---: |
| Balance, January 1, as reported | $5,130,000 |
| Correction for overstatement of net income in prior period (depreciation error) | 180,000 |
| Balance, January 1, as adjusted | 4,950,000 |
| Add: Net income | 2,000,000 |
| | 6,950,000 |
| Less: Cash dividends | 250,000 |
| Balance, December 31 | $6,700,000 |

*Related exercise material:* BE15–4 and E15–8.

# CORPORATION INCOME STATEMENTS

Income statements for **corporations are the same as the statements for proprietorships or partnerships except for the reporting of income taxes.** For income tax purposes, corporations are considered to be a separate legal entity. As a result, **income taxes (or income tax expense)** are reported in a separate section of the corporation income statement before net income. The condensed income statement for Leads Inc. in Illustration 15-17 shows a typical presentation. Note that income before income taxes is reported before income tax expense.

**4**
STUDY
OBJECTIVE
Describe the form and content of corporation income statements.

| LEADS INC.<br>Income Statement<br>For the Year Ended December 31, 1999 | | |
| --- | ---: | ---: |
| Sales | | $800,000 |
| Cost of goods sold | | 600,000 |
| Gross profit | | 200,000 |
| Operating expenses | | 50,000 |
| Income from operations | | 150,000 |
| Other revenues and gains | | 10,000 |
| Other expenses and losses | | 4,000 |
| **Income before income taxes** | | 156,000 |
| **Income tax expense** | | 46,800 |
| Net income | | $109,200 |

**ILLUSTRATION 15-17**

*Income statement with income taxes*

**HELPFUL HINT**
Corporations may also use the single-step form of income statement discussed in Chapter 5.

Income tax expense and the related liability for income taxes payable are recorded as part of the adjusting process preceding financial statement preparation. Using the data above for Leads Inc., the adjusting entry for income tax expense at December 31, 1999, would be as follows:

| | | |
| --- | ---: | ---: |
| Income Tax Expense | 46,800 | |
|     Income Taxes Payable | | 46,800 |
|       (To record income taxes for 1999) | | |

| A | = | L | + | SE |
| --- | --- | --- | --- | --- |
| | | +46,800 | | −46,800 |

Another illustration of income taxes is presented in the income statement of Kellogg Company in Appendix A.

# ACCOUNTING IN ACTION
## Business Insight

Net income and its components reported in the income statement measure a company's performance. The amount and trend of net income (earnings) are, therefore, of vital importance to management, stockholders, and creditors. Net income provides an indication of the amount of dividends that a company may distribute, and it results in an increase in retained earnings.

Reported net income has a major effect on the market price of a company's stock at a given point in time. For example, when IBM announced that its net income would be 7.7% lower, the price of its stock dropped $3.875 per share in one day. Conversely, when Eljer Industries Inc. (a Dallas-based maker of plumbing, heating, and ventilation products) reported a sharp improvement in its earnings, the market price of its stock increased 14% in one day.

The income statements we have studied so far provide considerable insight into a company's income-related activities. In studying such statements, the user may ask: (1) Are the results typical for this company? (2) Are the results a reasonable indicator of the company's future earnings?

To provide answers to these questions, accountants have concluded that additional sections should be added to the income statement to **report material items not typical of regular operations**. These items are reported in the income statement immediately before net income. The nontypical items include (1) discontinued operations, (2) extraordinary items, and (3) changes in accounting principle. All these irregular items are reported net of income taxes. That is, the applicable income tax expense or tax savings is shown for income before income taxes and for each of the listed irregular items. The general concept is "let the tax follow income or loss."

# Discontinued Operations

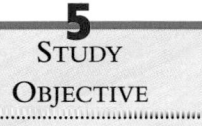

**STUDY OBJECTIVE**

Indicate the statement presentation of material items not typical of regular operations.

**Discontinued operations** refers to the disposal of a **significant segment** of a business, such as the cessation of an entire activity or the elimination of a major class of customers. Thus, Kmart's decision to terminate its interest in four business activities, including PACE Membership Warehouse and PayLess Drug Stores Northwest, was reported as discontinued operations. On the other hand, the phasing out of a model such as the GM Chevette or part of a line of business is not considered to be a disposal of a segment.

When the disposal of a significant segment occurs, the income statement should report both income from continuing operations and income (or loss) from discontinued operations. **The income (loss) from discontinued operations consists of the income (loss) from operations and the gain (loss) on disposal of the segment.** To illustrate, assume that during 1999 Acro Energy Inc. has income before income taxes of $800,000. During 1999 the company discontinued and sold its unprofitable chemical division. The loss in 1999 from chemical operations (net of $60,000 taxes) was $140,000, and the loss on disposal of the chemical division (net of $30,000 taxes) was $70,000. Assuming a 30% tax rate on income before income taxes, the income statement presentation is shown on the next page.

ILLUSTRATION 15-18
Statement presentation of discontinued operations

ACRO ENERGY INC.
Income Statement (partial)
For the Year Ended December 31, 1999

Income before income taxes		$800,000
Income tax expense		240,000
Income from continuing operations		560,000
Discontinued operations		
Loss from operations of chemical division, net of $60,000 income tax saving	$140,000	
Loss from disposal of chemical division, net of $30,000 income tax saving	70,000	210,000
Net income		$350,000

HELPFUL HINT
Observe the dual disclosures: (1) the results of operations of the discontinued division must be eliminated from the results of continuing operations, and (2) the disposal of the operation.

Note that the caption "Income from continuing operations" is used and that a section "Discontinued operations" is added. **Within the new section, both the operating loss and the loss on disposal are reported net of applicable income taxes.** This presentation clearly indicates the separate effects of continuing operations and discontinued operations on net income.

Extraordinary Items

Extraordinary items are events and transactions that meet two conditions: they are (1) **unusual in nature and** (2) **infrequent in occurrence**. To be considered unusual, the item should be abnormal and be only incidentally related to the customary activities of the entity. To be regarded as infrequent, the event or transaction should not be reasonably expected to recur in the foreseeable future. Both criteria must be evaluated in terms of the environment in which the entity operates. Thus, Weyerhaeuser Co. reported the $36 million in damages to its timberland caused by the volcanic eruption of Mount St. Helens as an extraordinary item because the event was both unusual and infrequent. In contrast, Florida Citrus Company does not report frost damage to its citrus crop as an extraordinary item because frost damage is not viewed as infrequent. Illustration 15-19 shows the appropriate classification of extraordinary and ordinary items.

ACCOUNTING IN ACTION

Business Insight

In the recession of the early 1990s, many companies closed some of their plants and reduced the size of their work forces. The costs incurred in these activities, called plant restructuring costs, are reported as other expenses and losses in the income statement. These costs are not considered to be an extraordinary item because plant closings are neither unusual nor infrequent in many industries. Plant restructuring costs often have a significant effect on net income as illustrated by the following:

Union Pacific Corp.	$585 million after-tax charge, of which $492 million applies to the disposal of 7,100 miles of the Union Pacific Railroad.
Borden, Inc.	$71.6 million before-tax charge for business reorganization costs as well as severance, relocation, and other employee-related expenses.

**ILLUSTRATION 15-19**

*Examples of extraordinary and ordinary items*

**Extraordinary items**

1. Effects of major casualties (acts of God), if rare in the area.

2. Expropriation (takeover) of property by a foreign government.

3. Effects of a newly enacted law or regulation, such as a condemnation action.

**Ordinary items**

1. Effects of major casualties (acts of God), frequent in the area.

2. Write-down of inventories or write-off of receivables.

3. Losses attributable to labor strikes.

4. Gains or losses from sales of property, plant, or equipment.

**Extraordinary items are reported net of taxes in a separate section of the income statement immediately below discontinued operations.** To illustrate, assume that in 1999 a revolutionary foreign government expropriated property held as an investment by Acro Energy Inc. If the loss is $70,000, before applicable income taxes of $21,000, the income statement presentation will show a deduction of $49,000 as shown in Illustration 15-20.

As illustrated, the caption "Income before extraordinary item" is added immediately before the section for the extraordinary item. This presentation clearly indicates the effect of the extraordinary item on net income. If there are no discontinued operations, the third line of the income statement in Illustration 15-20 would be labeled "Income before extraordinary item."

If a transaction or event meets one (but not both) of the criteria for an extraordinary item, it is reported under either "Other revenues and gains" or "Other expenses and losses" at its gross amount (not net of tax). This is true, for example, of gains (losses) resulting from the sale of property, plant, and equipment, as explained in Chapter 10.

## Change in Accounting Principle

For ease of comparison, financial statements are expected to be prepared on a basis **consistent** with that used for the preceding period. That is, where a choice of accounting principles is available, the principle initially chosen should be con-

**ILLUSTRATION 15-20**

*Statement presentation of extraordinary items*

| ACRO ENERGY INC.<br>Income Statement (partial)<br>For the Year Ended December 31, 1999 | | |
|---|---:|---:|
| Income before income taxes | | $800,000 |
| Income tax expense | | 240,000 |
| Income from continuing operations | | 560,000 |
| Discontinued operations | | |
| Loss from operations of chemical division, net of $60,000<br>income tax saving | $140,000 | |
| Loss from disposal of chemical division, net of $30,000<br>income tax saving | 70,000 | 210,000 |
| Income before extraordinary item | | 350,000 |
| **Extraordinary item** | | |
| **Expropriation of investment, net of $21,000 income tax<br>saving** | | **49,000** |
| Net income | | $301,000 |

sistently applied from period to period. A change in an accounting principle occurs when the principle used in the current year is different from the one used in the preceding year. A change is permitted, when (1) management can show that the new principle is preferable to the old principle, and (2) the effects of the change are clearly disclosed in the income statement. Examples of a change in accounting principle include a change in depreciation methods (e.g., declining-balance to straight-line) and a change in inventory costing methods (e.g., FIFO to average cost).

When a change in an accounting principle has occurred,

1. The new principle should be used in reporting the results of operations of the current year.
2. The cumulative effect of the change on all prior year income statements should be disclosed net of applicable taxes in a special section immediately preceding net income.

To illustrate, we will assume that at the beginning of 1999, Acro Energy Inc. changes from the straight-line method of depreciation to the declining-balance method for equipment purchased on January 1, 1996. The cumulative effect on prior year income statements (statements for 1996–1998) is to increase depreciation expense and decrease income before income taxes by $24,000. Assuming a 30% tax rate, the net of tax effect of the change is $16,800 ($24,000 × 70%). The income statement presentation is shown in Illustration 15-21 on page 652.

The income statement for Acro Energy will also show depreciation expense for the current year. The amount is based on the new depreciation method. In this case the caption "Income before extraordinary item and cumulative effect of change in accounting principle" is inserted immediately following the effects of discontinued operations. This presentation clearly indicates the cumulative effect of the change on prior years' income. If a company does not have either discontinued operations or extraordinary items, the label, "Income before cumulative effect of change in accounting principle" is used in place of "Income from continuing operations." A complete income statement showing all material items not typical of regular operations is illustrated in the Demonstration Problem (pp. 655–56).

**ETHICS NOTE**

Changes in accounting principles should result in financial statements that are more informative for statement users. They should not be used to artificially improve the reported performance and financial position of the corporation.

**ILLUSTRATION 15-21**

*Statement presentation of cumulative effect of change in accounting principle*

| ACRO ENERGY INC.<br>Income Statement (partial)<br>For the Year Ended December 31, 1999 | | |
|---|---:|---:|
| Income before income taxes | | $800,000 |
| Income tax expense | | 240,000 |
| Income from continuing operations | | 560,000 |
| Discontinued operations | | |
| Loss from operations of chemical division, net of $60,000 income tax saving | $140,000 | |
| Loss from disposal of chemical division, net of $30,000 income tax saving | 70,000 | 210,000 |
| Income before extraordinary item and cumulative effect of change in accounting principle | | 350,000 |
| Extraordinary item | | |
| Expropriation of investment, net of $21,000 income tax saving | | 49,000 |
| **Cumulative effect of change in accounting principle** | | |
| **Effect on prior years of change in depreciation method, net of $7,200 income tax saving** | | 16,800 |
| Net income | | $284,200 |

## ACCOUNTING IN ACTION
### Business Insight

Sometimes a change in accounting principle is mandated by the Financial Accounting Standards Board. An example is the change in accounting for interperiod income taxes required by Statement of Financial Accounting Standards 109. Such changes can significantly affect net income. For example, in a recent income statement, Consolidated Natural Gas Company reported an increase in income of $17,422,000 under "Cumulative Effect of Accounting Change." An accompanying note explained that the increase in income resulted from a required "change from the deferred method to an asset and liability approach for accounting for and reporting of income taxes."

## BEFORE YOU GO ON . . .

### Review It

1. What is the unique feature of a corporation income statement?
2. What are the similarities and differences in reporting material items not typical of regular operations?
3. Did Kellogg report any of the three types of irregular items in its 1997 income statement? The answer to this question is provided on p. 673.

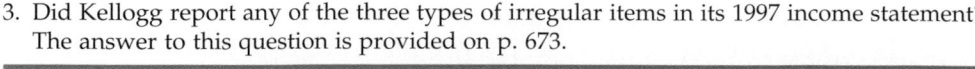

### Do It

In its proposed 1999 income statement, AIR Corporation reports income before income taxes $400,000, extraordinary loss from fire $100,000, income taxes (30%) $90,000, and net income $210,000. Prepare a correct income statement, beginning with income before income taxes.

*Reasoning:* The income tax effect of each component is disclosed in the income statement. Thus, the extraordinary loss should be reported net of income taxes.

*Solution:*

| AIR CORPORATION<br>Income Statement (partial) | |
| --- | --- |
| Income before income taxes | $400,000 |
| Income tax expense (30%) | 120,000 |
| Income before extraordinary item | 280,000 |
| Extraordinary loss from fire, net of $30,000 income tax saving | 70,000 |
| Net income | $210,000 |

*Related exercise material:* BE15–6, BE15–7, BE15–8, E15–12, and E15–13.

# EARNINGS PER SHARE

**6**
STUDY
OBJECTIVE
Compute earnings per share.

Earnings per share data are frequently reported in the financial press and are widely used by stockholders and potential investors in evaluating the profitability of a company. Investors, especially, attempt to link earnings per share to the market price per share.[2] **Earnings per share (EPS)** indicates the net income earned by each share of outstanding common stock. Thus, **earnings per share is reported only for common stock**. The formula for computing earnings per share is as follows:

**ILLUSTRATION 15-22**

*Earnings per share formula*

For example, if Modem Inc. has net income of $200,000 and 50,000 shares of common stock outstanding for the year, earnings per share is $4 ($200,000 ÷ 50,000).[3]

Because of the importance of earnings per share (EPS), most companies are required to report it on the face of the income statement. Generally this amount is simply reported below net income on the statement. For Modem Inc. the presentation would be:

---

[2]The ratio of the market price per share to the earnings per share is referred to as the *price-earnings (P/E) ratio.* This ratio is reported in *The Wall Street Journal* and other newspapers for common stocks listed on major stock exchanges.

[3]The calculation of the weighted average of common shares outstanding is discussed in advanced accounting courses.

**ILLUSTRATION 15-23**

*Basic earnings per share disclosure*

| MODEM INC. |
| :---: |
| **Income Statement (partial)** |

| | |
| --- | ---: |
| Net income | $200,000 |
| **Earnings per share** | **$ 4.00** |

## Preferred Stock Dividends

Earnings per share relates to earnings per share of **common stock**. When a corporation has both preferred and common stock outstanding, the current year's dividend declared on preferred stock is subtracted from net income to arrive at **income available to common stockholders**. The formula for computing EPS in such a case is:

**ILLUSTRATION 15-24**

*Expanded earnings per share formula*

To illustrate, assume that Rally Inc. reports net income of $211,000 on its 102,500 weighted average common shares. During the year it also declares a $6,000 dividend on its preferred stock. Therefore, Rally has $205,000 ($211,000 − $6,000) available for common stock dividends. Earnings per share is $2 ($205,000 ÷ 102,500). If the preferred stock is cumulative, the dividend for the current year is deducted whether or not it is declared.

## Irregular Items

When the income statement contains any of the three additional sections that report irregular items described earlier in the chapter, EPS should be disclosed for each component. Assuming that Acro Energy had 100,000 shares of common stock outstanding during the year, the additional EPS disclosures for the income statement shown in Illustration 15-21 would be as shown below.

**ILLUSTRATION 15-25**

*Additional earnings per share disclosures*

| ACRO ENERGY INC. |
| :---: |
| **Income Statement (partial)** |
| **For the Year Ended December 31, 1999** |

| | |
| --- | ---: |
| Net income | $284,200 |
| Earnings per share | |
|    **Income from continuing operations** | **$5.60** |
|    **Loss from discontinued operations** | **(2.10)** |
|    **Income before extraordinary item and cumulative effect of change in accounting principle** | 3.50 |
|    **Extraordinary loss** | **(.49)** |
|    **Cumulative effect of change in accounting principle** | **(.17)** |
|    **Net income** | **$2.84** |

These disclosures enable decision makers to recognize the effects on EPS of income from continuing operations, as distinguished from income or loss from material items not typical of regular operations. **Earnings per share from continuing operations is generally the most useful per share amount**, because it represents the results of continuing and ordinary business activity. Thus, it provides the best basis for predicting future operating results.

## BEFORE YOU GO ON . . .

### Review It

1. Explain the components of the formula for computing earnings per share when there is only common stock and outstanding shares are unchanged during the year.
2. What effects may preferred stock have on the formula for computing earnings per share?

## A LOOK BACK AT OUR FEATURE STORY

To answer the following questions, refer to the opening story.

1. Nike's stock has split numerous times in recent years. What is the likely reason for these splits?
2. Prepare the quarterly journal entry (accounts and amount) recorded by a Nike shareholder when he or she receives a dividend of $1,000 from Nike.
3. Nike has increased its cash dividend per share every year for the past 10 years. What issues must it consider when deciding the level of the divided payment?

*Solution:*

1. In recent years Nike's stock has experienced a rapid increase in value. To keep the stock in an affordable price range for the average investor, management has split the stock a number of times.
2. The entry to record receipt of a dividend each quarter is:

| | | |
|---|---|---|
| Cash | 1,000 | |
|     Dividend Revenue | | 1,000 |
|         (To record quarterly dividend revenue) | | |

THE
NAVIGATOR

3. Nike should consider the adequacy of its cash, the adequacy of its retained earnings, the level of its future earnings, and its ability to maintain the dividend level in the future.

## DEMONSTRATION PROBLEM

The events and transactions of the Dever Corporation for the year ending December 31, 1999, resulted in the following data:

| | |
|---|---|
| Cost of goods sold | $2,600,000 |
| Net sales | 4,400,000 |
| Other expenses and losses | 9,600 |
| Other revenues and gains | 5,600 |
| Selling and administrative expenses | 1,100,000 |
| Income from operations of plastics division | 70,000 |
| Gain on sale of plastics division | 500,000 |
| Loss from tornado disaster (extraordinary loss) | 600,000 |
| Cumulative effect of changing from the straight-line depreciation to double-declining-balance (increase in depreciation expense) | 300,000 |

Analysis reveals that:

1. All items are before the applicable income tax rate of 30%.
2. The plastics division was sold on July 1.
3. All operating data for the plastics division have been segregated.
4. There were 100,000 shares of common stock outstanding during the year.

*Instructions*

Prepare an income statement for the year, including the presentation of earnings per share data.

**PROBLEM-SOLVING STRATEGIES**

1. Remember that material items not typical of operations are reported in separate sections net of taxes.
2. Income taxes should be associated with the item that affects the taxes.
3. A corporation income statement will have income tax expense when there is income before income tax.
4. All data presented in determining income before income taxes are the same as for unincorporated companies.

## SOLUTION TO DEMONSTRATION PROBLEM

### DEVER CORPORATION
### Income Statement
### For the Year Ended December 31, 1999

| | | |
|---|---:|---:|
| Net sales | | $4,400,000 |
| Cost of goods sold | | 2,600,000 |
| Gross profit | | 1,800,000 |
| Selling and administrative expenses | | 1,100,000 |
| Income from operations | | 700,000 |
| Other revenues and gains | $ 5,600 | |
| Other expenses and losses | 9,600 | 4,000 |
| Income before income taxes | | 696,000 |
| Income tax expense ($696,000 × 30%) | | 208,800 |
| Income from continuing operations | | 487,200 |
| Discontinued operations | | |
|    Income from operations of plastics division, net of | | |
|       $21,000 income taxes ($70,000 × 30%) | 49,000 | |
|    Gain on sale of plastics division, net of $150,000 | | |
|       income taxes ($500,000 × 30%) | 350,000 | 399,000 |
| Income before extraordinary item and cumulative effect of | | |
|   change in accounting principle | | 886,200 |
| Extraordinary item | | |
|    Tornado loss, net of income tax saving $180,000 | | |
|      ($600,000 × 30%) | | 420,000 |
| Cumulative effect of change in accounting principle | | |
|    Effect on prior years of change in depreciation method, | | |
|      net of $90,000 income tax saving ($300,000 × 30%) | | 210,000 |
| Net income | | $ 256,200 |
| | | |
| Earnings per share | | |
|   Income from continuing operations | | $4.87 |
|   Gain from discontinued operations | | 3.99 |
|   Income before extraordinary item and cumulative effect | | |
|     of change in accounting principle | | 8.86 |
|   Extraordinary loss | | (4.20) |
|   Cumulative effect of change in accounting principle | | (2.10) |
|   Net income | | $2.56 |

THE NAVIGATOR

## SUMMARY OF STUDY OBJECTIVES

**1. Prepare the entries for cash dividends and stock dividends.** Entries for both cash and stock dividends are required at the declaration date and the payment date. At the declaration date the entries are: Cash dividend—debit Retained Earnings and credit Dividends Payable; small stock dividend—debit Retained Earnings, credit Paid-in Capital in Excess of Par (or Stated) Value, and credit Common Stock Dividends Distributable. At the payment date, the entries for cash and stock dividends, respectively, are debit Dividends Payable and credit Cash, and debit Common Stock Dividends Distributable and credit Common Stock.

**2. Identify the items that are reported in a retained earnings statement.** Each of the individual debits and credits to retained earnings should be reported in the retained earnings statement. Additions consist of net income and prior period adjustments to correct understatements of prior years' net income. Deductions consist of net loss, adjustments to correct overstatements of prior years' net income, cash and stock dividends, and some disposals of treasury stock.

**3. Prepare and analyze a comprehensive stockholders' equity section.** A comprehensive stockholders' equity section includes all stockholders' equity accounts. It consists of two sections: paid-in capital and retained earnings. It should also include notes to the financial statements that explain any restrictions on retained earnings and any dividends in arrears. One measure of profitability is the return on common stockholders' equity. It is calculated by dividing income available to common stockholders by average common stockholders' equity.

**4. Describe the form and content of corporation income statements.** The form and content of corporation income statements are similar to the statements of proprietorships and partnerships with one exception: Income taxes or income tax expense must be reported in a separate section before net income in the corporation's income statement.

**5. Indicate the statement presentation of material items not typical of regular operations.** Material items not typical of regular operations are reported net of taxes in sections on the income statement immediately before net income. These items include (a) discontinued operations, (b) extraordinary items, and (c) changes in accounting principle.

**6. Compute earnings per share.** Earnings per share is computed by dividing net income by the number of common shares outstanding during the period. An additional problem arises when preferred stock dividends exist.

THE NAVIGATOR

# GLOSSARY

**Cash dividend** A pro rata distribution of cash to stockholders. (p. 634).

**Change in accounting principle** The use of a principle in the current year that is different from the one used in the preceding year. (p. 650).

**Declaration date** The date the board of directors formally declares the dividend and announces it to stockholders. (p. 635).

**Deficit** A debit balance in retained earnings. (p. 642).

**Discontinued operations** The disposal of a significant segment of a business. (p. 648).

**Dividend** A distribution by a corporation to its stockholders on a pro rata (proportional) basis. (p. 634).

**Earnings per share** The net income earned by each share of outstanding common stock. (p. 653).

**Extraordinary items** Events and transactions that are unusual in nature and infrequent in occurrence. (p. 649).

**Liquidating dividend** A dividend declared out of paid-in capital. (p. 635).

**Payment date** The date dividend checks are mailed to stockholders. (p. 636).

**Prior period adjustment** The correction of an error in previously issued financial statements. (p. 644).

**Record date** The date when ownership of outstanding shares is determined for dividend purposes. (p. 636).

**Retained earnings** Net income that is retained in the business. (p. 642).

**Retained earnings restrictions** Circumstances that make a portion of retained earnings currently unavailable for dividends. (p. 643).

**Retained earnings statement** A financial statement that shows the changes in retained earnings during the year. (p. 644).

**Return on common stockholders' equity** A measure of profitability that shows how many dollars of net income were earned for each dollar invested by the owners; computed as net income divided by average common stockholders' equity. (p. 646)

**Stock dividend** A pro rata distribution of the corporation's own stock to stockholders. (p. 638).

**Stockholders' equity statement** A statement that shows the changes in each stockholders' equity account and in total stockholders' equity during the year. (p. 646).

**Stock split** The issuance of additional shares of stock to stockholders according to their percentage ownership, accompanied by a reduction in the par or stated value per share. (p. 640).

# APPENDIX  STOCKHOLDERS' EQUITY STATEMENT

**7**

**STUDY OBJECTIVE**

Describe the use and content of the stockholders' equity statement.

When balance sheets and income statements are presented by a corporation, changes in the separate accounts comprising stockholders' equity should also be disclosed. Disclosure of such changes is necessary to make the financial statements sufficiently informative for users. The disclosures may be made in an additional statement or in the notes to the financial statements.

Many corporations make the disclosures in a stockholders' equity statement. The statement shows the changes in **each** stockholders' equity account and in **total** stockholders' equity during the year. As shown in Illustration 15A-1 the stockholders' equity statement is prepared in columnar form, with columns for each account and for total stockholders' equity. The transactions are then identified and their effects are shown in the appropriate columns.

In practice, additional columns are usually provided to show the number of shares of issued stock and treasury stock. The stockholders' equity statement for Kellogg Company, for a three-year period, is shown in Appendix A. **When this statement is presented, a retained earnings statement is not necessary** because the retained earnings column explains the changes in this account.

**ILLUSTRATION 15A-1**

*Stockholders' equity statement*

| | Common Stock ($5 Par) | Paid-in Capital in Excess of Par | Retained Earnings | Treasury Stock | Total |
|---|---|---|---|---|---|
| **HAMPTON CORPORATION** Stockholders' Equity Statement For the Year Ended December 31, 1999 | | | | | |
| Balance January 1 | $300,000 | $200,000 | $650,000 | $(34,000) | $1,116,000 |
| Issued 5,000 shares of common stock at $15 | 25,000 | 50,000 | | | 75,000 |
| Declared a $40,000 cash dividend | | | (40,000) | | (40,000) |
| Purchased 2,000 shares for treasury at $16 | | | | (32,000) | (32,000) |
| Net income for year | | | 240,000 | | 240,000 |
| Balance December 31 | $325,000 | $250,000 | $850,000 | $(66,000) | $1,359,000 |

# SUMMARY OF STUDY OBJECTIVE FOR APPENDIX

**7. Describe the use and content of the stockholders' equity statement.** Corporations must disclose changes in stockholders' equity accounts and may choose to do so by issuing a separate stockholders' equity statement. This statement, prepared in columnar form, shows changes in each stockholders' equity account and in total stockholders' equity during the accounting period. When this statement is presented, a retained earnings statement is not necessary.

*Note: All asterisked Questions, Exercises, and Problems relate to material in the appendix to the chapter.

# SELF-STUDY QUESTIONS

Answers are at the end of the chapter.

(SO 1)  1. Entries for cash dividends are required on the:
  a. declaration date and the payment date.
  b. record date and the payment date.
  c. declaration date, record date, and payment date.
  d. declaration date and the record date.

(SO 1)  2. Which of the following statements about small stock dividends is true?
  a. A debit to Retained Earnings for the par value of the shares issued should be made.
  b. A stock dividend decreases total stockholders' equity.
  c. Market value per share should be assigned to the dividend shares.
  d. A stock dividend ordinarily will have no effect on book value per share of stock.

(SO 2)  3. All *but one* of the following is reported in a retained earnings statement. The exception is:
  a. cash and stock dividends.
  b. net income and net loss.
  c. some disposals of treasury stock below cost.
  d. sales of treasury stock above cost.

(SO 2)  4. A prior period adjustment is:
  a. reported in the income statement as a nontypical item.
  b. a correction of an error that is made directly to retained earnings.
  c. reported directly in the stockholders' equity section.
  d. reported in the retained earnings statement as an adjustment of the ending balance of retained earnings.

(SO 3)  5. In the stockholders' equity section, Stock Dividends Distributable is reported as a(an):
  a. deduction from total paid-in capital and retained earnings.
  b. addition in additional paid-in capital.
  c. deduction from retained earnings.
  d. addition in capital stock.

(SO 4)  6. Corporation income statements may be the same as the income statements for unincorporated companies *except* for:
  a. gross profit.
  b. income tax expense.
  c. operating income.
  d. net sales.

7. The return on common stockholders' equity is defined (SO 3) as:
  a. Net income divided by total assets.
  b. Cash dividends divided by average common stockholders' equity.
  c. Income available to common stockholders divided by average common stockholders' equity.
  d. None of these is correct.

8. In reporting discontinued operations, the income state- (SO 5) ment should show in a special section:
  a. gains and losses on the disposal of the discontinued segment.
  b. gains and losses from operations of the discontinued segment.
  c. Both (a) and (b).
  d. Neither (a) nor (b).

9. The Rand Corporation has income before taxes of (SO 5) $400,000 and an extraordinary loss of $100,000. If the income tax rate is 25% on all items, the income statement should show income before extraordinary items and extraordinary items, respectively, of:
  a. $325,000 and $100,000.
  b. $325,000 and $75,000.
  c. $300,000 and $100,000.
  d. $300,000 and $75,000.

10. The income statement for Nadeen, Inc., shows income (SO 6) before income taxes $700,000, income tax expense $210,000, and net income $490,000. If Nadeen has 100,000 shares of common stock outstanding throughout the year, earnings per share is:
  a. $7.00.
  b. $4.90.
  c. $2.10.
  d. no correct answer given.

*11. When a stockholders' equity statement is presented, it (SO 7) is not necessary to prepare a(an):
  a. retained earnings statement.
  b. balance sheet.
  c. income statement.
  d. All of the above must be prepared.

THE NAVIGATOR

# QUESTIONS

1. (a) What is a dividend? (b) "Dividends must be paid in cash." Do you agree? Explain.

2. Ruth Hoadley maintains that adequate cash is the only requirement for the declaration of a cash dividend. Is Ruth correct? Explain.

3. (a) Three dates are important in connection with cash dividends. Identify the dates and explain their significance to the corporation and its stockholders.
   (b) Identify the accounting entries that are made for a cash dividend and the date of each entry.

4. Null Inc. declares a $40,000 cash dividend on December 31, 1999. The required annual dividend on preferred stock is $12,000. Determine the allocation of the dividend to preferred and common stockholders assuming the preferred stock is cumulative and dividends are one year in arrears.

5. Contrast the effects of a cash dividend and a stock dividend on a corporation's balance sheet.

6. Laura Fultz asks, "Since stock dividends don't change anything, why declare them?" What is your answer to Laura?

7. Juno Corporation has 20,000 shares of $10 par value common stock outstanding when they announce a 2-for-1 split. Before the split, the stock had a market price of $140 per share. After the split, how many shares of stock will be outstanding, and what will be the approximate market price per share?

8. The board of directors is considering a stock split or a stock dividend. They understand that total stockholders' equity will remain the same under either action. However, they are not sure of the different effects of the two types of actions on other aspects of stockholders' equity. Explain the differences to the directors.

9. What is a prior period adjustment, and how is it reported in the financial statements?

10. ABC Corporation has a retained earnings balance of $210,000 on January 1. During the year, a prior period adjustment of $90,000 is recorded because of the understatement of depreciation in the prior period. Show the retained earnings statement presentation of these data.

11. What is the purpose of a retained earnings restriction? Identify the possible causes of retained earnings restrictions.

12. How are retained earnings restrictions generally reported in the financial statements?

13. Identify the events that result in credits and debits to retained earnings.

14. Ping Liu believes that both the beginning and ending balances in retained earnings are shown in the stockholders' equity section. Is Ping correct? Discuss.

15. Helen Louk, who owns many investments in common stock, says, "I don't care what a company's net income is. The balance sheet tells me everything I need to know!" How do you respond to Helen?

16. What is the unique feature of a corporation income statement? Illustrate this feature, using assumed data.

17. Why is it important to report discontinued operations separately from income from continuing operations?

18. You are considering investing in Alou Transportation, which reports 1999 earnings per share of $6.50 on income before extraordinary items and $4.75 on net income. Which EPS figure would you consider more relevant to your investment decision? Why?

19. Gray Inc. reported 1998 earnings per share of $3.20 and had no extraordinary items. In 1999, EPS on income before extraordinary items was $2.99, and EPS on net income was $3.49. Is this a favorable trend?

20. Indicate which of the following items would be reported as an extraordinary item in Embry Corporation's income statement.
    (a) Loss from damages caused by volcano eruption.
    (b) Loss from sale of temporary investments.
    (c) Loss attributable to a labor strike.
    (d) Loss caused when manufacture of a product was prohibited by the Food and Drug Administration.
    (e) Loss from flood damage. (The nearby Black River floods every two to three years.)
    (f) Write-down of obsolete inventory.
    (g) Expropriation of a factory by a foreign government.

21. When studying for an accounting test, a fellow student says, "Changes in accounting principle are reported in the retained earnings statement." Is your friend correct, or should he study harder?

22. Why must preferred stock dividends be subtracted from net income in computing earnings per share?

*23. What is the purpose of a stockholders' equity statement?

# BRIEF EXERCISES

*Prepare entries for a cash dividend.*
(SO 1)

**BE15–1** The Giles Corporation has 20,000 shares of common stock outstanding. It declares a $2 per share cash dividend on November 1 to stockholders of record on December 1. The dividend is paid on December 31. Prepare the entries on the appropriate dates to record the declaration and payment of the cash dividend.

**BE15–2**  Romano Corporation has 80,000 shares of $10 par value common stock outstanding. It declares a 10% stock dividend on December 1 when the market value per share is $15. The dividend shares are issued on December 31. Prepare the entries for the declaration and payment of the stock dividend.

*Prepare entries for a stock dividend.*
*(SO 1)*

**BE15–3**  The stockholders' equity section of Herrera Corporation consists of common stock ($10 par) $1,000,000 and retained earnings $300,000. A 10% stock dividend (10,000 shares) is declared when the market value per share is $16. Show the before and after effects of the dividend on (a) the components of stockholders' equity, (b) shares outstanding, and (c) book value per share.

*Show before and after effects of a stock dividend.*
*(SO 1)*

**BE15–4**  For the year ending December 31, 1999, Fritz Inc. reports net income $162,000 and dividends $85,000. Prepare the retained earnings statement for the year assuming the balance in retained earnings on January 1, 1999, was $220,000.

*Prepare a retained earnings statement.*
*(SO 2)*

**BE15–5**  Tara Corporation reported net income of $170,000, declared dividends on common stock of $50,000, and had an ending balance in retained earnings of $360,000. Stockholders' equity was $700,000 at the beginning of the year and $800,000 at the end of the year. Compute the return on common stockholders' equity.

*Compute return on common stockholders' equity.*
*(SO 3)*

**BE15–6**  An inexperienced accountant for Ervay Corporation showed the following in the income statement: Income before income taxes and extraordinary item is $300,000, and Extraordinary loss from flood (before taxes) is $70,000. The extraordinary loss and taxable income are both subject to a 30% tax rate. Prepare a correct income statement.

*Prepare income statement including extraordinary items.*
*(SO 5)*

**BE15–7**  On June 30, Ingram Corporation discontinued its operations in Mexico. During the year, the operating loss was $300,000 before taxes. On September 1, Ingram disposed of the Mexico facility at a pretax loss of $160,000. The applicable tax rate is 30%. Show the discontinued operations section of the income statement.

*Prepare discontinued operations section of income statement.*
*(SO 5)*

**BE15–8**  On January 1, 1999, Jimenez Inc., changed from the straight-line method of depreciation to the declining-balance method. The cumulative effect of the change was to increase prior years' depreciation by $60,000 and 1999 depreciation by $8,000. Show the change in accounting principle section of the 1999 income statement, assuming the tax rate is 30%.

*Prepare change in accounting principle section of income statement.*
*(SO 5)*

**BE15–9**  Klumpe Corporation's income statement shows: Income from continuing operations $580,000, Loss from discontinued operations $200,000, Extraordinary loss $90,000, and Cumulative effect of a change in accounting principle that increases net income $30,000. Show the earnings per share data in the income statement, assuming there are 100,000 shares of common stock outstanding at December 31.

*Show earnings per share data in income statement.*
*(SO 6)*

**BE15–10**  Lumley Corporation reports net income of $360,000 and a weighted average of 200,000 shares of common stock outstanding for the year. Compute the earnings per share of common stock.

*Compute earnings per share.*
*(SO 6)*

**BE15–11**  Income and common stock data for Lumley Corporation are presented in BE15–10. Assume also that Lumley has cumulative preferred stock dividends for the current year of $20,000 that were declared and paid. Compute the earnings per share of common stock.

*Compute earnings per share with cumulative preferred stock.*
*(SO 6)*

**\*BE15–12**  On January 1, 1999, MaGee Corporation had the following stockholders' equity balances: Common Stock $200,000, Paid-in Capital in Excess of Stated Value $300,000, and Retained Earnings $250,000. During 1999, it earned net income of $90,000 and declared a cash dividend of $30,000. Prepare a stockholders' equity statement for the year.

*Prepare stockholders' equity statement.*
*(SO 7)*

# EXERCISES

**E15–1**  On January 1, Neill Corporation had 75,000 shares of no-par common stock issued and outstanding. The stock has a stated value of $5 per share. During the year, the following occurred:

Apr.  1   Issued 15,000 additional shares of common stock.
June 15   Declared a cash dividend of $1 per share to stockholders of record on June 30.
July 10   Paid the $1 cash dividend.
Dec.  1   Issued 2,000 additional shares of common stock.
     15   Declared a cash dividend on outstanding shares of $1.50 per share to stockholders of record on December 31.

*Journalize cash dividends and indicate statement presentation.*
*(SO 1)*

*Instructions*
(a) Prepare the entries, if any, on each of the three dividend dates.
(b) How are dividends and dividends payable reported in the financial statements prepared at December 31?

*Allocate cash dividends to preferred and common stock.*
*(SO 1)*

**E15–2** The Orear Corporation was organized on January 1, 1998. During its first year, the corporation issued 2,000 shares of $50 par value preferred stock and 100,000 shares of $10 par value common stock. At December 31, the company declared the following cash dividends: 1998 $6,000, 1999 $12,000, and 2000 $28,000.

*Instructions*
(a) Show the allocation of dividends to each class of stock, assuming the preferred stock dividend is 8% and not cumulative.
(b) Show the allocation of dividends to each class of stock assuming the preferred stock dividend is 10% and cumulative.
(c) Journalize the declaration of the cash dividend at December 31, 2000, under part (b).

*Journalize stock dividends.*
*(SO 1)*

**E15–3** On January 1, 1999, Panek Corporation had $1,000,000 of common stock outstanding that was issued at par and retained earnings of $750,000. The company issued 50,000 shares of common stock at par on July 1 and earned net income of $400,000 for the year.

*Instructions*
Journalize the declaration of a 10% stock dividend on December 10, 1999, for the following independent assumptions:
1. Par value is $10 and market value is $16.
2. Par value is $5 and market value is $20.

*Compare effects of a stock dividend and a stock split.*
*(SO 1)*

**E15–4** On October 31, the stockholders' equity section of Rathke Company consists of Common stock $800,000 and Retained earnings $1,000,000. Rathke is considering the following two courses of action: (1) declaring a 10% stock dividend on the 80,000 $10 par value shares outstanding or (2) effecting a 2-for-1 stock split that will reduce par value to $5 per share. The current market price is $14 per share.

*Instructions*
Prepare a tabular summary of the effects of the alternative actions on the components of stockholders' equity, outstanding shares, and book value per share. Use the following column headings: Before Action, After Stock Dividend, and After Stock Split.

*Compute book value per share and indicate account balances after a stock dividend.*
*(SO 1, 3)*

**E15–5** On October 1, Savino Corporation's stockholders' equity is as follows:

| | |
|---|---|
| Common stock $10 par value | $200,000 |
| Paid-in capital in excess of par value | 25,000 |
| Retained earnings | 75,000 |
| Total stockholders' equity | $300,000 |

On October 1, Savino declares and distributes a 10% stock dividend when the market value of the stock is $18 per share.

*Instructions*
(a) Compute the book value per share (1) before the stock dividend and (2) after the stock dividend. (Round to two decimals.)
(b) Indicate the balances in the three stockholders' equity accounts after the stock dividend shares have been distributed.

*Indicate the effects on stockholders' equity components.*
*(SO 1, 2, 3)*

**E15–6** During 1999, Toso Corporation had the following transactions and events:
1. Declared a cash dividend.
2. Issued par value common stock for cash at par value.
3. Completed a 3-for-1 stock split in which $15 par value stock was changed to $5 par value stock.
4. Declared a stock dividend when the market value was higher than par value.
5. Made a prior period adjustment for overstatement of net income.
6. Issued the shares of common stock required by the stock dividend declaration in no. 4 above.
7. Paid the cash dividend in no. 1 above.
8. Issued par value common stock for cash above par value.

## Instructions
Indicate the effect(s) of each of the foregoing items on the subdivisions of stockholders' equity. Present your answer in tabular form with the following columns. Use (I) for increase, (D) for decrease, and (NE) for no effect. Item 1 is given as an example.

| | Paid-in Capital | | |
| | Capital | | Retained |
| Item | Stock | Additional | Earnings |
| --- | --- | --- | --- |
| 1. | NE | NE | D |

**E15–7**   Before preparing financial statements for the current year, the chief accountant for O'Dell Company discovered the following errors in the accounts:

*Prepare correcting entries for dividends and a stock split.*
*(SO 1)*

1. The declaration and payment of $25,000 cash dividend was recorded as a debit to Interest Expense $25,000 and a credit to Cash $25,000.
2. A 10% stock dividend (1,000 shares) was declared on the $10 par value stock when the market value per share was $14. The only entry made was: Retained Earnings (Dr.) $10,000 and Dividend Payable (Cr.) $10,000. The shares have not been issued.
3. A 4-for-1 stock split involving the issue of 400,000 shares of $5 par value common stock for 100,000 shares of $20 par value common stock was recorded as a debit to Retained Earnings $2,000,000 and a credit to Common Stock $2,000,000.

## Instructions
Prepare the correcting entries at December 31.

**E15–8**   On January 1, 1999, Mayes Corporation had Retained Earnings of $550,000. During the year, Mayes had the following selected transactions:

*Prepare a retained earnings statement.*
*(SO 2)*

1. Declared cash dividends $120,000.
2. Corrected overstatement of 1998 net income because of depreciation error $20,000.
3. Earned net income $310,000.
4. Declared stock dividends $60,000.

## Instructions
Prepare a retained earnings statement for the year.

**E15–9**   The following accounts appear in the ledger of Osaki Inc. after the books are closed at December 31.

*Prepare a stockholders' equity section.*
*(SO 3)*

| | |
| --- | --- |
| Common Stock, no par, $1 stated value, 400,000 shares authorized; | |
| 300,000 shares issued | $ 300,000 |
| Common Stock Dividends Distributable | 75,000 |
| Paid-in Capital in Excess of Stated Value—Common Stock | 1,200,000 |
| Preferred Stock, $5 par value, 8%, 40,000 shares authorized; | |
| 30,000 shares issued | 150,000 |
| Retained Earnings | 700,000 |
| Treasury Stock (10,000 common shares) | 60,000 |
| Paid-in Capital in Excess of Par Value—Preferred Stock | 244,000 |

## Instructions
Prepare stockholders' equity section at December 31, assuming retained earnings is restricted for plant expansion in the amount of $100,000.

**E15–10**   This financial information is available for Mary Jo Corporation:

*Calculate ratios to evaluate earnings performance.*
*(SO 3, 6)*

| | 1999 | 1998 |
| --- | --- | --- |
| Average common stockholders' equity | $1,200,000 | $900,000 |
| Dividends paid to common stockholders | 50,000 | 30,000 |
| Dividends paid to preferred stockholders | 10,000 | 10,000 |
| Net income | 200,000 | 140,000 |
| Market price of common stock | 20 | 15 |

The weighted average number of shares of common stock outstanding was 80,000 for 1998 and 100,000 for 1999.

## Instructions
Calculate earnings per share and return on common stockholders' equity for 1999 and 1998.

*Calculate ratios to evaluate earnings performance.*
*(SO 3, 6)*

**E15–11**   This financial information is available for Fountain City Corporation:

|  | 1999 | 1998 |
|---|---|---|
| Average common stockholders' equity | $1,800,000 | $1,900,000 |
| Dividends paid to common stockholders | 90,000 | 70,000 |
| Dividends paid to preferred stockholders | 10,000 | 15,000 |
| Net income | 230,000 | 180,000 |
| Market price of common stock | 20 | 25 |

The weighted number of shares of common stock outstanding was 180,000 for 1998 and 150,000 for 1999.

*Instructions*
Calculate earnings per share and return on common stockholders' equity for 1999 and 1998.

*Prepare a correct income statement.*
*(SO 4, 5)*

**E15–12**   For its fiscal year ending October 31, 1999, Lorenz Corporation reports the following partial data:

| | |
|---|---|
| Income before income taxes | $640,000 |
| Income tax expense (30% × $550,000) | 165,000 |
| Income before extraordinary items | 475,000 |
| Extraordinary loss from fire | 90,000 |
| Net income | $385,000 |

The fire loss is considered an extraordinary item. The income tax rate is 30% on all items.

*Instructions*
(a) Prepare a correct income statement, beginning with income before income taxes.
(b) ▭▭▭▶ Explain in memo form why the income statement data are misleading.

*Prepare income statement.*
*(SO 4, 5)*

**E15–13**   Kelso Corporation has income from continuing operations of $240,000 for the year ended December 31, 1999. It also has the following items (before considering income taxes): (1) an extraordinary fire loss of $80,000, (2) a gain of $50,000 on the discontinuance of a division, (3) a cumulative change in an accounting principle that resulted in an increase in prior years' depreciation of $30,000, and (4) a correction of an error in last year's financial statements that resulted in a $20,000 understatement of 1998 net income. Assume all items are subject to income taxes at a 30% tax rate.

*Instructions*
(a) Prepare an income statement, beginning with income from continuing operations.
(b) Indicate the statement presentation of any item not included in (a) above.

*Compute earnings per share under different assumptions.*
*(SO 6)*

**E15–14**   At December 31, 1999, Heimer Corporation has 2,000 shares of $100 par value, 8%, preferred stock outstanding and 100,000 shares of $10 par value common stock issued. Heimer's net income for the year is $500,000.

*Instructions*
Compute the earnings per share of common stock under the following independent situations. (Round to two decimals.)

1. The dividend to preferred stockholders was declared, and there has been no change in the number of shares of common stock outstanding during the year.
2. The dividend to preferred stockholders was not declared. The preferred stock is cumulative. Heimer held 10,000 shares of common treasury stock throughout the year.

*Prepare stockholders' equity statement.*
*(SO 7)*

**\*E15–15**   Jaeger, Inc. has the following stockholders' equity balances at January 1, 1999: Common Stock ($5 par) $600,000, Paid-in Capital in Excess of Par Value $230,000, and Retained Earnings $160,000. In 1999, the following transactions and events occurred:

1. Issued 15,000 additional shares of common stock for $120,000.
2. Declared and paid a cash dividend of $30,000.
3. Net income was $100,000.

*Instructions*
Prepare a stockholders' equity statement for the year ended December 31, 1999.

# PROBLEMS: SET A

**P15–1A**  On January 1, 1999, O'Brien Corporation had the following stockholders' equity accounts:

*Prepare dividend entries and stockholders' equity section.*
*(SO 1, 3)*

| | |
|---|---:|
| Common Stock ($10 par value, 80,000 shares issued and outstanding) | $800,000 |
| Paid-in Capital in Excess of Par Value | 200,000 |
| Retained Earnings | 540,000 |

During the year, the following transactions occurred:

Jan. 15  Declared a $1 cash dividend per share to stockholders of record on January 31, payable February 15.

Feb. 15  Paid the dividend declared in January.

Apr. 15  Declared a 10% stock dividend to stockholders of record on April 30, distributable May 15. On April 15, the market price of the stock was $13 per share.

May 15  Issued the shares for the stock dividend.

July  1  Announced a 2-for-1 stock split. The market price per share prior to the announcement was $15. (The new par value is $5.)

Dec.  1  Declared a $.50 per share cash dividend to stockholders of record on December 15, payable January 10, 2000.

   31  Determined that net income for the year was $250,000.

**Instructions**

(a) Journalize the transactions and the closing entry for net income.

(b) Enter the beginning balances and post the entries to the stockholders' equity accounts. (*Note:* Open additional stockholders' equity accounts as needed.)

(c) Prepare a stockholders' equity section at December 31.

**P15–2A**  The stockholders' equity accounts of Rodriguez, Inc., at January 1, 1999, are as follows:

*Journalize and post transactions, and prepare retained earnings statement and stockholders' equity section.*
*(SO 1, 2, 3)*

| | |
|---|---:|
| Preferred Stock, $100 par, 9% | $400,000 |
| Common Stock, $5 par | 900,000 |
| Paid-in Capital in Excess of Par Value—Preferred Stock | 100,000 |
| Paid-in Capital in Excess of Par Value—Common Stock | 200,000 |
| Retained Earnings | 500,000 |

During 1999, the company had the following transactions and events:

July  1  Declared a $.50 cash dividend on common stock.

Aug.  1  Discovered a $72,000 overstatement of 1998 depreciation. Ignore income taxes.

Sept. 1  Paid the cash dividend declared on July 1.

Dec.  1  Declared a 10% stock dividend on common stock when the market value of the stock was $12 per share.

   15  Declared a 9% cash dividend on preferred stock payable January 31, 2000.

   31  Determined that net income for the year was $350,000.

**Instructions**

(a) Journalize the transactions and the closing entry for net income.

(b) Enter the beginning balances in the accounts and post to the stockholders' equity accounts. (*Note:* Open additional stockholders' equity accounts as needed.)

(c) Prepare a retained earnings statement for the year.

(d) Prepare a stockholders' equity section at December 31, 1999.

**P15–3A**  The ledger of Quandt Corporation at December 31, 1999, after the books have been closed, contains the following stockholders' equity accounts:

*Prepare retained earnings statement and stockholders' equity section, and compute earnings per share.*
*(SO 1, 2, 3, 6)*

| | |
|---|---:|
| Preferred Stock (10,000 shares issued) | $1,000,000 |
| Common Stock (400,000 shares issued) | 2,000,000 |
| Paid-in Capital in Excess of Par Value—Preferred | 200,000 |
| Paid-in Capital in Excess of Par Value—Common | 1,200,000 |
| Common Stock Dividends Distributable | 100,000 |
| Retained Earnings | 2,340,000 |

A review of the accounting records reveals the following:

1. No errors have been made in recording 1999 transactions or in preparing the closing entry for net income.
2. Preferred stock is 10% $100 par value, noncumulative, and callable at $125. Since January 1, 1998, 10,000 shares have been outstanding; 20,000 shares are authorized.
3. Common stock is no-par with a stated value of $5 per share; 600,000 shares are authorized.
4. The January 1 balance in Retained Earnings was $2,200,000.
5. On October 1, 100,000 shares of common stock were sold for cash at $8 per share.
6. A cash dividend of $600,000 was declared and properly allocated to preferred and common stock on November 1. No dividends were paid to preferred stockholders in 1998.
7. On December 31, a 5% common stock dividend was declared out of retained earnings on common stock when the market price per share was $7.
8. Net income for the year was $880,000.
9. On December 31, 1999, the directors authorized disclosure of a $100,000 restriction of retained earnings for plant expansion. (Use Note A.)

**Instructions**
(a) Reproduce the retained earnings account (T-account) for the year.
(b) Prepare a retained earnings statement for the year.
(c) Prepare a stockholders' equity section at December 31.
(d) Compute the earnings per share of common stock using 325,000 as the weighted average shares outstanding for the year.
(e) Compute the allocation of the cash dividend to preferred and common stock.

*Prepare income statement with discontinued operations and an extraordinary loss, and compute earnings per share.*
*(SO 4, 5, 6)*

**P15–4A** Patel Corporation owns a number of travel agencies and a chain of motels in the Northwest. Its condensed operating results for 1999 show the following:

| | |
|---|---|
| Operating revenues | $14,580,000 |
| Operating expenses | 10,600,000 |
| Income from operations | $ 3,980,000 |

An additional analysis of the data indicate that the travel agencies are very profitable but the motel chain has been unprofitable. Through September 30, the motels lost $500,000 from operating revenues of $4,200,000 and operating expenses of $4,700,000. On October 1, the motel operation was discontinued and sold at a loss of $1,000,000 before taxes. The motel operating results are included in income from operations, but the loss on disposal is not included in the operating results shown above. During the year, the corporation had other expenses and losses of $80,000, which are not included in the operating results. In November, a condemnation action was taken against the company to obtain property for a new national park. As a result, the corporation suffered an extraordinary loss of $800,000 before taxes which is not included in the operating results. The corporation is in a 30% tax bracket.

**Instructions**
(a) Prepare a condensed income statement for the year.
(b) Compute all of the earnings per share amounts that should appear on the income statement. Assume weighted average shares of stock equaled 400,000. (Round to two decimals.)

*Prepare expanded income statement, and compute earnings per share data.*
*(SO 4, 5, 6)*

**P15–5A** The ledger of Mesa Corporation at December 31, 1999, contains the following summary data:

| | | | |
|---|---|---|---|
| Net sales | $1,500,000 | Cost of goods sold | $800,000 |
| Selling expenses | 110,000 | Administrative expenses | 140,000 |
| Other revenues and gains | 40,000 | Other expenses and losses | 30,000 |

Your analysis reveals the following additional information that is not included in the above data.

1. The entire ceramics division was discontinued on August 31. The loss from operations for this division before income taxes was $150,000. The ceramics division was sold at a gain of $60,000 before income taxes.
2. On July 12, a fire occurred in one plant that resulted in an extraordinary loss of $90,000 before income taxes.

3. During the year, Mesa changed its depreciation method from straight-line to declining balance. The cumulative effect of the change on prior years' net income was a decrease of $30,000 before taxes. (Assume that depreciation under the new method is correctly included in the ledger data.)

4. The income tax rate on all items is 30%.

*Instructions*

(a) Prepare an income statement for the year ended December 31, 1999, using the format illustrated in the Demonstration Problem (p. 656).

(b) Prepare the earnings per share data that should appear in the income statement, assuming there were 100,000 shares of common stock outstanding throughout the year.

**\*P15–6A**  On January 1, 1999, Leiker Inc. had the following stockholders' equity balances:

*Prepare stockholders' equity statement.*
*(SO 7)*

| | |
|---|---|
| Common Stock (500,000 shares issued) | $1,000,000 |
| Paid-in Capital in Excess of Par Value | 500,000 |
| Stock Dividends Distributable | 100,000 |
| Retained Earnings | 600,000 |

During 1999, the following transactions and events occurred:

1. Issued 50,000 shares of $2 par value common stock as a result of 10% stock dividend declared on December 15, 1998.
2. Issued 40,000 shares of common stock for cash at $5 per share.
3. Purchased 20,000 shares of common stock for the treasury at $6 per share.
4. Declared and paid a cash dividend of $100,000.
5. Sold 5,000 shares of treasury stock for cash at $6 per share.
6. Earned net income of $300,000.

*Instructions*

Prepare a stockholders' equity statement for the year.

# PROBLEMS: SET B

**P15–1B**  On January 1, 1999, Stengel Corporation had the following stockholders' equity accounts:

*Prepare dividend entries and stockholders' equity section.*
*(SO 1, 3)*

| | |
|---|---|
| Common Stock ($20 par value, 60,000 shares issued and outstanding) | $1,200,000 |
| Paid-in Capital in Excess of Par Value | 200,000 |
| Retained Earnings | 600,000 |

During the year, the following transactions occurred:

Feb.  1  Declared a $1 cash dividend per share to stockholders of record on February 15, payable March 1.

Mar.  1  Paid the dividend declared in February.

Apr.  1  Announced a 4-for-1 stock split. Prior to the split, the market price per share was $36.

July  1  Declared a 5% stock dividend to stockholders of record on July 15, distributable July 31. On July 1, the market price of the stock was $13 per share.

    31  Issued the shares for the stock dividend.

Dec.  1  Declared a $.50 per share dividend to stockholders of record on December 15, payable January 5, 2000.

    31  Determined that net income for the year was $350,000.

*Instructions*

(a) Journalize the transactions and the closing entry for net income.

(b) Enter the beginning balances and post the entries to the stockholders' equity accounts. (*Note:* Open additional stockholders' equity accounts as needed.)

(c) Prepare a stockholders' equity section at December 31.

*Journalize and post transactions, and prepare retained earnings statement and stockholders' equity section.*
*(SO 1, 2, 3)*

**P15–2B**  The stockholders' equity accounts of Fryman Company at January 1, 1999, are as follows:

| Preferred Stock, 9%, $50 par | $300,000 |
| --- | --- |
| Common Stock, $2 par | 500,000 |
| Paid-in Capital in Excess of Par Value—Preferred Stock | 200,000 |
| Paid-in Capital in Excess of Par Value—Common Stock | 300,000 |
| Retained Earnings | 600,000 |

During 1999, the company had the following transactions and events:

July  1  Declared a $.50 cash dividend on common stock.

Aug.  1  Discovered $45,000 understatement of 1998 depreciation. Ignore income taxes.

Sept. 1  Paid the cash dividend declared on July 1.

Dec.  1  Declared 10% stock dividend on common stock when the market value of the stock was $18 per share.

15  Declared a 9% cash dividend on preferred stock payable January 15, 2000.

31  Determined that net income for the year was $385,000.

31  Recognized a $200,000 restriction of retained earnings for plant expansion.

*Instructions*
 (a) Journalize the transactions, events, and closing entries.
 (b) Enter the beginning balances in the accounts and post to the stockholders' equity accounts. (*Note:* Open additional stockholders' equity accounts as needed.)
 (c) Prepare a retained earnings statement for the year.
 (d) Prepare a stockholders' equity section at December 31, 1999.

*Prepare retained earnings statement and stockholders' equity section, and compute earnings per share.*
*(SO 1, 2, 3, 6)*

**P15–3B**   The post-closing trial balance of Javier Corporation at December 31, 1999, contains the following stockholders' equity accounts:

| Preferred Stock (15,000 shares issued) | $  750,000 |
| --- | --- |
| Common Stock (250,000 shares issued) | 2,500,000 |
| Paid-in Capital in Excess of Par Value—Preferred | 250,000 |
| Paid-in Capital in Excess of Par Value—Common | 500,000 |
| Common Stock Dividends Distributable | 200,000 |
| Retained Earnings | 803,000 |

A review of the accounting records reveals the following:

1. No errors have been made in recording 1999 transactions or in preparing the closing entry for net income.
2. Preferred stock is $50 par, 10%, and cumulative. 15,000 shares have been outstanding since January 1, 1998.
3. Authorized stock is 20,000 shares of preferred, 500,000 shares of common with a $10 par value.
4. The January 1 balance in Retained Earnings was $920,000.
5. On July 1, 20,000 shares of common stock were sold for cash at $16 per share.
6. On September 1, the company discovered an understatement error of $60,000 in computing depreciation in 1998. The net of tax effect of $42,000 was properly debited directly to Retained Earnings.
7. A cash dividend of $250,000 was declared and properly allocated to preferred and common stock on October 1. No dividends were paid to preferred stockholders in 1998.
8. On December 31, an 8% common stock dividend was declared out of retained earnings on common stock when the market price per share was $16.
9. Net income for the year was $495,000.
10. On December 31, 1999, the directors authorized disclosure of a $200,000 restriction of retained earnings for plant expansion. (Use Note X.)

*Instructions*
 (a) Reproduce the retained earnings account for the year.
 (b) Prepare a retained earnings statement for the year.
 (c) Prepare a stockholders' equity section at December 31.
 (d) Compute the earnings per share of common stock using 240,000 as the weighted average shares outstanding for the year.
 (e) Compute the allocation of the cash dividend to preferred and common stock.

**P15–4B**  Lau Corporation owns a number of cruise ships and a chain of hotels. The hotels, which have not been profitable, were discontinued on September 1, 1999. The 1999 operating results for the company were as follows:

*Prepare income statement with discontinued operations and extraordinary loss, and compute earnings per share.*
*(SO 4, 5, 6)*

| Operating revenues | $12,600,000 |
|---|---|
| Operating expenses | 8,600,000 |
| Operating income | $ 4,000,000 |

Analysis discloses that these data include the operating results of the hotel chain, which were: operating revenues $3,000,000 and operating expenses $4,000,000. The hotels were sold at a gain of $500,000 before taxes. This gain is not included in the operating results. During the year, Lau suffered an extraordinary fire loss of $800,000 before taxes which is not included in the operating results. In 1999, the company had other revenues and gains of $100,000, which are not included in the operating results. The corporation is in the 30% income tax bracket.

**Instructions**
(a)  Prepare a condensed income statement.
(b)  Compute the earnings per share data that should appear in the income statement. Assume weighted average shares of stock equaled 440,000. (Round to two decimals.)

**P15–5B**  The ledger of Yevak Corporation at December 31, 1999, contains the following summary data:

*Prepare income statement with nontypical items, and compute earnings per share data.*
*(SO 4, 5, 6)*

| Net sales | $1,800,000 | Cost of goods sold | $1,000,000 |
|---|---|---|---|
| Selling expenses | 120,000 | Administrative expenses | 130,000 |
| Other revenues and gains | 20,000 | Other expenses and losses | 28,000 |

Your analysis reveals the following additional information that is not included in the above data.

1. The entire puzzles division was discontinued on August 31. The gain from operations for this division before income taxes was $50,000. The puzzles division was sold at a loss of $70,000 before income taxes.
2. On May 15, company property was expropriated for an interstate highway. The settlement resulted in an extraordinary gain of $90,000 before income taxes.
3. During the year, Yevak changed its depreciation method from double-declining balance to straight-line. The cumulative effect of the change on prior years' net income was an increase of $60,000 before taxes. (Assume that depreciation under the new method is correctly included in the ledger data.)
4. The income tax rate on all items is 30%.

**Instructions**
(a)  Prepare an income statement for the year ended December 31, 1999, using the format illustrated in the Demonstration Problem (p. 656).
(b)  Prepare the earnings per share data that should appear in the income statement, assuming there were 100,000 shares of common stock outstanding throughout the year.

# BROADENING YOUR PERSPECTIVE

# FINANCIAL REPORTING AND ANALYSIS

**FINANCIAL REPORTING PROBLEM: Kellogg Company**

**BYP15–1**  The financial statements of Kellogg Company are presented in Appendix A.

**Instructions**
Refer to Kellogg's financial statements and answer the following questions:

(a)  What was Kellogg's dividend paid per share in 1997? What was the total dividend paid? What percentage of Kellogg's December 31, 1997, retained earnings did this dividend represent? What percentage of reported net income did this dividend represent? What percentage of cash and cash equivalents did this dividend represent?

(b) Kellogg reported nonrecurring charges in its income statement. What was the nature of these nonrecurring charges in 1997? How did these items differ from discontinued operations?

(c) The Selected Financial Data table in the Management Discussion and Analysis section has a footnote describing accounting changes enacted by Kellogg. In what way does adoption of a new standard affect the ability to analyze Kellogg's results over the past 10 years?

## COMPARATIVE ANALYSIS PROBLEM: Kellogg Company vs. General Mills

**BYP15–2**   Kellogg's financial statements are presented in Appendix A; General Mills's financial statements are presented in Appendix B.

*Instructions*

(a) Compute earnings per share and return on common stockholders' equity for both companies for 1997. Assume Kellogg's weighted average shares were 414,100,000 and General Mills's weighted average shares were 158,200,000. Can these measures be used to compare the profitability of the two companies? Why or why not?

(b) What was the total amount of dividends paid by each company in 1997? What fraction of net income did the dividend represent for each company?

(c) Did either company report one of the three types of irregular items on its income statement? If so, what was the nature of the irregular item?

## RESEARCH ASSIGNMENT

**BYP15–3**   The October 3, 1994, issue of *Barron's* includes an article by Shirley A. Lazo entitled "Split Decision: One Way to Lift Shares."

*Instructions*
Read the article and answer the following questions:

(a) Why might a stock dividend/split have a positive effect on shareholder wealth?

(b) Why might a stock dividend/split have a negative effect on shareholder wealth?

(c) According to the study described in the article, what happens to the stock prices of banks during the month following a stock dividend/split?

(d) What conclusion was drawn from the study?

## INTERPRETING FINANCIAL STATEMENTS: BFGoodrich Company

**BYP15–4**   The BFGoodrich Company is a diversified manufacturer of tires, vinyl products, specialty chemicals, and aerospace products. Selected financial data, in millions of dollars, for a recent two-year period were as follows.

|  | Current Year | Prior Year |
|---|---|---|
| Sales | $2,416.7 | $2,023.5 |
| Total operating income | 298.0 | 200.7 |
| Income from continuing operations | 209.9 | 83.6 |
| Income (loss) from discontinued operations (net of taxes) | (16.9) | (4.4) |
| Extraordinary items (net of taxes) |  | 25.8 |
| Cumulative effect of change in method of accounting for taxes | 2.7 |  |
| Net income | 195.7 | 105.0 |
| Dividends on preferred stock | 8.8 | 9.8 |
| Dividends on common stock | 43.3 | 37.0 |
| Income retained in the business at end of year | 548.9 | 405.3 |

The notes to the company's financial statements indicate that the weighted average number of common shares outstanding (in thousands of shares) were 25,179 for the current year and 23,651 for the prior year. In addition, the stockholders' equity section of the balance sheet shows that at December 31 of the current year there were 25,554,627 shares of common stock issued and 352,396 shares of common stock held in the treasury.

*Instructions*
  (a)  Present the earnings per share data for the company for each year.
  (b)  Comment on the relative importance of material nontypical items in each year.
  (c)  Discuss how you would factor these nontypical items into your prediction of next year's net income for BFGoodrich.
  (d)  Prepare a retained earning statement for the current year.
  (e)  What was the total dividend per share of common stock for the current year?

## REAL-WORLD FOCUS: Diebold, Inc.

**BYP15–5   Diebold, Inc.,** is a world leader in financial self-service transaction systems, security products, and customer service. The company develops, manufactures, sells, and services automated teller machines (ATMs), electronic and physical security systems, and bank facility equipment. It also designs and markets related application software and integrated systems for global financial and commercial markets. Headquartered in Canton, Ohio, Diebold has offices in five countries and manufacturing facilities in the United States and in China.

The following note related to stockholders' equity was recently reported in Diebold's annual report:

### DIEBOLD, INC.
### Notes to the Financial Statements

On February 1, 1994, the Board of Directors declared a 3-for-2 stock split, distributed on February 22, 1994, to shareholders of record on February 10, 1994. Accordingly, all numbers of common shares, except authorized shares and treasury shares, and all per share data have been restated to reflect this stock split in addition to the 3-for-2 stock split declared on January 27, 1993, distributed on February 26, 1993, to shareholders of record on February 10, 1993.

On the basis of amounts declared and paid, the annualized quarterly dividends per share were $0.80 in 1993, $0.75 in 1992, and $0.71 in 1991.

*Instructions*
  (a)  What is the significance of the date of record and the date of distribution?
  (b)  Why might Diebold have declared a 3-for-2 stock split?
  (c)  What impact does Diebold's stock split have on (1) total stockholders' equity; (2) total par value; (3) outstanding shares, and (4) book value per share?

# CRITICAL THINKING
## GROUP DECISION CASE

**BYP15–6**   General Dynamics develops, produces, and supports innovative, reliable, and highly sophisticated military and commercial products. In July of a recent year, the corporation announced that its Quincy Shipbuilding Division (Quincy) will be closed following the completion of the Maritime Prepositioning Ship construction program.

Prior to discontinuance, the operating results of Quincy were net sales $246.8 million, income from operations before income taxes $28.3 million, and income taxes $12.5 million. The corporation's loss on disposition of Quincy was $5.0 million, net of $4.3 million income tax benefits.

From its other operating activities, General Dynamics' financial results were net sales $8,163.8 million, cost of goods sold $6,958.8 million, and selling and administrative expenses $537.0 million. In addition, the corporation had interest expense of $17.2 million and interest revenue of $3.6 million. Income taxes were $282.9 million.

General Dynamics had an average of 42.3 million shares of common stock outstanding during the year.

**Instructions**

With the class divided into groups, answer the following:

(a) Prepare the income statement for the year, assuming that the year ended on December 31, 1999. Show earnings per share data on the income statement. All dollars should be stated in millions, except for per share amounts. (For example, $8 million would be shown as $8.0.)

(b) In the preceding year, Quincy's earnings were $51.6 million before income taxes of $22.8 million. For comparative purposes, General Dynamics reported earnings per share of $0.61 from discontinued operations for Quincy in the preceding year.

    1. What was the average number of common shares outstanding during the preceding year?

    2. If earnings per share from continuing operations was $7.47, what was income from continuing operations during the preceding year? (Round to two decimals.)

## COMMUNICATION ACTIVITY

**BYP15–7**  In the past year, Alameda Corporation declared a 10% stock dividend, and Butte, Inc., announced a 2-for-1 stock split. Your parents own 100 shares of each company's $50 par value common stock. During a recent phone call, your parents ask you, as an accounting student, to explain the difference between the two events.

**Instructions**

Write a letter to your parents that explains the effects of the two events to them as stockholders and the effects of each event on the financial statements of each corporation.

## ETHICS CASE

**BYP15–8**  Flambeau Corporation has paid 60 consecutive quarterly cash dividends (15 years). The last 6 months, however, have been a cash drain on the company, as profit margins have been greatly narrowed by increasing competition. With a cash balance sufficient to meet only day-to-day operating needs, the president, Vince Ramsey, has decided that a stock dividend instead of a cash dividend should be declared. He tells Flambeau's financial vice president, Janice Rahn, to issue a press release stating that the company is extending its consecutive dividend record with the issuance of a 5% stock dividend. "Write the press release convincing the stockholders that the stock dividend is just as good as a cash dividend," he orders. "Just watch our stock rise when we announce the stock dividend; it must be a good thing if that happens."

**Instructions**

(a) Who are the stakeholders in this situation?

(b) Is there anything unethical about Ramsey's intentions or actions?

(c) What is the effect of a stock dividend on a corporation's stockholders' equity accounts? Which would you rather receive as a stockholder—a cash dividend or a stock dividend? Why?

# SURFING THE NET

**BYP15–9**  Use the stockholders' equity section of an annual report and identify the major components.

**Address:** http://www.reportgallery.com

**Steps:**

1. From Report Gallery Homepage, choose **Viewing Library.**
2. Select a particular company.
3. Choose Annual Report.
4. Follow instructions below.

*Instructions*
Answer the following questions:

(a) What is the company's name?
(b) What classes of capital stock has the company issued?
(c) For each class of stock:
   (1) How many shares are authorized, issued, and/or outstanding?
   (2) What is the par value?
(d) What are the company's retained earnings?
(e) Has the company acquired treasury stock? How many shares?

---

*Answers to Self-Study Questions*
1. a    2. c    3. d    4. b    5. d    6. b    7. c    8. c    9. d    10. b    *11. a

---

*Answer to Kellogg Review It Question 3, p. 652*
In its 1997 income statement Kellogg reported a cumulative effect of accounting change.

 **Remember to go back to the Navigator box on the chapter-opening page
and check off your completed work.**

**Before studying this chapter, you should know or, if necessary, review:**

a. What is a long-term liability? a current liability? (Ch. 4, pp. 159–160 and Ch. 11, p. 470).

b. How to record adjusting entries for interest expense and payable. (Ch. 3, pp. 104–105).

c. How to record entries for the issuance of notes payable and related interest expense. (Ch. 11, p. 471).

THE NAVIGATOR

## FEATURE STORY

# UK Builds with Bonds

Every year, hundreds of colleges around the country build new buildings. Where do most schools get the money for these expensive projects? From long-term bonds, which are obligations in which the issuer of the bond promises to repay the loan amount plus interest on or before a specified date.

The University of Kentucky (UK) has issued "revenue" bonds to build buildings on the 23,000-student Lexington campus, and on 14 community colleges throughout the state. These bonds pledge the school's revenues as collateral to guarantee payment of the bonds. At one time the outstanding debt on the Lexington campus buildings was $137 million. The total debt on the community college buildings equaled $121 million. The bonds generally have maturities ranging from 10 to 20 years.

Additional "guarantees" for bond purchasers are the ratings given the bonds by professional rating agencies. "Our bonds are rated AA− by Standard & Poor's Corp.," says Henry Clay Owen, UK's treasurer. "That's well above investment grade," he says. "We always have a very good market for our bonds. People in Kentucky identify very closely with the university. Even though the bonds are rated AA−, they trade at AAA [the top bond rating] because they're so easy to sell."

One advantage for investors: the bonds' interest revenue is exempt from federal income tax and from state tax for in-state investors. So, an issue offering 6% is the equivalent of 10% to those individuals in the top tax bracket. "I would feel very comfortable buying UK bonds because it's inconceivable to me that there would ever be a default," says Owen.

THE NAVIGATOR

# CHAPTER 16

# LONG-TERM LIABILITIES

## THE NAVIGATOR ✔

- ■ Understand *Concepts for Review* ☐
- ■ Read *Feature Story* ☐
- ■ Scan *Study Objectives* ☐
- ■ Read *Preview* ☐
- ■ Read text and answer *Before You Go On*
  p. 681 ☐ p. 688 ☐ p. 691 ☐ p. 697 ☐
- ■ Work *Demonstration Problems* ☐
- ■ Review *Summary of Study Objectives* ☐
- ■ Answer *Self-Study Questions* ☐
- ■ Complete assignments ☐

## STUDY OBJECTIVES

**After studying this chapter, you should be able to:**

1. *Explain why bonds are issued.*
2. *Prepare the entries for the issuance of bonds and interest expense.*
3. *Describe the entries when bonds are redeemed or converted.*
4. *Indicate the entries required for a bond sinking fund.*
5. *Describe the accounting for long-term notes payable.*
6. *Contrast the accounting for operating and capital leases.*
7. *Identify the methods for the presentation and analysis of long-term liabilities.*

THE NAVIGATOR

*A*s you can see from the opening story, the University of Kentucky has chosen to issue long-term bonds to fund its building projects. The UK bonds are classified as long-term liabilities because they are obligations that are expected to be paid after one year. In this chapter we will explain the accounting for the major types of long-term liabilities reported on the balance sheet. These liabilities may be bonds, long-term notes, or lease obligations. The content and organization of the chapter are as follows:

THE
NAVIGATOR

# BOND BASICS

Bonds are a form of interest bearing notes payable issued by corporations, universities, and governmental agencies. Bonds, like common stock, are sold in small denominations (usually a thousand dollars or multiples of a thousand dollars). As a result, bonds attract many investors.

## Why Issue Bonds?

**1**

STUDY
OBJECTIVE
........................
Explain why bonds are
issued.

A corporation may use long-term financing other than bonds, such as notes payable and leasing. However, these other forms of financing involve one individual, one company, or a financial institution. Notes payable and leasing are therefore seldom sufficient to furnish the funds needed for plant expansion and major projects like new buildings. To obtain **large amounts of long-term capital**, corporate management usually must decide whether to issue bonds or to use equity financing (common stock).

From the standpoint of the corporation seeking long-term financing, bonds offer the following advantages over common stock:

**ILLUSTRATION 16-1**

*Advantages of bond financing over common stock*

| Bond Financing | Advantages |
|---|---|
|  | 1. **Stockholder control is not affected.** Bondholders do not have voting rights, so current owners (stockholders) retain full control of the company. |
|  | 2. **Tax savings result.** Bond interest is deductible for tax purposes; dividends on stock are not. |
|  | 3. **Earnings per share on common stock may be higher.** Although bond interest expense reduces net income, earnings per share on common stock often is higher under bond financing because no additional shares of common stock are issued. |

To illustrate the potential effect on earnings per share, assume that Microsystems, Inc., is considering two plans for financing the construction of a new $5 million plant: Plan A involves issuance of 200,000 shares of common stock at the current market price of $25 per share. Plan B involves issuance of $5 million, 12% bonds at face value. Income before interest and taxes on the new plant will be $1.5 million; income taxes are expected to be 30%. Microsystems currently has 100,000 shares of common stock outstanding. The alternative effects on earnings per share are shown in Illustration 16-2.

**ILLUSTRATION 16-2**

*Effects on earnings per share—stocks vs. bonds*

|  | Plan A Issue Stock | Plan B Issue Bonds |
|---|---|---|
| Income before interest and taxes | $1,500,000 | $1,500,000 |
| Interest (12% × $5,000,000) | — | 600,000 |
| Income before income taxes | 1,500,000 | 900,000 |
| Income tax expense (30%) | 450,000 | 270,000 |
| Net income | $1,050,000 | $ 630,000 |
| Outstanding shares | 300,000 | 100,000 |
| **Earnings per share** | $ 3.50 | $ 6.30 |

Note that net income is $420,000 ($1,050,000 − $630,000) less with long-term debt financing (bonds). However, earnings per share is higher because there are 200,000 fewer shares of common stock outstanding.

**The major disadvantages resulting from the use of bonds are that interest must be paid on a periodic basis and the principal (face value) of the bonds must be paid at maturity.** A company with fluctuating earnings and a relatively weak cash position may experience great difficulty in meeting interest requirements in periods of low earnings.

**INTERNATIONAL NOTE**

The priority of bondholders' versus stockholders' rights varies across countries. In Japan, Germany, and France stockholders and employees are given priority, with liquidation of the firm to pay creditors seen as a last resort. In Britain creditors' interests are put first—the courts are quick to give control of the firm to creditors.

## Types of Bonds

Bonds may have many different features. Some types of bonds commonly issued are described in the following sections:

### Secured and Unsecured Bonds

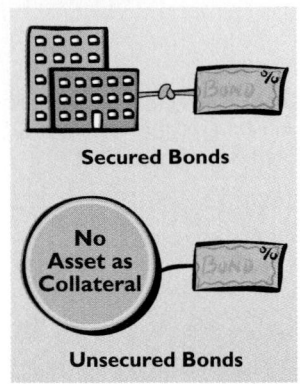

**Secured Bonds**

**Unsecured Bonds**

Secured bonds have specific assets of the issuer pledged as collateral for the bonds. A bond secured by real estate, for example, is called a mortgage bond. A bond secured by specific assets set aside to retire the bonds is called a sinking fund bond. (This type of bond is discussed later in the chapter.) Unsecured bonds are issued against the general credit of the borrower. These bonds, called debenture bonds, are used extensively by large corporations with good credit ratings. For example, in a recent annual report, DuPont reported over $2 billion of debenture bonds outstanding.

### Term and Serial Bonds

Bonds that are due for payment (mature) at a single specified future date are called term bonds. In contrast, bonds that mature in installments are called serial bonds. For example, Caterpillar Inc. debentures due in 2007 are term bonds, and their debentures due between 1999 and 2007 are serial bonds.

### Registered and Bearer Bonds

**Convertible Bonds**

**Callable Bonds**

Bonds issued in the name of the owner are called registered bonds; interest payments on registered bonds are made by check to bondholders of record. Bonds not registered are called bearer (or coupon) bonds; holders are required to send in coupons to receive interest payments. Coupon bonds may be transferred directly to another party. In contrast, the transfer of registered bonds requires cancellation of the bonds by the corporation and the issuance of new bonds. With minor exceptions, most bonds issued today are registered bonds.

### Convertible and Callable Bonds

Bonds that can be converted into common stock at the bondholder's option are called convertible bonds. Bonds subject to retirement at a stated dollar amount prior to maturity at the option of the issuer are known as callable bonds.

## Issuing Procedures

State laws grant corporations the power to issue bonds. Within the corporation, formal approval by both the board of directors and stockholders is usually required before bonds can be issued. **In authorizing the bond issue, the board of directors must stipulate the total number of bonds to be authorized, total face value, and the contractual interest rate.** The total bond authorization often exceeds the number of bonds originally issued. This is done intentionally to help ensure that the corporation will have the flexibility it needs to meet future cash requirements.

The face value is the amount of principal due at the maturity date. The contractual interest rate, often referred to as the **stated rate**, is the rate used to determine the amount of cash interest the borrower pays and the investor receives. Usually the contractual rate is stated as an annual rate, and interest is generally paid semiannually.

The terms of the bond issue are set forth in a legal document called a bond indenture. In addition to the terms, the indenture summarizes the respective rights and privileges of the bondholders and their trustees, as well as the obligations and commitments of the issuing company. The **trustee** (usually a financial institution) keeps records of each bondholder, maintains custody of unissued bonds, and holds conditional title to pledged property.

# ACCOUNTING IN ACTION

## Business Insight

Although bonds are generally secured by solid, substantial assets like land, buildings, and equipment, exceptions occur. For example Trans World Airlines Inc. (TWA) at one time decided to issue $300 million of high-yielding 5-year bonds. TWA's bonds would be secured by a grab bag of assets, including some durable spare parts, but also a lot of disposable items that TWA had in its warehouses, such as light bulbs and gaskets. Some called the planned TWA bonds "light bulb bonds." As one financial expert noted: "You've got to admit that some security is better than none." However, another noted, "They're digging pretty far down the barrel."

After the bond indenture is prepared, **bond certificates** are printed. The indenture and the certificate are separate documents. As shown in Illustration 16-3, a bond certificate provides information such as the following: name of the issuer, the face value of the bonds, the contractual interest rate, and the maturity date of the bonds. Bonds are generally sold through an investment company that specializes in selling securities. In most cases, the issue is underwritten by the investment company. Under an underwriting arrangement, the company sells the bonds to the investment company, which, in turn, sells the bonds to individual investors.

**ILLUSTRATION 16-3**

*Bond certificate*

*Bond certificate illustration with labels: Issuer of bonds, Maturity date, Trustee, Face or par value, Contractual interest rate.*

INTERNATIONAL MINERALS & CHEMICAL CORPORATION
11.875% SINKING FUND DEBENTURE DUE MAY 1, 2005

No.    $5000

11.875% DUE 2005    11.875% DUE 2005

FIVE THOUSAND DOLLARS

CUSIP 459884 AC 6
SEE REVERSE FOR CERTAIN DEFINITIONS

## Bond Trading

Corporate bonds, like capital stock, are traded on national securities markets. Thus, bondholders have the opportunity to convert their holdings into cash at any time by selling the bonds at the current market price.

**Bond prices are quoted as a percentage of the face value of the bond, which is usually $1,000.** Thus, a $1,000 bond with a quoted price of 97 means that the selling price of the bond is 97% of face value, or $970 in this case. Bond prices and trading activity are published daily in newspapers and the financial press, as illustrated by the following:

**ILLUSTRATION 16-4**

*Market information for bonds*

| Bonds | Current Yield | Volume | Close | Net Change |
|-------|---------------|--------|-------|------------|
| Kmart 8⅜ 17 | 8.4 | 35 | 100¼ | +⅞ |

**HELPFUL HINT**
(1) What is the price of a $1,000 bond trading at 95¼?
(2) What is the price of a $1,000 bond trading at 101⅞?
Answers: (1) $952.50 and
(2) $1,018.75.

The information in Illustration 16-4 indicates that Kmart Corporation has outstanding 8⅜%, $1,000 bonds maturing in 2017 and currently yielding an 8.4% return. In addition, 35 bonds were traded on this day; and at the close of trading, the price was 100¼% of face value, or $1,002.50. The net change column indicates the difference between the day's closing price and the previous day's closing price.

Transactions between a bondholder and other investors **are not journalized by the issuing corporation**. If Tom Smith sells bonds that are bought by Faith Jones, the issuing corporation does not journalize the transaction (although it does keep records of the names of bondholders in the case of registered bonds). A corporation makes journal entries only when it issues or buys back bonds, and when bondholders convert bonds into common stock.

## Determining the Market Value of Bonds

If you were an investor interested in purchasing a bond, how would you determine how much to pay? To be more specific, assume that Coronet, Inc., issues a zero-interest bond (pays no interest) with a face value of $1,000,000 due in 20 years. For this bond, the only cash you receive is a million dollars at the end of 20 years. Would you pay a million dollars for this bond? We hope not, because a million dollars received 20 years from now is not the same as a million dollars received today. The reason you would not pay a million dollars relates to what is called the **time value of money.** If you had a million dollars today, you would invest it and earn interest such that at the end of 20 years, your investment would be worth much more than a million dollars. Thus, if someone is going to pay you a million dollars 20 years from now, you would want to find its equivalent today, or its **present value.** In other words, you would want to determine how much must be invested today at current interest rates to have a million dollars in 20 years.

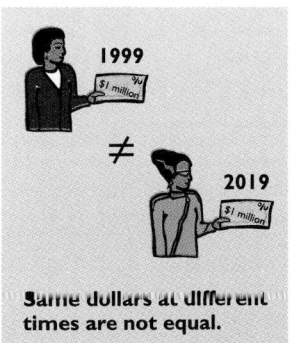

Same dollars at different times are not equal.

The market value (present value) of a bond is, therefore, a function of three factors: (1) the dollar amounts to be received, (2) the length of time until the amounts are received, and (3) the market rate of interest. The market interest rate is the rate investors demand for loaning funds to the corporation. The process of finding the present value is referred to as **discounting** the future amounts.

To illustrate, assume that Kell Company on January 1, 1999, issues $100,000 of 9% bonds, due in 5 years, with interest payable annually at year-end. The purchaser of the bonds would receive the following two cash payments: (1) **principal** $100,000 to be paid at maturity, and (2) five $9,000 **interest payments**

($100,000 × 9%) over the term of the bonds. The time diagram depicting both cash flows is shown below:

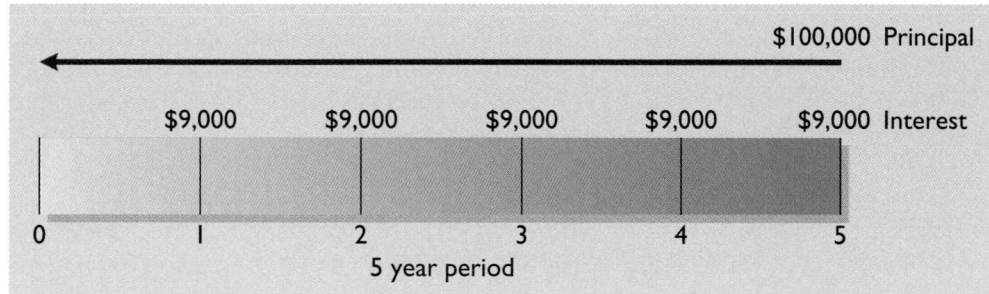

ILLUSTRATION 16-5

*Time diagram depicting cash flows*

The present values of these amounts are as shown in Illustration 16-6.

| | |
|---|---|
| Present value of $100,000 received in 5 years | $ 64,993 |
| Present value of $9,000 received annually for 5 years | 35,007 |
| **Market price of bonds** | **$100,000** |

ILLUSTRATION 16-6

*Computing the market price of bonds*

Tables are available to provide the present value numbers to be used, or these values can be determined mathematically.[1] Further discussion of time value of money computations is provided in Appendix C near the end of the book.

## BEFORE YOU GO ON . . .

### Review It

1. What are the advantages of bond versus stock financing?
2. What are secured versus unsecured bonds, term versus serial bonds, registered versus bearer bonds, and callable versus convertible bonds?
3. Explain the terms face value, contractual interest rate, and bond indenture.
4. Explain why you would prefer to receive $1 million today rather than 5 years from now.

THE
NAVIGATOR

# ACCOUNTING FOR BOND ISSUES

Bonds may be issued at face value, below face value (discount), or above face value (premium). They also are sometimes issued between interest dates.

## Issuing Bonds at Face Value

To illustrate the accounting for bonds, assume that Devor Corporation issues 1,000, 10-year, 9%, $1,000 bonds dated January 1, 1999, at 100 (100% of face value). The entry to record the sale is:

| | | | |
|---|---|---|---|
| Jan. 1 | Cash | 1,000,000 | |
| | Bonds Payable | | 1,000,000 |
| | (To record sale of bonds at face value) | | |

**2**
STUDY
OBJECTIVE

Prepare the entries for the issuance of bonds and interest expense.

| A | = | L | + | SE |
|---|---|---|---|---|
| +1,000,000 | | +1,000,000 | | |

[1]For those knowledgeable in the use of present value tables, the computations in this example are: $100,000 × .64993 = $64,993, and $9,000 × 3.88965 = $35,007 (rounded).

Bonds payable are reported in the long-term liability section of the balance sheet because the maturity date is January 1, 2009 (more than one year away).

Over the term (life) of the bonds, entries are required for bond interest. Interest on bonds payable is computed in the same manner as interest on notes payable, as explained in Chapter 11. Assuming that interest is payable semiannually on January 1 and July 1 on the bonds described above, interest of $45,000 ($1,000,000 × 9% × 6/12) must be paid on July 1, 1999. The entry for the payment, assuming no previous accrual of interest, is:

|  |  |  |  |
|---|---|---|---|
| A = L + SE | July 1 | Bond Interest Expense | 45,000 |
| −45,000    −45,000 |  |     Cash |  45,000 |
|  |  |     (To record payment of bond interest) |  |

At December 31, an adjusting entry is required to recognize the $45,000 of interest expense incurred since July 1. The entry is:

|  |  |  |  |
|---|---|---|---|
| A = L + SE | Dec. 31 | Bond Interest Expense | 45,000 |
|  +45,000  −45,000 |  |     Bond Interest Payable |  45,000 |
|  |  |     (To accrue bond interest) |  |

**Bond interest payable is classified as a current liability**, because it is scheduled for payment within the next year. When the interest is paid on January 1, 2000, Bond Interest Payable is debited and Cash is credited for $45,000.

## Discount or Premium on Bonds

The previous illustrations assumed that the interest rate paid on bonds, often referred to as the contractual (stated) interest rate and the market (effective) interest rate were the same. The contractual interest rate is the rate applied to the face (par) value to arrive at the interest paid in a year. The market interest rate is the rate investors demand for loaning funds to the corporation. When the contractual interest rate and the market interest rate are the same, bonds sell at face value.

However, market interest rates change daily. They are influenced by the type of bond issued, the state of the economy, current industry conditions, and the company's individual performance. As a result, the contractual and market interest rates often differ and therefore bonds sell below or above face value.

To illustrate, suppose that investors have one of two options: purchase bonds that have a market rate of interest of 10% or purchase bonds that have a contractual rate of interest of 8%. Assuming that the bonds are of equal risk, investors will select the 10% investment. To make the investments equal, investors will demand a rate of interest higher than the contractual interest rate on the 8% bonds. Because investors cannot change the contractual interest rate, they will pay less than the face value for the bonds. By paying less for the bonds, they can obtain the market rate of interest. In these cases, **bonds sell at a discount**.

Conversely, if the market rate of interest is **lower** than the contractual interest rate, investors will have to pay more than face value for the bonds. That is, if the market rate of interest is 8%, but the contractual interest rate is 9%, the issuer will require more funds from the investor. In these cases, **bonds sell at a premium**. These relationships are shown graphically in Illustration 16-7.

Issuance of bonds at an amount different from face value is quite common. By the time a company prints the bond certificates and markets the bonds, it will be a coincidence if the market rate and the contractual rate are the same. Thus, the issuance of bonds at a discount does not mean that the financial strength of the issuer is suspect. Conversely, the sale of bonds at a premium does not indicate that the financial strength of the issuer is exceptional.

**ILLUSTRATION 16-7**

*Interest rates and bond prices*

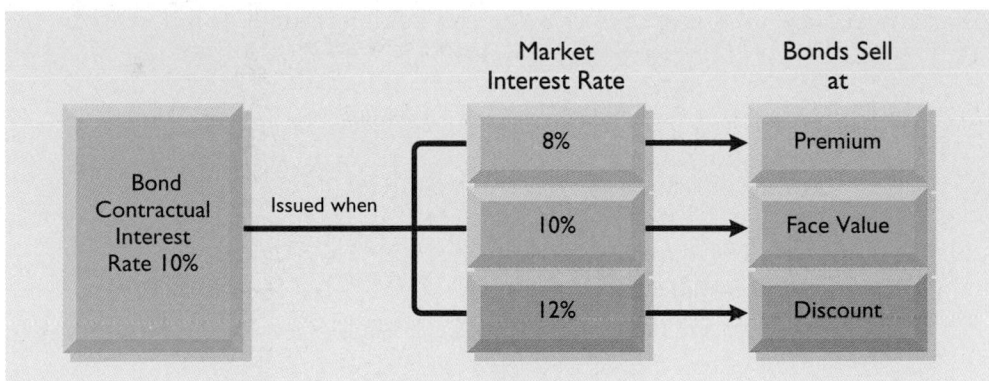

**HELPFUL HINT**

Discount on Bonds Payable

| Increase<br>Debit | Decrease<br>Credit |
|---|---|
| ↓ | |
| Normal | |
| Balance | |

## Issuing Bonds at a Discount

To illustrate the issuance of bonds at a discount, assume that on January 1, 1999, Candlestick, Inc., sells $1 million, 5-year, 10% bonds at 98 (98% of face value) with interest payable on July 1 and January 1. The entry to record the issuance is:

| | | | |
|---|---|---|---|
| Jan. 1 | Cash | 980,000 | |
| | Discount on Bonds Payable | 20,000 | |
| |     Bonds Payable | | 1,000,000 |
| |       (To record sale of bonds at a discount) | | |

| A | = | L | + | SE |
|---|---|---|---|---|
| +980,000 | | − | 20,000 | |
| | | | +1,000,000 | |

Although Discount on Bonds Payable has a debit balance, **it is not an asset.** Rather it is a **contra account,** which is **deducted from bonds payable** on the balance sheet, as illustrated below:

**ILLUSTRATION 16-8**

*Statement presentation of discount on bonds payable*

| CANDLESTICK, INC.<br>Balance Sheet (partial) | | |
|---|---|---|
| Long-term liabilities | | |
|   Bonds payable | $1,000,000 | |
|   **Less: Discount on bonds payable** | **20,000** | $980,000 |

The $980,000 represents the **carrying (or book) value** of the bonds. On the date of issue this amount equals the market price of the bonds.

**HELPFUL HINT**

Carrying value (book value) of bonds issued at a discount is determined by subtracting the balance of the discount account from the balance of the Bonds Payable account.

    The issuance of bonds below face value causes the total cost of borrowing to differ from the bond interest paid. That is, at maturity the issuing corporation must pay not only the contractual interest rate over the term of the bonds, but also the face value (rather than the issuance price). Therefore, the difference between the issuance price and face value of the bonds—the discount—is an **additional cost of borrowing that should be recorded as bond interest expense over the life of the bonds.** The total cost of borrowing $980,000 for Candlestick, Inc., is $520,000, computed as follows:

**ILLUSTRATION 16-9**

*Total cost of borrowing— bonds issued at a discount*

| Bonds Issued at a Discount | |
|---|---|
| Semiannual interest payments | |
|     ($1,000,000 × 10% × ½ = $50,000; $50,000 × 10) | $500,000 |
| Add: Bond discount ($1,000,000 − $980,000) | 20,000 |
| **Total cost of borrowing** | **$520,000** |

Alternatively, the total cost of borrowing can be determined as follows:

**ILLUSTRATION 16-10**

*Alternative computation of total cost of borrowing— bonds issued at a discount*

| Bonds Issued at a Discount | |
|---|---:|
| Principal at maturity | $1,000,000 |
| Semiannual interest payments ($50,000 × 10) | 500,000 |
| Cash to be paid to bondholders | 1,500,000 |
| Cash received from bondholders | 980,000 |
| **Total cost of borrowing** | **$ 520,000** |

## Amortizing Bond Discount

To comply with the matching principle, it follows that bond discount should be allocated systematically to each accounting period benefiting from the use of the cash proceeds.

One method, the **straight-line method of amortization**, allocates the same amount to interest expense in each interest period.[2] The amount is determined as shown in Illustration 16-11:

**ILLUSTRATION 16-11**

*Formula for straight-line method of bond discount amortization*

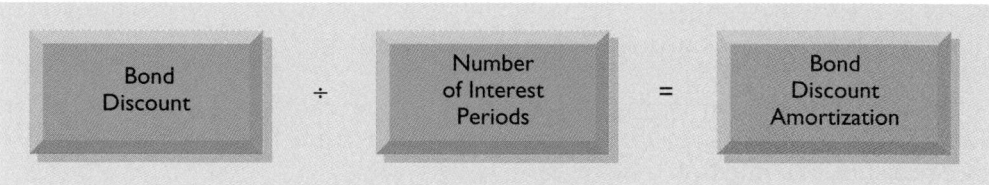

In this example, the bond discount amortization is $2,000 ($20,000 ÷ 10). The entry to record the payment of bond interest and the amortization of bond discount on the first interest date (July 1, 1999) is:

| A | = | L | + | SE |
|---|---|---|---|---|
| −50,000 | | +2,000 | | −52,000 |

| July 1 | Bond Interest Expense | 52,000 | |
|---|---|---|---|
| |     Discount on Bonds Payable | | 2,000 |
| |     Cash | | 50,000 |
| |     (To record payment of bond interest and | | |
| |     amortization of bond discount) | | |

At December 31, the adjusting entry is:

| A | = | L | + | SE |
|---|---|---|---|---|
| | | + 2,000 | | −52,000 |
| | | +50,000 | | |

| Dec 31 | Bond Interest Expense | 52,000 | |
|---|---|---|---|
| |     Discount on Bonds Payable | | 2,000 |
| |     Bond Interest Payable | | 50,000 |
| |     (To record accrued bond interest and | | |
| |     amortization of bond discount) | | |

**ALTERNATIVE TERMINOLOGY**
The amount in the Discount on Bonds Payable account is often referred to as *Unamortized Discount on Bonds Payable*.

Over the term of the bonds, the balance in Discount on Bonds Payable will decrease annually by the same amount until it has a zero balance at the maturity date of the bonds. Thus, the carrying value of the bonds at maturity will be equal to the face value of the bonds.

Preparing a bond discount amortization schedule as shown in Illustration 16-12 is useful to determine interest expense, discount amortization and the car-

---

[2]Another method, the effective-interest method, is discussed in the appendix at the end of this chapter.

rying value of the bond. As indicated, the interest expense recorded each period is $52,000. Also note that the carrying value of the bond increases $2,000 each period until it reaches its face value $1,000,000 at the end of period 10.

**ILLUSTRATION 16-12**

*Bond discount amortization schedule*

| Semiannual Interest Periods | (A) Interest to Be Paid (5% × $1,000,000) | (B) Interest Expense to Be Recorded (A) + (C) | (C) Discount Amortization ($20,000 ÷ 10) | (D) Unamortized Discount (D) − (C) | (E) Bond Carrying Value ($1,000,000 − D) |
|---|---|---|---|---|---|
| Issue date | | | | $20,000 | $ 980,000 |
| 1 | $ 50,000 | $ 52,000 | $ 2,000 | 18,000 | 982,000 |
| 2 | 50,000 | 52,000 | 2,000 | 16,000 | 984,000 |
| 3 | 50,000 | 52,000 | 2,000 | 14,000 | 986,000 |
| 4 | 50,000 | 52,000 | 2,000 | 12,000 | 988,000 |
| 5 | 50,000 | 52,000 | 2,000 | 10,000 | 990,000 |
| 6 | 50,000 | 52,000 | 2,000 | 8,000 | 992,000 |
| 7 | 50,000 | 52,000 | 2,000 | 6,000 | 994,000 |
| 8 | 50,000 | 52,000 | 2,000 | 4,000 | 996,000 |
| 9 | 50,000 | 52,000 | 2,000 | 2,000 | 998,000 |
| 10 | 50,000 | 52,000 | 2,000 | –0– | 1,000,000 |
| | $500,000 | $520,000 | $20,000 | | |

Column **(A)** remains constant because the face value of the bonds ($1,000,000) is multiplied by the semiannual contractual interest rate (5%) each period.

Column **(B)** is computed as the interest paid (Column A) plus the discount amortization (Column C).

Column **(C)** indicates the discount amortization each period.

Column **(D)** decreases each period by the same amount until it reaches zero at maturity.

Column **(E)** increases each period by the amount of discount amortization until it equals the face value at maturity.

## Issuing Bonds at a Premium

The issuance of bonds at a premium can be illustrated by assuming the Candlestick, Inc., bonds described above are sold at 102 (102% of face value) rather than at 98.

The entry to record the sale is:

| | | | |
|---|---|---|---|
| Jan. 1 | Cash | 1,020,000 | |
| | Bonds Payable | | 1,000,000 |
| | Premium on Bonds Payable | | 20,000 |
| | (To record sale of bonds at a premium) | | |

```
A      =      L     +    SE
+1,020,000  +1,000,000
                +     20,000
```

Premium on bonds payable is **added to bonds payable** on the balance sheet, as shown below:

**ILLUSTRATION 16-13**

*Statement presentation of bond premium*

---

**CANDLESTICK, INC.**
**Balance Sheet (partial)**

| | | |
|---|---|---|
| Long-term liabilities | | |
| Bonds payable | $1,000,000 | |
| Add: Premium on bonds payable | 20,000 | $1,020,000 |

The sale of bonds above face value causes the total cost of borrowing to be **less than the bond interest paid**, because the borrower is not required to pay the bond premium at the maturity date of the bonds. Thus, the premium is considered to be **a reduction in the cost of borrowing** that should be credited to Bond Interest Expense over the life of the bonds. The total cost of borrowing $1,020,000 for Candlestick, Inc., is $480,000, computed as follows:

**ILLUSTRATION 16-14**

*Total cost of borrowing—bonds issued at a premium*

| Bonds Issued at a Premium | |
|---|---|
| Semiannual interest payments | |
| ($1,000,000 × 10% × ½ = $50,000; $50,000 × 10) | $500,000 |
| Less: Bond premium ($1,020,000 − $1,000,000) | 20,000 |
| **Total cost of borrowing** | **$480,000** |

Alternatively, the cost of borrowing can be computed as follows:

**ILLUSTRATION 16-15**

*Alternative computation of total cost of borrowing—bonds issued at a premium*

| Bonds Issued at a Premium | |
|---|---|
| Principal at maturity | $1,000,000 |
| Semiannual interest payments ($50,000 × 10) | 500,000 |
| Cash to be paid to bondholders | 1,500,000 |
| Cash received from bondholders | 1,020,000 |
| **Total cost of borrowing** | **$ 480,000** |

## Amortizing Bond Premium

The formula for determining bond premium amortization under the straight-line method is presented in Illustration 16-16.

**ILLUSTRATION 16-16**

*Formula for straight-line method of bond premium amortization*

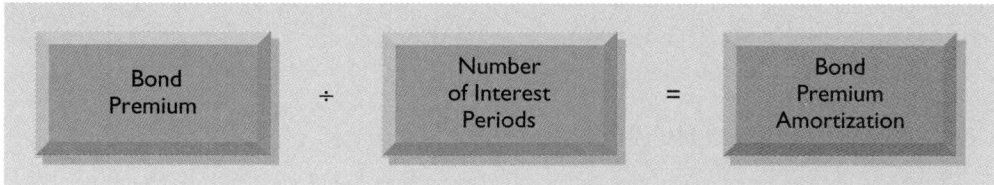

Thus, in our example, the premium amortization for each interest period is $2,000 ($20,000 ÷ 10). The entry to record the first payment of interest on July 1 is:

| A | = | L | + | SE |
|---|---|---|---|---|
| −50,000 | | −2,000 | | −48,000 |

| July 1 | Bond Interest Expense | 48,000 | |
|--------|------------------------|--------|--------|
| | Premium on Bonds Payable | 2,000 | |
| |    Cash | | 50,000 |
| |     (To record payment of bond interest and | | |
| |     amortization of bond premium) | | |

At December 31, the adjusting entry is:

| A | = | L | + | SE |
|---|---|---|---|---|
| | | − 2,000 | | −48,000 |
| | | +50,000 | | |

| Dec. 31 | Bond Interest Expense | 48,000 | |
|---------|------------------------|--------|--------|
| | Premium on Bonds Payable | 2,000 | |
| |    Bond Interest Payable | | 50,000 |
| |     (To record accrued bond interest and | | |
| |     amortization of bond premium) | | |

Over the term of the bonds, the balance in Premium on Bonds Payable will decrease annually by the same amount until it has a zero balance at maturity.

Preparing a bond premium amortization schedule as shown in Illustration 16-17 is useful to determine interest expense, premium amortized, and the carrying value of the bond. As indicated, the interest expense recorded each period is $48,000. Also note that the carrying value of the bond decreases $2,000 each period until it reaches its face value $1,000,000 at the end of period 10.

**ILLUSTRATION 16-17**

*Bond premium amortization schedule*

| Semiannual Interest Periods | (A) Interest to Be Paid (5% × $1,000,000) | (B) Interest Expense to Be Recorded (A) − (C) | (C) Premium Amortization ($20,000 ÷ 10) | (D) Unamortized Premium (D) − (C) | (E) Bond Carrying Value ($1,000,000 + D) |
|---|---|---|---|---|---|
| Issue date | | | | $20,000 | $1,020,000 |
| 1 | $ 50,000 | $ 48,000 | $ 2,000 | 18,000 | 1,018,000 |
| 2 | 50,000 | 48,000 | 2,000 | 16,000 | 1,016,000 |
| 3 | 50,000 | 48,000 | 2,000 | 14,000 | 1,014,000 |
| 4 | 50,000 | 48,000 | 2,000 | 12,000 | 1,012,000 |
| 5 | 50,000 | 48,000 | 2,000 | 10,000 | 1,010,000 |
| 6 | 50,000 | 48,000 | 2,000 | 8,000 | 1,008,000 |
| 7 | 50,000 | 48,000 | 2,000 | 6,000 | 1,006,000 |
| 8 | 50,000 | 48,000 | 2,000 | 4,000 | 1,004,000 |
| 9 | 50,000 | 48,000 | 2,000 | 2,000 | 1,002,000 |
| 10 | 50,000 | 48,000 | 2,000 | −0− | 1,000,000 |
| | $500,000 | $480,000 | $20,000 | | |

Column **(A)** remains constant because the face value of the bonds ($1,000,000) is multiplied by the semiannual contractual interest rate (5%) each period.

Column **(B)** is computed as the interest paid (Column A) less the premium amortization (Column C).

Column **(C)** indicates the premium amortization each period.

Column **(D)** decreases each period by the same amount until it reaches zero at maturity.

Column **(E)** decreases each period by the amount of premium amortization until it equals the face value at maturity.

## Issuing Bonds between Interest Dates

Bonds are often issued between interest payment dates. **When this occurs, the issuer requires the investor to pay the market price for the bonds plus accrued interest since the last interest date.** At the next interest date, the corporation will return the accrued interest to the investor by paying the full amount of interest due on outstanding bonds.

To illustrate, assume that Deer Corporation sells $1,000,000, 9% bonds at face value plus accrued interest on March 1. Interest is payable semiannually on July 1 and January 1. The accrued interest is $15,000 ($1,000,000 × 9% × 2/12). The total proceeds on the sale of the bonds, therefore, are $1,015,000, and the entry to record the sale is:

| Mar. 1 | Cash | 1,015,000 | |
| | Bonds Payable | | 1,000,000 |
| | Bond Interest Payable | | 15,000 |
| | (To record sale of bonds at face value plus accrued interest) | | |

A = L + SE
+1,015,000 +1,000,000
       +    15,000

At the first interest date, it is necessary to eliminate the bond interest payable balance and to recognize interest expense for the 4 months (March 1–June 30) the bonds have been outstanding. Interest expense in this example is, therefore, $30,000 ($1,000,000 $\times$ 9% $\times$ 4/12). The entry on July 1 for the $45,000 interest payment is:

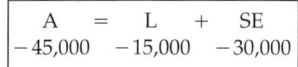

|  |  | A | = | L | + | SE |
|---|---|---|---|---|---|---|
|  |  | −45,000 | | −15,000 | | −30,000 |

| July 1 | Bond Interest Payable | 15,000 | |
|---|---|---|---|
|  | Bond Interest Expense | 30,000 | |
|  |    Cash | | 45,000 |
|  |    (To record payment of bond interest) | | |

Why does Deer Corporation collect interest at the time of issuance and then return this interest at the time of payment? The rationale: Collection of accrued interest at the issuance date allows the company to pay a full period's interest to all bondholders at the next interest payment date. Deer Corporation does not have to determine the individual amount of interest due each holder based on the time each bond has been outstanding during the interest period.

In other words, if bonds are not sold "with accrued interest," Deer Corporation would have to keep track of the purchaser and the dates that the bonds were purchased. This procedure would be necessary to ensure that each bondholder received the correct amount of interest. By selling the bonds "with accrued interest," Deer does not have to maintain detailed records and cost savings occur.

# BEFORE YOU GO ON . . .

## Review It

1. What entry is made to record the issuance of bonds payable of $1 million at 100? at 96? at 102?
2. Why do bonds sell at a discount? at a premium? at face value?
3. Explain the accounting for bonds sold between interest dates.

## Do It

A bond amortization table shows (a) interest to be paid $50,000, (b) interest expense to be recorded $52,000, and (c) amortization $2,000. Answer the following questions: (1) Were the bonds sold at a premium or a discount? (2) After recording the interest expense, will the bond carrying value increase or decrease?

*Reasoning:* To answer the questions you need to know the effects that the amortization of bond discount and bond premium have on bond interest expense and on the carrying value of the bonds. Bond discount amortization increases both bond interest expense and the carrying value of the bonds. Bond premium amortization has the reverse effect.

*Solution:* The bond amortization table indicates that interest expense is $2,000 greater than the interest paid. This difference is equal to the amortization amount. Thus, the bonds were sold at a discount. The interest entry will decrease Discount on Bonds Payable and increase the carrying value of the bonds.

THE NAVIGATOR

*Related exercise material:* BE16–2, BE16–3, BE16–4, BE16–5, E16–2, E16–3, E16–4, and E16–5.

# ACCOUNTING FOR BOND RETIREMENTS

Bonds may be retired either when they are purchased (redeemed) by the issuing corporation or when they are converted into common stock by bondholders. The appropriate entries for these transactions are explained in the following sections.

## Redeeming Bonds at Maturity

Regardless of the issue price of bonds, the book value of the bonds at maturity will equal their face value. This can be seen in Illustrations 16-12 and 16-17 where the carrying value of the bonds at the end of their 10-year life ($1 million) is equal to the face value of the bonds.

Assuming that the interest for the last interest period is paid and recorded separately, the entry to record the redemption of the Candlestick bonds at maturity is:

| | | |
|---|---|---|
| Bonds Payable | 1,000,000 | |
|    Cash | | 1,000,000 |
|      (To record redemption of bonds at maturity) | | |

| A | = | L | + | SE |
|---|---|---|---|---|
| −1,000,000 | | −1,000,000 | | |

## Redeeming Bonds before Maturity   (callible Bond)

Bonds may be redeemed before maturity. A company may decide to retire bonds before maturity to reduce interest cost and remove debt from its balance sheet. A company should retire debt early only if it has sufficient cash resources. When bonds are retired before maturity, it is necessary to: (1) eliminate the carrying value of the bonds at the redemption date, (2) record the cash paid, and (3) recognize the gain or loss on redemption. The carrying value of the bonds is the face value of the bonds less unamortized bond discount or plus unamortized bond premium at the redemption date.

To illustrate, assume at the end of the eighth period Candlestick, Inc. (having sold its bonds at a premium, per Illustration 16-17) retires its bonds at 103 after paying the semiannual interest. The carrying value of the bonds at the redemption date, as shown in the bond premium amortization schedule, is $1,004,000. The entry to record the redemption at the end of the eighth interest period (January 1, 2003) is:

| Jan. 1 | Bonds Payable | 1,000,000 | |
|---|---|---|---|
| | Premium on Bonds Payable | 4,000 | |
| | Loss on Bond Redemption | 26,000 | |
| |    Cash | | 1,030,000 |
| |      (To record redemption of bonds at 103) | | |

| A | = | L | + | SE |
|---|---|---|---|---|
| −1,030,000 | | −1,000,000 | | −26,000 |
| | | − 4,000 | | |

Note that the loss of $26,000 is the difference between the cash paid of $1,030,000 and the carrying value of the bonds of $1,004,000. Losses (gains) on bond redemption are reported in the income statement as extraordinary items as required by the accounting profession.

## Converting Bonds into Common Stock

Convertible bonds have features that are attractive both to bondholders and to the issuer. The conversion often gives bondholders an opportunity to benefit if the market price of the common stock increases substantially. Furthermore, until conversion, the bondholder receives interest on the bond. For the issuer, the bonds sell at a higher price and pay a lower rate of interest than comparable debt securities that do not have a conversion option. Many corporations, such as USAir, USX Corp., and Daimler-Chrysler Corporation, have convertible bonds outstanding.

When bonds are converted into common stocks and the conversion is recorded, the current market prices of the bonds and the stock are ignored. Instead, the **carrying value** of the bonds is transferred to paid-in capital accounts, and **no gain or loss is recognized**. To illustrate, assume that on July 1 Saunders Associates converts $100,000 bonds sold at face value into 2,000 shares of $10 par value common stock. Both the bonds and the common stock have a market value of $130,000. The entry to record the conversion is:

| A | = | L | + | SE |
|---|---|---|---|---|
| | | − 100,000 | | + 20,000 |
| | | | | + 80,000 |

| July 1 | Bonds Payable | 100,000 | |
|--------|---------------|---------|---|
| | Common Stock | | 20,000 |
| | Paid-in Capital in Excess of Par Value | | 80,000 |
| | (To record bond conversion) | | |

Note that the current market price of the bonds and stock ($130,000) is not considered in making the entry. This method of recording the bond conversion is often referred to as the **carrying (or book) value method**.

## Using a Bond Sinking Fund

Many bond issues require the borrower to make periodic cash contributions to a sinking (redemption) fund over the life of the bonds. A sinking fund is cash or other assets set aside to retire debt. In other words, it is like a savings account that is used to pay back bondholders. **A sinking fund makes the bonds more attractive to investors, because it enhances the likelihood that the bonds will be redeemed at maturity.** For example, Texaco and Alcoa have sinking funds for their debenture bonds. Such bonds are often referred to as **sinking fund bonds**.

Sinking funds are usually under the control of a trustee, such as a bank or a trust company. The trustee may be permitted to invest the periodic deposits in high-quality income-producing securities. **It is expected that the deposits plus the earnings from the investments will equal the face value of the bonds at maturity.** Shortly before the maturity date, the trustee sells the securities and uses the total cash in the fund to redeem the bonds. Any excess cash in the fund is returned to the bond issuer.

To illustrate, assume that Bountiful Corporation issues $1 million face value, 5-year bonds on January 1. The terms of the bond indenture indicate that Bountiful must make annual deposits with a sinking fund trustee, starting at the end of the first year. The amount of the annual cash contribution is $215,000. The entry to record this contribution by Bountiful Corporation at the end of the first year is as follows:

| A | = | L | + | SE |
|---|---|---|---|---|
| + 215,000 | | | | |
| − 215,000 | | | | |

| Dec. 31 | Bond Sinking Fund | 215,000 | |
|---------|-------------------|---------|---|
| | Cash | | 215,000 |
| | (To record annual contribution) | | |

At the end of the second year, Bountiful Corporation records actual earnings on the assets in the sinking fund of $16,500. The entry to record this revenue and the required contribution to the fund is as follows:

| A | = | L | + | SE |
|---|---|---|---|---|
| + 231,500 | | | | + 16,500 |
| − 215,000 | | | | |

| Dec. 31 | Bond Sinking Fund | 231,500 | |
|---------|-------------------|---------|---|
| | Bond Sinking Fund Revenue | | 16,500 |
| | Cash | | 215,000 |
| | (To record sinking fund revenue and annual contribution) | | |

At the maturity date, sinking fund assets are used to redeem the bonds. The entry to record the redemption, assuming that the sinking fund has $985,000 in cash, is as follows:

| Jan. 1 | Bonds Payable | 1,000,000 | |
| | Bond Sinking Fund | | 985,000 |
| | Cash | | 15,000 |
| | (To redeem bonds at maturity) | | |

| A | = | L | + | SE |
|---|---|---|---|---|
| −985,000 | | −1,000,000 | | |
| −15,000 | | | | |

In this case, Bountiful Corporation had to make up for the deficiency by paying an additional $15,000. If the sinking fund had excess cash, it would be returned to Bountiful.

**The bond sinking fund is reported as a single amount in the investment section of the balance sheet.** Bond sinking fund revenue is classified as other revenues and gains in the income statement.

The bond contract may also require the corporation to establish a restriction on its retained earnings. As explained in Chapter 15, this restriction is reported as a note in the financial statements.

# ACCOUNTING IN ACTION
## International Insight

Now that you have read about bonds, you may be beginning to realize how significant bond financing can be. A dramatic example of bond financing—which literally changed the course of history—is seen in Britain's struggle for supremacy in the eighteenth and nineteenth centuries. With only a fraction of the population and wealth of France, Britain ultimately humbled its mightier foe through the use of bonds. Because of its effective central bank and a fair system of collecting taxes, Britain developed the capital markets that enabled its government to issue bonds. Britain was able to borrow money at almost half the cost paid by France, and was able to incur more debt as a proportion of the economy than could France. Britain thus could more than match the French navy, raise an army of its own, and lavishly subsidize other armies, eventually destroying Napoleon and his threat to Europe.

*Source:* "How British Bonds Beat Back Bigger France," *Forbes*, March 13, 1995.

# BEFORE YOU GO ON . . .
## Review It

1. Explain the accounting for redemption of bonds at maturity, before maturity by payment in cash, and by conversion into common stock.
2. Did Kellogg Company redeem any of its debt during 1997? (*Hint:* To find information related to this question, examine Kellogg Company's statement of cash flows. The answer to this question is provided on page 719.)
3. What is the purpose of the bond sinking fund? Where is a bond sinking fund reported in the financial statements?

## Do It

R & B Inc. issued $500,000, 10-year bonds at a premium. Prior to maturity, when the carrying value of the bonds is $508,000, the company retires the bonds at 102. Prepare the entry to record the redemption of the bonds.

*Reasoning:* In recording the redemption of bonds before maturity, it is necessary to (1) eliminate the carrying value of the bonds, (2) recognize the cash paid, and (3) recognize the gain or loss equal to the difference between (1) and (2).

*Solution:* There is a loss on redemption because the cash paid, $510,000 ($500,000 × 102), is greater than the carrying value of $508,000. The entry is:

| | | |
|---|---:|---:|
| Bonds Payable | 500,000 | |
| Premium on Bonds Payable | 8,000 | |
| Loss on Bond Redemption | 2,000 | |
|     Cash | | 510,000 |
|     (To record redemption of bonds at 102) | | |

*Related exercise material:* BE16–6, E16–3, E16–4, and E16–6.

THE
NAVIGATOR

# ACCOUNTING FOR OTHER LONG-TERM LIABILITIES

Other common types of long-term obligations are notes payable and lease liabilities. The accounting for these liabilities is explained in the following sections.

## Long-Term Notes Payable

**5**
STUDY
OBJECTIVE
Describe the accounting for long-term notes payable.

The use of notes payable in long-term debt financing is quite common. Long-term notes payable are similar to short-term interest-bearing notes payable except that the terms of the notes exceed one year. In periods of unstable interest rates, the interest rate on long-term notes may be tied to changes in the market rate for comparable loans. Examples are the 8.03% adjustable rate notes issued by General Motors and the floating rate notes issued by American Express Company.

A long-term note may be secured by a document called a **mortgage** that pledges title to specific assets as security for a loan. Mortgage notes payable are widely used in the purchase of homes by individuals and in the acquisition of plant assets by many small and some large companies. For example, approximately 18% of McDonald's long-term debt relates to mortgage notes on land, buildings, and improvements. Like other long-term notes payable, the mortgage loan terms may stipulate either a fixed or an adjustable interest rate. Typically, the terms require the borrower to make installment payments over the term of the loan. Each payment consists of (1) interest on the unpaid balance of the loan, and (2) a reduction of loan principal. The interest decreases each period, while the portion applied to the loan principal increases.

Mortgage notes payable are recorded initially at face value, and entries are required subsequently for each installment payment. To illustrate, assume that Porter Technology Inc. issues a $500,000, 12%, 20-year mortgage note on December 31, 1999, to obtain needed financing for the construction of a new research laboratory. The terms provide for semiannual installment payments of $33,231 (not including real estate taxes and insurance). The installment payment schedule for the first 2 years is as follows:

**ILLUSTRATION 16-18**
*Mortgage installment payment schedule*

| Semiannual Interest Period | (A) Cash Payment | (B) Interest Expense (D) × 6% | (C) Reduction of Principal (A) − (B) | (D) Principal Balance (D) − (C) |
|---|---|---|---|---|
| Issue date | | | | $500,000 |
| 1 | $33,231 | $30,000 | $3,231 | 496,769 |
| 2 | 33,231 | 29,806 | 3,425 | 493,344 |
| 3 | 33,231 | 29,601 | 3,630 | 489,714 |
| 4 | 33,231 | 29,383 | 3,848 | 485,866 |

**HELPFUL HINT**
Electronic spreadsheet programs can create a schedule of installment loan payments. This allows you to put in the data for your own mortgage loan and get an illustration that really hits home.

The entries to record the mortgage loan and first installment payment are as follows:

| Dec. 31 | Cash | 500,000 | |
| |     Mortgage Notes Payable | | 500,000 |
| |       (To record mortgage loan) | | |

| A | = | L | + | SE |
|---|---|---|---|---|
| +500,000 | | +500,000 | | |

| June 30 | Interest Expense | 30,000 | |
| | Mortgage Notes Payable | 3,231 | |
| |     Cash | | 33,231 |
| |       (To record semiannual payment on mortgage) | | |

| A | = | L | + | SE |
|---|---|---|---|---|
| −33,231 | | −3,231 | | −30,000 |

**In the balance sheet, the reduction in principal for the next year is reported as a current liability, and the remaining unpaid principal balance is classified as a long-term liability.** At December 31, 2000, the total liability is $493,344 of which $7,478 ($3,630 + $3,848) is current, and $485,866 ($493,344 − $7,478) is long-term.

## Lease Liabilities

As indicated in Chapter 10, a lease is a contractual arrangement between the lessor (owner of the property) and a lessee (renter of the property) that grants the right to use specific property for a period of time in return for cash payments. Leasing is big business. For example, an estimated $125 billion of capital equipment was leased in a recent year. This represents approximately one-third of equipment financed that year. The two most common types of leases are operating leases and capital leases.

**6**
STUDY OBJECTIVE
Contrast the accounting for operating and capital leases.

## ACCOUNTING IN ACTION
### Business Insight

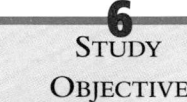 As an excellent example of the magnitude of leasing, leased planes account for nearly 40% of the U.S. fleet of commercial airlines. The reasons for leasing include favorable tax treatment, increased flexibility, and low airline income. As passenger volume is expected to double in the next 20 years, some industry analysts estimate that approximately $400 billion in airplanes will be needed, and it is anticipated that much of the financing will be done through leasing. Leasing is particularly attractive to lessors because airplanes have relatively long lives, a ready secondhand market, and a significant resale value. Or take the commercial truck fleet—over one-third of heavy-duty trucks are presently leased.

## Operating Leases

The renting of an apartment and the rental of a car at an airport are examples of operating leases. **In an operating lease the intent is temporary use of the property by the lessee with continued ownership of the property by the lessor.** The lease (or rental) payments are recorded as an expense by the lessee and as revenue by the lessor. For example, assuming that a sales representative for Western Inc. leases a car from Hertz Car Rental at the Los Angeles airport and that Hertz charges a total of $275, the entry by the lessee, Western Inc., is:

| A | = | L | + | SE |
|---|---|---|---|---|
| −275 | | | | −275 |

| | | |
|---|---|---|
| Car Rental Expense | 275 | |
|     Cash | | 275 |
|       (To record payment of lease rental charge) | | |

In addition, the lessee may incur other costs during the lease period. For example, in the case above, the lessee may be required to pay for gas and oil. These costs are also reported as an expense.

## Capital Leases

**HELPFUL HINT**

A capital lease situation is one in which although it is legally a rental case, it is *in substance* an installment purchase by the lessee. Accounting standards require that substance over form be used in such a situation.

In most lease contracts, a periodic payment is made by the lessee and is recorded as rent expense in the income statement. However, in some cases, the lease contract transfers substantially all the benefits and risks of ownership to the lessee, so that the lease is in effect a purchase of the property. This type of lease is called a capital lease because the present value of the cash payments for the lease are capitalized and recorded as an asset. Illustration 16-19 indicates the major difference between an operating and a capital lease.

**ILLUSTRATION 16-19**

*Types of leases*

In addition to the conditions below:

The lessee must record the lease **as an asset**—that is, as a capital lease—if any **one** of the following conditions exists:

1. **The lease transfers ownership of the property to the lessee.** *Rationale:* If during the lease term, the lessee receives ownership of the asset, the leased asset should be reported as an asset on the lessee's books.
2. **The lease contains a bargain purchase option.** *Rationale:* If during the term of the lease, the lessee can purchase the asset at a price substantially below its fair market value, the lessee will obviously exercise this option. Thus, the lease should be reported as a leased asset on the lessee's books.
3. **The lease term is equal to 75% or more of the economic life of the leased property.** *Rationale:* If the lease term is for much of the asset's useful life, the asset should be recorded by the lessee.
4. **The present value of the lease payments equals or exceeds 90% of the fair market value of the leased property.** *Rationale:* If the present value of the lease payments is equal to or almost equal to the fair market value of the asset, the lessee has essentially purchased the asset. As a result, the leased asset should be recorded on the books of the lessee.

To illustrate, assume that Gonzalez Company decides to lease new equipment. The lease period is 4 years; the economic life of the leased equipment is estimated to be 5 years. The present value of the lease payments is $190,000 which is equal to the fair market value of the equipment. There is no transfer of ownership during the lease term nor is there any bargain purchase option.

In this example, Gonzalez has essentially purchased the equipment. Conditions 3 and 4 have been met: First, the lease term is 75% or more of the economic life of the asset, and second, the present value of cash payments is equal to the equipment's fair market value. The entry to record the transaction is as follows:

| | | |
|---|---|---|
| Leased Asset—Equipment | 190,000 | |
|   Lease Liability | | 190,000 |
|     (To record leased asset and lease liability) | | |

| A | = | L | + | SE |
|---|---|---|---|---|
| + 190,000 | | + 190,000 | | |

The leased asset is reported on the balance sheet under plant assets. The lease liability is reported as a liability on the balance sheet. **The portion of the lease liability expected to be paid in the next year is reported as a current liability. The remainder is classified as a long-term liability.**

Most lessees do not like to report leases on their balance sheets. The reason is that the lease liability increases the company's total liabilities. This, in turn, may make it more difficult for the company to obtain needed funds from lenders. As a result, companies attempt to keep leased assets and lease liabilities off the balance sheet by not meeting any one of the four conditions mentioned above. This procedure of keeping liabilities off the balance sheet is often referred to as **off-balance sheet financing.**

# STATEMENT PRESENTATION AND ANALYSIS

## Presentation

Long-term liabilities are reported in a separate section of the balance sheet immediately following current liabilities, as shown on the next page.

**STUDY OBJECTIVE 7**

Identify the methods for the presentation and analysis of long-term liabilities.

| **LAX CORPORATION** | | |
| :---: | :---: | :---: |
| **Balance Sheet (partial)** | | |
| Long-term liabilities | | |
| Bonds payable 10% due in 2009 | $1,000,000 | |
| Less: Discount on bonds payable | 80,000 | $ 920,000 |
| Mortgage notes payable, 11%, due in 2015 and secured by plant assets | | 500,000 |
| Lease liability | | 540,000 |
| Total long-term liabilities | | $1,960,000 |

Alternatively, summary data may be presented in the balance sheet with detailed data (such as interest rates, maturity dates, conversion privileges, and assets pledged as collateral) shown in a supporting schedule. The current maturities of long-term debt should be reported under current liabilities if they are to be paid from current assets.

## Analysis

Long-term creditors and stockholders are interested in a company's long-run solvency, particularly its ability to pay interest as it comes due and to repay the face value of the debt at maturity. Debt to total assets and times interest earned are two ratios that provide information about debt-paying ability and long-run solvency.

The **debt to total assets ratio** measures the percentage of the total assets provided by creditors. It is computed, as shown in the formula below, by dividing total debt (both current and long-term liabilities) by total assets. The higher the percentage of debt to total assets, the greater the risk that the company may be unable to meet its maturing obligations.

The **times interest earned ratio** provides an indication of the company's ability to meet interest payments as they come due. It is computed by dividing income before income taxes and interest expense by interest expense.

To illustrate these ratios, we will use data from Kellogg Company's annual report which disclosed total liabilities of $3,880.1 million, total assets of $4,877.6 million, interest expense of $108.3 million, income taxes of $340.5 million, and net income of $546.0 million. Kellogg's debt to total assets ratio and times interest earned ratio are shown graphically below, along with their computations.

| Total Debt | ÷ | Total Assets | = | Debt to Total Assets |
| :---: | :---: | :---: | :---: | :---: |
| $3,880.1 | ÷ | $4,877.6 | = | 79.6% |
| Income before Income Taxes and Interest Expense | ÷ | Interest Expense | = | Times Interest Earned |
| $546.0 + $340.5 + $108.3 | ÷ | $108.3 | = | 9.2 times |

Even though Kellogg Company has a relatively high debt to total assets percentage of 79.6%, its interest coverage of 9.2 times appears very safe.

# BEFORE YOU GO ON . . .

## Review It

1. Explain the accounting for long-term mortgage notes payable.
2. What is the difference in accounting for an operating lease versus a capital lease? Explain the four conditions used to determine whether the lease contract transfers substantially all the benefits and risks of ownership.
3. What ratios may be computed to analyze a company's long-run solvency?

## A LOOK BACK AT OUR FEATURE STORY

Refer to the opening story and answer the following questions:

1. The University of Kentucky's bonds are rated AA– by Standard & Poor's and A1 by Moody's Investor Service. Why is it important to the University of Kentucky that its bonds have a high bond rating?
2. Explain the meaning of the tax-exempt status of the University of Kentucky bonds. What does it mean to say that "a recent issue offering 6% is the equivalent of 10% to those individuals in the top tax bracket"?
3. Why does the state use bonds to finance the buildings rather than taking the funds out of general revenues?

*Solution:*

1. Having a high (good) bond rating is as important to a university as it is to a business corporation. A high bond rating indicates that the bonds are less risky, and thus more attractive, to purchasers of the bonds. Hence a lower interest rate results, and the cost to the issuer of the bonds is less.
2. Because the University of Kentucky bonds are tax exempt, holders of the bonds do not have to pay federal income tax on the interest received on the bonds. To earn an after-tax return of 6%, a person in the maximum tax bracket would have to receive interest equal to approximately 10% on taxable bonds [10% − (40% × 10%)].
3. Financing the buildings through the issuance of bonds spreads the cost of the buildings over many years and more equitably distributes the costs to a broader base of taxpayers. Future taxpayers pay for the buildings as the buildings are used, rather than the taxpayers of one year absorbing the total cost out of general revenues in the year of construction.

THE
NAVIGATOR

## DEMONSTRATION PROBLEM

Snyder Software Inc. has successfully developed a new spreadsheet program. However, to produce and market the program, the company needed $2.0 million of additional financing. On December 31, 1999, Snyder borrowed money as follows:

1. Snyder issued $500,000, 11%, 10-year convertible bonds. The bonds sold at face value and pay semiannual interest on January 1 and July 1. Each $1,000 bond is convertible into 30 shares of Snyder's $20 par value common stock.
2. Snyder issued $1.0 million, 10%, 10-year bonds for $885,301. Interest is payable semiannually on January 1 and July 1. Snyder uses the straight-line method of amortization.
3. Snyder also issued a $500,000, 12%, 15-year mortgage note payable. The terms provide for semiannual installment payments of $36,324 on June 30 and December 31.

*Instructions*

1. For the convertible bonds, prepare journal entries for:
   (a) the issuance of the bonds on January 1, 2000.

    (b) interest expense on July 1 and December 31, 2000.

    (c) the payment of interest on January 1, 2001.

    (d) the conversion of all bonds into common stock on January 1, 2001, when the market value of the common stock was $67 per share.

2. For the 10-year, 10% bonds:

    (a) journalize the issuance of the bonds on January 1, 2000.

    (b) prepare a bond discount amortization schedule for the first six interest periods.

    (c) prepare the journal entries for interest expense and amortization of bond discount in 2000.

    (d) prepare the entry for the redemption of the bonds at 101 on January 1, 2003, after paying the interest due on this date.

3. For the mortgage note payable:

    (a) prepare the entry for the issuance of the note on December 31, 1999.

    (b) prepare a payment schedule for the first four installment payments.

    (c) indicate the current and noncurrent amounts for the mortgage note payable at December 31, 2000.

## SOLUTION TO DEMONSTRATION PROBLEM

**PROBLEM-SOLVING STRATEGIES**

1. Interest is usually paid semiannually. Be careful to use only 6 months' interest in your computations.

2. Upon conversion, the book (carrying) value of the bonds is removed from the liability accounts and recorded as common stock and related paid-in capital.

1. (a) 2000

| | | | | |
|---|---|---|---|---|
| Jan. 1 | Cash | | 500,000 | |
| |     Bonds Payable | | | 500,000 |
| |     (To record issue of 11%, 10-year convertible bonds at face value) | | | |

(b) 2000

| | | | | |
|---|---|---|---|---|
| July 1 | Bond Interest Expense | | 27,500 | |
| |     Cash ($500,000 × 0.055) | | | 27,500 |
| |     (To record payment of semiannual interest) | | | |
| Dec. 31 | Bond Interest Expense | | 27,500 | |
| |     Bond Interest Payable | | | 27,500 |
| |     (To record accrual of semiannual bond interest) | | | |

(c) 2001

| | | | | |
|---|---|---|---|---|
| Jan. 1 | Bond Interest Payable | | 27,500 | |
| |     Cash | | | 27,500 |
| |     (To record payment of accrued interest) | | | |

(d) Jan. 1

| | | | | |
|---|---|---|---|---|
| | Bonds Payable | | 500,000 | |
| |     Common Stock | | | 300,000* |
| |     Paid-in Capital in Excess of Par Value | | | 200,000 |
| |     (To record conversion of bonds into common stock) | | | |
| |     *($500,000 ÷ $1,000 = 500 bonds; 500 × 30 = 15,000 shares; 15,000 × $20 = $300,000) | | | |

2. (a) 2000

| | | | | |
|---|---|---|---|---|
| Jan. 1 | Cash | | 885,301 | |
| | Discount on Bonds Payable | | 114,699 | |
| |     Bonds Payable | | | 1,000,000 |
| |     (To record issuance of bonds at a discount) | | | |

(b)

| Semiannual Interest Period | Interest to Be Paid | Interest Expense to Be Recorded | Discount Amortization | Unamortized Discount | Bond Carrying Value |
|---|---|---|---|---|---|
| Issue date | | | | $114,699 | $885,301 |
| 1 | $50,000 | $55,735 | $5,735 | 108,964 | 891,036 |
| 2 | 50,000 | 55,735 | 5,735 | 103,229 | 896,771 |
| 3 | 50,000 | 55,735 | 5,735 | 97,494 | 902,506 |
| 4 | 50,000 | 55,735 | 5,735 | 91,759 | 908,241 |
| 5 | 50,000 | 55,735 | 5,735 | 86,024 | 913,976 |
| 6 | 50,000 | 55,735 | 5,735 | 80,289 | 919,711 |

(c) 2000

| | | | | |
|---|---|---|---|---|
| July 1 | Bond Interest Expense | | 55,735 | |
| | Discount on Bonds Payable | | | 5,735 |
| | Cash | | | 50,000 |
| | (To record payment of semiannual interest and amortization of bond discount) | | | |
| | | | | |
| Dec. 31 | Bond Interest Expense | | 55,735 | |
| | Discount on Bonds Payable | | | 5,735 |
| | Bond Interest Payable | | | 50,000 |
| | (To record accrual of semiannual interest and amortization of bond discount) | | | |

(d) 2003

| | | | | |
|---|---|---|---|---|
| Jan. 1 | Bonds Payable | | 1,000,000 | |
| | Loss on Bond Redemption | | 90,289* | |
| | Discount on Bonds Payable | | | 80,289 |
| | Cash | | | 1,010,000 |
| | (To record redemption of bonds at 101) | | | |
| | *($1,010,000 − $919,711) | | | |

3. (a) 1999

| | | | | |
|---|---|---|---|---|
| Dec. 31 | Cash | | 500,000 | |
| | Mortgage Notes Payable | | | 500,000 |
| | (To record issuance of mortgage note payable) | | | |

(b)

| Semiannual Interest Period | Cash Payment | Interest Expense | Reduction of Principal | Principal Balance |
|---|---|---|---|---|
| Issue date | | | | $500,000 |
| 1 | $36,324 | $30,000 | $6,324 | 493,676 |
| 2 | 36,324 | 29,621 | 6,703 | 486,973 |
| 3 | 36,324 | 29,218 | 7,106 | 479,867 |
| 4 | 36,324 | 28,792 | 7,532 | 472,335 |

(c) Current liability      $14,638 ($7,106 + $7,532)
    Long-term liability      $472,335

---

**PROBLEM-SOLVING STRATEGIES**

1. Discount on bonds payable is a contra liability account.

2. Amortization of bond discount increases bond interest expense.

3. Bond interest expense is the same each period when the straight-line method is used.

4. Loss on bond redemption occurs when the cash paid is greater than the bond carrying value.

**PROBLEM-SOLVING STRATEGIES**

1. Interest expense decreases each period because the principal is decreasing each period.

2. Each payment consists of (1) interest on the unpaid loan balance and (2) a reduction of the loan principal.

THE NAVIGATOR

# SUMMARY OF STUDY OBJECTIVES

1. *Explain why bonds are issued.* Bonds may be sold to many investors, and they offer the following advantages over common stock: (a) stockholder control is not affected, (b) tax savings result, (c) earnings per share of common stock may be higher.

2. *Prepare the entries for the issuance of bonds and interest expense.* When bonds are issued, Cash is debited for the cash proceeds and Bonds Payable is credited for the face value of the bonds. In addition, Bond Interest Payable is credited if there is accrued interest, and the accounts Premium on Bonds Payable or Discount on Bonds Payable are used to show the bond premium or bond discount. Bond discount and bond premium are amortized by the straight-line method.

3. *Describe the entries when bonds are redeemed or converted.* When bonds are redeemed at maturity, Cash is credited and Bonds Payable is debited for the face value of the bonds. When bonds are redeemed before maturity, it is necessary to (a) eliminate the carrying value of the bonds at the redemption date, (b) record the cash paid, and (c) recognize the gain or loss on redemption. When bonds are converted to common stock, the carrying (or book) value of the bonds is transferred to appropriate paid-in capital accounts, and no gain or loss is recognized.

4. *Indicate the entries required for a bond sinking fund.* Entries are required for a bond sinking fund to record (a) periodic contributions, (b) annual revenue, and (c) redemption of the bonds.

5. *Describe the accounting for long-term notes payable.* Each payment consists of (1) interest on the unpaid balance of the loan, and (2) a reduction of loan principal. The interest decreases each period, while the portion applied to the loan principal increases each period.

6. *Contrast the accounting for operating and capital leases.* For an operating lease, lease (or rental) payments are recorded as an expense by the lessee (renter). For a capital lease, the lessee records the asset and related obligation at the present value of the future lease payments.

7. *Identify the methods for the presentation and analysis of long-term liabilities.* The nature and amount of each long-term debt should be reported in the balance sheet or in schedules in the notes accompanying the statements. Stockholders and long-term creditors are interested in a company's long-run solvency, particularly its ability to pay interest as it comes due and to repay the face value of the debt at maturity. Debt to total assets and times interest earned are two ratios that provide information about debt-paying ability and long-run solvency.

# GLOSSARY

**Bearer (coupon) bonds**    Bonds not registered. (p. 678).

**Bond certificate**    A legal document that indicates the name of the issuer, the face value of the bonds, and such other data as the contractual interest rate and maturity date of the bonds. (p. 679).

**Bond indenture**    A legal document that sets forth the terms of the bond issue. (p. 678).

**Bonds**    A form of interest bearing notes payable issued by corporations, universities, and governmental entities. (p. 676).

**Callable bonds**    Bonds that are subject to retirement at a stated dollar amount prior to maturity at the option of the issuer. (p. 678).

**Capital lease**    A contractual arrangement that transfers substantially all the benefits and risks of ownership to the lessee so that the lease is in effect a purchase of the property. (p. 694).

**Convertible bonds**    Bonds that permit bondholders to convert them into common stock at their option. (p. 678).

**Contractual interest rate**    Rate used to determine the amount of interest the borrower pays and the investor receives. (p. 678).

**Debenture bonds**    Bonds issued against the general credit of the borrower. Also called unsecured bonds. (p. 678).

**Debt to total assets ratio**    A solvency measure that indicates the percentage of total assets provided by creditors, computed as total debt divided by total assets. (p. 696).

**Face value**    Amount of principal due at the maturity date of the bond. (p. 678).

**Long-term liabilities**    Obligations expected to be paid after one year. (p. 676).

**Market interest rate**    The rate investors demand for loaning funds to the corporation. (p. 680).

**Mortgage bond**    A bond secured by real estate. (p. 678).

**Mortgage note payable**    A long-term note secured by a mortgage that pledges title to specific units of property as security for the loan. (p. 692).

**Operating lease**    A contractual arrangement giving the lessee temporary use of the property with continued ownership of the property by the lessor. (p. 694).

**Registered bonds**    Bonds issued in the name of the owner. (p. 678).

**Secured bonds**    Bonds that have specific assets of the issuer pledged as collateral. (p. 678).

**Serial bonds**    Bonds that mature in installments. (p. 678).

**Sinking fund**    Cash or other assets set aside to retire debt. (p. 690).

**Sinking fund bonds**   Bonds secured by specific assets set aside to retire them. (p. 678).

**Straight-line method of amortization**   A method of amortizing bond discount or bond premium that allocates the same amount to interest expense in each interest period. (p. 684).

**Term bonds**   Bonds that mature at a single specified future date. (p. 678).

**Times interest earned ratio**   A solvency measure that indicates a company's ability to meet interest payments, computed by dividing income before income taxes and interest expense by interest expense. (p. 696).

**Unsecured bonds**   Bonds issued against the general credit of the borrower. Also called debenture bonds. (p. 678).

# APPENDIX   EFFECTIVE-INTEREST AMORTIZATION

The straight-line method of amortization that you studied in the chapter has a conceptual deficiency: It does not completely satisfy the matching principle. Under the straight-line method, interest expense as a percentage of the carrying value of the bonds varies each interest period. This can be seen by using data from the first three interest periods of the bond amortization schedule that was shown in Illustration 16-12:

| Semiannual Interest Period | Interest Expense to Be Recorded (A) | Bond Carrying Value (B) | Interest Expense as a Percentage of Carrying Value (A) ÷ (B) |
|---|---|---|---|
| 1 | $52,000 | $980,000 | 5.31% |
| 2 | 52,000 | 982,000 | 5.29% |
| 3 | 52,000 | 984,000 | 5.27% |
| 10 | 52,000 | 998,000 | 5.21% |

**ILLUSTRATION 16A-1**

*Interest percentage rates under straight-line method*

Note that interest expense as a percentage of carrying value declines in each interest period. However, to completely comply with the matching principle, interest expense as a percentage of carrying value should not change over the life of the bonds. This percentage, referred to as the **effective-interest rate**, is established when the bonds are issued and remains constant in each interest period. The effective-interest method of amortization accomplishes this result.

Under the **effective-interest method**, the amortization of bond discount or bond premium results in periodic interest expense equal to a constant percentage of the carrying value of the bonds. The effective-interest method results in varying amounts of amortization and interest expense per period but a constant percentage rate; the straight-line method results in constant amounts of amortization and interest expense per period but a varying percentage rate.

The following steps are required under the effective-interest method:

1. Compute the **bond interest expense** by multiplying the carrying value of the bonds at the beginning of the interest period by the effective-interest rate.
2. Compute the **bond interest paid** (or accrued) by multiplying the face value of the bonds by the contractual interest rate.
3. Compute the **amortization amount** by determining the difference between the amounts computed in steps (1) and (2).

These steps are graphically depicted in Illustration 16A-2.

**8**

**STUDY OBJECTIVE**

Contrast the effects of the straight-line and effective-interest methods of amortizing bond discount and bond premium.

Both the straight-line and effective-interest methods of amortization result in the same total amount of interest expense over the term of the bonds. Furthermore, interest expense each interest period is generally comparable in amount. However, **when the amounts are materially different, the effective-interest method is required under generally accepted accounting principles (GAAP).**

# AMORTIZING BOND DISCOUNT

**ILLUSTRATION 16A-3**

*Bond discount amortization schedule*

To illustrate the effective-interest method of bond discount amortization, assume that Wrightway Corporation issues $100,000 of 10%, 5-year bonds on January 1,

## WRIGHTWAY CORPORATION
### Bond Discount Amortization
### Effective-Interest Method—Semiannual Interest Payments
### 10% Bonds Issued at 12%

| Semiannual Interest Periods | (A) Interest to Be Paid (5% × $100,000) | (B) Interest Expense to Be Recorded (6% × Preceding Bond Carrying Value) | (C) Discount Amortization (B) − (A) | (D) Unamortized Discount (D) − (C) | (E) Bond Carrying Value ($100,000 − D) |
|---|---|---|---|---|---|
| Issue date | | | | $7,361 | $ 92,639 |
| 1 | $ 5,000 | $ 5,558 (6% × $92,639) | $ 558 | 6,803 | 93,197 |
| 2 | 5,000 | 5,592 (6% × $93,197) | 592 | 6,211 | 93,789 |
| 3 | 5,000 | 5,627 (6% × $93,789) | 627 | 5,584 | 94,416 |
| 4 | 5,000 | 5,665 (6% × $94,416) | 665 | 4,919 | 95,081 |
| 5 | 5,000 | 5,705 (6% × $95,081) | 705 | 4,214 | 95,786 |
| 6 | 5,000 | 5,747 (6% × $95,786) | 747 | 3,467 | 96,533 |
| 7 | 5,000 | 5,792 (6% × $96,533) | 792 | 2,675 | 97,325 |
| 8 | 5,000 | 5,840 (6% × $97,325) | 840 | 1,835 | 98,165 |
| 9 | 5,000 | 5,890 (6% × $98,165) | 890 | 945 | 99,055 |
| 10 | 5,000 | 5,945* (6% × $99,055) | 945 | −0− | 100,000 |
| | $50,000 | $57,361 | $7,361 | | |

Column **(A)** remains constant because the face value of the bonds ($100,000) is multiplied by the semiannual contractual interest rate (5%) each period.

Column **(B)** is computed as the preceding bond carrying value times the semiannual effective-interest rate (6%).

Column **(C)** indicates the discount amortization each period.

Column **(D)** decreases each period until it reaches zero at maturity.

Column **(E)** increases each period until it equals face value at maturity.

*$2 difference due to rounding.

1999, with interest payable each July 1 and January 1. The bonds sell for $92,639 (92.639% of face value), which results in bond discount of $7,361 ($100,000 − $92,639) and an effective-interest rate of 12%. (Note that the $92,639 can be proven as shown in Appendix C at the end of this book.) Preparing a bond discount amortization schedule as shown in Illustration 16A-3 on the previous page facilitates the recording of interest expense and the discount amortization. Note that interest expense as a percentage of carrying value remains constant at 6%.

For the first interest period, the computations of bond interest expense and the bond discount amortization are as follows:

| | |
|---|---|
| Bond interest expense ($92,639 × 6%) | $5,558 |
| Contractual interest ($100,000 × 5%) | 5,000 |
| **Bond discount amortization** | **$ 558** |

**ILLUSTRATION 16A-4**

*Computation of bond discount amortization*

As a result, the entry to record the payment of interest and amortization of bond discount by Wrightway Corporation on July 1, 1999, is:

| | | | |
|---|---|---|---|
| July 1 | Bond Interest Expense | 5,558 | |
| | Discount on Bonds Payable | | 558 |
| | Cash | | 5,000 |
| | (To record payment of bond interest and amortization of bond discount) | | |

| A | = | L | + | SE |
|---|---|---|---|---|
| −5,000 | | +558 | | −5,558 |

For the second interest period, bond interest expense will be $5,592 ($93,197 × 6%), and the discount amortization will be $592. At December 31, the following adjusting entry is made:

| | | | |
|---|---|---|---|
| Dec. 31 | Bond Interest Expense | 5,592 | |
| | Discount on Bonds Payable | | 592 |
| | Bond Interest Payable | | 5,000 |
| | (To record accrued interest and amortization of bond discount) | | |

| A | = | L | + | SE |
|---|---|---|---|---|
| | | + 592 | | −5,592 |
| | | +5,000 | | |

Total bond interest expense for 1999 is $11,150 ($5,558 + $5,592). On January 1, payment of the interest is recorded by a debit to Bond Interest Payable and a credit to Cash.

# AMORTIZING BOND PREMIUM

The amortization of bond premium by the effective-interest method is similar to the procedures described for bond discount. As an example, assume that Wrightway Corporation issues $100,000, 10%, 5-year bonds on January 1, 1999, with interest payable on July 1 and January 1. In this case, the bonds sell for $108,111, which results in bond premium of $8,111 and an effective-interest rate of 8%. The bond premium amortization schedule is shown in Illustration 16A-5.

**HELPFUL HINT**
When a bond sells for $108,111, it is quoted as 108.111% of face value. Note that $108,111 can be proven as shown in Appendix C.

**ILLUSTRATION 16A-5**

*Bond premium amortization schedule*

### WRIGHTWAY CORPORATION
### Bond Premium Amortization
### Effective-Interest Method—Semiannual Interest Payments
### 10% Bonds Issued at 8%

| Semiannual Interest Periods | (A) Interest to Be Paid (5% × $100,000) | (B) Interest Expense to Be Recorded (4% × Preceding Bond Carry Value) | (C) Premium Amortization (A) − (B) | (D) Unamortized Premium (D) − (C) | (E) Bond Carrying Value ($100,000 + D) |
|---|---|---|---|---|---|
| Issue date | | | | $8,111 | $108,111 |
| 1 | $ 5,000 | $ 4,324 (4% × $108,111) | $ 676 | 7,435 | 107,435 |
| 2 | 5,000 | 4,297 (4% × $107,435) | 703 | 6,732 | 106,732 |
| 3 | 5,000 | 4,269 (4% × $106,732) | 731 | 6,001 | 106,001 |
| 4 | 5,000 | 4,240 (4% × $106,001) | 760 | 5,241 | 105,241 |
| 5 | 5,000 | 4,210 (4% × $105,241) | 790 | 4,451 | 104,451 |
| 6 | 5,000 | 4,178 (4% × $104,451) | 822 | 3,629 | 103,629 |
| 7 | 5,000 | 4,145 (4% × $103,629) | 855 | 2,774 | 102,774 |
| 8 | 5,000 | 4,111 (4% × $102,774) | 889 | 1,885 | 101,885 |
| 9 | 5,000 | 4,075 (4% × $101,885) | 925 | 960 | 100,960 |
| 10 | 5,000 | 4,040* (4% × $100,960) | 960 | –0– | 100,000 |
| | $50,000 | $41,889 | $8,111 | | |

Column (A) remains constant because the face value of the bonds ($100,000) is multiplied by the semiannual contractual interest rate (5%) each period.

Column (B) is computed as the carrying value of the bonds times the semiannual effective-interest rate (4%).

Column (C) indicates the premium amortization each period.

Column (D) decreases each period until it reaches zero at maturity.

Column (E) decreases each period until it equals face value at maturity.

*$2 difference due to rounding.

For the first interest period, the computations of bond interest expense and the bond premium amortization are:

**ILLUSTRATION 16A-6**

*Computation of bond premium amortization*

| | |
|---|---|
| Bond interest expense ($108,111 × 4%) | $4,324 |
| Contractual interest ($100,000 × 5%) | 5,000 |
| Bond premium amortization | $ 676 |

The entry on the first interest date is:

| A | = | L | + | SE |
|---|---|---|---|---|
| −5,000 | | −676 | | −4,324 |

| | | | | |
|---|---|---|---|---|
| July 1 | Bond Interest Expense | | 4,324 | |
| | Premium on Bonds Payable | | 676 | |
| | Cash | | | 5,000 |
| | (To record payment of bond interest and amortization of bond premium) | | | |

For the second interest period, interest expense will be $4,297, and the premium amortization will be $703. Total bond interest expense for 1999 is $8,621 ($4,324 + $4,297).

# TECHNOLOGY IN ACTION

The amortization schedule is an excellent example of an accounting computation efficiently and effectively performed by an electronic spreadsheet. Once the selling price, face amount, contractual rate of interest, effective rate of interest, and number of interest periods are determined and entered into the spreadsheet, all of the computations until maturity can be performed by the computer. Note that all data needed for the adjusting entries can be taken directly from the amortization schedule.

## DEMONSTRATION PROBLEM

Gardner Corporation issues $1,750,000, 10-year, 12% bonds on January 1, 1999, at $1,820,000 to yield 10%. The bonds pay semiannual interest July 1 and January 1. Gardner uses the effective-interest method of amortization.

### Instructions

(a)  Prepare the journal entry to record the issuance of the bonds.
(b)  Prepare the journal entry to record the payment of interest on July 1, 1999.

**PROBLEM-SOLVING STRATEGIES**

1. Bond carrying value at beginning of period times effective-interest rate equals interest expense.
2. Credit to cash (or bond interest payable) is computed by multiplying the face value of the bonds by the contractual interest rate.
3. Bond premium or discount amortization is the difference between (1) and (2).
4. Interest expense increases when the effective-interest method is used for bonds issued at a discount. The reason is that a constant percentage is applied to an increasing book value to compute interest expense.

### SOLUTION TO DEMONSTRATION PROBLEM

(a) 1999

| | | | |
|---|---|---|---|
| Jan. 1 | Cash | 1,820,000 | |
| | Bonds Payable | | 1,750,000 |
| | Premium on Bonds Payable | | 70,000 |
| | (To record issuance of bonds at a premium) | | |
| 1999 | | | |
| July 1 | Bond Interest Expense | 91,000* | |
| | Premium on Bonds Payable | 14,000** | |
| | Cash | | 105,000 |
| | (To record payment of semiannual interest and amortization of bond premium) | | |
| | *($1,820,000 × 5%) | | |
| | **($105,000 − $91,000) | | |

## SUMMARY OF STUDY OBJECTIVE FOR APPENDIX

**8. *Contrast the effects of the straight-line and effective-interest methods of amortizing bond discount and bond premium.*** The straight-line method of amortization results in a constant amount of amortization and interest expense per period but a varying percentage rate. In contrast, the effective-interest method results in varying amounts of amortization and interest expense per period but a constant percentage rate of interest. The effective-interest method generally results in a better matching of expenses with revenues. When the difference between the straight-line and effective-interest method is material, the use of the effective-interest method is required under GAAP.

# GLOSSARY FOR APPENDIX

**Effective-interest method of amortization**  A method of amortizing bond discount or bond premium that results in periodic interest expense equal to a constant percentage of the carrying value of the bonds. (p. 701).

**Effective-interest rate**  Rate established when bonds are issued that remains constant in each interest period. (p. 701).

*Note: All asterisked Questions, Exercises, and Problems relate to material in the appendix to the chapter.

# SELF-STUDY QUESTIONS

Answers are at the end of the chapter.

(SO 1)  1. The term used for bonds that are unsecured is:
   a. callable bonds.
   b. indenture bonds.
   c. debenture bonds.
   d. bearer bonds.

(SO 2)  2. Karson Inc. issues 10-year bonds with a maturity value of $200,000. If the bonds are issued at a premium, this indicates that:
   a. the contractual interest rate exceeds the market interest rate.
   b. the market interest rate exceeds the contractual interest rate.
   c. the contractual interest rate and the market interest rate are the same.
   d. no relationship exists between the two rates.

(SO 2)  3. On January 1, Hurley Corporation issues $500,000, 5-year, 12% bonds at 96 with interest payable on July 1 and January 1. The entry on July 1 to record payment of bond interest and the amortization of bond discount using the straight-line method will include a:
   a. debit to Interest Expense, $30,000.
   b. debit to Interest Expense, $60,000.
   c. credit to Discount on Bonds Payable, $4,000.
   d. credit to Discount on Bonds Payable, $2,000.

(SO 2)  4. For the bonds issued in question 3, above, what is the carrying value of the bonds at the end of the third interest period?
   a. $486,000
   b. $488,000
   c. $472,000
   d. $464,000

(SO 2)  5. When the interest payment dates of a bond are May 1 and November 1, and a bond issue is sold on June 1, the amount of cash received by the issuer will be:
   a. decreased by accrued interest from June 1 to November 1.
   b. decreased by accrued interest from May 1 to June 1.
   c. increased by accrued interest from May 1 to June 1.
   d. increased by accrued interest from June 1 to November 1.

(SO 3)  6. Gester Corporation retires its $100,000 face value bonds at 105 on January 1, following the payment of semiannual interest. The carrying value of the bonds at the redemption date is $103,745. The entry to record the redemption will include a:
   a. credit of $3,745 to Loss on Bond Redemption.
   b. debit of $3,745 to Premium on Bonds Payable.
   c. credit of $1,255 to Gain on Bond Redemption.
   d. debit of $5,000 to Premium on Bonds Payable.

(SO 3)  7. Colson Inc. converts $600,000 of bonds sold at face value into 10,000 shares of common stock, par value $1. Both the bonds and the stock have a market value of $760,000.

What amount should be credited to Paid-in Capital in Excess of Par as a result of the conversion?
   a. $10,000
   b. $160,000
   c. $600,000
   d. $590,000

8. Sanger Company has a bond sinking fund in the amount (SO 4) of $400,000. Where should this amount be reported on the balance sheet?
   a. investments section
   b. current asset section
   c. current liability section
   d. long-term liability section

9. Andrews Inc. issues a $497,000, 10% 3-year mortgage (SO 5) note on January 1. The note will be paid in three annual installments of $200,000, each payable at the end of the year. What is the amount of interest expense that should be recognized by Andrews Inc. in the second year?
   a. $16,567
   b. $49,740
   c. $34,670
   d. $347,600

10. Lease A does not contain a bargain purchase option, but (SO 6) the lease term is equal to 90 percent of the estimated economic life of the leased property. Lease B does not transfer ownership of the property to the lessee by the end of the lease term, but the lease term is equal to 75 percent of the estimated economic life of the leased property. How should the lessee classify these leases?

|  | Lease A | Lease B |
|---|---|---|
| a. | Operating lease | Capital lease |
| b. | Operating lease | Operating lease |
| c. | Capital lease | Operating lease |
| d. | Capital lease | Capital lease |

*11. On January 1, Besalius Inc. issued $1,000,000, 9% bonds (SO 8) for $939,000. The market rate of interest for these bonds is 10%. Interest is payable annually on December 31. Besalius uses the effective interest method of amortizing bond discount. At the end of the first year, Besalius should report unamortized bond discount of:
   a. $54,900.
   b. $57,100.
   c. $51,610.
   d. $51,000.

*12. On January 1, Dias Corporation issued $1,000,000, 14%, (SO 8) 5-year bonds with interest payable on July 1 and January 1. The bonds sold for $1,098,540. The market rate of interest for these bonds was 12%. On the first interest date, using the effective-interest method, the debit entry to Bond Interest Expense is for:
   a. $60,000.
   b. $76,898.
   c. $65,912.
   d. $131,825.

THE NAVIGATOR

# QUESTIONS

1. (a) What are long-term liabilities? Give three examples. (b) What is a bond?

2. (a) As a source of long-term financing, what are the major advantages of bonds over common stock? (b) What are the major disadvantages in using bonds for long-term financing?

3. Contrast the following types of bonds: (a) secured and unsecured, (b) term and serial, (c) registered and bearer, and (d) convertible and callable.

4. The following terms are important in issuing bonds: (a) face value, (b) contractual interest rate, (c) bond indenture, and (d) bond certificate. Explain each of these terms.

5. Describe the two major obligations incurred by a company when bonds are issued.

6. Assume that Shinn Inc. sold bonds with a par value of $100,000 for $104,000. Was the market interest rate equal to, less than, or greater than the bonds' contractual interest rate? Explain.

7. Connie Black and Dan Sells are discussing how the market price of a bond is determined. Connie believes that the market price of a bond is solely a function of the amount of the principal payment at the end of the term of a bond. Is she right? Discuss.

8. If a 10%, 10-year, $800,000 bond is issued at par and interest is paid semiannually, what is the amount of the interest payment at the end of the first semiannual period?

9. If the Bonds Payable account has a balance of $900,000 and the Discount on Bonds Payable account has a balance of $60,000, what is the carrying value of the bonds?

10. Explain the straight-line method of amortizing discount and premium on bonds payable.

11. Darby Corporation issues $300,000 of 8%, 5-year bonds on January 1, 1999, at 104. Assuming that the straight-line method is used to amortize the premium, what is the total amount of interest expense for 1999?

12. Which accounts are debited and which are credited if a bond issue originally sold at a premium is redeemed before maturity at 97 immediately following the payment of interest?

13. Mai Corporation is considering issuing a convertible bond. What is a convertible bond? Discuss the advantages of a convertible bond from the standpoint of (a) the bondholders and (b) the issuing corporation.

14. The financial statements of Landis Inc. disclose that it has a bond sinking fund. What is a bond sinking fund? What is its purpose?

15. Dan Foley, a friend of yours, has recently purchased a home for $125,000, paying $25,000 down and the remainder financed by a 10.5%, 20-year mortgage, payable at $998.38 per month. At the end of the first month, Dan receives a statement from the bank indicating that only $123.38 of principal was paid during the month. At this rate, he calculates that it will take over 67 years to pay off the mortgage. Is he right? Discuss.

16. (a) What is a lease agreement? (b) What are the two most common types of leases? (c) Distinguish between the two types of leases.

17. Seminole Company rents a warehouse on a month-to-month basis for the storage of its excess inventory. The company periodically must rent space when its production greatly exceeds actual sales. What is the nature of this type of lease agreement, and what accounting treatment should be accorded it?

18. Alvarez Company entered into an agreement to lease 12 computers from Estes Electronics Inc. The present value of the lease payments is $186,300. Assuming that this is a capital lease, what entry would Alvarez Company make on the date of the lease agreement?

19. In general, what are the requirements for the financial statement presentation of long-term liabilities?

*20. Janet Hashmi is discussing the advantages of the effective-interest method of bond amortization with her accounting staff. What do you think Janet is saying?

*21. Mobley Corporation issues $500,000 of 9%, 5-year bonds on January 1, 1999, at 104. If Mobley uses the effective-interest method in amortizing the premium, will the annual interest expense increase or decrease over the life of the bonds? Explain.

# BRIEF EXERCISES

**BE16-1** Mayo Inc. is considering two alternatives to finance its construction of a new $2 million plant:

*Compare bond versus stock financing.*
(SO 1)

   (a) Issuance of 200,000 shares of common stock at the market price of $10 per share.
   (b) Issuance of $2 million, 8% bonds at par.

Complete the following table and indicate which alternative is preferable.

| | Issue Stock | Issue Bond |
|---|---|---|
| Income before interest and taxes | $800,000 | $800,000 |
| Interest expense from bonds | | |
| Income before income taxes | $ | $ |
| Income tax expense (30%) | | |
| Net income | $ | $ |
| Outstanding shares | | 700,000 |
| Earnings per share | | |

*Prepare entries for bonds issued at face value.*
*(SO 2)*

**BE16–2**  Kaiser Corporation issued 1,000, 8%, 5-year, $1,000 bonds dated January 1, 1999, at 100. (a) Prepare the journal entry to record the sale of these bonds on January 1, 1999. (b) Prepare the journal entry to record the first interest payment on July 1, 1999 (interest payable semiannually), assuming no previous accrual of interest. (c) Prepare the adjusting journal entry on December 31, 1999, to record interest expense.

*Prepare entries for bonds issued at a discount.*
*(SO 2)*

**BE16–3**  Cruyen Company issues $2 million, 10-year, 9% bonds at 97, with interest payable on July 1 and January 1. The straight-line method is used to amortize bond discount. (a) Prepare the journal entry to record the sale of these bonds on January 1, 1999. (b) Prepare the journal entry to record interest expense and bond discount amortization on July 1, 1999, assuming no previous accrual of interest.

*Prepare entries for bonds issued at a premium.*
*(SO 2)*

**BE16–4**  Wiggins Inc. issues $5 million, 5-year, 10% bonds at 102, with interest payable on July 1 and January 1. The straight-line method is used to amortize bond premium. (a) Prepare the journal entry to record the sale of these bonds on January 1, 1999. (b) Prepare the journal entry to record interest expense and bond premium amortization on July 1, 1999, assuming no previous accrual of interest.

*Prepare entries for bonds issued between interest dates.*
*(SO 2)*

**BE16–5**  Quarry Inc. has outstanding $1 million, 10-year, 9% bonds with interest payable on July 1 and January 1. The bonds were dated January 1, 1999, but were issued on May 1, 1999, at face value plus accrued interest. (a) Prepare the journal entry to record the sale of the bonds on May 1, 1999. (b) Prepare the journal entry to record the interest payment on July 1, 1999.

*Prepare entry for redemption of bonds.*
*(SO 3)*

**BE16–6**  The balance sheet for Lopez Company reports the following information on July 1, 1999:

| Long-term liabilities | | |
|---|---|---|
| Bonds payable | $1,000,000 | |
| Less: Discount on bonds payable | 60,000 | $940,000 |

Lopez decides to redeem these bonds at 103 after paying semiannual interest. Prepare the journal entry to record the redemption on July 1, 1999.

*Prepare entries for bond sinking fund.*
*(SO 4)*

**BE16–7**  Pasco Company establishes a sinking fund for its $1 million, 5-year bonds. On January 1, 1999, it makes its first annual cash contribution of $180,000. At the end of 1999, the sinking fund had earned $12,000. (a) Prepare the journal entry to record the contribution made into the sinking fund on January 1, 1999. (b) Prepare the journal entry to record the revenue earned in the sinking fund in 1999.

*Prepare entries for long-term notes payable.*
*(SO 5)*

**BE16–8**  O'Neill Inc. issues a $400,000, 10%, 10-year mortgage note on December 31, 1999, to obtain financing for a new building. The terms provide for semiannual installment payments of $32,097. Prepare the entry to record the mortgage loan on December 31, 1999, and the first installment payment.

*Contrast accounting for operating and capital lease.*
*(SO 6)*

**BE16–9**  Prepare the journal entries that the lessee should make to record the following transactions:

1. The lessee makes a lease payment of $70,000 to the lessor in an operating lease transaction.
2. Lloyd Company leases a new building from Chang Construction, Inc. The present value of the lease payments is $600,000. The lease qualifies as a capital lease.

*Prepare statement presentation of long-term liabilities.*
*(SO 7)*

**BE16–10**  Presented below are long-term liability items for Malik Company at December 31, 1999. Prepare the long-term liabilities section of the balance sheet for Malik Company.

| | |
|---|---|
| Bonds payable, due 2001 | $800,000 |
| Lease liability | 50,000 |
| Notes payable, due 2003 | 80,000 |
| Discount on bonds payable | 45,000 |

**\*BE16–11** Presented below is the partial bond discount amortization schedule for Sauer Corp. Sauer uses the effective-interest method of amortization.

*Use effective-interest method of bond amortization.*
*(SO 8)*

| Semiannual Interest Periods | Interest to Be Paid | Interest Expense to Be Recorded | Discount Amortization | Unamortized Discount | Bond Carrying Value |
|---|---|---|---|---|---|
| Issue date | | | | $62,311 | $937,689 |
| 1 | $45,000 | $46,884 | $1,884 | 60,427 | 939,573 |
| 2 | 45,000 | 46,979 | 1,979 | 58,448 | 941,552 |

**Instructions**
(a) Prepare the journal entry to record the payment of interest and the discount amortization at the end of period 1.
(b) ▭▭▭▷ Explain why interest expense is greater than interest paid.
(c) Explain why interest expense will increase each period.

# EXERCISES

**E16–1** National Airlines is considering two alternatives for the financing of a purchase of a fleet of airplanes. These two alternatives are:

*Compare two alternatives of financing—issuance of common stock vs. issuance of bonds.*
*(SO 1)*

1. Issue 60,000 shares of common stock at $45 per share. (Cash dividends have not been paid nor is the payment of any contemplated.)
2. Issue 13%, 10-year bonds at par for $2,700,000.

It is estimated that the company will earn $600,000 before interest and taxes as a result of this purchase. The company has an estimated tax rate of 30% and has 90,000 shares of common stock outstanding prior to the new financing.

**Instructions**
Determine the effect on net income and earnings per share for these two methods of financing.

**E16–2** On January 1, Madden Company issued $80,000, 10%, 10-year bonds at par. Interest is payable semiannually on July 1 and January 1.

*Prepare entries for issuance of bonds and payment and accrual of bond interest.*
*(SO 2)*

**Instructions**
Present journal entries to record:

(a) The issuance of the bonds.
(b) The payment of interest on July 1, assuming that interest was not accrued on June 30.
(c) The accrual of interest on December 31.

**E16–3** Kang Company issued $200,000, 9%, 20-year bonds on January 1, 1999, at 103. Interest is payable semiannually on July 1 and January 1. Kang uses straight-line amortization for bond premium or discount.

*Prepare entries to record issuance of bonds, payment of interest, amortization of premium, and redemption at maturity.*
*(SO 2, 3)*

**Instructions**
Prepare the journal entries to record:

(a) The issuance of the bonds.
(b) The payment of interest and the premium amortization on July 1, 1999, assuming that interest was not accrued on June 30.
(c) The accrual of interest and the premium amortization on December 31, 1999.
(d) The redemption of the bonds at maturity, assuming interest for the last interest period has been paid and recorded.

**E16–4** Cortez Company issued $180,000, 11%, 10-year bonds on December 31, 1998, for $170,000. Interest is payable semiannually on June 30 and December 31. Cortez uses the straight-line method to amortize bond premium or discount.

*Prepare entries to record issuance of bonds, payment of interest, amortization of discount, and redemption at maturity.*
*(SO 2, 3)*

**Instructions**
Prepare the journal entries to record:

(a) The issuance of the bonds.
(b) The payment of interest and the discount amortization on June 30, 1999.
(c) The payment of interest and the discount amortization on December 31, 1999.
(d) The redemption of the bonds at maturity, assuming interest for the last interest period has been paid and recorded.

*Prepare entries to record issuance of bonds between interest dates, and payment and accrual of interest.*
(SO 2)

**E16–5**  On April 1, Jantz Company issued $80,000, 10%, 10-year bonds dated January 1 at par plus accrued interest. Interest is payable semiannually on July 1 and January 1.

**Instructions**
Present journal entries to record:

 (a) The issuance of the bonds.
 (b) The payment of interest on July 1, assuming that interest was not accrued on June 30.
 (c) The accrual of interest on December 31.

**E16–6**  Presented below are three independent situations:

*Prepare entries for redemption of bonds and conversion of bonds into common stock.*
(SO 3)

 1. Noble Corporation retired $130,000 face value, 12% bonds on June 30, 1999, at 102. The carrying value of the bonds at the redemption date was $107,500. The bonds pay semiannual interest and the interest payment due on June 30, 1999, has been made and recorded.
 2. Vargas, Inc. retired $150,000 face value, 12.5% bonds on June 30, 1999, at 96. The carrying value of the bonds at the redemption date was $151,000. The bonds pay semiannual interest and the interest payment due on June 30, 1999, has been made and recorded.
 3. Lennon Company has $80,000, 8%, 12-year convertible bonds outstanding. These bonds were sold at face value and pay semiannual interest on June 30 and December 31 of each year. The bonds are convertible into 30 shares of Lennon $2 par value common stock for each $1,000 worth of bonds. On December 31, 1999, after the bond interest has been paid, $20,000 face value bonds were converted. The market value of Lennon common stock was $44 per share on December 31, 1999.

**Instructions**
For each independent situation above, prepare the appropriate journal entry for the redemption or conversion of the bonds.

*Prepare entries to record sinking fund deposit, revenue earned on fund assets, and redemption of bonds.*
(SO 4)

**E16–7**  Tabaras Co. decides to establish a sinking fund for its $6,000,000, 20-year bonds that are outstanding. The trustee indicates that an annual contribution of $165,000 should be made at the end of each year. The sinking fund earned $9,700 in the second year. At the maturity date, the sinking fund had a balance of $5,980,000.

**Instructions**
Prepare the journal entries to record:

 (a) The first contribution by Tabaras Co.
 (b) The actual earnings in the second year and the second contribution.
 (c) The redemption of the bonds at maturity.

*Prepare entries to record mortgage note and installment payments.*
(SO 5)

**E16–8**  Neumann Co. receives $120,000 when it issues a $120,000, 10%, mortgage note payable to finance the construction of a building at December 31, 1999. The terms provide for semiannual installment payments of $8,000 on June 30 and December 31.

**Instructions**
Prepare the journal entries to record the mortgage loan and the first two installment payments.

**E16–9**  Presented below are two independent situations.

*Prepare entries for operating lease and capital lease.*
(SO 6)

 1. Speedy Car Rental leased a car to Leach Company for one year. Terms of the operating lease agreement call for monthly payments of $500.
 2. On January 1, 1999, Knapp Inc. entered into an agreement to lease 20 computers from Guinn Electronics. The terms of the lease agreement require three annual rental payments of $90,000 (including 10% interest) beginning December 31, 1999. The present value of the three rental payments is $223,816. Knapp considers this a capital lease.

**Instructions**
 (a) Prepare the appropriate journal entry to be made by Leach Company for the first lease payment.
 (b) Prepare the journal entry to record the lease agreement on the books of Knapp Inc. on January 1, 1999.

*Prepare long-term liabilities section.*
(SO 7)

**E16–10**  The adjusted trial balance for Vowell Corporation at the end of the current year contained the following accounts:

| | |
|---|---:|
| Bond Interest Payable | $ 9,000 |
| Lease Liability | 59,500 |
| Bonds Payable, due 2007 | 140,000 |
| Premium on Bonds Payable | 32,000 |
| Bond Sinking Fund | 241,600 |

**Instructions**

(a) Prepare the long-term liabilities section of the balance sheet.

(b) Indicate the proper balance sheet classification for the account(s) listed above that do not belong in the long-term liabilities section.

*E16–11   Pfeifer Corporation issued $390,000, 9%, 10-year bonds on January 1, 1999, for $365,698. This price resulted in an effective interest rate of 10% on the bonds. Interest is payable semiannually on July 1 and January 1. Pfeifer uses the effective-interest method to amortize bond premium or discount.

*Prepare entries for issuance of bonds, payment of interest, and amortization of discount using effective-interest method.*
*(SO 8)*

**Instructions**

Prepare the journal entries to record (round to the nearest dollar):

(a) The issuance of the bonds.

(b) The payment of interest and the discount amortization on July 1, 1999, assuming that interest was not accrued on June 30.

(c) The accrual of interest and the discount amortization on December 31, 1999.

*E16–12   Nieto Company issued $360,000, 11%, 10-year bonds on January 1, 1999, for $382,432. This price resulted in an effective interest rate of 10% on the bonds. Interest is payable semiannually on July 1 and January 1. Nieto uses the effective-interest method to amortize bond premium or discount.

*Prepare entries for issuance of bonds, payment of interest, and amortization of premium using effective-interest method.*
*(SO 8)*

**Instructions**

Prepare the journal entries (rounded to the nearest dollar) to record:

(a) The issuance of the bonds.

(b) The payment of interest and the premium amortization on July 1, 1999, assuming that interest was not accrued on June 30.

(c) The accrual of interest and the premium amortization on December 31, 1999.

# PROBLEMS: SET A

•••••••••••••••••••••••••••••••••••••••••••••••••••••••••••••

P16–1A   Lorenzo Company sold $4,000,000, 9%, 20-year bonds on January 1, 1999. The bonds were dated January 1, 1999, and pay interest on January 1 and July 1. Lorenzo Company uses the straight-line method to amortize bond premium or discount. The bonds were sold at 98. Assume no interest is accrued on June 30.

*Prepare entries to record issuance of bonds, interest accrual, and amortization for 2 years.*
*(SO 2, 7)*

**Instructions**

(a) Prepare the journal entry to record the issuance of the bonds on January 1, 1999.

(b) Prepare a bond discount amortization schedule for the first four interest periods.

(c) Prepare the journal entries for interest and the amortization of the discount in 1999 and 2000.

(d) Show the balance sheet presentation of the bond liability at December 31, 2000.

P16–2A   Cockrill Corporation sold $1,500,000, 8%, 10-year bonds on January 1, 1999. The bonds were dated January 1, 1999, and pay interest on July 1 and January 1. Cockrill Corporation uses the straight-line method to amortize bond premium or discount. Assume no interest is accrued on June 30.

*Prepare entries to record issuance of bonds, interest, and amortization of bond premium and discount.*
*(SO 2, 7)*

**Instructions**

(a) Prepare all the necessary journal entries to record the issuance of the bonds and bond interest expense for 1999, assuming that the bonds sold at 103.

(b) Prepare journal entries as in part (a) assuming that the bonds sold at 96.

(c) Show balance sheet presentation for each bond issue at December 31, 1999.

*Prepare entries to record interest payments, discount amortization, and redemption of bonds.*
*(SO 2, 3)*

**P16–3A**    The following is taken from Emig Corp. balance sheet:

### EMIG CORPORATION
### Balance Sheet (partial)
### December 31, 1999

| | | |
|---|---|---|
| Current liabilities | | |
| Bond interest payable (for 6 months | | |
| from July 1 to December 31) | | $132,000 |
| Long-term liabilities | | |
| Bonds payable, 11%, due | | |
| January 1, 2010 | $2,400,000 | |
| Less: Discount on bonds payable | 90,000 | $2,310,000 |

Interest is payable semiannually on January 1 and July 1. The bonds are callable on any semi-annual interest date. Emig uses straight-line amortization for any bond premium or discount. From December 31, 1999, the bonds will be outstanding for an additional 10 years or 120 months.

**Instructions**
(Round all computations to the nearest dollar.)

(a) Journalize the payment of bond interest on January 1, 2000.
(b) Prepare the entry to amortize bond discount and to pay the interest due on July 1, 2000, assuming that interest was not accrued on June 30.
(c) Assume that on July 1, 2000, after paying interest, Emig Corp. calls bonds having a face value of $800,000. The call price is 102. Record the redemption of the bonds.
(d) Prepare the adjusting entry at December 31, 2000, to amortize bond discount and to accrue interest on the remaining bonds.

*Prepare installment payments schedule and journal entries for a mortgage note payable.*
*(SO 5)*

**P16–4A**    Kinyae Electronics issues a $600,000, 10%, 10-year mortgage note on December 31, 1999, to help finance a plant expansion program. The terms provide for semiannual installment payments, not including real estate taxes and insurance of $48,145. Payments are due June 30 and December 31.

**Instructions**
(a) Prepare an installment payments schedule for the first 2 years.
(b) Prepare the entries for (1) the mortgage loan and (2) the first two installment payments.
(c) Show how the total mortgage liability should be reported on the balance sheet at December 31, 2000.

*Analyze three different lease situations and prepare journal entries.*
*(SO 6)*

**P16–5A**    Presented below are three different lease transactions in which Foyle Enterprises engaged in 1999. Assume that all lease transactions start on January 1, 1999. In no case does Foyle receive title to the properties leased during or at the end of the lease term.

| | Lessor | | |
|---|---|---|---|
| | Kasnic Associates | Dieker Co. | Irwin Inc. |
| Type of property | Bulldozer | Truck | Furniture |
| Bargain purchase option | None | None | None |
| Lease term | 4 years | 6 years | 3 years |
| Estimated economic life | 8 years | 7 years | 5 years |
| Yearly rental | $13,000 | $ 6,000 | $ 4,000 |
| Fair market value of leased asset | $80,000 | $29,000 | $27,500 |
| Present value of the lease rental payments | $48,000 | $25,000 | $12,000 |

**Instructions**
(a) Identify the leases above as operating or capital leases. Explain.
(b) How should the lease transaction for Dieker Co. be recorded on January 1, 1999?
(c) How should the lease transactions for Irwin Inc. be recorded in 1999?

**\*P16–6A**  On July 1, 1999, Gordon Satellites issued $1,800,000 face value, 9%, 10-year bonds at $1,687,840. This price resulted in an effective-interest rate of 10% on the bonds. Gordon uses the effective-interest method to amortize bond premium or discount. The bonds pay semi-annual interest July 1 and January 1.

*Prepare entries to record issuance of bonds, payment of interest, and amortization of bond discount using effective-interest method.*
*(SO 8)*

**Instructions**
(Round all computations to the nearest dollar.)
  (a)  Prepare the journal entry to record the issuance of the bonds on July 1, 1999.
  (b)  Prepare the journal entry to record the accrual of interest and the amortization of the discount on December 31, 1999.
  (c)  Prepare the journal entry to record the payment of interest and the amortization of the discount on July 1, 2000, assuming that interest was not accrued on June 30.
  (d)  Prepare the journal entry to record the accrual of interest and the amortization of the discount on December 31, 2000.
  (e)  Prepare an amortization table through December 31, 2000 (three interest periods) for this bond issue.

**\*P16–7A**  On July 1, 1999, Crose Chemical Company issued $3,000,000 face value, 12%, 10-year bonds at $3,373,868. This price resulted in a 10% effective-interest rate on the bonds. Crose uses the effective-interest method to amortize bond premium or discount. The bonds pay semiannual interest on each July 1 and January 1.

*Prepare entries to record issuance of bonds, payment of interest, and amortization of premium using effective-interest method. In addition, answer questions.*
*(SO 8)*

**Instructions**
  (a)  Prepare the journal entries to record the following transactions:
    (1)  The issuance of the bonds on July 1, 1999.
    (2)  The accrual of interest and the amortization of the premium on December 31, 1999.
    (3)  The payment of interest and the amortization of the premium on July 1, 2000, assuming no accrual of interest on June 30.
    (4)  The accrual of interest and the amortization of the premium on December 31, 2000.
  (b)  Show the proper balance sheet presentation for the liability for bonds payable on the December 31, 2000, balance sheet.
  (c)  ▨▨▨▨▷  Provide the answers to the following questions in letter form.
    (1)  What amount of interest expense is reported for 2000?
    (2)  Would the bond interest expense reported in 2000 be the same as, greater than, or less than the amount that would be reported if the straight-line method of amortization were used?
    (3)  Determine the total cost of borrowing over the life of the bond.
    (4)  Would the total bond interest expense be greater than, the same as, or less than the total interest expense if the straight-line method of amortization were used?

# PROBLEMS: SET B
• • • • • • • • • • • • • • • • • • • • • • • • • • • • • • • • • • • • • • • • • • • • •

**P16–1B**  Grabowski Electric sold $2,000,000, 10%, 10-year bonds on January 1, 1999. The bonds were dated January 1 and pay interest July 1 and January 1. Grabowski Electric uses the straight-line method to amortize bond premium or discount. The bonds were sold at 104. Assume no interest is accrued on June 30.

*Prepare entries to record issuance of bonds, interest accrual, and amortization for 2 years.*
*(SO 2, 7)*

**Instructions**
  (a)  Prepare the journal entry to record the issuance of the bonds on January 1, 1999.
  (b)  Prepare a bond premium amortization schedule for the first four interest periods.
  (c)  Prepare the journal entries for interest and the amortization of the premium in 1999 and 2000.
  (d)  Show the balance sheet presentation of the bond liability at December 31, 2000.

**P16–2B**  O'Meara Company sold $1,500,000, 12%, 10-year bonds on July 1, 1999. The bonds were dated July 1, 1999, and pay interest July 1 and January 1. O'Meara Company uses the straight-line method to amortize bond premium or discount. Assume no interest is accrued on June 30.

*Prepare entries to record issuance of bonds, interest, and amortization of bond premium and discount.*
*(SO 2, 7)*

*Instructions*

   (a) Prepare all the necessary journal entries to record the issuance of the bonds and bond interest expense for 1999, assuming that the bonds sold at 104.

   (b) Prepare journal entries as in part (a) assuming that the bonds sold at 98.

   (c) Show balance sheet presentation for each bond issue at December 31, 1999.

**P16–3B** The following is taken from the Whitfield Company balance sheet:

*Prepare entries to record interest payments, premium amortization, and redemption of bonds.*
*(SO 2, 3)*

### WHITFIELD COMPANY
### Balance Sheet (partial)
### December 31, 1999

| | | |
|---|---|---|
| Current liabilities | | |
|   Bond interest payable (for 6 months | | |
|     from July 1 to December 31) | | $ 216,000 |
| Long-term liabilities | | |
|   Bonds payable, 12% due January 1, 2010 | $3,600,000 | |
|   Add: Premium on bonds payable | 200,000 | $3,800,000 |

Interest is payable semiannually on January 1 and July 1. The bonds are callable on any semi-annual interest date. Whitfield uses straight-line amortization for any bond premium or discount. From December 31, 1999, the bonds will be outstanding for an additional 10 years (120 months).

*Instructions*

   (a) Journalize the payment of bond interest on January 1, 2000.

   (b) Prepare the entry to amortize bond premium and to pay the interest due on July 1, 2000, assuming no accrual of interest on June 30.

   (c) Assume that on July 1, 2000, after paying interest, Whitfield Company calls bonds having a face value of $1,800,000. The call price is 101. Record the redemption of the bonds.

   (d) Prepare the adjusting entry at December 31, 2000, to amortize bond premium and to accrue interest on the remaining bonds.

*Prepare installment schedule and journal entries for a mortgage note payable.*
*(SO 5)*

**P16–4B** Evans Electronics issues a $400,000, 12%, 10-year mortgage note on December 31, 1998. The proceeds from the note are to be used in financing a new research laboratory. The terms of the note provide for semiannual installment payments, exclusive of real estate taxes and insurance, of $34,874. Payments are due June 30 and December 31.

*Instructions*

   (a) Prepare an installment payments schedule for the first 2 years.

   (b) Prepare the entries for (1) the loan and (2) the first two installment payments.

   (c) Show how the total mortgage liability should be reported on the balance sheet at December 31, 1999.

*Analyze three different lease situations and prepare journal entries.*
*(SO 6)*

**P16–5B** Presented below are three different lease transactions that occurred for Beck Inc. in 1999. Assume that all lease contracts start on January 1, 1999. In no case does Beck receive title to the properties leased during or at the end of the lease term.

| | Lessor | | |
|---|---|---|---|
| | **Choi Delivery** | **Duncan Co.** | **Cagle Auto** |
| Type of property | Computer | Delivery equipment | Automobile |
| Yearly rental | $ 8,000 | $ 4,200 | $ 3,700 |
| Lease term | 6 years | 4 years | 2 years |
| Estimated economic life | 7 years | 7 years | 5 years |
| Fair market value of lease asset | $44,000 | $19,000 | $11,000 |
| Present value of the lease rental | | | |
|   payments | $41,000 | $13,000 | $ 6,400 |
| Bargain purchase option | None | None | None |

**Instructions**

(a) Which of the leases above are operating leases and which are capital leases? Explain.

(b) How should the lease transaction for Duncan Co. be recorded in 1999?

(c) How should the lease transaction for Choi Delivery be recorded on January 1, 1999?

**\*P16–6B**  On July 1, 1999, Keller Corporation issued $2,500,000 face value, 12%, 10-year bonds at $2,811,556. This price resulted in an effective-interest rate of 10% on the bonds. Keller uses the effective-interest method to amortize bond premium or discount. The bonds pay semi-annual interest July 1 and January 1.

*Prepare entries to record issuance of bonds, payment of interest, and amortization of bond premium using effective-interest method.*
*(SO 2)*

**Instructions**

(Round all computations to the nearest dollar.)

(a) Prepare the journal entry to record the issuance of the bonds on July 1, 1999.

(b) Prepare the journal entry to record the accrual of interest and the amortization of the premium on December 31, 1999.

(c) Prepare the journal entry to record the payment of interest and the amortization of the premium on July 1, 2000, assuming no accrual of interest on June 30.

(d) Prepare the journal entry to record the accrual of interest and the amortization of the premium on December 31, 2000.

(e) Prepare an amortization table through December 31, 2000 (three interest periods) for this bond issue.

**\*P16–7B**  On July 1, 1999, Shawnee Company issued $2,000,000 face value, 10%, 10-year bonds at $1,770,592. This price resulted in an effective-interest rate of 12% on the bonds. Shawnee uses the effective-interest method to amortize bond premium or discount. The bonds pay semiannual interest July 1 and January 1.

*Prepare entries to record issuance of bonds, payment of interest, and amortization of discount using effective-interest method. In addition, answer questions.*
*(SO 2, 8)*

**Instructions**

(a) Prepare the journal entries to record the following transactions.

(1) The issuance of the bonds on July 1, 1999.

(2) The accrual of interest and the amortization of the discount on December 31, 1999.

(3) The payment of interest and the amortization of the discount on July 1, 2000, assuming no accrual of interest on June 30.

(4) The accrual of interest and the amortization of the discount on December 31, 2000.

(b) Show the proper balance sheet presentation for the liability for bonds payable on the December 31, 2000, balance sheet.

(c) ▭▭▭▭▶ Provide the answers to the following questions in letter form.

(1) What amount of interest expense is reported for 2000?

(2) Would the bond interest expense reported in 2000 be the same as, greater than, or less than the amount that would be reported if the straight-line method of amortization were used?

(3) Determine the total cost of borrowing over the life of the bond.

(4) Would the total bond interest expense be greater than, the same as, or less than the total interest expense that would be reported if the straight-line method of amortization were used?

# BROADENING YOUR PERSPECTIVE

# FINANCIAL REPORTING AND ANALYSIS
· · · · · · · · · · · · · · · · · · · · · · · · · · · · · · · · · · · · · · · · · · · · · · · · · · · · · · ·

## FINANCIAL REPORTING PROBLEM: Kellogg Company

**BYP16–1**  Refer to the financial statements of Kellogg Company and the Notes to Consolidated Financial Statements in Appendix A.

*Instructions*

Answer the following questions:

(a) What was Kellogg's total long-term debt at December 31, 1997? What was the increase/decrease in Kellogg's total long-term debt (excluding other liabilities) from the prior year?

(b) What were the components of total long-term debt (excluding other liabilities) on December 31, 1997?

(c) What is the amount of leases that are reported as part of long-term debt?

## COMPARATIVE ANALYSIS PROBLEM: Kellogg Company vs. General Mills

**BYP16–2**  Kellogg's financial statements are presented in Appendix A; General Mills's financial statements are presented in Appendix B.

*Instructions*

(a) Based on the information contained in these financial statements, compute the following 1997 ratios for each company:

   (1) Debt to total assets

   (2) Times interest earned

(b) What conclusions concerning the companies' long-run solvency can be drawn from these ratios?

## RESEARCH ASSIGNMENT

**BYP16–3**  The November 6, 1995, edition of *The Wall Street Journal* contains an article by Linda Sandler entitled "Kmart Is Pressured Over Obscure Bond 'Puts,' Which Stir Worries Amid Tough Retail Times."

*Instructions*

Read the article and answer these questions:

(a) What is the total dollar amount of the bond issue in question? Who purchased these bonds?

(b) What right does the "put option" give to bondholders?

(c) What amount is available under Kmart's bank lines? Why can't Kmart borrow under these lines to purchase the bonds? What is the most likely solution to the problem?

(d) Were the terms of the put bonds adquately disclosed?

## INTERPRETING FINANCIAL STATEMENTS: Texas Instruments

**BYP16–4**  Texas Instruments designs and produces devices that use semiconductor technology. You may have one of its calculators on your desk. Because it is in a high-tech industry, the company must constantly invest in new technology, which requires considerable financing. During 1995 Texas Instruments' current liabilities and its long-term liabilities increased by about $1 billion each. Here is additional information (in millions) from Texas Instruments' 1995 annual report:

|  | 1995 | 1994 |
|---|---|---|
| Current assets | $ 5,518 | $ 4,017 |
| Total assets | 9,215 | 6,980 |
| Current liabilities | 3,188 | 2,199 |
| Total liabilities | 5,120 | 3,950 |
| Stockholders' equity | 4,095 | 3,030 |
| Sales revenue | 13,128 | 10,315 |
| Income taxes | 531 | 351 |
| Interest expense | 48 | 45 |
| Net income | 1,088 | 691 |

Maturities (in millions) of long-term debt due during the 4 years subsequent to December 31, 1996, are:

| 1997 | $14 | 1999 | $168 |
|---|---|---|---|
| 1998 | 18 | 2000 | 19 |

*Instructions*
Address each of these questions related to the liabilities of Texas Instruments:

(a) Using both working capital and the current ratio as indicators, evaluate the change in the company's liquidity from 1994 to 1995. Working capital and the current ratio are discussed in Chapter 11.

(b) Using both the debt to total assets ratio and the times interest earned ratio, evaluate the change in the company's solvency from 1994 to 1995.

(c) What are the implications of the information provided about the maturities of the company's long-term debt?

## REAL-WORLD FOCUS: Apache Corporation

**BYP16–5** **Apache Corporation** is an international, independent energy enterprise engaged in the exploration, development, production, gathering, processing, and marketing of natural gas and crude oil. Its corporate headquarters are located in Houston, Texas, and it has operations in North America, Australia, Egypt, Poland, People's Republic of China, Indonesia, and the Ivory Coast.

The 1994 annual report of Apache Corporation disclosed the following information in its management discussion section:

### APACHE CORPORATION
### Management Discussion

In May 1994, Apache issued 9.25% bonds due 2002 in the principal amount of $100 million. The proceeds of $99 million from the offering were used to reduce bank debt, to pay off the 9.5% convertible debentures due 1996, and for general corporate purposes. In December 1994, the company privately placed 3.93% convertible notes due 1997 in the principal amount of $75 million. The notes are not redeemable before maturity and are convertible into Apache common stock at the option of the holders at any time prior to maturity, at a conversion price of $27 per share. Proceeds from the sale of the notes were used for the repayment of bank debt.

*Instructions*

(a) Identify the face amount, contractual interest rate, and selling price of the newly issued bonds due in 2002. Explain whether the bonds sold at a premium or a discount.

(b) For what purposes has Apache Corporation been incurring more debt?

# CRITICAL THINKING
•••••••••••••••••••••••••••••••••••••••••••••••••••••••••••••••••••••••••••••••••••••••••••••
## GROUP DECISION CASE

**BYP16–6** On January 1, 1998, Marsh Corporation issued $1,200,000 of 5-year, 8% bonds at 96; the bonds pay interest semiannually on July 1 and January 1. By January 1, 2000, the market rate of interest for bonds of risk similar to those of Marsh Corporation had risen. As a result the market value of these bonds was $1,000,000 on January 1, 2000—below their carrying value. Tom Marsh, president of the company, suggests repurchasing all of these bonds in the open market at the $1,000,000 price. To do so the company will have to issue $1,000,000 (face value) of new 10-year, 12% bonds at par. The president asks you, as controller, "What is the feasibility of my proposed repurchase plan?"

*Instructions*
With the class divided into groups, answer the following:

(a) What is the carrying value of the outstanding Marsh Corporation 5-year bonds on January 1, 2000? (Assume straight-line amortization.)

(b) Prepare the journal entry to retire the 5-year bonds on January 1, 2000. Prepare the journal entry to issue the new 10-year bonds.

(c) Prepare a short memo to the president in response to his request for advice. List the economic factors that you believe should be considered for his repurchase proposal.

## COMMUNICATION ACTIVITY

**BYP16–7** Dane Ely, president of the Briley Corporation, is considering the issuance of bonds to finance an expansion of his business. He has asked you to (1) discuss the advantages of bonds over common stock financing, (2) indicate the type of bonds he might issue, and (3) explain the issuing procedures used in bond transactions.

*Instructions*
Write a memorandum to the president, answering his request.

## ETHICS CASE

**BYP16–8** Ron Gant is the president, founder, and majority owner of Newman Medical Corporation, an emerging medical technology products company. Newman is in dire need of additional capital to keep operating and to bring several promising products to final development, testing, and production. Ron, as owner of 51% of the outstanding stock, manages the company's operations. He places heavy emphasis on research and development and on long-term growth. The other principal stockholder is Judy Costello who, as a nonemployee investor, owns 40% of the stock. Judy would like to deemphasize the R&D functions and emphasize the marketing function, to maximize short-run sales and profits from existing products. She believes this strategy would raise the market price of Newman's stock.

All of Ron's personal capital and borrowing power is tied up in his 51% stock ownership. He knows that any offering of additional shares of stock will dilute his controlling interest because he won't be able to participate in such an issuance. But, Judy has money and would likely buy enough shares to gain control of Newman. She then would dictate the company's future direction, even if it meant replacing Ron as president and CEO.

The company already has considerable debt. Raising additional debt will be costly, will adversely affect Newman's credit rating, and will increase the company's reported losses due to the growth in interest expense. Judy and the other minority stockholders express opposition to the assumption of additional debt, fearing the company will be pushed to the brink of bankruptcy. Wanting to maintain his control and to preserve the direction of "his" company, Ron is doing everything to avoid a stock issuance and is contemplating a large issuance of bonds, even if it means the bonds are issued with a high effective-interest rate.

*Instructions*

(a) Who are the stakeholders in this situation?
(b) What are the ethical issues in this case?
(c) What would you do if you were Ron?

# SURFING THE NET

**BYP16–9** Bond or debt securities pay a stated rate of interest. This rate of interest is dependent on the risk associated with the investment. Moody's Investment Service provides ratings for companies that issue debt securities.

**Address:** http://www.moodys.com/index.shtml

**Steps:** From Moody's homepage choose **SiteMap.**

*Instructions*
Answer the following questions:

    (a)  What year did Moody's introduce the first bond rating?
    (b)  List three basic principles Moody's uses in rating bonds.
    (c)  What is the definition of Moody's Aaa rating on long-term taxable debt?

---

*Answers to Self-Study Questions*
1. c    2. a    3. d    4. a    5. c    6. b    7. d    8. a    9. c    10. d    *11. b
*12. c

---

*Answer to Kellogg Review It Question 2, p. 691*

An examination of Kellogg Company's statement of cash flows indicates the following reductions of debt: reductions of notes payable, with maturities less than or equal to 90 days ($374.7 million); reductions of notes payable, with maturities greater than 90 days ($14.1 million), and reductions of long-term debt ($507.9 million).

**Remember to go back to the Navigator box on the chapter-opening page and check off your completed work.**

**Before studying this chapter, you should know or, if necessary, review:**

a. How to record the issuance of bonds. (Ch. 16, pp. 681–688)

b. How to compute and record interest. (Ch. 3, pp. 104–5, Ch. 8, p. 340, and Ch. 16, pp. 684–88)

c. How to record amortization of bond discount and bond premium using the straight-line method. (Ch. 16, pp. 684–87)

d. Where temporary and long-term investments are classified on a balance sheet. (Ch. 4, pp. 157–58)

THE NAVIGATOR

## FEATURE STORY

# Is There Anything Else We Can Buy?

In a rapidly changing world you must change rapidly or suffer the consequences. In business, to change means to invest. A case in point is found in the entertainment industry. Technology is bringing about new innovations so quickly that it is nearly impossible to guess which technologies will last and which will soon fade away. For example, consider the publishing industry. Will paper newspapers and magazines be replaced by online news via the World Wide Web? If you are a publisher, you have to make your best guess about what the future holds and invest accordingly.

Time Warner Corporation lives at the center of this arena. It is not an environment for the timid, and Time Warner's philosophy is anything but timid. It might be characterized as "If we can't beat you, we will buy you." Its mantra is "invest, invest, invest." An abbreviated list of Time Warner's holdings gives an idea of its reach. Magazines: *People, Time, Life, Sports Illustrated, Fortune.*

Book publishers: Time-Life Books, Book-of-the-Month Club, Little, Brown & Co. Music: Warner Bros., Reprise, Atlantic, Rhino. Television and movies: Warner Bros. ("ER" and "Friends"), HBO, and movies like *Batman Forever.* And, in 1996 Time Warner merged with Turner Broadcasting, so it now owns TNT, CNN, and Turner's library of thousands of classic movies. Even before the Turner merger, Time Warner owned more information and entertainment copyrights and brands than any other company in the world.

So what has Time Warner's aggressive acquisition spree meant for the bottom line? It has left Time Warner with huge debt and massive interest costs. In addition, some of the acquisitions have not come cheap, resulting in large amounts of reported goodwill and goodwill amortization. As a consequence, since the merger of Time and Warner in 1988, the combined corporation has reported net losses in all but two years through 1997, and many analysts expect losses for some time longer. With so much investing by Time Warner and so little profit to show for it, one is reminded of one more of its companies, Looney Tunes cartoons—"That's all, folks."

THE NAVIGATOR

*On the World Wide Web*
http://www.timewarner.com

# CHAPTER 17

## THE NAVIGATOR ✔

- Understand *Concepts for Review*  ☐
- Read *Feature Story*  ☐
- Scan *Study Objectives*  ☐
- Read *Preview*  ☐
- Read text and answer *Before You Go On*
  p. 725 ☐ p. 730 ☐ p. 736 ☐
- Work *Demonstration Problems*  ☐
- Review *Summary of Study Objectives*  ☐
- Answer *Self-Study Questions*  ☐
- Complete assignments  ☐

# INVESTMENTS

## STUDY OBJECTIVES

**After studying this chapter, you should be able to:**

1. *Identify the reasons corporations invest in stocks and debt securities.*
2. *Explain the accounting for debt investments.*
3. *Explain the accounting for stock investments.*
4. *Describe the purpose and usefulness of consolidated financial statements.*
5. *Indicate how debt and stock investments are valued and reported on the financial statements.*
6. *Distinguish between temporary and long-term investments.*

THE NAVIGATOR

*T*ime Warner's management believes in a policy of aggressive growth through investing in the stock of existing companies. In addition to purchasing stock, companies also purchase other securities such as debt securities issued by corporations or by governments. Investments can be purchased for a short or long period of time, as a passive investment, or with the intent to control another company. As you will see later in the chapter, the way in which a company accounts for its investments is determined by a number of factors.

The content and organization of this chapter are as follows:

THE NAVIGATOR

# WHY CORPORATIONS INVEST

Corporations purchase investments in debt or equity securities generally for one of three reasons. First, a corporation may **have excess cash** that it does not need for the immediate purchase of operating assets. For example, many companies experience seasonal fluctuations in sales. A Cape Cod marina has more sales in the spring and summer than in the fall and winter, whereas the reverse is true for an Aspen ski shop. Thus, at the end of an operating cycle, many companies may have cash on hand that is temporarily idle pending the start of another operating cycle. Until the cash is needed, these companies may invest the excess funds to earn, through interest and dividends, a greater return than they would get by just holding the funds in the bank. The role played by such temporary investments in the operating cycle is depicted in Illustration 17-1.

A second reason some companies purchase investments is that they generate **a significant portion of their earnings from investment income.** Although banks make most of their earnings by lending money, they also generate earnings by investing in debt and equity securities. Banks purchase investment securities because loan demand varies both seasonally and with changes in the economic climate. Thus, when loan demand is low, a bank must find other uses for its cash. Investing in securities also allows banks to diversify some of their risk. Bank

**ILLUSTRATION 17-1**

*Temporary investments and the operating cycle*

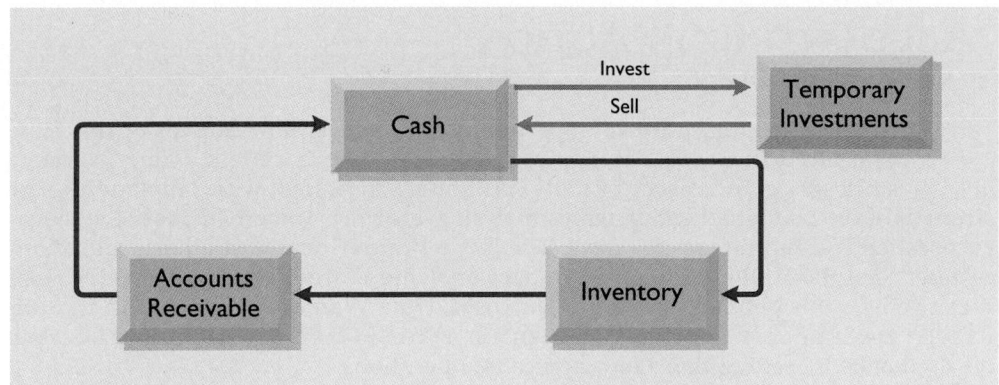

regulators severely limit the ability of banks to invest in common stock; therefore, most investments held by banks are debt securities.

Pension funds and mutual funds are corporations that also regularly invest to generate earnings. However, they do so for **speculative reasons**; that is, they are speculating that the investment will increase in value and thus result in positive returns. Therefore, they invest primarily in the common stock of other corporations. These investments are passive in nature; the pension fund or mutual fund does not usually take an active role in controlling the affairs of the companies in which they invest.

A third reason why companies invest is for **strategic reasons**. A company may purchase a noncontrolling interest in another firm in a related industry in which it wishes to establish a presence. For example, Time Warner initially purchased an interest of less than 20% in Turner Broadcasting to have a stake in Turner's expanding business opportunities. Similarly, Canadian giant Seagram purchased a significant interest in Time Warner. (Thus, not even a huge corporation like Time Warner is at the top of the corporate "food chain.") Alternatively, a company can exercise some influence over one of its customers or suppliers by purchasing a significant, but not controlling, interest in that company.

In summary, businesses invest in other companies for the reasons shown in Ilustration 17-2.

**ILLUSTRATION 17-2**

*Why corporations invest*

| Reason | Typical Investment |
|---|---|
| To house excess cash until needed | Low-risk, high-liquidity, short-term securities such as government-issued securities |
| To generate earnings | Debt securities (banks and other financial institutions); and stock securities (mutual funds and pension funds) |
| To meet strategic goals | Stocks of companies in a related industry or in an unrelated industry that the company wishes to enter |

## ACCOUNTING IN ACTION
### Business Insight

In the 2 months prior to approval by the federal government of the Time Warner/Turner deal, as approval appeared more certain, Time Warner's stock price increased by 30%. Although investors were applauding the strength of the combined entity, many analysts were very concerned about the mega-corporation's ability to control costs. The Time Warner deal and other acquisitions resulted in a $17.5 billion mountain of debt on Time Warner's balance sheet. Unless it can reduce this debt and control other costs, Time Warner will not return to profitability any time soon. One possible scenario is that $8 billion in debt could be taken off the books by selling the company's cable operations.

Observers were also interested to see how the two corporate cultures would merge. Ted Turner had been openly critical of Time Warner's management for running a loose ship, with far too much being spent on unnecessary extravagances such as corporate jets. Time Warner executives privately responded that if Mr. Turner was really concerned, he might consider taking a cut in his salary of $10 millon a year.

# ACCOUNTING FOR DEBT INVESTMENTS

**2**
STUDY
OBJECTIVE

Explain the accounting for debt investments.

Debt investments are investments in government and corporation bonds. In accounting for debt investments, entries are required to record (1) the acquisition, (2) the interest revenue, and (3) the sale.

## Recording Acquisition of Bonds

**At acquisition, the cost principle applies.** Cost includes all expenditures necessary to acquire these investments, such as the price paid plus brokerage fees (commissions), if any. Assume, for example, that Kuhl Corporation acquires 50 Doan Inc. 12%, 10-year, $1,000 bonds on January 1, 1999, for $54,000, including brokerage fees of $1,000. The entry to record the investment is:

```
A    =   L   +   SE
+54,000
-54,000
```

| Jan. 1 | Debt Investments | 54,000 | |
|---|---|---|---|
| |     Cash | | 54,000 |
| |     (To record purchase of 50 Doan Inc. bonds) | | |

## Recording Bond Interest

The bonds pay interest of $3,000 semiannually on July 1 and January 1 ($50,000 × 12% × ½). The entry for the receipt of interest on July 1 is:

```
A    =   L   +   SE
+3,000           +3,000
```

| July 1 | Cash | 3,000 | |
|---|---|---|---|
| |     Interest Revenue | | 3,000 |
| |     (To record receipt of interest on Doan Inc. bonds) | | |

If Kuhl Corporation's fiscal year ends on December 31, it is necessary to accrue the interest of $3,000 earned since July 1. The adjusting entry is:

```
A    =   L   +   SE
+3,000           +3,000
```

| Dec. 31 | Interest Receivable | 3,000 | |
|---|---|---|---|
| |     Interest Revenue | | 3,000 |
| |     (To accrue interest on Doan Inc. bonds) | | |

Interest Receivable is reported as a current asset in the balance sheet; Interest Revenue is reported under Other Revenues and Gains in the income statement. When the interest is received on January 1, the entry is:

| Jan. 1 | Cash | 3,000 | |
| | Interest Receivable | | 3,000 |
| | (To record receipt of accrued interest) | | |

| A | = | L | + | SE |
|---|---|---|---|---|
| +3,000 | | | | |
| −3,000 | | | | |

A credit to Interest Revenue at this time is incorrect because the interest revenue was earned and accrued in the preceding accounting period.

## Recording Sale of Bonds

When the bonds are sold, it is necessary to credit the investment account for the cost of the bonds. Any difference between the net proceeds (sales price less brokerage fees) from sale and the cost of the bonds is recorded as a gain or loss. Assume, for example, that Kuhl Corporation receives net proceeds of $58,000 on the sale of the Doan Inc. bonds on January 1, 2000, after receiving the interest due. Since the securities cost $54,000, a gain of $4,000 has been realized. The entry to record the sale is:

| Jan. 1 | Cash | 58,000 | |
| | Debt Investments | | 54,000 |
| | Gain on Sale of Debt Investments | | 4,000 |
| | (To record sale of Doan Inc. bonds) | | |

| A | = | L | + | SE |
|---|---|---|---|---|
| +58,000 | | | | |
| −54,000 | | | | +4,000 |

The gain on sale of debt investments is reported under Other Revenues and Gains in the income statement.

The accounting for temporary debt investments and for long-term debt investments is similar. The major exception is when bonds are purchased at a premium or discount. For temporary investments, the bond premium or discount is not amortized to interest revenue because the bonds are held for a short period of time and a misstatement of interest revenue for such a period is not considered material. For long-term investments, however, any bond premium or discount is amortized to interest revenue over the remaining term of the bonds. Like the issuer of the bonds, the investor uses either the straight-line or the effective-interest method of amortization. The effective-interest method is required under generally accepted accounting principles when the annual amounts of the two amortization methods are materially different.

## BEFORE YOU GO ON . . .

### Review It

1. Why might a company purchase debt or equity investments?
2. What entries are required in accounting for debt investments?
3. How does the accounting for a temporary debt investment differ from that for a long-term debt investment?

### Do It

The Waldo Corporation had the following transactions pertaining to debt investments:

Jan. 1   Purchased 30 10%, $1,000 Hillary Co. bonds for $30,000 plus brokerage fees of $900. Interest is payable semiannually on July 1 and January 1.
July 1   Received semiannual interest on Hillary Co. bonds.
July 1   Sold 15 Hillary Co. bonds for $15,000 less $400 brokerage fees.

(a) Journalize the transactions, and (b) prepare the adjusting entry for the accrual of interest on December 31.

*Reasoning:* Bond investments are recorded at cost. Interest is recorded when received and/or accrued. When bonds are sold, the investment account is credited for the cost of the bonds. Any difference between the cost and the net proceeds is recorded as a gain or loss.

*Solution:*

| | | | | |
|---|---|---|---|---|
| (a) Jan. 1 | Debt Investments | | 30,900 | |
| |     Cash | | | 30,900 |
| |       (To record purchase of 30 Hillary Co. bonds) | | | |
| July 1 | Cash | | 1,500 | |
| |     Interest Revenue ($30,000 × .10 × 6/12) | | | 1,500 |
| |       (To record receipt of interest on Hillary Co. bonds) | | | |
| July 1 | Cash | | 14,600 | |
| | Loss on Sale of Debt Investments | | 850 | |
| |     Debt Investments ($30,900 ÷ 15/30) | | | 15,450 |
| |       (To record sale of 15 Hillary Co. bonds) | | | |
| (b) Dec. 31 | Interest Receivable | | 750 | |
| |     Interest Revenue ($15,000 × .10 × 6/12) | | | 750 |
| |       (To accrue interest on Hillary Co. bonds) | | | |

*Related exercise material:* BE17–1 and E17–1.

THE NAVIGATOR

# ACCOUNTING FOR STOCK INVESTMENTS

**3**

STUDY
OBJECTIVE

Explain the accounting for stock investments.

**Stock investments** are investments in the capital stock of corporations. When a company holds stock (and/or debt) of several different corporations, the group of securities is identified as an **investment portfolio**. The accounting for investments in common stock is based on the extent of the investor's influence over the operating and financial affairs of the issuing corporation (commonly called the **investee**) as shown in Illustration 17-3. In some cases, depending on the degree of investor influence, net income of the investee is considered to be income to the investor.

INTERNATIONAL NOTE

A recent study demonstrated the peril of investing overseas. For the same company under different reporting systems, income was $84,600, $260,600, $240,600, and $10,402 in the United States, the United Kingdom, Australia, and West Germany, respectively.

The presumed influence may be negated by extenuating circumstances. For example, a company that acquires a 25% interest in another company in a "hostile" takeover may not have any significant influence over the investee.[1] In other words, companies are required to use judgment instead of blindly following the guidelines. On the following pages we will explain and illustrate the application of each guideline.

---

[1]Among the factors that should be considered in determining an investor's influence are whether (1) the investor has representation on the investee's board of directors, (2) the investor participates in the investee's policy-making process, (3) there are material transactions between the investor and investee, and (4) the common stock held by other stockholders is concentrated or dispersed.

**ILLUSTRATION 17-3**

*Accounting guidelines for stock investments*

| Investor's Ownership Interest in Investee's Common Stock | Presumed Influence on Investee | Accounting Guidelines |
|---|---|---|
| Less than 20% | Insignificant | Cost method |
| Between 20% and 50% | Significant | Equity method |
| More than 50% | Controlling | Consolidated financial statements |

## Holdings of Less Than 20%

In accounting for stock investments of less than 20%, the cost method is used. Under the cost method, the investment is recorded at cost and revenue is recognized only when cash dividends are received.

### Recording Acquisition of Stock Investments

At acquisition, the cost principle applies. Cost includes all expenditures necessary to acquire these investments, such as the price paid plus brokerage fees (commissions), if any. Assume, for example, that on July 1, 1999, Sanchez Corporation acquires 1,000 shares (10% ownership) of Beal Corporation common stock at $40 per share plus brokerage fees of $500. The entry for the purchase is:

| | | | |
|---|---|---|---|
| July 1 | Stock Investments | 40,500 | |
| |     Cash | | 40,500 |
| |       (To record purchase of 1,000 shares of Beal Corporation common stock) | | |

$$A = L + SE$$
$$+40{,}500$$
$$-40{,}500$$

### Recording Dividends

During the time the stock is held, entries are required for any cash dividends received. Thus, if a $2.00 per share dividend is received by Sanchez Corporation on December 31, the entry is:

| | | | |
|---|---|---|---|
| Dec. 31 | Cash (1,000 × $2) | 2,000 | |
| |     Dividend Revenue | | 2,000 |
| |       (To record receipt of a cash dividend) | | |

$$A = L + SE$$
$$+2{,}000 \qquad +2{,}000$$

Dividend Revenue is reported under Other Revenues and Gains in the income statement. Unlike interest on notes and bonds, dividends do not accrue. Therefore, adjusting entries are not made to accrue dividends.

### Recording Sale of Stock

When stock is sold, the difference between the net proceeds (sales price less brokerage fees) from the sale and the cost of the stock is recognized as a gain or a loss. Assume, for instance, that Sanchez Corporation receives net proceeds of $39,500 on the sale of its Beal stock on February 10, 2000. Because the stock cost $40,500, a loss of $1,000 has been incurred. The entry to record the sale is:

<table>
<tr><td>A</td><td>=</td><td>L</td><td>+</td><td>SE</td></tr>
<tr><td>+39,500</td><td></td><td></td><td></td><td>−1,000</td></tr>
<tr><td>−40,500</td><td></td><td></td><td></td><td></td></tr>
</table>

| Feb. 10 | Cash | 39,500 | |
| | Loss on Sale of Stock Investments | 1,000 | |
| | Stock Investments | | 40,500 |
| | (To record sale of Beal common stock) | | |

**HELPFUL HINT**
The entries for investments in common stock also apply to investments in preferred stock.

The loss account is reported under Other Expenses and Losses in the income statement, whereas a gain on sale is shown under Other Revenues and Gains.

# Holdings between 20% and 50%

When an investor company owns only a small portion of the shares of stock of another company (the investee), the investor cannot exercise control over the company. When an investor owns between 20% and 50% of the common stock of a corporation, however, it is generally presumed that the investor has significant influence over the financial and operating activities of the investee. The investor probably has a representative on the investee's board of directors. With a representative on the board, the investor begins to exercise some control over the investee—and the investee company in some sense really becomes part of the investor company.

For example, even prior to purchasing all of Turner Broadcasting, Time Warner owned 20% of Turner. Because it exercised significant control over major decisions made by Turner, Time Warner used an approach called the equity method. Under the equity method, **the investor records its share of the net income of the investee in the year when it is earned.** To delay recognizing the investor's share of net income until a cash dividend is declared ignores the fact that the investor and investee are, in some sense, one company, so the investor is better off by the investee's earned income.

**HELPFUL HINT**
Revenue is recognized under the equity method on the accrual basis—i.e., when it is earned by the investee.

Under the equity method, the investment in common stock is initially recorded at cost, and the investment account is **adjusted annually** to show the investor's equity in the investee. Each year, the investor (1) increases (debits) the investment account and increases (credits) revenue for its share of the investee's net income[2] and (2) decreases (credits) the investment account for the amount of divideds received. The investment account is reduced for dividends received because the net assets of the investee are decreased when a dividend is paid.

## Recording Acquisition of Stock Investments

Assume that Milar Corporation acquires 30% of the common stock of Beck Company for $120,000 on January 1, 1999. The entry to record this transaction is:

<table>
<tr><td>A</td><td>=</td><td>L</td><td>+</td><td>SE</td></tr>
<tr><td>+120,000</td><td></td><td></td><td></td><td></td></tr>
<tr><td>−120,000</td><td></td><td></td><td></td><td></td></tr>
</table>

| Jan. 1 | Stock Investments | 120,000 | |
| | Cash | | 120,000 |
| | (To record purchase of Beck common stock) | | |

## Recording Revenue and Dividends

For 1999, Beck reports net income of $100,000 and declares and pays a $40,000 cash dividend. Milar is required to record (1) its share of Beck's income, $30,000 (30% × $100,000) and (2) the reduction in the investment account for the dividends received, $12,000 ($40,000 × 30%). The entries are:

(1)

<table>
<tr><td>A</td><td>=</td><td>L</td><td>+</td><td>SE</td></tr>
<tr><td>+30,000</td><td></td><td></td><td></td><td>+30,000</td></tr>
</table>

| Dec. 31 | Stock Investments | 30,000 | |
| | Revenue from Investment in Beck Company | | 30,000 |
| | (To record 30% equity in Beck's 1999 net income) | | |

---

[2]Conversely, the investor increases (debits) a loss account and decreases (credits) the investment account for its share of the investee's net loss.

(2)

| Dec. 31 | Cash | 12,000 | |
| | Stock Investments | | 12,000 |
| | (To record dividends received) | | |

| A | = | L | + | SE |
|---|---|---|---|---|
| + 12,000 | | | | |
| − 12,000 | | | | |

After posting the transactions for the year, the investment and revenue accounts will show the following:

| Stock Investments | | | | Revenue from Investment in Beck Company | | |
|---|---|---|---|---|---|---|
| Jan. 1 | 120,000 | Dec. 31 | 12,000 | | Dec. 31 | 30,000 |
| Dec. 31 | 30,000 | | | | | |
| Dec. 31 Bal. | 138,000 | | | | | |

**ILLUSTRATION 17-4**
*Investment and revenue accounts after posting*

During the year, the investment account has increased by $18,000. This $18,000 is Milar's 30% equity in the $60,000 increase in Beck's retained earnings ($100,000 − $40,000). In addition, Milar will report $30,000 of revenue from its investment, which is 30% of Beck's net income of $100,000. Note that the difference between reported income under the cost method and reported revenue under the equity method can be significant. For example, Milar would report only $12,000 of dividend revenue (30% × $40,000) if the cost method were used.

## Holdings of More Than 50%

A company that owns more than 50% of the common stock of another entity is known as the parent company. The entity whose stock is owned by the parent company is called the subsidiary (affiliated) company. Because of its stock ownership, the parent company has a controlling interest in the subsidiary company.

When a company owns more than 50% of the common stock of another company, consolidated financial statements are usually prepared. Consolidated financial statements present the assets and liabilities controlled by the parent company and the aggregate profitability of the subsidiary companies. They are prepared **in addition to** the financial statements for each of the individual parent and subsidiary companies. As noted earlier, prior to acquiring all of Turner Broadcasting, Time Warner accounted for its investment in Turner using the equity method. Time Warner's net investment in Turner was reported in a single line item—Other Investments. After the merger, Time Warner instead consolidated Turner's results with its own. Under this approach, the individual assets and liabilities of Turner are included with those of Time Warner; its plant and equipment are added to Time Warner's plant and equipment, its receivables are added to Time Warner's receivables, and so on.

**Consolidated statements are especially useful to the stockholders, board of directors, and management of the parent company.** Moreover, consolidated statements inform creditors, prospective investors, and regulatory agencies as to the magnitude and scope of operations of the companies under common control. For example, regulators and the courts undoubtedly used the consolidated statements of AT&T to determine whether a breakup of AT&T was in the public interest. Listed at the top of page 730 are three companies that prepare consolidated statements and some of the companies they have owned. Note that one, Disney, is Time Warner's arch rival.

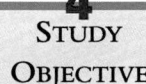

**4**
**STUDY OBJECTIVE**
................................
Describe the purpose and usefulness of consolidated financial statements.

**HELPFUL HINT**
If parent (A) has three wholly owned subsidiaries (B, C, & D), there are four separate legal entities, but only one economic entity from the viewpoint of the shareholders of the parent company.

| Beatrice Foods | American Brands, Inc. | The Walt Disney Company |
|---|---|---|
| Tropicana Frozen Juices | American Tobacco Company | Capital Cities/ABC, Inc. |
| Switzer Candy Company | Master Lock Company | Disneyland, Disney World |
| Samsonite Corporation | Pinkerton's Security Service | Mighty Ducks |
| Dannon Yogurt Company | Titleist Golf Company | Anaheim Angels |
| | | ESPN |

# ACCOUNTING IN ACTION
## Business Insight

Time Warner, Inc., owns 100% of the common stock of Home Box Office (HBO) Corporation. The common stockholders of Time Warner elect the board of directors of the company, who, in turn, select the officers and managers of the company. The board of directors controls the property owned by the corporation, which includes the common stock of HBO. Thus, they are in a position to elect the board of directors of HBO and, in effect, control its operations. These relationships are graphically illustrated here:

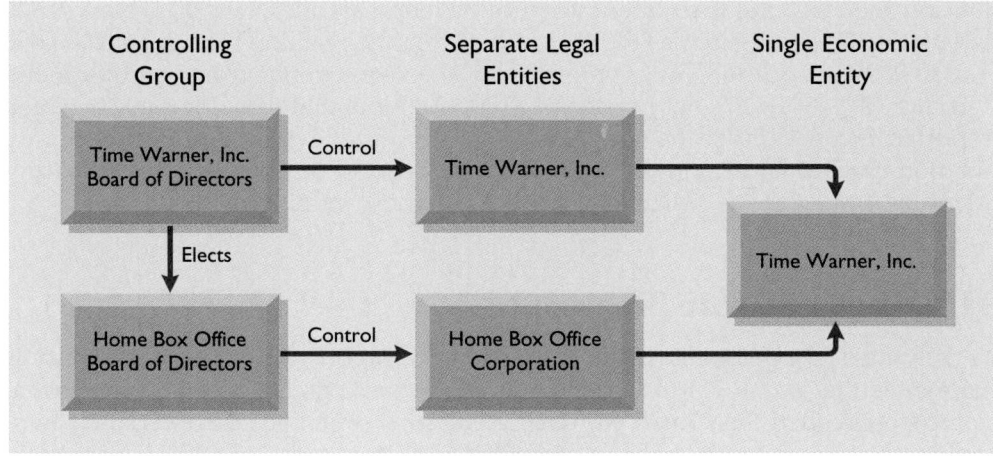

# BEFORE YOU GO ON . . .
## Review It

1. What are the accounting entries for investments in stock for which ownership is less than 20%?
2. What entries are made under the equity method when (a) the investor receives a cash dividend from the investee and (b) the investee reports net income for the year?
3. What is the purpose of consolidated financial statements?
4. What does Kellogg Company state regarding its accounting policy involving consolidated financial statements? The answer to this question is provided on page 751.

## Do It

Presented below are two independent situations:

1. Rho Jean Inc. acquired 5% of the 400,000 shares of common stock of Stillwater Corp. at a total cost of $6 per share on May 18, 1999. On August 30, Stillwater declared and paid a $75,000 dividend. On December 31, Stillwater reported net income of $244,000 for the year.

2. Debbie, Inc., obtained significant influence over North Sails by buying 40% of North Sails' 60,000 outstanding shares of common stock at a cost of $12 per share on January 1, 1999. On April 15, North Sails declared and paid a cash dividend of $45,000. On December 31, North Sails reported a net income of $120,000 for the year.

Prepare all necessary journal entries for 1999 for (1) Rho Jean Inc. and (2) Debbie, Inc.

*Reasoning:* When an investor owns less than 20% of the common stock of another corporation, it is presumed that the investor has relatively little influence over the investee. As a result, net income earned by the investee is not considered a proper basis for recognizing income from the investment by the investor. For investments of 20%–50%, significant influence is presumed and therefore the investor's share of the net income of the investee should be recorded.

*Solution:*

| | | | | |
|---|---|---|---|---|
| (1) May 18 | Stock Investments (20,000 × $6) | | 120,000 | |
| | Cash | | | 120,000 |
| | (To record purchase of 20,000 shares of Stillwater Co. stock) | | | |
| | | | | |
| Aug. 30 | Cash | | 3,750 | |
| | Dividend Revenue ($75,000 × 5%) | | | 3,750 |
| | (To record receipt of cash dividend) | | | |
| | | | | |
| (2) Jan. 1 | Stock Investments (60,000 × 40% × $12) | | 288,000 | |
| | Cash | | | 288,000 |
| | (To record purchase of 24,000 shares of North Sails' stock) | | | |
| | | | | |
| Apr. 15 | Cash | | 18,000 | |
| | Stock Investments ($45,000 × 40%) | | | 18,000 |
| | (To record receipt of cash dividend) | | | |
| | | | | |
| Dec. 31 | Stock Investments ($120,000 × 40%) | | 48,000 | |
| | Revenue from Investment in North Sails | | | 48,000 |
| | (To record 40% equity in North Sails' net income) | | | |

THE NAVIGATOR

*Related exercise material:* BE17-2, BE17-3, E17-1, E17-2, E17-3, E17-4, and E17-5.

# VALUING AND REPORTING INVESTMENTS

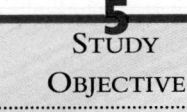
**5**
STUDY OBJECTIVE

Indicate how debt and stock investments are valued and reported on the financial statements.

The value of debt and stock investments may fluctuate greatly during the time they are held. For example, in one 12-month period, the stock of Digital Equipment Corporation hit a high of 76½ and a low of 28⅜. In light of such price fluctuations, how should investments be valued at the balance sheet date? Valuation could be at cost, at fair value (market value), or at the lower of cost or market value. Many people argue that fair value offers the best approach because it represents the expected cash realizable value of securities. **Fair value** is the amount for which a security could be sold in a normal market. Others counter that, unless a security is going to be sold soon, the fair value is not relevant because the price of the security will likely change again.

# Categories of Securities

For purposes of valuation and reporting at a financial statement date, debt and stock investments are classified into three categories of securities:

1. **Trading securities** are securities bought and held primarily for sale in the near term to generate income on short-term price differences.
2. **Available-for-sale securities** are securities that may be sold in the future.
3. **Held-to-maturity securities** are debt securities that the investor has the intent and ability to hold to maturity.

The valuation guidelines for these securities are shown in Illustration 17-5. These guidelines apply to all debt securities and all stock investments where the holdings are less than 20%.

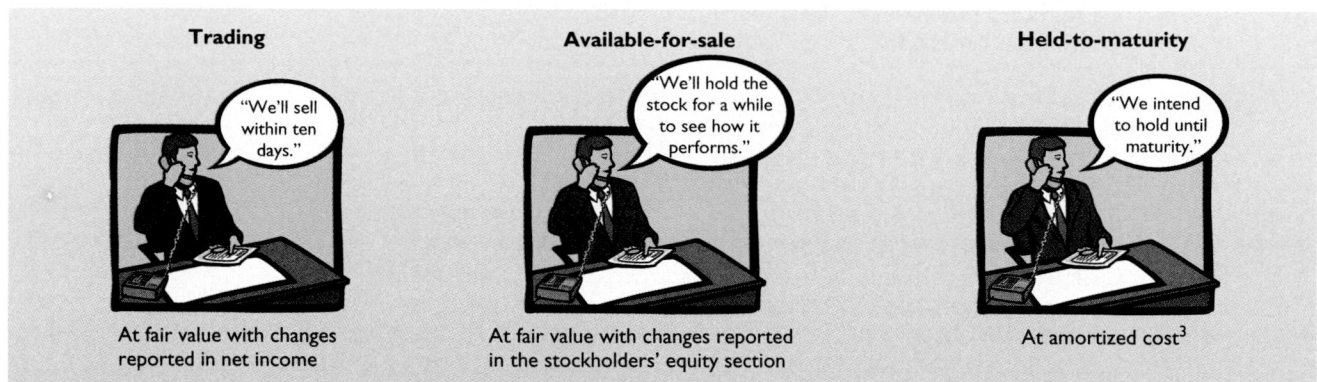

| Trading | Available-for-sale | Held-to-maturity |
| --- | --- | --- |
| "We'll sell within ten days." | "We'll hold the stock for a while to see how it performs." | "We intend to hold until maturity." |
| At fair value with changes reported in net income | At fair value with changes reported in the stockholders' equity section | At amortized cost[3] |

**ILLUSTRATION 17-5**

*Valuation guidelines*

## Trading Securities

Trading securities are held with the intention of selling them in a short period of time (generally less than a month). Trading means frequent buying and selling. As indicated in Illustration 17-5, trading securities are reported at fair value, and changes from cost are reported as part of net income. The changes are reported as **unrealized gains or losses** because the securities have not been sold. The unrealized gain or loss is the difference between the **total cost** of the securities in the category and their **total fair value**.

As an example, Illustration 17-6 shows the cost and fair values for investments classified as trading securities for Pace Corporation on December 31, 1999. Pace Corporation has an unrealized gain of $7,000 because total fair value ($147,000) is $7,000 greater than total cost ($140,000).

**ILLUSTRATION 17-6**

*Valuation of trading securities*

| Trading Securities, December 31, 1999 | | | |
| --- | --- | --- | --- |
| Investments | Cost | Fair Value | Unrealized Gain (Loss) |
| Yorkville Company bonds | $ 50,000 | $ 48,000 | $(2,000) |
| Kodak Company stock | 90,000 | 99,000 | 9,000 |
| Total | $140,000 | $147,000 | $ 7,000 |

---

[3]This category is provided for completeness. The accounting and valuation issues related to held-to-maturity securities are discussed in more advanced accounting courses.

The fact that trading securities are a short-term investment increases the likelihood that they will be sold at fair value (the company may not be able to time their sale) and the likelihood that there will be an unrealized gain or loss. Fair value and unrealized gain or loss are recorded through an adjusting entry at the time financial statements are prepared. In the entry, a valuation allowance account, Market Adjustment—Trading, is used to record the difference between the total cost and the total fair value of the securities. The adjusting entry for Pace Corporation is:

| Dec. 31 | Market Adjustment—Trading | 7,000 | |
|---|---|---|---|
| |     Unrealized Gain—Income | | 7,000 |
| |       (To record unrealized gain on trading | | |
| |       securities) | | |

**HELPFUL HINT**
An unrealized gain or loss is reported in the income statement because of the likelihood that the securities will be sold at fair value since they are a short-term investment.

| A | = | L | + | SE |
|---|---|---|---|---|
| +7,000 | | | | +7,000 |

The use of a Market Adjustment–Trading account enables the company to maintain a record of the investment cost. Actual cost is needed to determine the gain or loss realized when the securities are sold. The Market Adjustment–Trading balance is added to the cost of the investments to arrive at a fair value for the trading securities.

**The fair value of the securities is the amount reported on the balance sheet.** The unrealized gain is reported on the income statement in the Other Revenues and Gains section. The term income is used in the account title to indicate that the gain affects net income. When the total cost of the trading securities is greater than total fair value, an unrealized loss has occurred. In such a case, the adjusting entry is a debit to Unrealized Loss—Income and a credit to Market Adjustment—Trading. The unrealized loss is reported under Other Expenses and Losses in the income statement.

The market adjustment account is carried forward into future accounting periods. No entries are made to this account during the period. At the end of each reporting period, the balance in the account is adjusted to the difference between cost and fair value. The Unrealized Gain or Loss–Income account is closed at the end of the reporting period.

## Available-for-Sale Securities

As indicated earlier, available-for-sale securities are held with the intent of selling them sometime in the future. If the intent is to sell the securities within the next year or operating cycle, the securities are classified as current assets in the balance sheet. Otherwise, they are classified as long-term assets in the investments section of the balance sheet.

Available-for-sale securities are also reported at fair value. The procedure for determining fair value and the unrealized gain or loss for these securities is the same as for trading securities. To illustrate, assume that Elbert Corporation has two securities that are classified as available-for-sale. Illustration 17-7 provides information on cost, fair value, and the amount of the unrealized gain or loss. For Elbert Corporation, there is an unrealized loss of $9,537 because total cost ($293,537) is $9,537 more than total fair value ($284,000).

**ETHICS NOTE**
Some managers appear to hold their available-for-sale securities that have experienced losses, while selling those that have gains, thus increasing income. Do you think this is ethical?

**ILLUSTRATION 17-7**
*Valuation of available-for-sale securities*

### Available-for-Sale Securities, December 31, 1999

| Investments | Cost | Fair Value | Unrealized Gain (Loss) |
|---|---|---|---|
| Campbell Soup Corporation | | | |
|   8% bonds | $ 93,537 | $103,600 | $ 10,063 |
| Hersey Corporation stock | 200,000 | 180,400 | (19,600) |
| Total | $293,537 | $284,000 | $ (9,537) |

Both the adjusting entry and the reporting of the unrealized gain or loss from available-for-sale securities differ from those illustrated for trading securities. The differences result because these securities are not going to be sold in the near term. Thus, prior to actual sale there is a much greater likelihood of changes in fair value that may reverse either unrealized gains or losses. Accordingly, an unrealized gain or loss is not reported in the income statement. Instead, it is reported as a **separate component of stockholders' equity.** In the adjusting entry, the market adjustment account is identified with available-for-sale securities, and the unrealized gain or loss account is identified with stockholders' equity. The adjusting entry for Elbert Corporation to record the unrealized loss of $9,537 is as follows:

| A | = | L | + | SE |
|---|---|---|---|---|
| −9,537 | | | | −9,537 |

| Dec. 31 | Unrealized Loss—Equity | 9,537 | |
|---|---|---|---|
| | Market Adjustment—Available-for-Sale | | 9,537 |
| | (To record unrealized loss on available-for-sale securities) | | |

If total fair value exceeds total cost, the adjusting entry would have a debit to the market adjustment account and a credit to an unrealized gain account.

For available-for-sale securities, the unrealized gain or loss account is carried forward to future periods. At each future balance sheet date, it is adjusted with the market adjustment account to show the difference between cost and fair value at that time.

## Balance Sheet Presentation

For balance sheet presentation, investments are classified as either temporary or long-term.

### Temporary Investments

**6**
STUDY
OBJECTIVE
••••••••••••••••••••••••••••••
Distinguish between temporary and long-term investments.

**Temporary investments** are securities held by a company that are (1) **readily marketable** and (2) **intended to be converted into cash** within the next year or operating cycle, whichever is longer. Investments that do not meet **both criteria** are classified as **long-term investments.** In a recent survey of 600 large U.S. companies, over 400 reported temporary investments.

**Readily Marketable.** **An investment is readily marketable when it can be sold easily whenever the need for cash arises.** Short-term paper[4] meets this criterion because it can be sold readily to other investors. Stocks and bonds traded on organized securities markets, such as the New York Stock Exchange, are readily marketable because they can be bought and sold daily. In contrast, there may be only a limited market for the securities issued by small corporations and no market for the securities of a privately held company.

**HELPFUL HINT**
Trading securities are always classified as temporary. Available-for-sale securities can be either temporary or long-term.

**Intent to Convert.** **Intent to convert means that management intends to sell the investment within the next year or operating cycle, whichever is longer.** Generally, this criterion is satisfied when the investment is considered a resource that will be used whenever the need for cash arises. For example, a ski resort may invest idle cash during the summer months with the intent to sell the securities to buy supplies and equipment shortly before the next winter season.

---

[4]Short-term paper includes (1) certificates of deposits (CDs) issued by banks, (2) money market certificates issued by banks and savings and loan associations, (3) Treasury bills issued by the U.S. government, and (4) commercial paper issued by corporations with good credit ratings.

This investment is considered temporary even if lack of snow cancels the next ski season and eliminates the need to convert the securities into cash as intended.

Because of their high liquidity, temporary investments are listed immediately below Cash in the current asset section of the balance sheet. Temporary investments are reported at fair value. For example, Pace Corporation would report its trading securities as shown in Illustration 17-8.

| PACE CORPORATION Balance Sheet (partial) | |
|---|---|
| Current assets | |
| Cash | $ 21,000 |
| Temporary investments, at fair value | 147,000 |

**ILLUSTRATION 17-8**
*Presentation of temporary investments*

## Long-Term Investments

Long-term investments are generally reported in a separate section of the balance sheet immediately below Current assets, as shown later in Illustration 17-11. Long-term investments in available-for-sale securities are reported at fair value, and investments in common stock accounted for under the equity method are reported at equity.

# Presentation of Realized and Unrealized Gain or Loss

Gains and losses on investments, whether realized or unrealized, must be presented in the financial statements. In the income statement, gains and losses, as well as interest and dividend revenue, are reported in the nonoperating section under the categories listed in Illustration 17-9.

| Other Revenue and Gains | Other Expenses and Losses |
|---|---|
| Interest Revenue | Loss on Sales of Investments |
| Dividend Revenue | Unrealized Loss—Income |
| Gain on Sale of Investments | |
| Unrealized Gain—Income | |

**ILLUSTRATION 17-9**
*Nonoperating items related to investments*

As indicated earlier, an unrealized gain or loss on available-for-sale securities is reported as a separate component of stockholders' equity. To illustrate, assume that Dawson Inc. has common stock of $3,000,000, retained earnings of $1,500,000, and an unrealized loss on available-for-sale securities of $100,000. The statement presentation of the unrealized loss is shown in Illustration 17-10.

| DAWSON INC. Balance Sheet (partial) | |
|---|---|
| Stockholders' equity | |
| Common stock | $3,000,000 |
| Retained earnings | 1,500,000 |
| Total paid-in capital and retained earnings | 4,500,000 |
| Less: **Unrealized loss on available-for-sale** **securities** | (100,000) |
| Total stockholders' equity | $4,400,000 |

**ILLUSTRATION 17-10**
*Unrealized loss in stockholders' equity section*

Note that the presentation of the loss is similar to the presentation of the cost of treasury stock in the stockholders' equity section. An unrealized gain is added in this section. Reporting the unrealized gain or loss in the stockholders' equity section serves two important purposes: (1) It reduces the volatility of net income due to fluctuations in fair value, and (2) it informs the financial statement user of the gain or loss that would occur if the securities were sold at fair value.

A new accounting standard requires that items such as this, which affect stockholders' equity but are not included in the calculation of net income, must be reported as part of a more inclusive measure called *comprehensive income.* Comprehensive income is discussed in more advanced courses.

## Balance Sheet

Many sections of classified balance sheets have been presented in this and preceding chapters. The comprehensive balance sheet in Illustration 17-11 on page 737 includes such topics from previous chapters as the issuance of par value common stock, organization costs, restrictions of retained earnings, issuance of long-term bonds, and bond sinking funds. From this chapter, the statement includes (highlighted in red) temporary and long-term investments. The investments in temporary securities are considered trading securities; the long-term investments in stock of less than 20% owned companies are considered available-for-sale securities. Illustration 17-11 also includes a long-term investment reported at equity and descriptive notations within the statement, such as the basis for valuing merchandise and two notes to the statement.

# BEFORE YOU GO ON . . .

### Review It

1. What is the proper valuation and reporting of trading and available-for-sale securities on a balance sheet?
2. Explain how the unrealized gain or loss for both trading and available-for-sale securities is reported.
3. Explain where temporary and long-term investments are reported on a balance sheet.

# A LOOK BACK AT OUR FEATURE STORY

Refer back to the opening story about Time Warner Corporation, and answer the following questions:

1. For what reason(s) is Time Warner investing in equity securities?
2. Would you expect Time Warner to prepare consolidated financial statements for the many companies it owns? Explain your answer.
3. What has Time Warner's aggressive acquisition spree meant for its bottom line?

*Solution:*
1. Time Warner is investing for strategic reasons. As indicated in the feature story, the company's attitude is "If we can't beat you, we will buy you." Time Warner is diversifying because it is not sure what industry or set of industries will be successful in the future. As a result, Time Warner now owns more information and entertainment copyrights and brands than any other company in the world.
2. When a company owns more than 50% of the common stock of another company, consolidated financial statements are usually prepared. Because Time Warner owns over 50% of the companies mentioned in the opening story, Time Warner would consolidate these subsidiary companies with its own.
3. To date, Time Warner's acquisition spree has left it with huge debt and massive interest costs. In addition, some of the acquisitions have not come cheap, resulting in large amounts of reported goodwill and goodwill amortization. As a result, Time Warner has reported net losses in all but two years from 1989 through 1997.

THE NAVIGATOR

ILLUSTRATION 17-11

*Comprehensive balance sheet*

## PACE CORPORATION
### Balance Sheet
### December 31, 1999

#### Assets

| | | | |
|---|---|---|---|
| **Current assets** | | | |
| Cash | | | $ 21,000 |
| Temporary investments, at fair value | | | 147,000 |
| Accounts receivable | | $ 84,000 | |
| Less: Allowance for doubtful accounts | | 4,000 | 80,000 |
| Merchandise inventory, at FIFO cost | | | 43,000 |
| Prepaid insurance | | | 23,000 |
| Total current assets | | | 314,000 |
| **Investments** | | | |
| Bond sinking fund | | 100,000 | |
| Investments in stock of less than 20% owned companies, at fair value | | 50,000 | |
| Investment in stock of 20–50% owned company, at equity | | 150,000 | |
| Total investments | | | 300,000 |
| **Property, plant, and equipment** | | | |
| Land | | 200,000 | |
| Buildings | $800,000 | | |
| Less: Accumulated depreciation | 200,000 | 600,000 | |
| Equipment | 180,000 | | |
| Less: Accumulated depreciation | 54,000 | 126,000 | |
| Total property, plant, and equipment | | | 926,000 |
| **Intangible assets** | | | |
| Goodwill (Note 1) | | 100,000 | |
| Organization costs | | 70,000 | |
| Total intangible assets | | | 170,000 |
| Total assets | | | $1,710,000 |

#### Liabilities and Stockholders' Equity

| | | | |
|---|---|---|---|
| **Current liabilities** | | | |
| Accounts payable | | | $185,000 |
| Bond interest payable | | | 10,000 |
| Federal income taxes payable | | | 60,000 |
| Total current liabilities | | | 255,000 |
| **Long-term liabilities** | | | |
| Bonds payable, 10%, due 2010 | | $ 300,000 | |
| Less: Discount on bonds | | 10,000 | |
| Total long-term liabilities | | | 290,000 |
| Total liabilities | | | 545,000 |
| **Stockholders' equity** | | | |
| Paid-in capital | | | |
| Common stock, $10 par value, 200,000 shares authorized, 80,000 shares issued and outstanding | | 800,000 | |
| Paid-in capital in excess of par value | | 100,000 | |
| Total paid-in capital | | 900,000 | |
| Retained earnings (Note 2) | | 255,000 | |
| Total paid-in capital and retained earnings | | 1,155,000 | |
| **Add:** Unrealized gain on available-for-sale securities | | 10,000 | |
| Total stockholders' equity | | | 1,165,000 |
| Total liabilities and stockholders' equity | | | $1,710,000 |

**Note 1.** Goodwill is amortized by the straight-line method over 40 years.

**Note 2.** Retained earnings of $100,000 is restricted for plant expansion.

# DEMONSTRATION PROBLEM

In its first year of operations, the DeMarco Company had the following selected transactions in stock investments which are considered trading securities:

June  1   Purchased for cash 600 shares of Sanburg common stock at $24 per share plus $300 brokerage fees.

July  1   Purchased for cash 800 shares of Cey common stock at $33 per share plus $600 brokerage fees.

Sept. 1   Received a $1 per share cash dividend from Cey Corporation.

Nov.  1   Sold 200 shares of Sanburg common stock for cash at $27 per share less $150 brokerage fees.

Dec. 15   Received a $.50 per share cash dividend on Sanburg common stock.

At December 31, the fair values per share were: Sanburg $25 and Cey $30.

*Instructions*
(a) Journalize the transactions.
(b) Prepare the adjusting entry at December 31 to report the securities at fair value.

**PROBLEM-SOLVING STRATEGIES**

1. Cost includes the price paid plus brokerage fees.

2. Gain or loss on sales is determined by the difference between net selling price and the cost of the securities.

3. The adjustment to fair value is based on the total difference between cost and fair value of the securities.

## SOLUTION TO DEMONSTRATION PROBLEM

| | | | | | |
|---|---|---|---|---|---|
| (a) June | 1 | Stock Investments | | 14,700 | |
| | | Cash | | | 14,700 |
| | | (To record purchase of 600 shares of Sanburg common stock) | | | |
| July | 1 | Stock Investments | | 27,000 | |
| | | Cash | | | 27,000 |
| | | (To record purchase of 800 shares of Cey common stock) | | | |
| Sept. | 1 | Cash | | 800 | |
| | | Dividend Revenue | | | 800 |
| | | (To record receipt of $1 per share cash dividend from Cey Corporation) | | | |
| Nov. | 1 | Cash | | 5,250 | |
| | | Stock Investments | | | 4,900 |
| | | Gain on Sale of Stock Investments | | | 350 |
| | | (To record sale of 200 shares of Sanburg common stock) | | | |
| Dec. | 15 | Cash | | 200 | |
| | | Dividend Revenue | | | 200 |
| | | (To record receipt of $.50 per share dividend from Sanburg Corporation) | | | |
| (b) Dec. | 31 | Unrealized Loss—Income | | 2,800 | |
| | | Market Adjustment—Trading | | | 2,800 |
| | | (To record unrealized loss on trading securities) | | | |

| Investment | Cost | Fair Value | Unrealized Gain (Loss) |
|---|---|---|---|
| Sanburg common stock | $ 9,800 | $10,000 | $ 200 |
| Cey common stock | 27,000 | 24,000 | (3,000) |
| Totals | $36,800 | $34,000 | $(2,800) |

THE NAVIGATOR

# SUMMARY OF STUDY OBJECTIVES

**1. *Identify the reasons corporations invest in stocks and debt securities.*** Corporations invest for three primary reasons: (a) They have excess cash; (b) they view investments as a significant revenue source; or (c) they have strategic goals such as gaining control of a competitor or moving into a new line of business.

**2. *Explain the accounting for debt investments.*** Entries for investments in debt securities are required when the bonds are purchased, interest is received or accrued, and the bonds are sold. The accounting for long-term investments in bonds is the same as for temporary investments in bonds, except that bond premium and bond discount must be amortized.

**3. *Explain the accounting for stock investments.*** Entries for investments in common stock are required when the stock is purchased, dividends are received, and stock is sold. When ownership is less than 20%, the cost method is used. When ownership is between 20% and 50%, the equity method should be used. When ownership is more than 50%, consolidated financial statements should be prepared.

**4. *Describe the purpose and usefulness of consolidated financial statements.*** When a company owns more than 50%

of the common stock of another company, consolidated financial statements are usually prepared. These statements are especially useful to the stockholders, board of directors, and management of the parent company.

**5. *Indicate how debt and stock investments are valued and reported on the financial statements.*** Investments in debt and stock securities are classified as trading, available-for-sale, or held-to-maturity securities for valuation and reporting purposes. Trading securities are reported in current assets at fair value with changes from cost reported in net income. Available-for-sale securities are also reported at fair value with the changes from cost reported in stockholders' equity. Available-for-sale securities are classified as temporary or long-term depending on their expected realization.

**6. *Distinguish between temporary and long-term investments.*** Temporary investments are securities, held by a company, that are readily marketable and intended to be converted to cash within the next year or operating cycle, whichever is longer. Investments that do not meet both criteria are classified as long-term investments.

THE NAVIGATOR

# GLOSSARY

**Available-for-sale securities**   Securities that may be sold in the future. (p. 732)

**Consolidated financial statements**   Financial statements that present the assets and liabilities controlled by the parent company and the aggregate profitability of the affiliated companies. (p. 729)

**Controlling interest**   Ownership of more than 50% of the common stock of another entity. (p. 729)

**Cost method**   An accounting method in which the investment in common stock is recorded at cost and revenue is recognized only when cash dividends are received. (p. 727)

**Debt investments**   Investments in government and corporation bonds. (p. 724)

**Equity method**   An accounting method in which the investment in common stock is initially recorded at cost, and the investment account is then adjusted annually to show the investor's equity in the investee. (p. 728)

**Fair value**   Amount for which a security could be sold in a normal market. (p. 731)

**Held-to-maturity securities**   Debt securities which the investor has the intent and ability to hold to their maturity date. (p. 732)

**Investment portfolio**   A group of stocks in different corporations held for investment purposes. (p. 726)

**Long-term investments**   Investments that are not readily marketable or that management does not intend to convert into cash within the next year or operating cycle, whichever is longer. (p. 734)

**Parent company**   A company that owns more than 50% of the common stock of another entity. (p. 729)

**Stock investments**   Investments in the capital stock of corporations. (p. 726)

**Subsidiary (affiliated) company**   A company in which more than 50% of its stock is owned by another company. (p. 729)

**Temporary investments**   Investments that are readily marketable and intended to be converted into cash within the next year or operating cycle, whichever is longer. (p. 734)

**Trading securities**   Securities bought and held primarily for sale in the near term to generate income on short-term price differences. (p. 732)

# SELF-STUDY QUESTIONS

Answers are at the end of the chapter.

(SO 2) 1. Debt investments are initially recorded at:
  a. cost.
  b. cost plus accrued interest.
  c. fair value.
  d. None of the above.

(SO 2) 2. Hanes Company sells debt investments costing $26,000 for $28,000 plus accrued interest that has been recorded. In journalizing the sale, credits are:
  a. Debt Investments and Loss on Sale of Debt Investments.
  b. Debt Investments, Gain on Sale of Debt Investments, and Bond Interest Receivable.
  c. Stock Investments and Bond Interest Receivable.
  d. No correct answer given.

(SO 3) 3. Pryor Company receives net proceeds of $42,000 on the sale of stock investments that cost $39,500. This transaction will result in reporting in the income statement a:
  a. loss of $2,500 under Other Expenses and Losses.
  b. loss of $2,500 under Operating Expenses.
  c. gain of $2,500 under Other Revenues and Gains.
  d. gain of $2,500 under Operating Revenues.

(SO 3) 4. The equity method of accounting for long-term investments in stock should be used when the investor has significant influence over an investee and owns:
  a. between 20% and 50% of the investee's common stock.
  b. 20% or more of the investee's common stock.
  c. more than 50% of the investee's common stock.
  d. less than 20% of the investee's common stock.

(SO 4) 5. Which of the following statements is *not true*? Consolidated financial statements are useful to:
  a. determine the profitability of specific subsidiaries.
  b. determine the aggregate profitability of enterprises under common control.
  c. determine the breadth of a parent company's operations.
  d. determine the full extent of aggregate obligations of enterprises under common control.

(SO 5) 6. At the end of the first year of operations, the total cost of the trading securities portfolio is $120,000, and total fair value is $115,000. The financial statements should show:
  a. a reduction of an asset of $5,000 and a realized loss of $5,000.
  b. a reduction of an asset of $5,000 and an unrealized loss of $5,000 in the stockholders' equity section.
  c. a reduction of an asset of $5,000 in the current asset section and an unrealized loss in Other Expenses and Losses of $5,000.
  d. a reduction of an asset of $5,000 in the current asset section and a realized loss of $5,000 in Other Expenses and Losses.

(SO 5) 7. In the balance sheet, Unrealized Loss—Equity is reported as a:
  a. contra asset account.
  b. contra stockholders' equity account.
  c. loss in the income statement.
  d. loss in the retained earnings statement.

(SO 6) 8. Temporary debt investments must be readily marketable and be expected to be sold within:
  a. 3 months from the date of purchase.
  b. the next year or operating cycle, whichever is shorter.
  c. the next year or operating cycle, whichever is longer.
  d. the operating cycle.

THE
NAVIGATOR

# QUESTIONS

1. What are the reasons that corporations invest in securities?

2. (a) What is the cost of an investment in bonds?
   (b) When is interest on bonds recorded?

3. Sara Stine is confused about losses and gains on the sale of debt investments. Explain to Sara (a) how the gain or loss is computed, and (b) the statement presentation of the gains and losses.

4. Cline Company sells Hope's bonds costing $40,000 for $45,000, including $2,000 of accrued interest. In recording the sale, Cline books a $5,000 gain. Is this correct? Explain.

5. What is the cost of an investment in stock?

6. To acquire May Corporation stock, B. Mallon pays $60,000 in cash plus $1,500 broker's fees. What entry should be made for this investment, assuming the stock is readily marketable?

7. (a) When should a long-term investment in common stock be accounted for by the equity method? (b) When is revenue recognized under this method?

8. Marx Corporation uses the equity method to account for its ownership of 25% of the common stock of Welch Packing. During 1999 Welch reported a net income of $80,000 and declares and pays cash dividends of $10,000. What recognition should Marx Corporation give to these events?

9. What constitutes "significant influence" when an investor's financial interest is below the 50% level?

10. Distinguish between the cost and equity methods of accounting for investments in stocks.

11. What are consolidated financial statements?

12. What are the valuation guidelines for investments at a balance sheet date?

13. Kim Carley is the controller of Roarke, Inc. At December 31, the company's investments in trading securities cost $74,000 and have a fair value of $68,000. Indicate how Kim would report these data in the financial statements prepared on December 31.

14. Using the data in question 13, how would Kim report the data if the investment were long-term and the securities were classified as available-for-sale?

15. Colby Company's investments in available-for-sale securities at December 31 show total cost of $192,000 and total fair value of $205,000. Prepare the adjusting entry.

16. Using the data in question 15, prepare the adjusting entry assuming the securities are classified as trading securities.

17. What is the proper statement presentation of the account Unrealized Loss—Equity?

18. What purposes are served by reporting Unrealized Gains (Losses)—Equity in the stockholders' equity section?

19. Kiley Wholesale Supply owns stock in Sharp Corporation, which it intends to hold indefinitely because of some negative tax consequences if sold. Should the investment in Sharp be classified as a temporary investment? Why?

# BRIEF EXERCISES
•••••••••••••••••••••••••••••••••••••••••••••••••••••••••••••

**BE17–1** DeShields Corporation purchased debt investments for $41,500 on January 1, 1999. On July 1, 1999, DeShields received cash interest of $2,490. Journalize the purchase and the receipt of interest. Assume that no interest has been accrued.

*Journalize entries for debt investments.*
*(SO 2)*

**BE17–2** On August 1, Lolich Company buys 1,000 shares of Stead common stock for $36,000 cash plus brokerage fees of $600. On December 1, the stock investments are sold for $38,000 in cash. Journalize the purchase and sale of the common stock.

*Journalize entries for stock investments.*
*(SO 3)*

**BE17–3** Arkin Company owns 30% of Hines Company. For the current year Hines reports net income of $180,000 and declares and pays a $50,000 cash dividend. Record Arkin's equity in Hines's net income and the receipt of dividends from Hines.

*Record transactions under the equity method of accounting.*
*(SO 3)*

**BE17–4** Cost and fair value data for the trading securities of Mingo Company at December 31, 1999, are $64,000 and $59,000, respectively. Prepare the adjusting entry to record the securities at fair value.

*Prepare adjusting entry using fair value.*
*(SO 5)*

**BE17–5** For the data presented in BE17–4, show the financial statement presentation of the trading securities and related accounts.

*Indicate statement presentation using fair value.*
*(SO 5, 6)*

**BE17–6** Dexter Corporation holds available-for-sale stock securities costing $72,000 as a long-term investment. At December 31, 1999, the fair value of the securities is $68,000. Prepare the adjusting entry to record the securities at fair value.

*Prepare adjusting entry using fair value.*
*(SO 5)*

**BE17–7** For the data presented in BE17–6, show the financial statement presentation of the available-for-sale securities and related accounts. Assume the available-for-sale securities are noncurrent.

*Indicate statement presentation using fair value.*
*(SO 5, 6)*

**BE17–8** Thesh Corporation has the following long-term investments: common stock of Kubek Co. (10% ownership) held as available-for-sale securities, cost $108,000, fair value $110,000; common stock of Ely Inc. (30% ownership), cost $210,000, equity $250,000; and a bond sinking fund of $150,000. Prepare the investments section of the balance sheet.

*Prepare investment section of balance sheet.*
*(SO 5, 6)*

# EXERCISES
•••••••••••••••••••••••••••••••••••••••••••••••••••••••••••••

**E17–1** Greer Corporation had the following transactions pertaining to debt investments:

Jan. 1   Purchased 90 10%, $1,000 Ford Co. bonds for $90,000 cash plus brokerage fees of $900. Interest is payable semiannually on July 1 and January 1.
July 1   Received semiannual interest on Ford Co. bonds.
July 1   Sold 30 Ford Co. bonds for $32,000 less $400 brokerage fees.

*Journalize debt investment transactions and accrue interest.*
*(SO 2)*

*Instructions*
(a) Journalize the transactions.
(b) Prepare the adjusting entry for the accrual of interest at December 31.

*Journalize stock investment transactions.*
*(SO 3)*

**E17-2**  Jacobs Company had the following transactions pertaining to stock investments:

Feb. 1   Purchased 800 shares of Aber common stock (2%) for $9,000 cash plus brokerage fees of $200.
July 1   Received cash dividends of $1 per share on Aber common stock.
Sept. 1   Sold 300 shares of Aber common stock for $4,000 less brokerage fees of $100.
Dec. 1   Received cash dividends of $1 per share on Aber common stock.

**Instructions**
(a) Journalize the transactions.
(b) Explain how dividend revenue and the gain (loss) on sale should be reported in the income statement.

*Journalize transactions for investments in stocks.*
*(SO 3)*

**E17-3**  Crosby Inc. had the following transactions pertaining to investments in common stock:

Jan.  1   Purchased 1,000 shares of Hannah Corporation common stock (5%) for $70,000 cash plus $2,100 broker's commission.
July  1   Received a cash dividend of $9 per share.
Dec.  1   Sold 500 shares of Hannah Corporation common stock for $37,000 cash less $800 broker's commission.
Dec. 31   Received a cash dividend of $9 per share.

**Instructions**
Journalize the transactions.

*Journalize and post transactions and contrast cost and equity method results.*
*(SO 3)*

**E17-4**  On January 1 Howell Corporation purchased a 30% equity in Louise Corporation for $150,000. At December 31 Louise declared and paid a $60,000 cash dividend and reported net income of $200,000.

**Instructions**
(a) Journalize the transactions.
(b) Determine the amount to be reported as an investment in Louise stock at December 31.

*Journalize entries under cost and equity methods.*
*(SO 3)*

**E17-5**  Presented below are two independent situations:

1. Ritter Cosmetics acquired 10% of the 200,000 shares of common stock of Mai Fashion at a total cost of $13 per share on March 18, 1999. On June 30, Mai declared and paid a $75,000 dividend. On December 31, Mai reported net income of $122,000 for the year. At December 31, the market price of Mai Fashion was $15 per share. The stock is classified as available-for-sale.

2. Somer, Inc., obtained significant influence over Ortiz Corporation by buying 40% of Ortiz's 30,000 outstanding shares of common stock at a total cost of $9 per share on January 1, 1999. On June 15, Ortiz declared and paid a cash dividend of $35,000. On December 31, Ortiz reported a net income of $80,000 for the year.

**Instructions**
Prepare all the necessary journal entries for 1999 for (a) Ritter Cosmetics and (b) Somer, Inc.

*Prepare adjusting entry to record fair value and indicate statement presentation.*
*(SO 5, 6)*

**E17-6**  At December 31, 1999, the trading securities for Yanik, Inc., are as follows:

| Security | Cost | Fair Value |
|---|---|---|
| A | $17,500 | $16,000 |
| B | 12,500 | 14,000 |
| C | 23,000 | 21,000 |
| | $53,000 | $51,000 |

**Instructions**
(a) Prepare the adjusting entry at December 31, 1999, to report the securities at fair value.
(b) Show the balance sheet and income statement presentation at December 31, 1999, after adjustment to fair value.

*Prepare adjusting entry to record fair value and indicate statement presentation.*
*(SO 5, 6)*

**E17-7**  Data for investments in stock classified as trading securities are presented in E17-6. Assume instead that the investments are classified as available-for-sale securities with the same cost and fair value data. The securities are considered to be a long-term investment.

*Instructions*
(a) Prepare the adjusting entry at December 31, 1999, to report the securities at fair value.
(b) Show the statement presentation at December 31, 1999, after adjustment to fair value.
(c) ▣▬▬▶ M. Wise, a member of the board of directors, does not understand the reporting of the unrealized gains or losses. Write a letter to Mr. Wise explaining the reporting and the purposes that it serves.

**E17–8**   Quayle Company has the following data at December 31, 1999:

| Securities | Cost | Fair Value |
|---|---|---|
| Trading | $120,000 | $128,000 |
| Available-for-sale | 100,000 | 94,000 |

*Prepare adjusting entries for fair value and indicate statement presentation for two classes of securities.*
*(SO 5, 6)*

The available-for-sale securities are held as a long-term investment.

*Instructions*
(a) Prepare the adjusting entries to report each class of securities at fair value.
(b) Indicate the statement presentation of each class of securities and the related unrealized gain (loss) accounts.

# PROBLEMS: SET A

**P17–1A**   The following transactions related to long-term bonds occurred for Wolfe Corporation:

*Journalize transactions and show financial statement presentation.*
*(SO 2, 5, 6)*

**1999**
Jan. 1   Purchased $50,000 Lake Corporation 10% bonds for $50,000.
July 1   Received interest on Lake bonds.
Dec. 31   Accrued interest on Lake bonds.

**2000**
Jan. 1   Received interest on Lake bonds.
Jan. 1   Sold $25,000 Lake bonds for $26,500.
July 1   Received interest on Lake bonds.

*Instructions*
(a) Journalize the transactions.
(b) Assume that the fair value of the bonds at December 31, 1999, was $55,000. These bonds are classified as available-for-sale securities. Prepare the adjusting entry to record these bonds at fair value.
(c) Show the balance sheet presentation of the bonds and interest receivable at December 31, 1999, and indicate where any unrealized gain or loss is reported in the financial statements.

**P17–2A**   In January 1999, the management of Mann Company concludes that it has sufficient cash to purchase some temporary investments in debt and stock securities. During the year, the following transactions occurred:

*Journalize investment transactions, prepare adjusting entry, and show statement presentation.*
*(SO 2, 3, 5, 6)*

Feb. 1   Purchased 800 shares of SRI common stock for $32,000 plus brokerage fees of $800.
Mar. 1   Purchased 500 shares of FGH common stock for $15,000 plus brokerage fees of $300.
Apr. 1   Purchased 60 $1,000, 12% XYZ bonds for $60,000 plus $1,200 brokerage fees. Interest is payable semiannually on April 1 and October 1.
July 1   Received a cash dividend of $.60 per share on the SRI common stock.
Aug. 1   Sold 200 shares of SRI common stock at $42 per share less brokerage fees of $350.
Sept. 1   Received a $1 per share cash dividend on the FGH common stock.
Oct. 1   Received the semiannual interest on the XYZ bonds.
Oct. 1   Sold the XYZ bonds for $63,000 less $1,000 brokerage fees.

At December 31, the fair value of the SRI and FGH common stocks were $39 and $30 per share, respectively.

*Instructions*

   (a) Journalize the transactions and post to the accounts Debt Investments and Stock Investments. (Use the T-account form.)

   (b) Prepare the adjusting entry at December 31, 1999, to report the investments at fair value. All securities are considered to be trading securities.

   (c) Show the balance sheet presentation of investment securities at December 31, 1999.

   (d) Identify the income statement accounts and give the statement classification of each account.

*Journalize transactions and adjusting entry for stock investments.*
*(SO 3, 5, 6)*

**P17–3A** On December 31, 1999, Kern Associates owned the following securities that are held as long-term investments:

| Common Stock | Shares | Cost |
| --- | --- | --- |
| A Co. | 1,000 | $50,000 |
| B Co. | 6,000 | 36,000 |
| C Co. | 1,200 | 24,000 |

On this date, the total fair value of the securities was equal to its cost. The securities are not held for influence or control over the investees. In 2000, the following transactions occurred:

July  1  Received $1 per share semiannual cash dividend on B Co. common stock.

Aug.  1  Received $.50 per share cash dividend on A Co. common stock.

Sept.  1  Sold 500 shares of B Co. common stock for cash at $7 per share less brokerage fees of $100.

Oct.  1  Sold 400 shares of A Co. common stock for cash at $56 per share less brokerage fees of $600.

Nov.  1  Received $1 per share cash dividend on C Co. common stock.

Dec. 15  Received $.50 per share cash dividend on A Co. common stock.

     31  Received $1 per share semiannual cash dividend on B Co. common stock.

At December 31, the fair values per share of the common stocks were: A Co. $47, B Co. $6, and C Co. $19.

*Instructions*

   (a) Journalize the 2000 transactions and post to the account Stock Investments. (Use the T-account form.)

   (b) Prepare the adjusting entry at December 31, 2000, to show the securities at fair value. The stock should be classified as available-for-sale securities.

   (c) Show the balance sheet presentation of the investments at December 31, 2000. At this date, Kern Associates has common stock $2,000,000 and retained earnings $1,200,000.

*Prepare entries at cost and at equity and prepare memorandum.*
*(SO 3)*

**P17–4A** Jantz Concrete acquired 20% of the outstanding common stock of Hawes, Inc., on January 1, 1999, by paying $1,200,000 for 50,000 shares. Hawes declared and paid a $0.60 per share cash dividend on June 30 and again on December 31, 1999. Hawes reported net income of $800,000 for the year.

*Instructions*

   (a) Prepare the journal entries for Jantz Concrete for 1999 assuming Jantz cannot exercise significant influence over Hawes. (Use the cost method.)

   (b) Prepare the journal entries for Jantz Concrete for 1999, assuming Jantz can exercise significant influence over Hawes. (Use the equity method.)

   (c) ▭▭▭▭▷ The board of directors of Jantz Concrete is confused about the differences between the cost and equity methods. Prepare a memorandum for the board that (1) explains each method and (2) shows, in tabular form, the account balances under each method at December 31, 1999.

*Journalize stock transactions and show statement presentation.*
*(SO 3, 5, 6)*

**P17–5A** The following are in Hyatt Company's portfolio of long-term available-for-sale securities at December 31, 1999:

| | Cost |
| --- | --- |
| 500 shares of Aglar Corporation common stock | $26,000 |
| 700 shares of BAL Corporation common stock | 42,000 |
| 400 shares of Hicks Corporation preferred stock | 16,800 |

On December 31, the total cost of the portfolio equaled total fair value. Hyatt had the following transactions related to the securities during 2000:

Jan. 7 Sold 500 shares of Aglar Corporation common stock at $56 per share less brokerage fees of $700.

Jan. 10 Purchased 200 shares, $70 par value common stock of Miley Corporation at $78 per share, plus brokerage fees of $240.

26 Received a cash dividend of $1.15 per share on BAL Corporation common stock.

Feb. 2 Received cash dividends of $.40 per share on Hicks Corporation preferred stock.

10 Sold all 400 shares of Hicks Corporation preferred stock at $30.00 per share less brokerage fees of $180.

July 1 Received a cash dividend of $1.00 per share on BAL Corporation common stock.

Sept. 1 Purchased an additional 400 shares of the $70 par value common stock of Miley Corporation at $82 per share, plus brokerage fees of $400.

Dec. 15 Received a cash dividend of $1.50 per share on Miley Corporation common stock.

At December 31, 2000, the fair values of the securities were:

| BAL Corporation common stock | $64 per share |
| Miley Corporation common stock | $72 per share |

Hyatt uses separate account titles for each investment, such as Investment in BAL Corporation Common Stock.

*Instructions*
(a) Prepare journal entries to record the transactions.
(b) Post to the investment accounts. (Use T accounts.)
(c) Prepare the adjusting entry at December 31, 2000, to report the porfolio at fair value.
(d) Show the balance sheet presentation at December 31, 2000.

**P17–6A** The following data, presented in alphabetical order, are taken from the records of Lehman Corporation.

*Prepare a balance sheet.*
*(SO 5, 6)*

| | |
|---|---:|
| Accounts payable | $ 220,000 |
| Accounts receivable | 90,000 |
| Accumulated depreciation—building | 180,000 |
| Accumulated depreciation—equipment | 52,000 |
| Allowance for doubtful accounts | 6,000 |
| Bonds payable (10%, due 2012) | 400,000 |
| Bond sinking fund | 360,000 |
| Buildings | 900,000 |
| Cash | 92,000 |
| Common stock ($5 par value; 500,000 shares authorized, 300,000 shares issued) | 1,500,000 |
| Discount on bonds payable | 20,000 |
| Dividends payable | 50,000 |
| Equipment | 275,000 |
| Goodwill | 200,000 |
| Income taxes payable | 120,000 |
| Investment in Houston Inc, stock (30% ownership), at equity | 240,000 |
| Land | 500,000 |
| Temporary stock investment, at fair value | 185,000 |
| Merchandise inventory | 170,000 |
| Notes payable (due 2000) | 70,000 |
| Organization costs | 50,000 |
| Paid-in capital in excess of par value | 200,000 |
| Prepaid insurance | 16,000 |
| Retained earnings | 300,000 |

*Instructions*
Prepare a balance sheet at December 31, 1999.

# PROBLEMS: SET B

*Journalize transactions and show financial statement presentation.*
*(SO 2, 5, 6)*

**P17–1B**   The following transactions related to long-term bonds occurred for Gomez Corporation:

**1999**

Jan. 1   Purchased $100,000 Horton Corporation 9% bonds for $100,000.
July 1   Received interest on Horton bonds.
Dec. 31   Accrued interest on Horton bonds.

**2000**

Jan. 1   Received interest on Horton bonds.
Jan. 1   Sold $25,000 Horton bonds for $28,500.
July 1   Received interest on Horton bonds.

**Instructions**

(a) Journalize the transactions.
(b) Assume that the fair value of the bonds at December 31, 1999, was $96,000. These bonds are classified as available-for-sale securities. Prepare the adjusting entry to record these bonds at fair value.
(c) Show the balance sheet presentation of the bonds and interest receivable at December 31, 1999, and indicate where any unrealized gain or loss is reported in the financial statements.

*Journalize investment transactions, prepare adjusting entry, and show statement presentation.*
*(SO 2, 3, 5, 6)*

**P17–2B**   In January 1999, the management of the Norris Company concludes that it has sufficient cash to permit some temporary investments in debt and stock securities. During the year, the following transactions occurred:

Feb. 1   Purchased 600 shares of CBA common stock for $31,800 plus brokerage fees of $600.
Mar. 1   Purchased 800 shares of GHI common stock for $20,000 plus brokerage fees of $400.
Apr. 1   Purchased 50 $1,000, 12% UVW bonds for $50,000 plus $1,000 brokerage fees. Interest is payable semiannually on April 1 and October 1.
July 1   Received a cash dividend of $.60 per share on the CBA common stock.
Aug. 1   Sold 200 shares of CBA common stock at $58 per share less brokerage fees of $200.
Sept. 1   Received a $1 per share cash dividend on the GHI common stock.
Oct. 1   Received the semiannual interest on the UVW bonds.
Oct. 1   Sold the UVW bonds for $51,000 less $1,000 brokerage fees.

At December 31, the fair value of the CBA and GHI common stocks were $55 and $23 per share, respectively.

**Instructions**

(a) Journalize the transactions and post to the accounts Debt Investments and Stock Investments. (Use the T-account form.)
(b) Prepare the adjusting entry at December 31, 1999, to report the investment securities at fair value. All securities are considered to be trading securities.
(c) Show the balance sheet presentation of investment securities at December 31, 1999.
(d) Identify the income statement accounts and give the statement classification of each account.

*Journalize transactions and adjusting entry for stock investments.*
*(SO 3, 5, 6)*

**P17–3B**   On December 31, 1999, Milner Associates owned the following securities that are held as a long-term investment. The securities are not held for influence or control of the investee.

| Common Stock | Shares | Cost |
|---|---|---|
| X Co. | 2,000 | $90,000 |
| Y Co. | 5,000 | 45,000 |
| Z Co. | 1,500 | 30,000 |

On this date, the total fair value of the securities was equal to its cost. In 2000, the following transactions occurred.

July 1   Received $1 per share semiannual cash dividend on Y Co. common stock.
      8   Received 4,000 shares of X Co. common stock in a 3 for 1 stock split.

Aug.  1   Received $.50 per share cash dividend on X Co. common stock.

Sept.  1   Sold 700 shares of Y Co. common stock for cash at $8 per share less brokerage fees of $200.

Oct.  1   Sold 600 shares of X Co. common stock for cash at $17 per share less brokerage fees of $500.

Nov.  1   Received $1 per share cash dividend on Z Co. common stock.

Dec. 15   Received $.50 per share cash dividend on X Co. common stock.

     31   Received $1 per share semiannual cash dividend on Y Co. common stock.

At December 31, the fair values per share of the common stocks were: X Co. $16, Y Co. $8, and Z Co. $18.

### Instructions

(a)  Journalize the 2000 transactions and post to the account Stock Investments. (Use the T-account form.)

(b)  Prepare the adjusting entry at December 31, 2000, to show the securities at fair value. The stock should be classified as available-for-sale securities.

(c)  Show the balance sheet presentation of the investments at December 31, 2000. At this date, Milner Associates has common stock $1,500,000 and retained earnings $1,000,000.

**P17–4B**   Nayler Services acquired 30% of the outstanding common stock of Quinn Company on January 1, 1999, by paying $800,000 for the 40,000 shares. Quinn declared and paid $0.40 per share cash dividends on March 15, June 15, September 15, and December 15, 1999. Quinn reported net income of $360,000 for the year.

*Prepare entries under the cost and equity methods and tabulate differences.*
*(SO 3)*

### Instructions

(a)  Prepare the journal entries for Nayler Services for 1999 assuming Nayler cannot exercise significant influence over Quinn. (Use the cost method.)

(b)  Prepare the journal entries for Nayler Services for 1999, assuming Nayler can exercise significant influence over Quinn. (Use the equity method.)

(c)  In tabular form, indicate the investment and income statement account balances at December 31, 1999, under each method of accounting.

**P17–5B**   The following data, presented in alphabetical order, are taken from the records of Scheer Corporation:

*Prepare a balance sheet.*
*(SO 5, 6)*

| | |
|---|---:|
| Accounts payable | $ 270,000 |
| Accounts receivable | 140,000 |
| Accumulated depreciation—building | 180,000 |
| Accumulated depreciation—equipment | 52,000 |
| Allowance for doubtful accounts | 6,000 |
| Bonds payable (10%, due 2010) | 500,000 |
| Bond sinking fund | 150,000 |
| Buildings | 950,000 |
| Cash | 92,000 |
| Common stock ($10 par value; 500,000 shares authorized, 150,000 shares issued) | 1,500,000 |
| Dividends payable | 80,000 |
| Equipment | 275,000 |
| Goodwill | 200,000 |
| Income taxes payable | 120,000 |
| Investment in Dodge common stock (10% ownership), at cost | 278,000 |
| Investment in Huston common stock (30% ownership), at equity | 230,000 |
| Land | 500,000 |
| Market adjustment—available-for-sale securities (Dr) | 8,000 |
| Merchandise inventory | 170,000 |
| Notes payable (due 2000) | 70,000 |
| Organization costs | 50,000 |
| Paid-in capital in excess of par value | 200,000 |
| Premium on bonds payable | 40,000 |
| Prepaid insurance | 16,000 |
| Retained earnings | 213,000 |
| Temporary stock investment, at fair value | 180,000 |
| Unrealized gain—available-for-sale securities | 8,000 |

The investment in Dodge common stock is considered to be a long-term available-for-sale security.

*Instructions*
Prepare a balance sheet at December 31, 1999.

# BROADENING YOUR PERSPECTIVE

# FINANCIAL REPORTING AND ANALYSIS

### FINANCIAL REPORTING PROBLEM: Kellogg Company

BYP17–1   The annual report of Kellogg Company is presented in Appendix A.

*Instructions*
Answer the following questions:

(a) What information about investments is reported in the consolidated balance sheet?
(b) Based on the information in Note 1 accompanying the financial statements, what is the nature of Kellogg's short-term investments?
(c) How much was spent in acquisition of new businesses in 1997 compared with 1996?

### COMPARATIVE ANALYSIS PROBLEM: Kellogg Company vs. General Mills

BYP17–2   Kellogg's financial statements are presented in Appendix A; General Mills's financial statements are presented in Appendix B.

*Instructions*

(a) Based on the information contained in these financial statements, determine each of the following for each company:
    (1) Cash used in (by) investing (investment) activities during 1997 (from the Statement of Cash Flows).
    (2) Cash used for acquisitions and investments in businesses during 1997.
(b) Based on the information contained in the notes to the financial statements, explain the major acquisitions made by these two companies in the last two years.

### RESEARCH ASSIGNMENT

BYP17–3   The July 6, 1995, edition of *The Wall Street Journal* includes an article by Jim Carlton and David P. Hamilton, entitled "Packard Bell Sells 20% Stake to NEC for $170 Million; Deal Gives Japanese Firm Unprecedented Access to the U.S. PC Market."

*Instructions*
Read the article and answer the following questions:

(a) Why did Packard Bell sell shares to NEC?
(b) Identify a similar transaction between two other computer companies.
(c) Under U.S. GAAP, how would NEC account for its investment in Packard Bell?
(d) Packard Bell was considering a sale of common shares to the general public. Why didn't it select this option?

### INTERPRETING FINANCIAL STATEMENTS: Xerox Corporation

BYP17–4   Xerox Corporation has a 50% investment interest in a joint venture with the Japanese corporation Fuji, called Fuji Xerox. Xerox accounts for this investment using the equity method. The following additional information regarding this investment was taken from Xerox's 1995 annual report:

| | |
|---|---:|
| Investment in Fuji Xerox per balance sheet | $ 1,223 |
| Xerox's equity in Fuji Xerox net income | 88 |
| Xerox total assets | 25,969 |
| Xerox total liabilities | 21,328 |
| Fuji Xerox total assets | 6,603 |
| Fuji Xerox total liabilities | 4,153 |

*Instructions*

(a) What alternative approaches are available for accounting for long-term investments in stock? Discuss whether Xerox is correct in using the equity method to account for this investment.

(b) Under the equity method, how does Xerox reports its investment in Fuji Xerox? If Xerox owned a majority of Fuji Xerox, it then would have to consolidate Fuji Xerox instead of using the equity method. Discuss how this would change Xerox's financial statements. That is, in what way and by how much would assets and liabilities change?

(c) The use of 50% joint ventures is becoming a fairly common practice. Why might companies like Xerox prefer to participate in a joint venture rather than own a majority share?

## REAL-WORLD FOCUS: SPS Technologies, Inc.

**BYP17–5** **SPS Technologies, Inc.,** was formed in 1903 as Standard Pressed Steel. Today the company is engaged in the design, manufacture, and marketing of high-strength mechanical fasteners, superalloys, and magnetic materials for the aerospace, automotive, and off-highway equipment industries. The company owns plants in the United States, United Kingdom, Ireland, Australia, and Spain, and has minority interests in facilities in Brazil and India.

The following note to the financial statements appears in a recent SPS annual report:

### SPS TECHNOLOGIES
### Notes to the Financial Statements

**Investments:** The Company's investments in affiliates consist of a 16.75% interest in Precision Fasteners Ltd., Bombay, India; a 46.49% interest in Metalac S.A. Industria e Comercio, Sao Paulo, Brazil; a 51.0% interest in Pacific Products Limited, Guernsey, Channel Islands, United Kingdom; and a 51.0% interest in National-Arnold Magnetics Company, Adelanto, California, United States. Dividends received from these companies were $42,000, $44,000, and $66,000 in 1993, 1992 and 1991, respectively.

*Instructions*

(a) Does the investment in these companies represent short- or long-term investments? Are these investments in stocks or in bonds of these companies?

(b) The ownership percentages in these companies vary. Based upon the information given, which accounting method would appear appropriate for each company? What other information would you like to know before deciding how to account for each investment?

(c) What is the most likely method used to account for dividends received from Precision Fasteners? From National-Arnolds Magnetics Company?

# CRITICAL THINKING

## GROUP DECISION CASE

**BYP17–6** At the beginning of the question and answer portion of the annual stockholders' meeting of Powell Corporation, stockholder Cindy Olson asks, "Why did management sell the holdings in BMA Company at a loss when this company has been very profitable during the period its stock was held by Powell?"

Since president Tony Perez has just concluded his speech on the recent success and bright future of Powell, he is taken aback by this question and responds, "I remember we paid $1,100,000 for that stock some years ago, and I am sure we sold that stock at a much higher price. You must be mistaken."

Olson retorts, "Well, right here in footnote number 7 to the annual report it shows that 240,000 shares, a 25% interest in BMA, were sold on the last day of the year. Also, it states that BMA earned $550,000 this year and paid out $150,000 in cash dividends. Further, a summary statement indicates that in past years, while Powell held BMA stock, BMA earned

$1,240,000 and paid out $440,000 in dividends. Finally, the income statement for this year shows a loss on the sale of BMA stock of $180,000. So, I doubt that I am mistaken."

Red-faced, president Perez turns to you.

*Instructions*

With the class divided into groups, answer the following:

(a)  What dollar amount did Powell receive upon the sale of the BMA stock?

(b)  Explain why both stockholder Olson and president Perez are correct.

## COMMUNICATION ACTIVITY

**BYP17–7**   Ramariz Corporation has purchased two securities for its portfolio. The first is a stock investment in Thome Corporation, one of its suppliers. Ramariz purchased 10% of Thome with the intention of holding it for a number of years, but has no intention of purchasing more shares. The second investment was a purchase of debt securities. Ramariz purchased the debt securities because its analysts believe that changes in market interest rates will cause these securities to increase in value in a short period of time. Ramariz intends to sell the securities as soon as they have increased in value.

*Instructions*

Write a memo to Crus Carey, the chief financial officer, explaining how to account for each of these investments, and what the implications for reported income are from this accounting treatment.

## ETHICS CASE

**BYP17–8**   Kimble Financial Services Company holds a large portfolio of debt and stock securities as an investment. The total fair value of the portfolio at December 31, 1999, is greater than total cost, with some securities having increased in value and others having decreased. Ann Osborn, the financial vice president, and Sue Ling, the controller, are in the process of classifying for the first time the securities in the portfolio.

Osborn suggests classifying the securities that have increased in value as trading securities in order to increase net income for the year. She also wants to classify the securities that have decreased in value as long-term available-for-sale securities so that the decreases in value will not affect 1999 net income.

Ling disagrees. She recommends classifying the securities that have decreased in value as trading securities and those that have increased in value as long-term available-for-sale securities. Ling argues that the company is having a good earnings year and that recognizing the losses now will help to smooth income for this year. Moreover, for future years, when the company may not be as profitable, the company will have built-in gains.

*Instructions*

(a)  Will classifying the securities as Osborn and Ling suggest actually affect earnings as each says it will?

(b)  Is there anything unethical in what Osborn and Ling propose? Who are the stake-holders affected by their proposals?

(c)  Assume that Osborn and Ling properly classify the portfolio. Assume, at year-end, that Osborn proposes to sell the securities that will increase 1999 net income, and that Ling proposes to sell the securities that will decrease 1999 net income. Is this unethical?

# SURFING THE NET

**BYP17–9**   Bonds, similar to stocks, can be purchased by investors in an initial public offering or through a secondary market. Secondary markets can be reached via the Internet and provide users with investment information. Bonds Online is one site that provides a bond-specific glossary of terms.

**Address:** http://www.bondsonline.com

**Steps:**
1. From the Bonds Online homepage, choose **Bond Professor.**
2. Choose **Glossary.**

*Instructions*
Using the glossary, find the definition of:

  (a) discount rate.
  (b) capital market.
  (c) rating.

**BYP17–10**  Most publicly traded companies are analyzed by numerous analysts. These analysts often don't agree about a company's future prospects. In this exercise you will find analysts' ratings about companies and make comparisons over time and across companies in the same industry. You will also see to what extent the analysts experienced "earnings surprises." Earnings surprises can cause changes in stock prices.

**Address:** http://biz.yahoo.com/i (or go to the Wiley home page)

**Steps:**
1. Choose a company.
2. Use the index to find the company's name.
3. Choose **Research.**

*Instructions*
Answer the following questions:

  (a) How many brokers rated the company?
  (b) What percentage rated it a strong buy?
  (c) What was the average rating for the week?
  (d) Did the average rating improve or decline relative to last week?
  (e) How do the brokers rank this company among all the companies in its industry?
  (f) What was the amount of the earnings surprise during the last quarter (that is, to what extent were analysts' expectations of earnings incorrect)?
  (g) Are earnings expected to increase or decrease this quarter compared to last?

---

*Answers to Self-Study Questions*
1. a    2. b    3. c    4. a    5. a    6. c    7. b    8. c

---

*Answer to Kellogg Review It Question 4, page 730*
In Note 1, the following statement is made regarding the consolidation policy of Kellogg Company: "The consolidated financial statements include the accounts of Kellogg Company and its majority-owned subsidiaries. Intercompany balances and transactions are eliminated. Certain amounts in the prior year financial statements have been reclassified to conform to the current year presentation."

 **Remember to go back to the Navigator box on the chapter-opening page and check off your completed work.**

**Before studying this chapter, you should know or, if necessary, review:**

a.  The difference between the accrual basis and the cash basis of accounting.
    (Ch. 3, pp. 112–113)

b.  The major items included in a corporation's balance sheet.
    (Ch. 17, p. 737)

c.  The major items included in a corporation's income statement.
    (Ch. 15, p. 652)

THE
NAVIGATOR

---

# FEATURE STORY

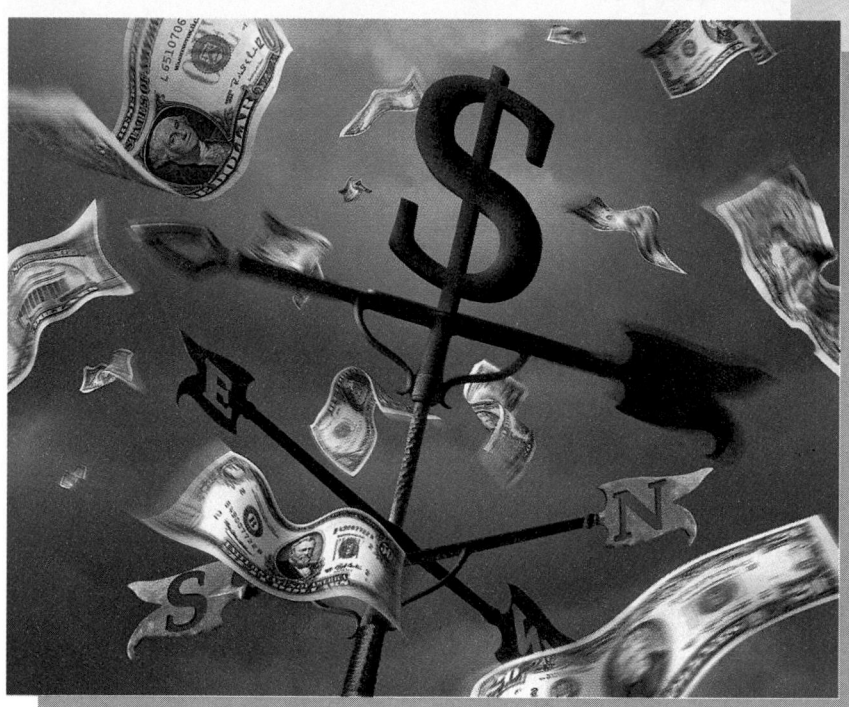

## "Cash Is Cash, and Everything Else Is Accounting"

For Gerald Biby, vice president and chief financial officer of Kilian Community College in Sioux Falls, South Dakota, the statement of cash flows was the difference between being able to refinance a mortgage and being turned down by six local banks. "We recently wanted to refinance a $125,000 mortgage on a piece of property that we own," he says. "It was the statement of cash flows that finally showed our lender that we had the cash flow to service the debt."

As he explains, the traditional financial statement for a not-for-profit, educational institution shows revenues and all expenditures, even the capital expenditures. According to this format, which the banks focused on initially, Kilian Community College was just breaking even. "In the business world, if we had spent $250,000 on a computer system, then we would have put that on a depreciation schedule. But in the non-profit arena, it's typical that the entire $250,000 is written off as an expense against the general fund." The statement of cash flows showed the bankers that one of the uses of funds was really the purchase of computer equipment that had several years of life.

The college's statement of cash flows has over 30 classifications including tuition, fees, bookstore revenues, and so on. The school has 250 students, charges $70 a credit hour (12 hours is a full-time schedule), and has five terms each year.

The bankers granted the refinancing when they saw that the college's sources of funds exceeded the loan repayments, including principal and interest, by a ratio of 3-to-1. Not only did the school get the loan, but it did so at a favorable rate. "We were able to cut the mortgage rate to prime plus 1% from prime plus 3%."

THE
NAVIGATOR

# CHAPTER 18

# THE STATEMENT
# OF CASH FLOWS

## THE NAVIGATOR

- Understand *Concepts for Review*
- Read *Feature Story*
- Scan *Study Objectives*
- Read *Preview*
- Read text and answer *Before You Go On*
  p. 761 ☐ p. 771 ☐ p. 784 ☐ p. 789 ☐
- Work *Demonstration Problems*
- Review *Summary of Study Objectives*
- Answer *Self-Study Questions*
- Complete assignments

## STUDY OBJECTIVES

**After studying this chapter, you should be able to:**

1. Indicate the primary purpose of the statement of cash flows.
2. Distinguish among operating, investing, and financing activities.
3. Prepare a statement of cash flows using the indirect method.
4. Prepare a statement of cash flows using the direct method.
5. Analyze the statement of cash flows.

THE
NAVIGATOR

*A*s the story about Kilian Community College indicates, the balance sheet, income statement, and retained earnings statement do not always show the whole picture of the financial condition of a company or institution. In fact, looking at the three traditional financial statements of some well-known companies, a thoughtful investor might have questions like the following: How did Eastman Kodak finance cash dividends of $649 million in a year in which it earned only $17 million? How could Delta Airlines purchase new planes costing $900 million in a year in which it reported a net loss of $86 million? How did Kohlberg Kravis Roberts finance its record-shattering $25 billion purchase of RJR Nabisco? Answers to these and similar questions can be found in this chapter, which presents the **statement of cash flows**. The content and organization of this chapter are as follows:

THE STATEMENT OF CASH FLOWS

OR

| The Statement of Cash Flows: Purpose and Format | Section 1: Indirect Method | Section 2: Direct Method | Analysis of the Statement of Cash Flows |
|---|---|---|---|
| • Purpose<br>• Meaning of "cash flows"<br>• Classifications<br>• Significant noncash activities<br>• Format<br>• Usefulness<br>• Preparation | • Determining net increase/decrease in cash<br>• Determining net cash provided/used by operating activities<br>• Determining net cash provided/used by investing and financing activities | • Determining net increase/decrease in cash<br>• Determining net cash provided/used by operating activities<br>• Determining net cash provided/used by investing and financing activities | • Current cash debt coverage ratio<br>• Cash return on sales ratio<br>• Cash debt coverage ratio |

THE NAVIGATOR

# THE STATEMENT OF CASH FLOWS: PURPOSE AND FORMAT

The three basic financial statements we've studied so far present only limited and fragmentary information about a company's cash flows (cash receipts and cash payments). For example, comparative balance sheets show the increase in property, plant, and equipment during the year, but they do not show how the additions were financed or paid for. The income statement shows net income, but it does not indicate the amount of cash generated by operating activities. Similarly, the retained earnings statement shows cash dividends declared but not the cash dividends paid during the year. None of these statements presents a detailed summary of the net change in cash as a result of operating, investing, and financing activities during the period.

## ACCOUNTING IN ACTION
### Business Insight

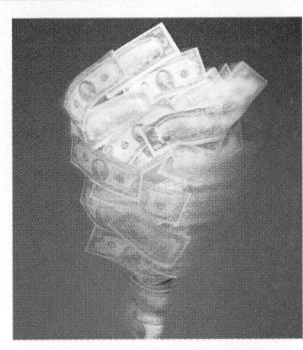

Libby-Owens-Ford (LOF) Company's mission statement in its annual report emphasizes the importance of cash flow as follows: "LOF stresses the importance of cash flow measurement and performance. Individual companies must analyze the cash flow effects of running their business. Where cash comes from and what cash is used for must be simply and clearly set forth."

## Purpose of the Statement of Cash Flows

The primary purpose of the statement of cash flows is to provide information about the cash receipts and cash payments of an entity during a period. A secondary objective is to provide information about the operating, investing, and financing activities of the entity during the period.[1] The statement of cash flows reports the cash receipts, cash payments, and net change in cash resulting from the operating, investing, and financing activities of an enterprise during a period in a format that reconciles the beginning and ending cash balances.

Reporting the causes of changes in cash is considered useful because investors, creditors, and other interested parties want to know what is happening to a company's most liquid resource—its cash. As the opening story about Kilian Community College demonstrates, a statement of cash flows helps us understand what is happening. It provides answers to the following simple, but important, questions about the enterprise:

1. Where did the cash come from during the period?
2. What was the cash used for during the period?
3. What was the change in the cash balance during the period?

**1**
STUDY
OBJECTIVE
..................................
Indicate the primary purpose of the statement of cash flows.

## Meaning of "Cash Flows"

The statement of cash flows is generally prepared using "**cash and cash equivalents**" as its basis. Cash equivalents are short-term, highly liquid investments that are both:

1. Readily convertible to known amounts of cash, and
2. So near their maturity that their market value is relatively insensitive to changes in interest rates.

Generally, only investments with original maturities of three months or less qualify under this definition. Examples of cash equivalents are Treasury bills, commercial paper (short-term corporate notes), and money market funds. All typically are purchased with cash that is in excess of immediate needs. Note that since cash and cash equivalents are viewed as the same, transfers between cash and cash equivalents are not treated as cash receipts and cash payments—i.e., they are not reported in the statement of cash flows. The term "cash" when used in this chapter includes cash and cash equivalents.

## Classification of Cash Flows

The statement of cash flows classifies cash receipts and cash payments by operating, investing, and financing activities. Transactions and other events char-

**2**
STUDY
OBJECTIVE
..................................
Distinguish among operating, investing, and financing activities.

---

[1]"Statement of Cash Flows," *Statement of Financial Accounting Standards No. 95* (Stamford, Conn.: FASB, 1987).

acteristic of each kind of activity are described in the list below and pictured in Illustration 18-1:

1. **Operating activities** include the cash effects of transactions that create revenues and expenses and thus enter into the determination of net income.
2. **Investing activities** include (a) acquiring and disposing of investments and productive long-lived assets, and (b) lending money and collecting the loans.
3. **Financing activities** include (a) obtaining cash from issuing debt and repaying the amounts borrowed, and (b) obtaining cash from stockholders and providing them with a return on their investment.

**ILLUSTRATION 18-1**

*Business activities shown on the statement of cash flows*

Operating activities    Investing activities    Financing activities

The category of operating activities is the most important because it shows the cash provided by company operations. This source of cash is generally considered to be the best measure of a company's ability to generate sufficient cash to continue as a going concern.

Illustration 18-2 on page 757 lists typical cash receipts and cash payments within each of the three classifications. Study the list carefully. It will prove very useful in solving homework exercises and problems.

As you can see, some cash flows relating to investing or financing activities are classified as operating activities. For example, **receipts of investment revenue (interest and dividends) and payments of interest to lenders are classified as operating activities because these items are reported in the income statement.**

Note that, generally, (1) operating activities involve income determination (income statement) items, (2) investing activities involve cash flows resulting from changes in investments and long-term asset items, and (3) financing activities involve cash flows resulting from changes in long-term liability and stockholders' equity items.

## Significant Noncash Activities

Not all of a company's significant activities involve cash. Examples of significant noncash activities are:

1. Issuance of common stock to purchase assets.
2. Conversion of bonds into common stock.
3. Issuance of debt to purchase assets.
4. Exchanges of plant assets.

**Significant financing and investing activities that do not affect cash are not reported in the body of the statement of cash flows.** However, these activities

**ILLUSTRATION 18-2**

*Typical receipts and payments classified by activity*

### Types of Cash Inflows and Outflows

**Operating activities**

Cash inflows:

From sale of goods or services.

From returns on loans (interest received) and on equity securities (dividends received).

Cash outflows:

To suppliers for inventory.

To employees for services.

To government for taxes.

To lenders for interest.

To others for expenses.

**Investing activities**

Cash inflows:

From sale of property, plant, and equipment.

From sale of debt or equity securities of other entities.

From collection of principal on loans to other entities.

Cash outflows:

To purchase property, plant, and equipment.

To purchase debt or equity securities of other entities.

To make loans to other entities.

**Financing activities**

Cash inflows:

From sale of equity securities (company's own stock).

From issuance of debt (bonds and notes).

Cash outflows:

To stockholders as dividends.

To redeem long-term debt or reacquire capital stock.

**HELPFUL HINT**
Operating activities generally relate to changes in current assets and current liabilities. Investing activities generally relate to changes in noncurrent assets. Financing activities relate to changes in noncurrent liabilities and stockholders' equity accounts.

are reported in either a separate schedule at the bottom of the statement of cash flows or in a separate note or supplementary schedule to the financial statements.

The reporting of these activities in a separate note or supplementary schedule satisfies the **full disclosure principle** because it identifies significant noncash investing and financing activities of the enterprise. In solving homework assignments you should present significant noncash investing and financing activities in a separate schedule at the bottom of the statement of cash flows. (See lower section of Illustration 18-3, on page 758, for an example.)

**HELPFUL HINT**
Do not include noncash investing and financing activities in the body of the statement of cash flows. Report this information in a separate schedule at the bottom of the statement.

# ACCOUNTING IN ACTION

## Business Insight

Differences between net income and net cash provided by operating activities are illustrated by the following results from recent annual reports for the same fiscal year (all data are in millions of dollars):

| Company | Net Income | Net Cash from Operations |
|---|---|---|
| Kmart Corporation | $ 296 | $ 76 |
| Wal-Mart Stores, Inc. | 2,681 | 2,906 |
| Gap Inc. | 452 | 845 |
| J.C. Penney Company, Inc. | 1,057 | 738 |
| Sears Roebuck & Co. | 1,454 | 1,930 |
| The May Department Stores Company | 782 | 999 |

Note the wide disparity among the companies that engaged in similar types of retail merchandising.

## Format of the Statement of Cash Flows

The three activities discussed previously—operating, investing, and financing—plus the significant noncash investing and financing activities constitute the general format of the statement of cash flows. A widely used form of the statement of cash flows is shown in Illustration 18-3.

**ILLUSTRATION 18-3**

*Format of statement of cash flows*

| COMPANY NAME<br>Statement of Cash Flows<br>Period Covered | | |
|---|---|---|
| **Cash flows from operating activities** | | |
| (List of individual items) | XX | |
| Net cash provided (used) by operating activities | | XXX |
| **Cash flows from investing activities** | | |
| (List of individual inflows and outflows) | XX | |
| Net cash provided (used) by investing activities | | XXX |
| **Cash flows from financing activities** | | |
| (List of individual inflows and outflows) | XX | |
| Net cash provided (used) by financing activities | | XXX |
| **Net increase (decrease) in cash** | | XXX |
| **Cash at beginning of period** | | XXX |
| **Cash at end of period** | | XXX |
| **Noncash investing and financing activities** | | |
| (List of individual noncash transactions) | | XXX |

As illustrated, the cash flows from operating activities section always appears first, followed by the investing activities and the financing activities sections. Also, **the individual inflows and outflows from investing and financing activities are reported separately**. Thus, cash outflow for the purchase of property, plant, and equipment is reported separately from the cash inflow from the sale of property, plant, and equipment. Similarly, the cash inflow from the issuance of debt securities is reported separately from the cash outflow for the retirement of debt. If a company did not report the inflows and outflows separately, it would obscure the investing and financing activities of the enterprise and thus make it more difficult to assess future cash flows.

The reported operating, investing, and financing activities result in either net cash **provided or used** by each activity. The net cash provided or used by each activity is totaled to show the net increase (decrease) in cash for the period. The net increase (decrease) in cash for the period is then added to or subtracted from the beginning-of-the-period cash balance to obtain the end-of-the-period cash balance. Finally, any significant noncash investing and financing activities are reported in a separate schedule at the bottom of the statement.

## Usefulness of the Statement of Cash Flows

The information in a statement of cash flows should help investors, creditors, and others assess various aspects of the firm's financial position:

1. **The entity's ability to generate future cash flows.** By examining relationships between such items as sales and net cash provided by operating activities, or cash provided by operations and increases or decreases in cash, investors and others can make predictions of the amounts, timing, and uncertainty of future cash flows better than from accrual basis data.

**ETHICS NOTE**

Many investors believe that "Cash is cash and everything else is accounting"—that is, cash flow is less susceptible to management manipulation and fraud than traditional accounting measures such as net income. Though we would discourage reliance on cash flows to the exclusion of accrual accounting, comparing cash from operations to net income can reveal important information about the "quality" of reported net income—that is, the extent to which net income provides a good measure of actual performance.

2. **The entity's ability to pay dividends and meet obligations.** Simply put, if a company does not have adequate cash, employees cannot be paid, debts settled, or dividends paid. Employees, creditors, stockholders, and customers should be particularly interested in this statement, because it alone shows the flows of cash in a business.

3. **The reasons for the difference between net income and net cash provided (used) by operating activities.** Net income is important, because it provides information on the success or failure of a business enterprise. However, some are critical of accrual basis net income because it requires many estimates; as a result, the reliability of the number is often challenged. Such is not the case with cash. Thus, many readers of the financial statement want to know the reasons for the difference between net income and net cash provided by operating activities. Then they can assess for themselves the reliability of the income number.

4. **The cash investing and financing transactions during the period.** By examining a company's investing activities and its financing transactions, a financial statement reader can better understand why assets and liabilities increased or decreased during the period. In summary, the information in the statement of cash flows is useful in answering the following questions:

> How did cash increase when there was a net loss for the period?
> How were the proceeds of the bond issue used?
> How was the expansion in the plant and equipment financed?
> Why were dividends not increased?
> How was the retirement of debt accomplished?
> How much money was borrowed during the year?
> Is cash flow greater or less than net income?

**HELPFUL HINT**
Income from operations and cash flow from operating activities are different. Income from operations is based on accrual accounting; cash flow from operating activities is prepared on a cash basis.

# ACCOUNTING IN ACTION
## Business Insight

Cash flow is also sometimes used to determine the price of a company. Page Net, a company in the telephone beeper business, had an initial public offering (IPO) in which $590 million of stock was sold. In December 1993 the stock had a market value of $1.5 billion. Yet Page Net reported losses in every quarter since it went public. However, its cash flow the year before the IPO was $39 million, $57 million in the IPO year, $75 million in 1992, and approximately $99 million in 1993. As one expert noted, "It is a classic example of a company valued by cash flow."

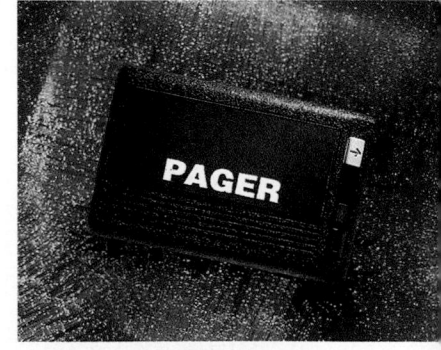

# Preparing the Statement of Cash Flows

The statement of cash flows is prepared differently from the three other basic financial statements. First, it is not prepared from an adjusted trial balance. Because the statement requires detailed information concerning the changes in account balances that occurred between two periods of time, an adjusted trial balance will not provide the necessary data for the statement. Second, the statement of cash flows deals with cash receipts and payments. As a result, **the accrual concept is not used in the preparation of a statement of cash flows**.

The information to prepare this statement usually comes from three sources:

**Comparative balance sheet.** Information in this statement indicates the amount of the changes in assets, liabilities, and stockholders' equities from the beginning to the end of the period.

**Current income statement.** Information in this statement helps the reader determine the amount of cash provided by or used by operations during the period.

**Additional information.** Additional information includes transaction data that are needed to determine how cash was provided or used during the period.

**ILLUSTRATION 18-4**

*Three major steps in preparing the statement of cash flows*

Preparing the statement of cash flows from these data sources involves three major steps, explained in Illustration 18-4.

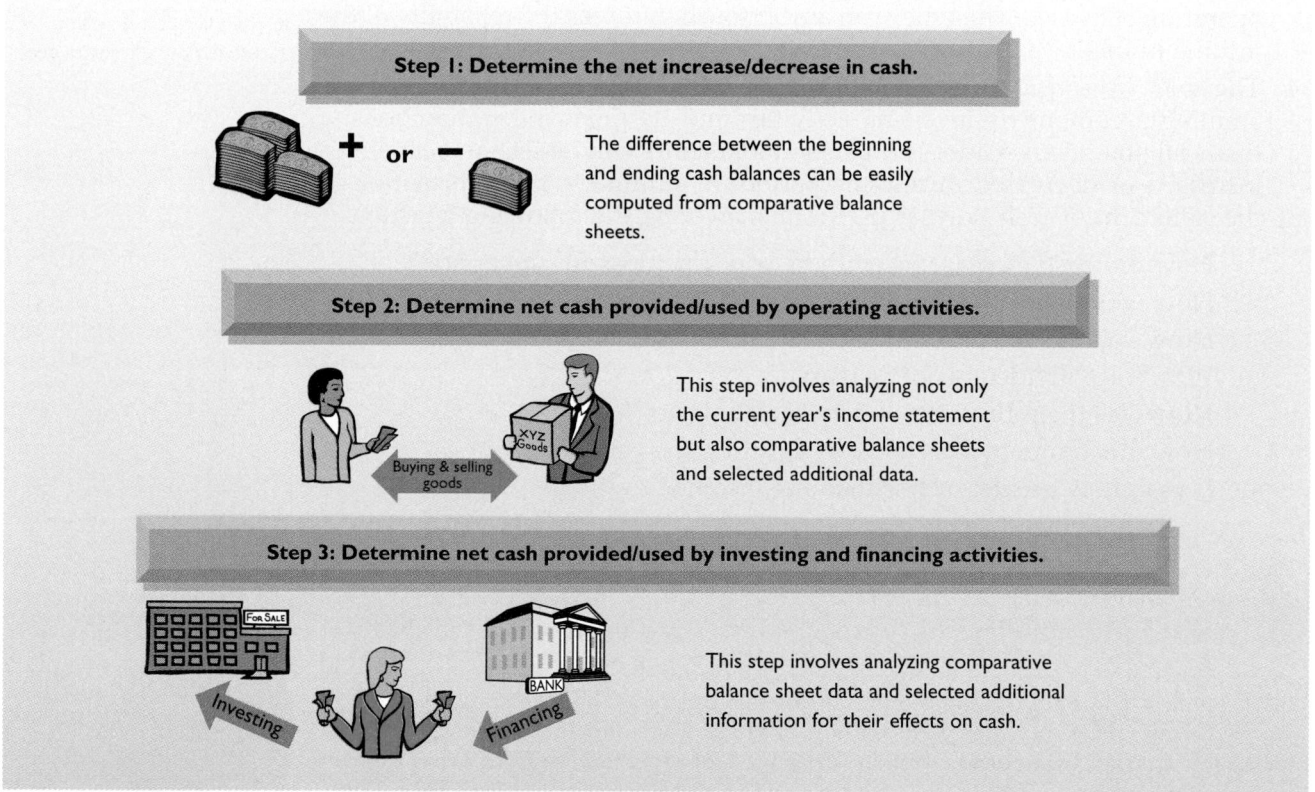

## Indirect and Direct Methods

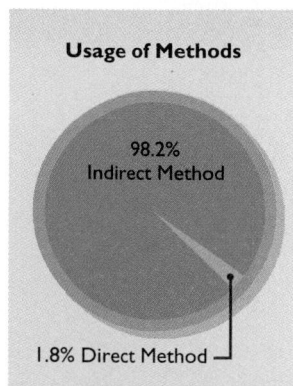

**Usage of Methods**

98.2% Indirect Method

1.8% Direct Method

In order to perform step 2, the operating activities section of the statement of cash flows **must be converted from an accrual basis to a cash basis**. This conversion may be done by either of two methods: (1) the indirect method or (2) the direct method. **Both methods arrive at the same total amount** for "Net cash provided by operating activities," but they differ in disclosing the items that comprise the total amount.

The indirect method is used extensively in practice, as shown in the nearby chart.[2] Companies (98%) favor the indirect method for two reasons: (1) it is easier to prepare, and (2) it focuses on the differences between net income and net cash flow from operating activities.

---

[2]*Accounting Trends and Techniques* survey of 600 companies indicated that 589 use the indirect method and 11 use the direct method.

Others, however, favor the direct method. The direct method shows operating cash receipts and payments. Thus, it is more consistent with the objective of a statement of cash flows. The FASB has expressed a preference for the direct method, but allows the use of either method. However, when the direct method is used, the net cash flow from operating activities as computed using the indirect method must also be reported in a separate schedule.

**INTERNATIONAL NOTE**

International accounting requirements are quite similar in most respects with regard to the cash flow statement. Some interesting exceptions: In Japan, operating and investing activities are combined; in Australia, the direct method is mandatory; in Spain, the indirect method is mandatory. Also, in a number of European and Scandinavian countries a cash flow statement is not required at all, although in practice most publicly traded firms provide one.

# BEFORE YOU GO ON . . .

## Review It

1. What is the primary purpose of a statement of cash flows?
2. What are the major classifications of cash flows on the statement of cash flows?
3. What are the three major steps in the preparation of a statement of cash flows?
4. Why is the statement of cash flows useful? What key information does it convey?

## Do It

During its first week of existence, Plano Molding Company had the following transactions:

1. Issued 100,000 shares of $5 par value common stock for $800,000 cash.
2. Borrowed $200,000 from Sandwich State Bank, signing a 5-year note bearing 8% interest.
3. Purchased two semi-trailer trucks for $170,000 cash.
4. Paid employees $12,000 for salaries and wages.
5. Collected $20,000 cash for services rendered.

Classify by type of cash flow activity each of these transactions.

*Reasoning:* All cash flows are classified into three types of activities for purposes of reporting cash inflows and outflows: operating activities, investing activities, and financing activities. Operating activities include the cash effects of transactions that create revenues and expenses and thus enter into the determination of net income. Investing activities include (a) acquiring and disposing of investments and productive long-lived assets, and (b) lending money and collecting the loans. Financing activities include (a) obtaining cash from issuing debt and repaying the amounts borrowed, and (b) obtaining cash from stockholders and providing them with a return on their investment.

*Solution:*
1. Financing activity.
2. Financing activity.
3. Investing activity.
4. Operating activity.
5. Operating activity.

*Related exercise material:* BE18–3, BE18–5, E18–1, and E18–6.

THE NAVIGATOR

On the following pages, in two separate sections, we describe the use of the two methods. Section 1 illustrates the indirect method, and Section 2 illustrates the direct method. These sections are independent of each other; *only one or the other* need be covered in order to understand and prepare the statement of cash flows. When you have finished the section assigned by your instructor, turn to the next topic, on page 786—"Analysis of the Statement of Cash Flows."

# SECTION 1    STATEMENT OF CASH FLOWS— INDIRECT METHOD

**3**
STUDY OBJECTIVE

Prepare a statement of cash flows using the indirect method.

To explain and illustrate the indirect method, we will use the transactions of the Computer Services Company for two years—1999 and 2000. Annual statements of cash flows will be prepared. Basic transactions will be used in the first year with additional transactions added in the second year.

## FIRST YEAR OF OPERATIONS—1999

Computer Services Company started on January 1, 1999, when it issued 50,000 shares of $1.00 par value common stock for $50,000 cash. The company rented its office space and furniture and performed consulting services throughout the first year. The comparative balance sheets at the beginning and end of 1999, showing increases or decreases, appear in Illustration 18-5.

**ILLUSTRATION 18-5**

*Comparative balance sheet, 1999, with increases and decreases*

**HELPFUL HINT**
Note that although each of the balance sheet items of Computer Services increased, their individual effects are not the same. Some of these increases are cash inflows, and some are cash outflows.

| COMPUTER SERVICES COMPANY Comparative Balance Sheet | | | |
|---|---|---|---|
| **Assets** | **Dec. 31, 1999** | **Jan. 1, 1999** | **Change Increase/Decrease** |
| Cash | $34,000 | $ –0– | $34,000 Increase |
| Accounts receivable | 30,000 | –0– | 30,000 Increase |
| Equipment | 10,000 | –0– | 10,000 Increase |
| Total | $74,000 | $ –0– | |
| **Liabilities and Stockholders' Equity** | | | |
| Accounts payable | $ 4,000 | $ –0– | $ 4,000 Increase |
| Common stock | 50,000 | –0– | 50,000 Increase |
| Retained earnings | 20,000 | –0– | 20,000 Increase |
| Total | $74,000 | $ –0– | |

The income statement and additional information for Computer Services Company are shown in Illustration 18-6.

**ILLUSTRATION 18-6**

*Income statement and additional information, 1999*

| COMPUTER SERVICES COMPANY Income Statement For the Year Ended December 31, 1999 | |
|---|---|
| Revenues | $85,000 |
| Operating expenses | 40,000 |
| Income before income taxes | 45,000 |
| Income tax expense | 10,000 |
| Net income | $35,000 |

**Additional information:**
(a) A dividend of $15,000 was declared and paid during the year.
(b) The equipment was purchased at the end of 1999. No depreciation was taken in 1999.

## Determining the Net Increase/Decrease in Cash (Step 1)

To prepare a statement of cash flows, the first step is **determining the net increase or decrease in cash**. This is a simple computation. For example, Computer Services Company had no cash on hand at the beginning of 1999, but had $34,000 on hand at the end of 1999. Thus, the change in cash for 1999 was an increase of $34,000.

## Determining Net Cash Provided/Used by Operating Activities (Step 2)

To determine net cash provided by operating activities under the indirect method, **net income is adjusted for items that did not affect cash**. A useful starting point in determining net cash provided by operating activities is to understand **why** net income must be converted. Under generally accepted accounting principles, most companies use the accrual basis of accounting. As you have learned, this basis requires that revenue be recorded when earned and that expenses be recorded when incurred. Earned revenues may include credit sales that have not been collected in cash and expenses incurred that may not have been paid in cash. Thus, under the accrual basis of accounting, net income does not indicate the net cash provided by operating activities. Therefore, under the indirect method, net income must be adjusted to convert certain items to the cash basis.

The indirect method (or reconciliation method) starts with net income and converts it to net cash provided by operating activities. In other words, **the indirect method adjusts net income for items that affected reported net income but did not affect cash**, as shown in Illustration 18-7. That is, noncash charges in the income statement are added back to net income and noncash credits are deducted to compute net cash provided by operating activities. A useful starting point in identifying the adjustments to net income is the current asset and current liability accounts other than cash. Those accounts—receivables, payables, prepayments, and inventories—should be analyzed for their effects on cash.

**HELPFUL HINT**
You may wish to insert the beginning and ending cash balances and the increase/decrease in cash necessitated by these balances immediately into the statement of cash flows. The net increase/decrease is the target amount. The net cash flows from the three classes of activity must equal the target amount.

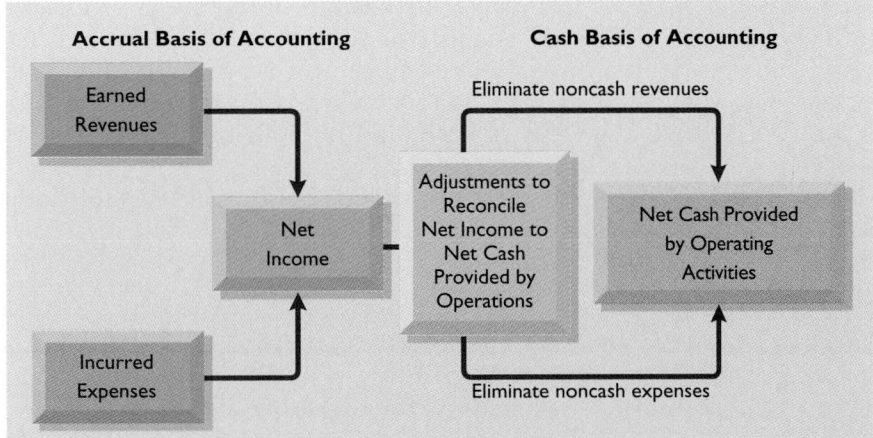

**ILLUSTRATION 18-7**

*Net income versus net cash provided by operating activities*

**Increase in Accounts Receivable.**   When accounts receivable increase during the year, revenues on an accrual basis are higher than revenues on a cash basis. In other words, operations of the period led to increased revenues, **but not all of these revenues resulted in an increase in cash**; some of the increase in revenues resulted in an increase in accounts receivable.

Illustration 18-8 shows that Computer Services Company had $85,000 in revenues, but it collected only $55,000 in cash. Therefore, to convert net income to net cash provided by operating activities, the increase of $30,000 in accounts receivable must be deducted from net income.

**ILLUSTRATION 18-8**

*Analysis of accounts receivable*

| Accounts Receivable | | | | |
|---|---|---|---|---|
| 1/1/99 | Balance | –0– | Receipts from customers | 55,000 |
| | Revenues | 85,000 | | |
| 12/31/99 | Balance | 30,000 | | |

**Increase in Accounts Payable.**   In the first year, operating expenses incurred on account were credited to Accounts Payable. When accounts payable increase during the year, operating expenses on an accrual basis are higher than they are on a cash basis. For Computer Services, operating expenses reported in the income statement were $40,000. However, since Accounts Payable increased $4,000, only $36,000 ($40,000 − $4,000) of the expenses were paid in cash. To adjust net income to net cash provided by operating activities, the increase of $4,000 in accounts payable must be added to net income.

A T-account analysis also indicates that payments to creditors are less than operating expenses.

**ILLUSTRATION 18-9**

*Analysis of accounts payable*

| Accounts Payable | | | | |
|---|---|---|---|---|
| Payments to creditors | 36,000 | 1/1/99 | Balances | –0– |
| | | | Operating expenses | 40,000 |
| | | 12/31/99 | Balance | 4,000 |

For Computer Services Company, the changes in accounts receivable and accounts payable were the only changes in current asset and current liability accounts. This means that any other revenues or expenses reported in the income statement were received or paid in cash. Thus, Computer Services' income tax expense of $10,000 was paid in cash, and no adjustment of net income is necessary.

The operating activities section of the statement of cash flows for Computer Services Company is shown in Illustration 18-10.

**ILLUSTRATION 18-10**

*Presentation of net cash provided by operating activities, 1999—indirect method*

| COMPUTER SERVICES COMPANY Partial Statement of Cash Flows—Indirect Method For the Year Ended December 31, 1999 | | |
|---|---|---|
| Cash flows from operating activities | | |
| Net income | | $35,000 |
| Adjustments to reconcile net income to net cash provided by operating activities: | | |
| Increase in accounts receivable | $(30,000) | |
| Increase in accounts payable | 4,000 | (26,000) |
| Net cash provided by operating activities | | $ 9,000 |

# Determining Net Cash Provided/Used by Investing and Financing Activities (Step 3)

The third and final step in preparing the statement of cash flows begins with a study of the balance sheet to determine changes in noncurrent accounts. The changes in each noncurrent account are then analyzed using selected transaction data to determine the effect, if any, the changes had on cash.

In Computer Services Company, the three noncurrent accounts are Equipment, Common Stock, and Retained Earnings, and all three have increased during the year. What caused these increases? No transaction data are given for the increases in Equipment of $10,000 and Common Stock of $50,000. In solving your homework, you can conclude that **any unexplained differences in noncurrent accounts involve cash**. Thus, the increase in equipment is assumed to be a purchase of equipment for $10,000 cash. This purchase is reported as a cash outflow in the investing activities section. The increase in common stock is assumed to result from the issuance of common stock for $50,000 cash. It is reported as an inflow of cash in the financing activities section of the statement of cash flows.

The reasons for the net increase of $20,000 in the Retained Earnings account are determined by analysis. First, net income increased retained earnings by $35,000. Second, the additional information provided below the income statement in Illustration 18-6 indicates that a cash dividend of $15,000 was declared and paid. The $35,000 increase due to net income is reported in the operating activities section. The cash dividend paid is reported in the financing activities section.

This analysis can also be made directly from the Retained Earnings account in the ledger of Computer Services Company as shown in Illustration 18-11:

| Retained Earnings | | | | |
|---|---|---|---|---|
| 12/31/99  Cash dividend | 15,000 | 1/1/99    Balance | –0– | |
| | | 12/31/99  Net income | 35,000 | |
| | | 12/31/99  Balance | 20,000 | |

**ILLUSTRATION 18-11**

*Analysis of retained earnings*

The $20,000 increase in Retained Earnings in 1999 is a **net** change. When a net change in a noncurrent balance sheet account has occurred during the year, it generally is necessary to report the causes of the net change separately in the statement of cash flows.

# Statement of Cash Flows—1999

Having completed the three steps above, we can prepare the statement of cash flows. The statement starts with the operating activities section, followed by the investing activities section, and then the financing activities section. The 1999 statement of cash flows for Computer Services is shown in Illustration 18-12.

Computer Services' statement of cash flows for 1999 shows that operating activities **provided** $9,000 cash; investing activities **used** $10,000 cash; and financing activities **provided** $35,000 cash. The increase in cash of $34,000 reported in the statement of cash flows agrees with the increase of $34,000 shown as the change in the cash account in the comparative balance sheet.

**ILLUSTRATION 18-12**

*Statement of cash flows, 1999—indirect method*

| COMPUTER SERVICES COMPANY<br>Statement of Cash Flows—Indirect Method<br>For the Year Ended December 31, 1999 | | |
|---|---:|---:|
| Cash flows from operating activities | | |
| Net income | | $35,000 |
| Adjustments to reconcile net income to net cash provided by operating activities: | | |
| Increase in accounts receivable | $(30,000) | |
| Increase in accounts payable | 4,000 | (26,000) |
| Net cash provided by operating activities | | 9,000 |
| Cash flows from investing activities | | |
| Purchase of equipment | (10,000) | |
| Net cash used by investing activities | | (10,000) |
| Cash flows from financing activities | | |
| Issuance of common stock | 50,000 | |
| Payment of cash dividends | (15,000) | |
| Net cash provided by financing activities | | 35,000 |
| Net increase in cash | | 34,000 |
| Cash at beginning of period | | –0– |
| Cash at end of period | | $34,000 |

# SECOND YEAR OF OPERATIONS—2000

Presented in Illustrations 18-13 and 18-14 is information related to the second year of operations for Computer Services Company.

**ILLUSTRATION 18-13**

*Comparative balance sheet, 2000, with increases and decreases*

| COMPUTER SERVICES COMPANY<br>Comparative Balance Sheet<br>December 31 | | | |
|---|---|---|---|
| **Assets** | **2000** | **1999** | **Change<br>Increase/Decrease** |
| Cash | $ 56,000 | $34,000 | $ 22,000 Increase |
| Accounts receivable | 20,000 | 30,000 | 10,000 Decrease |
| Prepaid expenses | 4,000 | –0– | 4,000 Increase |
| Land | 130,000 | –0– | 130,000 Increase |
| Building | 160,000 | –0– | 160,000 Increase |
| Accumulated depreciation—building | (11,000) | –0– | 11,000 Increase |
| Equipment | 27,000 | 10,000 | 17,000 Increase |
| Accumulated depreciation—equipment | (3,000) | –0– | 3,000 Increase |
| Total | $383,000 | $74,000 | |
| **Liabilities and Stockholders' Equity** | | | |
| Accounts payable | $ 59,000 | $ 4,000 | $ 55,000 Increase |
| Bonds payable | 130,000 | –0– | 130,000 Increase |
| Common stock | 50,000 | 50,000 | –0– |
| Retained earnings | 144,000 | 20,000 | 124,000 Increase |
| Total | $383,000 | $74,000 | |

ILLUSTRATION 18-14

*Income statement and additional information, 2000*

COMPUTER SERVICES COMPANY
**Income Statement**
**For the Year Ended December 31, 2000**

| | | |
|---|---:|---:|
| Revenues | | $507,000 |
| Operating expenses (excluding depreciation) | $261,000 | |
| Depreciation expense | 15,000 | |
| Loss on sale of equipment | 3,000 | 279,000 |
| Income from operations | | 228,000 |
| Income tax expense | | 89,000 |
| Net income | | $139,000 |

**Additional information:**
(a) In 2000, the company declared and paid a $15,000 cash dividend.
(b) The company obtained land through the issuance of $130,000 of long-term bonds.
(c) A building costing $160,000 was purchased for cash; equipment costing $25,000 was also purchased for cash.
(d) During 2000, the company sold equipment with a book value of $7,000 (cost $8,000, less accumulated depreciation $1,000) for $4,000 cash.

## Determining the Net Increase/Decrease in Cash (Step 1)

To prepare a statement of cash flows from this information, the first step is to **determine the net increase or decrease in cash**. As indicated from the information presented, cash increased $22,000 ($56,000 − $34,000).

## Determining Net Cash Provided/Used by Operating Activities (Step 2)

As in step 2 in 1999, net income on an accrual basis must be adjusted to arrive at net cash provided/used by operating activities. Explanations for the adjustments to net income for Computer Services in 2000 are as follows:

**Decrease in Accounts Receivable.**   Accounts receivable decreases during the period because cash receipts are higher than revenues reported on an accrual basis. To adjust net income to net cash provided by operating activities, the decrease of $10,000 in accounts receivable must be added to net income.

**Increase in Prepaid Expenses.**   Prepaid expenses increase during a period because cash paid for expenses is higher than expenses reported on an accrual basis. Cash payments have been made in the current period, but expenses (as charges to the income statement) have been deferred to future periods. To adjust net income to net cash provided by operating activities, the increase of $4,000 in prepaid expenses must be deducted from net income. An increase in prepaid expenses results in a decrease in cash during the period.

**Increase in Accounts Payable.**   Like the increase in 1999, the 2000 increase of $55,000 in accounts payable must be added to net income to convert to net cash provided by operating activities.

**Depreciation Expense.**   During 2000, Computer Services Company reported depreciation expense of $15,000. Of this amount, $11,000 related to the building and $4,000 to the equipment. These two amounts were determined by analyzing the accumulated depreciation accounts.

HELPFUL HINT
**Decrease in accounts receivable** indicates that cash collections were greater than sales. **Increase in accounts receivable** indicates that sales were greater than cash collections. **Increase in prepaid expenses** indicates that the amount paid for the prepayments exceeded the amount that was recorded as an expense. **Decrease in prepaid expenses** indicates that the amount recorded as an expense exceeded the amount of cash paid for the prepayments. **Increase in accounts payable** indicates that expenses incurred exceed the cash paid for expenses that period.

**Increase in Accumulated Depreciation—Building.**   As shown in Illustration 18-13, accumulated depreciation increased $11,000. This change represents the depreciation expense on the building for the year. **Because depreciation expense is a noncash charge, it is added back to net income** in order to arrive at net cash provided by operating activities.

**Increase in Accumulated Depreciation—Equipment.**   The increase in the Accumulated Depreciation—Equipment account was $3,000. This amount does not represent depreciation expense for the year because the additional information indicates that this account was decreased (debited $1,000) as a result of the sale of some equipment. Thus depreciation expense for 2000 was $4,000 ($3,000 + $1,000). This amount is added to net income to determine net cash provided by operating activities. The T-account below provides information about the changes that occurred in this account in 2000.

**ILLUSTRATION 18-15**

*Analysis of accumulated depreciation—equipment*

| Accumulated Depreciation—Equipment | | | |
|---|---|---|---|
| Accumulated depreciation on equipment sold | 1,000 | 1/1/00   Balance | –0– |
| | | Depreciation expense | 4,000 |
| | | 12/31/00  Balance | 3,000 |

Depreciation expense on the building of $11,000 plus depreciation expense on the equipment of $4,000 equals the depreciation expense of $15,000 reported on the income statement.

Other charges to expense that do not require the use of cash, such as the amortization of intangible assets and depletion expense, are treated in the same manner as depreciation. Depreciation and similar noncash charges are frequently listed in the statement of cash flows as the first adjustments to net income.

**Loss on Sale of Equipment.**   On the income statement, Computer Services Company reported a $3,000 loss on the sale of equipment (book value $7,000, less cash proceeds $4,000). The loss reduced net income but **did not reduce cash**. Thus the loss is **added to net income** in determining net cash provided by operating activities.[3]

As a result of the previous adjustments, net cash provided by operating activities is $218,000 as computed in Illustration 18-16.

## Determining Net Cash Provided/Used by Investing and Financing Activities (Step 3)

After finding net cash provided by operating activities, the next step involves analyzing the remaining changes in balance sheet accounts to determine net cash provided (used) by investing and financing activities.

---

[3]If a gain on sale occurs, a different situation results. To allow a gain to flow through to net cash provided by operating activities would be double-counting the gain—once in net income and again in the investing activities section as part of the cash proceeds from sale. As a result, a gain is deducted from net income in reporting net cash provided by operating activities.

ILLUSTRATION 18-16

*Presentation of net cash pro-
vided by operating activities,
2000—indirect method*

**COMPUTER SERVICES COMPANY**
**Partial Statement of Cash Flows—Indirect Method**
**For the Year Ended December 31, 2000**

| | | |
|---|---:|---:|
| Cash flows from operating activities | | |
| Net income | | $139,000 |
| Adjustments to reconcile net income to net cash provided | | |
| by operating activities: | | |
| Depreciation expense | $15,000 | |
| Loss on sale of equipment | 3,000 | |
| Decrease in accounts receivable | 10,000 | |
| Increase in prepaid expenses | (4,000) | |
| Increase in accounts payable | 55,000 | 79,000 |
| Net cash provided by operating activities | | $218,000 |

**Increase in Land.**   As indicated from the change in the Land account, land of $130,000 was purchased through the issuance of long-term bonds. Although the issuance of bonds payable for land has no effect on cash, it is a significant noncash investing and financing activity that merits disclosure. As indicated earlier, these activities are disclosed in a separate schedule at the bottom of the statement of cash flows.

**Increase in Building.**   As indicated in the additional data, an office building was acquired using cash of $160,000. This transaction is a cash outflow reported in the investing section.

**Increase in Equipment.**   The Equipment account increased $17,000. Based on the additional information, this was a net increase that resulted from two transactions: (1) a purchase of equipment of $25,000 and (2) the sale for $4,000 of equipment costing $8,000. These transactions are classified as investing activities, and each transaction should be reported separately. Thus the purchase of equipment should be reported as an outflow of cash for $25,000 and the sale should be reported as an inflow of cash for $4,000. The T-account below shows the reasons for the change in this account during the year.

ILLUSTRATION 18-17

*Analysis of equipment*

| Equipment | | | | |
|---|---:|---|---|---:|
| 1/1/00  Balance | 10,000 | | Cost of equipment sold | 8,000 |
| Purchase of equipment | 25,000 | | | |
| 12/31/00  Balance | 27,000 | | | |

The following entry shows the details of the equipment sale transactions:

| | | | |
|---|---:|---|---:|
| Cash | 4,000 | | |
| Accumulated Depreciation | 1,000 | | |
| Loss on Sale of Equipment | 3,000 | | |
| Equipment | | | 8,000 |

| A | = | L | + | OE |
|---|---|---|---|---|
| +4,000 | | | | −3,000 |
| +1,000 | | | | |
| −8,000 | | | | |

**Increase in Bonds Payable.**   The Bonds Payable account increased $130,000. As shown in the additional information, land was acquired from the issuance of these bonds. As indicated earlier, this noncash transaction is reported in a separate schedule at the bottom of the statement.

**Increase in Retained Earnings.**   Retained earnings increased $124,000 during the year. This increase can be explained by two factors: (1) net income of $139,000 increased retained earnings, and (2) dividends of $15,000 decreased retained earnings. Net income is adjusted to net cash provided by operating activities in the operating activities section. Payment of the dividends is a **cash outflow that is reported as a financing activity**.

## Statement of Cash Flows—2000

Combining the previous items, we obtain a statement of cash flows for 2000 for Computer Services Company as presented in Illustration 18-18.

**COMPUTER SERVICES COMPANY**
**Statement of Cash Flows—Indirect Method**
**For the Year Ended December 31, 2000**

| | | |
|---|---:|---:|
| Cash flows from operating activities | | |
| Net income | | $139,000 |
| Adjustments to reconcile net income to net cash | | |
|   provided by operating activities: | | |
|     Depreciation expense | $ 15,000 | |
|     Loss on sale of equipment | 3,000 | |
|     Decrease in accounts receivable | 10,000 | |
|     Increase in prepaid expenses | (4,000) | |
|     Increase in accounts payable | 55,000 | 79,000 |
|     Net cash provided by operating activities | | 218,000 |
| Cash flows from investing activities | | |
|   Purchase of building | $(160,000) | |
|   Purchase of equipment | (25,000) | |
|   Sale of equipment | 4,000 | |
|     Net cash used by investing activities | | (181,000) |
| Cash flows from financing activities | | |
|   Payment of cash dividends | (15,000) | |
|     Net cash used by financing activities | | (15,000) |
| Net increase in cash | | 22,000 |
| Cash at beginning of period | | 34,000 |
| Cash at end of period | | $ 56,000 |
| | | |
| **Noncash investing and financing activities** | | |
|   Issuance of bonds payable to purchase land | | $130,000 |

## Summary of Conversion to Net Cash Provided by Operating Activities—Indirect Method

As shown in the previous illustrations, the statement of cash flows prepared by the indirect method starts with net income and adds (or deducts) items not affecting cash to arrive at net cash provided by operating activities. The additions and deductions consist of (1) changes in specific current assets and current liabilities and (2) noncash charges reported in the income statement. A summary of the adjustments for current assets and current liabilities is provided in Illustration 18-19.

| | Adjustments to Convert Net Income to Net Cash Provided by Operating Activities | |
|---|---|---|
| Current Assets and Current Liabilities | Add to Net Income | Deduct from Net Income |
| Accounts receivable | Decrease | Increase |
| Inventory | Decrease | Increase |
| Prepaid expenses | Decrease | Increase |
| Accounts payable | Increase | Decrease |
| Accrued expenses payable | Increase | Decrease |

**HELPFUL HINT**
1. Increase in a current asset is deducted from net income.
2. Decrease in a current asset is added to net income.
3. Increase in a current liability is added to net income.
4. Decrease in a current liability is deducted from net income.

Adjustments for the noncash charges reported in the income statement are made as shown in Illustration 18-20.

| Noncash Charges | Adjustments to Convert Net Income to Net Cash Provided by Operating Activities |
|---|---|
| Depreciation expense | Add |
| Patent amortization expense | Add |
| Depletion expense | Add |
| Loss on sale of asset | Add |

# BEFORE YOU GO ON . . .

## Review It

1. What is the format of the operating activities section of the statement of cash flows using the indirect method?
2. Where is depreciation expense shown on a statement of cash flows using the indirect method?
3. Where are significant noncash investing and financing activities shown in a statement of cash flows? Give some examples.
4. Which method of computing net cash provided by operating activities does Kellogg use? What single item provided the largest amount of cash inflow for Kellogg in 1997? The answers to these questions are provided on page 816.

## Do It

Presented below is information related to Reynolds Company. Use it to prepare a statement of cash flows using the indirect method.

### REYNOLDS COMPANY
### Comparative Balance Sheet
### December 31

| Assets | 2000 | 1999 | Change Increase/Decrease |
|---|---|---|---|
| Cash | $ 54,000 | $ 37,000 | $ 17,000 Increase |
| Accounts receivable | 68,000 | 26,000 | 42,000 Increase |
| Inventories | 54,000 | –0– | 54,000 Increase |
| Prepaid expenses | 4,000 | 6,000 | 2,000 Decrease |
| Land | 45,000 | 70,000 | 25,000 Decrease |
| Buildings | 200,000 | 200,000 | –0– |
| Accumulated depreciation—buildings | (21,000) | (11,000) | 10,000 Increase |
| Equipment | 193,000 | 68,000 | 125,000 Increase |
| Accumulated depreciation—equipment | (28,000) | (10,000) | 18,000 Increase |
| Totals | $569,000 | $386,000 | |

| Liabilities and Stockholders' Equity | | | |
|---|---|---|---|
| Accounts payable | $ 23,000 | $ 40,000 | $ 17,000 Decrease |
| Accrued expenses payable | 10,000 | –0– | 10,000 Increase |
| Bonds payable | 110,000 | 150,000 | 40,000 Decrease |
| Common stock ($1 par) | 220,000 | 60,000 | 160,000 Increase |
| Retained earnings | 206,000 | 136,000 | 70,000 Increase |
| Totals | $569,000 | $386,000 | |

**HELPFUL HINT**
You may wish to insert the beginning and ending cash balances and the increase/decrease in cash necessitated by these balances immediately into the statement of cash flows. The net increase/decrease is the target amount. The net cash flows from the three classes of activities must equal the target amount.

### REYNOLDS COMPANY
### Income Statement
### For the Year Ended December 31, 2000

| | | |
|---|---|---|
| Revenues | | $890,000 |
| Cost of goods sold | $465,000 | |
| Operating expenses | 221,000 | |
| Interest expense | 12,000 | |
| Loss on sale of equipment | 2,000 | 700,000 |
| Income from operations | | 190,000 |
| Income tax expense | | 65,000 |
| Net income | | $125,000 |

**Additional information:**

(a) Operating expenses include depreciation expense of $33,000 and charges from prepaid expenses of $2,000.

(b) Land was sold at its book value for cash.

(c) Cash dividends of $55,000 were declared and paid in 2000.

(d) Interest expense of $12,000 was paid in cash.

(e) Equipment with a cost of $166,000 was purchased for cash. Equipment with a cost of $41,000 and a book value of $36,000 was sold for $34,000 cash.

(f) Bonds of $10,000 were redeemed at their book value for cash; bonds of $30,000 were converted into common stock.

(g) Common stock ($1 par) of $130,000 was issued for cash.

(h) Accounts payable pertain to merchandise suppliers.

*Reasoning:* As you have learned, the balance sheet and the income statement are prepared from an adjusted trial balance of the general ledger. The statement of cash flows is prepared from an analysis of the content and changes in the balance sheet and the income statement.

*Solution:*

HELPFUL HINT
To prepare the statement of cash flows:
1. Determine the net increase/decrease in cash.
2. Determine net cash provided/used by operating activities.
3. Operating activities generally relate to changes in current assets and current liabilities.
4. Determine net cash provided/used by investing and financing activities.
5. Investing activities generally relate to changes in noncurrent assets.
6. Financing activities generally relate to changes in noncurrent liabilities and stockholders' equity accounts.

### REYNOLDS COMPANY
### Statement of Cash Flows—Indirect Method
### For the Year Ended December 31, 2000

| | | |
|---|---:|---:|
| Cash flows from operating activities | | |
| Net income | | $125,000 |
| Adjustments to reconcile net income to net cash provided by operating activities: | | |
| Depreciation expense | $ 33,000 | |
| Increase in accounts receivable | (42,000) | |
| Increase in inventories | (54,000) | |
| Decrease in prepaid expenses | 2,000 | |
| Decrease in accounts payable | (17,000) | |
| Increase in accrued expenses payable | 10,000 | |
| Loss on sale of equipment | 2,000 | (66,000) |
| Net cash provided by operating activities | | 59,000 |
| Cash flows from investing activities | | |
| Sale of land | 25,000 | |
| Sale of equipment | 34,000 | |
| Purchase of equipment | (166,000) | |
| Net cash used by investing activities | | (107,000) |
| Cash flows from financing activities | | |
| Redemption of bonds | (10,000) | |
| Sale of common stock | 130,000 | |
| Payment of dividends | (55,000) | |
| Net cash provided by financing activities | | 65,000 |
| Net increase in cash | | 17,000 |
| Cash at beginning of period | | 37,000 |
| Cash at end of period | | $ 54,000 |
| | | |
| **Noncash investing and financing activities** | | |
| Conversion of bonds into common stock | | $ 30,000 |

*Related exercise material:* BE18–1, BE18–2, BE18–4, E18–2, E18–3, E18–4, and E18–5.

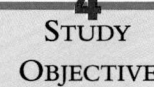

THE NAVIGATOR

Note: This concludes Section 1 on preparation of the statement of cash flows using the indirect method. Unless your instructor assigns Section 2, you should turn to the concluding section of the chapter, "Analysis of the Statement of Cash Flows," on page 786.

# SECTION 2  STATEMENT OF CASH FLOWS—
# DIRECT METHOD

To explain and illustrate the direct method, we will use the transactions of Juarez Company for two years, 1999 and 2000. Annual statements of cash flow will be prepared. Basic transactions will be used in the first year with additional transactions added in the second year.

**4**
STUDY
OBJECTIVE

Prepare a statement of cash flows using the direct method.

# FIRST YEAR OF OPERATIONS—1999

Juarez Company began business on January 1, 1999, when it issued 300,000 shares of $1 par value common stock for $300,000 cash. The company rented office and sales space along with equipment. The comparative balance sheet at the beginning and end of 1999 and the changes in each account are shown in Illustration 18-21. The income statement and additional information for Juarez Company are shown in Illustration 18-22.

**ILLUSTRATION 18-21**

*Comparative balance sheet, 1999, with increases and decreases*

### JUAREZ COMPANY
### Comparative Balance Sheet

| Assets | Dec. 31, 1999 | Jan. 1, 1999 | Change Increase/Decrease |
|---|---|---|---|
| Cash | $159,000 | $-0- | $159,000 Increase |
| Accounts receivable | 15,000 | -0- | 15,000 Increase |
| Inventory | 160,000 | -0- | 160,000 Increase |
| Prepaid expenses | 8,000 | -0- | 8,000 Increase |
| Land | 80,000 | -0- | 80,000 Increase |
| Total | $422,000 | $-0- | |
| **Liabilities and Stockholders' Equity** | | | |
| Accounts payable | $ 60,000 | $-0- | $ 60,000 Increase |
| Accrued expenses payable | 20,000 | -0- | 20,000 Increase |
| Common stock | 300,000 | -0- | 300,000 Increase |
| Retained earnings | 42,000 | -0- | 42,000 Increase |
| Total | $422,000 | $-0- | |

**ILLUSTRATION 18-22**

*Income statement and additional information, 1999*

### JUAREZ COMPANY
### Income Statement
### For the Year Ended December 31, 1999

| | |
|---|---|
| Revenues | $780,000 |
| Cost of goods sold | 450,000 |
| Gross profit | 330,000 |
| Operating expenses | 170,000 |
| Income before income taxes | 160,000 |
| Income tax expense | 48,000 |
| Net income | $112,000 |

**Additional information:**
(a) Dividends of $70,000 were declared and paid in cash.
(b) The accounts payable increase resulted from the purchase of merchandise.

The three steps cited on page 760 for preparing the statement of cash flows are used in the direct method.

## Determining the Net Increase/Decrease in Cash (Step 1)

The comparative balance sheet for Juarez Company shows a zero cash balance at January 1, 1999, and a cash balance of $159,000 at December 31, 1999. Thus, the change in cash for 1999 was a net increase of $159,000.

# Determining Net Cash Provided/Used by Operating Activities (Step 2)

Under the direct method, net cash provided by operating activities is computed by **adjusting each item in the income statement** from the accrual basis to the cash basis. To simplify and condense the operating activities section, **only major classes of operating cash receipts and cash payments are reported**. The difference between these major classes of cash receipts and cash payments is the net cash provided by operating activities as shown in Illustration 18-23.

**ILLUSTRATION 18-23**

*Major classes of cash receipts and payments*

An efficient way to apply the direct method is to analyze the revenues and expenses reported in the income statement in the order in which they are listed. Cash receipts and cash payments related to these revenues and expenses are then determined. The direct method adjustments for Juarez Company in 1999 to determine net cash provided by operating activities are presented in the following sections.

**Cash Receipts from Customers.** The income statement for Juarez Company reported revenues from customers of $780,000. To determine cash receipts from customers, it is necessary to consider the change in accounts receivable during the year. When accounts receivable increase during the year, revenues on an accrual basis are higher than cash receipts from customers. In other words, operations led to increased revenues, but not all of these revenues resulted in cash receipts. To determine the amount of cash receipts, the increase in accounts receivable is deducted from sales revenues. Conversely, a decrease in accounts receivable is added to sales revenues, because cash receipts from customers then exceed sales revenues.

For Juarez Company, accounts receivable increased $15,000. Thus, cash receipts from customers were $765,000, computed as follows:

| | |
|---|---|
| Revenues from sales | $780,000 |
| Deduct: Increase in accounts receivable | 15,000 |
| **Cash receipts from customers** | **$765,000** |

Cash receipts from customers may also be determined from an analysis of the Accounts Receivable account as shown in Illustration 18-25.

| Accounts Receivable | | | | |
|---|---|---|---|---|
| 1/1/99 | Balance | –0– | Receipts from customers | 765,000 |
| | Revenues from sales | 780,000 | | |
| 12/31/99 | Balance | 15,000 | | |

The relationships between cash receipts from customers, revenues from sales, and changes in accounts receivable are shown in Illustration 18-26.

**Cash Payments to Suppliers.** Juarez Company reported cost of goods sold on its income statement of $450,000. To determine cash payments to suppliers, it is first necessary to find purchases for the year. To find purchases, cost of goods sold is adjusted for the change in inventory. When inventory increases during the year, it means that purchases this year exceed cost of goods sold. As a result, the increase in inventory is added to cost of goods sold to arrive at purchases.

In 1999, Juarez Company's inventory increased $160,000. Purchases, therefore, are computed as follows.

| | |
|---|---|
| Cost of goods sold | $450,000 |
| Add: Increase in inventory | 160,000 |
| **Purchases** | **$610,000** |

After purchases are computed, cash payments to suppliers are determined by adjusting purchases for the change in accounts payable. When accounts payable increase during the year, purchases on an accrual basis are higher than they are on a cash basis. As a result, an increase in accounts payable is deducted from purchases to arrive at cash payments to suppliers. Conversely, a decrease in accounts payable is added to purchases because cash payments to suppliers exceed purchases. Cash payments to suppliers were $550,000, computed as follows:

| Purchases | $610,000 |
| Deduct: Increase in accounts payable | 60,000 |
| **Cash payments to suppliers** | **$550,000** |

**ILLUSTRATION 18-28**

*Computation of cash payments to suppliers*

Cash payments to suppliers may also be determined from an analysis of the Accounts Payable account as shown in Illustration 18-29.

| | **Accounts Payable** | | | |
|---|---|---|---|---|
| Payments to suppliers | 550,000 | 1/1/99 | Balance | –0– |
| | | | Purchases | 610,000 |
| | | 12/31/99 | Balance | 60,000 |

**ILLUSTRATION 18-29**

*Analysis of accounts payable*

**HELPFUL HINT**
The T-account shows that purchases less increase in accounts payable equals payments to suppliers.

The relationship between cash payments to suppliers, cost of goods sold, changes in inventory, and changes in accounts payable is shown in the following formula:

**ILLUSTRATION 18-30**

*Formula to compute cash payments to suppliers—direct method*

**Cash Payments for Operating Expenses.**   Operating expenses of $170,000 were reported on Juarez's income statement. To determine the cash paid for operating expenses, this amount must be adjusted for any changes in prepaid expenses and accrued expenses payable. For example, when prepaid expenses increased $8,000 during the year, cash paid for operating expenses was $8,000 higher than operating expenses reported on the income statement. To convert operating expenses to cash payments for operating expenses, the increase of $8,000 must be added to operating expenses. Conversely, if prepaid expenses decrease during the year, the decrease must be deducted from operating expenses.

Operating expenses must also be adjusted for changes in accrued expenses payable. When accrued expenses payable increase during the year, operating expenses on an accrual basis are higher than they are in a cash basis. As a result, an increase in accrued expenses payable is deducted from operating expenses to arrive at cash payments for operating expenses. Conversely, a decrease in accrued expenses payable is added to operating expenses because cash payments exceed operating expenses.

Juarez Company's cash payments for operating expenses were $158,000, computed as follows:

**HELPFUL HINT**
**Decrease in accounts receivable** indicates that cash collections were greater than sales. **Increase in accounts receivable** indicates that sales were greater than cash collections. **Increase in prepaid expenses** indicates that the amount paid for the prepayments exceeded the amount that was recorded as an expense. **Decrease in prepaid expenses** indicates that the amount recorded as an expense exceeded the amount of cash paid for the prepayments. **Increase in accounts payable** indicates that expenses incurred exceed the cash paid for expenses that period.

| Operating expenses | $170,000 |
| Add: Increase in prepaid expenses | 8,000 |
| Deduct: Increase in accrued expenses payable | (20,000) |
| **Cash payments for operating expenses** | **$158,000** |

**ILLUSTRATION 18-31**

*Computation of cash payments for operating expenses*

The relationships among cash payments for operating expenses, changes in prepaid expenses, and changes in accrued expenses payable are shown in the following formula:

**Cash Payments for Income Taxes.**   The income statement for Juarez shows income tax expense of $48,000. This amount equals the cash paid because the comparative balance sheet indicated no income taxes payable at either the beginning or end of the year.

   All of the revenues and expenses in the 1999 income statement have now been adjusted to a cash basis. The operating activities section of the statement of cash flows is as follows:

| JUAREZ COMPANY | | |
|---|---|---|
| **Partial Statement of Cash Flows—Direct Method** | | |
| **For the Year Ended December 31, 1999** | | |
| Cash flows from operating activities | | |
| Cash receipts from customers | | $765,000 |
| Cash payments: | | |
| To suppliers | $550,000 | |
| For operating expenses | 158,000 | |
| For income taxes | 48,000 | 756,000 |
| Net cash provided by operating activities | | $   9,000 |

## Determining Net Cash Provided/Used by Investing and Financing Activities (Step 3)

Preparing the investing and financing activities sections of the statement of cash flows begins with a determination of the changes in noncurrent accounts reported in the comparative balance sheet. The change in each account is then analyzed using the additional information to determine the effect, if any, the change had on cash.

**Increase in Land.**   No additional information is given for the increase in land. In such case, you should assume that the increase affected cash. You should also make the same assumption in solving homework problems when the cause of a change in a noncurrent account is not explained. The purchase of land is an investing activity. Thus, an outflow of cash of $80,000 for the purchase of land should be reported in the investing activities section.

**Increase in Common Stock.**   As indicated earlier, 300,000 shares of $1 par value stock were sold for $300,000 cash. The issuance of common stock is a financing activity. Thus, a cash inflow of $300,000 from the issuance of common stock is reported in the financing activities section.

**Increase in Retained Earnings.**   For the Retained Earnings account, the reasons for the net increase of $42,000 are determined by analysis. First, net income increased retained earnings by $112,000. Second, the additional information section indicates that a cash dividend of $70,000 was declared and paid. The adjustment of revenues and expenses to arrive at net cash provided by operations was done in step 2 above. The cash dividend paid is reported as an outflow of cash in the financing activities section.

This analysis can also be made directly from the Retained Earnings account in the ledger of Juarez Company as shown in Illustration 18-34.

**HELPFUL HINT**
It is the **payment** of dividends, not the declaration, that appears on the cash flow statement.

**ILLUSTRATION 18-34**
*Analysis of retained earnings*

| | | **Retained Earnings** | | | |
|---|---|---|---|---|---|
| 12/31/99 | Cash dividend | 70,000 | 1/1/99 | Balance | –0– |
| | | | 12/31/99 | **Net income** | **112,000** |
| | | | 12/31/99 | Balance | 42,000 |

The $42,000 increase in Retained Earnings in 1999 is a net change. When a net change in a noncurrent balance sheet account has occurred during the year, it generally is necessary to report the individual items that cause the net change.

## Statement of Cash Flows—1999

The statement of cash flows can now be prepared. The operating activities section is reported first, followed by the investing and financing activities sections. The statement of cash flows for Juarez Company for 1999 is shown in Illustration 18-35.

**ILLUSTRATION 18-35**
*Statement of cash flows, 1999—direct method*

| JUAREZ COMPANY<br>Statement of Cash Flows—Direct Method<br>For the Year Ended December 31, 1999 | | |
|---|---|---|
| Cash flows from operating activities | | |
| Cash receipts from customers | | $765,000 |
| Cash payments: | | |
| To suppliers | $550,000 | |
| For operating expenses | 158,000 | |
| For income taxes | 48,000 | 756,000 |
| Net cash provided by operating activities | | 9,000 |
| Cash flows from investing activities | | |
| Purchase of land | (80,000) | |
| Net cash used by investing activities | | (80,000) |
| Cash flows from financing activities | | |
| Issuance of common stock | 300,000 | |
| Payment of cash dividend | (70,000) | |
| Net cash provided by financing activities | | 230,000 |
| Net increase in cash | | 159,000 |
| Cash at beginning of period | | –0– |
| Cash at end of period | | $159,000 |

**HELPFUL HINT**
Note that in the investing and financing activities sections, positive numbers indicate cash inflows (receipts) and negative numbers indicate cash outflows (payments).

The statement of cash flows shows that operating activities provided $9,000 of the net increase in cash of $159,000. Financing activities **provided** $230,000 of cash, and investing activities **used** $80,000 of cash. The net increase in cash for the year of $159,000 agrees with the increase in cash of $159,000 reported in the comparative balance sheet.

# SECOND YEAR OF OPERATIONS—2000

Illustrations 18-36 and 18-37 present the comparative balance sheet, the income statement, and additional information pertaining to the second year of operations for Juarez Company.

**ILLUSTRATION 18-36**

*Comparative balance sheet, 2000, with increases and decreases*

### JUAREZ COMPANY
### Comparative Balance Sheet
### December 31

| Assets | 2000 | 1999 | Change Increase/Decrease |
|---|---|---|---|
| Cash | $191,000 | $159,000 | $ 32,000 Increase |
| Accounts receivable | 12,000 | 15,000 | 3,000 Decrease |
| Inventory | 130,000 | 160,000 | 30,000 Decrease |
| Prepaid expenses | 6,000 | 8,000 | 2,000 Decrease |
| Land | 180,000 | 80,000 | 100,000 Increase |
| Equipment | 160,000 | -0- | 160,000 Increase |
| Accumulated depreciation—equipment | (16,000) | -0- | 16,000 Increase |
| Total | $663,000 | $422,000 | |
| **Liabilities and Stockholders' Equity** | | | |
| Accounts payable | $ 52,000 | $ 60,000 | $  8,000 Decrease |
| Accrued expenses payable | 15,000 | 20,000 | 5,000 Decrease |
| Income taxes payable | 12,000 | -0- | 12,000 Increase |
| Bonds payable | 90,000 | -0- | 90,000 Increase |
| Common stock | 400,000 | 300,000 | 100,000 Increase |
| Retained earnings | 94,000 | 42,000 | 52,000 Increase |
| Total | $663,000 | $422,000 | |

**ILLUSTRATION 18-37**

*Income statement and additional information, 2000*

### JUAREZ COMPANY
### Income Statement
### For the Year Ended December 31, 2000

| | | |
|---|---|---|
| Revenues | | $975,000 |
| Cost of goods sold | $660,000 | |
| Operating expenses (excluding depreciation) | 176,000 | |
| Depreciation expense | 18,000 | |
| Loss on sale of store equipment | 1,000 | 855,000 |
| Income before income taxes | | 120,000 |
| Income tax expense | | 36,000 |
| Net income | | $ 84,000 |

**Additional information:**
(a) In 2000, the company declared and paid a $32,000 cash dividend.
(b) Bonds were issued at face value for $90,000 in cash.
(c) Equipment costing $180,000 was purchased for cash.
(d) Equipment costing $20,000 was sold for $17,000 cash when the book value of the equipment was $18,000.
(e) Common stock of $100,000 was issued to acquire land.

## Determining the Net Increase/Decrease in Cash (Step 1)

The comparative balance sheet shows a beginning cash balance of $159,000 and an ending cash balance of $191,000. Thus, there was a net increase in cash in 2000 of $32,000.

## Determining Net Cash Provided/Used by Operating Activities (Step 2)

**Cash Receipts from Customers.**   Revenues from sales were $975,000. Since accounts receivable decreased $3,000, cash receipts from customers were greater than sales revenues. Cash receipts from customers were $978,000, computed as follows:

| | |
|---|---:|
| Revenues from sales | $975,000 |
| Add: Decrease in accounts receivable | 3,000 |
| Cash receipts from customers | $978,000 |

**ILLUSTRATION 18-38**

*Computation of cash receipts from customers*

**Cash Payments to Suppliers.**   The conversion of cost of goods sold to purchases and purchases to cash payments to suppliers is similar to the computations made in 1999. For 2000, purchases are computed using cost of goods sold of $660,000 from the income statement and the decrease in inventory of $30,000 from the comparative balance sheet. Purchases are then adjusted by the decrease in accounts payable of $8,000. Cash payments to suppliers were $638,000, computed as follows:

| | |
|---|---:|
| Cost of goods sold | $660,000 |
| Deduct: Decrease in inventory | 30,000 |
| Purchases | 630,000 |
| Add: Decrease in accounts payable | 8,000 |
| Cash payments to suppliers | $638,000 |

**ILLUSTRATION 18-39**

*Computation of cash payments to suppliers*

**Cash Payments for Operating Expenses.**   Operating expenses (exclusive of depreciation expense) for 2000 were reported at $176,000. This amount is then adjusted for changes in prepaid expenses and accrued expenses payable to arrive at cash payments for operating expenses.

As indicated from the comparative balance sheet, prepaid expenses decreased $2,000 during the year. This means that $2,000 was allocated to operating expenses (thereby increasing operating expenses), but cash payments did not increase by that $2,000. To arrive at cash payments for operating expenses, the decrease in prepaid expenses is deducted from operating expenses.

Accrued operating expenses decreased $5,000 during the period. As a result, cash payments were higher by $5,000 than the amount reported for operating expenses. The decrease in accrued expenses payable is added to operating expenses. Cash payments for operating expenses were $179,000, computed as follows:

ILLUSTRATION 18-40

*Computation of cash payments for operating expenses*

| | |
|---|---|
| Operating expenses, exclusive of depreciation | $176,000 |
| Deduct: Decrease in prepaid expenses | (2,000) |
| Add: Decrease in accrued expenses payable | 5,000 |
| **Cash payments for operating expenses** | **$179,000** |

**Depreciation Expense and Loss on Sale of Equipment.**   Operating expenses are shown exclusive of depreciation. Depreciation expense in 2000 was $18,000. Depreciation expense is not shown on a statement of cash flows because it is a noncash charge. If the amount for operating expenses includes depreciation expense, operating expenses must be reduced by the amount of depreciation to determine cash payments for operating expenses.

The loss on sale of equipment of $1,000 is also a noncash charge. The loss on sale of equipment reduces net income, but it does not reduce cash. Thus, the loss on sale of equipment is not reported on a statement of cash flows.

Other charges to expense that do not require the use of cash, such as the amortization of intangible assets and depletion expense, are treated in the same manner as depreciation.

**Cash Payments for Income Taxes.**   Income tax expense reported on the income statement was $36,000. Income taxes payable, however, increased $12,000 which means that $12,000 of the income taxes have not been paid. As a result, income taxes paid were less than income taxes reported on the income statement. Cash payments for income taxes were, therefore, $24,000 as shown below.

ILLUSTRATION 18-41

*Computation of cash payments for income taxes*

| | |
|---|---|
| Income tax expense | $36,000 |
| Deduct: Increase in income taxes payable | 12,000 |
| **Cash payments for income taxes** | **$24,000** |

The relationships of cash payments for income taxes, income tax expense, and changes in income taxes payable are shown in the following formula:

ILLUSTRATION 18-42

*Formula to compute cash payments for income taxes— direct method*

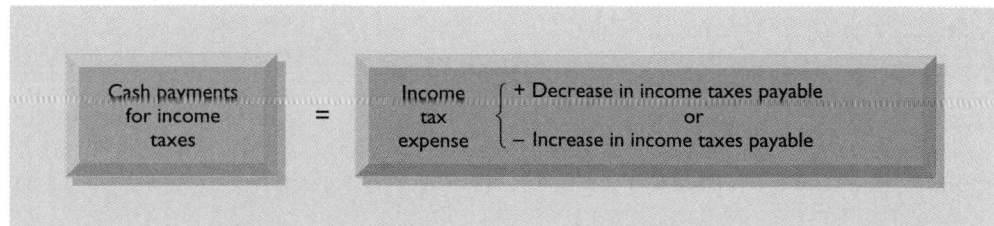

## Determining Net Cash Provided/Used by Investing and Financing Activities (Step 3)

**Increase in Land.**   Land increased $100,000. The additional information section indicates that common stock was issued to purchase the land. Although the issuance of common stock for land has no effect on cash, it is a **significant non-cash investing and financing transaction**. This transaction requires disclosure in a separate schedule at the bottom of the statement of cash flows.

**Increase in Equipment.**   The comparative balance sheet shows that equipment increased $160,000 in 2000. The additional information in Illustration 18-37 indicates that the increase resulted from two investing transactions: (1) equipment costing $180,000 was purchased for cash, and (2) equipment costing $20,000 was sold for $17,000 cash when its book value was $18,000. The relevant data for the statement of cash flows is the cash paid for the purchase and the cash proceeds from the sale. For Juarez Company, the investing activities section will show: Purchase of equipment $180,000, as an outflow of cash; and sale of equipment $17,000, as an inflow of cash. The two amounts **should not be netted** because one is an outflow of cash and the other is an inflow of cash; **both flows should be shown**.

The analysis of the changes in equipment should include the related Accumulated Depreciation account. These two accounts for Juarez Company are shown in Illustration 18-43.

**ILLUSTRATION 18-43**

*Analysis of equipment and related accumulated depreciation*

**Equipment**

| | | | | |
|---|---|---|---|---|
| 1/1/00 | Balance | –0– | Cost of equipment sold | 20,000 |
| | Cash purchase | 180,000 | | |
| 12/31/00 | Balance | 160,000 | | |

**Accumulated Depreciation—Equipment**

| | | | | |
|---|---|---|---|---|
| Sale of equipment | 2,000 | 1/1/00 | Balance | –0– |
| | | | Depreciation expense | 18,000 |
| | | 12/31/00 | Balance | 16,000 |

**Increase in Bonds Payable.**   Bonds Payable increased $90,000. The additional information in Illustration 18-37 indicates that bonds with a face value of $90,000 were issued for $90,000 cash. The issuance of bonds is a financing activity. For Juarez Company, there is an inflow of cash of $90,000 from the issuance of bonds.

**Increase in Common Stock.**   The Common Stock account increased $100,000. As indicated from the additional information, land was acquired from the issuance of common stock. This transaction is a **significant noncash investing and financing transaction** that should be reported in a separate schedule at the bottom of the statement.

**Increase in Retained Earnings.**   The net increase in Retained Earnings of $52,000 resulted from net income of $84,000 and the declaration and payment of a cash dividend of $32,000. **Net income is not reported in the statement of cash flows**

**under the direct method.** Cash dividends paid of $32,000 are reported in the financing activities section as an outflow of cash.

## Statement of Cash Flows—2000

The statement of cash flows for Juarez Company is shown in Illustration 18-44.

**ILLUSTRATION 18-44**

*Statement of cash flows, 2000—direct method*

**JUAREZ COMPANY**
**Statement of Cash Flows—Direct Method**
**For the Year Ended December 31, 2000**

| | | |
|---|---:|---:|
| Cash flows from operating activities | | |
| Cash receipts from customers | | $978,000 |
| Cash payments: | | |
| To suppliers | $638,000 | |
| For operating expenses | 179,000 | |
| For income taxes | 24,000 | 841,000 |
| Net cash provided by operating activities | | 137,000 |
| Cash flows from investing activities | | |
| Purchase of equipment | (180,000) | |
| Sale of equipment | 17,000 | |
| Net cash used by investing activities | | (163,000) |
| Cash flows from financing activities | | |
| Issuance of bonds payable | 90,000 | |
| Payment of cash dividends | (32,000) | |
| Net cash provided by financing activities | | 58,000 |
| Net increase in cash | | 32,000 |
| Cash at beginning of period | | 159,000 |
| Cash at end of period | | $191,000 |
| | | |
| **Noncash investing and financing activities** | | |
| Issuance of common stock to purchase land | | $100,000 |

# BEFORE YOU GO ON . . .

## Review It

1. What is the format of the operating activities section of the statement of cash flows using the direct method?
2. Where is depreciation expense shown on a statement of cash flows using the direct method?
3. Where are significant noncash investing and financing activities shown on a statement of cash flows? Give some examples.

## Do It

Presented below is information related to Reynolds Company. Use it to prepare a statement of cash flows using the direct method.

## REYNOLDS COMPANY
## Comparative Balance Sheet
## December 31

| Assets | 2000 | 1999 | Change Increase/Decrease |
|---|---|---|---|
| Cash | $ 54,000 | $ 37,000 | $ 17,000 Increase |
| Accounts receivable | 68,000 | 26,000 | 42,000 Increase |
| Inventories | 54,000 | –0– | 54,000 Increase |
| Prepaid expenses | 4,000 | 6,000 | 2,000 Decrease |
| Land | 45,000 | 70,000 | 25,000 Decrease |
| Buildings | 200,000 | 200,000 | –0– |
| Accumulated depreciation—buildings | (21,000) | (11,000) | 10,000 Increase |
| Equipment | 193,000 | 68,000 | 125,000 Increase |
| Accumulated depreciation—equipment | (28,000) | (10,000) | 18,000 Increase |
| Totals | $569,000 | $386,000 | |

**Liabilities and Stockholders' Equity**

| | 2000 | 1999 | Change Increase/Decrease |
|---|---|---|---|
| Accounts payable | $ 23,000 | $ 40,000 | $ 17,000 Decrease |
| Accrued expenses payable | 10,000 | –0– | 10,000 Increase |
| Bonds payable | 110,000 | 150,000 | 40,000 Decrease |
| Common stock ($1 par) | 220,000 | 60,000 | 160,000 Increase |
| Retained earnings | 206,000 | 136,000 | 70,000 Increase |
| Totals | $569,000 | $386,000 | |

## REYNOLDS COMPANY
## Income Statement
## For the Year Ended December 31, 2000

| | | |
|---|---|---|
| Revenues | | $890,000 |
| Cost of goods sold | $465,000 | |
| Operating expenses | 221,000 | |
| Interest expense | 12,000 | |
| Loss on sale of equipment | 2,000 | 700,000 |
| Income from operations | | 190,000 |
| Income tax expense | | 65,000 |
| Net income | | $125,000 |

**Additional information:**
(a) Operating expenses include depreciation expense of $33,000 and charges from prepaid expenses of $2,000.
(b) Land was sold at its book value for cash.
(c) Cash dividends of $55,000 were declared and paid in 2000.
(d) Interest expense of $12,000 was paid in cash.
(e) Equipment with a cost of $166,000 was purchased for cash. Equipment with a cost of $41,000 and a book value of $36,000 was sold for $34,000 cash.
(f) Bonds of $10,000 were redeemed at their book value for cash; bonds of $30,000 were converted into common stock.
(g) Common stock ($1 par) of $130,000 was issued for cash.
(h) Accounts payable pertain to merchandise suppliers.

*Reasoning:* The indirect and the direct methods differ primarily in their presentation of the cash flows from the operating activities. The direct method reports cash receipts less cash payments to arrive at net cash provided by operating activities.

Solution:

**REYNOLDS COMPANY**
**Statement of Cash Flows**
**For the Year Ended December 31, 2000**

| | | |
|---|---:|---:|
| Cash flows from operating activities | | |
| Cash receipts from customers | | $848,000[a] |
| Cash payments: | | |
| To suppliers | $536,000[b] | |
| For operating expenses | 176,000[c] | |
| For interest expense | 12,000 | |
| For income taxes | 65,000 | 789,000 |
| Net cash provided by operating activities | | 59,000 |
| Cash flows from investing activities | | |
| Sale of land | 25,000 | |
| Sale of equipment | 34,000 | |
| Purchase of equipment | (166,000) | |
| Net cash used by investing activities | | (107,000) |
| Cash flows from financing activities | | |
| Redemption of bonds | (10,000) | |
| Sale of common stock | 130,000 | |
| Payment of dividends | (55,000) | |
| Net cash provided by financing activities | | 65,000 |
| Net increase in cash | | 17,000 |
| Cash at beginning of period | | 37,000 |
| Cash at end of period | | $ 54,000 |
| | | |
| **Noncash investing and financing activities** | | |
| Conversion of bonds into common stock | | $ 30,000 |

Computations:

[a]$848,000 = $890,000 − $42,000
[b]$536,000 = $465,000 + $54,000 + $17,000
[c]$176,000 = $221,000 − $33,000 − $2,000 − $10,000
Technically, an additional schedule reconciling net income to net cash provided by operating activities should be presented as part of the statement of cash flows when using the direct method.

*Related exercise material:* BE18–6, BE18–7, BE18–8, E18–7, E18–8, E18–9, and E18–10.

THE
NAVIGATOR

Note: This concludes Section 2 on preparation of the statement of cash flows using the direct method. You should now turn to the next—and concluding—section of the chapter, "Analysis of the Statement of Cash Flows."

**5**
STUDY
OBJECTIVE

Analyze the statement of cash flows.

# ANALYSIS OF THE STATEMENT OF CASH FLOWS

The statement of cash flows provides information about a company's financial health that is not evident from analysis of the balance sheet or the income statement. Bankers, creditors, and other users of the statement of cash flows are as concerned with cash flow from operations as they are with net income because they are interested in a company's ability to pay its bills. Does accrual accounting conceal cash flow problems? What can be learned about a company and its management from the statement of cash flows?

In the following discussion of cash flow analysis, we use financial information from the fiscal 1997 annual report of Gap Inc. (manufacturer and retailer of Gap, Banana Republic, and Old Navy brands). Gap Inc. reported the following relevant information:

**Gap Inc.**
Gap
Banana Republic
Old Navy

**Gap Inc.**

| ($ in millions) | Fiscal 1997 | Fiscal 1996 |
| --- | --- | --- |
| Current liabilities | $ 992 | $ 775 |
| Total liabilities | 1,754 | 973 |
| Net sales | 6,508 | 5,284 |
| Net cash provided by operating activities | 845 | 835 |

**ILLUSTRATION 18-45**

*Gap Inc. data used in cash flow analysis*

As with the balance sheet and the income statement, ratio analysis of the statement of cash flows can evaluate Gap Inc.'s liquidity, profitability, and solvency. Three cash flow ratios that contribute to these evaluations are (a) the current cash debt coverage ratio, (b) the cash return on sales ratio, and (c) the cash debt coverage ratio. Each of these ratios uses net cash provided by operating activities as the numerator.

## Current Cash Debt Coverage Ratio

A disadvantage of the current ratio is that it employs year-end balances of current asset and current liability accounts. These year-end balances may not be representative of what the company's current position was during most of the year. A ratio that partially corrects for this problem is the ratio of net cash provided by operating activities to average current liabilities, referred to as the current cash debt coverage ratio. Because it uses net cash provided by operating activities during the period, rather than a balance at a point in time, it may provide a better representation of **liquidity**. Using Gap Inc.'s financial data, the current cash debt coverage ratio is computed as follows:

**HELPFUL HINT**
Recall that the current ratio is current assets divided by current liabilities.

**ILLUSTRATION 18-46**

*Current cash debt coverage ratio*

This ratio indicates that for every dollar of debt due during the year, $0.96 of cash was generated from operations to pay that debt.

## Cash Return on Sales Ratio

One measure of profitability using accrual accounting is the profit margin ratio. This ratio is defined as net income divided by net sales and measures net income generated by each dollar of sales. The cash-based ratio that is the counterpart of the profit margin ratio is the cash return on sales ratio (sometimes referred to as "cash flow margin"), computed by dividing net cash provided by operating activities by net sales. For Gap Inc, this ratio is computed as follows:

**ILLUSTRATION 18-47**

*Cash return on sales ratio*

Although differences are expected between cash and accrual accounting, significant differences should be investigated. When Gap Inc.'s "cash flow margin"—its cash return on sales—of 13% is compared with its profit margin of 5.3%, it appears that Gap Inc. is very efficient at turning sales into cash—since its cash flow margin is more than double its profit margin (accrual basis).

## Cash Debt Coverage Ratio

In Chapter 16 we introduced the debt to total assets ratio as one measure of long-term **solvency**. The cash basis measure of solvency is the cash debt coverage ratio—the ratio of net cash provided by operating activities to average total liabilities. This ratio demonstrates a company's ability to repay its liabilities from net cash provided by operating activities, without having to liquidate the assets employed in its operations. Gap Inc.'s cash debt coverage ratio is computed as follows:

**ILLUSTRATION 18-48**

*Cash debt coverage ratio*

The three cash-based ratios illustrated above show that Gap Inc. is efficiently generating cash, and its cash flow coverage ratios are in line with industry averages. These ratios indicate that the company is liquid, profitable, and solvent.

# BEFORE YOU GO ON . . .

## Review It

1. Why might an analyst want to supplement accrual-based ratios with cash-based ratios?
2. What cash-basis ratios may be prepared to evaluate liquidity, profitability, and solvency?

## A LOOK BACK AT OUR FEATURE STORY

Refer to the opening story of Gerald Biby's attempt to refinance Kilian Community College's mortgage, and answer the following questions:

1. How was the purchase of the $250,000 computer system presented on the "traditional educational institution financial statement" so that it negatively affected Biby's ability to refinance the mortgage?
2. How was the purchase of the $250,000 computer system presented on the statement of cash flows? How did the preparation of the statement of cash flows aid Biby in securing the refinancing of the mortgage?

*Solution:*

1. A traditional financial statement for a not-for-profit, educational institution reports receipts as revenues and expenses all expenditures, even capital expenditures such as the $250,000 computer system. That is, the traditional financial statement reported the entire $250,000 as an expense in one year, making it look like the college was just breaking even.
2. When the computer purchase was classified as an investing activity, the statement of cash flows showed the bankers that one of the uses of funds was really the purchase of computer equipment that had several years of life. In addition, the bankers noted from the statement of cash flows "that the college's sources of funds exceeded the loan repayments, including principal and interest, by a ratio of 3-to-1."

THE
NAVIGATOR

## DEMONSTRATION PROBLEM

The income statement for the year ended December 31, 1999, for John Kosinski Manufacturing Company contains the following condensed information:

### JOHN KOSINSKI MANUFACTURING COMPANY
### Income Statement

| | | |
|---|---:|---:|
| Revenues | | $6,583,000 |
| Operating expenses (excluding depreciation) | $4,920,000 | |
| Depreciation expense | 880,000 | 5,800,000 |
| Income before income taxes | | 783,000 |
| Income tax expense | | 353,000 |
| Net income | | $  430,000 |

Included in operating expenses is a $24,000 loss resulting from the sale of machinery for $270,000 cash. Machinery was purchased at a cost of $750,000. The following balances are reported on Kosinski's comparative balance sheet at December 31:

### JOHN KOSINSKI MANUFACTURING COMPANY
### Balance Sheet (partial)

| | 1999 | 1998 |
|---|---|---|
| Cash | $672,000 | $130,000 |
| Accounts receivable | 775,000 | 610,000 |
| Inventories | 834,000 | 867,000 |
| Accounts payable | 521,000 | 501,000 |

Income tax expense of $353,000 represents the amount paid in 1999. Dividends declared and paid in 1999 totaled $200,000.

*Instructions*
(a) Prepare the statement of cash flows using the indirect method.

OR

(b) Prepare the statement of cash flows using the direct method.

**PROBLEM-SOLVING STRATEGY**
This demonstration problem illustrates both the direct and indirect methods using the same basic data. Note the similarities and the differences between the two methods. Both methods report the same information in the investing and financing activities sections. The cash flow from operating activities section reports different information, but the amount—net cash provided by operating activities—is the same for both methods.

# SOLUTION TO DEMONSTRATION PROBLEM

(a)
### JOHN KOSINSKI MANUFACTURING COMPANY
### Statement of Cash Flows—Indirect Method
### For the Year Ended December 31, 1999

| | | |
|---|---:|---:|
| Cash flows from operating activities | | |
| Net income | | $ 430,000 |
| Adjustments to reconcile net income to net cash provided by operating activities: | | |
| Depreciation expense | $880,000 | |
| Loss on sale of machinery | 24,000 | |
| Increase in accounts receivable | (165,000) | |
| Decrease in inventories | 33,000 | |
| Increase in accounts payable | 20,000 | 792,000 |
| Net cash provided by operating activities | | 1,222,000 |
| Cash flows from investing activities | | |
| Sale of machinery | 270,000 | |
| Purchase of machinery | (750,000) | |
| Net cash used by investing activities | | (480,000) |
| Cash flows from financing activities | | |
| Payment of cash dividends | | (200,000) |
| Net increase in cash | | 542,000 |
| Cash at beginning of period | | 130,000 |
| Cash at end of period | | $672,000 |

(b)
### JOHN KOSINSKI MANUFACTURING COMPANY
### Statement of Cash Flows—Direct Method
### For the Year Ended December 31, 1999

| | | |
|---|---:|---:|
| Cash flows from operating activities | | |
| Cash collections from customers | | $6,418,000 * |
| Cash payments: | | |
| For operating expenses | $4,843,000 ** | |
| For income taxes | 353,000 | 5,196,000 |
| Net cash provided by operating activities | | 1,222,000 |
| Cash flows from investing activities | | |
| Sale of machinery | $270,000 | |
| Purchase of machinery | (750,000) | |
| Net cash used by investing activities | | (480,000) |
| Cash flows from financing activities | | |
| Payment of cash dividends | | (200,000) |
| Net increase in cash | | 542,000 |
| Cash at beginning of period | | 130,000 |
| Cash at end of period | | $ 672,000 |

*Direct Method Computations:*

| | | |
|---|---|---:|
| * | Computation of cash collections from customers: | |
| | Revenues per the income statement | $6,583,000 |
| | Less increase in accounts receivable | 165,000 |
| | Cash collections from customers | $6,418,000 |

| ** | Computation of cash payments for operating expenses: | |
|---|---|---|
| | Operating expenses per the income statement | $4,920,000 |
| | Deduct loss from sale of machinery | (24,000) |
| | Deduct decrease in inventories | (33,000) |
| | Deduct increase in accounts payable | (20,000) |
| | Cash payments for operating expenses | $4,843,000 |

# SUMMARY OF STUDY OBJECTIVES

**1. Indicate the primary purpose of the statement of cash flows.** The primary purpose of the statement of cash flows is to provide information about the cash receipts and cash payments of an entity during a period. A secondary objective is to provide information about the operating, investing, and financing activities of the entity during the period.

**2. Distinguish among operating, investing, and financing activities.** Operating activities include the cash effects of transactions that enter into the determination of net income. Investing activities involve cash flows resulting from changes in investments and long-term asset items. Financing activities involve cash flows resulting from changes in long-term liability and stockholders' equity items.

**3. Prepare a statement of cash flows using the indirect method.** The preparation of a statement of cash flows involves three major steps: (1) determine the net increase or decrease in cash; (2) determine net cash provided (used) by operating activities; and (3) determine net cash flows provided (used) by investing and financing activities. Under the indirect method, accrual basis net income is adjusted to net cash provided by operating activities.

**4. Prepare a statement of cash flows using the direct method.** The preparation of the statement of cash flows involves three major steps: (1) determine the net increase or decrease in cash; (2) determine net cash provided (used) by operating activities; and (3) determine net cash flows provided (used) by investing and financing activities. The direct method reports cash receipts less cash payments to arrive at net cash provided by operating activities.

**5. Analyze the statement of cash flows.** Ratio analysis of the statement of cash flows can evaluate liquidity, profitability, and solvency by computing (a) the current cash debt coverage ratio, (b) the cash return on sales ratio, and (c) the cash debt coverage ratio.

# GLOSSARY

**Cash debt coverage ratio**  A cash-basis measure of solvency, computed as net cash provided by operating activities divided by average total liabilities. (p. 788)

**Cash return on sales ratio**  A cash-basis measure of profitability, computed as net cash provided by operating activities divided by net sales. Also called *cash flow margin.* (p.788)

**Current cash debt coverage ratio**  A cash-basis measure of liquidity, computed as net cash provided by operating activities divided by average current liabilities. (p.787)

**Direct method**  A method of determining the "net cash provided by operating activities" by adjusting each item in the income statement from the accrual basis to the cash basis. (p. 775)

**Financing activities**  Cash flow activities that include (a) obtaining cash from issuing debt and repaying the amounts borrowed and (b) obtaining cash from stockholders and providing them with a return on their investment. (p. 756)

**Indirect method**  A method of preparing a statement of cash flows in which net income is adjusted for items that did not affect cash, to determine net cash provided by operating activities. (p. 763)

**Investing activities**  Cash flow activities that include (a) acquiring and disposing of investments and productive long-lived assets and (b) lending money and collecting on those loans. (p. 756)

**Operating activities**  Cash flow activities that include the cash effects of transactions that create revenues and expenses and thus enter into the determination of net income. (p. 756)

**Statement of cash flows**  A basic financial statement that provides information about the cash receipts and cash payments of an entity during a period, classified as operating, investing, and financing activities, in a format that reconciles the beginning and ending cash balances. (p. 755)

# APPENDIX USING A WORK SHEET TO PREPARE THE STATEMENT OF CASH FLOWS—INDIRECT METHOD

**STUDY OBJECTIVE**

Explain the guidelines and procedural steps in using a work sheet to prepare the statement of cash flows.

When numerous adjustments of net income are necessary, **a work sheet is often used to assemble and classify the data that will appear on the statement of cash flows.** The work sheet is merely a device that aids in the preparation of the statement; its use is optional. The skeleton format of the work sheet for preparation of the statement of cash flows is shown in Illustration 18A-1.

### XYZ COMPANY
### Work Sheet
### Statement of Cash Flows
### For the Year Ended . . .

| Balance Sheet Accounts | End of Last Year Balances | Reconciling Items Debits | Reconciling Items Credits | End of Current Year Balances |
|---|---|---|---|---|
| Debit balance accounts | XX | XX | XX | XX |
|  | XX | XX | XX | XX |
| Totals | XXX |  |  | XXX |
| Credit balance accounts | XX | XX | XX | XX |
|  | XX | XX | XX | XX |
| Totals | XXX |  |  | XXX |
| **Statement of Cash Flows Effects** |  |  |  |  |
| Operating activities |  |  |  |  |
| Net income |  | XX |  |  |
| Adjustments to net income |  | XX | XX |  |
| Investing activities |  |  |  |  |
| Receipts and payments |  | XX | XX |  |
| Financing activities |  |  |  |  |
| Receipts and payments |  | XX | XX |  |
| Totals |  | XXX | XXX |  |
| Increase (decrease) in cash |  | (XX) | XX |  |
| Totals |  | XXX | XXX |  |

**ILLUSTRATION 18A-1**

*Format of work sheet*

The following guidelines are important in using a work sheet:

1.  In the balance sheet accounts section, **accounts with debit balances are listed separately from those with credit balances.** This means, for example, that Accumulated Depreciation is listed under credit balances and not as a contra account under debit balances. The beginning and ending balances of each account are entered in the appropriate columns. The transactions that caused the change in the account balance during the year are entered as reconciling items in the two middle columns. After all reconciling items have been entered, each line pertaining to a balance sheet account should "foot across." That is, the beginning balance plus or minus the reconciling item(s) must equal the ending balance. When this agreement exists for all balance sheet accounts, all changes in account balances have been reconciled.

2. The bottom portion of the work sheet consists of the operating, investing, and financing activities sections. Accordingly, it provides the information necessary to prepare the formal statement of cash flows. **Inflows of cash are entered as debits in the reconciling columns, and outflows of cash are entered as credits in the reconciling columns.** Thus, in this section, the sale of equipment for cash at book value is entered as a debit under investing activities. Similarly, the purchase of land for cash is entered as a credit under investing activities.

3. **The reconciling items shown in the work sheet are not entered in any journal or posted to any account.** They do not represent either adjustments or corrections of the balance sheet accounts. They are used only to facilitate the preparation of the statement of cash flows.

# PREPARING THE WORK SHEET

As in the case of work sheets illustrated in earlier chapters, the preparation of a work sheet involves a series of prescribed steps. The steps in this case are:

1. Enter in the balance sheet accounts section the balance sheet accounts and their beginning and ending balances.
2. Enter in the reconciling columns of the work sheet the data that explain the changes in the balance sheet accounts other than cash and their effects on the statement of cash flows.
3. Enter on the cash line and at the bottom of the work sheet the increase or decrease in cash. This entry should enable the totals of the reconciling columns to be in agreement.

To illustrate the preparation of a work sheet, we will use the 2000 data for Computer Services Company. Your familiarity with these data should help you understand the use of a work sheet. For ease of reference, the comparative balance sheets, income statement, and selected data for 2000 are presented in Illustrations 18A-2 and 18A-3.

**ILLUSTRATION 18A-2**

*Comparative balance sheet, 2000, with increases and decreases*

| | | | Change |
|---|---|---|---|
| **Assets** | **2000** | **1999** | **Increase/Decrease** |
| Cash | $ 56,000 | $34,000 | $ 22,000 Increase |
| Accounts receivable | 20,000 | 30,000 | 10,000 Decrease |
| Prepaid expenses | 4,000 | –0– | 4,000 Increase |
| Land | 130,000 | –0– | 130,000 Increase |
| Building | 160,000 | –0– | 160,000 Increase |
| Accumulated depreciation—building | (11,000) | –0– | 11,000 Increase |
| Equipment | 27,000 | 10,000 | 17,000 Increase |
| Accumulated depreciation—equipment | (3,000) | –0– | 3,000 Increase |
| Totals | $383,000 | $74,000 | |
| **Liabilities and Stockholders' Equity** | | | |
| Accounts payable | $ 59,000 | $ 4,000 | 55,000 Increase |
| Bonds payable | 130,000 | –0– | 130,000 Increase |
| Common stock | 50,000 | 50,000 | –0– |
| Retained earnings | 144,000 | 20,000 | 124,000 Increase |
| Totals | $383,000 | $74,000 | |

**COMPUTER SERVICES COMPANY**
**Comparative Balance Sheet**
**December 31**

**COMPUTER SERVICES COMPANY**
**Income Statement**
**For the Year Ended December 31, 2000**

| | | |
|---|---:|---:|
| Revenues | | $507,000 |
| Operating expenses (excluding depreciation) | $261,000 | |
| Depreciation expense | 15,000 | |
| Loss on sale of equipment | 3,000 | 279,000 |
| Income from operations | | 228,000 |
| Income tax expense | | 89,000 |
| Net income | | $139,000 |

**Additional information:**
(a) In 2000, the company declared and paid a $15,000 cash dividend.
(b) The company obtained land through the issuance of $130,000 of long-term bonds.
(c) A building costing $160,000 was purchased for cash; equipment costing $25,000 was also purchased for cash.
(d) During 2000, the company sold equipment with a book value of $7,000 (cost $8,000, less accumulated depreciation $1,000) for $4,000 cash.

## Determining the Reconciling Items

Several approaches may be used to determine the reconciling items. For example, the changes affecting net cash provided by operating activities could be completed first and then the effects of financing and investing transactions could be determined. Alternatively, the balance sheet accounts can be analyzed in the order in which they are listed on the work sheet. We will follow this latter approach for Computer Services, except for cash. As indicated above, **cash is handled last.**

**Accounts Receivable.** The decrease of $10,000 in accounts receivable means that cash collections from revenues are higher than the revenues reported in the income statement. To convert net income to net cash provided by operating activities, the decrease of $10,000 is added to net income. The entry in the reconciling columns of the work sheet is:

| | | | |
|---|---|---:|---:|
| (a) | Operating—Decrease in Accounts Receivable | 10,000 | |
| | Accounts Receivable | | 10,000 |

**Prepaid Expenses.** An increase of $4,000 in prepaid expenses means that expenses deducted in determining net income are less than expenses that were paid in cash. Thus, the increase of $4,000 must be deducted from net income in determining net cash provided by operating activities. The work sheet entry is:

| | | | |
|---|---|---:|---:|
| (b) | Prepaid Expenses | 4,000 | |
| | Operating—Increase in Prepaid Expenses | | 4,000 |

**Land.** The increase in land of $130,000 resulted from a purchase through the issuance of long-term bonds. This transaction should be reported as a significant noncash investing and financing activity. The work sheet entry is:

| | | | |
|---|---|---:|---:|
| (c) | Land | 130,000 | |
| | Bonds Payable | | 130,000 |

**Building.** The cash purchase of a building for $160,000 is an investing activity cash outflow. The entry in the reconciling columns of the work sheet is:

| (d) | Building | 160,000 | |
| | Investing—Purchase of Building | | 160,000 |

**Equipment.** The increase in equipment of $17,000 resulted from a cash purchase of $25,000 and the sale of equipment costing $8,000. The book value of the equipment was $7,000, the cash proceeds were $4,000, and a loss of $3,000 was recorded. The work sheet entries are:

| (e) | Equipment | 25,000 | |
| | Investing—Purchase of Equipment | | 25,000 |

| (f) | Investing—Sale of Equipment | 4,000 | |
| | Operating—Loss on Sale of Equipment | 3,000 | |
| | Accumulated Depreciation—Equipment | 1,000 | |
| | Equipment | | 8,000 |

**Accounts Payable.** The increase of $55,000 in accounts payable must be added to net income to obtain net cash provided by operating activities. The following work sheet entry is made:

| (g) | Operating—Increase in Accounts Payable | 55,000 | |
| | Accounts Payable | | 55,000 |

**Bonds Payable.** The increase of $130,000 in this account resulted from the issuance of bonds for land. This is a significant noncash investing and financing activity. Work sheet entry (c) above is the only entry necessary.

**Accumulated Depreciation—Building, and Accumulated Depreciation—Equipment.** The increases in these accounts of $11,000 and $4,000, respectively, resulted from depreciation expense. Depreciation expense is a **noncash charge that must be added to net income** in determining net cash provided by operating activities. The work sheet entries are:

| (h) | Operating—Depreciation Expense—Building | 11,000 | |
| | Accumulated Depreciation—Building | | 11,000 |

| (i) | Operating—Depreciation Expense—Equipment | 4,000 | |
| | Accumulated Depreciation—Equipment | | 4,000 |

**Retained Earnings.** The $124,000 increase in retained earnings resulted from net income of $139,000 and the declaration of a $15,000 cash dividend that was paid in 2000. Net income is included in net cash provided by operating activities, and the dividends are a financing activity cash outflow. The entries in the reconciling columns of the work sheet are:

| (j) | Operating—Net Income | 139,000 | |
| | Retained Earnings | | 139,000 |

| (k) | Retained Earnings | 15,000 | |
| | Financing—Payment of Dividends | | 15,000 |

**Disposition of Change in Cash.** The firm's cash increased $22,000 in 2000. The final entry on the work sheet, therefore, is:

| (l) | Cash | 22,000 | |
| | Increase in cash | | 22,000 |

As shown in the work sheet, the increase in cash is entered in the reconciling credit column as a **balancing** amount. This entry should complete the reconciliation of the changes in the balance sheet accounts. In addition, it should permit the totals of the reconciling columns to be in agreement. When all changes have been explained and the reconciling columns are in agreement, the reconciling columns are ruled to complete the work sheet. The completed work sheet for Computer Services Company is shown in Illustration 18A-4.

**ILLUSTRATION 18A-4**

*Completed work sheet—
indirect method*

## COMPUTER SERVICES COMPANY
## Work Sheet
## Statement of Cash Flows
## For the Year Ended December 31, 2000

| Balance Sheet Accounts | Balance 12/31/99 | Reconciling Items Debit | | Reconciling Items Credit | | Balance 12/31/00 |
|---|---|---|---|---|---|---|
| **Debits** | | | | | | |
| Cash | 34,000 | (l) | 22,000 | | | 56,000 |
| Accounts receivable | 30,000 | | | (a) | 10,000 | 20,000 |
| Prepaid expenses | –0– | (b) | 4,000 | | | 4,000 |
| Land | –0– | (c) | 130,000* | | | 130,000 |
| Building | –0– | (d) | 160,000 | | | 160,000 |
| Equipment | 10,000 | (e) | 25,000 | (f) | 8,000 | 27,000 |
| Total | 74,000 | | | | | 397,000 |
| **Credits** | | | | | | |
| Accounts payable | 4,000 | | | (g) | 55,000 | 59,000 |
| Bonds payable | –0– | | | (c) | 130,000* | 130,000 |
| Accumulated depreciation—building | –0– | | | (h) | 11,000 | 11,000 |
| Accumulated depreciation—equipment | –0– | (f) | 1,000 | (i) | 4,000 | 3,000 |
| Common stock | 50,000 | | | | | 50,000 |
| Retained earnings | 20,000 | (k) | 15,000 | (j) | 139,000 | 144,000 |
| Total | 74,000 | | | | | 397,000 |

**Statement of Cash Flows Effects**

| | | Debit | | Credit | |
|---|---|---|---|---|---|
| Operating activities | | | | | |
| Net income | (j) | 139,000 | | | |
| Decrease in accounts receivable | (a) | 10,000 | | | |
| Increase in prepaid expenses | | | (b) | 4,000 | |
| Increase in accounts payable | (g) | 55,000 | | | |
| Depreciation expense—building | (h) | 11,000 | | | |
| Depreciation expense—equipment | (i) | 4,000 | | | |
| Loss on sale of equipment | (f) | 3,000 | | | |
| Investing activities | | | | | |
| Purchase of building | | | (d) | 160,000 | |
| Purchase of equipment | | | (e) | 25,000 | |
| Sale of equipment | (f) | 4,000 | | | |
| Financing activities | | | | | |
| Payment of dividends | | | (k) | 15,000 | |
| Totals | | 583,000 | | 561,000 | |
| Increase in cash | | | (l) | 22,000 | |
| Totals | | 583,000 | | 583,000 | |

*Significant noncash investing and financing activity.

# PREPARING THE STATEMENT

The statement of cash flows is prepared primarily from the data that appear in the work sheet under Statement of Cash Flows Effects. The reconciling columns should also be scanned for any asterisked items that designate significant non-cash activities. The formal statement was shown in Illustration 18-18.

## SUMMARY OF STUDY OBJECTIVE FOR APPENDIX

**6. *Explain the guidelines and procedural steps in using a work sheet to prepare the statement of cash flows.*** When there are numerous adjustments, a work sheet can be a helpful tool in preparing the statement of cash flows. Key guidelines for using a work sheet are: (1) list accounts with debit balances separately from those with credit balances; (2) in the reconciling columns in the bottom portion of the work sheet, show cash inflows as debits and cash outflows as credits; (3) do not enter reconciling items in any journal or account but use them only to help prepare the statement of cash flows.

The steps in preparing the work sheet are: (1) enter beginning and ending balances of balance sheet accounts; (2) enter debits and credits in reconciling columns; (3) enter the increase or decrease in cash in two places as a balancing amount.

**\*Note:** All asterisked Questions, Exercises, and Problems relate to material in the appendix to the chapter.

# SELF-STUDY QUESTIONS

Answers are at the end of the chapter.

(SO 1)  1. Which of the following is *incorrect* about the statement of cash flows?
   a. It is a fourth basic financial statement.
   b. It provides information about cash receipts and cash payments of an entity during a period.
   c. It reconciles the ending cash account balance to the balance per the bank statement.
   d. It provides information about the operating, investing, and financing activities of the business.

(SO 2)  2. The statement of cash flows classifies cash receipts and cash payments by the following activities:
   a. operating and nonoperating.
   b. investing, financing, and operating.
   c. financing, operating, and nonoperating.
   d. investing, financing, and nonoperating.

(SO 2)  3. An example of a cash flow from an operating activity is:
   a. payment of cash to lenders for interest.
   b. receipt of cash from the sale of capital stock.
   c. payment of cash dividends to the company's stockholders.
   d. none of the above.

(SO 2)  4. An example of a cash flow from an investing activity is:
   a. receipt of cash from the issuance of bonds payable.
   b. payment of cash to repurchase outstanding capital stock.
   c. receipt of cash from the sale of equipment.
   d. payment of cash to suppliers for inventory.

5. Cash dividends paid to stockholders are classified on (SO 2) the statement of cash flows as:
   a. operating activities.
   b. investing activities.
   c. a combination of the above.
   d. financing activities.

6. An example of a cash flow from a financing activity is: (SO 2)
   a. receipt of cash from sale of land.
   b. issuance of debt for cash.
   c. purchase of equipment for cash.
   d. none of the above.

7. Which of the following about the statement of cash (SO 2) flows is *incorrect*?
   a. The direct method may be used to report cash provided by operations.
   b. The statement shows the cash provided (used) for three categories of activity.
   c. The operating section is the last section of the statement.
   d. The indirect method may be used to report cash provided by operations.

**Questions 8 and 9 apply only to the indirect method.**

8. Net income is $132,000, accounts payable increased (SO 3) $10,000 during the year, inventory decreased $6,000 during the year, and accounts receivable increased $12,000 during the year. Under the indirect method, net cash provided by operations is:

a. $102,000.
b. $112,000.
c. $124,000.
d. $136,000.

(SO 3) 9. Noncash charges that are added back to net income in determining cash provided by operations under the indirect method do *not* include:
a. depreciation expense.
b. an increase in inventory.
c. amortization expense.
d. loss on sale of equipment.

**Questions 10 and 11 apply only to the direct method.**

(SO 4) 10. The beginning balance in accounts receivable is $44,000, and the ending balance is $42,000. Sales during the period are $129,000. Cash receipts from customers are:
a. $127,000.
b. $129,000.
c. $131,000.
d. $141,000.

11. Which of the following items is reported on a cash flow (SO 4) statement prepared by the direct method?
a. Loss on sale of building.
b. Increase in accounts receivable.
c. Depreciation expense.
d. Cash payments to suppliers.

12. The statement of cash flows should *not* be used to eval- (SO 3) uate an entity's ability to:
a. earn net income.
b. generate future cash flows.
c. pay dividends.
d. meet obligations.

*13. In a work sheet for the statement of cash flows, a de- (SO 5) crease in accounts receivable is entered in the reconciling columns as a credit to Accounts Receivable and a debit in the:
a. investing activities section.
b. operating activities section.
c. financing activities section.
d. none of the above.

# QUESTIONS

1. (a) What is the statement of cash flows? (b) Alice Weiseman maintains that the statement of cash flows is an optional financial statement. Do you agree? Explain.

2. What questions about cash are answered by the statement of cash flows?

3. What are "cash equivalents"? How do cash equivalents affect the statement of cash flows?

4. Distinguish among the three types of activities reported in the statement of cash flows.

5. What are the major sources (inflows) of cash in a statement of cash flows? What are the major uses (outflows) of cash?

6. Why is it important to disclose certain noncash transactions? How should they be disclosed?

7. Wilma Flintstone and Barny Rublestone were discussing the presentation format of the statement of cash flows of Stone Candy Co. At the bottom of Stone Candy's statement of cash flows was a separate section entitled "Noncash investing and financing activities." Give three examples of significant noncash transactions that would be reported in this section.

8. Why is it necessary to use comparative balance sheets, a current income statement, and certain transaction data in preparing a statement of cash flows?

9. Contrast the advantages and disadvantages of the direct and indirect methods. Are both methods acceptable? Which method is preferred by the FASB? Which method is more popular?

10. When the total cash inflows exceed the total cash outflows in the statement of cash flows, how and where is this excess identified?

11. Describe the indirect method for determining net cash provided by operating activities.

12. Why is it necessary to convert accrual based net income to cash basis income when preparing a statement of cash flows?

13. The president of Styx Company is puzzled. During the last year, the company experienced a net loss of $800,000, yet its cash increased $300,000 during the same period of time. Explain to the president how this situation could occur.

14. Identify five items that are adjustments to reconcile net income to net cash provided by operating activities under the indirect method.

15. Why and how is depreciation expense reported in a statement prepared using the indirect method?

16. Why is the statement of cash flows useful?

17. During 1999, James Brown Company converted $1,600,000 of its total $2,000,000 of bonds payable into common stock. Indicate how the transaction would be reported on a statement of cash flows, if at all.

18. Describe the direct method for determining net cash provided by operating activities.

19. Give the formulas under the direct method for computing (a) cash receipts from customers and (b) cash payments to suppliers.

20. Sharon Stone Inc. reported sales of $2 million for 1999. Accounts receivable decreased $100,000 and accounts payable increased $325,000. Compute cash receipts from customers, assuming that the receivable and payable transactions related to operations.

21. Why is depreciation expense not reported in the direct-method cash flow from operating activities section?

22. Give an example of one accrual-based ratio and one cash-based ratio to measure these characteristics of a company: (a) liquidity, (b) solvency, and (c) profitability.

*23. Why is it advantageous to use a work sheet when preparing a statement of cash flows? Is a work sheet required to prepare a statement of cash flows?

# BRIEF EXERCISES

**BE18–1**   DiCaprio Co., reported net income of $2.5 million in 1999. Depreciation for the year was $280,000, accounts receivable decreased $350,000, and accounts payable decreased $310,000. Compute net cash provided by operating activities using the indirect approach.

*Compute cash provided by operating activities—indirect method.*
*(SO 3)*

**BE18–2**   The net income for Kate Winslet Co. for 1999 was $280,000. For 1999, depreciation on plant assets was $60,000, and the company incurred a loss on sale of plant assets of $10,000. Compute net cash provided by operating activities under the indirect method.

*Compute cash provided by operating activities—indirect method.*
*(SO 3)*

**BE18–3**   Each of the following items must be considered in preparing a statement of cash flows for Matt Damon Co. for the year ended December 31, 1999. For each item, state how it should be shown in the statement of cash flows for 1999.

*Indicate statement presentation of selected transactions.*
*(SO 2)*

  (a) Issued bonds for $200,000 cash.
  (b) Purchased equipment for $180,000 cash.
  (c) Sold land costing $20,000 for $20,000 cash.
  (d) Declared and paid a $50,000 cash dividend.

**BE18–4**   The comparative balance sheet for the Amistad Company shows the following changes in noncash current asset accounts: accounts receivable decrease $95,000, prepaid expenses increase $12,000, and inventories increase $30,000. Compute net cash provided by operating activities using the indirect method assuming that net income is $220,000.

*Compute net cash provided by operating activities using indirect method.*
*(SO 3)*

**BE18–5**   Classify the following items as an operating, investing, or financing activity. Assume all items involve cash unless there is information to the contrary.

*Classify items by activities.*
*(SO 2)*

  (a) Purchase of equipment.      (d) Depreciation.
  (b) Sale of building.           (e) Payment of dividends.
  (c) Redemption of bonds.        (f) Issuance of capital stock.

**BE18–6**   Julie Christie Co. has accounts receivable of $14,000 at Janury 1, 1999, and $24,000 at December 31, 1999. Sales revenues were $490,000 for the year 1999. What is the amount of cash receipts from customers in 1999?

*Compute receipts from customers using direct method.*
*(SO 4)*

**BE18–7**   Joe Pesci Company reported income taxes of $90,000 on its 1999 income statement and income taxes payable of $12,000 at December 31, 1998, and $9,000 at December 31, 1999. What amount of cash payments was made for income taxes during 1999?

*Compute cash payments for income taxes using direct method.*
*(SO 4)*

**BE18–8**   Titanic Company reports operating expenses of $100,000 excluding depreciation expense of $15,000 for 1999. During the year prepaid expenses decreased $6,600 and accrued expenses payable increased $4,400. Compute the cash payments for operating expenses in 1999.

*Compute cash payments for operating expenses using direct method.*
*(SO 4)*

**BE18–9**   The T-accounts for Equipment and the related Accumulated Depreciation for Kim Bassinger Company at the end of 1999 are as follows:

*Determine cash received in sale of equipment.*
*(SO 3, 4)*

| Equipment | | | | Accumulated Depreciation | | | |
|---|---|---|---|---|---|---|---|
| Beg. bal. | 80,000 | Disposals | 22,000 | Disposals | 5,500 | Beg. bal. | 44,500 |
| Acquisitions | 41,600 | | | | | Depr. | 12,000 |
| End. bal. | 99,600 | | | | | End. bal. | 51,000 |

In addition, Kim Bassinger Company's income statement reported a loss on the sale of equipment of $6,900. What amount was reported on the statement of cash flows as "cash flow from sale of equipment"?

*Identify financing activity transactions.*
*(SO 2)*

**BE18–10**    The following T-account is a summary of the cash account of Robin Williams Company.

### Cash (Summary Form)

| | | | |
|---|---|---|---|
| Balance, 1/1/99 | 8,000 | | |
| Receipts from customers | 364,000 | Payments for goods | 200,000 |
| Dividends on stock investments | 6,000 | Payments for operating expenses | 140,000 |
| Proceeds from sale of equipment | 36,000 | Interest paid | 10,000 |
| Proceeds from issuance of bonds | | Taxes paid | 8,000 |
| payable | 100,000 | Dividends paid | 45,000 |
| | | | |
| Balance, 12/31/99 | 111,000 | | |

For Robin Williams Company what amount of net cash provided (used) by financing activities should be reported in the statement of cash flows?

*Calculate cash-based ratios.*
*(SO 5)*

**BE18–11**    Alice Weiseman Company reported cash from operations of $300,000, net sales $1,500,000, average current liabilities of $150,000 and average total liabilities of $225,000. Calculate these ratios:
(a) Current cash debt coverage ratio.
(b) Cash debt coverage ratio.
(c) Cash return on sales ratio.

*Indicate entries in work sheet.*
*(SO 6)*

**\*BE18–12**    Using the data in BE18–8, indicate how the changes in prepaid expenses and accrued expenses payable should be entered in the reconciling columns of a work sheet. Assume that beginning balances were: prepaid expenses, $18,600 and accrued expenses payable, $8,200.

# EXERCISES

*Classify transactions by type of activity.*
*(SO 2)*

**E18–1**    Depeche Mode Corporation had the following transactions during 1999:

1. Issued $50,000 par value common stock for cash.
2. Collected $16,000 of accounts receivable.
3. Declared and paid a cash dividend of $25,000.
4. Sold a long-term investment with a cost of $15,000 for $15,000 cash.
5. Issued $200,000 par value common stock upon conversion of bonds having a face value of $200,000.
6. Paid $18,000 on accounts payable.
7. Purchased a machine for $30,000, giving a long-term note in exchange.

*Instructions*
Analyze the transactions above and indicate whether each transaction resulted in a cash flow from (a) operating activities, (b) investing activities, (c) financing activities, or (d) noncash investing and financing activities.

*Prepare the operating activities section—indirect method.*
*(SO 3)*

**E18–2**    Burt Reynolds Company reported net income of $195,000 for 1999. Reynolds also reported depreciation expense of $45,000, and a loss of $5,000 on the sale of equipment. The comparative balance sheet shows an increase in accounts receivable of $15,000 for the year, an $8,000 increase in accounts payable, and a decrease in prepaid expenses $4,000.

*Instructions*
Prepare the operating activities section of the statement of cash flows for 1999. Use the indirect method.

**E18-3**    The current sections of Greg Kinnear Co. balance sheets at December 31, 1998 and 1999, are presented below.

*Prepare the operating activities section—indirect method.*
*(SO 3)*

**GREG KINNEAR CO.**
**Balance Sheet (partial)**
**December 31**

|  | 1999 | 1998 |
|---|---|---|
| Current assets |  |  |
| Cash | $105,000 | $ 99,000 |
| Accounts receivable | 110,000 | 89,000 |
| Inventory | 171,000 | 186,000 |
| Prepaid expenses | 27,000 | 32,000 |
| Total current assets | $413,000 | $406,000 |
|  |  |  |
| Current liabilities |  |  |
| Accrued expenses payable | $ 15,000 | $ 5,000 |
| Accounts payable | $ 85,000 | $ 92,000 |
| Total current liabilities | $100,000 | $ 97,000 |

Kinnear's net income for 1999 was $153,000. Depreciation expense was $24,000.

**Instructions**
Prepare the net cash provided by operating activities section of Kinnear's statement of cash flows for the year ended December 31, 1999, using the indirect method.

**E18-4**    Presented below are three accounts that appear in the general ledger of Anthony Hopkins Co. during 1999:

*Prepare a partial statement of cash flows—indirect method.*
*(SO 3)*

**Equipment**

| Date |  | Debit | Credit | Balance |
|---|---|---|---|---|
| Jan. 1 | Balance |  |  | 160,000 |
| July 31 | Purchase of equipment | 70,000 |  | 230,000 |
| Sept. 2 | Cost of equipment constructed | 53,000 |  | 283,000 |
| Nov. 10 | Cost of equipment sold |  | 45,000 | 238,000 |

**Accumulated Depreciation—Equipment**

| Date |  | Debit | Credit | Balance |
|---|---|---|---|---|
| Jan. 1 | Balance |  |  | 71,000 |
| Nov. 10 | Accumulated depreciation on equipment sold | 30,000 |  | 41,000 |
| Dec. 31 | Depreciation for year |  | 24,000 | 65,000 |

**Retained Earnings**

| Date |  | Debit | Credit | Balance |
|---|---|---|---|---|
| Jan. 1 | Balance |  |  | 105,000 |
| Aug. 23 | Dividends (cash) | 14,000 |  | 91,000 |
| Dec. 31 | Net income |  | 67,000 | 158,000 |

**Instructions**
From the postings in the accounts above, indicate how the information is reported on a statement of cash flows by preparing a partial statement of cash flows using the indirect method. The loss on sale of equipment was $6,000.

**E18-5**    A comparative balance sheet for Rupert Everett Company is presented below.

*Prepare a statement of cash flows—indirect method.*
*(SO 3, 5)*

**RUPERT EVERETT COMPANY**
**Balance Sheet**
**December 31**

| Assets | 1999 | 1998 |
|---|---|---|
| Cash | $ 63,000 | $ 22,000 |
| Accounts receivable | 85,000 | 76,000 |
| Inventories | 180,000 | 189,000 |
| Land | 75,000 | 100,000 |
| Equipment | 260,000 | 200,000 |
| Accumulated depreciation | (66,000) | (42,000) |
| Total | $597,000 | $545,000 |

| Liabilities and Stockholders' Equity | | |
|---|---|---|
| Accounts payable | $ 34,000 | $ 47,000 |
| Bonds payable | 150,000 | 200,000 |
| Common stock ($1 par) | 214,000 | 164,000 |
| Retained earnings | 199,000 | 134,000 |
| Total | $597,000 | $545,000 |

Additional information:

1. Net income for 1999 was $105,000.
2. Cash dividends of $40,000 were declared and paid.
3. Bonds payable amounting to $50,000 were redeemed for cash $50,000.
4. Common stock was issued for $50,000 cash.
5. Depreciation expense was $24,000.
6. Sales for the year were $978,000.

*Instructions*

(a) Prepare a statement of cash flows for 1999 using the indirect method.
(b) Compute the following cash-basis ratios:
   (1) Current cash debt coverage ratio.
   (2) Cash return on sales ratio.
   (3) Cash debt coverage ratio.

*Classify transactions by type of activity.*
*(SO 2)*

**E18–6** An analysis of comparative balance sheets, the current year's income statement, and the general ledger accounts of Kevin Spacey Corp. uncovered the following items. Assume all items involve cash unless there is information to the contrary.

(a) Issuance of capital stock.
(b) Amortization of patent.
(c) Issuance of bonds for land.
(d) Payment of interest on notes payable.
(e) Conversion of bonds into common stock.
(f) Sale of land at a loss.
(g) Receipt of dividends on investment in stock.
(h) Purchase of land.
(i) Payment of dividends.
(j) Sale of building at book value.
(k) Exchange of land for patent.
(l) Depreciation.
(m) Redemption of bonds.
(n) Receipt of interest on notes receivable.

*Instructions*

Indicate how the above items should be classified in the statement of cash flows using the following four major classifications: operating activity (indirect method), investing activity, financing activity, and significant noncash investing and financing activity.

*Compute cash provided by operating activities—direct method.*
*(SO 4)*

**E18–7** Judi Dench Company has just completed its first year of operations on December 31, 1999. Its initial income statement showed that Judi Dench had revenues of $157,000 and operating expenses of $88,000. Accounts receivable and accounts payable at year-end were $42,000 and $33,000, respectively. Assume that accounts payable related to operating expenses. Ignore income taxes.

*Instructions*

Compute net cash provided by operating activities using the direct method.

**E18–8** The income statement for Helen Hunt Company shows cost of goods sold $355,000 and operating expenses (exclusive of depreciation) $250,000. The comparative balance sheet for the year shows that inventory increased $6,000, prepaid expenses decreased $6,000, accounts payable (merchandise suppliers) decreased $8,000, and accrued expenses payable increased $8,000.

*Compute cash payments— direct method. (SO 4)*

**Instructions**
Using the direct method, compute (a) cash payments to suppliers and (b) cash payments for operating expenses.

**E18–9** The 1999 accounting records of Helena Bonham Co. reveal the following transactions and events.

*Compute cash flow from operating activities— direct method. (SO 2, 4)*

| | | | |
|---|---|---|---|
| Payment of interest | $ 6,000 | Collection of accounts receivable | $180,000 |
| Cash sales | 48,000 | Payment of salaries and wages | 68,000 |
| Receipt of dividend revenue | 14,000 | Depreciation expense | 18,000 |
| Payment of income taxes | 15,000 | Proceeds from sale of aircraft | 812,000 |
| Net income | 38,000 | Purchase of equipment for cash | 22,000 |
| Payment of accounts payable for | | Loss on sale of aircraft | 3,000 |
| merchandise | 90,000 | Payment of dividends | 14,000 |
| Payment for land | 74,000 | Payment of operating expenses | 20,000 |

**Instructions**
Prepare the cash flows from operating activities section using the direct method. (Not all of the above items will be used.)

**E18–10** The following information is taken from the 1999 general ledger of Robert Duvall Company:

*Calculate cash flows—direct method. (SO 4)*

| | | |
|---|---|---|
| Rent | Rent expense | $ 33,000 |
| | Prepaid rent, January 1 | 5,900 |
| | Prepaid rent, December 31 | 3,000 |
| Salaries | Salaries expense | $ 54,000 |
| | Salaries payable, January 1 | 5,000 |
| | Salaries payable, December 31 | 8,000 |
| Sales | Revenue from sales | $180,000 |
| | Accounts receivable, January 1 | 12,000 |
| | Accounts receivable, December 31 | 9,000 |

**Instructions**
In each of above cases, compute the amount that should be reported in the operating activities section of the statement of cash flows applying the direct method.

**E18–11** Presented here is information for two companies in the same industry: Morgan Corporation and Cole Corporation.

*Compare two companies by using cash-based ratios. (SO 5)*

| | Morgan Corporation | Cole Corporation |
|---|---|---|
| Cash provided by operations | $200,000 | $200,000 |
| Average current liabilities | 50,000 | 100,000 |
| Average total lilibities | 200,000 | 250,000 |
| Net income | 200,000 | 200,000 |
| Sales | 400,000 | 800,000 |

**Instructions**
Using the cash-based ratios presented in this chapter, compare the (a) liquidity, (b) solvency, and (c) profitability of the two companies.

***E18–12** Information for Rupert Everett Company is presented in E18–5.

*Prepare a work sheet. (SO 6)*

**Instructions**
Use the data in E18–5 to prepare a work sheet for a statement of cash flows for 1999. Enter the reconciling items directly on the work sheet, identifying the entries alphabetically.

# PROBLEMS: SET A

......................................................................................

*Prepare the operating activities section—indirect method.*
*(SO 3)*

**P18–1A**    The income statement of Oprah Winfrey Company is shown below:

## OPRAH WINFREY COMPANY
### Income Statement
### For the Year Ended November 30, 1999

| | | |
|---|---:|---:|
| Sales | | $6,900,000 |
| Cost of goods sold | | |
|    Beginning inventory | $2,000,000 | |
|    Purchases | 4,300,000 | |
|    Goods available for sale | 6,300,000 | |
|    Ending inventory | 1,600,000 | |
|    Cost of goods sold | | 4,700,000 |
| Gross profit | | 2,200,000 |
| Operating expenses | | |
|    Selling expenses | 450,000 | |
|    Administrative expenses | 700,000 | 1,150,000 |
| Net income | | $1,050,000 |

Additional information:

1. Accounts receivable decreased $290,000 during the year.
2. Prepaid expenses increased $150,000 during the year.
3. Accounts payable to suppliers of merchandise decreased $300,000 during the year.
4. Accrued expenses payable decreased $100,000 during the year.
5. Administrative expenses include depreciation expense of $90,000.

**Instructions**
Prepare the operating activities section of the statement of cash flows for the year ended November 30, 1999, for Oprah Winfrey Company using the indirect method.

*Prepare the operating activities section—direct method.*
*(SO 4)*

**P18–2A**    Data for the Oprah Winfrey Company are presented in P18–1A.

**Instructions**
Prepare the operating activities section of the statement of cash flows using the direct method.

*Prepare the operating activities section—direct method.*
*(SO 4)*

**P18–3A**    Pierce Brosnan Company's income statement for the year ended December 31, 1999, contained the following condensed information:

| | | |
|---|---:|---:|
| Revenue from fees | | $900,000 |
| Operating expenses (excluding depreciation) | $624,000 | |
| Depreciation expense | 60,000 | |
| Loss on sale of equipment | 26,000 | 710,000 |
| Income before income taxes | | 190,000 |
| Income tax expense | | 40,000 |
| Net income | | $150,000 |

Brosnan's balance sheet contained the following comparative data at December 31:

| | 1999 | 1998 |
|---|---:|---:|
| Accounts receivable | $47,000 | $55,000 |
| Accounts payable | 41,000 | 33,000 |
| Income taxes payable | 4,000 | 9,000 |

(Accounts payable pertains to operating expenses.)

*Prepare the operating activities section—indirect method.*
*(SO 3)*

**Instructions**
Prepare the operating activities section of the statement of cash flows using the direct method.

**P18–4A**    Data for Pierce Brosnan Company are presented in P18–3A.

## Instructions

Prepare the operating activities section of the statement of cash flows for Pierce Brosnan Company using the indirect method.

**P18–5A**   The financial statements of Joan E. Robinson Company appear below:

*Prepare a statement of cash flows—indirect method.*
*(SO 3, 5)*

### JOAN E. ROBINSON COMPANY
### Comparative Balance Sheet
### December 31

| Assets | 1999 | 1998 |
|---|---|---|
| Cash | $ 29,000 | $ 13,000 |
| Accounts receivable | 28,000 | 14,000 |
| Merchandise inventory | 25,000 | 35,000 |
| Property, plant, and equipment | 60,000 | 78,000 |
| Accumulated depreciation | (20,000) | (24,000) |
| Total | $122,000 | $116,000 |

| Liabilities and Stockholders' Equity | | |
|---|---|---|
| Accounts payable | $ 29,000 | $ 23,000 |
| Income taxes payable | 5,000 | 8,000 |
| Bonds payable | 27,000 | 33,000 |
| Common stock | 18,000 | 14,000 |
| Retained earnings | 43,000 | 38,000 |
| Total | $122,000 | $116,000 |

### JOAN E. ROBINSON COMPANY
### Income Statement
### For the Year Ended December 31, 1999

| | | |
|---|---|---|
| Sales | | $220,000 |
| Cost of goods sold | | 180,000 |
| Gross profit | | 40,000 |
| Selling expenses | $14,000 | |
| Administrative expenses | 10,000 | 24,000 |
| Income from operations | | 16,000 |
| Interest expense | | 2,000 |
| Income before income taxes | | 14,000 |
| Income tax expense | | 4,000 |
| Net income | | $ 10,000 |

The following additional data were provided:

1. Dividends declared and paid were $5,000.
2. During the year equipment was sold for $8,500 cash. This equipment cost $18,000 originally and had a book value of $8,500 at the time of sale.
3. All depreciation expense is in the selling expense category.
4. All sales and purchases are on account.

## Instructions

(a) Prepare a statement of cash flows using the indirect method.
(b) Compute the following cash-basis ratios:
   (1) Current cash debt coverage ratio.
   (2) Cash return on sales ratio.
   (3) Cash debt coverage ratio.

*Prepare a statement of cash flows—direct method.*
*(SO 4, 5)*

**P18–6A**   Data for the Joan E. Robinson Company are presented in P18–5A. Further analysis reveals the following:

1. Accounts payable pertain to merchandise suppliers.
2. All operating expenses except for depreciation were paid in cash.

*Instructions*

(a) Prepare a statement of cash flows for Joan E. Robinson Company using the direct method.

(b) Compute the following cash-basis ratios:
   (1) Current cash debt coverage ratio.
   (2) Cash return on sales ratio.
   (3) Cash debt coverage ratio.

*Prepare a statement of cash flows—indirect method.*
*(SO 3)*

**P18–7A**   The financial statements of Charlie Brown Company appear below:

## CHARLIE BROWN COMPANY
### Balance Sheet
### December 31

| Assets | 1999 | 1998 |
|---|---|---|
| Cash | $ 25,000 | $ 11,000 |
| Accounts receivable | 22,000 | 33,000 |
| Merchandise inventory | 20,000 | 29,000 |
| Prepaid expenses | 15,000 | 13,000 |
| Land | 40,000 | 40,000 |
| Property, plant, and equipment | 210,000 | 225,000 |
| Less: Accumulated depreciation | (55,000) | (67,500) |
| Total | $277,000 | $283,500 |

| Liabilities and Stockholders' Equity | | |
|---|---|---|
| Accounts payable | $ 11,000 | $ 18,500 |
| Accrued expenses payable | 9,500 | 7,500 |
| Interest payable | 1,000 | 1,500 |
| Income taxes payable | 3,000 | 2,000 |
| Bonds payable | 50,000 | 80,000 |
| Common stock | 125,000 | 105,000 |
| Retained earnings | 77,500 | 69,000 |
| Total | $277,000 | $283,500 |

## CHARLIE BROWN COMPANY
### Income Statement
### For the Year Ended December 31, 1999

| | | |
|---|---|---|
| Revenues | | |
| Sales | $600,000 | |
| Gain on sale of plant assets | 2,500 | $602,500 |
| Less: Expenses | | |
| Cost of goods sold | $500,000 | |
| Operating expenses (excluding depreciation) | 60,000 | |
| Depreciation expense | 7,500 | |
| Interest expense | 5,000 | |
| Income tax expense | 9,000 | 581,500 |
| Net income | | $ 21,000 |

Additional information:

1. Plant assets were sold at a sales price of $37,500.
2. Additional equipment was purchased at a cost of $40,000.
3. Dividends of $12,500 were paid.
4. All sales and purchases were on account.
5. Bonds were redeemed at face value.
6. Additional shares of stock were issued for cash.

**Instructions**

Prepare a statement of cash flows for Charlie Brown Company for the year ended December 31, 1999, using the indirect method.

**P18–8A** Data for Charlie Brown Company is presented in P18–7A. Further analysis reveals the following:

*Prepare a statement of cash flows—direct method.*
*(SO 4)*

1. Accounts payable relates to merchandise creditors.
2. All operating expenses, except depreciation expense, were paid in cash.

**Instructions**

Prepare a statement of cash flows for Charlie Brown Company for the year ended December 31, 1999, using the direct method.

**P18–9A** Presented below is the comparative balance sheet for Karin Weigle Company as of December 31:

*Prepare a statement of cash flows—indirect method.*
*(SO 3, 5)*

### KARIN WEIGLE COMPANY
### Comparative Balance Sheet
### December 31

| Assets | 1999 | 1998 |
|---|---|---|
| Cash | $ 41,000 | $ 45,000 |
| Accounts receivable | 47,500 | 52,000 |
| Inventory | 151,450 | 142,000 |
| Prepaid expenses | 16,780 | 21,000 |
| Land | 100,000 | 130,000 |
| Equipment | 228,000 | 155,000 |
| Accumulated depreciation—equipment | (45,000) | (35,000) |
| Building | 200,000 | 200,000 |
| Accumulated depreciation—building | (60,000) | (40,000) |
| | $679,730 | $670,000 |
| | | |
| **Liabilities and Stockholders' Equity** | | |
| Accounts payable | $ 43,730 | $ 40,000 |
| Bonds payable | 250,000 | 300,000 |
| Common stock, $1 par | 200,000 | 150,000 |
| Retained earnings | 186,000 | 180,000 |
| | $679,730 | $670,000 |

Additional information:

1. Operating expenses include depreciation expense of $42,000.
2. Land was sold for cash at book value.
3. Cash dividends of $32,000 were paid.
4. Net income for 1999 was $38,000.
5. Equipment was purchased for $95,000 cash. In addition, equipment costing $22,000 with a book value of $10,000 was sold for $8,100 cash.
6. Bonds were converted at face value by issuing 50,000 shares of $1 par value common stock.
7. Net sales for 1999 totaled $420,000.

**Instructions**

(a) Prepare a statement of cash flows for the year ended December 31, 1999, using the indirect method.
(b) Compute the following cash-basis ratios for 1999:
   (1) Current cash debt coverage ratio.
   (2) Cash return on sales ratio.
   (3) Cash debt coverage ratio.

**\*P18–10A** Data for Charlie Brown Company are presented in P18–7A.

*Prepare a work sheet.*
*(SO 6)*

*Instructions*
Prepare a work sheet for a statement of cash flows for 1999. Enter the reconciling entries directly on the work sheet, identifying the entries alphabetically.

# PROBLEMS: SET B

......................................................................................

*Prepare the operating activities section—indirect method.*
*(SO 3)*

**P18–1B**   The income statement of Emma Thompson Company is shown below:

### EMMA THOMPSON COMPANY
### Income Statement
### For the Year Ended December 31, 1999

| | | |
|---|---:|---:|
| Sales | | $7,100,000 |
| Cost of goods sold | | |
|   Beginning inventory | $1,700,000 | |
|   Purchases | 5,430,000 | |
|   Goods available for sale | 7,130,000 | |
|   Ending inventory | 1,920,000 | |
|   Cost of goods sold | | 5,210,000 |
| Gross profit | | 1,890,000 |
| Operating expenses | | |
|   Selling expenses | 380,000 | |
|   Administrative expense | 525,000 | |
|   Depreciation expense | 75,000 | |
|   Amortization expense | 30,000 | 1,010,000 |
| Net income | | $ 880,000 |

Additional information:

1. Accounts receivable increased $510,000 during the year.
2. Prepaid expenses increased $170,000 during the year.
3. Accounts payable to merchandise suppliers increased $50,000 during the year.
4. Accrued expenses payable decreased $180,000 during the year.

*Instructions*
Prepare the operating activities section of the statement of cash flows for the year ended December 31, 1999, for Emma Thompson Company using the indirect method.

*Prepare the operating activities section—direct method.*
*(SO 4)*

**P18–2B**   Data for the Emma Thompson Company are presented in P18–1B.

*Instructions*
Prepare the operating activities section of the statement of cash flows using the direct method.

*Prepare the operating activities section—direct method.*
*(SO 4)*

**P18–3B**   The income statement of Kanapilei International Co. for the year ended December 31, 1999, reported the following condensed information:

| | |
|---|---:|
| Revenue from fees | $470,000 |
| Operating expenses | 280,000 |
| Income from operations | 190,000 |
| Income tax expense | 47,000 |
| Net income | $143,000 |

Kanapilei's balance sheet contained the following comparative data at December 31:

| | 1999 | 1998 |
|---|---:|---:|
| Accounts receivable | $50,000 | $40,000 |
| Accounts payable | 30,000 | 41,000 |
| Income taxes payable | 6,000 | 4,000 |

Kanapilei has no depreciable assets. (Accounts payable pertains to operating expenses.)

*Instructions*

Prepare the operating activities section of the statement of cash flows using the direct method.

**P18–4B**  Data for Kanapilei International Co. are presented in P18–3B.

*Instructions*

Prepare the operating activities section of the statement of cash flows using the indirect method.

*Prepare the operating activities section—indirect method.*
(SO 3)

**P18–5B**  The financial statements of Adam Sandler Company appear below:

*Prepare a statement of cash flows—indirect method.*
(SO 3, 5)

## ADAM SANDLER COMPANY
### Comparative Balance Sheet
### December 31

| Assets | | 1999 | | 1998 |
|---|---|---|---|---|
| Cash | | $ 26,000 | | $ 13,000 |
| Accounts receivable | | 18,000 | | 14,000 |
| Merchandise inventory | | 38,000 | | 35,000 |
| Property, plant, and equipment | $70,000 | | $78,000 | |
| Less accumulated depreciation | (30,000) | 40,000 | (24,000) | 54,000 |
| Total | | $122,000 | | $116,000 |

| Liabilities and Stockholders' Equity | | | | |
|---|---|---|---|---|
| Accounts payable | | $ 29,000 | | $ 33,000 |
| Income taxes payable | | 15,000 | | 20,000 |
| Bonds payable | | 20,000 | | 10,000 |
| Common stock | | 25,000 | | 25,000 |
| Retained earnings | | 33,000 | | 28,000 |
| Total | | $122,000 | | $116,000 |

## ADAM SANDLER COMPANY
### Income Statement
### For the Year Ended December 31, 1999

| | | |
|---|---|---|
| Sales | | $240,000 |
| Cost of goods sold | | 180,000 |
| Gross profit | | 60,000 |
| Selling expenses | $24,000 | |
| Administrative expenses | 10,000 | 34,000 |
| Income from operations | | 26,000 |
| Interest expense | | 2,000 |
| Income before income taxes | | 24,000 |
| Income tax expense | | 7,000 |
| Net income | | $ 17,000 |

The following additional data were provided:

1. Dividends of $12,000 were declared and paid.
2. During the year equipment was sold for $10,000 cash. This equipment cost $15,000 originally and had a book value of $10,000 at the time of sale.
3. All depreciation expense, $11,000, is in the selling expense category.
4. All sales and purchases are on account.
5. Additional equipment was purchased for $7,000 cash.

*Instructions*

(a) Prepare a statement of cash flows using the indirect method.
(b) Compute the following cash-basis ratios:
   (1) Current cash debt coverage ratio.
   (2) Cash return on sales ratio.
   (3) Cash debt coverage ratio.

*Prepare a statement of cash flows—direct method.*
*(SO 4, 5)*

**P18–6B** Data for the Adam Sandler Company are presented in P18–5B. Further analysis reveals the following:

1. Accounts payable pertains to merchandise creditors.
2. All operating expenses except for depreciation are paid in cash.

**Instructions**

(a) Prepare a statement of cash flows using the direct method.
(b) Compute the following cash-basis ratios:
 (1) Current cash debt coverage ratio.
 (2) Cash return on sales ratio.
 (3) Cash debt coverage ratio.

*Prepare a statement of cash flows—indirect method.*
*(SO 3)*

**P18–7B** Condensed financial data of Dan Aykroyd Company appear below:

## DAN AYKROYD COMPANY
### Comparative Balance Sheet
### December 31

| Assets | 1999 | 1998 |
| --- | --- | --- |
| Cash | $ 96,700 | $ 47,250 |
| Accounts receivable | 86,800 | 57,000 |
| Inventories | 121,900 | 102,650 |
| Investments | 84,500 | 87,000 |
| Plant assets | 250,000 | 205,000 |
| Accumulated depreciation | (49,500) | (40,000) |
| | $590,400 | $458,900 |
| **Liabilities and Stockholders' Equity** | | |
| Accounts payable | $ 52,700 | $ 48,280 |
| Accrued expenses payable | 12,100 | 18,830 |
| Bonds payable | 100,000 | 70,000 |
| Common stock | 250,000 | 200,000 |
| Retained earnings | 175,600 | 121,790 |
| | $590,400 | $458,900 |

## DAN AYKROYD COMPANY
### Income Statement Data
### For the Year Ended December 31, 1999

| | | |
| --- | --- | --- |
| Sales | | $297,500 |
| Gain on sale of plant assets | | 8,750 |
| | | 306,250 |
| Less: | | |
| Cost of goods sold | $99,460 | |
| Operating expenses (excluding depreciation expense) | 14,670 | |
| Depreciation expense | 49,700 | |
| Income taxes | 7,270 | |
| Interest expense | 2,940 | 174,040 |
| Net income | | $132,210 |

Additional information:

1. New plant assets costing $92,000 were purchased for cash during the year.
2. Investments were sold at cost.
3. Plant assets costing $47,000 were sold for $15,550, resulting in a gain of $8,750.
4. A cash dividend of $78,400 was declared and paid during the year.

*Instructions*
Prepare a statement of cash flows using the indirect method.

**P18–8B**   Data for Dan Aykroyd Company are presented in P18–7B. Further analysis reveals that accounts payable pertains to merchandise creditors.

*Prepare a statement of cash flows—direct method.*
*(SO 4)*

*Instructions*
Prepare a statement of cash flows for Dan Aykroyd Company using the direct method.

**P18–9B**   Presented below is the comparative balance sheet for Andy Garcia Company at December 31:

*Prepare a statement of cash flows—indirect method.*
*(SO 3, 5)*

### ANDY GARCIA COMPANY
### Comparative Balance Sheet
### December 31

| Assets | 1999 | 1998 |
|---|---|---|
| Cash | $ 40,000 | $ 57,000 |
| Accounts receivable | 77,000 | 64,000 |
| Inventory | 132,000 | 140,000 |
| Prepaid expenses | 12,140 | 16,540 |
| Land | 125,000 | 150,000 |
| Equipment | 200,000 | 175,000 |
| Accumulated depreciation—equipment | (60,000) | (42,000) |
| Building | 250,000 | 250,000 |
| Accumulated depreciation—building | (75,000) | (50,000) |
| | $701,140 | $760,540 |

| Liabilities and Stockholders' Equity | 1999 | 1998 |
|---|---|---|
| Accounts payable | $ 33,000 | $ 45,000 |
| Bonds payable | 235,000 | 265,000 |
| Common stock, $1 par | 280,000 | 250,000 |
| Retained earnings | 153,140 | 200,540 |
| | $701,140 | $760,540 |

Additional information:

1. Operating expenses include depreciation expense of $70,000 and charges from prepaid expenses of $4,400.
2. Land was sold for cash at cost.
3. Cash dividends of $74,290 were paid.
4. Net income for 1999 was $26,890.
5. Equipment was purchased for $65,000 cash. In addition, equipment costing $40,000 with a book value of $13,000 was sold for $14,000 cash.
6. Bonds were converted at face value by issuing 30,000 shares of $1 par value common stock.
7. Net sales in 1999 were $367,000.

*Instructions*

(a) Prepare a statement of cash flows for 1999 using the indirect method.
(b) Compute the following cash-basis ratios for 1999:
  (1) Current cash debt coverage ratio.
  (2) Cash return on sales ratio.
  (3) Cash debt coverage ratio.

**\*P18–10B**   Data for Dan Aykroyd Company are presented in P18–7B.

*Prepare a work sheet*
*(SO 6)*

*Instructions*
Prepare a work sheet for a statement of cash flows. Enter the reconciling items directly in the work sheet columns, identifying the debit and credit amounts alphabetically.

## BROADENING YOUR PERSPECTIVE

# FINANCIAL REPORTING AND ANALYSIS

### FINANCIAL REPORTING PROBLEM: Kellogg Company

**BYP18–1**   Refer to the financial statements of Kellogg Company, presented in Appendix A and answer the following questions:

(a) What was the amount of net cash provided by operating activities for the year 1997? For the year 1996?

(b) What was the amount of increase or decrease in cash and cash equivalents for the year 1997? For the year 1996?

(c) Which method of computing net cash provided by operating activities does Kellogg use?

(d) From your analysis of the 1997 statement of cash flows, did the change in accounts receivable require or provide cash? Did the change in inventories require or provide cash? Did the change in accounts payable require or provide cash?

(e) What was the net outflow or inflow of cash from investing activities for 1997?

(f) What was the amount of interest paid in 1997? What was the amount of income taxes paid in 1997?

### COMPARATIVE ANALYSIS PROBLEM: Kellogg Company vs. General Mills

**BYP18–2**   Kellogg's financial statements are presented in Appendix A; General Mills's financial statements are presented in Appendix B.

*Instructions*

(a) Based on the information contained in these financial statements, compute the following 1997 ratios for each company:
   (1) Current cash debt coverage ratio
   (2) Cash return on sales ratio
   (3) Cash debt coverage ratio

(b) What conclusions concerning the management of cash can be drawn from these data?

### RESEARCH ASSIGNMENT

**BYP18–3**   The March 25, 1996, issue of *Barron's* includes an article by Harry B. Ernst and Jeffrey D. Fotta, entitled "Weary Bull."

*Instructions*
Read the article and answer the following questions:

(a) The article describes a cash flow-based model used by investors. Identify the model and briefly describe its purpose.

(b) How does the model classify a firm's cash flows?

(c) Identify one way in which the cash flow classifications described in the article differ from those under GAAP.

(d) How can the model be used to predict stock prices?

### INTERPRETING FINANCIAL STATEMENTS: Vermont Teddy Bear Co.

**BYP18–4**   Founded in the early 1980s, the Vermont Teddy Bear Co. designs and manufactures American-made teddy bears and markets them primarily as gifts called Bear-Grams or Teddy Bear-Grams. Bear-Grams are personalized teddy bears delivered directly to the recipient for special occasions such as birthdays and anniversaries. The Shelburne, Vermont, company's primary markets are New York, Boston, and Chicago. Sales have jumped dramatically in recent years, exceeding 50% increases in several consecutive years prior to 1994. Such dramatic growth has significant implications for cash flows. Provided below are the company's cash flow statements for 1993 and 1994.

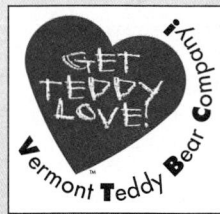

| VERMONT TEDDY BEAR CO.<br>Comparative Statement of Cash Flows<br>For the Years Ended December 31 | | |
| --- | --- | --- |
| | **1994** | **1993** |
| Cash flows from operating activities | | |
| Net income | $ 17,523 | $ 838,955 |
| Adjustments to reconcile net income to net cash provided by operating activities | | |
| Deferred income taxes | (69,524) | (146,590) |
| Depreciation and amortization | 316,416 | 181,348 |
| Changes in assets and liabilities | | |
| Accounts receivable, trade | (38,267) | (25,947) |
| Inventories | (1,599,014) | (1,289,293) |
| Prepaid and other current assets | (444,794) | (113,205) |
| Deposit and other assets | (24,240) | (83,044) |
| Accounts payable | 2,017,059 | (284,567) |
| Accrued expenses | 61,321 | 170,755 |
| Accrued interest payable, debentures | — | (58,219) |
| Other | — | (8,960) |
| Income taxes payable | — | 117,810 |
| Net cash provided by (used for) operating activities | 236,480 | (700,957) |
| Net cash used for investing activities | (2,102,892) | (4,422,953) |
| Net cash (used for) provided by financing activities | (315,353) | 9,685,435 |
| Net change in cash and cash equivalents | $(2,181,765) | $ 4,561,525 |
| Other information: | | |
| | **1994** | **1993** |
| Current liabilities | $ 4,055,465 | $ 1,995,600 |
| Total liabilities | 4,620,085 | 2,184,386 |
| Net sales | 20,560,566 | 17,025,856 |

**Instructions**

(a) Note that net income in 1994 was only $17,523 compared to 1993 income of $838,955, but cash flow from operations was $236,480 in 1994 and a negative $700,957 in 1993. Explain the causes of this apparent paradox.

(b) Evaluate Vermont Teddy Bear's liquidity, solvency, and profitability for 1994 using cash-based ratios.

## REAL-WORLD FOCUS: Praxair Incorporated

**BYP18–5  Praxair** was founded in 1907 as Linde-Air Products Company and was a pioneer in separating oxygen from air. It was purchased and run as a division of Union Carbide. In 1992 Praxair became an independent public company. Today, the company is one of the top three largest suppliers of industrial gases worldwide. Praxair has operations in all regions of the world, with half of its sales occurring outside of the United States.

The following management discussion was included in a recent annual report:

## PRAXAIR INCORPORATED
## Management Discussion and Analysis

**Liquidity, Capital Resources and Other Financial Data:** This year, Praxair changed its presentation of the Statement of Cash Flows to the direct method to report major classes of cash receipts and payments from operations. Praxair believes the direct method more clearly presents its operating cash flows. Prior years' cash flow information has been reclassified to conform to the current year presentation.

*Instructions*

(a) What method has Praxair changed from?
(b) What will the newly prepared cash flow statement show that the former one did not?
(c) Will the cash flows from investing and financing appear any differently under the new method of preparation than they did under the old method?

# CRITICAL THINKING

## GROUP DECISION CASE

**BYP18–6**   Greg Rhoda and Debra Sondgeroth are examining the following statement of cash flows for K.K. Bean Trading Company for the year ended January 31, 1998.

### K.K. BEAN TRADING COMPANY
### Statement of Cash Flows
### For the Year Ended January 31, 1998

| | |
|---|---:|
| Sources of cash | |
| From sales of merchandise | $370,000 |
| From sale of capital stock | 420,000 |
| From sale of investment (purchased below) | 80,000 |
| From depreciation | 55,000 |
| From issuance of note for truck | 20,000 |
| From interest on investments | 6,000 |
| Total sources of cash | 951,000 |
| Uses of cash | |
| For purchase of fixtures and equipment | 340,000 |
| For merchandise purchased for resale (all sold) | 258,000 |
| For operating expenses (including depreciation) | 160,000 |
| For purchase of investment | 75,000 |
| For purchase of truck by issuance of note | 20,000 |
| For purchase of treasury stock | 10,000 |
| For interest on note payable | 3,000 |
| Total uses of cash | 866,000 |
| Net increase in cash | $ 85,000 |

Greg claims that K.K. Bean's statement of cash flows is an excellent portrayal of a superb first year with cash increasing $85,000. Debra replies that it was not a superb first year—but rather, that the year was an operating failure, that the statement was incorrectly presented, and that $85,000 is not the actual increase in cash. The cash balance at the beginning of the year was $140,000.

*Instructions*

With the class divided into groups, answer the following:

(a) With whom do you agree, Greg or Debra? Explain your position.
(b) Using the data provided, prepare a statement of cash flows in proper form using the indirect method. The only noncash items in the income statement are depreciation and the gain from the sale of the investment.

## COMMUNICATION ACTIVITY

**BYP18–7** Arnold Byte, the owner-president of Computer Services Company, is unfamiliar with the statement of cash flows which you, as his accountant, prepared. He asks for further explanation.

*Instructions*

Write him a brief memo explaining the form and content of the statement of cash flows as shown in Illustration 18-18 on page 770.

## ETHICS CASE

**BYP18–8** Puebla Corporation is a medium-sized wholesaler of automotive parts. It has 10 stockholders, who have been paid a total of $1 million in cash dividends for 8 consecutive years. The policy of the Board of Directors requires that in order for this dividend to be declared, net cash provided by operating activities as reported in Puebla's current year's statement of cash flows must be in excess of $1 million. President and CEO Phil Monat's job is secure so long as he produces annual operating cash flows to support the usual dividend.

At the end of the current year, controller Rick Rodgers presents president Monat with some disappointing news—the net cash provided by operating activities is calculated by the indirect method to be only $970,000. The president says to Rick, "We must get that amount above $1 million. Isn't there some way to increase operating cash flow by another $30,000?" Rick answers, "These figures were prepared by my assistant. I'll go back to my office and see what I can do." The president replies, "I know you won't let me down, Rick."

Upon close scrutiny of the statement of cash flows, Rick concludes that he can get the operating cash flows above $1 million by reclassifying a $60,000, 2-year note payable listed in the financing activities section as "Proceeds from bank loan—$60,000." He will report the note instead as "Increase in payables—$60,000" and treat it as an adjustment of net income in the operating activities section. He returns to the president saying, "You can tell the Board to declare their usual dividend. Our net cash flow provided by operating activities is $1,030,000." "Good man, Rick! I knew I could count on you," exults the president.

*Instructions*

(a) Who are the stakeholders in this situation?
(b) Was there anything unethical about the president's actions? Was there anything unethical about the controller's actions?
(c) Are the Board members or anyone else likely to discover the misclassification?

# SURFING THE NET

**BYP18–9** Bonds, similar to stocks, can be purchased by investors in an initial public offering or through a secondary market. Secondary markets can be reached via the Internet and provide users with investment information. Bonds Online is one site that provides a bond-specific glossary of terms.

**Address:** http://www.bondsonline.com

**Steps:**
1. From the Bonds Online homepage, choose **Bond Professor.**
2. Choose **Glossary.**

*Instructions*
Using the glossary, find the definition of:

    (a) discount rate.
    (b) capital market.
    (c) rating.

---

*Answers to Self-Study Questions*

1. c    2. b    3. a    4. c    5. d    6. b    7. c    8. d    9. b    10. c    11. d
12. a    13. b

---

*Answer to Kellogg Review It Question 4, p. 771*

4. Kellogg uses the indirect method of computing net cash provided by operating activities. The largest single item of cash flow for Kellogg in 1997 is "Issuance of long-term debt, $1 billion."

**Remember to go back to the Navigator box on the chapter-opening page and check off your completed work.**

## CONCEPTS FOR REVIEW

**Before studying this chapter, you should know or, if necessary, review:**

a. The contents and classification of a corporate balance sheet.
   (Ch. 4, pp. 157–162)

b. The contents and classification of a corporate income statement.
   (Ch. 5, pp. 200–202, 207–210)

c. Who are the various users of financial statement information.
   (Ch. 1, pp. 3–5)

d. How to compute earnings per share (EPS). (Ch. 15, p. 653–55)

e. How the liquidity of a company is determined. (Ch. 4, p. 160)

## FEATURE STORY

# Just Fooling Around?

The information superhighway added a new lane recently when two brothers, Tom and David Gardner, created an online investor service called the Motley Fool. The name comes from Shakespeare's *As You Like It*. The fool in Shakespeare's plays was the only one who could speak unpleasant truths to kings and queens without being killed. Tom and David view themselves as 20th-century "fools," revealing the "truths" of Wall Street to the small investor, who they feel has been taken advantage of by Wall Street insiders. They provide a bulletin board service where America Online subscribers can exchange information and insights about companies that may be of interest to investors.

One company, Iomega, has captured the interest of Motley Fool subscribers more than all others. Iomega makes a new kind of computer disk drive called a Zip drive. In less than one year, Iomega's stock price soared by a multiple of 16; that is, a $1,000 investment was suddenly worth $16,000! Many people suggest that this tremendous run-up in price (one of the highest increases experienced by any U.S. company during that period) was caused by the attention the stock received on the Motley Fool bulletin board. Supporters of the Motley Fool say that this is an example of how the Internet can be used by small investors to make the kind of returns that the "big guys" make. Participants share any information they can find about the company and its product: Are Zip drive users happy with the product? How quickly are Zip drives moving off store shelves? How full is the employee parking lot at Iomega on Sundays?

Critics, however, contend that the bulletin board is merely a high-tech rumor mill that has built a speculative house of cards. One potentially troubling aspect of the bulletin board is that participants on the board don't have to give their identities. Consequently, there is little to stop people from putting misinformation on the board to influence the price in the direction they desire.

As information services such as Motley Fool proliferate, gathering information will become easier, and evaluating it will become the harder task.

*On the World Wide Web:*
http://fool.yahoo.com
http://www.iomega.com

# CHAPTER 19

# FINANCIAL STATEMENT ANALYSIS

**THE NAVIGATOR** ✔

- Understand *Concepts for Review* ☐
- Read *Feature Story* ☐
- Scan *Study Objectives* ☐
- Read *Preview* ☐
- Read text and answer *Before You Go On*
  p. 827 ☐  p. 844 ☐  p. 845 ☐
- Work *Demonstration Problems* ☐
- Review *Summary of Study Objectives* ☐
- Answer *Self-Study Questions* ☐
- Complete assignments ☐

## STUDY OBJECTIVES

**After studying this chapter, you should be able to:**

1. *Discuss the need for comparative analysis.*
2. *Identify the tools of financial statement analysis.*
3. *Explain and apply horizontal analysis.*
4. *Describe and apply vertical analysis.*
5. *Identify and compute ratios and describe their purpose and use in analyzing a firm's liquidity, profitability, and solvency.*
6. *Recognize the limitations of financial statement analysis.*

THE NAVIGATOR

*I*f you are thinking of purchasing Iomega Corporation stock, or the stock of any company, how can you determine the worth of the stock? How can you determine the company's financial soundness or its profitability? How does Iomega compare financially with other companies in the high-tech industry of computer disk-drive manufacturers? To answer these types of questions, it is helpful for you to understand how to analyze financial statement information.

Financial statement analysis, the topic of this chapter, enhances the usefulness of published financial statements in making decisions about a company. The content and organization of this chapter are shown below.

THE NAVIGATOR

# BASICS OF FINANCIAL STATEMENT ANALYSIS

Analyzing financial statements involves evaluating three characteristics of a company: its liquidity, its profitability, and its solvency. For example, a **short-term creditor**, such as a bank, is primarily interested in the ability of the borrower to pay obligations when they come due. The liquidity of the borrower in such a case is extremely important in evaluating the safety of a loan. A **long-term creditor**, such as a bondholder, however, looks to indicators such as profitability and solvency that indicate the firm's ability to survive over a long period of time. Long-term creditors consider such measures as the amount of debt in the company's capital structure and the ability to meet interest payments. Similarly, **stockholders** are interested in the profitability and solvency of the enterprise when they assess the likelihood of dividends and the growth potential of the stock.

## Need for Comparative Analysis

Every item reported in a financial statement has significance. For example, when Iomega Corporation reports cash of $108 million on its balance sheet, we know the company had that amount of cash on the balance sheet date. However, we do not know whether the amount represents an increase over prior years or whether the amount is adequate in relation to the company's need for cash. To obtain this information, it is necessary to compare the amount of cash with other financial statement data.

Comparisons can be made on a number of different bases—three are illustrated in this chapter:

1. **Intracompany basis.** This basis compares an item or financial relationship **within a company** in the current year with the same item or relationship in one or more prior years. For example, a comparison of Iomega's cash balance at the end of the current year with last year's balance will show the amount of the increase or decrease. Likewise, Iomega can compare the percentage of cash to current assets at the end of the current year with the percentage in one or more prior years. Intracompany comparisons are useful in detecting changes in financial relationships and significant trends.
2. **Industry averages.** This basis compares an item or financial relationship of a company with **industry averages** (or **norms**) published by financial ratings organizations such as Dun & Bradstreet, Moody's, and Standard & Poor's. For example, Iomega's net income can be compared with the average net income of all companies in the computer hard-drive and storage solutions industry. Comparisons with industry averages provide information as to a company's relative performance within the industry.
3. **Intercompany basis.** This basis compares an item or financial relationship of one company with the same item or relationship in **one or more competing companies**. The comparisons are made on the basis of the published financial statements of the individual companies. For example, Iomega's total sales for the year can be compared with the total sales of its major competitors such as IBM and Nomai. Intercompany comparisons are useful in determining a company's competitive position.

## Tools of Financial Statement Analysis

Various tools are used to evaluate the significance of financial statement data. Three commonly used tools are these:

**Horizontal analysis** is a technique for evaluating a series of financial statement data over a period of time.

**Vertical analysis** is a technique for evaluating financial statement data that expresses each item in a financial statement in terms of a percent of a base amount.

**Ratio analysis** expresses the relationship among selected items of financial statement data.

Horizontal analysis is used primarily in intracompany comparisons. Two features in published financial statements facilitate this type of comparison: First, each of the basic financial statements is presented on a comparative basis for a minimum of two years. Second, a summary of selected financial data is presented for a series of 5 to 10 years or more. Vertical analysis is used in both intra- and intercompany comparisons. Ratio analysis is used in all three types of compar-

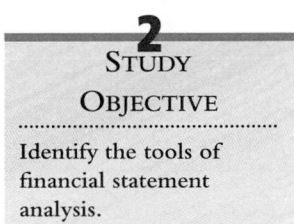

isons. In the following sections, we will explain and illustrate each of the three types of analysis.

# HORIZONTAL ANALYSIS

Horizontal analysis, also called **trend analysis**, is a technique for evaluating a series of financial statement data over a period of time. Its purpose is to determine the increase or decrease that has taken place, expressed as either an amount or a percentage. For example, the recent net sales figures of Sears, Roebuck and Co. are as follows (yes, that's $41 **billion** 296 million in 1997):

**ILLUSTRATION 19-1**

*Sears, Roebuck's net sales*

| SEARS, ROEBUCK AND CO. Net Sales (in millions) | | | | |
| --- | --- | --- | --- | --- |
| **1997** | **1996** | **1995** | **1994** | **1993** |
| $41,296 | $38,064 | $34,835 | $33,110 | $30,518 |

If we assume that 1993 is the base year, we can measure all percentage increases or decreases from this base period amount as follows:

**ILLUSTRATION 19-2**

*Formula for horizontal analysis of changes since base period*

$$\text{Change since base period} = \frac{\text{Current year amount} - \text{Base year amount}}{\text{Base year amount}}$$

For example, we can determine that net sales for Sears, Roebuck increased approximately 8.5% [($33,110 − $30,518) ÷ $30,518] from 1993 to 1994. Similarly, we can determine that net sales increased over 35.3% [($41,296 − $30,518) ÷ $30,518] from 1993 to 1997.

Alternatively, we can express current year sales as a percentage of the base period by dividing the current year amount by the base year amount, as shown below:

**ILLUSTRATION 19-3**

*Formula for horizontal analysis of current year in relation to base year*

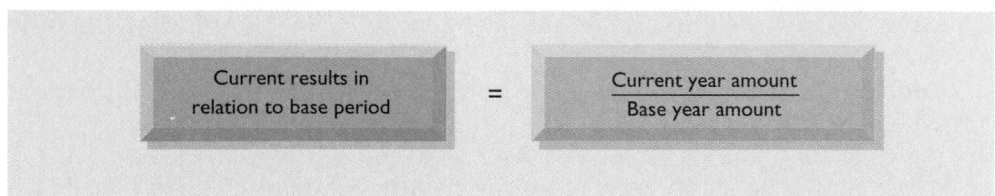

$$\text{Current results in relation to base period} = \frac{\text{Current year amount}}{\text{Base year amount}}$$

Illustration 19-4 presents this analysis for Sears for a 5-year period using 1993 as the base period.

| | SEARS, ROEBUCK AND CO.<br>Net Sales (in millions)<br>in relation to base period 1993 | | | |
|---|---|---|---|---|
| 1997 | 1996 | 1995 | 1994 | 1993 |
| $41,296 | $38,064 | $34,835 | $33,110 | $30,518 |
| 135% | 125% | 114% | 108% | 100% |

## Balance Sheet

To further illustrate horizontal analysis, we will use the financial statements of Quality Department Store Inc., a downtown full-line department store in a southeastern city of 55,000 population. Its 2-year condensed balance sheets for 1997 and 1996 showing dollar and percentage changes are presented in Illustration 19-5.

**ILLUSTRATION 19-5**

*Horizontal analysis of a balance sheet*

### QUALITY DEPARTMENT STORE INC.
### Condensed Balance Sheet
### December 31

| | 1997 | 1996 | Increase or (Decrease)<br>during 1997 | |
|---|---|---|---|---|
| | | | Amount | Percent |
| **Assets** | | | | |
| Current assets | $1,020,000 | $ 945,000 | $ 75,000 | 7.9% |
| Plant assets (net) | 800,000 | 632,500 | 167,500 | 26.5% |
| Intangible assets | 15,000 | 17,500 | (2,500) | (14.3%) |
| Total assets | $1,835,000 | $1,595,000 | $240,000 | 15.0% |
| **Liabilities** | | | | |
| Current liabilities | $ 344,500 | $ 303,000 | $ 41,500 | 13.7% |
| Long-term liabilities | 487,500 | 497,000 | (9,500) | (1.9%) |
| Total liabilities | 832,000 | 800,000 | 32,000 | 4.0% |
| **Stockholders' Equity** | | | | |
| Common stock, $1 par | 275,400 | 270,000 | 5,400 | 2.0% |
| Retained earnings | 727,600 | 525,000 | 202,600 | 38.6% |
| Total stockholders' equity | 1,003,000 | 795,000 | 208,000 | 26.2% |
| Total liabilities and<br>stockholders' equity | $1,835,000 | $1,595,000 | $240,000 | 15.0% |

**HELPFUL HINT**
It is difficult to comprehend the significance of a change when only the dollar amount of change is examined. When the change is expressed in percentage form, it is easier to grasp the true magnitude of the change.

The comparative balance sheet in Illustration 19-5 shows that a number of significant changes have occurred in Quality Department Store's financial structure from 1996 to 1997. In the asset section, plant assets (net) increased $167,500, or 26.5%. In the liabilities section, current liabilities increased $41,500, or 13.7%. In the stockholders' equity section, we find that retained earnings increased $202,600, or 38.6%. This suggests that the company expanded its asset base during 1997 and financed this expansion primarily by retaining income in the business rather than assuming additional long-term debt.

## Income Statement

Presented in Illustration 19-6 is a 2-year comparative income statement of Quality Department Store Inc. for the years 1997 and 1996, in a condensed format.

**ILLUSTRATION 19-6**

*Horizontal analysis of an income statement*

| QUALITY DEPARTMENT STORE INC. Condensed Income Statement For the Years Ended December 31 | | | Increase or (Decrease) during 1997 | |
|---|---|---|---|---|
| | 1997 | 1996 | Amount | Percent |
| Sales | $2,195,000 | $1,960,000 | $235,000 | 12.0% |
| Sales returns and allowances | 98,000 | 123,000 | (25,000) | (20.3%) |
| Net sales | 2,097,000 | 1,837,000 | 260,000 | 14.2% |
| Cost of goods sold | 1,281,000 | 1,140,000 | 141,000 | 12.4% |
| Gross profit | 816,000 | 697,000 | 119,000 | 17.1% |
| Selling expenses | 253,000 | 211,500 | 41,500 | 19.6% |
| Administrative expenses | 104,000 | 108,500 | (4,500) | (4.1%) |
| Total operating expenses | 357,000 | 320,000 | 37,000 | 11.6% |
| Income from operations | 459,000 | 377,000 | 82,000 | 21.8% |
| Other revenues and gains | | | | |
| Interest and dividends | 9,000 | 11,000 | (2,000) | (18.2%) |
| Other expenses and losses | | | | |
| Interest expense | 36,000 | 40,500 | (4,500) | (11.1%) |
| Income before income taxes | 432,000 | 347,500 | 84,500 | 24.3% |
| Income tax expense | 168,200 | 139,000 | 29,200 | 21.0% |
| Net income | $ 263,800 | $ 208,500 | $ 55,300 | 26.5% |

**HELPFUL HINT**

Note that while the amount column is additive (the total is $55,300), the percentage column is not additive (26.5% is not the total). A separate percentage has been calculated for each item.

Horizontal analysis of the income statements shows the following changes:

1. Net sales increased $260,000, or 14.2% ($260,000 ÷ $1,837,000).
2. Cost of goods sold increased $141,000, or 12.4% ($141,000 ÷ $1,140,000).
3. Total operating expenses increased $37,000, or 11.6% ($37,000 ÷ $320,000).

Overall, gross profit and net income were up substantially. Gross profit, for example, increased 17.1% and net income 26.5%. It appears, therefore, that Quality's profit trend is favorable.

## Retained Earnings Statement

Quality Department Store's comparative retained earnings statement for the years 1997 and 1996 is presented in Illustration 19-7. Analyzed horizontally, net income increased $55,300, or 26.5%, whereas dividends on the common stock increased only $1,200, or 2%. Ending retained earnings, as shown in the horizontal analysis of the balance sheet, increased 38.6%. As indicated earlier, Quality Department Store Inc. retained a significant portion of its net income to finance expenditures for additional plant facilities.

ILLUSTRATION 19-7

*Horizontal analysis of a
retained earnings statement*

**QUALITY DEPARTMENT STORE INC.**
**Retained Earnings Statement**
**For the Years Ended December 31**

| | 1997 | 1996 | Increase or (Decrease) during 1997 Amount | Percent |
|---|---|---|---|---|
| Retained earnings, Jan. 1 | $525,000 | $376,500 | $148,500 | 39.4% |
| Add: Net income | 263,800 | 208,500 | 55,300 | 26.5% |
| | 788,800 | 585,000 | 203,800 | |
| Deduct: Dividends | 61,200 | 60,000 | 1,200 | 2.0% |
| Retained earnings, Dec. 31 | $727,600 | $525,000 | $202,600 | 38.6% |

The measurement of changes from period to period in terms of percentages is relatively straightforward and is quite useful. However, complications can result in making the computations. For example, if an item has no value in a base year or preceding year and a value in the next year, no percentage change can be computed. Similarly, if a negative amount appears in the base or preceding period and a positive amount exists the following year, or vice versa, no percentage change can be computed.

# VERTICAL ANALYSIS

Vertical analysis, sometimes referred to as **common size analysis**, is a technique for evaluating financial statement data that expresses each item within a financial statement in terms of a percent of a base amount. For example, on a balance sheet we might say that current assets are 22% of total assets (total assets being the base amount). Or on an income statement, we might say that selling expenses are 16% of net sales (net sales being the base amount).

## Balance Sheet

Presented in Illustration 19-8 on page 826 is the comparative balance sheet of Quality Department Store Inc. for 1997 and 1996, analyzed vertically. The base for the asset items is **total assets**, and the base for the liability and stockholders' equity items is **total liabilities and stockholders' equity**.

In addition to showing the relative size of each category on the balance sheet, vertical analysis may show the **percentage change** in the individual asset, liability, and stockholders' equity items. In this case, even though current assets increased $75,000 from 1996 to 1997, they decreased from 59.2% to 55.6% of total assets. Plant assets (net) have increased from 39.7% to 43.6% of total assets, and retained earnings have increased from 32.9% to 39.7% of total liabilities and stockholders' equity. These results reinforce the earlier observations that Quality is choosing to finance its growth through retention of earnings rather than through the issuance of additional debt.

## Income Statement

Vertical analysis of the comparative income statements of Quality, shown in Illustration 19-9, reveals that cost of goods sold as a percentage of net sales de-

**ILLUSTRATION 19-8**

*Vertical analysis of a balance sheet*

## QUALITY DEPARTMENT STORE INC.
## Condensed Balance Sheet
### December 31

| | 1997 Amount | 1997 Percent | 1996 Amount | 1996 Percent |
|---|---|---|---|---|
| **Assets** | | | | |
| Current assets | $1,020,000 | 55.6% | $ 945,000 | 59.2% |
| Plant assets (net) | 800,000 | 43.6% | 632,500 | 39.7% |
| Intangible assets | 15,000 | .8% | 17,500 | 1.1% |
| Total assets | $1,835,000 | 100.0% | $1,595,000 | 100.0% |
| **Liabilities** | | | | |
| Current liabilities | $ 344,500 | 18.8% | $ 303,000 | 19.0% |
| Long-term liabilities | 487,500 | 26.5% | 497,000 | 31.2% |
| Total liabilities | 832,000 | 45.3% | 800,000 | 50.2% |
| **Stockholders' Equity** | | | | |
| Common stock, $1 par | 275,400 | 15.0% | 270,000 | 16.9% |
| Retained earnings | 727,600 | 39.7% | 525,000 | 32.9% |
| Total stockholders' equity | 1,003,000 | 54.7% | 795,000 | 49.8% |
| Total liabilities and stockholders' equity | $1,835,000 | 100.0% | $1,595,000 | 100.0% |

**HELPFUL HINT**
The formula for calculating these balance sheet percentages is:

$$\frac{\text{Each item on B/S}}{\text{Total assets}} = \%$$

clined 1% (62.1% vs. 61.1%) and total operating expenses declined 0.4% (17.4% vs. 17.0%). As a result, it is not surprising to see net income as a percent of net sales increase from 11.4% to 12.6%. As indicated from the horizontal analysis, Quality appears to be a profitable enterprise that is becoming even more successful.

**ILLUSTRATION 19-9**

*Vertical analysis of an income statement*

## QUALITY DEPARTMENT STORE INC.
## Condensed Income Statement
### For the Years Ended December 31

| | 1997 Amount | 1997 Percent | 1996 Amount | 1996 Percent |
|---|---|---|---|---|
| Sales | $2,195,000 | 104.7% | $1,960,000 | 106.7% |
| Sales returns and allowances | 98,000 | 4.7% | 123,000 | 6.7% |
| Net sales | 2,097,000 | 100.0% | 1,837,000 | 100.0% |
| Cost of goods sold | 1,281,000 | 61.1% | 1,140,000 | 62.1% |
| Gross profit | 816,000 | 38.9% | 697,000 | 37.9% |
| Selling expenses | 253,000 | 12.0% | 211,500 | 11.5% |
| Administrative expenses | 104,000 | 5.0% | 108,500 | 5.9% |
| Total operating expenses | 357,000 | 17.0% | 320,000 | 17.4% |
| Income from operations | 459,000 | 21.9% | 377,000 | 20.5% |
| Other revenues and gains | | | | |
| Interest and dividends | 9,000 | 0.4% | 11,000 | 0.6% |
| Other expenses and losses | | | | |
| Interest expense | 36,000 | 1.7% | 40,500 | 2.2% |
| Income before income taxes | 432,000 | 20.6% | 347,500 | 18.9% |
| Income tax expense | 168,200 | 8.0% | 139,000 | 7.5% |
| Net income | $ 263,800 | 12.6% | $ 208,500 | 11.4% |

**HELPFUL HINT**
The formula for calculating these income statement percentages is:

$$\frac{\text{Each item on I/S}}{\text{Net sales}} = \%$$

An associated benefit of vertical analysis is that it enables you to compare companies of different sizes. For example, Quality's main competitor is a Sears store in a nearby town. Using vertical analysis, the condensed income statements of the small local retail enterprise, Quality Department Store Inc., can be more meaningfully compared with the 1997 income statement of the giant international retailer, Sears, Roebuck and Co., as shown in Illustration 19-10.

**ILLUSTRATION 19-10**

*Intercompany income statement comparison*

| Condensed Income Statements (in thousands) | | | | |
|---|---|---|---|---|
| | Quality Department Store Inc. | | Sears, Roebuck and Co.[1] | |
| | Dollars | Percent | Dollars | Percent |
| Net sales | $2,097 | 100.0% | $41,296,000 | 100.0% |
| Cost of goods sold | 1,281 | 61.1% | 26,769,000 | 64.8% |
| Gross profit | 816 | 38.9% | 14,527,000 | 35.2% |
| Selling and administrative expenses | 357 | 17.0% | 10,649,000 | 25.8% |
| Income from operations | 459 | 21.9% | 3,878,000 | 9.4% |
| Other expenses and revenues (including income taxes) | 195 | 9.3% | 2,690,000 | 6.5% |
| Net income | $ 264 | 12.6% | $ 1,188,000 | 2.9% |

Although Sears' net sales are 19,693 times greater than the net sales of relatively tiny Quality Department Store, vertical analysis eliminates this difference in size. The percentages show that Quality's and Sears' gross profit rates were somewhat comparable at 38.9% and 35.2%, although the percentages related to income from operations were significantly different at 21.9% and 9.4%. This disparity can be attributed to Quality's selling and administrative expense percentage (17%) which is much lower than Sears' (25.8%). Although Sears earned net income more than 4,500 times larger than Quality's, Sears' net income as a **percent of each sales dollar** (2.9%) is only 23% of Quality's (12.6%).

# BEFORE YOU GO ON . . .

## Review It

1. What are the different tools that might be used to compare financial information?
2. What is horizontal analysis?
3. What is vertical analysis?
4. Identify the specific sections in Kellogg's 1997 Annual Report where horizontal and vertical analysis of financial data is presented. The answer to this question is provided on page 866.

## Do It

Summary financial information for Rosepatch Company is as follows:

| | December 31, 1999 | December 31, 1998 |
|---|---|---|
| Current assets | $234,000 | $180,000 |
| Plant assets (net) | 756,000 | 420,000 |
| Total assets | $990,000 | $600,000 |

---

[1]Sears, Roebuck and Co., *1997 Annual Report* (Hoffman Estates, Illinois).

Compute the amount and percentage changes in 1999 using horizontal analysis, assuming 1998 is the base year.

*Reasoning:* Since 1998 is the base year, the percentage change is found by dividing the amount of the increase by the 1998 amount.

*Solution:*

| | Increase in 1999 | |
| --- | --- | --- |
| | **Amount** | **Percent** |
| Current assets | $ 54,000 | 30% [($234,000 − $180,000) ÷ $180,000] |
| Plant assets (net) | 336,000 | 80% [($756,000 − $420,000) ÷ $420,000] |
| Total assets | $390,000 | 65% [($990,000 − $600,000) ÷ $600,000] |

THE NAVIGATOR

*Related exercise material:* BE19–1, BE19–3, BE19–4, BE19–6, E19–1, E19–3, and E19–4.

**5**
STUDY
OBJECTIVE

Identify and compute ratios and describe their purpose and use in analyzing a firm's liquidity, profitability, and solvency.

HELPFUL HINT
Each of these is illustrated in the following sections.

# RATIO ANALYSIS

Ratio analysis expresses the relationship among selected items of financial statement data. A ratio expresses the mathematical relationship between one quantity and another. The relationship is expressed in terms of either a percentage, a rate, or a simple proportion. To illustrate, recently Nike, Inc., had current assets of $3,830 million and current liabilities of $1,867 million. The relationship is determined by dividing current assets by current liabilities. The alternative means of expression are:

**Percentage:**   Current assets are 205% of current liabilities.
**Rate:**   Current assets are 2.05 times greater than current liabilities.
**Proportion:**   The relationship of current assets to liabilities is 2.05:1.

## TECHNOLOGY IN ACTION

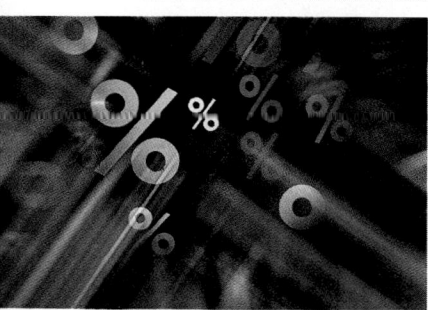

Many general ledger accounting programs include the generation of financial ratios as routine output. All the ratio computations presented in this chapter can be done with electronic spreadsheets as well. There are also many programs written specifically for financial statement analysis. These packages are written for both general purpose use and use in specific industries. For example, financial institutions routinely use over 60 ratios geared specifically to the banking industry.

For analysis of the primary financial statements, ratios can be classified as pictured in Illustration 19-11.

Ratios can provide clues to underlying conditions that may not be apparent from inspection of the individual components of a particular ratio. However, a single ratio by itself is not very meaningful. Accordingly, in the following discussion we will use:

1. **Intracompany comparisons** covering 2 years for the Quality Department Store.

**ILLUSTRATION 19-11**

*Financial ratio classifications*

**Liquidity Ratios**

Measures of short-term ability of the enterprise to pay its maturing obligations and to meet unexpected needs for cash

**Profitability Ratios**

Measures of the income or operating success of an enterprise for a given period of time

**Solvency Ratios**

Measures of the ability of the enterprise to survive over a long period of time

2. **Industry average comparisons** based on Dun & Bradstreet's median ratios for department stores and Robert Morris Associates' median ratios for department stores.

3. **Intercompany comparisons** based on Sears, Roebuck and Co. as Quality Department Store's principal competitor.

## Liquidity Ratios

Liquidity ratios measure the short-term ability of the enterprise to pay its maturing obligations and to meet unexpected needs for cash. Short-term creditors such as bankers and suppliers are particularly interested in assessing **liquidity**. The ratios that can be used to determine the enterprise's short-term debt-paying ability are the current ratio, the acid-test ratio, the current cash debt coverage ratio, receivables turnover, and inventory turnover.

### 1. Current Ratio

The current ratio is a widely used measure for evaluating a company's liquidity and short-term debt-paying ability. The ratio is computed by dividing current assets by current liabilities. It is sometimes referred to as the **working capital ratio** because **working capital** is the excess of current assets over current liabilities. The current ratio is a more dependable indicator of liquidity than working capital. Two companies with the same amount of working capital may have significantly different current ratios. The 1997 and 1996 current ratios for Quality Department Store and comparative data are shown in Illustration 19-12 on page 830.

What does the ratio actually mean? The 1997 ratio of 2.96:1 means that for every dollar of current liabilities, Quality has $2.96 of current assets. Quality's current ratio has decreased in the current year. However, compared to the industry average of 3.2:1, and Sears' 1.94:1 current ratio, Quality appears to be reasonably liquid.

The current ratio is only one measure of liquidity. It does not take into account the composition of the current assets. For example, a satisfactory current ratio does not disclose the fact that a portion of the current assets may be tied up in slow-moving inventory. A dollar of cash is more readily available to pay the bills than is a dollar of slow-moving inventory.

**HELPFUL HINT**

Can any corporation operate successfully without working capital? Yes, if it has very predictable cash flows and solid earnings. A surprising number of companies, including Whirlpool, American Standard, and Campbell's Soup, are pursuing this goal. The rationale: Less money tied up in working capital means more money to invest in the business.

## 2. Acid-Test Ratio

**ALTERNATIVE TERMINOLOGY**

The acid-test ratio is also called the *quick ratio.*

The **acid-test ratio** is a measure of a company's immediate short-term liquidity, computed by dividing the sum of cash, marketable securities, and net receivables by current liabilities. Thus, it is an important complement to the current ratio. For example, assume that the current assets of Quality Department Store for 1997 and 1996 consist of the following items:

**ILLUSTRATION 19-13**

*Current assets of Quality Department Store*

| **QUALITY DEPARTMENT STORE INC.** | | |
|---|---|---|
| **Balance Sheet (partial)** | | |
| | 1997 | 1996 |
| Current assets | | |
| **Cash** | $ 100,000 | $155,000 |
| **Marketable securities** | 20,000 | 70,000 |
| **Receivables (net)** | 230,000 | 180,000 |
| Inventory | 620,000 | 500,000 |
| Prepaid expenses | 50,000 | 40,000 |
| Total current assets | $1,020,000 | $945,000 |

# ACCOUNTING IN ACTION
## Business Insight

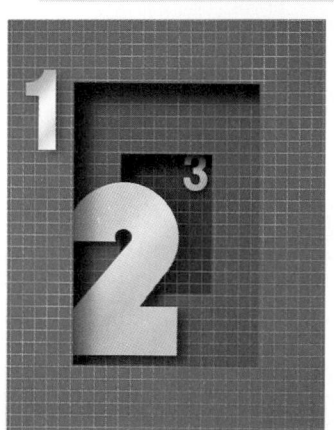

The apparent simplicity of the current ratio can have real-world limitations because an addition of equal amounts to both the numerator and the denominator causes the ratio to decrease. Assume, for example, that a company has $2,000,000 of current assets and $1,000,000 of current liabilities; its current ratio is 2:1. If it purchases $1,000,000 of inventory on account, it will have $3,000,000 of current assets and $2,000,000 of current liabilities; its current ratio will decrease to 1.5:1. If, instead, the company pays off $500,000 of its current liabilities, it will have $1,500,000 of current assets and $500,000 of current liabilities, and its current ratio will increase to 3:1. Thus, any trend analysis should be done with care, since the ratio is susceptible to quick changes and is easily influenced by management.

Cash, marketable securities (short-term), and receivables (net) are highly liquid compared to inventory and prepaid expenses. The inventory may not be readily saleable and the prepaid expenses may not be transferable to others.

Thus, the acid-test ratio measures **immediate** liquidity. The 1997 and 1996 acid-test ratios for Quality Department Store and comparative data are as follows:

ILLUSTRATION 19-14

*Acid-test ratio*

$$\text{ACID-TEST RATIO} = \frac{\text{CASH} + \text{MARKETABLE SECURITIES} + \text{RECEIVABLES (NET)}}{\text{CURRENT LIABILITIES}}$$

Quality Department Store

| 1997 | 1996 |
|---|---|
| $\dfrac{\$100,000 + \$20,000 + \$230,000}{\$344,500} = 1.0{:}1$ | $\dfrac{\$155,000 + \$70,000 + \$180,000}{\$303,000} = 1.3{:}1$ |
| Industry average<br>1.3:1 | Sears, Roebuck and Co.<br>1.5:1 |

Is an acid-test ratio of 1.0:1 adequate? The ratio has declined in 1997. However, when compared with the industry median of 1.3:1 and Sears' of 1.5:1, Quality's acid-test ratio seems adequate.

## 3. Current Cash Debt Coverage Ratio

A disadvantage of the current and acid-test ratios is that they use year-end balances of current asset and current liability accounts. These year-end balances may not be representative of what the company's current position was during most of the year. A ratio that partially corrects for this problem is the ratio of net cash provided by operating activities to average current liabilities, referred to as the current cash debt coverage ratio. Because it uses net cash provided by operating activities rather than a balance at a point in time, it may provide a better representation of liquidity.

To illustrate the computation of this ratio, assume that Quality Department Store's statement of cash flows shows net cash flows provided by operating activities of $404,000 in 1997 and $340,000 in 1996 and that current liabilities at January 1, 1996, are $290,000. The current cash debt coverage ratio for Quality Department Store and comparative data are as follows:

ILLUSTRATION 19-15

*Current cash debt coverage ratio*

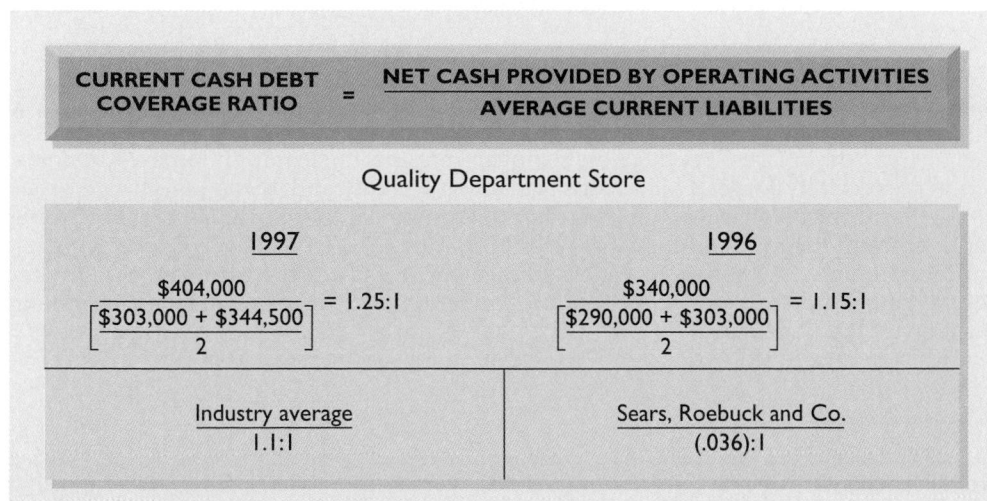

$$\begin{matrix}\text{CURRENT CASH DEBT} \\ \text{COVERAGE RATIO}\end{matrix} = \frac{\text{NET CASH PROVIDED BY OPERATING ACTIVITIES}}{\text{AVERAGE CURRENT LIABILITIES}}$$

Quality Department Store

| 1997 | 1996 |
|---|---|
| $\dfrac{\$404,000}{\left[\dfrac{\$303,000 + \$344,500}{2}\right]} = 1.25{:}1$ | $\dfrac{\$340,000}{\left[\dfrac{\$290,000 + \$303,000}{2}\right]} = 1.15{:}1$ |
| Industry average<br>1.1:1 | Sears, Roebuck and Co.<br>(.036):1 |

The ratio has increased in 1997. Is the coverage adequate? Probably so. Quality's operating cash flow coverage of average current liabilities is slightly greater than the industry average. Sears' current cash debt coverage ratio in 1997 was (.036):1. It was negative because operating activities **used** (as opposed to provided) net cash.

## 4. Receivables Turnover

Liquidity may be measured by how quickly certain assets can be converted to cash. How liquid, for example, are the receivables? The ratio used to assess the liquidity of the receivables is the receivables turnover ratio. This ratio measures the number of times, on average, receivables are collected during the period. The receivables turnover ratio is computed by dividing net credit sales (net sales less cash sales) by the average net receivables during the year. Unless seasonal factors are significant, average net receivables outstanding can be computed from the beginning and ending balance of the net receivables.[2]

Assuming that all sales are credit sales and the balance of accounts receivable (net) at the beginning of 1996 is $200,000, the receivables turnover ratio for Quality Department Store and comparative data are shown in Illustration 19-16. Quality's receivables turnover improved in 1997. The turnover of 10.2 times compares quite favorably with Sears' 2.11 times and the department store industry's average of 7.0 times.

**ILLUSTRATION 19-16**

*Receivables turnover*

$$\text{RECEIVABLES TURNOVER} = \frac{\text{NET CREDIT SALES}}{\text{AVERAGE NET RECEIVABLES}}$$

Quality Department Store

| 1997 | 1996 |
|------|------|
| $\dfrac{\$2,097,000}{\left[\dfrac{\$180,000 + \$230,000}{2}\right]} = 10.2 \text{ times}$ | $\dfrac{\$1,837,000}{\left[\dfrac{\$200,000 + \$180,000}{2}\right]} = 9.7 \text{ times}$ |
| Industry average 7.0 times | Sears, Roebuck and Co. 2.11 times |

## ACCOUNTING IN ACTION
### Business Insight

In some cases, receivables turnover may be misleading. Some companies, especially large retail chains, encourage credit and revolving charge sales, and they slow collections in order to earn a healthy return on the outstanding receivables in the form of interest at rates of 18% to 22%. This may explain why Sears' turnover is only 2.11 times. In general, however, the faster the turnover, the greater the reliance that can be placed on the current and acid-test ratios for assessing liquidity.

---

[2]If seasonal factors are significant, the average receivables balance might be determined by using monthly amounts.

A popular variant of the receivables turnover ratio is to convert it into an **average collection period** in terms of days. This is done by dividing the receivables turnover ratio into 365 days. For example, the receivables turnover in 1997 of 10.2 times is divided into 365 days to obtain approximately 35.8 days. This means that the average collection period for receivables is 36 days, or approximately every 5 weeks. The average collection period is frequently used to assess the effectiveness of a company's credit and collection policies. The general rule is that the collection period should not greatly exceed the credit term period (i.e., the time allowed for payment).

### 5. Inventory Turnover

The inventory turnover ratio measures the number of times on average the inventory is sold during the period. Its purpose is to measure the liquidity of the inventory. The inventory turnover is computed by dividing cost of goods sold by the average inventory during the period. Unless seasonal factors are significant, average inventory can be computed from the beginning and ending inventory balances. Assuming that the inventory balance for Quality Department Store at the beginning of 1996 was $450,000, its inventory turnover and comparative data are as shown in Illustration 19-17. Quality's inventory turnover declined slightly in 1997. The turnover ratio of 2.3 times is relatively low compared with the industry average of 3.4 and Sears' 5.5. Generally, the faster the inventory turnover, the less cash that is tied up in inventory and the less the chance of inventory obsolescence.

**ILLUSTRATION 19-17**

*Inventory turnover*

A variant of the inventory turnover ratio is the **average days to sell the inventory**. For example, the inventory turnover in 1997 of 2.3 times divided into 365 is approximately 159 days. An average selling time of 159 days is also relatively high compared with the industry average of 107 days (365 ÷ 3.4) and Sears' 66 days (365 ÷ 5.5).

## Profitability Ratios

Profitability ratios measure the income or operating success of an enterprise for a given period of time. Income, or the lack of it, affects the company's ability to obtain debt and equity financing, the company's liquidity position, and the com-

# ACCOUNTING IN ACTION
## Business Insight

Inventory turnover ratios vary considerably among industries. For example, grocery store chains have a turnover of 10 times and an average selling period of 37 days. In contrast, jewelry stores have an average turnover of 1.3 times and an average selling period of 281 days. Within a company there may be significant differences in inventory turnover among different types of products. Thus, in a grocery store the turnover of perishable items such as produce, meats, and dairy products will be faster than the turnover of soaps and detergents.

pany's ability to grow. As a consequence, creditors and investors alike are interested in evaluating earning power (profitability). Profitability is frequently used as the ultimate test of management's operating effectiveness.

## 6. Profit Margin

**ALTERNATIVE TERMINOLOGY**
The profit margin ratio is also called the *rate of return on sales*.

The profit margin ratio is a measure of the percentage of each dollar of sales that results in net income. It is computed by dividing net income by net sales for the period. Quality Department Store's profit margin ratios and comparative data are shown in Illustration 19-18.

**ILLUSTRATION 19-18**

*Profit margin ratio*

$$\text{PROFIT MARGIN ON SALES} = \frac{\text{NET INCOME}}{\text{NET SALES}}$$

Quality Department Store

| 1997 | 1996 |
|---|---|
| $\dfrac{\$263,800}{\$2,097,000} = 12.6\%$ | $\dfrac{\$208,500}{\$1,837,000} = 11.4\%$ |
| Industry average 3.6% | Sears, Roebuck and Co. 2.9% |

Quality experienced an increase in its profit margin from 1996 to 1997. Its profit margin is unusually high in comparison with the industry average of 3.6% and Sears' 2.9%.

High-volume (high inventory turnover) enterprises such as grocery stores (Safeway or Kroger) and discount stores (Kmart or Wal-Mart) generally experience low profit margins, whereas low-volume enterprises such as jewelry stores (Tiffany & Co.) or airplane manufacturers (Boeing Aircraft) have high profit margins.

## 7. Cash Return on Sales Ratio

The profit margin ratio discussed above is an accrual-based ratio using net income as the numerator. The cash-basis counterpart to that ratio is the cash return on sales ratio which uses net cash provided by operating activities as the numerator and net sales as the denominator. The difference between these two ratios should be explainable as differences between accrual accounting and cash-basis accounting, i.e., differences in the timing of revenue and expense recognition. Using net cash provided by operating activities of $404,000 in 1997 and $340,000 in 1996, Quality Department Store's cash return on sales ratios are computed as follows:

ILLUSTRATION 19-19

*Cash return on sales ratio*

Quality's cash return on sales is considerably higher than its profit margin on sales. The difference of 6.7% (19.3% − 12.6%) in 1997 is due to excess noncash charges over noncash credits to the income statement. Quality appears to have a very healthy cash return on sales.

## 8. Asset Turnover

The asset turnover ratio measures how efficiently a company uses its assets to generate sales. It is determined by dividing net sales by average assets for the period. The resulting number shows the dollars of sales produced by each dollar invested in assets. Unless seasonal factors are significant, average total assets can be computed from the beginning and ending balance of total assets. Assuming that the total assets at the beginning of 1996 were $1,446,000, the 1997 and 1996 asset turnover ratios for Quality Department Store and comparative data are as follows:

ILLUSTRATION 19-20

*Asset turnover*

The asset turnover ratio shows that Quality generated sales of $1.22 in 1997 for each dollar it had invested in assets. The ratio changed little from 1996 to 1997. Quality's asset turnover ratio is below the industry average of 2.2 times and above Sears' ratio of 1.1 times.

Asset turnover ratios vary considerably among industries. For example, a large utility company like Consolidated Edison (New York) has a ratio of 0.49 times, and the large grocery chain Kroger Stores has a ratio of 4.3 times.

## 9. Return on Assets Ratio

An overall measure of profitability is the return on assets ratio. This ratio is computed by dividing net income by average assets. The 1997 and 1996 return on assets for Quality Department Store and comparative data are shown below.

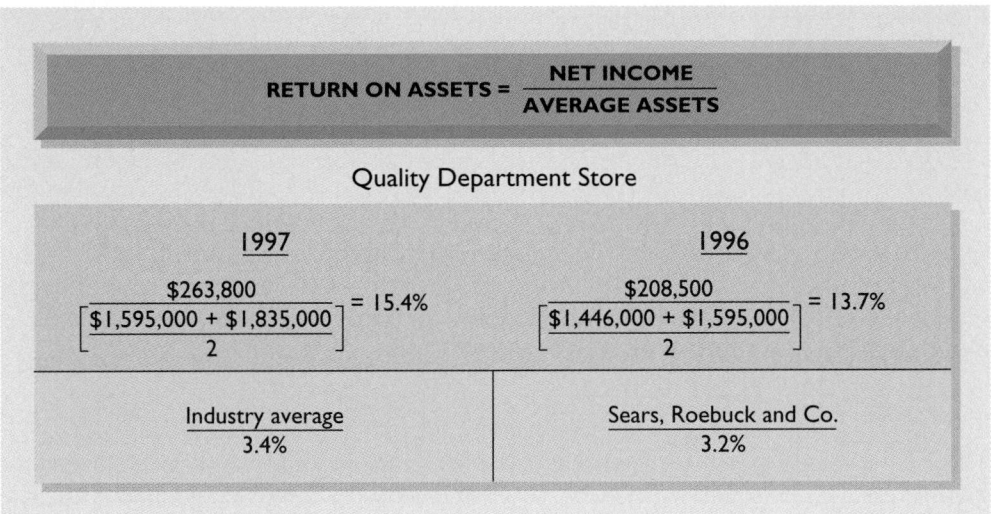

Quality's return on assets improved from 1996 to 1997. Its return of 15.4% is very high, compared with the department store industry average of 3.4% and Sears' 3.2%.

## 10. Return on Common Stockholders' Equity

Another widely used ratio that measures profitability from the common stockholder's viewpoint is return on common stockholders' equity. This ratio shows how many dollars of net income were earned for each dollar invested by the owners. It is computed by dividing net income by average common stockholders' equity. Assuming that common stockholders' equity at the beginning of 1996 was $667,000, the 1997 and 1996 ratios for Quality Department Store and comparative data are shown in Illustration 19-22.

Quality's rate of return on common stockholders' equity is unusually high at 29.3%, considering an industry average of 12.9% and a rate of 22% for Sears.

When preferred stock is present, **preferred dividend** requirements are deducted from net income to compute income available to common stockholders.

**ILLUSTRATION 19-22**

*Return on common stock-holders' equity*

$$\frac{\text{RETURN ON COMMON}}{\text{STOCKHOLDERS' EQUITY}} = \frac{\text{NET INCOME}}{\text{AVERAGE COMMON STOCKHOLDERS' EQUITY}}$$

**Quality Department Store**

| 1997 | 1996 |
|------|------|
| $\dfrac{\$263,800}{\left[\dfrac{\$795,000 + \$1,003,000}{2}\right]} = 29.3\%$ | $\dfrac{\$208,500}{\left[\dfrac{\$667,000 + \$795,000}{2}\right]} = 28.5\%$ |
| Industry average<br>12.9% | Sears, Roebuck and Co.<br>22% |

Similarly, the par value of preferred stock (or call price, if applicable) must be deducted from total stockholders' equity to arrive at the amount of common stock equity used in this ratio. The ratio then appears as follows:

$$\text{Rate of return on common stockholders' equity} = \frac{\text{Net income} - \text{Preferred dividends}}{\text{Average common stockholders' equity}}$$

Note that Quality's rate of return on stockholders' equity (29.3%) is substantially higher than its rate of return on assets (15.38%). The reason is that Quality has made effective use of leverage or **trading on the equity** at a gain. Trading on the equity at a gain means that the company has borrowed money through the issuance of bonds or notes at a lower rate of interest than it is able to earn by using the borrowed money. Leverage is using money supplied by nonowners to increase the return to the owners. A comparison of the rate of return on total assets with the rate of interest paid for borrowed money indicates the profitability of trading on the equity. Quality Department Store earns more on its borrowed funds than it has to pay in the form of interest. Thus the return to stockholders exceeds the return on the assets, benefiting from the positive leveraging.

**ALTERNATIVE TERMINOLOGY**

Trading on the equity is also called *leveraging*.

## 11. Earnings per Share (EPS)

**Earnings per share** of stock is a measure of the net income earned on each share of common stock. It is computed by dividing net income by the number of weighted average common shares outstanding during the year. Reducing net income earned to a per share basis provides a useful perspective for determining profitability. Assuming that there is no change in the number of outstanding shares during 1996 and that the 1997 increase occurred midyear, the net income per share for Quality Department Store for 1997 and 1996 is computed as shown in Illustration 19-24 on page 838.

Note that no industry or Sears data are presented. Such comparisons are not meaningful because of the wide variations in the number of shares of outstanding stock among companies. Quality's earnings per share increased 20 cents per

**ILLUSTRATION 19-24**

*Earnings per share*

share in 1997. This represents a 26% increase over the 1996 earnings per share of 77 cents.

When the term "net income per share" or "earnings per share" is used, it refers to the amount of net income applicable to each share of **common stock**. Therefore, in computing net income per share, if there are preferred dividends declared for the period, they must be deducted from net income to arrive at income available to the common stockholders.

## 12. Price-Earnings Ratio

The price-earnings ratio is an oft-quoted statistic that measures the ratio of the market price of each share of common stock to the earnings per share. The price-earnings (PE) ratio reflects investors' assessments of a company's future earnings. It is computed by dividing the market price per share of the stock by earnings per share. Assuming that the market price of Quality Department Store Inc. stock is $8 in 1996 and $12 in 1997, the price-earnings ratio is computed as follows:

**ILLUSTRATION 19-25**

*Price-earnings ratio*

In 1997 each share of Quality's stock sold for 12.4 times the amount that was earned on each share. Quality's price-earnings ratio is significantly lower than the industry average of 32 times, and it is less than the ratio of 17 times for Sears. The average price-earnings ratio for the stocks that constitute the Dow-Jones industrial average on the New York Stock Exchange in March 1998 was an unusually high 21 times.

# ACCOUNTING IN ACTION

## Business Insight

For the stock of some companies, investors are willing to pay over 20 times the current per-share earnings because they feel the future growth in earnings will provide an adequate return on the investment. Examples of companies with price-earnings ratios over 20 are America Online (101), Microsoft (54), Coca-Cola (41), and Gillette Co. (40). Examples of companies with low price-earnings ratios are Ford Motor (9), General Motors (8), and Northwest Airlines (7).

## 13. Payout Ratio

The **payout ratio** measures the percentage of earnings distributed in the form of cash dividends. It is computed by dividing cash dividends by net income. Companies that have high growth rates are characterized by low payout ratios because they reinvest most of their net income into the business. The 1997 and 1996 payout ratios for Quality Department Store are computed as follows:

**ILLUSTRATION 19-26**

*Payout ratio*

$$\text{PAYOUT RATIO} = \frac{\text{CASH DIVIDENDS}}{\text{NET INCOME}}$$

### Quality Department Store

| 1997 | 1996 |
|------|------|
| $\frac{\$61,200}{\$263,800} = 23.2\%$ | $\frac{\$60,000}{\$208,500} = 28.8\%$ |
| Industry average | Sears, Roebuck and Co. |
| N/A | 30.8% |

Quality's payout ratio is lower than Sears' payout ratio of 30.8%. As indicated earlier, the company has apparently decided to fund its purchase of plant assets through retention of earnings.

# ACCOUNTING IN ACTION

## Business Insight

Many companies with stable earnings have high payout ratios. For example, Baltimore Gas and Electric has had an 84% payout ratio over the last 5 years, and Omega Healthcare's dividends exceeded net income over the same period. Conversely, companies that are expanding rapidly, such as Toys 'R' Us, Microsoft, and Telecommunications Inc. (TCI) have never paid a cash dividend.

## Solvency Ratios

Solvency ratios measure the ability of the enterprise to survive over a long period of time. Long-term creditors and stockholders are interested in a company's long-run solvency, particularly its ability to pay interest as it comes due and to repay the face value of the debt at maturity. Debt to total assets, times interest earned, and cash debt coverage are three ratios that provide information about debt-paying ability.

### 14. Debt to Total Assets Ratio

The **debt to total assets ratio** measures the percentage of the total assets provided by creditors (this ratio indicates the degree of leveraging). It is computed by dividing total debt (both current and long-term liabilities) by total assets. This ratio provides some indication of the company's ability to withstand losses without impairing the interests of creditors. The higher the percentage of debt to total assets, the greater the risk that the company may be unable to meet its maturing obligations. The 1997 and 1996 ratios for Quality Department Store and comparative data are as follows:

**ILLUSTRATION 19-27**

*Debt to total assets*

$$\text{DEBT TO TOTAL ASSETS} = \frac{\text{TOTAL DEBT}}{\text{TOTAL ASSETS}}$$

**Quality Department Store**

| 1997 | 1996 |
|------|------|
| $\dfrac{\$832,000}{\$1,835,000} = 45.3\%$ | $\dfrac{\$800,000}{\$1,595,000} = 50.2\%$ |

| Industry average | Sears, Roebuck and Co. |
|------|------|
| 38% | 85% |

A ratio of 45.3% means that creditors have provided 45.3% of Quality Department Store's total assets. Quality's 45.3% is above the industry average of 38%, but it is considerably below the incredibly high 85% ratio of Sears. The lower the ratio, the more equity "buffer" there is available to the creditors if the company becomes insolvent. Thus, from the creditors' point of view, a low ratio of debt to total assets is usually desirable.

The adequacy of this ratio is often judged in the light of the company's earnings. Generally, companies with relatively stable earnings, such as public utilities, have higher debt to total assets ratios than cyclical companies with widely fluctuating earnings, such as many high-tech companies. (See *Accounting in Action* for examples of debt to total assets ratios for selected companies.)

# ACCOUNTING IN ACTION
### Business Insight

Examples of debt to total assets ratios for selected companies are:

|  | Total Debt to Total Assets as a Percent |
| --- | --- |
| Advanced Micro Devices | 19% |
| Ford Motor Company | 42% |
| Merck | 9% |
| Caterpillar | 37% |
| Bob Evans Farms | 0% |
| Revlon | 56% |

Another means used in practice to measure this same leverage phenomenon is the debt to equity ratio. It shows the relative use of borrowed funds (total liabilities) as compared to resources invested by the owners. Because this ratio may be computed in several ways, care should be taken when making comparisons. Debt may be defined to include only the noncurrent portion of the liabilities, and intangible assets may be excluded from owners' equity (resulting in tangible net worth).

## 15. Times Interest Earned Ratio

The **times interest earned ratio** provides an indication of the company's ability to meet interest payments as they come due. It is computed by dividing income before interest expense and income taxes by interest expense. The 1997 and 1996 ratios for Quality Department Store and comparative data are shown in Illustration 19-28. Note that the times interest earned ratio uses income before income taxes and interest expense, because this amount represents the amount available to cover interest. For Quality Department Store the 1997 amount of $468,000 is computed by taking the income before income taxes of $432,000 and adding back the $36,000 of interest expense. The interest expense of Quality is well covered at 13 times relative to the industry average of 2.7 times and Sears' 2.49 times.

**ALTERNATIVE TERMINOLOGY**
The times interest earned ratio is also called the *interest coverage ratio*.

**ILLUSTRATION 19-28**
*Times interest earned*

$$\text{TIMES INTEREST EARNED} = \frac{\text{INCOME BEFORE INCOME TAXES AND INTEREST EXPENSE}}{\text{INTEREST EXPENSE}}$$

### Quality Department Store

| 1997 | 1996 |
| --- | --- |
| $\dfrac{\$468,000}{\$36,000} = 13 \text{ times}$ | $\dfrac{\$388,000}{\$40,500} = 9.6 \text{ times}$ |
| Industry average 2.7 times | Sears, Roebuck and Co. 2.49 times |

# TECHNOLOGY IN ACTION

In terms of the types of financial information that are available and the ratios used by various industries, you should be aware that what can be practically covered in this textbook gives you only the "Titanic approach." That is, you are seeing only the tip of the iceberg compared to the vast data bases and different types of ratio analysis that are available on computers. The availability of information is not a problem. The real trick is to be discriminating enough to perform relevant analysis and to select pertinent comparative data.

## 16. Cash Debt Coverage Ratio

The ratio of net cash provided by operating activities to average total liabilities, referred to as the cash debt coverage ratio, is a cash-basis measure of **solvency**. This ratio demonstrates a company's ability to repay its liabilities from cash generated from operating activities, without having to liquidate the assets employed in its operations. Using Quality's net cash provided by operating activities of $404,000 in 1997 and $340,000 in 1996 and assuming total liabilities of $740,000 on January 1, 1996, the cash debt coverage ratios are computed as follows:

**ILLUSTRATION 19-29**

*Cash debt coverage ratio*

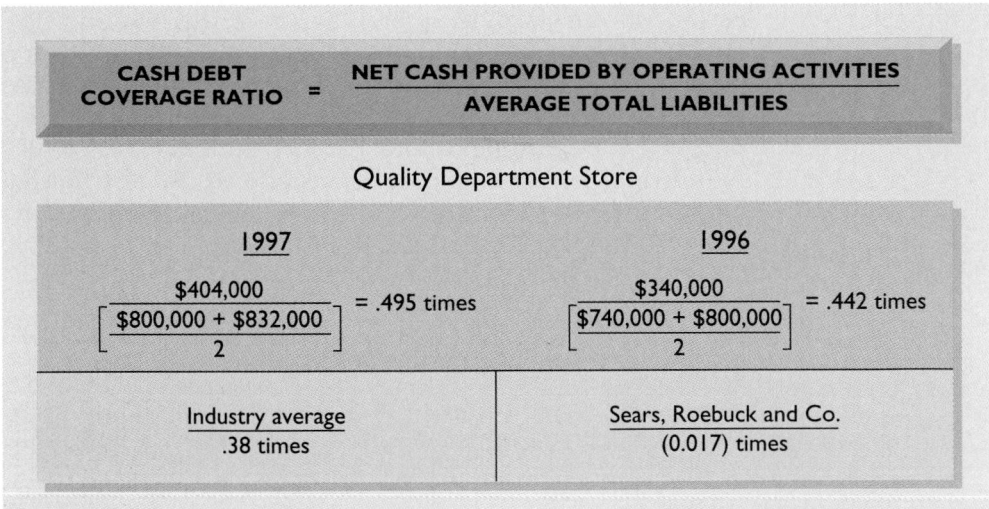

Based on net cash generated from operations in 1997, it would take Quality approximately 2 years to generate enough cash to pay off all its liabilities (assuming all of the net cash generated were used for that purpose only). Its ratio is also superior to that of the retail industry and Sears. (Sears' ratio is negative because its operating activities **used** net cash during 1997.)

## Summary of Ratios

A summary of the ratios discussed in the chapter is presented in Illustration 19-30. The summary includes the formula and purpose or use of each ratio.

**ILLUSTRATION 19-30**

*Summary of liquidity, profit-
ability, and solvency ratios*

| Ratio | Formula | Purpose or Use |
|---|---|---|
| **Liquidity Ratios** | | |
| 1. Current ratio | $\dfrac{\text{Current assets}}{\text{Current liabilities}}$ | Measures short-term debt-paying ability. |
| 2. Acid-test or quick ratio | $\dfrac{\text{Cash + marketable securities + receivables (net)}}{\text{Current liabilities}}$ | Measures immediate short-term liquidity. |
| 3. Current cash debt coverage ratio | $\dfrac{\text{Net cash provided by operating activities}}{\text{Average current liabilities}}$ | Measures short-term debt-paying ability (cash basis). |
| 4. Receivables turnover | $\dfrac{\text{Net credit sales}}{\text{Average net receivables}}$ | Measures liquidity of receivables. |
| 5. Inventory turnover | $\dfrac{\text{Cost of goods sold}}{\text{Average inventory}}$ | Measures liquidity of inventory. |
| **Profitability Ratios** | | |
| 6. Profit margin | $\dfrac{\text{Net income}}{\text{Net sales}}$ | Measures net income generated by each dollar of sales. |
| 7. Cash return on sales ratio | $\dfrac{\text{Net cash provided by operating activities}}{\text{Net sales}}$ | Measures the net cash flow generated by each dollar of sales. |
| 8. Asset turnover | $\dfrac{\text{Net sales}}{\text{Average assets}}$ | Measures how efficiently assets are used to generate sales. |
| 9. Return on assets | $\dfrac{\text{Net income}}{\text{Average assets}}$ | Measures overall profitability of assets. |
| 10. Return on common stockholders' equity | $\dfrac{\text{Net income}}{\text{Average common stockholders' equity}}$ | Measures profitability of owners' investment. |
| 11. Earnings per share | $\dfrac{\text{Net income}}{\text{Weighted average common shares outstanding}}$ | Measures net income earned on each share of common stock. |
| 12. Price-earnings ratio | $\dfrac{\text{Market price per share of stock}}{\text{Earnings per share}}$ | Measures the ratio of the market price per share to earnings per share. |
| 13. Payout ratio | $\dfrac{\text{Cash dividends}}{\text{Net income}}$ | Measures percentage of earnings distributed in the form of cash dividends. |
| **Solvency Ratios** | | |
| 14. Debt to total assets | $\dfrac{\text{Total debt}}{\text{Total assets}}$ | Measures the percentage of total assets provided by creditors. |
| 15. Times interest earned | $\dfrac{\text{Income before income taxes and interest expense}}{\text{Interest expense}}$ | Measures ability to meet interest payments as they come due. |
| 16. Cash debt coverage ratio | $\dfrac{\text{Net cash provided by operating activities}}{\text{Average total liabilities}}$ | Measures the long-term debt-paying ability (cash basis). |

## BEFORE YOU GO ON . . .

### Review It

1. What are liquidity ratios? Explain the current ratio, acid-test ratio, current cash debt coverage ratio, receivables turnover ratio, and inventory turnover ratio.
2. What are profitability ratios? Explain the profit margin ratio, cash return on sales ratio, asset turnover ratio, return on assets ratio, return on common stockholders' equity ratio, earnings per share, price-earnings ratio, and payout ratio.
3. What are solvency ratios? Explain the debt to total assets ratio, times interest earned ratio, and cash debt coverage ratio.

### Do It

Selected financial data for Drummond Company at December 31, 1999, are as follows: cash $60,000; receivables (net) $80,000; inventory $70,000; current liabilities $140,000. Compute the current and acid-test ratios.

*Reasoning:* The formula for the current ratio is: current assets ÷ current liabilities. The formula for the acid-test ratio is: cash + marketable securities + receivables (net) ÷ current liabilities.

*Solution:* The current ratio is 1.5:1 ($210,000 ÷ $140,000). The acid-test ratio is 1:1 ($140,000 ÷ $140,000).

*Related exercise material:* BE19–7, BE19–8, BE19–9, BE19–10, BE19–11, E19–5, E19–6, and E19–7.

THE
NAVIGATOR

---

# LIMITATIONS OF FINANCIAL STATEMENT ANALYSIS

**6**

STUDY

OBJECTIVE

Recognize the limitations of financial statement analysis.

Significant business decisions are frequently made using one or more of the three analytical tools illustrated in this chapter. However, you should be aware of some of the limitations of these tools and of the financial statements on which they are based.

## Estimates

Financial statements contain numerous estimates. Estimates, for example, are used in determining the allowance for uncollectible receivables, periodic depreciation, the costs of warranties, and contingent losses. To the extent that these estimates are inaccurate, the financial ratios and percentages are inaccurate.

## Cost

Traditional financial statements are based on cost and are not adjusted for price-level changes. Comparisons of unadjusted financial data from different periods may be rendered invalid by significant inflation or deflation. For example, a 5-year comparison of Sears' revenues might show a growth of 36%. But this growth trend would be misleading if the general price-level had increased significantly during the same 5-year period.

## Alternative Accounting Methods

Variations among companies in the application of generally accepted accounting principles may hamper comparability. For example, one company may use the

FIFO method of inventory costing, whereas another company in the same industry may use LIFO. If inventory is a significant asset to both companies, it is unlikely that their current ratios are comparable. For example, if General Motors Corporation had used FIFO instead of LIFO in valuing its inventories, its inventories would have been 26% higher, significantly affecting the current ratio (and other ratios as well). In addition to differences in inventory costing methods, differences also exist in reporting such items as depreciation, depletion, and amortization. Although these differences in accounting methods might be detectable from reading the notes to the financial statements, adjusting the financial data to compensate for the different methods is difficult, if not impossible in some cases.

## Atypical Data

Fiscal year-end data may not be typical of the financial condition during the year. Firms frequently establish a fiscal year-end that coincides with the low point in operating activity or in inventory levels. Therefore, certain account balances (cash, receivables, payables, and inventories) may not be representative of the balances in the accounts during the year.

## Diversification of Firms

Diversification in American industry also limits the usefulness of financial analysis. Many firms today are so diversified that they cannot be classified by a single industry—they are true conglomerates. Others appear to be comparable but are not.

**INTERNATIONAL NOTE**

In many industries competition is global: To evaluate a firm's standing, an investor or analyst must make comparisons to firms from other countries. However, given the many differences in accounting practices, these comparisons can be both difficult and misleading.

**ETHICS NOTE**

When investigating diversified firms, investors are often most interested to learn about the results of particular divisions. Firms are required to disclose the results of distinct lines of business separately if they are a material part of operations. Unfortunately, shifting revenues and expenses across divisions to achieve desired results reduces the usefulness of this information for financial statement analysis.

# BEFORE YOU GO ON . . .

### Review It

1. What are some limitations of financial statement analysis?
2. Give examples of alternative accounting methods that hamper comparability.
3. In what way does diversification limit the usefulness of financial statement analysis?

## A LOOK BACK AT OUR FEATURE STORY

Refer to the opening story and answer the following questions:

1. How is the Motley Fool bulletin board like the fool in Shakespeare's plays?
2. What makes the Motley Fool bulletin board attractive to Internet subscribers?
3. What are the dangers of using the Motley Fool bulletin board for investment purposes?

*Solution:*

1. The fool in Shakespeare's play was the only one who could speak unpleasant truths to kings and queens without being killed. The creators of the Motley Fool bulletin board view themselves as twentieth-century "fools," revealing the "truths" of Wall Street to the small investor, who the Gardner brothers believe has been taken advantage of by Wall Street insiders. That is, both Shakespeare's fools and the Motley Fool are irreverent attacks on the establishment.
2. The Motley Fool provides a bulletin board service where America Online subscribers can exchange information and insights about companies of interest to investors and potential investors. The information sources are endless (grassroots, insiders, anyone), worldwide, and nearly costless.

3. Critics contend that the bulletin board is nothing more than a high-tech rumor mill that tends to build a speculative house of cards. Participants on the board don't have to give their identities. Consequently, there is little to stop people from putting mis-information on the board to influence stock prices in the direction they want. Much of the information is soft and stands in sharp contrast to the data and ratios provided by analysis of financial statements as illustrated in this chap-ter.

THE NAVIGATOR

# DEMONSTRATION PROBLEM

The condensed financial statements of The Estée Lauder Companies, Inc., for the years ended June 30, 1997 and 1996, are presented below:

## THE ESTÉE LAUDER COMPANIES, INC.
### Balance Sheet
### June 30

|  | (in millions) | |
| Assets | 1997 | 1996 |
| --- | --- | --- |
| Current assets | | |
| Cash and cash equivalents | $ 255.6 | $ 254.8 |
| Accounts receivable (net) | 471.7 | 434.0 |
| Inventories | 440.6 | 452.8 |
| Prepaid expenses and other current assets | 143.2 | 148.8 |
| Total current assets | 1,311.1 | 1,290.4 |
| Property, plant, and equipment (net) | 265.0 | 229.3 |
| Investments | 25.9 | 24.7 |
| Intangibles and other assets | 271.1 | 235.0 |
| Total assets | $1,873.1 | $1,779.4 |
| | | |
| **Liabilities and Stockholders' Equity** | | |
| Current liabilities | $759.5 | $822.9 |
| Long-term liabilities | 565.9 | 562.3 |
| Stockholders' equity—common | 547.7 | 394.2 |
| Total liabilities and stockholders' equity | $1,873.1 | $1,779.4 |

## THE ESTÉE LAUDER COMPANIES, INC.
### Income Statement
### For the Year Ended June 30

|  | (in millions) | |
|  | 1997 | 1996 |
| --- | --- | --- |
| Revenues | $3,381.6 | $3,194.5 |
| Costs and expenses | | |
| Cost of goods sold | 765.1 | 731.0 |
| Selling and administrative expenses | 2,224.6 | 2,116.0 |
| Interest expense and royalties | 52.4 | 92.0 |
| Total costs and expenses | 3,042.1 | 2,939.0 |
| Income before income taxes | 339.5 | 255.5 |
| Income tax expense | 165.3 | 152.6 |
| Net income | $ 174.2 | $ 102.9 |

*Instructions*

Compute the following ratios for 1997 and 1996.

(a) Current ratio.

(b) Inventory turnover (Inventory 6/30/95, $437.4).

(c) Profit margin ratio.

(d) Return on assets (Assets 6/30/95, $1,701.4).

(e) Return on common stockholders' equity (Equity 6/30/95, $335.1).

(f) Debt to total assets.

(g) Times interest earned.

## SOLUTION TO DEMONSTRATION PROBLEM

|  | 1997 | 1996 |
|---|---|---|
| (a) Current ratio: |  |  |
| $1,311.1 ÷ $759.5 = | 1.7:1 |  |
| $1,290.4 ÷ $822.9 = |  | 1.6:1 |
| (b) Inventory turnover: |  |  |
| $765.1 ÷ [($440.6 + $452.8) ÷ 2] = | 1.7 times |  |
| $731.0 ÷ [($452.8 + $437.4) ÷ 2] = |  | 1.6 times |
| (c) Profit margin: |  |  |
| $174.2 ÷ $3,381.6 = | 5.2% |  |
| $102.9 ÷ $3,194.5 = |  | 3.2% |
| (d) Return on assets: |  |  |
| $174.2 ÷ [($1,873.1 + $1,779.4) ÷ 2] = | 9.5% |  |
| $102.9 ÷ [($1,779.4 + $1,701.4) ÷ 2] = |  | 5.9% |
| (e) Return on common stockholders' equity: |  |  |
| $174.2 ÷ [($547.7 + $394.2) ÷ 2] = | 37% |  |
| $102.9 ÷ [($394.2 + $335.1) ÷ 2] = |  | 28% |
| (f) Debt to total assets: |  |  |
| $1,325.4 ÷ $1,873.1 = | 70.8% |  |
| $1,385.2 ÷ $1,779.4 = |  | 77.8% |
| (g) Times interest earned: |  |  |
| ($174.2 + $165.3 + $52.4) ÷ $52.4 = | 7.5 times |  |
| ($102.9 + $152.6 + $92.0) ÷ $92.0 = |  | 3.8 times |

**PROBLEM-SOLVING STRATEGIES**

1. Remember that the current ratio includes all current assets; acid-test ratio uses only cash, marketable securities, and net receivables.

2. Use average balances for turnover ratios like inventory, receivables, and assets.

3. Return on assets is greater or smaller than return on common stockholders' equity depending on cost of debt.

THE NAVIGATOR

## SUMMARY OF STUDY OBJECTIVES

**1. Discuss the need for comparative analysis.** There are three bases of comparison: (1) Intracompany, which compares an item or financial relationship with other data within a company. (2) Industry, which compares company data with industry averages. (3) Intercompany, which compares an item or financial relationship of a company with data of one or more competing companies.

**2. Identify the tools of financial statement analysis.** Financial statements may be analyzed horizontally, vertically, and with ratios.

**3. Explain and apply horizontal (trend) analysis.** Horizontal analysis is a technique for evaluating a series of data over a period of time to determine the increase or decrease that has taken place, expressed as either an amount or a percentage.

**4. Describe and apply vertical analysis.** Vertical analysis is a technique that expresses each item within a financial statement in terms of a percentage of a relevant total or a base amount.

**5. Identify and compute ratios and describe their purpose and use in analyzing a firm's liquidity, profitability, and solvency.** The formula and purpose of each ratio is presented in Illustration 19-30.

**6. Recognize the limitations of financial statement analysis.** The usefulness of analytical tools is limited by the use of estimates, the cost basis, the application of alternative accounting methods, atypical data at year-end, and the diversification of firms.

THE NAVIGATOR

# GLOSSARY

**Acid-test ratio** A measure of a company's immediate short-term liquidity, computed by dividing the sum of cash, marketable securities, and (net) receivables by current liabilities. (p. 830).

**Asset turnover ratio** A measure of how efficiently a company uses its assets to generate sales, computed by dividing net sales by average assets. (p. 835).

**Cash debt coverage ratio** A cash-basis measure of long-term debt-paying ability, computed as net cash provided by operating activities divided by average total liabilities. (p.842).

**Cash return on sales ratio** A measure of the cash generated by each dollar of sales, computed as net cash provided by operating activities divided by net sales. (p.834).

**Current cash debt coverage ratio** A cash-basis measure of short-term debt-paying ability, computed as net cash provided by operating activities divided by average current liabilities. (p.831).

**Current ratio** A measure used to evaluate a company's liquidity and short-term debt-paying ability, computed by dividing current assets by current liabilities. (p. 829).

**Debt to total assets ratio** Measures the percentage of total assets provided by creditors, computed by dividing total debt by total assets. (p. 840).

**Earnings per share** The net income earned by each share of common stock, computed by dividing net income by the weighted average common shares outstanding. (p. 837).

**Horizontal analysis** A technique for evaluating a series of financial statement data over a period of time to determine the increase (decrease) that has taken place, expressed as either an amount or a percentage. (p. 822).

**Inventory turnover ratio** A measure of the liquidity of inventory, computed by dividing cost of goods sold by average inventory. (p. 833).

**Liquidity ratios** Measures of the short-term ability of the enterprise to pay its maturing obligations and to meet unexpected needs for cash. (p. 829).

**Payout ratio** Measures the percentage of earnings distributed in the form of cash dividends, computed by dividing cash dividends by net income. (p. 839).

**Price-earnings ratio** Measures the ratio of the market price of each share of common stock to the earnings per share, computed by dividing the market price of the stock by earnings per share. (p. 838).

**Profitability ratios** Measures of the income or operating success of an enterprise for a given period of time. (p. 833).

**Profit margin ratio** Measures the percentage of each dollar of sales that results in net income, computed by dividing net income by net sales. (p. 834).

**Ratio** An expression of the mathematical relationship between one quantity and another. The relationship may be expressed either as a percentage, a rate, or a simple proportion. (p. 828).

**Ratio analysis** A technique for evaluating financial statements that expresses the relationship among selected financial statement data. (p. 828).

**Receivables turnover ratio** A measure of the liquidity of receivables, computed by dividing net credit sales by average net receivables. (p. 832).

**Return on assets ratio** An overall measure of profitability, computed by dividing net income by average assets. (p. 836).

**Return on common stockholders' equity** Measures the dollars of net income earned for each dollar invested by the owners, computed by dividing net income by average common stockholders' equity. (p. 836).

**Solvency ratios** Measures of the ability of the enterprise to survive over a long period of time. (p. 840).

**Times interest earned ratio** Measures a company's ability to meet interest payments as they come due, computed by dividing income before interest expense and income taxes by interest expense. (p. 841).

**Trading on the equity (leverage)** Borrowing money at a lower rate of interest than can be earned by using the borrowed money. (p. 837).

**Vertical analysis** A technique for evaluating financial statement data that expresses each item within a financial statement in terms of a percent of a base amount. (p. 825).

# SELF-STUDY QUESTIONS

Answers are at the end of the chapter.

(SO 1) 1. Comparisons of data within a company are an example of the following comparative basis:
   a. Industry averages.
   b. Intracompany.
   c. Intercompany.
   d. Both (b) and (c).

2. In horizontal analysis, each item is expressed as a percentage of the: (SO 2)
   a. net income amount.
   b. stockholders' equity amount.
   c. total assets amount.
   d. base year amount.

(SO 4)  3. In vertical analysis, the base amount for depreciation expense is generally:
a. net sales.
b. depreciation expense in a previous year.
c. gross profit.
d. fixed assets.

(SO 4)  4. The following schedule is a display of what type of analysis?

| | Amount | Percent |
|---|---|---|
| Current assets | $200,000 | 25% |
| Property, plant, and equipment | 600,000 | 75% |
| Total assets | $800,000 | |

a. Horizontal analysis.
b. Differential analysis.
c. Vertical analysis.
d. Ratio analysis.

(SO 3)  5. Leland Corporation reported net sales of $300,000, $330,000, and $360,000 in the years 1997, 1998, and 1999, respectively. If 1997 is the base year, what is the trend percentage for 1999?
a. 77%.
b. 108%.
c. 120%.
d. 130%.

(SO 5)  6. Which of the following measures is an evaluation of a firm's ability to pay current liabilities?

a. Acid-test ratio.
b. Current ratio.
c. Both (a) and (b).
d. None of the above.

7. A measure useful in evaluating the efficiency in man- (SO 5) aging inventories is:
a. inventory turnover ratio.
b. average days to sell inventory.
c. Both (a) and (b).
d. None of the above.

8. Which of the following is *not* a liquidity ratio?     (SO 5)
a. Current ratio.
b. Asset turnover.
c. Inventory turnover.
d. Receivables turnover.

9. Plano Corporation reported net income $24,000, net (SO 5) sales $400,000, and average assets $600,000 for 1999. The 1999 profit margin was:
a. 6%.
b. 12%.
c. 40%.
d. 200%.

10. Which of the following is generally *not* considered to be (SO 6) a limitation of financial analysis?
a. Use of estimates.
b. Use of ratio analysis.
c. Use of cost.
d. Use of alternative accounting methods.

# QUESTIONS

1. (a) Tara Goff believes that the analysis of financial statements is directed at two characteristics of a company: liquidity and profitability. Is Tara correct? Explain.
   (b) Are short-term creditors, long-term creditors, and stockholders interested primarily in the same characteristics of a company? Explain.

2. (a) Distinguish among the following bases of comparison: (1) intracompany, (2) industry averages, and (3) intercompany.
   (b) Give the principal value of using each of the three bases of comparison.

3. Two popular methods of financial statement analysis are horizontal analysis and vertical analysis. Explain the difference between these two methods.

4. (a) If Roy Company had net income of $480,000 in 1999 and it experienced a 24.5% increase in net income for 2000, what is its net income for 2000?
   (b) If six cents of every dollar of Roy's revenue is net income in 1999, what is the dollar amount of 1999 revenue?

5. What is a ratio? What are the different ways of expressing the relationship of two amounts? What information does a ratio provide?

6. Name the major ratios useful in assessing (a) liquidity and (b) solvency.

7. Bob Thebeau is puzzled. His company had a profit margin of 10% in 1999. He feels that this is an indication that the company is doing well. Loren Foelske, his accountant, says that more information is needed to determine the firm's financial well-being. Who is correct? Why?

8. What do the following classes of ratios measure? (a) Liquidity ratios. (b) Profitability ratios. (c) Solvency ratios.

9. What is the difference between the current ratio and the acid-test ratio?

10. Payne Company, a retail store, has a receivables turnover ratio of 4.5 times. The industry average is 12.5 times. Does Payne have a collection problem with its receivables?

11. Which ratios should be used to help answer the following questions?
    (a) How efficient is a company in using its assets to produce sales?
    (b) How near to sale is the inventory on hand?
    (c) How many dollars of net income were earned for each dollar invested by the owners?
    (d) How able is a company to meet interest charges as they fall due?

12. The price-earnings ratio of General Motors (automobile builder) was 9, and the price-earnings ratio of Microsoft (computer software) was 49. Which company did the stock market favor? Explain.

13. What is the formula for computing the payout ratio? Would you expect this ratio to be high or low for a growth company?

14. Holding all other factors constant, indicate whether each of the following changes generally signals good or bad news about a company:
    (a) Increase in profit margin.
    (b) Decrease in inventory turnover.
    (c) Increase in the current ratio.
    (d) Decrease in earnings per share.
    (e) Increase in price-earnings ratio.
    (f) Increase in debt to total assets ratio.
    (g) Decrease in times interest earned.
    (h) Increase in book value per share.

15. The return on total assets for Matson Corporation is 7.6%. During the same year Matson's return on common stockholders' equity is 12.8%. What is the explanation for the difference in the two rates?

16. Which two ratios do you think should be of greatest interest to:
    (a) A pension fund considering the purchase of 20-year bonds?
    (b) A bank contemplating a short-term loan?
    (c) A common stockholder?

17. (a) What is meant by trading on the equity?
    (b) How would you determine the profitability of trading on the equity?

18. Kiser Inc. has net income of $210,000, weighted average shares of common stock outstanding of 50,000, and preferred dividends for the period of $40,000. What is Kiser's earnings per share of common stock? Jim Akins, the president of Kiser Inc., believes the computed EPS of the company is high. Comment.

19. Identify and briefly explain five limitations of financial analysis.

20. Explain how the choice of one of the following accounting methods over the other raises or lowers a company's net income during a period of continuing inflation:
    (a) Use of FIFO instead of LIFO for inventory costing.
    (b) Use of a 6-year life for machinery instead of a 9-year life.
    (c) Use of straight-line depreciation instead of accelerated declining-balance depreciation.

21. What three ratios are partially dependent on cash-basis data, that is, data from the statement of cash flows?

# BRIEF EXERCISES*

••••••••••••••••••••••••••••••••••••••••••••••••••••••••••••••••••••••••••

*Prepare horizontal analysis.*
(SO 3)

**BE19–1**  Using the following data from the comparative balance sheet of Jackie Remmers Company, illustrate horizontal analysis:

|  | December 31, 2000 | December 31, 1999 |
|---|---|---|
| Accounts receivable | $ 500,000 | $ 400,000 |
| Inventory | $ 840,000 | $ 600,000 |
| Total assets | $3,220,000 | $2,800,000 |

*Prepare vertical analysis.*
(SO 4)

**BE19–2**  Using the same data presented above in BE19–1 for Jackie Remmers Company, illustrate vertical analysis.

*Calculate percentage of change.*
(SO 3)

**BE19–3**  Net income was $500,000 in 1998, $400,000 in 1999, and $504,000 in 2000. What is the percentage of change from (1) 1998 to 1999 and (2) 1999 to 2000? Is the change an increase or a decrease?

*Calculate net income.*
(SO 3)

**BE19–4**  If Hal Adelman Company had net income of $662,500 in 2000 and it experienced a 25% increase in net income over 1999, what was its 1999 net income?

*Calculate change in net income.*
(SO 4)

**BE19–5**  Vertical analysis (common size) percentages for Domingo Company's sales, cost of goods sold, and expenses are shown below:

| Vertical Analysis | 2000 | 1999 | 1998 |
|---|---|---|---|
| Sales | 100.0 | 100.0 | 100.0 |
| Cost of goods sold | 59.5 | 61.4 | 64.5 |
| Expenses | 25.0 | 26.6 | 28.5 |

*Follow the rounding procedures used in the chapter.

Did Domingo's net income as a percent of sales increase, decrease, or remain unchanged over the 3-year period presented above? Provide numerical support for your answer.

**BE19–6**   Horizontal analysis (trend analysis) percentages for Foltz Company's sales, cost of goods sold, and expenses are shown below:

*Calculate change in net income.*
*(SO 3)*

| Horizontal Analysis | 2000 | 1999 | 1998 |
|---|---|---|---|
| Sales | 96.2 | 106.8 | 100.0 |
| Cost of goods sold | 102.0 | 97.0 | 100.0 |
| Expenses | 110.6 | 95.4 | 100.0 |

Did Foltz's net income increase, decrease, or remain unchanged over the 3-year period presented above?

**BE19–7**   Selected condensed data taken from a recent balance sheet of Jensen Farms are as follows:

*Calculate liquidity ratios.*
*(SO 5)*

### JENSEN FARMS
### Balance Sheet (partial)

| | |
|---|---|
| Cash | $ 8,241,000 |
| Marketable securities | 1,947,000 |
| Accounts receivable | 12,545,000 |
| Inventories | 14,814,000 |
| Other current assets | 5,371,000 |
| Total current assets | $42,918,000 |
| Total current liabilities | $45,844,000 |

What are the (1) working capital, (2) current, and (3) acid-test ratios?

**BE19–8**   Hawkins Corporation has net income of $12 million and net revenue of $100 million in 1999. Its assets were $12 million at the beginning of the year and $18 million at the end of the year. What are (a) the Hawkins' asset turnover ratio and (b) profit margin ratio? (Round to two decimals.)

*Calculate profitability ratios.*
*(SO 5)*

**BE19–9**   The following data are taken from the financial statements of Geitz Company:

*Evaluate collection of accounts receivable.*
*(SO 5)*

| | 2000 | 1999 |
|---|---|---|
| Accounts receivable (net), end of year | $ 560,000 | $ 540,000 |
| Net sales on account | 4,400,000 | 3,100,000 |
| Terms for all sales are 1/10, n/60. | | |

Compute for each year (1) the receivables turnover and (2) the average collection period. What conclusions about the management of accounts receivable can be drawn from these data? At the end of 1998, accounts receivable (net) was $490,000.

**BE19–10**   The following data were taken from the income statements of Lester Fredrick Company:

*Evaluate management of inventory.*
*(SO 5)*

| | 2000 | 1999 |
|---|---|---|
| Sales | $6,420,000 | $6,240,000 |
| Beginning inventory | 980,000 | 860,000 |
| Purchases | 4,440,000 | 4,661,000 |
| Ending inventory | 1,020,000 | 980,000 |

Compute for each year (1) the inventory turnover ratio and (2) the average days to sell the inventory. What conclusions concerning the management of the inventory can be drawn from these data?

**BE19–11**   McCarty Company has owners' equity of $400,000 and net income of $60,000. It has a payout ratio of 20% and a rate of return on assets of 16%. How much did McCarty pay in cash dividends, and what were its average assets?

*Calculate profitability ratios.*
*(SO 5)*

**BE19–12**   Selected data taken from the 1999 financial statements of Shirley Denson Manufacturing Company are as follows:

*Calculate cash-basis liquidity, profitability, and solvency ratios. (SO 5)*

| | |
|---|---|
| Net sales for 1999 | $6,860,000 |
| Current liabilities, January 1, 1999 | 180,000 |
| Current liabilities, December 31, 1999 | 240,000 |
| Net cash provided by operating activities | 760,000 |
| Total liabilities, January 1, 1999 | 1,500,000 |
| Total liabilities, December 31, 1999 | 1,300,000 |

Compute the following ratios at December 31, 1999: (a) the current cash debt coverage ratio, (b) the cash return on sales ratio, and (c) the cash debt coverage ratio.

# EXERCISES*

*Prepare horizontal analysis.*
*(SO 3)*

**E19–1**  Financial information for Lister Inc. is presented below:

| | December 31, 2000 | December 31, 1999 |
|---|---|---|
| Current assets | $125,000 | $100,000 |
| Plant assets (net) | 400,000 | 330,000 |
| Current liabilities | 91,000 | 70,000 |
| Long-term liabilities | 144,000 | 95,000 |
| Common stock, $1 par | 155,000 | 115,000 |
| Retained earnings | 135,000 | 150,000 |

**Instructions**
Prepare a schedule showing a horizontal analysis for 2000 using 1999 as the base year.

*Prepare vertical analysis.*
*(SO 4)*

**E19–2**  Operating data for Khan Corporation are presented below:

| | 2000 | 1999 |
|---|---|---|
| Sales | $800,000 | $600,000 |
| Cost of goods sold | 464,000 | 378,000 |
| Selling expenses | 120,000 | 72,000 |
| Administrative expenses | 80,000 | 54,000 |
| Income tax expense | 38,400 | 25,200 |
| Net income | 97,600 | 70,800 |

**Instructions**
Prepare a schedule showing a vertical analysis for 2000 and 1999.

*Prepare horizontal and vertical analyses.*
*(SO 3, 4)*

**E19–3**  The comparative balance sheets of Barkley Corporation are presented below:

**BARKLEY CORPORATION**
**Comparative Balance Sheets**
**December 31**

| | 2000 | 1999 |
|---|---|---|
| Assets | | |
| Current assets | $ 76,000 | $ 80,000 |
| Property, plant, & equipment (net) | 99,000 | 90,000 |
| Intangibles | 25,000 | 40,000 |
| Total assets | $200,000 | $210,000 |
| Liabilities & stockholders' equity | | |
| Current liabilities | $ 45,800 | $ 48,000 |
| Long-term liabilities | 138,000 | 150,000 |
| Stockholders' equity | 16,200 | 12,000 |
| Total liabilities & stockholders' equity | $200,000 | $210,000 |

*Follow the rounding procedures used in the chapter.

*Instructions*

(a) Prepare a horizontal analysis of the balance sheet data for Barkley Corporation using 1999 as a base. (Show the amount of increase or decrease as well.)

(b) Prepare a vertical analysis of the balance sheet data for Barkley Corporation in columnar form for 2000.

**E19–4**   The comparative income statements of LaGalle Corporation are shown below:

*Prepare horizontal and vertical analyses.*
*(SO 3, 4)*

### LaGalle Corporation
### Comparative Income Statements
### For the Years Ended December 31

|  | 2000 | 1999 |
|---|---|---|
| Net sales | $550,000 | $500,000 |
| Cost of goods sold | 440,000 | 420,000 |
| Gross profit | 110,000 | 80,000 |
| Operating expenses | 57,200 | 44,000 |
| Net income | $ 52,800 | $ 36,000 |

*Instructions*

(a) Prepare a horizontal analysis of the income statement data for LaGalle Corporation using 1999 as a base. (Show the amounts of increase or decrease.)

(b) Prepare a vertical analysis of the income statement data for LaGalle Corporation in columnar form for both years.

**E19–5**   Nordstrom, Inc., operates department stores in numerous states. Selected financial statement data in millions of dollars for a recent year are as follows:

*Compute liquidity ratios and compare results.*
*(SO 5)*

### Nordstrom, Inc.
### Balance Sheet (partial)

|  | End-of-Year | Beginning-of-Year |
|---|---|---|
| Cash and cash equivalents | $ 33 | $ 91 |
| Receivables (net) | 676 | 586 |
| Merchandise Inventory | 628 | 586 |
| Prepaid expenses | 61 | 52 |
| Total current assets | $1,398 | $1,315 |
| Total current liabilities | $690 | $627 |

For the year, net sales were $3,894 and cost of goods sold was $2,600. Net cash provided by operating activities was $800.

*Instructions*

(a) Compute the five liquidity ratios at the end of the current year.

(b) Using the data in the chapter, compare Nordstrom's liquidity with (1) Sears, Roebuck and (2) the industry averages for department stores.

**E19–6**   Fargo Incorporated had the following transactions occur involving current assets and current liabilities during February 1999:

*Perform current and acid-test ratio analysis.*
*(SO 5)*

Feb.  3   Accounts receivable of $15,000 are collected.

7   Equipment is purchased for $25,000 cash.

11   Paid $3,000 for a 3-year insurance policy.

14   Accounts payable of $14,000 are paid.

18   Cash dividends are declared, $6,000.

Additional information:

1. As of February 1, 1999, current assets were $120,000 and current liabilities were $50,000.

2. As of February 1, 1999, current assets included $15,000 of inventory and $5,000 of prepaid expenses.

*Instructions*

(a) Compute the current ratio as of the beginning of the month and after each transaction.

(b) Compute the acid-test ratio as of the beginning of the month and after each transaction.

*Compute selected ratios.*
*(SO 5)*

**E19–7**   Georgette Company has the following comparative balance sheet data:

**GEORGETTE COMPANY**
**Balance Sheet**
**December 31**

| | 1999 | 1998 |
|---|---|---|
| Cash | $ 20,000 | $ 30,000 |
| Receivables (net) | 65,000 | 60,000 |
| Inventories | 60,000 | 50,000 |
| Plant assets (net) | 200,000 | 180,000 |
| | $345,000 | $320,000 |
| | | |
| Accounts payable | $ 50,000 | $ 60,000 |
| Mortgage payable (15%) | 100,000 | 100,000 |
| Common stock, $10 par | 140,000 | 120,000 |
| Retained earnings | 55,000 | 40,000 |
| | $345,000 | $320,000 |

Additional information for 1999:

1. Net income was $25,000.
2. Sales on account were $420,000. Sales returns and allowances amounted to $20,000.
3. Cost of goods sold was $198,000.
4. Net cash provided by operating activities was $44,000.

*Instructions*
Compute the following ratios at December 31, 1999:

(a) Current.
(b) Acid-test.
(c) Receivables turnover.
(d) Inventory turnover.

(e) Cash return on sales.
(f) Cash debt coverage.
(g) Current cash debt coverage.

*Compute selected ratios.*
*(SO 5)*

**E19–8**   Selected comparative statement data for Meng Products Company are presented below. All balance sheet data are as of December 31.

| | 2000 | 1999 |
|---|---|---|
| Net sales | $800,000 | $720,000 |
| Cost of goods sold | 480,000 | 40,000 |
| Interest expense | 7,000 | 5,000 |
| Net income | 64,000 | 42,000 |
| Accounts receivable | 120,000 | 100,000 |
| Inventory | 85,000 | 75,000 |
| Total assets | 600,000 | 500,000 |
| Total common stockholders' equity | 450,000 | 310,000 |

*Instructions*
Compute the following ratios for 2000:

(a) Profit margin.
(b) Asset turnover.
(c) Return on assets.
(d) Return on common stockholders' equity.

**E19–9**   The income statement for Cheryl Countryman, Inc., appears below.

*Compute selected ratios.*
*(SO 5)*

### CHERYL COUNTRYMAN, INC.
### Income Statement
### For the Year Ended December 31, 1999

| | |
|---|---:|
| Sales | $400,000 |
| Cost of goods sold | 230,000 |
| Gross profit | 170,000 |
| Expenses (including $20,000 interest and $24,000 income taxes) | 100,000 |
| Net income | $ 70,000 |

Additional information:

1. Common stock outstanding January 1, 1999, was 35,000 shares.
2. The market price of Cheryl Countryman, Inc., stock was $15 in 1999.
3. Cash dividends of $21,000 were paid, $5,000 of which were to preferred stockholders.
4. Net cash provided by operating activities $98,000.

*Instructions*
Compute the following ratios for 1999.

(a) Earnings per share.     (d) Times interest earned.
(b) Price-earnings.     (e) Cash return on sales.
(c) Payout.

**E19–10**   Perez Corporation experienced a fire on December 31, 2000, in which its financial records were partially destroyed. It has been able to salvage some of the records and has ascertained the following balances:

*Compute amounts from ratios.*
*(SO 5)*

| | December 31, 2000 | December 31, 1999 |
|---|---:|---:|
| Cash | $ 30,000 | $ 10,000 |
| Receivables (net) | 72,500 | 126,000 |
| Inventory | 200,000 | 180,000 |
| Accounts payable | 50,000 | 90,000 |
| Notes payable | 30,000 | 60,000 |
| Common stock, $100 par | 400,000 | 400,000 |
| Retained earnings | 115,000 | 101,000 |

Additional information:

1. The inventory turnover is 3.8 times.
2. The return on common stockholders' equity is 22%. The company had no additional paid-in capital.
3. The receivables turnover is 8.4 times.
4. The return on assets is 20%.
5. Total assets at December 31, 1999, were $605,000.

*Instructions*
Compute the following for Perez Corporation:

(a)  Cost of goods sold for 2000.
(b)  Net sales for 2000.
(c)  Net income for 2000.
(d)  Total assets at December 31, 2000.

# PROBLEMS*

**P19–1**   Comparative statement data for Eller Company and Foley Company, two competitors, appear below. All balance sheet data are as of December 31, 2000, and December 31, 1999.

*Prepare vertical analysis and comment on profitability.*
*(SO 4, 5)*

*Follow the rounding procedures used in the chapter.

|  | Eller Company | | Foley Company | |
|---|---|---|---|---|
|  | **2000** | **1999** | **2000** | **1999** |
| Net sales | $1,549,035 |  | $339,038 |  |
| Cost of goods sold | 1,080,490 |  | 238,006 |  |
| Operating expenses | 302,275 |  | 79,000 |  |
| Interest expense | 6,800 |  | 1,252 |  |
| Income tax expense | 51,030 |  | 6,650 |  |
| Current assets | 325,975 | $312,410 | 83,336 | $ 79,467 |
| Plant assets (net) | 521,310 | 500,000 | 139,728 | 125,812 |
| Current liabilities | 66,325 | 75,815 | 35,348 | 30,281 |
| Long-term liabilities | 108,500 | 90,000 | 29,620 | 25,000 |
| Common stock, $10 par | 500,000 | 500,000 | 120,000 | 120,000 |
| Retained earnings | 172,460 | 146,595 | 38,096 | 29,998 |

*Instructions*
(a) Prepare a vertical analysis of the 2000 income statement data for Eller Company and Foley Company in columnar form.
(b) �▶ Comment on the relative profitability of the companies by computing the return on assets and the return on common stockholders' equity ratios for both companies.

*Compute ratios from balance sheet and income statement.* (SO 5)

**P19–2** The comparative statements of Dorothy Fleming Company are presented below:

## DOROTHY FLEMING COMPANY
### Income Statement
### For the Year Ended December 31

|  | **1999** | **1998** |
|---|---|---|
| Net sales | $1,818,500 | $1,750,500 |
| Cost of goods sold | 1,005,500 | 996,000 |
| Gross profit | 813,000 | 754,500 |
| Selling and administrative expense | 506,000 | 479,000 |
| Income from operations | 307,000 | 275,500 |
| Other expenses and losses |  |  |
|   Interest expense | 18,000 | 19,000 |
| Income before income taxes | 289,000 | 256,500 |
| Income tax expense | 86,700 | 77,000 |
| Net income | $ 202,300 | $ 179,500 |

## DOROTHY FLEMING COMPANY
### Balance Sheet
### December 31

| Assets | **1999** | **1998** |
|---|---|---|
| Current assets |  |  |
|   Cash | $ 60,100 | $ 64,200 |
|   Marketable securities | 54,000 | 50,000 |
|   Accounts receivable (net) | 107,800 | 102,800 |
|   Inventory | 123,000 | 115,500 |
|     Total current assets | 344,900 | 332,500 |
| Plant assets (net) | 625,300 | 520,300 |
| Total assets | $970,200 | $852,800 |

| Liabilities and Stockholders' Equity | 1999 | 1998 |
|---|---|---|
| Current liabilities | | |
| Accounts payable | $150,000 | $145,400 |
| Income taxes payable | 43,500 | 42,000 |
| Total current liabilities | 193,500 | 187,400 |
| Bonds payable | 210,000 | 200,000 |
| Total liabilities | 403,500 | 387,400 |
| Stockholders' equity | | |
| Common stock ($5 par) | 280,000 | 300,000 |
| Retained earnings | 286,700 | 165,400 |
| Total stockholders' equity | 566,700 | 465,400 |
| Total liabilities and stockholders' equity | $970,200 | $852,800 |

On April 1, 1999, 4,000 shares were repurchased and canceled. All sales were on account. Net cash provided by operating activities for 1999 was $280,000.

*Instructions*
Compute the following ratios for 1999:

(a) Earnings per share.
(b) Return on common stockholders' equity.
(c) Return on assets.
(d) Current.
(e) Acid-test.
(f) Receivables turnover.
(g) Inventory turnover.

(h) Times interest earned.
(i) Asset turnover.
(j) Debt to total assets.
(k) Current cash debt coverage.
(l) Cash return on sales.
(m) Cash debt coverage.

**P19–3**  Condensed balance sheet and income statement data for Roland Carlson Corporation appear below:

*Perform ratio analysis.*
(SO 5)

### ROLAND CARLSON CORPORATION
### Balance Sheet
### December 31

| | 2000 | 1999 | 1998 |
|---|---|---|---|
| Cash | $ 25,000 | $ 20,000 | $ 18,000 |
| Receivables (net) | 50,000 | 45,000 | 48,000 |
| Other current assets | 90,000 | 85,000 | 64,000 |
| Investments | 75,000 | 70,000 | 45,000 |
| Plant and equipment (net) | 400,000 | 370,000 | 358,000 |
| | $640,000 | $590,000 | $533,000 |
| Current liabilities | $ 75,000 | $ 80,000 | $ 70,000 |
| Long-term debt | 80,000 | 85,000 | 50,000 |
| Common stock, $10 par | 340,000 | 300,000 | 300,000 · |
| Retained earnings | 145,000 | 125,000 | 113,000 |
| | $640,000 | $590,000 | $533,000 |

### ROLAND CARLSON CORPORATION
### Income Statement
### For the Years Ended December 31

| | 2000 | 1999 |
|---|---|---|
| Sales | $740,000 | $700,000 |
| Less: Sales returns and allowances | 40,000 | 50,000 |
| Net sales | 700,000 | 650,000 |
| Cost of goods sold | 420,000 | 400,000 |
| Gross profit | 280,000 | 250,000 |
| Operating expenses (including income taxes) | 230,000 | 215,000 |
| Net income | $ 50,000 | $ 35,000 |

Additional information:

1. The market price of Carlson's common stock was $4.00, $5.00, and $7.95 for 1998, 1999, and 2000, respectively.
2. All dividends were paid in cash.
3. On July 1, 2000, 4,000 shares of common stock were issued.

*Instructions*

(a) Compute the following ratios for 1999 and 2000:
   (1) Profit margin.
   (2) Asset turnover.
   (3) Earnings per share.
   (4) Price-earnings.
   (5) Payout.
   (6) Debt to total assets.
(b) ▉▉▉▊═▶ Based on the ratios calculated, discuss briefly the improvement or lack thereof in financial position and operating results from 1999 to 2000 of Roland Carlson Corporation.

*Compute ratios, commenting on overall liquidity and profitability.*
*(SO 5)*

**P19–4**   Financial information for Callaway Company is presented below:

### CALLAWAY COMPANY
### Balance Sheet
### December 31

| Assets | 2000 | 1999 |
|---|---|---|
| Cash | $ 60,000 | $ 55,000 |
| Short-term investments | 45,000 | 40,000 |
| Receivables (net) | 94,000 | 90,000 |
| Inventories | 130,000 | 125,000 |
| Prepaid expenses | 25,000 | 23,000 |
| Land | 140,000 | 140,000 |
| Building and equipment (net) | 190,000 | 175,000 |
| | $684,000 | $648,000 |

| Liabilities and Stockholders' Equity | 2000 | 1999 |
|---|---|---|
| Notes payable | $100,000 | $100,000 |
| Accounts payable | 45,000 | 42,000 |
| Accrued liabilities | 40,000 | 40,000 |
| Bonds payable, due 2003 | 150,000 | 150,000 |
| Common stock, $10 par | 200,000 | 200,000 |
| Retained earnings | 149,000 | 116,000 |
| | $684,000 | $648,000 |

### CALLAWAY COMPANY
### Income Statement
### For the Years Ended December 31

| | 2000 | 1999 |
|---|---|---|
| Sales | $850,000 | $790,000 |
| Cost of goods sold | 610,000 | 570,000 |
| Gross profit | 240,000 | 220,000 |
| Operating expenses | 194,000 | 180,000 |
| Net income | $ 46,000 | $ 40,000 |

Additional information:

1. Inventory at the beginning of 1999 was $115,000.
2. Receivables at the beginning of 1999 were $88,000.
3. Total assets at the beginning of 1999 were $630,000.
4. No common stock transactions occurred during 1999 or 2000.
5. All sales were on account.

## Instructions

(a) Indicate, by using ratios, the change in liquidity and profitability of Callaway Company from 1999 to 2000. (Note: Not all profitability ratios can be computed.)

(b) Given below are three independent situations and a ratio that may be affected. For each situation, compute the affected ratio (1) as of December 31, 2000, and (2) as of December 31, 2001, after giving effect to the situation. Net income for 2001 was $45,000. Total assets on December 31, 2001, were $700,000.

| Situation | Ratio |
| --- | --- |
| 1. 18,000 shares of common stock were sold at par on July 1, 2001. | Return on common stockholders' equity |
| 2. All of the notes payable were paid in 2001. | Debt to total assets |
| 3. Market price of common stock was $9 and $12.80 on December 31, 2000, and 2001, respectively. | Price-earnings ratio |

**P19–5**  Selected financial data of two intense competitors in a recent year are presented below in millions of dollars.

*Compute selected ratios and compare liquidity, profitability, and solvency for two companies.*
*(SO 5)*

| | Kmart Corporation | Wal-Mart Stores, Inc. |
| --- | --- | --- |
| **Income Statement Data for Year** | | |
| Net sales | $34,025 | $82,494 |
| Cost of goods sold | 25,992 | 65,586 |
| Selling and administrative expenses | 7,701 | 12,858 |
| Interest expense | 494 | 706 |
| Other income (net) | 572 | 918 |
| Income taxes | 114 | 1,581 |
| Net income | $   296 | $ 2,681 |
| **Balance Sheet Data (End-of-Year)** | | |
| Current assets | $ 9,187 | $15,338 |
| Property, plant, and equipment (net) | 7,842 | 17,481 |
| Total assets | $17,029 | $32,819 |
| Current liabilities | $ 5,626 | $ 9,973 |
| Long-term debt | 5,371 | 10,120 |
| Total stockholders' equity | 6,032 | 12,726 |
| Total liabilities and stockholders' equity | $17,029 | $32,819 |
| **Beginning-of-Year Balances** | | |
| Total assets | $17,504 | $26,441 |
| Total stockholders' equity | 6,093 | 10,753 |
| **Other Data** | | |
| Average net receivables | $ 1,570 | $   695 |
| Average inventory | 7,317 | 12,539 |
| Net cash provided by operating activities | 351 | 3,106 |

## Instructions

(a) For each company, compute the following ratios:

(1) Current
(2) Receivables turnover
(3) Inventory turnover
(4) Profit margin
(5) Asset turnover
(6) Return on assets

(7) Return on common stockholders' equity
(8) Debt to total assets
(9) Times interest earned
(10) Current cash debt coverage
(11) Cash return on sales
(12) Cash debt coverage

(b) Compare the liquidity, profitability, and solvency of the two companies.

*Compute numerous ratios.*    **P19–6**    The comparative statements of Swanson Company are presented below:
*(SO 5)*

## SWANSON COMPANY
## Income Statement
### For Year Ended December 31

|  | 2000 | 1999 |
|---|---|---|
| Net sales (all on account) | $650,000 | $520,000 |
| Expenses |  |  |
| Cost of goods sold | 415,000 | 354,000 |
| Selling and administrative | 150,800 | 114,800 |
| Interest expense | 7,200 | 6,000 |
| Income tax expense | 18,000 | 14,000 |
| Total expenses | 591,000 | 488,800 |
| Net income | $ 59,000 | $ 31,200 |

## SWANSON COMPANY
## Balance Sheet
### December 31

| Assets | 2000 | 1999 |
|---|---|---|
| Current assets |  |  |
| Cash | $ 41,000 | $ 18,000 |
| Marketable securities | 18,000 | 15,000 |
| Accounts receivable (net) | 92,000 | 74,000 |
| Inventory | 84,000 | 70,000 |
| Total current assets | 235,000 | 177,000 |
| Plant assets (net) | 403,000 | 383,000 |
| Total assets | $638,000 | $560,000 |
| **Liabilities and Stockholders' Equity** |  |  |
| Current liabilities |  |  |
| Accounts payable | $112,000 | $110,000 |
| Income taxes payable | 23,000 | 20,000 |
| Total current liabilities | 135,000 | 130,000 |
| Long-term liabilities |  |  |
| Bonds payable | 130,000 | 80,000 |
| Total liabilities | 265,000 | 210,000 |
| Stockholders' equity |  |  |
| Common stock ($5 par) | 150,000 | 150,000 |
| Retained earnings | 223,000 | 200,000 |
| Total stockholders' equity | 373,000 | 350,000 |
| Total liabilities and stockholders' equity | $638,000 | $560,000 |

**Additional data:**
The common stock recently sold at $19.50 per share.

*Instructions*
Compute the following ratios for 2000:

(a) Current.
(b) Acid-test.
(c) Receivables turnover.
(d) Inventory turnover.
(e) Profit margin.
(f) Asset turnover.
(g) Return on assets.

(h) Return on common stockholders' equity.
(i) Earnings per share.
(j) Price-earnings.
(k) Payout.
(l) Debt to total assets.
(m) Times interest earned.

**P19–7**   Presented below is an incomplete income statement and an incomplete comparative balance sheet of Vickers Corporation:

*Compute missing information given a set of ratios.*
*(SO 5)*

### VICKERS CORPORATION
### Income Statement
### For the Year Ended December 31, 2000

| | |
|---|---:|
| Sales | $12,000,000 |
| Cost of goods sold | ? |
| Gross profit | ? |
| Operating expenses | 2,665,000 |
| Income from operations | ? |
| Other expenses and losses | |
| Interest expense | ? |
| Income before income taxes | ? |
| Income tax expense | 580,000 |
| Net income | $    ? |

### VICKERS CORPORATION
### Balance Sheet
### December 31

| Assets | 2000 | 1999 |
|---|---:|---:|
| **Current assets** | | |
| Cash | $   440,000 | $   375,000 |
| Accounts receivable (net) | ? | 950,000 |
| Inventory | ? | 1,720,000 |
| Total current assets | ? | 3,045,000 |
| Plant assets (net) | 4,550,000 | 3,955,000 |
| Total assets | $    ? | $7,000,000 |
| **Liabilities and Stockholders' Equity** | | |
| Current liabilities | $    ? | $   825,000 |
| Long-term notes payable | ? | 2,800,000 |
| Total liabilities | ? | 3,625,000 |
| Common stock, $1 par | 3,000,000 | 3,000,000 |
| Retained earnings | 400,000 | 375,000 |
| Total stockholders' equity | 3,400,000 | 3,375,000 |
| Total liabilities and stockholders' equity | $    ? | $7,000,000 |

Additional information:

1. The receivables turnover for 2000 is 10 times.
2. All sales are on account.
3. The profit margin for 2000 is 15%.
4. Return on assets is 25% for 2000.
5. The current ratio on December 31, 2000, is 3:1.
6. The inventory turnover for 2000 is 5 times.

**Instructions**

Compute the missing information given the ratios above. Show computations. (Note: Start with one ratio and derive as much information as possible from it before trying another ratio. List all missing amounts under the ratio used to find the information.)

## BROADENING YOUR PERSPECTIVE

# FINANCIAL REPORTING AND ANALYSIS

### FINANCIAL REPORTING PROBLEM: Kellogg Company

**BYP19–1**   Your parents are considering investing in Kellogg Company, Inc., common stock. They ask you, as an accounting expert, to make an analysis of the company for them. Fortunately, excerpts from a current annual report of Kellogg are presented in Appendix A of this textbook. Note that all amounts omit 000,000's (i.e., all dollar amounts are in millions).

*Instructions*
(Follow the approach in the chapter for rounding numbers.)

(a) Make a 5-year trend analysis, using 1993 as the base year, of (1) net sales and (2) operating profit. Comment on the significance of the trend results.

(b) Compute for 1997 and 1996 the (1) profit margin, (2) asset turnover, (3) return on assets, and (4) return on common stockholders' equity. How would you evaluate Kellogg's profitability? Total assets at December 31, 1995, were $4,414.6, and total stockholders' equity at December 31, 1995, was $1,590.9.

(c) Compute for 1997 and 1996 the (1) debt to total assets and (2) times interest earned ratio. How would you evaluate Kellogg's long-term solvency?

(d) What information outside the annual report may also be useful to your parents in making a decision about Kellogg Company?

### COMPARATIVE ANALYSIS PROBLEM: Kellogg Company vs. General Mills

**BYP19–2**   Kellogg's financial statements are presented in Appendix A; General Mills's financial statements are presented in Appendix B.

*Instructions*

(a) Based on the information contained in these financial statements, determine each of the following for each company:
   1. The percentage increase (decrease) in (i) net sales and (ii) net income from 1996 to 1997.
   2. The percentage increase in (i) total assets and (ii) total stockholders' (shareholders') equity from 1996 to 1997.
   3. The earnings per share and price-earnings ratio for 1997. General Mills's common stock had a market price of $64.25 at the end of 1997.

(b) What conclusions concerning the two companies can be drawn from these data?

### RESEARCH ASSIGNMENT

**BYP19–3**   The chapter stresses the importance of comparing an individual firm's financial ratios to industry norms. Robert Morris Associates (RMA), a national association of bank loan and credit officers, publishes industry-specific financial data in its *Annual Statement Studies*. This publication includes common-size financial statements and various ratios classified by four-digit SIC code. (Note: An alternative source is Dun & Bradstreet's *Industry Norms and Key Business Ratios*.)

   Obtain the 1997 edition of *Annual Statement Studies* (covering fiscal years ended 4/1/96 through 3/31/97) and the 1997 (or 1998) Annual Report of Wal-Mart Stores, Inc.

*Instructions*

(a) Prepare a 1997 common-size (vertical analysis) balance sheet and income statement for Wal-Mart.

(b) Calculate those 1997 ratios for Wal-Mart which are covered by RMA. (Note: The specific ratio definitions used by RMA are described in the beginning of the book. Use ending values for balance sheet items.)

(c) What is Wal-Mart's SIC code? Use your answers from parts (a) and (b) to compare Wal-Mart to the appropriate current industry data. How does Wal-Mart compare to its competitors? (Note: RMA sorts current-year data by firm assets and sales, while five years of historical data are presented on an aggregate basis.)

(d) How many sets of financial statements did RMA use in compiling the current industry data sorted by sales?

## INTERPRETING FINANCIAL STATEMENTS: Manitowoc Company and Caterpillar Corp.

**BYP19–4** The Manitowoc Company and Caterpillar Corporation are both producers and sellers of large fixed assets. Caterpillar is substantially larger than Manitowoc. Financial information taken from each company's financial statements is provided below.

| Financial highlights | Caterpillar (in millions) | | Manitowoc (in thousands) | |
|---|---|---|---|---|
| | 1995 | 1994 | 1995 | 1994 |
| Cash and short-term investments | $ 638 | $ 419 | $ 16,635 | $ 16,163 |
| Accounts receivable | 4,285 | 4,290 | 51,011 | 29,500 |
| Inventory | 1,921 | 1,835 | 52,928 | 36,793 |
| Other current assets | 803 | 865 | 14,571 | 14,082 |
| Current assets | 7,647 | 7,409 | 135,145 | 96,538 |
| Total assets | 16,830 | 16,250 | 324,915 | 159,465 |
| Current liabilities | 6,049 | 5,498 | 110,923 | 54,064 |
| Total liabilities | 13,442 | 13,339 | 243,254 | 84,408 |
| Total stockholders' equity | 3,388 | 2,911 | 81,661 | 75,057 |
| Sales | 15,451 | | 313,149 | |
| Cost of goods sold | 12,000 | | 237,679 | |
| Interest expense | 191 | | 1,865 | |
| Income tax expense | 501 | | 8,551 | |
| Net income | 1,136 | | 14,569 | |
| Cash provided from operations | 2,190 | | 16,367 | |

*Instructions*

(a) Calculate the following liquidity ratios and provide a discussion of the relative liquidity of the two companies.
   1. Current ratio
   2. Quick or acid-test ratio
   3. Current cash debt coverage
   4. Accounts receivable turnover
   5. Inventory turnover
(b) Calculate the following profitability ratios and provide a discussion of the relative profitability of the two companies.
   1. Asset turnover
   2. Profit margin on sales
   3. Return on assets
   4. Return on common equity
(c) Calculate the following solvency ratios and provide a discussion of the relative solvency of the two companies.
   1. Debt to assets
   2. Times interest earned

## REAL-WORLD FOCUS: The Coca-Cola Company and PepsiCo, Inc.

**BYP19–5** The Coca-Cola Company and PepsiCo, Inc., provides refreshments to every corner of the world. Both believe that great potential still exists—to satisfy the thirst of the world's population. Selected data from the consolidated financial statements for The Coca-Cola Company and for PepsiCo, Inc., are presented below. (All dollars are in millions.)

|  | Coca-Cola | PepsiCo |
|---|---|---|
| Total current assets (including cash, accounts receivable, and marketable securities totaling $3,056 and $3,539, respectively) | $ 5,205 | $ 5,546 |
| Total current liabilities | 6,177 | 5,230 |
| Net sales | 16,172 | 30,421 |
| Cost of goods sold | 6,167 | 14,886 |
| Net income | 2,554 | 1,606 |
| Average receivables for the year | 1,384 | 2,229 |
| Average inventories for the year | 1,048 | 1,011 |
| Average total assets | 12,947 | 25,112 |
| Average common stockholders' equity | 4,910 | 7,085 |
| Net cash provided by operating activities | 3,115 | 3,742 |
| Average current liabilities | 6,763 | 5,250 |
| Total assets | 13,873 | 25,432 |
| Total liabilities | 8,638 | 18,119 |
| Income before income taxes | 3,728 | 2,432 |
| Interest expense | 199 | 682 |

*Instructions*

(a) Compute the following liquidity ratios for Coca-Cola and for PepsiCo.:
   (1) Current
   (2) Acid-test
   (3) Current cash debt coverage
   (4) Receivables turnover
   (5) Inventory turnover
(b) Comment on the relative liquidity of the two competitors.
(c) Compute the following profitability ratios for the two companies:
   (1) Profit margin
   (2) Cash return on sales
   (3) Asset turnover
   (4) Return on assets
   (5) Return on common stockholders' equity
(d) Comment on the relative profitability of the two competitors.

# CRITICAL THINKING

## GROUP DECISION CASE

**BYP19–6**   As the CPA for L. Gonzalez Manufacturing Inc., you have been requested to develop some key ratios from the comparative financial statements. This information is to be used to convince creditors that L. Gonzalez Manufacturing Inc. is solvent and to support the use of going-concern valuation procedures in the financial statements.

The data requested and the computations developed from the financial statements follow:

|  | 2000 | 1999 |
|---|---|---|
| Current ratio | 3.1 times | 2.1 times |
| Acid-test ratio | .8 times | 1.4 times |
| Asset turnover | 2.8 times | 2.2 times |
| Sales to stockholders' equity | 2.3 times | 2.7 times |
| Net income | Up 32% | Down 8% |
| Earnings per share | $3.30 | $2.50 |
| Book value per share | Up 8% | Up 11% |

*Instructions*

With the class divided into groups, answer the following:

(a) L. Gonzalez Manufacturing Inc. asks you to prepare a list of brief comments stating how each of these items supports the solvency and going-concern potential of the business. The company wishes to use these comments to support its presentation of data to its creditors. You are to prepare the comments as requested, giving the implications and the limitations of each item separately, and then the collective inference that may be drawn from them about L. Gonzales's solvency and going-concern potential.

(b) What warnings should you offer these creditors about the limitations of ratio analysis for the purpose stated here?

## COMMUNICATION ACTIVITY

**BYP19–7**   Ken Powell is the Chief Executive Officer of Midwest Electronics. Powell is an expert engineer but a novice in accounting. Powell asks you, as an accounting major, to explain (1) the bases for comparison in analyzing Midwest's financial statements and (2) the limitations, if any, in financial statement analysis.

*Instructions*

Write a letter to Powell that explains the bases for comparison and the limitations of financial statement analysis.

## ETHICS CASE

**BYP19–8**   Ron Staub, president of Staub Industries, wishes to issue a press release to bolster his company's image and maybe even its stock price, which has been gradually falling. As controller, you have been asked to provide a list of twenty financial ratios along with some other operating statistics relative to Staub Industries' first quarter financials and operations.

Two days after you provide the ratios and data requested, you are asked by Manny Alomar, the public relations director of Staub, to prove the accuracy of the financial and operating data contained in the press release written by the president and edited by Manny. In the news release, the president highlights the sales increase of 25% over last year's first quarter and the positive change in the current ratio from 1.5:1 last year to 3:1 this year. He also emphasizes that production was up 50% over the prior year's first quarter. You note that the release contains only positive or improved ratios and none of the negative or deteriorated ratios. For instance, no mention is made that the debt to total assets ratio has increased from 35% to 55%, that inventories are up 89%, and that while the current ratio improved, the acid-test ratio fell from 1:1 to .5:1. Nor is there any mention that the reported profit for the quarter would have been a loss had not the estimated lives of Staub's plant and machinery been increased by 30%. Manny emphasized, "The Pres wants this release by early this afternoon."

*Instructions*

(a) Who are the stakeholders in this situation?

(b) Is there anything unethical in president Staub's actions?

(c) Should you as controller remain silent? Does Manny have any responsibility?

# SURFING THE NET

**BYP19–9**   The Management Discussion and Analysis (MD&A) section of an annual report addresses corporate performance for the year, and sometimes uses financial ratios to support its claims.

**Addresses:** http://www.ibm.com/financialguide
http://www.yahoo.com

**Steps:**
1. From IBM's Financial Guide, choose **Guides Contents.**
2. Choose **Anatomy of an Annual Report.**
3. Follow instruction (a).
4. From Yahoo Homepage, choose **Stock Quotes.**
5. Enter **GE.**
6. Choose **Get Quotes.**
7. Choose **SEC filing** (this will take you to Yahoo-Edgar Online).
8. Choose the most recent annual report.
9. Follow instructions (b)-(e).

*Instructions*

(a) Using IBM's Financial Guide, describe the contents of the Management Discussion and Analysis.
(b) In the overview section, GE's management discusses the company's performance. What were the net corporate earnings in the most recent year?
(c) Compare current year earnings with the previous year's earnings.
(d) What were management's reasons for the change in net earnings?

---

*Answers to Self-Study Questions*
1. b    2. d    3. a    4. c    5. c    6. c    7. c    8. b    9. a    10. b

---

*Answer to Kellogg Review It Question 4, p. 827.*
4. Kellogg presents horizontal analyses in its "Financial Highlights" section, its Management's Discussion and Analysis section, and its Note 13 on Operating Segments. Vertical analysis is used in schedules presented in the Management's Discussion and Analysis section.

**Remember to go back to the Navigator box on the chapter-opening page and check off your completed work.**

# APPENDIXES A – E

# SPECIMEN FINANCIAL STATEMENTS:
## Kellogg Company

........................................................................................................

# THE ANNUAL REPORT

Once each year a corporation communicates to its stockholders and other interested parties by issuing a complete set of audited financial statements. The **annual report**, as this communication is called, summarizes the financial results of its operations for the year and its plans for the future. Many such annual reports have become attractive, multicolored, glossy public relations ad pieces containing pictures of corporate officers and directors as well as photos and descriptions of new products and new buildings. Yet the basic function of every annual report is to report **financial information**, almost all of which is a product of the corporation's accounting system.

The content and organization of corporate annual reports have become fairly standardized. Excluding the public relations part of the report (pictures and products), the following items are the traditional financial portions of the annual report:

> Financial Highlights
> Letter to the Stockholders
> Auditor's Report
> Management Discussion and Analysis
> Financial Statements and Accompanying Notes
> Five- or Ten-Year Summary

In this appendix we illustrate current financial reporting with a comprehensive set of corporate financial statements that are prepared in accordance with generally accepted accounting principles and audited by an international independent certified public accounting firm. We are grateful for permission to use the actual financial statements and other accompanying financial information from the annual report of a large, publicly held company, Kellogg Company.

# FINANCIAL HIGHLIGHTS

The financial highlights section is usually presented inside the front cover or on the first two pages of the annual report. This section generally reports the total or per share amounts for five to ten financial items for the current year and one or more previous years. Financial items from the income statement and the balance sheet that typically are presented are sales, income from continuing operations, net income, net income per share, dividends per common share, and the amount of capital expenditures. The financial highlights section from Kellogg's Annual Report is shown below:

## FINANCIAL HIGHLIGHTS

| (millions, except per share data) | 1997 | Change | 1996 | Change | 1995 | Change |
|---|---|---|---|---|---|---|
| Net sales | $6,830.1 | +2% | $6,676.6 | -5% | $7,003.7 | +7% |
| Operating profit, excluding non-recurring charges (a) | 1,193.2 | +9% | 1,095.0 | -13% | 1,259.3 | +8% |
| Earnings, excluding non-recurring charges and other unusual items (a) and before cumulative effect of accounting change (b) | 704.5 | +8% | 651.1 | -14% | 761.6 | +8% |
| Earnings per share (basic and diluted), excluding non-recurring charges and other unusual items (a) and before cumulative effect of accounting change (b) (c) | 1.70 | +11% | 1.53 | -12% | 1.74 | +10% |
| Operating profit | 1,009.1 | +5% | 958.9 | +14% | 837.5 | -28% |
| Net earnings | 546.0 | +3% | 531.0 | +8% | 490.3 | -30% |
| Net earnings per share (basic and diluted) (c) | 1.32 | +6% | 1.25 | +12% | 1.12 | -29% |
| Net cash provided by operating activities | 879.8 | +24% | 711.5 | -32% | 1,041.0 | +8% |
| Capital expenditures | 312.4 | +2% | 307.3 | -3% | 315.7 | -11% |
| Average shares outstanding (c) | 414.1 | | 424.9 | | 438.3 | |
| Dividends per share (c) | $ .87 | +7% | $ .81 | +8% | $ .75 | +7% |
| Year-end stock price (c) | $ 49⅝ | +51% | $ 32¹³/₁₆ | -15% | $ 38⅝ | +33% |

(a) Refer to Management's Discussion and Analysis on pages A9-A14 and Notes 3 and 4 within the Notes to Consolidated Financial Statements for further explanation of non-recurring charges and other unusual items for years 1995 - 1997.

(b) Refer to Management's Discussion and Analysis on pages A9-A14 and Note 1 within the Notes to Consolidated Financial Statements for further explanation of cumulative effect of accounting change in 1997.

(c) Restated for two-for-one stock split effective August 22, 1997.

As shown above, Kellogg chose also to present the percent change from last year to the current year for each of the reported items.

# LETTER TO THE STOCKHOLDERS

Nearly every annual report contains a letter to the stockholders from the Chairman of the Board or the President (or both). This letter typically discusses the company's accomplishments during the past year and highlights significant

Arnold G. Langbo

Kellogg Company recorded solid growth in 1997, as we prepared to assume an even stronger leadership position among the global food companies of the 21st century.

Your Company's earnings per share increased 11 percent in 1997, excluding unusual items. Global volume was up 11 percent, helped by the strong performance of new products and the impact of our new Lender's Bagels business. Excluding Lender's, global volume was up 5 percent.

Kellogg Company stock split two-for-one, and our stock price advanced by 51 percent. The Kellogg dividend rose for the 41st straight year, with a split-adjusted increase of 6 cents per share to $.87.

We also continued our program of purchasing Kellogg shares. These purchases totaled $426 million in 1997, and the Board of Directors has authorized $389 million in additional purchases during 1998.

Building on a heritage of leadership and excellence, we are shaping Kellogg Company into a value-focused global growth company of the future. To reach that goal, we must:

- **Gain a clear competitive advantage** in certain critical aspects of our business; and
- **Build from strength**, taking full advantage of the equity assets that make Kellogg unique among the world's food companies.

I am pleased to report substantial progress in meeting these two requirements.

## TO OUR

### Gaining a Competitive Advantage

Kellogg Company's foundation for leadership in the 21st century will be clear competitive superiority in *innovation, cost structure*, and *global capabilities.*

**Innovation.** Leadership in innovation is leadership in ideas. One imperative of this leadership is knowing and understanding the vast diversity of consumers around the world and organizing Kellogg Company's resources to respond with high-value products.

To enhance our leadership in global food innovation, the W.K. Kellogg Institute for Food and Nutrition Research (WKKI) in Battle Creek, Michigan, began operations during 1997. At this world-class facility, we have brought together Kellogg research and development people from 23 nations. At the WKKI, we are strengthening our product development effort and building our capability to generate products for launch in multiple markets. This new system allows us to allocate resources to the highest-value ideas and take them to market rapidly around the world.

The success of three of our newest products – *Kellogg's® Honey Crunch Corn Flakes™* and *Kellogg's Cocoa Frosted Flakes™* cereals and *Kellogg's® Rice Krispies Treats™* squares – demonstrates the value of innovative product development. We also are optimistic about our events such as mergers and acquisitions, new products, operating achievements, business philosophy, changes in officers or directors, financing commitments, expansion plans, and future prospects. The letter to the stockholders signed by Arnold G. Langbo, Chairman of the Board and Chief Executive Officer of Kellogg, is shown on pages A4 to A7.

most-recent cereal launch, *Kellogg's®
Razzle Dazzle Rice Krispies™* Kellogg Company's consumer-focused thinking, backed by the WKKI's unmatched R&D facilities, is continuing to fill our new product pipeline for 1998 and beyond.

The European initiative reduced the number of plants from seven to four, while actually enhancing our ability to serve the pan-European marketplace.

As we continue to improve our supply chain, we expect additional savings and an increasingly advantaged cost structure.

decisions that create value for shareholders.

The Enterprise Business Applications (EBA) initiative, centerpiece of our business transformation, is currently under way for our supply chain, financial, and performance management processes.

# SHAREHOLDERS

Our quest to sustain our leadership in innovation extends to all aspects of our business. Examples are the mutually beneficial global relationships we are developing with major retailers and, in the U.S., our new *"Cereal. Eat it for Life.™"* television and print advertisements. Leading-edge efforts such as these will deliver value to consumers and to Kellogg shareholders.

**Cost structure.** A relentless commitment to be the low-cost producer of cereal and convenience foods enables us to offer *Kellogg's®* products at a competitive value advantage in diverse markets around the world.

To further strengthen our cost positioning, we are realigning what we call our global supply chain. This supply chain extends from the grain in the field through the purchasing, manufacturing, and distribution processes to the ultimate consumer.

Over the past two years, we have aggressively streamlined major parts of our supply chain. In 1996, we completed significant manufacturing efficiency initiatives in the U.S. and Australia. Then, in 1997, we restructured our European cereal manufacturing and distribution network.

**Global capabilities.** Leadership in the 21st century requires that we build greater global capabilities to fully leverage our worldwide resources and knowledge. Advances in information technology are enabling us to manage our business processes, people, and technology very differently to better serve our customers and consumers.

We are transforming the Company by engineering our major processes worldwide for improved effectiveness and efficiency. These processes, and the responsibilities of Kellogg people, will transcend today's functional and country boundaries. There will be greater collaboration and sharing of intellectual capital. Our people will have worldwide access to critical information to accelerate fact-based

**Building from Strength**
Our initiatives to assure long-term superiority in innovation, cost structure, and global capabilities have made this a time of dynamic change at Kellogg Company.

Our accomplishments from these initiatives are of great strategic importance.

Just as significant, however, is how your Company is using its unique strengths to deliver solid growth today and set the stage for consistent growth and superior returns to shareholders in the 21st century.

**Building on a commitment to nutrition.** This Company was founded on a belief in the dietary goodness of grain-based food. We continue to be driven by that same belief. An ever-growing base of scientific evidence provides a solid foundation for the Company's efforts to communicate the value of wheat-bran fiber, folic acid, and other attributes of our products in a healthy diet.

As we prepare to begin a new millennium, a 1997 meeting of scientists from around the world reached this consensus:

- A diet rich in high-fiber cereal is associated with a reduced risk of colo-rectal cancer.
- There is suggestive evidence that cereal fiber protects against breast cancer.
- There is good reason to examine the relationship between cereal fiber intake and the prevention of other cancers.

With further favorable reports expected in 1998, the health positioning of *Kellogg's®* products could well become an even stronger factor in our future growth.
**Building our two core product lines.** Our global strategic plan remains centered on Kellogg Company's two

immensely valuable core businesses: ready-to-eat cereal and grain-based convenience foods. We acted decisively in 1997 to further develop both.

To foster the continued growth of our cereal business, we opened an efficient new plant in Thailand, streamlined our European cereal infrastructure, and purchased cereal businesses in Ecuador and Brazil. We also adjusted our development strategies in emerging Asian markets to better respond to local taste preferences.

Our global roll-out of convenience foods accelerated with the highly successful introduction of *Kellogg's® Nutri-Grain®* cereal bars in the United Kingdom, the late-year launch of *Kellogg's® Rice Krispies Squares™* in the U.K., and the strong national introductions of *Kellogg's® Rice Bubbles Treats™* and four other cereal bars in Australia. Further convenience food launches are planned for 1998.

Continuing to develop our convenience foods infrastructure, we invested in a bagel business in the United Kingdom and reached agreement to purchase Day Dawn, a producer of wheat biscuit cereal, cereal bars, and other convenience foods in Australia. We also began construction of convenience foods capacity in Latin America and

carefully integrated the Lender's Bagels business, purchased in December 1996, into our U.S. operations.
**Building by understanding and responding to consumers.** Building on strength also means delivering products where and when consumers want them.

One of our biggest ongoing initiatives in 1997 was the expanded delivery of *Kellogg's®* products through new, non-traditional channels such as vending machines and kiosks, as well as convenience,

*Kellogg's Corn Flakes®* cereal, a family favorite around the world, is one of Kellogg Company's many growth equities. It is popular in diverse markets and in our growing single-serve business. The potential of the *Kellogg's Corn Flakes®* equity has been broadened by *Kellogg's® Honey Crunch Corn Flakes™* cereal, which has achieved exceptionally strong results in the United States since its introduction in 1996. International marketing of *Honey Crunch Corn Flakes™* begins in 1998.

*Dig 'Em™* the frog, and *Snap!® Crackle!®* and *Pop!®*; and the *Kellogg's®* name itself, associated worldwide with great taste, nutrition, quality, and value.

The pages that follow describe how we are taking increasing advantage of this equity base to enhance the growth and development of our business.

club, and general merchandise stores. Our introduction of *Nutri-Grain®* cereal bars in the U.K. marked the first presence of *Kellogg's®* products in nearly 30,000 additional food outlets, primarily convenience stores.

**Building on a strong equity base.** Perhaps the most important way Kellogg Company builds on strength is through our exceptionally powerful equity base. No other food company can match the Kellogg combination of internationally recognized brands such as *Kellogg's Frosted Flakes,® Rice Krispies,® Pop-Tarts,®* and *Special K®*; widely known and loved characters such as *Tony the Tiger,® Toucan Sam,® Corny™* the rooster,

## People: Our Most Important Advantage

As we grow globally, we continue to recognize, as did our founder W.K. Kellogg, that people represent Kellogg Company's greatest competitive advantage. Our global team turned in another strong performance during 1997 and is totally focused on delivering superior value to consumers and to Kellogg shareholders in the future. The wide-ranging talents and perspectives of our people are of great value to Kellogg Company, and we are strongly committed to diversity in our workforce.

Special recognition is due several members of the Kellogg family. Dolores D. Wharton and

Timothy P. Smucker left our Board of Directors in 1997 after 21 and 7 years, respectively, of dedicated service. We extend sincere thanks and best wishes to both Dolores and Tim.

Joining the Board during 1997 were Dr. Benjamin S. Carson, a world-renowned neurosurgeon, and Carleton (Carly) S. Fiorina, group president of Lucent Technologies' Global Service Provider Business.

Promotions among Kellogg Company officers during 1997 included William A. Camstra to vice chairman; Alan F. Harris to executive vice president and president – Kellogg Latin America; John R. Hinton to executive vice president – administration and chief financial officer; and Donna J. Banks to senior vice president – research and development.

Our fine team of Kellogg people is executing growth strategies that we believe are right for Kellogg Company and right for the future. We look forward with excitement to the challenges and global growth opportunities of 1998, 1999, and the new century.

Arnold G. Langbo
Chairman of the Board
Chief Executive Officer

# AUDITOR'S REPORT

All publicly held corporations, as well as many other enterprises and organizations (both profit and not-for-profit, large and small) engage the services of independent certified public accountants for the purpose of obtaining an objective, expert report on their financial statements. Based on a comprehensive examination of the company's accounting system and records, and of the financial statements, the outside CPA issues the auditor's report.

The standard auditor's report consists of three pieces of information, expressed in separate sentences or paragraphs: (1) a responsibilities statement, (2) a scope statement, and (3) the opinion. In the **responsibilities statement**, the auditor identifies who and what was audited and indicates the responsibilities of management and the auditor relative to the financial statements. In the **scope statement**, the auditor states that the audit was conducted in accordance with generally accepted auditing standards and discusses the nature and limitations of the audit. In the **opinion statement**, (which is first in Kellogg's auditor's report), the auditor expresses an informed opinion as to (1) the fairness of the financial statements and (2) their conformity with generally accepted accounting principles. The **Report of Price Waterhouse Independent Auditors** appearing in Kellogg's Annual Report is shown below:

## REPORT OF INDEPENDENT ACCOUNTANTS

### Price Waterhouse LLP

To the Shareholders and Board of Directors of Kellogg Company

In our opinion, the accompanying consolidated balance sheet and the related consolidated statements of earnings, of shareholders' equity and of cash flows present fairly, in all material respects, the financial position of Kellogg Company and its subsidiaries at December 31, 1997 and 1996, and the results of their operations and their cash flows for each of the three years in the period ended December 31, 1997, in conformity with generally accepted accounting principles. These financial statements are the responsibility of the Company's management; our responsibility is to express an opinion on these financial statements based on our audits. We conducted our audits of these statements in accordance with generally accepted auditing standards which require that we plan and perform the audit to obtain reasonable assurance about whether the financial statements are free of material misstatement. An audit includes examining, on a test basis, evidence supporting the amounts and disclosures in the financial statements, assessing the accounting principles used and significant estimates made by management, and evaluating the overall financial statement presentation. We believe that our audits provide a reasonable basis for the opinion expressed above.

As discussed in Note 1 to the financial statements, the Company changed its method of accounting for business process reengineering costs effective October 1, 1997.

*Price Waterhouse LLP*

Battle Creek, Michigan
January 30, 1998

The auditor's report above contains an additional paragraph wherein Price Waterhouse reports that Kellogg changed its method of accounting for business process reengineering costs as discussed in notes to the financial statements.

The auditor's report issued on Kellogg's financial statements is **unqualified** or "clean"; that is, it contains no qualifications or exceptions. In other words, the auditor conformed completely with generally accepted auditing standards in performing the audit, and the financial statements conformed in all material respects with generally accepted accounting principles.

When the financial statements do not conform with generally accepted accounting principles, the auditor must issue a **qualified** opinion and describe the exception. If the lack of conformity with GAAP is sufficiently material, the auditor is compelled to issue an **adverse** or negative opinion. An adverse opinion means that the financial statements do not present fairly the company's financial condition and/or the results of the company's operations at the dates and for the periods reported.

In circumstances where the auditor is unable to perform all the auditing procedures necessary to reach a conclusion as to the fairness of the financial statements, a **disclaimer** must be issued. In these rare instances, the auditor must report the reason for failure to reach a conclusion on the fairness of the financial statements.

Companies strive to obtain an unqualified auditor's report. Hence, only infrequently are you likely to encounter anything other than this type of opinion on the financial statements.

# MANAGEMENT DISCUSSION AND ANALYSIS

The **management discussion and analysis (MD&A)** section covers three financial aspects of a company: its results of operations, its ability to pay near-term obligations, and its ability to fund operations and expansion. Management must highlight favorable or unfavorable trends and identify significant events and uncertainties that affect these three factors. This discussion obviously involves a number of subjective estimates and opinions. The MD&A section of Kelloggs' annual report is presented on the following pages.

## Management's Discussion and Analysis

### Results of operations

#### Overview

Kellogg Company operates in a single industry – manufacturing and marketing grain-based convenience food products, including ready-to-eat cereal, toaster pastries, frozen waffles, cereal bars, and bagels, throughout the world. The Company leads the global ready-to-eat cereal category, with an estimated 39% annualized share of worldwide volume. Additionally, the Company is the North American market leader in the toaster pastry, cereal/granola bar, frozen waffle, and pre-packaged bagel categories.

During 1997, the Company returned to growth in earnings per share (excluding unusual items, discussed below), as management continued with its global strategy of brand-differentiated pricing, investment in new product research, brand-building marketing activities, and cost structure reduction initiatives. Results for 1997 were significantly improved over 1996, a year in which earnings were negatively impacted by competitive conditions in the Company's major markets.

For the full year of 1997, Kellogg Company reported net earnings and earnings per share of $546.0 million and $1.32, respectively, compared to 1996 net earnings of $531.0 million and net earnings per share of $1.25. Net earnings and earnings per share for 1995 were $490.3 million and $1.12, respectively. (All per share amounts reflect the 2-for-1 stock split effective August 22, 1997. All earnings per share presented represent both basic and diluted earnings per share.)

During the current and prior years, the Company reported non-recurring charges and other unusual items that have been excluded from all applicable amounts presented below for purposes of comparison between years. Additionally, results for 1997 are presented before the cumulative effect of a change in the method of accounting for business process reengineering costs. Refer to the separate section below on non-recurring charges and other unusual items for further information.

### 1997 compared to 1996

Excluding non-recurring charges and other unusual items, the Company reported 1997 earnings per share of $1.70, an 11% increase over the prior-year results of $1.53. The year-over-year increase in earnings per share of $.17 resulted from $.12 of business growth, $.03 of common stock repurchases, and $.04 of favorable tax rate movements, partially offset by $.02 of unfavorable foreign currency movements. The business growth was principally attributable to cereal volume growth in the Company's U.S. and Latin American markets, continued double-digit growth in other convenience foods volume, and reductions in manufacturing and marketing costs. Foreign currency movements negatively impacted earnings by 2% in Europe, 3% in other non-U.S. areas, and 1% on a consolidated basis. The negative impact on 1997 earnings per share due to results of the Lender's Bagels business, acquired in December 1996, was approximately $.05.

The Company achieved the following volume growth during 1997:

|  | Change |
| --- | --- |
| Global cereal | +3.4% |
| U.S. cereal | +3.9% |
| Global total | +11.3% |
| Global total excluding Lender's (a) | +5.0% |

(a) Lender's Bagels business acquired in December 1996.

Within the U.S. market, the Company recovered cereal volume declines of the prior year, and slightly exceeded 1995 results. Growth in most other non-U.S. cereal markets offset softness in the Company's United Kingdom, Canada, and Australia volume. The Company's Latin American region achieved record annual volume results. Other convenience foods volume continued to increase at a double-digit rate, even after excluding sales from the Lender's Bagels business.

On an annualized basis, regional volume share of the ready-to-eat cereal category remained strong during the year, at approximately 34% in North America, 44% in Europe, 43% in Asia-Pacific, and 60% in Latin America.

Consolidated net sales increased 2% for 1997. The favorable impact of strong volumes was partially offset by unfavorable pricing and product mix movements, and a negative foreign currency impact of 2%. Excluding the Lender's business, consolidated net sales were even with the prior year. On a geographic basis, net sales versus the prior year were:

| Net sales by geographic area – 1997 vs. 1996 % change | | | | |
| --- | --- | --- | --- | --- |
|  | U.S. | Europe | All other | Consolidated |
| Business | +5% | +2% | +6% | +4% |
| Foreign currency impact | — | -5% | -4% | -2% |
| **Total change** | **+5%** | **-3%** | **+2%** | **+2%** |

Margin performance for 1997 was:

|  | 1997 | 1996 | Change |
| --- | --- | --- | --- |
| Gross margin | 52.1% | 53.2% | -1.1% |
| SGA%(a) | -34.6% | -36.8% | +2.2% |
| Operating margin | 17.5% | 16.4% | +1.1% |

(a) Selling, general, and administrative expense as a percentage of net sales.

Gross margin performance for 1997 benefited from volume increases and year-over-year operational cost savings. However, these favorable factors were outweighed by the negative impact of prior-year pricing actions. The improvement in SGA% primarily reflects reduced promotional spending in the U.S. market, in line with the Company's integrated pricing strategy.

Operating profit results on a geographic basis were:

| Operating profit by geographic area – 1997 vs. 1996 | | | | |
| --- | --- | --- | --- | --- |
| (millions) | U.S. | Europe | All other | Consolidated |
| 1997 operating profit as reported | $706.8 | $158.9 | $143.4 | $1,009.1 |
| Non-recurring charges | 35.2 | 119.1 | 29.8 | 184.1 |
| **1997 operating profit excluding non-recurring charges** | **$742.0** | **$278.0** | **$173.2** | **$1,193.2** |
| 1996 operating profit as reported | $611.2 | $204.4 | $143.3 | $958.9 |
| Non-recurring charges | 24.1 | 76.5 | 35.5 | 136.1 |
| **1996 operating profit excluding non-recurring charges** | **$635.3** | **$280.9** | **$178.8** | **$1,095.0** |
| % change – 1997 vs. 1996 excluding non-recurring charges: | | | | |
| Business | +17% | +3% | +1% | +11% |
| Foreign currency impact | — | -4% | -4% | -2% |
| **Total change** | **+17%** | **-1%** | **-3%** | **+9%** |

Gross interest expense, prior to amounts capitalized, increased 70% versus the prior year to $117.9 million. The higher interest expense resulted from increased debt levels to fund the Lender's Bagels business acquisition and the Company's common stock repurchase program.

Excluding the impact of non-recurring charges and other unusual items, the effective income tax rate was 35.3%, 1.5 percentage points lower than the prior-year rate. The lower effective tax rate is primarily due to enactment of a 2% statutory rate reduction in the United Kingdom, effective April 1, 1997, as well as favorable adjustments in other jurisdictions. The effective income tax rate based on reported earnings (before cumulative effect of accounting change) was 37.6% in 1997 and 38.2% in 1996. For both 1997 and 1996, the higher reported rate (as compared to the rate excluding the impact of unusual items) primarily relates to certain non-recurring charges for which no tax benefit was provided, based on management's assessment of the likelihood of recovering such benefit in future years.

## 1996 compared to 1995

The Company's 1996 results were negatively impacted by competitive conditions in the U.S. ready-to-eat cereal market, in which significant price reductions were undertaken by all major competitors during the year. In an effort to improve the brand value proposition to the consumer, the Company implemented several pricing actions in 1996, most notably reductions announced June 10, 1996, averaging 19% on brands comprising approximately two-thirds of its U.S. cereal business. Following an integrated strategy, the Company combined its price reductions with reduced marketing expenditures, while competitors continued heavy deep-discount promotional spending during most of the year. As a result, the Company reported a 12% decline in 1996 earnings per share (excluding non-recurring charges and other unusual items) to $1.53, versus $1.74 in 1995. The $.21 decrease was comprised of $.22 in business decline and $.03 in unfavorable foreign currency movements, mitigated by $.03 of common stock repurchases, and $.01 from a lower effective tax rate. Foreign currency movements negatively impacted earnings by 3% in Europe, 4% in other non-U.S. areas, and 1% on a consolidated basis.

The Company experienced the following volume results during 1996:

|  | Change |
| --- | --- |
| Global cereal | -.7% |
| U.S. cereal | -3.6% |
| Global total | +1.2% |

Total volume growth was led by strength in the Company's Asia-Pacific and Latin American ready-to-eat cereal shipments and low double-digit growth in other convenience foods volume. These volume gains offset softness in the Company's U.S. and United Kingdom ready-to-eat cereal markets.

Net sales were down 5%, primarily reflecting the price reductions, ready-to-eat cereal volume loss, and unfavorable product mix and foreign currency movements. On a geographic basis, net sales versus the prior year were:

| Net sales by geographic area – 1996 vs. 1995 % change | | | | |
| --- | --- | --- | --- | --- |
|  | U.S. | Europe | All other | Consolidated |
| Business | -7% | -1% | +8% | -4% |
| Foreign currency impact | — | -3% | -3% | -1% |
| Total change | -7% | -4% | +5% | -5% |

Margin performance for 1996 was:

|  | 1996 | 1995 | Change |
| --- | --- | --- | --- |
| Gross margin | 53.2% | 54.6% | -1.4% |
| SGA% | -36.8% | -36.6% | -.2% |
| Operating margin | 16.4% | 18.0% | -1.6% |

The decline in gross profit margin reflected the price reductions, partially offset by the effect of operational cost savings. The SGA% was maintained at nearly a constant level versus the prior year despite the relatively high level of spending related to the Company's 90th Anniversary promotional programs, implementation costs associated with pricing actions, and competitive conditions in the U.S. cereal market.

Operating profit results on a geographic basis were:

| Operating profit by geographic area – 1996 vs. 1995 | | | | |
| --- | --- | --- | --- | --- |
| (millions) | U.S. | Europe | All other | Consolidated |
| **1996 operating profit excluding non-recurring charges** | **$635.3** | **$280.9** | **$178.8** | **$1,095.0** |
| 1995 operating profit as reported | $ 443.1 | $ 293.6 | $ 100.8 | $ 837.5 |
| Non-recurring charges | 325.0 | 38.4 | 58.4 | 421.8 |
| **1995 operating profit excluding non-recurring charges** | **$768.1** | **$332.0** | **$159.2** | **$1,259.3** |
| % change – 1996 vs. 1995 excluding non-recurring charges: | | | | |
| Business | -17% | -11% | +16% | -11% |
| Foreign currency impact | — | -4% | -4% | -2% |
| **Total change** | **-17%** | **-15%** | **+12%** | **-13%** |

Gross interest expense prior to amounts capitalized was $69.4 million, compared to $69.8 million in 1995. Despite an increase in debt during the year, total interest expense was maintained at prior-year levels due to the favorable effect of lower rates on short-term borrowings.

Other expense for 1996 included a charge of $35.0 million for a contribution to the Kellogg's Corporate Citizenship Fund, a private trust established for charitable donations. Excluding this unusual item, other income, net, decreased $19.5 million to $1.6 million, primarily due to foreign currency losses in Latin American markets and lower interest income during 1996.

Excluding the impact of non-recurring charges and other unusual items, the effective income tax rate was 36.8%, .7 percentage points lower than the prior-year rate, primarily due to favorable audit settlements in foreign jurisdictions and country mix.

## Liquidity and capital resources

The Company's financial condition remained strong throughout 1997. A strong cash flow, combined with a program of issuing commercial paper and maintaining worldwide credit facilities, provides adequate liquidity to meet the Company's operational needs.

Net cash provided by operating activities during 1997 was $879.8 million, compared to $711.5 million in 1996, with the increase due principally to higher earnings, lower benefit plan contributions, and favorable working capital movements. The ratio of current assets to current liabilities was .9 at December 31, 1997, compared to .7 at December 31, 1996.

Net cash used in investing activities was $329.3 million, principally comprised of $312.4 million in property additions. Net cash used in investing activities decreased significantly from the prior year, in which the Company paid $466 million to purchase the Lender's Bagels business.

Net cash used in financing activities was $607.3 million, primarily related to common stock repurchases of $426.0 million and dividend payments of $360.1 million, partially offset by a net increase in total debt of $108.1 million. The Company's total 1997 per share dividend payment was $.87, a 7.4% increase over the prior-year payment of $.81.

On August 1, 1997, the Company's Board of Directors approved a 2-for-1 stock split to shareholders of record at the close of business August 8, 1997, effective August 22, 1997, and also authorized retirement of 105.3 million common shares (pre-split) held in treasury. All per share and shares outstanding data have been restated retroactively to reflect the stock split.

Under existing plans authorized by the Company's Board of Directors, management spent $426.0 million during 1997 to repurchase 10.9 million shares (on a post-split basis) of the Company's common stock at an average price of $39 per share. The open repurchase authorization, which extends through December 31, 1998, was $389.1 million at year-end 1997.

Notes payable consist principally of commercial paper borrowings in the United States. Associated with these borrowings, during September 1997, the Company purchased a $225 million notional, four-year fixed interest rate cap. Under the terms of the cap, if the Federal Reserve AA composite rate on 30-day commercial paper increases to 6.33%, the Company will pay this fixed rate on $225 million of its commercial paper borrowings. If the rate increases to 7.03% or above, the cap will expire. As of year end 1997, the rate was 5.65%.

To reduce short-term borrowings, on February 4, 1998, the Company issued $400 million of three-year 5.75% fixed rate U.S. Dollar Notes. Accordingly, an equivalent amount of commercial paper borrowings was classified as long-term debt in the December 31, 1997, balance sheet. These Notes were issued under an existing "shelf registration" with the Securities and Exchange Commission, and provide an option to holders to extend the obligation for an additional four years at a predetermined interest rate of 5.63% plus the Company's then-current credit spread. Concurrent with this issuance, the Company entered into a $400 million notional, three-year fixed-to-floating

interest rate swap, indexed to the Federal Reserve AA composite rate on 30-day commercial paper.

As of December 31, 1997, current maturities of long-term debt primarily consisted of $200 million of five-year notes due October 1998. Management currently intends to replace these notes with new long-term debt issuances as of the maturity date and, as of year-end 1997, had entered into $25 million notional amount of interest rate hedges to effectively fix the U.S. Treasury rate on which an equivalent amount of future issuances would be priced. Subject to market conditions, management intends to gradually increase the notional amount of interest rate hedges to $200 million, prior to the maturity date of the notes.

On January 29, 1997, the Company issued $500 million of seven-year 6.625% fixed rate Euro Dollar Notes. This debt was issued primarily to fund the purchase of the Lender's Bagels business, acquired in December 1996. In conjunction with this issuance, the Company settled $500 million notional amount of interest rate forward swap agreements, which effectively fixed the interest rate on the debt at 6.354%. Associated with this debt, during September 1997, the Company entered into a $225 million notional, 4 ½-year fixed-to-floating interest rate swap, indexed to the three-month London Interbank Offered Rate (LIBOR). Under the terms of the swap, if three-month LIBOR decreases to 4.71% or below, the swap will expire. At year-end 1997, three-month LIBOR was 5.81%.

To replace other long-term debt maturing during the year, the Company issued $500 million of four-year 6.125% Euro Dollar Notes on August 5, 1997. In conjunction with this issuance, the Company settled $400 million notional amount of interest rate forward swap agreements that effectively fixed the interest rate on the debt at 6.4%. Associated with this debt, during September 1997, the Company entered into a $200 million notional, four-year fixed-to-floating interest rate swap, indexed to three-month LIBOR.

The ratio of total debt to market capitalization at December 31, 1997, was 10%, down from 14% at December 31, 1996, principally due to an increase in the market price of the Company's stock since that date.

## Non-recurring charges and other unusual items

From 1995 to the present, management has commenced major productivity and operational streamlining initiatives in an effort to optimize the Company's cost structure and move toward a global business model. The incremental costs of these programs have been reported throughout 1995-1997 as non-recurring charges.

In addition to the non-recurring charges reported during 1995-1997 for streamlining initiatives, the Company incurred charges for other unusual items. Furthermore, net earnings for 1997 included a cumulative effect of accounting change related to business process reengineering costs. In summary, the following charges were excluded from reported results for purposes of comparison within the "Results of operations" section above:

| **Non-recurring charges & other unusual items** | | | | |
| Impact on (millions, except per share data): | Operating profit | Earnings before income taxes and cumulative effect of accounting change | Net earnings | Net earnings per share |
| --- | --- | --- | --- | --- |
| **1997:** | | | | |
| Streamlining initiatives | $161.1 | $161.1 | | |
| Impairment losses | 23.0 | 23.0 | | |
| **Total non-recurring charges** | **$184.1** | **$184.1** | **$140.5** | **$.34** |
| **Cumulative effect of accounting change** | — | — | **$ 18.0** | **$.04** |
| **1996:** | | | | |
| Streamlining initiatives | $121.1 | $121.1 | | |
| Litigation provision | 15.0 | 15.0 | | |
| Private trust contribution (a) | — | 35.0 | | |
| **Total** | **$136.1** | **$171.1** | **$120.1** | **$.28** |
| **1995:** | | | | |
| Streamlining initiatives | $348.0 | $348.0 | | |
| Impairment losses | 73.8 | 73.8 | | |
| **Total** | **$421.8** | **$421.8** | **$271.3** | **$.62** |

(a) Recorded in other income (expense), net.

The 1997 charges for streamlining initiatives relate principally to management's plan to optimize the Company's pan-European operations, as well as ongoing productivity programs in the United States and Australia. A major component of the pan-European initiatives was the late 1997 closing of manufacturing plants and separation of employees in Riga, Latvia; Svendborg, Denmark; and Verola, Italy.

Approximately 50% of the total 1997 streamlining charges consist of manufacturing asset write-downs, with the balance comprised of current and anticipated cash outlays for employee separation benefits, equipment removal, production redeployment, associated management consulting, and similar costs. Related primarily to the pan-European initiatives, streamlining programs begun in 1997 will result in employee headcount reductions of approximately 600 and are expected to deliver annual pre-tax savings of approximately $60 million when fully implemented. Total cash outlays for streamlining initiatives were approximately $85 million during 1997 and are expected to be approximately $50 million in 1998. Refer to Note 3 within Notes to Consolidated Financial Statements for additional information.

The streamlining programs commenced since 1995, including the aforementioned pan-European initiatives, are expected to result in the elimination of approximately 3,000 employee positions by the end of 1998, with approximately 90% of this reduction already achieved. These programs are expected to deliver average annual pre-tax sav-

ings in excess of $200 million by the year 2000, with approximately 75% of that amount being realized currently. These savings are not necessarily indicative of current and future incremental earnings due to management's commitment to invest in competitive business strategies, new markets, and growth opportunities.

Also included in the 1997 charges are $23.0 million of asset impairment losses, which result from evaluation of the Company's ability to recover components of its investments, based on management's ongoing strategic assessment of local conditions, in the emerging markets of Asia-Pacific.

In addition to the non-recurring charges reported during 1995 and 1996 for streamlining initiatives, the Company incurred charges for the following unusual items:

- During 1996, the Company included in non-recurring charges a provision of $15.0 million for the potential settlement of certain litigation.

- During 1996, the Company included in other expense a charge of $35.0 million for a contribution to the Kellogg's Corporate Citizenship Fund, which is expected to satisfy the charitable-giving plans of this private trust through the year 2000.

- During 1995, the Company included in non-recurring charges $73.8 million of asset impairment losses that resulted from the evaluation of the Company's ability to recover asset costs given changes in local market conditions, sourcing of products, and other strategic factors in its North American and Asia-Pacific operations.

The foregoing discussion of streamlining initiatives contains forward-looking statements regarding headcount reductions, cash requirements, and realizable savings. Actual amounts may vary depending on the final determination of important factors, such as identification of specific employees to be separated from pre-determined pools, actual amounts of asset removal and relocation costs, dates of asset disposal and costs to maintain assets up to the date of disposal, proceeds from asset disposals, final negotiation of third party contract buy-outs, and other items.

On November 20, 1997, the Emerging Issues Task Force (EITF) of the Financial Accounting Standards Board reached a consensus in Issue 97-13 that the costs of business process reengineering activities are to be expensed as incurred. This consensus also applies to business process reengineering activities that are part of an information technology project. Beginning in 1996, the Company has undertaken an Enterprise Business Applications (EBA) initiative that combines design and installation of business processes and software packages to achieve global best practices. Under the EBA initiative, the Company had capitalized certain external costs associated with business process reengineering activities as part of the software asset. EITF Issue 97-13 prescribes that previously capitalized business process reengineering costs should be expensed and reported as a cumulative effect of a change in accounting principle. Accordingly, for the fourth quarter of 1997, the Company reported a charge of $18.0 million (net of tax benefit of $7.7 million) or $.04 per share for write-off of business process reengineering costs. Such costs were expensed as incurred during the fourth quarter of 1997, and were insignificant.

### 1998 outlook

Management is not aware of any adverse trends that would materially affect the Company's strong financial position. Should suitable investment opportunities or working capital needs arise that would require additional financing, management believes that the Company's strong credit rating, balance sheet, and earnings history provide a base for obtaining additional financial resources at competitive rates and terms. Based on the expectation of continued cereal volume growth, and strong results from product innovation and the global introduction of other convenience foods, management believes the Company is well-positioned to deliver sales and earnings growth for the full year 1998. The Company will continue to identify and pursue streamlining and productivity initiatives to optimize its cost structure.

Additional expectations for 1998 include a gross profit margin of 53-54%, an SGA% of 35-36%, an effective income tax rate of 36-37%, capital spending of approximately $400 million, common stock repurchase activity of $390 million, and an increase in interest expense of 10%.

To address the millennium date change issue (the inability of certain computer software, hardware, and other equipment with embedded computer chips to properly process two-digit year-date codes after 1999), the Company formed a global task force to perform a risk assessment, and develop and execute action plans, as necessary. The global risk assessment is substantially complete. Remediation and testing activities for critical business operations are under way, with completion scheduled by year-end 1998. Remediation and testing of non-critical business operations will continue, as necessary, throughout 1999. Management currently believes that the total cost of becoming Year 2000 compliant will not be significant to the Company's financial results, partly due to other significant systems initiatives currently under way. While the Company believes all necessary work will be completed, there can be no guarantee that all systems will be in compliance by the year 2000 or that the systems of other companies and government agencies on which the Company relies will be converted in a timely manner. Such failure to complete the necessary work by the year 2000 could result in material financial risk.

The foregoing projections of volume growth, profitability, capital spending, and common stock repurchase activity are forward-looking statements that involve risks and uncertainties. Actual results may differ materially due to the impact of competitive conditions, marketing spending, and/or incremental pricing actions on actual volumes and product mix; the levels of spending on system initiatives, properties, business opportunities, continued streamlining initiatives, and other general and administrative costs; raw material price and labor cost fluctuations; foreign currency exchange rate fluctuations; changes in statutory tax law; interest rates available on short-term financing; the impact of stock market conditions on common stock repurchase activity; and other items.

## FINANCIAL STATEMENTS AND ACCOMPANYING NOTES

The standard set of financial statements consists of: (1) a comparative income statement (statement of earnings) for 3 years, (2) a comparative balance sheet for 2 years, (3) a comparative statement of cash flows for 3 years, (4) a statement of retained earnings (or stockholders' equity) for 3 years, and (5) a set of accompanying notes that are considered an integral part of the financial statements. The auditor's report, unless stated otherwise, covers the financial statements and the accompanying notes. The financial statements and accompanying notes plus some supplementary data for Kellogg Company appear on the following pages.

Kellogg Company and Subsidiaries

# CONSOLIDATED STATEMENT OF EARNINGS

Year ended December 31,

| (millions, except per share data) | 1997 | 1996 | 1995 |
|---|---|---|---|
| **Net sales** | **$6,830.1** | $6,676.6 | $7,003.7 |
| Cost of goods sold | **3,270.1** | 3,122.9 | 3,177.7 |
| Selling and administrative expense | **2,366.8** | 2,458.7 | 2,566.7 |
| Non-recurring charges | **184.1** | 136.1 | 421.8 |
| **Operating profit** | **1,009.1** | 958.9 | 837.5 |
| Interest expense | **108.3** | 65.6 | 62.6 |
| Other income (expense), net | **3.7** | (33.4) | 21.1 |
| **Earnings before income taxes and cumulative effect of accounting change** | **904.5** | 859.9 | 796.0 |
| Income taxes | **340.5** | 328.9 | 305.7 |
| **Earnings before cumulative effect of accounting change** | **564.0** | 531.0 | 490.3 |
| Cumulative effect of accounting change (net of tax) | **(18.0)** | — | — |
| **Net earnings** | **$ 546.0** | $ 531.0 | $ 490.3 |
| **Per share amounts (basic and diluted):** | | | |
| **Earnings before cumulative effect of accounting change** | **$ 1.36** | $ 1.25 | $ 1.12 |
| Cumulative effect of accounting change | **(0.04)** | — | — |
| **Net earnings per share** | **$ 1.32** | $ 1.25 | $ 1.12 |

Refer to Notes to Consolidated Financial Statements.

Kellogg Company and Subsidiaries

# CONSOLIDATED STATEMENT OF SHAREHOLDERS' EQUITY

| (millions, except per share data) | Common stock shares | amount | Capital in excess of par value | Retained earnings | Treasury stock shares | amount | Currency translation adjustment | Total shareholders' equity |
|---|---|---|---|---|---|---|---|---|
| Balance, January 1, 1995 | 310.4 | $ 77.6 | $ 68.6 | $ 3,801.2 | 88.7 | ($ 1,980.6) | ($ 159.3) | $ 1,807.5 |
| Stock options exercised | .7 | .2 | 36.6 | | | | | 36.8 |
| Common stock repurchases | | | | | 5.7 | (374.7) | | (374.7) |
| Net earnings | | | | 490.3 | | | | 490.3 |
| Dividends | | | | (328.5) | | | | (328.5) |
| Currency translation adjustments | | | | | | | (34.6) | (34.6) |
| Other | | | | | — | (5.9) | | (5.9) |
| **Balance, December 31, 1995** | **311.1** | **77.8** | **105.2** | **3,963.0** | **94.4** | **(2,361.2)** | **(193.9)** | **1,590.9** |
| Stock options exercised | .4 | .1 | 18.7 | | | | | 18.8 |
| Common stock repurchases | | | | | 7.4 | (535.7) | | (535.7) |
| Net earnings | | | | 531.0 | | | | 531.0 |
| Dividends | | | | (343.7) | | | | (343.7) |
| Currency translation adjustments | | | | | | | 27.6 | 27.6 |
| Other | | | | | .1 | (6.5) | | (6.5) |
| **Balance, December 31, 1996** | **311.5** | **77.9** | **123.9** | **4,150.3** | **101.9** | **(2,903.4)** | **(166.3)** | **1,282.4** |
| Stock options exercised (pre-split) | .6 | .1 | 31.9 | | (.1) | 2.1 | | 34.1 |
| Common stock repurchases (pre-split) | | | | | 3.9 | (290.9) | | (290.9) |
| Other (pre-split) | | | | | .1 | (6.0) | | (6.0) |
| Retirement of treasury stock | (105.3) | (26.3) | (55.8) | (3,095.8) | (105.3) | 3,177.9 | | — |
| Two-for-one stock split | 206.8 | 51.7 | (51.7) | | .5 | — | | — |
| Stock options exercised (post-split) | 1.2 | .3 | 44.3 | | (.1) | 2.1 | | 46.7 |
| Common stock repurchases (post-split) | | | | | 3.1 | (135.1) | | (135.1) |
| Net earnings | | | | 546.0 | | | | 546.0 |
| Dividends | | | | (360.1) | | | | (360.1) |
| Currency translation adjustments | | | | | | | (115.6) | (115.6) |
| Other (post-split) | | | | | .1 | (4.0) | | (4.0) |
| **Balance, December 31, 1997** | **414.8** | **$103.7** | **$ 92.6** | **$1,240.4** | **4.1** | **($ 157.3)** | **($281.9)** | **$ 997.5** |

Refer to Notes to Consolidated Financial Statements.

Kellogg Company and Subsidiaries

# CONSOLIDATED BALANCE SHEET

At December 31,

| (millions, except share data) | 1997 | 1996 |
|---|---|---|
| **Current assets** | | |
| Cash and cash equivalents | $ 173.2 | $ 243.8 |
| Accounts receivable, less allowances of $7.5 and $6.6 | 587.5 | 592.3 |
| Inventories | 434.3 | 424.9 |
| Other current assets | 272.7 | 267.6 |
| **Total current assets** | 1,467.7 | 1,528.6 |
| **Property, net** | 2,773.3 | 2,932.9 |
| **Other assets** | 636.6 | 588.5 |
| **Total assets** | $4,877.6 | $5,050.0 |
| | | |
| **Current liabilities** | | |
| Current maturities of long-term debt | $ 211.2 | $ 501.2 |
| Notes payable | 368.6 | 652.6 |
| Accounts payable | 328.0 | 335.2 |
| Other current liabilities | 749.5 | 710.0 |
| **Total current liabilities** | 1,657.3 | 2,199.0 |
| **Long-term debt** | 1,415.4 | 726.7 |
| **Other liabilities** | 807.4 | 841.9 |
| **Shareholders' equity** | | |
| Common stock, $.25 par value, 500,000,000 shares authorized<br>  Issued: 414,823,142 shares in 1997 and 311,524,437 in 1996 | 103.7 | 77.9 |
| Capital in excess of par value | 92.6 | 123.9 |
| Retained earnings | 1,240.4 | 4,150.3 |
| Treasury stock, at cost:<br>  4,143,124 shares in 1997 and 101,876,325 in 1996 | (157.3) | (2,903.4) |
| Currency translation adjustment | (281.9) | (166.3) |
| **Total shareholders' equity** | 997.5 | 1,282.4 |
| **Total liabilities and shareholders' equity** | $4,877.6 | $5,050.0 |

Refer to Notes to Consolidated Financial Statements.

Kellogg Company and Subsidiaries

# CONSOLIDATED STATEMENT OF CASH FLOWS

Year ended December 31,

| (millions) | 1997 | 1996 | 1995 |
|---|---|---|---|
| **Operating activities** | | | |
| Net earnings | $ **546.0** | $ 531.0 | $ 490.3 |
| Items in net earnings not requiring (providing) cash: | | | |
| Depreciation and amortization | **287.3** | 251.5 | 258.8 |
| Deferred income taxes | **38.5** | 58.0 | (78.7) |
| Non-recurring charges, net of cash paid | **133.8** | 90.6 | 385.3 |
| Other | **9.5** | 14.5 | 9.1 |
| Pension and other postretirement benefit contributions | **(114.5)** | (156.8) | (74.5) |
| Changes in operating assets and liabilities | **(20.8)** | (77.3) | 50.7 |
| **Net cash provided by operating activities** | **879.8** | 711.5 | 1,041.0 |
| **Investing activities** | | | |
| Additions to properties | **(312.4)** | (307.3) | (315.7) |
| Acquisitions of businesses | **(25.4)** | (505.2) | — |
| Property disposals | **5.9** | 11.6 | 6.3 |
| Other | **2.6** | 14.1 | .5 |
| **Net cash used in investing activities** | **(329.3)** | (786.8) | (308.9) |
| **Financing activities** | | | |
| Net issuances (reductions) of notes payable, with maturities less than or equal to 90 days | **(374.7)** | 906.6 | (86.8) |
| Issuances of notes payable, with maturities greater than 90 days | **4.8** | 137.0 | — |
| Reductions of notes payable, with maturities greater than 90 days | **(14.1)** | (79.0) | — |
| Issuances of long-term debt | **1,000.0** | — | — |
| Reductions of long-term debt | **(507.9)** | (3.4) | (.4) |
| Net issuances of common stock | **70.7** | 12.2 | 31.2 |
| Common stock repurchases | **(426.0)** | (535.7) | (374.7) |
| Cash dividends | **(360.1)** | (343.7) | (328.5) |
| **Net cash provided by (used in) financing activities** | **(607.3)** | 94.0 | (759.2) |
| Effect of exchange rate changes on cash | **(13.8)** | 3.2 | (17.3) |
| Increase (decrease) in cash and cash equivalents | **(70.6)** | 21.9 | (44.4) |
| Cash and cash equivalents at beginning of year | **243.8** | 221.9 | 266.3 |
| **Cash and cash equivalents at end of year** | $ **173.2** | $ 243.8 | $ 221.9 |

Refer to Notes to Consolidated Financial Statements.

# Notes to Consolidated Financial Statements
Kellogg Company and Subsidiaries

## Note 1 Accounting policies

### Consolidation
The consolidated financial statements include the accounts of Kellogg Company and its majority-owned subsidiaries. Intercompany balances and transactions are eliminated.

Certain amounts in the prior year financial statements have been reclassified to conform to the current year presentation.

### Cash and cash equivalents
Highly liquid temporary investments with original maturities of less than three months are considered to be cash equivalents. The carrying amount approximates fair value.

### Inventories
Inventories are valued at the lower of cost (principally average) or market.

### Property
Fixed assets are recorded at cost and depreciated over estimated useful lives using straight-line methods for financial reporting and accelerated methods for tax reporting. Cost includes an amount of interest associated with significant capital projects.

### Advertising
The costs of advertising are generally expensed as incurred.

### Stock compensation
The Company follows Accounting Principles Board Opinion (APB) #25, "Accounting for Stock Issued to Employees," in accounting for its employee stock options and other stock-based compensation. Under APB #25, because the exercise price of the Company's employee stock options equals the market price of the underlying stock on the date of the grant, no compensation expense is recognized. As permitted, the Company has elected to adopt the disclosure provisions only of Statement of Financial Accounting Standards (SFAS) #123, "Accounting for Stock-Based Compensation." (Refer to Note 7 for further information.)

### Net earnings per share
Basic net earnings per share is determined by dividing net earnings by the weighted average number of common shares outstanding during the period. Weighted average shares outstanding, in millions, were 414.1, 424.9, and 438.3 for the years 1997, 1996, and 1995, respectively. Diluted net earnings per share is similarly determined except that the denominator is increased to include the number of additional common shares that would have been outstanding if all dilutive potential common shares had been issued. Dilutive potential common shares are principally comprised of employee stock options issued by the Company and had an insignificant impact on the computation of diluted net earnings per share during the periods presented.

### Change in accounting principle
On November 20, 1997, the Emerging Issues Task Force (EITF) of the Financial Accounting Standards Board reached a consensus in EITF 97-13 that the costs of business process reengineering activities are to be expensed as incurred. This consensus also applies to business process reengineering activities that are part of an information technology project. Beginning in 1996, the Company has undertaken an Enterprise Business Applications (EBA) initiative that combines design and installation of business processes and software packages to achieve global best practices. Under the EBA initiative, the Company had capitalized certain external costs associated with business process reengineering activities as part of the software asset. EITF Issue 97-13 prescribes that previously capitalized business process reengineering costs should be expensed and reported as a cumulative effect of a change in accounting principle. Accordingly, for the fourth quarter of 1997, the Company reported a charge of $18.0 million (net of tax benefit of $7.7 million) or $.04 per share for write-off of business process reengineering costs. Such costs were expensed as incurred during the fourth quarter of 1997, and were insignificant.

### Common stock split
On August 1, 1997, the Company's Board of Directors approved a 2-for-1 stock split to shareholders of record at the close of business August 8, 1997, effective August 22, 1997, and also authorized retirement of 105.3 million common shares (pre-split) held in treasury. All per share and shares outstanding data in the Consolidated Statement of Earnings and Notes to Consolidated Financial Statements have been retroactively restated to reflect the stock split.

### Use of estimates
The preparation of financial statements in conformity with generally accepted accounting principles requires management to make estimates and assumptions that affect the reported amounts of assets and liabilities and disclosure of contingent assets and liabilities at the date of the financial statements and the reported amounts of revenues and expenses during the reporting period. Actual results could differ from those estimates.

## Note 2 Acquisition
On December 16, 1996, the Company purchased certain assets and liabilities of the Lender's Bagels business from Kraft Foods, Inc. for $466 million in cash, including related acquisition costs. The acquisition was accounted for as a purchase. The assets and liabilities of the acquired business are included in the consolidated balance sheet as of December 31, 1996. The results of Lender's operations from the date of the acquisition to December 31, 1996, were not significant. The acquisition was initially financed through commercial paper borrowings that were replaced with long-term debt in January 1997.

The components of intangible assets included in the allocation of purchase price, along with the related straight-line amortization periods, were:

|  | Amount (millions) | Amortization period (yrs.) |
|---|---|---|
| Trademarks and tradenames | $150.0 | 40 |
| Non-compete covenants | 20.0 | 5 |
| Goodwill | 179.0 | 40 |
| Total | $349.0 | |

The unaudited pro forma combined historical results, as if the Lender's Bagels business had been acquired at the beginning of fiscal 1996 and 1995, respectively, are estimated to be:

| (millions, except per share data) | 1996 | 1995 |
|---|---|---|
| Net sales | $6,873.1 | $7,219.4 |
| Net earnings | $ 524.3 | $ 489.3 |
| Net earnings per share | $ 1.23 | $ 1.12 |

The pro forma results include amortization of the intangibles presented above and interest expense on debt presumed issued to finance the purchase. The pro forma results are not necessarily indicative of what actually would have occurred if the acquisition had been completed as of the beginning of each of the fiscal periods presented, nor are they necessarily indicative of future consolidated results.

## Note 3 Non-recurring charges
Operating profit for 1997 includes non-recurring charges of $184.1 million ($140.5 million after tax or $.34 per share), comprised of $161.1 million for streamlining initiatives and $23.0 million for asset impairment losses.

Operating profit for 1996 includes non-recurring charges of $136.1 million ($97.8 million after tax or $.23 per share), comprised of $121.1 million for streamlining initiatives and $15.0 million for potential settlement of certain litigation.

Operating profit for 1995 includes non-recurring charges of $421.8 million ($271.3 million after tax or $.62 per share), comprised of $348.0 million for streamlining initiatives and $73.8 million for asset impairment losses.

### Streamlining initiatives
From 1995 to the present, management has commenced major productivity and operational streamlining initiatives in an effort to optimize the Company's cost structure and move toward a global business model. The incremental costs of these programs have been reported throughout 1995-1997 as non-recurring charges.

The 1997 charges for streamlining initiatives relate principally to management's plan to optimize the Company's pan-European operations, as well as ongoing productivity programs in the United States and Australia. A major component of the pan-European initiatives was the late-1997 closing of plants and separation of employees in Riga, Latvia; Svendborg, Denmark; and Verola, Italy. Approximately 50% of the total 1997 streamlining charges consist of manufacturing asset write-downs, with the balance comprised of current and anticipated cash outlays for employee separation benefits, equipment removal, production redeployment, associated management consulting, and similar costs. Principally related to the pan-European initiatives, streamlining programs commenced in 1997 will result in employee headcount reductions of approximately 600. Total cash outlays during 1997 for streamlining initiatives were approximately $85 million.

The 1996 and 1995 charges for streamlining initiatives result from management's actions to consolidate and reorganize operations in the United States, Europe, and other international locations. Cash outlays for streamlining initiatives were approximately $120 million in 1996 and $40 million in 1995. The streamlining programs commenced since 1995, including the aforementioned pan-European initiatives, are expected to result in the elimination of approximately 3,000 employee positions by the end of 1998, with approximately 90% of this headcount reduction already achieved.

The components of the streamlining charges, as well as reserve balances remaining at December 31, 1997, 1996, and 1995, were:

| (millions) | Employee retirement & severance benefits (a) | Asset write-offs | Asset removal | Other costs | Total |
|---|---|---|---|---|---|
| 1995 streamlining charges | $183.6 | $106.5 | $39.5 | $ 18.4 | $348.0 |
| Amounts utilized during 1995 | (126.1) | (106.5) | (3.0) | (18.4) | (254.0) |
| Remaining reserve at December 31, 1995 | 57.5 | — | 36.5 | — | 94.0 |
| 1996 streamlining charges (b) | 31.4 | 37.5 | 13.5 | 38.7 | 121.1 |
| Amounts utilized during 1996 | (65.0) | (37.5) | (19.6) | (38.7) | (160.8) |
| Remaining reserve at December 31, 1996 | 23.9 | — | 30.4 | — | 54.3 |
| 1997 streamlining charges | 22.4 | 78.1 | 19.3 | 41.3 | 161.1 |
| Amounts utilized during 1997 | (22.7) | (78.1) | (21.4) | (41.3) | (163.5) |
| Remaining reserve at December 31, 1997 | $ 23.6 | $ — | $28.3 | $— | $ 51.9 |

(a) Includes approximately $100 and $5 of pension and postretirement health care curtailment losses and special termination benefits recognized in 1995 and 1996, respectively. (Refer to Notes 8 and 9.)

(b) Includes $23 of reversals of prior-year reserves due to lower than expected employee severance payments and asset removal costs, and other favorable factors.

### Other

In addition to the non-recurring charges reported for streamlining initiatives, the Company incurred charges for the following unusual items:

- During 1997, asset impairment losses of $23.0 million, which resulted from evaluation of the Company's ability to recover components of its investments, based on management's ongoing strategic assessment of local conditions, in the emerging markets of Asia-Pacific.

- During 1996, a provision of $15.0 million for the potential settlement of certain litigation.

- During 1995, asset impairment losses of $73.8 million which resulted from the evaluation of the Company's ability to recover asset costs given changes in local market conditions, sourcing of products, and other strategic factors in its North American and Asia-Pacific operations.

## Note 4  Other income and expense

Other income and expense includes non-operating items such as interest income, foreign exchange gains and losses, and charitable donations.

Other expense for 1996 includes a charge of $35.0 million ($22.3 million after tax or $.05 per share) for a contribution to the Kellogg's Corporate Citizenship Fund, a private trust established for charitable donations. This contribution is expected to satisfy the charitable-giving plans of this trust through the year 2000.

## Note 5  Leases

Operating leases are generally for equipment and warehouse space. Rent expense on all operating leases was $38.6 million in 1997, $37.9 million in 1996, and $32.0 million in 1995. At December 31, 1997, future minimum annual rental commitments under non-cancelable operating leases totaled $68 million consisting of (in millions): 1998-$17; 1999-$12; 2000-$9; 2001-$8; 2002-$7; 2003 and beyond-$15.

## Note 6  Debt

Notes payable consist principally of commercial paper borrowings in the United States at the highest credit rating available and, to a lesser extent, bank loans of foreign subsidiaries at competitive market rates. U.S. borrowings at December 31, 1997 (including $400 million classified in long-term debt, as discussed in (f) below), were $744.2 million with an effective interest rate of 5.7%. U.S. borrowings at December 31, 1996 (including $500 million classified in long-term debt, as discussed in (f) below), were $1.12 billion with an effective interest rate of 5.4%. Associated with these borrowings, during September 1997, the Company purchased a $225 million notional, four-year fixed interest rate cap. Under the terms of the cap, if the Federal Reserve AA composite rate on 30-day commercial paper increases to 6.33%, the Company will pay this fixed rate on $225 million of its commercial paper borrowings. If the rate increases to 7.83% or above, the cap will expire. As of year-end 1997, the rate was 5.65%. At December 31, 1997, the Company had $775.1 million of short-term lines of credit, of which $749.4 million were unused and available for borrowing on an unsecured basis.

Long-term debt at year-end consisted of:

| (millions) | 1997 | 1996 |
|---|---|---|
| (a) Seven-Year Notes due 2004 | $ 500.0 | $ — |
| (b) Four-Year Notes due 2001 | 500.0 | — |
| (c) Five-Year Notes due 1998 | 200.0 | 200.0 |
| (d) Three-Year Notes due 1997 | — | 200.0 |
| (e) Five-Year Notes due 1997 | — | 299.9 |
| (f) Commercial paper | 400.0 | 500.0 |
| Other | 26.6 | 28.0 |
| | 1,626.6 | 1,227.9 |
| Less current maturities | (211.2) | (501.2) |
| Balance, December 31 | $1,415.4 | $ 726.7 |

(a) In January 1997, the Company issued $500 of seven-year 6.625% fixed rate Euro Dollar Notes. In conjunction with this issuance, the Company settled $500 notional amount of interest rate forward swap agreements, which effectively fixed the interest rate on the debt at 6.354%. Associated with this debt, during September 1997, the Company entered into a $225 notional, 4½-year fixed-to-floating interest rate swap, indexed to the three-month London Interbank Offered Rate (LIBOR). Under the terms of the swap, if three-month LIBOR decreases to 4.71% or below, the swap will expire. At year-end 1997, three-month LIBOR was 5.81%.

(b) In August 1997, the Company issued $500 of four-year 6.125% Euro Dollar Notes. In conjunction with this issuance, the Company settled $400 notional amount of interest rate forward swap agreements which effectively fixed the interest rate on the debt at 6.4%. Associated with this debt, during September 1997, the Company entered into a $200 notional, four-year fixed-to-floating interest rate swap, indexed to three-month LIBOR.

(c) In October 1993, the Company issued $200 of five-year 6.25% Euro Canadian Dollar Notes which were swapped into 4.629% fixed rate U.S. Dollar obligations for the duration of the five-year term.

(d) In September 1994, the Company issued $200 of three-year debt consisting of both 8.125% Euro Canadian Dollar Secured Notes and 5.25% Swiss Franc Secured Notes. These Notes were swapped into U.S. Dollar obligations, with a variable rate indexed to the Federal Reserve AA composite rate on 30-day commercial paper, for the duration of the three-year term.

(e) In July 1992, the Company issued $300 of five-year 5.9% U.S. Dollar obligations.

(f) At December 31, 1997, $400 of the Company's commercial paper was classified as long-term, based on the Company's intent and ability to refinance as evidenced by an issuance of $400 of three-year 5.75% fixed rate U.S. Dollar Notes on February 4, 1998. These Notes were issued under an existing "shelf registration" with the Securities and Exchange Commission, and provide an option to holders to extend the obligation for an additional four years at a predetermined interest rate of 5.63% plus the Company's then-current credit spread. Concurrent with this issuance, the Company entered into a $400 notional, three-year fixed-to-floating interest rate swap, indexed to the Federal Reserve AA composite rate on 30-day commercial paper.

At December 31, 1996, $500 of the Company's commercial paper was classified as long-term, based on the Company's intent and ability to refinance as evidenced by the issuance described in (a) above.

The $200 million of five-year notes will mature during the fourth quarter of 1998 and are classified in current maturities as of December 31, 1997. Management currently intends to replace these borrowings with new long-term debt issuances as of the maturity date and, as of year-end 1997, had entered into $25 million notional amount of interest rate forward swap agreements to pay fixed and receive variable interest, effectively fixing the U.S. Treasury rate on which an equivalent amount of future issuances would be priced.

Scheduled principal repayments on long-term debt are (in millions): 1998-$211; 1999-$2; 2000-$1; 2001-$901; 2002-$5; 2003 and beyond-$507.

Interest paid was $85 million for 1997 and approximated interest expense for 1996 and 1995. Interest expense capitalized as part of the construction cost of fixed assets was (in millions): 1997- $9.6; 1996-$3.8; 1995-$7.2.

## Note 7 Stock options

The Key Employee Long-Term Incentive Plan provides for benefits to be awarded to executive-level employees in the form of stock options, performance shares, performance units, incentive stock options, restricted stock grants, and other stock-based awards. Options granted under this plan generally vest over two years and, prior to September 1997, vested at the date of grant. The Bonus Replacement Stock Option Plan allows certain key executives to receive stock options that generally vest immediately in lieu of part or all of their respective bonus. Options granted under this plan are issued from the Key Employee Long-Term Incentive Plan. The Kellogg Employee Stock Ownership Plan is designed to offer stock and other incentive awards based on Company performance to employees who are not eligible to participate in the Key Employee Long-Term Incentive Plan or the Bonus Replacement Stock Option Plan. Options awarded under the Kellogg Employee Stock Ownership Plan are subject to graded vesting over a five-year period. Under these plans (the "stock option plans"), options are granted with exercise prices equal to the fair market value of the Company's common stock at the time of grant, exercisable for a 10-year period following the date of grant, subject to vesting rules.

The Key Employee Long-Term Incentive Plan contains an accelerated ownership feature ("AOF"). An AOF option is granted when Company stock is surrendered to pay the exercise price of a stock option. The holder of the option is granted an AOF option for the number of shares surrendered. For all AOF options, the original expiration date is not changed, but the options vest immediately.

As permitted by SFAS #123 "Accounting for Stock-Based Compensation," the Company has elected to account for the stock option plans under APB #25 "Accounting for Stock Issued to Employees." Accordingly, no compensation cost has been recognized for these plans.

For purposes of pro forma disclosures, the estimated fair value of the options is amortized to expense over the options' vesting period. Had compensation cost for the stock option plans been determined based on the fair value at the grant date consistent with SFAS #123, the Company's net earnings and earnings per share for employee stock options granted after December 31, 1994, are estimated as follows:

| (millions, except per share data) | 1997 | 1996 | 1995 |
|---|---|---|---|
| Net earnings | | | |
| As reported | $546.0 | $531.0 | $490.3 |
| Pro forma | $520.8 | $514.1 | $476.4 |
| Net earnings per share (basic and diluted) | | | |
| As reported | $ 1.32 | $ 1.25 | $ 1.12 |
| Pro forma | $ 1.26 | $ 1.21 | $ 1.09 |

The fair value of each option grant was estimated at the date of grant using a Black-Scholes option pricing model with the following weighted average assumptions:

| | 1997 | 1996 | 1995 |
|---|---|---|---|
| Risk-free interest rate | 6.31% | 6.16% | 6.89% |
| Dividend yield | 1.97% | 2.30% | 2.30% |
| Volatility | 19.83% | 19.16% | 21.45% |
| Average expected term (years) | 3.52 | 3.34 | 3.02 |
| Fair value of options granted | $7.48 | $6.32 | $5.47 |

Under the Key Employee Long-Term Incentive Plan, options for 13.2 million and 15.5 million shares were available for grant at December 31, 1997 and 1996, respectively. Under the Kellogg Employee Stock Ownership Plan, options for 6.9 million and 8.3 million shares were available for grant at December 31, 1997 and 1996, respectively. Transactions under these plans were:

| (millions, except per share data) | 1997 | 1996 | 1995 |
|---|---|---|---|
| Under option, January 1 | 11.2 | 8.4 | 7.6 |
| Granted | 6.0 | 5.2 | 4.8 |
| Exercised | (4.5) | (2.1) | (3.8) |
| Cancelled | (.3) | (.3) | (.2) |
| Under option, December 31 | 12.4 | 11.2 | 8.4 |
| Exercisable, December 31 | 8.1 | 7.6 | 6.1 |
| Shares available, December 31, for options that may be granted | 20.1 | 23.8 | 27.4 |
| | Average prices per share | | |
| Under option, January 1 | $33 | $30 | $28 |
| Granted | 36 | 38 | 31 |
| Exercised | 33 | 30 | 28 |
| Cancelled | 34 | 30 | 27 |
| Under option, December 31 | $35 | $33 | $30 |
| Exercisable, December 31 | $36 | $35 | $31 |

Employee stock options outstanding and exercisable under these plans as of December 31, 1997, were:

| (millions, except per share data) | Outstanding | | | Exercisable | |
|---|---|---|---|---|---|
| Range of exercise prices | Number of options | Weighted average exercise price | Weighted average remaining contractual life (yrs.) | Number of options | Weighted average exercise price |
| $15 – 34 | 6.4 | $31 | 8.0 | 3.4 | $31 |
| 35 – 39 | 4.7 | 38 | 8.3 | 3.4 | 38 |
| 40 – 44 | .7 | 44 | 9.8 | .7 | 44 |
| 45 – 50 | .6 | 48 | 9.7 | .6 | 48 |
| | 12.4 | | | 8.1 | |

## Note 8 Pension benefits

The Company has a number of U.S. and foreign pension plans to provide retirement benefits for its employees. Benefits for salaried employees are generally based on salary and years of service, while union employee benefits are generally a negotiated amount for each year of service. Plan funding strategies are influenced by tax regulations. Plan assets consist primarily of equity securities with smaller holdings of bonds, real estate, and other investments. Investment in Company common stock represented 4.2% and 6.8% of consolidated plan assets at December 31, 1997, and 1996, respectively.

The components of pension expense were:

| (millions) | 1997 | 1996 | 1995 |
|---|---|---|---|
| Service cost | $ 29.9 | $ 27.6 | $ 27.4 |
| Interest cost | 79.6 | 72.8 | 66.0 |
| Actual return on plan assets | (210.4) | (102.8) | (163.3) |
| Net amortization and deferral | 118.0 | 19.7 | 100.3 |
| Curtailment loss and special termination benefits expense | — | 4.0 | 77.7 |
| Pension expense – Company plans | 17.1 | 21.3 | 108.1 |
| Pension expense – multiemployer plans | 1.9 | 2.0 | 1.8 |
| Total pension expense | $ 19.0 | $ 23.3 | $109.9 |

The worldwide weighted average actuarial assumptions were:

| | 1997 | 1996 | 1995 |
|---|---|---|---|
| Discount rate | **7.6%** | 7.9% | 7.5% |
| Long-term rate of compensation increase | **4.9%** | 5.2% | 5.1% |
| Long-term rate of return on plan assets | **10.5%** | 10.5% | 9.6% |

Reconciliation of funded status of the plans at year-end was:

| | Underfunded | | Overfunded | |
|---|---|---|---|---|
| (millions) | **1997** | 1996 | **1997** | 1996 |
| Accumulated benefit obligation: | | | | |
| Nonvested | **$ 6.6** | $ 6.0 | **$ 60.0** | $ 46.9 |
| Vested | **62.5** | 41.5 | **926.3** | 845.2 |
| Total | **69.1** | 47.5 | **986.3** | 892.1 |
| Projected salary increases | **18.0** | 17.4 | **60.0** | 79.3 |
| Projected benefit obligation | **87.1** | 64.9 | **1,046.3** | 971.4 |
| Plan assets at fair value | **15.4** | — | **1,193.6** | 1,048.7 |
| Assets (less) greater than | | | | |
| projected benefit obligation | **(71.7)** | (64.9) | **147.3** | 77.3 |
| Unrecognized net (gain) loss | **14.4** | 15.0 | **(7.0)** | 28.8 |
| Unrecognized transition amount | **2.6** | (2.8) | **1.8** | .6 |
| Unrecognized prior service cost | **3.9** | 3.4 | **43.3** | 49.3 |
| Minimum liability adjustment | **(10.7)** | (5.7) | **—** | — |
| Prepaid (accrued) pension | **($61.5)** | ($55.0) | **$ 185.4** | $ 156.0 |

Curtailment losses and special termination benefits expense recognized in 1996 and 1995 relate to operational workforce reduction initiatives undertaken during these years and are recorded as a component of non-recurring charges. (Refer to Note 3 for further information.)

The amount of intangible assets related to underfunded pension plans was $10.7 million and $5.7 million at year-end 1997 and 1996, respectively. All gains and losses, other than curtailment losses, are recognized over the average remaining service period of active employees.

Certain of the Company's subsidiaries sponsor 401(k) or similar savings plans for active employees. Expense related to these plans was (in millions): 1997-$16; 1996-$17; 1995-$18.

## Note 9  Nonpension postretirement benefits

Certain of the Company's North American subsidiaries provide health care and other benefits to substantially all retired employees, their covered dependents, and beneficiaries. Generally, employees are eligible for these benefits when one of the following service/age requirements is met: 30 years and any age; 20 years and age 55; 5 years and age 62.

Components of postretirement benefit expense were:

| (millions) | 1997 | 1996 | 1995 |
|---|---|---|---|
| Service cost | **$ 9.6** | $11.2 | $11.8 |
| Interest cost | **37.2** | 40.2 | 41.5 |
| Actual return on plan assets | **(23.0)** | — | — |
| Net amortization and deferral | **2.9** | .3 | (.6) |
| Curtailment loss | **—** | 1.0 | 26.3 |
| Postretirement benefit expense | **$26.7** | $52.7 | $79.0 |
| Discount rate used for accumulated benefit obligation | **7.25%** | 7.75% | 7.25% |

The assumed health care cost trend rate was 7.0% for 1997, decreasing gradually to 4.5% by the year 2003 and remaining at that level thereafter. These trend rates reflect the Company's prior experience and management's expectation that future rates will decline. Increasing the assumed health care cost trend rates by 1 percentage point in each year would increase the accumulated postretirement benefit obligation as of December 31, 1997, by $63.5 million and postretirement benefit expense for 1997 by $6.8 million. All gains and losses, other than curtailment losses, are recognized over the average remaining service period of active plan partici-

pants. Curtailment losses recognized in 1996 and 1995 relate to operational workforce reduction initiatives undertaken during these years and were recorded as a component of non-recurring charges. (Refer to Note 3 for further information.) Since December 1996, the Company has contributed to a voluntary employee benefit association (VEBA) trust for funding of its nonpension postretirement benefit obligations. Plan assets consist primarily of equity securities with smaller holdings of bonds.

The accrued postretirement benefit cost included in the balance sheet at year-end was:

| (millions) | 1997 | 1996 |
|---|---|---|
| Accumulated benefit obligation: | | |
| Retirees | **$347.4** | $305.9 |
| Active plan participants | **175.9** | 188.2 |
| | **523.3** | 494.1 |
| Plan assets at fair value | **(150.7)** | (81.0) |
| Accumulated benefit obligation greater than assets | **372.6** | 413.1 |
| Unrecognized experience gain | **86.5** | 95.1 |
| Unrecognized prior service adjustments | **8.1** | 8.6 |
| Accrued postretirement benefit cost | **$467.2** | $516.8 |

## Note 10  Income taxes

Earnings before income taxes and cumulative effect of accounting change, and the provision for U.S. federal, state, and foreign taxes on these earnings, were:

| (millions) | 1997 | 1996 | 1995 |
|---|---|---|---|
| Earnings before income taxes and cumulative effect of accounting change: | | | |
| United States | **$576.4** | $516.7 | $430.9 |
| Foreign | **328.1** | 343.2 | 365.1 |
| | **$904.5** | $859.9 | $796.0 |
| Income taxes: | | | |
| Currently payable: | | | |
| Federal | **$129.4** | $130.6 | $205.2 |
| State | **29.6** | 21.9 | 34.7 |
| Foreign | **143.0** | 118.4 | 144.5 |
| | **302.0** | 270.9 | 384.4 |
| Deferred: | | | |
| Federal | **50.2** | 45.7 | (81.0) |
| State | **4.0** | 11.4 | (10.7) |
| Foreign | **(15.7)** | .9 | 13.0 |
| | **38.5** | 58.0 | (78.7) |
| Total income taxes | **$340.5** | $328.9 | $305.7 |

The difference between the U.S. federal statutory tax rate and the Company's effective rate was:

| | 1997 | 1996 | 1995 |
|---|---|---|---|
| U.S. statutory rate | **35.0%** | 35.0% | 35.0% |
| Foreign rates varying from 35% | **.1** | .7 | .2 |
| State income taxes, net of federal benefit | **2.4** | 2.5 | 2.0 |
| Net change in valuation allowance | **1.6** | (.1) | 1.9 |
| Statutory rate changes, deferred tax impact | **(.5)** | — | .4 |
| Other | **(1.0)** | .1 | (1.1) |
| Effective income tax rate | **37.6%** | 38.2% | 38.4% |

The 1997 increase in valuation allowance on deferred tax assets and corresponding impact on the effective income tax rate, as presented above, primarily result from management's assessment of the Company's ability to utilize certain operating loss and tax credit carryforwards. Total tax benefits of carryforwards at year-end 1997 were $30.4 million and principally expire after the year 2002.

The 1995 increase in valuation allowance on deferred tax assets and corresponding impact on the effective income tax rate, as presented above, primarily relate to asset impairment losses recorded as non-recurring charges (refer to Note 3) for which no tax benefit was provided, based on management's assessment of the likelihood of recovering such benefit in future years.

The deferred tax assets and liabilities included in the balance sheet at year-end were:

| (millions) | Deferred tax assets 1997 | 1996 | Deferred tax liabilities 1997 | 1996 |
|---|---|---|---|---|
| **Current:** | | | | |
| Promotion and advertising | **$ 65.0** | $ 78.4 | **$ 10.5** | $  6.7 |
| Wages and payroll taxes | **13.8** | 13.8 | **—** | — |
| Health and postretirement benefits | **15.7** | 17.2 | **2.4** | 6.3 |
| State taxes | **8.1** | 8.6 | **—** | — |
| Operating loss and credit carryforwards | **2.1** | .1 | **—** | — |
| Other | **24.2** | 23.4 | **12.3** | 23.3 |
| | **128.9** | 141.5 | **25.2** | 36.3 |
| Less valuation allowance | **(4.1)** | (2.5) | **—** | — |
| | **124.8** | 139.0 | **25.2** | 36.3 |
| **Noncurrent:** | | | | |
| Depreciation and asset disposals | **18.8** | 25.6 | **326.0** | 337.0 |
| Health and postretirement benefits | **163.5** | 179.6 | **56.2** | 43.0 |
| Capitalized interest | **3.5** | 3.3 | **32.3** | 31.5 |
| State taxes | **—** | .9 | **2.6** | — |
| Operating loss and credit carryforwards | **28.3** | 1.4 | **—** | — |
| Other | **26.6** | 26.3 | **5.8** | .7 |
| | **240.7** | 237.1 | **422.9** | 412.2 |
| Less valuation allowance | **(41.8)** | (29.1) | **—** | — |
| | **198.9** | 208.0 | **422.9** | 412.2 |
| Total deferred taxes | **$323.7** | $347.0 | **$448.1** | $448.5 |

At December 31, 1997, foreign subsidiary earnings of $1.3 billion were considered permanently invested in those businesses. Accordingly, U.S. income taxes have not been provided on these earnings. Foreign withholding taxes of approximately $64 million would be payable upon remittance of these earnings. Subject to certain limitations, the withholding taxes would then be available for use as credits against the U.S. tax liability.

Cash paid for income taxes was (in millions): 1997-$332; 1996-$281; 1995-$404.

## Note 11  Financial instruments and credit risk concentration

The fair values of the Company's financial instruments are based on carrying value in the case of short-term items, quoted market prices for derivatives and investments, and, in the case of long-term debt, incremental borrowing rates currently available on loans with similar terms and maturities. The carrying amounts of the Company's cash, cash equivalents, receivables, notes payable, and long-term debt approximate fair value.

The Company is exposed to certain market risks which exist as a part of its ongoing business operations and uses derivative financial and commodity instruments, where appropriate, to manage these risks. In general, instruments used as hedges must be effective at reducing the risk associated with the exposure being hedged and must be designated as a hedge at the inception of the contract. Deferred gains or losses related to any instrument 1) designated but ineffective as a hedge of existing assets, liabilities, or firm commitments, or 2) designated as a hedge of an anticipated transaction which is no longer likely to occur, are recognized immediately in the statement of earnings.

For all derivative financial and commodity instruments held by the Company, changes in fair values of these instruments and the resultant impact on the Company's cash flows and/or earnings would generally be offset by changes in values of underlying exposures. The impact on the Company's results and financial position of holding derivative financial and commodity instruments was insignificant during the periods presented.

### Foreign exchange risk

The Company is exposed to fluctuations in foreign currency cash flows primarily related to third party purchases, intercompany product shipments, and intercompany loans. The Company is also exposed to fluctuations in the value of foreign currency investments in subsidiaries and cash flows related to repatriation of these investments. Additionally, the Company is exposed to volatility in the translation of foreign currency earnings to U.S. Dollars.

The Company assesses foreign currency risk based on transactional cash flows and enters into forward contracts of generally less than twelve months duration to reduce fluctuations in net long or short currency positions. Foreign currency contracts are marked-to-market with net amounts due to or from counterparties recorded in accounts receivable or payable. For contracts hedging firm commitments, mark-to-market gains and losses are deferred and recognized as adjustments to the basis of the transaction. For contracts hedging subsidiary investments, mark-to-market gains and losses are recorded in the currency translation adjustment component of shareholders' equity. For all other contracts, mark-to-market gains and losses are recognized currently in other income or expense.

The notional amounts of open forward contracts were $143.2 million and $80.0 million at December 31, 1997, and 1996, respectively. Refer to Supplemental Financial Information on page 33 for further information regarding these contracts.

### Interest rate risk

The Company is exposed to interest rate volatility with regard to future issuances of fixed rate debt and existing issuances of variable rate debt. The Company uses interest rate caps, and currency and interest rate swaps, including forward swaps, to reduce interest rate volatility and funding costs associated with certain debt issues, and to achieve a desired proportion of variable versus fixed rate debt, based on current and projected market conditions.

Interest rate forward swaps are marked-to-market with net amounts due to or from counterparties recorded in interest receivable or payable. Mark-to-market gains and losses are deferred and recognized over the life of the debt issue as a component of interest expense. For other caps and swaps entered into concurrently with the debt issue, the interest or currency differential to be paid or received on the instrument is recognized in the statement of earnings as incurred, as a component of interest expense. If a position were to be terminated prior to maturity, the gain or loss realized upon termination would be deferred and amortized to interest expense over the remaining term of the underlying debt issue or would be recognized immediately if the underlying debt issue was settled prior to maturity.

The notional amounts of currency and interest rate swaps were $875.0 million and $1.05 billion at December 31, 1997, and 1996, respectively. Refer to Note 6 and Supplemental Financial Information on page 33 for further information regarding these swaps.

### Price risk

The Company is exposed to price fluctuations primarily as a result of anticipated purchases of raw and packaging materials. The Company uses the combination of long cash positions with vendors, and exchange-traded futures and option contracts to reduce price fluctuations in a desired percentage of forecasted purchases over a duration of generally less than one year. Commodity contracts are marked-to-market with net amounts due to or from brokers recorded in accounts receivable or payable. Mark-to-market gains and losses are deferred and recognized as adjustments to the basis of the underlying material purchases.

### Credit risk concentration

The Company is exposed to credit loss in the event of nonperformance by counterparties on derivative financial and commodity contracts. This credit loss is limited to the cost of replacing these contracts at current market rates. Management believes that the probability of such loss is remote.

Financial instruments which potentially subject the Company to concentrations of credit risk are primarily cash, cash equivalents, and accounts receivable. The Company places its investments in highly rated financial institutions and investment grade short-term debt instruments, and limits the amount of credit exposure to any one entity. Concentrations of credit risk with respect to accounts receivable are limited due to the large number of customers, generally short payment terms, and their dispersion across geographic areas.

## Note 12  Quarterly financial data (unaudited)

| (millions, except per share data) | Net sales 1997 | 1996 | Gross profit 1997 | 1996 |
|---|---|---|---|---|
| First | $1,688.9 | $1,785.9 | $ 860.9 | $ 995.5 |
| Second | 1,719.7 | 1,651.4 | 908.9 | 876.2 |
| Third | 1,803.8 | 1,681.6 | 944.4 | 865.6 |
| Fourth | 1,617.7 | 1,557.7 | 845.8 | 816.4 |
| | $6,830.1 | $6,676.6 | $3,560.0 | $3,553.7 |

| | Earnings before cumulative effect of accounting change (a) 1997 | 1996 | Earnings per share before cumulative effect of accounting change (a)(b) 1997 | 1996 |
|---|---|---|---|---|
| First | $160.6 | $206.1 | $.38 | $.48 |
| Second | 163.6 | 78.1 | .39 | .18 |
| Third | 207.2 | 159.5 | .50 | .38 |
| Fourth | 32.6 | 87.3 | .08 | .21 |
| | $564.0 | $531.0 | | |

| | Net earnings (a) 1997 | 1996 | Net earnings per share (a)(b) 1997 | 1996 |
|---|---|---|---|---|
| First | $160.6 | $206.1 | $.38 | $.48 |
| Second | 163.6 | 78.1 | .39 | .18 |
| Third | 207.2 | 159.5 | .50 | .38 |
| Fourth | 14.6 | 87.3 | .04 | .21 |
| | $546.0 | $531.0 | | |

(a) The quarterly results of 1997 and 1996 include the following non-recurring charges, other unusual items, and cumulative effect of accounting change. (Refer to Notes 1, 3, and 4 for further information.)

| | Earnings 1997 | 1996 | Earnings per share 1997 | 1996 |
|---|---|---|---|---|
| Non-recurring charges and other unusual items: | | | | |
| First | $ — | ($ 6.1) | $— | ($.01) |
| Second | (8.0) | (16.9) | (.02) | (.04) |
| Third | (6.6) | (21.3) | (.02) | (.05) |
| Fourth | (125.9) | (75.8) | (.31) | (.18) |
| Earnings before cumulative effect of accounting change | (140.5) | (120.1) | | |
| Cumulative effect of accounting change - Fourth | (18.0) | — | (.04) | — |
| Net earnings | ($158.5) | ($120.1) | | |

(b) Earnings per share presented represent both basic and diluted earnings per share.

The principal market for trading Kellogg shares is the New York Stock Exchange (NYSE). The shares are also traded on the Boston, Chicago, Cincinnati, Pacific, and Philadelphia Stock Exchanges. At year-end 1997, the closing price (on the NYSE) was $49 5/8 and there were 25,305 shareholders of record.

Dividends paid and the quarterly price ranges on the NYSE during the last two years were:

| 1997 – Quarter | Dividend | Stock Price High | Low |
|---|---|---|---|
| Fourth | $.225 | $50.38 | $40.00 |
| Third | .225 | 50.38 | 42.00 |
| Second | .210 | 43.44 | 32.00 |
| First | .210 | 36.38 | 32.06 |
| | $.870 | | |
| 1996 – Quarter | | | |
| Fourth | $.210 | $34.56 | $31.00 |
| Third | .210 | 38.69 | 32.81 |
| Second | .195 | 37.88 | 33.69 |
| First | .195 | 40.31 | 36.25 |
| | $.810 | | |

## Note 13  Operating segments

The Company operates in a single industry – manufacturing and marketing grain-based convenience food products including ready-to-eat cereal, toaster pastries, frozen waffles, cereal bars, and bagels throughout the world. The following table describes operations by geographic area. Geographic operating profit includes allocated corporate overhead expenses. Corporate assets are comprised principally of cash and cash equivalents held for general corporate purposes.

| (millions) | 1997 | % change | 1996 | % change | 1995 | % change |
|---|---|---|---|---|---|---|
| **Net sales** | | | | | | |
| United States | $3,961.8 | +5 | $3,779.5 | −7 | $4,080.3 | +6 |
| % of total | 58% | | 57% | | 58% | |
| Europe | 1,702.0 | −3 | 1,749.6 | −4 | 1,829.1 | +9 |
| % of total | 25% | | 26% | | 26% | |
| Other areas | 1,166.3 | +2 | 1,147.5 | +5 | 1,094.3 | +5 |
| % of total | 17% | | 17% | | 16% | |
| Consolidated | $6,830.1 | +2 | $6,676.6 | −5 | $7,003.7 | +7 |
| **Operating profit (a)** | | | | | | |
| United States | $ 706.8 | +16 | $ 611.2 | +38 | $ 443.1 | −37 |
| % of total | 70% | | 64% | | 53% | |
| Europe | 158.9 | −22 | 204.4 | −30 | 293.6 | +2 |
| % of total | 16% | | 21% | | 35% | |
| Other areas | 143.4 | — | 143.3 | +42 | 100.8 | −39 |
| % of total | 14% | | 15% | | 12% | |
| Consolidated | $1,009.1 | +5 | $ 958.9 | +14 | $ 837.5 | −28 |
| **Identifiable assets** | | | | | | |
| United States | $2,819.9 | +1 | $2,785.9 | +27 | $2,194.8 | −1 |
| % of total | 58% | | 55% | | 50% | |
| Europe | 1,160.2 | −8 | 1,258.2 | −1 | 1,269.4 | −1 |
| % of total | 24% | | 25% | | 29% | |
| Other areas | 882.3 | −9 | 973.3 | +5 | 929.7 | −1 |
| % of total | 18% | | 19% | | 21% | |
| Corporate assets | 15.2 | −53 | 32.6 | +57 | 20.7 | +9 |
| % of total | — | | 1% | | — | |
| Consolidated | $4,877.6 | −3 | $5,050.0 | +14 | $4,414.6 | −1 |

(a) Operating profit includes the following non-recurring charges, by geographic area. (Refer to Note 3 for further information.)

| | 1997 | 1996 | 1995 |
|---|---|---|---|
| United States | ($ 35.2) | ($ 24.1) | ($325.0) |
| Europe | (119.1) | (76.5) | (38.4) |
| All other | (29.8) | (35.5) | (58.4) |
| Consolidated | ($184.1) | ($136.1) | ($421.8) |

## Note 14  Supplemental financial statement data

*(millions)*

| Consolidated Statement of Earnings | 1997 | 1996 | 1995 |
|---|---|---|---|
| Research and development expense | $106.1 | $ 84.3 | $ 72.2 |
| Advertising expense | $780.4 | $778.9 | $891.5 |

| Consolidated Statement of Cash Flows | 1997 | 1996 | 1995 |
|---|---|---|---|
| Accounts receivable | $   5.1 | $ 10.9 | ($ 25.6) |
| Inventories | (8.1) | (35.4) | 19.6 |
| Other current assets | (11.0) | (.5) | (33.7) |
| Accounts payable | (8.7) | (41.0) | 36.3 |
| Other current liabilities | 1.9 | (11.3) | 54.1 |
| **Changes in operating assets and liabilities** | **($ 20.8)** | ($ 77.3) | $ 50.7 |

| Consolidated Balance Sheet | 1997 | 1996 |
|---|---|---|
| Raw materials and supplies | $  135.0 | $  135.2 |
| Finished goods and materials in process | 299.3 | 289.7 |
| **Inventories** | **$  434.3** | $  424.9 |
| | | |
| Deferred income taxes | $  113.4 | $  117.9 |
| Prepaid advertising and promotion | 95.2 | 83.4 |
| Other | 64.1 | 66.3 |
| **Other current assets** | **$  272.7** | $  267.6 |
| | | |
| Land | $   49.0 | $   52.4 |
| Buildings | 1,213.8 | 1,226.1 |
| Machinery and equipment | 3,434.7 | 3,464.1 |
| Construction in progress | 283.1 | 277.5 |
| Accumulated depreciation | (2,207.3) | (2,087.2) |
| **Property, net** | **$2,773.3** | $2,932.9 |
| | | |
| Goodwill | $  194.3 | $  193.7 |
| Other intangibles | 191.2 | 186.6 |
| Other | 251.1 | 208.2 |
| **Other assets** | **$  636.6** | $  588.5 |
| | | |
| Accrued income taxes | $   30.5 | $   50.5 |
| Accrued salaries and wages | 99.7 | 84.6 |
| Accrued advertising and promotion | 308.8 | 336.8 |
| Other | 310.5 | 238.1 |
| **Other current liabilities** | **$  749.5** | $  710.0 |
| | | |
| Nonpension postretirement benefits | $  444.1 | $  494.2 |
| Deferred income taxes | 237.7 | 226.3 |
| Other | 125.6 | 121.4 |
| **Other liabilities** | **$  807.4** | $  841.9 |

# Supplemental Financial Information

## Quantitative & qualitative disclosures related to market risk sensitive instruments

The Company is exposed to certain market risks which exist as a part of its ongoing business operations and uses derivative financial and commodity instruments, where appropriate, to manage these risks. The Company, as a matter of policy, does not engage in trading or speculative transactions. Refer to Note 11 within Notes to Consolidated Financial Statements for further information on accounting policies related to derivative financial and commodity instruments.

### Foreign exchange risk

The Company is exposed to fluctuations in foreign currency cash flows related to third party purchases, intercompany product shipments, and intercompany loans. The Company is also exposed to fluctuations in the value of foreign currency investments in subsidiaries and cash flows related to repatriation of these investments. Additionally, the Company is exposed to volatility in the translation of foreign currency earnings to U.S. Dollars. Primary exposures include the U.S. Dollar versus functional currencies of the Company's major markets, i.e. British Pound, German Deutchmark, French Franc, Australian Dollar, Canadian Dollar, and Mexican Peso, and in the case of inter-subsidiary transactions, the British Pound versus other European currencies. The Company assesses foreign currency risk based on transactional cash flows and enters into forward contracts of generally less than twelve months duration to reduce fluctuations in net long or short currency positions.

The tables below summarize forward contracts held at year-end 1997. All contracts are valued in U.S. Dollars using year-end 1997 exchange rates, are hedges of anticipated transactions (unless indicated otherwise), and mature in 1998.

### Contracts to sell foreign currency

| Currency sold | Currency received | Notional value (millions) | Exchange rate (fc/1US$) | Fair value (millions) |
|---|---|---|---|---|
| Belgian Franc | British Pound | $ 11.7 | 35.19 | $ .5 |
| Swiss Franc | German Deutchmark | 3.9 | 1.46 | — |
| French Franc | German Deutchmark | 4.3 | 6.08 | — |
| French Franc | Danish Kroner | .6 | 6.06 | — |
| Danish Kroner | British Pound | 5.4 | 6.67 | .1 |
| Belgian Franc | French Franc | 1.0 | 36.87 | — |
| French Franc | British Pound | 48.0 | 5.70 | 2.3 |
| Irish Punt | British Pound | 27.4 | .66 | 1.7 |
| Spanish Peseta | British Pound | 1.3 | 134.72 | .2 |
| Swedish Kroner | Danish Kroner | 16.0 | 7.89 | .1 |
| | Total | $119.6 | | $4.9 |

### Contracts to purchase foreign currency

| Currency purchased | Currency exchanged | Notional value (millions) | Exchange rate (fc/1US$) | Fair value (millions) |
|---|---|---|---|---|
| Swiss Franc (a) | British Pound | $ 4.7 | 1.42 | ($.1) |
| German Deutchmark (a) | British Pound | .3 | 1.72 | — |
| German Deutchmark | British Pound | 18.6 | 1.71 | ( .8) |
| | Total | $23.6 | | ($.9) |

(a) Designated as hedge of firm committment.

### Interest rate risk

The Company is exposed to interest rate volatility with regard to future issuances of fixed rate debt and existing issuances of variable rate debt. Primary exposures include movements in U.S. Treasury rates, London Interbank Offered rates (LIBOR), and commercial paper rates. The Company uses interest rate caps, and currency and interest rate swaps, including forward swaps, to reduce interest rate volatility and funding costs associated with certain debt issues, and to achieve a desired proportion of variable versus fixed rate debt, based on current and projected market conditions.

The tables below provide information on the Company's significant debt issues and related hedging instruments at year-end 1997. For foreign currency-denominated debt, the information is presented in U.S. Dollar equivalents. Variable interest rates are based on effective rates or implied forward rates as of year-end 1997. Refer to Note 6 within the Notes to Consolidated Financial Statements for further information.

### Significant debt issues

| Debt characteristics | Principal by year of maturity (millions) 1998 | 2001 | 2004 | Fair value (millions) |
|---|---|---|---|---|
| Euro Canadian Dollar | $200.0 | | | $186.6 |
| fixed rate | 6.25% | | | |
| Euro Dollar | | $500.0 | | $502.6 |
| fixed rate | | 6.125% | | |
| effective rate (a) | | 6.400% | | |
| Euro Dollar | | | $500.0 | $515.3 |
| fixed rate | | | 6.625% | |
| effective rate (a) | | | 6.354% | |
| U.S. commercial paper (b) | $744.2 | | | $744.2 |
| weighted av. variable | 5.74% | | | |

(a) Effective fixed interest rate paid, as a result of settlement of forward interest rate swap at date of debt issuance.

(b) $400 million of commercial paper classified in long-term debt as of year-end 1997. Refer to Note 6 within Notes to Consolidated Financial Statements for further information.

### Interest & currency swaps & caps

| Instrument characteristics | | Year of maturity (millions) 1998 | 2001 | 2002 | Fair value (millions) |
|---|---|---|---|---|---|
| Mixed swap – currency/interest – pay/receive fixed – hedge of existing debt issue | Notional amt. | $200.0 | | | ($10.8) |
| | Pay | US$/4.629% | | | |
| | Receive | C$/6.250% | | | |
| Interest rate swap – pay variable/receive fixed – hedge of existing debt issue | Notional amt. | | $200.0 | | 1.3 |
| | Pay | | 5.96% | | |
| | Receive | | 6.40% | | |
| Interest rate swap – pay variable/receive fixed – hedge of existing debt issue (a) | Notional amt. | | | $225.0 | 1.2 |
| | Pay | | | 5.600% | |
| | Receive | | | 6.354% | |
| Interest rate forward swap – pay fixed/receive variable – hedge of future debt issue | Notional amt. | $25.0 | | | ( .1) |
| | Pay | 5.8125% | | | |
| | Receive | 5.7730% | | | |
| Interest rate cap – pay fixed if 30-day C.P. rate rises to strike rate – hedge of U.S. commercial paper (b) | Notional amt. | | | $225.0 | ( .4) |
| | Strike | | | 6.33% | |
| | Reference | | | 5.65% | |

(a) Under the terms of this swap, if three-month LIBOR falls to 4.71% or below, the swap will expire. At year-end 1997, three-month LIBOR was 5.81%.

(b) Under the terms of this cap, if the Federal Reserve AA composite rate on 30-day commercial paper increases to 7.83% or above, the cap will expire. At year-end 1997 the rate was 5.65%.

### Price risk

The Company is exposed to price fluctuations primarily as a result of anticipated purchases of raw and packaging materials. Primary exposures include corn, wheat, soybean oil, sugar, and other ingredients for the Company's grain-based convenience food products. The Company uses the combination of long cash positions with vendors, and exchange-traded futures and option contracts to reduce price fluctuations in a desired percentage of forecasted purchases over a duration of generally less than one year. The fair values of commodity contracts held at year-end 1997 were insignificant, and potential near-term changes in commodity prices are not expected to have a significant impact on the Company's future earnings or cash flows.

For all derivative financial instruments presented in the tables above, changes in fair values of these instruments and the resultant impact on the Company's cash flows and/or earnings would generally be offset by changes in values of underlying transactions and positions. Therefore, it should be noted that the exclusion of certain of the underlying exposures from the tables above may be a limitation in assessing the net market risk of the Company.

# FIVE- OR TEN-YEAR SUMMARY

Usually presented in close proximity to the audited financial statements is a 5- or 10-year summary of selected financial data. From such a summary, one can determine trends and growth patterns over a fairly long period of time. Kellogg

## Value-Focused Global Growth

Kellogg Company has a governing objective of creating shareholder value by maximizing economic profit.* Applying value-based management principles, with economic profit as a key measure, to our exceptionally strong brand equities will be our foundation for future growth. Management strongly believes stock price appreciation is linked to growth in economic profit. To align our people behind this objective, Kellogg managers have incentive components of their compensation linked directly to value creation. Also, employees are strongly encouraged to become shareholders.

This value-focused formula has clearly delivered historic wealth creation for Kellogg shareholders. Over the past ten years, your Company's equity market value has increased from $6 billion to $20 billion. In this same time period, equity book value has remained unchanged at $1 billion, mainly due to our aggressive share repurchase program. As a result, market value added, which measures the wealth created for shareholders, has increased at a compound annual growth rate of 14%. In 1997, you received a 54% total return on your investment (stock appreciation plus reinvested dividends).

Management remains committed to finding new and innovative ways to leverage our global resources in pursuit of value-focused global growth and long-term shareholder value.

**Market Value Added**
(billions)

Compound Annual Growth Rate 14%

$20

$6

$1     $1

1987          1997

☐ Market Value of Equity   ☐ Book Value of Equity

*Defined as net operating profit after tax (excluding non-recurring charges), less a financing charge for capital utilization.

## SELECTED FINANCIAL DATA

*(millions, except per share data and number of employees)*

|  | Net sales | % Growth | (a) Operating profit | % Growth |
|---|---|---|---|---|
| 10-year compound growth rate | 6% |  | 4% |  |
| **1997** | **$6,830.1** | **2%** | **$1,009.1** | **5%** |
| 1996 | 6,676.6 | (5) | 958.9 | 14 |
| 1995 | 7,003.7 | 7 | 837.5 | (28) |
| 1994 | 6,562.0 | 4 | 1,162.6 | 16 |
| 1993 | 6,295.4 | 2 | 1,004.6 | (5) |
| 1992 | 6,190.6 | 7 | 1,062.8 | 3 |
| 1991 | 5,786.6 | 12 | 1,027.9 | 16 |
| 1990 | 5,181.4 | 11 | 886.0 | 21 |
| 1989 | 4,651.7 | 7 | 732.5 | (8) |
| 1988 | 4,348.8 | 15 | 794.1 | 15 |
| 1987 | 3,793.0 | 14 | 691.2 | 7 |

|  | Total assets | Return on average assets | Shareholders' equity | Return on average equity |
|---|---|---|---|---|
| **1997** | **$4,877.6** | **11%** | **$ 997.5** | **49%** |
| 1996 | 5,050.0 | 11 | 1,282.4 | 37 |
| 1995 | 4,414.6 | 11 | 1,590.9 | 29 |
| 1994 | 4,467.3 | 16 | 1,807.5 | 40 |
| 1993 | 4,237.1 | 16 | 1,713.4 | 37 |
| 1992 | 4,015.0 | 11 | 1,945.2 | 21 |
| 1991 | 3,925.8 | 16 | 2,159.8 | 30 |
| 1990 | 3,749.4 | 14 | 1,901.8 | 28 |
| 1989 | 3,390.4 | 14 | 1,634.4 | 30 |
| 1988 | 3,297.9 | 16 | 1,483.2 | 36 |
| 1987 | 2,680.9 | 17 | 1,211.4 | 38 |

(a) Operating profit for 1997 includes non-recurring charges of $184.1 ($140.5 after tax or $.34 per share). Operating profit for 1996 includes non-recurring charges of $136.1 ($97.8 after tax or $.23 per share). Earnings before accounting change for 1996 include a charge of $35.0 ($22.3 after tax or $.05 per share) for a contribution to the Kellogg's Corporate Citizenship Fund. Operating profit for 1995 includes non-recurring charges of $421.8 ($271.3 after tax or $.62 per share). Operating profit for 1993 includes non-recurring charges of $64.3 ($41.1 after tax or $.09 per share). Refer to Management's Discussion and Analysis on pages 18-22 and Notes 3 and 4 within Notes to Consolidated Financial Statements for further explanation of non-recurring charges and other unusual items for years 1995-1997.

presents selected financial data that includes operating data, financial position data, and selected statistics and ratios. In addition, it provides a discussion of its value-based management principles.

| | | | Per Common Share Data (c) | | | | | | |
|---|---|---|---|---|---|---|---|---|---|
| (a)(b) Earnings before accounting change | % Growth | Average shares outstanding(c) | (a)(b) Earnings before accounting change | Cash dividends | (d) Price/ earnings ratio | Stock price range | Net cash provided by operating activities | Net cash provided by/ (used in) financing activities | Common stock repurchases |
| 4% | | | 5% | 11% | | | | | |
| $564.0 | 6% | 414.1 | $1.36 | $.87 | 36 | $32-50 | $ 879.8 | $(607.3) | $426.0 |
| 531.0 | 8 | 424.9 | 1.25 | .81 | 26 | 31-40 | 711.5 | 94.0 | 535.7 |
| 490.3 | (30) | 438.3 | 1.12 | .75 | 34 | 26-40 | 1,041.0 | (759.2) | 374.7 |
| 705.4 | 4 | 448.6 | 1.57 | .70 | 18 | 24-30 | 966.8 | (559.5) | 327.3 |
| 680.7 | — | 463.0 | 1.47 | .66 | 19 | 23-34 | 800.2 | (464.2) | 548.1 |
| 682.8 | 13 | 477.7 | 1.43 | .60 | 23 | 27-37 | 741.9 | (422.6) | 224.1 |
| 606.0 | 21 | 482.4 | 1.26 | .54 | 26 | 17-33 | 934.4 | (537.7) | 83.6 |
| 502.8 | 19 | 483.2 | 1.04 | .48 | 18 | 14-19 | 819.2 | (490.9) | 86.9 |
| 422.1 | (12) | 488.4 | .87 | .43 | 20 | 14-20 | 533.5 | (143.2) | 78.6 |
| 480.4 | 21 | 492.8 | .98 | .38 | 16 | 12-17 | 492.3 | 52.1 | 33.6 |
| 395.9 | 24 | 494.8 | .80 | .32 | 16 | 9-17 | 523.5 | (130.5) | 22.6 |

| Property, net | Capital expenditures | Depreciation and amortization | Long-term debt | (e) Debt to market capitalization | Pretax interest coverage (times) | Current ratio | Advertising expense | R&D expense | Number of employees |
|---|---|---|---|---|---|---|---|---|---|
| $2,773.3 | $312.4 | $287.3 | $1,415.4 | 10% | 9 | .9 | $780.4 | $106.1 | 14,339 |
| 2,932.9 | 307.3 | 251.5 | 726.7 | 14 | 13 | .7 | 778.9 | 84.3 | 14,511 |
| 2,784.8 | 315.7 | 258.8 | 717.8 | 5 | 12 | 1.1 | 891.5 | 72.2 | 14,487 |
| 2,892.8 | 354.3 | 256.1 | 719.2 | 8 | 23 | 1.2 | 856.9 | 71.7 | 15,657 |
| 2,768.4 | 449.7 | 265.2 | 521.6 | 7 | 27 | 1.0 | 772.4 | 59.2 | 16,151 |
| 2,662.7 | 473.6 | 231.5 | 314.9 | 3 | 33 | 1.2 | 782.3 | 56.7 | 16,551 |
| 2,646.5 | 333.5 | 222.8 | 15.2 | 3 | 17 | .9 | 708.3 | 34.7 | 17,017 |
| 2,595.4 | 320.5 | 200.2 | 295.6 | 7 | 10 | .9 | 648.5 | 38.3 | 17,239 |
| 2,406.3 | 508.7 | 167.6 | 371.4 | 10 | 10 | .9 | 611.4 | 42.9 | 17,268 |
| 2,131.9 | 538.1 | 139.7 | 272.1 | 9 | 14 | .9 | 560.9 | 42.0 | 17,461 |
| 1,738.8 | 478.4 | 113.1 | 290.4 | 7 | 14 | .9 | 486.9 | 40.0 | 17,762 |

(b) Earnings before accounting change for 1997 exclude the effect of a charge of $18.0 after tax ($.04 per share) to write off business process reengineering costs in accordance with guidance issued by the Emerging Issues Task Force of the FASB. Earnings before accounting change for 1992 and 1989 exclude the effect of adopting the following Statements of Financial Accounting Standards (SFAS): in 1992, a charge of $251.6 ($.53 per share) net of $144.6 of income tax benefit for the transition effect of SFAS #106, "Employers' Accounting for Postretirement Benefits Other Than Pensions," and, in 1989, a gain of $48.1 ($.10 per share) for SFAS #96 "Accounting for Income Taxes".

(c) All share data retroactively restated to reflect 2-for-1 stock splits in 1997 and 1991. All earnings per share presented represent both basic and diluted earnings per share.

(d) The price/earnings ratio was calculated based on year-end stock price divided by earnings before the accounting changes referred to in note (b). These earnings include the non-recurring charges and other unusual items referred to in note (a). Excluding the impact of these unusual items, the price/earnings ratio in 1997, 1996, 1995, and 1993 would have been 29, 21, 22, and 19, respectively.

(e) Debt to market capitalization was calculated based on year-end total debt balance divided by market capitalization. Market capitalization was calculated based on year-end stock price multiplied by the number of shares outstanding at year-end.

# APPENDIX B

# SPECIMEN FINANCIAL STATEMENTS:
# General Mills, Inc.

## Continuing Operations

**Reported Sales**
dollars in billions

4.96 | 5.14 | 5.33 | 5.03 | 5.42 | 5.61
92 | 93 | 94 | 95 | 96 | 97

**Earnings per Share**
dollars

2.39 | 2.71 | 2.69 | 2.35 | 3.00 | 3.00
2.52 | 2.14 | 1.64 | 2.82
92 | 93 | 94 | 95 | 96 | 97

━●━ Results including unusual items

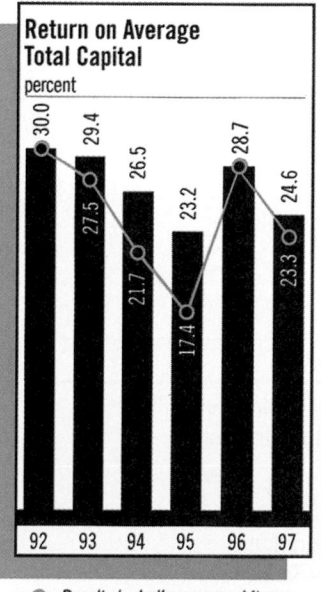

**Return on Average Total Capital**
percent

30.0 | 29.4 | 26.5 | 23.2 | 28.7 | 24.6
27.5 | 21.7 | 17.4 | 23.3
92 | 93 | 94 | 95 | 96 | 97

━●━ Results including unusual items

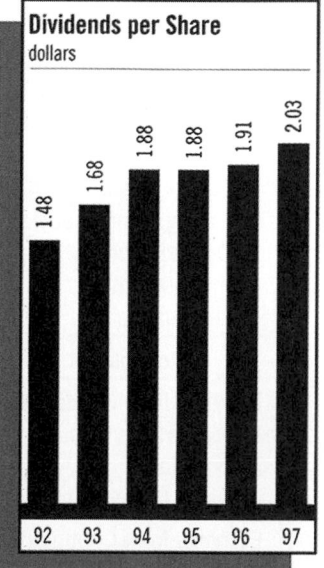

**Dividends per Share**
dollars

1.48 | 1.68 | 1.88 | 1.88 | 1.91 | 2.03
92 | 93 | 94 | 95 | 96 | 97

# Financial Highlights

| Dollars In Millions, Except per Share Data; Fiscal Year Ended | May 25, 1997 | May 26, 1996 | May 28, 1995 |
|---|---|---|---|
| **Continuing Operations** | | | |
| Sales | $5,609.3 | $5,416.0 | $5,026.7 |
| Earnings after Taxes | 445.4 | 476.4 | 259.7 |
| Earnings per Share | 2.82 | 3.00 | 1.64 |
| Return on Average Total Capital | 23.3% | 28.7% | 17.4% |
| **Results After Discontinued Operations** | | | |
| Discontinued Operations after Taxes | $     – | $     – | $   107.7 |
| Net Earnings | 445.4 | 476.4 | 367.4 |
| Net Earnings per Share | 2.82 | 3.00 | 2.33 |
| Average Shares Outstanding | 158.2 | 158.9 | 158.0 |
| Dividends per Share | $    2.03 | $    1.91 | $    1.88 |

# Consolidated Statements of Earnings

| In Millions, Except per Share Data, Fiscal Year Ended | May 25, 1997 | May 26, 1996 | May 28, 1995 |
|---|---|---|---|
| Continuing Operations: | | | |
| Sales | $5,609.3 | $5,416.0 | $5,026.7 |
| Costs and Expenses: | | | |
| Cost of sales | 2,328.4 | 2,241.0 | 2,123.0 |
| Selling, general and administrative | 2,239.2 | 2,128.3 | 2,008.3 |
| Depreciation and amortization | 182.8 | 186.7 | 191.4 |
| Interest, net | 100.5 | 101.4 | 101.2 |
| Unusual items | 48.4 | – | 183.2 |
| Total Costs and Expenses | 4,899.3 | 4,657.4 | 4,607.1 |
| Earnings from Continuing Operations before Taxes and Earnings (Losses) of Joint Ventures | 710.0 | 758.6 | 419.6 |
| Income Taxes | 258.3 | 279.4 | 153.3 |
| Earnings (Losses) from Joint Ventures | (6.3) | (2.8) | (6.6) |
| Earnings from Continuing Operations | 445.4 | 476.4 | 259.7 |
| Discontinued Operations after Taxes | – | – | 107.7 |
| Net Earnings | $  445.4 | $  476.4 | $  367.4 |
| Earnings per Share: | | | |
| Continuing operations | $    2.82 | $    3.00 | $    1.64 |
| Discontinued operations | – | – | .69 |
| Net Earnings per Share | $    2.82 | $    3.00 | $    2.33 |
| Average Number of Common Shares | 158.2 | 158.9 | 158.0 |

# Consolidated Balance Sheets

| In Millions | May 25, 1997 | May 26, 1996 |
|---|---|---|
| **Assets** | | |
| Current Assets: | | |
| Cash and cash equivalents | $ 12.8 | $ 20.6 |
| Receivables, less allowance for doubtful accounts of $4.1 in both 1997 and 1996 | 419.1 | 337.8 |
| Inventories | 364.4 | 395.5 |
| Prepaid expenses and other current assets | 107.3 | 132.6 |
| Deferred income taxes | 107.7 | 108.6 |
| Total Current Assets | 1,011.3 | 995.1 |
| Land, Buildings and Equipment, at cost | 1,279.4 | 1,312.4 |
| Other Assets | 1,611.7 | 987.2 |
| Total Assets | $3,902.4 | $3,294.7 |
| **Liabilities and Equity** | | |
| Current Liabilities: | | |
| Accounts payable | $ 599.7 | $ 590.7 |
| Current portion of long-term debt | 139.0 | 75.4 |
| Notes payable | 204.3 | 141.6 |
| Accrued taxes | 97.0 | 124.3 |
| Accrued payroll | 129.4 | 124.7 |
| Other current liabilities | 123.1 | 135.2 |
| Total Current Liabilities | 1,292.5 | 1,191.9 |
| Long-term Debt | 1,530.4 | 1,220.9 |
| Deferred Income Taxes | 272.1 | 250.0 |
| Deferred Income Taxes – Tax Leases | 143.7 | 157.5 |
| Other Liabilities | 169.1 | 166.7 |
| Total Liabilities | 3,407.8 | 2,987.0 |
| Stockholders' Equity: | | |
| Cumulative preference stock, none issued | – | – |
| Common stock, 204.2 shares issued | 578.0 | 384.3 |
| Retained earnings | 1,535.4 | 1,408.6 |
| Less common stock in treasury, at cost, shares of 44.3 in 1997 and 45.2 in 1996 | (1,501.9) | (1,367.4) |
| Unearned compensation and other | (58.0) | (61.2) |
| Cumulative foreign currency adjustment | (58.9) | (56.6) |
| Total Stockholders' Equity | 494.6 | 307.7 |
| Total Liabilities and Equity | $3,902.4 | $3,294.7 |

# Consolidated Statements of Cash Flows

| In Millions, Fiscal Year Ended | May 25, 1997 | May 26, 1996 | May 28, 1995 |
|---|---|---|---|
| Cash Flows – Operating Activities: | | | |
| Earnings from continuing operations | $ 445.4 | $ 476.4 | $ 259.7 |
| Adjustments to reconcile earnings to cash flow: | | | |
| Depreciation and amortization | 182.8 | 186.7 | 191.4 |
| Deferred income taxes | 20.9 | 42.4 | 59.0 |
| Change in current assets and liabilities, net of effects | | | |
| from business acquired | (86.4) | (25.9) | (227.8) |
| Unusual expenses | 48.4 | – | 183.2 |
| Other, net | (17.0) | (3.2) | (8.1) |
| Cash provided by continuing operations | 594.1 | 676.4 | 457.4 |
| Cash provided (used) by discontinued operations | (6.8) | (16.6) | 210.1 |
| Net Cash Provided by Operating Activities | 587.3 | 659.8 | 667.5 |
| Cash Flows – Investment Activities: | | | |
| Purchases of land, buildings and equipment | (162.5) | (128.8) | (156.5) |
| Investments in businesses, intangibles and affiliates, net of dividends | (42.0) | (40.0) | (48.8) |
| Purchases of marketable securities | (8.0) | (21.6) | (21.7) |
| Proceeds from sale of marketable securities | 47.7 | 22.5 | 49.1 |
| Proceeds from disposal of land, buildings and equipment | 2.6 | 6.2 | 1.2 |
| Proceeds from disposition of businesses | 6.5 | – | 188.3 |
| Other, net | (29.9) | (11.3) | (27.5) |
| Discontinued operations investment activities, net (primarily new restaurants) | – | – | (357.5) |
| Net Cash Used by Investment Activities | (185.6) | (173.0) | (373.4) |
| Cash Flows – Financing Activities: | | | |
| Increase (decrease) in notes payable | 312.7 | (42.4) | (330.4) |
| Issuance of long-term debt | 76.2 | 42.3 | 135.0 |
| Payment of long-term debt | (167.0) | (164.7) | (117.2) |
| Common stock issued | 60.5 | 38.0 | 24.3 |
| Purchases of common stock for treasury | (361.8) | (35.6) | (57.7) |
| Dividends paid | (320.7) | (303.6) | (297.2) |
| Other, net | (9.4) | (13.2) | (13.6) |
| Pre spin-off borrowings by Darden (Note Three) | – | – | 347.9 |
| Net Cash Used by Financing Activities | (409.5) | (479.2) | (308.9) |
| Increase (Decrease) in Cash and Cash Equivalents | (7.8) | 7.6 | (14.8) |
| Cash and Cash Equivalents – Beginning of Year | 20.6 | 13.0 | 27.8 |
| Cash and Cash Equivalents – End of Year | $  12.8 | $  20.6 | $  13.0 |
| Cash Flow from Changes in Current Assets and Liabilities: | | | |
| Receivables | $ (80.0) | $ (59.5) | $ (11.9) |
| Inventories | 45.0 | (23.7) | (52.7) |
| Prepaid expenses and other current assets | 2.5 | (6.3) | (11.9) |
| Accounts payable | (27.8) | 93.2 | (18.1) |
| Other current liabilities | (26.1) | (29.6) | (133.2) |
| Change in Current Assets and Liabilities | $ (86.4) | $ (25.9) | $(227.8) |

# Consolidated Statement of Stockholders' Equity

| In Millions, Except per Share Data | $.10 Par Value Common Stock (One Billion Shares Authorized) | | | | Retained Earnings | Unearned Compensation and Other | Cumulative Foreign Currency Adjustment | Total |
|---|---|---|---|---|---|---|---|---|
| | Issued | | Treasury | | | | | |
| | Shares | Amount | Shares | Amount | | | | |
| Balance at May 29, 1994 | 204.2 | $251.0 | (45.7) | $(1,334.4) | $2,457.9 | $(160.2) | $(63.1) | $1,151.2 |
| Unrealized gain, net of income taxes of $14.0, on available-for-sale securities at May 30, 1994 | | | | | | 22.0 | | 22.0 |
| Net earnings | | | | | 367.4 | | | 367.4 |
| Cash dividends declared ($1.88 per share), net of income taxes of $3.1 | | | | | (294.1) | | | (294.1) |
| Stock option, profit sharing and ESOP plans | – | 10.0 | .4 | 17.2 | | | | 27.2 |
| Shares purchased via puts, or on open market | | | (1.0) | (57.7) | | | | (57.7) |
| Put option premium/settlements, net | – | (3.5) | – | 2.8 | | | | (.7) |
| Transfer of put options | – | 122.0 | | | | | | 122.0 |
| Unearned compensation related to restricted stock awards | | | | | | (5.6) | | (5.6) |
| Earned compensation and other | | | | | | 11.0 | | 11.0 |
| Change in unrealized gain, net of income taxes of $3.7, on available-for-sale securities | | | | | | 5.8 | | 5.8 |
| Amount charged to gain on sale of foreign operations | | | | | | | 3.6 | 3.6 |
| Translation adjustments, net of income tax benefit of $.2 | | | | | | | 7.6 | 7.6 |
| Transfer of equity components to Darden prior to spin-off | | | | | | 69.1 | 10.1 | 79.2 |
| Distribution of equity to stockholders from spin-off of Restaurant operations | | | | | (1,297.9) | | | (1,297.9) |
| Balance at May 28, 1995 | 204.2 | 379.5 | (46.3) | (1,372.1) | 1,233.3 | (57.9) | (41.8) | 141.0 |
| Net earnings | | | | | 476.4 | | | 476.4 |
| Cash dividends declared ($1.91 per share), net of income taxes of $2.5 | | | | | (301.1) | | | (301.1) |
| Stock option, profit sharing and ESOP plans | – | 4.6 | 1.7 | 40.3 | | | | 44.9 |
| Shares purchased on open market | | | (.6) | (35.6) | | | | (35.6) |
| Put option premium/settlements, net | – | .2 | | | | | | .2 |
| Unearned compensation related to restricted stock awards | | | | | | (6.5) | | (6.5) |
| Earned compensation and other | | | | | | 7.1 | | 7.1 |
| Change in unrealized gain, net of income taxes of $2.0, on available-for-sale securities | | | | | | (3.1) | | (3.1) |
| Minimum pension liability adjustment | | | | | | (.8) | | (.8) |
| Translation adjustments, net of income tax benefit of $.2 | | | | | | | (14.8) | (14.8) |
| Balance at May 26, 1996 | 204.2 | 384.3 | (45.2) | (1,367.4) | 1,408.6 | (61.2) | (56.6) | 307.7 |
| Net earnings | | | | | 445.4 | | | 445.4 |
| Cash dividends declared ($2.03 per share), net of income taxes of $2.1 | | | | | (318.6) | | | (318.6) |
| Shares issued in acquisition | – | 181.4 | 5.4 | 173.0 | | | | 354.4 |
| Stock option, profit sharing and ESOP plans | – | 9.3 | 1.7 | 57.4 | | | | 66.7 |
| Shares purchased via puts, or on open market | | | (6.2) | (368.0) | | | | (368.0) |
| Put and call option premium/settlements, net | – | 3.0 | – | 3.1 | | | | 6.1 |
| Unearned compensation related to restricted stock awards | | | | | | (7.9) | | (7.9) |
| Earned compensation and other | | | | | | 13.1 | | 13.1 |
| Change in unrealized gain, net of income taxes of $.1, on available-for-sale securities | | | | | | (.1) | | (.1) |
| Minimum pension liability adjustment | | | | | | (1.9) | | (1.9) |
| Amount removed on disposition of foreign operation | | | | | | | 6.1 | 6.1 |
| Translation adjustments | | | | | | | (8.4) | (8.4) |
| **Balance at May 25, 1997** | **204.2** | **$578.0** | **(44.3)** | **$(1,501.9)** | **$1,535.4** | **$ (58.0)** | **$(58.9)** | **$ 494.6** |

# APPENDIX C

# PRESENT VALUE CONCEPTS

Business enterprises borrow and invest large sums of money. Both of these types of transactions involve the use of **present value computations**. A present value computation is based on the concept of the **time value of money**. For example, would you rather be given $1,000 today or be given $1,000 a year from today? If you get the $1,000 today and invest it to earn 10% per year, the $1,000 will accumulate to $1,100 ($1,000 plus the $100 interest) one year from today. The $1,000 received today is the present value amount that is equivalent to $1,100 one year from now. The present value, therefore, is based on three variables: (1) the dollar amount to be received (the future amount), (2) the length of time until the amount is received (the number of periods), and (3) the interest rate (the discount rate). The process of determining the present value is referred to as **discounting the future amount**. The relationship of these fundamental variables is depicted in the following time diagram:

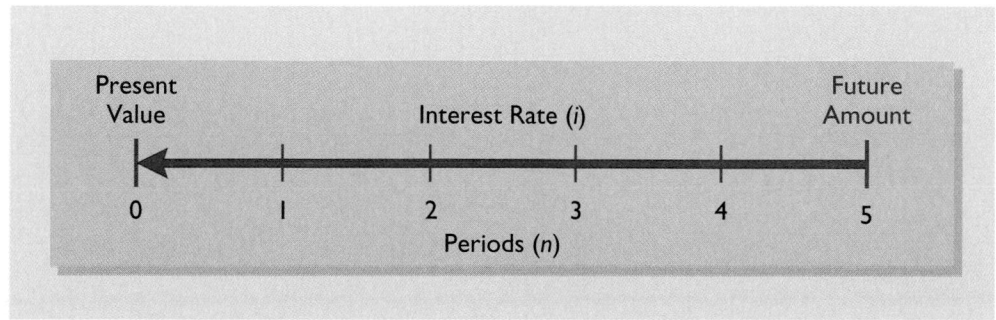

**ILLUSTRATION C-1**

*Time diagram*

To better understand the variables involved in present value analysis, we encourage you to use time diagrams such as the one in Illustration C-1.

In this textbook, present value computations are used in measuring several items. For example, in Chapter 16, to determine the market price of a bond, the present value of the principal and interest payments is computed. In addition, the determination of the amount to be reported for notes payable and lease liability involves present value computations. And, in Chapter 27, the discounted cash flow technique and the net present value method are used to make capital budget decisions.

# PRESENT VALUE OF A SINGLE FUTURE AMOUNT

To illustrate present value concepts, assume that you are willing to invest a sum of money that will yield $1,000 at the end of one year. In other words, what amount would you need to invest today to have $1,000 one year from now? If you want a 10% rate of return, the investment or present value is $909.09 ($1,000 ÷ 1.10). The computation of this amount is shown in Illustration C-2.

**ILLUSTRATION C-2**

*Present value computation—$1,000 discounted at 10% for 1 year*

Present value × (1 + interest rate) = Future amount
Present value × (1 + 10%)         = $1,000
Present value                     = $1,000 ÷ 1.10
**Present value**                 = **$909.09**

The future amount ($1,000), the discount rate (10%), and the number of periods (1) are known. The variables in this situation can be depicted in the following time diagram:

**ILLUSTRATION C-3**

*Finding present value if discounted for one period*

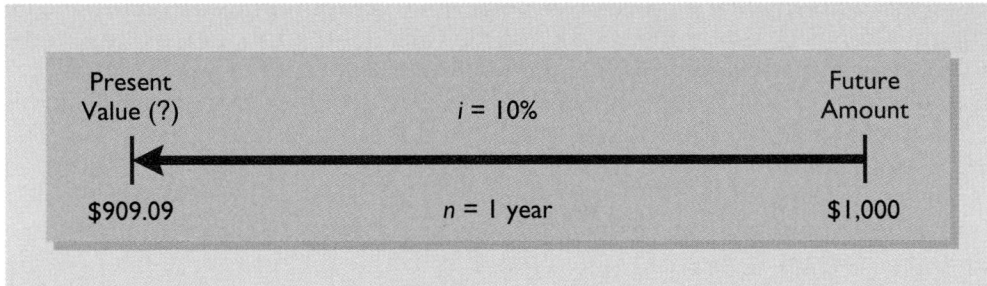

If the single future amount of $1,000 is to be received **in 2 years** and discounted at 10%, its present value is $826.45 [($1,000 ÷ 1.10) ÷ 1.10], depicted as follows:

**ILLUSTRATION C-4**

*Finding present value if discounted for two periods*

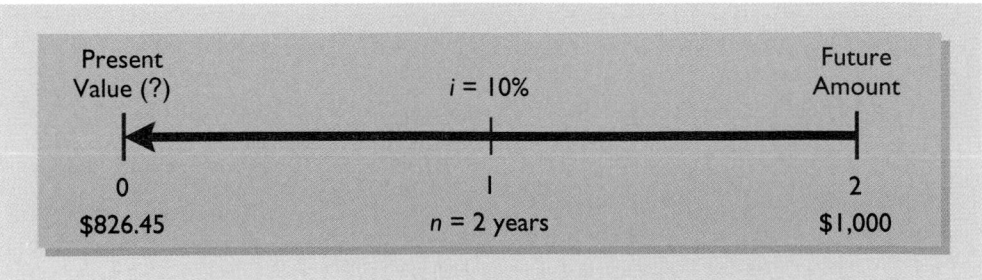

The present value of 1 may also be determined through tables that show the present value of 1 for $n$ periods. In Table C-1 on page C3, $n$ is the number of discounting periods involved. The percentages are the periodic interest rates or discount rates, and the 5-digit decimal numbers in the respective columns are the factors for the present value of 1.

When Table C-1 is used, the future amount is multiplied by the present value factor specified at the intersection of the number of periods and the discount rate. For example, the present value factor for 1 period at a discount rate of 10% is .90909, which equals the $909.09 ($1,000 × .90909) computed in Illustration C-2.

### TABLE C-1
### Present Value of 1

| (n) Periods | 4% | 5% | 6% | 8% | 9% | 10% | 11 % | 12% | 15% |
|---|---|---|---|---|---|---|---|---|---|
| 1 | .96154 | .95238 | .94340 | .92593 | .91743 | .90909 | .90090 | .89286 | .86957 |
| 2 | .92456 | .90703 | .89000 | .85734 | .84168 | .82645 | .81162 | .79719 | .75614 |
| 3 | .88900 | .86384 | .83962 | .79383 | .77218 | .75132 | .73119 | .71178 | .65752 |
| 4 | .85480 | .82270 | .79209 | .73503 | .70843 | .68301 | .65873 | .63552 | .57175 |
| 5 | .82193 | .78353 | .74726 | .68058 | .64993 | .62092 | .59345 | .56743 | .49718 |
| 6 | .79031 | .74622 | .70496 | .63017 | .59627 | .56447 | .53464 | .50663 | .43233 |
| 7 | .75992 | .71068 | .66506 | .58349 | .54703 | .51316 | .48166 | .45235 | .37594 |
| 8 | .73069 | .67684 | .62741 | .54027 | .50187 | .46651 | .43393 | .40388 | .32690 |
| 9 | .70259 | .64461 | .59190 | .50025 | .46043 | .42410 | .39092 | .36061 | .28426 |
| 10 | .67556 | .61391 | .55839 | .46319 | .42241 | .38554 | .35218 | .32197 | .24719 |
| 11 | .64958 | .58468 | .52679 | .42888 | .38753 | .35049 | .31728 | .28748 | .21494 |
| 12 | .62460 | .55684 | .49697 | .39711 | .35554 | .31863 | .28584 | .25668 | .18691 |
| 13 | .60057 | .53032 | .46884 | .36770 | .32618 | .28966 | .25751 | .22917 | .16253 |
| 14 | .57748 | .50507 | .44230 | .34046 | .29925 | .26333 | .23199 | .20462 | .14133 |
| 15 | .55526 | .48102 | .41727 | .31524 | .27454 | .23939 | .20900 | .18270 | .12289 |
| 16 | .53391 | .45811 | .39365 | .29189 | .25187 | .21763 | .18829 | .16312 | .10687 |
| 17 | .51337 | .43630 | .37136 | .27027 | .23107 | .19785 | .16963 | .14564 | .09293 |
| 18 | .49363 | .41552 | .35034 | .25025 | .21199 | .17986 | .15282 | .13004 | .08081 |
| 19 | .47464 | .39573 | .33051 | .23171 | .19449 | .16351 | .13768 | .11611 | .07027 |
| 20 | .45639 | .37689 | .31180 | .21455 | .17843 | .14864 | .12403 | .10367 | .06110 |

For 2 periods at a discount rate of 10%, the present value factor is .82645, which equals the $826.45 ($1,000 × .82645) computed previously.

Note that **a higher discount rate produces a smaller present value.** For example, using a 15% discount rate, the present value of $1,000 due one year from now is $869.57 versus $909.09 at 10%. It should also be recognized that **the further removed from the present the future amount is, the smaller the present value.** For example, using the same discount rate of 10%, the present value of $1,000 due **in five years** is $620.92 versus the present value of $1,000 due in **one** year, which is $909.09.

The following two demonstration problems (Illustrations C-5 and C-6) illustrate how to use Table C-1.

**ILLUSTRATION C-5**

*Demonstration Problem—*
*Using Table C-1 for PV of 1*

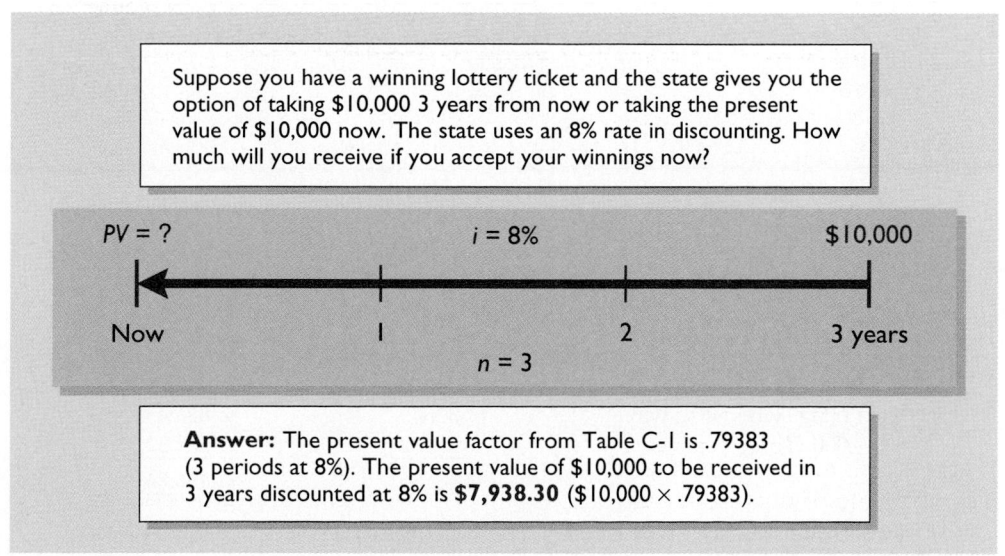

Suppose you have a winning lottery ticket and the state gives you the option of taking $10,000 3 years from now or taking the present value of $10,000 now. The state uses an 8% rate in discounting. How much will you receive if you accept your winnings now?

PV = ?          i = 8%          $10,000

Now          1          2          3 years

n = 3

**Answer:** The present value factor from Table C-1 is .79383 (3 periods at 8%). The present value of $10,000 to be received in 3 years discounted at 8% is **$7,938.30** ($10,000 × .79383).

ILLUSTRATION C-6

*Demonstration Problem—*
*Using Table C-1 for PV of 1*

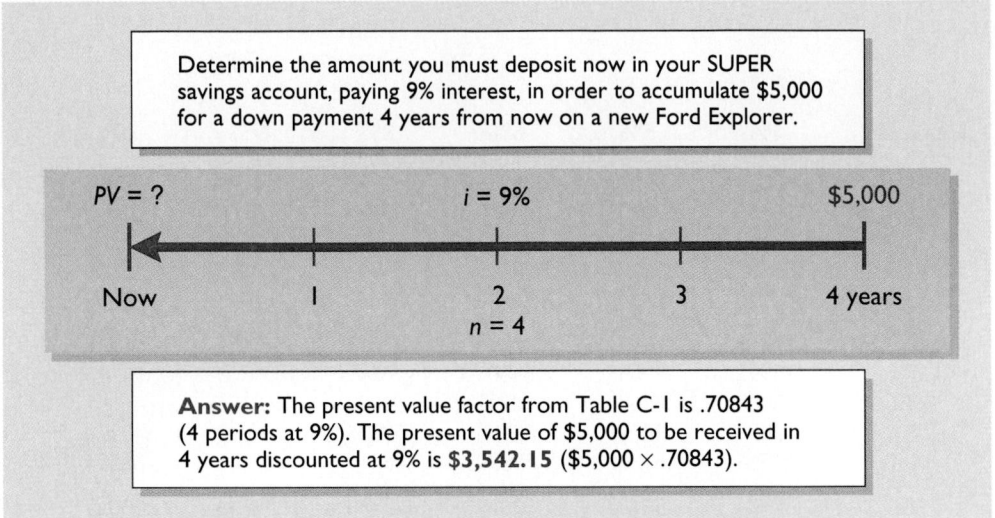

> Determine the amount you must deposit now in your SUPER savings account, paying 9% interest, in order to accumulate $5,000 for a down payment 4 years from now on a new Ford Explorer.

PV = ?               i = 9%                  $5,000

Now        1        2        3      4 years
                  n = 4

> **Answer:** The present value factor from Table C-1 is .70843 (4 periods at 9%). The present value of $5,000 to be received in 4 years discounted at 9% is **$3,542.15** ($5,000 × .70843).

# PRESENT VALUE OF A SERIES OF FUTURE AMOUNTS (ANNUITIES)

The preceding discussion involved the discounting of only a single future amount. Businesses and individuals frequently engage in transactions in which a series of equal dollar amounts are to be received or paid periodically. Examples of a series of periodic receipts or payments are loan agreements, installment sales, mortgage notes, lease (rental) contracts, and pension obligations. These series of periodic receipts or payments are called **annuities**. In computing the present value of an annuity, it is necessary to know the (1) discount rate, (2) the number of discount periods, and (3) the amount of the periodic receipts or payments. To illustrate the computation of the present value of an annuity, assume that you will receive $1,000 cash annually for 3 years and the discount rate is 10%. This situation is depicted in the following time diagram:

ILLUSTRATION C-7

*Time diagram for a 3-year*
*annuity*

PV = ?          $1,000          $1,000          $1,000
                       i = 10%

Now        1              n = 3        2        3 years

The present value in this situation may be computed as follows:

ILLUSTRATION C-8

*Present value of a series of*
*future amounts computation*

| Future Amount | × | Present Value of 1 Factor at 10% | = | Present Value |
|---|---|---|---|---|
| $1,000 (One year away) | | .90909 | | $ 909.09 |
| 1,000 (Two years away) | | .82645 | | 826.45 |
| 1,000 (Three years away) | | .75132 | | 751.32 |
| | | 2.48686 | | **$2,486.86** |

This method of calculation is required when the periodic cash flows are not uniform in each period. However, when the future receipts are the same in each period, there are two other ways to compute present value. First, the annual cash flow can be multiplied by the sum of the three present value factors. In the example above, $1,000 × 2.48686 equals $2,486.86. Second, annuity tables may be used. As illustrated in Table C-2 below, these tables show the present value of 1 to be received periodically for a given number of periods.

### TABLE C-2
### Present Value of an Annuity of 1

| (n) Periods | 4% | 5% | 6% | 8% | 9% | 10% | 11 % | 12% | 15% |
|---|---|---|---|---|---|---|---|---|---|
| 1 | .96154 | .95238 | .94340 | .92593 | .91743 | .90909 | .90090 | .89286 | .86957 |
| 2 | 1.88609 | 1.85941 | 1.83339 | 1.78326 | 1.75911 | 1.73554 | 1.71252 | 1.69005 | 1.62571 |
| 3 | 2.77509 | 2.72325 | 2.67301 | 2.57710 | 2.53130 | 2.48685 | 2.44371 | 2.40183 | 2.28323 |
| 4 | 3.62990 | 3.54595 | 3.46511 | 3.31213 | 3.23972 | 3.16986 | 3.10245 | 3.03735 | 2.85498 |
| 5 | 4.45182 | 4.32948 | 4.21236 | 3.99271 | 3.88965 | 3.79079 | 3.69590 | 3.60478 | 3.35216 |
| 6 | 5.24214 | 5.07569 | 4.91732 | 4.62288 | 4.48592 | 4.35526 | 4.23054 | 4.11141 | 3.78448 |
| 7 | 6.00205 | 5.78637 | 5.58238 | 5.20637 | 5.03295 | 4.86842 | 4.71220 | 4.56376 | 4.16042 |
| 8 | 6.73274 | 6.46321 | 6.20979 | 5.74664 | 5.53482 | 5.33493 | 5.14612 | 4.96764 | 4.48732 |
| 9 | 7.43533 | 7.10782 | 6.80169 | 6.24689 | 5.99525 | 5.75902 | 5.53705 | 5.32825 | 4.77158 |
| 10 | 8.11090 | 7.72173 | 7.36009 | 6.71008 | 6.41766 | 6.14457 | 5.88923 | 5.65022 | 5.01877 |
| 11 | 8.76048 | 8.30641 | 7.88687 | 7.13896 | 6.80519 | 6.49506 | 6.20652 | 5.93770 | 5.23371 |
| 12 | 9.38507 | 8.86325 | 8.38384 | 7.53608 | 7.16073 | 6.81369 | 6.49236 | 6.19437 | 5.42062 |
| 13 | 9.98565 | 9.39357 | 8.85268 | 7.90378 | 7.48690 | 7.10336 | 6.74987 | 6.42355 | 5.58315 |
| 14 | 10.56312 | 9.89864 | 9.29498 | 8.24424 | 7.78615 | 7.36669 | 6.98187 | 6.62817 | 5.72448 |
| 15 | 11.11839 | 10.37966 | 9.71225 | 8.55948 | 8.06069 | 7.60608 | 7.19087 | 6.81086 | 5.84737 |
| 16 | 11.65230 | 10.83777 | 10.10590 | 8.85137 | 8.31256 | 7.82371 | 7.37916 | 6.97399 | 5.95424 |
| 17 | 12.16567 | 11.27407 | 10.47726 | 9.12164 | 8.54363 | 8.02155 | 7.54879 | 7.11963 | 6.04716 |
| 18 | 12.65930 | 11.68959 | 10.82760 | 9.37189 | 8.75563 | 8.20141 | 7.70162 | 7.24967 | 6.12797 |
| 19 | 13.13394 | 12.08532 | 11.15812 | 9.60360 | 8.95012 | 8.36492 | 7.83929 | 7.36578 | 6.19823 |
| 20 | 13.59033 | 12.46221 | 11.46992 | 9.81815 | 9.12855 | 8.51356 | 7.96333 | 7.46944 | 6.25933 |

From Table C-2 it can be seen that the present value factor of an annuity of 1 for three periods at 10% is 2.48685.[1] This present value factor is the total of the three individual present value factors as shown in Illustration C-8. Applying this amount to the annual cash flow of $1,000 produces a present value of $2,486.85.

The following demonstration problem (Illustration C-9) illustrates how to use Table C-2.

---

[1]The difference of .00001 between 2.48686 amd 2.48685 is due to rounding.

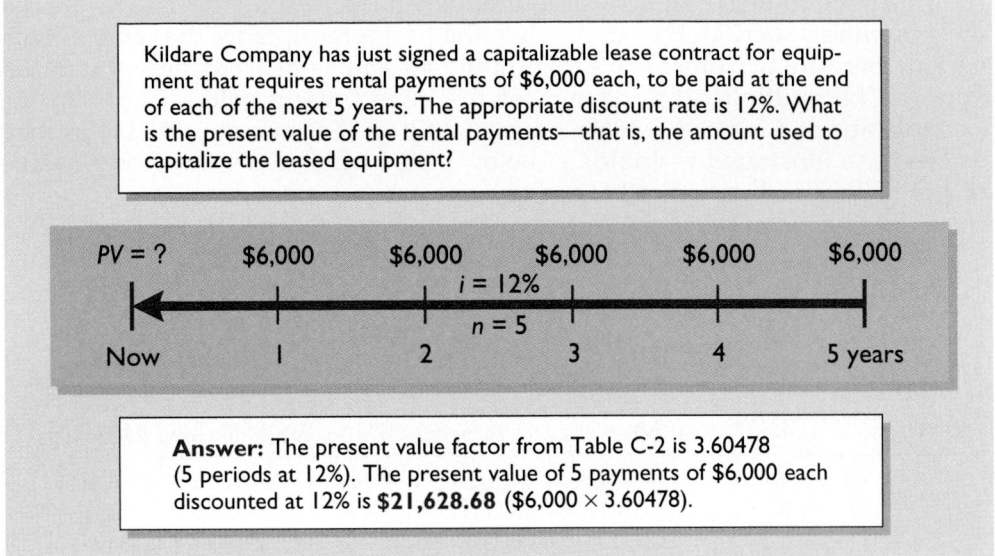

Kildare Company has just signed a capitalizable lease contract for equipment that requires rental payments of $6,000 each, to be paid at the end of each of the next 5 years. The appropriate discount rate is 12%. What is the present value of the rental payments—that is, the amount used to capitalize the leased equipment?

**Answer:** The present value factor from Table C-2 is 3.60478 (5 periods at 12%). The present value of 5 payments of $6,000 each discounted at 12% is **$21,628.68** ($6,000 × 3.60478).

# TIME PERIODS AND DISCOUNTING

In the preceding calculations, the discounting has been done on an annual basis using an annual interest rate. Discounting may also be done over shorter periods of time such as monthly, quarterly, or semiannually. When the time frame is less than one year, it is necessary to convert the annual interest rate to the applicable time frame. Assume, for example, that the investor in Illustration C-8 received $500 **semiannually** for 3 years instead of $1,000 annually. In this case, the number of periods becomes 6 (3 × 2), the discount rate is 5% (10% ÷ 2), the present value factor from Table C-2 is 5.07569, and the present value of the future cash flows is $2,537.85 (5.07569 × $500). This amount is slightly higher than the $2,486.86 computed in Illustration C-8 because interest is computed twice during the same year; therefore interest is earned on the first half year's interest.

# COMPUTING THE PRESENT VALUE OF A BOND

The present value (or market price) of a bond is a function of three variables: (1) the payment amounts, (2) the length of time until the amounts are paid, and (3) the discount rate.

The first variable (dollars to be paid) is made up of two elements: (1) a series of interest payments (an annuity) and (2) the principal amount (a single sum). To compute the present value of the bond, both the interest payments and the principal amount must be discounted—two different computations. The time diagrams for a bond due in 5 years are shown in Illustration C-10.

When the investor's discount rate is equal to the bond's contractual interest rate, the present value of the bonds will equal the face value of the bonds. To

**ILLUSTRATION C-10**

*Time diagram for the present value of a bond*

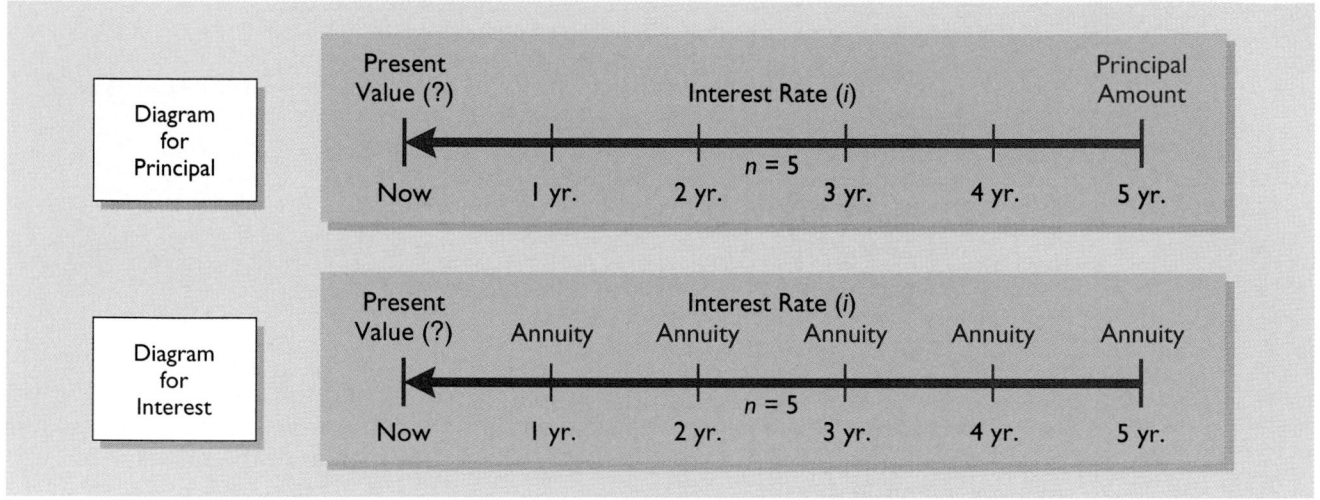

illustrate, assume a bond issue of 10%, 5-year bonds with a face value of $100,000 with interest payable **semiannually** on January 1 and July 1. If the discount rate is the same as the contractual rate, the bonds will sell at face value. In this case, the investor will receive (1) $100,000 at maturity and (2) a series of ten $5,000 interest payments [($100,000 × 10%) ÷ 2] over the term of the bonds. The length of time is expressed in terms of interest periods, in this case, 10, and the discount rate per interest period, 5%. The following time diagram (Illustration C-11) depicts the variables involved in this discounting situation:

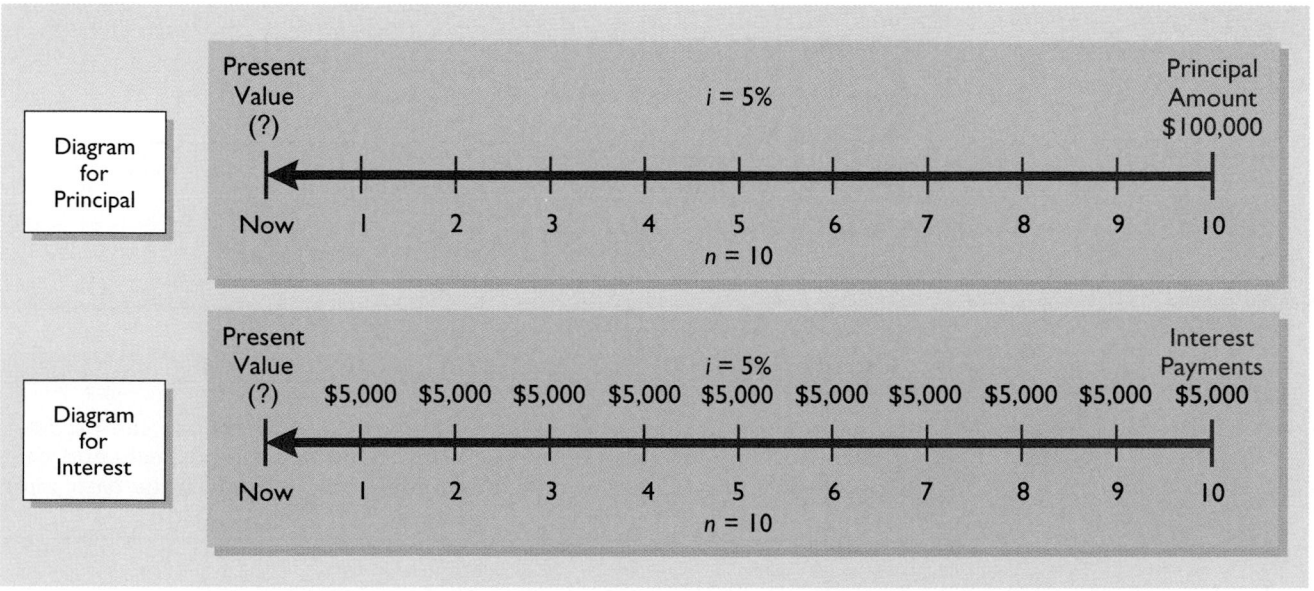

The computation of the present value of these bonds is shown below.

**ILLUSTRATION C-12**

*Present value of principal and interest (face value)*

| 10% Contractual Rate—10% Discount Rate | |
| --- | ---: |
| Present value of principal to be received at maturity | |
| $100,000 × PV of 1 due in 10 periods at 5% | |
| $100,000 × .61391 (Table C-1) | $ 61,391 |
| Present value of interest to be received periodically | |
| over the term of the bonds | |
| $5,000 × PV of 1 due periodically for 10 periods at 5% | |
| $5,000 × 7.72173 (Table C-2) | 38,609* |
| Present value of bonds | $100,000 |

*(Rounded).

Now assume that the investor's required rate of return is 12%, not 10%. The future amounts are again $100,000 and $5,000, respectively, but now a discount rate of 6% (12% ÷ 2) must be used. The present value of the bonds is $92,639, as computed below:

**ILLUSTRATION C-13**

*Present value of principal and interest (discount)*

| 10% Contractual Rate—12% Discount Rate | |
| --- | ---: |
| Present value of principal to be received at maturity | |
| $100,000 × .55839 (Table C-1) | $55,839 |
| Present value of interest to be received periodically | |
| over the term of the bonds | |
| $5,000 × 7.36009 (Table C-2) | 36,800 |
| Present value of bonds | $92,639 |

Conversely, if the discount rate is 8% and the contractual rate is 10%, the present value of the bonds is $108,111, computed as follows:

**ILLUSTRATION C-14**

*Present value of principal and interest (premium)*

| 10% Contractual Rate—8% Discount Rate | |
| --- | ---: |
| Present value of principal to be received at maturity | |
| $100,000 × .67556 (Table C-1) | $ 67,556 |
| Present value of interest to be received periodically | |
| over the term of the bonds | |
| $5,000 × 8.11090 (Table C-2) | 40,555 |
| Present value of bonds | $108,111 |

## TECHNOLOGY IN ACTION

 As discussed in this appendix, the selling price of the bonds can be determined by present value formulas. Many computer spreadsheets and computer programs can perform the discounting functions given the basic information of the situation.

The above discussion relied on present value tables in solving present value problems. Electronic hand-held calculators may also be used to compute present values without the use of these tables. Some calculators, especially the "business" or "financial" type calculators, have present value (PV) functions that allow you to calculate present values by merely punching in the proper amount, discount rate, periods, and pressing the PV key.

# BRIEF EXERCISES
## (Use Tables to Solve Exercises)

**BEC–1**  For each of the following cases, indicate (a) to what interest rate columns and (b) to what number of periods you would refer in looking up the discount rate.

*Using present value tables.*

1. In Table C-1 (present value of 1):

|  | Annual Rate | Number of Years Involved | Discounts Per Year |
|---|---|---|---|
| a. | 12% | 6 | Annually |
| b. | 10% | 15 | Annually |
| c. | 8% | 8 | Semiannually |

2. In Table C-2 (present value of an annuity of 1):

|  | Annual Rate | Number of Years Involved | Number of Payments Involved | Frequency of Payments |
|---|---|---|---|---|
| a. | 12% | 20 | 20 | Annually |
| b. | 10% | 5 | 5 | Annually |
| c. | 8% | 4 | 8 | Semiannually |

**BEC–2**  (a) What is the present value of $10,000 due 8 periods from now, discounted at 8%? (b) What is the present value of $10,000 to be received at the end of each of 6 periods, discounted at 9%?

*Determining present values.*

**BEC–3**  Smolinski Company is considering an investment that will return a lump sum of $500,000 5 years from now. What amount should Smolinski Company pay for this investment in order to earn a 15% return?

*Compute the present value of a single-sum investment.*

**BEC–4**  Pizzeria Company earns 11% on an investment that will return $875,000 8 years from now. What is the amount Pizzeria should invest now in order to earn this rate of return?

*Compute the present value of a single-sum investment.*

**BEC–5**  Shake-A-Soda Company sold a 5-year, noninterest-bearing $27,000 note receivable to Valley Inc. Valley wishes to earn 12% over the remaining 4 years of the note. How much cash will Shake-A-Soda receive upon sale of the note?

*Compute the present value of a single-sum noninterest-bearing note.*

**BEC–6**  Roberto Company issues a 3-year, zero-interest-bearing $66,000 note. The interest rate used to discount the zero-interest-bearing note is 8%. What are the cash proceeds that Roberto Company should receive?

*Compute the present value of a single-sum noninterest-bearing note.*

**BEC–7**  Kilarny Company is considering investing in an annuity contract that will return $20,000 annually at the end of each year for 15 years. What amount should Kilarny Company pay for this investment if it earns a 6% return?

*Compute the present value of an annuity investment.*

**BEC–8**  Zarita Enterprises earns 11% on an investment that pays back $110,000 at the end of each of the next 4 years. What is the amount Zarita Enterprises invested to earn the 11% rate of return?

*Compute the present value of an annuity investment.*

**BEC–9**  Hernandez Railroad Co. is about to issue $100,000 of 10-year bonds paying a 12% interest rate, with interest payable semiannually. The discount rate for such securities is 10%. How much can Hernandez expect to receive for the sale of these bonds?

*Compute the present value of bonds.*

**BEC–10**  Assume the same information as BEC–9 except that the discount rate is 12% instead of 10%. In this case, how much can Hernandez expect to receive from the sale of these bonds?

*Compute the present value of bonds.*

**BEC–11**  Caledonian Taco Company receives a $50,000, 6-year note bearing interest of 11% (paid annually) from a customer at a time when the discount rate is 12%. What is the present value of the note received by Caledonian?

*Compute the present value of a note.*

*Compute the present value of bonds.*

**BEC–12**   Galway Bay Enterprises issued 10%, 8-year, $2,000,000 par value bonds that pay interest semiannually on October 1 and April 1. The bonds are dated April 1, 1999, and are issued on that date. The discount rate of interest for such bonds on April 1, 1999, is 12%. What cash proceeds did Galway Bay receive from issuance of the bonds?

*Compute the value of a machine for purposes of making a purchase decision.*

**BEC–13**   Barney Googal owns a garage and is contemplating purchasing a tire retreading machine for $16,280. After estimating costs and revenues, Barney projects a net cash flow from the retreading machine of $2,790 annually for 8 years. Barney hopes to earn a return of 11% on such investments. What is the present value of the retreading operation? Should Barney Googal purchase the retreading machine?

*Compute the present value of a note.*

**BEC–14**   Hung-Chao Yu Company issues a 10%, 6-year mortgage note on January 1, 1999, to obtain financing for new equipment. Land is used as collateral for the note. The terms provide for semiannual installment payments of $112,825. What were the cash proceeds received from the issuance of the note?

*Compute the maximum price to pay for a machine.*

**BEC–15**   Ramos Company is considering purchasing equipment. The equipment will produce the following cash flows: Year 1, $30,000; Year 2, $40,000; Year 3, $50,000. Ramos requires a minimum rate of return of 15%. What is the maximum price Ramos should pay for this equipment?

*Compute the interest rate on a single sum.*

**BEC–16**   If Kerry Rodriquez invests $1,827 now, she will receive $10,000 at the end of 15 years. What annual rate of interest will Kerry earn on her investment? (Hint: Use Table C-1.)

*Compute the number of periods of a single sum.*

**BEC–17**   Maloney Cork has been offered the opportunity of investing $24,719 now. The investment will earn 15% per year and at the end of that time will return Maloney $100,000. How many years must Maloney wait to receive $100,000? (Hint: Use Table C-1.)

*Compute the interest rate on an annuity.*

**BEC–18**   Annie Dublin purchased an investment for $11,469.92. From this investment, she will receive $1,000 annually for the next 20 years, starting one year from now. What rate of interest will Annie's investment be earning for her? (Hint: Use Table C-2.)

*Compute the number of periods of an annuity.*

**BEC–19**   Andy Sanchez invests $8,851.37 now for a series of $1,000 annual returns, beginning one year from now. Andy will earn a return of 8% on the initial investment. How many annual payments of $1,000 will Andy receive? (Hint: Use Table C-2.)

# APPENDIX D

# COMPLETING THE ACCOUNTING CYCLE UNDER THE PERIODIC INVENTORY SYSTEM

In Chapter 5, the **perpetual inventory method** was explained and illustrated. That presentation, using a merchandising firm, demonstrated the use of a work sheet and closing entries. Our presentation of the **periodic inventory method** in Chapter 9 did not include these steps. The purpose of this appendix is to explain these two steps.

Under a periodic inventory system the ending inventory and the cost of goods sold are determined at the end of the period. And, once determined, the ending inventory replaces the beginning inventory in the general ledger. There are two ways to record the newly determined ending inventory: (1) as part of the closing process, or (2) as part of the adjusting process. We demonstrate both ways, using a work sheet.

## SECTION I CLOSING ENTRY METHOD FOR MERCHANDISE INVENTORY

## USING A WORK SHEET

As indicated in Chapters 4 and 5, a work sheet enables financial statements to be prepared before the adjusting entries are journalized and posted. The work sheet for Highpoint Electronic, shown in Illustration D-1, contains all the income statement data explained in Chapter 9 plus other noninventory data from Chapter 5. The unique accounts for a merchandising company using a periodic inventory system are shown in capital letters in red.

### Trial Balance Columns

Data for the trial balance are obtained from the ledger balances of Highpoint Electronic at December 31. The amount shown for Merchandise Inventory, $36,000, is the beginning inventory.

**HIGHPOINT ELECTRONIC**
**Work Sheet**
**For the Year Ended December 31, 1999**

| | Trial Balance | | Adjustments | | Adjusted Trial Balance | | Income Statement | | Balance Sheet | |
|---|---|---|---|---|---|---|---|---|---|---|
| | Dr. | Cr. | Dr. | Cr. | Dr. | Cr. | Dr. | Cr. | Dr. | Cr. |
| Cash | 9,500 | | | | 9,500 | | | | 9,500 | |
| Accounts Receivable | 16,100 | | | | 16,100 | | | | 16,100 | |
| MERCHANDISE INVENTORY | 36,000 | | | | 36,000 | | 36,000 | 40,000 | 40,000 | |
| Prepaid Insurance | 3,800 | | | (a) 2,000 | 1,800 | | | | 1,800 | |
| Store Equipment | 80,000 | | | | 80,000 | | | | 80,000 | |
| Accumulated Depreciation | | 16,000 | | (b) 8,000 | | 24,000 | | | | 24,000 |
| Accounts Payable | | 20,400 | | | | 20,400 | | | | 20,400 |
| R. A. Lamb, Capital | | 83,000 | | | | 83,000 | | | | 83,000 |
| R. A. Lamb, Drawing | 15,000 | | | | 15,000 | | | | 15,000 | |
| SALES | | 480,000 | | | | 480,000 | | 480,000 | | |
| SALES RETURNS AND ALLOWANCES | 12,000 | | | | 12,000 | | 12,000 | | | |
| SALES DISCOUNTS | 8,000 | | | | 8,000 | | 8,000 | | | |
| PURCHASES | 325,000 | | | | 325,000 | | 325,000 | | | |
| PURCHASE RETURNS AND ALLOWANCES | | 10,400 | | | | 10,400 | | 10,400 | | |
| PURCHASE DISCOUNTS | | 6,800 | | | | 6,800 | | 6,800 | | |
| FREIGHT-IN | 12,200 | | | | 12,200 | | 12,200 | | | |
| Freight-out | 7,000 | | | | 7,000 | | 7,000 | | | |
| Advertising Expense | 16,000 | | | | 16,000 | | 16,000 | | | |
| Rent Expense | 19,000 | | | | 19,000 | | 19,000 | | | |
| Store Salaries Expense | 40,000 | | (c) 5,000 | | 45,000 | | 45,000 | | | |
| Utilities Expense | 17,000 | | | | 17,000 | | 17,000 | | | |
| Totals | 616,600 | 616,600 | | | | | | | | |
| Insurance Expense | | | (a) 2,000 | | 2,000 | | 2,000 | | | |
| Depreciation Expense | | | (b) 8,000 | | 8,000 | | 8,000 | | | |
| Salaries Payable | | | | (c) 5,000 | | 5,000 | | | | 5,000 |
| Totals | | | 15,000 | 15,000 | 629,600 | 629,600 | 507,200 | 537,200 | 162,400 | 132,400 |
| Net Income | | | | | | | 30,000 | | | 30,000 |
| Totals | | | | | | | 537,200 | 537,200 | 162,400 | 162,400 |

Key: (a) Insurance expired, (b) Depreciation expensed, (c) Salaries accrued.

**ILLUSTRATION D-1**

*Work sheet for merchandising company using a periodic inventory system*

## Adjustments Columns

After all adjustment data are entered on the work sheet, the equality of the adjustment column totals is established. The balances in all accounts are then extended to the adjusted trial balance columns.[1]

---

[1]Conceptually, it can be argued that the change between the beginning and ending inventory balances should be shown on the work sheet as an adjustment. The adjusting entry approach is explained and illustrated in Section II of this appendix.

## Adjusted Trial Balance

The adjusted trial balance shows the balance of all accounts after adjustment at the end of the accounting period. **Note that beginning inventory was not adjusted.** Therefore, it is extended to the adjusted trial balance in the amount of $36,000.

## Income Statement Columns

The accounts and balances that affect the income statement are transferred from the adjusted trial balance columns to the income statement columns. For Highpoint Electronic, Sales of $480,000 is shown in the credit column whereas the contra revenue accounts, Sales Returns and Allowances of $12,000 and Sales Discounts of $8,000, are shown in the debit column. Thus, the difference of $460,000 is the net sales shown on the income statement. Similarly, Purchases of $325,000 and Freight-in of $12,200 are extended to the debit column. The contra purchase accounts, Purchase Returns and Allowances of $10,400 and Purchase Discounts of $6,800, are extended to the credit columns.

The work sheet procedures for the account Merchandise Inventory merit specific comment. The procedures are:

1. The beginning balance, $36,000, is extended from the adjusted trial balance column to the **income statement debit column**. From there it can be used (added) in reporting cost of goods available for sale in the income statement.
2. The ending inventory, $40,000, is added to the work sheet by an **income statement credit and a balance sheet debit**. The credit makes it possible to deduct ending inventory from the cost of goods available for sale in the income statement to determine cost of goods sold. The debit means the ending inventory can be reported as an asset on the balance sheet.

These two procedures are specifically illustrated below:

|  | Income Statement | | Balance Sheet | |
|---|---|---|---|---|
|  | Dr. | Cr. | Dr. | Cr. |
| Merchandise Inventory | (1) 36,000 | 40,000 ←—(2)—→ 40,000 | | |

**ILLUSTRATION D-2**

*Work sheet procedures for inventories—periodic inventory system*

The computation for cost of goods sold, taken from the income statement columns in Illustration D-1, is as follows:

| Debit Column | | Credit Column | |
|---|---|---|---|
| Beginning inventory | $ 36,000 | Ending inventory | $40,000 |
| Purchases | 325,000 | Purchase returns and allowances | 10,400 |
| Freight-in | 12,200 | Purchase discounts | 6,800 |
| Total debits | 373,200 | Total credits | $57,200 |
| Less: Total credits | 57,200 | | |
| Cost of goods sold | $316,000 | | |

**ILLUSTRATION D-3**

*Computation of cost of goods sold from work sheet columns*

## Balance Sheet Columns

For Highpoint Electronic, the ending inventory amount of $40,000 is shown in the balance sheet debit column (see Illustration D-2).

# PREPARING FINANCIAL STATEMENTS

Financial statements for a merchandising company are prepared from the financial statement columns of the work sheet. The income statement for Highpoint Electronic has already been illustrated (see Illustration 9-6, page 375). The owner's equity statement (see Illustration 5-12, page 203) and the balance sheet (see Illustration 5-13, page 204) appear as already reported in Chapter 5.

## Closing Entries

All accounts (including beginning and ending inventory under a periodic inventory system) that affect the determination of net income are closed to Income Summary. Data for the preparation of closing entries may be obtained from the income statement columns of the work sheet. In journalizing, all debit column amounts are credited, and all credit column amounts are debited.

The closing of merchandise inventory is included with other closing entries, as shown below for Highpoint Electronic.

| Dec. 31 | Merchandise Inventory (Dec. 31) | 40,000 | |
| | Sales | 480,000 | |
| | Purchase Returns and Allowances | 10,400 | |
| | Purchase Discounts | 6,800 | |
| |    Income Summary | | 537,200 |
| |      (To record ending inventory and close accounts with credit balances) | | |

| 31 | Income Summary | 507,200 | |
| |   Merchandise Inventory (Jan. 1) | | 36,000 |
| |   Sales Returns and Allowances | | 12,000 |
| |   Sales Discounts | | 8,000 |
| |   Purchases | | 325,000 |
| |   Freight-in | | 12,200 |
| |   Store Salaries Expense | | 45,000 |
| |   Rent Expense | | 19,000 |
| |   Freight-out | | 7,000 |
| |   Advertising Expense | | 16,000 |
| |   Utilities Expense | | 17,000 |
| |   Depreciation Expense | | 8,000 |
| |   Insurance Expense | | 2,000 |
| |     (To close beginning inventory and other income statement accounts with debit balances) | | |

| 31 | Income Summary | 30,000 | |
| |   R. A. Lamb, Capital | | 30,000 |
| |     (To transfer net income to capital) | | |

| 31 | R. A. Lamb, Capital | 15,000 | |
| |   R. A. Lamb, Drawing | | 15,000 |
| |     (To close drawings to capital) | | |

# SECTION II    ADJUSTING ENTRY METHOD FOR MERCHANDISE INVENTORY

As previously stated, the change between the beginning and ending inventory balances may be made through adjusting entries rather than through closing entries. Some favor this method because they believe that changes in merchandise inventory should receive the same accounting treatment as changes in the cost of supplies on hand between two points in time. The adjusting entry method is just as acceptable as the closing entry method, and it accomplishes the same objective.

The adjusting entry method affects several steps in the accounting cycle, beginning with the use of a work sheet. Again, these effects are explained and illustrated using Highpoint Electronic as an example.

# USING A WORK SHEET

In Illustration D-4, you will see a work sheet similar to the work sheet presented in Section I (Illustration D-1). The major difference in these two work sheets relates to merchandise inventory. In Illustration D-4, the accounting for merchandise inventory uses the adjusting entry method. In Illustration D-1, the closing entry method was used. The unique accounts for the adjusting entry method are shown in capital letters in red.

## Trial Balance Columns

The trial balance columns are self-explanatory. The inventory before adjustment is the beginning inventory.

## TECHNOLOGY IN ACTION

The adjusting entry method is used in most computerized systems since the programming logic involved is more straightforward. That is, in a computerized system, the command to close the books will close all the temporary accounts to Income Summary. However, if the inventory has not been adjusted, it will not be up-to-date and therefore a misstatement can occur. Some accountants favor the adjusting entry method in manual systems as well.

## Adjustments Columns

In the adjustments columns of Illustration D-4, you will see two adjusting entries related to inventory. The objective of preparing adjusting entries for merchandise inventory is to adjust the asset balance to the cost of goods on hand at the balance sheet date. To accomplish this objective for merchandise inventory, two adjusting entries are made: (1) the beginning inventory amount is removed from merchandise inventory, and (2) the ending inventory amount is recorded in merchandise inventory. The adjusting entries, using the inventory data for Highpoint Electronic, are shown below the worksheet on page D6.

## HIGHPOINT ELECTRONIC
## Work Sheet
## For the Year Ended December 31, 1999

| | Trial Balance Dr. | Trial Balance Cr. | Adjustments Dr. | Adjustments Cr. | Adjusted Trial Balance Dr. | Adjusted Trial Balance Cr. | Income Statement Dr. | Income Statement Cr. | Balance Sheet Dr. | Balance Sheet Cr. |
|---|---|---|---|---|---|---|---|---|---|---|
| Cash | 9,500 | | | | 9,500 | | | | 9,500 | |
| Accounts Receivable | 16,100 | | | | 16,100 | | | | 16,100 | |
| MERCHANDISE INVENTORY | 36,000 | | (e) 40,000 | (d) 36,000 | 40,000 | | | | 40,000 | |
| Prepaid Insurance | 3,800 | | | (a) 2,000 | 1,800 | | | | 1,800 | |
| Store Equipment | 80,000 | | | | 80,000 | | | | 80,000 | |
| Accumulated Depreciation | | 16,000 | | (b) 8,000 | | 24,000 | | | | 24,000 |
| Accounts Payable | | 20,400 | | | | 20,400 | | | | 20,400 |
| R. A. Lamb, Capital | | 83,000 | | | | 83,000 | | | | 83,000 |
| R. A. Lamb, Drawing | 15,000 | | | | 15,000 | | | | 15,000 | |
| SALES | | 480,000 | | | | 480,000 | | 480,000 | | |
| SALES RETURNS AND ALLOWANCES | 12,000 | | | | 12,000 | | 12,000 | | | |
| SALES DISCOUNTS | 8,000 | | | | 8,000 | | 8,000 | | | |
| PURCHASES | 325,000 | | | | 325,000 | | 325,000 | | | |
| PURCHASE RETURNS AND ALLOWANCES | | 10,400 | | | | 10,400 | | 10,400 | | |
| PURCHASE DISCOUNTS | | 6,800 | | | | 6,800 | | 6,800 | | |
| FREIGHT-IN | 12,200 | | | | 12,200 | | 12,200 | | | |
| Freight-out | 7,000 | | | | 7,000 | | 7,000 | | | |
| Advertising Expense | 16,000 | | | | 16,000 | | 16,000 | | | |
| Rent Expense | 19,000 | | | | 19,000 | | 19,000 | | | |
| Store Salaries Expense | 40,000 | | (c) 5,000 | | 45,000 | | 45,000 | | | |
| Utilities Expense | 17,000 | | | | 17,000 | | 17,000 | | | |
| Totals | 616,600 | 616,600 | | | | | | | | |
| Insurance Expense | | | (a) 2,000 | | 2,000 | | 2,000 | | | |
| Depreciation Expense | | | (b) 8,000 | | 8,000 | | 8,000 | | | |
| Salaries Payable | | | | (c) 5,000 | | 5,000 | | | | 5,000 |
| INCOME SUMMARY | | | (d) 36,000 | (e) 40,000 | 36,000 | 40,000 | 36,000 | 40,000 | | |
| Totals | | | 91,000 | 91,000 | 669,600 | 669,600 | 507,200 | 537,200 | 162,400 | 132,400 |
| Net Income | | | | | | | 30,000 | | | 30,000 |
| Totals | | | | | | | 537,200 | 537,200 | 162,400 | 162,400 |

Key: (a) Insurance expired, (b) Depreciation expensed, (c) Salaries accrued, (d) Beginning merchandise inventory, (e) Ending merchandise inventory.

**ILLUSTRATION D-4**

*Work sheet—adjusting inventory method*

| Dec. 31 | Income Summary | 36,000 | |
| | Merchandise Inventory | | 36,000 |
| | (To remove beginning inventory) | | |
| | | | |
| 31 | Merchandise Inventory | 40,000 | |
| | Income Summary | | 40,000 |
| | (To record ending inventory) | | |

These entries are identified as adjustments (d) and (e), respectively, in the work sheet.

After posting, the accounts will show:

| Merchandise Inventory | | Income Summary | |
|---|---|---|---|
| Jan.  1 Bal.  36,000 | Dec.31 Adj.  36,000 | Dec. 31  Adj.  36,000 | Dec. 31  Adj.  40,000 |
| Dec.31 Adj.  40,000 | | | |
| Dec. 31 Bal.  40,000 | | | |

## Adjusted Trial Balance Columns

In Illustration D-4, the merchandise inventory amount is extended to the adjusted trial balance debit column. **This amount is the ending inventory for the period.** Both amounts reported in Income Summary are transferred to the adjusted trial balance columns to ensure that these two amounts are reported in the income statement columns. Therefore the net amount, in this case, $4,000 ($40,000 − $36,000), is not reported.

## Financial Statement Columns

Complete financial statements are prepared directly from the income statement and balance sheet columns of the work sheet. The use of the financial statement columns should be familiar to you. One difficult subject is the treatment of merchandise inventory and income summary adjustments. A partial work sheet showing just these two items is presented below:

| | Trial Balance | | Adjustments | | Adjusted Trial Balance | | Income Statement | | Balance Sheet | |
|---|---|---|---|---|---|---|---|---|---|---|
| | Dr. | Cr. | Dr. | Cr. | Dr. | Cr. | Dr. | Cr. | Dr. | Cr. |
| Merchandise Inventory | 36,000 | | (e) 40,000 | (d) 36,000 | 40,000 | | | | 40,000 | |
| Income Summary | | | (d) 36,000 | (e) 40,000 | 36,000 | 40,000 | 36,000 | 40,000 | | |

In the merchandise inventory line, the $40,000 in the balance sheet debit column is the ending inventory. In the income summary line, the debit in the income statement column indicates the cost of the beginning inventory, and the credit in the income statement column shows the cost of the ending inventory. Complete financial statements are then prepared directly from the income statement and balance sheet columns of the work sheet.

# JOURNALIZING AND POSTING CLOSING ENTRIES

When the adjusting entry method is followed, merchandise inventory is not part of the closing process. As a result, entries to close the books are as follows:

| Dec. 31 | Sales | 480,000 | |
|---|---|---|---|
| | Purchase Returns and Allowances | 10,400 | |
| | Purchase Discounts | 6,800 | |
| |    Income Summary | | 497,200 |
| |      (To close income statement accounts with | | |
| |      credit balances) | | |

| Dec. 31 | Income Summary | 471,200 | |
|---|---|---|---|
| | Sales Returns and Allowances | | 12,000 |
| | Sales Discounts | | 8,000 |
| | Purchases | | 325,000 |
| | Freight-in | | 12,200 |
| | Store Salaries Expense | | 45,000 |
| | Rent Expense | | 19,000 |
| | Freight-out | | 7,000 |
| | Advertising Expense | | 16,000 |
| | Utilities Expense | | 17,000 |
| | Depreciation Expense | | 8,000 |
| | Insurance Expense | | 2,000 |
| | (To close income statement accounts with debit balances) | | |

These entries produce a credit balance in the Income Summary account of $30,000. This amount equals the net income reported for Highpoint Electronic using the closing method. The postings to Income Summary are as follows:

**ILLUSTRATION D-7**

*Postings to Income Summary*

| | Income Summary | | | | |
|---|---|---|---|---|---|
| Dec. 31 | **Adj.** | **36,000** | Dec. 31 | **Adj.** | **40,000** |
| 31 | Close | 471,200 | 31 | Close | 497,200 |
| 31 | to Cap. | 30,000 | | | |
| | | 537,200 | | | 537,200 |

Both the closing entry method and the adjusting entry method result in the same accounts and amounts reported in the financial statements. It is a matter of personal preference which method is used.

# QUESTIONS

1. Assuming the closing entry method is used, indicate the columns of the work sheet in which (a) the beginning merchandise inventory, and (b) the ending merchandise inventory will be shown.

2. Prepare the closing entries for the merchandise inventory account, assuming the closing entry method is used with a beginning inventory of $48,000 and an ending inventory of $58,000.

3. What merchandising account(s) will appear in the post-closing trial balance (assume the closing entry method is used)?

4. Assuming the adjusting entry method is used, indicate the columns of the work sheet in which (a) the beginning merchandise inventory, and (b) the ending merchandise inventory will be shown.

5. Prepare the adjusting entry for the merchandise inventory account, assuming the adjusting entry method is used with a beginning inventory of $48,000 and an ending inventory of $58,000.

6. What merchandising account(s) will appear in the post-closing trial balance (assume the adjusting entry method is used)?

# BRIEF EXERCISES

*Identify work sheet columns for selected accounts.*

**BED-1** Presented below is the format of the work sheet presented in the chapter.

| Trial Balance | | Adjustments | | Adjusted Trial Balance | | Income Statement | | Balance Sheet | |
|---|---|---|---|---|---|---|---|---|---|
| Dr. | Cr. | Dr. | Cr. | Dr. | Cr. | Dr. | Cr. | Dr. | Cr. |

Assuming the closing entry method is used, indicate where the following items will appear on the work sheet: (a) cash, (b) beginning inventory, (c) purchases, (d) ending inventory. *Example:*

Cash: Trial balance debit column; Adjusted trial balance debit column; and Balance sheet debit column.

**BED–2**   Pema Company has the following merchandise account balances: Sales $180,000, Sales Discounts $2,000, Purchases $120,000, Purchase Returns and Allowances $30,000. In addition, it has a beginning inventory of $50,000 and an ending inventory of $30,000. Assuming the closing entry method is used, prepare the entries to record the closing of these items to Income Summary.

*Prepare closing entries for merchandise accounts.*

**BED–3**   Using the information from BED–1, indicate how these four items are presented on the work sheet if the adjusting entry method is used.

*Adjusting entry method.*

# EXERCISES

**ED–1**   The adjusted trial balance of Cecilie Company shows the following data pertaining to sales at the end of its fiscal year October 31, 1999: Sales $900,000, Freight-out $12,000, Sales Returns and Allowances $24,000, Sales Discounts $2,000, beginning inventory $155,000, and ending inventory $176,000. The closing entry method is used.

*Prepare sales revenues section and closing entries, using the closing entry method.*

**Instructions**

(a)  Prepare the sales revenues section of the income statement.

(b)  Prepare the closing entries for Cecilie Company.

**ED–2**   On June 10, L. Pele Company purchased $5,000 of merchandise from R. Duvall Company FOB shipping point, terms 2/10, n/30. L. Pele pays the freight costs of $300 on June 11. Damaged goods totaling $300 are returned to R. Duvall for credit on June 12. On June 19, L. Pele pays R. Duvall Company in full, less the purchase discount. Pele had a beginning inventory of $25,000, sales of $40,000, and ending inventory of $10,000.

*Prepare purchase entries and closing entries, using the closing entry method.*

**Instructions**

(a)  Prepare separate entries for each purchase related transaction on the books of L. Pele Company.

(b)  Using the closing entry method, prepare separate closing entries on June 30 for the temporary accounts with (1) debit balances, and (2) credit balances.

**ED–3**   The trial balance of G. Garbo Company at the end of its fiscal year, August 31, 1999, includes the following accounts: Merchandise Inventory $17,200, Purchases $142,400, Sales $190,000, Freight-in $4,000, Sales Returns and Allowances $3,000, Freight-out $1,000, and Purchase Returns and Allowances $2,000. The ending merchandise inventory is $26,000. Garbo uses the closing entry method for inventory.

*Prepare cost of goods sold section and closing entries, using the closing entry method.*

**Instructions**

(a)  Prepare a cost of goods sold section for the year ending August 31.

(b)  Prepare the closing entries for all accounts.

(c)  Post the closing entries to Merchandise Inventory.

**ED–4**   Use the information provided in ED-3 to complete the following instructions; assume Garbo uses the adjusting entry method for inventory.

*Prepare cost of goods sold section and adjusting and closing entries, using the adjusting entry method.*

**Instructions**

(a)  Prepare a cost of goods sold section for the year ending August 31.

(b)  Prepare the adjusting entries for inventory.

(c)  Prepare the closing entries for all accounts.

**ED–5**   Presented on page D10 are selected accounts for B. Milia Company as reported in the work sheet at the end of May 1999. Ending merchandise inventory is $72,000.

*Complete work sheet and identify accounts for post-closing trial balance, using the closing entry method.*

| Accounts | Adjusted Trial Balance | | Income Statement | | Balance Sheet | |
|---|---|---|---|---|---|---|
| | Dr. | Cr. | Dr. | Cr. | Dr. | Cr. |
| Cash | 9,000 | | | | | |
| Merchandise Inventory | 80,000 | | | | | |
| Purchases | 240,000 | | | | | |
| Purchase Returns and Allowances | | 30,000 | | | | |
| Sales | | 450,000 | | | | |
| Sales Returns and Allowances | 10,000 | | | | | |
| Sales Discounts | 5,000 | | | | | |
| Rent Expense | 42,000 | | | | | |

**Instructions**

(a) Complete the work sheet by extending amounts reported in the adjusted trial balance to the appropriate columns in the work sheet. The closing entry method is used to account for merchandise inventory. Do not total individual columns.

(b) Identify the merchandising account(s) that are in the post-closing trial balance.

# PROBLEMS

* * * * * * * * * * * * * * * * * * * * * * * * * * * * * * * * * * * * * * * * * * * * * * * *

*Complete accounting cycle beginning with a work sheet, using the closing entry method.*

**PD–1** The trial balance of Mesa Wholesale Company contained the following accounts at December 31, the end of the company's fiscal year. Mesa uses the closing entry method for inventory.

**MESA WHOLESALE COMPANY**
**Trial Balance**
**December 31, 1999**

| | Debit | Credit |
|---|---|---|
| Cash | $ 33,400 | |
| Accounts Receivable | 37,600 | |
| Merchandise Inventory | 62,400 | |
| Land | 92,000 | |
| Buildings | 197,000 | |
| Accumulated Depreciation—Buildings | | $ 54,000 |
| Equipment | 83,500 | |
| Accumulated Depreciation—Equipment | | 42,400 |
| Notes Payable | | 50,000 |
| Accounts Payable | | 37,500 |
| G. Mesa, Capital | | 267,800 |
| G. Mesa, Drawing | 10,000 | |
| Sales | | 886,100 |
| Sales Discounts | 4,600 | |
| Purchases | 725,100 | |
| Purchase Discounts | | 16,000 |
| Freight-in | 12,400 | |
| Salaries Expense | 69,800 | |
| Utilities Expense | 9,400 | |
| Repair Expense | 5,900 | |
| Gas and Oil Expense | 7,200 | |
| Insurance Expense | 3,500 | |
| | $1,353,800 | $1,353,800 |

Adjustment data:

1. Depreciation is $10,000 on buildings and $9,000 on equipment. (Both are administrative expenses.)
2. Interest of $7,000 is due and unpaid on notes payable at December 31.

Other data:

1. Merchandise inventory on hand at December 31, 1999, is $90,000.
2. Salaries are 80% selling and 20% administrative.
3. Utilities expense, repair expense, and insurance expense are 100% administrative.
4. $15,000 of the notes payable are payable next year.
5. Gas and oil expense is a selling expense.

**Instructions**

(a) Enter the trial balance on a work sheet and complete the work sheet.
(b) Prepare a multiple-step income statement and owner's equity statement for the year, and a classified balance sheet at December 31, 1999.
(c) Journalize the adjusting entries.
(d) Journalize the closing entries.
(e) Prepare a post-closing trial balance.

**PD-2**  The trial balance of Ivanna Fashion Center contained the following accounts at November 30, the end of the company's fiscal year. Ivanna uses the closing entry method for inventory.

*Complete accounting cycle beginning with a work sheet, using the closing entry method.*

### IVANNA FASHION CENTER
### Trial Balance
### November 30, 1999

|  | Debit | Credit |
|---|---|---|
| Cash | $ 16,700 | |
| Accounts Receivable | 33,700 | |
| Merchandise Inventory | 38,000 | |
| Store Supplies | 5,500 | |
| Store Equipment | 85,000 | |
| Accumulated Depreciation—Store Equipment | | $ 18,000 |
| Delivery Equipment | 48,000 | |
| Accumulated Depreciation—Delivery Equipment | | 6,000 |
| Notes Payable | | 51,000 |
| Accounts Payable | | 48,500 |
| L. Ivanna, Capital | | 110,000 |
| L. Ivanna, Drawing | 12,000 | |
| Sales | | 746,600 |
| Sales Returns and Allowances | 4,200 | |
| Purchases | 503,600 | |
| Purchase Returns and Allowances | | 6,900 |
| Purchase Discounts | | 3,700 |
| Freight-in | 10,800 | |
| Salaries Expense | 140,000 | |
| Advertising Expense | 26,400 | |
| Utilities Expense | 14,000 | |
| Repair Expense | 12,100 | |
| Delivery Expense | 16,700 | |
| Rent Expense | 24,000 | |
| | $990,700 | $990,700 |

Adjustment data:

1. Store supplies on hand totaled $3,500.
2. Depreciation is $9,000 on the store equipment and $7,000 on the delivery equipment.
3. Interest of $11,000 is accrued on notes payable at November 30.

Other data:

1. Merchandise inventory on hand at November 30, 1999 is $45,000.
2. Salaries expense is 70% selling and 30% administrative.
3. Rent expense and utilities expense are 80% selling and 20% administrative.
4. $30,000 of notes payable are due for payment next year.
5. Repair expense is 100% administrative.

*Instructions*

(a) Enter the trial balance on a work sheet and complete the work sheet.
(b) Prepare a multiple-step income statement and owner's equity statement for the year and a classified balance sheet as of November 30, 1999.
(c) Journalize the adjusting entries.
(d) Journalize the closing entries.
(e) Prepare a post-closing trial balance.

*Complete a work sheet using the adjusting entry method, prepare adjusting and closing entries and post to some accounts.*

**PD–3**  The trial balance of World Enterprises for the year ending December 31, 1999, is shown below. World Enterprises uses the adjusting entry method for inventory.

**WORLD ENTERPRISES**
**Trial Balance**
**December 31, 1999**

|  | Debit | Credit |
|---|---|---|
| Cash | $ 14,000 | |
| Accounts Receivable | 27,600 | |
| Merchandise Inventory | 27,500 | |
| Prepaid Insurance | 1,800 | |
| Store Equipment | 42,000 | |
| Accumulated Depreciation—Store Equipment | | $  9,000 |
| Accounts Payable | | 31,200 |
| R. Roger, Capital | | 50,300 |
| Sales | | 238,500 |
| Sales Returns and Allowances | 4,600 | |
| Sales Discounts | 3,900 | |
| Purchases | 172,000 | |
| Freight-in | 5,000 | |
| Purchase Returns and Allowances | | 1,200 |
| Purchase Discounts | | 2,000 |
| Salaries Expense | 27,700 | |
| Utilities Expense | 6,100 | |
|  | $332,200 | $332,200 |

Other data:

1. Merchandise inventory on hand at December 31, $38,600.
2. Insurance expired $800.
3. Depreciation expense, $3,000.
4. The company uses the adjusting entry method for merchandise inventory.

*Instructions*

(a) Enter the trial balance on a work sheet and complete the work sheet using the adjusting entry method.
(b) Journalize the adjusting entries.
(c) Prepare the closing entries.
(d) Post the entries in (b) and (c) to Merchandise Inventory and Income Summary.

# STANDARDS OF ETHICAL CONDUCT FOR MANAGEMENT ACCOUNTANTS

Management accountants have an obligation to the organizations they serve, their profession, the public, and themselves to maintain the highest standards of ethical conduct. In recognition of this obligation, the Institute of Management Accountants, formerly the National Association of Accountants, has published and promoted the following standards of ethical conduct for management accountants. Adherence to these standards is integral to achieving the *Objectives of Management Accounting.*[1] Management accountants shall not commit acts contrary to these standards nor shall they condone the commission of such acts by others within their organizations.

## COMPETENCE

Management accountants have a responsibility to:
- Maintain an appropriate level of professional competence by ongoing development of their knowledge and skills.
- Perform their professional duties in accordance with relevant laws, regulations, and technical standards.
- Prepare complete and clear reports and recommendations after appropriate analyses of relevant and reliable information.

## CONFIDENTIALITY

Management accountants have a responsibility to:
- Refrain from disclosing confidential information acquired in the course of their work except when authorized, unless legally obligated to do so.

[1]Institute of Management Accountants, formerly National Association of Accountants, *Statements on Management Accounting: Objectives of Management Accounting,* Statement No. 1B, June 17, 1982.

- Inform subordinates as appropriate regarding the confidentiality of information acquired in the course of their work and monitor their activities to assure the maintenance of that confidentiality.
- Refrain from using or appearing to use confidential information acquired in the course of their work for unethical or illegal advantage either personally or through third parties.

# INTEGRITY

Management accountants have a responsibility to:
- Avoid actual or apparent conflicts of interest and advise all appropriate parties of any potential conflict.
- Refrain from engaging in any activity that would prejudice their ability to carry out their duties ethically.
- Refuse any gift, favor, or hospitality that would influence or would appear to influence their actions.
- Refrain from either actively or passively subverting the attainment of the organization's legitimate and ethical objectives.
- Recognize and communicate professional limitations or other constraints that would preclude responsible judgment or successful performance of an activity.
- Communicate unfavorable as well as favorable information and professional judgments or opinions.
- Refrain from engaging in or supporting any activity that would discredit the profession.

# OBJECTIVITY

Management accountants have a responsibility to:
- Communicate information fairly and objectively.
- Disclose fully all relevant information that could reasonably be expected to influence an intended user's understanding of the reports, comments, and recommendations presented.

# PHOTO CREDITS

Chapter 12
Page 514: Walter Geiersperger/Index Stock. Page 517: Donald Struthers/Tony Stone Images/New York, Inc. Page 519: Comstock, Inc. Page 525: Henry Sims/The Image Bank. Page 526: Comstock, Inc. Page 527: Andy Zito/The Image Bank. Page 531: Olney Vasan/Tony Stone Images/New York, Inc. Page 545: Courtesy Newcor, Inc.

Chapter 13
Page 548: Andy Washnik. Page 552: Jim Scruggs/Gamma Liaison. Page 553: Walter Bibikow/The Image Bank. Page 557: Robert Cattan/Index Stock.

Chapter 14
Page 588: Rick Graves/Tony Stone Images/New York, Inc. Page 593: Jaques Chenet/Woodfin Camp & Associates. Page 594: Courtesy Delaware State Travel Service. Page 596: Paul Van Riel/Black Star. Page 598: Dave Wilhelm/The Stock Market. Page 605: Courtesy Reebok International, Ltd. Page 609: Will Crocker/The Image Bank. Page 612: Courtesy Knight-Ridder.

Chapter 15
Page 632: Mike Powell/Tony Stone Images/New York, Inc. Page 635: Sandra Baker/Tony Stone Images/New York, Inc. Page 641: John Labbe/The Image Bank. Page 643 (top): Courtesy Lockheed Martin. Page 643 (bottom): Ken Whitmore/Tony Stone Images/New York, Inc. Page 648: Robert Kristofik/The Image Bank. Page 649: Rob Nelson/Black Star. Page 652: Mitchell Funk/The Image Bank. Page 671: Courtesy DIEBOLD, Inc.

Chapter 16
Page 674: Mark Burnside/Tony Stone Images/New York, Inc. Page 679: Steven Wilkes/The Image Bank. Page 691: Archiv/Photo Researchers. Page 693: Mitchell Funk/The Image Bank. Page 705: Ken Whitmore/Tony Stone Images/New York, Inc. Page 717: Courtesy Apache Corporation.

Chapter 17
Page 720: Sven Annstein/Photofest. Page 724: Steve Allen/Gamma Liaison. Page 749: Courtesy SPS Technologies.

Chapter 18
Page 752: John Lund/Tony Stone Images/New York, Inc. Page 755: R. Rathe/FPG International. Page 757: Jonathan Elderfield/Gamma Liaison. Page 759: Garry Gay/The Image Bank. Page 787: Courtesy Gap, Inc. Page 813: Courtesy The Vermont Teddy Bear Company. Page 814: Courtesy Praxair, Inc.

Chapter 19
Page 818: Jeanne Strongin. Page 828: D. Sarraute/The Image Bank. Page 830: Nora Good/Masterfile. Page 832: Christopher Morris/Black Star. Page 834: Phil Banko/Tony Stone Images/New York, Inc. Page 839 (top): Michael Skott/The Image Bank. Page 839 (bottom): Eric Sander/Gamma Liaison. Page 841: Vladimir Pcholkin/FPG International. Page 842: Tom Stewart/The Stock Market. Page 846: Jan Cobb/The Image Bank.

# INDEXES